ALSO BY LANCE RICHARDSON

House of Nutter: The Rebel Tailor of Savile Row

TRUE NATURE

Peter Matthiessen in Dolpo, Nepal, November 1973.

TRUE NATURE

The Pilgrimage
of Peter Matthiessen

LANCE RICHARDSON

PANTHEON BOOKS
New York

FIRST HARDCOVER EDITION
PUBLISHED BY PANTHEON BOOKS 2025

Copyright © 2025 by Lance Richardson

Penguin Random House values and supports copyright. Copyright fuels creativity, encourages diverse voices, promotes free speech, and creates a vibrant culture. Thank you for buying an authorized edition of this book and for complying with copyright laws by not reproducing, scanning, or distributing any part of it in any form without permission. You are supporting writers and allowing Penguin Random House to continue to publish books for every reader. Please note that no part of this book may be used or reproduced in any manner for the purpose of training artificial intelligence technologies or systems.

Published by Pantheon Books, a division of Penguin Random House LLC, 1745 Broadway, New York, NY 10019.

Pantheon Books and colophon are registered trademarks of Penguin Random House LLC.

Library of Congress Cataloging-in-Publication Data
Names: Richardson, Lance, [date]- author.
Title: True nature : the pilgrimage of Peter Matthiessen / Lance Richardson.
Description: First edition. | New York : Pantheon Books, [2025] |
Includes bibliographical references and index.
Identifiers: LCCN 2024046519 (print) | LCCN 2024046520 (ebook) |
ISBN 9781524748319 (hardcover) | ISBN 9781524748326 (ebook)
Subjects: LCSH: Matthiessen, Peter. | Authors, American—20th century—Biography.
Classification: LCC PS3563.A8584 Z86 2025 (print) |
LCC PS3563.A8584 (ebook) | DDC 813/.54 [B]—dc23/eng/20241214
LC record available at https://lccn.loc.gov/2024046519
LC ebook record available at https://lccn.loc.gov/2024046520

penguinrandomhouse.com | pantheonbooks.com
Book design by Cassandra J. Pappas

Printed in the United States of America
1st Printing

The authorized representative in the EU for product safety and compliance is Penguin Random House Ireland, Morrison Chambers, 32 Nassau Street, Dublin D02 YH68, Ireland, https://eu-contact.penguin.ie.

*To Donna and Murray, who always put us first;
and to Theo, who made this possible*

A pilgrimage distinguishes itself from an ordinary journey by the fact that it does not follow a laid-out plan or itinerary, that it does not pursue a fixed aim or a limited purpose, but that it carries its meaning in itself, by relying on an inner urge which operates on two planes: on the physical as well as on the spiritual plane. It is a movement not only in the outer, but equally in the inner space, a movement whose spontaneity is that of the nature of all life, i.e. of all that grows continually beyond its momentary form, a movement that always starts from an invisible inner core.

—Peter Matthiessen[1]

Contents

Introduction	*xi*

PART I · 1927–1956

1. Home Waters	3
2. The Curly God	26
3. An Opening	44
4. Bird of Passage	64
5. Daily Themes	88
6. *The Paris Review*	101
7. People from Away	138

PART II · 1957–1973

8. Lost Americans	167
9. Unsurveyed and Unfathomed	188
10. War Games	209
11. In Paradisum	242
12. A Simple Man	265
13. Lions and Sharks	286
14. Ho Ko	314
15. Twenty Months	331

PART III · 1974–1990

16. At Crystal Mountain	355
17. Fool Day	365
18. Anthropology of the Unknown	383

19.	New Teachers	406
20.	*The Snow Leopard*	429
21.	Indian Energy	451
22.	Ten Thousand Islands	486

PART IV · 1991–2014

23.	Muryo Sensei	513
24.	The Watson Years	530
25.	Homegoing	567
	Epilogue	590
	Acknowledgments	595
	Notes	601
	Index	675

Introduction

There was a moment during the writing of this biography when I thought I might be in serious trouble. We had taken our time climbing to Shey Gompa, a Tibetan Buddhist monastery in the shadow of the Crystal Mountain, high in the Himalayas of Nepal, but my body had refused to properly acclimatize. As we ascended to a pass at 17,550 feet above sea level, I'd started finding blood in my nose, and developed a dry cough and chest rattle that suggested, a doctor later told me, the onset of pulmonary edema. Sitting alone at night in my tent near the monastery, I could count the minutes between coughing fits that left me doubled over, aching from the strain. Tomorrow we would need to leave Shey earlier than anticipated (after years of planning, after coming so far) to rapidly descend, retracing a path through the mountains that few foreigners had ever followed, though hundreds of thousands have read about it in a remarkable book.

I first discovered *The Snow Leopard*, by Peter Matthiessen, in my mid-twenties. A friend lent me her beat-up Penguin paperback, and I opened it expecting to learn something about a part of the world, with its vast snow-capped peaks, that I had always found hard to imagine while growing up in hot, flat Australia. The book took the form of an expedition journal, and it began conventionally enough: "In late September of 1973, I set out with GS on a journey to the Crystal Mountain, walking west under Annapurna and north along the Kali Gandaki River, then west and north again, around the Dhaulagiri peaks and across the Kanjiroba, two hundred and fifty miles or more to the Land of Dolpo, on the Tibetan Plateau."[1] But then the book made an unexpected turn. While Matthiessen was accompanying a field biologist, George Schaller, to study the Himalayan blue sheep in its natural habitat, he described this scientific survey as "a true pilgrimage, a journey of the heart." Matthiessen's wife had recently died of cancer, and he seemed to be using the expedition as an opportunity to search for something more elusive, a kind of enlightenment. Reading on, I found crystalline descriptions of landscapes, wildlife, and environmental change—receding glaciers—that now sound like early warning signs we had chosen to ignore. But I also found digressions into Zen Buddhism, mystical experience, and "a primordial memory of Creation."[2]

What struck me about *The Snow Leopard* is the same thing, I think, that has struck so many readers over the past five decades that the book has attained the status of a modern classic. It is steeped in science *and* spirituality; Matthiessen moves between these seemingly incompatible modes of thought with startling ease. Sentences grounded in empirical observation— "the basio-occipital bone at the base of the skull is goatlike, and so are the large dew claws and the prominent markings on the fore sides of the legs"[3]— share space with ecstatic declarations like: "I know this mountain because I am this mountain."[4] At one point, he uses geology to explain the formation of Phoksundo Lake, then immediately offers another explanation involving an enraged Bon demoness. In the journal entry for November 4, while performing a sutra chanting service in front of a Buddha statue, he pauses his ritual to identify a bird: "the bill is slim in a pale-gray head, and it has a rufous breast and a white belly. This is the robin accentor (*Prunella*)."[5] He draws on ecology, divinity, ornithology, metaphysics, sometimes in the same paragraph.

There is an interview online where Matthiessen can be seen discussing, with Betsy Gaines Quammen, what he calls the relative and absolute. "The relative would be the scientific," he explains, and the absolute would be "traditional" forms of knowledge, like religion and myth. Raising his arms above his head and extending his fingers, he describes the two like "arrow points that touch high in the air": "It's a wonderful idea, I mean, the delicacy of that—they are together, but they're also separate."[6] It seems to me that a great deal of *The Snow Leopard* exists at that delicate touching point.

We live in a time of diminishing vocabularies. The English writer and naturalist Helen Macdonald recently lamented the limits of our "secular lexicon," which comes up short when dealing with the numinous or sublime, "times in which the world stutters, turns and fills with unexpected meaning."[7] Yet Matthiessen attempted to overcome this limitation in *The Snow Leopard*, a work of voracious open-mindedness. There is something Thoreauvian in the book's reach; Henry David Thoreau, as Philip Hoare has observed about *Walden*, sometimes spoke "with the voice of angels, sometimes with earthbound science."[8] Refusing to limit himself to a single register, Matthiessen used a syncretic language to explain what he saw and experienced in the mountains of Nepal. In a lecture given the same year *The Snow Leopard* was published (1978), he suggested this approach was vital to his life: "As [Archie Fire] Lame Deer says, white man sees only with one eye. What he means,

I think, is that the white man sees only the reality before his eye. Just one description of the universe."⁹ A more holistic description was needed, Matthiessen insisted, "if we are going to survive." He said this as a longtime observer of the violence being inflicted by humanity on the natural world. He understood that our "fragmented and compartmentalized" culture was condemning us all to a grim future.

I found *The Snow Leopard* thrilling on that first read. I still find it provocative for the possibilities it suggests about thick, layered descriptions that draw just as much from Indigenous knowledge, or spiritual traditions, as they do from the sciences. You could call Matthiessen a poet-scientist; the mystical naturalist. He had blind spots, of course, but his way of seeing tended to be bold, capacious, and hopeful. I initially set out to write this biography because I wanted to understand how he evolved that enviable sensibility. Where did he start, and where did his journey take him? Did he ever find the enlightenment he'd gone looking for in the Himalayas?

THE GENERATION OF American writers who came of age during World War II and its atomic aftermath was an extraordinary one: James Baldwin, Truman Capote, William Gass, Norman Mailer, Flannery O'Connor, James Salter, Gore Vidal, Richard Yates. William Styron, another prominent member, once remarked that his cohort was "the most mistrustful of power and the least nationalist of any generation that America had produced."¹⁰ That certainly describes Peter Matthiessen, though in most other respects he stood apart from his literary peers.

He was best known as a nature writer, publishing fifteen books of fine-tuned prose about shorebirds and great white sharks, Antarctica and East Africa. He was an elegist, penning funereal laments for disappearing species, and a polemicist angry that a species should *ever* disappear. By the time the modern environmental movement gained momentum in the 1960s, he had already documented a continent's worth of human abuses in *Wildlife in America*. Matthiessen's work, as Bill McKibben has noted, constitutes "key parts of the canon of emergent environmental writing in the twentieth century."¹¹ Barry Lopez, responsible for significant additions to the canon himself, once wrote Matthiessen a humble fan letter: "I have been reading you since I was in high school, and if one has distant mentors you certainly have been one for me.... I don't wish to make you self-conscious, but these things, these courtesies of spiritual indebtedness are not often enough observed. I wish simply to state my gratitude, and my pleasure that you write."¹²

Matthiessen actually resented being labeled a nature writer, even, as Styron put it, "the finest writer on nature since John Burroughs."¹³ All those nonfiction books were, by his own estimation, second-tier achievements. He insisted on identifying as a *fiction* writer—"I think fiction is the heart of my work"[14]—responsible for prize-winning novels about missionaries, Caymanian turtle fishermen, frontier outlaws in the Florida Everglades.

Yet the novels were only another fraction of what he got up to in his eighty-six years. He cofounded, while an undercover agent for the fledgling CIA, a little magazine called *The Paris Review*. A few years later, he floated through Peru on a balsawood raft searching for a prehistoric fossil in the Amazon rainforest. He was a member of the 1961 Harvard-Peabody Expedition to Netherlands New Guinea—the one preceding the unsolved disappearance of Michael Rockefeller. He established himself as a strident social activist alongside Cesar Chavez, and then again with the American Indian Movement. His incendiary book defending Leonard Peltier, *In the Spirit of Crazy Horse*, triggered two long-running libel suits adding up to more than $49 million. There was also his yeti and bigfoot fixation: Matthiessen spent decades hunting for irrefutable proof in forests and swamps, and even convinced *The New Yorker* to briefly fund his adventures in cryptozoology. The list could go on, though perhaps it should end with his commitment to Zen, so ardent that he ultimately became a roshi in a spiritual lineage said to stretch all the way back to the Buddha.

"People are always asking me to introduce them to Peter Matthiessen," James Salter once said at a literary conference, "but the thing that is hard to know is which Peter Matthiessen they would like to meet."[15]

Many have tried to capture him in a few pithy words. "A traditional earthbound explorer in the space age."[16] "A cross between Solzhenitsyn and Scott of the Antarctic."[17] "A kind of Thoreau-on-the-Road."[18] "The Man of Experience who has Done It All."[19] Maybe "the only writer to have ever won the National Book Award for both fiction and nonfiction" counts as another often used example. The editor Terry McDonell once compiled a list of applicable titles for Matthiessen (boat captain, shark hunter, LSD pioneer . . .), then threw up his hands in exasperation: "It seemed as if what I had written was for a sixth-grade report, trying too hard not to miss anything—a list impossibly naïve in its comprehensiveness. Peter wasn't there at all."[20]

Peter, it should be said, did not make himself easy to find. He was a tangle of contradictions. Though he was rightfully renowned as a vocal champion of Indigenous rights, his attitudes around race and "the Indian" were sometimes complicated. He could be incredibly supportive of other writers, women writers, Native American writers; he could also be brutal if a writer's work failed to reach his own high standards. He once wrote to the poet and novelist Jim Harrison, after reading a manuscript for *Legends of the Fall*:

"why do you settle for this prime-time media mock-up tough-sensitive wine-tasting hard-fucking killer-killing Hemingway cum James Bond spitback who infests all three stories to one degree or another?"[21] Matthiessen would *never* settle. But nor would he tolerate such blunt criticism himself; he had a fragile ego for a Zen priest who liked to preach that ego is just an illusion.

Friends often felt they were only ever afforded glimpses of his inner life. His three wives, each subjected to a degree of misogynistic disregard, felt the same way. To his children he was a confusing parent, frequently absent for weeks or months at a stretch. "I love my kids, they're wonderful and they're a great blessing to me, but I don't necessarily think I should have had children," he confessed to the writer and filmmaker Jeff Sewald in 2006, before cutting himself off with an embarrassed laugh as he realized what he had just said on camera.[22]

Matthiessen was absent because he was always doing something somewhere far-flung: battling the Tellico Dam in Tennessee; interviewing Cree elders in Manitoba; observing cranes in the Korean Demilitarized Zone. There are few figures in American letters who led such an *eventful* life during the past hundred years. So why is he less famous than other writers of his generation? A case could be made that his work was too idiosyncratic, too niche—those novels written in Caribbean dialects and backcountry cracker slang—for a mainstream readership. And that is certainly part of it. But a more notable reason might be Matthiessen's refusal to fit into tidy boxes. He was, and remains, impossible to categorize. He wrote about too many different things, in too many disparate styles. As Pico Iyer put it for *Time* in 1993: "he juggles so many balls that it's hard for his audience to follow the high, clear arc of any one."[23] Matthiessen knew this was a handicap. He once complained to Jim Harrison (who thought his friend deserved the Nobel Prize in Literature), "Sometimes I think I make the New York critics very uneasy because they can't place me, and they kind of wish I would go away, or at least stick to nature writing where I belong."[24]

OF ALL THE PEOPLE who have struggled to get a handle on Peter Matthiessen, none have struggled more than Matthiessen himself. This is a major theme in *The Snow Leopard:*

> Upstream, in the inner canyon, dark silences are deepening by the roar of stones. Something is listening, and I listen, too: who is it that intrudes here? Who is breathing? I pick a fern to see its spores, cast it away, and am filled in that instant with misgiving: the great sins, so the Sherpas say, are

to pick wild flowers and to threaten children. My voice murmurs its regret, a strange sound that deepens the intrusion. I look about me—who is it that spoke? And who is listening? Who is this ever-present "I" that is not me?[25]

Matthiessen hoped to shed his ego in the Himalayas, thus apprehending "what Zen Buddhists call our own 'true nature.'"[26] Yet this pilgrimage would take far longer than the two months he spent walking to and from Shey Gompa; it would take his whole life. As a young child growing up in gilded circumstances, he felt a fundamental conflict between the "Peter" he thought he was and the "Peter" his patrician parents expected him to be. As an old man nearly nine decades later, he wondered what would endure once the "I" was finally extinguished by death. In between those points, obsessing over ontological questions about being and existence, he yearned to "simplify," to regain a "lost paradise," which often took the form of an imagined "island" where he could dispense with responsibilities and be his original self. This inner journey determined the choices he made throughout his long life; it is the string on which the various beads of his career were strung. It is also the organizing focus of this biography.

I began my research in late 2017, a little more than three years after Matthiessen died of acute myeloid leukemia. He remained a vivid presence for family members, friends, colleagues, neighbors, lovers. I conducted more than two hundred interviews, and some of these people shared correspondence that had not yet entered archival collections. Matthiessen's first serious girlfriend produced an enormous pile of letters sent by him from Pearl Harbor in 1945 and '46. Maria, his widow, granted access to two boxes filled with intimate notes spanning four decades, along with a hard drive containing an unfinished memoir and confessional CIA notes. One woman even opened a silver locket and tweezered out a tiny oval photograph: Peter on horseback, aged nineteen. She no longer needed the memento of her distant past.

The Peter Matthiessen Papers are housed at the Harry Ransom Center, which is part of the University of Texas at Austin. Nearly half the material had yet to be catalogued when I started sifting through what now fills 227 document boxes. It took me eleven months just to photograph the moldy typescripts and almost indecipherable journals. Any biography is a mammoth commitment, but few take a biographer to places as disparate as the Hamptons, an Indian reservation, a bird sanctuary, mosquito-infested swamps, and a Zen monastery for days of sutra chanting and zazen on a black cushion.

In May 2022, I set out with Gavin Anderson, a Scotsman who runs an ethical trekking company called Nomadic Skies, and James Appleton, an English photographer, to walk from Juphal to Shey Gompa, the Crystal Monastery in Nepal, one of those "lost paradises" where Matthiessen found a fleeting sense of contentment. We were joined by two guides, Dawa Gyalpo Baiji and Nurbu Lama, and four local men who organized the kitchen tent and minded our pack animals. As our expedition trudged through dusty gorges and along hair-raising cliffs, I noticed how much had changed since Matthiessen and Schaller had come this way in 1973—everything from the blue tin roofs that now decorated villages to the villagers' economic dependence on *yarsagumba*, a caterpillar fungus dug out of alpine meadows and sold to Chinese merchants as a potent aphrodisiac. But I was also amazed at how much had not changed. There were times when Matthiessen's description of a hermitage, or a shallow cave off the trail, rang with the rightness of a struck bell.

Though I would gradually recover my health as we descended from the mountains, that evening up at Shey Gompa when I was plagued by coughing fits was an alarming experience for everyone, my companions listening to the painful cacophony from their own tents. I slipped into my thermal sleeping bag and tried to steady my breaths. As a distraction, I opened a copy of *The Snow Leopard* that showed, on its cover, the same monastery bluff where we were presently camped. I had read the book so many times that I knew passages by heart, but now I let Matthiessen read it to me. In 2012, toward the end of his life, he'd recorded an abridged audiobook, which I had also brought on the trek; his deep, gravelly voice was a ghostly echo in this "spare, silent place"[27] he had once loved.

PART I

1927–1956

Once asked for a self-portrait to be published in
The Paris Review, Matthiessen offered his "original face,"
a sly reference to a famous koan (Case 23)
from the *Mumonkan*.

1

Home Waters

> Nothing begins the way we think we see it, there is no real beginning or end to anything, all is memory and change and process. Everything is right here now, remember?
>
> —PM, untitled *teisho* (September 26, 2000)[1]

For four decades, whenever he wanted to write, Peter Matthiessen stepped through the back door of his house in Sagaponack, on the East End of Long Island, walked past a grove of apple trees that had never borne edible fruit, and unlocked an ivy-covered shack that was once a child's playhouse. Inside, a musty smell emanated from rough-hewn woodwork—the long L-shaped desk, which took up most of a small room. Drawers were full of maps, magazine clippings, well-thumbed drafts, and the walls were flaking with pictures of his wife, his friends, the Dalai Lama, the Sasquatch. Somebody had sent him a copy of *The Snow Leopard* that had been ceremonially burned in the Himalayas; he kept the ashes pinned above the desk in a Ziploc bag. A window ledge nearby functioned as a kind of altar, cluttered with mementos charged with talismanic significance: slate from the Klamath River; a dried snake found on a beach in Baja; a carved praying mantis nose ornament acquired from a tribe in Netherlands New Guinea. Outside, visible through the window, a small stone Buddha meditated on a tree stump.

For all those years, Matthiessen had come to his office almost every day he was home and worked for up to twelve hours straight. He'd emerged to eat lunch, prepared by his wife, Maria, and then gone back inside again. He'd come out for dinner, also prepared by Maria, and then, if the words were flowing, returned to his desk. Interruptions and social calls were mostly forbidden. A small sign near the door demanded SILENCE. To be in his office was to be projecting himself somewhere far away: Lake Baikal, or Mongolia, or the Selous Game Reserve in southern Tanzania. His writing studio was a sanctuary and an escape hatch—until the mold began to colonize his files, and until the cancer, blooming in his bones, made those mental wanderings increasingly difficult, stranding him in a chemo fog.

Twenty days before his death at the age of eighty-six, Matthiessen switched on a computer that had been hastily relocated to a spore-free bedroom in the main house. He stumbled through a maze of poorly organized drafts, searching for the latest iteration of his memoir. "I don't think I'm going to have time to do it," he'd told a journalist a few weeks earlier.[2] Now he was sure.

The Word document was fifty-eight pages long, nearly 23,000 words. Structureless and rough, much of it was comprised of words to jog various recollections, and questions to himself that still needed answers. But the first half concerned his childhood, and here he'd managed to get down some detailed vignettes. In a roundabout way, tentative as he pulled all the pieces together, these fragments were an attempt to portray a transition he'd been talking about since his embrace of Zen in the early 1970s. A young child is "a part of things," Matthiessen once wrote, "unaware of endings and beginnings, still in unison with the primordial nature of creation, letting all light and phenomena pour through." This state of innocence, as most people might call it, in which no boundary is perceived between the leaves, the trees, and the stars in the sky, is inevitably lost as "the 'I' begins to form."[3] Children come to understand their "selves" as something separate—*apart from*, rather than *a part of*. And when that estrangement happens, they stop perceiving reality directly and instead enter a dream world of ideas and delusions. Much of Matthiessen's life had been a concerted effort to wake up from the dream. But when had he fallen asleep? His memoir circled this universal mystery.

At the top of the first page, he typed: "ROUGH OUTLINE FOR A BIOGRAPHY (IF ANY)."[4] This would be among the last edits he ever made. He left two suggested epigraphs to frame what remained: one from Jorge Luis Borges, about the mystery of writing; and another adapted from something once said to Paul Auster by the poet George Oppen: "Rickety old person peering into the mirror: *What a terrible thing to have happened to a little boy!*"[5]

FISHERS ISLAND IS a ridge of low-slung hills, nine miles long and one mile wide, which sits in quiet solitude off the southeast coast of Connecticut. The waters surrounding it are treacherous, clotted with currents that form an unforgiving rip tide, and a lighthouse called Race Rock shines out above a reef to prevent any more shipwrecks. The island's distance from the mainland—two miles as the shorebird flies, seven by ferry—can make it hard to see clearly across Long Island Sound even on a good day. But if there is something mirage-like about the place, that is part of the appeal for the island's residents: Fishers was never meant to be reached by most Americans.

In the spring of 1925, a notice appeared in *The New York Times* for the "Fisher's [*sic*] Island Project." Spearheaded by Alfred and Henry L. Ferguson, second-generation majority owners of the island, this million-dollar scheme promised "not only new golf links and a 300-room hotel but also a new wharf and harbor facilities for the use of pleasure yachts."[6] Fishers already had history as an elite summer resort: by the turn of the century it could accommodate more than a thousand visitors seasonally.[7] That was limited, however, to a small settled section in the west, near the military installation of Fort H. G. Wright; the eastern two-thirds of the island remained virtually undeveloped, some 1,800 acres of rolling moors left to grazing livestock. The cows were now being evicted, and Frederick Law Olmsted Jr. was drawing up plans for a real estate subdivision. Construction soon began on a country club in the style of a giant Norman farmhouse. In the words of a later promotional brochure, this club would offer everything from "quiet lounges where one may loaf away tranquil summer days, to gay entertainments with all the friendliness one can only hope to find among one's own kind of people."[8]

Peter Matthiessen was born at Miss Lippincott's Sanitarium, in New York City, on May 22, 1927—two years after the Fishers Island Project was announced, and just one day (as he liked to point out) after Charles Lindbergh had flown across the Atlantic in the *Spirit of St. Louis*.[9] Miss Lippincott's combined the attentiveness and security of a hospital with the conveniences of a luxury hotel, which is why it was frequented by Sloanes, Prestons, Benjamins, and Rockefellers.[10] Elizabeth Matthiessen—"Betty"—stayed as a guest for two weeks. Then she checked out with her baby to join Erard Adolph Matthiessen, Peter's father, for a drive up to New London, where the three of them boarded the white SS *Fishers Island* to ferry back down across the state line. (Though Fishers Island is closer to Connecticut and Rhode Island, it is technically part of Suffolk County, New York.) Once ashore, they glided past a security gate that barred outsiders from the east end. Their driveway, snaking out of sight into a stand of trees, would one day be marked with the wrought iron silhouette of a Native American man, salvaged from an antiques store as an eye-catching signpost.

The Matthiessens had a longstanding family connection to Fishers: Erard's aunt and uncle had bought a place in the older section sometime before 1913.[11] Perhaps this was why "Matty," as Erard preferred to be called, became a paying member of the new club not long after the roll was opened.[12] Fortified with immense wealth, he felt comfortable settling his family in a place where "phone book" was a synonym for the *Social Register*. On Fishers, adults were served tea and cinnamon toast in a bathing pavilion on Chocomount Beach; they attended parties at the Big Club, as it came to be known, while the children learned how to swim, play tennis, or sail small boats at "their club," the Hay Harbor.

Peter would dwell in this rarefied milieu for most of his first fifteen summers, and the privilege inevitably leached into his self-understanding, his attitude toward others, his sense of class differences, even his manner of speaking and the words he used. Yet there was another aspect of Fishers that would prove far more influential for a sensitive child just opening his eyes to the world: its extraordinary natural splendor.

The vacation house that Matty designed and built for his growing family was two stories, clad in cedar shingles, with window boxes for geraniums and a screened-in porch full of heavy wicker furniture. The bedrooms were upstairs, and a separate servants' cottage sat opposite the kitchen door. Behind the house, twin paths meandered down a slope covered with myrtle and blackberry thickets, until they terminated at a private beach, little more than a crescent of kelp-encrusted sand, which faced the distant shore of Connecticut. Here, as Peter wrote in his memoir notes, he would "sit mystified by the water's unaccountable retreat just as it touched the entrance channel into my sandcastle."[13] Rockpools swirled like miniature galaxies at either end of the beach: he and Carey, his brother, "hunched like night herons," coaxed out crabs using broken mussel shells as bait. And then there were the birds: osprey, flycatchers, wood-warblers, plovers. Sometimes they used a decoy great horned owl, mounted on a pole on the island's highest hill, to tempt the hawks migrating south from Canada. It was wildness that animated many of Peter's earliest memories of "home," as he liked to call Fishers—untamed creatures, mercurial ocean, the island as a prelapsarian Eden:

> The sounds and odors and queer lights at evening are baked in, the sea wrack on white sand . . . body-surfing small waves coming fresh from the Atlantic . . . fishing for tautog and cunner from the old East Harbor dock near the Coast Guard Station; trolling for big bluefish in the Race.[14]

When Peter was twelve or so, Matty began taking him on boat trips from Fishers down around the promontory of Montauk Point, where the Gulf Stream washes in weakfish, bonita, striped bass, mackerel, and white marlin during the warmer months. Once they counted eighty dorsal fins on a single expedition, a shiver of sharks drifting through "all that emptiness." Because Peter was a weak adversary against anything of size ("my twiggy arms"), he left the fishing rods to his father's friends and mounted the cabin roof so he could survey the oily swell through binoculars. One day he spotted his first pelagic whales this way: finbacks, or maybe humpbacks, spouting mist in the distance. "I was so excited," he wrote in his notes, "that I never bent my knees to maintain balance in the slow rolling of the boat." Peter started to pitch overboard, and he would have gone were a seasick guest not alerted to his "cry of doom." Henry Pelham-Clinton-Hope, the Earl of Lincoln, reached out and grabbed the boy at the last moment.[15]

"NO WORD CONVEYS the eeriness of whale song," Matthiessen wrote in *Blue Meridian*, "tuned by the ages to a purity behind refining, a sound that man should hear each morning to remind him of the morning of the world."[16] Yet his own Danish forebears were whalers from the Frisian Islands in the North Sea—and not only whalers, but owners of a whaling school that trained others in the art of maritime slaughter. In the seventeenth and eighteenth centuries, their center of industry was Før, or "Föhr," a stray speck of Denmark, located off the west coast of Schleswig, which had once been colonized by Vikings. Despite a small population, this bucolic island of maize crops and sleepy hamlets was renowned for producing seafarers of exemplary daring; Dutch whaling ships dropped anchor to recruit workers on the way to Arctic fishing grounds.

One of the best was a man named Matthias Petersen, who was just sixteen when he went to work as assistant mate on a ship belonging to a Hamburg merchant. Within a few years, Matthias's talents had elevated him to commander of his own whaling vessel.[17] Uncanny good luck—fourteen whales on a single voyage out of Amsterdam—soon earned him a nickname: Matthias der Glückliche, "Matthias the Fortunate." While the luck would eventually run out, with Matthias being attacked by French privateers, by the time of his death in 1706 he'd hunted "373 balenas"—an "incredibili successu" that was immortalized in Latin on his gravestone.[18]

In addition to the wealth based on oil and baleen, Matthias bequeathed two other gifts to his descendants. The first was a coat of arms: Goddess Fortuna, to whom he attributed his "successu," balancing on one leg above a spouting whale. (Peter would dismiss this as a "truly unfortunate artistic juxtaposition.")[19] The second gift was a surname. Following a custom of patronyms, part of Matthias's name had been derived from his father: as the son of Peter Johnen, he was a Peter*sen*. Matthias's own sons were similarly named, and they would have been expected to pass on their own Christian names to the next generation. However, according to the family record, "the respect and reputation enjoyed by Commander Matthias rendered the retention of his name desirable."[20] Hunting all those bowheads had earned him considerable social capital, and his sons decided their own children ought to reap the benefits of association. The custom was therefore suspended. All members of the clan, for all future generations, were henceforth anointed *sens* of Matthias—the Matthiessens.

That an outspoken conservationist should carry such a bloody legacy in his own surname was an irony not lost on Peter. "I've been cleaning up after it my whole life," he once remarked wryly at a public lecture, casting his long environmental record as one of atonement.[21] Yet he found the association exciting, too. When the artist Paul Davis presented him with a portrait of himself styled as Captain Ahab, the ultimate whaler who seeks something both tangible and symbolic "over all sides of the earth" ("What say ye, men, will ye splice hands on it, now? I think ye do look brave"),[22] Peter hung the drawing in his house, stirred by the likeness.

BY THE TIME Peter was born, more than two hundred years had elapsed since the halcyon days of Matthias Petersen. To claim that the Matthiessen fortune "was made in whaling," as Peter sometimes did, is a romantic edit of history.[23] For his immediate family, it was more accurate to say that the Matthiessen fortune was made by three brothers who had emigrated to America in the middle of the nineteenth century. They came from Altona, a small town on the Elbe, just west of Hamburg, which is 120 miles from Föhr.

Ehrhard Adolph Matthiessen (five generations after Matthias) fled the First Schleswig War, which saw Denmark and the German Confederation fighting over control of Schleswig and Holstein. In August 1850, at the age of twenty-five, he arrived on the SS *Asia*, a sleek Cunard paddle steamer that paced the Atlantic between Liverpool and New York. Though an astronomer by training, Ehrhard turned his hand to a more lucrative profession in Manhattan, joining the banking house of German American financier August Belmont. During the Civil War—having escaped one conflict, he soon became witness to a larger one—Ehrhard was appointed the firm's managing head, then worked his way up to become a director while he was still the youngest clerk in the company. Meanwhile, his brother, Franz Otto Matthiessen, had arrived sometime around 1857. Franz went into the sugar business. He found employment as a superintendent at refineries in New York and Boston, then built his own, Matthiessen & Wiechers, across the Hudson River in Jersey City. Eventually this would merge into a sprawling national conglomerate, the American Sugar Refining Company, later known as Domino Sugar, and Franz, "considered by those in the business as knowing it as few others ever did," would amass a personal fortune of up to $20 million—more than half a billion dollars today.[24]

The third and youngest of the three brothers, Frederick Wilhelm Matthiessen, also arrived in 1857. His métier was zinc. After studying mining in

Freiburg and graduating as an engineer, he traveled to America with a fellow student, Edward C. Hegeler,* and began scouting for opportunities beyond the East Coast. They ended up in La Salle, Illinois, an important trading hub where canal boats from Chicago, ninety-six miles away, met steamboats traveling up from New Orleans, and where the new Illinois Central Railroad chugged through on its route from Cairo to Galena. Here on the bank of the Little Vermilion River, they cofounded the Matthiessen & Hegeler Zinc Company, which smelted Wisconsin ores using Illinois coal. A few years later, in 1862, "demand for zinc in ammunition provided a ready market for the plant output"—a company-handbook way of saying that business boomed by selling bullets to both sides in the war.[25] A rolling mill and sulfuric acid plant were added afterward, further enhancing profits. Frederick would try his hand at other pursuits over the years—mayor of La Salle; investor in alarm clocks—but these industrial works stood as his signature achievement.†

Frederick had a daughter, Eda Wilhelmina Sophie Matthiessen. Ehrhard had a son, Conrad Henry Matthiessen. In 1888, she was twenty-two years old, and he was twenty-three. First cousins, they nevertheless married in Cornwall-on-Hudson, New York—a union that was either strongly encouraged or strategically arranged to inaugurate a kind of Matthiessen dynasty in America.[26] The newlyweds each funneled part of the financial holdings of their powerful fathers; additionally, through their shared uncle Franz, Conrad would hold various executive roles in the glucose industry. "He received $75,000 a year," a newspaper later reported about one of these positions, "and at the time was regarded as the highest salaried official of any industrial concern in the country."[27] The marriage kept all this wealth in the family.

Eda and Conrad had something in common as the children of immigrants: they both lived in the overlap of two cultures. Eda was born in the Midwest, and she learned all the social graces expected of a young American lady; yet she also spoke German with her maids, adored Wagner and Beethoven, and

---

* In addition to his work with Frederick Matthiessen, Edward Hegeler also founded the Open Court Publishing Company, which sought to reconcile science and religion through open dialogues. In 1893, during the World Parliament of Religions in Chicago, the managing editor of Open Court (and Hegeler's son-in-law), Dr. Paul Carus, invited a formidable Japanese man named Soyen Shaku to make a side trip to the company's headquarters in La Salle. Soyen Shaku, who allegedly once said of himself, "My heart burns like fire but my eyes are as cold as dead ashes," was the very first Zen roshi to travel and teach in America. He would one day be described as the ancestor of American Zen. Peter Matthiessen liked to speculate that an encounter between Soyen Shaku and Frederick, as Hegeler's business partner, "almost certainly took place" on this landmark visit—an early family brush with a tradition that would one day define the shape of his own life. Nevertheless, such a meeting was at best "unpromising," Peter had to admit, "since it passed unrecorded in the annals on either side."
† Matthiessen & Hegeler is now a Superfund site. The U.S. Environmental Protection Agency placed it on the National Priorities List in 2003, having found elevated levels of cadmium, lead, and zinc in the soil, along with traces of pesticides and solvents. According to the EPA, a slag pile on the steep west bank of the Little Vermilion River poses "major environmental concerns."

insisted on elaborate Bavarian Christmases—a five-foot-long centerpiece of Sankt Nikolaus and his reindeer, "hand-wrought of mahogany and bone, and restaged each year with cotton-and-mica snow."[28*] Conrad was born in Cornwall, yet his father sent him abroad for school in Wiesbaden, then on to the Collège de Genève, before he was brought back to finish off what Nelson Aldrich Jr. once called the "curriculum" of American blue-bloods, meaning the right college (Yale) and the right affiliations (Sigma Delta Chi).[29]

An overlap of cultures was where the similarities ended, however. In temperament and personality, Conrad and Eda were a poor match from the start. To illustrate exactly how poor, Peter enjoyed recounting a story about Eda, who was his grandmother:

> [A]s a simple precaution, it is said, my grandfather [Conrad] had this good young woman followed by a private detective from the day of their marriage to the day of their inevitable divorce, many years later. (It is related in the family that my grandmother turned around one day on Madison Avenue to confront a little man, saying, "You have been following me, unless I'm very much mistaken." The embarrassed Pinkerton confessed that he had been following her for eight years and was deeply ashamed of it, whereupon she said, "There, there," and took him into Longchamps for an ice cream soda.)[30]

This is probably apocryphal, or at least exaggerated, but the underlying dynamic is accurate enough. Eda was sharp, sympathetic, and unfailingly proper. Her grandchildren—who called her "Muttie," from Mutti, German for "Mom"—would recall her as bountifully generous: concert seats at Carnegie Hall, "where the fierce baton of Arturo Toscanini would whip the New York Philharmonic to a brilliant froth," and gifts of rare stamps hailing from "crown colonies in turquoise southern seas."[31] Conrad, on the other hand, was mostly absent from the family narrative, and the few surviving traces of him in public records refer almost exclusively to business exploits, including conspiracy, antitrust, and bilked stockholders.[32]

After the wedding, Conrad and Eda settled in Chicago, in the affluent neighborhood of Kenwood. Servants outnumbered family members at a red-brick mansion on Ellis Avenue, and this would continue to be the case as the family expanded. Ralph Henry came first, followed by Conrad Henry,

---

* This ornate construction went up in smoke during the Christmas dinner of 1941, a dramatic event begun by a fallen candle that Matthiessen would fictionalize in his short story "The Centerpiece": "In the chaos of motion and voices I saw Madrina [i.e., Eda], the only person still seated, observing the destruction as if the ruin of this antiquated treasure was somehow fitting, as if she sensed that, like the tapestries and urns, it was far too venerable and vast to serve the New World Hartlingens [Matthiessens] again."

followed by Constance Eda, followed by Erard Adolph, named after his paternal grandfather, on May 27, 1902.

The same month that Erard—as in Matty, Peter's father—was born, Conrad made a substantial purchase back east in Irvington-on-Hudson, a village twenty miles north of New York City. Named in honor of Washington Irving, who died there in 1859, Irvington had started life as four adjoining tenant farms belonging to a Dutch slaveowner who used his land as a provisioning plantation; more recently, the farms had been transformed into sprawling estates for industrial tycoons, plus a small community of servants. Prominent residents had included Cyrus West Field, who installed the cable across the Atlantic seabed; Amzi Lorenzo Barber, "the Asphalt King," who paved the streets in dozens of American cities; and Franz Otto Matthiessen, who became a recluse there after an unexpected tragedy.[33]

Franz had bought a slice of Irvington with the intention of leaving it to his only daughter, Helen. But then Helen died of acute appendicitis during a visit to Italy—a shock so enormous that Franz repatriated her body and, according to a news report, kept it locked up in his home for months, "refusing to have it interred." When Franz had finally died himself in 1901, from diabetes, one of his closest friends told the press that "he was sure Mr. Matthiessen's death was precipitated by a broken heart."[34] Conrad bought the plot of land adjacent to his late uncle's estate: Tiffany Park, which had previously belonged to Charles Lewis Tiffany of Tiffany & Co. Two months after the sale, Franz's widow conveyed the land originally intended for Helen to Conrad and Eda, thereby uniting neighboring addresses into a single sprawling plot. This is how the Matthiessens came to own an enclave of some sixty-two acres, which they named Matthiessen Park.

IN ONE OF PETER'S BEST short stories, "Lumumba Lives," which he wrote in 1988, a retired CIA operative returns to the old family estate in Westchester County after living in Africa for more than two decades. The town is named Arcadia, and here "[h]is father's great-uncle, in the nineteenth century, had bought a large tract of valleyside and constructed a great ark of a house with an uplifting view of the magnificent Palisades across the river."[35] Over the years, the great-uncle's descendants had added "lesser houses"—still stately manors by most estimates—around the valley tract, and it was in one of these houses that the man had grown up. The estate has long since passed out of family hands when the story opens, but now the former agent intends to buy a piece back, to return to his roots and, by implication, to a time before his life became so complicated. He will "reassemble things—well, not 'things' so much as continuity."[36]

Like many of Matthiessen's fictions, this will all turn sour before the end of the tale, an explosion of violence denying the man's longed-for retreat to an idealized boyhood. Yet much of the buildup consists of Proustian flashes, memories resurrecting as he strolls around a landscape he once knew intimately. Here is the gardener's cottage, where he used to flee when his grandmother made her loathsome cambric tea. There are the train tracks where he'd once placed pennies so the face of "Honest Abe" would be squashed smooth by passing freight cars.

"Lumumba Lives" is a fictional response to an encounter Matthiessen once had with a mercenary pilot who likely helped in the assassination of Patrice Lumumba, the first prime minister of the independent Republic of the Congo. (What if the man went home decades later, Matthiessen wondered, and was forced, in a supposedly safe space, to reckon with his role in colonialism?) But the setting and memories are fact: "Arcadia" is Irvington, and many of the man's recollections belong to Matthiessen, which is why he copied out whole passages from the story into his memoir notes.

At the end of each summer, Betty and Matty closed up the house on Fishers Island and returned with the children to Matthiessen Park. From Broadway, a sinuous downhill drive ended in a carriage circle, where two weathered cannons stood sentinel by the front door. This handsome house of brick and stone—another of Matty's constructions—had multiple chimneys, a light-filled sunroom ("The world has changed since a private house had a room designed for sun and dancing"),[37] and a broad terrace in the rear from which one could watch the Day Line *Alexander Hamilton* steaming down the Hudson. Nearby were the other "lesser houses" owned by Matty's brother, Ralph, and assorted friends like the "Littlers, Sweetsers, Robbinses, etc."[38] Thomas McConaughey, the Scottish gardener, lived in the cottage behind a tall privet hedge. One of McConaughey's sons, also named Thomas, would become Peter's childhood companion; they founded a boys-only club together in an old chicken coop, its sole purpose being to collect the weekly allowance of other young members as "club dues," which they then spent at the confectionery on Main Street. The other McConaughey son, Jim, would one day become the family's chauffeur.

MATTY MATTHIESSEN NEVER SPOKE about his own early memories of Irvington. Conrad and Eda had relocated there from Chicago by 1903. That year, before Matty could walk or talk, his six-year-old sister Constance died for reasons that nobody recorded. In 1904, Eda then gave birth to another son, Matthies, who died after six days.

In the grim atmosphere of a double-bereavement, Matty was raised by nannies. He would see his mother at dinnertime, his father more rarely. As an adolescent, he was sent away to Hotchkiss for four years of boarding school; meanwhile, his two surviving brothers, both considerably older, went off to fight in the Great War. By graduation, his parents' marriage was approaching its inevitable denouement. It seems unlikely that they ever legally divorced, as Peter claimed, but Eda began spending much of her time down in Manhattan, in a luxurious eleventh-floor apartment on East 60th Street that looked over the horse broughams in Central Park South. Conrad stayed in Cornwall, or spent time in Kerhonkson near the Shawangunk Mountains. Eventually Eda would list herself as head of the household.

Peter once asked his father about the family background. Matty's reaction was "somewhat bemused."[39] He was uninterested in dwelling on the past, perhaps because thinking about it was painful. Matty's daughter, Mary (Peter's sister), would come to suspect he'd suffered from bouts of depression in his childhood, though specifics with Matty were always impossible to excavate. He was one of those men who carefully avoid anything that might summon up strong, unwieldy emotions like anxiety or loneliness. "I had always thought that I possessed a certain armor to protect me from things such as this," he wrote in a letter in 1977, stunned to find himself experiencing grief after the death of his wife.[40] This "armor" was as much cultural as personal, and it manifested as a demeanor of insouciant ease: "Matty," fitting over Erard like a sport coat.

Matty was described by Thomas Guinzburg, longtime president of the Viking Press and one of Peter's closest childhood friends, as looking like "a Marine Corps master sergeant," or like Burt Lancaster if the actor lost most of his hair.[41] He had a "massive head that reminded you of the ancients," another friend observed, and there was something "vaguely brutish" about his presence.[42] Tall and imposing, he could intimidate when he wanted, but Matty was also a consummate host who liked nothing more than to socialize at parties or on one of his motorboats, rubbing shoulders with people who were susceptible to being charmed. *Charm*, that ambiguous power which allows one to attract others while also maintaining a protective distance, was something both of Peter's parents wielded with expertise. "I didn't say they were lovely," Maria Matthiessen once clarified about her in-laws for a documentary filmmaker: "I said they were charming."[43]

Matty met Betty at a Yale dance. He was studying for a Bachelor of Science at the Sheffield Scientific School, a middling student (Cs and Ds) who seemed to expend most of his energy on extracurricular distractions like St. Anthony Hall, a fraternity and literary society.[44] Betty was working as a clerk in a New York department store, possibly Bonwit Teller; she had come up to New Haven on a visit with a friend. "She was a fabulous dancer," recalled Mary, "but god knows what she wore on her back because she didn't have a penny."⁴⁵

Elizabeth Bleecker Carey was born on August 28, 1903. She lived with her family in Short Hills, New Jersey, in circumstances that her strict and rather dour mother might have described as genteel poverty, though they still had enough resources to employ a Black housekeeper named Addie McLeod. Betty traced her paternal ancestry to Reverend William Norvell Ward, who had once been the friend and confidant of Robert E. Lee. In 1842, Reverend Ward had acquired a Federal-style farmhouse between the Potomac and the Rappahannock Rivers, in Richmond County, Virginia, named Bladensfield, which would remain the family seat for generations ("*our* old place," Peter once called it).⁴⁶ From Bladensfield during the Civil War, Reverend Ward had offered support to another friend, Jefferson Davis, while two of his sons died fighting what a family history book called the "Yankee raiders."⁴⁷ After hostilities ended with the Wards on the losing side, they were left with "one silver quarter and a heap of Confederate money, now not worth a dime."⁴⁸ The eldest of the Reverend's seven daughters, Martha Ward, soon moved to Baltimore, where she was widowed young and forced to make ends meet by taking in student boarders from Johns Hopkins. Martha's son, George Carey—Peter's grandfather—dreamed of returning to Bladensfield and transforming it into a prosperous farm, but his young wife vetoed that idea (too remote and dilapidated), so he settled for ill-suited odd jobs in her native New Jersey instead. This persuasive wife, Mary Seymour Jewett—Peter's grandmother—traced her own roots back to white Anglo-Saxon Protestants such as Horatio Seymour, the eighteenth governor of New York, and a man Peter would come to admire for having championed the rights of Native Americans in the nineteenth century.* Mary Seymour Jewett had no money either, just unimpeachable Victorian values, which she used to rule the Short Hills home like a tyrant.

Betty attended the Ethel Walker School on scholarship. After that early leg up, however, the rest was left to her. Photographs capture her glamorous profile, long and lithe like a Modigliani painting. Her beauty was paired with a fluty laugh, an idiosyncratic sense of propriety—a name like "Emma" was, in her estimation, only fit for a servant—and a belief, also probably

---

* Governor Horatio Seymour was quoted by Helen Hunt Jackson on the title page of her book *A Century of Dishonor* (1881): "Every human being born upon our continent, or who comes here from any quarter of the world, whether savage or civilized, can go to our courts for protection—except those who belong to the tribes who once owned this country. The cannibal from the islands of the Pacific, the worst criminals from Europe, Asia, or Africa, can appeal to the law and courts for their rights of person and property—all, save our native Indians, who, above all, should be protected from wrong." Matthiessen found this "unpopular opinion" deeply moving, and he would discuss Seymour at length in his own incendiary work, *In the Spirit of Crazy Horse*.

derived from her mother, that she was destined for a higher station in life. Betty made her debut in 1922. She did not go to college, though she would one day regret that decision as she strolled through Rome with a daughter who could tell her all the things she'd never learned. While she waited for what came next, she worked in the city and socialized at parties where people played games like the "peanut jab": "With hat pins each player in turn jabs for a peanut until he misses, when the next one tries."[49]

What ignited the spark between Betty and Matty? Here was another subject never discussed with the children. Matty was well-heeled; Betty had breeding and refinement; yet it was more than merely transactional. "She thought he was kind of a hoot," said Jeff Wheelwright, their grandson. "He wasn't a stuffed shirt. She liked that about him. I can see them in a room full of people on Fishers Island at a cocktail party, and he was the most relaxed, comfortable-in-his-skin fellow there. He was kind of a complete guy. Maybe *too* complete, because once the party was over, he was still being cool."[50]

More than five hundred people attended the wedding. Performed by Reverend Malcolm Douglas at Christ Episcopal Church in Short Hills, the ceremony was held on October 11, 1924. Betty had seven bridesmaids; Matty's best man was his brother, Conrad Henry Jr.[51]

The honeymoon, a two-month grand tour of Europe, began with a voyage to Southampton on the RMS *Majestic*, the largest ocean liner in the world, with a marble swimming pool and library containing some four thousand volumes. After excursions through England, the Netherlands, Belgium, France, and Italy, the newlyweds concluded with skating and skiing in Switzerland. "Although it's just been too perfect and we've had the most wonderful time," Betty wrote to a cousin, both she and Matty were looking forward to seeing "the good old U. S. A. again," where one didn't need to unpack and repack "every five minutes."[52]

As soon as they returned, Matty was admitted to Columbia University—an Avery Hall program that aimed to train architects who "fearlessly accept the modern problem; solve it in the modern way, but always conform to those elemental truths which have ever expressed that beauty and good taste which distinguishes all true art and has come down to us as our precious inheritance."[53] Betty had no desire to work now it was no longer necessary, so she joined committees and played bridge to raise money for the nearby hospital at Dobbs Ferry. She also began having the children: Mary Seymour was born eighteen months before Peter, on October 9, 1925; and George Carey (called "Carey" by all) was born fifteen months after, on August 15, 1928.

Lacking any example from his own upbringing, Matty struggled, by his own admission, to be "demonstrative" with his offspring.[54] And while Betty kept an eye on them, she followed the example of her friends by delegating the laborious child-rearing to nannies, preferring to prioritize the needs of her fickle husband instead. Leaving Mary, Peter, and Carey at home, they attended Sunday teas, tenpin bowling tournaments, suppers in the Crystal Room of the Ritz-Carlton. They watched the Harvard-Yale Regatta on the Thames River, and performed in revues at the Tarrytown Music Hall, where the Chorus Men (including Matty) competed against the Chorus Girls (including Betty) in elaborate comic routines.

Peter was two years old when Wall Street crashed in the fall of 1929, foreshadowing a decade in which nearly five out of ten white families and nine out of ten Black families would slip below the poverty line.[55] But not the Matthiessens. "The Depression had no serious effect on our well-insulated family," he later acknowledged in an essay for *Architectural Digest*.[56] The only notable adjustment seems to have been an increased sense of noblesse oblige. As dozens of Irvington townsfolk from "virtually every conceivable trade" began registering at town hall with a Mayor's Committee on Unemployment Relief, Matty doled out private jobs around Matthiessen Park.[57] Betty co-chaired a Ways and Means Committee "to bring about a SOLUTION of the present EMERGENCY," and she was singled out for praise in an *Irvington Gazette* editorial for combating a "WRONG ATTITUDE" among certain members of the community—"that there was no real need for any action."[58] Betty also worked to distribute several hundred milk bottles, which residents were encouraged to fill with silver coins for the relief funds.[59]

But Peter was gesturing toward something important when he chose the phrase "well-insulated," because for all their generosity, Matty and Betty maintained a buffer between themselves and the misery sweeping the nation. This would be a common theme for his parents, who treated money, like charm, as both a means of reaching out *and* as a defensive bulwark. If anything broke through the barricade to create an uncomfortable situation, they recoiled in disgust.

One Saturday afternoon in 1930, a deliveryman came to the house with new upholstered chairs from Carl von Schenk, a local furniture dealer. Matty and Betty were out, so a maid answered the door and then retreated to take a telephone call. As the deliveryman went about his business of unloading goods, a middle-aged woman followed him inside the house. By her "manner," a newspaper later reported, the woman conveyed to the man that she was "a member of the family."[60] Calmly, she headed upstairs to the second floor, then returned, a few minutes later, and told the deliveryman in a "cultured voice" that she was going to inspect the stock in his truck. She promptly disappeared. That evening, Betty came home to discover a ransacked dresser in the master bedroom: gone were assorted jewels—a rope of seed pearls, a diamond necklace—worth $13,260, or more than $240,000 today.[61]

Claire Ritchey was forty-four years old, a door-to-door saleswoman for Harford Frocks of Cincinnati. She was apprehended two days later in Leonia, New Jersey, having pawned some of Betty's larger pieces to a skeptical broker for just $300. In its coverage of this "unusual crime," the *Gazette* was quick to poke fun at the idea of a female burglar, labeling Ritchey's actions "a real broad daylight robbery." But little attention was paid to her motive. What drove a woman who was able to successfully sell dresses to Irvington housewives—meaning she presented as middle-class—and whose husband was a printer for the *New York Herald Tribune*, to commit a heist and then trade the loot for a pittance? "Mrs. Ritchey claims that this was her first offense and that she lost every sense of reason in committing such a crime."[62] She was desperate enough to have tried other houses first, though, including Ralph Matthiessen's. It is reasonable to suppose she was a casualty of the times.

At the district attorney's office in White Plains, Ritchey pleaded with Betty for forgiveness. Betty was "sympathetically inclined" after hearing all the details, *The New York Times* reported. But the violation was too upsetting. "Mrs. Matthiessen said she would press the charge of first degree grand larceny."[63] Matty signed the paperwork.

AT SIX YEARS OF AGE, dressed in gray flannel, red tie, and scuffed black shoes, Peter matriculated at the tony St. Bernard's School, which offered, in his words, "a British faculty, first-grade Latin, and strong Old World ideas about corporal punishment and other enlightenments not municipally approved in New York City."[64]

After graduating from Columbia, Matty had gone to work for Henry Otis Chapman & Son, an architecture firm responsible for bank buildings and upmarket private residences. Chapman & Son had an office in Midtown Manhattan, and he traveled back and forth from Irvington, which is less than an hour away by train. Once the children reached school age, however, the family moved for fall and spring terms to a leased apartment at 1165 Fifth Avenue. Central Park was directly across the street (the reservoir and meadows were visible from the living room windows); Brearley, where Mary enrolled, was a short drive or bus ride away; and St. Bernard's was right around the corner, four stories of brick and limestone on East 98th Street. Here "pink-kneed St. Bernard's boys," escorted by their nannies, would brush past "sullen youth of the more sallow neighborhoods" just a few blocks further north.[65] It was the closest Peter had yet come to the hard truths of poverty.

St. Bernard's was one of the best private schools in the city, and its purpose was to prepare boys for the best boarding schools in the country.[66] Founded in 1904 by an Englishman named John Card Jenkins, it was rigorous, Christian, and inherently conservative—the motto, *Perge Sed Caute*, means "Push on, but cautiously." Days were long (8 a.m. to 5 p.m.), and sportsmanship was prized almost as highly as scholarship. Many decades later, Peter, carousing with another "Old Boy" from St. Bernard's at a party, would still be able to sing the school's Football Song, which had been drummed into his head like the Hail Mary: "We do not mind the winter wind / Or weep o'er summer's bier, / Nor care a jot if cold or hot, / So long as football's here. . . ." The competitive spirit was encouraged each year at Sports Day, where students went up against one another in races, then watched from the sidelines as their chauffeurs took a turn.

In the classroom, Francis Ritchie's *First Steps in Latin* was a compulsory text, and students were expected to memorize poetry by the likes of John Masefield and Robert Browning. One master, Vere Manders, used Greek mythology to illustrate the fundamentals of storytelling. Peter excelled in history and reading comprehension, learning how to diagram complex sentences to tease out the grammatical function of every word, which was "invaluable for a career in writing," he later commented, appalled that his own college students (when he eventually became a teacher himself) were incapable of saying "what part of speech 'however' is."[67]

But all this learning paled, in his memory, when compared to the discipline. As veterans of the Great War, some faculty members seemed to treat the classrooms as extensions of the front line. Erasers were lobbed over desks at the inattentive; ears were grabbed and twisted; outstretched palms were slapped raw; and an aptly named Mr. Strange punctuated his points by applying a ruler to the base of Peter's skull.[68]

One morning, the young Matthiessen was escorted, with James W. Symington, a future chief of protocol of the United States and four-term member of the U.S. House of Representatives, to the school auditorium, where they were handed pairs of boxing gloves. A master then commanded them, as Peter recalled, to beat up "two sullen little boys, similarly dressed and gloved but scarcely half our size, just to give them a taste of what it felt like to be bullied." Peter and James protested, to no avail; then they "dabbed" at the little boys "unhappily," everyone teetering on the verge of tears.[69] That night, Peter confessed to Matty what had happened in the auditorium. Matty exploded in anger, growling that the British schoolmasters had broken every rule in the book. He threatened to report the teacher to the municipal authorities and withdraw both his sons from school. This response so unsettled Peter, being wildly out of character for his father, that he refrained, lest Matty carry through on the threat, from mentioning "bombardment," another supervised game in which students pummeled the weakest members of the class with soccer balls until they were pinned against the wall and pleading for mercy.

Like James Symington, several of Peter's classmates would grow up to become prominent public figures, including Arthur Ochs "Punch" Sulzberger, publisher of *The New York Times*. Some would remain lifelong friends with Peter, including the landscape painter Sheridan "Sherry" Lord, but none would loom as large in his future as the boy named George Ames Plimpton. Even at the age of eight, "George was gangly limbed and plummy voiced, an extroverted participant in school Pierrot shows and Shakespeare plays," and already possessed, Matthiessen wrote, of "that bright-eyed pointy-nosed expression found in woodland creatures on the point of mischief."[70] It would be years before their friendship bore its legendary fruit, *The Paris Review*, but the seed was planted at St. Bernard's. Peter coedited a newsletter, *The Weekly Blues*—"ORDER YOUR COPY OF THE BLUE AHEAD TO AVOID DISA POINTMENT"—and George was a colorful presence in its irregularly typewritten pages: "Plimpton forced home many runs with his wildness.... Third base Matthiessen played poorly.... All the outfielders were perfect in their role of day dreamers."[71]

Matthiessen later said that George Plimpton, like many children raised in strict but fortunate circumstances—his father was the prominent lawyer Francis T. P. Plimpton, a close friend of Adlai Stevenson—"had a naughty streak, which was one reason I liked him, being perpetually in trouble myself."[72] No doubt it helped that they lived in the same building.* This proximity meant that George quite possibly (Peter hedged on this point, his memory fuzzy) joined the Matthiessen brothers in committing acts of terrorism against pedestrians in the street below. The stratagem was simple: paper bags pilfered from the kitchen, which Peter and Carey, and maybe George, filled with water and then lobbed out the living room window, aiming for "a good splashy near-miss."

> I don't think George was there the day when, peering out the window, dripping bags at the ready, we saw a woman killed outright as she tried to cross Fifth Avenue to Central Park: the poor thing stepped out from

---

* For a while, anyway. Sometime around 1936, Matty relocated the family to another apartment in the fortress-like edifice of 1185 Park Avenue. Peter's memories of this building focused on the trains outside, which exited a subway tunnel "like dragons from beneath one's feet." The writer Anne Roiphe, who lived there at the same time, offers a more nuanced portrait in her book, *1185 Park Avenue*: "Doormen with white gloves and gold braid on their hats opened the taxi doors. Elevator men with Irish names and shining shoes pushed levers forward or backward.... In the large windowless basements with gray stone walls Negro laundresses washed clothes by hand in white enamel tubs.... From eight in the morning till six at night the steam rose from the heavy pressing irons, ten, twenty laundresses at a time bending, standing, the smell of human sweat mingling with soap powders hanging in the wet and heavy air."

between two parked cars. It was early in the morning and the taxis were going lickety-split—*wham!*[73]

Their nanny, Maisie O'Brien, yanked the brothers away from the carnage, but too late to stop them from absorbing the details. Flesh slamming against metal ("as if the woman had attacked the taxi")[74] was a sound that would echo through Peter's head for years, the first incursion of the real into a sheltered childhood.

A warmhearted Irish woman, Maisie was a doting surrogate parent. During the four school years the family resided in New York, she chaperoned Peter around the city to the Madison Avenue Armory, where he practiced his equestrian skills in the drill ring; to the American Museum of Natural History, where he liked to inspect the imposing skeleton of Tyrannosaurus rex; and to the Bronx Zoo, where lions and elephants kept "solitary counsel" in cages. ("I don't doubt that a lifelong interest in wild creatures, shared with my brother, Carey, had its inception in those lordly Victorian halls.")[75]

One afternoon, Maisie took her charge to the Ringling Bros. Circus at Madison Square Garden. Sitting amongst five thousand spectators, eating pink cotton candy from a paper cone, Peter watched, spellbound, as something went terribly wrong: "a missed 'catch' on the high trapeze, a small arching body, a split second of suspense, and once again that scary *thump*, much louder than sawdust striking a young woman's soft body could ever be thought to produce."[76] Here was another shock he would never forget: Miss America Olvera, who had declined to use a net, was rushed to hospital with facial lacerations and badly broken arms.[77]

TWO MONTHS SHY of Peter's tenth birthday, Matty made the surprise purchase of an old colonial house and forty-seven acres of land in rural Connecticut.[78] Stamford was a growing hub of American manufacturing—the company headquarters of Pitney Bowes, Clairol, and Schick Dry Shaver, Inc.—and it was home to some 45,000 residents. Matty's acquisition was near enough to reach the conveniences of Stamford, yet far enough away, five miles northwest, that it also felt secluded. Long Ridge, with its fallow hills and farmland, was so sparsely populated that number addresses were rarely used there. You could write a letter to "the Matthiessens on Riverbank Road" and it would inevitably find its target.

The house was shaded from the street by a line of prosperous conifers. A separate garage featured an upstairs apartment for staff. A dirt track climbed to a large barn, and a stream meandered its way across the property: a tributary of the Mianus River, shaded by a multitude of maples and oaks. A previous occupant had installed stonewall horse jumps on an open grassy course, maintained for foxhunting. The only conspicuous sign of modern times anywhere close by was the Merritt Parkway, then under construction just down the road.

There were several reasons why Matty and Betty might have felt compelled to make such a drastic change of scene. Even if the Depression had, as Peter said, no material impact on the Matthiessens, it transformed Irvington, which had already seen the Ardsley Club sold off and converted into the Hudson House Apartments. Vast private estates were fracturing into smaller lots, and even Matthiessen Park had undergone at least one significant subdivision. Matty would sell his last few acres in 1941, thereby abandoning the town at what was clearly an inflection point, cloistered privilege giving way to the commuter suburb that Irvington is today.[79]

But perhaps a more compelling reason was fatigue. "They were getting a little sick of their social life," Mary recalled—"or my mother was getting sick of Dad's social life." The excitement of being in Irvington or New York "wore off a bit, and maybe they thought it would be better for us to be in the country."[80] This aligns with a letter Betty had written to *The Irvington Gazette* in which she argued that play was "the most important means for the education of a child. If we do not allow children to have a normal childhood now, they can not come back and have it later."[81] A "normal childhood," at least as Betty understood it based on her own in Short Hills, was simple and unfettered—an easier proposition in rural Connecticut than it was on the Upper East Side of Manhattan in the 1930s.

Mary quickly adjusted to her new circumstances. She sunbathed, played tennis at the Field Club, and made a large group of friends around Bedford Hills, New Canaan, and Greenwich, including George H. W. "Poppy" Bush, who would go on to summarize her in a presidential biography as "very pretty, very flirty. Fine body. Cute sense of humor."[82] But for Peter and Carey, the move was nothing short of a revelation. They were enrolled in the Greenwich Country Day School but left alone on weekends to run wild. If Fishers Island was an Eden inhabited for a few months each summer, Long Ridge, with its frogs, turtles, and salamanders, offered the same blissful communion with nature year-round.

One day the brothers discovered a copperhead den on a rocky slope that Matty had cleared near the house. Thrilled, they pinned snakes behind the head using a forked tree branch, captured seven, carried them into the house, and christened them with fanciful names like Morgan le Fay. "You know the kind of desk that has cubbyholes?" said Cis Ormsby, a friend who would eventually marry Carey. "The snakes were in the cubbyholes."[83] The brothers acquired other species via mail order, or through their parents' social connections: Raymond Lee Ditmars, the esteemed herpetologist at the Bronx Zoo, presented Carey with the gift of an eastern indigo snake, which Peter later declared "a glorious addition to our rather drab local collection."[84] The boys let the serpents slither over their shoes, or hid them in heart-stopping pranks during Mary's sleepovers. ("They thought it was a riot," said Shirley Howard, a friend of Mary's who discovered a garter snake in her bed.)[85] The brothers also invited the neighborhood kids over to watch, for twenty-five cents a viewing, frogs and mice get swallowed whole. "Peter hoped you would appreciate his collection," said Tom Guinzburg. "He was almost like a little child showing his special dolls. He was very particular about what he had and what they seemed to mean to him." Other boys his age hoarded baseball paraphernalia: "His room was a repository of living things."[86] Eventually Betty, having decided the menagerie was too dangerous, ordered the boys to destroy all the snakes, but Peter just released them outside when she wasn't paying attention. He likely avoided drawing her attention to the venomous snakes he caught during family vacations on Captiva Island in Florida: Eastern diamondback rattlesnakes, coral snakes, pygmy rattlers, and water moccasins.*

Betty installed a large bird feeder in the yard, and this, too, became an object of fixation for her young sons. "I must have worn out a half dozen dog-eared copies of that small blue book," Peter once commented, referring to Roger Tory Peterson's *A Field Guide to the Birds*.[87] He convinced his father to install an elaborate coop up a narrow ladder in the barn. "In adolescence I needed a lot of solitude (and got somewhat more than I bargained for) and would perch up there under the eaves with the barn swallows and spiders, exulting in my dovecote for hours at a time, watching my pretty fliers come and go through the small entrance."[88] The question of where the doves went, liberated by flight, was fuel for a young boy's imagination.

Matty turned out to be as handy with tools as he was with his golf clubs, and the old social engagements were soon replaced with outdoor projects: cutting down trees, filling in ponds, digging new ponds. Having left Henry Otis Chapman & Son when the senior partner died, he now opened his own

---

* One spring when Matthiessen was in his twenties, he went birdwatching with a friend in a Gulf Coast bayou. The friend, a pilot, stepped on a water moccasin. "He jumped back, ashen-faced," Matthiessen recalled. "I was scared, too, but I wanted that snake for an undamaged specimen to take home. I found a strong stick, pressed it down right behind the snake's head—hard but not too hard—and while he was pinned, grabbed him at the neck, forefinger and thumb tip under the lower jaw as he writhed, mouth open to show the cotton-white interior. Back at the airstrip, I took a two-gallon jug, filled it with water, and slipped the snake in, still very much alive, making the pilot very nervous because the Piper was a two-seater and I held the jug on my lap; the landing at New Orleans was light as a flower petal to avoid breaking that jug. We left instructions to clean and refuel the plane, but next morning, we found four of the airport crew surrounding the untouched plane in horror, even though that snake [left inside] had died overnight."

architecture firm in Stamford, with a second office in Manhattan on East 53rd Street. Matthiessen, Johnson & Green specialized in luxury houses, private clubs—the Beach House on Fishers Island's Club Beach—and the occasional charity project. Matty had found his calling as a "society architect," which meant he mostly designed show homes for wealthy acquaintances such as John ("Jock") Hay Whitney, publisher, philanthropist, and president of the Museum of Modern Art.

One thing that didn't change in Connecticut was Matty's comportment toward the children. He absorbed his sons' enthusiasm for birds (he would later become a trustee of the Nature Conservancy, a vice president and board member of the Audubon Society), but he still had no idea how to relate to them. As Mary got older, she would sometimes sit next to her father at club dinners: "Some lovely lady would be on the other side, and I'd just look at his back the whole time. That really hurt. I struggled to talk to him, yet he came to life when some attractive, smart, young woman came along."[89]

Of course, Peter's mother noticed this, too, and the cumulative effect on Betty was ruinous. Depression already ran down the Carey line: George, her father, committed suicide by filling his pockets with stones and walking into a millpond not long after the Matthiessens moved to Connecticut. This predisposition was helped along in Betty by a growing realization that life with Matty was not going to be quite what she'd imagined for herself; that she would fight to keep up with her dynamo husband; that she *needed* to be charming to compete for attention; and that, even then, it would probably not be enough. Much later, Matty would admit that he and Betty differed in many ways, "in our views and our tastes, our temperaments and our very outlook on life."[90] But he was able to compartmentalize these differences and find satisfaction elsewhere. Betty, being primly traditional and subordinate to his whims, could not do that, so a bitter gloom began to engulf her. "In the lottery of life, I don't think she had a bad deal," said Rue Matthiessen, who became Betty's granddaughter after Peter adopted her during his second marriage to Deborah Love. "But she never contended with her bitterness. She was of that generation where you started drinking at five o'clock on a weekday, and ten o'clock in the morning on a weekend, and you drank continually in that WASPy way that must have functioned as a kind of numbing agent."[91]

Years hence, some of Betty's grandchildren would visit her bedroom in Long Ridge, where she liked to recline on a chaise longue, Dubonnet in hand, watching through the window as birds visited the feeder. Her sadness was palpable, and she could be warm or very cold depending on its severity. One day she had what was likely a transient ischemic attack—a brief stroke-like blackout. She awoke disoriented, speaking gibberish. When she finally recovered her wits, a grandson asked her where she'd gone. "My dear," Betty replied, "I went to the Valley of the Shadow."[92]

MUCH OF MATTHIESSEN'S WRITINGS in his memoir notes is inflected with a tone of ineffable longing. He recalls the landscapes of his childhood as a series of oases—but there is also an unmistakable note of self-flagellation. He accuses himself of being a "terrible sissy" who felt things more keenly than a boy properly should. This criticism is only partially elaborated in his surviving drafts, as though he'd delayed confronting the most painful parts of childhood: "Upchuck in assembly out of nerves"; "Red Riding Hood costume as a child—fearful of sissy rep"; spectacles that were "a mortal insult to vanity."[93] Yet there is one incident that he wrote about in particular detail, perhaps because it was the defining event of his early life.

Two types of water were visible from the family beach on Fishers Island. Nearest was what Peter called the "green water," six to ten feet deep over white sand. Beyond that, the sand dropped away to the sapphire depths of Fishers Island Sound, and this was thus the "blue water." He was untroubled by the green, could tolerate the blue, but the space in-between, where the colors merged in a liminal zone of "dark amorphous shapes shrouded by algae," filled him with terror: "those strange fronds straining toward the surface . . . might well conceal gigantic crabs and savage moray eels and monsters heretofore unknown to science."[94]

One Saturday morning, Matty stopped by the Hay Harbor Club to test the progress of his children's swimming lessons. Peter joined Mary and Carey aboard the *Puddleduck*, his father's boat, and they motored away from the shore. When Matty was satisfied they were far enough out, he cut the engine. Then he told the children to jump. Peter peeked over the side and realized they had stopped in the dreaded "shadow region." As Mary and Carey took the plunge, he refused. "Humiliated but very frightened, I disobeyed a direct command." In Peter's recollection, Mary, swimming blithely around the boat, pronounced him "silly," and Carey turned away in embarrassment. Then an exasperated Matty picked up his son and started to toss him overboard—"in effect, to cast me from his sight." Peter clutched at his father's shirt, which had the effect of shortening Matty's throw. As a result, Peter's forearm slammed into the gunwale before he hit the water, a "violation" that was so unexpected he was shouting as he surfaced. Sonofabitch! Dirty bastard! "The very worst swear words that in those gentle days a well-brought-up Wasp child might ever be heard to utter."

Back at the house, Peter was banished to the upstairs playroom. He sulked while waiting for his mother, who would "surely" rush to examine his outrageous injury. But Betty considered his language the more serious transgression. "On her way downstairs in a flowered bathing suit, Mum scarcely deigned to poke her curls around the door. *'We are so dreadfully ashamed of you!'* she said. And in the echo of that closed door, I was left alone with my throbbing arm and lacerated heart for the remainder of that endless summer day."

Peter would rehearse his version of these events for countless listeners over the decades. He would allude to it in public interviews with journalists: "I've been angry since I was about eight. And I had good reason to be angry, but I didn't realize until years later that it had actually seeped into my entire life."[95] He would even dredge up the memory during experimental drug therapy, wracked by phantom pains as he attempted to pinpoint the moment in his past when everything had started to go wrong. "Christ, my fucking hand hurts," he scribbled in a diary on June 15, 1969, tripping on 400 micrograms of LSD taken with a cup of coffee in Italy.[96] In his memoir notes, he wrote:

> I can still reconstitute the entire scene from start to finish, including the long white toy-chest bench I was kneeling on, peering out like a spook as the hum of the motor idling down there below the red geraniums in the window came to an end and the parade departed without me, abandoning the now fully certified sissy in the family to his shameful disgrace. But by that day's end, I was feeling less ashamed and frightened than lonely and betrayed, and even vengeful, nursing fantasies of murder. Though never much of a weeper, I may well have wept, in the deep instinct that these heretofore beloved grown-ups were not to be trusted, in fact never again.[97]

The sensitive child had been punished for feeling too much. Like a left-handed boy forced to contort his right hand around a pencil to satisfy a teacher, Peter was taught to suppress his inclinations in favor of performing the socially sanctioned role of a "well-brought-up Wasp child." To stumble in that performance was, as he put it, to risk being branded as something short of a real man. Manhood, or at least the kind represented by his gruff, inaccessible father, demanded he dissociate from his true self. Who Peter was, for Matty and Betty, was less important than who Peter *should* be. The ugly incident on the boat was his earliest memory of failing to live up to an impossible ideal. Nearly eight decades later, the event would remain, in Matthiessen's mind, a foundational trauma, "the opening skirmish in an absolutely pointless lifelong war" with his parents. He would still be raking through the wreckage on his deathbed.

2

The Curly God

> George felt unbearably oppressed. Yet he knew there was nothing unbearable in his life ... and the guilty paradox of his existence angered him. He had money and friends and position, everything his father had wrenched so bodily from life. . . . Was it a surfeit of things, or simply a deepening inevitable boredom?
>
> —*Race Rock* (1954)[1]

Peter's childhood rebellion began with incivility—talking back to elders, hiding outside when he was called in for dinner—and escalated, once he reached adolescence, into minor acts of delinquency. One summer he was entrusted with a .22-caliber rifle so he could go hunting with his father on Fishers Island. He stationed himself on the family beach, took aim at the house, and opened fire on an attic window. Another year he joined a friend whom many parents considered "criminal or crazy or ungovernable at the very least" and teed up more than fifty golf balls that belonged to the friend's father; these were socked, one by one, from a sea wall into Long Island Sound. Breaking rules felt "very exciting" to the two boys, yet after they were caught and sentenced to three days of dusty chores at a rock quarry in Connecticut, Peter found himself wondering what the point had been: "*Why* did I join him?"[2]

One reason was attention. He was desperate to be seen. The more he believed he was invisible or misunderstood, the more often he unleashed his frustration by turning into "that rotten Matthiessen kid."

In the house on Fishers Island, a hardwood hallway ran from the front door right through to the rear terrace. On a day when Betty and Matty were entertaining guests in the living room, Peter positioned himself near the front door and rolled, tenpin bowling style, a giant ball bearing down the length of the hallway. The bearing banged against the terrace door, and then Peter rolled it in reverse, banging the front door, back and forth, until Matty finally emerged from the party and kicked him outside.

As the cocktails resumed, Peter gathered up some rocks. He approached an "elegant mocha-colored roadster," which belonged to a guest named Maitland Griggs. Peter liked Mr. Griggs, his godfather, who had always been friendly toward him; but he was spoiling for a fight. He threw rocks at the car until Griggs rushed out and bellowed at him to stop. Matty reacted more forcefully, running up and administering a blow that sent Peter sprawling in the dirt. As Peter recalled the scene in his notes, Matty then struggled to speak, mortified that he'd lost his temper in front of guests. Having thus humiliated his father, Peter crept away to await "the lonely fate of martyrs."[3]

In 1975, Matty would write a letter to Peter that attempted to articulate their early relationship from his perspective: "You were just beginning to feel the power of that great mind of yours, and there was much that in my inexperience and lack of wisdom that I didn't understand. In a way I was working from the defensive position, making quick judgments, trying to preserve my status as pater f. and making a bit of a hash of it."[4] This remained unacknowledged during Peter's childhood, though every now and then one of Matty's friends would pull the boy aside to make a well-intentioned plea for his understanding. Matty Matthiessen, these friends insisted, was a generous, fair, honorable figure, and anyone would be lucky to have him as their father. Some of Peter's own friends felt the same way. John Nelson Cole, who, as Peter's college roommate, often visited the Matthiessens in Stamford, once published a tribute to Matty as the perfect role model: "His tall presence radiated good humor, a zest for life.... Matty could have asked me to become an account executive with Chase Manhattan, and I would have tried. I would have done anything he asked because he was, and had always been, one of the few among my older generation who gave me such good reasons to believe there could be life after youth."[5] Such encomiums would have struck Peter as risible while he was still living at home. "What Peter never got," recalled his sister, Mary, "was Dad's vulnerability and inner weakness, and his lack of self-confidence."[6]

Believing himself unfairly judged and insufficiently loved, Peter fixated on his father's failings as a form of retaliation. Matty was outraged, for instance, when the Fishers Island Club rejected a membership application from Bernard Baruch, the financier and philanthropist, on the grounds that Baruch was Jewish. Yet Matty refrained from voicing his liberal sympathies to other members of the club lest it impact his own social standing. "He went along with it," Mary said, "and *then* he'd come home and complain." Peter observed the disparity between his father's public persona and private convictions and refused to reconcile the two sides into a single person worthy of respect.

His lack of respect would become an important feature of his first published novel, *Race Rock*, in which an emotionally volatile young scion, George

McConville, struggles to understand what it means to be a man, largely as a product of his father's confusing influence. ("Do I suffer? Just decide to go someplace and suffer? Do I take responsibilities? . . . What does one ever do?")[7] George's father, Cyrus McConville, is an unmistakable caricature of Matty—though Peter insisted that the novel was *not* based on either of his parents when they confronted him, wounded, upon its publication in 1954. Cyrus is charismatic but conceited, incapable of self-reflection, and wedded to a status quo that elevates him while diminishing others.* He violently rejects George's "sensitive ideas" because he finds them threatening: "For a while there, if he'd said or done one more sensitive thing I'd have strangled him with my bare hands!"[8] For his part, George comes to see everything Cyrus stands for as hollow and inauthentic, his father's life a charade sustained by the delusory power of money. "[H]ow fatuous," he thinks at one point, "to fill the shoes of the man who has crushed by his own example the incentive to do so."[9] Words that could have been spoken, fairly or not, by the novel's author.

Sometime around the start of the 1940s, Peter and a friend took up position on either side of the Merritt Parkway, which had finally opened in June 1938. Armed with BB guns, they began to shoot into passing traffic. As Matthiessen later remembered the incident, a police car soon pulled up, two officers emerged, and there was a chase through the trees. "It was a bad scene," he said.[10] Not because of any legal consequences, or even because of the reform school representative who apparently knocked on the door the following morning to discuss his future; but because of his parents. "It was being reported in the *Greenwich Time*," meaning half of Connecticut would read about his disgrace. "Was anybody going to be embarrassed by what Peter did? With both our parents, that was their terrible weakness," Mary said. "They really didn't want their friends to be shocked or offended in any way."[11] Matty and Betty were furious because Peter's conduct reflected poorly on *them*, and Peter was disgruntled because he was once again cast as an inconvenience.

---

* Agnes McConville, Cyrus's wife, fares little better in the novel. Intractable when it comes to her principles, thinking she's cultured "for the simple reason of her ancestry," she simpers about not having enough servants at a hosted lunch, nearly cries over a spill on her Turkish rug, and holds up her hand, palm outward, when she's displeased, suggesting "reproof, or horror, or pointed dismissal of the incident, but most likely all three, as her face [assumes] an almost characteristic and favorite 'Dear, dear, dear, whatever will become of us!' expression." Betty was mortified by this description, although Peter publicly dismissed her concern. "She thought I was gunning for her," he recalled in an interview in 2005, adding, "I think parents are especially sensitive. They're not only sensitive to the fact that you may be portraying them, but also, what are their friends going to think?"

IN SEPTEMBER 1941, a long procession of black sedans rumbled to the top of a hill in northwest Connecticut, where several hundred young men were gathering in front of Georgian brick buildings, which were themselves gathered before a lake called Wononscopomuc. Among this horde of students, a group of freshmen wearing black ties peered around for the first time at the place they were expected to call home for much of the next four years. None of the Class of 1945, of which Peter was a member, had any idea that a third of them would never make it to graduation day at the Hotchkiss School—that some twenty students would be called up early to serve in the armed forces.[12]

Just three months later, Japanese naval planes launched their surprise attack on Pearl Harbor. "[W]e didn't quite know where it was," recalled John Luke, who was sitting in a Hotchkiss common room when reports of the bombings began to circulate; "nor could we appreciate the magnitude of what happened."[13] The situation became clearer the following day, on December 8, as the entire student body sat before a radio listening to President Roosevelt deliver his Infamy Speech: "There is no blinking at the fact that our people, our territory, and our interests are in grave danger. . . ."

Peter was fourteen when the United States joined the war. This was his first time at boarding school, and it became a transitional moment for both him and Hotchkiss, which mobilized to meet the demands of a strange new reality.[14] Some of the masters withdrew from teaching responsibilities so they could go off and fight; others began to take shifts as air raid wardens, watching the night sky for signs of the enemy. George Van Santvoord, the headmaster, tried to prevent the oldest students from absconding to enlist; he would eventually adjust the academic calendar to offer an extra summer session so boys could finish their studies before they turned eighteen, when the draft would get them anyway. A Victory Garden was planted on the school's extensive grounds, and certain sports were suspended so students could maintain it. Instead of running track on Baker Field, they might plant potatoes. Interscholastic competitions and away games were all canceled. "Maybe one football game, but that was it," remembered Blair Childs, one of Peter's classmates. "Especially in the first year there was very little interaction with anybody outside the school. We were basically in a bubble."[15]

Yet isolation was one of the points of Hotchkiss. Founded in 1891 by Maria Bissell Hotchkiss and opened the following year for an enrollment of just fifty students, the school was intended to cultivate gentlemen for Yale—future leaders who embodied Christian values and American self-sufficiency. The surest way to accomplish this goal, or so the reasoning went, was to remove all temptations for vice. Given that cities were widely considered to be breeding grounds for immorality, Hotchkiss was built a hundred miles north of New York, in the "bracing air" of the countryside near Salisbury.[16] From the top of Town Hill, where the Main Building was erected, one could look north toward Mount Greylock in Massachusetts; west toward the Catskills; and in any direction over American elms and white pines, with Lakeville, a small town and railway station, just a mile down below. "The contour of the mountains, contrasts of color which the seasons bring, the deep blue of the lake's surface, the play of light and shade upon the mountainsides, and the golden hues of the sunset—these are ours," wrote Walter Buell, a prior headmaster, in 1925. "Material possession belongs to others— ours is spiritual."[17]

This sentiment was shared by Peter. Six months after leaving Hotchkiss, he would recall nostalgically how he "used to go out and look at the world of the lake and the mountains when I felt depressed, on the dubious theory that the greatness of Creation would place your self-centered negligible worries in their proper perspective—it used to work pretty well for me. Church has somewhat the same effect, I find."[18] He was not conventionally religious (none of the Matthiessens were devout, though they described themselves on paper as Episcopalians), but something about the landscape reassured him, in the same way that a house of worship might still offer comfort to a nonbeliever. In the two days of fall and two days of spring that students were given free rein to do as they pleased on school-wide "holidays," Peter escaped on solitary hikes, wandering the trails of Beeslick Brook Woods.

The rest of the year, Hotchkiss's schedule did not permit much time for daydreaming. You woke up in the morning; you left your dormitory room for the maids to tidy; you went to mandatory chapel. Rushing up and down a hallway that was longer than a football field and decorated with everything from seasonal flowers to plaster casts of Parthenon statues, you worked through the day, played sport in the afternoon, attended study hall, ate dinner, and then retired to bed. As an inflexible routine, it was "lousy and tough,"[19] Peter thought, and he grumbled about his inability to keep up the pace in letters to a friend: "I'm so far behind in my work."[20] This would soon become "about four years behind on my work,"[21] and finally "a frantic attempt to do four years' work in as many days."[22]

A number of elite college-preparatory schools had reputations for exacting academic standards. Few were known to be as punitive as Hotchkiss. A boy could be expelled if he was caught smoking cigarettes; he could also be expelled for repeatedly reading a book under the covers after lights-out. Short of expulsion was "sequestration," a kind of shameful social quarantine that forced a student to endure a litany of mental and physical punishments, including five-mile runs around the school triangle.[23] As with St. Bernard's, the rationale for this regime was enshrined in the school motto, lifted from

Virgil's *Aeneid: Moniti Meliora Sequamur*, which means "Having been warned, let us follow better ways." (Today the school translates it as the much softer, "Guided by each other, let us seek better paths.") Hotchkiss was meant to correct naughty boys, in the same way that wild plants can be trained to grow in a more pleasing direction.

George Van Santvoord, the headmaster since 1926, was called "the Duke" by students. He would sometimes shout at them imperiously: "You're barbarians!"[24] Some students saw him as a prejudiced bully, but others described a more benevolent figure who encouraged the boys to become Renaissance men, taking as their purview everything under the sun.[25] As the school's most conspicuous representative, he became a focus of rumors in both the student body and parental community. Conservatives whispered that he was in contact with Franklin Roosevelt, that he was "a terrible radical" and "dangerous New Dealer."[26]

At least once a year, every student was expected to sit at the headmaster's table for dinner. "He would pepper you with questions about things that were completely off the wall," recalled Blair Childs.[27] Should golf be made into a twenty-hole game? Should Lake Wononscopomuc be filled with sharks? Should Mickey Mouse be granted a driver's permit?[28] Most students dreaded sitting near the Duke, who expected his dinner companions to engage fully in this layman's koan study. "But I think Peter really liked it," said Childs. "He thought Santvoord was a terrific guy."*

The headmaster seemed to like Peter, too, although he had a few reservations. "He is an attractive person, highly mature and intelligent," Van Santvoord wrote about the young Matthiessen in a report. "He is athletic, popular, and has engaged extensively in outside activities"—soccer, hockey, tennis, swimming, skiing, English Club, and the Pigeon Club. Yet Peter also had a "dubious scholastic record," and by graduation he would be ranked fortieth in a class of sixty-seven. "It seems to us that this was due to a certain lack of effort on his part, arising out of his interest in other matters."[29]

A taste of these "other matters" can be found in the Hotchkiss *Mischianza*, a yearbook which summarized the full experience of the Class of 1945. Matthiessen's natural habitat is listed as "In intrigue." His nicknames are given as "Pete," "Matt," "Matty," "Pietros," "Lucky Pierre," "Suavete," and most

---

* "I was surprised," the editor Lewis Lapham once recalled, "by the likeness of [Matthiessen's] interests and turns of mind to those of Mr. George Van Santvoord . . . with whom [he] seemed to share not only a love of words and nature but also the courage to lead an examined and examining life." Lapham first met Matthiessen on Fishers Island in 1949, when his mother introduced them so Lewis could get some advice about Hotchkiss, where he was just about to start as a freshman. But Peter had no interest in discussing "an ornamental pillar of the bourgeois *status quo*." Instead, he identified seabirds, offered up the Latin names of nearby snakes and crabs, and speculated about the catch aboard a fishing trawler they both could see drifting on the watery horizon—far more useful information.

evocatively, "The Curly God." In a class poll published in the school newspaper, *The Hotchkiss Record*, Peter scored highly as "Wittiest," "Best Dressed," "Biggest Sponge," and "Gets Away with Most."[30] By a considerable margin, he won the title of "Biggest Operator," or most skillfully manipulative, and "Biggest Buller"—horniest. "Forsooth," he mock-protested in a letter after reading these results: "Me, the paragon of youthful integrity."[31]

A photograph in the *Mischianza* shows him sitting on his bed, oblivious as he scribbles in a notebook, which was a pose he would be caught in repeatedly by photographers over the coming decades. Above his head, a sign says, "Smoking permitted in this car"—an advertisement of his disdainful attitude toward rules. Though potentially a good student, Peter was more focused on having a good time than in applying himself to studies. He was kicked out of math class for insubordination, then kicked out of choir for more mysterious reasons. (His memoir notes say "tablecloth," with no further elaboration.) He once participated in a prank where a bucket of slops was dropped on the head of a widely despised master. He is remembered by a friend as having dangled bottles of cider outside the dorm window until they fermented in the sun. By his own admission, he stole apple-cured tobacco from the snack bar in Lakeville, then took it back to school and chewed it all up, despite loathing the taste. "Nothing like indulging one's whims," he commented stubbornly in a letter.[32] He also smuggled in a five foot eleven pilot black snake ("entirely different [from] a regular blacksnake—much rarer, much prettier, and much more vicious") and named it Jules Obispo, in honor of a character from Aldous Huxley's *After Many a Summer Dies the Swan*.[33] The snake bit his friend, Charlie "Ears" Lord, and its fate was not recorded.

"I find myself extremely unpopular with the masters these days," Peter wrote in another letter. "One old geezer took me aside for ten minutes the other day, told me I'd flunk if he had anything to say about it (and he does, damnit)."[34] A few days later, Hotchkiss hosted a string quartet. "I was sitting in my seat and suddenly looked up to behold four of the most awful-looking creeps I have ever seen, all clutching violins, all with atrocious builds and faces, and all beaming down at us."[35] Peter broke into peals of derisive laughter, which spread like a contagion to the boys around him, although "it wasn't funny at all—we just could not stop, quivering shoulders up and down the rows." The quartet played on, ignoring the insult, but Van Santvoord began to comb the audience for an instigator. Peter was "very foxy" at this point. He leaned forward in his chair and glared around at his neighbors with theatrical, accusatory disgust, throwing the Duke off the scent—"I hope."

LATER IN LIFE, Peter Matthiessen would sometimes tell a story about Hotchkiss that he liked to link to the dawning of his social conscience.[36] When and where had he first felt the stirrings of "uneasiness about unearned privilege"?[37] He cited a penitentiary corridor on Second Floor Main, where he was assigned to sleep as a sophomore after courting so much trouble in his first year.

Main Building had living space for four masters and fifty-eight students. Some of these students were the rotten apples of Hotchkiss, but others were ill or had transferred to the school too late to find a bed in the regular dorms. One of these late arrivals was a small, studious New Yorker who was destined to get "wiped out" by thugs on the same floor.[38] Peter took pity and decided to offer some advice.

The boy had no muscles for self-defense, so Peter taught him how to do push-ups. Then he warned the bullies not to try anything. This reluctant guardianship ("lordly mercy," Matthiessen later dubbed it) went on for a few weeks, until the boy, aware he was being saved from daily bouts of humiliation, had become so indebted that he invited Peter to visit his Park Avenue apartment during the upcoming Christmas vacation.[39] Maybe they could go see a movie together, the boy suggested—provided his mother approved of the plan. Peter was not looking to make friends, but he agreed, then immediately put it out of mind.

The day before the vacation period began, the boy came running with some news. The visit to New York could go ahead; his mother had looked up the Matthiessens in the *Social Register*, and Peter was deemed "presentable."

Class at Hotchkiss was weighted in unexpected ways. The students were certainly aware of pedigree and wealth; it was hard to hide who had money and who didn't at Ma Dufour's shop down in Lakeville. Yet the social hierarchy was based more on age, popularity, and accomplishments, both academic and athletic. The boy was committing a faux pas by measuring Peter by his family background. In Peter's mind, it was nothing short of a grave insult. The Matthiessens were listed in the *Social Register*, alongside thirty thousand other "presentable" families, because of Matty and Betty. The small black book with orange lettering was a symbol of *their* desires, the social milieu that dictated *their* values, a WASP code that was notable, to Peter, mostly for its constraints and prohibitions. According to this code, failure was unacceptable; and so were flagrant displays of emotion. (At the age of nineteen, he would remark that he had yet to express "any feeling" in front of his family: "On the other hand, perhaps no one else has either, so that may not be strange.")[40] Being listed in the *Social Register* was to be publicly separated out from the hoi polloi into a supposedly superior echelon, but then strapped into a straitjacket.

In Matthiessen's telling, he immediately had "a fit of antisnob-snob outrage" and rejected the boy's conditional invitation to New York.[41] Then he went home to Stamford and demanded that his name be "stricken" from all future editions of the distasteful directory. "To their great credit, my parents acceded gracefully to this overexcited request," he wrote in an essay in 1989. This is where the story usually ended: with a successful swerve away from "plump beginnings." The truth, however, was a little more complicated. While Peter almost certainly asked his parents to redact his name, either Matty and Betty lied, changed their minds, forgot to file the "blank" (a form for amendments), or were ignored by the staff who maintained the index. "Peter & G Carey" would remain "at Hotchkiss" in the annual *Registers* for 1943, 1944, and 1945, and then with various other affiliations for years afterward. (In 1949, Peter was listed "at Sorbonne"—a piece of information unlikely to have come from any source except his parents.)[42] "I remember being present many years ago, in the 50's," William Styron once recalled, "when by chance he discovered his name was still in the Social Register. I remember his rage at finding it there, and his determination to get it out."[43] Matthiessen had not exiled himself quite as "gracefully" as he liked to suggest. Still, he narrated his tidy anecdote so often, and with such conviction, that it would be repeated as fact in his *New York Times* obituary.

ANOTHER HOTCHKISS STORY Matthiessen liked to tell concerned the "shock" that made him realize "there was something I did not understand about life."[44]

St. Luke's Society, the oldest student organization at Hotchkiss, was a charity club offering students the chance to give something back through volunteer work, like visiting the elderly or serving in a soup kitchen. One day, St. Luke's recruited counselors to attend a two-week summer camp for, as Matthiessen later put it, "little hellions out of the New Haven slums"—the New Haven Boys Club, which provided services for young immigrants and poor boys whose mothers were working in factories while their fathers fought on the front lines.[45] Peter signed up with a friend ("I said sure, let's do that"), probably after a nudge from Matty, who was adamant that his children do their part for the war effort. "We weren't allowed to slouch around," recalled Mary, who spent one of her own summers rolling bandages for the Red Cross and another working as a nurse's aide in Bellevue Hospital.[46]

Peter was only a year older than the New Haven boys he was charged with supervising. They were all housed together in a single small cabin—"tough kids with their own turf," and Peter, who felt outnumbered and unimpressive in his prescription glasses, "a real four-eyed wonder."[47] But something odd happened on the first night of camp. For dinner, the cook served a towering buffet of hamburgers, hot dogs, coleslaw, and corn on the cob. The boys devoured all of it, gorging as much food as they could fit on their plates. Then, back in the cabin, one of them threw up. Then another boy vomited, and so on, until "the whole camp was a symphony of upchucking." They had stuffed themselves sick. Peter was amazed by the turn of events: "I never realized what it must feel like to be brought up and never have enough."

He soon found his footing as a counselor. "I got my kids to stop fighting in the simplest way. Instead of yanking them apart and risking getting punched out myself, I just lay back on my bunk and watched them fight. I never said a word. I was like a Roman at the gladiator [arena]. And in an amazingly short time they stopped fighting, there were no more fights. It was all for show. . . . They were showing off for me."[48]

Yet he was haunted by "a really bad feeling" that he had missed, somewhere in his own childhood, an important lesson about inequality. That such a banal realization should come as a "shock" shows just how cosseted Peter was at the time. "I think people in power shelter themselves from poverty," he later observed, "because they really don't want to know about it."[49] Once *he* knew what lay outside the bubbles of Hotchkiss, Stamford, and Fishers Island, it was impossible to fully retreat into the numb ignorance that had been his element since birth. And so, he concluded, "I became more and more [of a] social activist within the terms of my existence."[50] Those terms were inevitably limited at a place like Hotchkiss, but evidence of the shift can perhaps be found in his earliest writing.

ALL GOOD WRITERS BEGIN as readers. Peter liked to devour dime novels about the Golden Age of Piracy, along with James Fenimore Cooper's *Leatherstocking Tales*, which he credited with inciting his interest in Native American culture. As a child he preferred "the true real strangeness of wild regions on the maps to the never-never realms of fairy tales and myths."[51] But he made an exception for anything about animals—A. A. Milne's *Winnie-the-Pooh*, and Beatrix Potter's stories of Squirrel Nutkin or Peter Rabbit. Then there was Kenneth Grahame's *The Wind in the Willows*, and particularly its seventh chapter, "The Piper at the Gates of Dawn," where Mole and Ratty go searching for a lost baby otter and discover it dozing at the feet of a flute-playing Pan:

> Then suddenly the Mole felt a great Awe fall upon him, an awe that turned his muscles to water, bowed his head, and rooted his feet to the ground. It was no panic terror—indeed he felt wonderfully at peace and happy—

but it was an awe that smote and held him and, without seeing, he knew it could only mean that some august Presence was very, very near. With difficulty he turned to look for his friend, and saw him at his side cowed, stricken, and trembling violently. And still there was utter silence in the populous bird-haunted branches around them; and still the light grew and grew.[52]

This chapter, Matthiessen once wrote, is "a more profound manifestation of mystical experience than almost anything to be found in the 'religious' literature."[53] It would remain one of his favorite pieces of writing as an adult, discussed in books (*The Snow Leopard*), speeches, articles, and roundtable discussions: "Pan is not simply a goat man with horns and a flute. He is the Universal Power, the air, the breath of being . . . the pure beauty of the life force that permeates everything, even a stone."[54]

Another childhood favorite was Rudyard Kipling. The adventures of Kipling's anthropomorphized menagerie were not only exciting but infused with "a feeling of the withheld and the unfathomable," which was a heady mix for a child prone to daydreams.[55] Because these adventures occurred outside the constraints of civilization, they suggested other ways to be and behave beyond the models presented by unimaginative parents. In "Toomai of the Elephants," a boy rides a wise old elephant named Kala Nag ("Black Snake") to a secret elephant dance deep in the Indian jungle; Matthiessen credited this "extraordinary scene" with giving him a "yearning for wild places and wild experience that was to become so important in my life." Only much later, in "more enlightened times," would he come to frown upon the colonial sensibility baked into Kipling's escapism, just as he would eventually critique the racism in another book that thrilled him as a child, *The Story of Little Black Sambo*, by Helen Bannerman, an Englishwoman living in India under the British Raj who "never bothered her head about useless distinctions between one group of dark-skinned 'natives' and another."[56]

After a few years at Hotchkiss, Peter's literary tastes had broadened considerably. "I seem to spend all my time around here reading instead of working," he wrote in one of several letters that included recommendations for novels by the likes of Louis Bromfield and Thomas Wolfe.[57] Somerset Maugham's *Of Human Bondage*, about "a sort of club-footed meatball" who dreams of becoming an artist before abandoning such romantic inclinations, was "really a very gripping book."[58] Meanwhile, Richard Wright's *Black Boy*, which Peter read within a month of its release, was "not as affective if more reasonable than his Native Son."[59]

In another letter, he singled out William Saroyan's *Dear Baby*, a collection of short stories, published in 1944, that included "The Story of the Young

Man and the Mouse." Toward the end of this vaguely surrealist sketch, there is a sentence—"The mouse watched the young man quietly for five days and five nights, and then it died"—which "should strike you after a bit right between the eyes," Peter wrote. "Sentiment of <u>this</u> kind has tremendous appeal for me."[60] The use of animals as conduits for complicated emotions was a narrative strategy he would later employ in his own work, once admitting that wildlife was "a metaphor and an evocative trigger to the imagination . . . to mystery, to strangeness."[61]

Peter began to write around the age of fifteen; he found himself scribbling compulsively with no clear sense of why he was doing it. "It's a disease," he later joked, before suggesting just the opposite: "It restores your balance and your sanity in some way."[62] In English classes at Hotchkiss, the master John McChesney pushed him to experiment with various forms and subjects. ("He opened my eyes to what was really happening in literature," the journalist John Hersey told historian Ernest Kolowrat of his own lessons with "Mr. Mac." "He got me out of Galsworthy and into Faulkner at a time when Faulkner had published only three novels and was far from famous.")[63] In one notable instance, Peter labored for three hours at a poem about the Renaissance, only to receive a "lousy" grade. Then he dashed off another in (he claimed) a little more than thirty minutes, "To the Beauty of Sun on Copper," about a copperhead snake:

> From varied scants of spring-waked life,
> Of rain-blown freshness, new-formed green,
> And hungry patter, woodland scene,
> Slides forth the subtle serpent lean,
> With wake of silence, writhing sheen,
> To edge of trees, to end of strife. [. . .][64]

Despite some clumsy phrases, the poem's vividly observed details ("markings of the hour-glass," "metal stare") earned it the highest grade given out that year. Which surprised Peter, because hadn't he worked six times harder on the Renaissance poem? When he approached Mr. Mac, the master explained that "poems were worthless to him unless <u>sincere</u>," and that he "didn't think the first to be sincere." Peter accepted this teaching and acknowledged that his earlier piece had come from intellect rather than the heart—but, he added in a letter afterward, "I wish I'd <u>known</u> this before wasting the time on it."[65]

In his third year at Hotchkiss, he was elected advertising manager of the *Mischianza*, alongside his friend Thornton "Gus" Lyttle (who would die in 1945 at the Battle of Iwo Jima); in his final year, Peter would be promoted to chairman. He also started experimenting with fiction—"an idea for a story is burgeoning in my dwarfed brain, creating a strange burning odor"[66]— and submitted several pieces to *The Lit*, a separate literary journal that published comic strips, short stories, and nonfiction reports by students. Some of Peter's pieces survive, and they are just as green as he later suggested. In "The Grave of Time," a young man gets fall-down drunk in New York and, having missed his train by three minutes and three seconds, plunges into a fugue state that becomes increasingly unhinged: "Above Grand Central is New York and so too is New York above and all around us, even in these faces, the small, drained faces peculiar to New York. Heavy-featured, painted and vulgar, furtive and impotent, morbid and vulpine, all with the common hue of the stale white or artificial red—face upon face, face within face and unnatural stream of unnatural humanity, of shame, confusion, depravity and staleness, always staleness . . ."[67] And so on, to an incoherent ending.

There is one piece of work from this period that stands apart from the rest. Written in the spring of 1944, when Peter was sixteen years old, it was his response to a series of articles in the *New York Herald Tribune* about a racially charged conflict that occurred in Great Meadows, New Jersey.[68] Over the protests of his neighbors, a man named Edward Kowalick had chosen to hire Japanese American laborers to work on his farm. Kowalick already had one employee, George Yamamoto, and he brought in an additional five men from the Gila River Relocation Center, in Arizona, via the War Relocation Authority. Kowalick's decision was seen by neighbors as almost treasonous, and somebody erected a sign on Route 6 pointing toward his farm: "To Little Tokio, 1 Mile." Four hundred members of the Great Meadows community had converged on the local school for a crisis meeting. When somebody mentioned "Christian values," another farmer responded: "We'll show them love with shotguns." Kowalick received threatening phone calls, and then his barn mysteriously caught on fire, incinerating seven tons of fertilizer. Eventually he caved to the pressure and released the workers. "A delegation of his neighbors visited him after the Japanese left at 11 a.m.," the *Herald Tribune* reported on April 14. "They gave Mr. Kowalick a box of cigars and turned the visit into a belated impromptu birthday celebration."

Peter read about the conflict, then crafted his own account of events, titled "The Rousing of the Rabble," which was far more animated than the reasonably objective reportage of the *Herald Tribune*. Borrowing quotes from the newspaper as raw material—and then adding some embroidery: burning the barn became "a coup d'etat on the Kowalick out-house"—he portrayed the townsfolk as reactionary buffoons "exuding sage comments and mouthing patriotic phrases."[69] For Peter, the aggrieved in this scenario were clearly the Japanese Americans, irrationally transformed from laborers into "evil forces" needing to be exorcised from the community. "As the news settled over New Jersey on Saturday night, the honest folk sighed happily as they sank into their musky beds," he wrote disdainfully of the outcome. "The danger was over, they had done well."

There was little in the way of serious analysis here, and no suggestion that he understood the politics of the situation. There was much, in fact, that was plainly juvenile, confusing sarcasm for trenchant criticism. Peter even included some racism for cheap laughs: a comment about how the laborers were all "substantially identical," all named George (a common name for second-generation Japanese Americans), and summaries of the townsfolk's "philosophies" that featured incendiary phrases like "little yellow babies" and "Lousy Japs!" He was not above deploying the kind of bigoted language then in common currency at Hotchkiss.* But his piece hummed with righteous indignation. Flexing his nascent skills as a writer, he sided with maligned outsiders against a more powerful authority, which was something he would one day do as an advocacy journalist for Long Island fishermen, California farmworkers, Alaska's Iñupiat people, and members of the American Indian Movement.

THREE MONTHS AFTER the attack on Pearl Harbor, Matty Matthiessen entered active service at the age of thirty-nine through the United States Naval Reserve. At the end of the war, he would be awarded an MBE—Member of the Most Excellent Order of the British Empire, an honor bestowed by King George VI in recognition of "distinguished service performed . . . in cooperation with British armed forces."[70] Despite this international recognition, the service happened almost entirely in New York, in the South Ferry Terminal Building, where the Armed Guard Gunnery School offered courses for guardsmen in the use of antiaircraft and antisubmarine guns so they could better protect the merchant ships of Atlantic supply convoys. The school welcomed not only American but British, Norwegian, Dutch, French, Polish, Russian, and Greek seamen. It also pioneered ordnance equipment and sixteen ingenious training devices: a simulator, for example, that combined four projectors and four replica guns, all of which rumbled realistically with compressed air hammers as a team of

---

* Hotchkiss was almost exclusively white. Asian American students were few and far between, and the school would not see a single Black student until the fall of 1951—a controversial development even then. However, during the war years when Peter was enrolled, a more immediate issue was anti-Semitism. Because of "anti-Jewish feeling," some students were targeted for harassment in the corridors. Decades later, one of these students would recall the day a newsreel shown before the Saturday movie included the first public images of the Holocaust: "The entire school cheered."

men "fired" at Me 109s gliding across a composite panorama.[71] (Not for nothing, an official history described the school as "a kind of wonderland for the Navy gunner.")[72] The design of these devices and tools, some of which were adopted by the British and saved Allied lives, are where Matty made his contribution, having turned out to be a canny engineer. "He had a good war," Peter later said, enviously.[73]

In the summer of 1944, not long after D-Day, Lieutenant Commander Matthiessen shipped out for six weeks to the European theater. Before he left, he signed a consent form for his son to spend two months in the Coast Guard Reserve between his junior and senior years at Hotchkiss. Peter had no idea how to operate depth charges or translate Morse code, but he had "a liking for sea duty," he wrote on his application, and he hoped "to enter service of this type upon completion of school."[74] He was also competitive with his father and angling, perhaps, for Matty's approval, though he would never admit it. The Coast Guard Reserve was as close as he could get to the actual Navy while he was still only seventeen years old.

On July 9, Peter turned up for training at Manhattan Beach in Brooklyn. He was assigned to the Coast Guard Temporary Reserve, a civilian force of unpaid volunteers who filled gaps left by the regular Coast Guard, which was now stretched thin on every front. Temporary Reservists reported on anything that did not appear "right," from an accidental fire to sightings of a German U-boat. (Hundreds of vessels were sunk by foreign submarines off the Atlantic Coast from 1942 onward.) Reservists also responded to distress calls, recovered bodies from wrecks, controlled access to piers, and kept shipping channels open for the swift passage of troops. Mostly, though, they just monitored more than 21,000 miles of waterfront, for tens of thousands of hours—crucial but monotonous work.[75] "I must journey forth into the night to stand a four-hour sentry watch, the incredible boredom of which appalls me," Peter wrote in a letter from Eatons Neck, Long Island, where he was stationed from late July.[76] Whatever he'd expected from the job, the reality turned out to be less than fulfilling. "I think, as a matter of fact, that the next person who steps near the post I shall belay around the head with a blunt instrument, unless it should be the chief, in the event of which I will bring the cannon into play and shoot."[77]

In early August, he expressed his discontent by greeting a superior with a Nazi salute. As punishment, he was transferred to Mattituck, on the North Fork of Long Island, a "sedentary ghost town," in Peter's words, full of "corrupt 'first' families, New Jersey vacationers, dogs, fanned-out harlots, beach workers, phlegmatic decay."[78] At the public dock, he was assigned to a picket boat, which set out for routine patrols of the nearby shoreline. This, at least, turned out to be an improvement, because now he was doing something on the water. In his downtime, he found off-duty work moonlighting as a bartender in a local saloon.

Every ten days, Peter was granted a "48"—two days of liberty—and he hitchhiked by way of Riverhead and Flanders down to the Hamptons, "a paradisal place for a young man in uniform whose life revolved around hunting and fishing, birding, tennis, hard drink, and the mysteries of young women."[79]

It was an unusual summer on the South Fork. Since Fishers Island had been closed by the Navy for coastal defense purposes, many people from the island were now renting in East Hampton. But the village felt empty compared to its prewar days, with overgrown lawns and bullbriers everywhere. Bicycles were ubiquitous, gas having been rationed. And since the older boys had gone off to fight, many of the girls had shifted their attention to a slightly younger crowd; Peter found himself in unfamiliar demand on the long, windswept beaches. He befriended Jackie and Lee Bouvier. He stayed with his school friends, Charlie and Sherry Lord, until their parents threw him out after some late-night shenanigans with a niece. He met a girl named Wendy Burden at a "silly little dance," hit on her with an "old, flip line," and kissed her in the backseat of a car.[80] Then he wrote Wendy a bashful letter asking her to play tennis with him—a proper date. "I am scheduled to appear over the horizon next Saturday afternoon, clad in sailor suit and Long Island dirt."[81] Wendy Burden was strikingly beautiful, an aspiring actress who would one day be photographed by Richard Avedon for the cover of *Life*. It was "a toss up," Peter told her, in another of the more than one hundred letters he would send over the course of their turbulent romance, who he wanted to see more that August: Wendy or his father, who had just arrived home from England.[82]

Here was a rare admission of affection for Matty Matthiessen; Peter missed him. However, Peter would come to tell a very different story as an adult about his two-month tenure in the Coast Guard—a story in which he dropped out of Hotchkiss, lied about his age to enlist as a Reservist, and ran away without telling anybody his plans, forcing Matty to track him down through military channels and then persuade the authorities that his errant son still needed to finish school. None of that was exactly true, judging by the archival evidence (including a photo of Peter posing in uniform alongside his family), though he did neglect to keep his mother apprised of his whereabouts, causing her considerable anxiety.

That summer, the final straw turned out to be his younger brother. Carey had evolved into a very different species from Peter: cooperative, reasonable, lighthearted, and adored as "an angel" by virtually everyone—except Peter, who rolled his eyes at Carey's "Gee whiz, it's good to see ya!" demeanor. So when Carey suddenly asked for his own name to be removed from the *Social Register*, Matty and Betty were surprised. When he was discovered drunk on the floor just inside the front door, they were scandalized. When he tried to mount the pugnacious defense that "beer is a food," they knew who to blame. Matty informed Peter that until he tamed his "insolence, absenteeism, excessive use of stimulants, speeding tickets, and chronic disruption of the social order," upsetting his mother and corrupting his impressionable brother, there was no longer space for him at Stamford.[83] "My father really told me I wasn't welcome," Matthiessen would recall decades later, still marveling that he somehow managed to get expelled not from school, but from home.[84]

EVEN AS A YOUNG MAN, Peter knew he was being wayward. Just a few months after graduating from Hotchkiss, he would send a letter to Wendy Burden that included a remarkably clear-eyed assessment of his own behavior:

> The realization has come to me that I've been about as inconsiderate of Mum and Dad and as ungrateful as I could possibly be and not get killed by a bolt of heaven's wrath. They've been wonderfully understanding and given me a free hand, but I can tell that they're secretly disappointed when I take advantage of it as much as I do, which has been quite a good deal.... These last four years have been one long individualistic bat, and they were beginning to think that there was a mistake in my ancestry somewhere or that someone had pulled a fast one at the hospital and spirited Erard's true heir away, leaving a misfire behind.[85]

The problem, as he saw it, would eventually be diagnosed in another candid letter to Wendy:

> I'll have to learn to at least keep them happy, but I don't believe I'll ever really gratify them, especially Dad. He believes me capable (and innately) of being an exceptionally fine person—of the "Pres-of-the-Class" variety—and a pillar of society, so to speak. I am not and will not be, either. Carey will. And Mary would, if she were a man. And I would, perhaps, if I were bored. But God, I'm anything but bored! For me, being model takes concentration, and anything as important as that which needs concentration needs time, and I'd spend that time laughing at myself ... in brief, I'd be two persons, and you know the one that would kick the other to death. So do I. I loathe a farce, and I'm not crazy enough about myself as it is, without trying that. It is and always has been either me or the "me" the

folks want, always a choice, and since I usually chose incorrectly, always a conflict.[86]

Matty and Betty wanted their son to succeed in life, but their definition of success hinged on social respectability. Peter (sounding a lot like Holden Caulfield) was exhausted by their expectations, which required him to perform a version of "Peter" that was so phony he found it almost violently objectionable. The split between him and his parents was mirrored, in a sense, by a split within himself. It was "either me or the 'me' the folks want," but he had spent so much time rebelling against the parental ideal that the real "me" remained uncharted territory. Who was Peter Matthiessen, really? His letters to Wendy were testimonies of self-alienation. "I get touchy, lose confidence in myself," he wrote. "I'm very confused and am in constant indecision."[87]

3

An Opening

> Invariably he would pause at the Pali Pass, high up in the Koolau Range, overlooking the north shore of Oahu. . . . From the mountain heights the great dark cloud shadows crept out across the valley toward the sunny shore, and, beyond, the ocean rolled away forever toward the Tropic of Cancer and the continent of home, toward the Golden Gate and Ensenada.
>
> —*Raditzer* (1961)[1]

"Some little mole crawled up and stamped REJECTED on my goddamn paper," Matthiessen wrote on January 8, 1945.[2] The problem was his eyesight. Hoping to join the Enlisted Reserve Corps when he turned eighteen, he'd traveled down to New York for the requisite physical exam. He understood what he was up against with his poor vision, so he'd devised a plan to cheat the test: "I listened with flapping ears to the three elves ahead of me, and by the time I seated my fair, white one in the chair, I had the chant down cold." When the medic asked him to read lines off the Snellen chart, Matthiessen recited the letters from memory. But then the medic asked him to read from the *other* chart. Matthiessen paused, scrutinizing some vague smudges on the opposite wall. Finally, the medic asked him to just point at Chart B. Afterward, on his way out the door, he put on his glasses and examined what he'd pointed at: "Exit to 47th St."

That, at least, is the story he told Wendy Burden—likely embellished to make her laugh, although it was not outside the realm of possibility. Matthiessen had bilateral myopia, 20/100 vision; he needed to be as close as twenty feet to see what a person with perfect vision could see at a hundred. The implications of this condition for a young man just five months from service age during a world war were more than a little alarming. "The draft," Matthiessen quipped, "would take me with open armpits." Anything even moderately selective was, however, a more formidable challenge, including sea duty in the Navy, which he listed as his preference in the Hotchkiss

Mischianza. His summer training in the Coast Guard Reserve counted for nothing; his hopes of transferring into the regular Coast Guard were already dashed after an earlier exam had exposed his weak spot. An ophthalmologist ("the 'seeing-without-glasses' boy") only offered more bad news: nothing could be done, medically speaking, to improve his military status.³

The previous October, Matthiessen had given himself an ultimatum. "What I think I will do, if worse comes to worst, is join the U.S.M.S. (Merchant Marine)."⁴ Now the worst had seemingly come to pass. "I'll be damned if I'll be drafted," he told Wendy. "Merchant Marines, here I come."⁵

ONE NIGHT AT THE END of February, after a student concert at a convalescent hospital in Pawling, New York, Matthiessen drifted into reverie during the drive back to Hotchkiss. Staring out the window at a shadowy landscape, he found himself thinking about "school and writing and Northport at night under the lighthouse and E[ast] H[ampton] and people I know and military service and when I was little and Fishers Island in a storm and deep-sea fishing every weekend on our old cruises, and various other things."⁶ He was increasingly anxious about his future, about what was going to happen to him during the war. And what about afterward, assuming he survived? Did he really need to settle down like his parents suggested—like his sister, Mary, already seemed to be doing? He thought about Wendy, and about how he'd never imagined falling in love so young.

Wendy Burden was just two weeks older than Peter. She attended the Garrison Forest School near Baltimore, and lived the rest of the year in Bedford, New York, on a sprawling family estate called Crowfields. Peter had started addressing her as "Darling" not long after their meeting on Long Island, trying out a pet name for the first time. He liked that Wendy was a fan of frozen daiquiris, that she carried box purses from Bonwit and wore two-piece bathing suits to the beach. He appreciated her sincerity, too, and the fact she was willing to forgive his drunken boorishness at a recent New Year's party—"I felt and feel quite skunklike about it"⁷—not to mention his tendency to make remarks that were stunningly tactless, even when he was intending to give a compliment. "You being so damned 'nice,' agreeable, generally sweet and non-bitchy constitutes much of your appeal," he told her. "You are the only girl I have ever liked beyond the first 'denouement.'"⁸

Peter also liked Wendy's father, William Douglas Burden, a naturalist, conservationist, and trustee of the American Museum of Natural History. In 1926, Burden had traveled with his then-wife, Katherine "Babs" Burden—Wendy's mother, who trained as a photographer for the expedition—to the island of Komodo in the East Indies, where he'd become the first foreigner to capture the endemic "dragon lizards," *Varanus komodoensis*. Burden had returned to New York with fourteen Komodo dragons in cargo (two living, twelve dead), as well as several thousand other species and a baby honey bear that Babs christened John Bear of Malaya.[9] (This was let loose at Crowfields as a family pet, until it learned how to swipe through fly screens to invade the house.) "Certainly my father and Peter had much in common," Wendy later recalled: "the passion for wilderness and wildlife, and a powerful need to test themselves."[10] Douglas Burden regaled Peter with tales of his unusual exploits: the oceanarium he had cofounded in Florida with Leo Tolstoy's grandson; an amoeba he contracted in the jungle of Nicaragua that was left undiagnosed for so long it permanently damaged his health. Peter was enchanted by the older man, and shared his dream to write for *The New Yorker*, which Burden encouraged with some words of advice.

"I've thought about it for a long time," Peter told Wendy about his literary ambitions.[11] But he was scared of rejection, and wrote out a sample letter to illustrate his greatest fear:

> Dear kid; what are you trying to pull off, anyhow? Here we are, trying to run a satirical sheet, and you, you freak, little bastard, have to go and send in utter tripe like this. If I had my way, you'd be taken out and shot for wasting our precious time, d'ya hear me? One more occurrence like this, and I'll write your father a letter, get me? Now go back to the nursery and dry off—
>
> (Signed) (by secretary—of course)
> Jack Glotz, Sub. Ass. Ed.

Having thus saved the magazine the trouble of turning him down, Peter added, about submitting material: "I might do it, though, there is always that possibility."

Wendy was tickled by his self-deprecating humor. She also thought he was extremely handsome: stork-like at six foot one, with a wave of blondish brown hair that crashed across a high forehead and glacial blue eyes. He could be charming, in the manner of his parents, and his letters, which flowed in a torrent between Lakeville and Baltimore, were playful and seductive, full of story fragments, snatches of dialogue, as the writer tested his newfound abilities by showing off for an enthusiastic audience. But there were also red flags—if Wendy was willing to heed them. Peter professed his love for her within the first few months of their correspondence; then he provided regular updates, as though this love, once discovered, was a variable to be measured like barometric pressure. One day he worshipped "the terra firma" she walked on.[12] Three days later, he loved her but was not "in love" with her, if she could understand the subtle difference.[13] And then briefly during Christmas vacation, "because of a temporary 'call of the wild' in me," he wasn't in love or much interested at all.[14]

The key to this volatility, which left Wendy insecure and seeking constant reassurances, came in a letter responding to an offhanded jab she had made about him being "conventional." "Great God!" Peter snapped. "That is the first statement of its kind I have ever heard, although opinions to the contrary have been frequent indeed. I nearly fell over, I mean it." He continued, "As my parents and others would be delighted to inform you, convention is hardly my forte."[15] In fact it was she, in Peter's opinion, who was the conventional one. Wendy was the kind of girl who had a "coming out" party at the River Club with a Meyer Davis band, one of those lavish cotillions where, as he later wrote, "lilting young things as pink as shrimps were presented on silver platters to society."[16] His attraction to her was real, and he enjoyed their epistolary courting, but he also suggested that what he really needed in a woman was something different, someone less safe—certainly someone less inclined to an early marriage. "The chances of you having met the person you're going to marry already are relatively slight," he wrote Wendy by way of warning. What they were doing was "just an experiment in search of the perfect formula."[17]

THREE WEEKS BEFORE Peter Matthiessen's eighteenth birthday, Adolf Hitler shot himself in his Führerbunker in Berlin.

By May 8, the Nazis had capitulated across Europe, and millions of people on both sides of the Atlantic swarmed city streets to celebrate V-E Day. As rain fell on Hotchkiss, Matthiessen found time between rehearsals of *Macbeth* to record his thoughts on the historic occasion: "The idea's nice [meaning the Nazis' surrender], but it's like an overlong play after the climax has been attained."[18]

On his birthday, May 22, he registered for the draft, having decided against the Merchant Marine. (Or perhaps it was decided for him: there is no record explaining the change of heart.) Then he waited to receive an order to report for induction. In the meantime, graduation came in late May; he was awarded the Teagle Prize for the best essay on Books and Reading. He also received word that he'd been accepted by Yale.

As spring warmed into summer, he made up his mind that he wasn't in love with Wendy Burden after all. "Bang just like that," he notified her in a letter. "Only it's not—I think it's awful, perfectly awful, and I'm just the biggest fool ever."[19] He then continued to write her letters as he started dating other girls, including the daughter of Mets cofounder Joan Whitney Payson (who *The New York Times* once described as "a merry, cherubic woman who inherited $100-million in the nineteen-twenties and lived in royal splendor").[20] Payne Whitney Payson met Peter through a friend, Lois Baldwin; along with Charlie Lord, who was courting Lois at the time, the four of them romped around the streets of New York, the two men trying to impress their dates by climbing up lampposts.

At the beginning of August, Matthiessen had another physical exam at an induction station in New Haven. Despite receiving the same diagnosis of myopia, he was accepted on the spot into the U.S. Navy as an apprentice seaman. Years later in his memoir notes, he would attribute this sudden reversal of fortune to "bluff and bluster": pleading "vast sea experience" and "a stern family sea-dog tradition," he supposedly talked his way "clean out of the Army."[21] But while there may have been some skillful rhetoric involved with the recruiting officer, the credit more properly belonged to Lieutenant Commander Matthiessen, who seems to have called in a favor for his son. "Made Navy by grace of Dad," Peter confessed in another letter to Wendy: "Close shave."[22]

The Naval Training Center in Sampson, New York, was a makeshift city. Conjured from nothing in just 270 days, it covered more than two thousand acres and four and a half miles of shoreline along Seneca Lake.[23] By the time Matthiessen arrived a few days after his induction, hundreds of thousands of men had already broken in the parade grounds, gymnasiums, and multiple rifle ranges. Matthiessen was sent to the hospital for inoculations, then assigned to one of twenty-two barracks, where his pillow smelled worse than "a Canal Street flophouse." Petty officers shouted that he was nothing but six feet of shit, and his head was shorn bare, by Matthiessen's count, in "29.8 seconds flat."[24] But he was thrilled to be at Sampson. He wrote to New Haven deferring his Yale enrollment until after he was discharged. Then his thoughts drifted down to Stamford. What did his parents make of his new trajectory? *Were* they thinking about him? "I have yet to inform the old folks at home that I am still alive," he wrote Payne, doing a poor job of disguising his hurt. "What a goddamned surprise that's going to be! I can just see them all hunched over the phone, rubbing their scaly palms together in gleeful anticipation of a War Dept. telegram."

Matthiessen had been at Sampson for four days when America dropped its "Little Boy" on Hiroshima. The destruction of Nagasaki followed thereafter, precipitating an unconditional surrender by the Empire of Japan. On August 14, celebrations broke out everywhere from Honolulu to New York, where tickertape and torn bits of paper showered down from open skyscraper windows, and where people danced until the early hours of the morning beneath a fifteen-ton replica of Lady Liberty in Times Square.

Matthiessen took a break from training to record his thoughts across several letters. "We were told tonight that the war is over," he wrote Payne. "On the surface, joy reigns supreme at Sampson, but it is a rather frantic joy, which exists because joy should exist in such a situation and not because of the feeling behind it."[25]

He was ruffled by the news and its implications for his immediate future. "I'm not quite sure what I'm doing here now," he told Wendy, "beyond the obvious purpose of replacing somebody who got in the war as a war and as a sailor and whom I should be glad not to have been a contemporary of because I am spared all the horror and destruction."[26] *Should* be glad, and yet: "I <u>know</u> I'm not." It was a "selfish point of view," and he felt "silly" for committing it to paper, but after years of anticipation he'd expected at least an opportunity to test his mettle, like all the older boys at Hotchkiss who had marched away before him.

"It's not over for us by a long shot," he added morosely. "Two-and-a-half-years minimum, they tell us." Two-and-a-half years of what, exactly? Matthiessen reported for his sentry watch. He went to double-time drills beneath a blazing sun. Five men fainted in the August heat.

SEPTEMBER BEGAN WITH another unexpected setback in his naval career. Somebody at Sampson had noticed his poor eyesight and reassigned him, without any discussion, to the U.S. Naval Construction Battalions—the Seabees (CBs), as they were popularly known. Represented by a Disney-esque insignia of a cartoon bee wearing a Dixie cap and clutching a hammer, wrench, and submachine gun, the Seabees built the necessary infrastructure of war, the bases and airstrips and pontoon causeways. Over the previous few years, they'd become so instrumental in advancing American forces across the Pacific, from island to atoll, that John Wayne had made a movie about them (*The Fighting Seabees*), and more than two thousand Purple Hearts had been awarded for sacrifices made under enemy fire. It was the Seabees who'd guarded the secret new weapon on Tinian before it was loaded into the *Enola Gay*.[27] Nevertheless, Matthiessen dreaded "the hideous threat of the Seabees,"[28] and when the threat became reality he took the reassignment as a low blow: "shore job in some forgotten place, pick & shovel duty."[29] He transferred begrudgingly to Camp Endicott, in Davisville, Rhode Island, for several weeks of basic training. One of the first things he did there was graffiti the toilet in a fit of pique:

> ENLISTED MEN ARE FORBIDDEN TO DRINK
> OUT OF THE URINALS[30]

Matthiessen's final period of leave came in late October. He traveled to Stamford to see Matty and Betty, then drove on to Bedford to bid farewell to Wendy. By this point, his involvement with Payne had grown more serious: "Am completely convinced, now that the shooting has died down, that I love you very much," he'd told her in late September, to which Payne had replied with a satisfactory, if not quite as effusive, expression of attachment.[31] However, Peter now took one look at Wendy in Bedford and was overcome with regret. "I was horrified," he later confessed, "my plans, my revolutions, PwP [Payne Whitney Payson]—everything crashing into the dust."[32] He spent the Sunday talking with Wendy and felt "nostalgic as all hell." Two days later, he wrote her a note: "Do you ever feel that you would like to yell or sing at the top of your lungs with contentment, or find yourself grinning idiotically at nothing at all and stifling little barks of elation?"[33]

In another letter, sent just before he headed west, he tried to explain exactly what Wendy had meant to him during their time together:

> Firstly, you taught me a respect for girls as people, an idea which I had not previously shared. I had always looked upon them as a sort of natural phenomenon which existed, somewhat pointlessly, for the benefit of a man's comfort.... Aside from thinking them inconceivably stupid, artificial, mentally worthless, the idea had not occurred to me that I should ever attach more importance to one than to myself. In those days I attached no small amount of importance to myself. From this, darling, you are intended to infer that such is no longer the case.... You taught me to say what I meant when with girls instead of diplomatic frippery, lines, general artifice. You taught me ... that the important thing was for you to think me attractive, not vice-versa. That love is a beautiful thing and that its beauty lies in its spontaneity and not in what can be made out of it.... That I was a bastard in its figurative sense and had better change pretty damn fast before you found out from experience.[34]

He said this with "sincerity, darling, because I mean all of it," yet this extraordinary confession, written with the chauvinism of a young man who has just spent his formative years at an all-male prep school, was surely motivated, to some extent, by last-minute jitters. Faced with an imminent posting somewhere abroad, Peter was nervous. Letters can be a way of tethering to familiar ground; receiving them is to reaffirm a connection with home. For this reason, he wanted Wendy to keep writing to him for as long as he was away. He would write to both her *and* Payne, simultaneously, until the day he returned; in fact, he would copy phrases or sentences from one letter to another, so the women would read roughly the same thing at approximately the same time. The letters they sent in return (almost none of which survive) would help him digest the strange events he was experiencing. He would come to rely on these letters, even expect them. But he would never stop to question whether he was leading one, or both, of the women on by continuing to write.

"I'm going to miss you," he told Payne from Camp Endicott. "But ce n'est pas la guerre."[35]

THE TROOP SLEEPER CRAMMED six into a space that a regular Pullman car would have reserved for four. At night, all windows shut tight, the carriage filled up with the ripe exhalations of open-mouthed men, and Matthiessen felt like he was trapped in a locker room after a vigorous basketball game. Restless in his berth, he tried to write as his pencil slipped with every jolt of the train. Beside him were poker dice and a pile of Russian classics, the syllabus he'd set for himself: *Anna Karenina*, *The Brothers Karamazov*, Chekhov's short stories. Outside, America slid by in an indistinguishable blur, New Haven giving way to Syracuse, Cleveland, St. Louis, the monotonous Midwest. Eventually the "Caravan of the Betrayed," as he christened it, crossed over the Rockies; he stared in awe at the snowcapped range. Only then did he feel truly far away from home. Vegas was "Sodom and Gomorrah and Greenwich Village all rolled into one." California was "luxurious" when it came into view, particularly the San Joaquin Valley backed by a horizon of misty mountains.[36]

Matthiessen's original order had been to offload at Port Hueneme, by Oxnard; from there, he and his fellow Seabees were to set out for Guam, or maybe the Philippines. Instead, a boiler had burst somewhere in the vicinity of Topeka, Kansas, and during the long delay that ensued an updated order had come through that rerouted them all to Treasure Island, near San Francisco. When the train finally arrived, conditions at the naval station turned out to be far from ideal. Down below the Oakland Bay Bridge, Matthiessen complained that "400 of us exist in 1 regulation barracks, which is surrounded by a high barbed-wire fence."[37] Treasure Island permitted no phone calls, no incoming mail, and no liberty—except for the newly freed German POWs, who seemed to come and go unsupervised, singing blissfully as the American seamen sat and brooded in their own version of Alcatraz.

Finally, on November 6, Matthiessen went to sea. His ship, the USS *Joseph T. Dickman*, had been an ocean liner before the War Department requisitioned her in October 1940, though it was difficult to tell that from all the artillery studding the decks. As Matthiessen put it, "She carries 3 40mm guns [actually four] and bristles with anti-aircraft, has seen 6 invasions and laid 3 German attackers low, and serves the worst coffee I have ever tasted."[38] Now her belly was filled with row after row of claustrophobic canvas bunks, and she was on her way to Pearl Harbor for Operation Magic Carpet, in which she would ferry active-duty troops back to Seattle for discharge.

Even before the ship passed the Farallon Islands, it was clear to the ninety or so passengers onboard—a mix of Seabees, Navy, Coast Guard, and Marines—that they were heading into an ocean storm. The temperature plummeted, and Matthiessen began wearing two shirts, a sweater, a windbreaker, and a pea coat whenever he ventured abovedeck. This chill was accompanied by a fierce gale, which ushered in heavy rain. Then there were waves the fathomless blue of "fresh-landed marlin or swordfish," rocking the ship into queasy submission.

Within a day, the constant pitching and yawing made seasickness epidemic: there was vomit "every moment, everywhere, in everything."[39] All were afflicted except a few lucky men like Matthiessen, who prided himself on an immunity to mal de mer; those trips with Matty down around Montauk Point had hardened his stomach to rough seas. As the living quarters became "a trickle-down hell of . . . dim-lit airless holds and haunted half-starved faces working up the nerve to risk the stench of the ship's mess," he escaped up a ladder for fire watch at the bow.[40] Opening and closing the fo'c's'le hatch, helping others climb out for gulps of fresh air, made him feel "positively fatherly." One seaman, after exiting the hatch, vomited straight onto an ensign who was waiting to enter; Matthiessen watched as they both lunged for the rails, "a touching picture of that old officer-crew camaraderie as they bent together in common struggle against the elements."[41]

Despite the wry commentary of his letters, he was made thoroughly miserable by the "painfully grotesque, macabre circus."[42] The idea of fire watch during a squall seemed senseless to him. Because of his fortitude—and because the men who were meant to relieve him were too stricken to move—he stood watch for twenty-six hours in three days, then another four the following and final night. His clothes were soaked, and he lit cigarette after shaky cigarette. At one point the waves were sluicing over the sides; he sought shelter beneath a landing craft lashed across the foredeck, where something strange happened, a brush with the sublime that left him reeling in confusion.

Many writers, after a mystical experience, have tried to find the words to adequately capture their impressions. Long before Kenneth Grahame and his "Gates of Dawn," Ralph Waldo Emerson recounted his sensation of walking in the Massachusetts woods: "Standing on the bare ground—my head bathed by the blithe air and uplifted into infinite space—all mean egotism vanishes. I become a transparent eyeball; I am nothing; I see all; the currents of the Universal Being circulate through me; I am part or particle of God."[43] Henry David Thoreau had a similar moment at Walden Pond during a rain shower, when "Every little pine needle expanded and swelled with sympathy and befriended me. I was so distinctly made aware of the presence of something kindred to me, even in scenes which we are accustomed to call wild and dreary . . . that I thought no place could ever be strange to me again."[44] More recently, Edward Abbey, passing two seasons in the parched wilderness of Arches National Park in Utah, had dreamed of "a hard and brutal mysticism in which the naked self merges with a non-human world."[45] Abbey was roused by "the shock of the real" as he admired the Delicate Arch and Rainbow Bridge—"For a little while we are again able to see, as the child sees, a world of marvels."[46] Annie Dillard, in a related fashion, sat by Tinker Creek in Virginia's Roanoke Valley, squinted her eyes, and sensed her self and surroundings lose all distinction: "Something broke and something opened. I filled up like a new wineskin. I breathed an air like light; I saw a light like water. I was the lip of a fountain the creek filled forever; I was ether, the leaf in the zephyr; I was flesh-flake, feather, bone."[47]*

Seeing in this way, outside the lines we draw around ourselves, is largely the purview of saints, Dillard wrote, or of monks who dedicate their whole lives to disciplined practice. And yet undisciplined glimpses can be also found in the work of William Blake, Allen Ginsberg, Hermann Hesse, Alfred, Lord Tennyson, Walt Whitman, Ludwig Wittgenstein, and Virginia Woolf. It was William James, in *The Varieties of Religious Experience*, who labeled glimpses of the numinous "mystical states," and who claimed they were common enough to identify four defining characteristics. A mystical state of mind is ineffable, beyond articulation. It has a noetic quality, in that it seems to impart knowledge not attainable by more rational means. It is transient, fading fast and leaving only imperfect memories. And the person feels an overwhelming sense of passivity throughout, as though gripped and directed by—or subsumed into—a higher/greater force. Others have preferred the phrase "cosmic consciousness" to discuss this state, or "oceanic feeling" (per Romain Rolland in a letter to Freud), or a vision of the Absolute, or a vision

---

* In January 2006, Annie Dillard wrote a letter to Matthiessen in which she admitted to seeing glimpses of the "light" many times "since I began studying ultimate things seriously." Dillard went on, "Like everyone else, I don't know why I get them—it's always when I'm alert + thinking of nothing in particular. Most often it's seeing chloroplasts streaming in translucent leaves. This vegetative business is amazingly common; I run into it everywhere in wildly random books, including near-contemporary poetry. If you read The Idea of the Holy, Rudolph Otto, you feel subhuman not to receive these extraordinary moments often. Receiving them is not + has never been the point. They only demonstrate what you're dealing with. It is conscious, if not consciousness itself."

of God. Alan Watts, writing in 1960, proposed the deliberately imprecise "It," as in, "This is *It*"—"this simplest of words because we have no word for it."[48]

Watts, of course, meant no word in the West. There is an elegant one in Zen Buddhism: *kensho*, "the liberation of seeing into [one's] true nature."[49] Kensho, a sudden, miraculous apprehension of the self in relation to the universe—sometimes called an "opening"[50]—is how Matthiessen would one day understand what he experienced while huddled beneath the landing craft.*

Here is how he recalled the moment in *The Snow Leopard*:

> One night in 1945, on a Navy vessel in Pacific storm, my relief on bow watch, seasick, failed to appear, and I was alone for eight hours in a maelstrom of wind and water, noise and iron; again and again, waves crashed across the deck, until water, air, and iron became one. Overwhelmed, exhausted, all thought and emotion beaten out of me, I lost my sense of self, the heartbeat I heard was the heart of the world, I breathed with the mighty risings and declines of earth, and this evanescence seemed less frightening than exalting.[51]

And here is the moment as it appears in *Raditzer*, his third novel, written nearly a decade before his embrace of Zen:

> He exulted in his solitude, in his long days in the wild isolated realm of wind and water. And one night, as time blurred about him, he thought he sensed the wax and wane of his own burning, a rhythm deeper and more inward still than the pulse of blood which filled his heart. This rhythm somehow aligned itself with the blind, mighty risings and declines of tides and winds and seasons, and he felt, as never before, at one with the earth whirling about him, whirling him out and away from the orderly adjustments of his life. . . .[52]

---

* In 2001, in a talk for his Zen students, he would explain the concept like this: "Mind and body fall away in the sudden outward-and-inwards opening or collapse into so-called Emptiness that we call kensho or satori, and we realize, like Shakyamuni under the bo tree, that I alone, above Heaven and below Earth, have the Buddha Nature. In short, that I and the whole universe are one. That is Realization, that is Enlightenment. . . . All the universe becomes enlightened in that moment, and all sentient beings, too." More generally, Matthiessen was fascinated by the "universality" of mystical experience, and he agreed with William James that most people have a brush with it at some point in their lives. However, at a lecture at UC Santa Barbara ("Literature and Mysticism," given on November 9, 1978), he suggested that there was a widespread tendency to repress or dismiss such experiences, "perhaps in fear that we might be losing our wits. In other words, losing our notion of a separate self, of 'Me, me, me, me.'"

This fleeting experience would become vital to Matthiessen, referenced repeatedly in his work and various interviews. Overcome with awe, he had sensed "another way of seeing the world,"[53] a continuity with something far more powerful than his own alienated self. And yet there was no mention of this impression in letters to Wendy or Payne; at the time it seemed too "bizarre," he later said, to try articulating his experience for anybody else.[54] All that remained afterward was a vague impression of loss, though loss of *what*, he couldn't yet say.

RADITZER WAS PUBLISHED by the Viking Press in 1961, sixteen years after the crossing of the *Joseph T. Dickman*. As Matthiessen's war novel, it opens with a strikingly faithful re-creation of his own voyage, from the departure beneath the Golden Gate to the cold, tempestuous fits of wind and men immobilized by illness. The novel's protagonist, Charles Stark, is another of Matthiessen's stand-ins: sensitive and introspective, he turns to the Navy "to flee" a suffocating milieu, though he is self-aware enough to know that he has it pretty good in comparison to most people. ("Perhaps that was part of it, the fatness of it all, the comfortable assumptions, the infallibility of 'good family.'")[55] Stark also struggles with a handicap—a bad knee—that makes the brass skeptical of his ability to serve. During the voyage out from California, he has fire watch at the bow, sees a man vomit on another man's shoes, and finds himself hypnotized by waves while sheltering beneath a landing craft. But there is a significant difference between Matthiessen's history and the novel's setup. The "USS *General Pendleton*" leaves in October 1944, which means Stark arrives on O'ahu when the Territory of Hawaii is still swelling with troops for major offensives like the Battle of Okinawa. Matthiessen, arriving there a full year later, witnessed exactly the opposite. "Aiea is the Casablanca of the Navy," he wrote from the receiving barracks behind Pearl Harbor—"everyone [is] hanging around waiting for a passport out."[56]

O'ahu was transformed by the events of December 7, 1941.[57] In the aftermath of the attack, as the *Arizona* plumed oil from its watery tomb, bomb shelters were constructed in private backyards, and the military started to requisition land. Where once there were unbroken sugarcane plantations, tent cities sprang up to accommodate thousands of soldiers. Previously tranquil spots were converted into training camps, the forests echoing with practice fire. Lei makers stopped buying flowers and started making camouflage nets to drape over gun emplacements. New roads were steamrolled to radar stations hidden at the top of Mount Ka'ala, and tunnels were bored under Diamond Head for ammunition storage. At the height of war in the

Pacific, the Army occupied around one-third of O'ahu, while the Navy controlled most of the acreage surrounding Pearl Harbor. The island turned from balmy backwater into a military fortress where the civilian population was ruled by more than a hundred edicts, which regulated everything from blackouts to the bowling alleys.[58]

By the time Matthiessen arrived, martial rule had expired, and the barbed wire barricades had been pulled off Waikīkī Beach. But deep scars marred the landscape in every direction. "Perhaps I was a trifle hard on Treasure Island and spoiled by Endicott," he wrote from the Aiea Barracks. On a clear day he looked out across the island to admire its "high, brilliant fields of sugar cane, green against the purple swell of the hills in the mist of a rainbow glow"—and found his eye caught by "the regimented squalor of ugly huts."[59] To make matters worse, much of this construction was now being hastily abandoned, creating an atmosphere of desolation that would only deepen as weeds began to sprout.

The first ship to head for home, the USS *Saratoga*, had left on September 9 carrying 3,800 men for discharge.[60] Since then, enormous crowds had bid aloha to many thousands more. These departures continued weekly, although some servicemen, frustrated that their own turn to get off "the Rock" was not coming fast enough, had started to brawl while they waited. In one incident that happened just two days after Matthiessen arrived, naval officers and enlisted men numbering either 500 or 1,000 or 1,500 (depending on the source) rioted for three hours in the Damon Tract of Honolulu, overturning two automobiles and causing a seventy-five-year-old local to die from a stress-induced heart attack.[61] "The blood," Matthiessen observed dryly, "flows like wine."[62] This was especially true if a woman happened to be involved; bored sailors had taken to following them around at a ratio, Matthiessen estimated, of three to every one. (He compared the spectacle to a necktie framing a pretty face.) These sailors were highly competitive and quick to lose their cool if they felt they were being usurped: "One amorous gesture less discreet than the long, low whistle, and you have about as much chance as a snowflake in hell of coming out of it with your head, much less your life."

Matthiessen was also restless, though he was less anxious than most to learn about his fate. As one week in the Aiea Receiving Barracks stretched into a second, he was assigned interim work as a street cleaner, butcher, then kitchen assistant.

To kill time, he read *Karamazov* ("there is no proper adjective to describe Dostoyevsky") and *I, Claudius* by Robert Graves ("sordid" but "excellently written").[63] He explored Honolulu, the honky-tonk district around Hotel Street, where signs for hamburgers and Coca-Cola competed with other, now obsolete ones reminding visitors that LOOSE TALK ONLY HELPS THE ENEMY. "The people here are very delicate and small-boned and tend to bump their noses on your navel," he observed of the Japanese residents.[64] Curio shops seemed to stand on every corner, all of them peddling overpriced tchotchkes and postcards of grass-skirted Native Hawaiian girls in improbable poses, with "even more improbable bosoms." These were, in Matthiessen's words, "somewhat startling at first glance to an ingenue weaned on the staid Polly girl of the US."

On Thanksgiving, he retreated to a church for some peace and quiet, gazing at the stained-glass windows for a few hours while a pastor fumbled through a service. Then his company was ordered, that very afternoon, back to the Personnel Staging Center at Pearl Harbor. For the second time he found himself reassigned with no warning, now out of the Seabees and back into the regular ranks of the U.S. Navy. This unlikely reprieve was no cause for celebration, however: Matthiessen stood by as man after man was assigned sea duty over him, including a major who'd been so sick on the *Dickman* that he'd sworn off ocean travel for the rest of his life. "<u>Every</u> one of my friends went out," Matthiessen groaned in a letter to Wendy.[65] Because of his nearsightedness, he was given shore duty at Moanalua Ridge, just a mile down the road from Aiea, where the Navy had centralized its demobilization efforts since September. "I regret to relate that I was assigned to the laundry," he wrote Payne a few days later. "I work a machine called an extractor, which extracts water out of a substance mostly called B.V.D.s"—a brand of men's underwear. "I then extract the remains from the extractors and deliver them to a youth . . . [who] is called a presser but whom you have my eager permission to call whatever you please." In case his ire wasn't clear here, Matthiessen added: "I hereby swear that if this goddam outfit hands me one more decrease [meaning demotion], I shall personally engineer Pearl Harbor #2, and if they don't catch me, Pearl Harbor #3. Then I shall flee to Nizhny Novgorod, and you AMERIKANISCH swine will grovel under the oppression of my O'Sullivan Cat's Paw heel."[66]

In *Raditzer*, Charlie Stark's request for sea duty is refused on account of his weak knee. He is forced to watch, "not without bitterness," as other passengers from the *General Pendleton* are given assignments that will likely see them sent into battle.[67] "Stark had desired the experience of the sea and, potentially, of combat, for motives more personal than patriotic."[68] He yearns to prove he can survive outside the safe room of his family; indeed, his self-respect depends upon it. Yet his wartime experience is restricted to a Navy laundry on O'ahu, "loading and unloading from harmless round machines the soiled raiments of authentic warriors in transit through the staging center."[69] The key word here is "authentic": to go to sea and confront mortal challenges is to do something *real* as a man; to stay behind, even unwillingly, is to defer life, risk nothing, become insignificant and emasculated.

In all the months Matthiessen spent in the Moanalua Ridge laundry, washing the underwear of those "authentic warriors" who were now waiting for their passage home, his proudest achievement, he later claimed in his memoir notes, in what sounds like an attempt to wring some retrospective dignity out of a sorry situation, was learning how to transfer a stogie from one corner of his mouth to the other without using wet hands.[70]

IN THE FIRST WEEK of January, Peter sat down to write Wendy a letter that was really, after its throat-clearing preamble, a letter to himself. "You may be interested to learn that I, Peter Conrad* Matthiessen, hereby exist, in this, the nineteenth year of my existence and 1946th year of Jesus Christ, our Lord. I do not live—I exist. In my case there is a great difference between life and existence—and a very small difference between existence and the mental vacuum of death. I think it would be terrible to be afraid to die, but it would be infinitely more terrible to be afraid to live. I'm all for it, myself. I'm as fond of life as the next mass of molecules. But I look at myself and I say, 'You are Peter Matthiessen, through no fault of your own, and it is not well with you. Why do you exist? . . . Why do you not live?'"[71] He longed to shake off the shackles placed on him by his parents and the U.S. Navy—to take control of his life.

When he did secure a weekend of liberty, he located a stable and rented a horse for a ride around Diamond Head, which lifted his spirits considerably. Then he sunbathed on Waikīkī, strolled past the pink pile of the Royal Hawaiian, and sat through a movie at the "most modern and beautiful" theater he'd ever seen, with huge palm trees framing an Art Deco stage.[72] Afterward, he fell in with three drunk sailors who offered him whiskey. Not having tasted it in months, he grabbed the bottle and drank deeply, becoming so drunk in the process that he had to be rolled out of a cab at the gate to Moanalua Ridge.

Another weekend, wanting to get away from the salty language and shooting galleries and hunts for "non-existent brothels" that preoccupied his colleagues, Matthiessen borrowed a car from some local friends and went for a drive. He headed up through the middle of the island to the sleepy North

---

* "Conrad" was an old Matthiessen family name, though it was never officially given to Peter. The name appealed to him because of Joseph Conrad, one of the two writers he most admired as a young man (the other was Dostoyevsky). Matthiessen would later adopt "Pierre Conrad" as a nom de plume in the inaugural issue of *The Paris Review*. He would also give it to his son, Lucas Conrad Matthiessen.

Shore, then made his way east around to Punalu'u, where there was a small community of fishermen typical, in his view, "of the lovely Hawaii that is so blasphemed by the over-civilized squalor of Pearl City and Honolulu."[73] (*Blasphemed*, as though Hawaii was holy in its untrammeled state. Years later, in *Raditzer*, Matthiessen would write that "Punaluu was as vivid as the setting of a dream.")[74] The owners of the car also had a small beach house in a nearby grove of coconut palms; Matthiessen stayed there alone for the night playing Sergei Prokofiev's orchestral suite for *Lieutenant Kijé* on a record player.[75] At sunrise, a strong wind was blowing off the ocean, and rough surf pounded a fringing reef. He wandered down a deserted beach searching for the green glass fishing floats that sometimes washed up from as far away as Hokkaido.

Out in the lagoon, a fisherman was hauling a gill net. Matthiessen realized the man was struggling. The boat turned haphazardly in the surf, while the man's heavy net, maybe three hundred feet long, appeared to be tangled up with chunks of coral. Matthiessen climbed down some rocks and waded out a quarter of a mile. Then he spoke a few Japanese words to the man, who replied in English. The tide was working against them; choppy water winded Matthiessen as he climbed into the boat and helped to haul the net. Finally it was in, revealing an unprofitable catch: mullet, lobster, and a few silver papio. But the fisherman encouraged Matthiessen to dive down to the bottom of the lagoon, which he did: tiny iridescent coral fish were swimming all around them. When he surfaced, the fisherman was waiting to ferry him back to shore. Matthiessen noticed black frigatebirds carving lines across the sky. It was the happiest he'd felt since leaving home.

ON APRIL 1, 1946, more than two thousand miles north of O'ahu, a large section of seabed shifted during an earthquake deep in the Aleutian Trench near Unimak Island, Alaska.[76] It was the early hours of the morning, and the five guardsmen at Scotch Cap Lighthouse were probably asleep when a wave surged more than a hundred feet up the Unimak cliffs and killed them all.

Without Scotch Cap, there would be no warning for anyone else. The shock radiated south, under the surface of the sea, as fast as a jet plane. If it passed beneath cargo ships, nobody on board felt anything, and it was only as the shock approached land that a telltale swell began to rise. Later, after the effects were reported everywhere from Peru to New Zealand, a small boat operator in Princeton, California, would say that "people thought an atomic bomb had been dropped in the Pacific."[77]

Hilo, on Hawaii, the Big Island, was a picturesque town of waterfalls, brackish ponds, and more sugarcane plantations. Because of a quirk in geography—a northeastern-facing bay, which tapers inward to downtown Hilo like a broad funnel—the tsunami struck here with spectacular force. Preceded by a noise like "a big wind," the first wave arrived at 7 a.m., some five hours after the earthquake, and it pushed fifty feet past the waterfront, flooding warehouses and parkland as people fled to higher ground.[78] A few minutes later, a second, larger wave pulverized boats, automobiles, storefronts, cottages, and tenements. A third wave, towering some twenty feet high, then slammed into the city with enough force to all but erase whatever remained around the Keaukaha section. Out of roughly a hundred homes that had been standing on an old lava flow, as few as six remained unscathed.[79]

Hiromi "Skeeter" Tsutsumi, a young boy who lived in Hilo, awoke to the sound of his sisters shouting, "Tidal wave, tidal wave"—to which he responded, "April Fool!"[80] Over on O'ahu, Matthiessen saw the early headline—"10 DEAD IN HILO! OAHU LOSS HEAVY"—and found it similarly implausible. "I'm a survivor," he joked in a letter written to Wendy that evening. "I read about it in the Honolulu Advertiser, after I survived. Some time after, as a matter of fact."[81]

Four days later, he had learned enough to adjust his attitude. "The Tidal Wave turned out to be very serious," he wrote to Wendy. "Two people I know had their houses washed away, and they were among hundreds of others."[82] The dead were still being fished out of Hilo's harbor, and the toll throughout the territory had already climbed to a "terrible" ninety-nine. (It would eventually reach 159, with Hilo hit hardest.) "You may have read all about it in the papers, but the place is truly in a mess along the north shore of the whole chain." Matthiessen then listed some details, including the news that had really brought home the devastation: "The Russells' beach house at Punaluu was in a wave pocket and comparatively untouched, but most of Punaluu was washed away." More than 1,800 residents from Punalu'u and nearby Hau'ula were now sheltering at a former Army training camp after losing everything in the worst day the islands had seen since 1941.[83]

The desecration of Punalu'u only deepened Matthiessen's lassitude. ("Life had carried him on so swiftly, and now Punaluu was lost to him forever," he would write in *Raditzer*; "like remote places one glimpses on a journey and, staring backward through small windows, realizes one will never see again.")[84] As the tsunami cleanup continued into May, O'ahu had never seemed more godforsaken, he told Payne: "The one thing worse than death is being somewhere where you can't leave."[85]

Matthiessen's mood swings became increasingly pronounced. One day he felt "so strongly about living and loving and beauty and the future that I startle myself," he wrote.[86] He daydreamed about a reunion with Wendy on the road between Bedford and Stamford, both of them stopping their cars to do a running embrace like Jeanne Crain and Dana Andrews at the end of *State Fair*. But then other days he swung in the opposite direction, down into "one of those slumps of melancholy inertia in which you barely have strength to breathe."[87] These "black moods," as he called them, could come on with no provocation, and they made him as volatile as an electrical storm. One night at Aiea, a sailor showing off for some friends declared that all women were "whores." Matthiessen turned around and struck him in the face. "I make no claims to being the defender of women—denials in fact," he explained in a letter to Wendy (which must have raised her eyebrows), "but that is just a case in point: any excuse to take out my mood on somebody."

By the middle of June, his spells of ennui had reached such "outlandish proportions" that he received news of his sister Mary's marriage to Henry Jefferds Wheelwright Jr., a medical student from Bangor, Maine, "as phlegmatically as I might a damp piece of bread."[88] This, Peter acknowledged to Payne, was a "terrible confession." But there was one recent development that he did manage to muster at least a little enthusiasm about. At the start of June, after three interminable months in the laundry, then another three months in the laundry's front office fielding irate telephone calls about missing articles of clothing, he had finally been given a decent assignment.

Matthiessen was moved into Recreation and Morale Activities—the District Athletics Office. This position came with some enviable perks: "a lot of driving around, lying around, pool, eau-de-vie." Yet the most important thing "by far" was an opportunity to write. As the man in charge of an All-Navy fight team, which had entered the local Golden Gloves boxing tournament, it was Matthiessen's job to report on their bouts at the Civic Auditorium. His brief dispatches were then printed in *The Honolulu Advertiser*: "Out of nineteen entries in last week's three smokers, only four managed to gain the nod; a preponderance of TKO's made it only too plain to the fans that the sailors weren't in good physical condition."[89] There was no byline on the columns, and they passed without much notice, but it was progress, for Matthiessen, in a promising professional direction. He made a clipping and folded it into his papers.

AS EARLY AS FEBRUARY, sailors had started to whisper that the Navy was planning to close Moanalua Ridge and ship everyone stateside. Matthiessen kept careful track of each new rumor, which he weighed in his letters for plausibility and likelihood. It was said, for example, that Captain Homer Jones ("the 'old man' around these parts") was putting in for retirement and wanted everybody else gone before him. Matthiessen presumed this rumor was based on the idea that a captain should be "the last to leave a sinking ship."[90]

Every time a story gained too much traction, the Navy would issue an official denial, but the men continued to gossip anyway. Were they going home in July? Or maybe September? Somebody claimed that fifty enlisted men were going to be marooned at Pearl Harbor for another full *year*. That rumor was "horrifyingly reasonable,"Matthiessen wrote.[91] In fact, he would arrive home in early August, but there was one final problem to be faced before then—"one rather large blemish," as he put it.[92]

Just a few days after he assumed his post in the District Athletics Office, Peter wrote a letter to Wendy summarizing the drama. "The Shore Patrol has seen fit to apprehend Mr. Morton Levy (of the Bayonne, N.J., Levys) and myself, and we are booked under the following charges, awaiting some form of captain's mast and eventually court martial: 1) use of unauthorized vehicle; 2) presence in an off-limits establishment . . . [in] Aiea Town; 3) out of uniform, i.e., in dungarees; 4) A.W.O.L." Put another way, Matthiessen had used his new privileges to commandeer a jeep. Then he'd driven with Mort Levy to a Japanese bar. A group of humorless patrolmen had intercepted them either on the way to the bar or after they'd ordered a round of drinks. The only saving grace, Peter told Payne, trying to make light of the serious trouble he now found himself in, was that the patrolmen hadn't demanded to inspect his billfold: "3 different I.D. cards, eight liberty cards, chow passes for 3 mess halls, a faked overnight permit, a faked driver's license, and a ticket to Rahway, New Jersey."[93]

Matthiessen and Levy reported to the Shore Patrol headquarters and pleaded for leniency. When that didn't work, they pressed an insider for a favor. "He managed to get the whole works ready to tear up the slips, all but one fat, loathsome lout of a loser who said, and I shall <u>not</u> quote, to hell with the bastards, give 'em the ticket."[94] By July, the charges against them remained active, though the Navy had yet to take any disciplinary actions. Matthiessen interpreted the quiet as a promising sign that the whole affair might just blow over. He would continue to believe he was safe as he boarded a troopship at Pearl Harbor, crossed the Pacific, boarded a sleeper train, crossed the breadth of America, and arrived at the separation center at Lido Beach, Long Island, on August 6. Only then would he discover that he was being denied a promotion to petty officer third class, and that his pay was being docked in belated punishment. While he would receive an honorable discharge from the Navy, unofficially he'd leave under a storm cloud.

Two weeks before that happened, however, Matthiessen flew to Maui for a last weekend of liberty with Joe Cooke, an old friend from Hotchkiss who was also stationed in the islands. Their excursion was not exactly "kosher"; Matthiessen was traveling without valid leave papers or an out-of-bounds permit, which meant, when they arrived in Wailuku, that the Grand Hotel refused to accommodate them.[95] The men shrugged off the snub, rented a truck, and raced out into the cane fields, where Matthiessen changed into slippers and a pair of Levi's as golden plovers scattered around him. Then they drove on to Haleakalā.

"Haleakala," he wrote afterward, "deserves its own paragraph. It is a huge mountain, occupying the entire eastern half of Maui and the third highest in the islands—10,000 feet." At its top is a vast erosional valley dotted with cinder cones, which was formed between 145,000 and 120,000 years ago. The entire mountain is an active shield volcano, and its Hawaiian name means "house of the sun."

In 1946, reaching the Haleakalā summit crater meant ascending a sandy road which wound "above the timberline and cloud fields and into the clear sky and sun." Joe Cooke's grandmother happened to own a ramshackle vacation house somewhere along the road, a house with a sloping lawn and towering eucalyptus trees. The two men stopped in her yard, checked there was nobody home, and then assembled camp near an overgrown garden of orchids and dahlias. Matthiessen was astounded by the view: "Through a great break in the trees, the central Maui plain stretch[es] out, with the western range of mountains and valleys dark above Wailuku, its light shallow water green and surf-fringed against the black cliffs in the windward headlands." He looked into the blue expanse, crickets chirping all around him, a scent of guava and wild ginger on the air, and didn't say anything "for a long time."

4

Bird of Passage

> I had a lot of Puritanism to deal with. I was educated in the conventional WASP way, but not in life; not in all sorts of ways that I found interesting; not in pleasure—oh! The dirtiest word in the language! So, Paris for me was a whole new thing.
>
> —PM, Undated Paris notes[1]

THERE WAS NEVER any question that Peter Matthiessen would go to Yale. His father, grandfather, and three uncles were alumni, which meant his own attendance was all but preordained. "My chief purpose in gaining a higher education is to acquire an intellectual foundation for a career in journalism or writing of one kind or another," he'd written on his application while still at Hotchkiss. "In short, I should like to know far more than I do now about everything."[2] The Navy had delayed this ambition but in no way derailed it. Once he was discharged from service, Matthiessen reapplied to college, using his earlier acceptance, on September 27, 1946. The next day he sat for a personal interview in New Haven. To show he was still serious about his studies, he explained that he'd done "a lot of reading" during his months in Hawaii, and taken ten weeks of night classes in Russian at the Pearl Harbor Navy College. The admissions officer made notes while Matthiessen talked about himself: "Tall, intellectual, blond curly hair, glasses, almost on the feminine side, but virile enough to escape that criticism."[3]

Because he was too late to enroll for the fall semester, he was told to come back in four months for spring. Tensions were already flaring at home with his parents, so waiting in Stamford for that length of time was an alarming prospect. "It's pathetically obvious from their letters that they're fondest of me when I'm away," he'd complained from Hawaii, and what he perceived as their desire for "a completely different person" had led to him lashing out upon his return.[4] Matty and Betty were annoyed to have a moody son stalking around their house; it was mutually agreed that it was best for Peter to take up temporary residence in New York with Betty's sweet, relaxed, and open-minded Aunt Bess.

Back during his senior year at Hotchkiss, Matthiessen had treated Manhattan as a playground for "rich-boy fun, brushing past the street poor with the cool callousness one must cultivate to avoid the discomforts of guilt, pity or distress."[5] His vision of the city was characterized by boxing matches and hockey games, the jazz clubs around West 52nd Street ("Coleman Hawkins and the rest . . . lined up on *top* of a Broadway bar, playing disconsolately for drunks and tourists"), and cheap restaurants like the Russian Tea Room, where he'd liked to order borscht and blinis, "perhaps nine dollars for two, with wine thrown in." It was this footloose hedonism that he planned to resume from his base in the East Eighties.

But it soon became clear that something had changed. Matthiessen was nineteen years old now, and his "formerly uproarious and heedless"[6] nature had turned unaccountably darker. Instead of being energized by Manhattan, he felt adrift as he wandered through Midtown. He realized his months in Hawaii had awoken "romantic longings." He ached for "unfettered 'real life,'" which seemed to be somewhere out *there*, in "faraway destinations,"[7] far from the high-rises and bleating traffic on Fifth Avenue.

With most of his friends either still in the military or already at college, Matthiessen searched around for some kind of distraction. He read books in cafés and tried his hand at piano lessons. He audited lectures at the New School for Social Research: "The Individual in Society," "The Twentieth Century Novel." Also at the New School, he attended lectures by W. H. Auden, who would win the Pulitzer Prize for Poetry in 1948, and the anthropologist Ruth Benedict, who had just published her controversial study of Japanese culture, *The Chrysanthemum and the Sword*.

One freezing night he passed an alley off 12th Street, not far from University Place, and noticed a man slumped alone in the shadows. Trying to shake the man awake so he could offer something warm, soup or perhaps coffee, Matthiessen realized he was touching a corpse. Instead of alerting the police, he left the alley—"abandoned" the man, he later admitted, to be discovered by another passing citizen who "might be more thrilled than myself to be first with the news of a dead body"—and continued on his way, feeling "more uneasy than ever."[8]

Betty Matthiessen had written to her son while he was at Moanalua Ridge floating the idea of psychoanalysis. Peter had been skeptical at the time ("hell, I know what's wrong and it's just up to me to fix it"),[9] but now he agreed to a trial. He lasted for two sessions. Then he went to see Florence Powdermaker, a psychiatrist who'd devoted much of her career to, as *The New York Times* put it, "making children feel secure in society," and who was currently pioneering group therapy sessions for war-shocked merchant seamen.[10] Peter was hardly war-shocked, and he was not cut out for group sharing, which is perhaps why Dr. Powdermaker was also abandoned.

The most effective analyst he met in New York turned out to be the elevator operator in Aunt Bess's apartment building. One morning when Aunt Bess was out of town, Matthiessen returned carrying several bottles of alcohol:

> This kind tough man had noticed my erratic comings and goings, which did not seem to include shopping for groceries, and he stopped his elevator between floors to poke his nose into my clinking paper bag, then chew me out. *Ya wanna roon yaself? Shame on ya!* he shouted in sincere anger. *A kid like you, all the advantages, fa Chris sweet sake! Think you got problems, kid? You ain't!* And he cited the real and painful problems of an uneducated poor man who longed to educate his children, making me ashamed of all my privilege and soft sheltered assumptions, my disgusting self-indulgent melancholia, my childish need to flout authority and seeming inability to quell destructive impulses, stay out of trouble.[11]

The operator nudged Matthiessen out of his bubble and challenged him to see his place in a larger, less gilded world. Not long after this sobering lecture, Matthiessen swallowed his pride and called up his parents, asking if they could collect him from the Stamford train station.

IN ALL THE MONTHS Peter was away in Hawaii, Wendy Burden had waited patiently for his return. In letter after letter, he'd given her reasons to be hopeful, spinning a vision of his future that featured her in a starring role: "If I'm a writer, I shall <u>not</u> be a homebody. I <u>shall</u> be irascible, but not to you. You'll probably starve to death in a garret, but you won't be bored. Right now I'm all for a career for you, as long as it doesn't support the house."[12] These flights of fancy were far from serious, but they had the ring of a feasible plan, which is how Wendy chose to interpret them, even as Peter muddied things by reiterating his aversion to an early marriage. "I am of the firm belief I shall ask you," he wrote. "But frankly, I don't believe you'll hold out that long, and I don't blame you, either. It wouldn't be the thing to do at all, would it? And that is my chief dread, and it tempts me to get married a lot sooner than I want."[13] What he wanted was to get married when he was twenty-eight years old. In the meantime, it would be wonderful if he could carry her around in his duffel bag, he said, "just you and not your body—just your character, yourself, so to speak. Picturesque notion. Then I could go all over the world and never need to come home hardly—lovely thought."[14]

When Peter did come home from the Navy, Wendy was studying at Finch College in Manhattan. Determined to make it as an actress and singer, she auditioned for the Barter Theatre, a repertory company in Abingdon, Virginia, whose alumni included Gregory Peck and Patricia Neal. She beat out several hundred other young hopefuls, but turned down the life-changing opportunity because she didn't want to leave New York while Peter was around. For the same reason, she also turned down an offer to attend the Curtis Institute of Music in Philadelphia. "I wasn't going to leave wherever *he* was," she recalled.[15]

At one point Betty, observing Wendy's steadfast and increasingly self-destructive commitment, pulled her aside for a talk about how "difficult" Peter could be. Wendy listened to the warning, yet she also listened to her own mother, Babs, who suggested exactly the opposite, that she'd regret it all her life if she didn't have an "affair" with a man she was so crazy about. That winter, Wendy's mother even arranged an opportunity. "It was an excitement around Crowfields," recalled Jill Fox (née Fuller), Wendy's cousin, who also lived on the family estate, "because it seemed that it was advertised, almost: Aunt Babs was setting up a time when Wendy and Peter could do the *thing*."[16] The couple was left alone in a drafty house for an evening, but the expectation killed the mood. "We were both tense, and it was impossible," Wendy recalled. "However, after that difficult night, we continued to see each other, and finally, without a 'plan,' it happened to my huge joy and relief."[17] By May 6, 1947, Peter could write to Wendy: "Can't get over what a ripky-pipky time we had Friday, not to mention sundry portions of Saturday. The past two times have been such a sort of relief after that series of depressed, dark evenings in the winter, don't you think?"[18]

What Peter did not write to Wendy about was Payne Whitney Payson. He had mentioned Payne in his Navy letters, mostly to affirm that there was nothing going on beyond a brief summertime spark that had subsided into the warm glow of a long-distance friendship. But he now failed to disclose that Payne had called him up, not long after he arrived home in Connecticut, and invited him on a vacation to Georgia.

Joan Whitney Payson and Jock Whitney, Payne's mother and uncle, co-owned the Greenwood Plantation, an 1838 Greek Revival mansion with some five thousand acres of land in the Red Hills region near Thomasville. In the 1930s, Jock had secured the screen rights to Margaret Mitchell's *Gone with the Wind*, and it was said by at least one journalist that Greenwood served as "a model of southern elegance for the movie."[19] (The journalist added, "if you're a guy who has driven up and down and back and forth through the tobacco fields and coastal marshes and dreary savannas and piney wastes, you wouldn't believe there was such a lovely town as Thomasville in all the South.") It was a Whitney family tradition to ride horses and go shooting at Greenwood just after Christmas, and once the girls came of age, they were encouraged to bring dates. Payne thought Peter might like the birds. He traveled down by train to join her just before New Year's.

The vacation was not exactly romantic, as there were few opportunities to be alone at Greenwood. The entire house woke up early. A small crew motored across the lake to a hunting blind on stilts about the size of a bathroom, where talking was forbidden lest it startle the ducks. After breakfast, the same crew changed into field jackets and khakis. Horses were saddled up, and they rode out to shoot turkeys and bobwhite quail, aided by an entourage of English pointers. Peter was amazed, as Payne had predicted, by the abundance of birdlife—"the air appears to be choked with hurtling brown balls,"[20] he later wrote of the quail hunt—although it took him several days to regain his efficiency with a shotgun after falling out of practice in the Navy. He also took an interest in the dogs; the resident trainer, who was white, and the man's subordinate workers, who were all Black, formed a tableau of tense dependency that Matthiessen would soon explore in his breakout short story, "Sadie."

Despite the constant company and distractions, Payne nevertheless sensed the attraction reignite between herself and Peter. So did her father, Charles Shipman Payson. "He could see that *something* was going on," Payne recalled, "and though he never spoke up, he was clearly unhappy about us taking the overnight train back to New York together."[21] With good reason, as it turned out: "We discovered we were in love on that train." While Payne refused to have sex for the reasonable fear of pregnancy, they kissed in her cabin, then agreed to start seeing each other again. By April 16, 1947, Peter could write to her, after a long weekend visit: "C'est un voyage, ma vie, dans l'Hiver et dans la nuit, sans vos caresses admirables. Il y a trois jours, je suis le plus heureux des hommes et maintenant—p-ff-t! d'existence de chien ai-je plus envie de passer, au lieu de celle-ci." (Translated as, "My life is a journey through winter and night without your estimable caresses. Three days ago, I was the happiest of men, and now—p-ff-t! I'd take a dog's life over what I'm currently experiencing.")[22]

"Everyone had a crush on Peter," said Tom Guinzburg, his childhood friend who would also be a contemporary at Yale. "He was a figure in everyone else's first novel. He was almost a Fitzgeraldian character."[23]

THE THREE SEMESTERS THAT Matthiessen spent at Yale before decamping to Paris for his junior year—the spring and fall of 1947, then the spring of 1948—were a period of relative stasis in his life. For the college, however, they represented a watershed. Protocols had been put in place by the university leadership on the understanding that the military would demobilize troops slowly, over the course of a few years. Instead, the boys came home in a "rip-roaring flood," in the grimacing words of Edward Boyes, dean of admissions, and Yale was forced to revise its strategy at the eleventh hour.[24] Some nine hundred men had left Yale when America joined the war: all were entitled to return. Fifteen hundred more had been offered a place but deferred to fight first, study later: all were entitled to pick up where they'd left off. And then there were nonveteran candidates who were simply coming of age: Yale was loath to turn them away and risk damaging relationships with feeder schools.[25] This meant the Class of 1950, which began in the fall of 1946, would include 1,767 students—a 65 percent increase over usual enrollment, and the largest cohort in Yale's history.[26] That figure only grew in the spring when another few hundred stragglers were admitted, including Matthiessen, who would catch up on what he'd missed during the first summer break.

So many matriculating students caused tremendous headaches in New Haven. The halls and Gothic dormitories of Old Campus were not designed to accommodate anywhere near that number of freshmen. Single rooms were transformed into doubles, and two-man suites were retrofitted for four. The overflow was housed in an old hospital in Allingtown, three miles from New Haven, and in Ray Tompkins House, a building usually reserved for visiting athletic teams. When that was still not enough space, the gymnasium was filled with bunks until a barracks could be completed on Whitney Avenue. Married students found themselves living in corrugated iron Quonset huts, many of them erected on a square near the Yale Bowl. The strain of so many new mouths affected the dining halls, which extended meal hours and swapped the friendly waitresses and white linen tablecloths for cafeteria lines. Class sizes, too, exploded, and the deans scrambled to hire enough teachers. "I found myself being taught economics by a freshman in the Law School," recalled William F. Buckley Jr. (who would go on to torch the place in his withering 1951 book, *God and Man at Yale*), "and the following year I, along with two other undergraduates, was teaching Spanish."[27] On the bright side, the sudden influx meant the campus had never been more diverse, filled with men who'd seen something of the world, something of themselves, and who felt that tradition bound them less tightly than any of their predecessors.

As Tom Guinzburg remembered, "The postwar Yale was totally

seductive—high profile extracurricular activities, fraternities, societies—[and] the code was easy to comprehend."[28] It was possible to become "a fairly big shot" on campus if you were committed to making a name for yourself. "But Peter had no such intention," Guinzburg said.[29] Matthiessen was uninterested in being tapped for a secret society such as Skull and Bones. "That separated him from all the rest of us who were kind of competing for recognition." He was going to "maintain his individuality."

This was evident in Matthiessen's proposed program of study, which was so irregular the board of admissions initially rejected it. He selected Advanced French, English ("Chaucer to Eliot"), Philosophy (Ethics), and Ornithology. "As far as we can determine from your record you have never studied Biology," Edward Boyes wrote him regarding the latter choice.[30] Rather than picking an alternative, however, Matthiessen drove to New Haven and convinced the registrar by demonstrating his birding prowess. After that, he was permitted to take a variety of courses in the natural sciences with no further questions asked.

Language would prove to be the toughest challenge once his studies properly began. "My French is horrible—2 to 3 hour assignments each day, plus a 300-word French paper and an 8 minute French speech per week," he grumbled to Wendy in February. "The effort of pronunciation causes hives on my gums and barnacles on the back of my teeth."[31] He started skipping classes almost immediately—ten by April, including four days in a single week ("and the Dean is taking offense"). Instead of lectures, he went wandering through the woods on "bird-and-snake" walks with his roommate, which were excursions he justified in letters—and to himself—by invoking the Yale Peabody Museum of Natural History: "The museum, of course, was enchanted with our huge catch—the biggest they've ever had."[32]

Though Matthiessen was a freshman, the overcrowding on campus meant he was assigned a room in Ray Tompkins House with a junior, John Nelson Cole, who had temporarily left Yale to fly over Europe in the Eighth Air Force. Cole had grown up between New York and East Hampton, where his father was a founding member of the Maidstone Club, so he already knew Matthiessen socially. In fact, they were similar in several ways. Cole had a strained relationship with his father; he was ambivalent about his fortunate circumstances; and he sought "a kind of escape," as he put it, from the pressure to conform through a rowboat named the *Emma*, poking at snapping turtles in Georgica Pond as he tended to homemade eel pots.[33] Just as Matthiessen would rather wrangle wild snakes than conjugate French verbs, John Cole preferred to study sailor's knots over Theodore Meyer Greene's *The Arts and the Art of Criticism*. This made them a good match, and in the fall semester they began coauthoring a column for the *Yale Daily News*, "Two in the Bush," which was a public declaration of their shared interest in the outdoors. While many students were focused on the Wall Street emissaries who traveled up to scout recruits for the big city firms, the duo were offering extremely specific advice about hunting decoys "constructed of papier mâché and burnt waffles." ("The latter may separate the men from the boys in hawk circles but mean very little to crows, who are smarter than we to start with.")[34]

Soon after arriving at Yale, Matthiessen joined the swimming team. In fall he was elected, alongside Tom Guinzburg, to the Fence Club, where they drank dry martinis and played pool in a basement bar off York Street. ("Boozing, BS-ing, dining, and drooling," is how another fellow member summarized the evenings.)[35] But much of what survives from this period is, to a remarkable extent, focused on birds. "One has only to consider the life force packed tight into that puff of feathers to lay the mind wide open to the mysteries—the order of things, the why and the beginning," Matthiessen would later write in *The Shorebirds of North America*.[36] The foundation for this lofty idea was already being laid in his first year at Yale, when birdwatching seems to have functioned as another form of escapism.

One day during semester break, Charlie Lord brought his new girlfriend, Margaret Plunkett, to visit Matthiessen at Stamford. Lord was probably going to propose to Plunkett, and he wanted her to meet his old friend from Hotchkiss. They sat at a big wooden table in the kitchen, where "it was all very warm, very relaxed," Peggy Lord (as she indeed soon became) recalled. But Matthiessen wasn't there. "He'd heard that a snowy owl had been seen on a beach at Stamford, and he *had* to see this snowy owl. We had lunch without him."[37]

For Payne Whitney Payson, a fixation that had seemed perfectly reasonable in Georgia was slightly harder to deal with when Peter came to visit her at Sarah Lawrence College in Bronxville. "I didn't want him to know I wore glasses. So off I go birdwatching, I don't know a canary from a robin, and I can barely see a thing."[38]

For Wendy, it was even more vexing. During the summer between Peter's freshman and sophomore years, she went to stay with the Matthiessens at their house on Fishers Island. One morning before dawn, the whole family rose to inspect a black-crowned night heron's nest with some newly hatched chicks. Wendy didn't much care about herons, but she trudged out politely behind them—a scene that Peter would sculpt, years later, into a self-effacing anecdote about the cost of his preoccupation: "I became obsessed with birds . . . until my girlfriend, fed up with the whitening experience of being dragged all day through a night heron rookery, pushed me off a dock into a harbor."[39] This is true. "He was ignoring me," Wendy explained. "Maybe he was embarrassed to have me with his family. Whatever it was, he was not nice. I became very cross. I don't know how I managed to push him into the water and keep his glasses safe."[40] Then, feeling guilty, she jumped into the water after him. The next day, back home at Crowfields, Wendy was greeted by a delivery of two dozen red roses. Peter penned an apology in which he noted that she had "never looked prettier" than when she rose up angrily from the depths of East Harbor. Still, he couldn't help needling her a little: "I think I shall fall in love this weekend in retaliation, okay?"[41]

Not long after, Wendy discovered Peter *had* fallen in love with somebody else—Payne Whitney Payson. And that was how things ended between them. "I realized that it was time to call it quits," Wendy later wrote in a memoir.[42] Peter was far too restless to be a serious suitor. "He was clearly too young to marry and was dedicated to starting his writing career."

IN AUGUST 1948, Joseph A. Barry, a journalist and critic, made an intriguing declaration in *The New York Times:* "Ever since there have been Americans, they have dreamed a dream and called it Paris."[43] Barry had been friends with Gertrude Stein in the years before her death, and his article proposed to sketch "the American" in postwar Paris, partly through observation and partly by contrasting "him" (always a he) with members of the Lost Generation—the legendary expat community that had once counted among its members not only Stein but Hemingway, the Fitzgeralds, Dos Passos, Ezra Pound, and Sylvia Beach. Barry argued that rather than trying to ignore his Americanness, as most of those figures had done in various ways, the new pilgrim came to Paris and proclaimed it openly. Then the pilgrim spent his time pursuing French culture for personal edification; he was seeking "a set of values," Barry wrote, not looking "to fight the shadows of childhood or of war." Instead of Surrealism or Dadaism, his prevailing interest was Existentialism, which was *dans le vent*—fashionable, with its focus on meaning created by the individual.

If there was much about this sketch that was overly generalized, Barry was on firmer ground when he identified a commonality between the generations. Hemingway and his compatriots had found Paris offered freedoms not readily available in the United States—the freedom to drink, think, paint, write, and publish whatever they wanted. "It's not so much what Paris gives you," Stein wrote in her 1940 memoir, "as what it doesn't take away."[44] That freedom *from*, just as much as the freedom *to*, remained a major goal of the younger generation, which Barry illustrated by conducting several interviews. A young American artist living off the largess of the G.I. Bill told him that coming to Paris "felt like coming home. I could breathe." Meanwhile, the writer Richard Wright, who'd moved to the city in 1946 with the assistance of Stein, told Barry that Paris offered respite from America's white supremacy problem: "there is more freedom in one square block of Paris than in all the United States," he said.[45]

For Peter Matthiessen, the freedom promised by Paris would have nothing to do with racism and everything to do with puritanism and class pressures. Nobody knew him in Paris, which meant nobody could remind him of his parents' expectations. Unfettered, he could finally try living as *he* wanted to live.

The opportunity to go presented itself in early 1948, toward the end of his sophomore year at Yale, when a bulletin appeared on campus announcing a "Junior Year in France under the auspices of Sweet Briar College." Tucked away in pristine white oak forest near Lynchburg, Virginia, Sweet Briar was (and remains) a private women's college, but its new "Junior Year in France" program—this would be the inaugural run—was coeducational. For qualified students from any participating college or university, the program offered a year of supervised study at the Sorbonne. "[T]he colleges have an essential and all-important responsibility to help bring the peoples of the world together in mutual understanding and lasting peace," said Martha B. Lucas, president of Sweet Briar, in a statement of support that connected the program thematically with the ideals of UNESCO.[46]

Yale was so enthusiastic about the JYF that it contributed its own director of undergraduate studies, Theodore Andersson, an associate professor of French, to be "Professor-in-charge," the authority figure who'd chaperone the students to Paris for the academic year. It was likely Andersson who sold the program to Matthiessen, along with the thirteen other Yalies who were deemed to meet the requirements: two years of pre-college French, two years of college French, strong general scholarship, seriousness of purpose, and an "excellent character." Also financial security, because the program cost a minimum of $1,807 (some $23,000 today), and this sum did not include spending money or factor in any of the innumerable items students were encouraged to bring in their luggage, including enough soap, powdered milk, chocolate, and bouillon cubes to last the full year. "There are no tidbits which can be bought in Paris in the way of candy or cookies in the afternoon," a program information pack warned about the postwar rationing.[47]

The initial Sweet Briar proposal to students elicited 240 inquiries, then 82 applications from around the country; 71 were approved, and 67 students ultimately went. Divided almost exactly between men and women, the final group was remarkably mixed in terms of background. There was a girl from Puerto Rico and a man from Hawaii, a Powers model who attended Barnard while trying to make it in magazines and a veteran who would do the whole trip accompanied by his wife and baby.

Arrangements were made by Sweet Briar for the students to travel to France in tourist class accommodation on the RMS *Mauretania*, sailing from New York on August 28. When departure day finally arrived, they wore their Sunday best and waved ecstatically as the ship pulled away from the pier. Many of the young women had never left the country before; many of the men had only left on troopships.

But Matthiessen was not aboard the *Mauretania*. He was so eager to reach Europe—or, more accurately, to leave America—that he had set out more than six weeks earlier, on July 9. His ship, the SS *Leerdam*, took twelve days to cross from New York to Antwerp; he passed the time by learning how "to play and dislike bridge," and by marveling at skua flying far from any landmass. "Trip very enjoyable," he noted in a black journal newly purchased so he could document his time abroad. "No sleep to speak of and, again, too much recourse to the fated flask."[48]

Matthiessen's arrival in Paris, via a train from Belgium on July 23, coincided with a moment when its nickname, the "City of Light," which dates back to the days of Louis XIV, had never seemed both more and less appropriate. The Grande Nuit de Paris, coming at the end of June, was supposed to be a morale boost for the city, and an enticement for tourists to return with their precious spending money. In the first major gala to happen since the war, monuments and buildings that had languished in darkness were brilliantly illuminated: Napoleon, dressed as Caesar atop his column in the Place Vendôme, "shone like an enormous lamp on what is left of Ritz society," wrote Janet Flanner, Paris correspondent for *The New Yorker*.[49] The Palais de Chaillot, where the U.N. General Assembly was scheduled to convene in September, was lit up like a giant birthday cake. Just across the Seine, the Eiffel Tower had never looked more dazzling, not only for its white lights but also for the elephants performing down between its legs as part of the Cirque d'Hiver-Bouglione. Fireworks had leapt off the Pont d'Iéna, and people had celebrated on the labyrinthine slopes of Montmartre until the sun peeped over the rooftops.

However, the Grande Nuit de Paris was an "advertisement," Flanner astutely pointed out; it showed "what Paris used to be like and may one day be again."[50] As with most advertisements, real life did not quite match the choreographed stage show. The lights stayed on at the Place de la Concorde, but power cuts, both scheduled and unscheduled, were common elsewhere in the city. Shops along the rue du Faubourg Saint-Honoré featured window displays of jewels or fresh fruit, yet few Parisians could afford the prices their local grocers chalked on miniature blackboards.[51] Butter remained scarce, as did coffee and, for a while, plain white bread. Though no longer rationed by the summer of 1948, wine was often "baptized" with water to make it go further.[52] A steak was still an unthinkable extravagance for most residents, and restaurants remained woefully empty compared to their prewar trade; people made do with whatever they could scrounge up for dinner at home. A few months before Matthiessen, Arthur Miller had arrived during winter and checked into a hotel on the rue du Bac. The hotel's concierge had nicks on his face from shaving with cold water, Miller noticed, and once a day the man rushed out to feed his pet rabbits, the only dependable source of protein for his family. "Rabbits," Miller wrote, "were saving a lot of people."[53]

If Matthiessen noticed anything similar—the daily strikes and political upheaval discussed in *Le Monde;* the trucks run on wood-burning engines; the old ladies in mismatched clothes riding rusted bicycles to avoid paying Métro fare—he never wrote it down in his journal. Art Buchwald, who would soon become a foreign correspondent for the *New York Herald Tribune,* once recalled of his own time in Paris that "one of the joys of being an American . . . was that you felt no responsibility for what happened there, as long as it did not interfere with the price of oysters."[54] This insouciance was shared by Matthiessen, who was, to be fair, just twenty-one years old, a young exchange student thrilled to find himself in a strange new city. His surviving letters from 1948 unsurprisingly focus on "the beauty" of Paris, its "openness and freshness and trees and open markets and the Seine and the dancing girls" of the Folies Bergère.[55] Because the French government had just devalued the franc in January, he discovered he was "rich" with the allowance from his parents, plus whatever remained of his weekly benefits under the G.I. Bill. Flush with American dollars, he could even sidestep the gas ration.

After one night in a hotel on the Place Vendôme, he traveled down to the Latin Quarter on the Left Bank, where a soft pink building at 1, rue Gît-le-Coeur overlooked the quai des Grands-Augustins. In the foyer was a Rodin statue and a two-person elevator; he ascended to the penthouse of the American railroad heiress Alice Antoinette DeLamar. Her two-floor apartment was "furnished like a country home in Westchester," in the words of Ludwig Bemelmans, who had once rented it and spent weeks on the roof terrace sketching a "sweeping panorama of the city" (and observing a homeless man push a fox terrier around the Pont Neuf in a pram).[56] Matthiessen's pal from back home, Peter Thacher, knew DeLamar as a family friend; he was already settled into the apartment for a few weeks of vacation. Also in residence was Thacher's stepbrother, Blair Fuller, who, at Matthiessen's encouragement, had taken a year away from Harvard to attend the JYF himself. Back in New York, Fuller lived on the Crowfields estate in Bedford alongside Wendy Burden, his cousin; he and Matthiessen had first bonded in their mid-teens over literature and a shared sense of disillusionment with their families. ("Our parents' suburban lives did not appeal to either of us," Fuller recalled. "We wanted adventures, to know things our parents could not explain to us.")[57] Now the three of them—Peter, Peter, and Blair—would use DeLamar's penthouse until the start of the academic year.

In the weeks that followed, Matthiessen explored Central Europe by rail. "Switzerland at first glance: a collection of healthy dullards playing with beautiful toys in a calendar," he wrote as he passed through Lucerne.[58] In Milan, his binoculars were purloined by a pickpocket, which made him write off the place as a "dreadful town, the worst since Troy, N.Y." Venice was "lovely in [a] garish, operatic way." Florence was "most impressive." Lake Como was relaxing, even if he was thoroughly trounced at tennis by a man Matthiessen referred to in his journal as "a colored saxophone player." Back in France, he traveled down to Saint-Jean-de-Luz, where the girls were the "most beautiful" he'd ever seen, and a bullfight was "macabre" and "overpowering," just as Hemingway had written.

Yet no trip made as much of an impression as a long weekend to Brittany and Normandy. "Peter [Thacher] and I left Gare du Montparnasse for Port Blanc. Took two days on train, bus, truck, bicycle, and foot (when we forgot to change & hiked 3 miles back down the track after stopping the Autorail).... Made every mistake it was possible to make and several which weren't, but very amusing and good for French."[59] During their first evening in Port-Blanc, a stark coastal village with a chapel built on a rocky outcrop, they crossed paths with a pretty blond woman named Marie-Claude Jallu, and a brunette of luminous intensity, Nathalie de Salzmann, who Matthiessen found "much the most remarkable person met in years . . . Truly admirable in every way and an instant friend who I feel sure will contribute substantially to everything I can derive from the coming year." The four of them headed east to Mont-Saint-Michel, the island abbey surrounded by tidal flats. It was drizzling rain, nearly dark when it came into view, which only added to the surreal effect: Matthiessen struggled to describe its "strength, majesty, mystery," or the impression it gave him of "other-worldliness." Early next morning, he was drawn out onto *les sables mouvants*—the waterlogged sand, where he identified seabirds and gathered small colored clam shells until the tide began to swallow his footsteps.

At nearby Pontorson, the foursome narrowly missed a train back to Paris. Sitting down for lunch before the next scheduled departure, they witnessed a grotesque spectacle. Matthiessen would remember the details decades later during an interview:

I was sitting in a café . . . and saw a guy who was accused of being a Nazi collaborator beaten in a square and left unconscious. When he came to, he came over to this café where all of these big guys who had beaten him up were sitting. There was a picket fence surrounding the terrace of the restaurant, and this poor guy started pounding his fists on the sharp pickets; with each blow, he shrieked, "C'est vous qui un lâche! C'est vous et vous et vous et vous!" He was turning his hands into hamburger. The men realized that the onlookers were horrified that they had beaten him in such a cowardly way, and they went out to shut him up. He was reeling around and this big man came at him and hit him so hard, he practically took his head off. Laid him out flat in the dirt again. It was a hateful scene. The whole country was full of shame and guilt about what they had done during the occupation murdering people, humiliating people, and how many of them behaved any better than that broken man?[60]

A younger, more callow Matthiessen briefly noted some of the same details in his journal, but then turned it back to himself, adding that it was the "sole incident to disturb . . . the enormous relaxation and easiness I seem to have achieved in Europe."[61]

REID HALL, IN MONTPARNASSE, was located at 4, rue de Chevreuse, just around the corner from Le Dôme Café, where writers and artists liked to debate the meaning of life through a pungent haze of cigarette smoke. Unassuming from the outside, Reid Hall was easy to overlook: four stories of buff-colored stone, with dormer windows and two large wooden doors. Behind those doors, however, a tranquil courtyard gave way to an iron gate, which opened onto a secret walled garden of lilacs and rhododendrons, maple and poplar trees. The eighteenth-century manor had once been a hunting lodge for the Duc de Chevreuse—then converted, variously, into a porcelain factory, a Protestant school (attended by André Gide), a girls' boardinghouse, a Red Cross military hospital (the Grand Salle becoming an operating theater), and a refuge during the German occupation, when people burned the furniture to endure winter. Now, in the fall of 1948, it was the center of student life for Americans in Paris, and headquarters for the Sweet Briar JYF. Visitors could step across the threshold and find young people reading Voltaire or Marivaux in dappled sunshine, particularly on Fridays and Saturdays when there was no electricity indoors.

While Reid Hall offered dormitory accommodation for several dozen *pensionnaires*, only women in the program were permitted to claim a bed when the group finally arrived from the *Mauretania*. They would share facilities with women from an almost identical program run by Smith College in Massachusetts. The men of the JYF were placed, promised a Sweet Briar report, with "carefully selected French families in the higher economic brackets who can afford to buy unrationed wood fuel when the scanty coal allotment has been exhausted."[62] Or they made their own arrangements, as Matthiessen did at the absolute last minute. "Pound pavements every day for rooms near Place St. Michel, unsuccessful," he wrote in early September. "At end of week locate Mme Bardel, 107, Malesherbes—most satisfactory if far away and unatmospheric."[63] His new address was in the 8th arrondissement, on the Right Bank, which meant a lengthy daily trek down across the river.

Before students could enroll in classes at the Sorbonne, they had a compulsory six-week preliminary period at Reid Hall. The purpose of this orientation was twofold: to polish language skills through grammar classes, phonetics, and *explication de texte*; and to introduce the students, as a buffer against culture shock, to the sweeping social and economic changes that had transformed life in France since 1939. Four to five seminars a week—some by candlelight, a lesson in itself—were devoted to subjects like "Present Day Problems" (the black market, le Parti communiste français), and "The Reconstruction of [the] French Economy and the Marshall Plan," which was augmented with an uninspiring guest appearance by U.S. Secretary of State George Marshall, in Paris to visit the U.N. General Assembly. ("He was *not* an orator," recalled Mary Booth, twenty years old and very bored as she sat in the audience as a student at Reid Hall.)[64] The relevance of these courses soon became clear to the young Americans when, for example, their fingers numbed around their pencils as the weather turned cold and the heating remained shut off; or when a girl got swept up in a communist street demonstration. Others found themselves criticized by resentful Parisians for their good teeth, or for the Marshall Plan, as though they were directly responsible for the so-called imperialist project.

Matthiessen's verdict on the introductory seminars was that they ranged "from excellent to ridiculous." He dutifully attended them, along with scheduled group visits to sites including Fontainebleau Palace ("like all museums, enervating as hell to me").[65] At the same time, he kept himself aloof from most of the other JYF students, declining to join the cliques that dominated Reid Hall.

In the first days of October, he went for drinks with Nathalie de Salzmann, the brunette he'd met in Brittany. She was twenty-nine—nearly eight years older than Peter—with three small children and a husband she was either currently divorcing or already divorced from. Peter found her so beguiling that he ignored these details, though, and listened as she narrated a "fascinating life history."

Nathalie's father, Alexandre de Salzmann, had been an Art Nouveau painter and part of the Jugendstil art movement in Germany. Her mother, Jeanne Allemand, was a dancer who trained in eurhythmics with Émile Jaques-Dalcroze. Both Alexandre and Jeanne were spiritual seekers—"searching for something in yourself, something that is missing in your usual state,"[66] Jeanne said—and in 1919, the year Nathalie was born, they'd fallen into the orbit of a charismatic Greek-Armenian mystic named George Ivanovitch Gurdjieff. Joining his study group in Tiflis (now Tbilisi), in Georgia, the Salzmanns had become ardent disciples of "the Work"—Gurdjieff's proprietary system for self-realization. From Georgia, the family had then followed him to Constantinople, Germany, and finally France, where they'd helped establish his "monastery" at the Château le Prieuré, in Fontainebleau-Avon, called the Institute for the Harmonious Development of Man. Alexandre began to proselytize, and when he died in 1934 Jeanne took responsibility for his pupils and relocated to Paris. In the years leading up to the war, Madame de Salzmann had become Gurdjieff's most trusted, most admired, and most widely known deputy, "living proof of the transmissibility of his Work."[67] As for Madame de Salzmann's children, Nathalie's entire life had been steeped in Gurdjieffian philosophy, and she now described it for Peter with the unblinking conviction of a true believer.

G. I. Gurdjieff was an enigmatic figure, revered by some as a visionary and derided by others as a charlatan. In an impossible tangle of fact and fiction, he claimed to have spent twenty years learning from "remarkable men" in religious sects across Central Asia and the Middle East. His system was immensely complex, a blend of everything from Buddhism to Gnosticism, with marked similarities to Theosophy. In brief, Gurdjieff taught that most people are asleep, barely conscious automatons who float through their lives without ever fully living them. We confront stimuli as a machine does, unthinkingly, programmed by habit to react. And in this state of passive sleepwalking, we mistake our mechanical reactions for who we think we are: a singular, unchanging "me." But in reality we are a multiplicity of "I's," all of them different parts of a dormant true self. To rouse from this condition, to integrate the "I's," to inhabit the world as a fully conscious organism with *free will* rather than mechanical reactions: this is the aim of Gurdjieff's Work. The intention is not to "transform oneself into something else," Michel de Salzmann, Nathalie's brother, once explained to a journalist. "It is to become what one is."[68]

80 · TRUE NATURE

A few days after their drinks, Nathalie took Peter to meet her mother and brother on the rue du Bac. "Spiritualist soirée chez Mme. De Salzmann," he wrote in his journal: "fascinating discussion with some forty people."[69]

That Matthiessen was intrigued by what he heard is hardly surprising. He had come to think of his self as fragmented long before he arrived in Paris. Gurdjieff not only taught that feeling this way was normal, because we *are* fragmented, but his system suggested that Matthiessen, in recognizing his own confused nature, was already on the path toward becoming an integrated whole. Matthiessen had identified the symptoms of his discontent; here was a potential cure. Gurdjieffians called it "self-remembering," a practice of heightened, effortful self-consciousness which Matthiessen would eventually describe in *The Snow Leopard*, emphasizing its similarity to Zen, as "paying attention to the present moment instead of wandering the ephemeral worlds of past and future."[70]

With Nathalie as his guide, he began to probe the "spiritualist" literature further that fall. While his classmates contemplated "Aspects of the French Countryside" after lectures at Reid Hall, he attended discussion groups to learn about P. D. Ouspensky, the Russian esotericist and a key explicator of Gurdjieff's Work.

Eventually Nathalie took him to the Salle Pleyel, a concert hall not far from the Arc de Triomphe, where Gurdjieff liked to hold private lessons in a rehearsal room. The mystic was not present—it is unclear whether Matthiessen ever met Gurdjieff, who died in October 1949—but Madame de Salzmann was seated at a piano. Matthiessen watched from the wall as a troupe of pupils, likely dressed in white, assembled in lines to practice "Les Mouvements," sacred, trance-like dances, resembling coordinated calisthenics or semaphore without the flags, that were intended to harmonize the body, mind, and emotions. "Fascinating," Matthiessen noted again in his journal.[71] Led by Nathalie, he soon returned to the Salle Pleyel to try these "appealing" Movements for himself.

AFTER THE PRELIMINARY PERIOD at Reid Hall, Matthiessen decided to spend the two-week break on a reporting trip—the first in his life. He was considering a career after Yale in journalism, and he figured this was as good a time as any to get some experience.

One of the biggest stories in the world that year was the February coup d'état in Czechoslovakia; Soviet-backed communists had seized control of the last remaining democracy in Eastern Europe, a major development in the burgeoning Cold War. Matthiessen knew relatively little about foreign politics, but he hatched a plan for a "wonderful, complicated" road trip from

Paris to Prague, where he would survey the situation and perhaps write a dispatch.[72] Blair Fuller agreed to split the driving duties in a Peugeot they had just bought together for 880 francs. The American embassy, informed of the plan, suggested it was a terrible idea—the men would be on their own in the event of an emergency—but Matthiessen decided to go anyway. "Blair and I and our little car are going to invade the Iron Curtain," he announced in a letter home.[73]

In mid-October, the friends drove to Steinbourg, in northeastern France, where they stopped for the night. The next morning they headed to Vienna, a long day of driving through countryside that was "comparatively rich," Matthiessen noted, and cities that were "shells, bleak and bitter."[74] When they skirted Dachau near Munich, Fuller observed an enormous crematorium chimney framed by "a field of tall grass waving peacefully in the wind."[75] Boys threw stones at their car, and they decided against stopping for a closer look.

In Vienna, Fuller left the itinerary to his friend and stared at the soldiers who were still patrolling the city streets in jeeps. Matthiessen soon dragged him off to the Musikverein Wien, for Beethoven's string quartets; to a performance of "Vetrate di chiesa," by Ottorino Respighi; and to one of "Eine Alpensinfonie," by Richard Strauss, which they both agreed was "boring."[76] Two locals they met along the way, Ernst and Emma Hartmann, took them to an Egon Schiele exhibition and up into the Vienna Woods so they could admire the view from Kahlenberg. Matthiessen thought Vienna was "charming, old, quite battered. Full of American and Russian personnel, no tourists. We were [a] curiosity." Ernst told him that "80% of people" hated the Americans, which was a statistic Matthiessen found hard to believe based on his own experience. Nevertheless, a few days later he read about Irving Ross, an American official involved with administering the Marshall Plan in Vienna, just discovered on the city outskirts beaten to death, reportedly by Soviets, with forty-five blows from the butt of a rifle.[77]

From Vienna, the Peugeot crossed the border into Czechoslovakia. After a brief breakdown, during which Matthiessen was more interested in some coots than in fixing the engine, they arrived in Prague on October 24. The typical touristic revelry ensued: hot dogs in the street, two drunk girls, an impromptu dance at the Embassy Bar. But other moments were a little more unusual, like when the Americans found themselves at an enormous rally in Wenceslas Square, where red, white, and blue flags had been unfurled down the National Museum façade to celebrate the thirtieth anniversary of the Republic. Matthiessen would later remember figures with submachine guns silhouetted along the rooftops, giant portraits of Stalin and Klement Gottwald, and propaganda bellowed from a rostrum. He also witnessed a brief flicker of resistance ("a wonderful thing") when an old woman began selling folding triptych photographs of the "patriot leaders of her country": Jan Masaryk; former president Tomáš Masaryk (his father); and former president Edvard Beneš.[78] "Those nearby erupted in cheers and laughter; she was bought out in minutes." Then the police swept in and the "gleeful throng" closed ranks to protect her, spiriting her away down a side street where she suddenly vanished.

Less than a year before, in New York, an acquaintance named Priscilla Preston had invited Matthiessen to after-dinner drinks with her "good friend," the foreign minister of Czechoslovakia Jan Masaryk. It was winter then, and Masaryk had been visiting the U.S. on a fruitless mission to secure support for his country against an imminent threat from the Soviet Union. He was "a big bald affable man," Matthiessen recalled, "intelligent and highly amusing." They got on well despite an age difference of decades, and when Matthiessen finally set down his whiskey glass and stood up to leave, Masaryk inscribed a photograph as a parting gift—himself in a dark suit, seated and leaning forward, arms folded across his lap. The minister had smiled as he handed it over, assuring the younger man that the photo was used "as an advertisement by his former in-laws, American owners of the Crane porcelain company, a foremost manufacturer of toilets."[79] (This was almost certainly a joke, though Masaryk's ex-wife was indeed Frances Crane Leatherbee.)

In Prague, Matthiessen now took a taxi to Černín Palace. Pulling up outside the enormous Baroque pile that served as the Czech Foreign Ministry, he asked the driver to point out the spot where Masaryk's body had been found on March 10, when he'd reportedly committed suicide by jumping out the bathroom window of his ministerial apartment. The driver indicated a place by a low wall, a short distance from the building. Matthiessen looked and was unconvinced; remembering the warm encounter in New York, he reached a different conclusion: Masaryk was "thrown." This was a widespread assumption at the time, with Matthiessen joining many Czechs who believed the order had come from Moscow. But while police finally closed the case in 2004, ruling murder based on forensic evidence, Jan Masaryk's death continues to be debated as an enduring mystery of the Cold War.

Matthiessen and Fuller circled back through Germany—"Nuremberg obviously once lovely; not now"—to Reims, France, where they inspected the red-brick schoolhouse recently renamed the Musée de la Reddition, in honor of the day just three years before when the Nazis had signed the document here that ended the European conflict. ("Extraordinary detail of war plans; very impressive.")[80] Then the friends returned to Paris, and

Matthiessen began writing his dispatch. Though the article is now lost, his impressions of the world beyond the Iron Curtain—the dark medievalism; the slogans, lies, and purges of decent men—would resurface in his second published novel, *Partisans*.

THE MAIN PROGRAM of the JYF began in early November. Matthiessen enrolled in five classes: two in French drama offered through Smith College and Sweet Briar at Reid Hall; two Cours de Civilisation, on literature and composition, offered by the Sorbonne; and one at the École du Louvre, about the history of French painting since the nineteenth century, which was partly taught by Jean Cassou, director of the Musée National d'Art Moderne. This was a heavy workload, but the intention was for students to settle down after two months of leisurely induction. Nevertheless, on November 8, Matthiessen wrote "Lectures etc." in his journal; then he barely mentioned any of his classes again until the following March, by which time he was averaging Bs and Cs: "Dreadful art paper. Should be ashamed."[81]

Proust and Baudelaire were swell, but an equally valuable education, in his view, could be found beyond the lecture halls in the bistros and *boîtes* and public gardens of Paris. He was "constantly more attached" to the city: birds and flowers at the market on Île de la Cité; Picassos at the Jeu de Paume; cocktail hour (an American import) at the Hôtel de Crillon, followed by plays at one of several theaters, including the Théâtre de l'Athénée, where Molière's *Dom Juan* was "excellent."

Women featured prominently in Matthiessen's extracurricular activities. Officially, he had never stopped seeing Payne Whitney Payson before departing for Europe. She'd waved him off at the pier, and they had continued to exchange letters for months afterward. But a friend, Walter Denegre Sohier, then bumped into Payne at a fancy-dress party in Manhasset, Long Island. While dancing together, Sohier, who had crossed paths with Matthiessen on his own continental travels, told Payne she was "a fool" for thinking Peter would ever marry her: "He's over there in Paris and he's got three girls crazy about him."[82] Payne was drunk, and she reacted to this shattering revelation by jumping into a pond so violently that her brother-in-law had to carry her upstairs and call for a doctor. The next day, she wrote a letter to Peter breaking it off. He replied with a note full of bitter truths, saying Sohier was right: "if you permit me to enter into your plans in the smallest way, you are indeed a fool, Payney darling, because you have no intention of waiting four or five years for me nor, as you have said, of marrying me under any circumstances other than those of my being ready for marriage in general, ready enough and mature enough not to resent the restriction."[83] Privately, in his journal, he berated himself for a repeat of the Wendy situation: "Can't seem to learn not to make the same mistakes twice."[84]

His relationship with Payne ended in late September; by November, he had escalated his involvement with Nathalie de Salzmann. "Armagnac, bath, and good old-fashioned sex," he wrote after visiting her apartment on rue Perceval.[85] But there were several American women he had also been seeing since the voyage on the SS *Leerdam*—Hope Dillion, for example, though she quickly dropped out of the picture, and Polly Winton, who years later would tell *Vanity Fair*, of Peter Matthiessen, that there was "something terribly glamorous about such a loner. Glamorous but tough—a combination of grace and raw rogue energy that's very rare."[86] Meanwhile, Mary "Piedy" Bailey had first met him in Connecticut, and here in Paris (she was part of the Smith College program) they went for cocktails together around the Place Pigalle. These raucous nights ended with him trying to boost her discreetly over the garden wall into Reid Hall, or with him blurting out an insult after one too many drinks. Piedy would become a lifelong friend, though she thought Peter could be a mean drunk sometimes: "I remember sitting in a bar in Paris, and him telling me that I was 'a rat sniveling in a corner,' or something that doesn't make you feel good. He didn't mean any harm, but he had a hurt heart, and it just turned nasty with the greatest of ease."[87]

And then there was "P. Southgate," as he wrote in his journal. Patricia Brigham Southgate—"Patsy"—was also in Paris studying literature through the Smith College program, and she would have a little more lasting power than the other women. Patsy first came to Peter's attention during a party at the rue Gît-le-Coeur apartment, likely for the same reason she would eventually receive one of the most lascivious obituaries ever published in *The New York Times:* "A clean-cut American beauty whose finely chiseled features were set off by surprisingly full lips generally framing a dazzling, inviting smile, Miss Southgate, whose animated beauty generally confounded the camera, was blond to her eyelids and had such a steady, open gaze it was said that to look into her deep blue eyes was to fall in love."[88] The fact Patsy seemed totally unaware of how she looked—Frank O'Hara would liken her to Grace Kelly—only made her more spellbinding.

Peter saw Patsy for a second time at the Ritz Bar. As he later remembered the autumn evening, there was "instant knowledge on both sides that this was It," and they blew off their friends "in favor of romantic supper w. each other and violins and La Boheme"—a swooning claim that might be overstating things a little.[89] His journal shows that he thought Patsy was "intelligent, humorous, broad-minded," and that their "fine rapport" developed over a whole series of dates: horse rides in the Bois, strolls along the Seine, a piano recital by Wilhelm Backhaus. Yet he also found her "neurotic" and "childish," even though she was only eight months younger than he was, and "fixed in her ideas"—unwilling, in other words, to concede that his own were superior.[90] Another annoyance was the fact that Patsy was still a virgin, at least until they had "lots of sauce" and addressed the situation ("phew"). The unsteady waltz of their early relationship would eventually become a topic of amusement among friends. One story about a heated disagreement, told by George Plimpton and repeated in print by the editor Terry McDonell, had Peter turning up at Patsy's door with "a single, perfect peach" as a peace offering.[91] Another story, told by Peter himself, had Patsy yelling at him on the phone, then trudging "all the way across Paris" with a conciliatory orange.[92]

This is how he spent much of that fall and early winter when he wasn't studying with the Gurdjieffians. "Our existence here continues in its usual extraordinary fashion—full, exciting, extremely stimulating and amusing, and very tiring indeed," he wrote in another letter to Wendy (with whom he was still corresponding, despite everything). "From time to time 'dull sloth' creeps over me, bringing with it a powerful desire for bird books, binoculars, guns, & Fishers Island, but in general we seem to be rushing crazily along in a wonderful wave of things, so fast as to make a decent perspective impossible, so furiously that only now have we begun to realize how little we knew before."[93]

WHEN THE RUSH BECAME *too* furious, he vowed to scale back his social engagements. "Would like to narrow social life down to N[athalie] and P. Southgate or somebody like her," he wrote in December.[94] Yet it was not until the middle of February that anything really changed, and only then because Nathalie de Salzmann announced over dinner one night that she was pregnant.

Peter was shocked. "I don't know [how] I'll straighten this out with myself," he wrote in his journal. He was even more shocked, however, by Nathalie's mention of abortion, which he'd been raised to consider a great taboo: "Jesus, what a disgusting thing." Feeling nervous and, he allowed, "perhaps guilty," he raised the idea of marriage ("Have made all the proper offers"). Nathalie likely recognized that his suggestion came from a tepid sense of duty rather than any genuine desire, because she turned him down. "Never will be this kind again," Peter told himself, "but wouldn't be otherwise with her."

Uncertain of what to say or do, he decided that the best course of action was to press on with his life as though nothing was amiss. He took Patsy to the Jardin des Plantes; they saw *La Tosca* by Victorien Sardou; they made plans to go skiing in Megève before the snow melted.

When he did return to Nathalie, he quietly hoped that the situation might simply have resolved itself. Perhaps the baby would just . . . go away. Natalie told him the baby was "doing fine." This was disappointing ("damnit"), and it made him worry about the next steps. Abortion was still illegal in France; an abortionist named Marie-Louise Giraud had been executed by guillotine as recently as 1943. There was not much chance of that happening to Nathalie de Salzmann, but what *would* happen remained an open question. The question seemed especially urgent after they consulted a woman who appears to have read their tarot cards, or palms, or even their tea leaves (the journal is vague): Peter was told he was going to get married when he was twenty-seven and lead a long, contented life; Nathalie was told it was "quite likely" she'd commit suicide at the age of forty.*

After that alarming consult, Peter refrained from recording any further details about the situation. His journal abruptly ended the following week, on March 11, 1949, with Nathalie de Salzmann departing with a friend "for Maroc.—" The baby was never born.

In *Race Rock*, written just a few years later, the protagonist's girlfriend, Evelyn Murray, also falls unexpectedly pregnant. When she gingerly broaches the subject one night in bed ("what would you do if I were to have a baby?"), George McConville's first inclination is to joke about rolling the baby down the stairs, and his second is to pretend that he hasn't understood—"to pretend, to pretend."[95] George is horrified when Eve suggests that she could have a doctor "arrange something,"[96] but then perhaps, he concedes, the alternative is worse. He leaves her to deal with the details ("stepping suddenly, melodramatically, from her bed and quitting the apartment, the glory of the gesture like a brief flame on a mounting pile of ash") while he battles with himself during a long weekend of soul-searching. The abortionist is a short, dandyish creep straight out of German Expressionist cinema, Doktor Rudolf Lichenstein, who wears a bright tweed topcoat and one of his collar points directed out "like an accusing finger."[97] He sets the price for an operation at $500.

"That's much too much," Eve says.

"Excuse me, I know it is, but my clients do not think so."

All of which is fiction, of course, though it suggests how deeply the scenario had settled into Matthiessen's consciousness. For Eve, the pregnancy

---

* In fact, Nathalie de Salzmann moved to Venezuela in 1950; married Jacques Regis Etievan in 1954; promoted Gurdjieff throughout South America, from Ecuador to Argentina; opened several schools based on Gurdjieffian pedagogy; wrote a book called *A Sense of Wonder When I Do Not Know*; and died, in 2007, one month before her eighty-eighth birthday.

is presented as a physical problem, to be solved through a ghoulish "crime." For George, the dilemma is framed in existential terms: "I am twenty-eight, he thought, educated, intelligent, a veteran of one war and several women, and still I am a boy."[98]

"I CAN'T DESCRIBE the feeling of relaxation and complete ease which is partly based on France itself and partly on escaping from those endless messes and complications at home," Peter had written Wendy Burden soon after his arrival in Paris.[99] Now, almost a year later, not even the drama with Nathalie could shake his conviction that everything was better for him here. Being in Paris meant a new mode of being: "there was no time-sense; living from hand to mouth."[100] When he ran out of francs, he hocked his watch and ordered another bottle of champagne. It was easy, thanks to the next infusion of funds from Connecticut, to drop everything and dash off to Corsica, stay in an old mansion atop the harbor battlements in Calvi. "Whenever I leave [Paris], I am relieved to get back, and every time I get back, I discover something strange and wonderful in its atmosphere that I hadn't been aware of before."[101] Inspired by the city, he began to draft short stories again. He took up watercolors ("I have confined myself to date to compelling interpretations of birds") and dabbled with poetry for the first time since Hotchkiss: fifteen shaky lines, entitled "Bird of Passage," about a great skua that "Floats restless, sober, lawless / On the February ocean."[102]

The Junior Year in France ended in June 1949. Like many young Americans who'd read Ernest Hemingway, Matthiessen set off for Spain, drifted through the villages of Navarre, and washed up in Pamplona for the festival of San Fermín—a last hurrah before he headed back to finish up at Yale. But Paris had shown him that it was possible to forget what his parents wanted him to be; that it was possible to forget what he, as the progeny of WASPs, was supposed to want for himself. Paris gave him a "queer feeling (as a result of my peace of mind, perhaps) that this is the only place I have ever lived,"[103] as opposed to just existing, and he would seize the first opportunity to return.

5

Daily Themes

> What interests me most is the working through from book to book of some recurrent obsession or at least preoccupation, a reverberation from within, which may burst the work wide at any moment, though it often seems half-hidden from the writer.
>
> —PM, "The Art of Fiction No. 157," *The Paris Review* (1999)[1]

MATTHIESSEN'S SENIOR YEAR at Yale, the year he found his footing as a writer, began in September 1949 with a class called Daily Themes. Organized by Professor Benjamin Nangle to, as Matthiessen put it, "weed out gut-course specialists and assorted pretenders,"[2] the class was infamously demanding, requiring at least one page of prose every weekday throughout the full semester. "Theme" did not mean *theme* so much as part of a short story, a scene, character sketch, or evocation of mood. Plot was beside the point. So were trick endings and any attempts at exposition. Undergraduates were encouraged to scour their everyday lives for material, transforming mundane events or moments of drama—"being approached by a homosexual," one instructor said, was a popular example—into a few sturdy paragraphs.[3] The pressure to submit something fresh every morning could sometimes cause mid-semester anguish, as John Downey, who graduated the year after Matthiessen, later recalled: "Our supplies of disgusting roommates, faithless maidens, callous parents were running low. In the later stages of the course we took to wandering the streets of New Haven late nights, in the hope that something, anything, might occur to furnish a page."[4]

Matthiessen had no shortage of inspiration for Daily Themes. He could draw on his new living arrangement at Davenport College: a four-man apartment he shared with Tom Guinzburg, Sherry Lord, Frederick "Freck" Vreeland (son of Diana), and a stray cat who adopted them because they offered food and were easily accessible via a narrow ledge outside the top-floor window.[5]

Or he could write about the Yale Peabody Museum, where he found work that fall preparing duck skins for Sidney Dillon Ripley, the esteemed ornithologist who had just discovered the spiny babbler in the Middle Hills of Nepal, an endemic bird presumed extinct since the mid-nineteenth century. (Matthiessen dreamed of joining one of Ripley's expeditions.)

Or he could write about the Gurdjieffians, with whom he'd continued studying after arriving home from Paris, until he spontaneously decided that Gurdjieff's methods were "too esoteric" for long-term commitment, "that despite an evident strength among the leaders"—meaning Nathalie de Salzmann and her mother—"too few among the rest of us were meant to follow."[6]

Or he could even write about Patsy Southgate, and how he traveled up to visit her at Smith College in Northampton, Massachusetts, almost every opportunity he got, collecting a fistful of speeding tickets along the way. Matthiessen's "pussyfooting around New England,"[7] as he labeled these romantic escapades, led to so much absenteeism that he swore he'd spend at least one full weekend in New Haven before the end of the calendar year, just to prove he was capable. He could write about how a friend foiled this virtuous plan by getting him drunk and driving them down to New York, and how he "more or less" came to in the Stork Club.[8]

The point of Daily Themes was to help students improve their writing through close reading and criticism. What an author intended something to mean was less important, as the New Critics said, than how the story worked, how a mellifluous phrase or evocative symbol could impact the texture of the whole. Certain precepts were handed down by the class instructors: Individualize by Specific Detail; Vivify by Range of Appeal; Characterize by Speech and Gesture. Students were trained to look—really *look* at their subject—as a painter might scrutinize a life model. Exactly how old was an "old man"? What made the "pretty girl" pretty? Precision of expression was important, vagueness was anathema (though not to be confused with ambiguity), and the goal was always to illustrate through the kind of action that revealed something deeper about the scene or character than just what was written on the page. An expertly crafted piece of work could transcend the limitations of its length and subject, grazing universal truths.

For forty years, the Yale English department had produced a bound book of the best Daily Themes from each class, which also represented a time capsule of the student experience. In 1949—the last year before rising printing costs ended the tradition—the collection was filled with references to the armed services ("How G.I. can one guy be?"), class jealousies ("You're just rationalizing, you lazy bastard. You were born into the society and the contacts. It's no work for you."), and numerous instances of alcohol abuse: nickel beers, daiquiris, and martinis gulped so fast "they hurt on the way down."[9]

Matthiessen's contribution to the book was a fictional snapshot, though it concerned a family whose interpersonal dynamics were strikingly familiar. Elianne, prostrate with depression and some undefined, possibly psychosomatic illness, broods from her sickbed about three young children who "weren't enough for her, nor she for them." Elianne's husband, Philip, has vanished from the scene, depriving the house of its "last smell of masculinity." Elianne's daughter and youngest son do their best to cheer her up by offering a stuffed one-eyed penguin to accompany her convalescence. Yet it's the middle child, Michael, a "girlish" nine-year-old, who mostly occupies Elianne's thoughts. After hearing him torment his little brother, she calls out to him angrily. Michael shuffles into her room and up to the bed:

> She watched him come, watched him kiss her without looking at her eyes, and the artifice was so brazen that she slapped him. Immediately he cried, full, easy tears, and hopelessly she told him all over again about responsibility, and did not clutch him to her, did not kiss him where she had slapped him, did not cry.[10]

The withholding of maternal affection; a haughty demand for responsibility; a sensitive little boy, his temperament interpreted by an unhappy mother as weakness when compared to his stoic father, who is all but a ghost in their lives—this was the example Peter Matthiessen selected as his representative theme.

OF THE FOUR INSTRUCTORS who shared the load in Daily Themes, the most important for Matthiessen was Charles A. Fenton, a thirty-year-old PhD candidate from Springfield, Massachusetts. Charlie Fenton was described by the *Yale Daily News* as "a new bright light among bright lights in the English department,"[11] although his curly hair and round, boyish face made him look more like another undergraduate than a member of the faculty. From his first seminar in October, Fenton was a figure of curiosity among the students, who traded (true) rumors about his past exploits: that he'd been shot down during the war while flying as a tail gunner for the Royal Canadian Air Force; that he'd won a prize for an unpublished novel in New York; that he'd worked for a spell on the editorial staff at *Life* before quitting to pursue advanced studies in English. Fenton "had done and was doing the things we ourselves yearned to do," wrote Scott Donaldson, a fellow student in Matthiessen's class, in a biography of their teacher entitled *Death of a Rebel*. "We admired that, and admired the way he carried himself with the side-of-the-mouth offhand wit and irreverent stance of the hardened warrior and newspaperman. Young as he was, he'd been around barracks and city rooms long enough to acquire a free and easy skepticism that made him dubious about all received wisdom and distrustful of anyone who dispensed it."[12]

Matthiessen was drawn to Fenton's iconoclasm, which mirrored his own wary attitude toward authority figures and anything Establishment. He was particularly tickled by a story about Fenton's undergraduate days at Yale. In 1940, Fenton had infiltrated the sacred ritual of Tap Day, during which hopeful juniors gathered in Branford Court to be tapped on the shoulder for membership in one of the secret societies. Fenton was contemptuous of the whole self-important affair (just as Matthiessen told Tom Guinzburg that the societies were "plain nonsense"),[13] and he'd caused chaos by randomly tapping twenty or so boys for Skull and Bones—much to the horror of legitimate Bonesmen, who then tried to have him expelled.

Matthiessen saw Fenton as a model and mentor, worldly, literate, and uninterested in paying his dues through conventional avenues; but they also became friends when they started drinking together. Fenton evidently trusted Matthiessen, eight years younger than he was, because he soon revealed that he'd gone AWOL in England during the war and done sixty days in the Darland Detention Barracks—not something he volunteered lightly to anyone. Matthiessen came for dinner with Fenton's wife, Gwendolyn. ("Their relationship wasn't so great," he noticed.)[14] On another occasion, the two men, accompanied by a student named James Stevenson, who would go on to find success as an illustrator at *The New Yorker*, got roaringly drunk and descended into the New Haven sewer system for a reckless midnight ramble. Matthiessen's "fondest memory of undergraduate life" was, he later claimed, escaping through a manhole somewhere on the west side of the city at dawn: "Hours before, we had run out of Zippo lighter fuel, the only source of illumination in our long wanderings."[15]

Fenton was in the early stages of a dissertation on Ernest Hemingway, which put him somewhat at odds with a conservative English department that had little respect for any writer working more recently than Mark Twain. Nevertheless, he was well liked by the other faculty members, and his popularity among students was impossible to ignore. On the strength of his reception in Daily Themes, Fenton was tasked by the department with running a creative writing workshop in the spring of 1950. A seminar on short stories was something new for Yale, and Matthiessen signed up immediately.

According to Scott Donaldson, Fenton's approach to the class was necessarily idiosyncratic. One of the first things he did was consult Wallace Stegner, who had founded the Stanford Creative Writing Program in 1946.

Stegner believed that "[m]inds grow by contact with other minds. The bigger the better, as clouds grow toward thunder by rubbing together."[16] Yet he struggled to offer concrete advice about how to teach the art of fiction. Stegner's letter to Fenton was full of banal pointers that already defined the Daily Themes approach: work from the student's manuscript as much as possible, and "look at it with an eye to seeing anything of value the manuscript may contain."[17] Beyond that, Fenton would have to make it up as he went along. He did so by leaning on the American authors he most admired. He read out and analyzed the deceptively simple opening of *A Farewell to Arms*. He advocated restraint, a Hemingway hallmark, and disapproved of "fancy" or "fine" writing, although that criticism did not apply to the kind of prose exemplified by F. Scott Fitzgerald. Anything pretentious was "lugubrious," Fenton liked to tell his students.[18] He did not think highly of John Steinbeck, or William Faulkner—two writers whom Matthiessen was reading extensively at the time and liked very much. Indeed, in Matthiessen's contrarian view, Steinbeck was free of the self-conscious "and therefore intrusive"[19] style that had begun to bother him in Hemingway's fiction, not to mention, as he would later put it, Hemingway's "sententious machismo . . . with its latent self-pity."[20] And Faulkner was an expert at finding "that one detail, that one scrap of dialogue, one color or smell, that brings the whole scene to life"— a Carolina wren, for example, singing its unsettling song in the opening pages of *Sanctuary* (1931).[21]

Decades later, Matthiessen would be mostly unforgiving about his earliest forays into fiction during Fenton's workshop. A novice skier, he once explained, doesn't catch the lift to the summit of a mountain and ski flawlessly down to the bottom on the first try. "You make a lot of mistakes, go off at angles, do pratfalls."[22]

One pratfall was "Martin's Beach," in which two young brothers become obsessed with a snowy owl near their house, until the eldest boy (who happens to be intellectually disabled) follows the owl onto a frozen pond, slips through overnight ice, and drowns. "I had some metaphor for modern life in mind," Matthiessen said. "I don't quite know what it was."[23]*

Another stumble was "October in Valhalla," his wildly unsuccessful bid to inhabit the psyche of a ninety-two-year-old fishing captain in Montauk:

> Cap Wall thought a great deal about important matters but only on rainy days. When he thought, he really hauled off and thought, but he never changed his mind about anything. He was away past midstream and

---

* An edited version of "Martin's Beach" would appear in the literary journal *Botteghe Oscure* in 1952. Despite the distinctive title, the story has no obvious connection to "The Horror at Martin's Beach," written by H. P. Lovecraft and Sonia Greene in 1922.

crowding the far shore now, as he said, and he wouldn't leave his horse, "was it goin' down for the last time."[24]

"I went right from retarded youth to aged relic," Matthiessen later explained. "Which you do when you're a new writer. These things strike you; you're struck by the strangeness, and maybe a little bit nervous."[25] Nevertheless, there is a word in Zen, *shoshin*, which means "beginner's mind." Because a beginner is unburdened by a full understanding of rules and techniques, his or her mind is open to serendipitous accidents. ("In the beginner's mind there are many possibilities," as Shunryu Suzuki famously put it; "but in the expert's mind there are few.")[26] Most of what Matthiessen wrote under Fenton's guidance was disposable apprentice work, but he also managed to produce a story that would become one of the most lauded he'd ever write at any point in his life.

"Sadie" is presented as memory, Les Webster recalling two occasions he visited a stable yard in rural Georgia to inquire about some hunting dogs. In the first memory, Webster interacts with one of the workers, a laconic white man named Dewey Floyd, who orders around a Black underling while rolling cigarettes with one hand. Floyd is tightly wound, and Webster observes him cautiously: "There was something funny about the way he moved, just like the way he talked—sort of soft and quiet and not really getting anyplace, and that stick switching back and forth, slow, like the tail on a cat."[27]

At a fallow cornfield down the road, Webster meets up with the dog trainer Joe Pentland, and together they watch as Floyd gives a shooting demonstration with a "lemon bitch pointer" called Sadie. But the real spectacle is the simmering rivalry between Pentland and Floyd, who turn out to be related by marriage. Pentland loathes Floyd—and fears him, too. He believes his brother-in-law is no better than "black folks," and tells Webster that Floyd, a former bird poacher, should "stay in the woods with the rest of the animals." Floyd is aware of these insults, but his speech remains slow and steady as he wanders over, his thoughts guarded until he whips his stick across the rump of a horse and sends it—and its Black rider—bolting. "I believe he'd as soon take that stick to himself if he couldn't find no other place to use it," Webster thinks.

The second memory, dated to a few weeks later, has Webster returning to the stable yard to buy the best three dogs Pentland is selling. But Pentland announces that Sadie is no longer available: Floyd, in a drunken stupor, has beaten her to death. This memory ends with Floyd muttering to Webster that he "jes don't know rightly what it was, how I could come to doin it." The only thing he could beat to death while sober, he says, is another man: "Times come, I reckon I could do that easier'n nothing." Unsettled, Webster watches as the stick switches back and forth; watches as Floyd runs his tongue along the edge of a cigarette paper, squinting out from under his wide-brimmed hat.

The twist of the story is that a man *has* been beaten to death—the dog trainer Joe Pentland. Webster is revisiting his memories of the stable yard because something doesn't add up in what people are saying about the murder. "Hell, it ain't the nigger beat Pentland to death," Webster tells the reader—"it's Floyd. Dewey Floyd, sure as anything." The implication is that a wolfish white man has enacted the bloody execution of his rival, yet society has scapegoated the innocent Black bystander.

"Sadie" was inspired by Matthiessen's visit to the Greenwood Plantation near Thomasville, Georgia. It is far from perfect as a short story. The use of "cracker" dialect is inconsistent, so Webster's narration can read, as a critic once noted, "a little like a collaboration between William Faulkner and Henry James."[28] The use of racial slurs is also extravagant, with Matthiessen relying on them too much to sketch the ugly edges of his characters. Meanwhile, the only significant Black figure in the story, Buster, is notably child-like and talks like Jim from *Huckleberry Finn*: "Whuffo' he wan' go foolin' Bustuh? He ain' got no call to do dat."

As a young man, Matthiessen's attitude toward Black people—staff, mostly—was paternalistic but never, in the surviving letters, deliberately hostile or derogatory. He would likely have defended the racism in "Sadie" on the grounds of verisimilitude: he was trying to capture how white rural Georgians *did* see and speak about their Black workers, and how they would have represented Black speech. (All of Buster's minstrel dialogue comes through Pentland's distorting narration.) Even so, Matthiessen understood what the N-word connoted in 1950, its repugnant, dehumanizing power, and it is difficult to argue that he didn't exploit the slur for shock value, which is a dubious rhetorical strategy. Webster's first use of it appears less than halfway through the story's very first sentence, hitting the reader like a snake bite.[*]

Despite its fraught treatment of race, however, "Sadie" is remarkable for its economy and pacing, its superb deployment of Faulknerian details, and for how it prefigures so much in Matthiessen's mature fiction, including his determination to imagine experiences through subjectivities completely different from his own. "Sadie" hints at his fascination with the dialectic of civilization and wildness; and with the ways in which power and class—and

---

[*] The version of "Sadie" that appears in *On the River Styx* (1989) was edited by Matthiessen when he was an older, more experienced writer. Some phrases were deleted from the original story, softening the overall violence, and the reveal of Pentland's death and Buster's scapegoating was moved from the beginning to near the end, along with the incendiary opening line.

race—can be catalysts for conflict in homosocial relationships. As the title suggests, being the name of a dog, "Sadie" also shows his interest in how animals might draw out and illuminate complicated emotions, particularly from men who are unable to express themselves through the heavy armor of their own masculinity. Then there is the tone of the story, a sweltering strangeness, and its central figure of an intense outsider—a living id—who challenges the assumptions of all who are unlucky enough to encounter him. As a manifestation, perhaps, of the author's own untamable impulses, Dewey Floyd would reappear in different guises throughout much of Matthiessen's fiction: as Cady Shipman, Raditzer, Lewis Meriwether Moon, Miguel Moreno Smith, and finally as Edgar "Jack" Watson.

When "Sadie" was published in Matthiessen's short story collection, *On the River Styx*, in 1989, a *New York Times* reviewer remarked that "[e]very young would-be writer of Mr. Matthiessen's generation . . . dreamed of writing such a story."[29] This was probably true as much for the story itself as for the almost immediate effect it had on Matthiessen's trajectory. Not long after he finished the draft (there was only one), it fell into the hands of John Farrar, cofounder of the literary house Farrar, Straus and Company, which was then publishing writers such as Carlo Levi and Shirley Jackson. Charlie Fenton liked to invite guest speakers into his creative writing workshop; it is possible that Farrar, himself a Yale alumnus, stopped by to share some advice about the vagaries of the New York publishing world. Farrar read Matthiessen's piece and thought it was "a very fine story indeed"; he admired its "skill, authenticity, atmosphere, [and] restraint."[30] There was little he could do with it himself, but sometime that spring or summer, he wrote a note to Edward Weeks, editor of *The Atlantic Monthly*, recommending "Sadie" for the magazine.

BEFORE WEEKS RESPONDED, Matthiessen turned twenty-three and graduated from Yale. For the first time in his life, he was faced with a prospect of genuine choice. There was no longer a draft board waiting to conscript him, and all nagging expectations that he finish his education had now been satisfied. He could become a journalist in New York, or maybe seek out that "unfettered 'real life'" in "faraway destinations."

Instead, Matthiessen made two decisions that show just how uncertain he was about his future. First, at the persuasive nudging of Charlie Fenton, he agreed to stay on in New Haven for another year. Professor A. Dwight Culler, a scholar of Victorian literature, had just become a Fulbright Fellow and was temporarily abandoning his teaching obligations; to fill the gap, Matthiessen was offered—and accepted—a part-time position as an assistant in instruction, teaching Daily Themes in the first semester and a writing course in the second for a salary of $1,000.

The second decision was more surprising, and far more consequential. After years of vehemently insisting that he had no intention of getting married until his late twenties ("Heaven can wait, so to speak"),[31] and of grousing that his friends were "falling like flies"[32] as they rushed to the altar, Peter suddenly proposed to his girlfriend.

It was easy to underestimate Patsy Southgate. She was often objectified for how she looked—one Smith College professor would go to the campus pool just to watch her dive[33]—or she was measured by the yardstick of her background, then written off as just another debutante who would one day make an obliging hostess, like her mother, Lila Southgate (née Lancashire), a prominent socialite in Washington, D.C.

Patsy's father, Richard Southgate, had started his career in the State Department in 1917. He had served in the diplomatic corps in Paris, Rome, Guatemala, Constantinople, and Havana, before leaving to enter the banking business in Chicago, where he worked for the Continental Illinois National Bank and Trust Company. Not long after Patsy was born, on February 11, 1928, Richard had returned to the State Department in the role of assistant chief of protocol, then ascended to chief of protocol of the United States in 1935. While Patsy was growing up in the D.C. neighborhood of Kalorama Heights, her parents had dined with the Roosevelts, and attended music recitals in the East Room of the White House. Their own cocktail parties sometimes made the pages of the Washington *Evening Star:* "Not only were there borders of heavenly pastel-colored tulips around the garden, but Lila told us that all the flowers used in the drawing room had been freshly cut from their own flower beds that morning."[34] Patsy had attended the Potomac School in McLean, Virginia, then the college-preparatory boarding school of Chatham Hall. In 1946, she'd graduated just weeks before her father, recently retired from a role with the Office of Strategic Services, died of a heart condition at the age of fifty-three. Three months after the loss of Richard Southgate, Patsy had enrolled at Smith.

Accounts suggest she was funny, gracious, and fastidiously tidy, which is why Terry Southern christened her "Pat Perfect."[35] But there was grit below the polished surface, along with a deep vein of frustration at being so frequently misjudged. As the painter Jane Freilicher once observed, "With her golden hair, bright blue eyes, and soft-spoken voice, it came as a surprise to find that she had a mind like a steel trap—she didn't suffer fools gladly."[36] One of those "fools" was her own mother; Lila was unable to "boil an egg, drive a car, or anything," Patsy once told a biographer contemptuously.[37] Of course, this was socially conditioned ineptitude (why would a woman like Lila Southgate need to boil an egg?), but Patsy was not inclined to be sympathetic. Her animosity, which was shared by her siblings—"I think all three children resented her," recalled Sarita Southgate of their mother[38]—had crystallized sometime around the age of six, when a favorite French governess disappeared from their lives without so much as an adieu. Lila had dismissed the governess out of jealousy, Patsy suspected, because she knew Patsy loved the governess more. This unforgivable betrayal by Lila was the likely root of Patsy's Francophilia, which also functioned as a form of revenge: a constant reminder that Patsy's love for the governess had not been extinguished but only grown more expansive. "She spent much of her life longing for her imagined mother, the true mother of her invented French soul," wrote the writer and performer Patti Smith (who once taped a picture of Patsy to her wall alongside Renée Jeanne Falconetti, Edie Sedgwick, and Jean Seberg—"the girls of my day").[39]

Like Peter, Patsy aspired to write, and in the decades ahead she'd try her hand at fiction, nonfiction, playwriting, poetry, and translation. She was fully aware of what society expected her to be, yet the more pressure she felt to play her part, the more she'd adopt subversion as a psychological lifeline. Other than her beauty, the stories that survive about Patsy Southgate focus on her rebelliousness. How she wrote children's stories as well as pornography, and how she claimed the only difference between the two was a matter of emphasis. How she'd walk around the house bare-breasted and chain-smoking, even in front of her children's friends (a "beatnik nudist," her seven-year-old son called her).[40] How she'd think nothing of heckling a golfer—"Fore, asshole!"—as she sped past links on the highway. How she had Mae West's gift for wicked turns of phrase: yellow forsythia was "the vomit of spring." How she once slept with Frank O'Hara, then wondered in an essay if a desire dwelled in the hearts of all women "to convert a homosexual, a sort of female version of the male dream of seducing a virgin."[41]

A nascent feminist in the 1950s, Patsy resented the privileged position automatically extended to men in America, the resurgent puritanism that had rolled back the freedoms women gained for a few short years during the war. Yet she also struggled with an internalized idea that a husband's happiness was her rightful duty. Nor was she immune to vanity and competitiveness when it came to other women. Cis Ormsby, who would marry Peter's brother, Carey Matthiessen, in 1952, had known Patsy in Washington when they were both little girls. "She was jolly and a little bit overweight, and we were best friends. We did all sorts of naughty things around Georgetown, putting milk bottles full of water against people's doors so they'd open the door and the water would spill everywhere. And then we lost touch, practically, until Peter started courting her. I remember we met at the Matthiessens' house. I rushed up to give her a big hug, and she was really strange. Just completely different. In walked this beautiful woman who had no use for me at all."[42]

PETER WAS "mad for Patsy," he said, because she was so different from any girl he'd ever dated. She was a rare bird, in other words, and he was worried she might fly away if he didn't make it official. But then she accepted his proposal, and somewhere in between the elated announcements to family and friends, he felt a twinge of regret: "Much as I loved that beautiful girl, I also knew that I was setting aside, perhaps forever, a strong desire to travel light and see the world."[43] The twinge grew into ambivalence, then swelled into a kind of wounded resentment. Eventually he would claim that he'd been "sucked into the system" before he was "ready," as though marriage had not really been his idea but something that just happened to him.[44]

The engagement party, in late June, was held at Gloucester in Massachusetts, where Lila had relocated after her husband's death. Peter, whether he'd planned to or not, approached the festivities like a saboteur. As he later recalled the day, it began with Patsy's aunt: he knocked off her lavender hat and veil by throwing up his hands "in an expansive Gallic gesture."[45] Then he was discovered in an inebriated "open-mouth smooch" with the maid of honor, who supposedly waylaid him in the larder. After the guests had all left, he denounced Lila Southgate from the foot of the stairs because the liquor cabinet was locked, "until she came out, affrighted, in her nightgown and threw down the key." Finally, he too departed, without a thank-you or apology, at dawn, abandoning his fiancée to go on a six-week birding expedition with his old friend Sherry Lord in Quebec.

Bonaventure Island is a speck in the Gulf of St. Lawrence, off the Gaspé Peninsula. Matthiessen would give an extraordinary description of the island's four-hundred-foot cliffs in *Wildlife in America*:

> The birds swarm ceaselessly in spring and summer, drifting in from the ocean in flocks like long wisps of smoke and whirring upward from the water to careen clumsily along the ledges. Above, on the crest, the magnificent white gannets nest, and the kittiwakes and larger gulls patrol the face, their sad cries added to a chittering and shrieking which pierce the booming of the surf in the black sea caves below. At the base of the cliff the visitor, small in a primeval emptiness of ocean, rock, and sky, feels simultaneously exalted and diminished; the bleak bird rocks of the northern oceans will perhaps be the final outposts of the natural profusion known to early voyagers, and we moderns, used to remnant populations

of creatures taught to know their place, find this wild din, this wilderness of life, bewildering."[46]

Matthiessen and Lord stayed with a young cod fisherman named Walter Paget. Each day, they admired songbirds in the island's uphill spruce forest. Each evening, with no television or radio to disrupt the peace, they browsed guidebooks, took notes, and drank. If birdwatching was a way of retreating from the world, Bonaventure was the perfect setting in which to do it.

But then Patsy appeared, motoring across from the nearby coastal village of Percé. Grim and officious, she haunted Peter for a single evening in July, which was all the time she needed to call off their engagement. He pleaded with her to reconsider; confronted with the facts of his caddish behavior, he was "heart-broken, truly, and filled with bitter shame."[47] But Patsy departed the island "steadfast and courageous," which only emphasized what he'd just gambled away through his selfishness.

Walter Paget owned a nineteen-foot fishing smack that Matthiessen had been eyeing since he arrived. It had a single-cylinder Acadia engine with a flywheel, a dysfunctional steadying sail, and a double hull of soft yellow pine that still had some bark stuck to it. The deck was so shallow, owing to the numerous codfish hatches, that it was easy to fall into the freezing Atlantic. Matthiessen had already committed to buying the vessel, with a foolhardy plan to sail it around Nova Scotia and down along New England all the way to Long Island, while Lord drove the car back to New York. "Such an adventure," he had reasoned, "would be just what was needed to reconcile me to an early marriage."[48] Now the voyage was reconceived as a desperate ploy to show Patsy the seriousness of his devotion. He christened the boat the *Maudite*, which means "Cursed."

On the first morning, as the blue sea "seemed to grow higher every minute,"[49] Matthiessen realized that he needed to tie a fishing line around his ankle to the sparkplug wire; if he happened to fall overboard, this would kill the engine so he could save himself from drowning. He also realized, too late, that he was woefully inexperienced as a navigator, and that a bout of bad weather would probably spell his doom.

Fishermen at Grande-Rivière, slightly south of Percé, told him he was crazy to attempt the Nova Scotia coastline in a vessel that could barely manage six knots an hour. After two days of minimal progress through turbulent seas, he was inclined to agree. At the end of the third day, he entered the outer harbor of Port Daniel, navigated beneath a low bridge, and sheared off the mast in a violent collision. As a crowd of onlookers showered him with laughter, he beached the wreck and stepped overboard, sinking up to his crotch in viscous mud. Thus ended the voyage of the *Maudite*, less than eighty nautical miles from Bonaventure Island. Exhausted and humiliated, Matthiessen found a drunk in a local bar who agreed to winch the smack onto his truck for a ride as far south as Massachusetts.

FOR THE REST of the summer, Patsy rebuffed all attempts at a rapprochement. She was unimpressed by the aborted voyage. She was skeptical that what Peter felt was genuine remorse, given his convincingly cruel performance at the Gloucester party. But he continued to plead his case anyway, mostly from New York, where he landed a temporary job as a slush pile reader for the Viking Press through his friend Tom Guinzburg, whose father, Harold K. Guinzburg, had cofounded the publishing house in 1925. And by early September, Patsy seemed to be gradually coming around.

Matthiessen returned to New Haven to prepare as an instructor for Daily Themes. Not long after classes started back, in October, he received a letter from Boston. "Sadie," with its controlled calm disguising a savage power, had impressed every one of the *Atlantic*'s editors, wrote Edward Weeks: "I am accepting it with pleasure as an Atlantic First."[50] The story would appear in an upcoming issue of the magazine.

This was a major achievement for someone so early in their career, the kind of high-profile validation that would flag him for agents and editors as a fiction writer of exceptional promise. Thrilled with the letter—at least *something* was going right for him—Matthiessen showed it off to his new students as a way of establishing authority over a group of young men who knew him better for drunken capers around campus than for literary talent.[51] Then, in his spare time, he started to type up a few more short stories, along with the first tentative pages of a novel.

6

The Paris Review

In the pale pink dawn of Paris, chill with new autumn air, he listened to his footsteps ringing out behind him, like some persistent second self of solitude.

—*Partisans* (1955)[1]

For decades, whenever somebody asked Peter Matthiessen about the nature of his involvement with the CIA, he was liable to respond with an evasiveness that could flare, if challenged even slightly, into tart frustration. In 1977, *The New York Times* outed him as a former undercover agent in a long exposé by John M. Crewdson, titled "Worldwide Propaganda Network Built by the C.I.A."[2] Though he was only passingly mentioned in the article, Matthiessen spent the rest of his life dealing with its implications, largely by refusing to deal with them at all. He declined, for many years, to answer any detailed questions. Or he offered up partial answers and then insisted they were distractions, unimportant, not worth discussing further. Sometimes he became tense during interviews, his gaze narrowing into two pinpricks of fiery caution. "It hit you the way a headmaster in an old school used to look at you," recalled the writer David Michaelis, who was still in college when he tried to excavate the history of *The Paris Review*—"as in: 'I know exactly what you've just been doing, and actually, for the reputation and benefit of the school, I'm going to be restrained about it, but I'm letting you know that not only are you under surveillance and probation, but morally, you are a corrupted human being, and you are cinder in my eyes, and you are nothing in this universe.' "[3]

There were several good reasons why Matthiessen wanted to avoid discussing his clandestine activities. Not least, they were classified during his lifetime (and remain so today: the CIA rejected multiple requests by this biographer through the Freedom of Information Act and through the Office of Public Affairs).[4] Without authorization to "roll back" his cover, Matthiessen was, in his own words, "legally prohibited from acknowledging an intelligence agency association."[5] He worried, too, about the impact any public disclosure might have on his more sensitive associates. From 1968, he was closely involved with the United Farm Workers of America, led by Cesar Chavez, and then later with the American Indian Movement, both of which were subject to covert surveillance (or interference) by the FBI. The revelation that Matthiessen himself had history as a spy threatened to damage his reputation as a trustworthy ally, particularly among the AIM leaders, who, "from long hard experience," as he put it, were "especially paranoid about infiltration by government agents."[6] Indeed, Matthiessen would avoid talking about his past deeds with Leonard Peltier, the subject of his 1983 book, *In the Spirit of Crazy Horse*, until 2008, when he wrote an agonized letter to Peltier in prison: "This CIA business has *nothing* to do with your case and nothing to do with the FBI. . . . [It] doesn't mean you should ever doubt my loyalty and support for you and the Indian struggle."[7]

But perhaps the biggest reason for Matthiessen's reticence was simply embarrassment. Embarrassment that he spied on some decent people, maybe even friends. Embarrassment that he played a role, however minor, in an organization that was later involved with "ugly stuff"[8] like attempted assassinations, human rights abuses, and the undermining of democratically elected governments ("so foreign to what I believe and how I've led my life"). And embarrassment that the truth eventually slipped out of his control; that instead of stifling curiosity, his unwillingness to speak up about what happened in Paris, early and honestly, only allowed rumors to ossify around one of the most prestigious literary journals in the English-speaking world. "Long, long, long ago I should have simply typed out the right chronology and gotten it straight," Matthiessen lamented to *The New York Times* a few years before his death, when it was already too late.[9]

As it happens, he did type out a chronology, or personal narrative—several, with titles like "THE PARIS REVIEW v. THE CIA: My Half-life as a Capitalist Running Dog."[10] Left unpublished alongside his memoir notes, these accounts are surprising, illuminating, confounding, elliptical, and in many respects impossible to corroborate: the testimonies of a raconteur who was not always reliable when it came to the more shadowy recesses of his own history. Still, in the absence of any official government records, these documents represent the fullest story yet available of what Matthiessen preferred to dismiss as "the one adventure of my life that I regret."[11]

THE MAN WHO STARTED the whole affair, at Yale in the fall of 1950, was a forty-one-year-old assistant professor who wore finely tailored suits and walked with a limp, the lingering effect of a childhood infection in his hip-bone. Matthiessen had first encountered Norman Holmes Pearson in his senior year, when he submitted a final paper on Faulkner and was summoned into Pearson's office. "Where the hell have you been for the last three years?" Pearson demanded to know. "You could have won the English prize!"[12] When Matthiessen then returned to Yale to work as an instructor in Daily Themes, the two became friendly, sometimes ribbing one another with lighthearted insults. Both men were active members of the Elizabethan Club, a campus literary society that served afternoon tea in a series of genteel rooms, perfect for private conversation, that were organized around a gargantuan walk-in safe containing a Shakespeare First Folio and a first edition of Milton's *Paradise Lost*.[13]

To Matthiessen, Pearson was a gentle, generous presence in the English department, a teacher willing to surrender his time even as he labored beneath some intimidating commitments, including an ongoing study of Nathaniel Hawthorne and the five-volume *Poets of the English Language*, which he was coediting with W. H. Auden. Pearson was responsible for American Studies at Yale, a relatively new program dedicated to "a broad understanding of American civilization—its origins, evolution and present world relationships."[14] He was also connected, both professionally and socially, to every modernist poet from Ezra Pound to Wallace Stevens. One day Pearson showed Matthiessen a letter from Stevens concerning the lauded author of *American Renaissance*, F. O. Matthiessen—Peter's second cousin, who, after being smeared in the press as a communist sympathizer, had shocked academe by jumping out the twelfth-floor window of the Hotel Manger in Boston.*

What Peter would not have known, at least at first, was what Pearson did under the code name "Puritan" during the war. Pearson had been recruited from Yale to work in the Office of Strategic Services, and more specifically in the top secret counterintelligence branch, X-2. Collaborating closely with the British, Pearson had acted as the principal liaison for the OSS on all matters "Ultra," a designation used to cover codebreaking activities at Bletchley Park. As acting chief, then chief, of X-2 in London, Pearson had watched the Germans bomb the city while he managed a network of spies spread across

---

* F. O. Matthiessen's depression was also linked to the death of his lover, the painter Russell Cheney, five years earlier. Peter only met his second cousin once, at a family funeral in 1936, but he did write a sympathetic sketch about the closeted gay scholar: "F. O.'s father, Frederick William Jr., known in the family as 'Wild Bill,' was my grandmother's scapegrace brother.... Like his brother-in-law [meaning Peter's grandfather, Conrad], Bill did not trust his wife and doubted his own role in the production of his bright, sensitive son whom he finally disowned and drove out of the house. Even years later, this insensitive old man disdained a scheduled reconciliation with the now eminent Rhodes scholar and Harvard professor upon learning that the Jameses so interesting to 'that sissy' were William and Henry, not Frank and Jessie, who were real men after his own heart."

Europe. A brilliant, indefatigable organizer, he started briefings, according to his biographer Robin Winks, "without notes, from behind his desk; soon he would sit upon it, and then he would progress to the top of a safe, to the windowsill, in constant movement, a huge foulard handkerchief hanging down his chest, witty and complex material flowing from him."[15]

Pearson had departed the successor to the OSS, the Central Intelligence Group, in 1946, and by all outward appearances he was settled into civilian life by the time Matthiessen met him. But American Studies was not quite what it seemed; the program would double as an ideological cudgel wielded against communism during the Cold War. And Pearson still maintained a relationship with what was now being called the Central Intelligence Agency—as did several of his colleagues: academic talent spotters who'd collectively become known as the CIA's "P source" ("P" for "Professor"). Sid Lovett, who eventually organized an alumni group for the Class of 1950, estimated that "at least twenty-five" of his and Matthiessen's peers were secretly recruited by their teachers.[16] This included William F. Buckley Jr., referred to the CIA by a conservative professor of political philosophy named Willmoore Kendall;[17] and Frederick Vreeland, one of Matthiessen's roommates at Davenport College. As Vreeland recalled, "It was many years later—when all of them except yours truly had left the Agency and were pursuing other careers—that I learned how many of my classmates had been recruited while at college, and via faculty members."[18]

It is tempting to imagine what Pearson saw when he looked at Matthiessen: a polished young man unsure of himself and what he wanted out of life; a young man deferring decisions while he stumbled around in search of guidance. It is tempting, too, to imagine how Matthiessen experienced the sales pitch: over tea sandwiches in a quiet corner of the Elizabethan Club, beneath the portrait of Walter Raleigh; or perhaps in Pearson's office, the older man closing the door and clearing his throat. Matthiessen would remember an appeal to his sense of "patriotic duty."[19] It was an appeal that opened him up "like an oyster."[20]

Nearly five years after leaving the Navy, Matthiessen remained self-conscious about his lackluster war record. Now someone was offering a second chance to become one of those "authentic warriors" whose underwear he'd scrubbed in the Moanalua laundry. It also sounded like an adventure: Pearson told him the workload would be so light that he'd have the time and money (via a stipend) to focus on his writing, and that he could do it all in Paris, "crossroads of international espionage."[21] The promise of Paris was particularly alluring given that it remained, for both himself and Patsy Southgate, the city they'd longed to call home since the "spiritual vacation"[22] of their year abroad. As Matthiessen once explained in a letter to his friend, the *Washington Post* executive editor Ben Bradlee: "When you're 23, it seems pretty romantic to go to Paris with yr beautiful young wife to serve as an intelligence agent and write the Great American Novel into the bargain. Weren't you ever as young and dumb as that?"[23]

As for the political implications, Matthiessen gave them little thought. Nobody he knew would have frowned upon him working for the CIA, which had not yet acquired the more troubling caveats to its reputation. Indeed, people from across the political spectrum worked for the Agency in its earliest days, united by a shared belief that they all were defending democracy. Matthiessen had "no politics to speak of nor even a clear understanding of the politics of the CIA," other than the fact it was a "new sprout off the old stump of the wartime OSS."[24] He was just a naive "young Yalie," he later maintained: "I'm always in the club drinking martinis, what did I know from politics?"[25]

Yet perhaps he was not quite as apolitical as he liked to suggest. In 1946, in Hawaii, he'd written a long, meandering rant to Wendy Burden about the tense relationship between Russia and America. "I don't blame Russia," he said. "I do blame us—after all, Russia may be sabotaging the peace, but we're sabotaging ourselves, our prestige, even our men; both those who fought and those who will fight, and for what?"[26] More recently, he'd read about the blacklisting of Paul Robeson, who, while supportive of the Soviet Union, had criticized the racial hypocrisy of the United States at an international peace conference in 1949, only to have his passport revoked. Matthiessen had decided that Robeson "got a shitty deal." ("I felt really bad at the time, and I loved it that he had the courage as a Black man to come out and be so vocal.")[27] Matthiessen had also read *The God That Failed* (1949), a collection of six autobiographical essays by writers who'd been attracted to, and then disillusioned by, communism, including Richard Wright and Arthur Koestler. Rather than being persuaded by the book's anticommunist thesis, he had been "stirred" by Koestler's early beliefs: "I think everyone at that young age, almost anyone of right mind, has Communist leanings, even if only seeing the startling parallel between communist doctrine and the teachings of Jesus Christ."[28]

Matthiessen's politics, like his sense of self, were still far from coherent when Pearson first approached him. Knee-jerk opinions, filtered through ambivalence about his family background, had yet to be assembled into anything close to an ideology. But perhaps his sympathies were already radical *enough* that, had the CIA been using a rigorous recruitment process—more rigorous, at any rate, than the hunches of some Ivy League professors—he might have been weeded out, flagged as too unreliable, and the entire business might have ended there.

"I VAGUELY RECALL a large Quonset hut in the late autumn woods south of the Potomac," Matthiessen wrote in one of his CIA narratives.[29] The figure who welcomed him into a windowless, paper-strewn office, standing up to stretch his hand across a cluttered desk, was known to him only as Pearson's protégé from Yale and the OSS. He was very cordial, Matthiessen noted, "a cadaverous, hawk-boned man with dark hair, large elfin ears, and a lively intelligent face behind black horn-rimmed glasses."[30] His name was James Angleton.

As chief of CIA counterintelligence from 1954 until 1974, Angleton would prove so influential—and so notorious—that he eventually became a figure of spy mythology: the master of deception who was obsessed, with his encyclopedic knowledge of Soviet operations, with unearthing KGB "moles" in the Agency's ranks.[31] In 1950, however, Angleton was still head of staff for the Office of Special Operations (OSO), which was responsible for foreign intelligence, counterintelligence, and espionage. Its tasks were to protect American secrets from the country's enemies, and to acquire foreign secrets wherever possible. Gathering and assessing information was the mandate—not action. Those covert operations the CIA is known to have carried out in its early years (election interference; paramilitary activities like sabotage and the support of anticommunist guerrilla groups) were largely the doings of another outfit, the Office of Policy Coordination (OPC), which was run by Frank G. Wisner. The distinction is important. Members of the OSO were sometimes compared by their critics to librarians with a "card file mentality,"[32] excavating mountains of documents for a lead. Members of the OPC were compared by *their* critics to cowboys with "missionary zeal in their eyes,"[33] using "dirty tricks"[34] in reckless missions that sometimes went catastrophically wrong. In 1950, the two offices had separate chains of command and were locked in organizational rivalry, refusing to share intelligence or staff as they operated independently in many of the same locations around the world. Given Pearson's background and Angleton's role at the time, Matthiessen was almost certainly being recruited for the OSO—not, as has sometimes been assumed, for Wisner's more gung ho OPC.[35]

After some "pleasant talk," perhaps about poetry, which was one of Angleton's passions (he too was a member of the Elizabethan Club), Matthiessen was taken for a drive through Northwest Washington on a "roundabout route."[36] He knew that Angleton was evaluating him out of the corner of his eye, and he knew that he'd passed when Angleton told him Paris was a good place to be posted. He would need to move to Washington for immediate training. But Matthiessen objected to the idea: "an abrupt three-month remove to Washington . . . would blow my 'cover' before I even had one."[37] And so it was agreed, as Matthiessen recalled it, that he would instead train in New York, where he could easily weave an excuse to justify his presence. With that settled, he returned to New Haven and withdrew from teaching in the spring semester.

AT THE START OF 1951, "Sadie" appeared in *The Atlantic Monthly* beneath a banner of mermaids flanking the title, "An Atlantic 'First.'" As a public introduction of Peter Matthiessen—"A veteran of the Navy now in his twenty-fourth year . . ."—it was impressive and flattering, and the story garnered immediate attention in publishing and media. William Maxwell, a fiction editor at *The New Yorker*, wrote a letter of compliments and then phoned up Matthiessen to suggest they meet for lunch.[38] Cass Canfield, the chairman of Harper & Brothers (and stepfather to Matthiessen's close friend, Blair Fuller), praised what he considered an "extraordinarily acute" portrait of Southern characters and scenes. "Doubtless a number of publishers are writing or have written you expressing interest in a novel on the basis of this story," Canfield added. "At all events I feel like doing so on behalf of Harpers, and hope that you will keep this firm in mind when the time comes for you to make publishing arrangements."[39]

Still, the most significant development was that it landed Matthiessen "the toughest agent in town," as he later described Bernice Baumgarten.[40] Head of the book department at the Brandt & Brandt literary agency, on Park Avenue, where she'd worked her way up from a secretary, Baumgarten was indeed formidable: "Hey, you better drop that *Bernice*," she once told her assistant. "It's *Miss Baumgarten*."[41] Small and neat, with a "straight, reflecting, considered look,"[42] in the words of Mary McCarthy, she was renowned as a shrewd bargainer and master of contract negotiations. Over the years her client list had included Thomas Mann, John Dos Passos, E. E. Cummings, Edna St. Vincent Millay, Raymond Chandler (who sacked her in 1952 for daring to suggest that Philip Marlowe in *The Long Goodbye* was "too Christlike and sentimental"),[43] and Shirley Jackson, who remarked admiringly that there was nothing Baumgarten liked better "than getting someone . . . by the throat."[44] Matthiessen thought her husband, the Pulitzer Prize–winning novelist James Gould Cozzens, was something of a joke; but he held Baumgarten's bluntness, business acumen, and piercing editorial eye in reverential awe. Years later, he would tell an anecdote, possibly embroidered, about how, when an editor returned one of his pieces to her office, she sent it right back with a curt note: "I think you've made a mistake. Read this story again. Yrs, Bernice."[45]

In the wake of "Sadie," which was soon awarded the *Atlantic* Prize, Matthiessen forwarded a stockpile of stories to Brandt & Brandt, hoping Baumgarten might prolong his taste of success with a string of acceptances in similar magazines.

And then he got married. The wedding was held at the Leslie Lindsey Memorial Chapel, part of the Emmanuel Episcopal Church in Boston, on February 17. Having finally forgiven her fiancé, Patsy Southgate was given away by an uncle, Umberto Coletti, and she looked like a Pre-Raphaelite painting in an ivory satin gown and needlepoint appliqué veil, her hands filled with Eucharis lilies.[46] As Peter's parents watched, he was supported by his brother, Carey, and a phalanx of his closest friends, including John Cole, Charlie and Sherry Lord, Blair Fuller, and Tom Guinzburg. The reception was held in the French Room of the Ritz-Carlton. A honeymoon, coming immediately after, was spent on Sanibel Island, Florida, and only slightly sullied by the discovery that Patsy's former schoolmaster was staying in the cottage next door.

Sometime in March or early April, the newlyweds moved into an apartment at 10 Mitchell Place, adjacent to East 49th Street in Manhattan. The address was chosen for convenience. Five days a week, Matthiessen stepped out the front door and ceased to be himself; he became nobody, his identity concealed behind a pseudonym. Going to a nearby "safe house"[47]—a private residence whose owners had an arrangement with the CIA—he met with an officer who taught him the skills for intelligence gathering. There was no personal talk, no chitchat, only tradecraft, which Matthiessen thought was "great fun." He would have learned, for example, how to tail somebody without getting caught; how to photograph documents; how to recognize surveillance; and how to conduct a persuasive interview with a reticent subject to extract desirable information.

In 1961, C. D. Edbrook (an alias) published "Principles of Deep Cover" in the CIA journal *Studies in Intelligence*. An operative working under "nonofficial cover" poses as a private citizen, Edbrook explained, "with such authenticity that their intelligence sponsorship would not be disclosed even by an intensive and determined investigation."[48] Establishing this kind of cover requires "not the mechanical efficiency of the assembly-line worker, but the patient inventiveness of the artisan." As an act of long-term embodied creativity, it is convincing enough to avoid arousing suspicion, but flexible enough to allow the agent to improvise as they carry out their tasks. This was the kind of cover that Matthiessen was now being prepared to assume in Paris. "Cover," Edbrook wrote, "should always be considered in relation to the intelligence objective, and insofar as possible it should provide legitimate access to the targets being attacked. The ideal solution is achieved when the activities of the agent in doing his cover job provide the basis for the operational contacts desired."

Patsy was aware of her husband's involvement with the CIA. She would have known approximately where he was going each morning, but probably not the details—the *what*, or *who*, or ultimate goal, which Peter was not supposed to divulge to anyone. As the wife of an undercover agent, she was meant to offer support without questioning her own exposure.

At the same time, Patsy was also expected to commiserate when the progress of Peter's writing career suddenly stalled. Bernice Baumgarten began to forward the rejections almost immediately. Katharine White, another editor at *The New Yorker*, found one of his stories overwrought and immature: "It's the kind of story the young dream up, I guess, in lieu of any actual knowledge of tragedy on which to base a story, and yet it has a promise of good things to come."[49] An editor at *Harper's Magazine* was less restrained about a different piece: "I always detest sending back a story because it's 'unpleasant' but when it seems an old and familiar story as well to which nothing much seems to have been added, I guess I'll have to."[50] Even Edward Weeks, at *The Atlantic Monthly*, sent his apologies at least once, though the magazine did accept "The Fifth Day," about a college student and a fisherman trawling the ocean for a missing corpse ("Joe said he'd pop up like a rubber ball on the fifth day"), which would appear in the September 1951 issue.

But the most stinging rejection came directly from Baumgarten. Matthiessen had typed thirty-five pages of "Wilderness" when he decided it was a masterpiece begging to be shared. The novel-in-progress concerned a thinly fictionalized version of Fishers Island: *Further* Island, "so-named because it lies further from the New England coast than the first colonists cared to go."[51] The plot (shaky) followed a wellborn marine biologist (two-dimensional) as he returns to the Edenic landscape of his youth, where antipathy is growing between a preservationist—the scientist's wealthy father, who owns much of the island and wants it protected as a wildlife reserve—and working-class locals siding with a tourism developer who promises them prosperity and comfort. Once Baumgarten had the pages, Matthiessen waited breathlessly for her verdict, fantasizing about a lucrative offer from Hollywood. Baumgarten soon put an end to that: "Dear Peter, James Fenimore Cooper wrote this 150 years ago, only he wrote it better. Yrs, Bernice."[52] This no-nonsense letter, which was presumably referencing Cooper's 1823 novel *The Pioneers*, humbled Matthiessen so completely that he memorized every word. "She beat me up," he later said with grudging appreciation. "She was like a Zen teacher."[53]

Back at the safe house, weeks of training culminated in a final test. For security reasons, Matthiessen had never been told his trainer's real name, just as the trainer had only learned Matthiessen's alias. But could they both figure out the other man's true identity from clues dropped inadvertently along the way? Matthiessen went home and thought the challenge over. Then he returned, as he later recalled, and explained how, step by step, he might go about unmasking his colleague. The officer stopped him: his training was complete.

On June 16, a perfect summer day in New York, the Matthiessens gathered their luggage and headed to a Hell's Kitchen pier to meet the SS *Liberté*, a stately ocean liner preparing to make a six-day crossing to Le Havre. Their departure was recorded by officials on an outward-bound passenger list. In response to the prompt, "Length of Time Passenger Intends to Remain Abroad," most other passengers had indicated weeks, or a period at most of between one and four months. For Peter and Patsy, who was now pregnant with their first child, the answer was "Indefinite."[54]

IN 1948, Matthiessen had behaved in Paris like a runaway prince, confident that his nationality gave him license to do whatever he pleased. Now, three years later, the easy life was still available—*bifteck, pommes frites*, and a carafe of wine for less than two dollars—but Paris was no longer so willing to tolerate every whim of *les Américains*. An editorial in *Le Monde* bewailed the American gum wrappers littering Paris boulevards, the imported Du Pont stockings sheathing Parisienne legs.[55] Coca-Cola was deplored as a symbol of creeping American materialism: the Coca-colonization of France. The French were "tired of being occupied, even if for their own welfare," explained Janet Flanner in *The New Yorker*, "and especially of being occupied by Americans who, in their own phrase, 'never had it so good.'"[56] In 1952, Flanner would compile a laundry list of major reasons behind the surge of anti-Americanism, the most striking of which was "our hysterical hunts for a few hidden Communists, 'like moths in an office carpet.'"[57]

As Senator Joseph McCarthy stoked an inquisition in the United States, and as a new conflict flared in Korea, the communists remained remarkably influential in France. In the June 1951 legislative election, which unfolded while the Matthiessens were crossing the Atlantic, the Parti communiste français secured nearly five million out of nineteen million votes, or 26.27 percent, which was the most of any single party.[58] A rival right-wing coalition, the Third Force, would ultimately secure the parliamentary majority, but the result was a testament to the PCF's appeal across political lines. Culturally, French communists were often associated with the Resistance fighters who'd battled Nazism during the war. The PCF leveraged this heroic prestige, stoked popular resentments through sloganeering, and targeted citizens, both communist and noncommunist, who dreaded being dragged into yet another bloody struggle.[59]

American officials watched the French scene from Washington, D.C., with growing trepidation. France was strategically crucial in the Cold War, and the PCF's popularity was seen as a serious impediment to American foreign policy goals and the ongoing security of Western Europe. An intervention to mitigate the communists' successful messaging was therefore deemed a priority. In April 1951, President Truman created a subcommittee called the Psychological Strategy Board, which was tasked with overseeing psychological warfare—anticommunist offensives that could "influence men's minds and wills."[60] In the struggle against Moscow, France would become one of the first soft power campaigns.

This "psywar," a war of propaganda intended to tilt public opinion in a more pro-American direction, was still in its early stages when the *Liberté* docked at Le Havre. For most of the blithe young men Matthiessen would soon become acquainted with in Paris, it would never be more than something that happened in the background, a culture battle that (they believed) had nothing to do with them. But even they could sense the new atmosphere in the city: "a subdued yet tense quality," William Styron called it, "as of a people pushed very close to the breaking point, or as of one hysterical woman who, if you so much as dropped a pin behind her, would break out in screams. 'U.S. Go Home.'"[61]

RUE PERCEVAL WAS HOME to an obscure row of artist studios, tucked between the open railroad tracks of the Gare Montparnasse, on one side, and the bustling rue de l'Ouest, where fragrant stalls sold everything "from celery root to blackbirds."[62] The concierge at 14, rue Perceval was "a little black stump of an old countrywoman from Dordogne," Matthiessen recalled, and she kept chickens out back that were apt to make even more of a racket than the trains. Matthiessen was already familiar with the address because it had once been Nathalie de Salzmann's place. Now that Nathalie was living in Venezuela, she was subletting it to him for just twenty-seven dollars a month.

The apartment was located at the top of four flights of dark stairs, and it needed to be heated by lumps of coal dust that were hauled up from the basement in buckets and then fed into a dyspeptic stove. But it was romantic in a way, with its huge living room, balcony bed, chipped bathtub, and sunny terrace offering a view of the neighborhood. Over time it would become a slightly fantastical setting for tales told about the *The Paris Review* crowd, transforming into a meeting place akin to "Gertrude Stein's apartment in the twenties," as Gay Talese once put it: "On one wall was a Foujita* painting of a gigantic head of a cat. The other wall was all glass, and there were large trees against the glass and wild growth crawling up it, and visitors to this apartment often felt that they were in a monstrous fishbowl, particularly by 6 p.m., when the room was floating with Dutch gin and absinthe and the cat's head seemed bigger, and a few junkies would wander in, nod, and settle softly, soundlessly in the corner."[63] That was probably overstating things somewhat, though the atelier was certainly "bohemian," Patsy once acknowledged to another writer—"just what you wanted if you were twenty-three years old and living in Paris."[64]

After Matthiessen finished unpacking, he rode the Métro to the Place de la Concorde and walked into the Jeu de Paume. The museum, which just a few years before had been used by Nazis as a sorting house for art stolen from Jewish families, was now filled with crowds of tourists. Matthiessen drifted past Cézannes and Renoirs, Monets and Manets, until he found the man he would come to think of as his "handler,"[65] a low-key veteran of the OSS. Together, they headed outside to stroll in the Jardin des Tuileries, where they discreetly discussed the new recruit's assignments.

What Matthiessen did, day to day for the CIA, remains something of a mystery. His written narratives glide over the gritty details of counterintelligence. "They promised me Paris was a hotbed of intrigue, and it was at that time,"[66] he once acknowledged to *Men's Journal*, yet he tended to downplay his own part to friends and journalists, who then repeated what he told them. He was "just running errands and carrying messages and false passports between agents in Paris."[67] Or he was "sending in reports of national gasoline consumption, that sort of thing."[68] Or he was reading Party literature like *L'Humanité*—an organ of the PCF that was "wrong-headed, ill-written, rhetorical, and boring to a crazed degree, like a stuck record," he said[69]—to keep his eye on communist "enemies."[70]

Perhaps his most candid admission came during an awkward exchange on *Charlie Rose* in 2008, when the host cornered his guest while the cameras were rolling. What was he doing for the CIA in Paris?

"Well, I think we'll just have to go to the rest of the show," Matthiessen replied. "It wasn't very much. It was pretty paltry, really. What it really was doing . . . Know what I was doing, spending my day doing? Deceiving people. That's all it is."

---

* Léonard Tsuguharu Foujita was a flamboyant Japanese-French artist known for his meticulous studies of cats. Foujita lived in Montparnasse for years, but he'd abandoned Paris by the time the Matthiessens arrived. They became friends with Foujita's ex-wife, Youki (Lucie Badoud), who was now with Henri Espinouze, another artist whose works the Matthiessens collected.

"Deceiving people as to—?"

"As to who you are, your identity, what you're up to, what you want to know [...]"

"Were you looking for people you can convert? Were you looking to expose people?"

"No, I was getting information on people."[71]

Those "people"—French left-wingers and communists, as well as expatriate Americans who'd caught the CIA's attention as potential subversives—were "inevitably so uninteresting that fifty years later, I have all but forgotten who they were or what they did," Matthiessen wrote elsewhere.[72] This was an ambiguous statement that was intended to suggest any further inquiry was a wild-goose chase.

Was Matthiessen watching Richard Wright, as the journalist Joel Whitney has speculated?[73] Wright publicly broke with the Communist Party in 1944, but the FBI was still monitoring his movements in Paris through military channels, the U.S. Information Agency, and the Foreign Liaison Service. The CIA, too, was keeping an eye on him. Wright's partially declassified CIA file includes a three-page memo documenting comments he made at a conference in the Club de l'Observateur on April 27, 1951—barely seven weeks before Matthiessen arrived in the city.[74] Given the CIA was already gathering intelligence, it is hard to believe that Matthiessen, who soon became acquainted with the writer through their overlapping social circles, did not at least mention Wright to his handler.

After *The New York Times* revealed Matthiessen's CIA role in 1977, Irwin Shaw questioned whether *he* had been on the Agency's watchlist. The thirty-eight-year-old playwright, short story writer, and critically acclaimed author of *The Young Lions* was on the same June voyage of the *Liberté*, and he and his wife, Marian, soon grew close with the Matthiessens in Paris. Indeed, Peter and Patsy became front-row spectators to the Shaws' marital dramas: Patsy watched Marian "regularly taking off her wedding ring and throwing it across the restaurant, or onto the tracks of an oncoming train, or casting it into the surf. Irwin was always buying her new wedding rings. It was sort of a running joke."[75] With his literary fame and Hollywood money, Shaw would assume the role of paterfamilias, or "a kind of scout master,"[76] over Peter and his troop of friends in Paris—"Tall Young Men" who, Shaw assumed, were just "going through a period of Gallic slumming for the fun of it."[77]

One of the reasons Irwin Shaw had sailed to Europe was to put some distance between himself and the searchlights of the House Un-American Activities Committee. Suggestions that he was either a communist or a fellow traveler had dogged him since 1947, when Jack Warner of Warner Bros. accused him of spiking his screenplays with "un-American doctrines."[78]

While Shaw had avoided the Hollywood blacklist, he'd recently been named in *Red Channels*, a right-wing pamphlet that alleged widespread communist manipulation of the media and entertainment industries. He had also been forced to withdraw one of his old plays, *Bury the Dead*, after communist groups co-opted it as antiwar propaganda.[79] So it was not entirely far-fetched to think he might have been a person of interest to the U.S. government. Yet when Shaw eventually raised this with Matthiessen—asking, effectively, *Did you spy on me in Paris?*—Matthiessen dismissed the idea out of hand: Shaw "styled himself without much cause as a political fugitive exiled by the media witch-hunts at home."[80] Nevertheless, the older man could be "snide about it in his cups in later years," which suggests Shaw was never entirely convinced by the denial.

Whoever Matthiessen was "getting information on" during his first few months in Paris, the pace was breakneck, work and life blending into an unbroken streak of social engagements. If he and Patsy were not out at dinner or a party, they were watching Senegalese dancers at La Vieille Rose Rouge, smoking cigarettes at the Chaplain bar, where the haze was so thick you could almost write your name in it, or playing cards until the early hours of the morning in Montparnasse cafés, then stumbling up the dim stairs to their flat.

Toward the end of summer, this ceaseless tempo exacted a sudden, horrifying toll: Patsy went into early labor. She was rushed to the American Hospital in Neuilly-sur-Seine, where she delivered a boy several months before his due date. "Though he only lived about 12 hours," Peter later remembered, "Thomas looked like the star of that incubator batch, at least to me."[81] In his book *Nine-Headed Dragon River*, he would write: "Years ago in Paris I said goodbye to my infant son by touching kissed fingers to his forehead, at a small service in the hospital yard conducted by a wine-spotted cleric and two conscripted witnesses, still clutching brooms."[82]

Patsy was devastated by their loss. She was also furious, though it would take time for the anger at Peter and herself to seep through the shock. Lila and Sarita, her mother and younger sister, flew over from Massachusetts, but in the immediate aftermath the concierge at rue Perceval offered a few words of comfort: "Mais vous êtes jeune! Il n'y a que fabriquer un autre." ("But you are young! You just have to make another.")[83] This didn't help. Nor did Peter. According to a friend, he observed his wife's heartbreak and struggled to offer an adequate response. What to do in such a wretched situation? He suggested a drink at the Ritz Bar, but Patsy refused to leave the apartment.[84]

MATTHIESSEN'S SECOND ATTEMPT at a novel, begun around this time, was tentatively titled "Signs of Winter," which he borrowed from a translation of Rilke's *Duino Elegies:*

> O Trees of life, what are your signs of winter?
> We're not at one. We've no instinctive knowledge,
> like migratory birds. Outstript and late,
> we force ourselves on winds and find no welcome
> from ponds where we alight.[85]

Writing the novel was supposed to be his cover in Paris, and he made considerable progress in marathon sessions at his typewriter. The problem was that nobody could see it—a writer's labor is largely imperceptible to the outside world. As Matthiessen recalled, "early on, my CIA 'handler' and I agreed that my literary life was going to require a more visible public activity in order to be plausible to the ever-inquisitive French police or any other agency that wanted to know what young foreigners of ambiguous occupation were really up to."[86]

A solution presented itself in late September. One afternoon, Matthiessen was sitting in Le Dôme when a man walked up and announced that they had previously met in Pamplona in 1949.

Harold Louis Humes Jr.—"Doc" Humes—was a twenty-five-year-old American eccentric, known for waltzing around Paris with a Homburg hat and silver-headed cane. He had bags under his eyes, a scruffy beard, and a tendency "to orate at length," as Tom Guinzburg once noted, "climaxing his remarks with a 'I guess we are all agreed on that,' the only certain entente being that the Café Dubonnet serves a lousy lunch."[87] Some people suspected Humes was "crazy,"[88] or maybe a mad genius; the "Doc" nickname had been derived during high school from "Doc" Elias Huer, the polymath scientist in *Buck Rogers*.[89] Matthiessen found him "remarkable," looming over his table in Le Dôme: Humes was wearing a cape, had a deep, infectious laugh, and seemed "appealing, aggressive, warm-hearted, curious, yet with convictions on every subject . . . all of which made him impossible."[90]

After a few early years in Arizona, Humes had grown up in Westfield, New Jersey, the son of middle-class Christian Scientists. He had done a stint in the Navy during the war, and then returned to study at MIT in Cambridge. In 1948, he had caught a freighter to Europe with the intention of getting a different sort of education. "I went to Paris because Paris is where you go when you want to think," he later explained to Gay Talese. "I wanted to hide out and think, and maybe learn." Acutely conscious of the racism and class exploitation in his "native land," he had also left because he couldn't stand watching "the rape of justice and murder of decency." As he told Talese, "I left America because the alternative to leaving was suicide or madness."[91] In Paris, he was a methods and procedures expert for the Marshall Plan under Ambrose Chambers; an art dealer who acquired paintings on the French market; a chess hustler in cafés, where he managed to pocket a few thousand francs per session; and a "remittance man," receiving small sums of money from his father as an encouragement not to come home again. He also walked dogs.

But the part that was relevant to Matthiessen was Humes's position as a magazine publisher. Several American periodicals had been planted and bloomed—and in many cases withered—in the creatively fecund climate of postwar Paris, including *Points, ID, Janus, New-Story,* and *Zero.* Humes had been inspired (reports vary) either by *Points,* created by Sindbad Vail, the *bon viveur* son of Peggy Guggenheim, or by *Zero,* which was cofounded by George Solomos, a pugnacious Greek American who edited under the pen name Themistocles Hoetis. (The inaugural issue of *Zero,* published in spring 1949, featured a scorching essay titled "Everybody's Protest Novel," by a twenty-four-year-old James Baldwin.) Wanting in on the action, Humes had purchased his own magazine for $600, the *Paris News Post.*

Humes thought Matthiessen was "suave, inquisitive, quite handsome. Peter and Patsy were *the* attractive young couple around Paris, possessing something of the same sort of allure . . . as did the Crosbys [Harry and Caresse] in the twenties."[92] If Matthiessen could be a little sharp sometimes, "riding" him with critical comments, Humes scratched it up to insecurity: "Peter needs to do this even if only as a ritual jest," he said. "If he doesn't do it, he'll start working on himself. He'll start drinking too hard, maybe."[93] (This was a shrewd observation.) After a few meetings, he asked if Matthiessen might be interested in becoming fiction editor for the *Paris News Post.* Matthiessen was hesitant; he flicked through a copy of the magazine and concluded it was little more than a feeble guide to restaurants and social events, like a Paris *Cue.** But then he agreed, because it was also the kind of alibi he needed: "a public place of work, editors and writers coming and going, manuscripts, mail, identification on a masthead would all bolster the cover provided by the novel."[94]

---

* In 2001, Immy Humes, in an interview for her documentary about her father (*Doc,* 2008), handed Matthiessen an old copy of the *Paris News Post.* Surprised, he leafed through the pages, then said, "I revise my opinion. They were quite nice." Indeed, dismissing the *News Post* as a *Cue* or *New Yorker* knockoff is not really fair; the magazine had inventive art direction, some amusing cartoons, and features that were, at the very least, informative and far-ranging: modern farming methods; the odd delicacies sold at Hédiard (shark fins, reindeer tongues); and Christian Dior's transgressive experiments with hemlines ("This year you *add* rather than scissor those inches").

Matthiessen appealed to friends and acquaintances to furnish him with material. James Baldwin, whom he'd met at a poker game and didn't much like ("I never could locate him, find his center"),[95] promised something but then failed to deliver. Blair Fuller mailed a story from America, "Markle and the Mouse," which made the cut. And Matthiessen published at least one of his own manuscripts, "The Replacement," an uncanny war tale about a German officer confronting an enemy prisoner who turns out to be a kind of doppelgänger:

"You're frightened. Perhaps you will be more frightened when I tell you that, with a story like that one, you will have to be shot as a spy."
"But I'm not a spy," the boy said, moaning a little.[96]

At the same time Matthiessen was finding his way as an editor, he was also dealing with the fiction editors at *The New Yorker*. Katharine White wrote Bernice Baumgarten about a story called "The Novices" in September: "[T]he first four and a half pages of the manuscript seem to be pretty badly written; quite a few of the sentences come apart in your hands if you try to analyze them and I think he has tried a little too hard to make them 'poetic.' . . . Also, all through the story there seem to be holes—places he has skipped or slighted, ellipses that are not clear. . . . I hope you will forgive all this and that you and Mr. Matthiessen will understand that if we were not interested in his writing, I would not criticize it so severely."[97] Matthiessen attempted a hasty rewrite based on her feedback, but White thought he only made it worse. "There are writers who just cannot revise with success and perhaps he is one of them," she said.[98] Baumgarten submitted a few other stories—"The Midget Football," "Late in the Season"—but White sent those back, too. "This time I won't bother you with our reasons for rejection, but what I said in my last letter about Mr. Matthiessen's work still holds true."[99]

What is interesting is how White's criticisms—painful, because they confirmed the fears about rejection he'd once confided to Wendy Burden—were then metabolized into Matthiessen's own editorial judgment for the *Paris News Post*. Sometime around the start of 1952, he received a submission from Britain titled "The Luna Moth." "Generally speaking, this sort of story is not precisely my dish of gooseberry fool," he wrote to the sender in reply. "Perhaps this is because I myself have had no luck with Miss Baumgarten on a similar theme and have been infected by a general feeling among agents and editors that the decadent child is anathema to the Amurkan reading public, or damn well should be if it isn't." Still, there was "a modicum of truth in it," he wrote—even if nobody else could see the pathos in a dissatisfied scion, *he* certainly could—before adding: "I should probably submit it before a final decision to the idiots in control. However, I am sure they will dance for joy and that GP can count on being published if he is willing to leave his fee (10,000 fr.) in abeyance, not only for the moment but perhaps forever."[100]

"GP" was George Plimpton, his boyhood pal from St. Bernard's, who was finishing up his studies in Cambridge.

THE SHORT STORY THAT brought about the sale of the *Paris News Post* was written by Terry Southern, yet another young American expatriate loafing around the Left Bank. Southern was "going through a rather mind-altering substance phase,"[101] Matthiessen recalled—he would laugh with a characteristic *snee snee snee*, and sort of "lean" back into a conversation—but his work was surreal and sophisticated in equal measure. "The Sun and the Still-Born Stars," an allegorical story about a Texas farmer and his wife battling a monstrous "sea-hog" that crawls out of the Gulf, was simply too good, in Matthiessen's opinion, to be wasted on the *Paris News Post*. When he saw it printed in "this dinky little magazine," he pulled Humes aside and made a suggestion.[102] What if they ditched the *News Post* and created something better?

Humes replied, "I'll do it if you do it,"[103] although he would later claim that starting a new publication had been *his* idea, just carefully planted in Matthiessen's head, like a cuckoo's egg laid in another bird's nest.*

Before anything substantial could come of this new scheme, a distraction turned up in the form of William Clark Styron Jr.—literally turned up, on the fourth-floor landing at rue Perceval, clutching a letter of introduction from a mutual friend. It was the second half of April, and Styron had just taken a circuitous twenty-two-hour train trip from Copenhagen. Matthiessen seemed "a trifle cold,"[104] Styron thought, as he stood in the doorway: "He presents to strangers an aloof and hollow-eyed reserve which is apt to be defined as either puritanically humorless or frostily cavalier."[105] But this impression subsided when Matthiessen invited him inside for whisky. Then, with Patsy accompanying, they relocated around the corner to a small Breton restaurant for Belon oysters—*huîtres*, a word derived, Matthiessen

---

* "No one can know the organizing dream, the planning, the scheming, the long conversations, the step-by-step learning, which had to precede the event," Humes explained to George Plimpton in 1953. "No one ever saw me step into the dark street and click my heels in the air in a mad little dance one morning at 5 a.m. That was the night that Peter had first suggested that maybe we should junk the Paris News Post and start a new magazine.... I played reluctant, unconvinced. It was necessary—for Peter to convince me, before he'd really convinced himself." If this sounds a little far-fetched, it is also difficult to disprove. When reminded of Humes's claim five decades later, Matthiessen's reactions would range from "bullshit" to "it's possible."

announced, "from the sound made when one's first oyster is spat across the room: hweet-tre!"[106] The three of them ate and drank until Styron turned suddenly lachrymose, overcome by exhaustion. He slumped forward into the debris of his dinner. "Ah ain' got no mo' ree-sistance to change than a *snow-flake*. Ah'm goin home to the James Rivuh an' grow *pee*-nuts."[107] Matthiessen would quote this strange declaration back at Styron, in a faux Tidewater accent, for the rest of his life, and even describe it in Styron's eulogy as "the heart-rending cry which as a metaphor will echo down the ages."[108]

Bill Styron, from Newport News, Virginia, was the precocious son of a shipyard engineer. He was on his way to Rome as winner of the Prix de Rome from the American Academy of Arts and Letters, which came with a year-long residency and stipend. Styron's first novel, *Lie Down in Darkness*, published in September 1951, had been a breakout success in America. Styron had ascended the bestseller list after receiving more than a hundred mostly favorable reviews, some of which compared him to Faulkner while also suggesting he was a spokesman for the new Lost Generation.

Reports of Styron's glory had yet to reach France; Matthiessen knew nothing about him as they sat in the bistro. But Styron was an engaging fellow, confident and well informed, and Matthiessen discovered they had a great deal in common despite their very different backgrounds. Both tended, for example, to be ruled by emotions, particularly the depressive kind "in a subterranean way," as Styron once phrased it.[109] Both had cheated on eye exams during the war, Styron with considerably more luck—he concealed a congenital cataract and bluffed his way into the Marine Corps.[110] And both valued writing above everything else in the world. "We were swept up in the very midst of a postwar literary fever," Styron later recalled. "Peter had not yet written a book . . . but he was, after all, barely twenty-five; he had time to burn and I remember telling him so, from the senior and authoritative vantage point of a writer who was two years older."[111]

In the next few days, the Matthiessens moved Styron from his Right Bank tourist dive into the sunny Hôtel Liberia, near Reid Hall in Montparnasse. Then they set about showing him a good time. Irwin Shaw was introduced: "honest, gentle, witty," Styron decided; "not at all the sort of Brooklyn wise-guy that he's made out to be."[112] Irwin crammed them all into a convertible, along with Marian, and drove out of the city to a wayside inn, where they lounged in a rose garden eating langoustines and strawberry shortcake. On other days the men picnicked on the banks of the Marne, or drifted around St.-Germain-des-Prés, where Styron spotted Truman Capote looking "perfectly furious that no one recognized him."[113] Matthiessen even took his new friend to visit Tristan Tzara, one of the founders of the Dada movement: Styron reported home in a letter that Tzara was "a fabulous old gent who rather wistfully lives off the memories of past grandeur but whose apartment is absolutely crammed with original Picassos.... He's a communist, like most left-bank* French intellectuals, but withal quite reasonable."[114] The likely reason for this surprising social call did not occur to Styron, who would not learn about Matthiessen's covert job for years.

While Styron and Matthiessen were enjoying themselves, much of the rest of central Paris was preoccupied with a month-long contemporary arts festival called "Masterpieces of the Twentieth Century." The festival was a lavish celebration of Euro-American culture, offering a full schedule of operas, ballets, symphonies, exhibitions, lectures, and roundtable debates. It was organized by the Congress for Cultural Freedom, which was subsidized and guided by the CIA. "Masterpieces" was intended to promote a vibrant, attractive alternative to the cultural barrenness of totalitarian regimes. As Nicolas Nabokov, the festival's director and a major Cold War propagandist, explained in February: "It is not necessary for us to confine ourselves to polemics about artistic freedom. We have only to exhibit the products of that freedom to win our argument."[115]

There is no evidence that either Styron or Matthiessen attended any of the festival's events. But the Matthiessens knew Nabokov well enough to invite him over to rue Perceval for drinks, and Peter was also in contact with the festival's principal benefactor, Julius Fleischmann Jr., who happened to be an old family friend. The heir to a vast yeast manufacturing fortune in Cincinnati, Ohio, Fleischmann had made a name for himself as a patron of the arts; he was a member of committees for the Metropolitan Opera, the Yale School of Drama, and the Ballet Russe de Monte-Carlo. According to *The New York Times*, he had raised "about $500,000" to float "Masterpieces of the Twentieth Century."[116] This money had come from private sources like the Farfield Foundation—a pass-through, in reality, for the CIA's sponsorship, with Fleischmann an enthusiastic front man for the Agency. During their conversation, Matthiessen explained his idea for a new Paris-based literary review, buttering up the "Cincinnati Maecenas"[117] for a funding proposal.

"JUST A GRISLY REMINDER that publisher's row back here is agog with news that you are nearing completion of your novel," John Appleton, an editor at Harper & Brothers, wrote to Matthiessen in May.[118] The letter was a confidence booster, and Matthiessen replied to Appleton (an old friend) a

---

* Tzara lived on the Right Bank, on avenue Junot, in a striking modern house designed by Adolf Loos, surrounded by his extensive collection of African and Oceanic art, as well as the Picassos, Miros, Chiricos, and Utrillos.

few days later with enthusiasm: "I don't know quite what to report about the novel except that it is of unparalleled merit. It is also 40 pp. along in the second draft, and I should imagine it will be finished around November, although that may be optimistic, especially since there is such a plethora of unprincipled rumpots in this neck of the woods.... Styron helped me celebrate my birthday last night, and today is like every other day, I have something really quite special in the way of a hangover."[119]

Accomplishing much of anything was a challenge when there were so many distractions. Styron, in a letter to his father, complained about the "treacherous" atmosphere in Paris, "so lulling and lazy that one is content to sit for hours and hours drinking a beer in a café, and to do nothing more, no work, just sit."[120]

The new magazine idea was making only glacial progress. But seductive indolence was not the only challenge; another was Doc Humes. In their initial talks, Humes had told Matthiessen that he wanted to be the head of it, whatever "it" turned out to be. Matthiessen had agreed at the time, because he was content to oversee the fiction while he poked at his novel and went about his other work. Yet Humes, though undeniably brilliant and imaginative—an unstoppable font of ideas—was not particularly interested in deadlines, schedules, or in supervising the details once the conceptual phase was over, making him a poor fit as editor-in-chief. Before Humes sold the *News Post* to an intense English woman (whereupon it promptly folded), the staff had been "ready to mutiny," according to Matthiessen.[121] "I too wanted to kill him half the time, although I remained very fond of him."

That spring, what saved the inchoate venture from a premature end was Matthiessen's friend in Cambridge. George Plimpton did not invent *The Paris Review*, but his exuberance and dedication would bring it to life. "I'm the Father of the Magazine," Humes once proclaimed. "George is the Mother."[122]

When Matthiessen phoned Plimpton in England to suggest he take over the editorship, Plimpton was adrift, having no firm idea of what to do with his life. He was twenty-five years old, charismatic, debonair, and highly educated: after St. Bernard's there'd been Phillips Exeter (from which, according to one story, he'd been expelled for pointing a musket at a housemaster and saying, "Bang bang! You're dead");[123] then Harvard, where he took creative writing classes with Archibald MacLeish and edited *The Harvard Lampoon;* and now King's College in Cambridge, where he was studying English. Yet all that learning had not given him a sense of direction. Plimpton had considered becoming a writer, but he was not sure he was talented enough: "I thought that everybody around me at Cambridge wrote better than I did."[124] He had wondered if television, "the new big thing" in America, offered a viable pathway instead. While he considered his opinions, a brief vacation to Paris at Easter had left a lasting impression. Matthiessen had invited him to a party at rue Perceval, and Plimpton had been enchanted by the freedoms he observed there: "people at work with their books and ideas and shoutings about life and this magazine they were planning."[125] With this tableau in mind, and nothing else on the immediate horizon, he agreed to be editor-in-chief.

Plimpton's decision was received by Matthiessen as "cheering intelligence indeed"[126] (a choice of words that reads, as Joel Whitney has noted, like a Freudian slip). But Plimpton was reluctant to migrate across the English Channel until after he'd marched in his commencement, so they were forced to make plans via correspondence. "I have had a long letter from Humes, presently in Portugal, full of bright ideas, and if we can lure Guinzburg into the trap, which I think we can, all will be well," Matthiessen wrote. Plimpton replied that he was cajoling a contribution out of E. M. Forster, an acquaintance of acquaintances at Cambridge. "Tip top, in fact peachy keeno," Matthiessen said.[127] Styron was happy to toss in a manuscript, and Humes claimed that Randall Jarrell would pen them a thematic preface to set the tone (which never materialized). William Pène du Bois, the son of Guy Pène du Bois and a well-regarded children's book illustrator—he'd won a Newbery Medal in 1948—soon came on as art editor. Plimpton was able to find a poetry editor, too, in the able form of Donald Hall, an American student at Oxford who had just been awarded the Newdigate Prize for best English verse. By the start of summer in 1952, a remarkable number of ingredients were either already assembled or teetering on the edge of the basket, including, Matthiessen hinted, "a wealthy backer" (i.e., Julius Fleischmann), though "a great deal more must be done in this distasteful direction."[128]

Plimpton arrived in Paris in the last week of June. "Sure, it was an escape," Tom Guinzburg recalled a decade later. "This was the last fling, in a sense. We always said, 'This magazine will be good just as long as we're good and we're young.'"[129] It was not meant to last forever. But George Plimpton, never finding anything that gave him a stronger sense of purpose in life, would remain editor of the magazine for the next fifty years, until his death in 2003 at the age of seventy-six.

IN JULY 1963, Gay Talese published what he called a "painting" of *The Paris Review* crowd, "Looking for Hemingway," in *Esquire*. The long article was a group portrait of "the witty, irreverent sons of a conquering nation,"[130] written in a witty, irreverent style that was intended to capture the esprit of an era. Talese had a talent for waggish descriptions; Plimpton, for instance, "was made editor-in-chief, and soon he could be seen strolling through the streets of Paris with a long woolen scarf flung around his neck, cutting a figure reminiscent of Toulouse-Lautrec's famous lithograph of Aristide Bruant, that dashing litterateur of the nineteenth century."[131] If there was a streak of acid through the painting—caustic references to entitlement, wealth, and a self-centered desire on the part of the men to never grow up, to remain in a "free, frolicsome world" untroubled by adult responsibilities—the overall effect was nevertheless to elevate the crowd into the realm of romantic legend.

Matthiessen loathed Talese's article, complaining to Plimpton that it reduced his part in the magazine's founding to "a tall, thin Yalie who owned a nice apartment."[132]

Plimpton hated it, too, though his objection had more to do with what he saw as certain "inaccuracies." After the feature appeared on newsstands, he fired off a letter to Talese questioning his ethics as a journalist. Horrified, Talese wrote a long, piqued response, and then another even longer response addressing Plimpton's "20,000-word attacks."[133] "[S]ince you did not like the painting, you are naturally entitled to throw eggs at my painting," Talese said. But he refused to swallow a charge of sloppy reporting. "[Y]ou must understand that, in my interviews with other Paris Review people, I got different versions of the same thing, different recollections of the way things were in Paris in those days." Talese had created a "painting," he said, because a "photograph" was impossible—there were too many conflicting accounts for anything approaching objective truth.

One of the sources Talese had consulted was Patsy Southgate, whose own memories of Paris had, by 1963, become steeped in bitterness. "I fell into *The Paris Review*," she told him during an interview in New York. "It never occurred to me whether it was something I really wanted to be doing."[134]

Following the death of her baby in the autumn of 1951, Patsy had found Paris to be a far lonelier place than the one she'd fallen in love with a few years earlier. Peter had his novel, his short stories, his machinations with Humes (and with the CIA); Patsy had no occupation *except* her husband, though she had begun going into restaurant kitchens so she could learn how to cook through observation. "She really wanted to be a writer," recalled her sister, Sarita. "But I think she was so dominated by Peter that she didn't feel she could get in there. So cooking is a womanly thing, and Parisian cooking is top drawer."[135] In fact, her literary aspirations were mostly ignored by Matthiessen and his "boys club,"[136] as Patsy nicknamed the gang who converted her home into their makeshift office. None of them were interested in her ideas or opinions. "Peter used to tell me to lower my voice, and I was practically inaudible," she told Talese.[137] Nor would she be considered a founder of their magazine despite her dependable presence at foundational meetings. It is worth noting that Patsy, as "Patricia Southgate," was the only woman to contribute to the first issue of *The Paris Review*—an elegant translation of "Death on the Avenue de Ségur," by Antoine Blondin—yet she believed her main contribution had been as a servant. "*I* was a Stepin Fetchit in that crowd, getting them tea at four, and sandwiches at ten."

Patsy became a sharp observer as she waited on the men at rue Perceval. Humes and Styron would come around in the early evenings, she told Talese, and drink Dutch gin and play word games, then talk for hours about where they should all go out to dinner. Their discussion was amusing, Patsy thought, "but not entertaining." They all spoke with an affected stammer, using phrases like "'Now see here,' or 'old fellow,' 'old boy,' and 'tip-top!'" They all embraced the "ineffable impact of the understatement." Some of them downplayed their family money and security. It was part of the game to pretend they were destitute.[138]

Warming up to her theme, Patsy confided to Talese what she believed was behind all this posturing: "Those people, I think, never accomplished anything during the war." They were masquerading as bohemians to compensate for a sense of something missing in their lives. "I think they're very insecure about their maleness," she continued, including Peter in her assessment. "I think they're all bugged about their maleness."[139] From her perspective, *The Paris Review* was the product of macho insecurity.

In "Looking for Hemingway," Talese quoted Patsy as saying that "there was something very *manqué* about [the *Paris Review* crowd]."[140] Yet in one of his defensive responses to Plimpton, he noted that he'd left her "most violent quotes" out of his article as a "gracious gesture" to the gentlemen she effectively eviscerated.[141] However, since Plimpton was now being so rude as to denigrate his methods and accuracy ("challenging everything I am"), Talese chose to share some choice extracts from Patsy's interview: "They're a bunch of reactionaries; their idea of a radical step is to eliminate the co[m]ma. . . . They're not disturbed enough ever to have a mental breakdown or to go to an analyst [*sic*]. . . . Plimpton has arranged to have things happen around him but I don't think that anything has happened to him."[142]

"So this is how Patsy 'saw' the Crowd," Talese told Plimpton, serving up a sharp counter-history of the magazine's founding: "her portrait is quite different from mine, and from yours; but it is how she remembered it."

WHO CAME UP WITH the name, *The Paris Review*? Plimpton claimed that he did, during a stroll one evening on the Île Saint-Louis.[143] Styron thought that Matthiessen was responsible, having suggested it sometime after a fruitless brainstorming session involving two green bottles of absinthe.[144] Humes, too, credited Matthiessen for the title, though in a roundabout way: "The Paris-American Review" had been registered by him, he said, at the Palais de Justice on October 3, 1951, and then planted in Matthiessen's head along with the rest of the magazine idea. ("PARIS REVIEW C'EST MOI!." he told Talese.)[145] John P. C. Train insisted that Matthiessen had wanted to call the magazine "Baccarat"—"crystalline perfection, no doubt, à la Théophile Gautier"—and that *he* had proposed the name because it was logical: "Paris" for the slightly exotic appeal, and "Review" because "that's what it was."[146]

John Train was a Harvard graduate and former editor of the *Lampoon* who'd moved to Paris to earn a doctorate at the Sorbonne, then dropped out after deciding that Comparative Literature was too divorced from real life. An acerbic figure, though never, Matthiessen said, "quite as formidable as the prickly personality he projected,"[147] Train was the business manager for the new magazine, but his unofficial role for much of the first year was managing editor.

It was Train, Matthiessen, Plimpton, Humes, Styron, Billy Pène du Bois, and Patsy, in the kitchen, who gathered at rue Perceval to thrash out the details of what *The Paris Review* should be. (Tom Guinzburg, also credited as a founder, would not fly over from New York until November.) These meetings varied wildly in terms of productivity. One session, as Plimpton later recounted, went off the rails when everybody indulged in hashish cookies: "Even someone *starting* to say something would get us laughing helplessly."[148] Another meeting was dedicated to just the masthead: "who was to be arranged in which way."[149] Yet another session saw the conception of the "Art of Fiction" interview series—an innovative format in which established writers discuss their influences and working habits. Debate at these meetings could get wildly passionate, Styron said, plans going forward "in euphoria, in kennel snarls of bickering, in buoyant certitude, in schism and in total despair"; Humes broke at least one glass with spirited emotion.[150] "We were prima donnas," Matthiessen later admitted. "Every goddamn one of us was a prima donna. We had no down-the-middle work-a-day guy. We had no Eisenhower."[151]

In a note to his parents, Plimpton explained that "what we are doing that's new is presenting a literary quarterly in which the emphasis is more on fiction than on criticism."[152] Unlike other literary quarterlies like *Partisan Review*, cultural commentary and critical theory was, if not forbidden, then to be relegated somewhere near the back of the book. *The Paris Review* would focus on new writing by young(ish) writers. It would not be politically *engagé*. It "beat no drum for anything," as Styron put it in the letter that eventually served as the magazine's credo.[153] Nor, with a few notable exceptions like Samuel Beckett and Jack Kerouac, would the fiction writers it did promote be especially avant-garde (unlike the rival *Merlin*, also published in Paris). Indeed, the *Review*'s commitment—meaning Matthiessen's and Plimpton's commitment—to the traditional, well-crafted short story in its early years would stir one critic to complain that "the significance of the magazine is limited to those who will eventually fit into the suave pages of the *New Yorker*. It is too much like a chic miscellany; there is no sign of a fresh development of writing to express our very changed conditions."[154]

Most of the conceptual decisions were made by the second half of July. Plimpton turned his attention to troublesome logistics: assembling a prospectus for potential backers plucked out of a New York *Social Register*; negotiating with typesetters on the rue de la Sablière; decoding French copyright rules as they pertained to a periodical to be published in English and exported to the United States. Leaving him to this "baptism by fire,"[155] Styron and Humes climbed into a musty blue Volkswagen and headed for Saint-Tropez, where, after multiple delays owing to a broken axle, they arrived at the sprawling, shrapnel-damaged estate of a French movie star. Meanwhile, the Matthiessens departed for a few weeks of vacation in French Basque Country.

In Bayonne, near Biarritz, they joined the foreign correspondent Art Buchwald to watch the annual bullfights. Buchwald wrote a dispatch for the *New York Herald Tribune* in which Matthiessen became "the Old Lady," channeling Jake Barnes: "'Will it be a good bullfight?' we asked the Old Lady. 'It depends,' she replied. 'If the bulls are brave and the matadors are brave and the picadors are brave and the banderilleros are brave we should see some good fights. Are you afraid?'"[156]

In Hendaye, on the border with Spain, Matthiessen talked his way onto a commercial fishing vessel and watched men scoop tuna from the Bay of Biscay: "each hurtling fish, knocked off its barbless hook when it struck the cabin side behind the fisherman, would fall into a makeshift chute leading down into the fish hatch aft—terrific!"[157] Another day in Hendaye, he wandered the tidal flats at the harbor mouth, and learned from a local how to catch razor clams using a small-caliber bullet nose affixed to the top of a metal tine from a broken umbrella. These simple activities, meditative in their physicality, reminded him of how much he'd come to miss the ocean while living in Paris.

The rest of the holiday was spent in Saint-Jean-de-Luz, where the Matthiessens found accommodation in a rooming house not far from the hilltop villa where Irwin and Marian Shaw were holding court. At sunset drinks overlooking the village, and at formal dinners served by a small platoon of waitstaff, they found themselves talking to film people like Harry Kurnitz,

Martin Gabel, and Anatole Litvak. "Nearly all of the Shaws' friends that summer drove Jaguars," Patsy told the biographer Michael Shnayerson.[158] When she attempted to reciprocate the Shaws' hospitality by hosting a dinner party of her own, she produced an overcooked roast beef that turned a "desperate" shade of gray: "Marian suggested I slice it and serve it cold with chutney, but it was beyond hope."

Between afternoon martinis and swims in the Atlantic, Matthiessen dashed off letter after letter to Plimpton, who was subletting the rue Perceval flat for a dollar a day. These notes started off playful—a hope that he might find "a little companion" to keep him company in their "Balcony Suite"[159]—but then took on a more imperious tone. Plimpton mentioned that he planned to go to press in two weeks, and that a second issue was being prepared for as soon as October. "Surely you have gone mad," Matthiessen wrote. "I have a terrible feeling that, alone in the Paris heat, you two [Plimpton and du Bois] are threatening to capsize the whole business." He added, "I know this does not come well from the lips of one who is rehabilitating on the seashore while you two work, and for this reason, I am more than willing to go along with the great majority of the very fine deeds (I mean this most sincerely) you have accomplished. On the other hand, I do not want to be responsible for a second issue of 9 pp. which lands us up to our crotches in debt."[160]

Money was a problem. While "terribly excited about this avalanche we've started," Matthiessen had yet to send his proposal to Julius Fleischmann, mostly because Humes had taken his typewriter to St. Tropez.

> Dear Mr. Fleischmann
>   Here at last is a prospectus of the fine new literary review I mentioned to you in June: I sincerely believe, as do all who have seen the material, that it will be the best literary quarterly since the TRANSITION of the Hemingway-Pound-Gertrude Stein era. You will see that we have already the interest and contributions (unpaid-for) of many fine writers, as well as of the promising younger people with whom the magazine is chiefly concerned. It is a question now, quite frankly, of sufficient sponsorship, until the magazine is able to pay for itself.
>   I hope the brochure will interest you in what we are trying to do . . .[161]

This undated draft by Matthiessen, handwritten in pencil on letterhead paper, is arguably the most contentious document in the *Paris Review* archive. The founders obtained start-up funds from twenty-three sources, including their wealthy parents (Humes, not coming from money, submitted an IOU); their parents' friends, like Ellen Barry, widow of the playwright Philip Barry; Lila Southgate, via Patsy; Mr. and Mrs. Walter Sohier—i.e., Wendy Burden, who had married Sohier in 1949; and Princess Andrée Aga Khan, whose son, Prince Sadruddin Aga Khan, had been a classmate of Plimpton's at Harvard.[162] Did Matthiessen also solicit funding from the CIA?

In 2007, he responded to questions posed by the *Nation* journalist Scott Sherman, stating "flatly" that the "chronic rumors" about CIA influence on the *Review* are "simply untrue."[163] Matthiessen added, "To the best of my knowledge—it's not provable, alas—the corollary rumors about CIA funding and/or sponsorship of the *Review* are untrue, as well, but for the record it should probably be acknowledged that the water here is slightly murky." He claimed to have had no idea that Julius Fleischmann was a CIA front man. As far as he knew, Fleischmann was just a wealthy Midwesterner who liked to drink highballs with his father on motorboats in Nassau. He'd targeted this old family friend for a prospectus because Fleischmann was an easily accessible arts aficionado who just so happened to have a documented interest in patronizing American cultural initiatives abroad.

Matthiessen never wavered from this testimony, and it is plausible, if not entirely satisfying. As Frances Stonor Saunders wrote in *The Cultural Cold War*, Fleischmann was a "fully roped-up member of Wisner's OPC from its earliest days"[164]—a member of the Office of Policy Coordination, the group likened by its critics to a posse of cowboys. Because Matthiessen was almost certainly employed in the rival OSO under the command of James Angleton, who enforced a sharp division of operations—one only knew what one needed to know—it is unlikely he was privy to the truth of Fleischmann's role or the secret purpose of the Congress for Cultural Freedom.

Nevertheless, the Congress was in the business of sponsoring magazines as part of its anticommunist offensive: *Preuves* and *Encounter* were both started with strong CIA backing around the same time as *The Paris Review*. Setting aside the question of Matthiessen's knowledge, what remains "slightly murky" is whether Fleischmann's donation was part of the Congress's campaign—whether, in other words, Fleischmann recognized the *Review* as an opportunity for pro-Western propaganda and then contributed CIA money via the Farfield Foundation. For his part, Matthiessen claimed not to think so: "It seems to me that a brand new, utterly unknown, and apolitical magazine of laughable potential circulation was a pretty unlikely target for international manipulation, and so far as I know, Fleischmann's donation of one thousand dollars was a private one."[165] Private or not, the check arrived in April 1953, and it was deposited, withdrawn, and exhausted immediately on overdue bills. Money would remain a "pressing problem" long after Fleischmann's modest grant.[166] (*Encounter*, to put this in perspective, received $40,000 in its first year through the Farfield Foundation.)[167]

The specter of CIA funding has long haunted *The Paris Review*, because it raises the discomforting idea that the magazine was used as an ideological weapon in the "cultural Cold War." While it is impossible to rule out the possibility, there is another explanation. The *Review* was intended by Matthiessen to be his primary cover in Paris, but it was shaky while the finances remained a mess. Perhaps the OSO asked the OPC to extend a small grant through its front man for a little relief and reinforcement. Matthiessen was just about to embark on a new assignment for the CIA; he needed the strongest cover he could manage.

This would also explain why Fleischmann declined any further support after his initial investment. In early 1955, Plimpton would make a further appeal to the Cincinnati philanthropist, only to have Fleischmann's secretary respond with regrets: "He doesn't feel that he can do anything for The Paris Review as he has too many other commitments."[168] If the CIA was seriously interested in *The Paris Review* as cultural propaganda, why deny the request? The only thing that had changed was Matthiessen's status as a contract agent. By 1955, *The Paris Review* was no longer useful as his cover.

"ALSO, OFF THE RECORD, Patsy finds she is pregnant again," Matthiessen added in one of his letters to Plimpton.[169] This surprise development demanded a few adjustments to their lives in the fall: no more alcohol binges or late nights spent in smoke-filled bars, and no more hikes up four flights of dark stairs. Peter turned suddenly solicitous toward his wife. "After her misfortune last year, I want to get her someplace where she can relax, have a maidservant, etc."[170] The doctor predicted a difficult pregnancy, which is why it was suggested they move somewhere closer to the ground. Peter wanted Left Bank, Saint-Germain area, but soon after they arrived back in Paris, he started searching the Right Bank, too, until he found a second-floor apartment with central heating at 18, rue de Chazelles, just across from the site of the former workshop and forge where the Statue of Liberty had been constructed. It was quiet and private, perfect for Patsy and baby; and Peter suspected he could get some serious work done on his novel there. Friends, however, were less satisfied with the change: "in spite of the neighboring strumpets," Styron wrote him from Rome, "the street which you describe sounds mightily cheerless compared to dear old Perceval, which will live on in all of our memories as the finest rue there is anywhere."[171]

Meanwhile, the magazine was relocated to more professional headquarters at 8, rue Garancière, directly north of the Jardin du Luxembourg. Because of French law, for *The Paris Review* to operate as a limited liability company (Société à Responsabilité Limitée), with shareholders, it required a French legal representative called a *gérant*. Before he'd moved to Italy, Styron had introduced Plimpton and Matthiessen to Colette Duhamel, the vivacious editor of a conservative bimonthly magazine, *La Table Ronde*, which was put out by the publishing house Librairie Plon. Duhamel agreed to act as gérant in a quid pro quo arrangement: they would include translations of her French writers in *The Paris Review*, thereby introducing them to English-speaking readers; and she, in addition to becoming their legal representative, would share her extensive knowledge of French magazine production and provide a workspace in the Plon building.

As Plimpton later recalled, "The editors of Plon worked in the kind of silence one associated with clerking in 19th century London banking institutions."[172] But things were far more anarchic in the *Review* office, which was a room so small that editors often evacuated to do work—and play the pinball machines—in cafés like the Flore or Tournon.* Letters, manuscripts, and invoices cascaded over the desk and three chairs, and the only typewriter available was missing its "A" key because Plimpton had accidentally burned it off with a cigarette.[173] A procession of young American women just graduated from Radcliffe, Barnard, or Vassar, collectively dubbed "Miss Aptecker,"† fought to impose order on the space, with little success. The

---

* One day, Plimpton discovered Humes slacking off, reading *Huckleberry Finn*, in Le Dôme; he exploded in frustration. Humes explained that this was a deliberate strategy to make Plimpton stand on his own two feet. Humes then announced that he was returning to America to take up studies at Harvard—and promptly went, too, participating so little in the production process of *The Paris Review* that the other founders demoted him on the masthead. Unsurprisingly, this offended Humes, who believed (rightly) that the magazine only existed in the first place because of him. In February 1953, when copies finally arrived on a dock in New York, he was waiting there to greet them. He pressed a large rubber stamp onto many of the title pages: "Editorial Representative (USA)—H. L. Humes." He then wrote to Matthiessen, "I left George a small moral problem: should he stamp my name and the NY address in the balance of the copies I left undone?"
† The origin of this unusual title for secretaries (along with its correct spelling: Aptecker, Apthecker, or Apothecker) is another *Paris Review* myth, impossible to confirm with any certainty. Both Guinzburg and Matthiessen suggested it was invented to spare the women from the bureaucratic nightmare of obtaining French work papers, one woman just assuming the identity of her predecessor. Gay Talese, however, suggested John Train coined the moniker because "so many young women came and went" that it was "ridiculous to try to remember all their names." Either way, one of the first Miss Apteckers, Louisa Noble, believed it meant "menial person" in Greek. "They treated us like maids," Noble said of the male editors, referring to herself and Jacqueline de Chalain, another Miss Aptecker. In 1983, *Esquire* reprinted Talese's article, and Noble, having kept quiet the first time it was published, fired off a long letter in a bid to finally correct the public record. Far from being "forgetful" and losing manuscripts, as the article claimed, *she* was the one who'd kept the office from falling apart: "My job was to . . . follow up on subscription orders, bank the checks, pay the bills, file, clean, distribute Paris Review posters all over Paris (except where it said: 'Defense d'Afficher'!) and, eventually, sell ads. It was I who started the page of ads which in Issue 3 we called 'Along the Rue de Seine' and later 'Sous les Toits de Paris.' I would stagger out into the Left Bank streets of Paris with my faltering French and inhibiting shyness and force myself to attempt my little ad-selling speech at every single store in the rue de Seine area [a chore for which Matthiessen insisted she be paid]. . . . I also sharpened pencils. I would arrive in the

mess was only exacerbated by unannounced visits by writer friends who were pursuing their own moveable feasts, including Max Steele, Bee Dabney, Evan S. Connell, John Marquand Jr., and Eugene Walter, a young Alabamian who the editors called "Tum-te-Tum," after the sound he made when one of his stories was accepted. Every evening at six-thirty, the concierge locked the doors to the courtyard below; legend has it that anyone trapped inside was forced to open the office window, hang by their fingertips, and drop into the rue Garancière with a prayer.

For the next few months, Matthiessen moved between Patsy, slow and cautious at home, and the *Paris Review* office, where the first issue was gradually taking shape. He read fiction submissions and mailed out rejection notices. He courted Graham Greene for a craft interview. He corresponded with Guinzburg in New York about advertising, the subscription drive—based on their parents' Christmas card lists—and the impending presidential election. "If IKE does win everyone you know will be scrambling out of the country—we'll all be named communists anyway," Guinzburg wrote.[174]

Matthiessen was careful to conceal his CIA activities from the other editors, none of whom had any idea their pet project was serving an ulterior function. This subterfuge required some elaborate ruses. On one occasion, Plimpton mentioned that a Harvard friend was eager to join them from America; Matthiessen, suspicious, passed the friend's name along to his handler to be checked, saying that he didn't want another novice agent "poaching on my cover."[175] Plimpton was confused when the friend then dropped out, and Matthiessen found himself having to play dumb.

At some point around this time, his covert duties suddenly escalated. Later in life, when Matthiessen sat down to record his memories of Paris, he considered revealing the identity of the figure who now became his most significant assignment. Ultimately, he would settle on a pseudonym: "Monsieur X." According to his narrative accounts, which, again, are one-sided

---

office and find a note from Train which would read: 'Kindly sharpen these pencils.' So I would kindly sharpen them!"

As an act of courtesy, Noble, in 1983, forwarded a duplicate of her *Esquire* complaint to George Plimpton, along with an anxious note: "Those years are engraved upon my memory as if they were yesterday; I have tried in my letter to report the part I played at the Paris Review as truthfully as possible." Plimpton was unsympathetic, though, and dismissed her correction as "vindictive." "Frankly, I think you've gone overboard with all this," he wrote in response. Noble protested, but Plimpton only doubled down: "your letter was one I could not support . . . it seemed hasty, full of conjecture and hypothesis, full of ruth (as my grandmother used to say), and unprintably long." He added, somewhat condescendingly, "If Esquire does not respond by publishing your present letter, I'd write them a somewhat more concise version." It is worth pointing out that Plimpton was not above throwing a secretary under the bus in the early days of the magazine. In 1953, Terry Southern raged after Plimpton censored the word "shit" from his issue one story, "The Accident." Uncertain how to handle Southern's ire, Plimpton wrote to Matthiessen with an idea: "Can't we put the blame on, say, an overly-sensitive Miss Aptecker?"

and incomplete, he met X through "bohemian French friends on the Blvd St. Germain." Then he approached the communist alone after his handler deemed the contact "exciting," and to be "hotly pursued."

Matthiessen's descriptions of X were deliberately vague: "a well-known French writer" who'd also made films; an older Jewish man who was committed to Stalin despite the virulent anti-Semitism in the Soviet Union; a Party faithful who was known to peddle *L'Humanité* on weekends. Hazarding a guess from unverifiable details is difficult, but one possible candidate (though not a perfect fit) is Tristan Tzara, the Dadaist poet and essayist Matthiessen had visited with Styron, and whom he once mentioned to Plimpton as a potential *Paris Review* contributor, to write on his "comrade" Pablo Neruda.[176] Born as Samuel Rosenstock in 1896, in Romania, Tzara had lived in Paris since 1920. He was responsible for books, films, cabarets, and little magazines, and he was a respected member of the Parti communiste français who supported its "Salon of Books" on Saturday afternoons.[177] He also played chess with Doc Humes.

At his handler's urging, Matthiessen met with X at a café on the boulevard Saint-Germain. He was nervous about the encounter; X, he wrote, was "a suspicious man and a very hard one." They ordered red wine and began to talk. The CIA was hungry for information about the inner workings of the PCF; it was Matthiessen's job to extract that information. One could not simply come out and *ask*, of course, so he approached X with a plan, presenting himself as "a young American writer who was openly disgusted—convincing because true—by the Cold War hysteria and witch hunts gathering momentum in the U.S." He wanted X to see him as a budding radical who might be exploited in the anti-American propaganda campaign still being waged by the Party across France.

Once properly introduced in this fashion, Matthiessen then, in his telling, proposed something daring. "My story was that I needed this man's advice as a veteran Communist agitator about a new left-wing political novel based in Spain and Paris." To gather intel about the PCF, he would put into practice what he'd learned about writing fiction. He unfurled the plot of a fake novel that he was supposedly working on, and then asked X to help him make it "more effective" from his highly partisan point of view. As X gave some feedback, Matthiessen scoured his comments "like a jackdaw," gathering morsels of intel.

This was a strange method, but Matthiessen claimed in his notes that it was an effective one: X agreed to additional meetings. And so he expanded his "novel" into several scribbled pages of an outline. While these original pages are lost, in some rudimentary form they concerned an American journalist who works for a wire service in Paris. Though still idealistic at twenty-nine, the journalist feels himself losing the strong quality of his conscience, growing gradually less angry at injustices in the world. The abrasive indignation he once possessed as a student, his willingness to speak up and say something, is smoothing down to complacency; his lucid moral vision is becoming clouded as he settles into a rhythm that in no way deviates from the status quo. Knowing this fills him with self-loathing, and he is fixated on his own weakness when word suddenly arrives that the PCF has just purged one of its most prominent revolutionaries. Years before, in Spain, at the outbreak of civil war, the journalist, then aged fourteen, had encountered the very same Marxist revolutionary while fleeing the country with his mother and father, a callous American diplomat. In a long conversation at a fairground, the revolutionary had dazzled him as a man certain about the righteousness of his cause—a man who was unafraid to fight authorities, majorities, or anything that got in his way, like a twentieth-century John Brown. Now, in Paris, the journalist sets out to track down and interview the revolutionary, plunging into the Paris underworld in the hope of reorienting his own life and clearing up his political and philosophical confusion.

If there is much about this outline that sounds suspiciously autobiographical, that's because it was. "I had to recognize," Matthiessen wrote, "that the slow-dawning opinions about politics and social justice attributed to the young narrator in my bogus novel were troubling reflections of my own."

Matthiessen claimed to have been deeply rattled by his meetings with X. Like many of the French communists he'd met during his undercover work for the CIA, X was "a near fanatic." Yet the man's sincerity of purpose and dedication to a more equitable social order were impossible to miss. The Party rhetoric was ludicrous, but X's personal convictions, explained across the café table, challenged Matthiessen to articulate his own. After two years of intense reading and political education in Paris, what *did* he believe in? Were his past flirtations with the left just a token gesture of rebellion meant to provoke his parents? Was he the same as his father, comfortable with a so-called natural order, people in a hierarchy, those at the top consoling themselves about human misery by occasional acts of noblesse oblige; or did he acknowledge the moral necessity for change? In an ironic reversal, and quite unwittingly, the "enemy" he was supposed to be interrogating made him "pause to consider my beliefs and ask myself what I really thought I was doing on this job." He ended up interrogating himself.

SOMETIME IN THE FIRST few months of 1953, Matthiessen, his account continues, was summoned to an unfamiliar Right Bank apartment to see three or four higher-ups from the CIA, including "a well-known theatrical entrepreneur of Eastern European origin whose role at this meeting was of course withheld from the lowly spy."[178] There was considerable excitement about the information he'd managed to extract from X, and he was "strongly encouraged" to pursue his new relationship further, in the hope that X might invite him to pledge support for the PCF. Then, the thinking went, he would continue his work from within the Party ranks as a penetration agent, or mole.

During this briefing, Matthiessen pondered the risks of his unusual situation. The new address on rue de Chazelles had turned out to be a little *too* quiet. Without the comings and goings of *The Paris Review* crowd to provide a distraction, the Matthiessens had been noticed as a solitary American couple—noticed by whom, nobody could say for sure, though Matthiessen suspected it was French police—and placed under surveillance. Climbing into his car in front of the building, he'd noticed vehicles in the rearview mirror pulling out behind him; he suspected he was being tailed all over Paris. Meanwhile, Patsy, as her pregnancy progressed, had become all but confined to bed, and she found herself on the receiving end of troubling phone calls, the silent kind that suggested their apartment was being checked to see if it was empty for a search. Friends would visit to play board games, trying to keep up her spirits, but she was growing increasingly nervous for reasons she was not permitted to share with them. A short story Matthiessen wrote in this period, "Lina," about a Jewish woman who comes unglued as she hides in Tuscany during the war, seems to capture something of his wife's mental state: "Despite her safety at the villa, she felt in her heart that in some way she was fated, that it was only a matter of time before the Fascisti would find her out and she would be taken away."[179] As Matthiessen later recalled, "Patsy was going nuts. She told me I had to stop doing this, because every time we left the apartment, people were after us."[180]

What if they lost another baby? The possibility weighed on him as he contemplated going deeper with the communists. But there was also the matter of his own ethical adjustment, which was pronounced enough that friends could tell that something was going on. "You've only recently learned to stand on your own feet and you're unsteady, uncertain, insecure, perhaps?" Humes wrote in a lacerating billet doux (as he called it). "You no longer feel the sharp difference between good and evil. If the truths were publicly available: you are I think a little more than unsettled over the recent discovery that you have a muddy and grey soul, like soggy ashes."[181]

Matthiessen had spent the better part of two years practicing "serial lying" for the CIA, largely on the assumption that there were good guys and bad guys, and that he was indisputably on the side of light. Yet deceiving friends had never felt particularly virtuous, was "nerve-wracking" and "disagreeable," "petty and pointless," and after his eye-opening interviews with X, he'd come to see the political situation on the ground as far more ambiguous. His bosses in the Right Bank apartment now struck him as no different than Senator McCarthy or any of the other Red-baiting reactionaries back home, "smug, sheltered people . . . who knew nothing of life, for all their cynicism."[182] And so Matthiessen refused, as he told it, their request that he burrow into the PCF:

> right there, on that very day, I quit my first job with the CIA, telling these men that I would not submit my pregnant wife to further distress . . . and also that, while I could be trusted to keep my mouth shut about the very little that I knew . . . they could no longer trust my politics because I had moved left. Of course they protested, made mild threatening noises about our govt contract, etc etc; but by and large, they accepted what I said in fairly good grace, having no choice: they knew I meant business, so they could not trust me anymore, not even if I changed my mind . . .[183]

This explanation is not entirely convincing; telling the CIA that you sympathize with communists in 1953, at the height of the Red Scare, seems like an invitation to your own investigation. But in other notes Matthiessen acknowledged that he might have been remembering what he *wanted* to say, rather than what he *did* say to his bosses that day: "I'd like to claim credit for making clear in ringing tones that I'd lost faith in my job and was quitting on moral principle, but alas, I can't really be certain of that fifty-four years later: Patsy's situation was essentially the reason given."[184]

Whatever was said, it is difficult to underestimate the significance of Matthiessen's decision to quit the CIA. As he approached his twenty-sixth birthday, he remained, as much to himself as to others, slippery and enigmatic as a person. But here was something he was absolutely *not*. By placing himself in opposition to the Agency and its ideological goals, he was, in addition to moving left, starting to stake out a personal philosophy based on the idea that an individual's own moral principle should be heeded above all else, regardless of the consequences. In his brazen choice, it is possible to see the faint silhouette of the man who would one day march in antiwar demonstrations; vocally condemn oil, gas, and mining interests with ties to the government; propagandize for Mexican American farmworkers on California picket lines; and petition a sitting U.S. president (in the West Wing, no less) for the pardon of an Anishinaabe-Dakota man convicted for murdering two FBI agents. The outspoken social and environmental activist, unafraid to take controversial positions and put his reputation on the line for what he believed in, could perhaps trace his development backward through time to this particular moment.

Matthiessen's resignation coincided with a larger culture shift at the CIA. Rumors that the OSO and OPC were going to merge had surfaced as early as 1950, with the appointment of Walter Bedell Smith, the decorated general and diplomat, as CIA director, but it was not until late 1952 that the process properly began. The librarians and cowboys were now being yoked together, intelligence collection wedded to covert action, which was a "momentous move," one agent recalled, that "may not have led straight to the Bay of Pigs, but it helped speed us on our way."[185] The coup d'état in Iran, orchestrated by the CIA, would happen just five months after Matthiessen quit, followed by another in Guatemala in 1954. On the ground in Paris, he'd sensed a sea change in the organization through his handler. The "cool laconic" OSS veteran he'd met at the Jeu de Paume, a man he liked and trusted, was suddenly and inexplicably replaced by a suit—"innocuous, pleasant, more polished, perhaps, but not, I sensed, a man to be counted on in a crisis."[186]

MATTHIESSEN BAILED FROM the CIA at almost exactly the moment the inaugural issue of *The Paris Review* appeared in America, its cover ablaze in red, with graceful drawings by Billy Pène du Bois: La Renommée, or Fame, atop the winged Pegasus as she sounds her trumpet (a silhouette of the statue by Antoine Coysevox); and an eagle clutching a pen in its talons while wearing a Phrygian cap, which was a symbol of *liberté* from the French Revolution. "The little magazines still come and go, and some of them don't go a moment too soon, but the past week brought a promising reminder of the old days when the Left Bank was headquarters for a whole department of world letters," the *New York Herald Tribune* noted in March.[187] After so much stumbling, the finished product managed to be both beautiful and assured: fiction by Antoine Blondin, Matthiessen, and Terry Southern; an interview with E. M. Forster; poetry by Donald Hall and Robert Bly; a commentary on death by Henry de Montherlant. But it was just a preview of the quality to come in future issues that would make it so famous. "At the moment the young editors are modest enough to realize that they have a bit further to go before they attain the standard of excellence they first envisioned," Styron acknowledged in *Harper's Bazaar*. "They have, however, made a notable beginning."[188]

That same month, Bernice Baumgarten sold Matthiessen's first novel to Harper & Brothers for an advance of $2,000.[189] John Appleton shared the news in a rapturous telegram, then followed up with a letter: "it's hard to put into words exactly how enthusiastic we feel about SIGNS OF WINTER without sounding almost giddy. . . . It's wonderful to know that your career between hard covers will get off to such a spectacular start."[190] Matthiessen waited for official confirmation from Baumgarten before he allowed himself to respond; when he did, his appreciative note to Appleton was bundled with another big announcement: "the happy tidings came right on the heels of one Lucas Matthiessen, who had to put up quite a diminutive struggle for top honors that week."[191]

Lucas "Luke" Conrad Matthiessen was born at the American Hospital on March 24, 1953, weighing a healthy seven pounds, one ounce. As Peter celebrated three promising debuts and one very welcome ending, Patsy exhaled with relief, sending letters to her friends back home in which she sounded "gayer and more typically PBS"—Patsy Brigham Southgate—than she had "in ages."[192]

7

People from Away

> When the snake is shedding, before it drops that extraordinary skin, it has a hell of a time getting it off in most cases. They struggle for a long, long time. That old skin! They don't eat, they're irritable. They're kind of hungry. Ill-tempered. They can't see. The scale over the eye, the eye-scale, also goes, and it's quite opaque. They can't see through it, so they're threatened by that. And those are the times you don't want to be near a poisonous snake, when they're shedding. . . . And that's the way I feel about this stage we go through. We have this bright, shiny, new person in there, but it can't get out yet, and we're stuck with our old habits and old disgusting ways.
>
> —PM, in conversation with Howard Norman (1990s)[1]

MATTHIESSEN "grew to hate" Paris, he recalled in an interview with the editor Nelson Aldrich Jr.[2] The reason was the rising tide of anti-Americanism, and the tipping point came one day when he was driving around the city in his Simca. A car in front of him braked without warning, causing him to slam into its rear. There was no question who was to blame—at least, from Matthiessen's perspective—but the other driver jumped out and, noticing Matthiessen's nationality, started to shout xenophobic slurs. This attracted a crowd, which then joined in with more pointed insults. Finding himself the focus of a mob, Matthiessen denounced the driver for making a scene, which had the unintended effect of turning the mob in his favor. "First they're shrieking *'Yankee, go home!'* and then they were shrieking abuse at this man." The sudden volte-face disturbed him. And that was what did it: not the loss of his CIA stipend, or the ceaseless demands of *The Paris Review*, but the barely suppressed rage of a people who were still processing war and the occupation. It was impossible to reconcile such confused currents of trauma with his youthful fantasy of the city as a refuge of frictionless liberty and the good life.

He drove home to Patsy and said, "I've had enough of this."

AT THE BEGINNING of May, Matthiessen flew to Rome in response to an indignant letter from Irwin Shaw: "What do you mean you're not coming to Bill's wedding? Don't you realize a man only gets married two or three times in his entire life?"[3]

Styron had first met the poet Rose Burgunder ("a most ravishing creature")[4] during a writing seminar at Johns Hopkins in 1951. While touring through Europe the following year, Rose had left an impulsive note in his mailbox at the American Academy in Rome. This initiated a dizzying romance—"[she] loves me as hotly as I love her," Styron had written to Matthiessen after just a few weeks—and they had been engaged by the middle of December. But Rose was from an old family in Baltimore, and her mother, Selma, was not convinced the match was acceptable. (How did a novelist make any *money*?) At Christmas, Bill and Rose had visited the Matthiessens in Paris, where they found an agitated letter waiting for them from William Styron Sr.: a "gumshoe," the letter announced, was questioning all the Styrons' neighbors in Newport News. Just what kind of trouble was Bill in, exactly? With dawning horror, Rose realized (this had happened before to the Burgunder children) that Selma had hired a private detective to dig up dirt on her daughter's fiancé. Rose said to Bill, "I can't let you marry into a family that does this." And Bill replied, "You're right."[5]

After Christmas, the couple had returned to Rome and ended things unhappily. Rose moved on to Florence, trying to cheer herself up with art, while Bill spiraled into depressed hypochondria: pains in his legs, which he self-diagnosed as evidence of blood clots. Then a mutual friend had reminded them both that *their* feelings should overrule family objections. This had been enough of a nudge to convince them to reinstate the engagement. Rose had returned to Rome in the middle of March, and Bill wrote home to his father requesting his late mother's engagement ring, along with some black-eyed peas for good luck at the wedding.[6]

Matthiessen arrived just in time for the ceremony on May 4, 1953. The Styrons were married "in truly gala style," in the Piazza del Campidoglio.[7] Afterward, the Shaws, who were staying in town so Irwin could work as a screenwriter on Mario Camerini's *Ulysses*, hosted a reception at their apartment, followed by dinner at a restaurant that served up mountains of fettuccine and chicken alla diavola.

Luke was too young to travel yet, so Patsy excused herself from the wedding. But mother and baby, accompanying Peter, would go on the Styrons' honeymoon, because it doubled as a final European sojourn for the Matthiessens. In late June, they arrived with their luggage in Ravello, on the

Amalfi Coast, which Bill had warned was enough to "make the blood run out of your ears, as they say in Virginia, it's so beautiful."[8] Perched on hills and cliffs more than a thousand feet above the Tyrrhenian Sea, the villas, churches, and lemon groves looked out over emerald water "all awash in a sort of gold dust light." Though Ravello was already a resort town, it had yet to be completely overrun by tourists; the Styrons had managed to rent two floors of the huge, partially modernized twelfth-century Palazzo Confalone for just $100 a month. They'd also driven in "a new English Austin heavily carapaced with birdshit," as Bill put it in a letter, which allowed them to cruise along the coast and descend to a beach whenever they felt the urge for sunbathing.[9]

The Matthiessens stayed for several weeks in Ravello, eating, swimming, and playing tennis with the newlyweds. Coming off three months of voluntary abstinence, Peter fell hard for the local rosé, and he (as "Pete-man") and Bill (now and forevermore "Porter," for reasons lost to time) sparred over drunken games of chess. As Matthiessen later recalled the rules: "no more than three pieces could be maneuvered simultaneously," and "a player upsetting or vomiting upon the board more than once during the course of any one game was penalized one rook and two *coups de rouge*."[10]

At some point during the visit, conversation between the men drifted inevitably to work. Back in Paris, Matthiessen had been hugely impressed when he got around to reading *Lie Down in Darkness*. And he'd been flattered when Styron asked him to comment on the draft of a new novella called "Like Prisoners, Waking." ("I thought it was very fine but suggested the plainer and less literary title 'The Long March.'")[11] In Ravello, Styron now agreed to return the favor, cementing a tradition of "supportive but blunt criticism" that would become a valued part of the writing process for both men.[12] Matthiessen handed over some pages. Styron, having no idea that he'd just been given the fragments of a bogus novel created for an aborted CIA operation, read them, liked them, and encouraged Pete-man to finish the book. "Pleasantly surprised," Matthiessen decided to do just that; over the next year, because of Styron's vote of confidence, he would flesh out the fake story into a very real and deeply personal manuscript titled "The Partisans."[13]

In the final version of the novel, which would drop the definite article to be called just *Partisans*, Edwin Baring "Barney" Sand, the idealistic American journalist, sets out to interview the Marxist revolutionary Jacobi by submitting himself to a surreal tour of Paris. In a bid to find himself—"he had counted on Jacobi to clarify the disordered pattern of his concepts"[14]— Barney agrees to lose himself in a labyrinth first. His guide in the underworld is Marat (named after Jacques-Louis David's *The Death of Marat*), a Party zealot who attempts to indoctrinate Barney by dragging him through scenes of the oppressed proletariat: an abattoir, slums, a pauper's cemetery, and hotels for prostitutes. As days and weeks begin to lose distinction, Barney stumbles after Marat "from one stark revelation to another, unshaven, dirty, scarcely thinking, peering into the mirrors of public toilets for some sign of his past existence, past scale of values."[15] By the time he finally reaches Jacobi, who has been imprisoned by the PCF after being purged from its upper ranks, Barney is ensnared in a trap, with the communists convinced he's an American spy.

What makes *Partisans* worth considering at the moment Matthiessen was about to leave Europe behind is how the novel makes meaning from his years of experiences there. "[You are] speaking primarily to yourself," an editor would tell him, astutely, after reading the draft.[16] Matthiessen's 1948 road trip to Czechoslovakia, for instance, becomes a scarring first exposure for Barney to communism in action. A pot-infused party—one that sounds suspiciously like the soirées attended by the *Paris Review* crowd—is a vision of manic desperation: "They don't know what they are doing in their life, these people; they are afraid and lost," a character tells Barney. "They think they are really living, only they are really dying."[17] Even something as small and insignificant as the Rodin statue in the foyer at 1, rue Gît-le-Coeur, where Matthiessen had stayed when he first arrived in the city, reappears as a symbol of how the "true beauty" of Paris is hidden away from the world.[18]

At the center of the novel are two competing paternal figures: Consul Sand, Barney's actual father, who is an American capitalist committed to following government protocol; and the charismatic guerrilla Jacobi, a passionate communist who holds Consul Sand in contempt. According to Matthiessen's notes, Jacobi was modeled on Monsieur X, the Party member who, as Matthiessen told it, triggered his self-interrogation in the Paris cafés. Consul Sand, by contrast, espouses the same beliefs as his former CIA bosses, and notably resembles Matty Matthiessen. Like Peter, Barney finds himself tugged between two dogmatic positions—until he decides the men are not so different after all. "Their causes," Barney concludes, "seemed remote and unimportant, like accounts of distant happenings in small, cold print."[19] What *is* important is an individual's ethics, the decisions a man makes for himself about what constitutes righteous action.

Partisans dramatizes the choice Matthiessen made in Paris to reject ideology in favor of his own moral principles. Barney returns to America determined to live a meaningful life, to keep trying—"And perhaps that trying would come to something in the end, though he might never see the sense in it."²⁰*

THE MATTHIESSENS DEPARTED NAPLES on the SS *Andrea Doria* and arrived in New York at the end of July. Patsy continued on to Massachusetts to introduce her son to his grandmother Lila, while Peter remained in New York to consult with Harper & Brothers about "Signs of Winter," and to figure out the next move for his family.

Though he was "more or less glad"²¹ to be back, he had no desire to assume a place in what the economist John Kenneth Galbraith would soon label the "affluent society." America was not as grim as Matthiessen had expected to find it after living in France, but Eisenhower was now president, and his election still represented the ascendancy of small-town thinking and sexual repression, not to mention a galloping consumerism that manifested, in 1953, as more than nineteen million television sets.²² (According to David Halberstam, "Studies showed that when a popular program was on, toilets flushed all over certain cities, as if on cue, during commercials or the moment the program was over.")²³ Matthiessen could have bought a house in the new suburbia, sent his wife to shop at one of the gleaming new supermarkets. He could have taken a white-collar job and spent his paychecks on the many luxurious appliances just coming into vogue. He could have *settled*, which was the hope of his parents, who now presented him with the homecoming gift of a green Chevrolet station wagon. Instead, he had something else in mind, so unconventional that even a few of his friends would find it hard to understand.

At the start of September, Peter drove Patsy and Luke a hundred miles east, almost to the end of Long Island. "I don't feel too easy at home and am happier away, which is why I've formed an almost unnatural attachment [to] E. H., in place of home. For there I can start from scratch and be natural, for no one can interpret my words or actions according to the past."²⁴ He had written these lines about East Hampton in 1946, but they remained true seven years later. If "home"—meaning New York City as much as Stamford, Connecticut—was contaminated by a long history of familial drama and suffocating social constraints, then the East End of Long Island felt like neutral

---

* Despite the obvious existentialism in Matthiessen's early novels, he denied any direct influence by Jean-Paul Sartre, whom he used to see in Paris drinking on the rue du Bac: "If I absorbed his influence, it was by osmosis—certainly nothing conscious, far less thought through." Matthiessen read Albert Camus much more closely, and admired his work, "but I couldn't pinpoint any direct influence from Camus either."

ground. Here was a tranquil territory that he would one day rhapsodize in a book called *Men's Lives:*

> I loved the quiet of the summer bay, the blue water and the hot sand shores with their acrid horsefoot smell and windrows of stout quarterdecks* and light gold jingle shell that in other days was gathered up for oyster cultch; the gulls plucking scallops from the shallows, swooping upward, and dropping them on the old erratic boulders carried down out of the north by the great glaciers that formed the high moraines of "fish-shaped Pommanocc"; the ospreys lugging glinting fish across the sky, the bright lobster buoys and white sails, the yelp and crying of the nesting gulls, the screech of terns . . .[25]

Matthiessen did not stop in the village of East Hampton, with its clipped privet hedges and residences which, in Patsy's words, "would have tempted Gatsby."[26] He pushed a few miles further northeast into the hamlet of Springs, located in a tangle of scrub oaks and pitch pines near the tidal marsh of Accabonac Harbor.† Once the domain of a tribe known as the Accabonacs, by 1953 Springs was home to fewer than seven hundred people, many of whom could trace their ancestry back to the fisherman-farmers who'd built their houses there in the seventeenth and eighteenth centuries—and who, for their proud self-sufficiency and peculiar dialect ("Yes yes, bub," a remnant of their Kentish and Dorset forebears) had earned the tag "Bonacs": i.e., Bonackers. Unlike East Hampton, Springs was not a prosperous place. Many of the residents were dirt poor, although they rarely thought of themselves that way because they could gather almost everything they needed from the land. "The poorest person, in my opinion, is the one who in an emergency or everyday life can actually do nothing," declared Ferris Talmage, a Bonacker, summing up the ethos of his people.[27] Some of their houses had been built with mortar made from ground-up shells, sand, and handfuls of cow hair. In the old days, they'd dragged ice from the ponds using long-toothed saws and horses, and sometimes paid the doctor in vegetables or milk.

Yet to many members of the summer crowd who frequented East Hampton, the Bonackers were rednecks, all cousins of cousins and all named Talmage, Bennett, King, Parsons, Miller, or Lester. Springs was spoken of as

---

* A quarterdeck is the shell of a sea snail, *Crepidula fornicata,* sometimes called the Atlantic slipper shell.
† The town of East Hampton, founded in 1648, includes the main village plus several adjoining hamlets: Amagansett, Montauk, Napeague, Springs, and Wainscott. East Hampton shares jurisdiction of Sag Harbor with the town of Southampton.

"below the bridge," and "on the wrong side of the tracks" (literally: the Long Island Rail Road bisected the community). To the Bonackers, the village of East Hampton was "up-street," and the colony consisted of "people from away." The artists who had started to move into Springs were also "people from away." It took many years not to be "from away."[28]

Matthiessen rented a rustic cottage on Springs Fireplace Road, just west of a horse and cattle farm owned by George Sid Miller. Years later, he would recall the setting as "a peaceful and very pretty place of meadowlands and cedar fields and a quiet lead of water, widening out eastward past Tick Island to the sand spit at Louse Point and Gardiners Bay."[29] In her recollections, Patsy would focus on the derelict house across the road: "It was like a welfare house. . . . The place was all full of old shoes and overcoats."[30]

Matthiessen had chosen Springs because the rents were low. Not only that, but it was also the adopted home of John Cole, his roommate from Yale, and John's wife, Cynthia Waterbury, who had studied at both Chatham Hall and Smith College alongside Patsy, her good friend. The Coles had a newborn son, Marshall, who was almost exactly the same age as Luke; the couples were at similar points in their lives and marriages. After Yale, John had worked as a captain for the Fishers Island Country Club, at the invitation of Matty Matthiessen. He'd then done time as a stock boy at a St. Louis department store, Scruggs, Vandervoort and Barney, followed by a stint as a "writer-public relations man" for News Contacts, Inc., a small outfit in New York financed by Jock Whitney, which introduced him to a legion of glamorous young women. This had prompted his father to remark, "John, the only two things you care about are fishing and fucking."[31]

As if to prove his father right, John had quit News Contacts the following year and moved out to the East End with a vow to make an honest living from the sea. With a like-minded friend, Jim Reutershan (also from "up-street"), he'd acquired a dory named the *Blue Peril,* done some hasty repairs, and filled her with gill nets. After a season of hard labor, this had proved so fruitless that Cynthia, who married him in 1951, suggested he try something else to conjure up an income. John flatly refused: "I would not surrender my life with the water; I would never deny my mistress."[32] Instead, he adjusted his methodology, took up scalloping, which *was* profitable, and joined a crew of Bonacker fishermen, or baymen, to go haul-seining off the beaches for striped bass, which the baymen sold commercially. "I never thought about much of anything because I was living a dream," he later reflected, "my dream of ecstasy on earth."[33]

Matthiessen found the dream so enchanting that he decided to adopt it for himself. To make ends meet, he would follow Cole's example in the spring, summer, and fall months, with a series of seasonal jobs, and then write on bad weather days and during the slower season of winter.

One of the first things Matthiessen did after arriving in Springs was to fetch the *Maudite* from her berth on Fishers Island—the codfish boat he'd bought and promptly crashed in Quebec. He rechristened her the *Vop-Vop*, in honor of the *pop* made by her one-cylinder engine, and because *Maudite* ("Cursed") was a poor name for a fishing vessel. Soon he and Cole could be spotted pop-popping together around the Three Mile and Northwest Harbors. "I remember the two of them . . . in the basin at Promised Land," Everett Rattray, editor of *The East Hampton Star*, wrote in 1978. "Young summer colony types, we thought, fooling around with fishing aboard a little double-ender from Nova Scotia powered by a lawnmower engine."[34]

Cole and Matthiessen spent the fall searching the eelgrass for scallops, which they sold by the bushel; as the season progressed, they prospected farther and farther afield. This was a satisfying way to pass the days, almost a spiritual experience for both men. On boats, as Matthiessen once said, "you have to pare everything down to the bare necessities, and there you are . . . without a shelter, without a past, without future hopes."[35]

And yet, it is possible to pare things down beyond the bare necessities. By mid-October, when the engine suddenly died, they were floating off the western shore of Gardiners Island. To reach safety, they unfurled the canvas sail and aimed for land, but a hard gale pushed them into rough chop. The mast broke, just as it had in Canada, and they were immobilized with no radio communication. To stop the boat from drifting any further into the ocean, they dropped anchor. Night set in, and they swallowed raw scallops in the autumn chill. The next morning, a Coast Guard plane appeared overhead and dropped a message on a fluorescent ribbon. Were they in trouble? If so, stand up and wave. Their wives had raised the alarm on their behalf—an inauspicious start to Matthiessen's career as a bayman.[36]

IN NOVEMBER, Matthiessen helped out on a small haul-seine rig owned by Cole's friend, Jim Reutershan: "we were beginners, and we made one dry haul after another, standing around the limp and forlorn bag as if puzzling out an oracle."[37] However, he soon put a pause on the lean outdoor life and sat down at his desk to catch up on writing. *Partisans* still needed work, and there were final details to address in "Signs of Winter," which was now being published under the title *Race Rock*. He also continued to tinker with a few short stories, having managed to place more in journals like *Botteghe Oscure* ("Martin's Beach"), *Cornhill Magazine* ("Tower of the Four Winds," about travels in Spain), and *New World Writing* ("Late in the Season," in which a loveless couple encounters a snapping turtle and the husband shoots at it with a gun, turning the animal into a repository for all the frustration and discontent he cannot express to his wife).

The return to this more familiar rhythm could not have come soon enough for George Plimpton, who derided Matthiessen's new "valueless occupation" in a letter to Irwin Shaw.[38] When Matthiessen failed to do a planned phone interview for *The Paris Review* with the Anglo-Irish writer Joyce Cary, Plimpton suspected either "shere [sic] laziness or perhaps a bumper day of mussel fishing."[39] He complained to Matthiessen directly from Paris:

> I have a feeling that the joy of stalking the Hudsonian Curlew through the rushes of the Easthampton [sic] dunes is a compelling one, and that the LIRR carries one P. Matthiessen to New York 'bout once a blue moon, [when] the recluse looks at the city lights with startled eyes. Judging from the lonely ring of the title RACE ROCK I suspect that future titles will be along equivalent lines, born of lonely years on the seashore, the kelp of the Sargossa [sic] Sea, with the companionship of Scoter* and maybe an occasional tamed shore-bird, not a pretty picture for the literary editor of this cosmopolitan smash—The Paris Review.[40]

The successful launch of the magazine, by now in its third issue, had not quelled the chaos that characterized its founding. If anything, Matthiessen's decision to move to Long Island, and Tom Guinzburg's simultaneous return to New York, where he'd opened a *Review* office at 2 Columbus Circle ("used mostly for storage, mail, and so forth"),[41] had only made the turbulence worse. Subscribers were not receiving their copies. Fiction manuscripts were being lost in the mail, which threatened to ruin relationships with literary agents. Communication between editors—a problem even when they were living in the same city—struggled to surmount the challenge posed by the Atlantic Ocean. "PLEASE ANSWER MY QUESTIONS, GEORGE," Matthiessen pleaded to Paris.[42] "Such a lackadaisical attitude seems to shroud the N.Y. office that it's all we can do to get questions answered at all," Plimpton wrote in an angry note on a "wretched rain-soaked day."[43] Cash flow, too, continued to cause confused recriminations. The New York office was spending far too much money; or else the New York office was not spending "one red

---

* Matthiessen adopted a black Labrador and named it "Scoter" after the species of sea duck. When Scoter developed a penchant for stalking chickens and infuriating the neighbors, Matthiessen wrote to Plimpton: "He has so much buckshot in him that his ass is dragging, but on he goes, with the heart of a lion, and I may make a present of him to his two-legged prototype, Senator McCarthy."

cent": Matthiessen and Guinzburg claimed they were shouldering the "considerable" burden of long-distance phone calls, postage, and transportation costs.[44] It was Plimpton who was being profligate—or perhaps Plimpton was being miserly, out to (as Plimpton put it himself, sarcastically) "bugger the entire clan of writers right up to the hilt."[45]

At one point Matthiessen seemed on the verge of securing a $20,000 infusion of capital—"if the magazine is well enough set up."[46] The editors braced themselves for some much needed good news. But then the prospective benefactor, Matty Matthiessen ("for it is no less a person than he"), balked after realizing *The Paris Review* would probably never pay a healthy dividend.[47] So here was yet another thing to sour Peter's relationship with his father. "Of course I had assumed all along that the sum was to be a combination pat-on-the-head and tax dodge, pretty much as a present," he wrote to Paris by way of apology. Plimpton replied: "I can't say that a more depressing document has ever been received by this office. . . . I'm just as happy as a spring cricket over the state of our affairs."[48]

Still, underlying all the petty squabbles—over cover design; over issue contents; over whether Saul Bellow, fresh off *The Adventures of Augie March*, would attract them more attention than "that soggy little midinette Capote"[49]—was a more fundamental conflict. Now the magazine was out in the world, with contributors and subscribers expecting four fresh issues a year, what were the long-term plans? Plimpton made it clear that he wanted *The Paris Review* to steadily increase its scope and ambition. He wanted, for instance, to dedicate an entire issue to Ernest Hemingway, "an outrageous old man" whom he would soon follow to Pamplona, trying to score an interview.[50] He wanted *Life* to reprint a *Review* feature on the *livres d'Or* of Paris, restaurant guest books with original doodles by the likes of Picasso, Matisse, Jean Cocteau, and Toulouse-Lautrec. He wanted the publicity this would inevitably bring because he'd already made an emotional investment; for George Plimpton, *The Paris Review* was a crutch that would leave him unsteady should it suddenly drop away. For Matthiessen, however, the magazine was never more than a diversion: "a bloody labor of love," he called it, with a strictly limited engagement. "When he came back and went into the shrimp boat business, he pretty much left the *Review* to George," Tom Guinzburg once told the filmmaker Jeff Sewald—an exaggeration, though not by much.[51]

IN ONE OF HIS typed letters to Plimpton, Matthiessen included a brief sketch of his domestic situation in Springs. "Lucas now will laugh at even the poorest joke and as a result is being put up for the Knickerbocker Club. . . . Patsy and I are bucolic and well, she spends her days hunched over a game called LABYRINTSPEL, in which a small ball is maneuvered past a series of likely-looking holes."[52] This joke suggests how Peter saw—or failed to see—the labor of a mother caring for a nine-month-old baby.

Springs could be a forbidding place in the winter. Salt ice rimed the shore of Accabonac Harbor. Frigid winds swept down through gray skeletal trees into houses which, in many cases, had no heating except for a Franklin stove and cannel coal. The twisting country roads, barely illuminated at night, became perilous gauntlets after heavy snowfall. It was enough to grate on anyone's nerves, and to a young woman accustomed to the stimulations of Paris, it must have seemed almost purgatorial.

Patsy "hunched over" the Labyrintspel because she was lonely in her new isolation; lonely and bored. Certainly she was not the only wife in Springs to feel that way. Cynthia Cole, with her ravenous curiosity and desire for international travel, had wanted to be a foreign correspondent; she'd talked with John about living in Sausalito, near San Francisco, or maybe as far away as New Zealand. Instead, she found herself married to a man who drank too much and who could barely hold a conversation over the meals she prepared. "John's whole vocabulary at the time consisted of ten words, all of which had to do with fishing," Cynthia later said.[53] Cile Downs, an artist who moved to Springs with Matthiessen's school friend, the painter Sherry Lord, in 1954, would feel similarly diminished by her husband and his friends: "If you told them anything about your life, they would go on to the next subject immediately. It was like, 'Oh shoot, *your* life!'"[54] The East End may have represented freedom to men who sought unorthodox living arrangements, but their views on a woman's role remained largely in sync with the society they'd tried to leave behind. "Wives got shoved aside," said Downs, "because the men wanted to be important."

On the days when Patsy became particularly restless, she put Luke in a stroller and pushed him half a mile down Springs Fireplace Road, to an old Victorian farmhouse with a large, light-filled barn overlooking the harbor. Lee Krasner and Jackson Pollock had bought the house eight years earlier, for $5,000, and it had proven so cold the first winter that they'd needed to thaw the toilet water using a blowtorch. Now it was insulated and shingled, its rooms cluttered with books, shells, jars of pigment, and revolutionary works of art. For Patsy, introduced to the abstract expressionists by Cynthia Cole, it offered a refuge of color in the middle of so much white silence. "I was so interested in role models," she later recalled. "I would check on how Lee did her cooking and her gardening, painting, her general life—this type of thing. She and Jackson just loved Luke."[55]

Jackson Pollock—who the art critic Clement Greenberg had not long before compared to Mondrian and Picasso, predicting he would "compete for recognition as the greatest American painter of the twentieth century"[56]—was now in the vise grip of alcoholism, dealing with a string of failed shows and feeling, as he told a friend, like "a clam without a shell."[57] His reputation for genius had become rivaled by a reputation for self-destructive capriciousness: he acted, Matthiessen once said, like a man who had "a hand grenade in his pocket"[58] that threatened to detonate at any moment.* But Patsy was drawn to his status as an enfant terrible, and they engaged, on her visits with Luke, in what she would later describe as a "Socratic dialogue" about art.[59] Eventually Patsy came to understand Pollock by way of Baudelaire and Rimbaud: "Romantics used their lives as kind of horror stories to plumb their emotions, in particular Baudelaire, who used the expression, 'Plunge to the bottom of the abyss,' or 'the bottom of the pit'—'*Plonger au fond du gouffre.*'... Jackson, in a way, was the first real live person like that, that I'd met.... Jackson gave us his guts. He also gave up his guts, gave up that security of life. That was his impact on art, I think."[60]

If Pollock transformed Patsy's understanding of aesthetics that winter, Lee Krasner made no less of an impression. Like her husband, she was in a state of personal collapse, gaunt from colitis, unsure of her place in the New York art scene, and burnt out after years of trying to mollify Pollock. She had traded away her own ambitions so *he* could create, which was a sacrifice Patsy understood all too well, as she told two of Pollock's biographers: "That was what we thought we had to do in those days—be nurturing.... It was masochism, all right, but for turning out a Hemingway or a Pollock, it was well worth the candle."[61] Or was it? Lee had obviously exceeded her limit, and Patsy was disturbed by the toll it had taken on her new friend. As she would explain to yet another Pollock biographer: "I took Lee's side strongly from the point of view of This Woman Is Not Being Treated Fairly. I mean literally, Lee had two pairs of britches to her name, was trapped in the house, and didn't know how to drive. Jackson didn't want her to, but he had mobility. He would go off, had this large studio, this person making delicious food,

---

* One night it *did* detonate, as Matthiessen recalled in an unpublished fragment in his archive. Having become blind drunk at a party given by the *New Yorker* writer Berton Roueché, who also lived in the area, Pollock yanked his knees up to his chest and kicked the windshield out of Matthiessen's car as they sped down the road between Amagansett and Springs. Matthiessen regained control of the vehicle, then berated Pollock for his "childishness." But this only made matters worse. Back at Pollock's house, Matthiessen and Roueché watched in horror as "Jackson all but destroyed his valuable record collection by shying his records out the window, through the window, into the stove, and increasingly, in the direction of his friends; he then picked up a carving knife and began stabbing it into the kitchen table as close as possible to our hands. When Berton jumped up, Jackson, who was much bigger, began to shove him around, and at this point, fed up, I stood up and socked him on the point of the jaw. He went down hard against the wall, where he lay dazed, staring at me. 'Nobody ever stopped me before,' he said finally. Drunk as he was, he was now quiet and calm, and told us we could go home, he would be fine."

and pretty much do whatever he wanted. And so before I knew what was happening, I undertook to teach her how to drive and in return she was to teach me how to paint."[62]

Patsy ushered Lee into the Chevy sedan and gave instructions from the passenger seat. When that didn't work—Lee had no confidence as a driver—she employed a more experimental approach. Patsy drove them a mile from her house, climbed out of the car, and walked off alone, abandoning Lee with the baby in a bassinet. "She realized that if I was willing to leave Luke in the car with her, then I must know that she was a good driver."[63] Lee inched the car homeward. She then went on to earn her license, and thus her liberation, much to Jackson's chagrin.

Patsy's art lessons did not go so well, however. "I took [my canvas] over to Lee and said, 'I think we both had to admit that I have no talent at all.'"[64] But that happened, according to Cynthia Cole, only *after* it had already caused tension in the Matthiessen household. When Patsy picked up a brush with Lee's encouragement, "the following day Peter was painting something. . . . There was a history of this kind of competition and her giving into it."[65] While Patsy had helped Lee claw back her independence, she had yet to find a good way to reassert her own.

"PETER MATTHIESSEN IS an author who owes nothing to literary cults or fashions," declared the book jacket for *Race Rock*, which was published by Harper & Brothers in March 1954. Yet this novel of "confused young people emerging from a confused adolescence into a confused world," as Matthiessen's editor, Elizabeth Lawrence, elegantly summarized it, was very much a product of its moment.[66] Alienation and anomie, neurosis and disillusionment, questions of identity, legitimacy, and innocence—many flavors of *Race Rock* were already familiar to readers who'd tasted *Lie Down in Darkness* or *The Catcher in the Rye*, or perhaps even *Augie March*. Matthiessen's novel also included commentary on the same kind of WASP preoccupations satirized by John P. Marquand in *The Late George Apley*. But while Marquand had been gentle with his jabs at blue bloods, Matthiessen was making an aggressive frontal assault. "I am assured that the Prescotts, Gannetts, Gissens, and Wests of the world, if they should deign to look at it, cannot help but hate it," he wrote to Plimpton, with obvious relish, in the week before *Race Rock*'s release.[67] Matthiessen knew his book was likely to be interpreted as an attack by a group that prized discretion above all else, and he soon received telephone calls "from nervous family members fearing social ostracization."[68]

Like Barney Sand in *Partisans*, George McConville is conflicted about his background, the pointlessness of expensive schools and pompous Christmas dances. Because of his pampered childhood and his father's overbearing influence, George feels poorly equipped to tackle the challenges of life: "It's just hard to know *what* to do in these mixed-up times."[69] After his girlfriend Eve shares the shocking news of her pregnancy, he is forced out of his complacent wallowing, however, and arranges to go duck shooting with an old friend at his family's New England summer house. "We'll go down to Shipman's Crossing and see things in the light of the past," he announces to Sam Rubicam, a painter who has recently returned from Paris.[70] The house is a sanctuary, "home in all the childhood connotations of the word," as much a dreamscape as a physical place on a headland overlooking the Atlantic.[71] But the men are unexpectedly joined there by Cady Shipman, a brooding sadist (and another version of Dewey Floyd from "Sadie"). If painter Sam is "the culmination of civilized man," Cady is the untamed opposite. And George is caught somewhere in between, allied with Sam but attracted to Cady's unusual "force," or charisma: "He doesn't compromise every two seconds like the rest of us, he does what he pleases."[72]

When the novel is not lurching into flashbacks about stuffy Sunday lunches, much of the narrative is a slow climb toward an inevitable confrontation. An ominous storm gathers over Shipman's Crossing. George, Sam, and Cady play Russian roulette with a pistol. The Pequot caretaker, Daniel Barleyfield, drowns in a freak accident off the beach. There is violence and a great deal of shouting. George emerges from the weekend, as if from a great ordeal, having found a balance between Sam and Cady, between the two competing parts of himself. Swearing never to return to the house, which now reminds him of "a lie . . . that childhood would go on forever," he prepares to confront responsibility.[73] "[T]his was the end of youth," he says to Eve in a dream.[74]

Matthiessen made it clear, during the editing process for *Race Rock*, that he wasn't particularly interested in realism.* "I would like to get away with as much coincidence and symbolism as I can without making the story silly," he told the team at Harper & Brothers.[75] This symbolism ranged from the obvious (the storm), to the elasticity of time in the novel; George's transformation occurs over the unlikely span of just three days. "That is because I do not believe in 'logical' or 'normal' arrival at maturity," Matthiessen explained, "so much as in maturity arrived at by a strength of character more

---

* "[M]y fiction," he once noted, "is realistic only in the most superficial sense; someone has called it *surreal*, in the sense of intensely or *wildly* real, and I think this is correct. At least, the idea attracts me, because in the intensity of true reality—as opposed to 'realism'—lie the greatest mysteries of all."

or less responsive to the test of events." He felt, from personal experience, that character is forged through the exposure to tests, and that maturity is something a person earns.

Matthiessen's ambition for the symbolism in *Race Rock* can be glimpsed in the title. After discarding "Signs of Winter," from Rilke, he considered calling the novel "A Man Among Others," "Pride's Crossing," or "Prevailing Wind," the latter rejected because "it sounds like a book about families carrying on their salty traditions in Old Nantucket."[76] "Race Rock" was borrowed from the dangerous reef surrounded by rip tides off the western end of Fishers Island. Matthiessen told Plimpton that it was "too complicated"[77] to explain his reasoning for the choice, though he wrote Elizabeth Lawrence that, "[i]n some obscure way which I don't quite understand myself, it seems to suit the mood of the book."[78] Just before publication, he inserted a new passage into the opening pages to justify the choice:

> Once he himself had clutched at a green glass ball only to see this unsinkable thing drift down from the light into the shadows of water rushing hard upon Race Rock, and had wondered if the glass would shatter on the Rock or lie in a crevice until the current swept it up again. More particularly, and refusing beforehand to recognize such a possibility, he asked himself if he, who had seen it sink, would be there when it reappeared. George could not account for this idea nor for the uneasiness it gave him, any more than he could account for his conviction that the glass float would remain forever in the Race.[79]

The green glass ball—a stray fishing float—gestures at a more metaphysical concern permeating *Race Rock*; it shows Matthiessen attempting to articulate his still nascent thoughts about the sublime, mortality, and transcendence.* In an early draft of *The Snow Leopard*, he would cite this passage when discussing the "strange pangs of loss" he'd experienced during the Pacific storm on the *Joseph T. Dickman* in 1945. But it is just one of several places in *Race Rock* where George turns from grounded concerns to contemplate the larger universe and his own place in it. Standing before the ocean, his feet submerged in waves (as Matthiessen's were on the *Dickman*), the young man is transfixed by "nothingness," and loses himself as he might

---

* Decades later, during a public lecture, he would explain that the green float was based on a memory of fishing near the Race Rock lighthouse: "It suddenly appeared. It came up seemingly from below. It came up and broke the surface. Very rough water. And then it rolled under again. And then it appeared again. I don't know why. I kept saying, 'What is this thing telling me?' I shouldn't have been subjective about it. It's just an old netball, green glass and rope. And yet, being there and the strangeness of it—it didn't belong on that coast, and how did it get there? There were so many mysteries for me tied up in that ball."

before flames, or a wind-blown forest, or "anything moving in a rhythm deeper than his own."[80] George yearns to "feel at peace, at one with simple existence," because "[t]o be a part of things was not to be lonely"—and he gets his wish for a moment toward the end of the novel, when he strips naked in a skiff and senses "the strokes of the oars building a harmony with the ocean rhythm, the vast invisible world."[81]

The numinous imagery in *Race Rock*, which would reappear, greatly elaborated, in Matthiessen's later work as he became more explicitly interested in "simple existence" and "the vast invisible world," is the novel's most notable achievement. But *Race Rock*, on the whole, is overstuffed and overwritten, cluttered with purple metaphors and awkward jump cuts into the past that arrive in the middle of a sentence to simulate the fractured quality of memory. Self-absorbed characters do not speak so much as emote ("At least I *feel*"), which only adds to an atmosphere of sweltering melodrama. John K. Hutchens, writing about the book in the *New York Herald Tribune*, observed that Matthiessen "will not have read many reviews of his first novel before he is good and tired of the word 'sensitive.'"[82] Joe Fox was less diplomatic. As a reader at Knopf, he'd inspected the manuscript before it was even bought by Harper and declared it "stank on ice": "We had great hopes for this guy on the basis of a few short stories but Matthiessen is still a painfully immature writer who needs to write a great deal more."[83] (Matthiessen got hold of this scathing report and held it against the editor for more than a decade.)

Between March and April, the reviews that appeared in newspapers and magazines were largely positive, if qualified. "He has a way of creating suspense, of telling a story that keeps the reader on edge—suspense, but not pleasurable suspense,"[84] said a critic in *The Boston Globe*. The critic for *Harper's Magazine* seemed to concur: "The story is written with such power that one reads even when repelled by the violence."[85] Orville Prescott, writing for *The New York Times*, praised the novel of "Northern decadence"—"It is time the South enjoyed a breathing spell"—but noted that, while its emotional impact was considerable, the craftsmanship behind it all was "uncomfortably cold-blooded."[86]

Race Rock sold poorly, and editors at Harper soon wrote it off as a disappointment. After a brief spell of euphoria for having finally ascended to the rank of published novelist, Matthiessen turned critical toward his own work. "I was never satisfied with it as an entity," he told Norman Holmes Pearson just a few months after publication—"at the very least, I failed to accomplish what I had in mind."[87] This belief would only harden over time, until he came to feel embarrassed by any discussion of his first two novels, *Race Rock* and *Partisans*, companion bildungsromans that "mercifully," as he told a friend in 1980, "no-one has ever read."[88]

ONE OF THE MORE noteworthy aspects of *Race Rock* is its idealization of the working class. George, with his hands "soft as dough,"[89] sees himself as the offspring of weakness and dissipation, heir to an estate that should rightfully belong to more deserving owners. When it comes to the hunters, carpenters, and fishermen who live in the village near Shipman's Crossing, he is "a canary among crows in his flannels and Paisley tie," lacking confidence and jealous of their easy belonging.[90] Characters like Cady Shipman (working-class), or Daniel Barleyfield (working-class and Native), are "on closer terms with life than he had ever been."[91] This idea in particular, that privation and hard physical work, oriented toward nature, is a more authentic existence than the privileged one he's been conditioned to lead, haunts George so persistently that even his girlfriend can sense it. "Isn't he the other person you wish you were," Eve says to him of Cady: "the craggy outdoor type, the breath of the woods, the hard-bitten, laconic sage of the swampland[?]"[92] For George McConville, whether he wants to acknowledge it or not ("I've never seen you so bitchy," he snaps back at Eve), these working-class "types" represent an enviable way of being.

Much the same could have been said for the novel's author. Two months after *Race Rock* was published, in early May, Matthiessen joined John Cole for a rainy predawn visit to Amagansett, where a cluster of modest houses with yards full of fishing paraphernalia had earned the nickname Fish Gut Alley, or Poseyville, after its inhabitants, the Posey Lesters. Matthiessen and Cole pulled into the driveway of Theodore Roosevelt Lester—Ted Lester, a forty-six-year-old Bonacker who introduced himself by pouring gasoline onto the sodden engine of a silver truck and setting it on fire. As Matthiessen recalled, Lester then said, after dousing the flames and starting the ignition with a wink, "There's a lot of shit built into them things, bub, and the more you kick out of 'em, the less is left in there to kick you back."[93]

A quick-tempered, disheveled man who haul-seined off the beaches of East Hampton and then sold what he caught to the Fulton Fish Market in New York, Ted Lester was something of an oddity among the local fishermen. While most Bonacker captains were hesitant to work with "people from away," Lester had no such reservation, supposedly—according to his detractors—because outsiders rarely questioned the ragged equipment he stubbornly refused to replace.[94] (Nor did they question his method of stuffing herring into the mouths of bass to increase the sale weight.) Provided Matthiessen and Cole were willing to pull when he yelled the order, they were welcome to join his five-man crew in exchange for a share of the earnings.

That spring, for six weeks, Matthiessen was assigned to the lowliest position in Lester's dory, on the middle oar. His first haul—two truckloads of striped bass—translated into something close to $200: "a very good week's pay," although subsequent hauls "scarcely made enough to pay for gas."[95] An elaborate ritual requiring strength, daring, and good fortune, ocean haul-seining was exhausting work, with a single attempt taking as much as two hours from start to finish.[96] It involved launching a dory from a truck down through the surf; feeding out a net (seine) with coils of lead line as the dory turned and traveled parallel with the beach, either east or west depending on the migratory season; and then heaving the dory back through the breakers. Finally, the two ends of the net were hauled simultaneously, in-shore and gradually toward one another along the beach, thereby creating a shrinking half-circle in the water that funneled the fish—striped bass, primarily, though as many as forty species could appear in the catch, including comical blowfish the Bonackers liked to call "Democrats"—into a central bag, or cod-end. Timing was crucial. Even tiny errors could mean a lost catch, or worse. One day Lester's son forgot to bring protective gloves and lost his grip when the jack line chafed his hands, so the incoming dory struck the beach on a steep gradient and did a forward somersault; Matthiessen, thrown onto the sand, escaped serious injury only because Lester scuttled in and caught the falling stern before it crashed down on top of him.

In his book about the baymen, *Men's Lives* (1986),* Matthiessen wrote that, as a seasonal participant with other sources of income, "I could afford to romanticize this life, to indulge myself in wondering why a veteran bayman such as Milt Miller would inveigh so vehemently against his lifelong occupation."[97] It was a striking admission, and an honest one, because he did romanticize the extent to which Bonackers valued their independence over security and their freedom over wealth. "Fishing wasn't a job, it was your station in life," a local once told him. "Like the old sayin goes, 'If you have saltwater in your blood, there ain't nothin you can do, you just gotta *do* it.'"[98] Matthiessen romanticized this certainty, the self-assured sense of what it meant to be a Bonacker; and he valued the feeling of solidarity that he discovered on Lester's crew.

The Matthiessens employed a Black housekeeper, Mrs. Davis, who lived in an area of Springs called Freetown, where the descendants of people freed from slavery had coexisted with the Montauketts in relative harmony since the early 1800s. Like many locals who were not Bonackers, Mrs. Davis considered the white fishermen to be her social inferiors, and she informed Patsy that "Mr. Matthiessen" was threatening her reputation in the community by

---

* The title was borrowed from Sir Walter Scott's *The Antiquary*: "It's no fish ye're buying—it's men's lives."

fraternizing with them. But Peter was more concerned with what the *fishermen* thought, and he went to incredible lengths to make the right impression. In 1963, Patsy would tell Gay Talese that Peter once became furious with her because she showed a visiting Bonacker into his study: "now the fisherman knew that Peter was not just another fisherman but was, indeed, a liter'y fellow," Talese wrote.[99] Similarly, Carol Southern, the wife of Terry Southern, would once recall that Peter used to make Patsy crouch down in the car whenever they passed a group of Bonackers, "so that he wouldn't be identified with this classy blonde."[100]

Matthiessen was not playacting here; he genuinely wanted to be accepted by these wary, insular people. Like George McConville, he aspired to erase the markings of his past and privilege. "Associated with working men, doing hard labor I enjoyed, I felt less malcontent than at any time in all my life," he wrote in his memoir notes.[101] However, Matthiessen's patrician intonations revealed his background far more readily than a writing study or a beautiful wife. The Bonackers were never really fooled. Nor were they romantics when it came to their own lot—none of the Lester dories even had names. At least one Bonacker, puzzled by Matthiessen's fascination with their lives, questioned why he wanted to work "like a donkey" when he could have been using his education to get ahead elsewhere, do something easier like "psycho-analyzin." As Milt Miller told him, "Boy, this life here is just one big mess, in case you ain't found that out yet!"[102]

IN LATER DECADES, whenever Matthiessen served up tales about his three years as a bayman alongside the Bonackers, he often joked that he would meet Patsy at social events still reeking of fish, then fall asleep at the dinner table.[103] But Patsy never found this behavior particularly amusing, and Peggy Lord, who dined with them on the East End, remembered her grimacing remarks about "always having to be home at nine o'clock," or "Peter always going to bed at nine o'clock."[104] When Sarita Southgate came to visit the Matthiessens in Springs, she found her brother-in-law locked in his study, and Patsy making do with quiet forbearance: "I think she thought of him as rather a prima donna."[105]

By the time Peter joined Ted Lester's crew, Patsy had been pregnant again for several months. For more space, the family moved to a renovated building on Stony Hill Farm, just north of Amagansett—a former chauffeur's apartment, with a garage below that had been converted into a living room. The hundred-acre farm belonged to Jeffrey Potter, a handsome, Groton-educated stage manager, who had bought it during a tax sale and now spent much of his time trying to make it profitable through rentals; and Jeffrey's wife, Penny, who had been forced to give up her life as an actress in New York, somewhat resentfully.

The Potters expanded Patsy's social circle, and so did Donald and Carol Braider, who ran the House of Books and Music on Main Street, in East Hampton, where they sold everything from encyclopedias to Le Creuset cookware. Though Carol also deferred to her husband, an aspiring novelist— "Your father was the picture and I was the frame," she later explained to their daughter, Susan—the Braiders were attractively bohemian, friends with Franz Kline and the de Koonings, and their store was a bright spot of cosmopolitanism. "They brought Paris to East Hampton," recalled Susan.[106] Through the Braiders, Patsy secured a part-time job at Books and Music, and she began passing her afternoons charming customers and eating chocolate-covered caramels. Running the store was another antidote to loneliness, much as visiting Pollock and Krasner had been in Springs. In August, she helped Lee arrange a one-day exhibition of work in a small gallery fashioned from the store's adjoining car shed.

Meanwhile, Matthiessen expanded his commitment to fishing. After the end of his season on Ted Lester's crew, during a brief visit to Rockport, Massachusetts, he spied a thirty-two-foot tuna harpoon boat with "the most beautiful lines" he'd ever seen, and a FOR SALE sign on the windshield.[107] He bought the *Keewatin* for a price he couldn't afford, then ran her down the coast past Salem and Boston, all the way to the Three Mile Harbor marina. Within days, alarmed at the financial burden he'd unthinkingly acquired, he recruited John Cole as first mate and launched a charter-boat business—without bothering to pass the test required by the Coast Guard for a captain's license. The *Merlin*, as he rechristened the boat after the species of falcon, spent that summer as an "outlaw vessel," ferrying parties of Chinese and Shinnecock men to the fishing grounds around Montauk Point.[108]

FOR MUCH OF the next year, Matthiessen coasted along in his arrangement, which felt to him like the closest he'd ever come to true freedom. His first daughter, Sara Carey Matthiessen, was born on November 1, 1954, in the middle of scallop and clamming season. He handed control of the *Vop-Vop* to John Cole and returned to the house on Stony Hill Farm, where he remained, poised above a typewriter, surrounded by the happy gurgles of his two young children, until the end of April. Then he dug out his black rubber waders and rejoined Ted Lester's crew for another six weeks: "the springtime filled me with well-being despite my drowsiness, despite sore hands, despite the prospect of a long hard day that, if we were lucky, would end long after dark in the cold freezer of Montauk Seafood, hosing down and packing and icing bass."[109] After haul-seining with the Bonackers, he put the *Merlin* back into service in June, for what turned out to be a busy and successful (and now legal) few months of chartering, until the scallop season came around again. With birdwatching and an occasional duck hunt at Napeague thrown in, this added up to what Matthiessen would nostalgically recall as "the best year-round working schedule that I ever devised."[110]

It was not all perfect, however. Throughout 1954 and 1955, *The Paris Review* continued to demand his attention. As fiction editor, Matthiessen read submissions whenever he found a spare moment, then sent his selections over to Plimpton in Paris. He also acted as a buffer between contributors and Plimpton, who could, Matthiessen thought, be "needlessly abrasive" in his feedback.[111] By the middle of 1955, Matthiessen had been involved in several major decisions that would determine the magazine's future: the recruitment of Prince Sadruddin Aga Khan, son of the forty-eighth hereditary Imam of the Shia Ismaili Muslims, as publisher, which solved the funding dilemma; the inauguration of an Aga Khan Prize for Fiction (which was awarded annually until 2004); and the appointment of a new managing editor, the brilliant Robert B. Silvers, who would soon assume control of the Paris office so Plimpton could return to New York.

But Matthiessen's letters were frequently filled with Sturm und Drang, and his irritation with the *Review* only became more acute as he succumbed to what he called "a general feeling of detachment from the whole operation."[112] When Plimpton failed to deal with a manuscript after months of needless delays, Matthiessen lost his temper: "I simply don't love the job enough to put up with this sort of thing, and if you should care to request my resignation, you'll have it by return mail."[113] The issue was quickly resolved, only to be followed a few weeks later by another problem, with Plimpton making unilateral decisions about the masthead. Offended, Matthiessen wrote to say so in prose so vivid that Plimpton denounced it as "irresponsible and insulting nonsense."[114] Plimpton claimed he would quit if no apology was forthcoming; instead, Matthiessen demanded that *Plimpton* apologize, "not to me but to the U.S. members of the PR." He offered a warning: "[T]he next repetition of the incident will be the last so far as I am concerned. I'll resign before you even have a chance."[115]

It is not entirely clear when he finally acted on these threats. Matthiessen's name mostly disappears from editorial correspondence dated after the summer of 1955, although there is an occasional note as late as 1957, and Plimpton once estimated that their "big fight" did not occur until "about 1960," in New York: "We had too much to drink one night during a meeting, and tempers began to flare. I kept trying to get people to stay on and work harder. I kept trying to hold them together, and I think they finally were impatient."[116]

Whenever the fight happened, Matthiessen, in the aftermath, wrote an undated note to Plimpton that was a little more than "impatient":

> I regret having become so overwrought the other evening, and doubtless the demon rum had a hand in the whole messy affair, but on reflection, I can't honestly say that my impression of it all has changed—to wit, that since I ventured to assail certain aspects of the PR which you appear to find personally embarrassing, you retaliated with the public inference . . . if not accusation, that my departure from the PR might be likened to the departure of a rat from a sinking ship. Since others have resigned, in effect, without owning up to it, and since the job I've done has been more or less acceptable, I find your bad sportsmanship a disheartening reward for these years of gratis labor, and a very poor recommendation for the privilege of working with you, or of your integrity. I didn't expect a testimonial gold pencil, but neither did I expect such a shabby exit as that, even from you, and God knows I ought to be hardened to your ways by now.[117]

As a founder, Matthiessen would remain on the board of *The Paris Review* until his death. But his direct involvement as editor ended early in the magazine's run, and his friendship with George Plimpton, resilient as it would prove to be, never shook a small, lingering note of mutual ambivalence.

IN SEPTEMBER 1955, Matthiessen marked the release of his second novel, *Partisans*, with an "autograph party" at Books and Music. Despite the enthusiasm of *The East Hampton Star*, which promoted the event by touting him as one of the finest young writers in America, it was a bittersweet occasion.[118]

When Bernice Baumgarten had read an early draft of the manuscript focused on communists in Paris, she was "full of misgivings" about what she interpreted as a heavy-handed allegory, and "not at all convinced" that Matthiessen should show it to Harper & Brothers.[119] He'd done so against her advice, hoping that his own enthusiasm for *Partisans* would persuade the editors. Yet the response had been overwhelmingly negative: "We do not see [fixing it] as an easy job,"[120] Elizabeth Lawrence told him, before adding, in another letter, "You understand that all I say to you is in a spirit of warm friendship. You're starting a long road. You will need all the truths any of us can give you."[121] Matthiessen had attempted a rewrite over several months; Lawrence had read it again and suggested he set it aside for a few years of fermentation. Matthiessen had then pulled the manuscript from Harper and taken it to Tom Guinzburg, who shared it with the writer and editor Malcolm Cowley, an adviser for the Viking Press. Cowley also had serious reservations. He'd appreciated the novel's theme and ambition, though, and he agreed to cast a vote in favor of acceptance should Matthiessen submit it to Viking for formal consideration. Which Matthiessen did, signing a contract for $1,500—25 percent less than his advance for *Race Rock*.[122]

While his faith in the work had pushed it through multiple lines of resistance, Matthiessen faltered once the fictionalization of his own ethical awakening was finally out in the world. Once again, he turned critical. A few weeks after the party at Books and Music, he sat for an interview with *The Saturday Review*. "What I am trying to do, what every other writer is trying to do, is write a very, very good book," he explained—"and I haven't yet. But I think I am capable of doing it, and I don't think anybody who isn't capable of doing it has any business being a writer."[123] He then talked about the "terrible miasmas of depression" a writer faces when he can't get across what he really wants to say. This was hardly the confident promotional statement his publisher was probably hoping for.

The reviews for *Partisans* were mixed. For every critic who applauded the novel's psychological suspense (like Graham Greene interpreted by Arthur Koestler, according to the *San Francisco Chronicle*), another critic pointed out its shaky plot, or the ways in which characters seemed more like "mouthpieces" for Ideas than real flesh-and-blood people.

The most incisive review came from Bill Styron, in a letter Matthiessen received in late December. Styron preferred the book to its predecessor, he wrote: "You've achieved an <u>ease</u>, which you didn't have in <u>Race Rock</u>, and by that I think I mean simply that, artistically, you've become much more sure of yourself."[124] There were "Dostoievski-like glimmerings" in the prose, and he admired Matthiessen's ability to enliven scenes through "one or two beautifully exact, extraneous observations"—the technique of deploying specific details that Matthiessen had learned from reading Faulkner. But Styron also thought the book was too buttoned up, or too anemic. *Partisans* read more like an extended outline than the expansive, unpredictable, risk-taking novel they'd discussed over wine in Ravello two years earlier. He continued, "I'd knock the piss out of anyone who said this to me (for my condescension by now must be sickening), but I think—such is my faith in your imagination, which you really <u>haven't</u> let loose—that if you were to sit down and, say, over a period of two or three or even four years really suffer over a scene and <u>let</u> it loose, you could make us all look like Harold Bell Wright"—a once bestselling author of negligible talent who had mostly been ignored since his death in 1944.

Matthiessen was holding back, still trying to find his voice and true subject. But if he could unleash his imagination, the result might be something extraordinary. "Shit you not," Styron wrote, trying to encourage his friend, "I don't think I've ever read a novel which, so skeletal as it seemed to me, impelled me to such famous conclusions."

WHILE MATTHIESSEN WAS processing the lukewarm reception of *Partisans*, John Cole, over in Springs, was attempting to salvage his relationship with Cynthia. Next year, he'd told himself, year after year, "I will arrive at an understanding of this compelling business of making a living on the sea."[125] Yet their debts had only continued to mount, and now Cynthia had finally tired of the fish guts caked into his clothes every evening. With pressure from her, John "surrendered to reality," he later wrote, and gave up on "selfish romanticism." In other words, he accepted a copywriting job in Dayton, Ohio, with a company that manufactured fire extinguishers. Matthiessen lost his first mate as suddenly as the fall of an axe, although he took no lesson from Cole's compromise. Perhaps it was already too late to save his own marriage.

The catalyst for Peter's breakup with Patsy was a terrible accident at the end of May 1955. Jeffrey Potter, their landlord, operated a landscaping and construction business in addition to Stony Hill Farm. One morning, he was driving a truck filled with topsoil down the Montauk Highway, and a seven-year-old boy, trying to reach his school bus, ran out from behind a parked car into the road. Potter hit the boy, dragged his body for fifteen feet, and then held him as he died.[126] Shellshocked, he returned home covered in blood, which he later recalled struggling to scrub off in the shower: "I kept thinking of Lady Macbeth. It was very strange the way it sunk into my skin. In the meantime, people had come out of sympathy—of course, they should have been going to the family of the child, but they didn't. And down comes Penny [Potter's wife], cheerfully, into this room full of people and says, 'Ah, let's all have a nice Bloody Mary.' And that was no help. And the next day I sort of stopped functioning."[127]

Potter's license was suspended pending the outcome of a police investigation. Patsy, because she was an early riser, volunteered to drive him to job sites around East Hampton. As his relationship with Penny fell apart, he came to rely on Patsy for emotional support. Then, at some point, they started an affair. "Patsy drove me to more than my jobs," Potter said. Luke Matthiessen would remember his mother's perspective in less crude terms: "Many years later, she told me flat out that she felt the reason she was attracted to him was because she knew that he loved her"—the implication being that she was no longer convinced her own husband did.[128]

Peter was certainly aware of Patsy's discontent. In "Nightfall in Another Country," a short story written at Stony Hill, a man living in a modest community of fishermen says to his wife, when she gently suggests he seek his fortune in the big city: "But aren't we happy where we are, poor creature, isn't life good to us here?"[129]

Peter, however, had developed the sort of tunnel vision that renders consequences mostly invisible. He could see the Bonackers, the *Merlin*, his writing projects—and almost everything else had slipped out of focus. This meant other people realized well before he did what was going on between his wife and their landlord. "The affair between Patsy Matthiessen and Jeff Potter was, with the help of the party-line, burning up the telephone wires in Amagansett, and spreading out from there to the growing community of abstractionists and their writer friends," recalled Anton Prohaska, a neighbor who was only a child at the time.[130]

Eventually Patsy just confessed to Peter, came clean about the affair, during what became a full season of sad endings. In August, Jackson Pollock crashed his Oldsmobile convertible on Springs Fireplace Road, killing himself and another passenger instantly, and injuring Ruth Kligman, his lover. Lee Krasner flew home from France—Patsy was part of the group that met her at the airport—and immediately went to pieces. Then, the day after Pollock's funeral, Donald Braider had a nervous breakdown and was committed to the Institute of Pennsylvania Hospital; Carol was forced to shutter the House of Books and Music.

In his memoir notes, Peter accepted full responsibility for the situation with Patsy. "I did not 'work at my marriage,'" he wrote. "[It was] my fault: long winters, stunted social life in summers due to commercial fishing." Also, when Patsy begged for forgiveness, he was "too macho + insecure" to see things from her point of view.[131] This was a clearheaded confession, but it didn't come until he'd had decades to consider his culpability from every angle.

In 1956, furious with his wife's betrayal, Peter walked out of the marriage. He left Patsy with Sara Carey, who was two years old, and Luke, who was three. "I was in therapy for a while," Luke later reflected, "and the therapist always tried to get me behind what he called 'the wall,' which was anything that happened before the age of five. And I just wouldn't do it. I *couldn't* do it. I still haven't, to this day. But my parents both told me that I was unusually distressed. That was their term: 'unusually distressed' over the breakup of their marriage."[132]

The following year, Patsy would publish her first short story, "A Very Important Lady," in the countercultural *Evergreen Review*—not, it should be noted, in *The Paris Review*. An "oblique, embittered response to her failed first marriage,"[133] as her friend Joe LeSueur once described it, the story concerns a woman who believes that all traces of herself have been effaced by her husband: "Even her own clothes, leaning against each other in her closet, did not hold the shape of her, in no way seemed to stand for her. They were, like everything else now, his."[134] The woman's husband had once been her "god," able to bestow a blessing through the briefest of smiles; she had bitten her lip at their wedding to stop herself from weeping with joy. But after years of neglect, she has come to imagine them both as enemies standing on either side of an open coffin, and if she looks down into the metaphorical casket, she will glimpse herself. "No one had dared put the lid on, yet, but it would have to be done soon." With its blistering resentment, this story captured the way Patsy Southgate would regard Peter Matthiessen until the end of her life. Even the mention of his name, Luke recalled, could elicit an involuntary physical reaction: "You could just feel her pull back a little bit, and a sort of sardonic grin might come across her face."[135]

In Amagansett, Peter immediately went about wrapping up unfinished business. Approached by Lewis Lester, Captain Ted's nephew, about joining a new haul-seine crew for a rig owned by a neighbor, he shook his head, saying that his days as a bayman were over. "[B]ut Lewis's words sent me on my way feeling much better," he wrote in *Men's Lives*. "I would never be a Bonacker, not if I lived here for a century, but apparently I was accepted as a fisherman."[136] With that consolation, he donated the *Vop-Vop* to a charity boys camp near Three Mile Harbor. He pulled the *Merlin* from the marina and had her stored indefinitely. He sold a parcel of land high on Stony Hill, which he'd bought with the intention of building a house. Then he went to New York and stayed with friends on the Upper East Side.

When his wounded pride finally healed, Peter, unlike Patsy, came to feel almost sanguine about the dissolution of their relationship. In twenty-nine years, he had rebelled against his parents and everything they stood for. He had served in the U.S. Navy, received an education at Yale, joined and then deserted the CIA, cofounded a literary journal in Paris, written award-winning short stories and two (middling) novels, and ingratiated himself with a closed community of fishermen. But he had not achieved a sense of satisfaction in life, or a robust understanding of who he really was. While leaving his wife was a failure, it was also, as Peter came to see it, a rare opportunity to start over, take a very different path in life. "I loved Patsy," he once told a journalist, "but it freed me."[137]

PART II

1957–1973

An illustration by Josiah Wood Whymper,
from Henry Walter Bates's *The Naturalist
on the River Amazons* (1863).

8

Lost Americans

The wild creatures of the open spaces, of clear water and green northern wilds, of gold prairie and huge sky, embody a human longing no less civilized for being primitive, no less real for being felt rather than thought.

—*Wildlife in America* (1959)[1]

IN NOVEMBER 1953, less than four months after the Matthiessens had arrived home from Europe on the *Andrea Doria*, a damp, pearly blanket of smog—or "smaze": nobody knew quite what to call it—settled over New York City and the adjacent counties of Nassau and Westchester.[2] Bridges between Manhattan and Brooklyn seemed to vanish halfway across the East River, and skyscrapers towered into the clouds. Flights into Idlewild were canceled due to safety concerns, while traffic on the New Jersey Turnpike slowed to an interminable crawl. Astronomers at the Hayden Planetarium peered through their telescopes to watch the transit of Mercury across the face of the sun—an event they'd awaited for fifty-nine years— only to see absolutely nothing. For six days, what *The New York Times* called an "eye-smarting, throat-irritating twilight gray" ruined sports games and sunset strolls, and temporarily marooned tourists on Liberty Island.[3] Even the pigeons seemed "sluggish and distressed" as they attempted to navigate an acrid soup of soot, fly ash, dust, tar, asphalt, grit, and sulfur dioxide, all of it trapped beneath a layer of unseasonably hot air. By the time a rainstorm finally washed the city clean, several hundred people had died, mostly from respiratory complications, although it would take another decade for anyone to correlate their deaths with the eerie phenomenon.[4]

What happened in New York was a disaster, but it was also a symptom of a more chronic environmental sickness that was still awaiting proper diagnosis in America. The 1950s were filled with such symptoms, so scattered and various that it was difficult for most people to see the underlying problem. In Colorado, ducks expired en masse from swimming in a basin laced with detergents. In Nevada, more than a hundred nuclear tests were conducted between Las Vegas and Reno over the course of several years, causing pinkish clouds to waft through the skies of southern Utah; after one particularly large explosion, sheep developed burn-like lesions on their faces, necks, and ears, and some had miscarriages. Meanwhile, beaches in California were condemned as too contaminated for recreational use: in 1948, San Francisco Bay had been described by one official as "the world's largest cesspool."[5] Synthetic pesticides—dichlorodiphenyltrichloroethane, or DDT, among others—were being sprayed indiscriminately to control insects, and poisoning, in the process, everything from salmon to bald eagles, which then laid eggs so thin they broke apart in their nests. As Peter Matthiessen would write after surveying the national scene:

> The true wilderness—the great woods and clear rivers, the wild swamps and grassy plains which once were the wonder of the world—has been largely despoiled, and today's voyager, approaching our shore through the oiled waters of the coast, is greeted by smoke and the glint of industry on our fouled seaboard, and an inland prospect of second growth, scarred landscapes, and sterile, often stinking, rivers of pollution and raw mud, the whole bedecked with billboards, neon lights, and other decorative evidence of mankind's triumph over chaos.[6]

That bitter "triumph over chaos" was official government policy under President Eisenhower, who acknowledged the environment, if he did so at all, largely in terms of economic utility. Conservation was not about "locking up and putting resources beyond the possibility of wastage or usage," he affirmed at a conference in 1953; it was about "the intelligent use of all the resources we have, for the welfare and benefit of all the American people."[7] This was the era of the Interstate Highway System, steamrolling lines across an unruly continent. Of the levees, floodgates, and canals draining the Everglades to make room for sugarcane. Of the Saint Lawrence Seaway, a sinuous route that connected the Atlantic Ocean and the Great Lakes, enabling ready access to cargo freighters—and to invasive species. The few environmental laws that Congress did pass, such as the Air Pollution Control Act of 1955, favored research over regulation, which was left up to individual states, and therefore mostly nonexistent. "We would not plan," lamented Stewart Udall in 1968, when he was secretary of the interior, looking back at a decade of ignorant damage: "We did not love the land."[8]

However, it was also the era when public attitudes began to evolve. As the historian Thomas R. Dunlap has illustrated, mass media, aided by advances in camera technology, exposed people to sides of nature they had rarely considered.⁹ Disney documentaries such as *The Living Desert* (1953) and *The Vanishing Prairie* (1954) captured "a story no dramatist could write," as one trailer announced, with flowers blooming in time-lapse and macro shots of scorpions engaged in a "frolicking love dance."¹⁰* The ascendancy of television made the wild real for viewers in a way that books could never do, by *showing* the community of relationships that existed in even the most inhospitable of places. At the same time, postwar prosperity meant that many Americans had more hours for leisure than ever before, which they increasingly spent outdoors, picnicking in a local park or camping in a national one beneath some Douglas firs. "The economic insecurity that had made them accept dirty air and stinking rivers as the price of progress was fading," Dunlap wrote. "They could afford, and now demanded, environmental 'amenities'—clean air and water and wilderness."¹¹

What became known as the environmental movement would not come into focus until after 1962, when Rachel Carson published *Silent Spring*, her legendary exposé about the hidden effects of pesticides. But the stirrings of a renewed appreciation for nature—as a site for recreation; as part of America's frontier heritage; as a salve for the human spirit, as John Muir once rhapsodized: "Nature's peace will flow into you as sunshine flows into trees"¹²—were already strong enough to lend groups like the Wilderness Society and the Sierra Club some political influence.

In 1950, the Bureau of Reclamation proposed a network of ten dams in the American West, collectively called the Colorado River Storage Project. One of the dams would be built in a remote corner of Utah's Dinosaur National Monument, at Echo Park, where the Yampa and Green Rivers converge in a canyon dominated by an enormous sandstone formation known as Steamboat Rock. Under the proposal, the dam would flood the canyon, effectively destroying it to provide water for a burgeoning population. When word of this plan got out, however, it triggered a fiery five-year debate.¹³ On one side of the Echo Park controversy were advocates with Eisenhower's mindset, like Interior Secretary Douglas McKay, who saw the canyon as a resource waiting to be developed; and on the other side were preservationists like Howard Zahniser, executive director of the Wilderness Society, who wanted to leave the canyon unmolested, valuing Echo Park in its pristine state. While Congress conducted a series of hearings about the Storage Project, a coalition of these preservationists—"punks," McKay called them¹⁴—appealed to

---

* Matthiessen thought the Disney documentaries were "phony" and "vulgar," but perhaps critical in saving species from extinction. "I think you can make an argument," he once told the writer Howard Norman, "that if it had not been for those early Walt Disney films, the whooping crane might not even exist now. As my father used to say when I was a boy, halitosis is better than no breath at all."

everyday Americans through films, newspaper editorials, books, and illustrated pamphlets (*"Will you DAM the Scenic Wild Canyons of Our National Park System?"*).¹⁵ The blitz of publicity was devastating, unrelenting, and ultimately effective—the preservationists won. In 1956, following a groundswell of opposition, the Colorado River Storage Project was approved by the Senate *minus* the Echo Park Dam. A milestone in the annals of conservation, it showed just how seriously public views on nature were shifting.

In the aftermath of the Echo Park standoff, Howard Zahniser picked up his son's grade school notebook and scribbled out the first longhand draft of a new wilderness bill. A passionate, persevering man who had grown up near the Allegheny National Forest in Pennsylvania, Zahniser believed that "[w]e have a profound, a fundamental need for areas of wilderness—a need that is not only recreational but spiritual, educational, scientific, essential to a true understanding of ourselves, our culture, our own natures, and our place in all nature."¹⁶ In drafting a bill that would place millions of acres beyond the reach of development, he was recognizing the moment as an opportunity to reckon with past and ongoing mistakes. Americans, Zahniser knew, were long overdue for some hard truths about their wildlands and wildlife: what they'd already lost through greed, vanity, or negligence; what they were in the process of losing right now; and what threatened to vanish tomorrow if society remained on its troubling trajectory.

PETER MATTHIESSEN REINVENTED himself as one of the preeminent "naturalist-writers" in America because he needed the money.¹⁷ Although he would identify as a novelist until the end of his life, fiction rarely paid a living wage, and certainly not in 1957. In February, he published "Travelin Man" in *Harper's Bazaar*, a haunting short story about a Black convict who escapes from a chain gang only to find himself hunted by a white poacher on a windswept barrier island off the coast of the Carolinas. Inspired by occasional visits Matthiessen made with his father to the Santee Gun Club, a duck hunting reserve just north of Charleston, which employed Black guides for its largely conservative white membership, the story was meant as an indictment "of the still-violent racial bigotry in our country."¹⁸ It would win him an O. Henry Prize, and George Pepper, the film producer, would develop it into *The Young One*, directed by Luis Buñuel.* Yet all Matthiessen received

---

* "Like many film-makers in the ugly red-baiting climate of the House Un-American Activities Committee in the late Fifties," Matthiessen recalled of Pepper and Buñuel, "they were both in political banishment, making low budget films in Mexico; under the circumstances, I was content to accept a modest $500 advance on a full payment of $1500 for the screen rights to my story." However, when *The Young One* was finished in 1960, Matthiessen caught an early screening in New York before it was entered in the Cannes Film Festival: "sitting alone in the back row, I felt

for his labor was a few hundred dollars—hardly enough to cover himself, let alone Patsy, Luke, and Sara Carey, all of whom remained his responsibility even though he was no longer living with them.

Nonfiction was a compromise: not what he wanted to do, but at least it was writing. In his head—and in interviews and public speeches, for years afterward—he was careful to make a distinction: while fiction was "art," nonfiction was more like "fashioning a cabinet. It can be elegant and very beautiful but it can never be sculpture."[19] He would explain his position further in *The Paris Review*:

> A good essay or article can and should have all the attributes of a good short story, including structure and design, pacing and effective placement of its parts—almost all the attributes of fiction except the creative imagination, which can never be permitted to enliven fact. The writer of nonfiction is stuck with objective reality, or should be; how his facts are arranged and presented is where his craft appears, and it can be dazzling when the writer is a good one. The best nonfiction has many, many virtues, among which simple truthfulness is perhaps foremost, yet its fidelity to the known facts is its fatal constraint.[20]

In writing fiction, Matthiessen had discovered that he could abandon himself "to the free creation of something never beheld on earth," and this exhilarated him "with a strange joy." Nonfiction, on the other hand, was a livelihood, and inherently earthbound: "I find it drains my batteries." From the very start of his career as a nature writer, he considered what he wrote necessary but lesser—an ironic view given the nonfiction would become his most famous achievement, largely for the ways in which his novelist's eye interpreted "the known facts."

Before he settled on nature writing, however, he made a few preliminary ventures into other genres to generate some income. Also in February, he published his first and only piece in *Holiday*, the glamorous travel magazine known for long, meandering articles by the likes of E. B. White, John Stein-

---

myself go crimson in the face." His stark, elemental drama of birdsong and crashing waves had been reduced, in his view, to a hothouse "travesty" about a Black jazz musician (Bernie Hamilton), on the run after a false accusation of rape, and a white game warden (Zachary Scott), who is more concerned with a nubile teenager than he is with the island's actual game. "Marvelously," Matthiessen noted, with withering sarcasm, the "cold-eyed" warden is hiding a "heart of gold" under his hardened exterior: "instead of murdering the black man, as in the story, he tells him gruffly to meet him at his boat for a ride back to the mainland, at which point the grateful [musician] nails down the upbeat ending by saying something like, 'Yay-hay, Man, like, I'm there aw-ready!'" To add insult to injury, George Pepper stiffed Matthiessen on the final $1,000 owed for the screen rights. Matthiessen would not see the rest of his money until sometime in the 1970s when Pepper's widow, going over her late husband's accounts, noticed the debt and mailed out a check—"for which I honor her," Matthiessen wrote.

beck, and Ian Fleming. Matthiessen's contribution, titled "Powerboat Cruising," was unmistakably his own: "A psychiatrist may see in the small boat a symbol of man's search for individuality," he wrote, summing up the last few years of his life; and most owners, he added, "will agree that the boat is the ideal vehicle of escape from whatever it is they wish to escape."[21] But there was no byline on the piece, because Matthiessen fell out with the editors when they asked him to delete a reference to Chris-Craft Boats, which he'd described as the worst that money could buy. "They said, 'We're not going to say that,'" he recalled—Chris-Craft was an advertiser in the magazine. "And I said, 'Well, I'm not going to sign it.' Then I said, 'I tell you what, I need the money, and I did the work. Why don't *you* sign it and just send me the money?' This was the unholy bargain we made."[22]

Around the same time, he finally gained traction in *The New Yorker*, although this, too, came with its share of drama. In 1956, while he was still living in Amagansett, he'd pitched multiple ideas to William Shawn, the magazine's editor: a piece about "a professional and very successful jewel thief, just out of prison"; a piece about Edward Haight, the mentally unbalanced young man who'd murdered two girls near Stamford in 1942, and was then sent to the electric chair ("I knew him and felt sorry for him and had, as did many people there, a bad conscience about him"); a piece about the Bladensfield Plantation in Virginia, where his mother traced her roots; and a piece about the Bonackers and ruinous sea bass regulation that had recently been proposed in Albany, "which has many overtones of the general problems of conservation, and not a few of its political undertones."[23]

But the idea that was accepted was one that Matthiessen had conceived all the way back in 1952, a Paris collaboration with Ben Bradlee, who was then just a press attaché at the American embassy. "Peter and I had become totally caught up in one of the great French cultural events," recalled Bradlee— "a *crime passionnel*, involving the dashing and politically promising young mayor of Orléans, Pierre Chevallier, a doctor, and his faithful but slightly drab wife, Yvonne, a nurse."[24] Madame Chevallier, upon discovering that her husband was having an affair, had shot him five times with a revolver. "The French press went crazy, throwing caution to the wind with police reports, court reports, sob sisters, psychiatrists, novelists, the works." Bradlee and Matthiessen had tracked this ravenous outrage with a view to writing about the scandal for *The New Yorker*; they'd spread hundreds of clippings across the floor of Bradlee's embassy office and coauthored a first draft. Yet the story had aroused little interest over in New York, so it was abandoned until Matthiessen, in 1957, tried his luck again through Bernice Baumgarten. This time the magazine said yes; "Five Bullets," renamed "Peut-être un Peu

Excessif," was accepted for the "Annals of Crime" series. The proposed fee of $1,800 was more than he'd received for *Partisans*.

The New Yorker refused to run shared bylines, so Bradlee, who contributed no new reporting for the revived draft, agreed to forgo credit in exchange for a third of the payment. *If* there was any payment. In March, Matthiessen read through the proofs and threatened to withdraw the article. "I regret very much that its editor did not consult me about what is, in effect, a complete revision," he fumed in a letter to William Shawn. "Throughout, the style seems at best uncertain, and at worst overwritten, arch, and labored. In any case, the writing is not mine, and I do not want my name attached to it."[25]

"Steam," Matthiessen later said, "was coming out of my ears and eyes." He called Baumgarten and announced that he was "going to bomb" *The New Yorker*. To which Baumgarten replied something like: "Count to ten. Count to a hundred. This is the first money you've ever earned. Don't be stupid and blow it."[26]

Shawn read the irate letter and then invited his new contributor to a meeting in the magazine's office on West 43rd Street. Matthiessen took a seat before the small, composed man, already a legend in American letters, and noticed the sun shining through his ears, a home-packed lunch perched on his desk in a brown paper bag. "I'm sure we can straighten all this out," Shawn said, as Matthiessen later recalled. "Mr. Vanderbilt likes your material very much, but you didn't put it in chronological order. He was just putting it back in chronological order."

"Well, I could have done that," Matthiessen said.

"I'm sure we can straighten it out. You just come in here tomorrow and work it out with him. Sit down together, and we'll work it out."

"I don't think we'll be able to work together very well after the letter I sent to you."

"Mr. Matthiessen, I took the precaution of not showing Mr. Vanderbilt your letter."[27]

Nevertheless, Sanderson Vanderbilt had received word of the impudent denunciation, which meant Matthiessen was forced to endure a few frigid weeks of back-and-forth as he revised his much-anticipated debut for *The New Yorker*.[28]

It was during this revision fracas that he sold the pitch that would change the direction of his life. Casting around for new material, Matthiessen had asked himself what topics interested him that might also appeal to the audience of a middlebrow magazine: "I knew about animals and birds, so I started with that."[29] Like many writers, he sensed his story before he understood its shape and parameters. It was "almost instinctive," the feeling that "something was out of balance."[30] Years later, he would explain what he meant by referencing a letter Rachel Carson ("a heroine of mine") once sent to a friend, Lois Crisler, in which she wrote: "Of course I felt a special sympathy with your thoughts on 'the secret tension between love and despair' so that 'no carefree love of the planet is now possible.'"[31] Having observed the degradation of shorelines she adored, Carson "awoke with a kind of sadness every day," Matthiessen said; "it took her a little while to kind of get her spirits back up again." Like Carson, he intuited that *now* was a prime moment to draw people's attention to the imperiled natural world.

On March 15, 1957, he received a commissioning letter from *Sports Illustrated* for a three-part series on extinct fauna, historical movements toward conservation, and the contemporary status of American wildlife.[32] The magazine offered $1,000 for each part, with up to $500 for travel expenses. The same week, he signed a contract with the Viking Press for a book-length adaptation of the series, securing an additional advance of $2,000.[33] This added up to a respectable commitment of $5,500 (around $60,000 today), the most he'd ever received for a single project.

In the original Viking contract, the working title for his first nonfiction book is "Lost Americans," an ambiguous name that might be interpreted in two different ways. Was Matthiessen referring to the lost American fauna? Or was it perhaps the American people who were "lost," having so profoundly misunderstood the natural riches of the continent since the earliest days of white dominion? By the time the book was published in 1959, Viking had adjusted the title to *Wildlife in America*, a toothless choice for something filled with so much bite.

THROUGHOUT THE EARLY DECADES of the nineteenth century, a species called the "artist-explorer" fanned out across the landscape with sketchbooks and watercolors, determined to paint the New World. "As it has fallen to my lot to be the biographer of the feathered tribes of the United States," wrote Alexander Wilson in 1809, "I am solicitous to do full justice to every species; and I would not conceal one good quality that any one of them possesses."[34] A poet and illustrator as well as a naturalist, Wilson roamed from New England to Tennessee, enduring fetid swamps, dysentery, and a tornado to finish his nine-volume *American Ornithology*, with its painstaking depictions of orioles, mockingbirds, and scarlet tanagers. Wilson was soon followed by John James Audubon, who traveled just as widely for *The Birds of America*, published serially between 1827 and 1838. And then there were figures such as Prince Maximilian of Wied-Neuwied, an ethnologist, who took the Swiss-born painter Karl Bodmer on an expedition up the Missouri River in 1832; and George Catlin, who journeyed some four hundred miles up the Missouri himself, then spent years painting bison, grizzly bears, and stirring portraits of Native American people, including members of the Blackfoot, Cheyenne, Crow, Pawnee, and Ojibwe tribes.[35]

Matthiessen, with his new book, was also proposing to be a kind of artist-explorer. But his cross-country travels had the intention of highlighting the majesty and diversity that had *vanished* since European colonization.

There was a personal dimension to the travels as well. Sometime in the early spring of 1957, he packed a green Ford convertible with a down sleeping bag, a 20-gauge shotgun, and armloads of birding books by writers such as Arthur C. Bent and Roger Tory Peterson.[36] This was the same year that Jack Kerouac published *On the Road*, and Matthiessen saw the highway in similar terms of personal liberation. An ambitious research trip presented an opportunity to put some serious distance between himself and his failed marriage, and to try out the nomadic life to see if it suited his temperament. "The gun was for protection," he later told the historian Douglas Brinkley. "Perhaps I thought I might need it to shoot a bird to eat in the Mojave or Sonora."[37]

Matthiessen left no record of his particular driving route around the contiguous United States—or *routes*, because he likely made multiple trips during the approximately eighteen months it took him to research and write *Wildlife in America*. But there are traces of stops he made along the way (photographs and notes), which offer a sense of how far he roamed with his Ford. In Louisiana, he dropped by the Audubon Zoo in New Orleans, paying respects to two captive whooping cranes, Josephine and Crip, who lived in a "sad, cramped pen" as representatives of a species on the brink of extinction. From there, he continued west through Houston, Texas, to the Aransas National Wildlife Refuge, near Rockport, where an Audubon tour boat brought him close to the last wild whoopers—just twenty-six birds*—as they searched salt meadows and boggy lagoons of the barrier island marshland for blue crabs. "Dwarfing the heron and egrets, they stalked like avengers over dark green spartina."[38]

In Arizona, he drove up mountains that erupted from the desert floor "like islands from the sea," and marveled at how a valley can seamlessly transition

---

* There were once around fifteen thousand whooping cranes in North America. Human interference—hunting, egg theft, and the drainage of prime habitat—reduced this number to a nadir in 1941 of just fifteen migratory birds, plus six that lived year-round in Louisiana. In the decades since, conservation efforts have helped stabilize the migratory flock, which winters at Aransas and then flies some 2,600 miles north to breed in the remote fastness of Canada's Wood Buffalo National Park, on the border of Alberta and the Northwest Territories. Though *Grus americana* remains endangered, today there are more than five hundred in the wild.

into sage foothills, then painted canyons, then deciduous woods, then sweet-smelling forests of ponderosa pine, before finally topping out as snowy peaks. "The wide range of habitats to be found within a few thousand perpendicular feet shelter everything from cactus wrens to chickadees," he observed, "but here, too, overgrazing of the spare grassland has encouraged blight and a serious decline of the game birds of the border region."[39]

In Southern California, he watched white-tailed kites from the tranquility of an orange grove. Then he headed north to the Los Padres National Forest, where he hiked up a trail to scan clouds for endangered California condors. Two promising shapes appeared in the distance, "coming on swiftly, unswerving" over the high country: "A mile away, they no longer can be eagles, and the heart stops."[40]

Further up the coast, he stood at Point Lobos, near Monterey, and spied a large herd of sea otters lolling by the shore, as well as breaching whales and flights of cormorants: "The din of the rookeries is muffled in the ocean wash, and the random bark which rises above the groaning of the herd is whirled away quickly on the sea wind, but facing seaward with one's back to civilization, one senses the wild quality of a scene many thousands of years old."[41]

Civilization proved slightly harder to ignore in Wyoming, at Yellowstone National Park, where a young naturalist showed Matthiessen the grizzly bears by directing him to Hayden Valley and thence to Trout Creek dump. Matthiessen counted thirty-seven grizzlies as they lumbered in at dusk, scaring away the timid black bears. Soon they were brawling, hurling barrels of trash, and sniffing around the Ford convertible, "doubtless wondering whether the human contents, plucked out squeaking like a marmot, might not prove more wholesome, if less tasty, than the feast of offal all about."[42] The vision of grizzlies gorging on human garbage in the nation's premier national park was one of the most shameful spectacles he had ever seen.

Another day, driving down a lonely road in Indian country, New Mexico, Matthiessen noticed a hitchhiker and pulled over to offer a ride. The young man was Diné, and Matthiessen, always curious about Native people, began to ask questions as they drove. "White people are so eager to make contact, be liked, and so I went through all that stuff," he later recalled.[43] The man remained mute in the passenger seat, however, ignoring him as they sped through the desert. Perhaps it was shyness, or perhaps his English was poor, but the man also radiated hostility, which made Matthiessen uneasy. Unsure of what to do, he fell silent, too, and they remained that way, saying nothing, for hundreds of miles, all the way into Nevada. Suddenly the man tapped on the window with his knuckle; Matthiessen pulled up at a crossroads. The Diné man got out and walked away with no apparent destination. Matthiessen drove on, feeling embarrassed and guilty about the tense encounter: "I could not get that kid to warm up, and it bothered me." The "kid" had refused to assuage a white man's desire for connection, and Matthiessen would recall this as the moment he began to recognize the extent of his own ignorance, how "conditioned" he'd been by "stereotypes," how little he really knew about the Indigenous peoples of North America.[44]

AT WILDLIFE REFUGES, Matthiessen interviewed the U.S. Fish and Wildlife Service field staff. He spoke to, or corresponded with, oceanographers, ichthyologists, herpetologists, and mammologists at various museums, universities, and independent research institutes. Not being a trained scientist himself, he went to considerable lengths to consult the appropriate experts—including his own brother, Carey, now a marine biologist—which was a practice he'd maintain on nonfiction projects for the rest of his career.

Sometime toward the end of May 1957, he flew to Alaska. The territory had not yet joined the union as the forty-ninth state (that would happen on January 3, 1959), and Anchorage retained the character of a frontier outpost, however much it may have aspired to Main Street respectability with town chimes that played "Some Enchanted Evening." Matthiessen wandered through pawnshops stocked with snowshoes and hides, and drank in saloons thronging with oil prospectors.[45]

Roads were unreliable beyond the city limits, so he arranged with the Fish and Wildlife Service office to accompany its agents as they flew between scattered settlements and fishing camps. Light aircraft was a mode of traveling through the wilderness that was convenient but hair-raising, given the changeable weather conditions and frequent reports of accidents. "Pilots constantly crashed," Matthiessen later said, exaggerating only mildly: "They'd break a shoulder blade but walk off relatively unscathed."[46] He took his first flight down the Kenai Peninsula, spotted some moose, and managed to return to Anchorage in one piece.

At the town of Bethel, in southwest Alaska, he met an agent whose area of patrol, the entire Yukon-Kuskokwim delta, was larger than New England. It was a blustery day when they took off in a floatplane heading downriver toward the Bering Sea. Below, in Matthiessen's words, was "a remote, foggy world of dark tundra pools, bleak, faceless shore, and isolated volcanic peaks rising mysteriously above the waste"; he looked out the window and noticed the white tents of the Yupik people.[47] The plane's destination was Nunivak Island, a permafrost-covered wildlife refuge, where Matthiessen hoped to view the muskoxen that had been reintroduced there in the mid-1930s, from Greenland, after the original population was extirpated from mainland Alaska. But thick fog soon descended, and the pilot was forced down at the village of Quinhagak. After three days of being stranded ("eating the last pickled pigs' feet in the larder of the local missionary"),[48] they tried to reach Nunivak for a second time, with no more luck: though the coast was now so clear they could make out the white heads of emperor geese against the tundra, roiling mist offshore deflected the plane to a salmon station at Akulurak.

Having failed to reach the muskoxen, Matthiessen consoled himself by taking notes on the game agent's negotiation with the Yupik, whose subsistence lifestyle chafed against government rules about hunting. The agent confiscated a wolverine pelt that had been taken out of season, then gave the community a lecture on the Migratory Bird Treaty Act of 1918. The people responded by insisting they *needed* the geese to prevent starvation before the arrival of king salmon, which they caught in the river and dried on wooden racks. What were their children supposed to eat? "The agent counsels them obliquely against waste, repeats the letter of the law, and smiles," Matthiessen wrote. "Immediately the fishermen smile, too, and remember the pidgin English they had forgotten so long as his presence posed a threat. One asks him in a sing-song voice, 'Why is it the birds go away so many in the fall of the year, and come back to us so few?' "[49]

A few days later, Matthiessen arrived in Fairbanks, several hundred miles north of Anchorage, and caught a flight over the Brooks Range to Barrow (now Utqiaġvik) on the Arctic coast. Despite being a settlement of no more than a few thousand people, Barrow already showed "a certain sophistication," as he later put it: unsheathing his camera as he stepped off the plane, Matthiessen was met by Iñupiat locals snapping photographs of their own. He watched a dance, "Grandmother is Still Chewing Seal-skin," and poked through some handicrafts. Then he turned his attention to the ice pack, which had yet to retreat from the nearby shore.

Because the ground was frozen solid, the Barrow townsfolk were unable to dig holes to bury their tins and cartons and other inorganic waste. Instead, they discarded the garbage in heaps on the ice until it melted down through the crust, sinking to the bottom of the Beaufort Sea. Matthiessen wandered past mounds of refuse, including huskies that had been strangled to death with wire: "these are old, weak, inefficient or otherwise excess sled dogs, killed off each spring in the most economical manner in order that food not be thrown away on them over the summer."[50] Pressing on, he walked until the trash disappeared, the houses of Barrow diminished to a "tawdry" smudge on the horizon, and he found "that blue-white world of ice and sky."[51]

Nature, to Peter Matthiessen, represented a salve for the excesses of civilization. The great woods and clear rivers, the swamplands and grassy plains—these were a "non-material need" for anyone who felt hopelessly "entrapped by the apparatus of [their] own progress."[52] To walk in the wild was to be freed of that "apparatus," to shake off the encrustations of life in industrialized America, to feel the unencumbered self revert, at least for a moment, to a simpler state that was more real because it was also our original state.

Alone on the ice, he strode toward the open sea, "exalted" as he watched Arctic terns and guillemots overhead. Then his eye was caught by a flicker of color in a shallow ice pool. He headed for it, bracing to discover "some natural phenomenon of the far north."[53] But when he reached the edge of the pool, he gazed down in astonishment. In the water was the fleshy face of a movie star, Victor Mature, staring up at him—the underside of an ice-cream Dixie Cup, which had been flung out into the wilderness.

BACK IN NEW YORK, Matthiessen combined his field notes with a wide-ranging literature review that reached all the way back to the Saga of Erik the Red, from the thirteenth century. He sifted through early accounts of life in America for references to "smale birdes" and "wild beastes." He scrutinized claims by naturalists including Wilson and Audubon, Mark Catesby, Thomas Pennant, and William Bartram, who once forwarded the bizarre notion that "swallows, instead of migrating, [hibernate] in the mud of frozen ponds."[54] Matthiessen also examined the writings of James Fenimore Cooper, and musings about Nature and "wildness" by Emerson and Thoreau. He read classic testimonies by Lewis and Clark; by "Buffalo Bill" Cody, the hunter-turned-showman; and by Theodore Roosevelt, a "strenuous partisan of the outdoor life."[55] He surveyed everything from the history of the conservation movement—including the Echo Park Dam controversy—to the account of the man who rediscovered masked bobwhite quail, presumed extinct, in a cage behind a Mexican cantina, which had intended to cook them. Over weeks and months, *Wildlife in America* gradually took form as a prodigious feat of assimilated research.

"It is odd, one reflects after reading this book, that what it does has never been done before," Richard Pough, the ornithologist and founding president of the Nature Conservancy, wrote in an introduction. "We have long needed a historical survey that would give us the whole story of the white man's effect on wildlife . . . from the earliest records to the present day."[56] Much of the material Matthiessen collected had been available for years, but nobody had ever tried to arrange it into a comprehensive narrative that doubled as a critical natural history of the continent.

Wildlife in America tells many stories, but the most significant is a story of paradise lost. Precolonial North America,* as Matthiessen evoked it, not entirely accurately, was once a place of such unbroken wilderness that an "ambitious gray squirrel" could scamper across forests from the Atlantic to the Mississippi River "without ever setting paw to the ground."[57] (In fact, the forest was more like a patchwork quilt, with pieces missing due to fires, insect outbreaks, and human intervention.)[58] The ocean was swarming with whales, and there were so many passenger pigeons that they could darken the midday sky. Mountain lions, bobcats, and beavers—"a sedentary, civic-minded rodent"[59]—were widespread and abundant. Moose lived on Long Island, wolves on Cape Cod. Tens of millions of bison trampled the Great Plains in herds that were "almost certainly" the largest animal congregations anywhere on earth. Meanwhile, the Native people left few lasting signs of their presence, save for a few groups like the Puebloans in the Southwest; the rest, Matthiessen wrote, also with overstatement, "moved softly through the wilderness like woodland birds, rarely remaining long enough in one locality to mar it."[60] (The rotational "slash-and-burn" method of agriculture used by many tribes allowed the land to regenerate, but evidence suggests plenty of ground was also cleared permanently by Native groups.)[61]

Then the Europeans arrived. It is notable that one of the epigraphs in *Wildlife in America* is Jeremiah 2:7: "And I brought you into a plentiful country, to eat the fruit thereof and the goodness thereof; but when ye entered, ye defiled my land, and made mine heritage an abomination."

If North America was, in Matthiessen's telling, a new Canaan, the defilers have been numerous. Much of the book, which is arranged geographically and starts with the outlying Atlantic islands, is a catalogue of sins by waves of colonizers. Breton fishermen, in the early sixteenth century, sought cod in the cold waters off modern-day Newfoundland, and their "incidental persecution" of pelagic birds is what Matthiessen fingered as the first major act of European aggression against the animal kingdom.[62] After the Bretons, there were the Spaniards in *La Florida*, so anxious for gold that they barely took notice of the fauna except to eat it; and then the English, French, and Dutch, whose fur trades devoured beavers as a starter. The English colonists put bounties on the heads of wolves and cougars, and they cut down forests because they feared "the dark monotone of trees, the wild beasts and savages they concealed, the wind-borne, whispered reminder of wilderness unconquered."[63] As the frontier moved inexorably westward in the following centuries, across prairies, mountains, and deserts, so, too, did the violence: the shooting, trapping, poisoning, burning, clearing, fencing, and reckless

---

* Matthiessen defined this for his book as the continent north of the U.S.-Mexico border, including offshore islands and the oceanic islands of Bermuda.

collecting by oologists, who coveted rare eggs. In *Wildlife in America*, Matthiessen wrote elegies for the Carolina parakeet, the heath hen, the sea mink, and the Merriam's elk—all driven to extinction in "man's dark shadow." Of the once seemingly indestructible passenger pigeon, which disappeared forever in 1914, he wrote:

> The season, commencing in April, was profitable for only a month, and by June the markets were glutted, the pigeons were scattered, and the hunters had largely departed, leaving behind a rancid wasteland of ground white with guano, of broken trees, nests, eggs, and blue-feathered, fly-blown forms too shattered to ship, of starving squabs, of maggots and silent fur-clawed and beaked prowlers.[64]

The barely controlled disgust of this visceral passage[*] recalls an important precursor to Matthiessen's book: *Our Vanishing Wildlife: Its Extermination and Preservation*, by William Temple Hornaday. A former trophy hunter and taxidermist, Hornaday had become first director of the New York Zoological Park (now the Bronx Zoo) in 1896, as well as a combative, contradictory conservationist. Hornaday had thought nothing of shooting several of the last Great Plains bison to mount in a museum display, yet his efforts to breed the animal in captivity were instrumental in rescuing the species from oblivion. *Our Vanishing Wildlife*, published in 1913, was a strident, moralistic condemnation of American bloodlust. "To-day, the thing that stares me in the face every waking hour, like a grisly spectre with bloody fang and claw, is *the extermination of species*," Hornaday wrote. "To me, that is a horrible thing. It is wholesale murder, no less."[65]

Matthiessen read *Our Vanishing Wildlife* closely, and he found it an exciting and "excited" work, with Hornaday "not given to mincing his words."[66] He shared the older man's frustration, along with his belief in communal responsibility and the need for some sort of cultural atonement. But there were key differences between Hornaday's and Matthiessen's approaches that highlight what made *Wildlife in America* such a landmark in nature writing. Hornaday, for example, had focused exclusively on game animals in his book, from antelope to the whooping crane, and he placed much of the blame for

---

[*] A more elaborate version would appear more than three decades later in *Killing Mister Watson*, spoken by the character Bill House: "It's the dead silence after all the shooting that comes back today, though I never stuck around to hear it; I kind of remember it when I am dreaming. Them ghostly white trees and dead white ground, the sun and silence and the dry stink of guano, the squawking and shrieking and flopping of dark wings, and varmints hurrying with no sound—coons, rats, and possums, biting and biting, and the ants flowing up all them pale trees in dark snaky ribbons to bite at them raw scrawny things that's backed up to the edge of the nest, gullet pulsing and mouth open wide for the food and water that ain't never going to come."

their reduction on "gentleman hunters" and "gunners who kill to the limit." Matthiessen's vision was capacious enough to encompass rare, unsung species like the Devils Hole pupfish and San Marcos salamander; he understood, too, that the problems wildlife faced went beyond greedy hunters to include misguided government policy and the widespread use of industrial poisons. Hornaday was a shameless white supremacist who dedicated whole chapters to haranguing the "Italian and negro bird-killers." Matthiessen reproduced a petition from 1789, written by the Mohegans of Connecticut, that lamented how "the White People" had "turn'd everything upside down."[67]

Matthiessen also filled his work with references to ecology, the web-like relationships between organisms and their environments. This eluded Hornaday, but ecological concepts were not widely understood even in the late 1950s. Something that might seem self-evident today—"Forests, soil, water, and wildlife are mutually interdependent, and the ruin of one element will mean, in the end, the ruin of them all"[68]—would have struck some of Matthiessen's readers as startlingly novel. As would the words of Aldo Leopold, whom Matthiessen quoted, approvingly, years before Leopold was justly recognized as a prophet of environmental ethics: "Everyone knows that the autumn landscape in the north woods is the land, plus a red maple, plus a ruffed grouse. In terms of conventional physics, the grouse represents only a millionth of either the mass or the energy of an acre. Yet subtract the grouse and the whole thing is dead."[69]

Wildlife in America was groundbreaking for its content, but there is also the matter of its style. Here, Matthiessen likely owed a debt to Rachel Carson, whose sea trilogy—*Under the Sea-Wind* (1941), *The Sea Around Us* (1951), and *The Edge of the Sea* (1955)—he'd already read "with the greatest pleasure and admiration."[70] Carson, with her background in marine biology, had worked as an editor for the Fish and Wildlife Service before leaving to write full-time, and her work balanced scientific precision with a strong, open-minded lyricism that enabled her to range from cool analysis to moments of rapturous contemplation. Her goal as a writer, in the years before *Silent Spring*, was to show people a world that was "full of wonder," she said.[71] Her sea books succeeded at this by detailing the lives of marine creatures in glorious specificity, and by describing the ocean in often soaring terms: a place where man, "alone in this world of water and sky . . . feels the loneliness of his earth in space."[72]

In *Wildlife in America*, Matthiessen took a similar approach, deferring to science while also making room for moments of deep, philosophical reflection. But he shifted the emphasis from wonder to horror. In the arresting opening pages, for instance, the last pair of great auks are butchered by hunters Jón Brandsson and Sigurður Ísleifsson on the island of Eldey, near Iceland, in 1844, while a solitary egg is smashed to pieces by Ketill Ketilsson. Matthiessen imagines ("with misgivings") the gruesome final moments in a novelistic present tense that renders the scene immediate and unforgettable. The hunters hurl the dead birds into their longboat. Then they depart Eldey, "the hollow thump of oars against wood tholepins unreal in the prevailing fogs of June." Meanwhile, left behind, "the last, pathetic generation of great auks gleams raw and unborn on the rock." Gulls squall overhead, until they alight on the rock to yank at the "loose embryo." A fragment of shattered shell slips into the tide, spirals downward, and comes to rest on a ledge near a snail, *Littorina littorea:* "The periwinkle scours it, spits the calcified bits away. The current takes the particles, so small as to be all but invisible, and they are borne outward, drifting down at last to the deeps of the sea out of which, across slow eons of the Cenozoic era, the species first evolved."[73]

Wildlife in America thrums with the indignation of Hornaday, the ecological consciousness of Leopold, the scientific poetry of Carson. It builds upon a long tradition of nature writing, although Matthiessen was never fond of that label. "I think it's too narrow," he once said during a public conversation with the poet Gary Snyder; "and it's also too soft."[74] If the older, genteel nature writing—John Burroughs, Henry Beston—was largely descriptive, or "passive," as Matthiessen claimed, his work was intended as a vigorous call to arms. *Wildlife in America* marshaled politics, economics, philosophy, science, emotion, and an acknowledgment of Indigenous wisdom as it prodded readers to reconsider the needless destruction of an interconnected natural world. In this sense, the book was an early example of a new kind of nature writing that would begin to hit its stride in the following decade: *environmental* writing. From the start, Matthiessen clarified, he was always "an environmental writer, and an environmental activist," which, from his perspective, amounted to much the same thing.[75]

WILDLIFE IN AMERICA WAS PUBLISHED by the Viking Press in October 1959. It featured 150 line drawings of hawks, Gila monsters, and ungulates by the artist Bob Hines, who had also illustrated Carson's *The Edge of the Sea*. The endpapers—sketches, symbols, and animal totems—were borrowed from George Catlin, who had collected them from various Native groups during his own travels.

The book was a major departure for Matthiessen, but so elegantly executed that some family members suggested he give up on the novel writing to focus exclusively on nonfiction. Matthiessen refused; he was determined, he later told a friend, to keep writing fiction until he got it "right," so the world could see that he was "also a novelist."[76] Meanwhile, the reviews were almost universally effusive. At *The Atlantic Monthly*, Edward Weeks, who had given Matthiessen his break with "Sadie" in 1951, but then sniffed at the "disagreeable" *Race Rock* a few years later, hailed his nonfiction debut as "the first modern and comprehensive record of our wildlife."[77] Archie Carr, a herpetologist known for his work on sea turtles, praised it in *The New York Times* as "a dramatic, unsettling story, skillfully told," adding that "[i]f his book is as widely read as it deserves to be, our descendants may be much in debt to Peter Matthiessen."[78] Alfred Ames, in the *Chicago Tribune*, found it to be "an impressive and beautiful memorial . . . not sentimental or unfair."[79] And Rae Brooks, in *Harper's Magazine*, was moved by "the author's genuine love for every creature he writes about, by his sorrow at the loss of one, or his joy at the sight of another."[80] Roger Tory Peterson, the ornithologist whose field guides to birds Matthiessen had adored since childhood, praised *Wildlife in America*, much to Matthiessen's pleasure, as "the number one source volume for everyone who embraces the philosophy of conservation—for every ethical person who thinks about the future."[81]

One dissenting opinion appeared in *The Sacramento Bee*. The book was a fine work, wrote Philip C. Freshwater, but it was fatally damaged by Matthiessen's "intemperate" scolding. "He is so firmly on the side of the wild that he will not concede that man cannot, if he is to survive and develop his own life, permit the wild to go undomesticated." This was a curious line of critique that ignored much of the conservation movement, but Freshwater dug in his heels. The bison, "one of the most dangerous of American great animals," needed to make way if the country was to progress, he argued: "The railroads knew what they were about when they sent hunters out to destroy that wave."[82]

Behind the scenes, the National Audubon Society refused to endorse the book because Matthiessen had included passages that questioned the organization's conservation record, as well as discussions of some "unfortunate conflicts" involving key society members. The Audubon president, John H. Baker, felt *Wildlife in America* did not show the society "in the proper light," he explained in a note to Matthiessen, with "warm regards."[83]

But the most surprising reaction came from *Sports Illustrated*. The editors hated the Viking book, which failed, they said, to live up to the idea's "original promise." They also hated the draft articles submitted by Matthiessen a year in advance for his three-part series, which "did not satisfy" their requirements, even after revisions.[84] Stunned by the poor reception, Matthiessen reacted by sending another hotheaded letter about editorial subterfuge and the mistreatment of contributors who produce "excellent material." Richard Johnston, an assistant managing editor, replied with far less sympathy than William Shawn had managed to muster at *The New Yorker*. "I am forced," Johnston wrote, "to respond to your own estimate of the worth of the material with the blunt statement that in our opinion a single article was the most that could be gotten out of it—and that with some difficulty. I was surprised to find how easily checked the article was—there seemed to be very little new or original material in it."[85] Indignant, Matthiessen then retorted that his book had received "strong endorsements" from Rachel Carson and Edwin Way Teale: naturalists and writers who, "if I may emulate that bluntness on which, apparently, you pride yourself," were "infinitely better qualified" than Johnston to pass judgment.[86]

With that bomb detonated, *Sports Illustrated* published a single article, "Slaughter and Salvation," in November 1959. The other two pieces were killed, and Matthiessen was paid just 70 percent of the original contract fee. Unsurprisingly, he never wrote for *Sports Illustrated* again.

READING *WILDLIFE IN AMERICA* TODAY, one can't help but notice a few shortcomings and obsolete passages. Certain species that Matthiessen flagged as imperiled (the roseate spoonbill) are no longer considered so, while others he overlooked (the Hawaiian duck, or koloa) have since become endangered. When he wrote in the late 1950s, island biogeography and conservation biology did not yet exist, and neither did the term "biodiversity." Over the years, significant developments in the study of ecology have meant biologists now have a far better understanding of habitat loss and its effects on wildlife than the men and women who advised Matthiessen during his travels. His comments, too, about Indigenous Americans moving as softly through the landscape as "woodland birds," and about precolonial North America as an Edenic wilderness, have dated, though these were mistakes he confronted in later decades. In notes made for proposed revisions to a 1987 edition of *Wildlife in America*, for example, Matthiessen would acknowledge that some theorists—i.e., the geoscientist Paul Martin, with his overkill hypothesis—believe certain megafauna species had been hunted to extinction by early Native groups toward the end of the Pleistocene. As for North America as a new Canaan, Matthiessen would offer a revised take on this "great myth" in 1992: "The 'New World' was not new, not virginal, nor was it a wilderness when Europeans came. For the Native Americans it was home—profoundly loved, respected, and honored; its geography intimately known; and its bountiful resources put to use in knowing ways by people fully inhabiting its spaces."[87] Indeed, the idea of a "pristine realm" was little more than a fantasy used by European settlers "to justify and to sustain the seizure of North and South America from native peoples."

But what remains striking about *Wildlife in America* is its extraordinary prescience. A year before the 8.9-million-acre Arctic National Wildlife Refuge was established, in 1960, Matthiessen was calling the territory "a splendid chance to demonstrate that the hard lessons of conservation have been learned."[88] Three years before Carson published *Silent Spring*, he was warning about wildlife mortalities in areas sprayed with chlorinated hydrocarbons.[89] Five years before Congress passed the Wilderness Act of 1964, he was championing Howard Zahniser's visionary bill as "crucial."[90] Seven years before the International Union for the Conservation of Nature released its Red Data Book, with profiles of threatened or endangered animals around the world, he was offering a more localized version as an appendix: "The Rare, Declining, and Extinct Vertebrate Animal Species of North America North of the Mexican Boundary." In 1967, Secretary of the Interior Stewart Udall issued a list of threatened species in the United States, in response to a new Endangered Species Preservation Act; of the seventy-eight mammals, birds, fish, reptiles, and amphibians gathered on the list, Matthiessen had already sounded the alarm over twenty-four in his appendix.[91] An additional seventeen he flagged would be added to the federal list later, either before or after the Endangered Species Act of 1973, which his book predated by fourteen years.

In the decades since its release, *Wildlife in America* has been admired by writers, environmentalists, and scientists including Barry Lopez, Terry Tempest Williams ("a Bible for me"),[92] David Quammen, and David S. Wilcove, a professor of ecology at Princeton University whose own 1999 book, *The Condor's Shadow*, was a direct response to "one of the most insightful and eloquent books ever written about wildlife."[93] Today, *Wildlife in America* may be less known to general readers than *Silent Spring*, perhaps because of the forgettable title, and because animal deaths are less alarming to most people than the prospect of human ones, but Matthiessen's jeremiad has never lost its force. Nor, given the escalating wildlife crisis of the Anthropocene, has it lost its relevance. The Cornell Lab of Ornithology recently estimated that three billion birds have disappeared in North America over the last fifty years.[94]

"The finality of extinction is awesome, and not unrelated to the finality of eternity," Matthiessen wrote in a somber introduction that could well have been written yesterday:

> Man, striving to imagine what might lie beyond the long light years of stars, beyond the universe, beyond the void, feels lost in space; confronted with the death of species, enacted on earth so many times before he came, and certain to continue when his own breed is gone, he is forced to face another void, and feels alone in time. Species appear and, left behind by a

changing earth, they disappear forever, and there is a certain solace in the inexorable. But until man, the highest predator, evolved, the process of extinction was a slow one. No species but man, so far as is known, unaided by circumstance or climatic change, has ever extinguished another, and certainly no species has devoured itself, an accomplishment of which man appears quite capable. There is some comfort in the notion that, however *Homo sapiens* contrives his own destruction, a few creatures will survive in that ultimate wilderness he will leave behind, going on about their ancient business in the mindless confidence that their own much older and more tolerant species will prevail.[95]

9

Unsurveyed and Unfathomed

> So long as he kept moving he would be all right. For men like himself the ends of the earth had this great allure: that one was never asked about a past or future but could live as freely as an animal, close to the gut, and day by day by day.
>
> —*At Play in the Fields of the Lord* (1965)[1]

Toward the end of June 1958, while he was still working on *Wildlife in America*, Matthiessen traveled to Reno, Nevada, and rented an apartment for more than six weeks, which was the minimum length of time required before a bona fide "resident" could file for divorce. The process was complicated back home in New York, and certainly less fun: the divorce capital of the world, as Reno was then known, offered a full calendar of entertainments while people ran down the clock, including dancing, drinking, and gambling at establishments such as the Golden Nugget. Matthiessen made the most of an unusual vacation, then appeared in the Second Judicial District Court, alongside his attorneys, on August 5. The grounds given for divorce were that "the defendant [Patsy] had treated the plaintiff [Peter] with extreme cruelty; that all of the acts of extreme cruelty on the part of the defendant were without cause or provocation and caused said plaintiff intense mental pain, anguish, and suffering, and seriously interfered with and impaired his health."[2]

Patsy didn't travel to Reno or contest the divorce, the details of which had been worked out several months earlier. She may have questioned the charge of "extreme cruelty," but by the time the judge signed the decree, she had already moved on with Michael Goldberg, a second-generation abstract expressionist whose riotously colorful canvases were just beginning to garner critical attention. Patsy would be married to Mike (whom she met through Lee Krasner) by the end of the year, although it was an uncommon arrangement from the start. Mike Goldberg was close with Joe LeSueur and the poet Frank O'Hara; as LeSueur later recalled, the Goldberg marriage would represent "[a] new spin on Noël Coward's triangular *Design for Living*, a quasi ménage à quatre."[3] Joe and Frank became honorary (platonic) members of the relationship, two gay friends balancing out Mike's "rough manner and bravado," and offering a welcome antidote to the kind of misogyny Patsy had become used to, LeSueur said, "in heterosexual circles dominated by sexist, egocentric males who thought of themselves as, to use Patsy's most damning epithet, 'entitled.'"[4] Years later, Patsy herself explained the new arrangement like this: "I really kind of canceled the rest of my life and started up this one with Frank and Joe and Mike and the whole works. My life with Peter Matthiessen had been sort of Uptown, and I considered this a move to Downtown."[5]

Her children moved Downtown, too, for better and worse. Some of Luke's earliest memories would be of gleeful summer tomato fights with O'Hara, and of mixing cocktails, at the age of six or seven, under the poet's gentle tutelage. (The boy's drinks were *perfect*, O'Hara announced to a party featuring the painters Joan Mitchell and Norman Bluhm.) Luke's earliest memory of his actual father, by contrast, was of Peter driving through the Connecticut woods, looking distant and "rather stern" at the wheel.[6]

For his part, Peter had also started seeing other women in between his research trips. One story he liked to tell in later decades, a story that suggests just how casually he approached most of these post-Patsy romances, concerned a party in Roxbury, Connecticut, at the farmhouse of Bill and Rose Styron. It was the Styrons' fifth wedding anniversary, and Norman Mailer was in attendance. "Norman had to make his own splash because Norman was about *himself*, always," Rose recalled. "So in addition to planting himself outside the entrance to our house, in the bushes, every time a man came up, he would challenge him to arm wrestling before he could go inside."[7] At some point during the party, Matthiessen got into a heated argument with Mailer, trading insults "bullshit-young-novelist-competitive-braggadocio-style."[8] The suggestion was made that they step outside to settle their differences in "an amicable manner." Before the brawl could begin, however, the young woman Matthiessen had brought along as his date intervened to reprimand him for not paying her enough attention. Then, as Matthiessen recalled (perhaps omitting some salient details here), she dashed a glass of champagne in his face. "I didn't blink, I did not wipe off one drop of champagne, but simply looked right through her and kept on talking with Norman as if she were invisible, was not standing there at all, had never arrived to interrupt things."

As Matthiessen told it, Mailer was impressed by the performance of icy hauteur: "'Pretty cool,' he chuckled quietly. 'Pretty damned good.'"*

AFTER RENO, Matthiessen returned to New York, although he had no fixed address in the city, and a friend soon complained that it was almost impossible to keep in touch with him. It was, in fact, a period of experimental flux; everything was up in the air. Even Matthiessen's literary agent had changed because Bernice Baumgarten, not long after selling *Wildlife in America*, announced her retirement from Brandt & Brandt. "I was very tough with you because I think you're very good, and I didn't want you to get a swollen head," she'd told him at their final meeting toward the end of 1957.[9] Matthiessen was now signed with Diarmuid Russell, the cofounder, with Henry Volkening, of the prestigious Russell & Volkening literary agency at 551 Fifth Avenue. An affable, slightly disheveled fifty-six-year-old Irishman who knew as much about wildflowers as he did about publishing, Russell decided which writers to represent—Eudora Welty, most prominently—based on his instinctual sense of a person's character.[10] Russell was a far more freewheeling and sociable agent than Baumgarten had ever been, writing letters like: "Isn't it time you came up for air and gave me a call so that we could have lunch together?"[11]

When *Wildlife in America* was released in the fall of 1959, Matthiessen was working on *Raditzer*, his short novel inspired by memories of the U.S. Navy. Yet alimony and child support remained a pressing concern—he needed money to stay out of "debtor's gaol," he told George Plimpton, "with the key in the hard hand of Pat Goldberg"[12]—so he visited *The New Yorker* for another meeting with William Shawn. He now had a track record with the magazine: "Peut-être un Peu Excessif" had finally been published the previous November. And writing *Wildlife*, poking around the untamed corners of California and Alaska, had given him a new idea.

In Matthiessen's opinion, *The New Yorker* was too focused on what he called "over-civilized"[13] places, or "fleshpots."[14] He told Shawn that "everybody" was covering New York and the cities of Europe—an exaggerated claim that ignored, for example, Emily Hahn and Norman Lewis, who were filing stories as far afield as Belize, Malaya, and Ghana.[15] But the point he was trying to make had to do with wilderness. Like the forests and swamps of North America, there were natural places in the wider world that were

---

* Matthiessen certainly thought so; he repurposed the episode for his 1997 novel *Lost Man's River*, changing the setting to a poker game and the champagne into whiskey. A "thin scratchy" woman throws a glass of it into her husband's face: "Kept right on studyin the cards with the whiskey runnin off his cheeks like nothing happened, like that hard little blonde weren't even there."

increasingly threatened by economic development and industrial growth. "All these wildernesses are going downhill and nobody's paying any attention," Matthiessen argued.[16] If *Wildlife* had examined a so-called paradise after the fall, he now proposed to visit several that retained, in his view, a vestige of their prelapsarian splendor. "I wanted to see wild creatures, wild places, people, life unspoiled by pollution," he later told a journalist. "I've always had a longing for the primeval place, a primordial yearning for the lost paradise."[17] This was as much a personal project as a journalistic one— a chance, perhaps, to explore radical alternatives to the society that caused him so much dissatisfaction. To Matthiessen's surprise, William Shawn approved his proposal for multiple articles, which would eventually run in *The New Yorker* under the series title "The Last Wilderness." Worried that Shawn might change his mind if he had time to think the project over, Matthiessen quickly forwarded an ambitious provisional itinerary outlining five months of hard travel on planes, trains, buses, and freighter ships that would take him from backcountry Brazil all the way to the Belgian Congo in Africa.[18]

PETER HAD STARTED seeing a woman in Reno named Lisa Barclay Bigelow, a great beauty (she would model on the covers of *Vogue* and *Harper's Bazaar*) who'd been in Nevada to secure a divorce of her own. Lisa lived in New York, and on November 19, Peter took her and his two children to the Coney Island aquarium, which had recently installed an Amazon River scene complete with piranhas and live tropical birds. Along the way, they all stopped at Pier B in Red Hook to examine the MV *Venimos*, which would soon ferry Peter to the genuine Amazon. "I don't think I've ever been around the world," Luke said after hearing the plan.[19] Peter pointed out that his seven-year-old son was nevertheless a world traveler of sorts, having sailed from Italy on the *Andrea Doria*, which was now at the bottom of the Atlantic after sinking near Nantucket in 1956. Sara Carey, aged five, listened to this shocking news, then warned her father that he, too, would end up at the bottom of the ocean if he tried to go around the world, and sharks have "very sharp teeth." She did not believe he was really leaving on the MV *Venimos*. Peter could barely believe it himself, though he showed no sign of trepidation. The next day at the pier, he said goodbye to Bill Styron, who'd come to bid him bon voyage. Styron was struck by his friend's equanimity: "his spectacles planted with scholarly precision on his long angular face, he might have been going no farther than Staten Island, so composed did he seem, rather than to uttermost jungle fastnesses where God knows what beast and dark happening would imperil his hide."[20]

Traveling by freighter was already something of an anachronism in 1959.

Just over a year earlier, Pan Am had begun offering its first commercial flights on the Boeing 707 (New York to Paris Le Bourget), marking the start of the Jet Age in America. This development only encouraged what was already a booming tourism industry worth billions of dollars annually.[21] In pitching his series to *The New Yorker*, Matthiessen had taken advantage of the national hunger for all things foreign; but he never saw his own journey in the context of mass tourism. Instead, his reference points were nineteenth- and early-twentieth-century British explorers. While he squirmed at the word *expedition*—"I could scarcely apply that term to any trip sponsored by myself"[22]—it was old expedition accounts that he turned to for inspiration about South America: *The Naturalist on the River Amazons*, by Henry Walter Bates, published in 1863; and *The Sea and the Jungle*, by Henry Major Tomlinson, published in 1912. Bates had explored Amazonia over a period of eleven years, four of them with Alfred Russel Wallace, collecting specimens of more than fourteen thousand species along the way. Tomlinson had crossed from England to Brazil on a tramp steamer named the *Capella*, then meandered up the Amazon and Madeira Rivers, writing vibrant, often metaphysical descriptions of a "soft and benignant Eden."* For *The New Yorker*, Matthiessen positioned himself in the same tradition, albeit with a modern American sensibility. He would cite both men in his work, alongside others such as Colonel Percy Fawcett, the British explorer who'd vanished in 1925 while scouring the jungle for what he called the City of Z.

After a delay of more than five hours, at 8:32 p.m., a stevedore untied the last rope on the pier, and a tugboat nudged the *Venimos* away from the Brooklyn shore. In a large hardcover notebook with numbered yellow pages, Matthiessen made his first journal entry of the voyage. Manhattan loomed out of the harbor "like the Seven Cities of Cibola," he wrote, and as the lights slipped away he felt "a little homesick."[23] Later, when he typed up these notes on a new Olivetti Lettera 22 to be submitted to the magazine, he clarified his state of mind: "Now the tug is gone, and there comes a sense of uncertainty, of loss. This is not entirely homesickness; a continuity has been broken with the desertion of that tug, as if life must now start up all over again."[24]

THE MS VENIMOS, of the Booth Steamship Company, was built in Hamburg in 1956, and she now operated out of a home port of Hamilton, Bermuda. Two hundred and sixty-five feet long, she had a wide gray deck and a

---

* Matthiessen once claimed that Tomlinson's *The Sea and the Jungle* features "the finest writing of the sea to be found anywhere in English literature, Conrad included." While that may be debatable, it certainly features one of the best dedications: "TO THOSE WHO DID NOT GO."

white superstructure, with most of the cargo hidden in the hold: a tractor, oil machinery, storage batteries, shotguns, rifles, and a consignment of Christmas trees destined for Trinidad. "Since she sails under the British flag, there is a temptation to anglicize the pronunciation of her name," Matthiessen wrote in his notes, "to imagine a scurvy hulk crewed by Malays and Lascars, hatching dark, mutinous stratagems in the fo'c's'le."[25] Yet this Conradian fantasy was wide of the mark. The food was good, the facilities were clean (nothing remotely "verminous," he joked), and the crew of twenty-five Brazilian and British men were polite and professional.

The *Venimos* was Matthiessen's base for more than five weeks. The ship would visit Bermuda, Haiti, the Windward Islands, Barbados, Trinidad and Tobago, British Guiana, and the city of Belém, Brazil, before navigating some 2,300 miles up the Amazon to the Peruvian port town of Iquitos.

From the first morning aboard (November 21), Matthiessen set out to record absolutely everything he saw in page after page of a loose pencil scrawl. "At eight this morning, over one hundred miles from land, there were ten herring gulls still with us, and at nine-thirty there were, astonishingly, three times that many." He documented wind speeds, cloud formations, and the deepening hues of the Gulf Stream. The ship appeared "to shrink in size under the vast engulfing sky," he wrote. One stormy evening, he was thrown around his berth "like a sack of custard." Another day, two large porpoises of a "cafe-au-lait color" swam by the stern. Overhead was "great, sprawling Orion, and red Betelgeuse, Sirius flashing like an oncoming comet."

He was just as interested in the other passengers on the *Venimos*, of which there were only two. Matthiessen studied them each evening across the dining table, these men he would soon immortalize in a short story called "Horace and Hassid."* "Hassid"—a pseudonym Matthiessen adopted even for his journal—was a dour Lebanese businessman, on his way to Belém, who complained incessantly about everything in his life and suffered from terrible seasickness. ("He turns a frightening shade of puce, at which times the suspense is such that I scarcely dare to breathe.") Meanwhile, "Horace" was a Baptist missionary of the New Tribes Mission, heading back to the village of Orizona, in the Brazilian state of Goiás, after undergoing a hemorrhoidectomy in New York. Horace's real name was Clayton Templeton, who was a native of Virginia. He wore a clip-on pink bow tie to dinners, and had "an odd, gravelly voice" and shrieking laugh. Templeton believed in demonology, Matthiessen noted—"or rather, demons, a faith he has acquired from the people he has set out to 'evangelize.' He has seen the 'proof' among his

---

* A revised version of the story appears in *On the River Styx* (1989) under the title "Horse Latitudes."

flock (though of course he cannot accept as proof the scientific evidence for such theories as evolution). And after all, he says, Our Lord was forever casting demons out Himself. Nevertheless, his demonology seems bizarre, contrasting with his intense pride in his new modern American shortwave radio. He hunches over this by the hour, invoking friendly voices from every corner of the globe." Templeton's contradictions were fascinating to Matthiessen, who considered himself agnostic ("for want of a better word"); the men spent hours talking on board about the nature of faith.

At Port-au-Prince, Haiti, Matthiessen went to watch a cockfight—"a tiresome and disheartening affair"—and then wandered through streets that had been terrorized into silence by the Dark Ages regime of François "Papa Doc" Duvalier. Dominica and St. Lucia made more favorable impressions, and Barbados, where he took a taxi into the countryside past sugarcane mills, surprisingly reminded him of North Dakota "on a long, blue afternoon of summer." In Bridgetown, the *Venimos* offloaded 450 tons of grain meal collected in Haiti; Matthiessen passed the time drinking rum in waterfront dive bars. On the first evening, he asked a Barbadian prostitute to tell him her life story. On the second evening, he was talking to another woman in the same bar when an English crew member from the *Venimos* interrupted to call her a "damn black whore." Matthiessen lunged at the man, and they had to be pried apart. Afterward, he made a self-righteous note in his journal that was not quite the insight he thought it was: "There is something unpleasant about the English attitude towards the Negro, at least when it goes awry, for it hasn't even the excuse of fear and guilt and economic threat, as in our South, but is purely gratuitous."

The coast of South America finally came into view on the afternoon of December 12, heralded by the appearance of royal terns and laughing gulls. But it was another five days, "identical in tone . . . apathetic, humid," before Matthiessen felt any real stirring of excitement. "We are off the [Araguari] River, in the wild Brazilian state of Amapá, and soon the jungle silt, borne miles out to sea by the huge Amazon, will signal our arrival at its mouth."

IN MATTHIESSEN'S FIRST PUBLISHED dispatch from South America for *The New Yorker*, which would appear in the July 8, 1961, issue of the magazine, he explained his journey's aim like this:

> In the extent of its unknowns, Amazonas might be compared to western North America in the early nineteenth century. In places, the land behind the riverbanks has never been seen by any man—white, black, or copper—and there are still lost cities, lost tribes, and strange animals to be discov-

ered. It is one of the world's last stretches of wilderness, and, as an amateur naturalist, I am travelling up the river in the hope of seeing as much of it as I can."[26]

The first "strange animal" appeared in Belém, as he was returning to the *Venimos* after a tour of the Parque Zoobotánico. Matthiessen was in the street when a French Canadian hailed him to ask if he worked for an American oil firm with local offices. Broke and stranded in the sunburnt port city, the man was looking for a job to tide him over until he could reach Paramaribo, in Suriname, where he planned to find a ship heading to Europe. Matthiessen said no, he was not affiliated with any oil firm—but he offered the man a beer and "a dollar for his sorrows."[27] The former merchant seaman's name was Jean Jacques "Johnny" Gauvin. In *The New Yorker*, Matthiessen would call him "Picquet." In the novel *At Play in the Fields of the Lord*, he would become Meriwether Lewis Moon.

Gauvin was thirty-eight years old, tall, thin, and weak from a recurrence of malaria. During World War II, he told Matthiessen, he'd been traveling on a freighter and fallen overboard when a shipment of lumber shifted during rough seas near Trinidad. He'd floated for eight hours in the ocean, expecting to die, before he was miraculously rescued by the USS *Barney*, a Navy destroyer escorting convoys between the British West Indies and Cuba. Then, when he reached dry land, he'd written a letter to his wife back in Canada saying that he'd discovered something was missing from his life, and that she could have the house because he was never coming home again: "Goodbye." Since then, he'd roamed as a pilgrim; the previous three years had been spent in South America, where he'd passed through every country except Paraguay. The most "fantastic trip," he said, was a long hike through the trackless wilds of Panama and Colombia, down into Ecuador and Peru, where he was forced to evade "dangerous Indians" and "Negro + Carib renegades," who may have been cannibals. "I figure I have about thirteen lives and have used up about seven. That leaves me six to go."[28]

That evening, Matthiessen wrote three full pages about Gauvin in his journal. (He would include several hundred words about "Picquet" in the *New Yorker* article.) He was impressed with Gauvin's ability to whittle his existence down to a single shirt, a jackknife, a safety razor in a wooden matchbox, a plastic pouch for maps and his passport. Matthiessen felt that Gauvin embodied the most extreme example of a philosophical search— "what is the meaning of life?"[29]—that he'd ever encountered. Yet he was also unnerved by the drifter. Gauvin's "catlike" indifference to other people reminded him of the Diné hitchhiker he'd picked up in New Mexico while reporting *Wildlife in America*. "It's a disturbing quality, and one that induces a certain self-consciousness about one's eye-glasses, say, or the gleam of one's new khaki pants."[30] In the hardened gaze of Johnny Gauvin, Matthiessen saw himself reflected back as an effete, bespectacled WASP. He didn't much like what he saw.

BELÉM (PORTUGUESE FOR BETHLEHEM) is located on the Pará River, a channel of the Amazon delta separated from the main river to the north by the Switzerland-sized Marajó Island, which sits in the mouth of the Amazon, as Matthiessen observed, "like a huge cork."[31]

The *Venimos* spent two days offloading cargo in Belém. "Hassid" and Clayton Templeton also disembarked, and they were replaced by an elderly Dutch lady Matthiessen dubbed "Miss X" in his journal, along with five Catholic missionaries heading home to Manaus. One of the missionaries—the one suffering from dysentery—was installed as Matthiessen's cabin mate.

In the early hours of the morning on December 19, the *Venimos* pushed away from port to take advantage of high tide in the estuary. Matthiessen awoke after sunrise to find himself surrounded by shifting walls of green. It soon struck him, as he watched the banks, that little had changed here since H. W. Bates conducted his monumental study of Amazonia in the 1850s. Bates's descriptions corresponded with what he could see from the ship: the ceibas and rubber trees, egrets and river swallows, huts that were sagging and seemingly abandoned. This impression of continuity—of eternity—made Matthiessen emit "little squeaks of pure excitement."[32] He was exhilarated by a prospect of what appeared to be pristine land: "It is difficult to accept that a wilderness of this dimension still exists, that, despite our airplane and machines, we cannot really enter it but only skirt its edges."[33] (The Trans-Amazonian highway, slicing through the heart of the wilderness and opening it up to Brazilian settlers and their cattle, would not be completed until 1972.) Matthiessen was determined to remain objective in his observations of the river and rainforest, to offer *facts* to a reader, but "awe of the Amazon is emotional, not intellectual," he later wrote.[34] He couldn't help but harbor a little romanticism. "At twilight pairs of parrots hurry down the sky about the treetops, their flight trembling and swift. Then sudden darkness, and the jungle is a wall again, a black misshapen silhouette towering above us on both sides, as if the ship were passing down a canyon in the River Styx."[35]

On December 21, the *Venimos* drifted past the town of Santarém, which sits at the confluence of the Amazon and the Tapajós Rivers. He thought about Fordlândia, a rubber plantation that had been established on the Tapajós by the Ford Motor Company in 1928, and then abandoned after just six years. On December 23, the *Venimos* arrived at Manaus, which sits at the confluence of the Amazon and the Negro Rivers. Matthiessen noticed the gold-domed Renaissance revival opera house, an incongruous remnant of the 1880s rubber boom, now decrepit and flecked with overgrowth.

Finding himself with a free afternoon in Manaus, he hailed a taxi and asked the driver to take him into the wilderness. He wanted to touch what he'd been straining to see from the ship's deck for a week. The arrival, when he got out of the car, was abrupt: "In New England one walks quite gradually into a wood, but not so in the jungle. One steps through the wall of the tropic forest, as Alice stepped through the looking glass; a few steps, and the wall closes behind."[36] He was accompanied by Miss X from the *Venimos*, who, after peering around at the trees, proved insufficiently respectful, in Matthiessen's view, "for this sort of cathedral."[37] The woman expressed her delight with little squeaks, until she realized her companion had affected a trance state ("not wholly false") and was ignoring her.

Matthiessen admired the brown wood butterflies and tree frogs, the defiant song of an unidentifiable bird. He stood next to a tree trunk and felt "like an insect at the leg of an elephant."[38] But it was a sudden downpour of rain that brought the whole scene together. He spotted a water snake, its throat distended from a recent kill, slipping away beneath a tangle of vegetation. "At this moment the jungle came into focus for me; suddenly I could feel it, hear it, smell it, could believe I was really there."[39] This is what he wrote in his journal that evening. Later, however, when he typed up his notes for *The New Yorker*, the sentence was amended in a small yet revealing way: "I could feel it, hear it, and smell it, all at once—could almost believe I was there."[40] *Almost* believe. The Amazon was not only a physical destination; it was also something imagined, as it had been for many people over the centuries: an idea of primeval purity that receded even as Matthiessen reached for it.

CHRISTMAS DAY WAS SPENT listening to carols on the captain's phonograph, and singing with officers on the ship's afterdeck. While Matthiessen had come to consider the crew friends, on December 30, when the *Venimos* reached its final destination of Iquitos, he was not sorry to say goodbye after forty days and nights aboard. For the next segment of his journey, he planned to buy passage on a riverboat bound for Pucallpa, six hundred miles up the Ucayali River. No departure was scheduled from Iquitos for nearly a week, though, so he talked his way onto a Peruvian military transport plane.

In 1960, Pucallpa was a quiet trading post of mud streets and thatched roofs, populated in part by Shipibo women wearing elaborately embroidered skirts called *chitontis*. Matthiessen passed a few days consulting with local missionaries about dangerous animals of the Amazon: the piranha, bushmaster, and jararaca, a highly venomous pit viper. Then he had a memorable encounter at the Gran Hotel Mercedes. Sitting in the bar was a plantation owner named Vargaray—known locally, Matthiessen wrote, as an "hombre muy serio," meaning the man was not one to exaggerate his stories.[41] This description was worth noting down because Señor Vargaray made a truly extraordinary claim: there was a prehistoric fossil jaw, so heavy that half a dozen men struggled to carry it, lying in the selva near the Inuya River, a tributary of Peru's powerful Urubamba River.

Matthiessen was skeptical. "Jungle legends are, in the main, absurd,"[42] he later wrote, and these legends are "augmented at every opportunity, not only by the Indians and settlers, but by the adventurers of all nations who drift in and out of the towns on this huge frontier, and by incautious writers like myself who venture within hearing distance."[43] Nevertheless, Vargaray became agitated when Matthiessen expressed doubt. And his conviction was certainly "impressive."[44] A second man, a cattle rancher on the Urubamba named César Cruz, then came forward to vouch for Vargaray—and to tell Matthiessen about an untouched ruin on another, more distant tributary called the Picha. Cruz suggested they mount a search party to claim both the *mandíbula* and the lost city. Matthiessen, rightly recognizing that he was expected to foot the bill for this impromptu caper, demurred. "I explained what was true, that my sponsors [i.e., *The New Yorker*] expected me to go to Africa directly from Buenos Aires, where I was to arrive the following month."[45] Neither Cruz nor Vargaray took this objection very seriously; perhaps they sensed what Matthiessen would later confess to his journal: "a nagging doubt, a fleeting impulse to scrape up the money and plunge off into those imperturbable green walls."[46]

Cruz said he knew a Machiguenga man who could act as their guide. Matthiessen sat with an "ironic smile" on his face, committing to nothing.[47] Over the next few days, however, he drank with Cruz, who proved adept at appealing to an overactive imagination. By January 7, when Matthiessen caught a flight from Pucallpa to Lima, he'd contracted "jungle fever," as he put it, and decided not to go to Africa at all. "I've gotten so fascinated by the wilder areas of this mysterious continent that I feel I want to see them more completely," he explained to William Shawn. "The material is here in abundance, and it is simply a question of determining how best to make use of it."[48] The letter to his editor contained a revised itinerary for the magazine's approval—an itinerary that struck Africa, and that included cryptic reference to a voyage "into the Amazon headwaters on a small boat," to happen sometime in spring, though this was "by no means certain as yet."

FOR THE NEXT SEVEN WEEKS, Matthiessen became exactly what he'd wanted to avoid in South America—a tourist. He lunched with dignitaries at an embassy in Lima, and swam in the pool of a private club named Waikiki. He visited Cusco in the Andes, comparing the "vulgar" colonial monuments to the Incan ingenuity at Sacsayhuaman. He crossed Lake Titicaca on a paddle steamer to reach La Paz in Bolivia, then made his way down to Argentina. He caught up on writing in Buenos Aires, which he likened to a poor man's Paris, before exploring the enormous region of Patagonia. He would later submit an article to *The New Yorker* about his travels in the Argentine province of Tierra del Fuego, at the southernmost tip of the continent, but it lacked the general interest and uncanny atmosphere of his "Amazonas Journal," and William Shawn killed it.

By the start of March, Matthiessen had circled up around to Brazil again. The second piece that Shawn did accept, titled "Brazilian Chronicle" (printed in the August 12, 1961, issue), was based on a tour through the relatively unpopulated states of Goiás and Mato Grosso.

From the federal capital of Brasília ("a brave new city cunningly disguised as a World's Fair"),[49] which was just six weeks out from its official inauguration, Matthiessen caught a bus southwest to Goiânia, then another heading east to the adobe brick village of Orizona, where Clayton Templeton lived and proselytized. The Baptist missionary from the *Venimos* was not expecting to see his recent travel companion, and they ran into each other at a transfer depot four hours outside Goiânia. Matthiessen then followed Templeton on errands all the way back to Anápolis, beyond Goiânia, before they returned once again to Orizona together. Along the way, Templeton encouraged his guest, who had gotten into a violent argument with a stranger in Brasília, to start carrying a gun if he planned to poke around the backcountry.

This unannounced visit was ostensibly about collecting information on the wildlife and Native people of the Brazilian interior. But Matthiessen was curious about the New Tribes Mission, too, which was financially supported by "various American Protestant sects."[50] Templeton lived with his wife and four children (a fifth was studying in the U.S.) in a large, converted store, one room of which was set aside as a rudimentary chapel. On the roof were two loudspeakers that Templeton had mounted to blare Baptist propaganda at the townsfolk, who, if they were any kind of Christians, tended to be Catholic, owing to the even more aggressive tactics of the opposition.

Matthiessen spent three days shadowing Templeton. He also accompanied Clayton's son, Vance, into the countryside on house calls. Matthiessen had no illusions about their evangelizing project. In his piece for the magazine, he would include a discussion with one candid missionary, Otto Austel, who admitted that (as Matthiessen paraphrased) "exposure of a primitive tribe to missionaries, however successful it may be . . . is followed more often than not by the tribe's extinction, through the subsequent exploitation, mixed breeding, alcohol, and disease that arrive, not with the advent of the Word but with the advent of civilization."[51] This was a damning assessment. Yet Matthiessen was never directly critical of the Templetons, and at moments he was even equivocal about their presence in Orizona. Clayton had been in the village for two years and amassed a following of forty-two believers. Matthiessen watched a meeting of the congregation and found himself at a loss: "It was hard to know what to make of the whole business, except that the Templetons took the villagers and their poverty seriously, and the villagers knew it."[52]

Perhaps another motivation for Matthiessen's visit was his own uncertainty around belief. He may have been compelled to seek out Templeton because their conversations on the *Venimos* had probed a source of the dissatisfaction in his own life: what the purpose of it was; what it really meant. It was confusing to have strangers praying for his soul in Orizona. "I kept thinking of Albert Camus"—who rejected religion for its attempts to impose meaning on the absurdity of existence—"with not quite such sympathy as usual, and without coming to any conclusions, either."[53] The faith of the missionaries was so strong and unwavering that Matthiessen found himself wondering if *he* was the deluded one with his stubborn existentialism.

After a few days in the village, he went with the Templetons to an airstrip back in Anápolis, where he'd arranged to catch a plane to a settlement on the Araguaia River. The pilot, another American, named George Glass, asked him to lead them all in a customary prayer before takeoff. Surprised, Matthiessen refused, saying he was unqualified; but then he felt "a sudden sense of inadequacy," and uncertainty, which he confided to his journal: "How serene these people are! As if religion were a state of shock, deep peaceful shock, that good men are driven to by the spectacle of life—or is it we, on the other cliff of the abyss, who do not want to give ourselves over to a higher power? For certainly . . . all temporal ambitions are insane. Yet I, for one, cling to them."[54] How *not* to "cling"? How to let go of "insane" worldly ambitions? How to confront the "spectacle of life" without retreating into reassuring stories? These were questions for a later date, though they were beginning to take shape in Matthiessen's mind.

George Glass flew him to the mission station at Macaúba. There, Matthiessen observed the Karajá people, who, despite the best efforts of the missionaries, maintained traditions like witchcraft and shamans. On this point, Matthiessen empathized with the Karajás; their "superstitions" seemed no more "incredible" than the holy miracles of Jesus Christ they were being asked to believe in instead.[55] Watching a group dance in the moonlight, he was stirred by the ecstatic movements of men in straw masks that represented the spirits they'd worshipped for countless generations.

Back in the Cessna, Glass navigated over the territory of a tribe that Matthiessen noted down as the "savage Canueiras."[56] (It is not clear which group he was referencing: "Canueira" is not a name in common usage.) Although these people were rumored to be violently hostile toward outsiders, Glass had never seen any trace of them on his missionary air runs. Now, however, he and Matthiessen peered out the window and spotted something down below: a hut in a clearing on the edge of a slough. Delighted at the prospect of potential new converts, Glass made several circles in the plane. But there was no sign of movement in the clearing, only a "breathless stillness," Matthiessen wrote, "as if the jungle here were petrified."[57]

A violent rainstorm erupted. Glass detoured west to escape a barrage of hail. When the low mountains of the highlands appeared in the distance, he turned the controls over to his passenger for a stretch. "I fly her south uncertainly," Matthiessen noted, "unable to get that one hut in the Canueira country out of my mind."[58] The silent clearing and its mysterious inhabitants, along with much of what he'd seen and struggled to process during his time with the Templetons—all this would reappear, carefully fictionalized, in *At Play in the Fields of the Lord*.

TEN DAYS LATER, in Lima, Peter was reunited with Lisa Barclay Bigelow, who had flown down from New York via Miami to see him. He suspended his journal as soon as she arrived in the city, which makes it impossible to know what they did for the next two weeks. The vacation concluded, however, with their amicable breakup after more than eighteen months of seeing one another. "[O]ur last week together, in Peru, was a very moving one, and ironically—these things are so pathetically ironic—we have never been closer, in a way," Peter wrote to George Plimpton.[59] Lisa wept at the airport, then poured out her feelings in a farewell letter written on the flight home. "Darling Peter, it breaks my heart—We don't reach each other in time—I see you suffering & stand by gaping."[60] Feeling depressed, he had woken her up to talk during their final night together. "I could only mumble," Lisa wrote in apology. But Peter barely understood how to handle these volatile moods either, or even what they signified. "I still seem to be pathologically restless in some way," he confessed to Plimpton, "and am no fit mate for anybody."[61] As soon as a woman got too close, he was overcome with an urge to push her away, or to run away himself.

IN 1961, Viking would release *The Cloud Forest: A Chronicle of the South American Wilderness*, which combined expanded versions of Matthiessen's *New Yorker* articles with material the magazine never published on his peregrinations in the Andes and down through Patagonia. The book was well received by critics: Matthiessen was compared to H. M. Tomlinson, as well as Peter Fleming, author of the 1933 classic *Brazilian Adventure* (and older brother of Ian Fleming). *Kirkus* called *The Cloud Forest* "an adventure story of the highest order," which shows "an experienced understanding of people and a fluid knowledge of the subject at hand."[62] Thomas Foster, writing in the *New York Herald Tribune*, thought it deserved "as long a life as the records of such earlier naturalists as Darwin, Bates and Hudson, who observed so much of South American wildlife in the last century."[63] Reviewing for *The New York Times*, Marston Bates, a zoologist who'd spent nearly a decade living in Villavicencio, on the eastern slopes of the Colombian Andes, said Matthiessen had shown "extraordinary perception": "[N]owhere in 'The Cloud Forest' did I come across a false note, or find occasion to raise my eyebrows at the reactions of a gringo tourist."[64]

None of the reviews pointed out the ethnocentrism in Matthiessen's account, though perhaps that is not surprising. When he described himself as a "hard-eyed modern" observing people who "until quite recently lived in the world of darkness and inarticulate fears,"[65] he was reproducing a view of the world that would have seemed natural to many American readers at the start of the 1960s. Alongside discussions of flora and fauna, *The Cloud Forest* features references most people would now consider racist—to "backward countries"[66] and dirty villages; to the "rapt faces" of "halfbreeds on the steaming bank";[67] to Indians who "can sleep standing up, like horses";[68] to Quechua who look "more slack-jawed and brutish than the most primitive man imaginable."[69] One of the reasons Matthiessen went to South America was to report on communities that were being steamrolled by misguided attempts to "develop" them.* He wrote about vanishing tribal practices, like facial tattoos; lamented the ruinous impact of alcohol on Native communities; and acknowledged the "fine" legacy of Cândido Mariano da Silva Rondon, a Brazilian colonel who'd spent much of his life condemning the extermination of Indigenous Brazilians. But Matthiessen had not yet confronted the extent of his own ingrained prejudices or his relationship with colonialism; nor had he recognized the limitations of relying on testimo-

---

* According to a statistical report published by Shelton H. Davis in 1957, more than eighty Indigenous tribes that had come into contact with "Brazilian national society" had been deculturated and destroyed since 1900. The population of Indigenous people during that same period plummeted from around one million to less than 200,000. Six tribes became entirely extinct due to agricultural expansion.

nies from people who looked exactly like himself. In "Brazilian Journal" for *The New Yorker*, he painted a nuanced, complicated portrait of the American missionary at work. He barely spoke to the Karajás, whose voices remained notably absent from his narrative.

In the decades since *The Cloud Forest* was published, one thing critics have pointed out is the significant tonal shift of the final section. The first two-thirds of the book, which cover everything up to Matthiessen's return to Lima (and Lisa), can be categorized as travel writing: aimless and impressionistic; a loosely structured assemblage of wry observations about whatever happened to cross the writer's field of view, from a morpho butterfly to a Bolivian insurrection. The last third of the book is something else entirely, however: a quest that takes on almost mythic overtones, like a hunt for the Holy Grail.

On April 8, Matthiessen flew from Lima back to Cusco. He'd decided to pursue the mandíbula and the rumored ruin on the Picha River, even though one of Peru's leading archaeologists, Rafael Larco Hoyle, told him the stories were probably false, and even though *The New Yorker* had yet to approve expenses for the outlandish digression to replace the Africa portion of his original itinerary. The plan was to join César Cruz, the rancher he'd met in the Pucallpa bar, at the confluence of the Urubamba and Yanatili Rivers. Matthiessen, Cruz, and a posse of Cruz's men would then descend the Urubamba in a small boat and canoe, passing through the fearsome rapids of the Pongo de Mainique, until they reached the Picha ruin; then, via a circuitous loop, they would scoop up the bone from the banks of the Mapuya tributary. The plan represented close to a thousand miles of remote river travel in Peru. In the clear sky high above the mountains, as Matthiessen approached Cusco, he wondered if he "had not lost my mind." The only comfort was the prospect of seeing the jungle up close "at last," which had "become important to me."[70]

Matthiessen was accompanied by Andrés Porras Cáceres, the brother of a friend in Lima who'd helped arrange some of the trip's logistics. Porras Cáceres would act as Matthiessen's interpreter and adviser. A "jungle veteran," he lent his partner a .38 revolver because, as Matthiessen put it, "one is never certain what manner of unfriendly beast one may encounter in the selva."[71] After three days of further outfitting in Cusco (snakebite medicine, malaria pills, machetes), the two men left to travel via Machu Picchu to Quillabamba.

Predictably, Cruz was nowhere to be found at the confluence of the Urubamba and Yanatili. Rather than abort the operation, though, Matthiessen walked for more than seven miles to the hacienda of a man named Lugarte, hoping to hear some encouraging news. Señor Lugarte advised him that the river was too dangerous to navigate in the wet season ("muy bravo, muy feo"), with the water the highest he'd ever seen it. "Though every other piece of information we had received had so far proved to be questionable or mistaken, I found this report extremely discouraging," Matthiessen wrote.[72] Yet Porras Cáceres, who was no stranger to river rapids, dismissed the warning as ignorance. So he and Matthiessen joined another landholder in an overloaded canoe, bailing water as they went, on the chance that Cruz might be waiting for them further downstream.

Matthiessen's account of everything that transpired from that point onward, an account that covers more than a hundred pages in *The Cloud Forest*, is increasingly deranged. At the mission of Coribene, a Dominican priest reaffirmed to the travelers that the river was unnavigable. Again, Matthiessen and Porras Cáceres pushed on anyway—the prospect of retreat was too humiliating—at first by the canoe, and then on foot. Porras Cáceres, in his early sixties, soon complained of a twinge in his heart; Matthiessen contemplated what it would mean to bury a body in the rainforest. After three grueling days of clambering through the overgrowth, with nights a torment of chicken lice, flies, and mosquitoes, they arrived at another hacienda. Several locals agreed to construct an eighteen-foot raft for them out of six balsa logs and lianas. Matthiessen christened this makeshift craft the *Happy Days*—"in a desperate attempt to amuse myself at this ominous moment."[73] On April 18, the *Happy Days*, steered by a Machiguenga man named Agostino, entered the Pongo de Mainique, a dark, sheer canyon characterized by Class III and IV rapids. "It is true that the approach is a magnificent sight," Matthiessen later wrote, "as the Gates of Hell must be, and the gaunt rocks and high waves at the entrance made a marked impression on me, to be sure, but after that I had but a tenuous grasp on my aesthetic vision. I don't say that everything went haywire, but my outlook was decidedly blurred, even when my head was not submerged."[74]*

Once safely through the rapids, the party abandoned the balsa raft at another mission populated by around forty Machiguengas. Matthiessen observed these "mission Indians" in their elevated huts and "cheap factory shirts," then reflected on the dispiriting contrast they made with the three "smiling, graceful boys" who'd just guided him through the Pongo—young

---

* In 1981, Werner Herzog traveled to the Pongo de Mainique to film key scenes for his film *Fitzcarraldo*. Herzog had visited Matthiessen in Sagaponack prior to the shoot—an awkward lunch that saw the director peeling off his shirt to exhibit a tattoo of Death crooning into a vintage microphone. While on location in Peru, he sent Matthiessen a letter saying that he thought often about *The Cloud Forest*, specifically the vivid description of the Pongo; and marveling at how insane it was that he (Herzog) was now trying to navigate an enormous steamboat across the rapids for his movie. Matthiessen did some light polishing on the *Fitzcarraldo* screenplay, and Herzog thanked him in the credits.

Erard "Matty" Matthiessen.

Elizabeth "Betty" Bleecker Carey.

Matty and Betty on their honeymoon in St. Moritz, Switzerland, 1924.

From ACME Newspictures, 1930: "Mrs. Erard Matthiessen, of New York society, pictured with her children, (left to right) Mary Seymour, George Carey, and Peter, as they spent the Labor Day holiday at the Fishers Island Club, N.Y., exclusive summer resort."

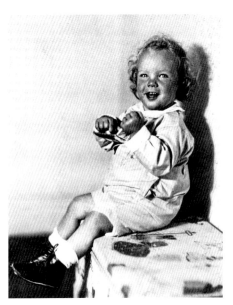

PM as an infant.

Carey and PM.

PM outside the Irvington house designed by his father, c. 1933.

Inga the Great Dane stands watch while PM and Carey duel.

Matty and his children aboard the *Puddleduck* at Fishers Island.

Baseball at the St. Bernard's School in New York, c. 1936.

PM's school photo at Hotchkiss, where he was known, among other names, as "Lucky Pierre" and "The Curly God."

Carey poses with a snake from the Matthiessen brothers' collection.

PM on the private Fishers Island family beach.

The Matthiessens outside their colonial house in Long Ridge, Connecticut, near Stamford—home from 1937.

The family war effort, 1945: Mary, between PM and Lieutenant Commander Matthiessen, is dressed as a nurse's aide.

PM's United States Navy ID card.

USS *Joseph T. Dickman*.

At the South Seas Club, Honolulu, which PM later fictionalized in *Raditzer* (1961): "They sat at the best table behind huge exotic drinks . . . and listened to songs like 'Princess Papooli Has Plenty Papaya.'"

PM's yearbook photo at Yale.

On horseback at the Greenwood Plantation in Thomasville, Georgia, December 1946. The photo was kept in a locket by Payne Whitney Payson.

Wendy Burden, PM's first serious girlfriend, 1947. "He was clearly too young to marry and was dedicated to starting his writing career," Wendy later recalled in a memoir.

Class of the Junior Year in France, 1948. PM is back row, fourth from the right.

Blair Fuller, an unknown friend, and PM with the bullfighter Antonio Ordóñez Araujo. Spain, 1949.

The Running of the Bulls in Pamplona: "The stupidest thing other than the Marine Corps I'd ever done," said Tom Guinzburg, who ran alongside PM.

Patricia "Patsy" Southgate, c. 1949.

PM and Patsy engaged, 1950.

PM and the *Maudite*, which he navigated from Nova Scotia to Massachusetts in the summer of 1950, trying to save his engagement.

Just married, with PM recently recruited into the CIA, in 1951.

Literary expats in Paris: Richard Wright, PM, and Max Steele, c. 1952.

Harold Louis "Doc" Humes Jr.

George Plimpton and William Pène du Bois—two of the founders of *The Paris Review*—with the writer Evan S. Connell.

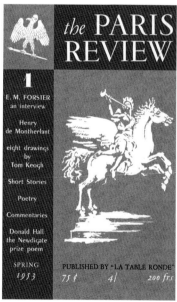

The Paris Review, No. 1, Spring 1953.

PM's card as a charter boat captain.

PM and William "Porter" Styron in Ravello, Italy, July 1953.

Haul-seining on the beaches of the Hamptons, c. 1955. PM is standing in the dory, back to camera.

With Lucas—"Luke"—and Sara Carey, his children with Patsy.

Patsy in Springs.

PM in Nevada with a pronghorn fawn, 1957.

Agostino steers the *Happy Days*, a balsawood raft, down the Urubamba River in Peru, April 1960.

Great Auk, by John James Audubon, an extinct species memorialized by PM in *Wildlife in America* (1959) and *Seal Pool* (1972).

PM, César Cruz, and the fossilized jaw of *Purussaurus brasiliensis*, dating to the late Miocene epoch, April 1960.

The Harvard-Peabody New Guinea Expedition, 1961. Standing from left: Polik and Wali, two Dugum Dani men; Navas; Wamamogen; Abututi; and Jusup Kakiay, the cook. Seated from left: Robert Gardner, expedition leader; Jan Broekhuijse; Eliot Elisofon; PM; Michael Rockefeller; and Karl Heider.

Eliot Elisofon takes a photo of Yosup, with Jan Broekhuijse (speaking) and Michael Rockefeller.

The Dugum Dani rush to meet their enemy on a grassy battlefield at the Warabara frontier.

PM's home in Sagaponack from 1960.

Deborah Love, c. 1964. "She has no mud on her soul," a friend remarked.

Deborah and PM.

PM with Rue, Deborah's daughter, whom he adopted, and young Alex.

With a muskox on Nunivak Island, Alaska, August 1964. Muskoxen "appear from the air like great boulders rolling, sprung to life out of the dark clay of the land," PM wrote in *Oomingmak* (1967).

Rue, Luke, and a despondent PM in County Galway, Ireland, August 1965.

PM and Alex at the Castello di Polgeto, in Umbria, Italy, c. 1968.

PM, Deborah, and a friend protesting the Vietnam War at one of the many public demonstrations during the 1960s.

Cesar Chavez breaking bread (after a 25-day fast) with Robert F. Kennedy, March 1968, less than three months before Kennedy was assassinated.

Ann Israel and PM talk to Cesar Chavez in Delano, California, August 1968. PM considered Chavez his "great hero"—a leader capable of ushering in a new American ethic that would turn people from consumers into citizens.

At work on *The Tree Where Man Was Born* (1972) in Tanzania, 1970.

PM suits up for the filming of Peter Gimbel and James Lipscomb's *Blue Water, White Death* (1971).

Divers during the *Blue Water* expedition, off the coast of South Australia, January, 1970. "I touched the massive thing," PM wrote of the great white shark: "it was like stroking one's own corpse, a spiritual, even metaphysical meeting."

men who, as far as Matthiessen could tell, were still following the old ways of their people.[75]

After acquiring a motorized canoe, Matthiessen and Porras Cáceres continued more than a hundred miles downstream to César Cruz's stud farm. Cruz was not exactly thrilled to see the American writer; he offered a feeble excuse for his absence back at Quillabamba. Nevertheless, Matthiessen had already paid Cruz an advance to cover the expedition costs, so a new agreement was now reached. They abandoned the idea of finding the Picha ruins in favor of heading straight for the mandíbula, on the nearby Mapuya River. The party set out in a canoe carved from a single forty-foot log, and they arrived at the site on April 26.

The fossil was real. "It appears to be the small upper jaw of an enormous herbivore," Matthiessen wrote (incorrectly) in his journal, "though of what age, and whether mammal or dinosaur, I am not equipped to say."[76] *Small* was an odd adjective to use given that, at twenty-four inches in diameter, the jaw was sizable enough for him to photograph Cruz sitting on it like a throne.

The men toasted the fossil with glasses of pisco and Peruvian vermouth. Yet this was not, as presented in *The Cloud Forest*, the true climax of Matthiessen's quest. That came the following morning when he set off to visit the place where Juan Pablo, an Indigenous man employed by a friend of César Cruz's, Victor Macedo, had originally found the fossil before it was lugged two miles down to the Mapuya riverbank. Matthiessen poked around a pristine stream, Quebrada Grasa, named after the natural oil that oozed out of its mud:

> Its still banks are laced with the tracks of tapir, capybara, and other creatures, and its clear water, running quietly on sandy shoals, sparkles with the flash of the pretty *sabalo*. In the bends the water runs beneath stone banks and is a pure, limpid green, and the trees which lend their leaf color to the water soar away in great white columns. . . . We paused to breakfast on a kind of nut, the Indian name for which has now escaped me, and I wondered why the stream itself was so much more exciting than the bones we had found in it—more exciting than the first sight of the great jaw itself the night before. And it occurred to me that, aside from the beauty—for it is precisely this inner, mysterious quality of the jungle, represented so well by this lost stream, that I have been searching for and feel I have found at last—there was an adventure here, an exploration, however timid.[77]

What to make of this striking passage from *The Cloud Forest*? In both the fiction and nonfiction of Peter Matthiessen, a reader stumbles repeatedly over references to a search for the lost paradise. But there are also moments when Matthiessen—or one of his protagonists—seems to *find* paradise, however fleetingly. These landscapes were sought out and celebrated by the writer for their "primordial" quality, civilization having yet to leave any indelible stains. As he wrote of Quebrada Grasa: "there is no mark of the white man's heavy hand upon it."[78] But paradise was more than just an unspoiled physical place; it was also the way these places made him *feel*. Paradise was a state of being. In paradise, Matthiessen believed, one can shed the illusions of ego, which is why he sometimes likened it to a return to earliest childhood. To be lifted into paradise, as one is lifted into awe upon glimpsing the sublime, is to experience the world once more as a young child does: directly, immediately, without the heavy burden of identity. In 1978, he would explain his idea in a slightly different way during a lecture titled "Literature and Mysticism":

> The Huichol Indians . . . of the western Sierra Madre, in Mexico, return each year to a sacred plateau, which is their paradise—a place beyond history, where linear time has not yet begun, a place where they can find their lives, refine their lives. Here, they say, "All is one; it is unity; it is ourselves." But most of us have no place outside ourselves where we may go to be reborn, renewed. And so we are filled with an obscure longing, all the more frustrating because it cannot be expressed.[79]

That "obscure longing" would remain a major preoccupation throughout the rest of his life. Yet in a place like the "lost stream" of Quebrada Grasa, the longing was briefly alleviated. The notion of "Peter Matthiessen" became meaningless in the depths of the Amazon rainforest. Unburdened of himself, a complicated man felt, at least for a moment, blissfully simple.

JUAN PABLO WAS PAID 530 soles for his discovery of the mandíbula. The fossil was loaded into the bow of Cruz's canoe, and the party set out to find the Ucayali River, which would carry them north to Pucallpa and the bar of the Gran Mercedes Hotel, bringing the expedition full circle.

When they reached Pucallpa on May 2, César Cruz was notified that Victor Macedo had registered a charge of theft with the police: Juan Pablo worked for *him*, Macedo said, and the fossil was rightfully his because it was discovered on the job. This was an unwelcome development, and Matthiessen spent a week in Pucallpa trying to mediate between Cruz and Macedo. As a distraction one evening with Cruz, he also sampled the psychedelic "jungle potion" ayahuasca, writing a minute-by-minute account of the experience, which started slowly (9:30 p.m.: "a vague disquietude, if that's a word") and then escalated into something so strange and revelatory it would soon inspire further experimentation with mind-altering drugs (10:20 p.m.: "Time for stomach pumps—BRING ON THE PUMPS, SHE SCREAMED, AND PUMP THE BEJESUS OUT OF ME").[80] At the end of the week, relations between Cruz and Macedo still at an impasse, Matthiessen threw up his hands and booked a flight home. His South American odyssey was over.

When "Peruvian Journal," detailing the dramatic voyage of the *Happy Days*, appeared in *The New Yorker* the following year in September, it included this "POSTSCRIPT":

> I have taken the photographs of the giant mandible to the American Museum of Natural History, where Dr. Charles Mook, the Museum's senior authority on fossil reptiles, has inspected them and tentatively identified the former owner of the jaw as a very large crocodilian that, in Dr. Mook's opinion, inhabited the earth at some period between five million and twenty-five million years ago. He was much interested in the discovery of this creature, which represents a species heretofore unknown to him, and said that the Museum would very much like to see the fossil and would pay for its shipment from Peru if I could obtain permission for its export.
>
> I have written a number of inquiries to Peru, where César Cruz has since become the defendant in a suit brought by his former friend Macedo, and where the ownership of the bone itself has been obscured for good under a mass of documents and memorandums. But for the written testimony of Allen Ginsberg [the poet, who, embarked on his own South America travels, visited Pucallpa not long after and wrote to Matthiessen about the "excellent monstrous fossil" impounded by the police], I might almost believe that the whole adventure of the jaw was the very sort of jungle hallucination against which I have often been warned. "Between the outer world and the secrets of ancient South America," the famous British explorer Colonel P. H. Fawcett once lamented, "a veil has descended." It now appears that the giant *mandíbula* will remain behind it, sinking slowly beneath man's detritus on the steaming banks of the Ucayali.[81]

Victor Macedo won his case, and César Cruz lost possession of the fossil. Macedo stored the jawbone with, and later sold it to, a man named Raul de los Ríos, who collected artifacts and mounted natural history exhibitions in Pucallpa and Lima. Sometime later, Raul de los Ríos lent it to a local doctor, Ulises Reategeci, who kept the jaw in his medical office, in a dusty wooden crate littered with gum wrappers. This is where Don Stap, the American author and poet, found it on a visit in 1987, as he reported in a letter to Matthiessen: "We took some photos, hung around a bit just looking at it, then made our way back to the hotel."[82] Matthiessen kept this letter as further proof he had not succumbed to jungle hallucinations, but it wasn't until 1997—thirty-seven years after his adventure to find a remnant of the "primeval place"—that the fossil was obtained by the Ucayali regional government and transferred to a museum in Pucallpa. Finally, paleontologists could validate the educated guess of Charles Mook. Here was the fossilized snout of a *Purussaurus brasiliensis*, a formidable caiman, capable of growing to more than thirty feet in length, that lived in Amazonian wetlands sometime between four and eight million years ago, during the late Miocene epoch.[83]

10

War Games

> The armies would take some time to form, and in the next hours, as the sun gained strength, a silence lay upon the fields. Only the black robin chat sang its sweet liquid song: this bird appears to have an affinity for war, for it perches commonly on the tips of spears implanted on the ground, or on the tops of kaios, and sings even in the midday hours, at the outskirts of a battle.
>
> —*Under the Mountain Wall* (1962)[1]

LESS THAN TWO MONTHS after Matthiessen returned home exhausted from South America, he received a letter from Robert Gardner, director of the small Film Study Center at the Peabody Museum of Archaeology and Ethnology, at Harvard University, that proposed an expedition no less extreme than the one he'd just endured on the Urubamba River. "I'll try to put in this letter some of the backlog of information and ideas that have accumulated since our talk," Gardner wrote.[2]

That talk had occurred the previous summer on Martha's Vineyard, where Matthiessen was staying in a shack for a few weeks to work on his manuscript for *Raditzer*. One Sunday, he'd been invited to lunch by the playwright Lillian Hellman—Matthiessen knew her through Bill and Rose Styron, who were also summering on the island—at Hellman's house overlooking the Vineyard Haven harbor. Gardner was another lunch guest, and they hit it off over drinks.

Robert Grosvenor Gardner was a ruggedly handsome thirty-three-year-old Boston Brahmin who, like Matthiessen, wore his elite family background with a great deal of discomfort. He had first sought an escape through art history, which took him to Europe and Anatolia; but then he'd read Ruth Benedict's *Patterns of Culture*, about the Zuñi, Dobu, and Kwakiutl peoples, and been so taken with Benedict's theories that he redirected his future toward anthropology. Combining the discipline with his passion for film, Gardner would eventually become a renowned pioneer of ethnographic cinema, even if he preferred to call himself a "reality filmmaker."³ While most academics in the field aimed to produce work that was objective, he was more like an artist with his interest in "intuitive, even subjective, casts of mind."⁴ He envisaged an anthropology that could reveal "the meaning of one's own life as well as, or even better than, the meaning of the lives of 'others.'" To Gardner, the study of humanity offered an instrument for studying the self.

Gardner had worked as an editor on John Marshall's *The Hunters* (1957), about the !Kung Bushmen of the Kalahari Desert. At Lillian Hellman's lunch, he told Matthiessen about a new project he was considering in Netherlands New Guinea. Leopold Pospíšil, the Yale anthropologist, had recently shot some footage there of two tribes of Kapauku (or Ekari) people waging war on one another. The footage was "a valiant effort," and "no doubt a valuable document," in Gardner's critical assessment, but it was technically inept: Pospíšil had "used a camera as if it were a flashlight... most everything scrambled and out of focus."⁵ Gardner was sure he could do better given the proper resources. Then a distant cousin at the National Research Council in Washington, D.C., had introduced him to Jean Victor de Bruijn, a Dutch ethnologist who worked with his government as director of the Kantoor voor Bevolkingszaken (Bureau of Native Affairs). De Bruijn had expressed a "profound concern"⁶ for the Indigenous people in Netherlands New Guinea at a moment when disputes were flaring around decolonization; the Dutch suddenly wanted self-determination for Papuans (after shuffling their feet on it for a decade), just as Indonesia was claiming rightful ownership over the territory. The politics were complicated—the U.N. and U.S. were also involved—but what was important to Gardner was de Bruijn's mention of financial assistance. If Gardner was serious about filming tribes of what he termed "neolithic warrior farmers,"⁷ the Netherlands government could help make it happen.

Over lunch, speculating about what an expedition to New Guinea might look like, Gardner told Matthiessen that besides anthropologists and camera operators, he would ideally take naturalists, photographers, writers, and maybe even a painter to capture multiple points of view, a plurality of interpretations both scientific and artistic. Matthiessen responded with enthusiasm to this broad nineteenth-century-style survey ("I was thrilled with the idea"),⁸ which made Gardner excited, too, as he later recalled: "I had read Peter's early novels, along with his work on North American birds [meaning *Wildlife in America*], and thought that I saw a sensibility attuned to the phenomenal world sympathetic to my own."⁹

In the months after that first talk on Martha's Vineyard, and for the duration of Matthiessen's travels in South America, Gardner had then set about turning his hypothetical expedition into reality. He disentangled himself from other commitments. He sought professional encouragement from "prominent figures on the cultural scene,"[10] including Margaret Mead, who warned him that Netherlands New Guinea was a challenging place to work. He also secured grants from several American foundations, plus a commitment for $6,500 from the Dutch government, which promised to supply interpreters, police protection in the field, and the services of Jan Broekhuijse, a district officer in New Guinea who could perform some preparatory fieldwork.

Following Ruth Benedict, Gardner believed that every society has "focal interests which tend to distinguish them from other social groups."[11] Because these "focal interests" hold the entire pattern of life together, they are worth studying closely. The focal interest he wanted to investigate most thoroughly in Netherlands New Guinea was intertribal warfare. He'd been drawn to the subject in a general way ever since he was a child, leafing through photos of the Great War in old issues of *The Illustrated London News:* "These photographs told me about the most exciting and terrible game anyone could possibly play."[12] Now he wondered if "a greater understanding about violence in men could be achieved if it was studied in a metaphysical context completely different from our own."[13] As his second wife, Adele Pressman, later explained: "It was very hard for Bob to connect with his own rage. Especially the old Freudian wish to murder your father. And so here was a group that, he felt, had ritualized their aggression, and in a way that not many people died from it. Nothing like our wars. That fascinated him."[14] Margaret Mead objected to the plan—making war the main subject of an anthropological study was "irresponsible," she told him—but Gardner was adamant.[15]

By the time he sent Matthiessen the letter with his backlog of information, the expedition was all but assured to be happening. "I have enclosed several things," Gardner wrote.[16] There was a government handbook with data on topography and demographics, as well as a pamphlet introducing New Guinea wildlife. There was an "extremely crude" map, much of it blank: the Grand Valley of the Baliem River in the Central Highlands, also called the Baliem Valley. And there were several eyewitness accounts that had been lifted from reports and letters sent by Protestant missionaries to their financial supporters over the past few years. One of these lurid extracts discussed "a hail of spears and arrows" directed at the missionaries, who were shaken by the reception but undeterred from their efforts to "save" the most recalcitrant of Baliem tribes: "we realize that our easy contacts in the past have been only gifts from His good hand, and that the strategy of Satan has assumed new directions."[17]

Matthiessen, having just visited the Templetons in backcountry Brazil, would have immediately recognized the fragility of the situation with the missionaries. Change was inevitable in the Baliem Valley; its agents were already "hammering at the gates."[18] But here was a rare opportunity to observe and perhaps preserve, on film and in writing, "a lost culture in the terrible beauty of its pure estate," as Matthiessen soon put it—an Indigenous culture *before* external pressures of religion and politics reduced its members to "no more than another backward people, crouched in the long shadow of the white man."[19] Of course he agreed to join the Harvard-Peabody New Guinea Expedition led by Robert Gardner.

IN THE SUMMER of 1960, Gardner set the rest of his team for the following spring. He found Karl Heider, a twenty-five-year-old PhD student, smoking on the front steps of the Peabody Museum—they sometimes smoked there together—and recruited him as an ethnographer and photographic assistant. "It sounded much more interesting than digging at old sites in Thailand, which is where I was going to do my dissertation," Heider recalled.[20] Gardner also invited the photojournalist Eliot Elisofon to tag along; Elisofon convinced *Life* magazine, his longtime employer, to release him for a month in exchange for a spread of original images. And then there was Michael Rockefeller, the youngest son of Nelson Rockefeller, incumbent governor of New York. Michael approached Gardner himself on the recommendation of his best friend, Samuel Putnam, a medical student who would join the expedition for a brief stint. Michael Rockefeller was twenty-two, wide-eyed, and looking for an adventure now he was finished with his studies at Harvard, though he appeared to have "no credentials," in Gardner's view, "beyond his modesty and an endless curiosity about a wider world, and especially about preliterate art."[21] Gardner challenged the young man to learn sound recording if he really wanted to contribute something. To practice, Rockefeller took a Nagra tape recorder to the 1960 Republican National Convention in Chicago.

Matthiessen's plan was to use the expedition to write another series of "Last Wilderness" chronicles for *The New Yorker*. He also hoped to produce a companion volume for the Viking Press on natural history and ecology in Netherlands New Guinea—or, as *The Berkshire Eagle* described it after an interview with him, on "head-hunters in their relationship to wild life."[22] But while Gardner arranged the team and went about compiling equipment to be shipped to Hollandia on the SS *Schie Lloyd*, Matthiessen's attention was mostly focused elsewhere for the time being, on his personal life.

It had been almost four years since he'd left Patsy and the children to adopt a nomadic lifestyle. There had been apartments in New York, women he stayed with occasionally, but nothing that could be considered a permanent abode. Now he returned to Springs on the East End of Long Island and rented a cabin near the Green River Cemetery, where Jackson Pollock was buried beneath a granite boulder. Hurricane Donna hit almost immediately, bringing 100 mph winds and six-foot tides; Matthiessen marveled, in the storm's aftermath, at birds that had been blown off their migratory courses: "'So this is the sea!' their expressions seemed to say."[23] Then he began to look for a house.

The property he purchased that fall was in Sagaponack, an old farming village nestled in the potato fields that separated Wainscott from Bridgehampton. Six acres of apple and catalpa trees, Japanese cherries and privet hedges, the property sat at the corner of Sagg Main and Bridge Lane, a quiet quarter-mile stroll past dune grass to the beach and the Atlantic Ocean. The farm across the road was one of the oldest in America, having been continuously cultivated by the same family (the Whites) since the seventeenth century. The property itself dated to a similar period, although its modern history began around 1900, when E. E. Miller, a cofounder of the Sagaponack Golf Club, constructed an impressive summer place he named "Deldune." Most recently, Deldune had belonged to the Russian-born art director of *Harper's Bazaar*, Alexey Brodovitch, and Alexey's wife, Nina—an unhappy couple (he was an alcoholic; their son was troubled) who were known by neighbors to expend considerable energy trying to destroy each other. In the winter of 1958, during a record-breaking blizzard, Deldune had burned to the ground before the Bridgehampton Fire Department could break through the snowdrifts to extinguish the blaze. When Matthiessen bought the property from Alexey two years later for $35,000 (a steal even then), he obtained the charred foundations of Deldune; a rudimentary garage with a chauffeur's apartment upstairs; an old horse stable; and a small outbuilding near the apple trees. He would never rebuild Deldune or replace it with another gilded mansion; instead, Matthiessen moved into the garage.

To visit his two children, he drove to Manhattan, where they now lived with Patsy and Mike Goldberg in a four-story house on West 11th Street. These visits also gave him the chance to catch up with friends, including Doc Humes, who had refashioned himself, since the founding of *The Paris Review*, as an acclaimed novelist (*The Underground City*), and as an impassioned political agitator who would soon be arrested in Washington Square Park for protesting a ban on folksinging.

One day in Greenwich Village, Matthiessen met up with Humes so they could take mescaline together. After his encounter with ayahuasca a few months earlier, Matthiessen had become intrigued by the therapeutic potential of psychedelics. Though the experience in Pucallpa had been alarming—his journal was filled with references to eerie voices and "church music," and to a sensation of slipping into "another world"[24]—it had also made clear "that this family of chemicals (the phenol alkaloids) might lead to another way of seeing, and not in the slow labor of ascetic discipline but in cool efficiency and speed, as in flight through air."[25] An interest in other ways of seeing, leading to other ways of *being*, had been a major motivation for his recent travels; and the idea of an expedition inward was no less attractive than one to South America or Netherlands New Guinea.[*]

Humes took Matthiessen to MacDougal Street, where the folksinger Mary Travers lived in a third-floor apartment with her husband, John Filler. At the last moment, Humes got cold feet and refused to participate, but Travers and Matthiessen dosed on mescaline, derived from the spineless peyote cactus, and lay down together on her bed. As Matthiessen recalled, they remained there, in an advanced state of narcosis, whispering as though they'd been "lovers for three years," until sunrise, when he stumbled into the street and discovered a "miracle": he could read all the street signs without wearing his glasses. Then the mescaline wore off.[26]

Later, Matthiessen would type a quotation from Aldous Huxley's *The Doors of Perception* (1954) onto a white notecard for easy reference. "To make biological survival possible, Mind at Large has to be funneled through the reducing valve of the brain and nervous system. What comes out at the other end is a measly trickle of the kind of consciousness which will help us to stay alive on the surface of this particular planet."[27] To take mescaline, Huxley suggested, was to open that "reducing value" and restore the unimpeded flow of one's consciousness.

After his night with Mary Travers, Matthiessen procured his own supply of mescaline so he could try it again. He offered to take Rose Styron on a trip, but Bill forbade it. ("Bill objected to any kind of substance use," Rose recalled.)[28] A more willing accomplice appeared one day in October, though, when Matthiessen was fishing on the beach at Sagaponack. A tall,

---

[*] Matthiessen sometimes referred to himself as one of the "early pioneers" of psychedelic drugs. This was certainly true in terms of presenting his experiences to a general readership. When he described *"aya huasca"* in "Peruvian Journal" in *The New Yorker* in 1961—"bitter stuff, which in appearance resembles opaque apple cider"—he joined the likes of Henri Michaux, who described mescaline in *The Paris Review* in 1956; and R. Gordon Wasson, who described psilocybin "magic" mushrooms for *Life* readers in 1957. Before Matthiessen, a few key figures had catalogued ayahuasca scientifically, including Richard Spruce, the English botanist, and Richard Evan Schultes, the American father of ethnobotany; but perhaps only William S. Burroughs had published subjective impressions of what it was like to, as Burroughs put it, "space time travel." Burroughs's vivid notes about imbibing ayahuasca—a letter to Allen Ginsberg, which he'd originally sent in 1953—had appeared in an issue of *The Black Mountain Review* in the spring of 1958. Matthiessen probably read this letter before he set out for South America the following year. After his own encounter with ayahuasca in Pucallpa, he carried a half-gallon of the brew back to Lima, where he handed it over to Allen Ginsberg, who had traveled to Peru with the express purpose of finally sampling the fabled jungle medicine for himself. Ginsberg drank it down, then wrote in his journal: "I have come home, I am the God, and I demand admittance thru the door."

dark-haired woman with a two-year-old girl wandered across the sand to introduce herself—to *reintroduce* herself. They had met at a party in Paris, in the early 1950s, when she was studying at the Sorbonne and he was caught up with *The Paris Review* crowd; the little girl was Rue, and her own name, she reminded him, was Deborah Love.

"D and I never considered ourselves 'seekers' when we first knew each other," Matthiessen would write in an early draft of *The Snow Leopard*—"although we both sensed that the guts were missing in the western concept of the 'pursuit of happiness,' and that the search for vital parts was the only game in town."[29] This joint "search" began on one of their first dates, when Deborah asked Peter to show her the psychedelics he kept mentioning. He gave her mescaline on "an autumn night of wind and rain," expecting a repeat of the warm communion he'd felt with Mary Travers in New York. Deborah, however, "freaked out."[30] She began to laugh uncontrollably, "and her mouth opened wide and she could not close it; her armor had cracked, and all of the night winds of the world went howling through." Turning to Peter for help, she watched as his flesh dissolved to reveal a grimacing skull.

After Aldous Huxley suffered through a bad mescaline trip, he compared the experience to the horror "overwhelming those who have come, too suddenly, face to face with some manifestation of the *Mysterium tremendum*."[31] Deborah was terrified by what was she was seeing, and Peter lacked the experience to guide her, so it was a rough journey until the hallucinations faded away. As he'd write in *The Snow Leopard*, looking back from a vantage point of far greater wisdom: "familiar things, losing the form assigned to them, begin to spin, and the center does not hold, because we search for it outside instead of in."[32]

THE VIKING PRESS RELEASED *Raditzer* in January 1961. Matthiessen's third novel, almost a novella, had a great deal in common with *Race Rock* and *Partisans:* another privileged young man, Charles Stark, struggling against an uncomprehending father; another attempt to flee the family influence, this time through the U.S. Navy; another disturbing encounter with a shadow self, the eponymous Raditzer, a cynical, insidious sailor who sends the hero hurtling toward crisis by forcing him to face "what he would not face ... a specter escaped from the dark attic of the mind."[33] But Matthiessen had improved as a writer since *Partisans*, and his preferred themes of nature (the untamed kind) versus civilization (bourgeois respectability), lost innocence, and the brittleness of identity, were assembled together in a more cohesive whole. If *Raditzer* was still not exactly first-rate fiction—"it's too pared down," Matthiessen later conceded; "[a] novel should have some sense of shambling looseness, unpredictability; it shouldn't be taut"[34]—it was nevertheless a step in the right direction. *Raditzer* displays a greater degree of self-awareness than anything he had previously written. Charlie Stark, for instance, is sustained by the art and Tahiti journal of Paul Gauguin; he is also drawn to "the freedom, the animal warmth," of an "unspoiled native girl," who seems to intuit the "artistic torment" raging behind the "big-nosed, balding exterior of Charles P. Stark, the weekend Gauguin."[35] By the end of the novel, this primitivism is exposed by Raditzer as a farcical delusion. Matthiessen gave Charlie the same habit his earlier protagonists had of romanticizing an "Other"—working-class roughs; the "unspoiled native"—but here he began to complicate that impulse. The result, an ambiguous meditation on the stories we tell ourselves about what it means to be a decent man, was closer to what he had in mind: "That was the first [novel] I thought showed signs of hope."[36]

The critical reception was reassuring. *Raditzer* "ought to bring this immensely talented young writer into the notice he deserves," declared Gene Baro in the *New York Herald Tribune*.[37] Raditzer, the spectral figure behind Charlie's awakening, was "one of the most astonishing scoundrels we have seen in a long time," said Charles Poore in *The New York Times*.[38] Writing in *The Nation*, Terry Southern gave his friend's book a wry stamp of approval while deftly pinpointing its central theme: "It is, in certain ways, as though a whole novel has been devoted to one of [Nelson] Algren's sideline freaks. . . . [But] perhaps what we see as 'ugly'—in nature, in life, in the human condition—is but the unhappily twisted reflection of a much closer source."[39]

Matthiessen read none of his reviews when they first appeared in January and February. Nor was he aware that MGM offered $15,000 for the screen rights in March, an offer his agent accepted on his behalf. By the time *Raditzer* was published, completing a loose coming-of-age trilogy, he had already left the country to join the Harvard-Peabody Expedition, taking the most circuitous route anyone could possibly devise.

TO REACH NETHERLANDS NEW GUINEA, Robert Gardner flew from New York to Honolulu; from Honolulu to Biak, an island in Melanesia; and from Biak to Hollandia (now Jayapura) on the northern New Guinea coast. Matthiessen flew in the opposite direction—to Rome. He gave mescaline to some Italian friends and advised them to consult *The Doors of Perception*. Then he departed for Egypt. Gardner had given him an around-the-world ticket, and he was determined to make the most of it.

From Cairo, he toured the pyramids at Giza. He followed the Nile past date palms and feluccas, all the way up to Abu Simbel, site of the rock-cut temples that were soon going to be drowned by the Aswan High Dam. A rescue plan to relocate the temples, which had originally been built by Ramesses II, had not yet been agreed upon in 1961, so Matthiessen approached the ancient site like a man paying his respects at a deathbed.

Crossing into Sudan through the Nubian Desert ("one imagines Dante wandering here"),[40] he traveled to the twin cities of Omdurman and Khartoum, where the White Nile meets the Blue Nile. Because the lands south of Khartoum were closed territories, a result of armed resistance by Nilotic tribesmen to the national Muslim government, he obtained a permit and promised to take no photographs of the "naked peoples." Then he paid for a ride on a merchant trading truck. He shared his "bed" of potatoes and tinware with sixteen Dinka, Nuer, and Shilluk men; a white South African student who was heading home the slow way; and Herb Cohen, from Los Angeles, who wore sunglasses and a gold earring beneath a beret, and who claimed to have fought the Palestinians on behalf of Israel.

Night had descended before the truck cleared Khartoum, "and a spray of stars froze on a blue-black sky," Matthiessen wrote in an account of the journey. "The vague track wandered south into a soft emptiness of cooling sand. . . . And farther onward, close to midnight, where the sands relented, came the birds of night—the African owl, and nightjars, and pale Senegal stone curlews whirling straight up into the dark like souls departing."[41] The first time the truck stopped, the driver and other merchants unrolled prayer rugs and bowed toward Mecca in the beam of the headlights. Another time, the driver became disoriented, drove in circles, and crashed into a ditch; everyone was forced to offload cargo and dig out the wheels.

A few days later, after transferring to a pickup at Malakal and passing through Juba, Matthiessen, Cohen, and the South African student arrived together in the town of Nimule, on the border with Uganda. Its small game reserve, which Theodore Roosevelt had visited in 1910, was home to a population of white rhinos, and Matthiessen accompanied two rangers to inspect them up close.

But something went wrong in Nimule. "There was yelling and shrieking through the village. And then we were taken into custody at the guard post there. It wasn't a matter of whether they were going to shoot us, it was when."[42]

On February 13, unbeknownst to Matthiessen in the desert, officials in the Republic of the Congo had publicly announced the death of Patrice Émery Lumumba, the independence leader who'd served as the country's first democratically elected prime minister. "I heard on the car radio today of Lumumba's death . . . and had a frightened and sick feeling," Deborah Love wrote in a letter Matthiessen wouldn't receive for weeks, describing Dag Hammarskjöld's "weary, cogent, and serious" voice as the secretary-general addressed his colleagues at the United Nations.[43] In the chaos that engulfed much of Sub-Saharan Africa, the Sudanese turned, as Matthiessen put it, "bitterly hostile" in Nimule.[44] As white people, he and his two companions became convenient targets for fury about the obscene assassination of an anticolonialism icon.

According to several consistent accounts he gave over the years, Matthiessen, trying to calm a situation he didn't understand, told Cohen and the student to harden their stomachs. Summoned to eat at a communal bowl thanks to the intercession of a sympathetic schoolteacher, he sensed they would need to accept the food to avoid an offense that might prove fatal. The South African student took a few bites of gamy tripe, then withdrew to vomit behind a hut; Matthiessen endured, scooping mouthfuls with his fingers as a show of respect. Cohen refused, ignoring all entreaties while making "strange ceremonial dipping motions with his hand."[45] This insane provocation put them all at risk, and Matthiessen scrambled to reassure their captors.

Then, just as quickly as the situation had deteriorated, it suddenly improved. In the morning, a truck passing through Nimule picked up the foreigners and shepherded them across the border into Uganda. "I'm still not sure why we were spared," Matthiessen said.[46]

In Kenya and Tanganyika, he tried to recover his wits by focusing on the wildlife. He took a Sunday air charter to the Serengeti National Park, where he spotted a leopard in the yellow-bark acacias along the Seronera River. "The wild creatures I had come to Africa to see are exhilarating in their multitudes and colors," he wrote a decade later, reflecting on the visit that sparked his love for East Africa, "and I imagined for a time that this glimpse of the earth's morning might account for the anticipation that I felt, the sense of origins, of innocence and mystery, like a marvelous childhood faculty restored."[47]

Yet the bloody realities of colonialism kept intruding into his reverie. On Matthiessen's flight out of Africa—Nairobi to Bombay (now Mumbai)—he found himself seated next to a drunk Australian pilot. The man's shirt was sweat-soaked, and "he started talking the minute I sat down," Matthiessen recalled. "I thought, Oh boy, this is going to be some flight."[48] The pilot had recently come from the Congo, where he'd witnessed atrocities that would haunt the rest of his days: "he described a recent episode in which some Africans had ordered him to fly a political prisoner to an airstrip in Katanga, where the prisoner was first beaten and then murdered."[49] In fact, the prisoner had been beaten while still on the plane to Elisabethville in

Katanga; the pilot recalled the brutal violence, and how he'd listened as soldiers promised the prisoner his wife would be raped. "It got to me," the pilot said. "This thing broke my spirit."⁵⁰ It was not until much later that Matthiessen connected the dots and realized the prisoner was almost certainly Patrice Lumumba.*

By comparison, the next few layovers were uneventful. In Delhi he had dinner with the novelist Ruth Prawer Jhabvala, who invited him to come back and stay just as soon as he'd "finished with the head-hunters."⁵¹ In Kathmandu, Nepal, he strolled through the Asan Bazaar, which was full of Tibetan refugees selling their religious icons to stay alive, and bought a bronze Akshobhya Buddha, the "Immovable One," associated with forbearance.

In Cambodia, he photographed the ruins at Angkor Wat, noting the bas-reliefs of dancing cranes. Then he paid for what he thought—what the seller claimed—was opium. Anticipating another expedition inward,† he tried the powder in a decrepit hotel on the edge of the forest: "After a first ecstatic rush, I was stricken, paralyzed, unable to get my breath; with no one to call to, unable to call, I imagined that the End had come in this dead silent room under slow fans."⁵² The "opium," he later claimed (though it is unclear how he reached this conclusion), was actually an unrefined form of heroin.

In a letter to Deborah Love sent en route to Netherlands New Guinea, where he finally arrived in April after nearly three months of travel, Matthiessen wondered whether he had a "death wish." Why did he court these perilous situations? And why did he feel such exhilaration afterward? "I think you ask for more life, not less," Deborah wrote back reassuringly. "I rather think that intimations of mortality come most clearly to the person most intensely alive, that very aliveness engendered by the knowledge (most people don't <u>know</u> they're going to die) that the next step, or the next, is dying. I don't think it curious, but quite reasonable you are supercharged with energy."⁵³ Putting a foot out over the abyss, in other words, was a way of waking oneself into a fuller apprehension of the present moment. Not a death wish but a life wish.

---

* Ludo De Witte's history, *The Assassination of Lumumba* (2001), is worth quoting here: "The DC-4 carrying Lumumba, Mpolo and Okito to Elisabethville was a large four-engined plane with seats for fifty passengers.... All the crew members subsequently stated that the prisoners were badly abused throughout the flight, which lasted several hours.... [The soldiers] tore out Lumumba's goatee and several tufts of his hair which they then forced him to swallow, a spectacle which apparently made one of the soldiers ill.... The crew repeatedly tried to restrain the soldiers, but they finally locked themselves in the cockpit from which they emerged only after landing in Elisabethville. In an interview with the *Durban Sunday Tribune* shortly after the transfer, the Australian co-pilot Jack Dixon said he tried in vain to keep the soldiers away from Lumumba and apparently told the unconcerned commissioners: 'Say, we have to hand Lumumba over alive.'"
† A second drug-related quote that Matthiessen typed onto a notecard, from Jean Cocteau: "Everything one does in life, even love, occurs in an express train racing towards death. To smoke opium is to get out of the train while it is still moving."

FLYING FROM HOLLANDIA to the Baliem Valley, 150 miles south, Matthiessen watched the rainforest vanish into clouds as the plane ascended the central mountain range of Netherlands New Guinea. "One has the feeling that, should the clouds close over, the sun would be seen no more, as if one had sunk into an underworld," he wrote in his journal.[54] But then the clouds suddenly parted, dissolving over a cavity forty miles long and eight miles wide, and he was confronted with a vista of "magnificent vastness": pandanus and banana trees, cultivated gardens and villages of round houses with neatly thatched roofs, all of it gathered around a river cascading out of mountains that encircled the valley floor like high walls of wet limestone.

People have lived in the Baliem for thousands of years. It was unknown to outsiders, however, until June 23, 1938, when a wealthy American zoologist named Richard Archbold stumbled upon it in a Grumman amphibious aircraft. Traveling under the aegis of the American Museum of Natural History, Archbold was astounded by what he saw below: "From the air the gardens and ditches and native-built walls appeared like the farming country of Central Europe," he wrote in a dispatch for *National Geographic*.[55] Several exploratory patrols soon entered the valley on foot to make first contact with the residents, one of whom was promptly shot by a trigger-happy Dutch officer.

During the war in the Pacific, American troops stationed in Hollandia took airborne sightseeing tours over the valley. In 1945, one of these planes, a Douglas C-47 Skytrain, slammed into a mountain, killing twenty-one passengers and stranding three survivors for more than six weeks. Because one of the three was an attractive young woman, Corporal Margaret Hastings, the international media became briefly obsessed with the (successful) rescue mission, dubbing the Baliem Valley "Shangri-La," and running installments of Hastings's sensational "Shangri-La Diary": "Gradually the natives slipped out of the jungle. They were still making that yapping sound. . . . They were jet black and over their shoulders hung stone axes. They were an ominous sight to three persons armed only with a jackknife."[56] Ominous, perhaps, but not hostile: the leader of Uwambo village, a man named Wimayuk Wandik, shook hands with the survivors.

After World War II, "Shangri-La" was all but left alone for a decade, until CAMA—the Christian and Missionary Alliance, headquartered in New York—entered the valley in April 1954. The CAMA fundraising pamphlets, sent to evangelical supporters around North America, announced optimistically that there was "a Light in this Valley";[57] the stories, however, suggested there was a great deal of tribal violence, too, which embarrassed Dutch administrators who wanted to project an image of order in their far-flung colony. At the end of 1956, the governor of Netherlands New Guinea dispatched a *controleur*, Frits Veldkamp, to establish the first administration post on the banks of the Baliem River, a post named Wamena. Pacification and development efforts began immediately, although a population of some sixty thousand individuals, "spread over an impossibly wide area, closely attached to their own traditions, and with no concept whatsoever of central authority," as Veldkamp acknowledged, meant that parts of the valley remained mostly unpacified even five years later.[58]

Matthiessen landed in Wamena—"[an] airstrip with its attendant shacks"[59]—on April 11, 1961. He was met by Robert Gardner and Jan Broekhuijse, the district officer and anthropologist-in-training (enrolled at Utrecht University) who was assigned by the government to assist the expedition. Because there were no roads beyond Wamena, the three of them loaded an outboard motorboat with the last of the expedition's supplies, which had also arrived on the plane; then they set off up the Aikhé, a tributary of the Baliem River, to join the rest of the team some fifteen miles northeast, far beyond the usual patrol route of the Dutch authorities.

Several hours into the journey, the skiff crossed an invisible border and entered the territory of the Dugum Dani.* "Four warriors with fifteen-foot spears appeared quite suddenly on the top of a steep grass bank, silhouetted on a dying sun."[60] This was Matthiessen's "startling" first impression of the people he would live with for the next four months, and he captured the moment in his journal: "They whooped in greeting, and ran ahead to the river bend where the skiff was to be unloaded." At the landing, "the men were excited, pressing around to touch me and take my hand. Ny-ak, ny-ak, they said, adding a grunt and squeeze by way of emphasis, and a sighed, rapturous Wah . . . Wah . . ." Other men and children began streaming across a field—the women held back—until a large group had gathered. Some of

---

* The Harvard-Peabody New Guinea Expedition of 1961 employed multiple names for the people it studied. The most common one, "Dani," is actually a sweeping term, first deployed by missionaries and Western explorers, that encompasses two ethnolinguistic groups in the Central Highlands. To be more specific, Karl Heider used "Dugum Dani" in his ethnographic monographs, which gestured to a small geographical area around Dugum Hill in the Baliem Valley. Elsewhere, Heider and Robert Gardner also referred to the people they filmed as members of the "Willigiman-Wallalua," which was a composite name (Willil:Haiman-Walilio:Alua) for a territorial and political confederation. Because "Willigiman-Wallalua" was cumbersome to say and inelegant on the page, Matthiessen, in *Under the Mountain Wall*, opted to use "Kurelu" instead, after the respected local leader—as in, "Kurelu's people," the Kurelu.

More recently, anthropologists have preferred the name "Hubula" when discussing residents of the Baliem Valley, because it is the name they use for themselves. Were I writing about Baliem Valley as it is today, I would use "Hubula." However, given that the valley's social composition has changed dramatically since 1961, and to avoid confusion with historical sources, I have adopted Heider's "Dugum Dani" when referencing the very particular group of people (320 of perhaps 60,000 valley residents) who were put in front of the lens by the Harvard-Peabody Expedition.

their bodies were daubed with red or yellow clay; all of them seemed to wear a protective coat of pig grease, blackened by dirt and fire smoke. The men, Matthiessen noticed, also wore ornamentations: armlets of dried pith; necklaces of white shells, or white egret feathers; and a long gourd (*horim*) sheathing the penis, which was held in place by woven strings of twig fiber tied around the chest and scrotum.

A chanting escort marched Matthiessen toward camp, which Gardner and the team had already established in a grove of araucaria pines well over a hundred feet tall. The Dugum Dani called the grove "Homuak," after a natural spring, and it was magnificent, with plenty of shade and enough space for multiple canvas tents. Karl Heider shared one of them with Michael Rockefeller. Broekhuijse would share his with Eliot Elisofon when the *Life* photographer arrived for the month of May. Matthiessen went in with Gardner, who owned the camp typewriter. There was also a dining fly with a large table, which was the domain of Jusup Kakiay, an Ambonese man from Sorong who'd been recommended as a cook to the expedition by Sidney Dillon Ripley at Yale.* Rounding out the crew was a security detail of two police, Navas and Abututi, the latter of whom, hailing from the south of Baliem Valley, also worked as a translator with Broekhuijse; and Abututi's young wife, Wamamogen. At first the Dutch government had wanted the expedition to take five guards for protection, but Gardner objected. Navas and Abututi were instructed to conceal their rifles in camp.

Deborah Love, in one of her letters from New York, had intuited a dread of transience that Matthiessen felt about his usual mode of travel. Despite the astonishing sights he'd witnessed over the past few years, he had rarely loitered long enough to get anything more than surface impressions. But perhaps this trip would be different. "You will live there," Deborah wrote, "not just peer at it."[61] There was a village on three sides of Homuak, with an important trading path snaking through the trees. Men crouched at the tent flaps and around fires they kindled on the campsite perimeter. The expedition was staked right at the crossroads of the Dugum Dani world.

THE DAY AFTER Matthiessen arrived in Homuak, the camp received several important visitors. Kurelu, a *kain*, or "big man," of the Dugum Dani, arrived with three lesser kains and a war chief of the allied Kossi-Alua. Kurelu was in his mid-forties, with graying hair and eyes that were "cold and deep, like

---

* The esteemed ornithologist S. Dillon Ripley, whom Matthiessen had prepared duck skins for while still at Yale, participated in the Denison-Crockett Expedition to Netherlands New Guinea in 1937–38. Jusup Kakiay's second job, after his kitchen duties were completed each day, was to collect exotic birds for Ripley.

small holes leading to infinity,"[62] and he walked with the bearing of a man who commanded the unhesitating respect of a large number of people.

The expedition team was eating a duck that Gardner had shot on the Aikhé River. Offered a plate, Kurelu declined to join them for lunch, pointing out that the stretch of water Gardner had hunted—Kurelu knew exactly where—belonged to the Wittaia, an enemy clan. The duck was thus "poisonous," Kurelu said, capable of blinding a man to a raiding party. He did accept a cigarette, however, "as much perhaps from politesse as desire," Gardner thought.[63] Then the group moved into Gardner and Matthiessen's tent. Kurelu sat on a wooden trunk; the other kains squatted on the bare ground. Matthiessen settled on his bedroll, observing the meeting with rapt attention. "It is safe to say that Kurelu is aware, and will continue to be aware, of every step we take," he wrote.[64] Indeed, Kurelu was already more knowledgeable about the white man than most of his fellow tribesmen. He had once seen Hollandia on the invitation of the Dutch governor.* He'd encountered Jan Broekhuijse, too, the previous October, when Broekhuijse had traveled to Kurelu's village to conduct a preliminary survey for the expedition and set up a small camp on the village outskirts. Kurelu had marched over and asked (as Matthiessen puckishly recounted the story) "how Broekhuyse [sic] would like it if he, Kurelu, were to come to Wamena and set up a house right in Broekhuyse's [sic] front yard."[65]

The meeting in Homuak went a little more smoothly. The team told Kurelu that they were neither missionaries nor agents of the Dutch government. They had no message to share, no advice to give, no demands to make of his people. They had a translator—Abututi—who could vouch for their motives. And they came bearing gifts. Gardner opened a box filled with several dozen sea snail shells of various sizes, which he'd purchased from a dealer in Massachusetts after learning the Dani considered them precious. "When he saw them," Gardner wrote in his journal, "Kurelu could hardly restrain his interest in possessing such marvels. I have the feeling he will do whatever he must in order to acquire even one of them. It is also my conviction that Kurelu is an important key to the unlocking of the Dani world and I intend to be mercilessly pragmatic in my use of the shells to engage his complicity."[66]

This rather blunt admission should be read as a response to the intimidating challenges facing the expedition in its earliest days. There were five

---

* The governor hoped to persuade Kurelu to lay down his weapons. According to both Matthiessen's and Gardner's journals, Kurelu had disliked the coastal climate in Hollandia, and found it pathetic that the governor only had one wife, while Kurelu had eleven. The most impressive thing, to Kurelu, had been "the great salt pond"—the Pacific Ocean—which was much larger than anything found in the Baliem Valley.

Westerners (six with Elisofon, or when Samuel Putnam came to visit afterward), surrounded by hundreds of Dugum Dani who had previously rebuffed the approach of all outsiders. A few concealed rifles and some tear gas guns wouldn't amount to much if the situation turned sour. ("It cannot help but occur to one," Matthiessen wrote, "how very simple it would be for the Wittaia to fill our chests with spears and arrows.")[67] Without coaxing, the Dugum men were shy in front of cameras, which they didn't understand. The Dugum women were shy in general: they tended to step off the trail and turn their faces away. And then there were logistical challenges: humidity, which affected the recording equipment, and the physical strain of lugging heavy loads across creeks and marshland. The expedition needed the cooperation of Kurelu if it was to produce anything of documentary value. Without him and the other kains on their side, a film, book, or ethnographic monograph would quickly prove impossible.

But Gardner soon realized that he didn't need to try very hard to ingratiate his team with the local community. Men and children pressed in to watch the pale strangers brush their teeth and spit out toothpaste. Boys crowded around an oil lamp to pull silly faces and wave at themselves in the reflective metal surface. Karl Heider showed one young warrior how to use a ballpoint pen, then encouraged him to doodle in a pocket notebook: "he did it stealthily, pleased with himself."[68] Confronted with objects such as matches and Rockefeller's red flannel blanket, the Dugum Dani were beguiled. "Probably none have had such a chance to study us and our material culture," Heider wrote in his field notes, not yet considering the problems this was bound to create.[69]

Heider was amazed by the "overwhelming friendly kindness" of the Dani. Gardner noted the same thing in his own journal: "The reception is almost too good to believe. Indeed, the logic of it quite escapes me."[70] The expedition team soon became known to all the Dugum Dani men, who translated their names into an easier local tongue: "Maik" (Michael); "Yan" (Jan); "Karuru" (Karl); "Bom" (Bob); and "Pe-tit" (Peter).

ON MATTHIESSEN'S FOURTH MORNING in Homuak, a chant started somewhere across the fields—*hoo, hoo, hoo, ua, ua*—and a man ran past the grove crying out urgently, "his voice a solitary echo of the wail from behind the mist."[71] The cry was taken up and passed through villages to the north, like bonfire signals along a ridge of mountains; warriors grabbed their weapons and headdresses and whitened their legs or shoulders with clay. There was to be a *weem* (war) with the neighboring Wittaia, and the Dugum Dani rushed to meet their enemy on a grassy battlefield called the Tokolik.

After breakfast, Gardner and Heider gathered their cameras and headed out to capture the scene. An earlier weem, just before Matthiessen arrived, had been "too overwhelming to comprehend," but Gardner hoped to make better sense of the spectacle this time around.[72] Several hundred men gathered on either end of the Tokolik, and as more warriors arrived, the groups hurled insults and brandished their spears. The weem's purpose was to restore balance through retribution: two months before, five Dugum Dani had been killed by rival Wittaia in an ambush, and the score needed settling to appease the ghosts of the slain. A few Wittaia now had to die on the battlefield. ("Unavenged ghosts bring sickness, unhappiness, and possibly disaster," Gardner would explain in his film *Dead Birds*.)[73] This ongoing cycle of murder and vengeance—of death—followed by a celebratory *etai*, or victory feast, was a governing factor of life here. The Dani fought because they saw it as necessary for religious reasons. But they also *liked* it, the ritual of the fight. Total annihilation of the enemy, or land acquisition, was never the goal, as it so often is in our wars. As limited engagements, the weems were more akin to group duels. One or two casualties was usually enough to send everyone back to their villages on any given day. Indeed, the Dani were content to cease fighting if it started to rain. Weems served social functions, in other words: they gave meaning and purpose to the men, something for them to focus on and talk about. They also offered a way to accrue prestige through the medium of combat—to become kains like Kurelu, the leaders who got to decide when and where the weems would happen.

Gardner and Heider began to film as lines of warriors dashed forward and back, prancing, dodging, and firing arrows into the enemy ranks with a casual lobbing motion. Matthiessen and Rockefeller stood off to the side near a large tree, making notes and taking photographs.

Shortly before noon, the appearance of Jan Broekhuijse caused a sudden lull in the fighting. Broekhuijse was returning from an overnight visit to his family in Wamena, and though he approached the Tokolik as a spectator, he carried a shotgun over his shoulder. The gun disturbed the warriors, Matthiessen wrote in his notes: it symbolized police "come to stop their wars, break their bows and spears, [and] take their war kains off to jail in Wamena."[74]

A hundred or so warriors converged around the expedition team. "The insects droned in the shimmering heat and a solitary robin-chat sang fitfully, and the black silent men observed us." Gardner was "irritable," Matthiessen continued, because Broekhuijse's blunder forced him to confront "a most unpleasant choice." In fact, it was the central ethical conundrum of the entire expedition. Did the team abandon the battlefield, and thus the chance to document warfare? Or did they tell the Dugum Dani that they had no objections to them killing Wittaia? Put another way, did they tell these men "to bloody well get on with it, and the quicker the better, in the name of color film"? Neither option seemed palatable, so the team decided to wait it out and see what happened. They sat under the tree, saying nothing, until the warriors spontaneously returned to the field. "If it seems heartless to remark that we felt relief, from several points of view, at the imminence of tribal blood-letting, it is the unhappy truth," Matthiessen confessed in his notes.[75] What he wrote next is remarkable:

> Unable to absorb what we were seeing, we all moved in a sort of trance behind the warriors, up to and beyond the shifting line where arrows fell. Though Weaklekek [a Dugum warrior] and others warned us, and finally forced us to withdraw, it was somehow impossible to accept the danger of what, for these people, was a kind of unholy game, and this despite the wounded men, the reality of blood. It was like finding oneself, quite suddenly, in the midst of a medieval tourney. Even when Michael Rockefeller had an arrow glance off the inside of his leg—I witnessed this newsworthy event myself, having just that moment turned to speak to him—we only laughed childishly in excitement, as the warriors themselves were laughing. It was only later, by the kerosene light in the grove of araucaria, that we were able to take in the extraordinary quality of the experience, and with it the degree of our irresponsibility, which included the impulse, in more than one of us, to seize up a bow and join in this wild game in which the combatants danced and laughed, in which nobody seemed to be killed—again, it recalled the primitive wild games of childhood.[76]

That the weem resembled a game was an impression shared by the rest of the team; Karl Heider, in his field journal, compared it to jousting. But Matthiessen's impulse to "seize up a bow" says more about Peter Matthiessen than it does about the Dugum Dani or their festivals of violence. What reminded *him* of "the primitive wild games of childhood" meant something very different to the actual participants, who really were trying to kill their enemies on the Tokolik, and several of whom, due to grievous injuries, had to be carried home "on the shoulders of comrades," as Gardner wrote in his camera notes.[77] Matthiessen's urge to "join in" with a bow, to play, was perhaps the desire to become a young boy again, unburdened of that same sense of responsibility which then troubled his conscience "by the kerosene light in the grove of araucaria."

"EVERYONE IS WELL and extremely busy," Gardner wrote to the director of the Peabody Museum in late April. "Peter is started on his book and seems vastly excited by this place."[78]

Each member of the expedition had a different focus and daily routine. Gardner spent most of his time filming in and around the villages; Heider busied himself with slowly learning the complex language, as he intended to write a full-scale ethnography of the Dugum Dani; and Rockefeller took photographs, made pencil sketches, and recorded hours of audio, everything from insect noises to a pair of men singing as they lazed together on a rock: "*Kere waliké keoe aho / Kere heriké oe / Kere heroké oe aho . . .*" ("We don't like to go far away / We like to roam around / Nearby, not far away . . .").[79]

Matthiessen's job was to compose a chronological account of the expedition. For this reason, he often accompanied Gardner, who was impressed by the "diligence" with which the writer went about his task. "It seemed he was intent on having his account finished on the day he departed, almost as if what he was doing was reportage. In some ways I think it was, especially in the extraordinary attention he gave to detail."[80] Matthiessen was also responsible for documenting the valley's flora and fauna in relation to the Dani, and to do this he began climbing a steep hill behind Homuak each morning because it offered a prospect of the villages—as well as an ideal vantage point for birdwatching. Heider noticed that Matthiessen, who dragged a tent up the hill to create a temporary research station, writing retreat, and blind, seemed to be "as interested in birds as he was in the Dani."[81]

However, to investigate the ecology of the Baliem in less than five months was an impractical ambition for any amateur naturalist. The camp was joined for two weeks by Chris Versteegh, a Dutch botanist who'd first seen the valley during the Archbold Expedition in 1938; Versteegh provided Matthiessen with a crash course in plant identification, although this was hardly enough to make him an expert. Jan Broekhuijse thought Matthiessen's literary aspirations were "naïve," as he wrote in a memoir published in 2019: "The Dani had their own vision of how the ecological system functioned. The casual connections they made on the basis of their own logic were incompatible with ours. . . . All that was far beyond Matthiessen's reach. . . . It was impossible for him to trace the way in which the Dani made use of, and understood, the nature that surrounded them. There was not enough time available. Nor was he equipped to do it."[82]

What saved Matthiessen from total failure was the same thing that saved Robert Gardner and his film, *Dead Birds*. Each evening the team came together for a meal in the dining fly. "Peter and Bob would tell stories about their lives, the intellectual and literary circles in Cambridge and New York,"

Heider recalled.[83] Then the team would exchange the information they'd gathered. "It was like a spy network covering the whole neighborhood. 'You want to see *that*, Peter? Oh, I saw that two days ago.' 'So-and-so is building a house over there.' 'They're just starting a garden.' 'They're constructing another watchtower here.' We'd all report in, whether there was a battle that day or nothing but weeding the sweet potatoes. In a sense, we were doing very basic ethnography." Doing it as a group meant a painstaking process was dramatically streamlined. "Each person was able to leverage the knowledge and experience of all the others."

Yet much of the advanced knowledge, the insights into rituals, taboos, and those ecological connections, came specifically through Jan Broekhuijse. Not only had Broekhuijse spent significant time before the expedition acquainting himself with Dani life elsewhere in the valley, but he was also the only one (until Heider became proficient) who could converse with the Dugum people via Abututi. Abututi translated from Dani into Malay; Broekhuijse translated from Malay into Dutch. Broekhuijse then brought his notebooks to the dining fly and served up "bite-sized chunks" to the Americans in English. He saw himself as a teacher; they were "listening as students."[84] Later, Matthiessen would publicly acknowledge his debt to Broekhuijse ("whose year of prior experience with other Baliem tribes proved invaluable in the gathering and assessment of information");[85] but privately, to Gardner, he fretted that he'd "exploited Jan" through this arrangement.[86] For his part, Broekhuijse would come to feel that he'd been too forthcoming during the expedition dinners, that the Americans had copied excessive amounts of his work into their own journals, though his ire, for decades afterward, was mostly directed at Gardner, who, as Broekhuijse saw it, barely acknowledged a debt at all.

Broekhuijse's position in the chain of translation meant he was sometimes forced to mediate between the Dugum Dani and the expedition team. In May, one of his Dugum informants, Wali, came to him "in despair."[87] Gardner had promised Wali he could have a *mikak* (shell) if the expedition was allowed to film the birth of Wali's child. Gardner had meant the actual birth, but Wali understood the request "in the context of his culture," which forbid men from being present during an *eak habatak*. Since such a request was plainly unthinkable, Wali assumed Gardner meant that he wanted to see the newborn. When the baby appeared, Gardner was disappointed. He decided Wali had cheated him and refused to give the mikak. This caused consternation among the Dani, "a kind of crisis of confidence," Broekhuijse recalled. After hearing Wali's perspective through Abututi, Broekhuijse approached Gardner and explained why the atmosphere of "spontaneity had changed into restraint." Gardner backed down and handed over the shell.

Before the expedition began, Gardner's intention—the entire team's intention—had been to leave no trace in Netherlands New Guinea. Yet the misunderstanding with the birth illustrates how easy it was to inflict accidental harm. It soon became clear, as Gardner wrote in his journal, "that the sort of community we are trying to make here in the Grand Valley means both permanent dwellers and impermanent visitors cannot escape learning from each other."[88] The mere presence of the expedition threatened to have a cumulative, irreversible influence on the Dani. Heider later compared it to quantum mechanics: "the closer one tries to observe, the more change one effects in the subject of observation."[89]

Most of these changes were passive and inadvertent. The Dani walked into Homuak and encountered foreign languages on the radio, or metal tools in the form of Jusup's kitchen knives. Wali picked up a copy of *Raditzer*, turned it over, and discovered Matthiessen's author photo: "I remember how profoundly disturbed he was by this 'double' that had suddenly appeared, like a ghost, to trouble him," Gardner later wrote.[90] The bizarre objects carried in by the expedition forced the Dugum Dani to reimagine the boundaries of their world.

Other changes were not so passive, though still unintended. Gardner's use of shells to elicit cooperation from the local kains, his exploitation of their desires, caused jealousy and arguments between clan leaders. "There is much kibitzing about who should get shells," he noted in his journal. "They have set their hearts on what they regard as great riches and there are many competing for a limited supply. So far only Wali and Wereklowé have been given the large diadema shells. Wali and Kurelu have each been promised one in the days ahead. They already know which shell is theirs and they come often to admire it, offering the thinnest imaginable excuses for happening by."[91] Individuals who were able to supply the camp with food or manual labor were also paid in shells (and salt), which gave them an edge over other tribesmen. The economic impact of the expedition was so focused in one geographical area, Heider later acknowledged, that it may have shifted the balance of political power in the mid-valley region.[92]

And then there were the moments when the expedition suspended its stance of theoretical neutrality to directly alter the course of events. These interventions were often medical, as Matthiessen once explained to the writer Howard Norman, who would interview him repeatedly over more than a decade about his life and career. The expedition team had made "a very hard-nosed decision" to refrain from assisting any of the warriors who were hurt during battles because, Matthiessen said, "if we touched one of these injured people, and then they died, we figured there was a chance we might die, too."[93] After the team witnessed its first weem, though, this rule was inconsistently applied. Gardner attempted a small operation to remove an arrow from a man's swollen foot; within a few weeks, warriors were approaching him to have their own wounds bandaged, requests he tried to discourage by saying he wasn't a doctor. But one day a boy got an arrow through his shoulder, and the wound became infected. As the son of a kain, the boy was an important ally to the expedition. So, when it seemed like he might die without treatment, Gardner and Matthiessen milked several ounces of pus from the wound and administered antibiotics. In his interviews with Howard Norman, Matthiessen recalled an "uncomfortable" consequence of this lifesaving decision:

> One day we were up in the forest, and we were making charcoal. . . . We got charcoal on our hands, and this young man [now recovered], he was so grateful—he came running along, and I remember he grabbed my wrist and started licking the charcoal off my hand. It was unpleasant. I said, "No, no!" And he said, "Black is bad! Black is bad!" Already, somehow, he'd gotten the idea that black was inferior. I thought, "Oh, boy." And I'm sure that if he felt that way, all the rest of them did too.[94]

The reason the young man had concluded black was "bad," Matthiessen surmised, was because the white people had guns and clothes and radios. The white people had penicillin, while the Dugum Dani did not. "What are they going to do when they get to civilization?" he found himself wondering at the time. Far from leaving no trace in New Guinea, was the expedition instilling the Dani with an "inferiority complex"?

ONE DAY A GROUP of boys passed through Homuak on their way to the Catholic mission at Simokak, a two-hour walk. The boys were dressed in dirty, Western-style clothes, and an older Malay man, their teacher, wore sneakers and a baseball cap. The Dugum Dani were intrigued by the boys' exotic outfits, but the expedition team was irritated by what they saw as a potential contaminant. Gardner asked the man not to pass through Homuak again because, as he wrote in his journal, "we didn't want the doctrines of Christianity confounding the people we were visiting."[95]

A few weeks later, a police patrol crossed the Dugum frontier. Missionaries, likely from the same group the teacher belonged to, had started complaining about active warfare in the area. The police warned the warriors they'd be taken to the Wamena jail if they insisted on fighting. Rattled by the threat, the warriors abandoned plans for another weem, and an atmosphere of sulking gloom settled over their villages. Days passed, and the expedition team began to worry that a central part of Dugum Dani life had become permanently inaccessible.

In May, Broekhuijse told Gardner that he had been summoned to Hollandia to face some serious allegations. Dutch officials had heard rumors, circulated by both Catholic and Protestant missionaries, that the Harvard-Peabody Expedition was not merely observing the Dani but *encouraging* them, or even *paying* them in steel axes, to kill one another for the cameras. Matthiessen later dismissed the charge as a deliberate manipulation: "The missionaries were very anxious to use us to get to those people. And when we refused to let them in, they attacked us [by spreading lies]."[96]

Gardner was already concerned the regional authorities might try to meddle with his expedition. For this reason, the team had chosen to conceal Rockefeller's arrow wound lest it be used as an excuse to expel them from the valley. Hearing about gossiping missionaries now made Gardner furious. On May 27, he left Matthiessen and the others, traveled to Wamena, and caught a flight to Hollandia to "straighten the matter out."[97] He had never informed the Bureau of Native Affairs that his film would probably focus on the very thing the administration was hoping to abolish—ritual warfare—so this was a delicate operation. The Dutch, Gardner had finally come to understand, were mostly preoccupied with "the goals of colonialism." Any emphasis on the warfare practiced by Papuan tribesmen would be treated as a source of embarrassment. None of the officials in Netherlands New Guinea had ever stopped to consider "what that warfare means to the people who make it and how they integrate it into their lives." That was the purview of an anthropologist; they were concerned with optics. "The most important issues," Gardner wrote in his journal, "have less to do with the destinies of the indigenous peoples of New Guinea than with the disappearing colonists of Europe."

He was prepared to fly to The Hague if necessary. In Hollandia, he met with an obedient government functionary ("reeking of cheap pomade") and laid out his argument. The missionaries did not understand the situation, Gardner insisted, and their reports were inaccurate. He pointed out that the Dutch government had promised him full independence for the duration of the expedition. He defended the intellectual basis of his film, along with the work of Matthiessen, Heider, et al., by stressing the value of the knowledge they would eventually disseminate internationally. And then he requested that the local authorities "disclaim jurisdiction" over the Dugum Dani, leaving them as they were, "unpatrolled and uncontrolled."[98]

This was a tall request, but somehow Gardner managed to persuade the official; he returned to Homuak "vastly relieved."[99] For the remainder of the expedition there would be no more visits from Dutch-directed police patrols.

The missionaries, however, were not so easily vanquished. They went to the media instead. In the months after the expedition concluded, a series of articles would appear in American and Australian newspapers with explosive headlines like "Harvard Group Accused of Inciting Native War." In most of these articles, a Reverend H. M. Lake, of the Christian and Missionary Alliance, denounced Gardner and his colleagues by claiming that ritual wars in the Baliem Valley had been "pretty well stopped" until the expedition whipped them back up again.[100] This was false. The expedition may have been ethically questionable in some pretty serious ways—Gardner obviously *wanted* the wars to happen, was *invested* in them for his documentary, and a case could be made that filming violence so enthusiastically was a kind of tacit approval—but the crew never incited a weem or explicitly encouraged conflict between the Dugum Dani and their neighbors, conflict which had not "pretty well stopped" before the Americans arrived.

Matthiessen was appalled by the missionaries' insinuations. And yet, he was also fascinated by the zealotry that motivated their tactics, the absolute conviction ("we have no doubt in our own minds," Reverend Lake told the press) that an enterprise like the Harvard-Peabody Expedition was wrong, while their evangelizing project was righteous, noble, and necessary, with an end that justified the means. It was an attitude of blind faith that Matthiessen would push to imaginative extremes in his next novel.

AS WEEKS TURNED into months, the expedition amassed a formidable documentary record: tens of thousands of photographs; countless hours of film; notebooks bulging with data; preserved birds and botanical specimens. Unsurprisingly, the relentless intensity began to wear on everybody's nerves. Observing the Dugum Dani was exciting work; it was also exhausting work, and often frustrating work, too. "I was so eager to tape sound, take pictures, and steer clear of Bob's movie camera, whose whereabouts I was not sure of, that I lost my head," Rockefeller wrote in notes to accompany his audio recordings.[101] Arguments broke out between Gardner and Broekhuijse, who made it clear that he thought Gardner was out of his depth. ("He wanted to go his own way.... He was tired of having to ask me everything.")[102] Tempers also flared between Gardner and Matthiessen, in part because of egos, and in part because Matthiessen liked to use the typewriter at night not far from Gardner's bedroll. And everyone became annoyed with Eliot Elisofon: the photographer, during his month in residence, staged elaborate artificial shoots and treated the Dugum Dani with a condescending dismissiveness that bordered on aggression. "He was a pain in the neck," Matthiessen said. "We had to put a guard on him to make sure he wouldn't transgress in a way that would get us all speared to death."[103] Elisofon jokingly called this his "anthropological straight-jacket,"[104] because the guard was Karl Heider. Elisofon, in Heider's words, "was a caricature of the *Life* photographer."

In later years, Matthiessen would remember his days in Homuak mostly with fondness. But he would also recall an undercurrent of "low-grade dread," which was connected to the suffocating intimacy of camp, both between members of the team and between the team and the ever-present Dugum Dani. "I tried to be alone, but with little success," Gardner complained to his journal. "Solitude is a condition contrary to the Dani sense of rightness in human society."[105]

This dread manifested in some striking ways. Rockefeller, according to Matthiessen's memoir notes, began having nightmares and spoke, with eerie prescience, about his own death. Gardner loaded a shotgun in the tent one evening for no reason except "a vague sense of disquiet."[106]

At a joint birthday celebration for Matthiessen and Rockefeller in late May, the two of them, plus Gardner and Elisofon, banged pots and pans with silverware, seemingly in response to percussive sounds made by the Dani around them. Rockefeller either covertly or accidentally recorded the group's conversation:

"I'll smash this machine if it's on!" said Elisofon. "I'll pour water all over it. Is it on, Michael?"

"No . . ."

"Tell the truth!"

"It's not on, look at it!"

"I don't know. I don't trust you. For all I know you're recording this infamous session."[107]

As Rockefeller did so, the men slipped into lingo ("you cats are so way out!"), and pretended to play improvised instruments as Charles Mingus, Thelonious Monk, Cannonball Adderley, and Oscar Peterson. The unsettling audio of this "infamous session," which sounds like a drunken minstrel show, suggests nothing so much as deep-seated racial anxieties rising suddenly to the surface. Here were four men accustomed to positions of power, now in an alien landscape and heavily outnumbered. Feeling uncertain, diminished, and perhaps afraid, these white men attempted to blow off steam, to dispel their insecurities, to regain symbolic authority, to "match" the Dugum Dani, by appropriating the inflections of familiar Black men from home. Matthiessen ("This is, wow, man, this is a gas! Like this is a gas, man, and we're going to go wild!") still had a long way to go in his quest to shake off the trappings of his cultural background.

His "dread," however, also had an existential dimension. Sometime in June, he typed out a short poem titled "Recognition": "In my own pupil, I perceive / The black hole of the universe / And grieve / That in its depth and splendor / There is nothing to believe."[108] Though not particularly good poetry, these lines captured the nihilistic despair that briefly overcame him in the strained atmosphere of the Baliem Valley.

In a letter to Deborah Love, sent not long before he wrote "Recognition," Matthiessen referred to "moments of terror" in the camp. The letter is lost, but Deborah's surviving reply is impressive for its insight. "These moments only come at a time of pressure & exhaustion when the defenses are down, as in mescaline," she suggested.[109] Then she drew a direct line between the "terror" and the alienation Peter had struggled to overcome since childhood, his sense of having a bifurcated self. Deborah advised him to embrace the uncertainty:

> The defenses are those of the social person, the conditioned social mechanical frame, and in such moments, the real man, the natural man, the universal man, takes over and is frightening to the social man. . . . I think such an experience is the beginning of realizing one's wholeness, and that you are not separate parts gripping together. Now is the moment to really let go and see how beautifully it all works—your being & its common boundary (implying the relationship) with everything—the air, the people, the stones, & be alive in the great yes + no of life.

EARLY ONE MORNING, Matthiessen received word there was a raid by the Assuk-Palek, another enemy of the Dugum Dani, unfolding in a sweet potato garden some distance to the northwest of Homuak. Racing to the scene across a long, slippery log bridging an irrigation ditch, his foot skidded off, he stumbled forward, and a pair of binoculars around his neck smashed into his face, leaving him with a broken tooth and a mouthful of blood.

Matthiessen typed up two pages about this day (May 26), but neither of them mentions his grisly accident, which forced him to seek medical assistance in Wamena. Nor do his seven pages about a walk to the salt well at Eluerainma (June 28) mention a narrowly avoided ambush that could have resulted in his and Gardner's murder.* None of his reportage, in fact, after the first few days of the expedition, mentions himself or his colleagues or their camp or the missionaries or the Dutch police patrols in any significant way.

---

* Jan Broekhuijse got wind of the ambush, instigated by strangers to the expedition, and dispatched a messenger with a warning scribbled on a piece of torn cardboard: "Bob, by Alum there is a [*sic*] ambush against us . . . wait!! Jan."

The erasure was deliberate, Matthiessen's solution to a literary predicament that went beyond a lack of knowledge about anthropology and ecological systems. "I recall my extreme exasperation at trying to catch in words, words, words that kind of ineffable simplicity that was so patently pictorial," he later wrote to Gardner.[110] "Do you remember how we felt in those first weeks, when we first *saw*?" How did a writer hope to communicate such a singular feeling—"the 'morning of time' sense of newness, freshness, mystery"—so a reader could feel it too?

Matthiessen might have written his account in the traditional way, which he called the *National Geographic* style of expedition writing. ("You know: 'Suddenly I heard a noise behind me.'")[111] This was essentially the style he'd adopted in South America, but it now seemed inadequate in the Baliem Valley. Including himself as a character meant introducing the entire expedition team, their idiosyncrasies and opinions. It meant positioning a group of interpreters between the reader and the Dugum Dani, interpreters who risked clouding the lens with ethnocentrism (as Matthiessen himself had done in *The Cloud Forest*). When he read over the early New Guinea material in which he was represented as an "I," he felt like a "sententious intruder."[112] He wanted to get out of the way so the Dani came properly into focus: their gallantry during weems, which were so unlike our own barbarous wars; the "tremendous amount of love and caring"[113] that existed in their culture, particularly when it came to their "touching" treatment of elders; and the way they'd learned to be perpetually vigilant, able to detect the slightest movement on a horizon of grass. The Dani had unparalleled perception, which made their days intense and full, Matthiessen thought, because it meant they were always present.

To honor the rhythms of life in the valley, he decided to adopt an experimental approach. He would hurl a reader into the middle of the Dugum culture, and he would remove the expedition completely, offering no authorial "I" to function as a reassuring tour guide. He would also prevent "any emotional identification with one character," as he later told the writer James Jones: "To give a true sense of what [Dani] life is like, I had to avoid the temptation of what might be called an 'easy impact' (not necessarily false, but easy) of reader identification with one strong but at all costs likable figure."[114] Put another way, he would provide no sympathetic protagonist to "carry the reader over the rough terrain." He intended to linger on the rough terrain, detailing "a kind of community spectrum of forces and interrelationships." His account would be disorienting, perhaps, but also illuminating, using techniques of fiction to create something greater than the sum of its facts.

Matthiessen sketched out his thinking in a letter to William Shawn, hoping to secure the editor's support:

Unlike the S. American stuff, this will be concentrated and in depth and, from a literary point of view, far superior: I am using a fly-on-the-wall approach at the moment (though without presuming to enter these people's extremely complex minds), a kind of day-to-day description of these people's lives, for I much dislike the "our brown brothers" approach of most Expedition writing, and am trying for a kind of purity of description suitable to the purity and spontaneity of existence here. This may well be the last chance a writer will ever have to treat a culture <u>completely</u> untouched by civilization (it is hard to imagine this until one sees it), for the missions are hard on our heels; the job cannot be done with too much care.[115]

He would gesture at the encroaching threat of civilization through a framing metaphor: the mountain rising behind the Dugum Dani, a barrier wall which would soon fail to prevent the outside world from spilling over the top and down into their gardens.

WHEN MATTHIESSEN CONCEIVED this literary approach, which William Shawn ultimately rejected as too radical for *The New Yorker*, he had no idea just how quickly the metaphorical wall would give way.

He completed his field notes and departed the expedition on August 7, traveling home via Australia (where he had his tooth fixed) and Tahiti with an unruly souvenir from the Baliem Valley: an eight-month-old puppy named Wisa, which means, in Dani, "invested with supernatural power." Robert Gardner then left Netherlands New Guinea three weeks later, satisfied with what he'd collected for his documentary. Michael Rockefeller flew out around the same time, and Jan Broekhuijse returned to his family in Wamena. Only Karl Heider remained behind in Homuak to continue fieldwork for his dissertation, which made him the sole eyewitness to what happened next to the Dugum Dani.

On October 4, Heider sent Gardner an alarmed letter: "All is not the same. They [the Dutch] have established a [police] post fifteen minutes away, toward the Elokhera. Jegé Asuk, who knows where the future lies, has joined. Even Uwar is now a police boy junior class—he has deserted Wubarainma. I can already feel things coming apart at the seams."[116]

On October 13, Heider wrote again: "Today the police held a great peace meeting on the [Tokolik]. Kurelu was there, apparently in charge.... So the Pax Hollandia has settled in."[117]

On October 19: "... now they are working on a road. Yes. Presumably to follow the trail of blood to the [Tokolik], then who knows—perhaps a tunnel under the swamp, then to Maxey's [missionary post]. . . . Everybody is working there now—Weyak, Wali."[118]

On November 2: "There is some sort of expert up from the city to weatherproof the Wamena strip—he plans to blow up a hill and use the rubble for base and cover it with asphalt."[119]

On November 15: "Things get worse and worse. The police have the Dani over a barrel. The only consolation is that when the Indonesians . . . take over, things will be much worse."[120]

Indonesia made its move in December. President Sukarno ordered his armed forces to mobilize against the Dutch, claiming that Dutch plans to grant Netherlands New Guinea self-determination amounted to little more than the creation of a Papuan puppet state. To "liberate" the disputed territory and thus "reunite" it with Indonesia, Sukarno approved a series of military incursions, by ship and by parachute, which continued until the middle of 1962. Meanwhile, the United States, worried that Indonesia might be falling under the sway of the Soviet Union, began pressuring the Dutch into a Cold War compromise. This ultimately led to the New York Agreement of August 1962, when the Netherlands ceded control of its colony to an interim U.N. administration, which, in May 1963, then handed "Irian Barat" to Indonesia, on the shared understanding that Papuans would get to vote on their own future sometime before the end of the decade.*

What all this meant for the Dugum Dani, oblivious in their corner of the Baliem Valley, was wave after wave of social upheaval: the end of ritual warfare; the influence of Christ and Christian ethics; the enforcement of laws dictated by outsiders with no understanding of—or interest in—age-old local customs. Introduced illnesses ravaged the villages, killing dozens of people with no immunity. Even the pines of Homuak were soon cut down and turned into lumber for the police post.

The Viking Press published Matthiessen's field notes from the expedition, *Under the Mountain Wall: A Chronicle of Two Seasons in the Stone Age*, in October 1962, not long after the New York Agreement was signed. The timing transformed a book that was intended to celebrate the texture of traditional Dani life into something of an elegy for it. The Dugum people would endure, of course, but not as the expedition had found them in the early months of 1961. The specific world Matthiessen described in his book—a world where the sun shines across a chaotic battlefield, its light glinting "on breastplates

---

* The Act of Free Choice, held between July 14 and August 2, 1969, was a sham referendum restricted to 1,025 men and women handpicked by Indonesian authorities. Unsurprisingly, these electors voted overwhelmingly *against* independence from Indonesia, and for this reason it is sometimes referred to sardonically as the "Act of No Choice." Today West Papua, as it is now known, is often rocked by violent conflicts between the Indonesian military and guerrilla members of the Organisasi Papua Merdeka (OPM)—the Free Papua Movement.

of white shells, on white headdresses, on ivory boars' tusks inserted through nostrils, on wands of white egret feathers twirling like batons"[121]—was already fractured by the time his readers turned to the first page.

Under the Mountain Wall is a singular achievement, beautiful and confounding; there is nothing else quite like it in American literature. It opens with a man named Weaklekek walking down a rain-soaked mountain path that is a "glutinous mire pocked by the hooves of pigs."[122] Weaklekek is on his way to war, and Matthiessen captures the weem with journalistic flair—the scars of an ancient fire on Kurelu's chest; the reflection of warriors "writhing on the windless water" of a pool.[123] But then the book turns to quotidian vignettes: women roasting sweet potatoes; a man hunting quail with a black dog; boys sparring with toy spears near Homuak. "In the dusk their thin bodies were no more than silhouettes, outlined against the distant hill called Siobara."[124] Matthiessen arranged the book with little regard for tension or narrative momentum; it is true to life in the sense that it feels almost random. Eventually a subtle pattern does begin to emerge, though, and it is the cyclical pattern of Dani culture. A weem is generally followed by a celebratory etai, or maybe a funeral, where "[t]he heavy smoke poured out across the sili, filming the crouched bodies of the women";[125] and then, after an indeterminate period signified by more scenes of work and play, there is a sudden raid, a brutal murder, which gives rise to another weem. In effect, the book offers pieces of a social mosaic, assembled to evoke an entire way of being.

Matthiessen went to great pains to emphasize the connectedness of the Dani with nature, how they were not estranged from their surroundings. "The ferns, like the mist hung on the cliffs, the squall of parrots echoing on the walls, the sun, the distant river, were part of him as he was part of them," he wrote of Weaklekek.[126] *Under the Mountain Wall* is filled with lovely descriptions of wildlife, and in scenes of human industry the focus often drifts to animals at the edge of the frame—bees buzzing next to a funeral, the whistle of cicadas audible behind a Dani chant. The tone is never sentimental; Matthiessen adopted a steady, detached voice that reports all details equally, everything from a friendly game of whirligig to a rape ("he was in haste and was already inside her when it came to her that he was not her husband").[127] Indeed, along with dancing and daydreaming in the forest, the book features domestic violence, abortion, torture, bride-theft, and the mutilation of young girls, their finger joints hacked off as a sign of mourning. But there is next to no critical commentary or ethical judgments. For the first time in his work, Matthiessen suppressed his own perspective to convincingly sketch a lifeworld utterly different from his own.

As for his goal of vanishing entirely, however, *Under the Mountain Wall* falls short in several ways. Despite the subtitle (*Two Seasons in . . .*) and occasional references to the passing months, time signifiers are deliberately minimized throughout the text, with the Dugum Dani presented in a perpetual ethnographic present—"experience," Matthiessen wrote, "was static in the valley."[128] This is a dubious claim: experience is never static, Dani culture evolved over thousands of years, and it was still evolving when the expedition arrived. Matthiessen's use of the term "Stone Age" (as in, "a Stone Age people") is similarly fraught: like "primitive," "Neolithic," or "backwards," "Stone Age" implies that the Dani, rather than being uniquely adapted to their circumstances, were living remnants from the past of their Atomic Age observers. Matthiessen was careful to show that the Dani were no less intelligent than Westerners, but some of his language reproduced a hierarchy, prevalent at the time, that put Westerners at the top of the cultural ladder and people like the Dani somewhere on a lower rung.

A more interesting flaw is a direct result of the experimental approach Matthiessen elected to use. Gardner once made a candid admission in his journal: "I am more and more certain we have begun the corruption of the Willigiman Wallalua [Dugum Dani]; they long for things that are only emblematic of our world. They crave many of our belongings and appurtenances and then give vent to their cravings by begging and even stealing. We are really not so different from the missionaries in long-term effect on the Dani. We cannot leave with clean hands."[129] By choosing to efface the expedition from *Under the Mountain Wall*, Matthiessen left himself little room to address its unintended role in cultural disintegration. A "fly-on-the-wall" approach may have enriched his depiction, making the book a dazzling triumph of empathic imagination; but the same approach leaves it incomplete as a chronicle of the two momentous, disruptive, end-of-an-era seasons he spent in the Baliem Valley.*

Like many works that challenge literary conventions, *Under the Mountain Wall* received mixed reviews upon release. The anthropologist and writer Loren Eiseley, writing in *The New York Times*, described it as "an engrossing human document that sheds light on the story of man."[130] Leopold Pospíšil called it "remarkable" in *American Anthropologist*, adding, "I had the feeling of walking through a gallery of paintings, each masterfully executed in a wealth of colorful rhetoric."[131] Yet Pospíšil and several other critics challenged certain stylistic choices, including Matthiessen's almost total erasure

---

* *Dead Birds* suffers from the same shortcoming. Despite the honest reckoning in his journal, Gardner's much lauded, even canonical ethnographical film effaces the expedition and offers no commentary on its lasting cultural impact. It would be decades before Gardner published his feelings of guilt, although he did acknowledge in *Gardens of War: Life and Death in the New Guinea Stone Age* (1969), cowritten with Karl Heider, that "All expeditions are to some extent invasions."

of himself and his colleagues. "[O]bviously they [the Dugum Dani] had to be under the observation of an outsider for the book to be written," Paul Pickrel noted in *Harper's Magazine*, "and the outsider's presence must have altered their behavior if only a little bit."[132] The *Washington Post*'s reviewer, Daniel Carleton Gajdusek (a medical researcher who would plead guilty in 1997 to sexually abusing boys from New Guinea and Micronesia), was so confused by Matthiessen's approach that he assumed the book was spurious: "It suffers from an unnecessary attempt to add scientific or journalistic respectability to a captivating work of fiction."[133]

Matthiessen found Gajdusek's takedown so disheartening that he dashed off a defensive response to Gardner. "[M]y approach seems to make people suspicious, since they do not know how to pigeonhole the book—what the hell is it? Well, I tell myself that all original approaches to *anything* are treated with suspicion, and I'm still convinced this approach was the best one. I really don't regret it. And it must be said that about one reviewer out of four gets the scent of what I'm after and goes into a raving fit; perhaps they will infect the rest."[134]

Because it was unclassifiable, *Under the Mountain Wall* would never find the recognition it probably deserved as a work of innovative nonfiction. One notable fan, however, was Truman Capote, who moved to Sagaponack in 1964. Matthiessen liked to recount that his new neighbor once pulled him aside to talk about experimental forms. Capote wanted "to establish a genre and he wanted to be the star of that genre," but he also wanted "a foundation for this new genre," examples of work that married the persuasiveness of fact with the poetics of fiction. According to Matthiessen—this is, unfortunately, impossible to corroborate—Capote told him *Under the Mountain Wall* was a "classic" nonfiction novel, as he was calling this supposedly new genre, and a "seminal" influence on *In Cold Blood*, which was serialized in *The New Yorker* in 1965. "A book on New Guinea influencing a book on Kansas—it was in his thinking about form," Matthiessen said. "It was nice of him to tell me that."[135]

UNDER THE MOUNTAIN WALL was dedicated to "Deborah, with love." But there was an additional note at the bottom of the page about Michael Rockefeller: "Though he did not live to see the achievement of the Expedition, his participation was crucial to its success."[136]

Rockefeller's disappearance has been well documented by the journalist Carl Hoffman.[137] How, after the expedition ended, he visited his family in New York, and then returned to New Guinea to look for art in the Asmat region. How a catamaran he was sharing with a Dutch anthropologist, René

Wassing, capsized in rough waves of the Arafura Sea. How, on November 19, 1961, after a day of drifting further from the coast on the overturned hull, he decided to swim for help. How Wassing watched him slip into shark-infested waters, two empty gasoline tanks tied to his waist for buoyancy. How his father, Nelson Rockefeller, chartered a Pan Am Boeing 707 for $38,000, filled it with reporters, political aides, Mary Strawbridge (Michael's twin sister), Eliot Elisofon, and Robert Gardner, and set out on a futile and largely performative search mission. How the young man's body was never found. How his fate was never officially confirmed.

Gardner always insisted that Rockefeller perished in the Arafura Sea. "Bob would get incredibly furious at the world whenever a new theory came out that Rockefeller had been eaten by cannibals," recalled his wife, Adele Pressman. "He would just go nuts."[138]

But Matthiessen disagreed with Gardner's conviction. Over the years he heard rumors, from anthropologists and missionaries, that seemed to him entirely plausible based on his own experiences and observations in the Baliem Valley. In 1958, a Dutch police patrol had gunned down several men in the Asmat village of Otsjanep. This created an imbalance of deaths, angry ghosts that needed to be avenged through ritual killing. "It was built into their thinking and tradition and history," Matthiessen said. "That was the [rationale for] all those tribal raids."[139] Perhaps Rockefeller had made it back to shore, had been spotted by the Otsjanep people, as the rumors suggested, and was speared to death by them in revenge, becoming an unfortunate victim of the conflict between tribal traditions and colonialism.

Matthiessen once raised the theory with one of the Rockefellers. The family didn't want to hear it. "But I'm afraid that's the truth," he affirmed during an interview in 1992. "I think that's what happened to Michael."[140]

11

In Paradisum

> Western culture is so starved for spiritual identity that we exploit and ruin everything authentic that we find. We romanticize nature in the same way, and this intensifies the very sense of separation we're trying to dissolve.
>
> —PM, in conversation with Jonathan White (1994)[1]

"I REMEMBER an April afternoon in 1962, when we had taken LSD together," Matthiessen wrote in *The Snow Leopard*.[2] He was standing on the lawn behind a country house, and Deborah stepped off the terrace and floated down toward him. "D had black hair and beautiful wide eyes; in the spring breeze and light of flowers, she looked bewitched." They had been "quarreling" in recent days, relations between them already tempestuous, but the closer she came, the more his grievances seemed to fade away to nothing. Neither of them needed to speak; both intuited what the other was going to say. It was a moment of "telepathy" when she stood next to him on the grass: "our mouths snapped shut at the same instant, then burst into smiles at the precise timing of this comic mime of our old fights." Laughing, he pulled her close. Their thoughts and emotions were not similar, he wrote, "but *just the same, one mind, one Mind,* even to this: that as we held each other, both bodies turned into sapling trees that flowed into each other, grew together in one strong trunk that pushed a taproot deeper and deeper into the ground."

Deborah would also write about this moment in some LSD notes, though her memory was different on one notable point: "Once under the tree with the swing, his arms were around me, our insides were the same, we were two trees grafted in the trunk, our legs rooted far away in the ground, our branches separate and lifted. He spoiled it by describing to me how we were trees. I had to stop being one and make a social response."[3] Rather than being fully *in* the moment, Peter was still standing outside it like an observer. As he himself admitted, "an 'I' remained, aware that something-was-happening. . . . At no time did the 'I' dissolve into the miracle."[4]

DEBORAH ANNE LOVE, the woman who became Peter Matthiessen's second wife, was born in St. Louis, Missouri, on July 11, 1927—a little more than seven weeks after him. Her father was John Allan Love, founder of the Prudential Savings and Loan Association of St. Louis, and a decorated Army officer in both world wars. John Love was good with money but despotic, conservative, and crude—"rough," as Peter liked to say with WASPy condescension. Deborah's mother, Mary Chauncey Potter, was one of the first women in St. Louis to head her own real estate firm, and the first woman director of the St. Louis County Real Estate Board; her success, however, was eclipsed by the ego of her husband, who liked to belittle her. They had six children—including one son from John's previous marriage—and Deborah was their second-eldest daughter. As an adult, she would struggle to recall much that was positive about her childhood. Her father's wrath and her mother's passivity left memories, dredged up by LSD, that were "dull and stiff and peopled with the unfamiliar, pale lifeless green in color, shockingly empty and boring."[5]

The Loves lived in a large house called Whitestone, on Ladue Road in prosperous Clayton, Missouri. They employed a cook, a housekeeper, a gardener, and a revolving cast of nannies. When the cook had a night off, Mary Love prepared macaroni and cheese—the limit of her domestic prowess. Deborah's parents (like Peter's) were present but removed, uninterested in the drudgery of raising children yet unsparing when it came to social expectations. Sons had freedom; daughters were groomed, through a series of onerous rituals such as the coming-out party, to be amenable wives.

From a young age, Deborah was "the tender one," in her father's estimation. (He adored her; she grew to despise him.) Timid and skittish, she was frightened of traffic and sudden loud noises. At least some of her sensitivity can be attributed to crippling self-consciousness, a side effect of eczema so terrible it qualified as a trauma. Deborah couldn't wear wool—too painful on the skin. She was the only one of the sisters to be given her own room for privacy. "[M]ost of my life has been preoccupied with this terrible thing," she later wrote in a diary.[6] The eczema made her perceive her own body as a kind of iron maiden, with some better version of herself imprisoned inside.

Deborah always vibrated at a high emotional frequency. "I could be an authority on the source, grade, and quality of various tear falls," she told Peter.[7] As a young person she proved incapable of developing the kind of defensive shell that most people use to protect themselves from feeling too much. Deborah would feel everything, all the time, and these feelings "tend to overwhelm me," she said. But her defenselessness—an emotional transparency—was paired with an advanced conceptual ability, which made her lean into whatever she was feeling, trying to articulate and thus comprehend it. She was lonely as a little girl, then asked: *Why am I alone?* "I asked my Catholic nurse for a rosary and kneeled beside my bed every night and said Our Fathers and Hail Marys until my knees couldn't bear it, and I went to bed wondering and sad. In summer I threw myself onto the earth and stretched out my arms to hug her and be hers, and then I sat up, unchanged and baffled with yearning."[8]

As Deborah grew older, small things would bloom almost reflexively into larger existential concerns. Once, hitting a dead animal on the road, she began crying so hard she had to pull over, which then gave way to contemplation of the "human condition . . . death."[9] "The outer limits kept calling her," said her daughter, Rue. "She wasn't completely on an earthly plane, and she couldn't realign herself with an earthly plane."[10] This state of otherworldliness could make everyday life seem inconsequential, "a bad dream of pestiferous events assuming monstrous proportions in an onrush of time," as Deborah once described the simple chores of buying a lamp and ordering a new slipcover for the sofa.[11]

A woman who was inclined to think and write at this pitch was never going to be content as a St. Louis debutante. Deborah had plenty of suitors, but her brother, Kennett Love, watched her tossing away boys like "corncobs over a fence."[12] She had no intention of settling for life as a genteel society wife.

Before she spied Peter on the Sagaponack beach in the fall of 1960, Deborah had already been married twice, although neither union was in any way conventional. The first came after years of education as she tried to find a meaningful path forward: an undergraduate degree at the University of Colorado, Boulder; international studies at the Université Grenoble Alpes and the Sorbonne; courses in dramatics at the academy and theater of the American Shakespeare Festival, and then at the Neighborhood Playhouse School of the Theatre in New York. In 1955, Deborah stopped studying to marry William T. Deacon III, the son of the president of Solvents & Plastic Co. in St. Louis. Their relationship had already run its course by then, but the reason was pregnancy. The reason for divorce, which followed soon after, was miscarriage. Nevertheless, Deborah would consider this brief arrangement the one that got her "out of the house," away from the rigid demands of her parents.

Her second marriage, in 1957, was to a writer named Clement W. Pollock Jr. "The news was contained in letters to Mr. and Mrs. Love," the *St. Louis Post-Dispatch* reported, which was a roundabout way of saying it was a shotgun wedding.[13] Clem was a friend from high school, and he had just published *The Victors* with Random House. ("A prurient first novel which grovels in gratuitous obscenities," *Kirkus* declared in a review.)[14] Deborah wanted somebody to help her escape St. Louis; Clem, who shared her background and thus understood her discontent, was handsome and maybe a genius, and he moved them up to Montreal. That Clem also happened to be a reckless nihilist only made him more alluring to Deborah. Once asked, "Why would you get together with a guy like that?" she replied, "It was like tying up a wild horse in my backyard."[15]

Clem Pollock may have been dissolute, but he helped Deborah reimagine the shape of herself, guiding her away from the country clubs in which they'd both been raised and toward a more literary and intellectual milieu. He also gave her a tool to address what she called, self-deprecatingly, her "exaggerated empathy." When Clem was in the Marines as a medical corpsman during the war, he'd trained himself to "mentally flip a switch" whenever he had to pick up body parts on the battlefield. Deborah adopted his coping strategy of dissociation, turning off every time she "didn't want to react."[16] Having thus found a salve for her hypersensitivity (which worked with varying levels of success), she thought she might be able to "understand more objectively" who she was and what she was supposed to be doing in her life. "My effort towards detachment was so that I could see," she told Peter.[17]

Deborah and Clem welcomed a daughter, Deborah Rue Pollock—"Rue"—on March 17, 1958. But Clem was an alcoholic, thoroughly unsuited to fatherhood, so Deborah left him to "study and understand and learn to live a full life all alone" with her baby.[18] She had two bohemian friends from St. Louis, John and Dorothy Sherry, who now lived on the East End of Long Island. Inspired by the elemental landscape around them ("the silence drew me"),[19] she decided to move nearby, into a modest cottage on Lumber Lane in Bridgehampton, not far from the farming hamlet of Sagaponack.

Deborah's earliest letters to Peter, written while he was traveling in Africa and Netherlands New Guinea, are the letters of somebody who is looking for guidance. She refers to herself as "an unformed being."[20] She signs her name and then draws an arrow to it: "I don't know who that is."[21] She describes a "hovering vacant gloom," a sadness that is not depression so much as a sensation "of having lost contact with something vital."[22]

Deborah approached Peter warily at first: "I tried to keep you out but you got me nevertheless & now it frightens me a little bit."[23] She had no intention of falling for another man so soon after Clem, but in her letters she feels "a great pull" toward Peter, misses him so much she can barely stand it.[24] She imagines walking with him down Sagg Main Beach, then listening to Mozart together in his new house, or throwing open the windows to welcome in the distant roar of the Atlantic. In one passionate letter, written later but reflecting on the beginning of their relationship, she describes Michelangelo's *The Creation of Adam*, a copy of which was pinned above her desk: "God's forefinger is extended to Adam's. From a distance the fingers look like they are touching but actually they are not. A desire and a gesture and the current flows into life. I feel now what I have felt so often—when I wrote you letters and didn't want to close but to write on to keep the circuit open—extending my finger for the current."[25]

Peter was drawn to Deborah Love for the same reasons many people were: her beauty and elegance, her obvious goodness. As one friend remarked, "She has no mud on her soul."[26] Though she could be guarded at times, there was an ethereal quality that inspired strangers to tell her she must be somebody special ("it seems odd," Deborah wrote, "that when I am shaking in my boots and my heart is pounding these people gather around with such curiosity & wonder").[27] For Peter, just as alluring was her intelligence—those satchels of books she carried everywhere—and her uncanny intuition. For years he'd struggled with a malaise he could barely comprehend, a sense of estrangement or "deep restlessness."[28] He'd blamed his parents for causing this condition, then looked for a cure in unfamiliar places, starting with "the Work" of G. I. Gurdjieff. In the process, he had developed romantic ideas of lost paradise, a primitive Edenic wilderness where he might feel whole and at peace. In *The Snow Leopard*, he would retroactively diagnose himself with what Kierkegaard once called "the sickness of infinitude": "wandering from one path to another with no real recognition that I was embarked upon a search. . . . I only knew that at the bottom of each breath there was a hollow place that needed to be filled."[29] But then Deborah Love appeared, "a girl . . . adrift on the same instinctive search."[30] Like Peter, Deborah felt postwar America was irredeemably hollow, and that the various forms of Christianity were ineffectual remedies. Like Peter, she desired simplicity, to simplify herself. ("For what? To feel a spirit tell me why I am.")[31] But unlike Peter, she was highly articulate when it came to her personal quest; she could express her discontent in ways that still eluded him.

Deborah Love would introduce Peter Matthiessen to new vocabularies of spirituality and mysticism, which he would then absorb and incorporate into his writing. Indeed, it is difficult to overestimate the influence she would have on his thinking during the eleven years they spent together. It was because of Deborah, because of where she led him, that he would come to define his restlessness as a search for "what Zen Buddhists call our own 'true nature.'"[32]

IN EARLY APRIL 1961, just as the Harvard-Peabody Expedition was getting underway in the Baliem Valley, Deborah traveled to Manhattan and checked into the Hotel George Washington for a weekend seminar. Alan Watts, the British autodidact, lapsed Episcopalian, and scholar of comparative mysticism, whose self-described vocation was to wonder about the inner workings of the universe, was already known for wide-ranging and largely improvised lectures. The title of this one was "The Marvelous Labyrinth," and it proposed to explore how the "labyrinth [i.e., life] is not a trap but the playful elaboration of the one original gesture." ("How does that strike your fancy?" Deborah wrote to Peter. "Is life a 'playful elaboration' for you? As for me, it's a maze in which I wander dazed and bleating.")[33] Inspired by Carl Jung, Watts liked to convene a small group of students in a private apartment for two days of intensive study, during which he alternated hour-long riffs on philosophy or Eastern religion with open discussion periods, when students were encouraged to share their own thoughts and impressions.

During one of these riffs, Watts raised the subject of psychedelics. His position would be summed up in a book he was then working on, *The Joyous Cosmology*: "Is there, in short, a medicine which can give us temporarily the sensation of being integrated, of being fully one with ourselves and with nature as the biologist knows us, theoretically, to be? If so, the experience might offer clues to whatever else must be done to bring about full and continuous integration. It might be at least the tip of an Ariadne's thread to lead us out of the maze in which all of us are lost from our infancy."[34]

The discussion excited Deborah so much that she stood up to recount the details of her bad mescaline trip with Peter before he'd left for the expedition. Watts listened carefully, then told her it was dangerous to fool around with peyote "for kicks." But if Deborah hadn't been so afraid, he said, or if a doctor or psychologist had been present to help her, she would have followed her feelings instead of fighting against them. Mescaline stripped you of your "protective devices," Watts said, making it possible for you to "see something else." He suggested she could have had a breakthrough—*did* have a breakthrough, in a way: "The insight gained was worth the pain."[35]

These comments validated what Deborah had already come to suspect. She needed to try again so that she might (as Matthiessen would write in *The Snow Leopard*) "free herself by living out the fear of death, the demoniac rage at one's own helplessness that drug hallucinations represent, and in that way let go of a life-killing accumulation of defenses."[36]

Alan Watts spoke of a substance that was still new enough that Deborah, in her report back to Peter, wrote out its full name: lysergic acid diethylamide. Watts had been introduced to LSD by Aldous Huxley and a former student, John Whittelsey, both of whom were in touch with the man conducting LSD research in the UCLA department of neuropsychiatry, Keith S. Ditman. Watts's first trip under Ditman's supervision, back in 1958, was "hilariously beautiful,"[37] and subsequent experiments had brought him "into an undeniably mystical state of consciousness."[38] In his essay "The New Alchemy," which Deborah devoured at the New York seminar and then enthusiastically recommended to Peter ("I wish you could read it all"),[39] Watts suggested that mescaline and LSD were the two chemicals "of most use in creating a change of consciousness conducive to spiritual experience."[40] Deborah and Peter had already tried to open their minds using mescaline; LSD became the logical next step.

In the years before "silly" Timothy Leary "wrecked" the whole scene, as Matthiessen once told *The Guardian*—"They used to say Timothy Leary was the only LSD patient whose ego was not soluble in LSD"[41]—the drug was the subject of serious scientific research. Albert Hofmann, a Swiss chemist, discovered LSD-25 in 1938, and then its effects on the brain in 1943, when he ingested 250 micrograms. Sandoz Pharmaceuticals, where Hofmann worked, began sending free samples to the U.S. in 1949, hoping somebody might alight on a clinical application, and for much of the 1950s, LSD was used in major American medical centers (and by the CIA) to replicate the symptoms of mental illness. A small but growing contingent of people began to argue, however, that the drug was better understood as a means of inducing transcendental states—as "mind-manifesting," which is the literal meaning of "psychedelic," a term that was only coined in 1956.[42]

By the end of the decade, LSD had entered the realm of psychotherapy, and interest among patients exploded after the actor Cary Grant gave an interview extolling the benefits of his own treatment. Meanwhile, some researchers started investigating the drug's effect on creativity, and dedicated institutes soon appeared, including the International Foundation for Advanced Study in Menlo Park, California, which catered to a clientele of scientists, architects, engineers, artists, and writers.

When Peter returned home from Netherlands New Guinea, he and Deborah read all the LSD literature they could get their hands on. But what they really wanted was a teacher. How they found one is unclear, although the most likely scenario involves a New York–based architect who Deborah befriended at another of Alan Watts's seminars; the architect introduced her to a psychiatrist who was dosing his patients. Matthiessen, in various interviews given over the decades, liked to refer to this "renegade shrink" with a pseudonym: "Dr. John the Night Tripper."[43] The man's real name was James Sutherland Watt. Jim Watt administered hallucinogenic substances in both New York and Menlo Park, where he was a staff member at the International Foundation for Advanced Study; Timothy Leary once described him as one of the "turned-on doctors—psychiatrists who had taken the trip, and came back hoping to fit the new potions into the medical game."[44] (Watt more than qualified as a "renegade shrink": in 1968, he was arrested in California for smuggling large quantities of LSD and methedrine aboard his yacht. In 2001, he pled guilty to criminally negligent homicide after treating a depressed woman with "gas therapy," a mixture of carbon dioxide, oxygen, and nitrous oxide that left her brain-dead.)

According to Matthiessen, Jim Watt first gave him Sandoz acid "out in Palo Alto,"[45] which is adjacent to Menlo Park.* As with ayahuasca and mescaline, Matthiessen found the LSD experience to be jarring but wonderful. "[Y]our ego is—*pshht!* It's gone; you're like a kid in a sandbox," he told a journalist. There were moments of "dissolving in white light, being one with the Universe," and moments when he believed he was "beginning to wipe the dust away, beginning to perceive."[46] After each trip he seemed to go "more lightly" on his way, "leaving behind old residues of rage and pain."[47] This sense of becoming gradually unburdened of the damage inflicted during his childhood was so welcome that Matthiessen would take LSD, he once estimated, some thirty-five times before the end of the decade.

More than a few of these trips occurred in the context of couples therapy. Peter and Deborah visited Jim Watt together, volunteering themselves as test subjects. Watt liked to play games with his patients, to incite reactions by, for example, holding up a box with a face drawn on it and announcing, "This is your mother." The goal of these games was to prod the patient to let go of their hang-ups and resentments.

The prospect of letting go was less intimidating to Peter than it was to Deborah, whose experiments with LSD mostly mirrored her first go with mescaline. While a few trips were positive experiences, the vast majority were unrelenting horror shows that left her feeling emotionally decimated. She responded to the misery by pushing herself harder, though, by taking *more* LSD in an effort to find her way through the shadows to a place of illumination. "In this search for the new man, for the realization of the self, undivided within, and inseparable from the world," she wrote in an unpublished essay, "we will fail over and over, we will cling to the fiction of our personal entities. But is there any other choice? I think it's the only game in town because it's the ultimate game."[48]

After joint therapy sessions, Deborah got in the habit of making detailed

---

* Did Matthiessen visit the International Foundation for Advanced Study? James Fadiman, a psychologist who conducted graduate research there until 1966, could not recall the writer ever checking in. "Jim Watts may have given [LSD] to him on the side," Fadiman conceded. "We had different doctors at different times, but Jim Watt was the only one who might have done that." Fadiman, too, described Jim Watt as a "renegade."

notes on what had transpired with Peter under the influence of LSD. One day, she saw him "frightened," and "pleading with anxious eyes" for her to push through "the circle of his anger" so it might finally break like a spell. "If I approached, relief shone from his face; if I didn't do what he wanted, it became hideous with self-pity. Where does he begin and I end? Can I see self-pity in him or only project it? Whose fangs does he see on me?"[49]

During another session, Peter tried to rouse Deborah from a vision in which her internal organs (kidneys, spleen, brain filled with blood vessels) were dancing before her. Deborah wrote in her notes:

> For a while he lay on top of me and I felt our skin had changed to warm yellow wax and was flowing in a river. . . . Then we went in to it, back to the unknown "problem." It turned out to be classic & very interesting, this hideous self-consciousness comes from having to pretend to [be] something he doesn't feel. . . . He kept looking to my expression for an answer to himself. He turned away saying it was all too horrible, he was tired. But I grabbed his hair and made him keep looking into my face and by that he was forced to look into his own. . . . And then it happened, the tears trickled out. He had wanted to cry for so long, and the only way he could repress the tears was the rigidity of anger. He worried about not being a man. He had been afraid as a child, and had been made to feel ashamed.[50]

It is not hard to understand why Peter, crying with relief, saw LSD as cathartic. The "unknown 'problem'" was given a familiar form: he was not living in accordance with his authentic self. And Deborah, despite her own discomfort with the acid, felt *needed* as his conduit to "an answer." Peter told her she was "the only friend" he'd ever had. She was his "pal," they were "pals together." Deborah also wept then, she confessed in her notes, "& said, 'That's all I ever wanted all my life.'"[51]

Convinced they could guide each other out of the maze, Peter Matthiessen and Deborah Love were married beneath the white spire of the Bridgehampton Presbyterian Church on May 16, 1963, six days before his thirty-sixth birthday.

THE TWO YEARS FOLLOWING the Harvard-Peabody Expedition were busy ones for Matthiessen as a writer. Immediately burying himself in work—a way of coping, perhaps, with being stationary in Sagaponack after so much invigorating travel—he polished his field notes and published *Under the Mountain Wall*, and then argued with his agent over foreign editions of *The Cloud Forest*. He accepted an award of merit for both books from the American Academy of Arts and Letters. He considered new projects—a biography of John James Audubon; an article on the Arabian Desert for *The New Yorker*—and pushed himself to try new forms. He sketched out a plan for an illustrated children's book about the extinct great auk.* He drafted a comic tragedy in two acts, "Monkey House," which climaxed with a chimpanzee being framed for a man's murder. He wrote a short story for *The Saturday Evening Post*, "Midnight Turning Gray," and a long appreciative essay on Atlantic coast landscapes from Maine to Florida for *The American Heritage Book of Natural Wonders*.

But the most significant thing was a new novel, which Matthiessen quickly recognized as the best piece of fiction he had yet produced. The manuscript had a number of provisional titles: "As it is in Heaven"; "Kingdom Come"; "Mare Imbrium"; "Culmination of Evils" (after the jungle mission in which much of the action takes place, Remate de Males); "The Trespassers," which was not bad; and Matthiessen's preference, "In Paradisum," borrowed from the Requiem Mass ("*In paradisum / deducant te Angeli . . .*"). The title that would ultimately stick, however, captured the essence of the story in one arresting phrase. "The fields of the Lord" refers to land that is metaphorically fallow, awaiting spiritual cultivation by people who are doing the Lord's good work—i.e., missionaries. *At Play in the Fields of the Lord* is sharply ironic, spoken in the novel over a radio ("I'm at play in the fields of the Lord . . . Repeat, at play in the fields of the Lord") by a nonbeliever who views "the Lord's work" with contempt, but who is nevertheless awed by a vast green world full of incomprehensible mysteries.

When Matthiessen wrote *Partisans* in the early 1950s, he used the novel to process what he'd gone through in Paris with the CIA. A decade later, *At Play in the Fields of the Lord* performed a similar function: it was a creative response to his travels in North America, South America, and Netherlands New Guinea. The narrative would feature many details he'd witnessed along the way—a wood moth with spots on its wings like two watchful eyes; a hotel bar that doubled as the town meeting place; a Bolivian uprising—and memorable people he'd encountered, including Clayton Templeton of the New Tribes Mission, and Jean Jacques Gauvin, the French Canadian drifter who carried little on his person besides a razor in a matchbox. The self-righteous obstinacy of the New Guinea missionaries, the sharp environmental aware-

---

* *Seal Pool* would be published by Doubleday in 1972, with illustrations by Matthiessen's former *Paris Review* associate William Pène du Bois. Set in Central Park Zoo, the short, whimsical book is full of talking animals ("The Bear remarked that New York was a dark and dingy place, though full of game"), and stars Matthiessen's two eldest children, Luke and Sara Carey. If the book was, as it seems to be, an attempt by the author to express paternal affection, it arrived a little late: Luke was nineteen and Sara Carey eighteen by the time it finally came out. Luke also struggled to recognize himself in the depiction of "two Upper East Side children, which we never were."

ness of the Dugum Dani, the troubling ethics of cross-cultural contact: all was jumbled together to create something original. Matthiessen may have evaded difficult questions in *Under the Mountain Wall*, but he would confront them directly through the medium of fiction.

He began with a feeling, "a secret, wonderful, exciting feeling," as he often did in his work. "The real seed of a novel is not an idea but this gritty, primordial feeling which is the most precious thing in the whole book. It is what I try to present to people, so that even after they have forgotten the characters and the people, they still remember the feel of the book."[52]

This feeling was connected to Amazonia. "I was stirred by the enormous *thickness* and extent of that great forest, the claustrophobia, and the long history of violence by civilized man against wild peoples. Also, a pervasive torpor and brutality in the river settlements, the mindless cruelty to dogs and other creatures. Cruelty and humorlessness pervade the miasmal atmosphere in backcountry South America—perhaps a reverberation of the Spanish conquests and the genocides of the rubber days when the Indians were enslaved."[53] The jungle both repulsed and intrigued him with a Conradian "air of violence, a heart-of-darkness atmosphere."[54] It also seemed porous enough to absorb a whole matrix of human behavior, anything and anyone a novelist might introduce to the setting.

At Play in the Fields of the Lord revolves around two Protestant missionary couples and their questionable attempts to convert a (fictional) Indigenous tribe of people called the Niaruna. In an unnamed country that resembles Peru, in a festering backwater of "Oriente State," Leslie and Andy Huben welcome the Quarrier family: Martin, his wife, Hazel, and their angelic nine-year-old son, Billy. Leslie Huben, who has been reporting his progress for months through a fundraising newsletter, *Mission Fields*, is an ex-athlete and real estate man from Minnesota ("I am enjoying the profits of a business deal I entered into with the Lord," he writes in one issue),[55] whose colorful Hawaiian shirts conceal a ruthless zealot. Huben would rather see the Niaruna die than remain in sin. His intention is to "infect" the Indians with "a need for cloth and beads, mirrors and ax heads," which would smooth the way for the Gospel, he believes, and thus make conversion "simply a matter of time."[56]

Martin Quarrier (inspired in a general way by Clayton Templeton) is different. When he arrives from North Dakota, where he had worked among the Sioux for more than ten unsuccessful years, he plans to start fresh in his remote mission station on the Río Espíritu. Quarrier objects to "rice Christians," meaning converts lured to worship by the promises of food and goods; he wants to lead the Niaruna out of their "darkness" through pure Christian example. Quarrier is supposed to assist Huben in a joint missionary effort, but they are temperamentally mismatched. Quarrier displays an alarming curiosity about Niaruna customs and beliefs—"You're not here as a sociologist, Martin," Huben snaps[57]—and a willingness to dispense with Church standards he finds superfluous, like insisting the Indians cover their nakedness with Western-style clothes around the mission. That Quarrier is grappling with a loss of evangelical zeal is pointed out by his own wife, Hazel, a pitiful woman whose fearfulness has made her even more of a fundamentalist than Huben. ("Why have we come here? she cried silently. What am I doing in this awful place? Jesus said: *In the world ye shall have tribulations: but be of good cheer; I have overcome the world*. Remembering this, she felt a little better.")[58] In fact, Quarrier is terrified that his faith might be slipping; to lose his God would be to lose the legible pattern of his life, which already feels to him like a failure.

When the novel opens, the missionaries come into immediate conflict with El Comandante Rufino Guzmán, the prefect of Oriente State. An "incensed executor of his own law, swollen and jovial with power,"[59] Guzmán has been charged by the federal government with pacifying the Niaruna so the region can be developed. Guzmán's preferred method for achieving pacification is violence: two American soldiers of fortune, indebted to him and unable to leave the area without their passports, which Guzmán is holding ransom, will drop bombs from a small plane over Niaruna territory, thereby killing the Indians, or at the very least driving them across the frontier and out of his jurisdiction. These are the stakes if the missionaries fail: the "Lord's unconquered fields,"[60] as Huben sees the rainforest, will be strafed.

Much of the narrative follows Quarrier's desperate efforts to evangelize the Niaruna, who are caught between gunpowder and the Gospels as preached by both the Protestant missionaries and by a Catholic padre named Father Xantes, "the Opposition." The pressure of the situation begins to mount, and the missionaries' tension grows like a fungus: "Their suspense and fear were made still worse by Hazel, who spoke wildly of the jungle and could talk of nothing else, describing obscenely the obscenity of the flowering and rot, the pale phallic trunks and dark soft caverns, the rampant hair, the slime and infestations."[61] Hazel goes mad because of the jungle, which looks to her like Satan's cathedral. Young Billy succumbs to blackwater fever. Martin loses his faith, and then finally his life at the hands of the missionaries' only "successful" convert, a conniving Tiro man named Uyuyu, or "Yoyo," who yo-yos between the would-be dominators—Protestant, Catholic, Guzmán—in an attempt to alleviate the self-loathing he's inherited from these foreigners who supposedly "saved" him.

Were this the extent of *At Play in the Fields of the Lord*, it would work as a blistering critique of colonialism, missionary idealism, American imperialism, and of various projects to "civilize" or subjugate Indigenous peoples in the name of progress. It would also resonate as a warning about the fragility of the Amazon rainforest. But this is only half of Matthiessen's novel.

The other half concerns the two American soldiers of fortune Guzmán attempts to blackmail into bombing the Niaruna. One of these men, Wolfie, with his dark glasses and gold earring, was based on the belligerent Jewish mercenary Matthiessen met while traveling through the Sudan in 1961. The other, more central character—Meriwether Lewis Moon—is an imaginative composite of three real-life people: the hostile Diné hitchhiker Matthiessen picked up while researching *Wildlife in America*; Jean Jacques Gauvin, the French Canadian; and Peter Matthiessen himself. Lewis Moon "is extremely angry and alienated and desperate, and I understood him pretty well," Matthiessen acknowledged a few years after the novel was published. "I think the important thing that I did not understand was that this angry, desperate, searching person was me."[62]

Like Matthiessen's earlier protagonists, Moon is a man at odds with his background. But here the alienation is emphasized along racial lines rather than class ones: Moon is part white, part Cheyenne and Choctaw. "[H]e's like a house cat somebody runs out on," Wolfie explains, "like turns out at the edge of some woods: he don't belong where he comes from and he don't belong where he is, so he keeps movin, and soon he's a wild animal that you don't never tame again."[63] Moon also embodies the intense outsider, the living id, or the "specter escaped from the dark attic of the mind" who haunts Matthiessen's prior fictions all the way back to "Sadie." This shadowy man unsettles everyone he looks at; Huben feels "exposed and wretched"[64] under Moon's gaze, while Quarrier senses that Moon can see through him to the doubt and lust he is struggling to conceal. Even Wolfie is ambivalent. "Moon is kind of like a threat," he says of his business partner. "He don't seem to care about nothin nobody else cares about, not even his own life hardly; so as long as a guy like that's around, the things you thought were so important, they begin to look kind of stupid."[65]

Lewis Moon is starved for meaning, but he catches a glimpse of something promising while he and Wolfie are flying reconnaissance for Guzmán. In a clearing in the jungle (like the one Matthiessen spotted in Brazil while flying over "Canueira country"), a Niaruna warrior steps out from the trees to fire a blue-and-yellow-feathered arrow at the plane. The sight of this "lone naked figure howling at the sky"[66] electrifies Moon as a symbol of something genuine. It is, he decides, just what he'd come to South America to find.*

---

* A book that Matthiessen read during the editing process for *At Play*, which may have influenced his characterization of Meriwether Lewis Moon, was *Ishi in Two Worlds* (1961), the anthropologist Theodora Kroeber's biography about the last known survivor of an exterminated Indian tribe (the

Back at the settlement of Madre de Dios, Moon procures a draught of ayahuasca. "*I* need it," he tells Wolfie; "it allows me to *see*."[67] His psychedelic trip, described over eighteen freewheeling pages in which the very paragraphs and sentences start to break apart, collapses past and present, and climaxes with a vision of childhood paradise—"a young animal among animals in a soft summer sunrise."[68]

Still under the influence, Moon smashes his watch, thereby repudiating the ordered, "civilized" world. Then he abandons Wolfie, commandeers their plane, runs down the gas, and parachutes from the gliding wreckage into Niaruna country, which now resembles an Eden: "a flight of parakeets shimmered downriver like a windburst of bright petals, and an alabaster egret burned his eye. He laughed with joy and sang."[69]

Moon infiltrates the Niaruna, masquerading as Kisu-Mu, the Great Spirit of the Rain, to ensure his acceptance and survival. He takes off his clothes and fastens his penis to his belly with string. He tries to toughen his feet by walking across rocks. "He had never envied anything so much as the identity of these people with their surroundings, nor realized quite so painfully how displaced he had always been."[70] Moon romanticizes the Niaruna as still living with "the true dignity of the Old Ways,"[71] as he puts it; they have an immediacy and awareness he thinks he has lost, and which he now hopes to regain. Soon, Moon convinces himself that he can help the Niaruna fend off Guzmán and the Protestant missionaries by forming an Indigenous confederacy of tribes more powerful than the Iroquois.

But the Niaruna are far from noble savages, and this is not a savior narrative. Moon's romantic primitivism, yet another form of colonialism, sits at deliberate odds with Matthiessen's nuanced and unsentimental portrait of the Niaruna, which is every bit as convincing as anything in *Under the Mountain Wall*. Moon's meddling with tribal governance triggers jealousies and fractious arguments among the leaders. And eventually his very presence proves ruinous. He spreads influenza to the Indians, causing a fatal epidemic that seals their extinction. He may have approached the Niaruna with admiration, to observe and then preserve their culture; but his actions make him little different, in the end, from the missionaries he claims to revile. Any form of sustained contact inflicts irreversible damage. Lewis Moon (like members of the Harvard-Peabody Expedition) cannot leave with clean hands.

At Play in the Fields of the Lord concludes with one of the finest scenes Matthiessen would ever write as a novelist. Malarial and hallucinating, Moon

---

Yahi), who was forced to make a new life in white society. Matthiessen also read Hermann Hesse's *Steppenwolf* (1927), from which he drew his novel's epigraph: "The way to innocence, to the uncreated and to God leads on, not back, not back to the wolf or to the child, but ever further into sin, ever deeper into human life."

floats in a canoe down the Río Espíritu—the Spirit River; the River Styx. He feels bereft, "though of what he did not know."[72] Having been disabused of his pastoral fantasies and lost nearly everything, he realizes he is "neither white nor Indian, man nor animal, but some mute, naked strand of protoplasm." This apprehension of his true self is presented as a moment of transcendence, the recovery, in a sense, of lost innocence. Moon is almost certainly doomed to die in the wilderness, but the final sentences show him approaching the peace of an enlightened being. "The wind was bright. Laid naked to the sun and sky, he felt himself open like a flower. Soon he slept. At dark he built an enormous fire, in celebration of the only man beneath the eye of Heaven."[73]

BOLD, ECCENTRIC, and often thrilling, Matthiessen's novel subverted old imperialist adventure tales by the likes of Edgar Rice Burroughs. The influence of Conrad was clear, along with Graham Greene and, perhaps, the existential despair of Paul Bowles's *The Sheltering Sky* (1949). At a time when many American writers were looking to cities for inspiration, or anatomizing despair-filled marriages in the new suburban sprawl, Matthiessen had found his element in sublime landscapes, in extreme emotional states, in people teetering on the edge of the ontological abyss.* The novel was a throwback in some ways, but it was also startlingly modern for its depiction of psychedelics as a pathway to freedom; for its cynicism about mainstream American society; for its ecological consciousness, its interest in Indigenous connections with the land; and for its admiring comments about Eastern religions, largely derived from Alan Watts, whom Matthiessen had started reading at Deborah's encouragement.

He forwarded the manuscript to his agent in May 1964. He was "awfully anxious to get settled quickly with a publisher," he told Diarmuid Russell, having decided to part ways for the time being with Viking. "Please make very clear [to acquiring editors] that this is not a finished draft by any means: there are still dead spots, over-statements of theme, under-developed characters, incomplete perceptions, etc. . . . But it's finished enough so that they will know how badly they want it."[74]

---

* One obvious comparison is Saul Bellow's *Henderson the Rain King* (1959), in which middle-aged Eugene Henderson travels to Africa in search of spiritual fulfillment. Matthiessen greatly admired the novel, though he thought Bellow had not pushed Henderson as far as he pushed Lewis Moon: "The entire book seems to build towards this epiphany, this liberation in a unifying vision. But Bellow, for whatever reason, does not break through, does not go all the way. This seems to me the one serious flaw in his best and most adventurous book. Like Beckett, he is exceptionally intellectual, cerebral, which makes it all the harder. Everything in their Western training would resist a leap into the unknown that transcends words or even thoughts. Yet both seem very aware of something beyond thought that holds astonishing significance."

Matthiessen had been courted in advance by Simon & Schuster, Harper, Scribner, Random House, Houghton Mifflin, McGraw-Hill, Atheneum, and Norton; Farrar, Straus was also requesting a look. Russell made copies of the manuscript and distributed them to a targeted list of editors. The reception, almost immediately, was gushing. "I think it is an extraordinary and powerful book," an editor at Scribner wrote to Matthiessen. "I cannot recall a contemporary novel that gives such a compelling sense of the primitive world, the outside and the inside of it both, the jungle and man's nature. And that is not all you do; you put the complications and contradictions of belief—the ideas and questions—in essential dramatic terms."[75] Paul Brooks at Houghton Mifflin thought the book was "one of the most beautiful and powerful novels that has been written in recent years," adding, "I think that you have succeeded in the most difficult task of wedding myth to realism—or rather, perhaps, in erasing the conventional line between the two."[76] Robert Gutwillig, executive editor of McGraw-Hill's trade book department, was even more effusive. "I am as of this moment so overwhelmed by the book that I fear I will sound more like an advertising copywriter than an editor. This is simply the best, most exciting, most beautiful novel by an American that I have read since, I guess, AUGIE MARCH."[77]

But the most rapturous response came from the same editor who had once declared that *Race Rock* "stank on ice." Joe Fox, at Random House, was a tall, shambling man who edited Truman Capote, Ralph Ellison, and Philip Roth. He was extremely well connected ("like an old courtier who understood and could arrange almost anything," said the writer James Salter),[78] gruff but affectionate, and highly excitable when he found an unpublished manuscript he admired. Matthiessen had known Fox for decades, ever since they were both stationed at Pearl Harbor at the end of the war, which is perhaps why the editor now felt emboldened to send sixteen different letters begging for *At Play in the Fields of the Lord*, some of them multiple pages long.

"I spent most of the weekend thinking about The Book," Fox wrote. "The thought of not being the editor of this book makes my stomach churn and my hands shake."[79]

"I warn you that you are going to be getting a letter from me every day until you sign a contract with us," he wrote. "The sooner you capitulate the sooner I'll stop nagging you. My determination can be compared to the effect of LSD: don't fight it, relax and enjoy it."[80]

"Why are you torturing me this way?" he wrote. "What have I ever done to you to deserve this—except turn down your first novel at a critical moment when you needed assurance, money and help?"[81]

"Reports filter in," he wrote. "I hear that Gutwillig is 'very enthusiastic.' [Robert] Gottlieb is also enthusiastic, but says he believes 'the book needs a lot of work.' Bah! Cross S&S off your list. Gottlieb is a great friend of mine, but I knife him in the back with no hesitation at all over this book."[82]

"On Saturday night we saw the Styrons," he wrote. "I told Bill how good your book was, and he was delighted. Since I have sometimes found him to be less than delirious on hearing the news that one of his peers has written a good book, I was warmed by his enthusiasm. He is a good friend to you, so why don't you follow his advice? He thinks that Random House is the place for you too."[83]

"I asked Diarmuid yesterday how much longer he thought it would be before you made up your mind," he wrote. "He said airily that he had no idea, and told me that the agony of waiting was good for my soul. If so, my soul is in better shape than it has ever been."[84]

In early June, Matthiessen caught a ride with Fox and Irwin Shaw to a surprise birthday party for Bill Styron in Connecticut. Matthiessen and Fox rode up front, Fox petitioning him the entire trip about the book; Shaw sat in the back, sullen and saying little until they reached the Styrons' farmhouse, at which point he jealously announced: "I want you both to know that I've had six sets of friends in my life, and I'm ready to start on my seventh."[85] (The men "sort of laughed it off," Fox later told Michael Shnayerson, but Shaw, who was already disgruntled with his publisher, left Random House "the next week.")

What made Matthiessen finally accept Fox's offer of $15,000—"I am still in something of a daze," Fox wrote; "I don't think I have ever been so pleased about publishing a book"[86]—was not the barrage of flattering attention. It was the editor's keen understanding of what *At Play in the Fields of the Lord* was really about. In a letter sent soon before release, Fox would explain to a colleague that the novel was, "despite its indictment of missionary ways, a very religious book, much concerned with the idea of God, and Moon seems to me to be a man who is searching for something to believe in."[87]

TO SAY JOE FOX WAS a meticulous editor is something of an understatement. He was known to get so absorbed in his work that ash from his cigarettes burned holes in his sweaters. Some colleagues at Random House thought he could be a bit of a fussbudget, but nobody doubted that his attention to detail made the books better. Fox told Matthiessen they'd go over every single page of *At Play* together, a process that would be "boring" but worth the effort. He began by editing a chapter each night and three on weekends. Once he started on a manuscript, he carried the pages everywhere in a small straw bag, including to weekly tennis games and on vacation in Wyoming. He then returned the manuscript in batches, annotated with lengthy critiques.

Some of his points were "lint-picking," as Fox himself acknowledged: paragraphs that went on too long, or Matthiessen's "inordinate fondness" for colons and pronouns.[88] Other edits were more substantial, and focused on the presentation of certain characters. Should Leslie Huben be likable in the beginning, so his cold-bloodedness hit harder when it was fully revealed to the reader? Should Lewis Moon be "shown more and less told about," or would that dilute the "kind of mystery that other people are drawn to/repelled by"?[89]

Fox encouraged Matthiessen to pay attention to tone. Sometimes the heightened language worked perfectly, as with the opening of chapter one: "At four miles above sea level, Martin Quarrier, on silver wings, was pierced by celestial light: to fall from such a height, he thought, would be like entering Heaven from *above*."[90] But in other places there was a "weightiness, occasionally a self-consciousness," Fox observed. "Sometimes your sentences seem too heavy for what you are saying."[91] The final chapter posed a particular tonal challenge: after a book packed with so much violent direct action, the sharp swerve to mysticism threatened to give readers whiplash.

Yet Fox's most significant edit had to do with the novel's structure. Matthiessen wrote in close third person; he followed individual characters for several chapters at a time, then switched to another character and rewound the clock to follow their experience. All this doubling back was less suspenseful than confusing and repetitious. To fix the issue, Fox studied the manuscript until he mastered its internal chronology; then he placed all twenty-seven chapters on his living room floor and reordered them. When he presented Matthiessen with the new structure (1, 2, 3, 4, 5, 6, 10, 11, 7, 12 . . .), which intercut between characters from chapter to chapter, Matthiessen said, "Huh. It works." And Fox replied, "You're damned right it works."[92]

Even after the manuscript was sent to the typesetters, Fox continued to circle words and slash out paragraphs. This was the same obsessive tinkering for which Matthiessen would become infamous among book editors, and perhaps it started with Fox's permissive influence. The ayahuasca trip was massively overhauled, made tighter and more thematically subtle, while the final chapter was rewritten, Matthiessen once estimated, more than thirty times, "and even then, it wasn't the way I wanted."[93]

Joe Fox was "the most dedicated and impassioned line editor I ever worked with," Matthiessen said in 1995.[94] Fox, too, found their collaboration highly satisfying, even if Matthiessen became argumentative at some of his suggestions. "The book is worth everything—and a good deal more—that you've put into it and the small amount of work I have done," Fox wrote with characteristic modesty. "I grow more convinced every day that this is a superb novel."[95] By the time they were finished, with no more changes, the editing had stretched on for nearly ten months.

Within Random House, excitement for *At Play in the Fields of the Lord* was enormous. The novel was positioned as a major upcoming release alongside John O'Hara's *The Lockwood Concern* and Truman Capote's *In Cold Blood* (which Fox was also working on). An internal reader's report called *At Play* "a 'Moby Dick' of the South American jungle," the kind of book that only comes along "once every 50 or 100 years."[96] But there was uncertainty about how to market such a peculiar story, and this uncertainty was only exacerbated by Matthiessen, who refused to write a summary explaining his novel to the marketing team. "His literary obliqueness simply prevents him from making such a statement," Fox advised in a winking memo. Matthiessen's only suggestion was that the publicist should avoid a "search for identity" angle, instead pushing the book as "an action novel, with overtones; he mentioned with amusement, but half seriously, Paul Goodman's joking catchphrase 'a jungle Dostoyevsky.' "[97]

What Matthiessen did provide was draft copy to go on the book jacket, which revealed his aspirations for *At Play:*

> P.M.'s last novel, Raditzer, was greatly admired by Kingsley Amis, Terry Southern, and many other writers . . . In our opinion, his achievement in APITFOTL . . . is much greater, and this opinion is shared by William Styron, Norman Mailer, Truman Capote, all of whom have seen this (supply own adj) book before its publication. As Styron? Mailer? Capote? says, "APITFOTL is far superior to anything we can expect from (check one) Mailer and Styron ☐ Mailer and Capote ☐ Capote and Styron ☐."[98]

The copy was a wry joke,* but his other request was not: "a clean dignified (and therefore original) jacket minus bio, quotes, purple prose, and all the rest of the gutless funky old MadAve formula treatment which has stunned readers with its naïveté for twenty years." If Random House *insisted* on including a bio, he wanted it to downplay his forays into nonfiction. "Let's avoid impression of gentleman naturalist trying his hand at a novel!" He was already worried that a reputation for nature writing might compromise his chances at achieving the kind of literary acclaim enjoyed by some of his peers.

---

* Not entirely. As Tom Guinzburg said during an interview in 2006, "Peter was furious with me once, thirty or forty years ago, when I said something like, 'You know, I think Styron is going to be the best of all you guys when it comes to fiction.' He didn't speak to me for about a year. Well, it may not have been quite *that* bad, but that was the tenor of [his competitiveness]."

Ironically, Matthiessen was still making the bulk of his income as a "gentleman naturalist" for *The New Yorker*. His letters to Random House were sent in between reporting trips to inspect new conservation initiatives around the country. For one article, "Sand and Wind and Waves," he accepted an invitation from the National Park Service to visit Assateague Island, off the coast of Maryland and Virginia, which the Johnson administration was declaring a National Seashore to protect it from private development. For another article, "Ovibos Moschatus," he traveled to Nunivak in Alaska—the same fog-shrouded island in the Bering Sea he'd failed to reach while researching *Wildlife in America*—and watched scientists capture several calves of the endangered muskox, which were then transferred to the mainland for an experimental breeding program near Fairbanks.[*]

Matthiessen needed this magazine work, especially now his family had just expanded again. On July 3, 1964, Deborah gave birth to "a fine boy"[99] named Alexander Farrar Love Matthiessen. Including Rue, whom Peter had legally adopted after marrying Deborah, this meant he now had four young children divided over two households. Fittingly, *At Play in the Fields of the Lord* was dedicated to "Luke and Carey / Rue and Alex."

BY 1965, Luke and Sara Carey were old enough to notice that their father had been away on expeditions for most of their lives. For his eldest son, now twelve, Peter was an inscrutable figure, and their interactions were "not quite fulfilled."[100] Luke resented having been abandoned when he was three, and he was confused about how he was supposed to relate to this man who appeared, from time to time, standing in the doorway. "Given the undefined nature of things, in a way his absence was kind of a relief." There was also the complicating factor of Mike Goldberg, Patsy's second husband, whom Luke had bonded with as a stepfather. Luke *preferred* Goldberg, in fact, to his birth father—"I fell in love with Mike," he recalled—which was a source of secret guilt whenever Peter came to visit him and his sister in New York.

On those rare occasions, Luke approached him warily. "One of the things that I developed as a child was the understanding that it was probably safer not to go there, because you were going to be disappointed. He was going to leave again."[101] At the same time, Luke longed for Peter's approval: "I thought the only way I could ever achieve self-esteem was by pleasing him, getting his sanction." Peter sensed the desire for paternal affirmation in his

---

[*] Matthiessen later edited this article into a slender book with photographs, *Oomingmak* (1967). The title is the Cup'ik word for muskox and means "bearded one." *Ovibos moschatus* is the scientific name.

young son, but he didn't seem to understand the hole it signified in their relationship, despite the exact same yearning for Matty in his own childhood. In a letter to Deborah, he wrote, cluelessly: "Sunday nite went down to hear Lukisse sing Fauré Requiem—great success. Luke was so pleased by praise that he kept waving hands frantically like someone imitating a dickie bird."[102]

In later years, Peter would be candid about his impatience, coldness, and lack of curiosity as a parent. "I think I'm a good father in the sense of being responsible," he said during an interview in 2010, meaning he would come through during a crisis—"but I'm not a good father in the conventional way of seeing it. A lot of that is because I've been [an] absentee, I've been away too much. And also because I don't think artists, by and large, are good parents."[103] He invoked this excuse on multiple occasions, the idea that creative acts for an artist always and unavoidably take precedence over family affairs. "I would love to be able to say I am a father first, but first I am a writer," he said.[104] To Luke, forced to internalize this difficult lesson at a young age, Peter was more accurately described as "the most self-centered man I've ever known."[105]

Deborah could be similarly selfish, though she justified her behavior by directly connecting it to her obligations as a mother. "My primary allegiance is to the health of my children and this cannot be without a relentless searching of myself," she once explained in a letter. "My drive is for an ambiance of clarity in which children can trust themselves; this requires things to be what they <u>seem</u> to be, and relationships natural and truthful."[106] Once again, however, her search for clarity and truthfulness looked very different from the perspective of her little girl, who just wanted to be fed at dinnertime. Deborah "wasn't able to compartmentalize," Rue recalled of her own childhood in Sagaponack. "*'We don't know where the universe ends and begins.' 'We don't know what happens when we die.'* These questions were looming in our house more largely than *'When do we need to do laundry next?'*" Deborah was not interested in the laundry. Rue was, because it was something she could hold on to, something grounded. "I became a pragmatic sort of person because I just had to say, 'Let's get here on the Earth, because man, we are flying off it all the time.'"[107]

By June 1965, *At Play* was with the designer at Random House, Guy Fleming, and Matthiessen was mentally preparing himself for the book's release in November. He and Deborah decided to spend the rest of summer in a secluded corner of County Galway, Ireland. Alex, eleven months old, was left in the care of Peter's parents and a nanny on Fishers Island ("I wished the baby were airmailed to me for a couple of hugs and kisses and sent away again," Deborah soon wrote);[108] but Rue, who was seven, came along for the trip, and so did Luke. Patsy's marriage to Mike Goldberg had just dramatically imploded, with Mike committed to a psychiatric ward and Patsy now struggling with alcohol addiction.* Carey was sent to a camp in Vermont. Luke needed closer supervision, though he went to Ireland unwillingly, aware of his mother's crisis and nonplussed about the prospect of spending months with people he barely knew, including his father.

Peter and Deborah crossed the Atlantic because they wanted to get away from the news about President Johnson's escalation of the war in Vietnam. Ireland was "not yet of the world, but belongs still to the earth, far more ancient and primitive and passionate," Deborah wrote.[109] The rental house was on an island, separated by an inlet from a crumbling thirteenth-century castle named Annaghkeen. There were no distractions, and no immediate lines of communication other than mail. "We pass long quiet days with never the sound of telephone or airplane or even car, only sheep and wind and lapping water," Peter rhapsodized in a letter to Joe Fox. "This week, for the first time, I have a sense of strength coming in instead of draining away—that awful and unpluggable leak after a book is finished."[110]

But the retreat to an island was not just for a break from the news cycle; it was also an attempt to heal a fissure that had opened in the marriage. One cause of the conflict was Deborah's "above-life quality," as Peter later termed it, which he found increasingly "maddening": "To live with a saint is not difficult, for a saint makes no comparisons, but saintlike aspirations present problems."[111] A much larger cause of conflict, though, was Peter's chronic unrest, his tendency to seek escape routes from every situation. "He is angry for being in love . . . for not being free," Deborah wrote in her journal.[112] He could not help himself, even in Ireland. He went for slow solo walks around Annaghkeen. He read books about Robert Falcon Scott's *Terra Nova* Expedition to the South Pole—another form of escapism. He stood for a long time gazing out to sea, which caused Luke to say to Deborah: "Dad is thinking of house sites I bet. Boy, he has a lot of dreams that won't come true."[113]

In July, a drive to Yeats country in Sligo erupted with recriminations. "We were estranged again," Deborah wrote. "Rue, in the back seat, put a hand on each of us and tried to press us toward each other. 'Stop the fight,' she

---

* Mike Goldberg had stolen ten paintings from their friend Willem de Kooning, forged de Kooning's signature, and then sold eight of the canvases for a tidy profit. As Patsy later told Frank O'Hara's biographer, Brad Gooch: "It finally all came out. . . . I managed to get de Kooning to agree not to prosecute, which wasn't easy because he had a very tough lawyer, Lee Eastman. He promised not to prosecute if I returned the paintings and Mike went to a psychiatric institute, which I managed to get him into. I had to sell a Pollock [which she had bought in Springs, and then kept during the divorce with Peter] and a Kline I owned to get them back. Mike was a psychopathic personality. . . . [The doctors] succeeded in making him into a fairly reputable person. But I could not be married to him after that." Compounding the loss for Patsy, Frank O'Hara, her great friend, would die after a freak accident on Fire Island in the summer of 1966.

chanted, 'remember you're husband and wife.' Unable to laugh, yet astonished and touched, we were silent and anger slowed to sorrow."[114] Peter wanted a wife and children. He once pricked Rue's finger, then his own, and pressed them together to affirm she was his daughter despite having different blood. But Deborah, Rue, and Luke (and Carey, back home) were often made to feel like rocks in his rucksack that he was desperate to offload.

At the start of August, after weeks of exhausting, frequently one-sided arguments ("as I sat with Rue cradled in my arms, a voice hissed epithets which went unanswered"),[115] Peter and Deborah left Luke and Rue for a few days with friends in Dublin. Then they drove southwest to Mount Melleray Abbey, a community of Cistercian monks in County Waterford. Deborah had discovered visitors could stay overnight and participate a little in monastic rituals. When she suggested that it might be good for them to go—maybe they would find some peace there—Peter agreed. "It interested him very much."[116] Both of them, in fact, had already spoken about entering monasteries once the children were grown, to devote themselves to "strange disciplines." Trying to explain the appeal, Deborah would later write:

> There is a therapy where the patient is put to bed in a room alone and at first finds it a blissful removal from the scene of his inadequacies. This brief rest turns to acute distress as the truth of one's behavior seeps unopposed into the vacuum. There is no relief; only the empty answers of pride. Endured, a sound barrier is broken, and one comes into being, humble and silent. The patient is now allowed into the garden, still without speech, and often sees for the first time, the blossoms, the leaves. Gradually words are allowed, and the patients may convey information to each other. . . . In this way, one comes to himself sensorily and finds the mind, the seat of speech, not the self, after all, but an integrator of the self, a tool, more complex than his hand.[117]

After a night at Mount Melleray, Deborah emerged from the ladies' guesthouse, feeling somewhat dissatisfied with the brief experience, to find Peter standing near their car beneath a tree. She drifted over and pulled him into a grateful embrace. "I'm very glad to see you," he said.[118] They drove south to the seaside resort town of Youghal, found a café, and ordered an indulgent breakfast of eggs, bacon, sausage, and cornflakes for twelve shillings.

12

A Simple Man

> I return often to that extraordinary suicide note from a Turgenev novel, *Fathers and Sons:* "I could not simplify myself." That note has always twisted my heart painfully. Why? Because I have bitter experience of that—the failure to simplify the self—and were I ever to commit suicide, that would be the reason.
>
> —PM, "Simplicity" teisho (undated)[1]

THE FIRST SIGNIFICANT REVIEW of *At Play in the Fields of the Lord* that Matthiessen read, in *Harper's Magazine*, left him seething with indignation. The problem was not so much the tepid verdict—"quite a lot of post-Maugham and post-Greene clichés"—as the fact that the critic, Roderick Cook, had skimmed the novel at most, and then invented a summary that bore only a cursory resemblance to the novel's actual plot.[2] Matthiessen wrote an outraged letter to the magazine's editor: "If Harper's rather than the helpless author were stuck with the gratuitous stupidities of its reviewers, I feel certain you would understand not only my personal discouragement but the general contempt among writers at large for book critics of this calibre."[3] The novel was "demeaned," he continued, by Cook's bizarre fabrications, "but so is Harper's, where writers should be able to expect a more responsible reception." After Bill Styron also sent a letter decrying the "supercilious dismissal of so fine a book,"[4] the magazine forced Cook to write a humiliating mea culpa, which was printed for all to see in a subsequent issue.

Other reviews of *At Play* were more scrupulous in their summaries, and a number of critics lauded the novel as one of the year's finest. It put Matthiessen "in the ranks of America's most perceptive writers."[5] It revived "one's faith in the future of fiction."[6] It was a "weird and engrossing" concoction of "sex, prayer, mosquitoes and vultures, jaguars and anacondas, man-eating ants and emerald parakeets."[7]

Vogue, *Life*, and *Time* were unrestrained with praise. *The New York Times* and *The New York Review of Books*, however, added a sprinkle of salt to their reviews. While the novel was filled with beautiful prose and ingenious plotting, wasn't it, in the end, just an old-fashioned adventure story? With their strong whiff of genre snobbery, these reviews elicited a stinging rebuke from Peter S. Prescott in his syndicated book column:

> Some reviewers who have grappled with Mr. Matthiessen's fourth novel are unable to deny its manifold merits, but they are oddly disturbed: this is, as they see it, a conservative novel; it cannot, therefore, be as good as it seems. These reviewers, anxious to build a new establishment on the literary left, criticize "At Play in the Fields of the Lord" because it was not written as Nabokov or Bellow would have written it—and indeed it was not. But in demanding that Mr. Matthiessen write in the only vein which they believe to be relevant to literature today, they are unable to appreciate the extent of what Mr. Matthiessen has actually accomplished.[8]

Privately, Matthiessen tried to shrug off the "nervous" New York critics. "The 'adventure' label might not hurt the sales," he reassured himself in some notes, "whatever its effect on my good temper."[9] He took comfort in Styron's assessment that he was finally writing at full capacity. He was heartened, too, by the congratulations and fan letters he received from various quarters. An ex-missionary who now worked for the Peace Corps told him that every trait, deed, and self-righteous utterance of his fictional missionaries was plausibly rendered, or even underplayed. The psychologist Ralph Metzner, editor of the *Psychedelic Review*, and an associate of Timothy Leary's, wrote to say that the ayahuasca chapter was one of the most brilliant descriptions of a psychedelic trip he had ever read.[10] Matthiessen even received a note from the Passaic County Jail, in New Jersey: a woman picked up on a fugitive warrant had discovered a copy of *At Play* in the jail library, then decided to seek out "dear Lewis Moon." Amused, Matthiessen replied to the letter, then kept up a correspondence with the woman for more than three years.

In one sense, at least, the reviews were irrelevant, along with the strong sales and selection by the Literary Guild Book Club. Before the novel was even released, it already constituted the single biggest financial success Matthiessen would ever have. The Random House advance ($15,000) didn't include international rights, which went to Heinemann in London for an additional fee. Nor did the original advance cover the reprint paperback rights, which were sold to the New American Library for $100,000. Meanwhile, the film rights were acquired by MGM, in a major deal brokered by the New York–based producer Stuart Millar, for $250,000.* In gross, before taxes, agent commissions, and Random House's cut of the reprint sale, *At Play in the Fields of the Lord* earned Matthiessen a modern-day equivalent of more than $3 million.

After signing the contracts, he set up trust funds to cover college tuition for his four children. Then, to celebrate his staggering turn of fortune, he purchased what he playfully called "success coats": otter skin for Deborah, and one in gray wool with a nutria collar for himself.

MATTHIESSEN'S WINDFALL AFFORDED him financial freedom as a writer. For the first time in his career, he was able to eschew all other work (those magazine articles) and focus exclusively on novels, which was what he'd always said he wanted. Nevertheless, he now chose to do exactly the opposite, temporarily setting the fiction aside.

The reason for this surprising decision was environmental. All around him in Sagaponack, the East End was transforming with astonishing speed. Sand dunes near the house had already been leveled for a parking lot, and tourist traffic now clogged the road to Sagg Main Beach. Real estate developers had begun to acquire the historic farms and replace them with garish private estates for wealthy people from away. Wetlands were being bulkheaded, or filled in entirely, depriving ducks of precious habitat; scrub oaks were being bulldozed in favor of irrigated lawns. *Silent Spring* may have started a national debate over pesticide use, but the effects of synthetic chemicals were still plainly apparent on the local landscape: the number of fiddler crabs in the spartina grass had plummeted, while osprey, which fed on contaminated fish, left nests on Gardiners Island and Cartwright Shoal that were omi-

---

* "I think this is going to be one of the great movies of all time," Millar told Matthiessen. What it turned out to be, for twenty-five years, was one of the most infamous examples of development hell in Hollywood. A whole book could be written about the convoluted film history of *At Play in the Fields of the Lord*, as the journalist Chip Brown once illustrated in a lengthy piece about that very subject for *Esquire*. "If the problem wasn't with the director," Brown wrote, "it was with the script, or the cast wasn't right, or the natives were restless, or the weather was too wet, or the budget was too big, or the studio's boss-of-the-month had his mind elsewhere." In 1965, Stuart Millar wanted Arthur Penn as director, and Warren Beatty in the role of Lewis Moon (which Matthiessen hated: "Beatty looks as Indian as Anita Ekberg, and has all the enigma of a hamburger," he told Joe Fox). But it was not until 1990 that another producer, Saul Zaentz, managed to mount a $30 million production in Belém, Brazil, with Héctor Babenco in the director's chair. Babenco showed the novel to some anthropologists, who told him that Matthiessen's fictional tribe was culturally accurate. Satisfied, Babenco then assembled a cast that included Tom Berenger (Lewis Moon), Aidan Quinn (Martin Quarrier), John Lithgow (Leslie Huben), Daryl Hannah (Andy Huben), Kathy Bates (Hazel Quarrier), Tom Waits (Wolfie), and an impressive legion of Indigenous Brazilians. When the three-hour movie finally arrived in cinemas, in December 1991, it received mixed reviews and bombed at the box office. Yet Matthiessen, who had tweaked some dialogue but otherwise remained uninvolved, thought it was a surprisingly solid effort. "It has the best Indian material I've ever seen," he said. "It makes *Dances with Wolves* look like kindergarten."

nously empty. Matthiessen began calling his children outside whenever a sea hawk flew overhead, worried that each sighting might be the last.[11]

"I am heartbroken," Deborah had written from Sagaponack in 1961. "This place is one of the last places and representative of what is happening to the world that human beings must occupy. It is being emptied inexorably and stuffed with stale inert matter and all the lovely potential of being human crowded into small pockets of lessening possibility."[12] A few years on, it was hard to deny the accuracy of her lament, and Matthiessen penned his own for the letters page of *The East Hampton Star*. "It is not a question of standing in the way of 'progress'; it is a question of understanding what true progress is. What progress is not is condemning one million acres of American land per year (our present rate) to asphalt; every year we have more highways (and more people) and every year we have fewer places left to go. 'Progress' is the last refuge of the speculator and the spoiler, just as 'patriotism is the last refuge of the scoundrel,'" he wrote, riffing on the famous adage by Samuel Johnson.[13]

On November 3, 1965, Matthiessen flew to Washington, D.C., for a job interview with the thirty-seventh United States secretary of the interior. As the plane banked around the Pentagon on its approach to Washington National Airport, he peered through the window in search of the spot where a Quaker man, just the day before, had set himself on fire and burned to death in a grim act of protest against the Vietnam War.

Secretary Stewart Udall—"a short, well-made man with plenty of spring in him," Matthiessen wrote in his notes from their first meeting[14]—was a major proponent of conservation. In the nearly five years Udall had already spent running the Department of the Interior, first under President Kennedy and now Johnson, he had established new national parks, seashores, monuments, and wildlife refuges around the country; addressed water pollution and urban renewal issues; helped pass the Wilderness Act of 1964; and convened the Committee on Rare and Endangered Wildlife Species, which advised the government on official designations and captive breeding programs.[15] Udall also considered himself to be something of a writer, having produced a book, *The Quiet Crisis* (1963), which praised "the land wisdom of the Indians" and called for an Aldo Leopold–inspired "land ethic for tomorrow." In his wood-paneled office, he pulled a copy of *Under the Mountain Wall* off the shelf, asking Matthiessen: "This is the expedition that young Rockefeller was on, isn't it?" Then he handed over a poem he'd written to commemorate an encounter with Nikita Khrushchev, first secretary of the Communist Party of the Soviet Union. "I appreciated this gesture," Matthiessen wrote in his notes, "which was designed to show me that we were in this literary game together, baby."

Secretary Udall had summoned Matthiessen to Washington because he was working on a new book and looking for "editorial aid." This was not a ghostwriting job—he would write the book himself—but he needed advice from someone who understood the challenges facing modern conservation, and who could help shape his arguments to give them more weight. Udall, Matthiessen wrote, "talked a little while about enlarging the concept of conservation . . . [which] should include such disparate problems as birth control and desalinization, wilderness and public beaches—in effect, the whole human environment." Udall wanted his new book to "deal openly" with controversial issues such as "the growth myth and the population explosion." He wanted, in other words, to mount a persuasive case for the realignment of America's values. Matthiessen understood what was being offered here: a chance to help craft "a fine, honest, and politically courageous program, crucial to the future of this country and the world."

As a special consultant ("I think that's what I'm called"), Matthiessen started commuting between New York and D.C. He was excited by the secretary's proposal; he thought Udall had the potential to become a conservation spokesman for the ages. He remained skeptical, however, that the book wouldn't be diluted by political exigencies. Washington was obviously a circus. Udall invited him, in a sleek black limousine, to public speeches and award ceremonies, to lunches with state fish-and-game directors, and to preliminary budget meetings where deep cuts were being made because of the runaway Vietnam expenditure. Matthiessen's notes were soon filled with savage commentary on the political scene. When Lady Bird Johnson smiled, "the corners of her mouth turn down, like the mouth of a galliform bird." When a politician entered a room, they invariably looked around for hands to shake: "All good politicians have this trait, which makes them infinitely predictable and therefore dull. Some are more colorful than others, but all of them, bright and dingy, keep circling restlessly around the tank, hunting out scraps." At a party one evening, Matthiessen was "stunned" when the host announced that *At Play in the Fields of the Lord* had just been nominated for the National Book Award; but his eye was fixed on Robert F. Kennedy, who was watching him during the celebratory toast: "He looks at moments like he might burst into tears, or snarl, or whine, in response to some inner agony that he doesn't understand himself. . . . [A] guy any tighter than this one seems to be would have trouble breathing."

For research, Udall dispatched his special consultant to Reston, Virginia, a new self-contained community conceived by Robert E. Simon (i.e., R.E.S.ton) in response to the Garden City movement. Reston was intended as a solution to urban sprawl, and Matthiessen was impressed by the pretty town of green spaces and bridle paths, with its untouched woodland of nearly two thousand acres. "When one realizes that this sort of town planning is just as efficient in terms of people housed as a comparable area of crowded makeshift 'development' which spoils the countryside, the case of the 'new towns' seems unassailable."

He was less impressed by what he saw in the Florida Everglades during a three-hour aerial survey in December. In a typed report for Udall—and later in a magazine piece for *Audubon*—he painted a grim picture of water mismanagement by the Army Corps of Engineers, "a once-proud name that is now almost synonymous with epic blundering."[16] Because of canals and levees trapping water for Miami, the national park was brown and wilted. The pilot, Ralph Miele, pointed out wells blasted by the Corps to provide survival pools for wildlife. "One hot day Ralph saw an alligator dragging itself across the burned-out land towards the nearest water," Matthiessen told Udall, "but the water was almost a mile away, and the vultures walking along beside the toiling beast were mute evidence that it was not going to make it."[17] He found the aerial survey so depressing—a glimpse of everything wrong with American attitudes toward the natural world—that he stopped by the Corkscrew Swamp Sanctuary to "console" himself by watching wood storks from the boardwalk. "In the big trees, the whine of progress is no longer heard, only the voice of creatures old before mankind was born."[18] And yet Corkscrew Swamp, Matthiessen knew, was also in peril.

In March 1966, he joined Udall in West Germany to inspect German solutions to air and water pollution, strip mining, and soil erosion. The trip turned out to be an unexpectedly important one, though not because of anything to do with the secretary or his book.

Matthiessen stopped over in London to catch up with Doc Humes, who was living there and recovering, in a way, from the dissolution of his marriage to Anna Lou Elianoff. Humes had recently suffered a breakdown after overdosing on LSD (supplied by Timothy Leary), and he'd been briefly institutionalized in Banstead Hospital. Matthiessen encouraged his old friend to come home for treatment, but he also took the opportunity to make a confession. A year or so earlier, he'd finally shared the backstory of the CIA and *The Paris Review* with George Plimpton. He now wanted Humes to know as well. "I thought if I leveled with him, it would be better," he later told Humes's daughter, explaining that he figured the truth might even be therapeutic, helping Doc to find a way forward after a paranoid episode in which he'd imagined his bedpost was bugged by the Queen.[19] In London, Matthiessen unfurled his tale as they walked down a street together. Humes appeared to take the revelation well; they had an "agreeable" evening afterward. "He came back to my hotel room and spent the night," Matthiessen recalled. "I suggested he take a bath, which he sorely needed, and he did. But he wasn't outraged. George says that he was outraged, I guess this was George's way of expressing outrage. *He* was the outraged one."[20]

Actually, Humes had more ambivalent feelings. After Matthiessen gave him some money to get back on his feet, then departed England for Germany, Humes sent Plimpton a letter that offered little evidence of the mental illness that would increasingly consume his life. "I believe Peter," he wrote, "when he says he is properly ashamed of involving the PR in his youthful folly," and "I think at this juncture he deserves full marks for having had the guts to speak up." Peter was not to be blamed "for a paranoid system that makes victims of its instruments." Still, it was shocking that, "in his own words, [he] used you as he used me, and frankly I am still sore as hell about it." More to the point, Humes was "hurt."[21]

He informed Plimpton that Matthiessen should make some kind of public statement, and he demanded his own name be removed from *The Paris Review* masthead until there was an article or press conference detailing the whole sorry affair. Plimpton responded by trying to persuade Humes *not* to resign, and to keep Matthiessen's confession a secret. In one of his replies to Humes's letters, Plimpton wrote, with barely stifled desperation: "What a paradox it would be if the magazine which stood up through that most tenuous CIA relationship in those early days was now destroyed when there is no relationship whatsoever!"[22] Of course, what risked being "destroyed," or at the very least tainted for readers, was the thing Plimpton had made the centerpiece of his life and literary reputation, and perhaps his identity. "I suppose," he wrote to Humes, carefully downplaying his own irritation about the whole Matthiessen matter, "every CIA agent must have a job of sorts. Otherwise his presence in a foreign city looks suspicious."[23] In a remarkable bit of self-rationalization, Plimpton added, "I'm not outraged by the thought of a CIA man selecting Tea at Le Gord for the mag."[*]

Matthiessen finished his tour with Udall in Munich. Then he returned home to deal with the crisis he'd created in London, with two friendships now on the line. He spoke to Plimpton, smoothing things over between them, and then wrote a calm note to Humes indicating he, too, would resign if Humes insisted on vacating the masthead. In conjunction with Plimpton's pleas, this seems to have done the trick: Humes dropped his demand for

---

[*] "Tea at Le Gord," by Sue Kaufman, was a short story selected by Matthiessen to appear in the third issue of *The Paris Review* (Autumn 1953). It follows a young American student, Madelaine, as she wrangles with an imperious French woman over the price of a homestay in Chartres. Plimpton meant to suggest that there was nothing remotely suspicious about Matthiessen's editorial choices for the magazine.

a public reckoning. It would be eleven more years before John Crewdson publicized the connection between *The Paris Review* and the CIA in *The New York Times*.

Almost immediately, Matthiessen's attention was drawn back to Washington because of another self-inflicted situation. During his government service, he'd remained steadfastly opposed to the "dishonorable" war in Vietnam. His private jottings were punctuated by biting asides about spending priorities, and about President Johnson: "If he were risking the whole world in Viet Nam, as I think he is, I'd hate his big flatulent patriotic guts even if he was certified as a saint from Saintsville."[24] Occasionally, while he was out doing the rounds with Udall, a chitchatting wife or political aide had asked for his thoughts on the conflict, and Matthiessen had expressed so much "heartfelt disgust" that the other person was left speechless. His candor was a faux pas in "diplomatic Washington"—Matthiessen knew this—as was his decision to join antiwar marches, where he held up signs with slogans like: "NO $$$ FOR BOMBING AND BURNING. STOP THE WAR NOW!"

Because of his participation in protest marches, Matthiessen received, according to his memoir notes, an anonymous letter that "encouraged" him to resign from the Department of the Interior.[25] Feeling that positive change was impossible under the circumstances, he quit after just four months of work. Stewart Udall's book, *1976: Agenda for Tomorrow*, was published two years later, with no acknowledgment of Matthiessen's brief involvement as special consultant. Its cultural impact was negligible.

IN 1966, the National Book Awards were held in the middle of March at the Philharmonic Hall in Lincoln Center, New York. More than a thousand writers, agents, publishers, editors, and librarians watched as Katherine Anne Porter won the fiction award for her *Collected Stories*.* "You'll be back," somebody reassured Matthiessen, who reacted to the loss by getting very drunk.[26]

A few weeks later, he flew to Grand Cayman to collect the material that would end up inspiring his next novel. As a child philatelist, one of his favorite stamps had shown an illustrated *tortuga* from the Cayman Islands. While writing *Wildlife in America*, he'd become intrigued anew by the green sea turtle (*Chelonia mydas*) because it was a living relic of a prehistoric age, and

---

* Other than Porter's *Collected Stories* and Matthiessen's *At Play in the Fields of the Lord*, the other finalists were *The Liberation of Lord Byron Jones*, by Jesse Hill Ford; *The (Diblos) Notebook*, by James Merrill; *Pericles on 31st Street*, by Harry Mark Petrakis; and *Everything That Rises Must Converge*, by Flannery O'Connor, who received a special tribute from the judges (Paul Horgan, J. F. Powers, and Glenway Wescott) in acknowledgment of her death in 1964.

"an ocean wanderer" whose "powers of navigation are even more awesome than those of birds."[27] As research for that book, he'd read Archie Carr's *The Windward Road* (1956), an award-winning account of the herpetologist's travels around the Caribbean in search of nesting sites. Carr described a schooner of Caymanian seafarers, operating under full sail on a seasonal hunt for an increasingly rare creature that had once sustained an entire industry. The description had burrowed into Matthiessen's consciousness, then resurfaced when he started writing "Last Wilderness" chronicles for *The New Yorker*.

In May 1964, Matthiessen had flown to Grand Cayman from Miami. Nobody he knew had ever been to the island ("the strongest sort of recommendation"), and he had no idea what he would find there, which turned out to be very little. (The Banks and Trust Company Law, which paved the way for an offshore banking industry, would not be passed until 1966.) He strolled along a deserted beach past bougainvillea and gumbo limbo trees, thinking about the "great flotillas of green turtles" that had long since vanished from the island's blue-green waters. In a bar over a glass of rum, he made a commitment to himself: "I would sail on a turtle voyage before it was too late; the green-turtle fishery and the turtle boats, the way the world was going, would soon pass, and their passing would end an epoch, on Grand Cayman and throughout the Caribbean."[28] He wanted to witness something "old and marvelous," just as he had in the Baliem Valley, before it, too, succumbed to the demands of "progress." Unfortunately, the one vessel still operating in the traditional style, two-masted, with no motor or shortwave radio—the *Lydia E. Wilson*—had already departed on the trade winds for the cays and reefs off Nicaragua.

In April 1965, Matthiessen had then returned to Grand Cayman with *The New Yorker*'s financial support. He contacted the *Wilson*'s captain, Cadie Ebanks, and expressed interest in accompanying the crew on a working voyage. Captain Ebanks seemed amenable to the idea, but when Matthiessen arrived at his house in a rental car, Ebanks admitted that he'd sent the schooner to Nicaragua again two days earlier. "He tried out one explanation," Matthiessen later wrote, "then another and another, speaking in a quiet voice, brow furrowed, toeing the warm ground, until, unable to contain it any longer, he gave way to an ultimate mirth that rolled up slowly from his belly until his body quaked with it and his eyes wept." The laugh was astonishing, and Matthiessen laughed, too, mostly out of incredulity. "The damned turtle trip is postponed until next year due to Nicaraguan govt and other absurd obstacles," he grumbled in a letter to Joe Fox, who was back in New York finalizing the pages for *At Play*.[29]

Now, in April 1966, Matthiessen tried for a third time. Thankfully, the *Lydia E. Wilson* had not yet set sail from her berth in George Town. Alarmingly, she no longer had many sails to speak of. In February, Ebanks had sent the ship, which was constructed in 1931 and weighed sixty-three tons, to the Bay Islands of Honduras to be outfitted with a diesel motor. She had returned with truncated spars, a deckhouse that made it impossible for the helmsman to see where he was steering, and myriad mechanical problems. "So that's the Wilson," Matthiessen said disapprovingly as he shook Ebanks's hand ("for I was angry with him, and angry with myself for having counted on him").[30] Ebanks told Matthiessen he was welcome to join a voyage to the hunting grounds off Nicaragua—for a fee, of course, which would help offset the expense of installing the new motor. Matthiessen was appalled. "Piracy," he observed aloud, was "not quite dead on Grand Cayman." Yet he met the captain's terms (*The New Yorker* paid), swallowing the ironic fact that in doing so he was funding the very modernization he had hoped to outpace.

The motor conversion of the *Lydia E. Wilson* meant this was a different kind of expedition from the one he'd accompanied to Netherlands New Guinea. There, the Dugum Dani had been standing on the threshold of change, but they had not yet been pushed over the edge by interfering outsiders. The Caymanian seafarers, whom Matthiessen also thought of as living a traditional lifestyle, had, by contrast, just stepped over the threshold willingly, and he would now watch as they tried to find their bearings.

On April 19, he loaded his gear aboard the *Wilson* and prepared for departure. The deck was a mess of anchors, chain, scraps of wood, and hundred-gallon drums filled with fuel and water; a tiny galley was lashed down "like a stray chicken coop."[31] He found a spot at the bow and settled in to observe the scene. As the schooner pulled away from George Town, the engine noise dissolved in ocean wind, and he tried to imagine himself on one of the sailing voyages of yore: "But there was no way to put aside the vibration underfoot, or the diesel smell that came in eddies on the salt sea air."

What followed was a profoundly uncomfortable journey. The deckhouse was small and poorly ventilated, and it lacked enough berths to accommodate everyone; Matthiessen was forced to sleep on the open deck. As the schooner moved through white-capped waves, the roll became so severe that he deflated the air mattress to stop himself from tumbling across the deck. When rains came, he held his bedding under a small overhang to keep it dry. Meanwhile, the food and coffee tasted of chemicals: the drum used for cooking water had once carried diesel. There was discomfort, too, in knowing that there were just two life preservers for a crew of nine, and that a "lurking" reef, leaking timber, or the wood-fire stove in the galley (also wood) could prove catastrophic in minutes. One evening some rotten rope snapped, sending the boom smashing into a pipe of the starboard engine and filling the air with acrid smoke. Another day, Matthiessen asked Ebanks why the radio-telephone didn't seem to work. Ebanks admitted he hadn't bothered to test it before they left George Town.

Despite the dangers, Matthiessen was excited to be heading for Nicaragua. "On a bright, fresh day at sea," he wrote in an account of the voyage, "the ocean wind against your cheek and the tropical sun on your bare feet can restore childhood's sense of being at the center of time, with no time passing."[32] As he reclined in the stern, he could hear the men talking in the deckhouse, and took notes on their stories of "old turtlers and turtle boats, of great storms on the Miskito Bank . . . and of the witchcraft called obeah, come to the Caymans from Jamaica."

The crew fascinated him with their idiosyncrasies and ambitions. Brown, for example, sported a sombrero, sideburns, and gold teeth in the style of a "Central American *bandito*." Alfred Buttrum, also known as "Speedy," planned to give up the sea and retire to Roatán with three cows once he'd earned enough money to support himself indefinitely. Matthiessen was moved, in the same way he'd been moved while working with the Bonackers, by the commitment of these men to a dangerous way of life. In a landscape where everything was weathered by sun, salt, and wind, the men seemed similarly stripped to their elements. At Edinburgh Reef, near Cape Gracias a Dios, he tagged along in a catboat to help them set the turtle nets; the Caymanians, he noticed, "move so beautifully in their small boats that they seem mere extensions of the wood and canvas."[33]

The green turtles were hoisted onto the *Wilson* by a bridle secured to the base of both fore flippers. Some of the animals were stored alive in the hold, upside-down on their shells, with flippers lashed together and a wooden pillow placed beneath their heads for support. Others were left above deck, where the crew stepped over or on them "as if they were part of the ship's machinery." Matthiessen admired the hunters, but he had nearly as much sympathy for the game: "the green turtle's air of innocence is troubling, and now and then one meets a turtle's eye and recalls the swift thing that flew so gracefully in the ocean."[34] He met the turtle's eye because there was one just three feet from his bedroll, leaking lubricating fluid like tears.

Matthiessen spent nearly two weeks on the *Wilson*, then disembarked at Puerto Cabezas when the ship stopped to obtain a hunting permit. Despite the brevity of the trip, the material he collected was so powerful that a magazine article seemed a little wasteful. He could present what he called the "factual linear relative truth"[35] to readers of *The New Yorker*: the history, geography, and moment-by-moment sequence of netting a turtle. But the "higher truth," or the "intuitive absolute truth" of the voyage—what this ramshackle schooner and its crew suggested about man's fate on earth, set against the sublime backdrop of the sea—demanded a more creative approach.*

Back in New York, he went to see William Shawn at *The New Yorker*. In a conversation he would often recall in later years because he found it so unusual, Matthiessen said to the editor something like: "Mr. Shawn, I can write you a fact piece, but I should tell you that I'm going to hold back the best stuff for a novel."[36] This was a bold declaration given the considerable expenses accrued on the magazine's account, but Shawn understood what he was saying. "Mr. Matthiessen," Shawn replied, with generosity that floored the writer, "you do what's best for your work."†

Within a year, the Nicaraguan government decided to expand its own turtle industry, revoking the permits it issued to Caymanians like Cadie Ebanks. This means the voyage described by Matthiessen in "To the Miskito Bank," which appeared in the October 28, 1967, issue of *The New Yorker*, may well have been the last hunt of the *Lydia E. Wilson*. In 1968, in the Barkers area of West Bay, Grand Cayman, the schooner caught fire and sank in mysterious circumstances. That detail, along with many of the others Matthiessen had collected in his notebook and on a tape recorder, would eventually find its way into a masterful novel called *Far Tortuga*.

ONE DAY IN THE FALL of 1966, Matthiessen received an invitation to a "Black and White Dance" to be held in honor of Katharine Graham, publisher of *The Washington Post*. He glanced at the invitation, embossed on an expensive cream card, and then phoned Truman Capote, who was throwing the ball, to say he couldn't attend because he would "only get drunk and lose the drift of things for two or three days."[37]

Work was his official excuse for skipping the party of the century, as it soon became known, but Matthiessen had no desire to don a tuxedo and hobnob with celebrities at the Plaza Hotel. Not long before, his name had appeared in *The New York Times* as part of a so-called "In Crowd": "an enormously influential social, intellectual and cultural élite" whose members— Jacqueline Kennedy, William Paley, Greta Garbo, Capote—supposedly

---

* Matthiessen's understanding of "intuitive absolute truth" was not dissimilar to what Werner Herzog would later term "ecstatic truth." As Matthiessen explained it in some notes for a lecture: "Mainly, I think, there is the urge to unify, make one, make universal our random and chaotic emotions and experiences, to find the resonance, the immanence implicit in the seemingly unmysterious particulars of the real event."

† In 1987, when William Shawn was unceremoniously nudged out of *The New Yorker*, Matthiessen wrote him a letter of "gratitude and thanks" in which he cited this exchange as an example of Shawn's brilliant editorial judgment. Shawn wrote back to say that he admired Matthiessen's work enormously: "You are not simply a marvellous nature writer; you are a marvellous writer."

drove Lincoln Continentals and wore Yves St. Laurent.³⁸ The article, which caused quite a stir, had made Matthiessen "depressed" with its aristocratic pretensions, and he'd written to Joe Fox: "I am <u>not</u> proud to be listed in that company, whose qualifications are not mine."³⁹ It was as though he'd found himself once again in the dreaded *Social Register*.

Because of his rising profile as a literary figure, Matthiessen was sometimes thrust into the spotlight—interviewed on television, say, where his patrician accent stiffened into something almost British. He appreciated the recognition, which he felt he'd earned, but fame was hardly a natural fit. He responded by becoming more private, less inclined to accept invitations like Capote's. While there were still boozy gatherings with an intimate circle—Bill Styron, Terry Southern, Sherry Lord—his new detachment, noticed by others, would cause Tom Guinzburg to accuse him of not "contributing" to their friendship. Why the hell didn't he "get off his ass," drive into New York, and sit down for "a couple of martinis" so they could properly catch up?⁴⁰ Capote registered his own complaint: "Cecil Beaton came all the way from London for my party, and you wouldn't even come in from Sagaponack."⁴¹*

Matthiessen spent long hours in his study tweaking a series of essays he'd been commissioned to write by Gardner Stout, an investment banker and amateur ornithologist who, in 1968, would become president of the American Museum of Natural History. The eleven essays concerned shorebirds—plovers, curlews, semipalmated sandpipers—and they were destined for a book, to accompany avian paintings by Robert Verity Clem, titled *The Shorebirds of North America*, which was probably a riff on Audubon's *Birds of America*. The prose was Matthiessen at his most technical: page after page devoted to taxonomy, phenotype, and species distribution. But he worked hard to balance the science with poetry, and inserted numerous passages where what he really seemed to be writing about was his own state of mind: "The restlessness of shorebirds, their kinship with the distance and swift seasons, the wistful signal of their voices down the long coastlines of the world make them, for me, the most affecting of wild creatures."⁴²

While Peter worked, Deborah was expected to maintain order in the house, which, thanks to the MGM money, had been extensively renovated to make it less like a garage and chauffeur's apartment and more like a family home. There were now floorboards instead of bare concrete, a new wing for

---

* In 1978, when an ex-girlfriend made a crack in a letter about Peter being a "Star," he shot back: "What's all that about? That's something in your head, not in mine. To be a star, you have to want to be a star, and I never have; I dodge all radio, TV, as many interviews as I can get away with, book-signings, the lot, and if anything, I live more quietly than ever. One reviewer [appraising *The Snow Leopard*] spoke of me as a 'socialite,' which made my friends laugh. I'm perfectly happy to agree that [as the ex-girlfriend had written] 'Bill Gaddis is a bigger star' than I am; he's a very nice guy and a terrific writer, and I suspect he'd be just as uncomfortable as I am with all this 'star' talk."

the children, and a spacious kitchen carved out of the old workshop. Deborah, however, had no interest in homemaking. She resented Peter's expectation that she would manage the family. This triggered more arguments when he emerged from his study, tense standoffs and unpredictable explosions, his heavy footfalls sounding, to the children, like those of an executioner. "Dad was an unbelievably frightening man when he was angry at you," said Alex, who would remember his father running his thumb back and forth across his fingers in an unconscious tic that signaled something bad was about to happen.[43] Peter was not usually violent in a physical sense (though he did once put his fist through a wall, creating a hole that Deborah left unpatched for months as a shameful reminder); instead, his rage came as ice-cold blasts of epithets. "He would use his unbelievable command of the English language to just tear you asunder," said Alex. This would happen, recalled Rue, "after he'd been writing all day."[44]

Deborah flirted with domesticity, trying to bake a loaf of bread or hand-paint some Easter eggs. What *she* wanted, though, was to continue her work of self-examination. That meant studying Alan Watts, or practicing yoga on the bathroom floor, or dropping acid—or writing, which Peter had encouraged her to do without quite realizing how much she would take to it. In between her struggles with Rue, who was difficult, and Alex, who was young, and housekeepers, who never seemed to stick around for very long, Deborah stole moments to write about the films of Fellini, which she adored; and about marriage, loneliness, disillusionment. In one undated, unpublished essay, she examined her situation using starkly analytical terms. "The game has backfired in both directions, both male and female becoming caught in the limitations of their own projections," she wrote. "Woman [i.e., Deborah] became the object of a partial man [Peter] whose fears (needs) she used to ensnare him. And man [Peter] was trapped in a mechanical life with the machine who was to provide for his needs, a sexual housekeeper [Deborah] whose dependence made him contemptuous, and most cruel, who bored him. She could not possibly remain sexy, when the mystery of the whole human entity had disappeared under the proscriptions of her role."[45]

At some point Peter, who described Deborah and himself in an LSD journal as two "bristling metallic scorpions"—"we carefully disengage, because if we ever touch, we will explode in self-destruction"[46]—began entertaining fantasies of abandoning everything. He daydreamed about an island not unlike the one near Annaghkeen; then he typed up a description of exactly what he was imagining, as if to write the fantasy into reality:

> my island would be large, and I would live at the far end of it, on the water. Ideally, the place would be an island, but a wooded neck would do

as well, with its own tidal creek for fish and duck shooting and a small boat to go down into the bay for crabs and oysters. . . . My house, close-chinked against the wind, with its pine fire and fat pile of drying wood, and good books and a store of food, and solitude (except, of course, [for] the beautiful and mysterious girl found walking the wild outer islands, in the rain) would be a most excellent place, inspiring the contentment that one draws from a wind-sheltered cove beyond rough water or a warm nest of tall sunlit grasses on a bright mountain field of autumn—such shelters are important to the soul.[47]

This indulgent vision left no room for a wife or children; Peter inhabited his island without them. The idea proved so alluring that he pitched a book to Joe Fox, tentatively titled "The Search for an Island," which would collect various nonfiction travel pieces into a narrative of vaguely defined pilgrimage. "Peter's most deep-felt interest is in finding a place isolated from the world—a retreat, so to speak," Fox noted in an internal Random House memo about the unrealized project.[48] Fox added, astutely, that "island" should be understood metaphorically: "the paradise on earth for which he is searching maybe [sic] in the middle of the Arctic tundra." Indeed, "island" was just another expression for the lost paradise Peter desired, which was emotional as much as physical: a state of being blissfully unencumbered, fully integrated, and as rapturously present as a young child.

AT THE START OF 1968, Matthiessen signed his name to the Writers and Editors War Tax Protest, refusing to pay a proposed 10 percent income tax surcharge that Congress wanted to implement so it could fund the ongoing conflict in Vietnam. In March, as the shock of the Tet Offensive came fully into focus, he signed his name to a list of supporters for Senator Eugene McCarthy—"FOR PRESIDENT and FOR PEACE."[49] Afterward, in early April, as the country rioted in response to the assassination of Martin Luther King Jr., he walked around Sagaponack encouraging his neighbors to embrace McCarthy and dump President Johnson, until one of them pointed out that Johnson had already dumped *himself* the week before. Matthiessen rarely watched anything on television except an occasional football game; he had missed Johnson's announcement about not seeking reelection for a second term.

Eugene McCarthy appealed to Matthiessen because the senator from Minnesota, who was a poet—and who had also spent time as a novice monk in a Benedictine abbey—had spoken out forcefully against the war, breaking ranks in the Democratic Party to question the decisions of an incumbent president. Yet Matthiessen's support was motivated just as much by his concerns about the future. Before the end of the century, he believed, there would be "an evolution in our values and the values of human society, not because man has become more civilized but because, on a blighted earth, he will have no choice."[50] In the two years since his work for Stewart Udall, he had become increasingly convinced that what was necessary was "a new order, a new politics,"[51] to help spur the evolution of values *right now*, before the country inched any further toward social and environmental collapse. This new order would treat "man and his habitat with respect."[52] Grounded in "human ecology," it would also center "humanity as its purpose and the economy as its tool, thus reversing the present order of the System," which—via American capitalism, the source of so many problems—cast people as consumers rather than citizens. To achieve the new order, however, Matthiessen thought the country needed more than "old-style machine candidates," who were mostly invested in maintaining the status quo. What the country needed was somebody motivated by conscience. Somebody who was prepared to move "in the bold and unpolitic directions that will be required in our damaged world environment."[53]

He had once hoped Udall would be that somebody. He turned to McCarthy—"a quiet revolutionary by comparison to Malcolm or Che Guevara"—with a similar wish. But McCarthy was not the figure he was looking for either. By the time the senator lost the Democratic nomination to Hubert Humphrey, in August, Matthiessen had decided that McCarthy's potential had probably been "illusory," and he'd found an even more promising leader to invest in: "an idealist unhampered by ideology, an activist with a near-mystic vision, a militant with a dedication to nonviolence ... [who] stands free of the political machinery that the election year 1968 made not only disreputable but irrelevant."[54]

Cesar Chavez came to his attention in June. Ann Israel, the young executive director of a New York–based organization called Spectemur Agendo, Inc.,* asked Matthiessen to edit an outline of insecticide abuses for possible inclusion in a newspaper ad supporting California farmworkers. (Having written about insecticides in *Wildlife in America*, he could speak to how growers were exposing their workers to toxic chemicals: "the broadcasting of these deadly and long-lived poisons ranks with the mass production of cars and highways as an ultimate expression of free enterprise run amok.")[55]

---

* Spectemur Agendo, Inc., was funded by the eccentric liberal philanthropist Stewart R. Mott, a major donor to Eugene McCarthy's presidential campaign, and an outspoken supporter of almost everything radical: abortion reform, feminism, civil liberties, gun control, gay rights. The name "Spectemur Agendo" came from the Mott family crest. It means: "Let us be known by our deeds."

Israel planned to visit the United Farm Workers Organizing Committee in Delano, California, to see exactly what Spectemur Agendo would be supporting with the newspaper ad; she invited Matthiessen along to meet the man responsible for the UFW.

Chavez, at that point in time, was famous but not legendary—not yet the civil rights icon whose bust would one day sit in the Oval Office behind President Joe Biden. Chavez had started with an improbable dream: to organize a labor union for the country's most impoverished workers. He'd then spent years learning how to inspire these (mostly Mexican American) farmworkers with a sense of solidarity. To force the agricultural overlords to recognize their right to collective bargaining, he'd joined a strike by Filipino American workers against table grape growers in 1965, then gradually built a consolidated labor movement which, as he wrote in a letter to potential picket line volunteers, "has the spirit of Zapata and the tactics of Martin Luther King."[56] He had refused to back down when the growers sprayed strikers with pesticide, and his defiance had inspired the devotion of young Anglo college students who, righteously furious about discrimination, flocked from the Bay Area to support *la causa*. In 1966, he'd marched three hundred miles from Delano to the state capitol at Sacramento, passing through laborer communities to encourage further resistance to appalling wages and poor working conditions. The march's slogan was "Peregrinación, Penitencia, Revolución."

More recently, Chavez had escalated the conflict with California agribusiness by declaring a consumer boycott on grapes from specific growers, targeting supermarket chains around the country. And he had reaffirmed his commitment to peaceful protest through an extended fast. For twenty-five days in February and March 1968, he'd frightened his friends by refusing all food—an act, inspired by Gandhi, that he likened to prayer. When he finally broke the fast during a meal with Robert F. Kennedy on March 10, he'd been too weak to speak, having lost more than thirty-three pounds, so a prepared statement was read out on his behalf. It concluded: "It is my deepest belief that only by giving our lives do we find life. I am convinced that the truest act of courage, the strongest act of manliness is to sacrifice ourselves for others in a totally non-violent struggle for justice. To be a man is to suffer for others. God help us to be men."[57]

Matthiessen was aware of the grape boycott, which had been expanded in May to target all California table grapes sold nationwide. (Perhaps he'd come across a copy of *Delano*, John Gregory Dunne's 1967 book about the early years of the strike.) He was intrigued by Cesar Chavez, because Chavez had managed to remain, despite all the attention, remarkably private. But the main reason he accepted Ann Israel's invitation was because the farmworkers' struggle seemed to encapsulate what he saw as America's "most serious afflictions: racism, poverty, environmental pollution, and urban crowding and decay—all of these compounded by the waste of war."[58]

Delano, between Bakersfield and Fresno in the San Joaquin Valley, was (and still is) a small town engulfed by acres of cotton, alfalfa, and table-grape vineyards. Matthiessen arrived with Israel at the beginning of August. They visited the UFW office to meet the staff: Dolores Huerta, union VP; Jerome Cohen and David Averbuck, union lawyers; LeRoy Chatfield, who ran the nonprofit Service Center; and Helen Chavez, Cesar's forbearing wife. Of Cesar himself, there was only the briefest glimpse. He welcomed them warmly to Delano, apologized for being so busy, and slipped out the door, saying, "I see you later, hey?"[59]

While Matthiessen waited for a proper conversation, he interviewed the grape growers to hear their side of the dispute. One of the growers, Bruno Dispoto, told him that Delano's grape pickers had a higher hourly wage, more benefits, and greater protections under the law than any other farmworkers in the country. Matthiessen was skeptical: "This is like saying that American blacks have no cause for dissatisfaction, since they own more clothes than those in Africa."[60] He also visited a strike at a vineyard southeast of Bakersfield, in the same landscape Steinbeck had described in *The Grapes of Wrath;* Matthiessen watched a procession of "ancient cars" arrive to form a picket line. "The flags were festive," he observed, "and in the air was that feeling of the arena which precedes a bugle note and the commencement of a blood sport."[61]

When he finally found Chavez, the short, sad-eyed man ("like a dark seraph")[62] was speaking with a delegation of high school students about racism and ethnic pride. "Mexican-American youth is just beginning to wake up," Chavez told them. "Five years ago we didn't have this feeling. Nobody wanted to be *chicanos*, they wanted to be anything but *chicanos*."[63] Matthiessen listened closely—"The newborn pride in being a *chicano*, in the opinion of most people, is due largely to Chavez himself," he later wrote—and then attached himself to the man like a shadow. For the better part of three days, he talked with Chavez in Chinese restaurants, during car trips, by a motel pool, after Sunday mass, and in a supermarket while Chavez searched for Diet Rite Cola. Early one morning, Matthiessen met him at his family home in Delano, kept deliberately low-key now that the leader was receiving death threats in the wake of Robert Kennedy's assassination in June. They hitched a ride to a construction site a few miles outside of town, where volunteers were slowly building a union compound called Forty Acres. "The first center for farm workers in history!"[64] Chavez said proudly as they surveyed the mud and discarded beer cans. Later he added, "It will be kind of a religious place, very restful, quiet. It's going to be nice here."[65]

Before flying to California, Matthiessen had expected to like Cesar Chavez. He had not expected to be "startled,"[66] to find a man he would come to regard as his "great hero."[67] He and Chavez were almost exactly the same age. They'd both served in the Navy, in the Pacific, at the end of World War II. But Chavez had none of the class privileges that Matthiessen relied upon to get ahead in life. He had little education, no money, no safety net, and no culture reassuring him at every moment of his importance and self-worth. The forces against him, as a union organizer, were overwhelming: "an enormously hostile Governor Reagan, university trustees, the railroads, agribusiness and everyone gaining from it."[68] Yet Chavez was tough, disciplined, and determined to best his enemies on every front so he could create better opportunities for farmworkers. "What welled out of him," Matthiessen wrote, with an admiration that would endure even after Chavez began to lose his way in the years ahead, "was a phenomenon much spoken of in a society afraid of its own hate, but one that I had never seen before—or not, at least, in anyone unswayed by drugs or aching youth: the simple love of man that accompanies some ultimate acceptance of oneself."[69]

Elsewhere, Matthiessen would praise Chavez as "a great spiritual teacher, in a way, because he was so quiet, and he drew so little attention to himself. He didn't pose at all."[70]

After nine days in California, taking notes and conducting interviews, Matthiessen flew back to New York and went, once again, to see William Shawn at *The New Yorker*. More than a decade earlier, Shawn had rejected a piece he'd written on East End Bonackers and the striped bass legislation that threatened their livelihood as too "grave, complicated, and partisan" for the "light and detached" magazine.[71] But times had changed dramatically since then, and so had *The New Yorker*. Recently, in an interview for *Women's Wear Daily*, Shawn had acknowledged that, given the parlous state of the world, "the magazine has come to have a greater social and political and moral awareness, and to feel a greater responsibility."[72] Taking advantage of this editorial shift, Matthiessen now pitched a grave, complicated, and partisan profile of Cesar Chavez. He would later boast that it was one of the first "social action" pieces *The New Yorker* ever accepted, the implication being that he'd finally breached the fortress and left a window open behind him for others to follow.

The writing took three months; Matthiessen took occasional breaks to visit union grape boycotts around the boroughs of New York, sometimes with Dolores Huerta and sometimes alone. Then, after Thanksgiving, he returned to California to consult with Chavez for fact-checking purposes. On the way, he stopped in Los Angeles to conduct an interview with the Reverend Chris Hartmire, one of Chavez's allies, who was picketing in a supermarket parking lot. Matthiessen put on a chest-board that read DON'T BUY GRAPES and tried to "inseminate" shoppers, in his words, with "grape-strike propaganda."[73]

Chavez was bedridden at St. Anthony's Seminary, in sunny Santa Barbara—the result of a chronic back condition that left him periodically immobilized in excruciating pain. Matthiessen sat beside him in a small building that resembled a horse stable. The two men caught up on news, then began to argue about overpopulation, which Matthiessen—though he later changed his mind—believed was a problem that required contraception initiatives. Chavez became so animated that he propped himself up to defend his more Catholic views. After a while, he requested that Matthiessen read the *New Yorker* article out loud. ("What is this, why do I have to read this?" Matthiessen wondered, before realizing that Chavez wanted to be able to tell illiterate members of the union that he'd never read the profile himself.)[74] Matthiessen obliged, narrating the long, unedited draft over the course of three or four days. Chavez was "amazed" and "pleased"[75] by what he heard, although he was conscious, too, that the more critical comments about his ruthlessness would be poorly received by some overprotective colleagues. "[He] told his aides to shove it when they criticized me for not making him 'perfect,'" Matthiessen later recalled.[76]

As a gesture of support, Matthiessen donated his entire fee from the magazine to the National Farm Workers Service Center. He also bought a washing machine for Helen Chavez, and discreetly gave an additional $900 so David Averbuck's Delano pool could be retrofitted with a water heater for Cesar's physical therapy.[77]

A few years later, some critics would ask whether Matthiessen had compromised his status as an objective observer. Was he too credulous with Chavez? Given the donations and "grape-strike propaganda," it is a reasonable question. But Matthiessen had never pretended to be an impartial reporter, even during his interviews with the growers: "Kovacevich, who was breathing hard, glared at me expectantly, and I said straight off that I was partisan to the Union, as no doubt Mr. Brosmer had told him, but that I was anxious to talk to as many growers as I could, to make certain that their side got a fair hearing."[78] When he discovered the farmworkers' movement, Matthiessen was already an advocate in search of a cause; he approached the union as an advocacy journalist, aiming to advance the reform in American values he'd been contemplating since he abandoned the work with Stewart Udall.

"I think this will interest you," he once wrote in a letter to Chavez, whom he periodically harangued with "impassioned speeches" on environmental problems.[79] Attached to the letter was a *New York Times* article summarizing a lecture given by Richard Anderson Falk, a professor of international law at Princeton who was working on a speculative research project about what the world order might look like in the 1990s. Matthiessen had underlined several quotes for emphasis, including a prescient warning by Falk: "The planet and mankind are in grave danger of irreversible catastrophe if the political structure that now prevails is not drastically changed during the next few decades."

The hope for "orderly change," Matthiessen would soon argue in *Sal Si Puedes*,* the book-length version of his *New Yorker* profile, "depends on men like Cesar Chavez, who, of all leaders now in sight, best represents the rising generations."[80]

---

* Sal Si Puedes—"Escape If You Can"—was the name of a barrio on the east side of San Jose, California, where Cesar Chavez had lived with his immigrant parents for a time during his youth. (A historic landmark now marks the spot on Scharff Avenue.) As Chavez explained to Matthiessen, the barrio acquired the name because "it was every man for himself, and not too many could get out of it, except to prison." Matthiessen repurposed "Sal Si Puedes" to symbolize Chavez's struggle and achievement.

13

Lions and Sharks

> That last afternoon I went exploring, coasting down below one hundred feet; here the last color, a brown-fringed overlapping coral like shelf fungi, died away. Beneath was bare dark dungeon-colored wall, the bastion of old reefs of other ages, and when, far above, clouds passed across the sun, this nether world was plunged into cold gloom.... I sank through rays of light like a particle in eternity, hearing the ring and tock of unknown voices and the closing and opening of my own heart. When apprehension eased, I would probe down again into the abyss. I did not know what I was searching for; nothing was there.
>
> —*Blue Meridian* (1971)[1]

MATTHIESSEN WAS SURPRISED, returning home from a trip to California, to find three "inscrutable small men"[2] standing in his Sagaponack driveway: Hakuun Yasutani, an eighty-three-year-old roshi whose teachings had been collected by Philip Kapleau in *The Three Pillars of Zen* (1965); Soen Nakagawa, a sixty-one-year-old roshi who seemed "entirely at ease and entirely aware at the same time, like a paused swallow"; and Eido Tai Shimano, a thirty-five-year-old monk with the poise and demeanor of a samurai. Soen Roshi and Tai-san (later known as Eido Roshi) would have an enormous influence on the direction of Matthiessen's life, though he would frame this first encounter with them, on August 12, 1968, as something of a farce. "The teachers were guests of my wife, Deborah Love, a new student of Zen, but I was ignorant of this as of much else on that long-ago summer day.... For years thereafter, Tai-san would relate how Soen and Yasutani, perceiving my unenlightened condition at a glance, had shaken their shining heads and sighed, 'Poor Debbo-lah.'"[3]

Deborah Love had turned to Zen Buddhism out of desperation. Back in 1966, when Sandoz Pharmaceuticals announced it would no longer supply LSD to American researchers because it was being abused, she had written an impassioned plea to the Swiss company defending the drug's "valuable therapeutic possibilities": "It can be a path to real sanity, not the conventions of civilized man. But it takes courage."⁴ Yet the toll of her harrowing trips had come to outweigh any obvious benefit, until one day it no longer made sense to keep trying. While Peter continued his sessions with psychedelics, Deborah started to look in another direction—to Charlotte Selver, the German educator known for teaching "sensory awareness" techniques. During one of Selver's classes in New York, probably in 1967, Deborah had met Mildred Johnstone, a philanthropist and needlepoint artist who'd already become deeply invested in Japanese tea ceremony. "Milly" had provided the commentary for a public demonstration of tea ceremony at the 1964 New York World's Fair; she had also founded a branch of the famous Urasenke tea school, from Kyoto, in a tower opposite the United Nations Headquarters. (It continues today at 153 East 69th Street.) Tea ceremony, as Johnstone once explained to *The New York Times*, "is an act of submission to the moment at hand. A way to empty your mind of distractions—and thus renew it with fresh energy."⁵

Deborah, through Milly Johnstone, had become enamored with tea ceremony, its lacquered boxes, bamboo whisks, and elaborate rituals performed over hours in near-total silence. The painstaking process of preparing and serving thick or thin tea could engender a state of *kotan*, where all extraneous thoughts fall away, leaving one with nothing but an "essential core."⁶ It could, in Johnstone's telling, be just as transporting as LSD: "The more you watch each little gesture the better your trip."⁷*

From Japanese tea ceremony, it is only a small step further to Zen, and Milly had introduced Deborah to the practice sometime in late 1967 or early 1968. The Zen Studies Society was still a fledgling organization then, and the zendo they visited was in a ground-floor apartment on West End Avenue at 81st Street, formerly a doctor's office. Eido Tai Shimano, who lived in the back rooms with his wife, Aiho Yasuko Shimano, had arrived in the city on

---

* Milly Johnstone used tea ceremony as a way of coping with personal tragedy. Her first husband, Oliver Holton, a trader of exotic animals, had kept a private zoo on their property in Middletown, New Jersey. On July 21, 1927, a supposedly tame timber wolf escaped from its enclosure, became disoriented, and lunged at their two-year-old son. A maid managed to rescue the boy and get him into the kitchen, but the wolf followed, as *The New York Times* reported (and as Johnstone corroborated in an anguished account of her own); the animal "leaped for little Tommie [*sic*], seized him up again and dragged him from the house. . . . Mrs. Mazza [the maid] grabbed a shotgun, but could find no shells, and so with the unloaded gun she ran out again. The wolf had gripped the little boy by the chest and was shaking and tossing him as a cat tosses a mouse. The woman, grasping the gun by the barrel, brought the stock down on the beast's head." Tommy was rushed to a hospital but soon died from his injuries. For Milly, tea ceremony was something akin to a mass for her little boy. She lit a candle on his birthday, folded the silk napkin over and over, wiped the bowl with a wheel-like motion, and whisked the tea into a jade froth, "froth on the tea like the things of this world—fleeting," she once wrote. "It was a way of celebrating the life of her son," said her friend Mira Nakashima. "It was a way of transforming the grief into something tolerable."

December 31, 1964, carrying nothing but a suitcase, a small Buddha statue, and a *keisaku*—a flat wooden stick about two feet long that is used to strike the shoulders of a person during meditation to discourage distracted mental states. Tai-san was part of a procession of Japanese Zen teachers, stretching back to the end of the nineteenth century, who had flocked to America as fertile ground for the "dharma to grow and evolve."[8] Many of these men—including Nyogen Senzaki and Shunryu Suzuki—had become disillusioned by the state of Zen in Japan, where it had calcified into a bureaucratic establishment riven by politics. Bringing Zen to the West was seen as a new start for old traditions.

Like a missionary, Tai-san had assembled his zendo out of found materials, sourcing a gong from an antique store and teaching his students how to sew black cloth for the round cushions called *zafus*.[9] By the time Deborah joined the New York *sangha*, or Zen community, it had grown so large that the monk was being forced to turn people away from daily practice until he could find a larger space. Those who did get in—a motley crowd of writers, artists, business executives—were united by a powerful sense of "being involved with something almost secret," as one member recalled, "almost like a political movement, only it was a spiritual movement that no one really knew about."[10] There were other zendos in San Francisco, Los Angeles, Honolulu, and Rochester, and plenty of lay readers had encountered the central ideas of Zen through Alan Watts, D. T. Suzuki, Hubert Benoit, Eugen Herrigel, or Jack Kerouac (*The Dharma Bums*). As a *practice*, though, Zen remained mostly unknown to the average American.

Deborah put on black robes, folded her legs into something approximating a lotus position, and chanted the Heart Sutra. She attempted to still the torrent of thoughts rushing through her mind. "We need ... to return to our original perfection, to see through the false image of ourselves as incomplete and sinful, and to wake up to our inherent purity and wholeness"— that, in the words of Yasutani Roshi, was the point of the sitting meditation known as zazen, not to achieve enlightenment but to reveal the enlightened being who is already there.[11] Deborah was primed to embrace this teaching, and once she found Zen, it became the center of her universe; everything else had to orbit around it. She was soon traveling to New York regularly to see Tai-san for zazen. She drove up to Litchfield, Connecticut, to Wisdom House, where the monk presided over multiday retreats of concentrated sitting called *sesshins*. She encouraged others to try tea ceremony as an introduction to Zen, or to jump with her straight into the deep end of ascetic discipline. "She came into my house one day with Rue," recalled her close friend Merete Galesi. "She said, 'You know what? This weekend I'm going to Litchfield for a three-day sesshin with Soen Roshi, and Yasutani Roshi, and Eido Roshi [Tai-san], and I want you to come, because this is for you! I know it's for you!' "[12]

Peter, however, was not invited to sesshin. The day he encountered the Zen masters standing in his driveway, relations between himself and his wife were strained almost to the breaking point. Deborah kept him "well away from her Zen practice," he later admitted, because she did not want to "contaminate the Zendo atmosphere with our dissension."[13]

That "dissension," which would delay his own embrace of Zen for another two years, was due to infidelity. It is not clear exactly when the affairs started, but Peter had been unfaithful to Deborah for years, perhaps since the very beginning. At the Harry Ransom Center in Austin, Texas, where the Peter Matthiessen Papers are housed, there is a box filled with letters, postcards, poems, photographs, pornographic sketches, and declarations of love scrawled on hotel stationery. While the dates on many of these items were deliberately effaced by Peter in a bid to scramble the chronology (to confuse a snooping wife) without actually destroying anything, the letters clearly cover decades—much of his adult life—and come from numerous women: fans, friends, colleagues, and students, all of them pining for "Darling," or "Black Pete," his "sweet self" and "sweet arms."

Matthiessen's charisma was a quality often noted by others. His attractiveness arose from some combination of his work (acclaimed), his adventures (exotic), his appearance (lean and craggily handsome, like Sir Edmund Hillary), and his aura of thinly veiled vulnerability, like a strong man superimposed onto a little boy. He understood his own allure and could deploy it deliberately, but he often took a position that was slyly passive when it came to women who were not his wives. He almost never pursued; instead, a woman showed interest in *him*, and he just did nothing to moderate the flirtation, letting it wash over him like a wave until he was in too deep to bother struggling. Perhaps this calculated passivity was a way of evading responsibility when he inevitably got caught.

The Snow Leopard is coy about his history of philandering. Yet he hints at an explanation when he writes that "in sexual abandon as in danger we are impelled, however briefly, into that vital present in which we do not stand apart from life."[14] Another explanation can be found in the LSD journal he kept from 1968 onward, a journal of self-inquiry in which he transcribed a quote from the Indian philosopher Jiddu Krishnamurti: "You escaped from loneliness through a person, used this person to cover it up. Your problem is not this relationship but rather it is the problem of your own emptiness. Escape is very dangerous because, like some drug, it hides the real problem. It is because you have no love inside you that you continually look for love to fill you from the outside."[15] Peter Matthiessen had an unquenchable need to be wanted and loved, which was perhaps a product of childhood insecurities about being neglected by his mother and his father—who, it is worth noting, also routinely engaged in extramarital affairs.

In trying to understand her husband's roving eye, Deborah made a connection between the infidelity and Peter's shaky sense of self. "I do believe that my inability to really settle down with your women"—to just accept his affairs as the price of admission—"is that they are a denial of my wholeness (as well as theirs) as a woman," she explained in a letter, adding, "I think they are equally a manifestation of your lack of wholeness."[16] In another letter, Deborah asked: "Do you think that by keeping me out of a great deal of your life it was a way of keeping me out of yourself because if you let me in and some day I walked away it would hurt so badly? And do you think perhaps getting involved with a new person is an insurance against letting somebody in?"[17] Peter, in Deborah's canny assessment, saw multiple women so he never needed to get close to any one of them; the affairs were a perverse form of self-preservation.

As she turned to Zen, Deborah was struggling with hurt and humiliation: she "writhed" when a neighbor made pitying reference to "Debby & her problems."[18] If she confronted Peter with evidence of his betrayals, he usually apologized, made assurances and promises, saying he did not "deserve" her. But sometimes he lashed out instead by declaring that he could have whomever he wanted—a remarkable claim given his own incensed reaction to Patsy's affair in 1956. "Did I drive you to your women?" Deborah demanded. "You used to make that case but is it really so?"[19]

More than once, in retaliation, Deborah pursued an affair of her own, although these never lasted long or gave her the satisfaction she craved. Trying to induce jealousy, she told Peter she preferred somebody else, or that, "very simply, with equanimity," she had given up and begun to lead her "own life."[20] She wrote anguished poetry: "The object is gone / And desire with no place of extinction / Hangs horrifyingly in the wind."[21] In a particularly dark moment, she even rationalized his behavior as a spiritual trial she had inflicted on herself. "In a peculiar way, you are a guru I have chosen to force me further and further onto the pathless path," she told him, citing a version of Torei Zenji's "Bodhisattva Vow": "I sincerely bow down in reverent belief that you are a merciful avatar of Buddha who uses devices to emancipate me from sinful karma that has been produced and accumulated upon myself by my own egotistical delusion and attachment."[22]

In January 1969, Deborah returned to Sagaponack with Rue and Alex from a skiing vacation in Sun Valley, Idaho. Peter had stayed home to work before heading off on a long trip, and he'd accidentally left out a photo of his "Florida girl." Deborah found it, then contacted a lawyer to request divorce papers. "I'm sorry I cannot play these games," she wrote Peter definitively.[23] But then she changed her mind, dropping all talk of separation. Having gone through two divorces already, she was desperate to avoid a third. She also loved her husband, both "'good' Pete and 'bad' Pete."[24] "She told me she would rather die than lose Peter," recalled Merete Galesi. "She'd prefer to die than lose him. She said that many times."[25]

The following month, Deborah sold her first book to the editor Nan Talese at Random House. "Going Home," as the manuscript was originally titled, would be published in 1970 as *Annaghkeen*, an account of the two-month trip to Ireland the Matthiessens had taken during the summer of 1965. The book was sensitively written, with passages of dazzling eloquence; Nancy Wilson Ross, in a blurb, called it "as beautiful and sad as Éire itself."[26] Deborah structured it as a journal, with dated entries full of picturesque descriptions and historical information on abbeys and castles. But the main subject was two spiritual seekers locked in an endless, cyclical crisis. It was the record of a woman sifting through the shards of a fractured marriage in search of something true. *The Snow Leopard*, written a few years later, would borrow (whether Matthiessen was conscious of it or not) thematic, structural, and stylistic elements from *Annaghkeen*; both books alchemize the pain of loss into crystalline observations about the messiness of relationships. To read them together, one after the other, is to hear both sides of an intimate conversation about life and death, about resentment and forgiveness, about fighting to hang on and finally learning to let go.

PETER'S DAYS WITH Deborah were "tainted with remorse," he would confess in *The Snow Leopard*. "I could not abide myself when near her, and therefore took advantage of my work to absent myself on expeditions all around the world."[27] Running away was easier than addressing the problem directly, and the next few years were filled with a staggering amount of foreign travel, often to places with poor communication where he could not be reached except by mail.

In 1969, he was away from Sagaponack for seven months straight, mid-January until early August. The opportunity for this extended absence came courtesy of John Owen, the director of Tanzania National Parks. A tall, blue-eyed British conservationist, born in Uganda to missionary parents, Owen had spent nearly a decade expanding the parks system within the young republic, adding nine new reserves while promoting wildlife to Tanzanians as an irreplaceable national treasure. At the same time, he had championed Tanzania's animals as a *world* treasure, and sought international funding for wildlife protection measures, as well as for ecological studies at the Serengeti

Research Institute, which informed conservation and management practices across the parks. In 1968, Owen had visited New York to commission an ad campaign ("Give a Lion a Home") that would solicit donations from nature-loving Americans. While in the city, he had met with Matthiessen on the recommendation of Truman Capote and Martha Gellhorn. Over lunch at the Williams Club on West 43rd Street, Owen made an extraordinary proposal. If Matthiessen was willing to write a profile-raising book about African wildlife, national parks, and the Research Institute at Seronera, a tiny settlement on the western side of the immense Serengeti plains, he could have his own quarters in the park as well as the loan of a Land Rover, with official permission to drive and walk and explore anywhere he pleased.

Matthiessen had accepted this offer immediately. Then, in the months following, he'd secured financial support from *The New Yorker* and padded out his itinerary by committing to three other expeditions, thus extending his absence from Sagaponack. Deborah was still skiing in Idaho with the children when he departed New York for Nairobi.

The last time Matthiessen had visited Kenya, in 1961, the country was still a British colony. Eight years on, Jomo Kenyatta was now president of an independent nation, and Matthiessen marveled at the "shining surface" of a rapidly expanding capital city. There were still the familiar tin-roofed Kikuyu slums, ramshackle bazaars, beggars and drifters in dusty streets, but the character of Nairobi had changed—and so, of course, had Matthiessen himself. Instead of rushing past the ugly realities of colonialism, as he had on his circuitous way to Netherlands New Guinea, he now paused to consider the situation as it currently stood. In the Long Bar, "a last redoubt of the old-style wardens and white hunters," he listened with distaste as talk turned to "the great days when the native knew his place." At least, Matthiessen noted, a few others present "understood that Independence had to come."[28]

After receiving cholera and typhoid vaccinations in Nairobi, he made his way across the border into Tanzania, which had been Tanganyika until it merged with Zanzibar and changed its name in 1964. He traveled to Seronera, more than two hundred miles from the nearest big town, Arusha, in a stark landscape of umbrella thorn acacias and sepia-tinted savanna. Seronera was home to a commercial game lodge as well as the Research Institute, but management staff and resident scientists lived apart from the tourists in prefabricated bungalows. Conditions were comfortable, if somewhat rudimentary: bottled gas; a generator for electricity at night; an artesian well for water. Until recently, toilet buckets from the lodge had been emptied into warthog burrows.[29] Matthiessen was given his own bungalow, although he lived just as much in the Land Rover, an enclosed truck with no backseats and a flat hood that was useful for preparing meals and pressing plants. Like a Swiss Army knife, the truck could be reconfigured to suit almost any situation. Hatches in the roof ensured safe animal watching, and loose boards in the rear were easily removed to make room for, at one time or another, "a whole butchered zebra, drying elephant ears, innumerable townspeople and tribesmen, tortoises, birds, chameleons, and a diseased baboon."[30] Matthiessen slept on a mattress beneath mosquito netting. With tools, books, maps, a machete, flashlights, cooking utensils, a rope-seat stool, and ample reserves of water, food, and gasoline, he was essentially self-sufficient.

As a much older man, he would describe the eight weeks he spent roaming in and around the Serengeti at forty-one years of age as "unquestionably . . . the most memorable of my life."[31] It was the season of the Great Migration, hundreds of thousands of wildebeest crossing the plains, with bull gnus "leaping, kicking, scampering, bucking, exploding crazy-legged in all directions as if in search of stones on which to dash their itching brains."[32] Here in the wilderness, Matthiessen would write, one could catch a "glimpse of the earth's morning"[33]—nature as it once was, without the pernicious rot of civilization. At the same time, somewhat paradoxically, he also felt that the African wilderness was a place where the past had been "left behind," and that being there was to return "into the present," a vital moment-by-moment existence.[34] Africa as an accessible past; Africa as the eternal present: both were variations on the romance of refuge.

He wandered alone across the Serengeti. He investigated a dead female Thomson's gazelle, slicing open her belly to see if she'd died while calving. He surprised and then trailed a honey badger, though not too closely: "in its dealings with man [it] is said to direct its attack straight at the crotch."[35] He took off his boots to feel the "hide" of the plains rubbing against his bare feet.

Sometimes he accompanied parks staff or the Seronera scientists on aerial surveys and field trips. Hans Kruuk, deputy director of the Research Institute, took him to inspect the animal that had earned Kruuk the nickname among African workers of "Bwana Fisi"—Mister Hyena. Myles Turner, the Serengeti warden, led Matthiessen on a three-day safari to the volcano Ol Doinyo Lengai, "Mountain of God," which they never quite reached because of treacherous terrain. Desmond Vesey-Fitzgerald, an Irish ecologist, taught him "bush botany" near the Momella Lakes, at the foot of Mount Meru. And Iain Douglas-Hamilton welcomed him ("Have you had tea?") to Lake Manyara National Park, where he was camped on the Ndala River with his mother. Douglas-Hamilton was a sprightly, devil-may-care British zoologist, writing a PhD thesis on elephants; he drove Matthiessen right up to the edge of a herd, which then responded with a vocal threat display. ("'Silly old things,' said Iain, scarcely looking up.")[36] With Douglas-Hamilton, Matthiessen also attended a conference in Tsavo East, back in Kenya, on what was being termed the "elephant problem": there were thought to be too many, causing too much habitat destruction, and representatives from both countries argued about the advisability of a cull.*

The most important scientist Matthiessen met at Seronera was George Beals Schaller. Though just thirty-five years old, Schaller was well on his way to becoming the world's leading field biologist, having already conducted a pioneering study of tigers in Kahna, India, and another on gorillas in the Virunga Mountains of Central Africa. While he was a diligent, exacting scientist, he was also a conservationist. "My love is being out and watching animals, but nobody can just sit and watch wildlife while it's disappearing," Schaller said.[37] He saw conservation as "the ethical criterion on which man's future depends; it is a religion based on moral, aesthetic, and practical values."[38] Uniting the scientific method with this "religion," he preferred to call himself a conservation biologist, or even an "ecological missionary," spreading a gospel of rigorous research. Later, he would also embrace "feral biologist"—someone who spends so much time with wild animals that returning to human society induces culture shock.[39]

Schaller had been living at Seronera with his wife, Kay, and their two young sons, Eric and Mark, since June 1966, an idyllic existence of family picnics and giraffes grazing just outside the kitchen window. Like Matthiessen, Schaller had come because of John Owen, who invited him to study lions in the Serengeti. Schaller had been "delighted" by the invitation because he found the lion fascinating as a predator, and because nobody had yet unraveled "the intricacies of its social system."[40] For nearly three years before Matthiessen's arrival, Schaller had been monitoring prides within a hundred square miles of Seronera, documenting all births, deaths, and social interactions he saw, along with—Schaller's main focus—the influence of lion predation on prey populations. This was the fieldwork that Matthiessen now accompanied him on.

---

* In the late 1960s there was an estimated concentration of twelve elephants to every square mile around Lake Manyara of Tanzania, and some forty thousand alone in Tsavo, Kenya. With Myles Turner, Matthiessen flew over a herd of four hundred marching across the Serengeti "like gray lava, leaving behind a ruined bog of mud and twisted trees." But then came devastating drought and the decades-long poaching crisis, and numbers dropped precipitously. In 1977, Iain Douglas-Hamilton counted 453 elephants in Lake Manyara National Park; ten years later, he counted just 181, most of them juveniles. Similarly, when Matthiessen visited the remote Selous in Tanzania in 1980—an expedition recounted in *Sand Rivers* (1981)—there were an estimated 110,000 elephants living in the game reserve; six years later, an aerial survey found half that number. By the time Matthiessen published *African Silences* (1991), the bleak final volume in a loose Africa trilogy, some 80 percent of elephants in East Africa had vanished, many of them slaughtered for the ivory trade. Today, the African forest elephant (*Loxodonta cyclotis*) is listed as critically endangered by the International Union for Conservation of Nature. The African savanna elephant (*Loxodonta africana*) is listed as endangered. As of 2021, there was an estimated combined population of 415,000 elephants remaining on the continent.

Schaller was not in the habit of driving people around in his truck. He preferred to "go out and concentrate and have nobody asking questions, be focused on the animals."[41] But he had read some of Matthiessen's books, including *Under the Mountain Wall*, which he thought was "terrific." He knew that Matthiessen possessed the skill to write "an informative, honest, and sensitive account" of life and death in the Serengeti.[42]

For his part, Matthiessen found the field biologist "single-minded, not easy to know."[43] Schaller showed integrity and dedication—Matthiessen admired his work enormously[*]—yet he was also taciturn, circumspect. He seemed more comfortable with animals than he did with other people. (Both men were loners not inclined to, as Schaller once put it, "buddy-buddy type interactions.")[44] "George is a stern pragmatist, unable to muster up much grace in the face of unscientific attitudes; he takes a hard-eyed look at almost everything," Matthiessen wrote.[45] This was an accurate assessment, but Schaller's stern pragmatism masked a depth of intuition and feeling. He was guided by his heart as well as his mind, and he considered the wilderness—Alaska, especially, where he'd made his professional start—to be a kind of spiritual home. "I view myself basically as a nineteenth-century wanderer with a scientific bent on an intangible and elusive search," he once explained, sounding a lot like his passenger in the Serengeti.[46]

One day the men were driving near a gorge when they spotted an emaciated lioness. The animal was covered in flies and swollen ticks. She struggled to stand upright as they approached, then slumped into the dirt. For mercy, and because he wanted to conduct an autopsy, Schaller shot her with an overdose of tranquilizer. But the lion kept moving; she stood, took a few shaky steps, and collapsed again. Schaller was aghast, as Matthiessen would write in *The Tree Where Man Was Born*:

> at this moment his boyish face was openly upset, more upset than I had ever thought to see him. The death of the lioness was painless, far better than being found by the hyenas, but it was going on too long; twice he returned to the Land Rover for additional dosage. We stood there in a kind of vigil, feeling more and more depressed, and the end, when it came at last, was shocking. The poor beast, her life going, began to twitch and

---

[*] "If you hadn't been a writer, what do you think your occupation would have been?" Michael Shapiro asked Matthiessen in 2003. Matthiessen replied, "There are so many other professions I would like to have tried. My brother is a marine biologist; I don't think I would work in his field, but certainly I would be a field biologist. I would want to work with wildlife and wild places. George Schaller, my partner on *the Snow Leopard* trip, not only does wonderful work in the field, but he also has been instrumental in establishing wildlife parks all around the world. That to me is terrific and exciting work. . . . That would be a wonderful combination of fieldwork and social benefit."

tremble. With a little grunt, she turned onto her back and lifted her hind legs into the air. Still grunting, she licked passionately at the grass, and her haunches shuddered in long spasms, and this last abandon shattered the detachment I had felt until that moment. I was swept by a wave of feeling, then a pang so sharp that, for a moment, I felt sick, as if all the waste and loss in life, the harm one brings to oneself and others, had been drawn to a point in this lonely passage between light and darkness.[47]

This paragraph illustrates an approach Matthiessen would use to brilliant effect when writing about the animals and landscapes of East Africa. He begins as the unsentimental observer attuned to minute details, which he re-creates with novelistic flair: the lion licking "passionately" at the grass. But in the process of looking so closely, his "detachment" falters; an objective stance gives way to feeling, and the tone turns philosophical. What begins as a straightforward description of Schaller's scientific fieldwork becomes, by the end, a kind of memento mori. This rhetorical movement of estrangement, from the particular to the universal, from empirical observations to contemplation of something abstract and infinitely large, is one of Matthiessen's hallmarks, present in almost all his nonfiction "nature" books. It is a movement that lends his work an extraordinary sense of immediacy and scale—and humility, too, because it approaches nature as something more than systems to be broken down and catalogued. Nature becomes a sublime conduit carrying the attentive, open-minded observer to glimpses of ultimate truths.

By March, the southeast monsoon had brought storms and bone-chilling winds to the Serengeti, but Matthiessen continued to explore with only brief bouts of loneliness. His two eldest children, Luke and Sara Carey, arrived for a visit during their spring break, and he drove them to the Olduvai Gorge where the Leakeys had discovered the famous hominin fossils.

Sara Carey hated the insects; she bickered incessantly with her father. But Luke, who was just days away from turning sixteen, had never felt so much affection as he did when they watched wildebeests together from the Land Rover. Peter, in Africa, was suddenly the man his son had always wanted him to be, attentive and interested. When Luke returned home to New York, he sat down to write a heartfelt letter: "I miss Africa more than I can say. Each day I miss it more. The whole time I felt like I was the first man to ever see it. I want to go back now, just us. That would be the ultimate appreciation of it. Thanks and I really wish I could see you. I really miss you, Dad." Re-reading this letter forty-five years later, Luke would be struck by "how much I yearned to have my father to myself. I can only speculate on what prompted this sentiment, but I believe Africa was the key. . . . I had him in

Africa, and he had me, but the note hints at an understanding that we had come as close to the 'ultimate appreciation' of each other as we ever would, and that this could only have happened in the short time we spent together in paradise."[48]

AFTER SEEING HIS CHILDREN off at the airport, Matthiessen gathered his things and departed Seronera almost immediately. To reach his next destination, he flew north to Addis Ababa, in Ethiopia, and then on to Asmara, the former capital of Italian Eritrea. From there, he headed overland to the sweaty port town of Massawa on the Red Sea, passing gutted oil trucks and burned-out buses—calling cards of the Eritrean Liberation Front. An expedition from Massawa to the Dahlak Archipelago, a group of 126 islands known for their pearl fisheries, had been organized by Frank Minot of the African Wildlife Leadership Foundation. The aim was to survey the archipelago for a proposed marine national park, and Matthiessen joined a team of biologists, ornithologists, and government representatives from Ethiopia.

An Imperial Ethiopian Navy patrol craft ferried the group southeast down the coast to Shumma, a sunburnt island of mangroves, coral banks, and feral goats. The team established camp and made plans for a survey of the neighboring islands. But then the expedition fell apart before it could even get properly underway. No naval vessel had been officially assigned to the project, and the Ethiopian Navy (or so the argument went) was not trained to navigate the coral maze of the Dahlak Archipelago anyway.

For eight days, Matthiessen found himself all but marooned on Shumma. "My own frustration about our exile passed quite quickly," he wrote in his notes on the failed expedition. "At dawn, I rose and washed in the tidal stream that disappeared under the mangroves. . . . Noisy reef herons and redshanks came and went, and the strange amphibious fish called the mud skipper climbed out of the white marly pools onto the mangrove roots and stared with elevated eyes at the creatures that had left the sea so long before."[49] Because the trip was a bust, the rest of the team settled down to rest each afternoon beneath acacia trees, but Matthiessen explored the beaches and black coral ledges, pausing to cool off in eye-stinging salt water. On the island's northern beach, furthest from camp, he came across a green turtle laying eggs in the sand. Astonished, he crawled up behind her and gingerly placed a hand on the barnacled shell. "Lying there beside the turtle, I peered into the ancient eye, and the eye gazed back, blind as the Universe."

There was no mail on Shumma, no telephone, no deadlines, no schedule. "There was only immersion in the island." At sunset, he peeled off his shorts and wrapped a hand-woven kikoi around his waist; his skin turned brown and his body "felt like flying." In the draft of a *New Yorker* article about the expedition that was edited but never published, Matthiessen rhapsodized that his time on Shumma before the team got ferried back to Massawa was "too much to contain": "In flight toward the cliffs and the burning sea, I had the sense I have had at other times, that the wind was blowing my life away, that I wanted not to struggle, but blow with it. Elation and madness come on the same wind, and there is no need to understand this well to know that it is true."

ON THE LAST DAY of March, Matthiessen flew to Durban, South Africa, for the first part of yet another expedition, this one to film great white sharks in the wild. For five days he traveled aboard the *Terrier VIII*, a former whaling ship chartered for the documentary project, descending periodically beneath the waves in a custom-built flotation cage. Then he took his leave, arranging to rejoin the crew in Madagascar for a longer stay at the end of June.

For a break from reporting, he traveled to Italy. Two American friends, John and Susan Abbot, owned a medieval castle near the village of Umbertide, in Umbria, a two-hour drive southeast of Florence. The Castello di Polgeto was straight out of a pastoral landscape painting: covered in ivy, surrounded by olive groves, vineyards, lemon and linden trees, with Monte Acuto rising blue in the background. John, an architect, had renovated the twelfth-century residence with all the modern conveniences; Matthiessen adored its "lovely corners and stone walls and sun and gardens and rain-smelling slates."[50] He also liked an Italian who lived nearby. "He was fascinated with the lady who would come and clean for us," recalled Susan. "She walked barefoot down this sandy path. He used to look out the window of the castle—it had a big glass window—at this simple woman, because that sort of thing was right up his alley, that primitive life."[51]

A girlfriend, Karen Yochim—the "Florida girl"—soon flew in to provide Peter with some company for a week or two. Karen had come to his attention back in 1966, when she'd sent him a fan letter about *At Play in the Fields of the Lord*—"such splendid writing that I can't quite believe there isn't a halo over your head in the jacket photograph."[52] He had responded to the flattering letter, and they'd begun seeing each other casually after meeting up in a tiny swamp town near the Everglades. Karen, from Sarasota, was young and free-spirited, the kind of woman who "traveled light" with "no baggage," as Peter told a nephew admiringly.[53] In Florida, they had driven on the highways together, which he called "running clouds," and in Italy they now took road trips to Florence and Rome. "Peter wanted to get away from his sophisticated world in New York," Karen later recalled. He told her about a dream he had to live somewhere "in the back of beyond," but Deborah wouldn't allow it: "He found that so tiresome." He wanted to forget about everything and everyone in America. He was disappointed when Karen admitted they had mutual acquaintances, including other writers. "It's like trying to brush wet rice off your hands," he told her. "No matter where I go, I can't get away from them."[54]

When he wasn't hosting his girlfriend, Matthiessen smoked pot at Polgeto, swam in the castle pool, and caught up on writing. He also took LSD, which was readily supplied by John Abbot. On a previous visit, Matthiessen had bought a small green notebook with "APPUNTI" stenciled on the cover—this became his LSD journal. One day, he added 300 micrograms of Sandoz LSD to a cup of coffee, put Fauré's "Requiem" on the stereo, and pushed through an onslaught of paranoid self-pity: "I pay attention, and I remain calm," he wrote.[55] Another day, he swallowed even more LSD—an extreme 500 micrograms—and stumbled through a procession of "hard" hallucinations: "I laugh but still feel negative: I shake with rage, trying to squeeze myself . . . squeeze out every last drop of rage . . . I shudder and shake with the violence of it." During a less intense session, he drove to Siena and wandered around the Piazza del Campo: "a fine wild funny day." He preferred to stay near Polgeto, though, where John and Susan could keep an eye on him when he was tripping. Once he dove into the pool, then started swimming laps without surfacing to breathe between strokes; Susan shouted a reminder that he was not as immortal as he seemed to imagine.[56]

The LSD journal is a fascinating document. Some of it is just the frenzied ranting of a man on acid: "CHEERS! I'M A MESS! AND I'M FUCKING WELL GOOD AND TIRED."[57] Some of it is almost incomprehensible: references to "funky David" and "a huge metal robot Goliath." But there are also dozens of pages devoted to sober quotations, because, as a complement to the LSD therapy, Matthiessen was also scouring books of psychology and philosophy at Polgeto, copying out passages that seemed to illuminate his discontent.

One of these books was *Neurosis and Human Growth* (1950), by Karen Horney, the German neo-Freudian who specialized in anxiety and neurosis. Horney placed particular emphasis on childhood trauma, arguing that a key source of anxiety is the experience of parental indifference. A child who feels overlooked or misunderstood loses touch with the full range of his or her emotions. The child might feel divided—an "ideal self" versus a "despised self"—and develop strategies to cope with anxiety, strategies which can then become compulsive and prevent healthy development, leading to neurosis. A neurotic adult views the world through the distorting lens of their ingrained coping strategies. Horney organized these strategies into three main groups, one of which was detachment, or withdrawal: the individual pulls away from others to avoid anxiety, prizing self-sufficiency and independence. It is not hard to understand why this theory resonated with Matthiessen. "Incapacity to love," he wrote in his journal. "Fear of rejection/dependency . . . Egocentricity (<u>not</u> self-love, but based on anxiety)." He asked himself some lacerating questions after reading Horney: "Are you clinging to role of child?" "Do I cling to illusion of independence, and thus <u>automatically</u> resent wife?" His answer to this one was "yes."[58]

Along with Horney's work, Matthiessen mined the old sermons of Meister Eckhart, the thirteenth-century Dominican mystic, as well as the gnomic pronouncements of Krishnamurti: "Freedom from confusion means awareness of the facts of confusion."[59] He took detailed notes on *The Wisdom of Insecurity*, by Alan Watts: "Whenever the past is dropped away and safely abandoned, life is renewed." He also dipped into Philip Kapleau's *Three Pillars of Zen*, perhaps in a bid to understand the new obsession that was giving his wife so much solace. Matthiessen still had little understanding of Zen, but his LSD journal shows him attempting to graft its vocabulary onto his problems:

KOAN: Do you still love DM [Deborah Matthiessen]?
ANSWER: The dog Mu[60]

This is a startling reference to the Mu koan from the *Mumonkan* ("The Gateless Gate"), a collection of forty-eight koans compiled by Wumen Huikai in the thirteenth century. A monk asks Joshu, a Chinese Ch'an master, whether a dog has Buddha Nature, and Joshu replies, "Mu!" Literally, Mu means "no," or "not," and Matthiessen may have meant it that way: *I do not still love Deborah Matthiessen.* But Mu is more properly translated as "nothingness," or perhaps "invalid," a blunt shutting-down of all logical discussion. "Try as it might, reasoning cannot gain even a toehold on Mu," Kapleau wrote in *The Three Pillars of Zen*. "In fact, trying to solve Mu rationally, we are told by the masters, is like 'trying to smash one's fist through an iron wall.'"[61] *Do you still love DM?* It is possible Matthiessen wrote Mu to flag the question as unanswerable, not fit to be asked in the first place.

One morning in May, he took LSD, and then, a few hours later, sat down in the garden to read a paper by Carl Jung. "The Development of Personality" is about self-realization, and it considers why some people are happy to follow conventions while others feel an impatient urge to go their own way, pursuing "a well-rounded psychic whole," or what Jung called personality—"the supreme realization of the innate idiosyncrasy of a living being." To develop personality and achieve wholeness, "consciously and with moral deliberation," is to reject conformity and embark on a "strange adventure":

> The fact that many a man who goes his own way ends in ruin means nothing. . . . He *must* obey his own law, as if it were a daemon whispering to him of new and wonderful paths. . . . If he hearkens to the voice, he is at once set apart and isolated, as he has resolved to obey the law that commands him from within. "His *own* law!" everybody will cry. But he knows better: it is *the* law, *the* vocation for which he is destined. . . . The only meaningful life is a life that strives for the individual realization—absolute and unconditional—of its own particular law.[62]

Matthiessen "actually yelled" and jumped out of his chair after reading this paper. He "floated free," he wrote in his journal: "After so many years of telling D. I was driven by something that had to work itself out, but not understanding it."[63] He was dazzled by the concept of *one's own law*, which Jung equated to Tao. ("To rest in Tao means fulfillment, wholeness, one's destination reached, one's mission done; the beginning, end, and perfect realization of the meaning of existence innate in all things.")[64] Matthiessen would include extracts from Jung's paper in *The Snow Leopard*, where he described it as "the first hard clue to the nature of my distemper."[65]

AFTER HIS SOJOURN in Italy, Matthiessen returned to Nairobi for a few days—another woman, Sara S., lived there—and then caught a flight to Antananarivo, Madagascar. He drove north to the harbor city of Diégo-Suarez (today called Antsiranana), where he rejoined the great white shark expedition on the first day of July.

The expedition's organizer was a tall, balding New Yorker named Peter Robin Gimbel, whom Matthiessen had known since his Hotchkiss days. A scion of the department store family, Gimbel (like Matthiessen; like Robert Gardner) had become disillusioned with a life of comfort and wealth. When his twin brother, David, committed suicide at the age of twenty-nine, Gimbel had treated the shock as a wake-up call, abandoning his job as an investment banker to refashion himself as a risk-taking gentleman adventurer.[*]

---

[*] "[W]hen David died, that triggered something—[Peter] wanted to make a move," Matthiessen said of Gimbel. "Many of us arrive at points in life when it would be perhaps appropriate to make a strong move out of the rut we have been in, do something else. It is very difficult. It takes a lot of guts. There is a lot of bloodshed and a lot of tearing, and generally we don't do it. Well, he did it. He really did it."

Gimbel had been the first person to dive through 225 feet of water to the *Andrea Doria* shipwreck, which he photographed for *Life* in 1956. Inspired by Matthiessen's *Cloud Forest*, he had parachuted into the Vilcabamba mountains, in the Peruvian Andes, to lead an eighty-nine-day mission sponsored by *National Geographic* and the New York Zoological Society. He had swum beneath Antarctic ice to film the Weddell seal, and shot a shaky documentary about blue sharks off the East End of Long Island. It was in Montauk, in fact, that he had first become intrigued by the great white shark, after noticing a set of monstrous jaws mounted on the wall of the bar at Salivar's Dock. "He stared at the great shark and brooded over it and even dreamed about it, until it became a small kind of obsession," Matthiessen wrote, making Gimbel sound something like Ahab; "he longed for the confrontation, if only to exorcise a dread that anyone else would have thought extremely healthy. And in this wish, his film idea was born."[66]

Gimbel's *Blue Water, White Death*—"white death" is a nickname for the great white shark—was funded by the CBS subsidiary Cinema Center Films. Gimbel invited Matthiessen to write an account of the documentary project, much as Gardner had asked him to cover the expedition in New Guinea. Matthiessen said yes, in Gimbel's case, because he already had plans to be traveling in Africa, and because he had never seen sharks underwater before. To address his lack of diving experience, he met Gimbel for a few days of scuba instruction in the Bahamas, in July 1968; the friends descended with a shark cage into the Lost Blue Hole near New Providence Island, a cave in the ocean floor, two hundred feet deep, that looks from the surface like a void.

Gimbel's expedition was not a scientific survey. He collected no data alongside his footage, and there were no marine biologists on the crew, just a small group of filmmakers and two Australian spearfishing champions, Ron and Valerie Taylor. "We came really, when you get right down to it," Gimbel announced in a moment of candor, "to see what the limits are, just how wildly—that's the wrong word—just how openly a man can expose himself in the water with excited sharks and still maintain control."[67] Contemplating this remark, Matthiessen suggested that Gimbel, "by confronting death over and over . . . might end some awful suspense about it, or dissipate it in some way." While Matthiessen could sympathize with the impulse, he was less enthusiastic about climbing into a cage that could crumple in the jaws of a determined great white. ("I'm not a brave person," he once insisted in an interview. "Something that takes nerve, I can muster it up for one occasion . . . [but] to let your nerves work in such a way that you will do it over and over again, that's real courage. I don't have that.")[68]

By the time Matthiessen rejoined the film crew in Madagascar, the expedition was not going exactly as planned. Gimbel had filmed some action in the waters off Durban, where a cage was suspended from the harpooned carcass of a sperm whale; more than forty sharks had torn into the "great cave of flesh," their tails "lashing in the bursts of gore that flowered in the sea."[69] But none of the sharks were great whites, and every dive since Durban had proved disappointing. While Matthiessen was relaxing in Italy, the *Terrier VIII* had visited the waters around Ceylon (now Sri Lanka): visibility was poor, there were no sharks at all, and Gimbel fell ill with an attack of the bends. On the passage from Ceylon to Madagascar, the seas had turned so rough he slipped over a rail and tumbled from the bridge ladder to the pilot deck, injuring his hip, elbow, and shoulder.

For the next nine days, Matthiessen accompanied the expedition around the Outer Islands of the Seychelles, north of Madagascar. The crew's luck did not improve. Though the reefs were rich in marine life—parrotfish, sweetlips, Moorish idols, and a green turtle "gliding down the sea cliff in the crystalline light like a great bird in a twilight canyon"[70]—there were no great whites, and the hammerheads the area was famous for remained stubbornly elusive. So there was *something* to film, Ron and Valerie Taylor gave a spearfishing demonstration, taking off their wetsuits to skin-dive. At Aldabra, a large coral atoll occupied by giant tortoises, Matthiessen was recruited to perform in front of the camera, too, a chore he carried out with much irritated grumbling. "As the ship's tame naturalist, I was to play opposite Valerie in her Adventures on a Desert Island, marveling at flightless rails, thumping tortoises, and wandering breathless through the magic wood."[71]

The Seychelles were a bust for the expedition, but the crew did see one thing that Matthiessen found moving for more personal reasons. On Astove, a coral atoll surrounded by a shallow lagoon, they encountered Mark Veevers-Carter, a Dutch man living in a palm-thatched house with his wife and two children. There to restore a copra plantation, the family had a menagerie of farm animals, an extensive vegetable garden, ready access to fresh seafood, and a variety of canned goods delivered by seafaring traders. Seeing these people living in a version of the "most excellent place" Matthiessen had fantasized about left him "stricken with longing for the solitude and peace of such an island, where I would live in a manner still more simple and self-sufficient than the one chosen by the Veevers-Carters."[72]

In *Blue Meridian*, his book about Gimbel's manic quest to confront the white death, Matthiessen described a conversation he had with Valerie Taylor on Astove. Did she ever long for a life like the one this family was leading, cut off from the outside world? Taylor told him she was "content" with her house in the Sydney suburbs; all she really lacked was children. While it would certainly be "an adventure" to live on a desert island, at thirty-three she felt "too old" to try. "She wasn't, of course," Matthiessen wrote, "but I realized that I was. With a forty-year accumulation of responsibilities, I would do it now for the wrong reason. For me, the life-long dream of my own island would no longer be adventure but escape."[73]

BECAUSE HE HAD no visa for Mozambique, where Gimbel was headed next, Matthiessen left the *Terrier VIII* in the Comoros. He flew once again to Nairobi, then made a long, exhausting journey to Maui, where he met a Hawaiian naturalist named John "Jack" Lind for a foray into the rainy wilderness of Kīpahulu Valley, on the windward slopes of Haleakalā. For four days, Matthiessen, Lind, and Lind's son, Terry, descended from the volcano's crater to the ocean, surveying pristine bird habitat that the Nature Conservancy hoped to purchase and donate to the Haleakalā National Park, thereby expanding its protective boundaries. Matthiessen was there to write about the potential acquisition for *Audubon* magazine, but he was poorly equipped for such a difficult hike: "I wear a borrowed jacket that no longer resists water. It is hard to believe that one could be cold in Maui in July, but I am shivering like a stunned fish."[74] As he persevered, he thought about a silver capsule somewhere above that was, at that very moment, carrying home the first men to walk on the moon.

In California, his final stop before arriving home himself, Matthiessen drove to Delano to check in with Cesar Chavez, who was still recovering from his bad back. Chavez asked him about the Kenyan labor leader Tom Mboya,* who had just been murdered outside a pharmacy in Nairobi, and about Julius Nyerere,† president of Tanzania, whose picture was now hanging in Chavez's office. They also discussed sharks, Chavez's earthworm farm ("the worms were prospering on a diet of oatmeal"), and an enormous spill in the Dos Cuadras Offshore Oil Field near Santa Barbara: "'I thought of you the minute it happened!' Cesar grinned, referring to my impassioned speeches on environmental pollution of the autumn before."[75] The topic of conversation didn't matter much to Matthiessen, who just enjoyed Chavez's company.

---

* Tom Mboya (1930–1969) was a significant figure in Kenya's independence movement. As that country's minister of economic planning and development—and a likely successor to Jomo Kenyatta—he was assassinated on July 5, 1969.
† Julius Nyerere (1922–1999) was the incumbent president of the United Republic of Tanzania. A proponent of African self-reliance, he instituted a socialist policy of cooperative economics (*ujamaa*) that involved, among other measures, the nationalization of major industries in Tanzania, mass literacy programs, and collectivized village farmlands. The failure of this "villagization" experiment was not yet apparent when Matthiessen and Chavez discussed Nyerere in Delano.

In early August, when he finally reappeared in Sagaponack, he was juggling a long feature for *Audubon* and three books at various stages of composition. This was a tremendous amount of work, but in one sense it was liberating, because it kept him removed from the domestic sphere. While he was physically present for Deborah and his children, while he went camping with them on Sagg Main Beach, sleeping next to Rue and Alex under the stars, mentally he never needed to fully return. His mind continued to roam between Africa, the Seychelles, Maui, Delano, and Grand Cayman.

The most pressing project was his extended profile of Chavez. *The New Yorker* had run a two-part version in June, which was "an important validation . . . of the cause of California farmworkers,"[76] according to Chavez's associate LeRoy Chatfield, and which "provided an enormous boost to Chavez's credibility and status on the East Coast,"[77] in the words of his biographer Miriam Pawel. Yet Matthiessen was frustrated with how the *New Yorker* articles came out: "I really don't like it."[78] He had originally written the two parts as three, but the magazine's editors decided to streamline the text. In the process, they had made the second article "too dense," in his opinion, and excised the "incendiary statements," meaning his more partisan commentary about Chavez. "[T]he whole damned thing is too safe and noncommittal," he complained in a letter to Ann Israel. He asked her to advise the union people to "wait for the book," which would restore cut material and be far more assertive in tone, as the full title suggested: *Sal Si Puedes: Cesar Chavez and the New American Revolution*. (For comparison, the *New Yorker* articles were meekly titled "Organizer~I," and "Organizer~II.")

Completed that fall, *Sal Si Puedes* was a significant departure from Matthiessen's previous books. There were familiar warnings of impending environmental catastrophe, with California—"which free enterprise has reduced from the most majestic of the states to the most despoiled"—described as a "blighted" landscape of ruined waterways and rank invasive weeds.[79] But equal or greater emphasis was given to labor exploitation, racism, corruption, and even musings on the stupidity of the Vietnam War. Matthiessen's experiences over the previous decade had taught him to step back and see the bigger picture, in which attitudes toward nature are indivisible from attitudes about economic, social, and political issues. "In a damaged human habitat, all problems merge," he wrote.[80] *Sal Si Puedes* was a portrait of a society in a crisis it had chosen to ignore: the book attempted to debunk the "carefully constructed legend"[81] of an American Way of Life. It was also a biography, almost a hagiography, of a man who offered, in Matthiessen's opinion, a stirring alternative to business as usual. Cesar Chavez was obviously focused on labor rights, but his grassroots movement, a "fight for a new ethic"[82] grounded in dignity and justice, was the kind of value shift, the book argued, that might counter the worrisome national trends of materialism, poverty, and ecological decline.

Sal Si Puedes was crafted using techniques that are now commonly associated with New Journalism. To show rather than tell what Chavez was doing with farmworkers in the San Joaquin Valley, Matthiessen describes a series of close encounters at union meetings and picket lines. He interviews the corporate growers and presents their hostile opposition to Chavez in scenes of unfiltered dialogue, where body language becomes an important part of what is being said. Chavez himself is portrayed as a complicated, idiosyncratic leader through his own statements, but also through the accumulation of seemingly insignificant details, like those used in fiction to sketch in a character: his annoyance at a discarded beer can; his fondness for matzos and Diet Rite Cola; his frightened, hands-to-head reaction when a glove compartment snaps open with a sound like a gunshot. And then there are Matthiessen's editorial asides, which, while ostensibly about Chavez, reveal something about the author's own preoccupations and hang-ups, projected onto the union leader: "He has what the Japanese call *hara*, or 'belly'—that is, he is centered in himself, he is not fragmented, he sits simply, like a Zen master."[83]

Matthiessen is candid about his sympathies; this is not the evenhanded reportage of a newspaper journalist. Indeed, the figure of "Peter Matthiessen" is presented in the narrative as a "long-haired" leftist who arouses the suspicion of Delano police (a fat officer who "appeared to be part of his machine, overflowing out of his front window like a growth").[84] Matthiessen even pauses to interrogate his own failings as a member of the country's (white) upper middle class. While reporting in California, he'd passed a broken-down car full of migrant workers and decided not to stop because he had a meeting, "and anyway, there was nothing I could do."[85] In *Sal Si Puedes*, he scrutinizes this decision, holding it up to the light: "It is not racists or rednecks or right-wingers who are the most formidable enemy of the poor, but 'responsible' people who back away at the first threat to their own convenience." It is difficult to imagine the aloof ironist who floats through *The Cloud Forest* offering such a damning self-critique. The "Matthiessen" in *Sal Si Puedes* is an older, wiser narrator, more able to push past easy cynicism in favor of optimism. "I really think that one day the world will be great," a Black migrant worker says, and Matthiessen agrees: "Cesar Chavez shares this astonishing hope of an evolution in human values, and I do too; it is the only hope we have."[86]

Sal Si Puedes lacks the literary distinction of something like Norman Mailer's *The Armies of the Night*, or Joan Didion's *Slouching Towards Beth-*

lehem, both published in 1968. But Matthiessen had no illusions about the quality of his book. It was "uncommon," he once said, "for a book to be artistically sound and also have an agenda. Occasionally it happens, as in Rachel Carson's *Silent Spring*, but it's rare. There's a choice you have to make."[87] The choice he made with *Sal Si Puedes* was to produce a text that comprehensively outlined all the challenges facing the United Farm Workers, which meant detailing esoteric union business and including a nine-page extract of the *Congressional Record* as an appendix.

He already made a value distinction between his fiction and nonfiction. After *Sal Si Puedes*, he would start to make a distinction *within* his nonfiction as well. Some of the books were written in response to a personal interest in wildlife or place, like *The Tree Where Man Was Born*; these began, to use his favored analogy, "with a tiny seed up in the ovary, then a progression, egg after egg, getting bigger and bigger, until finally one's ready to lay." And some of the books were written to support a cause he wanted to fight for: those originated "with some outside purpose or support system," and they inevitably ended up as "a frail child."[88]

In the coming decades, Matthiessen would devote entire years of his writing life to "cause" books, and when explaining why he made the sacrifice—why he wrote about Native American land rights or the Bonackers and striped bass legislation when he could have been working on another novel—he would often cite a comment made by Albert Camus at a lecture, "Create Dangerously," given at the University of Uppsala on December 14, 1957, less than two months after the French philosopher had won the Nobel Prize for Literature. The only justification for being a writer in the twentieth century, Camus said, "if indeed there be a justification, is to speak up, insofar as we can, for those who cannot do so."* This ethical imperative animated *Sal Si Puedes*, in which Matthiessen spoke up for Cesar Chavez and

---

* Matthiessen had this quote pinned to the wall of his writing studio for years, though he erroneously attributed it to Camus's Nobel Prize speech, which covered similar thematic territory. In 1985, at an annual meeting of the Association of Writers & Writing Programs (AWP), Matthiessen was supposed to give a keynote address on "literature and the land." Instead, he went rogue: "I think I'm just going to veer away from the topic and use this opportunity to say something I feel very strongly about American writing in general. I feel that as a group, American writers have not taken responsibility, politically, for the benefit of this country. I feel we've lost that position that, say, French writers like Sartre or Camus had in their countries. We have so many good writers who are really talented, but how many of them spend a measurable portion of their time writing on issues that are controversial, or for the public welfare? Camus said when he got the Nobel Prize that part of the writer's obligation was to speak for those who cannot speak for themselves.... I think in a sense we've avoided our responsibility here. We may have notoriety, we may even achieve fame at a certain point, but we have no power at all.... Wherever we are, wherever we're located in the country, there's some damned thing that ought to be written about forcefully.... We're interested in the lyrical possibilities and the literary possibilities, but I would love to see that literature applied, even at the risk of special pleading, even at the risk of being sued. I think that we owe at least part of our work to that."

the United Farm Workers of America. The book was packaged in red, with a black Aztec eagle on the front cover, making it resemble the union flag, and Chavez's smiling portrait occupied the space usually reserved for an author photo. By choice, Matthiessen was not pictured at all.

IN JANUARY 1970, the month Random House published *Sal Si Puedes* (which Chavez, receiving the very first copy, declared a "great treasure"),[89] Matthiessen flew to Australia to join Peter Gimbel on a last-ditch effort to film the great white shark. The crew had failed to find any in Africa, but Ron and Valerie Taylor were confident that at least one would turn up in the Spencer Gulf near Adelaide. Gimbel had convinced the executives at Cinema Center Films to provide additional funding so he could send his equipment to Port Lincoln in South Australia, where he hoped to capture a satisfying climax for his documentary.

The boat Gimbel chartered was a motor ketch called the *Saori*. For more than two weeks, the crew drifted aimlessly around Cape Catastrophe and Dangerous Reef, seeing nothing. "Day after day, sky and sea were the same oily gray, and the sea glimmered dimly like the old seal-polished stones," Matthiessen wrote.[90] But then a fin suddenly broke the surface—"My *God!*" Gimbel shouted—and they got their first glimpse of *Carcharodon carcharias*.

On January 28, a butchered horse was hanging from the stern as bait. Matthiessen pulled on a wetsuit that Valerie Taylor, at his request, had graffitied with red acrylic paint: DON'T BUY GRAPES, a bit of pro-Chavez boycott propaganda for Gimbel's rolling cameras.[91] Matthiessen and Gimbel sank together into one of the cages, which were already submerged off the side of the *Saori*. Soon a shape resolved in the murk beyond the steel bars: "first the slack jaw with the triangular splayed teeth, then the dark eye, impenetrable and empty as the eye of God, next the gill slits like knife slashes in paper, then the pale slab of the flank, aflow with silver rippling of light, and finally the thick short twitch of its hard tail."[92]

The great white rushed in to gulp the rotting horse flesh, and Matthiessen, as it brushed past the cage, reached out to trail his fingers down its flank. In a letter to the poet Jim Harrison, he would compare the experience to "stroking one's own corpse, a spiritual, even metaphysical meeting."[93]

Gimbel was pleased with the footage, which showed multiple sharks thrashing at the cages so violently some of their teeth broke off. *Blue Water, White Death*, released the following year, just after *Blue Meridian* was published, would be a visceral documentary that introduced many viewers to the fearsome power of the great white.* But a month after the Australia trip, when Matthiessen saw the filmmaker back in New York, Gimbel was already talking about a new extreme quest—a plan to crash-diet down to 170 pounds, just to see if he could do it. The diet "bothered" Matthiessen, perhaps because it reminded him of his own insatiable restlessness: "the search for the great white shark was at an end," he wrote, "but the search was not."[94]

THE DAY AFTER Peter flew to Australia, Deborah sat down to write him a letter while she waited for Rue to finish with a child psychologist. In a previous therapy session, Rue had apparently told the psychologist "that she knew [Peter] liked & respected her as a person, but not as a girl." This was disturbing news given that Rue was just eleven years old, but Deborah understood where her daughter was coming from. "Of course," she wrote to Peter, "that has always been my fight & my sadness with you. And reveals the split in both you & me. All these years you protested how much you admired & respected me—which was true enough, but at the same time you rejected the woman in me. And those women who provided the woman part of your life were not allowed to become manifest as persons."[95] Deborah insisted on recognizing Peter's women as "manifest." For her not to acknowledge them as real, for her to collaborate in his (self-)deceptions, would be a "kind of trampling on or patronizing of a valid person." She resented the mistresses but didn't blame them for her husband's bad behavior. They, too, deserved "an undivided relationship." "I would have liked the same thing myself," she wrote.[96]

One small source of comfort for Deborah was the understanding that

---

* *Blue Water, White Death* (1971) preceded Peter Benchley's *Jaws* by three years, and influenced that novel's depiction of the shark. (Benchley admitted this to his friend Peter Lake, a photographer on Gimbel's expedition.) In a letter sent to Joe Fox in 1975, Benchley also described *Blue Meridian* as "a splendid book, certainly the best non-fiction book ever written about Great White Sharks, and one of the very best books in the whole of shark literature." It is worth noting that Matthiessen didn't share this high opinion of his own work; he thought *Blue Meridian* was "not a great book." Parts of it are indeed mediocre—the listless pages about the Seychelles interlude, for instance—but the book also features a brilliant depiction of a whale hunt, which Matthiessen witnessed off the coast of Durban, South Africa, in 1969: "The dying whale has veered away to starboard, and the harpoon line shivers spray as it snaps taut; the white of the cachalot's toothed lower mandible flashes in the light as the beast rolls, and the first well of its blood spreads on the surface." As for Benchley's *Jaws*, Matthiessen had mixed feelings about the novel. In 2014, he told the writer Jonathan Meiburg that "I've always heard that Peter Benchley was a very nice man, so I have nothing against him except for *possibly* borrowing the mood of my white shark description in the beginning. But I thought it was—I mean, it's not my kind of book." He was amused, when he watched Steven Spielberg's blockbuster adaptation of *Jaws*, to spot a copy of *Blue Meridian* sitting in the cabin of Quint's boat. "That was to console me, I guess."

Peter's women were part of his travels. They existed, like Karen Yochim,* down in Florida; or like Sara S., over in Nairobi; or like Ann Israel—their collaboration on union matters had led to a brief romance—in Delano, California. They did not live in Sagaponack, which was Deborah's territory. When Peter was home, he belonged to her exclusively.

That had started to change by the start of 1970, though Deborah would not realize what was happening for months. In May, she threw a picnic to mark the dedication of her new tearoom. Rue's old upstairs bedroom had been remodeled with shoji screens and tatami mats and a *tokonoma*—an alcove for the Akshobhya Buddha Peter had purchased in Nepal, now perched on a throne of pine bark. Milly Johnstone was at the picnic, along with Hisashi Yamada, a certified tea master who led the Urasenke school in New York. Also present were Julian Koenig, the brilliant advertising copywriter responsible for naming "Earth Day" (which had just debuted in April), and Julian's beautiful, formidable, thirty-one-year-old wife, Maria.

Maria Koenig had grown up as the daughter of a German doctor in colonial Tanganyika, and she was old family friends with John Owen, the director of National Parks. In 1968, when Owen had visited New York, in part to work with Julian on the "Give a Lion a Home" fundraising campaign, she'd had dinner with him in the city and mentioned they were renting a summer house out in Sagaponack. Owen asked her if she knew anybody there, and Maria had said, "Not a soul." So he'd invited her to lunch with a writer he was scheduled to meet—a writer who happened to live in Sagaponack, and who Owen was planning to invite to the Serengeti. The lunch, of course, was the one with Peter Matthiessen at the Williams Club. "John Owen had those lovely English manners," Maria recalled. "He came to the door to meet me, and while he's leading me back to the table, I look around the room and see Peter. I said to myself, 'I hope it isn't him.' But it was. Coup de foudre."[97] Peter was similarly enchanted by the "very pretty girl"[98] with almond eyes who held herself like a lioness surveying the plains. "I'm in trouble," he thought, as Owen introduced them.

Nothing had happened for a while. Maria, solitary in Sagaponack (Julian worked in the city), became friendly with Deborah, who was also alone while Peter was traveling. Because Deborah struggled to control her willful daughter, Maria took Rue shopping for clothes and school supplies, and she also looked after Alex, along with her own two babies, while Deborah went to the zendo in New York. Through Deborah's influence, Maria had become

---

* Karen broke it off with Peter shortly after visiting him at Polgeto. "I think," she wrote in a letter, "that the strange way you shut me off in our separations is because you underneath feel that I'm not really alive when you're not here—that I'm in a state of suspension until you arrive and I begin ticking again."

a student of tea ceremony, too, which satisfied her penchant for order and precision. Hisashi Yamada would sit next to Maria at the Urasenke school, a fan folded into his robes, and adjust her cup an eighth of an inch—"and you could see that he was right."[99]

When something did happen with Peter, it was not like his other affairs. It was a companionable walk around the Central Park Reservoir, pausing at a bench so he could show her photos from his various expeditions. It was lunch in a dimly lit restaurant in New York, and then a rushed goodbye on Park Avenue as he sped away in a taxi to another appointment. It was a train ride on the LIRR from Babylon to Bridgehampton, laughing over "sedate drinks in plastic cups." It was a stroll along the beach, out of sight of "watching houses," their awkwardness giving way to a kiss, followed by mutual apologies "for cold wet noses."[100]

Maria was not the kind of woman to be seduced by a literary reputation; she read *At Play in the Fields of the Lord* and didn't like it very much. She was not reckless and impulsive, but a realist, no-nonsense and practical. Although she felt strongly for Peter, she worried about the pain they'd inevitably inflict on others if their attraction was allowed to grow into something more. "After tea ceremony [in Deborah's tearoom] I feel treacherous and so do you I expect," she wrote him in a letter. "But what is it that we feel treacherous about? A few talks on the beach? One pregnant lunch?" They had never slept together, and yet: "We have a relationship that has gone beyond any action of ours. I know it."[101]

That undefined "relationship" wafted through the Sagaponack air over spring and early summer, as Matthiessen worked on *Blue Meridian*. Then he headed back to Kenya in June to finish research for *The Tree Where Man Was Born*. "I hate it when you're away," Maria wrote. "But perhaps it's just as well."[102] Deborah, in a note of her own, sent Peter a snapshot of the home life he was once again leaving: "It is very quiet. . . . Rue is at the Klebnikovs for dinner & sleeping out in a tent. Alex is outside, his green pajamas among the green, shooting his water pistol. I'm going to wash my hair, eat dinner, and then work on my 'piece.' I started in again this morning. Then much later when Alex is asleep I will do za-zen."[103]

Matthiessen spent another three months in Kenya and Tanzania. He revisited Iain Douglas-Hamilton, the foolhardy elephant expert, in Lake Manyara National Park. While conducting research on foot, the men were charged by an old elephant that Douglas-Hamilton had nicknamed "Ophelia"; Matthiessen ran for his life while the zoologist waved his arms and shouted, "Bugger off!" (The elephant did so, "trumpeting angrily over her shoulder.")[104] Another day, Douglas-Hamilton stalled his open-top Land Rover beneath an acacia tree that was occupied by a pair of lions, and Matthiessen became paralyzed: "The intensity, the sun, the light were terrifically exciting—I hated it, but it was terrifically exciting. I felt unbearably *aware*. I think I smelled her but I can't remember; there is only the violent memory of lion-ness in all my senses."[105]

Near Lake Magadi in Kenya, he went on safari with Lewis Hurxthal, a biologist specializing in ostriches, and Hurxthal's wife, Nancy, who was four months pregnant. Some sixty miles into long-grass savanna, Nancy began having cramps. Worried she might be about to have a miscarriage, they passed a stressful afternoon and night in the wilderness, during which a rhino grazed against Matthiessen's tent, before driving—very carefully—to a game post to radio for emergency assistance. (Nancy and the baby were fine.) A few days later, Matthiessen's Land Rover spluttered to a halt in the middle of nowhere. Observed by a Maasai boy, he was forced to rig makeshift rope slings to keep the rotating engine shaft from scraping along the ground, then set off for safety at three miles an hour.

But the most dramatic event was undoubtedly the family vacation. The Matthiessens had arranged to visit the Serengeti and the Ngorongoro Crater together in July. Deborah would fly to Tanzania with Rue and Alex, meeting Peter in the town of Njombe, where they would all stay with Gottlieb Eckhart, Maria's father, because the Koenigs were coming on the holiday as well. Peter arrived at the appointed hour, but Deborah was inexplicably delayed in Dar es Salaam. "I was taken aback," Maria recalled. "We were expecting her. There was only one flight a week."[106] Deborah was delayed because she was stalling, having finally figured out that something was going on between Maria and her husband. Could she endure a safari with Peter and the Koenigs? The prospect must have been humiliating. In the end she went, because the children were expecting to go, and because everything was already paid for—but she was withdrawn and snappish the entire vacation. At one point by a lakeside, Rue pranked her mother by announcing that a herd of elephants was rushing up behind them; Deborah spun around and, seeing nothing, slapped Rue across the face.[107]

The Tanzania trip broke the friendship between Deborah and Maria, and it dissolved the "relationship" between Maria and Peter. In a poem written just after, Maria achingly described "A sickness of things spoilt. / Of situations rethought / Of pain felt and bestowed, above all bestowed on / undeserving victim."[108]

By late August, Peter was back at the Castello di Polgeto in Italy. As he powered through a "brute first draft"[109] of *The Tree Where Man Was Born*, he received another letter from Deborah. She had written six pages while preparing for sesshin with Tai-san. She hated all this "bother and preoccupation," she said, but there were some things she needed to get off her chest before she could focus on Zen:

> I think basically what so astonishes me and finally fills <u>me</u> with pity (when I'm not annoyed) is your absence of self-respect—not minding that your credibility rating must be about like [Lyndon] Johnson's. Telling me so easily the night I took you to the airport that there was nobody else. Telling me that you would never involve anybody in Sagaponack, or anyone that I knew. (How important it was to you that <u>I</u> didn't.) But then of course you have a double standard which is based on the assumption that women are so inferior that how can they be degraded? Or you rationalize that you thought I was <u>above</u> being humiliated, which gives you carte blanche to insult. And now you tell me, with pride in your progress, that two years ago you wouldn't have hesitated to continue your affair with the neighbor lady. Lies coming and going. . . . Well, never mind. I do sympathize too—with you both. You seem totally out of control Pete, pulled this way and that, and it is a sad and sorry thing to watch. . . . I do hope you're all right. You seem a man in 1000 pieces, running after each one.[110]

14

Ho Ko

> Circles of pain
> And circles within circles.
> And yet I love you so.
>
> —PM to Deborah Love (August 1971)[1]

Rue Matthiessen was twelve years old when she decided to get as far away from home as she could manage. School was miserable—she was unpopular, with poor grades—and home was not the sanctuary it was supposed to be. Her mother's perpetual existential breakdown, all but unfathomable to a young girl, was combined with a capriciousness that left Rue reeling with confusion. Sometimes Deborah held her daughter too close, was desperate with "ferocious need."[2] At other times, though, Deborah was distant and cold, like the day she told Rue matter-of-factly that she no longer loved her as much as she once had. Zen, from Rue's perspective, only made matters worse with its bowing strangers monopolizing her mother's attention, its loud foreign chanting alternated with a demand for absolute silence in the house. Deborah sat on her cushion for hours and hours, "dispersing and fragmenting into the air as she completely cleared her ego and all her attachments," including to the children.[3]

Then there was Peter, who, when he was even around, seemed more interested in Alex, his imperturbable little boy, than he did in a young woman in the early throes of puberty. Peter's own women—Rue had become aware of the affairs at a young age—swarmed around him like flies; Rue resented them for the way they made Deborah brittle and defensive. She also resented her father's "orientation to doom" when it came to animals, landscapes, and Indigenous peoples. The atmosphere he fostered at home was one of "great motivation and energy, but also sadness about a diminishing natural world." While this urgent sorrow instilled his children with a strong sense of moral responsibility, it was "difficult to grow up with."[4] As was the oppressive liberal guilt that Peter expected his family to shoulder for his privileged background.

Rue felt invisible in the eyes of both parents. (Her birth father, Clem Pollock, made only infrequent appearances.) "I think I learned to save myself," she recalled, "like many children with parents who are difficult, moody, or wedded to their art." She "saved" herself in the summer of 1970 when an older girl she admired gave her the phone number for a private boarding school in England. Rue waited until she was alone in the house, then called Cobham Hall, in Kent, to request admission as a student in the next academic year.

Peter and Deborah agreed to pay the hefty fees without asking any of the obvious questions. What motivated her request? Why *England*? Rue was stubborn and untamable; perhaps they saw British boarding school as a welcome solution. They arranged for a nanny to meet her at Heathrow Airport and buy her the necessary uniform at Harrods in Knightsbridge. But Rue would remember her mother's regretful anguish just before the flight, how Deborah stood at the bedroom door with tears in her eyes. Rue would also remember—a far more consequential moment, though she scratched it up at the time to hypochondria—Deborah pausing, confused, to scrutinize her own swollen belly in a mirror, and saying, "I'm not due for my period."[5]

In the weeks after Rue left the country, Deborah fell mysteriously ill. Peter was back from Polgeto, and they resumed their tense cohabitation in Sagaponack. While she tried to recuperate, he worked on the manuscript for *The Tree Where Man Was Born*. In a rare moment of fatherly support for his son, he gave a talk to students at the Hampton Day School, in Bridgehampton, on how a person can "fall off civilization's edge in but an instant,"[6] holding up a shark tooth he'd collected in South Australia to murmurs of awed appreciation.

By October, Deborah was feeling well enough for them both to give speeches at a luncheon hosted by the Friends of the South Huntington Public Library. "I think Peter told them his wife was an author too, thinking he could get out of it, but instead they snagged us both," she told her editor Nan Talese in a wry letter.[7] Peter lectured about his expeditions; Deborah talked about the universal search for meaning—"Each of us, in our way, seeks to be whole"—and challenged the audience with a somber reflection on mortality, which seemed to be on her mind. "Many people, when asked [what they would do] if they had a year left to live[,] give an answer that shows they are living a false life, with the lid on, for fear of exposure or punishment, and if released, would plunge from one gratification to another. Who among us can say, if the world were to last one more year, 'I'd continue doing exactly what I'm doing now'?"[8]

Sometime that winter, Deborah made a surprising suggestion to Peter. She had always rebuffed him when he "pestered her for inside information" about Zen, but now she changed her mind.⁹ She invited him to a weekend sesshin at the New York Zendo Shobo-ji, the Temple of True Dharma, an old carriage house on East 67th Street that Eido Shimano, using a sizable donation from Chester Carlson, inventor of the Xerox machine, had transformed into an oasis of tatami mats, oiled floors, and sandalwood incense. Unlike the cramped apartment on West End Avenue where Deborah had first met Tai-san through Milly Johnstone, the New York Zendo, which opened on September 15, 1968, was every bit as impressive as a church.

In *The Snow Leopard*, Matthiessen would offer a beautiful description of meditation:

> Meditation has nothing to do with contemplation of eternal questions, or of one's own folly, or even of one's navel, although a clearer view on all of these enigmas may result. It has nothing to do with thought of any kind— with anything at all, in fact, but intuiting the true nature of existence, which is why it has appeared, in one form or another, in almost every culture known to man. The entranced Bushman staring into fire, the Eskimo using a sharp rock to draw an ever-deepening circle into the flat surface of a stone achieves the same obliteration of the ego (and the same power) as the dervish or the Pueblo sacred dancer. . . . [I]n Zen, one seeks to empty out the mind, to return it to the clear, pure stillness of a seashell or a flower petal. When body and mind are one, then the whole being, scoured clean of intellect, emotions, and the senses, may be laid open to the *experience* that individual existence, ego, the "reality" of matter and phenomena are no more than fleeting and illusory arrangements of molecules.¹⁰

Matthiessen knew none of this when he walked into the New York Zendo. He had read about zazen in *The Three Pillars of Zen*, he had watched Deborah sitting alone in her upstairs tearoom, but he had no direct experience of how taxing it could be on the mind and body. The New York Zendo was deceptively beautiful, as a visiting Benedictine monk once observed: "It is not a hall of tranquility, but a furnace-room in which we work with all our might on the combustion of our egotistic delusions."¹¹ Robed students sat along dimly lit walls, facing one another with their legs folded into lotus, or half-lotus, or the *seiza* position (sitting on their knees); and with their hands in the *shashu* mudra, right hand holding the left thumb and the left hand covering the right hand. There everyone remained, except for meals, rest periods, and *kinhin*—walking meditation—for up to fourteen hours a day during sesshin. The only sound was a small bell or the thwack of a keisaku on somebody's shoulders, encouraging them to sit up straighter.

Matthiessen sat for the full weekend. The ache in his legs was "horrendous,"[12] he later said, and he was terrorized by boredom. As he struggled to return his mind to the pure stillness of a seashell, a monk ("a masochist, maybe a sadist") kept whispering to him, goading him on so he would "stick it out." Matthiessen got "stubborn and macho," gritted his teeth, and prayed for the next rest period.[13]

The brutality of that first sesshin—"I thought I had been hit by lightning"—made him wonder if Deborah had set him up to fail. Was she hoping to scare him away from Zen by entering him in a marathon before any basic training? His gut reaction was to dismiss the sangha members as "crazy," their sesshin as "barbaric." He swore the experience would never be repeated. Yet he also thought, despite himself, that he'd caught a glimpse of something beyond the frustration and eye-watering muscle pain. In an interview with the writer Lawrence Shainberg, for *Tricycle*, in 1993, Matthiessen would make a connection between his first tough experience at the New York Zendo and the experience on the troopship, en route to Hawaii, when he'd felt obliterated by crashing waves: "Something about zazen must have reawakened some primordial longing, though I didn't understand this at the time. I think most people who come to Zen practice have had an early glimmering, an opening, of mystical experience, like a glimpse of the lost paradise."[14] Rather than being scared away, Matthiessen sensed an "echo or reverberation" in the ringing silence of zazen, and it made him hungry to learn more.

TOWARD THE END of 1970, Deborah Love was diagnosed with ovarian cancer—a terrible shock. To stop it from spreading, she underwent a hysterectomy with bilateral salpingo-oophorectomy, which removed her uterus, ovaries, and fallopian tubes. The doctors were optimistic they'd caught all the cancer cells, but Deborah was deeply shaken.

To lift her spirits, in February, after she recovered from the procedure, Peter took her to visit Rue at Cobham Hall in England, then to Courchevel in the French Alps for a skiing vacation. With him being mindful of her ordeal, more considerate of her feelings than he had been in months, the time was a "happy" one for them both, long days on the slopes followed by a side trip to the thermal baths at Saint-Gervais-les-Bains. Peter saw "new hope" for a marriage that he'd long assumed was destined for failure. From Courchevel, they drove to Switzerland, where they strolled through the old town of Geneva. In an antique store, Deborah discovered a thirteenth-century bowl from Isfahan, Iran, which "seemed to float in the hands like an old leaf." The bowl was expensive, so they left it on the shelf, but Peter, moved by their tearful parting at the airport the next morning—Deborah was returning home while he continued to Italy—called the store and arranged to buy it anyway. The bowl would be "a symbol of a new beginning." He planned to present it to his wife on her forty-fourth birthday in July.[15]

The trip to Italy was damage control for an earlier purchase: Peter had, without consulting Deborah, acquired a three-bedroom farmhouse with twelve acres of land near the Castello di Polgeto. It was a stunning piece of property, recently renovated by John Abbot and affordable at just $45,000. But Deborah knew Peter had hosted at least one girlfriend in Polgeto, and she declined, on principle, to follow in the woman's footsteps. (In *The Snow Leopard*, Matthiessen mentions that D "refused to go" to Umbria but omits the reason why.)[16] As penance, Peter promised to sell the farmhouse; he went there to list it with an agency and to prepare an ad for the *Rome Daily American*—"stone, sunlight, flowers, mountain air, low taxes. Rare opportunity: American writer selling at cost."[17]

While he was in Italy, Matthiessen took the opportunity to get some writing done. He was nearly finished with *The Tree Where Man Was Born*, and the next project he wanted to look at was the "strange novel"[18] that had been gestating since the turtle voyage with Caymanian seafarers in 1966. But most of his time ended up being devoted to an original screenplay for Cesar Chavez. After *Sal Si Puedes*, Matthiessen had "committed entirely"[19] to a movie about California's farmworkers, a movie that was meant to dramatize the daily travails of life on "the gritty famished outskirts of American prosperity."[20] The plot concerned two fictional Mexican men, Hector Vega and Tomas Gutierrez, who illegally cross the border and travel to a small town in the Coachella Valley, where they find work picking grapes for racist, exploitative growers—until Hector, during a picket protest, pledges his allegiance to the United Farm Workers, followed thereafter by Tomas. Matthiessen spent several weeks on "The Valley," a propagandistic tragedy (it ends in gunfire) awash in a "surreal brown poisoned haze" of pesticides. Then he wrote a note to Chavez to say the scriptwriting was "going pretty well," and that, being in Italy, he had "naturally" contacted Federico Fellini about it.[21] Chavez seems to have taken the joke seriously, wondering in a response if Fellini "should be the man to direct our film!"[22]

Unlike on earlier visits, Matthiessen abstained from taking any LSD at Polgeto. His interest in psychedelics had waned over the previous twelve months, in part because his trips had become increasingly repetitive, and in part because he'd reached the conclusion that he was not seeing things "purely" while under the influence; the drug created another barrier that kept him from attaining genuine insight.[23] As he later explained, "Old mists may be banished, that is true, but the alien chemical agent forms another mist, maintaining the separation of the 'I' from the true experience of the

One."[24] Matthiessen could not dissolve his "self" into what he once called "the miracle." He wanted the trip without an alien chemical agent.

Instead of acid, he tried sitting at Polgeto—zazen, which proved more tolerable in shorter periods than it had been during a weekend sesshin. The full lotus position was beyond him, so he settled for a milder variation and began doing yoga to increase his flexibility. He also picked up *Zen Mind, Beginner's Mind*, a newly released collection of "informal talks" by Shunryu Suzuki, the soft-spoken Soto master who had established the San Francisco Zen Center in 1962. Suzuki Roshi was adept at translating esoteric Japanese teachings into an everyday American idiom, and his talks, recorded and edited by students, were eloquent, unpretentious introductions to the principles of Zen practice, covering everything from posture and breathing to "nonattachment" and "Emptiness." Matthiessen was so impressed by Suzuki's book that he copied a few lines into a letter home to Deborah: "For the moon there is the cloud. For the flower there is the wind."[25]*

PETER ADDRESSED THIS LETTER to "lovely Anne"—Deborah's middle name, used when he was feeling particularly affectionate. "I hope all of the above pleases you, and that you are very well. I miss you and I love you," he wrote.[26] Here was an expression of intimacy that suggests just how moved he had been by their time together in France and Switzerland. The solicitude, however, proved short-lived. Once he returned to Sagaponack in March, Peter began to exhibit familiar patterns of behavior. His conflict with Deborah flared up again—or, as she aptly put it, "the contradictions of 'our love' continue as the bombs keep dropping in the pursuit of peace."[27]

The resumption of hostilities seems to have been precipitated by Deborah's increasing independence, which Peter treated, consciously or not, as a threat to his position. By the spring of 1971, she had a book out (*Annaghkeen*) and a short story in *The Paris Review*, "One Winter," a fictionalized account of the lonely months she'd spent in Sagaponack while he was traveling to New Guinea. (At Peter's urging, she had submitted the story under a pseudonym, "Rose Kennett," to ensure an impartial reading by George Plimpton.) Deborah had also been asked by Tai-san to teach a course on Zen at

---

* The lines come from Suzuki's talk on "Calmness": "Before something happens in the realm of calmness, we do not feel the calmness; only when something happens within it do we find the calmness.... When we see a part of the moon covered by a cloud, or a tree, or a weed, we feel how round the moon is. But when we see the clear moon without anything covering it, we do not feel that roundness the same way we do when we see it through something else. When you are doing zazen, you are within the complete calmness of your mind; you do not feel anything. You just sit. But the calmness of your sitting will encourage you in your everyday life. So actually you will find the value of Zen in your everyday life, rather than when you sit."

the New School for Public Research, an honor she interpreted as "a chance to fulfill in part the Bodhisattva's vow . . . to save all sentient beings (in spite of being in the throes of trying to save myself)."[28] Nan Talese at Random House was supplying her with research books: *Zen in the Art of Archery*, *The Method of Zen*. There was even talk about Deborah writing one of her own for a general readership. In addition, and perhaps most egregiously to Peter, Deborah had taken a lover when she got home from Geneva, not to get his attention—he was fully focused on her for the first time in years—but because she felt like it. Having sacrificed so much to "accommodate" Peter's needs, she was now, in the aftermath of her cancer scare, making some choices for herself. *Who among us can say, if the world were to last one more year, "I'd continue doing exactly what I'm doing now?"*

While Peter kept reaffirming his love, the next few months, in Deborah's assessment, "consisted of almost unbroken anger and bullying to make me change 'my attitude to your work' . . . so you could feel safely in control of me, I guess."[29] He told her that *he* was being faithful, which was another mechanism of control—and another lie. If Deborah had the wrong "attitude" toward his work, if she was upending his preferred order of things, he found somebody else to reassure him of his place: Jane Stanton, the twenty-five-year-old daughter of a family friend, the actress and socialite Joan Stanton. Unlike Deborah, the doe-eyed Jane was "mesmerized" by Peter Matthiessen. "I wanted to be a writer, so Peter was like a god," she recalled. "I was just the little groupie disciple at his feet. He was twenty years older than I am. There was a lot of hero worship involved."[30] There was something else, too: "I think his unhappiness was almost like an aphrodisiac to a wounded woman, because there is a belief that you can help him, you can heal him." Peter was "a very troubled guy. He was really, probably, the unhappiest man I've ever met."[31] This ego-stroking affair—which Deborah never discovered despite the "hurricane of gossip"[32] it stirred up for friends and acquaintances on the East End—continued through the summer. By Deborah's birthday, the new beginning that Peter had imagined for their marriage was forgotten. He decided to withhold the Isfahan bowl.

Given his history of selfish choices, Deborah was understandably skeptical of her husband's newfound interest in Zen. She challenged him in a letter written that summer: "your work in Zen and participation in the tea ceremony . . . whose principles of harmony, respect, purity and tranquility are embodied in every gesture, every act, have not prevented you from making an enormous wave . . . even generated <u>out</u> of the tea room, which will not subside in the foreseeable future and whose subsidiary waves are endlessly unknown."[33] Nevertheless, Deborah thought Zen might finally "reach" Peter as "a living example of respect for people and things that naturally takes precedence over other needs and gratifications." Her hope for his eventual reform explains why she invited him to another weekend retreat, this one held in July at a remote site in the Catskill Mountains.

The opening of the New York Zendo Shobo-ji had been a major milestone for the Zen Studies Society: it now finally had a permanent home. However, Eido Shimano—Tai-san—had immediately instigated a search for another property outside the city for "a country Zendo," a place where students could train for three months in uninterrupted solitude.[34] The New York Zendo was perfect for daily practice and weekend sesshins, but a country zendo would focus on Zen as a whole way of life. For all intents and purposes, he wanted to build a monastery. This was crucial, Tai-san believed, if Zen was to become properly rooted in American soil—a next step in "the transmission of Buddhism from East to West."[35]

In the winter just passed, Tai-san had come across an advertisement in *The New York Times* for the perfect place: a slice of Beaverkill Valley in the Catskills, 140 miles northwest of Manhattan, far from highway noise and flight paths, yet already serviced by an access road and power lines. Encircled by mountains and state forest, the property was thick with birch, beech, and maple trees, and it included a dark body of water, Beecher Lake, named after former owner James Chaplin Beecher, the half-brother of abolitionist Harriet Beecher Stowe. In 1875, to "commune with the wild and picturesque scenery of tumbled nature,"[36] Reverend Beecher had erected a fourteen-room house for his family right on the lakeshore, a house which was conveniently still standing in 1971, and which could be adapted for use as a temporary zendo until an authentic monastery was constructed nearby.

The Zen Studies Society acquired the property in spring, using a massive donation from Dorris Carlson, Chester Carlson's widow. The Society also bought adjacent tracts to ensure privacy and prevent any future real estate development. In total, the parcel added up to some 1,400 acres of wilderness and former logging land. Once the purchase was finalized, Tai-san invited his own teacher, Soen Nakagawa, to visit from Mishima, Japan, where he was currently installed as abbot of Ryūtaku-ji. Soen Roshi stood by the lake and exclaimed, "This is like the site of an ancient temple!"[37] The two men decided to name the property Dai Bosatsu (Great Bodhisattva), after Mount Daibosatsu in Yamanashi Prefecture, where Soen had once dreamed of establishing a zendo when he was still a young monk. The new American monastery on Beecher Lake would be called, with a nod to its cross-cultural purpose, International Dai Bosatsu Zendo.

Starting from the long weekend of July 4, 1971, a few sangha members at a time were invited up from New York to tour the property and stay for *samu*, voluntary work practice. Deborah and Peter visited with Milly Johnstone and her husband, William, a vice president at Bethlehem Steel who was chairman of the Dai Bosatsu building committee. The couples found a hive of activity at Beecher Lake. Father Maxima, a Japanese artist and Greek Orthodox priest, was painting a mural in the old house depicting the Buddha's "Flower Sermon," when he transmitted the Dharma to his disciple Mahākāśyapa. Other people were clearing rocks so a new gatehouse could be built at the bottom of a logging road. Someone had even rowed a giant Buddha statue across the lake, and it now sat serenely observing the action from a rocky ledge on the far shore.

This weekend reconnaissance at Dai Bosatsu was the first time Matthiessen had spent any real time with Tai-san, the young monk who had so radically affected Deborah's outlook. It was also the first time since the brief encounter in his driveway, three years before, that he had seen Soen Roshi, who was small and unassuming in appearance yet fiercely intelligent, and an exceptional haiku poet—"considered the Basho of the Twentieth Century," according to Gary Snyder.[38] ("Do you or do you not know: / hidden in this bowl of tea is a secret / more secret than all of atomic science.")[39]

Matthiessen was particularly struck by Soen Roshi as they walked around the property. The older man, whose own search for meaning had brought him to Zen by way of Schopenhauer, had a deep, resonant voice, and sad eyes that could sparkle with mirth in an instant. "One felt a real egolessness in him," Matthiessen later said. "He was so light, no vanity, no arrogance. He was utterly free, completely wild and humorous, fearless. He wasn't hung up on how a Zen master should be."[40] Soen Roshi was contemptuous of "self-conscious spirituality," and he subverted expectations by hanging his underwear in the New York Zendo: nothing was sacred.[41] Matthiessen was so drawn to the man that he would later identify this weekend retreat as the true beginning of his practice. Soen Nakagawa "became my Zen teacher even before I realized that I was his student."[42]

After the visit to Dai Bosatsu, Matthiessen revised the rest of his summer plans. Because he was ineligible to attend the next sesshin in New York, not being a formal member of the sangha, he flew to San Francisco instead. Then he made his way to Carmel Valley and walked, "in a vague impulse towards pilgrimage,"[43] into the Los Padres National Forest, to Tassajara Hot Springs. The old resort, which sat at the end of a deep mountain canyon, had been purchased by the San Francisco Zen Center in 1966 and remodeled into the country's first Zen monastery, the Tassajara Zen Mountain Center, Zenshinji. As such, Tassajara was a laboratory for American Zen. Its residents had been forced to confront the most basic questions of form and schedule. Should they wear traditional robes as they go about their studies? Should they chant in English or Japanese? Should the organization of practice follow present-day customs in Japan, or perhaps some hybridized alternative that recognized the specific needs of American students?[44]

Matthiessen was curious to see what Dai Bosatsu might become. But this was mostly a test to gauge whether Zen practice suited him personally. It was probably also, to some extent, a competition—his attempt to outdo Deborah after being excluded from her New York Zendo visit. (She was going into Manhattan to sit for a long weekend? Well, he would walk miles through a forest to the oldest Zen monastery in America.) Deborah hinted at this in a letter, after they spoke on the phone one evening and his supposedly off-the-cuff remarks struck her as "preconceived."[45]

Still, he submitted himself to the routines of Tassajara: waking up at four to the beckon of a brass bell; doing two periods of zazen; eating a simple breakfast; going to work. His samu assignment was as a carpenter's assistant, and he helped install a new roof on a cottage for Shunryu Suzuki—a "lucky"[46] opportunity, as it brought him in direct contact with the remarkable man whose book of lectures Matthiessen had devoured in Italy. Suzuki Roshi would die in December from liver cancer. He was already frail, and one day Matthiessen watched as Suzuki's *jisha*, or attendant, a woman named Maggie Kress, "set down his teacup a little too hard in her rush to assist him at the doorway. 'Take care of my cup!' he warned her mildly. And when she protested that her only wish was to take care of her teacher, the roshi said, 'When you take care of my cup, you are taking care of me.'"[47] Matthiessen kept notes on Suzuki Roshi's comments, as though trying to decipher the riddles of an oracle: "If the work is only okay, Roshi says, 'Very good!' If he really likes it, he will find some small detail out of place: 'That is not good Zen practice!' That is the way he works, I think."[48]

Just after flying to San Francisco, Peter had written a letter to Deborah about the state of their marriage. Describing himself as a "crippled thing," he asked:

Why did you cry so when we parted in Geneva? And then you came home and took a lover. And now we have parted warmly on a summer morning, and you will no doubt greet me in September with news of our impending divorce. I am tormented, but where are you? "Never happier with Peter" (!), yet anxious to split. I understand less and less about us. On the plane I wrote a lot of disconnected verse, full of sadness, restlessness.... I hallucinate mildly at all times now.[49]

When he returned home from Tassajara in late August, he found a cooler, less self-pitying letter waiting for him from Deborah, who had gone to the lake house at Dai Bosatsu for another sesshin:

> [Y]ou not only turned down my proposal of a commitment to each other but also of a friendship including all our lovers . . . which would have required the utmost delicacy and frankness. (There could be no trust without frankness and truthfulness, with no need even for white lies.) Your need for secrecy and to withhold yourself I respect and accept. And I will try to invade your privacy as little as possible. . . .
>
> I hope to live as straight forward a life as I can manage. . . . I think the only thing we haven't tried is separating, which may truly be the greatest gift we have to bestow on each other.[50]

Deborah was not bluffing; she had finally reached a limit and chosen to prioritize the "vital" work of Zen. By the end of the summer, she and Peter made what he later called an "exhausted decision to divorce": "That decision was firm, we made it calmly and were both relieved."[51] Immediately, though, he felt an overwhelming urge to retract the white flag of surrender. He swore yet again to salvage their marriage. "I made a commitment to D, this time for good. She understood; sipping coffee in the sun, she merely nodded." This sentence from *The Snow Leopard* elides the fact that Deborah had proposed a frank and honest commitment *first*, which he rejected. It elides the fact that even as he made his own pledge, he was already breaking it: Jane Stanton remained an undisclosed secret. The sentence also contains more ambivalence than Matthiessen might have intended when he wrote it: in "merely" nodding, Deborah's acceptance seems inflected by a measure of doubt. There was, after all, no reason to believe the next go-around would be any different.

IN THE FALL OF 1971, Deborah began teaching at the New School for Social Research. She overcame her nerves—"I have never taught nor do I have the confidence or authority to hold a class's interest"[52]—to lecture for ninety minutes a week on a variety of topics, from basic Zen principles to "Zen in fairytale," including MGM's *The Wizard of Oz*, where Dorothy yearns to go "home" and Glinda, the Good Witch, tells her, "You've always had the power to go back to Kansas."

At the same time, Deborah was suffering from unexplained aches, which had surfaced in summer and only grown progressively worse. She rubbed her legs as though she was unable to get warm. She was losing weight and struggled with debilitating fatigue; sometimes she was confined to bed for an entire afternoon. "Peter was taking care of her," recalled Merete Galesi, who stopped by daily to check on her friend. "She called him 'Saint Peter' every time he came into the room. She said, 'This is Saint Peter,' like she was introducing a whole new person."[53]

Even before the diagnosis of ovarian cancer, death had been a constant topic of discussion in Sagaponack. Deborah and Peter argued over who would die first, a macabre game of "Me," "Nope, it will be me," right in front of the children.[54] Both of them had suspected they wouldn't make it past forty—"the idea doubtless a defense against chaos of some kind," Peter admitted to a journal in 1967. "Death at forty: I do not take the idea too seriously, but even so, I am conscious now of a certain restlessness, an apprehension: is the world dying, or is it me?"[55] For her part, Deborah was "fascinated with death," Luke observed in conversations with his stepmother. "There was a very morbid side to her."[56] And Rue noticed the same thing: "a morbidity, a sense that something was coming. And it came. I'm not a big one for 'the writing is on the wall,' but in this case it really seemed foretold."[57]

In late November, Peter was granted permission to attend another sesshin at the New York Zendo. Deborah didn't feel up to the full weekend, so she arranged to meet him at a small pied-à-terre they were renting on East 67th Street; she would join the sangha for a Sunday sit. In Matthiessen's telling, this was when he finally confronted the truth of what they were now facing: "On Saturday evening, meeting me at the door of our apartment, she stood there, smiling, in a new brown dress, but it was not the strange, transparent beauty in her face that took my breath away. I had been in zazen since before daybreak, and my mind was clear, and I saw Death gazing out at me from those wide, dark eyes. There was no mistaking it, and the certainty was so immediate and shocking that I could not greet her. In what she took as observance of sesshin silence, I pushed past quietly into the bathroom, to collect myself in order that I might speak."[58]

The realization was devastating, but it had an unexpected side effect. The next morning in the New York Zendo, Peter chanced to sit opposite Deborah for zazen, and as the group chanted the Kannon Sutra with mounting intensity, he focused on her and stopped paying attention to individual sounds. Then the group shouted "Mu," and he had an impression of swelling, "as if this 'I' were opening out into infinity."[59]

In a Dharma talk about death given in 2003, Matthiessen would offer the analogy of a tiger leaping into a zendo: here is a shock so severe that it can startle a person out of their wits. "In these terrible tiger moments we are suddenly confronted by a real live moment, a reality more real than real, a reality which is absolutely inevitable—NO ambiguity, NO choice, NO ESCAPE.... Paradoxically, because it is so powerful, it often serves to pierce our defensive armor of ideas and emotions and liberate us from all preconceptions, returning us to the realm of Emptiness, Not Knowing—the Lost Paradise of our True Nature, our Buddha Nature."[60] At the November sesshin, a "tiger" appeared in the guise of his dying wife. Fixating on Deborah, Peter was "pierced," and gave himself up to, as he put it, "immersion in all things, to a joyous *belonging* so overwhelming that tears of relief poured from my eyes. For the first time since unremembered childhood, I was not alone, there was no separate 'I.' Wounds, anger, ragged edges, hollow places were all gone, all had been healed; my heart was the heart of all creation."[61]

What Matthiessen was describing is, in Zen parlance, kensho: a "seeing into" (*ken*) "one's own nature" (*sho*), which is said to come as sparks of insight, visions of awakening. Trying to articulate the experience in his own words, he at first called it "the Smile": a smile that originated within and then expanded outward "like a huge shadow of my own Buddha form."[62] Be that as it may, there is something striking about this story, in which Deborah's diminishment is effectively subsumed into Peter's spiritual growth. Perhaps he was trying to salvage hope from the idea of her loss. Or perhaps he was comforting himself because he was afraid. But confronted with her visage of Death, what he saw, his overriding takeaway, was a clearer image of himself.

RUE RETURNED HOME for Thanksgiving from a boarding school in upstate New York, where she had enrolled, again at her request, after her year at Cobham Hall. Deborah spent mornings working in her study, but the pain meant she could only endure a few hours. Rue, for the duration of her break, was recruited as her mother's jisha, charged with keeping Deborah company, bringing her soft foods, and calling Peter from his studio (where he was finalizing *The Tree Where Man Was Born* before it went to the typist) if the pain escalated into agony. Later, Peter admitted to his daughter that this was a deliberate strategy to make her acknowledge the gravity of the situation. Rue's instinct was to turn away: "I refused to comprehend; I couldn't jump out of myself and start to think about her, about what it might be that I was seeing."[63]

At the end of November, Deborah was admitted to Roosevelt Hospital in New York for tests, including a bone biopsy. While they waited for results, Peter attended Rohatsu sesshin at the New York Zendo, an annual seven-day sitting that commemorates the Buddha's enlightenment. He came and went so he could keep an eye on Deborah, and the sangha dedicated the final morning service on December 8, Bodhi Day, to Deborah's health. "We were doing a lot of chanting," including the Avalokitesvara Sutra for Prolonging Life, recalled Shinge Roshi, then known as the student Roko Sherry Chayat. "We do it every day. We were doing it especially for her."[64] Meanwhile, at

Roosevelt Hospital, the doctors were baffled by Deborah's symptoms. "The tests have all come back negative and still the pain exists and the mystery with it," Milly Johnstone told a friend.[65] Peter was sure it was a recurrence of cancer; he informed Tai-san that Deborah was dying, "and that this knowing had come from no source subject to error."[66]

The bone biopsy took such a toll that Peter declined any further tests, which would have "subjected [her] uselessly to more pain."[67] He carried Deborah out of the hospital on December 9, and she went straight to bed in Sagaponack. Outside the bedroom, Peter attempted to create a semblance of normalcy for seven-year-old Alex: school, dinner, television, visits with friends.

After a few days, Deborah developed two small lumps under her skin—subcutaneous nodules, which can be signs of metastatic cancer. She went to see the family doctor in Sag Harbor, who ordered another biopsy. The result this time was unambiguous: adenocarcinoma. Taking a walk on the beach, Deborah and Peter cried together; their arguments seemed inconsequential in the light of such a poor prognosis. "[I]t turns out to be cancer, as we feared," he wrote in a letter to Jim Harrison. "I don't think her chances are very good at all, though I cling to hope. She is a very lovely and brave person—I haven't deserved her (truly)—and miraculously we are happy as well as sad."[68] Nevertheless, a complicating factor was again Jane Stanton, who did not entirely vanish from the picture even now. As Jane later remembered, "I would stay with my parents at their house in the winter and he would come to visit and talk obsessively about chemotherapy, this new thing that would make you lose your hair and have very severe side-effects. Obsessive because he didn't know whether she should do it. But he was willing to try anything to help her. Meanwhile, he's sleeping with me."[69]

Deborah told her friends about the cancer—"she knew I would take it hard," said Merete Galesi[70]—and Peter updated Tai-san, who received the news in silence, then offered the gift of a red fan decorated with Japanese calligraphy that translated as "Going home."

In mid-December, Peter drove Deborah to Memorial Hospital in Manhattan, where she was admitted to the Sloan-Kettering Institute for Cancer Research. This was the same week that President Nixon signed the National Cancer Act into law, declaring war on a group of diseases that were still essentially an enigma in 1971. The act designated Sloan-Kettering as one of three Comprehensive Cancer Centers in the country where cutting-edge research was being actively translated into clinical practice.

Deborah registered herself as a "Zen Buddhist," much to the surprise of her husband, who still didn't think of Zen as a religious marker like "Catholic." In her private room, she covered the bedside table with reading material for her New School class, determined to stay positive and make her stay at Sloan-Kettering a productive one. But the chemotherapy, begun immediately, decimated what little energy she still had in reserve. Within days, Deborah forgot about Herrigel and Wittgenstein. She would never finish teaching her class on Zen.

Peter drove to Sagaponack to put together an improvised Christmas for Rue, who was home on school vacation, and Alex, who was being minded by friends. The day after Christmas, he then returned to Sloan-Kettering for a small party in Deborah's suite with several members of the sangha, including Milly Johnstone and Tai-san. Someone had brought champagne and oysters; Tai-san produced a brown linen robe and a *rakusu*—a bib-like garment worn around the neck to signify a student has undergone lay ordination. Deborah, putting it on over her hospital gown, affirmed her commitment to Zen by receiving the ten Buddhist precepts in a makeshift *Jukai* ceremony. She was given a Dharma name: Ho Ko, which means "Dharma Light." "Under the covers, Ho Ko was already an old woman, her hips and beautiful legs collapsed, black and blue from needles," Matthiessen later wrote, "but she was still lovely when propped up in bed, and she wore her rakusu like a proud child."[71] When Rue came to visit, she noticed her mother's hospital suite had the same reverential atmosphere as the New York Zendo.

From Rue's perspective, Peter was never less than attentive once Deborah became terminally ill. "She needed him, and *this* time he came through. He was absolutely present for her illness, loving and concerned with her comfort and care."[72] Merete Galesi and Milly Johnstone kept Deborah company in the mornings, holding her hand or doing needlepoint by her bedside. Peter replaced them for the afternoon shift. "He would lift her into the bathtub so she could have a bath, and then lift her out," said Nan Talese. "And he brought her a Buddha"—the bronze statue from Kathmandu he'd purchased on the way to New Guinea.[73] He also controlled who, and what, was permitted to enter her field of view. A friend sent an aquarium so Deborah could watch the fish, but when one went belly-up in the tank, Peter banished the whole thing from the hospital: he "didn't want anything to die in front of her."[74] He even convinced the nurses to bend the rules so he could stay in the suite overnight.

"One day, knowing that she was dying," Matthiessen later recalled in *The Snow Leopard*, "D remarked, 'Isn't it queer? This is one of the happiest times in all my life.' And another day, she asked me shyly what would happen if she should have a miraculous recovery—would we love each other still, and stay together, or would the old problems rise again to spoil things as before? I didn't know, and that is what I said. We had tried to be honest, and anyway,

D would not have been fooled. I shrugged unhappily, she winced, then we both laughed."[75] But by the first weeks of 1972, Deborah had passed beyond laughter, and she became desperate for a show of proof that he really loved her. Peter remembered the Isfahan bowl. "I propped her up in bed, coaxing her to concentrate, then opened up the box and placed the bowl in her hands . . . she pressed it to her heart, lay back like a child, eyes shining, and in a whisper got one word out: 'Swit-zerland!' "[76]

Deborah's decline from that point was rapid and unsparing. She was soon gaunt, coughing up blood, her mind swamped by paranoid hallucinations. (An autopsy would find the cancer had spread to her brain.) She fought the nurses as though they were enemies, and failed to identify friends and family members, who turned red in the face or burst into tears when they walked into the room. But Zen people seemed to bring her peace, and a few women from the sangha—Sheila Curtis, Marsha Feinhandler, Kandida Boatwright—volunteered to help with her care "in the spirit of the Lotus Sutra."[77] One Sloan-Kettering nurse, watching the solemn procession from the New York Zendo, told Peter she had never seen so much support on the cancer ward: " 'I don't know what you Zen people do,' she said, 'but you're doing *something* right.' "[78] When Luke stopped by for a visit, however, he found the scene around Deborah to be surreal and unnerving: "Holding her emaciated arms above her head as if grasping for relief, she emitted small gasps of pain with each breath. Several Japanese monks in brown and green silk robes stood by her bed and chanted in base monotones over the beeping of the hospital monitors. The aroma of incense struggled for parity with the pervasive odors of disinfectant and the sweetly acrid smell of dying. I stood in the doorway, held there by an awkward uncertainty as much as a lack of room. My father sat in a chair across from the bed, silently holding his head in both hands."[79]

Less than a month after Deborah entered Sloan-Kettering, Peter demanded an end to the "obsessive tests and weighing."[80] Nothing more could be done to stop the inevitable. For the first time in two weeks, he drove home to Sagaponack to see Alex, who was being insulated from his mother's fate. Around this time, Peter also called Rue at her boarding school for an impossible conversation. "It was arranged for me to take the call in the science room in the basement, as there were no phones in the dorms," Rue wrote in a memoir. "I will never forget that room. The day's lesson was still on the blackboard. My father, sounding far away, was calling to tell me that Mom was 'very sick.' I asked him, 'Could she die?' And he said, yes, she could. I cried on the phone with him. He would not move from his words, he would not, he could not soften them."[81] Peter seems to have believed that

Rue was better off with her friends at the boarding school, because he left her there to process the terrible news; she, like Alex, would never see her mother alive again.

Deborah slipped into a coma. The doctors did not expect her to regain consciousness. Yet she did awaken, surprising everyone, for several days starting on January 22. Peter was in a sesshin at the New York Zendo, where Tai-san broke the silence to make an emotional speech about "our beloved sister Ho Ko": "The pain of your knees is nothing like the pain of *cancer*!"[82] After some intense morning zazen, Peter went to the hospital to discover Deborah "clear and lovely," with the strength to put her arms around his neck. ("It was hard to dissociate this transformation from the healing powers emanating from the zendo.")[83] Tai-san arrived with several students, all of whom Deborah could greet by name in an extraordinary resurgence of lucidity. She remained conscious the next day, albeit less focused, and on January 24, she smiled and whispered "Peter," according to his own account, then fell silent. Before she returned to the coma that afternoon, she appeared to be in a "blessed state," although this may have been a wishful projection by Peter; there was nothing blessed about her condition.[84]

Deborah lived two days longer than the doctors predicted. On the evening on January 26, when it was clear she was approaching the end, Peter and Tai-san grasped her hands and chanted the Four Great Bodhisattva Vows, over and over until shortly after midnight. Peter would later claim she had drawn her last breath during the third vow: HO MON MURYO SEI GAN GAKU ("Dharmas are boundless, I vow to perceive them").[85] "I am convinced that her zazen and mine, together with the support of Eido-shi and all the sangha, made a luminous death out of a very ugly one," he said in 1973, comforting himself in the same way a Christian takes comfort from a priest performing the last rites, the horrors of a deathbed made holy ("luminous") through the transformative power of prayer.[86]

Within days, the two men accompanied her body, dressed in the brown robe and rakusu, all the way to a crematorium in Queens, again chanting the Four Vows as mystified mortuary attendants watched on. By the time Deborah Love was gone, Peter Matthiessen was a committed follower of Zen Buddhism.

15

Twenty Months

The Roshi was pleased that there would be but two of us—this seemed to him a condition of true pilgrimage. He instructed me to recite the Kannon Sutra as I walked among the mountains, and gave me a *koan* (a Zen paradox, not to be solved by intellect, that may bring about a sudden dissolution of logical thought and clear the way for direct *seeing* into the heart of existence):
All the peaks are covered with snow—why is this one bare?

—*The Snow Leopard* (1978)[1]

> BECAUSE IT <u>ACCEPTS</u> ...
> BECAUSE <u>IT</u>
> BECAUSE!
>
> —PM's first attempt at an answer,
>   written in his Himalayas journal[2]

PETER WAS BATTERED by the stress, his face like "a pencil that's been shaved with a little knife," recalled Rose Styron, "because the ridges were so deep, the lines and layers were so obvious."[3] In the immediate aftermath of Deborah's death, he retreated into grief and refused to answer the telephone. Worried by the silence, Merete Galesi drove over to Sagaponack to let herself into the house; she found Peter slumped in a chair, doing nothing while his children slept at one o'clock in the afternoon. There were dishes piled in the kitchen, laundry covering the floor. He chided her for the intrusion, but she ignored him, got the children out of bed, and told them, "We've got to go on. Let's go and cry in the kitchen, but we've all got to go on."[4] Merete called a maid service and gave Peter a grocery list to get him up and moving. "He was so defensive about not writing," she later recalled. "*'I'm supposed to be writing and I can't, I'm falling apart.'* And he didn't want anybody to see it. He didn't want anybody to see how vulnerable and how out of it he was."

Over the following months, Matthiessen immersed himself in Zen. At a February sesshin in the New York Zendo, he chanted with the sangha for "Dai Shi [Great Teacher] Debby Hoko," who had been placed on the altar in an urn near some white carnations. He compiled a memorial booklet in her honor, with help from Nan Talese at Random House, filled with haiku, sutras, and Japanese ink paintings. During a seven-day retreat at Dai Bosatsu in March, he chose a place near a boulder by Beecher Lake and dug down through the snow and dirt to bury half of Deborah's ashes. He was so moved by zazen in the lake house that he sat through walking meditation, then through a full rest period, "welcoming the pain" in his legs.[5]

Some of his friends found his intense embrace of Zen perplexing. "I wouldn't have thought," said Rose Styron, "from what little I knew of Zen at the time, that he could have been a dedicated Buddhist."[6] He seemed too angry and restless, too *impulsive* for such a calm, disciplined practice. Some members of the New York sangha were similarly uncertain about his enthusiasm for their rituals. "He was always such an appealing guy," said Shinge Roshi (Roko Sherry Chayat). "But I think we had a kind of prejudice against him. Many of us just felt that, you know, it's maybe a little late? You could have done this while she was alive. It would have been a lot more helpful." He gave an impression of doing penance, trying to make it up to Deborah in some way: "He must have had a lot of regrets."[7]

After an April sesshin, he carried the rest of Deborah's ashes home to Sagaponack. In the old village cemetery just down the road from his house, he dug a grave while Alex watched; they planted it with heaths and marigolds. Tai-san and some Zen students traveled out from the city to conduct a small service, attended by Alex and Rue (who was numb with shock), and Luke and Sara Carey. The cemetery was supposed to be Deborah's final resting place, but Peter, not quite ready to let go, kept out a fragment of her bone, which he placed in the upstairs tearoom that he would now refer to as his zendo.

Four days after the memorial service, he sat down at his desk to type a letter. It was composed in response to an exchange he'd had with a gossiping acquaintance—somebody who'd suggested, indelicately, that he had been "madly in love all along with a girl [he] intended to marry as soon as Deborah was safely in the grave." The "girl" was Jane Stanton, and Peter now wrote to her directly because the rumor was suffocating him when "juxtaposed with the hard white stone in the Sagaponack cemetery." To set the record straight, he declared: "If I am in love with anybody, I am in love with D, despite all the evidence to the contrary, but actually I am increasingly suspicious of the term 'in love' and wonder if I will ever feel that way again. I very much doubt it." This was the respectable thing to say given the circumstances; but then, having said it, he shifted his tone, adding: "Not that this means we might not be good for each other at this time in our lives, if we were quiet and discreet and casual (it doesn't really matter what people say and speculate so long as one doesn't encourage them to intrude upon one's privacy by confirming it)."[8] He ended his note to Jane: "This is a love letter."

Peter's grief for Deborah was genuine; nobody doubted that he was shattered by her loss. Yet even as he did penance before the sangha and added her bone to his zendo altar, his need to feel wanted was so strong that he could compartmentalize his feelings from one sentence to the next. The thing he hated about himself could also be useful: he could split, on purpose, to become multiple "I's" simultaneously: bereft widower, willing lover.

MUCH OF THE WINTER and spring vanished in a "strange (also beautiful in a terrible way) gothic time lapse," Matthiessen told Jim Harrison.[9] As much as he was able, he focused on trying to "consolidate" the "home atmosphere" for the children, while simultaneously getting "my own head together."[10] Still, he did make time for one consequential meeting in either late April or early May: a dinner in New York with the field biologist George Schaller.

Schaller, whom Matthiessen had not seen since Tanzania in 1969, was in the process of relocating his family to Lahore, Pakistan, which he planned to use as a base for a series of scientific expeditions in and around the Himalayas. Just as he'd studied lions at Seronera, Schaller now hoped to unravel the secrets of "the world's greatest variety of sheep and goats, known by such obscure names as markhor, tahr, urial, argali, and bharal."[11] To this end, he'd already conducted several preliminary research trips, including to the highlands of southern India, where he observed the Nilgiri tahr. But the specific expedition he now proposed to Matthiessen—who had, as Schaller recalled, expressed interest in the Himalayas during one of their previous discussions—was one to Nepal. John Blower, a United Nations wildlife adviser to the Nepalese government, had recently shown Schaller some photographs of bharal, the blue sheep, taken in the valleys of Dolpo, a remote northern region of the country's large Dolpa District, near the edge of the Tibetan Plateau. The bharal were "tame" because the lama of an old Tibetan Buddhist monastery in Dolpo prohibited all hunting of them. Blower had suggested to Schaller that this eleventh-century monastery, named Shey Gompa, the Crystal Monastery, would not only make an ideal spot from which to study the bharal, but that it would, as Schaller paraphrased the invitation, "help the Nepal government if [he] were to make a wildlife survey and assess the potential of that area as a reserve."[12] Besides the bharal, the area was home to the elusive snow leopard, which preyed on the blue sheep. Getting there required an arduous trek over multiple mountain passes, yet the challenge would be worth it; here was a singular opportunity to survey a part of the world that was otherwise inaccessible to outsiders due to geographical and political impediments. Schaller asked Matthiessen, at dinner, if he "might like to join."[13]

In *The Snow Leopard*, Matthiessen offers several rationales for why he decided to walk more than 250 miles in high altitude to a valley he knew virtually nothing about. First, there was the chance to work with George Schaller again. Second, like all Matthiessen's previous expeditions, it was an opportunity to observe cultures, landscapes, and animals that were threatened with annihilation: Dolpo "was said to be the last enclave of pure Tibetan culture left on earth, and Tibetan culture was the last citadel of [quoting the lama Anagarika Govinda] 'all that present-day humanity is longing for, either because it has been lost or not yet been realized or because it is in danger of disappearing from human sight.'"[14] Third, there was the possibility of expanding his knowledge of Buddhism, a new interest that he flagged to Schaller by sending him a copy of *Zen Mind, Beginner's Mind* soon after their dinner. ("I've only browsed a bit so far," Schaller replied. "A lot of it seems most sensible, some of it less so, but I have to ponder things some more.")[15] And finally, there was a personal reason, which Matthiessen was hesitant to explain to others when they asked him about his goals: "One can't say, 'I am making a pilgrimage' without feeling like a fool, but that is the truth. I just want to go empty if I can into the mountains and see what happens."[16] He hoped the clarity of the Himalayas might induce some kind of spiritual insight, kensho, like he'd glimpsed in the New York Zendo.

In a letter following up on their dinner, Schaller recommended they schedule the trip to begin in either late September of '73 or '74, with the aim of finishing by mid-December of the same year, "in time to get home for Christmas," which was one of his wife, Kay's, "stipulations."[17] Matthiessen's reply is lost, but they would end up settling on the earlier date—twenty months after Deborah's death. "I made that pilgrimage for her sake as well as mine," he later said.[18]

OF ALL THE CONDOLENCE CALLS that Matthiessen fielded when he started answering the phone again, perhaps the most impactful came from Cesar Chavez, who heard the news about Deborah just as he was readying to drive to Arizona to protest new antiunion legislation that was about to be signed into law there by Governor Jack Williams. "In spite of his worries," Matthiessen noted appreciatively, Chavez called to "express his sorrow."[19] During the conversation, it occurred to them both that they hadn't seen each other for more than a year now: their last meeting, planned to coincide with Matthiessen's visit to Tassajara, had been aborted when an assassination plot sent Chavez into hiding for six weeks. On the phone, Chavez said that he hoped to see his friend sooner rather than later—"God willing." The comment, made just before they said goodbye, left a strong impression on Matthiessen. Chavez had spoken "without drama," he wrote in some notes, "but his final words reminded me once more that this man lived with the threat of death every day of his life in order to fulfill his hopes for other people."

In June, Matthiessen tried to resume a regular work routine. He dug out his long-gestating turtle novel, barely touched in months, and took on a new screenwriting job—a documentary feature for the Oscar-winning producers of *The Hellstrom Chronicle*.* But Chavez remained on his mind, until, in July, he set everything aside, left his children with a friend, and flew west to see the man in person.

Much had changed since the publication of *Sal Si Puedes*. In the summer of 1970, Chavez and the United Farm Workers had won a major victory when the prolonged boycott (DON'T BUY GRAPES) ended with more equitable labor contracts with growers. Chavez had held up these contracts, which included pay raises and pesticide regulation, as proof that nonviolent protests worked; one of the negotiating growers had called the agreement an "experiment in social justice," and a "revolution in agriculture."[20] Matthiessen had been ecstatic, writing to Chavez from Kenya, where he was traveling at the time: "Ann [Israel] has sent me all the clippings on all the new developments—congratulations to you all! By the time I get back in the fall, I suspect the whole agricultural empire of California will be crumbling, led by Tenneco [a farming subsidiary of the Houston-based oil company], I hope. And I'd like to write an end—A HAPPY END—to Sal Si Puedes."[21] In the two years since then, however, the victory had not translated into tangible quality-of-life improvements for many farmworkers. Further union initiatives had also aroused the ire of conservative national interest groups, including the American Farm Bureau Federation, and pro-agribusiness politicians such as President Nixon. Kansas and Idaho had passed laws to combat a union campaign against lettuce growers; other states were preparing their own legislation. Earl Butz, the U.S. secretary of agriculture, had even quipped that what the country really needed was to "take the Cesar out of salad."[22]

Chavez had responded to this upswell of hostility—to the taunts and

---

* The extremely weird project, titled "The Universe," mixed astronomy, Zen, Hindu mysticism, parapsychology, and a man hurtling into the void past Pluto. It never achieved liftoff.

intimidation tactics, and to a three-week stint in jail for violating an injunction against striking—by expanding his ambitions. By 1972, he wanted to take his union to the national stage. The farmworkers' plight, Matthiessen wrote in an unpublished update to *Sal Si Puedes*, had finally outgrown its California origins to become something much bigger: "a catalyst in the critical struggle between those citizens who sought an evolution in the nation's values and those content to be consumers." In this regard, la causa seemed closer than ever to becoming the transformative social movement Matthiessen had always believed it could be.

In Arizona, he joined a cavalcade of eighty cars, each flying the red union flag. The cars crossed through fields of cotton, cantaloupe, and lettuce to Yuma, Chavez's birthplace, for a rally of more than two thousand people. On the evening of July 24, in a big shed on the city's outskirts, "a sweating audience, brown, black, and white, waited for Chavez, who sat quietly in the front row." There was dancing and a mariachi band, and voices rose in unison to sing "Qué Viva Nuestra Union." Matthiessen observed the scene like a reporter, taking notes from his vantage point near the entrance door; but he was here as a volunteer, part of Chavez's security detail, on the watch for suspicious characters. "One has only to see the hope in the faces of people around him to know how precious Chavez is, and develop a hard watchful eye whenever he is out in public."

Matthiessen wore a red-and-black armband on his left sleeve that advertised his allegiance. After the rally, he forgot to take it off before entering a diner for a cup of coffee. Two policemen followed him inside with what he thought was "a funny look." Then three strangers—two local growers and a dealer in agricultural supplies, all hostile to the union—stood on either side of him at the counter. Realizing the men had clocked his armband, Matthiessen hid his "uneasiness" as best he could. He engaged them in conversation. "If Chavez was as bad as the Arizona media would claim, why did you attend the rally?" he asked. The growers shrugged. "Just wanted to see what he looked like, I guess," one of them said, according to Matthiessen's notes, before complaining about the threat the union posed to his bottom line. Matthiessen finished his coffee and quickly left the diner. On his way back to the motel, he checked all the dark corners to make sure nobody was waiting to jump him.

Later that night, he joined Chavez and a few associates—including Ann Israel, who, having married, now went by Anna Puharich, and who now worked for Chavez as an aide—for a nearly four-hundred-mile drive back to California. Matthiessen watched the desert slide past the car, those "strange ancient Joshua trees," and took the wheel once they reached Barstow. Thirty miles east of Bakersfield, he pulled up at a former tuberculosis sanatorium, recently transformed into a new headquarters for the union, which Chavez had christened Nuestra Señora Reina de la Paz (Our Lady Queen of Peace)—"La Paz," for short.* Matthiessen seized two hours of sleep in an empty room. Then he rose to write a rebuttal to a grower-backed initiative that was slated to appear on the California ballot in November. Proposition 22, if approved by voters, would ban consumer boycotts of lettuce across the state, thus crippling union-building efforts. Chavez was understandably anxious about the outcome of the vote. Matthiessen worked on the rebuttal all morning, and Chavez badgered him throughout the afternoon until a draft was completed. "I had plenty of my own work to do," Matthiessen recalled, "but Chavez has a genius for organizing efforts on the farm-workers' behalf without seeming to ask for it; anyone at hand will be put to use, and will work hard with minimal thanks, and what is more, will like it." And he did like it, because there was comfort in submitting to the charismatic leadership of Cesar Chavez, forgetting about his own situation for a few days.

Chavez was impressed with Matthiessen's rebuttal of Prop 22. He relaxed after reviewing the pages, and the men talked for several hours. Matthiessen had already noticed that speaking to Chavez was "like going to a source, a mountain spring; one comes away refreshed."[23] He drank deep at La Paz, stayed for another night, and then headed to Los Angeles to make his way home.

AUGUST SESSHIN WAS HELD at Wisdom House, an interfaith retreat center in Litchfield, Connecticut, in the foothills of the Berkshire Mountains. Fifty-seven people gathered in a white wood-frame building for an intensive week of zazen and to hear the Dharma presentations of Soen Nakagawa, who had recently arrived from Japan for another extended stay with Eido Shimano. Soen Roshi encouraged everyone to chant as loudly as they could. He gave his talks in the evenings: "True concentration IS true emancipation!"[24] He also met with students for *dokusan*, one-on-one formal interviews about some aspect of their practice. After Matthiessen rang the bell for his first interview, entered the dokusan room, and bowed, Soen spontaneously acknowledged Deborah's death. "It is all right," he said. "You live near ocean . . . the waves come and go, but the ocean is still there. You die, I die, it is all right, too. The ocean is still there."[25]

Matthiessen practiced writing haikus and went for quiet walks in the woods. He watched as Soen "shimmered and danced with a wild joy," and as the teacher pointed up at Orion and urged his students to "swallow the stars

---

* In 2012, President Barack Obama protected La Paz as the César E. Chávez National Monument.

until you are one with the universe."[26] On the final morning of the retreat, Matthiessen climbed the stairs for his last dokusan, and found Soen waiting for him on the landing. "He was standing at the window," recalled Shinge Roshi (Roko Sherry Chayat), who had the same experience. "I went over to him, and he gently positioned me so that I was looking out. There was an enormous, deep-red ball of the sun bursting over the horizon!"[27] It was, Matthiessen said, "roaring like fire through a tall black burning pine."[28] He was not the kind of man to readily express raw emotions in front of other people, but it was the end of a melancholy summer, and seven days of sesshin has the effect of making one's mind "very, very open."[29] The fiery vision came as a revelation. How often do we glimpse a tree or the sun without truly seeing the "treeness of the tree, or the sunness of the sun"?[30] Matthiessen wept "healing tears," standing next to Soen Roshi, "in the overwhelming clarity and simplicity of this moment."[31] He then cried through zazen, "the tears alternating with delicious silent laughter."

Come September, Matthiessen was feeling "better," he told Anna Puharich in a letter, but he was "not yet out of the woods."[32] The change of season left him stricken with a loneliness that nothing and nobody could effectively dispel. In this forlorn mood, he invited Soen Roshi and Eido Roshi—Tai-san had finally received *Inka Shomei* and been acknowledged as a Zen master, worthy of the roshi honorific—out to Sagaponack to hold another two memorial services for Deborah: one in the tearoom/zendo; and one at dawn where her ashes were buried in the Sagaponack cemetery.

As a gift, Soen Roshi presented his host with a polished plum pit, minutely etched with the ten-line Kannon Sutra—a talisman that Matthiessen would carry with him in the Himalayas. As another gift, Soen unfurled some blank scroll paper on the living room floor, and then, using brush and ink, dashed off a piece of Mu calligraphy for the zendo upstairs.

Just before October sesshin at the New York Zendo, Matthiessen received the ten Buddhist precepts and a rakusu with "Ishin" written on it—a Dharma name, meaning "One Mind," given to him by Soen Roshi. This was Matthiessen's own Jukai ceremony: "the turning point in your life," in the words of Eido Shimano, "where as a lay-student you unconditionally commit yourself to the practice of Buddha-Dharma. We take the precepts in the knowledge that we are committing to an endless path of transformation, a path that requires our constant vigilance and awareness. In a larger sense, you are committing your life to the realization of your True Nature."[33] Ishin Peter Matthiessen was honored to wear the rakusu over his robes. But after a few visits to the New York Zendo, he took it off and packed it away. Deborah had been a practitioner of Zen for nearly five years before the Jukai on her deathbed made her Ho Ko, "Dharma Light." Peter had been a sincere student for less than one year. He was not ready, he told a confused Eido Roshi during dokusan: "I had not earned lay ordination, being so scattered, so far from the condition of 'One Mind.'"[34]

THAT SAME OCTOBER, Matthiessen took a two-week sailing trip to the Galápagos Islands for *Audubon* magazine; the islands were "not beautiful," he wrote in a muted article, "yet their sparseness and simplicity and silence are very moving, and suit me in a spare and silent time in my own life."[35] E. P. Dutton also published *The Tree Where Man Was Born*, which he had completed just a day before Deborah first entered the hospital for tests, and which he now dedicated "in love and gratitude" to her memory.

The book was actually a combined effort: two books in one. Matthiessen's text was paired with ninety-two photographs by Eliot Porter, a collection separately, and confusingly, titled *The African Experience*. This collaboration between one of the world's leading nature writers and one of the best nature photographers alive—Porter was renowned for his landscapes—was the idea of the Dutton publisher, Jack Macrae. It was not, however, without creative friction. Porter was promised a higher percentage of the royalties than Matthiessen, despite spending far less time on the project (a few weeks versus several years); this struck Matthiessen as unfair. Each man was also given free rein to do as he pleased for the project without consulting the other, and Porter produced a series of accomplished yet predictable images: hippos wallowing by a waterhole; a Maasai herder with his cattle; zebras in the grass at Ngorongoro. Matthiessen thought they were lackluster. He wanted pictures that were "full of strange significations," with "emblematic angles, archetypal and remote."[36] He wanted the "virtual exclusion of 'animal portraits,' colorful natives, and the like except where an abstract quality is achieved that transcends the subject matter and makes it universal." Eliot Porter's photos were perfect for a coffee table book, but they were a mismatch, Matthiessen thought, for the "subtle and mysterious" essays that made up his half of the project. At least, that is what he told Porter in a letter.

His comments—which Porter politely rejected: "You were never expected to write a text designed to fit my visual insights, nor was I ever urged to produce illustrations of your literary concepts"[37]—indicate what Matthiessen was aiming to achieve with *The Tree Where Man Was Born*. The book was not intended to be the work of a foreign correspondent. Rather, it was "personal journalism, travel chronicle, belles lettres," lyrical, intimate, and impressionistic.[38] The essays showed East Africa as seen through the eyes of someone who had gone there, with all his baggage, in search of something elemental.

The book's title refers to the long-living baobab tree, which becomes, in

Matthiessen's presentation, both a mythic symbol of old Africa ("The tree where man was born, according to the Nuer, still stood within man's memory in the west part of the south Sudan"[39]), and a reminder of what was being lost in the difficult transition to the new Africa ("Today young baobab are killed by fires, set by the strangers who clear the country for their herds and gardens, and the tree where man was born is dying out"[40]). Matthiessen's ten chapters are digressive explorations of this world in flux. The book is filled with ekphrastic evocations of landscape, like living works of art; with trenchant questions about the costs of conservation in developing countries (how can "a shamba dweller" be expected to embrace the national parks when their "meagre existence" remains all but unaffected by tourist revenue?); and with moving laments for disappearing species and traditional ways of life—"the old ways," Matthiessen once again calls them.

The "personal" aspect of the book's journalism comes through his singular power of perception: the way he sits on a rocky outcrop overlooking a stream and sees not only the landscape and animals in crystalline detail (a Thomson's gazelle cocking its head "as if to shake a burr out of its ear"), but also himself and his own longing for an imagined Africa: "At my feet lay the reality, a litter of big lion droppings and a spat-up hair ball."[41]

The personal is reflected, too, in the book's curious structure, which takes the form of another quest. The first two chapters detail his overland trip from Cairo to Nairobi in 1961. The following seven, nonchronological, concern his African travels during 1969 and 1970, including his stay at Seronera and an expedition with Eliot Porter to Lake Rudolf (now Lake Turkana), in Kenya, where he hoped to catch "a glimpse of the vanishing hunters."[42] The final chapter, "At Gidabembe," documents a journey with the zoologist Peter Enderlein in Tanzania's Yaeda Valley.* As a climax to the quest, Matthiessen embeds with the Hadza people, a group of hunter-gatherers who had, when he visited them, not yet been infiltrated by missionaries or forcibly resettled by intolerant government forces. Admiring—and romanticizing—the "dignity and independence" of their nomadic lifestyle, and remembering what happened to the Dugum Dani in New Guinea, Matthiessen mounts a spirited defense of the autonomy of Native peoples, arguing that they should be left in peace "until a choice that they can make naturally is provided, for this people is acknowledged by all who have met them to be healthy and happy, with no history of epidemic or famine, and able to satisfy all needs in a few hours of each day."[43] But the self-sufficiency of the Hadza also spoke to his desire for simplicity, and Matthiessen claims to feel at home while staying

---

* Matthiessen made this journey in July 1970, immediately after his fraught vacation with Deborah and the Koenigs.

in their dry season camp called Gidabembe. Days are peaceful, slow, and spontaneous; there is "a ceremonial sense of order in which everything is in place, for the ceremony here is life itself."⁴⁴ In the end, *The Tree Where Man Was Born*, like much of Matthiessen's work, concerns the search for an island; Gidabembe is portrayed as a remnant paradise of old Africa on the verge of being lost through enforced modernization.

For the quality of its prose and the vividness of descriptions, Matthiessen considered *The Tree Where Man Was Born* to be one of his better nonfiction books. It is indeed stunning in places: "Even at rest the herd flowed in perpetual motion, the ears like delicate great petals, the ripple of the mud-caked flanks, the coiling trunks—a dream rhythm, a rhythm of wind and trees."⁴⁵ Many early readers were impressed, including William Shawn at *The New Yorker*: the magazine printed three long extracts over three consecutive weeks in September. John Owen, who had first planted the seed for the project with his invitation to the Serengeti Research Institute, wrote to Matthiessen to say that it surpassed his "highest expectations—great holding power, descriptive passages—it transported me back to the times when the world was young and free."⁴⁶ Elspeth Huxley, the British writer and journalist who had grown up in Kenya, admired a "dark thread of Greek tragedy" in the book, "the foreknowledge of doom, for we know that the beauty he writes of is condemned."⁴⁷ And Nancy Hurxthal, whose pregnancy Matthiessen had helped save during the ill-advised safari near Lake Magadi, marveled at his ability to capture a scene: "We remember being with you and wonder at the way in which you perceive and record these scales of experience, for, on the one hand, you seem to conduct your human affairs with total involvement and concentration, and yet to create a book such as this, a part of you must be quite distant and continually abstracting the moments."⁴⁸

One person who was less enamored was the Scottish anthropologist Colin Macmillan Turnbull, who had received an advance copy from Dutton because he had famously written *The Forest People* (1961), about Mbuti pygmies, and *The Lonely African* (1962), which considered African points of view during a period of massive sociocultural transition. Matthiessen admired *The Lonely African*; it had influenced his conclusions in *The Tree Where Man Was Born*. He expected Turnbull to respond approvingly to his work. Turnbull did not. The problem, the anthropologist explained in a regretful but unsparing letter, was what he detected as a "stereotype white-settler" attitude in many of the chapters. Matthiessen quoted colonial perspectives (like Elspeth Huxley) with insufficient critique, Turnbull said, and perhaps he'd failed to overcome his own ingrained prejudices. Indeed, Matthiessen seemed so focused on thinking of Africans as "different," and was so beholden to his "white patronage"—the scientists and park managers who'd hosted him in Kenya and Tanzania—that he never truly reckoned with the local people on their own terms. "At one point in the book he confesses to a lack of understanding," Turnbull wrote to Jack Macrae, "and I fear it remains throughout."[49]

Turnbull was not entirely wrong with his criticism; Matthiessen had relied almost exclusively on white guides to research his book, and his interactions with, and writing about, Maasai, Meru, El Molo, Samburu, and Rendille people were sometimes othering, punctuated by moments of awkwardness and incomprehension. But Matthiessen was justly "astonished" by the claim that he was promoting a white settler attitude. While parts of the book have aged poorly (all the unfortunate speculation about human origins and migratory routes), that is a matter of changing mores and Matthiessen's limited sources, not the deliberate boosting of racist viewpoints. To Turnbull, he defended himself vigorously "in the first such letter I have ever written to a serious person who criticized my work."[50] Though its tone was "quiet," he insisted, "the book's attitudes toward the colonial mentality, its smugness, venality, brutality, and folly, seem to me unmistakable, whether dealing with the 19th Century assumptions about Darkest Africa or the atrocities of the Kenya Regiment which were excused by vilification of 'Mau Mau' and Dedan Kimathi." The book's contempt for that mentality had been even more pronounced, he wrote, until Dutton asked him to dilute the acid of an early draft. Matthiessen continued:

> For better or worse, the book is an attempt to transcend the white myth and its literature, to perceive Africa and its people as best I can, which is to say, as honestly as I can, in the short time at my disposal, and I like to think that it moves steadily in this direction after traditional "history" is dispensed with in the early chapters, and that its essential spirit is expressed in the final chapter on the Hadza, where I came as close as I ever would to being in Africa among Africans.

Matthiessen was so "bewildered" by Turnbull's critique that he requested "some sort of clarification." Embarrassed to be put on the spot, Turnbull wrote a long, wincing reply that conceded he may have been a little brusque in his old age. Ultimately, though, he doubled down on his complaints. While Matthiessen clearly meant well—"I do know where your sympathies lie"[51]—the book was defined by the white settlers, who were peeking out, Turnbull felt, from virtually every page. Quoting their outdated views in any capacity only perpetuated those views further, he argued: "I fear your own personal views do NOT triumph as they should, except for those who already share them. Those that share the settler point of view will find as much to confirm them in their views."

Bruised by this rejection, Matthiessen let the matter drop; there was little to be gained by pressing his argument further. But then an even more alarming attack came from another quarter in late September.

Truman Capote stopped by the house to share some gossip. "What was interesting to me," Matthiessen later recalled about this impromptu visit from his neighbor, "was that he was very evidently torn on the one side by real delight, almost gleeful, but [on the other side] it was quite apparent that he was very concerned and upset for me. Right in front of my eyes, his face was kind of dancing with this split personality."[52] Capote revealed that Peter Beard, the American photographer and artist who lived part-time in Kenya, was planning to eviscerate *The Tree Where Man Was Born* in *The New York Times Book Review*.

Beard was the author of *The End of the Game* (1965), a pictorial study of the decline in African wildlife, particularly elephants, and a nostalgic history of big-game trophy hunters on the continent. Something of a hunter himself, as well as a playboy, Beard was a controversial figure in Kenya. He was known to have tied up and possibly tortured a poacher on his ranch near Nairobi, a crime for which he'd been sentenced to eighteen months in Kamiti Prison. ("Beard jail sentence probably just," Matthiessen had written to Jim Harrison in 1970: "he is said to be a morbid sort of psycho, much given to death and related pursuits, though this may be usual rancid E. Africa gossip."[53] Beard had evaded the sentence with help from some well-connected friends, including Jacqueline Onassis.) Capote's news that Beard now planned to review *The Tree Where Man Was Born* for "the paper of record" was extremely disturbing because, as Matthiessen reiterated to Harrison, the book "does not share his adoration of white colonials."[54]

Matthiessen notified Jack Macrae at Dutton. Could something be done to halt Beard's invidious critique? "I think we should avoid any <u>ad hominem</u> attacks on him in print, although his psychiatric record should certainly be used in trying to persuade the Times that it was irresponsible to assign Beard in the first place."[55] Macrae agreed and contacted John Leonard, executive editor at the *Book Review*, to plead for mercy. While he knew it was unwise, Macrae wrote in a letter, to dwell on Peter Beard's mental health issues or his vigilantism in East Africa, it was nevertheless alarming to hear that he intended to savage Matthiessen's book for territorial reasons. Was *The New York Times* so desperate for literary drama that it would knowingly sacrifice two authors (Eliot Porter as well!) and years of their work? This was a brazen intervention for a publisher to make, but John Leonard was apparently persuaded: Peter Beard's caustic review ("Peter Matthiessen swaggers around tourist lodges with celebrities, zoo directors, princelings and park authorities . . ."[56]) was never published.

The reviewer who replaced Beard for the *Times*, the writer and environmentalist Paul Shepard, was warmly complimentary about the book. As were most of the critics who passed judgment for various publications in October and November.

A few months later, *The Tree Where Man Was Born/The African Experience* was honored with a nomination for the National Book Award in the (now defunct) category of Sciences. This was Matthiessen's second nomination for an NBA, and it would also be his second loss. He was annoyed by the category designation: *Tree* was "anything but 'science.'"[57] But he could hardly fault the winner that year, which was the book he "would've voted for" if given the chance: *The Serengeti Lion: A Study of Predatory-Prey Relations*, by George B. Schaller.

PLANS FOR THE HIMALAYAS EXPEDITION began to come together in winter. Schaller applied to Nepal's Ministry of Foreign Affairs for travel permits to Dolpo, submitting his request to conduct a wildlife survey in the Shey Gompa area, which, he pointed out in the application, was "wisely" under consideration by His Majesty's Government for a new national park.* Schaller's work was sponsored by the National Geographic Society and the New York Zoological Society, and he asked for permission to take one "companion and assistant."[58] In a separate letter to Matthiessen, he explained the demotion in his job title: "I feel it might complicate matters to say you are a writer. Dolpo is sensitive because anti-Chinese bandits seek refuge there from Tibet, and Nepal does not want this advertised."[59]

For supplies, equipment, and expedition staff, Schaller turned to Mountain Travel in Kathmandu, a commercial trekking company (the world's first) founded by the mountaineer-explorer Lieutenant Colonel James Owen Merion Roberts. Mountain Travel would take care of Sherpas and tents, et cetera, but Matthiessen was told to bring everything personal from long johns to cough drops, plus quality padded boots with room for at least two pairs of socks to ward off the miserable cold of the mountains. With every new piece of correspondence, he became "more and more excited about the trip,"[60] although a contact at the American Museum of Natural History warned him that one of Schaller's former trekking companions had ended up with boots full of blood because the field biologist pushed them so hard. Perhaps to temper expectations, Matthiessen wrote to Schaller to say that "19,000 feet is an awful lot higher than I've ever climbed," and that he had "no experience of climbing, really, except an intense dislike of cliff edges and

---

* Shey Phoksundo National Park, established in 1984.

narrow, windswept ledges." Still, he was confident he could go the distance provided they didn't pick up dysentery (which was a reasonable fear): "I'll probably make it all right, as basically I have quite a lot of energy, and am stubborn, and my legs are in pretty good shape for 45 (years old)."

While Schaller figured out the logistics for their journey, Matthiessen was keeping himself busy with the turtle novel and various other projects. But his attention was routinely occupied by sesshins, which he attended every month without fail (except once, when Alex needed a tonsillectomy). These sesshins continued to be emotionally charged experiences: the tears flowed freely as Matthiessen's moods swung from one extreme to the other. At a dawn sitting, he felt "like a stone on the point of shattering," he wrote in some notes, "yet I am loose, as I used to feel back in the Sixties under LSD, entirely unbothered by noise, distractions, even pain: there is only this pervading intensity, this racing heart, this ringing—I am vibrating, like a tuning fork about to be struck."[61] Then the next day, during another period of zazen, he was "flat, a little sad; I had felt so close, and now feel faraway." That he was still grieving was plainly apparent to the people around him. Even a journalist, conducting an interview, noticed that he seemed to be in a "transitional state," his mind drifting somewhere "during the silences between sentences."[62] Matthiessen spoke openly to friends about Deborah visiting him as a "presence" in New York. One night when he was hosting a woman in the pied-à-terre, the presence seemed displeased (in a "teasing" way, he rationalized). Another night, when he was alone in bed, the presence was a "gentle" and "approving" glow. "Unafraid, I say softly, Who is it, though I think I mean, Who am I? What is It? But it gives no sign."[63]

The sesshin of January 1973 was held at Dai Bosatsu, in the guesthouse by Beecher Lake. It marked a full year since Deborah's death, and members of the sangha paid their respects at Ho Ko's resting place near the lake, while Matthiessen built a small snow Buddha on top of her memorial boulder.

Making this sesshin even more notable, Eido Roshi invited "Ishin" to address the sangha with a talk. Not about Deborah but about himself, about how he had reached this point in his life. Taking the invitation very seriously, Matthiessen prepared a long speech that traced the evolution of his spiritual inclinations. The speech reached all the way back to G. I. Gurdjieff and "les Mouvements" during his junior year abroad in Paris ("my first uncertain step toward finding a Way").[64] It included references to mystical experience, *The Wind in the Willows*, and Carlos Castaneda.* *At Play in the Fields of the*

---

* Matthiessen was inspired by *The Teaching of Don Juan: A Yaqui Way of Knowledge*, which he read soon after its publication in 1968. He would read all of Castaneda's "don Juan Matus" books, in fact, and then compile a thematic index to check the consistency of their claims, which he titled, "A Synthesis of the 'Don Juan' Teachings Presented by Castaneda." The question of Castaneda's

Lord, Matthiessen explained, was a novel about an alienated man in search of wholeness, unity, or "transcendental liberation," and a similar desire was behind his own experiment with psychedelics ("the 2nd Way that I abandoned"). Deborah, through tea ceremony, had discovered a third Way; and she had blown his mind open when she introduced him to Zen. "I'm not kidding myself any more. I need it," he said. "In fact, I can truthfully say that beginning last year, my zazen practice, unlike all those years of drugs, has made a profound change in my life." His tone for the speech was that of an addict who believes he has finally found relief from his demons: earnest, relieved, with an edge of desperation. Zen was cast as something akin to Narcotics Anonymous, and monthly sesshins were the meetings that kept him on track.

At Dai Bosatsu in January, Matthiessen sat for so long on his cushion that Eido Roshi felt compelled to offer some advice: "Pain and Mu are very good, but it is possible to be too intense, to expect too much."[65] Yet Matthiessen was determined to have another kensho experience, and the next day he sat for two hours straight without moving his legs from the lotus position. When he finally went to stand, the shock made his teeth chatter.

Back in his room, he opened a journal to make some notes about his "folly," and a photograph of Alex slipped out of the pages and onto his bed. Later, he would recall being "startled" by his young son's face, as though it was another ghostly apparition. Where were his children during all these sesshins, all this silent meditation? Where did they fit in the evolution of his spiritual inclinations? He chided himself in the third person: "Silly idiot, cracking his knees off for a glimpse of 'truth,' and here is truth smiling up at him from his own bed!"[66]

IN THE DECADES SINCE *The Snow Leopard* was published, many readers have wrestled with the same discomforting question about Alex Matthiessen. How could Peter have left an eight-year-old boy[*] who had recently lost his mother to go trekking in the mountains of Nepal? This question has led to some dubious speculation—perhaps Alex was a painful reminder of Deborah that Peter sought to escape?—and no small amount of censorious judgment.

---

credibility did not really interest Matthiessen. In endnotes for *The Snow Leopard*, he writes: "The 'authenticity' of this shaman [Don Juan] has been much debated, and the author [Castaneda] has chosen to abet the obfuscation—no matter. If 'Don Juan' is imaginary, then spurious ethnology becomes a great work of the imagination; whether borrowed or not, the teaching rings true." This was in keeping with his ideas about "intuitive absolute truth," which, in Matthiessen's understanding, rises above distinctions like *fiction* and *nonfiction*.

[*] Alex was actually nine at the time of the expedition. Matthiessen miscalculates dates in *The Snow Leopard* when he describes his son, who was born on July 3, 1964, as "only eight."

By missing Thanksgiving, which he'd promised to return for, Matthiessen was "failing his son," according to a writer in *The New Yorker*.[67] Another characteristic response described his choices using terms like "transgression," "betrayal," and "desertion."[68]

In an interview conducted in 2006, the writer and filmmaker Jeff Sewald put the question to Matthiessen directly. How did he justify leaving Alex behind to go on a pilgrimage in the Himalayas? Matthiessen admitted that, in retrospect, "it wasn't a great idea," adding: "I can't defend it, really."[69] But he was thin-skinned when confronted with sanctimonious criticism, and he did, in fact, try to defend himself on multiple occasions when it came to this question. He pointed out that he was honest in *The Snow Leopard* about the cost of his choices; the book documents the "stricken" remorse he felt about neglecting his children. He argued that he needed to travel for his livelihood: expedition writing was how he made the money to support his family. Nearly two years had elapsed since Deborah's death, he said: it was not like he flew to Nepal the day after her memorial service. Alex was left in the care of beloved friends, a family who temporarily moved into the Sagaponack house—"much more fun than the gloomy old widower!"[70] And Alex, Peter insisted, "seemed ok" at the time.[71] This was something he was claiming before the trek even began. "My little boy is in fine shape, and more and more independent," he told Schaller in February 1973.[72] Indeed, Alex seemed so "fine" and "independent" to him that he felt no compunction about flying to California that May to work again with Cesar Chavez,* or about flying to Japan in June for a sesshin with Soen Roshi at Ryūtaku-ji.

Yet Alex was not quite as untroubled as his father chose to believe. The loss of a parent cuts deep and unpredictably into a young child. Just after Deborah died, Peter had broken the news on the beach near their house, and Alex had replied: "If she was dead, I would be crying"—a poignant expression of denial he then held on to for months.[73] Luke was "very concerned" about how his little brother was coping (or not coping) with such a monumental loss. Rue was incensed when she discovered that kids at school were teasing him about their dead mother. "We became very close, wrapped around each other watching TV or reading," she later wrote. Alex seemed "small and vulnerable."[74] As the months passed, a few well-meaning women tried to offer

---

* At Chavez's request, Matthiessen went to write a magazine article about a new labor strike unfolding in the Coachella Valley, where members from the United Farm Workers were locked in a bitter conflict with the International Brotherhood of Teamsters. "The day I arrived, a 300lb brutote, as the chicanos say, punched our priest," Matthiessen soon reported in a letter to Maria Koenig. "How am I to keep a quiet N. Yorker tone?" He didn't; the magazine article would never materialize. Instead, he committed to cowriting, with Glen Pearcy and Luis Valdez, the script for a pro-union documentary about the Coachella strike, titled *Fighting for Our Lives*. Directed by Pearcy, the film was nominated for Best Documentary Feature at the 48th Academy Awards in 1976.

him comfort—including Merete Galesi, whom Peter had become involved with for a while after shared grief and Zen practice drew them together. And this, in part, was why the family moved into Sagaponack for the duration of his absence in Nepal. Mab Goldman had been a fierce defender of Deborah's during her final years. "One of the things that prompted her to stay in that house with Alex," recalled Mab's daughter Diana, "was that she didn't want just any other woman filling in for Deborah so soon after Deborah's death."[75] Mab was furious at Peter for his many affairs, and she moved in the Goldman clan (minus her husband, Bo, back in New York writing the screenplay for *One Flew Over the Cuckoo's Nest*) to provide some familiar company for her late friend's little boy. Peter thought Mab was a nuisance who had needlessly distressed Deborah on her deathbed by stirring up drama, but the arrangement was convenient.

As an adult, Alex's impulse would be to defend his father when somebody objected to the treatment of his younger self in *The Snow Leopard*. "You can imagine how many times I've heard my father 'abandoned' me to go to Nepal." In his view, his father had been offered an "extraordinarily important" professional and personal opportunity: "I understand how he might have made the decision to go knowing that there was going to be a trade-off."[76]

However, there was a limit to Alex's understanding. "I could look back on it and be even more comfortable with the decision he made to leave me behind at that tender moment *if* he had done the work in those twenty months to help me process my mother's death, and to grieve properly and openly." Peter Matthiessen was the product of an old-fashioned WASP upbringing: nannies and emotionally frigid parents who led separate lives from their children. This inevitably influenced how he approached his own offspring. ("As a parent I am uncertain of myself," he would confess in his Himalayas journal.)[77] "I got a signal early on," Alex recalled, "that the way I could be most helpful in dealing with my mother's loss, for all of us, was to be the 'good soldier,' to move forward, to not dwell on it, not be upset about it, not make too much of it. The message I got was that it was not okay to feel sadness, or to feel pain, or to feel lost." This atmosphere of repression in the months after Deborah's death, rather than Alex's "abandonment" for Schaller's expedition, would become the bigger source of resentment when he grew up. Because Peter never did "the work that you need to do with a child in that situation," Alex would retain almost no memories of his mother.

Rue, being six years older, would remember Deborah vividly. But she had her own struggles with Peter around communication. While he told her about the events leading up to her mother's illness, their endless cycle of fights and reconciliations, Rue had the impression that he was shaping a narrative, telling himself a reassuring story about love. His selective version of events left her with questions, but they were difficult to ask given how "unpredictable" he could be. "He had to be in a certain sort of rare mood for these kinds of conversations and initiate them himself. And there had to be time."[78] With Peter so preoccupied with work, with sesshins every month, and with preparations for the impending trek, there was very little to spare for his daughter (who, as an additional burden, was also processing the sudden death of Clem Pollock, which had come just two months after Deborah's). In late summer, Peter bought a new pair of hiking boots. Rue watched as he went for a long, solitary walk each day along Sagg Main Beach, trying to break them in.

MATTHIESSEN'S FIRST HIMALAYAS JOURNAL was a lined, spiral-bound notebook with a green plastic cover. He made his first entry on September 10, when he departed Sagaponack: "Clean clear day: monarchs and goldenrod and roses + shining pine needles . . . Parting with A. at school: very painful. With R. at noon, as well." The parting with Alex, on Alex's first day in the third grade, left Peter feeling as though he had "a slight concussion."[79]

In the city, he stopped by the New York Zendo to say goodbye to Eido Roshi, who gave him a koan to ponder as he walked toward Shey Gompa, and who advised him to "Expect nothing" from his pilgrimage. "The Roshi rose from his black cushion and, taking me by the shoulders, touched my forehead three times with his own, then smote my back, and sent me on my way with a great shout."[80]

That evening, Peter had dinner with Maria Koenig. In his journal, he described the meal as "a graceful ending," but it was considerably more complicated than that. Maria had reappeared in his life sometime toward the end of 1972. She was still married to Julian Koenig, and still dissatisfied; Julian worked in Manhattan during the week while she lived out in Bridgehampton with their two little girls. Peter's interest in Maria had not abated since their aborted, unconsummated "relationship" of two years earlier, and he was now single. They started talking again shortly before Christmas. Then they started sending letters to each other, using a friend's postbox so Julian wouldn't catch on. In one letter, Peter wrote: "I do love you, M: we do everything so well except be together."[81] And so it remained throughout the winter, spring, and summer—until August, when Peter had begun nudging Maria to tell Julian the truth. "I understand what you must be going through," he wrote in another letter, "and my heart aches for you. I love you and I trust you, whatever you decide. (And the decision will come quite naturally if you will just let in a little air, just move—not precipitously, impulsively, but just enough to let life in.)"[82] Increasing the pressure considerably, he also told her that he would "put an end to 'us'" if she failed to act by the time he returned from the Himalayas. Effectively given an ultimatum—was it Peter or Julian she wanted?—Maria agreed it was time to make a choice. The lying was "horrible," and Julian, a decent man who just wanted different things, deserved better either way.[83] But Peter was not convinced she would actually do anything to upend her comfortable arrangement. If their dinner in New York was a "graceful ending," as he put it, that was because he assumed she'd choose to stay with Julian Koenig. Nevertheless, he would keep nudging her anyway. "I think of you there in those gold and blue days," he soon wrote from Italy, "and hope you are moving, whatever becomes of us."[84]

Italy was Matthiessen's first stop on his way to Nepal. He flew to Rome on September 11, then made his way to Polgeto, where he'd scheduled a few days of downtime with his lover Jane Stanton. Peter had not mentioned this salient detail to Maria when he gave her the ultimatum. Indeed, if Maria had known about the other woman, she would "never have left Julian," she later said, and the rest of her life would have looked very different.[85]

In Italy, Peter and Jane went hiking so he could keep softening his boots. They swam in the pool, drove to Orvieto together, and had a Tarot reading—"need to get things in order before dealing w. . . . relationships,"[86] he wrote about his cards. At some point, Jane borrowed his journal and scribbled "I love you" on several blank pages, so he would stumble across her message in the Himalayas and think of her.

After a week at Polgeto, he continued to India alone. Varanasi was an "ant hill of decrepit streets," but he was fascinated by the cremation ghats on the Ganges, the sight and stench of death amid so much vitality. On the outskirts of the city, he visited Sarnath, the deer park where the Buddha had preached his first sermon to five disciples, thereby founding the original Buddhist sangha. A few days later, Matthiessen made his way by train to Bodh Gaya, where Siddhartha Gautama is said to have attained enlightenment beneath the Bodhi tree. Matthiessen stayed overnight at a nearby hotel, then woke before sunrise to walk to Mahabodhi under "limpid stars." The mostly deserted temple was unremarkable, with a "wailing old man," he reported in a letter to Maria, "but the place has enormous power of an ineffable kind—I felt fulfilled."[87]

He arrived in Kathmandu in the third week of September. George Schaller was waiting for him at the Hotel Shanker, an enormous neoclassical palace that, until 1964, had housed the Rana rulers of Nepal. The men talked for hours, going over plans for all possible contingencies, and then walked to a restaurant for a welcome dinner with Jeffrey McNeely, a young anthropologist who was working on a two-year wildlife survey in Nepal's relatively unknown Arun Valley, between Everest and Kanchenjunga. McNeely began the dinner, which was soon joined by Charles McDougal, a tiger ecologist, by placing a plaster cast of a mysterious footprint on the table. One of the aims of the Arun Valley project was to collect scientific data on the yeti, a creature frequently sighted (according to reports) by local villagers.[88] Perhaps the survey might capture a live specimen: McNeely had worked as a night zookeeper in Los Angeles, and he owned a tranquilizer rifle with the "necessary drug," phencyclidine hydrochloride.[89] Of the nine-inch plaster cast, which had been made in the snow just outside McNeely's tent, Matthiessen wrote in his journal: "Schaller exclaims at similarity to mtn gorilla ... more marked even than in Shipton photo.* It now appears certain that a [large] unknown creature exists—bipedal—probably a relic ape."[90] A few days later, Matthiessen and Schaller dined again with McNeely, who was accompanied this time by Edward W. Cronin Jr., a zoologist and head scientist of the Arun Valley Wildlife Expedition. In his journal, Matthiessen wondered why the two men ("attractive, easy-going—too easy-going, perhaps") hadn't followed the yeti tracks that were allegedly made right by their camp: "I would have followed them even if I had to go down into that jungle on my hands and knees!" Here were the first written references to something that would soon become an all-consuming obsession, influencing decades of Matthiessen's work.

The rain was torrential in Kathmandu. Schaller busied himself with last-minute errands around town: securing a visa extension from the inspector general of police; visiting the scientific library at Thyssen House; buying tennis shoes for the porters, boots for the Sherpa guides, sleeping bags, wicker baskets, and food; hiring another guide in case Matthiessen decided to leave the expedition early via a plane from Jumla; finalizing arrangements with the team at Mountain Travel; and obtaining, most important of all, those official government permits that granted them access to Dolpo.

Matthiessen and Schaller talked constantly as they went about their business. Some of this chatter, as Schaller wrote in his own journal, was "really a way of testing each other, to get an idea how the other will suit as a companion, to convey subtly one's ideas and preferences, the way one wants it to be."[91] Schaller tried to make it clear that each man should set his own hiking pace. "Peter indicated that he likes to meditate alone sometimes in the morning, but I noted that camp gets going at dawn and afternoons are often quiet times. I indicate that everyone should be free to do as he wishes once

---

* In 1951, while on the British Mount Everest reconnaissance expedition, Eric Shipton and Michael Ward photographed some oddly shaped footprints in the snow that appeared to be 12.5 inches long and 7.5 inches wide, with a heel as broad as the toe spread. The photographs triggered decades of scientific debate about the possible existence of yeti in the Himalayas.

base camp is set up etc. In this way one tests without saying 'I want . . . ' or 'This is the way it should be.'"

On September 25, Peter wrote another letter to Maria. "[W]e are off tomorrow to Pokhara, 100 mi west, by Land Rover, and on Friday begin an estimated 18-day trek west and north into the secrets of the mountains. I'll scribble a p.c. [postcard] from Pokhara (which may arrive if no one steals the stamps), and that will be the last mail for a while. . . . I do wish you were here—you are so far away, and I don't know where you are or where you are going."[92] The same day in Kathmandu, he received a note from Alex full of heartrending comments ("The cat and the dog are great, but I'm going to be sad when they die"), which reaffirmed Alex's hope that his father would make it home in time for Thanksgiving.[93] Peter tucked it into his bag and tried to clear his head. The next day, from Pokhara, he sent a final letter to his brother that would give Carey Matthiessen the impression he anticipated death, whereas what Peter hoped for was "rebirth."[94] His postcard to Maria included a list of the birds he'd spotted since arriving in Nepal: doves, hoopoes, the Egyptian vulture.

Matthiessen was revolted by the squalor of Pokhara, its "bad sweet smells" and ditches filled with stagnant water and human excrement. He was glad to get moving on September 28. The expedition gathered on the edge of town beneath a giant fig tree: fourteen Tamang, Gurung, Chhetri, and Sherpa porters, four Sherpa guides, and two Americans. There were no errands left to run; everything was finally ready. They set out after breakfast on a crude foot trail, heading west beneath a sky full of gathering clouds.

PART III

1974–1990

A *medret*, painted on cloth in Shey Gompa.

16

At Crystal Mountain

> Somewhere in the Bheri Gorge, I removed my watch—the time it tells is so irrelevant to the time here. Also, my instinct is to let things go, to depend on less and less, to <u>accumulate</u> less, to tear away veils, to simplify, to <u>see</u>.
>
> —PM, Himalayas journal (1973)[1]

To reach Shey Gompa today is, by any measure, a formidable undertaking. You begin by flying from Kathmandu to steamy Nepalgunj, on the Terai plains near the border with India, and from Nepalgunj, in a twenty-seat Twin Otter that climbs into the mountains, to Juphal, where the airstrip terminates in a sudden drop.[2]

The village of Juphal is perched above the Thuli Bheri River in Dolpo. Follow the flow east for a few miles, and you come to a confluence with the Suli Gad, its glacial blue water merging swiftly into the Thuli Bheri's brown. The Suli Gad valley, which stretches into the north, is sinuous and deep, with wild rose and cannabis plants that grow so high livestock can disappear amid the green. More villages are scattered on the valley slopes—Parilagaon, Rahagaon—and these are reached by precipitous trails that sparkle underfoot with mica. Another trail runs alongside the river through settlements that are occupied during winter months, when people from higher in Dolpo, the Dolpo-pa, migrate down to escape the unforgiving cold. Further up the Suli Gad River, at Chepka, a tea house has tsamba, roasted barley flour, dabbed on the fire-blackened ceiling like a constellation of stars. In a forest of pines and silver birch, *mani* stones are hand-carved with prayers and mandalas. The valley narrows the deeper you go; bridges crisscross the torrent, and the path threads beneath sheer, dripping cliffs of granite. Then the valley opens out beyond a second river confluence, and the trail switchbacks up to the rim of an enormous natural dam where a waterfall, deafening, spills through a crack to create a plume of mist among the boulders far below.

At the top of the waterfall is Ringmo, a settlement of low, flat-roofed stone houses, of stupas and prayer flags snapping in the wind. Women crush chilies in stone mortars using enormous pestles the length of javelins; men plant fields with rows of potatoes. There is a Bon monastery here, Thasung Tsholing, filled with painted panels depicting Tonpa Shenrab and other enlightened beings. But the most striking sight at Ringmo is Phoksundo Lake, which legend says was created by a demoness to drown an older village of people who foolishly betrayed her. The Y-shaped lake, fed by glaciers, is twelve thousand feet above sea level, nearly five hundred feet deep, and an uncanny shade of blue—slate, azure, or turquoise, depending on the changeable light. The only direct way around it, given boats are forbidden by the Lama of Thasung, is an alarming path etched high in the cliff along the western shore. You must share this path with mule trains, pressing against the rock to let them pass, and while being mindful of debris loosened by blue sheep that graze on the slopes above. Eventually, at the far end of the lake, you come to a windswept marsh of gravel bars and bent willows: the Phoksundo Khola, a river the Dolpo-pa call *nyomba*, "crazy," because it shifts course unpredictably, washing away bridges during the wet season. From the Kanjiroba massif, high overhead, comes a thunderous boom of avalanches.

Several miles up the crazy river is a side ravine carved by another stream, the Tok Kyaksa Khola. Shockingly steep, the ravine demands a breathless climb past patches of snow in permanent shade. Once above the treeline, it widens out into a gray bowl of talus. The trail continues up, up, up, into silence and fog; icy peaks appear and disappear like hallucinations caused by the rarefied air. The Kang La sits at 17,550 feet—a mountain pass in clouds. At the very top, snow devils dance near a cairn adorned with dozens of prayer flags, some so aged they have lost their color and turned transparent.

The descent on the other side of the pass is sharp, and the trail plummets into a more remote world. A frigid stream snakes through land resembling Arctic tundra. This further valley is stark but lovely, with scrub juniper, wildflowers, snow pigeons. Soon there is a profusion of quartz everywhere: the aptly named Crystal Mountain looms to the west. The stream becomes yet another river, and the air thickens with the steady loss of altitude. Not far ahead is an assembly of red and white buildings on a desolate hillside. For a weary pilgrim, this comes as a miraculous sight—the first glimpse of what, since the eleventh century, has been a sacred place according to Tibetan Buddhists.

IN 1973 there was no airport at Juphal, and the landing strip at Dhorpatan, a village to the south of Dolpo over the Dhaulagiri range, received planes so infrequently that George Schaller deemed it too unreliable to be used as a starting point for the trek to Shey Gompa. The expedition set out on foot from Pokhara, "the last outpost of the modern world,"[3] because it seemed like the best of limited options.

Challenges began to present themselves almost immediately. The monsoonal rain was unrelenting, causing lengthy delays and leaking through Matthiessen's cramped and ragged tent. His boots, despite all efforts to break them in, caused painful blisters, and he tried walking barefoot; he also damaged his glasses and had to mend them with tape. In a Tibetan refugee encampment outside Dhorpatan, a vicious dog slipped its chain and attacked, forcing Matthiessen and Schaller to defend themselves with sticks and logs. The porters were slow—mules were uncommon in 1973—and more than half gave up and abandoned the expedition within the first two weeks. Finding replacement porters proved hard during potato harvest season, and when the Sherpas (who remained loyal) did manage to find some, the new recruits also left at the first sign of difficulty. Schaller was impatient: "If we cannot go north, then the trip is over," he fretted in his journal.[4] "My knees are sore," Matthiessen noted in his, "toes, too, and back."[5] Then there were episodes of snow blindness, sunburn, and troubling dreams: Alex as a fox, neglected in a cage and "covered w. grime." Schaller and Matthiessen had hoped to reach Shey Gompa in seventeen days, but they walked for twenty-one days before they even reached the edge of Dolpo.

And yet morale was rarely a problem for long, because just being on the trail was enough to lift the spirits into "exaltation." As Matthiessen would later write in *The Snow Leopard*:

> In the clearness of this Himalayan air, mountains draw near, and in such splendor, tears come quietly to my eyes and cool on my sunburned cheeks. This is not mere soft-mindedness, nor am I all that silly with the altitude. My head has cleared in these weeks free of intrusions—mail, telephones, people and their needs—and I respond to things spontaneously, without defensive or self-conscious screens.[6]

Just after he had left Sagaponack en route to Kathmandu, Merete Galesi had written him a note of encouragement: "Don't worry about anything or anybody . . . the only important thing now is you going into the mountains empty."[7] To go into the mountains like this, without ideas or attachments, demanded mental preparation that Matthiessen expressed as a physical purge. He asked Schaller to shear off his hair, taking it close to the scalp. He removed a Turk's Head sailor bracelet he wore out of vanity—"my (ego) wristband," he called it—in order to make new sneaker laces.[8] He took off his wristwatch, too, the day after they crossed into Dolpo (as Lewis Moon removes his watch just before surrendering to the Amazon jungle in *At Play in the Fields of the Lord*). To travel light brings "intense energy and exhilaration," Matthiessen later wrote. "Simplicity is the whole secret of well-being."[9] To simplify the self as a spiritual ascetic does—as Siddhartha Gautama did on his path to becoming the Buddha—Matthiessen shed the signifiers of his prior life and opened himself up to happenstance.

As they walked, Schaller scrutinized the slopes for wildlife. "The first data in a month and a half!" he exclaimed after spotting bharal near the Seng Khola.[10] Matthiessen, by contrast, scrutinized absolutely everything, turning himself into an undiscriminating camera. He kept a small notebook in his pocket to record quick observations; he then expanded these jottings into detailed journal entries when he found the time. This system was part of "a Zen practice of close observation."[11] His own looking, in other words, was a form of meditation. He chanted *Om* while he walked to keep himself "one-pointed" as he attempted to really *see* what was passing in front of him.[12] There was pleasure in paying attention to small things on the trail—an unknown feather, the leaf of a fern—but deep concentration was another way of shedding the ego.

In Duhnai, a village near the confluence of the Thuli Bheri and Suli Gad that acts as an administrative center for the Dolpo region, Matthiessen and Schaller showed their permits to a local member of parliament. With permission, they set off up the Suli Gad by way of the villages perched high above the river. "I long for the snow mountains," Matthiessen wrote. "And entering the gorge of the Suli Gad is entering still another world—worlds within worlds. A strange expectant atmosphere is intensified."[13]

In Rahagaon, the crude wooden effigies and dead crows, hung by their feet as scarecrows in vegetable gardens, made him think of the Dark Ages, as though the walk into Dolpo was a literal walk back in time. And this impression only intensified the further they went. In Ringmo, at the top of the waterfall by Phoksundo Lake, Matthiessen wrote a letter to Maria Koenig: "every day that we travel back into the Middle Ages is pure delight, especially so now that the monsoon is broken and there have been 8 days in a row of unbroken almost cloudless sky, and such a light, so clear, that everything seems an illumination, for there is <u>no</u> air pollution here, no motor sound of any kind for 3 weeks, not even distant airplanes, only these clarifying silences and mighty landscapes out of fairy tales—one understands at once why the Tibetans are so mystical."[14] Ringmo itself, nestled at the center of a crown of mountains, "is so much like a village in a fairy-tale that it seems enchanted," he wrote in another letter to Alex and Rue, "and I feel enchanted, too, as if

I had wandered into another century, or into a dream."[15] Admitting that he wouldn't make it home for Thanksgiving due to unforeseen delays, he told his children: "Oh, I miss you two so much, and I have had lots of time to think about you, and realize how proud I am, and lucky I am to have such beautiful children, and will try to do my best in the future to deserve you."

The confession implicit in this letter—that he did not deserve them as things currently stood—was in keeping with the ruthless self-critique of his journal. Just as Matthiessen studied the trail before him, he also studied himself, and the view inward was decidedly less picturesque. He flagellated himself for buying a blanket ("another thing, another burden"[16]), and for "clinging" instead of letting go and obliterating all thought. He struggled with mood swings, a loss of confidence at crucial moments, and guilt about his spiritual ambition. Despite his best efforts to shed ideas and attachments, and despite the exhortation of Eido Roshi to "Expect nothing," he was hoping for a revelation in the mountains.

On the cliffside path above the lake, Matthiessen was reduced by fear to shuffling on his hands and knees. Beyond the pass, Phoksundo Khola, the crazy river, reminded him of Alaskan wilderness. The expedition camped on a cold gray beach where the river empties into the lake. Schaller had expanded the team by hiring some new porters in Ringmo, but they soon proved so intransigent, complaining about the weight of their loads and requesting more money, that he and Matthiessen dubbed them "robbers"—a hostile response to what was likely a cultural misunderstanding. (The people of Ringmo were proud agropastoralists who were not used to carrying luggage for foreigners like pack animals; Schaller and Matthiessen might have realized this if they'd stopped to speak with them in their houses.) As the expedition turned away from the river and ascended the steep side ravine toward the Kang La, the Ringmo porters became increasingly uncooperative, until finally they shrugged off their baskets and quit.

The last push to 17,550 feet was "extremely arduous."[17] Weighed down beneath sixty pounds of lentils, Matthiessen staggered to the top through a gauntlet of soft snow. "Peter is disgruntled," Schaller wrote in his journal, noting that "the hard physical labor and high altitude is having an effect on him."[18] But Peter was disgruntled at George, specifically, who had pushed ahead with Jang-bu, the head Sherpa, to survey conditions at Shey Gompa and to try to find more porters, leaving his partner to deal with the fourteen heavy loads that needed to be carried over the high pass. "Where the hell were GS + Jang-bu?" Matthiessen asked himself. "Why [haven't] they come back today to help us instead of firing off all these silly orders?"[19] (Schaller had left a note with brusque instructions.) Eventually Schaller did return to help—without porters—and the remaining loads were ferried up in a marathon of sweat. One of these loads, dropped imprudently at the top by Phu-Tsering, another Sherpa, tumbled down the far side of the pass, only missing Matthiessen as he descended the near-vertical drop because he scrambled instinctively to the left. "As my feet go out from under me, I punch my stick through the crust in time to stop my slide." Spread-eagled in shock, he pressed his forehead against the snow, "gasping for breath."[20]

SHEY GOMPA, the Crystal Monastery, is defined by its solitude. There are few inhabited places in the world so cut off from even the idea of a road. Everything around the monastery is immense and ancient, and the monastery's location, out on a bluff, is entirely exposed to the elements, permitting no visitor to escape from a feeling of insignificance. The bluff is like an altar decorated with stupas, and next to the main temple is a walled enclosure filled with tens of thousands of prayer stones, many eroded smooth by centuries of snow. Thousands more mani stones are piled up by the rivers, or in great collections on the lower slopes of Crystal Mountain, placed there by pilgrims on a *kora*, or circumambulation, of the holy peak. There are more prayer flags and miniature stupas in the hills, and prayers painted directly onto the sides of cliffs, and water mills that turn prayer wheels when the torrent is high enough to flood a man-made channel. The entire landscape is praying with the mantra of Avalokiteshvara: *om mani padme hum*—roughly, "The jewel is in the lotus."

When Schaller and Jang-bu arrived in Shey on forward reconnaissance, they found it deserted for the winter except for two women with infants, who shut themselves in a house for fear the strangers were bandits. The monastery, too, was locked up and silent. Schaller was untroubled because "there were sheep about and I could do my study."[21] But Matthiessen had planned to consult with the Lama of Shey, who was part of the Kagyu sect of Tibetan Buddhism, notable for "spare teachings" that were strikingly similar to those of Zen. "[W]ith the lama gone there is not much for him at Shey," Schaller noted in his journal. After thirty-five days of hard trekking, how would Matthiessen pass several weeks in such an empty place?

One answer to that question was scientific research. Schaller was determined to document the mating behavior of bharal, which would allow him to establish whether this "blue sheep" was actually a sheep or a goat—despite its common name, the animal exhibited a confusing blend of characteristics from both and occupied its own genus, *Pseudois*. Matthiessen helped Schaller observe the bharal herds near the monastery using binoculars and a telescope, and he also hunted for signs of local predators, going so far as to build a makeshift blind in the hope of spotting a snow leopard.

But science took up a relatively small part of his day. And the lack of other things to do at Shey Gompa meant he had no choice, for long periods, except to *be*. Instead of growing bored, Matthiessen embraced this enforced repose; he liked, as he later put it, "the contentment of doing one thing at a time: when I take my blue tin cup into my hand, that is all I do."[22] He went searching for juniper to feed the campfire. He studied stupa frescoes of elephants and the Pleiades. He scoured gravel by the rivers for marine fossils. He wrote snatches of poetry as he warmed himself in a hut the Sherpas had turned into a temporary kitchen:

> black pot   three stones
>   fire shadows
> who is this, who smells the lentil soup?[23]

At dawn, Matthiessen meditated in his sleeping bag: "I perform complete Shobo-ji morning service, which ends about 6:45 as the rising sun brings a glow to the tent."[24] He also meditated at a rocky outcrop that he arranged into a small, open-air zendo, where he recorded "glimmers of the Void." In his journal he wrote: "I think I understand the Void, 'Emptiness,' much better now. These rocks + mtns, all this matter, even the snow, the air, fairly resounds. All is moving, full of power, full of light."

Walking toward Dolpo, Matthiessen had sensed whispers of something "paradisal" in the landscape. This was familiar language for him, and Shey Gompa, where the whispers led, was a familiar target for his longing. Like Punalu'u, or Quebrada Grasa, or Gidabembe, or the coral atoll of Astove, the monastery was another "island," in his idiosyncratic use of the word—a primordial retreat from which to escape a complicated life.

He was stunned by Shey: "the emptiness and quiet are all one could wish for."[25] Part of him came to dread the return to Sagaponack, "where life unravels in details, where voices echo with the starkest kind of loneliness."[26] To dwell in this hidden valley was to retreat from everything that troubled him. "Though we talk little here, I am never lonely; I am returned into myself." It was like being a child again, as he suggested in a journal entry written after seventeen days of camping near the monastery:

> For the first time in this life, I sense that I have lived other lives, and that one of them was here, so strong is the feeling that these mountains are my home. But perhaps I have "home" confused with childhood, and Shey with

a fairy tale, with its flags and mythic beasts and remote snowy fastness, and what I feel is pain at the loss of eternity, of innocence, and a way of <u>seeing</u> that has nothing to do with eyesight, that all of us lose early in childhood.[27]

Shey, as Matthiessen came to understand it, was a place where one could free the mind of encrustations, find stillness, and perhaps regain the same kind of perception that people sought through contemplative practices like zazen—a way of seeing "ultimate reality," the true state of things beyond the veil of our projections, where the "I," alienated and alone, falls away into an ever-present, ceaselessly transforming emptiness, *sunyata*, the Void.[*] ("When we're little, we're not separate from light. Light going through us, the birds, everything like that. We have no ego, let alone zip codes, and social security numbers. . . . We are just free in the universe.")[28] That mountains might offer such spiritual liberation, might "serve as a mirror to one's own true being,"[29] is hardly a new concept: pilgrims have been seeking themselves and the divine in mountains since antiquity, and certain peaks, such as Kailash in Tibet, are still considered by many to be the abode of gods. Matthiessen was walking a well-worn path by pursuing transcendence in the Himalayas.

Exploring north one day, he had an encounter with Karma Tupjuk, the incarnate Lama of Shey, who turned out to be living not far from the monastery in a cliffside hermitage called Tsakang. Tupjuk was fifty-two years old—six years older than Matthiessen—and immobilized by arthritis. His twisted legs all but imprisoned him in Tsakang, because the hermitage was reached by a forbidding climb. Yet Tupjuk seemed "very happy" with his hermit's life of solitary meditation; he presented as a "holy man of great directness and simplicity."[30] Despite his confinement in a canyon with no view of anything except cold stone and sky, Tupjuk had attained the kind of calm acceptance that Matthiessen could only dream about.

A hermit's life was not, however, one that Matthiessen seriously considered for himself in the mountains. Even as he waxed lyrical about Shey, he couldn't help but fret about the possibility that snow on the high passes might block his exit from Dolpo. He refused to open some mail from home—

---

[*] Concepts like "Emptiness" and "Void" are notoriously difficult to pin down—thus the opacity of many Zen teachings. Shunryu Suzuki provides a vivid analogy in *Zen Mind, Beginner's Mind*: "Before we were born we had no feeling; we were one with the universe. . . . After we are separated by birth from this oneness [i.e., emptiness], as the water falling from the waterfall is separated by the wind and rocks, then we have feeling. You have difficulty because you have feeling. You attach to the feeling you have without knowing just how this kind of feeling is created. When you do not realize that you are one with the river, or one with the universe, you have fear. . . . When the water returns to its original oneness with the river, it no longer has any individual feeling to it; it resumes its own nature, and finds composure. How very glad the water must be to come back to the original river! . . . For us, just now, we have some fear of death, but after we resume our true original nature, there is Nirvana."

letters from Alex and Rue, and from Maria Koenig—for fear they might disturb the "special atmosphere" by making him "cling to a delusion of security, of permanence," but his thoughts drifted constantly to family and friends. "Peter has often been restless since his arrival at Shey," Schaller observed. "Although he finds contentment and spiritual solace at this Buddhist shrine, a part of him remains tense. Perhaps because of the recent death of his wife he is anxious to return to his children."[31] Shey was an island of tranquility, but Matthiessen would not abandon his real-world commitments to remain there indefinitely as an aspirant monk.

On November 18, he walked with Schaller east along the river and up a trail into the mountains. At the summit of another high pass, they shook hands twice and said goodbye. Trying to express his gratitude for the opportunity, Matthiessen choked up: "As you know, I have been very very moved."[32] Then he and a few of the Sherpas pressed on, while Schaller returned to camp to continue his wildlife survey until December.

They parted on good terms. Still, Schaller penned a reflection in his journal that illustrates the extent to which he and Matthiessen had been searching for very different things at Shey:

> Peter is gone, and I am sorry to lose his companionship. A pleasant person, though at times a little hard to take when he is a "writer." He thinks rather that only "he" feels and sees the beauty of a place or notices interesting details. Only he notices the snow slopes seemingly moving in midday heat waves. Every little thing is verbalized, unique, worth noting. And he always assumes that I have not seen things—because I don't comment on it. Finally Peter noted—to him a revelation—that I'm more relaxed at Shey than on the trip. . . . Actually Peter relaxed just as much as I. In the beginning he did not want his photo taken; at Shey, he asked to pose or was happy to do so. . . . Basically, here, he was on a sentimental journey, contact with Buddhism, remembrance of his wife, and he was more interested in looking at the scenery than really [becoming] acquainted with the area. He came out to watch sheep with me several times but after half an hour became restless and wandered off to "meditate." Perhaps this was all to the good for with each doing "our own thing," we did not clash. . . . Nothing major came up, and considering our dissimilar characters, it was rewarding how well we got along.[33]

The two men would reconnect in America, those minor irritations that inevitably accumulate over a long expedition left behind in the mountains. Schaller was an early reader of *The Snow Leopard*, and they remained friends for decades.

YEARS LATER, Matthiessen would refer to Dolpo as a "hidden kingdom of the mind." His journey to Shey was meaningful because he was "able to achieve that precious simplicity."[34]

Given how long he had been fixated on achieving a simple life, Shey represented something of a climax for him. Unsurprisingly, the descent in altitude that followed as he trekked down via Saldang and another two mountain passes was mirrored by a psychological crash. He vibrated from giddy joy—"My life, my work, my children . . . How lucky I am, how lucky!"[35]—to sudden grief—"I hear myself over the rush of the great river: 'Annie [Deborah], I miss you! I miss you!'" Despairing, he asked himself if he had left the monastery too early. Had he squandered a once-in-a-lifetime opportunity? Was he "disappointed" that he did not "gain" more from the trip, solve his koan, and pierce the illusion of "birth-and-death"? He chastised himself for wanting too much: "Just be sound, light, be a wind bell, be here, follow my breath—all day."

Matthiessen reached the village of Jumla on November 29. The next morning, waking early to catch a plane from the Jumla airstrip, he found himself in a terrible mood. "All the things I looked forward to I now see in the light of their accompanying problems," he wrote in his journal, before forcing himself to express some tepid optimism: "But this will change in a day or so, I'm sure. The mail at K[athmandu] will resolve something, and I'll go ahead from there, I hope, without remorse, moment by moment, truthfully—it is better to be truth-full than be ([or] appear) strong."

But nothing was resolved in Kathmandu, where he arrived later that afternoon. Indeed, everything seemed to be very wrong. The bath in his hotel room had no hot water. The staff at Indian Airlines were all on strike, meaning the status of his next flight was uncertain. He agreed to meet Tukten, the Sherpa he'd most connected with during the expedition, at the giant white Boudhanath, yet Tukten never showed up at the famous landmark. And news out of America—the Saturday Night Massacre; President Nixon declaring during a press conference that he was "not a crook"—suggested a disturbing turn of world events. "Now I am back in civilization," Matthiessen lamented in the final pages of his journal, "and the precious stillness I held at Shey is dissolving in my hands."[36]

17

Fool Day

> He a wind coptin, dass de trouble. He a sailin mon, and he used to de old-time way. All his life he been ziggin and zaggin, he don't know how to go straight.
>
> —*Far Tortuga* (1975)[1]

THE DAY AFTER MATTHIESSEN landed back in New York, he met up with Jim Harrison, who happened to be visiting the city from his home in Leelanau County, Michigan. They went for lunch at a restaurant on Lexington Avenue, and Harrison, peering across the table with his one good eye, noticed something strange about his friend. Not only was Matthiessen's body fat whittled down to almost nothing after weeks of trekking in the Himalayas, and not only was his skin a craggy brown from high-altitude UV exposure, but he appeared to be floating free, untethered from the usual human concerns. As Harrison later explained it in a letter: "you had none of the thrusts, wires, struts, arrogances that attach me to this earth."[2]

Matthiessen and Harrison had been writing to each other for several years by this point. Harrison, ten years younger, had initiated the correspondence by soliciting Matthiessen's thoughts about wolves; they had then moved on to the subject of poetry in long, discursive letters that referenced everyone from Apollinaire to García Lorca. Matthiessen admired Harrison's work. He was envious of poetry as a form of literary expression: "I meant to ask you how you would start, what you would read, if you were sick of all the furniture of prose and wished to try writing a poem."[3] Harrison thought Matthiessen was "among the few truly great prose writers alive," and encouraged him to stick to what he knew: "the functioning 'world' of poetry is a greasball [*sic*] pom-pom nightmare of mediocrities. Avoided easily through other preoccupations. Which you have in incredibly rich excess. You also may avoid the banknote comedown."[4] (Harrison was often broke.) "I suspect you are right," Matthiessen had replied to this argument, "but I am so bleeding sick of all the words. I want to cut away and cut away, in all departments."[5]

In early 1973, eight months before the Himalayas expedition, Harrison had traveled out to Sagaponack to write a profile of Matthiessen for *Sports Illustrated*. If this wasn't the first time the correspondents had met in person, it was no more than the second or third. They had certainly never discussed Zen Buddhism before, because Harrison was unnerved—"afraid" was the word he used—by the upstairs zendo, the "tea and sitting room."[6] He didn't understand what Zen was about, and he refrained from mentioning it in his profile, which leaned so heavily on an image of the older writer as swashbuckling adventurer that Matthiessen, when he read a draft that summer, protested its abundant "machismo cliché."[7]

Now, over lunch in New York, Harrison could no longer ignore the question of spirituality. Matthiessen had obviously had a profound experience in Dolpo. He seemed transformed. Harrison "perceived something"[8] vital about his friend for the first time.

In the following months, Harrison felt compelled to pick up Shunryu Suzuki's *Zen Mind, Beginner's Mind*. He went sniffing through the writings of Dōgen Zenji, Hakuin Ekaku, Bankei Yōtaku, Dajian Huineng. He sat in improvised zazen "for eight months," he admitted in another letter, and "got so burned away I was quite surprised anything was left."[9] What explained such a spontaneous, intense curiosity in Zen? "The right level of desperation and thirst have to be reached," Harrison explained. "So [I am] up here stumbling with books instead of a roshi. Trying to choke pride to death every moment to stay a beginner. Have no one really to speak about these matters but it's probably good. Thought I was batty several times but accepted 'batty' and it passed. . . . How tentative the tired bull is about entering a pasture big as the world."

DESPITE HARRISON'S IMPRESSION of a man liberated from "thrusts, wires, struts, arrogances," Matthiessen's own account suggests a more torturous return to life in America. "I had expected," he admitted in some notes, "the great clarity and insights of my snow mountains samadhi to culminate in an enlightened state."[10] He had expected transcendence in Dolpo, not quite understanding that expectation ensured the breakthrough would never happen. ("Expect nothing!") Instead of enlightened, Matthiessen came back confused. Something, as Harrison noticed, was different about him; he was not the same person who had set out from Pokhara at the end of September. But it would take him four more years of introspection to sort through his thoughts and feelings about the time spent at Shey Gompa, to arrange the rough, unfocused material of his Himalayas journal into the narrative of spiritual understanding that is presented with such startling clarity in *The Snow Leopard*.

In the months immediately following the expedition, Matthiessen's emotional crash continued. His spirits wandered "in some low, dark place."[11] They sank even further when his oldest son, Luke, was diagnosed with retinitis pigmentosa, a rare degenerative eye disease that would eventually leave him blind. Matthiessen struggled in group sesshins at the New York Zendo, which he continued to attend with "fierce" determination: "There are no tears in sesshin any more, not even when I truly grieve for Luke, for Ho Ko."[12] And he struggled with solo zazen in Sagaponack: his sitting was "weak, without exhilaration." He felt unmoored in a house that resounded with so many echoes of the past. Alex looked to be in good shape, "cheerful as a bird" after his time in the care of Mab Goldman.* But Peter was like "a sick bird,"[13] and he went through "the vague, dim motions" of running a household and being a father with even less enthusiasm than usual.

In March, at a Matthiessen family reunion in the Yucatán, his despondency manifested as paranoia. Everybody drank too much, and he bickered with his sister, Mary, over something insignificant. "I thought I was the injured party, but it seems I was the monster—the story of my life," he complained in a letter to Maria Koenig.[14] Touring with his parents, siblings, nieces, and nephews around the Mayan ruins of Uxmal, he wrestled with an "old gut feeling" that he was "not really part of this group, and not much liked by it, either, except on principle." It was the same complaint he'd made as a young man at Hotchkiss; despite being nearly forty-seven years old now, he still fretted that his family "resented" him for being too sensitive.

Maria's presence sustained him through the gray winter and spring. Back in September, before he left Kathmandu for Pokhara to begin the trek to Dolpo, he had written her again about their complicated entanglement. "I've given up my serious hope that you and I can be together openly by the time I get home, and I say that with no edge—I do understand—but perhaps the 'frank talk' [between Maria and Julian] . . . will have taken place at last, for better or for worse—do let me know."[15] In fact, Maria had let him know in mid-October, in a letter forwarded to Dolpo: "You will be amazed, or surprised, to hear that finally I had my talk with Julian," she wrote. "After a night and a half of sleepless talk and going forever backwards, I am a bit

---

* Alex's eventful few months, with few rules and much anarchy, was later fictionalized by Serena Rathbun, Mab's daughter, in the short film *Nonnie & Alex* (1995). The film follows a lonely eight-year-old boy whose unnamed father, played by Matthiessen look-alike Stephen McHattie, has just departed on a long journey. Alex and his young friend, Nonnie (Serena's childhood nickname), attempt to come to terms with the recent death of Alex's mother. *Nonnie & Alex* was the directorial debut of Todd Field while he was a graduate student at the AFI Conservatory.

frazzled around the edges." She continued, "Julian is deeply shocked and unhappy, but not surprised. As you can imagine it is all painful and raw at the moment and we shall have to do a great deal of talking through all this. I don't know how it will end yet. I see that my letter is stilted and formal; but you will understand. I have to do a lot of holding in at this point."[16]

This tormented note was one of the letters Peter had decided not to open at Shey Gompa lest it ruined the "special atmosphere." When he did read it, on his return journey to Kathmandu, he was stunned to learn that Maria had acted on his ultimatum. "I still don't think it will come to anything," he wrote in his journal, "but perhaps her husband inwardly is relieved to have a bad marriage come to an end, and he will finish it off. And then? After a month away I knew I did not want to create more bad karma, there are children involved, and at heart I feel that M. and I might fight like anything, for we are headed in different directions at the moment."[17] This sounds like a case of sudden cold feet—"I must say my heart sank when I read her letter," he added—but Peter recovered soon enough. Come December, he had started putting pressure on Maria to take the next step:

> You are married to a good man who is careful to provide no good rationale for leaving, and you have security, and a social situation that you like; to fly in the face of "reason" requires a passion and a need, a distaste for compromise and a willingness to risk, a trust in intuition over common sense, that simply isn't there. On the other hand, its seed is there, you can't quite forsake your situation, a certain "hope of life," because to do so is to die in some way, and so you will put off a decision, a choice, as long as those around you will tolerate it. So far I haven't found the courage to act for us, though I did make the decision in September, you recall, that if we were in the same old stagnant place when December came, I would put an end to "us." And of course we are still very much in that place, you are even still guilty and nervous about being seen with me; the only difference is that Julian is more upset about things than ever.[18]

In January, Peter warned, he would "extricate" himself from what had become an untenable situation. "I have no wish to harm your family, your household, if it can be made to work." He loved her "very much," he said. He was not interested in anybody else—Jane Stanton, again unmentioned, had fallen out of favor since his return from Nepal. He dreaded life in Sagaponack without Maria, without them together: "But what we have isn't life."

With its tone of grim finality, this letter had proved to be the decisive nudge for Maria. She loved Julian Koenig ("I wasn't *in love*, but I loved him"[19]), and she was ashamed of the hurt she'd already inflicted: "possibly the worst thing in the world is hurting somebody <u>else</u>," she told Peter.[20] And yet, to pass up a chance at genuine happiness in favor of a marriage that was merely *safe* felt like too much of a sacrifice. She was only thirty-four years old, not ready to give up hope for a more fulfilling future. And so, at the start of 1974, Maria had chosen Peter Matthiessen. This time he was thrilled with her decision, which arrived like a match struck in the dark of his depression. "Darling Maria Eckhart," he scribbled on a slip of paper, using her maiden name as though the marriage to Julian had never happened: "Why aren't we having dinner together, and a lovely wine? (I'd even promise to stop laughing.) You are still a part of my body"—they were finally sleeping together. "I love you, I love you."[21]

THE FIRST MAJOR PROJECT that Matthiessen became involved with in 1974 was the International Dai Bosatsu Zendo. Just four months after his walk to the Crystal Monastery, he devoted himself to the construction of a new Buddhist monastery in the Catskill Mountains.

The land for Dai Bosatsu had been acquired by the Zen Studies Society in 1971. A *Kai San Shiki*, or "Mountain Opening Ceremony," had followed in 1972: Eido Shimano, standing with a hundred people before an altar in the woods, read out a statement to the "deity" of the land asking forgiveness for the "destruction and pollution of all rocks, trees, grasses and mosses" that would inevitably occur during construction.[22] That same year, Eido Roshi had accompanied Davis Hamerstrom, an American architect, to Japan, where Hamerstrom toured monasteries and temples to find inspiration for an original design. His blueprints for Dai Bosatsu sprawled over four interconnected buildings and some 26,000 square feet. The complex featured everything from a Zazen Hall (for meditation) and Dharma Hall (for chanting) to a sewing room, tearoom, dining room, library, workshop, and infirmary. With its scalloped roof and *engawa*, a kind of wood porch, the design paid tribute to Japanese tradition, but it was American where it needed to be: private showers were provided for the fifty men and women who could fit in a coed residential wing.[23] A construction plan had been signed in May 1973 with contractors from the nearby town of Delhi, New York. By that fall, sangha members had cleared a hillside overlooking Beecher Lake, while workmen had excavated a hole and laid the monastery's concrete foundation.

In March 1974, Matthiessen inspected a construction site blanketed with heavy snow. He was attending another sesshin in the lake house, and during rest periods he wandered through the frozen woods, practiced tai chi, and visited Deborah's boulder. Soen Nakagawa was in attendance again, and one evening he joined Matthiessen in chanting over the grave. ("Take good care of yourself," the old man advised his student during their private interviews, sensing Matthiessen's unsettled mind.[24]) At the end of the week, Soen Roshi concluded the sesshin by leading a purification ceremony for the open construction site. In his own journal, he wrote in Japanese: "The dream of an international DAIBOSATSU ZENDO is at last about to come true."[25]

When the weather grew warmer, Matthiessen returned to the Catskills and rolled up his sleeves. By June, the monastery walls were erected, windows were going in, and ceramic shingles adorned the shapely roof. He helped install fiberglass insulation, "a dirty job that is extremely satisfactory."[26] On another visit, he unloaded heavy planks of Tasmanian oak destined for the monastery floor. The imported oak was expensive, and he questioned whether the indulgence was strictly necessary. Shouldn't a Zen monastery be modest? Matthiessen's distaste for the wood put him at odds with Eido Roshi, who had no problem surrounding himself with opulence.

Another disagreement between the two men concerned a few beavers that had recently built lodges on Beecher Lake. Eido Roshi wanted them killed to ensure the monastery would be aesthetically perfect, with no gnawed trees. Matthiessen took the side of the beavers. Thinking ecologically, he told his teacher, "respectfully," that nobody had the right to eradicate *Castor canadensis:* "They were here long before we were, with the mountains and the deer, and we should be happy they have returned with our own arrival, since they will bring new life to the deep lake by creating beaver pools and swampy edges."[27] The author of *Wildlife in America* challenged a proud Rinzai master who expected deference. A clash of egos was certainly part of it, as Matthiessen himself would readily admit: "The unquestionable obedience taken for granted by all Japanese teachers is very difficult for Western students, at least those like myself who are not devotional by nature and tend to resist figures of authority."[28] But their conflict stemmed from a difference in values. What sort of place should Dai Bosatsu be: meticulously ordered, or quite literally fringed by wildness?

Eido Roshi was disgruntled. Matthiessen refused to yield. Others in the sangha shared his view, too, and one man even threatened to quit as a student if any animals were harmed. The beavers were ultimately spared, and yet the "beaver episode," as Matthiessen called it, would linger between him and Eido as unresolved tension, an early warning sign of "much more serious trouble already on the way."[29]

According to a document titled "Donors to the Dai Bosatsu Zendo," three individuals gave more than $10,000 each to finance the monastery: Dorris Carlson, whose millions had also paid for the land; Libby Holman Schanker, the actress and blues singer who had given money before killing herself in 1971; and "Mrs. Deborah Matthiessen."[30] The final name suggests two possibilities: either Deborah arranged a generous gift for the Zen Studies Society in the months before her own death, or Peter made the gift in her honor and memory. Either way, the initial funding was expected to cover most, if not all, of the considerable construction costs. But then an oil crisis in the Middle East—an embargo led by Saudi Arabia to punish countries that had supported Israel during the Yom Kippur War—drove up the price of gas, and thus everything else, to astronomical levels. Dai Bosatsu suddenly became far more expensive than originally anticipated. A financial report in late summer found a shortfall in the building fund of some half a million dollars. Eido Roshi, distressed, encouraged the sangha to chant the Diamond Sutra, which is about cutting through illusions. "It was the first time in the history of American Zen that the Diamond Sutra had been chanted," recalled Shinge Roshi (Roko Sherry Chayat). "We were doing it day after day so we would move through this financial impasse."[31]

To raise the necessary funds for Dai Bosatsu Zendo Kongo-ji, as it was soon renamed, members of the sangha organized a series of events in Manhattan, including a sale of calligraphy and tea bowls at a SoHo art gallery, and an "evening" (Noh play, haiku reading, a staged demonstration of zazen) at the Japan Society. But it was Matthiessen who secured the most substantial infusion of capital. Since 1969, he had served on a conservation committee for the New York Zoological Society at the invitation of Laurance Rockefeller, a philanthropist with passionate interests in wildlife preservation, national parks—and, as it turned out, Buddhism. Matthiessen met with Rockefeller (uncle to the still missing Michael) and convinced him to pledge $75,000 to Dai Bosatsu.[32] Rockefeller's contribution was enough to make the monastery habitable. His tatami mats, taken from his tea house in Pocantico Hills and offered as a gift, helped make it beautiful.

Meanwhile, Matthiessen, working alongside Myoku Margot Wilkie and Roko Sherry Chayat, put together an informational brochure to solicit other donations. With its translated passages from the Tao Te Ching, moody photographs, and stately portraits of the two presiding roshis, the brochure functioned as a kind of prospectus and mission statement. Rising in the forest of a beautiful mountain, Dai Bosatsu would stand, the brochure's authors wrote, as "a response to the spiritual yearning of modern man in the midst of a failing materialist culture."[33]

IN BETWEEN TRIPS to Dai Bosatsu, Matthiessen received word that he was being inducted as a member into the American Academy of Arts and Letters, in recognition of distinguished work that was likely to have a lasting impact on the nation's literature. This was a major honor—there were only

242 members in the Academy then, all elected for life—and he shared the news in a letter to Jim Harrison that downplayed just how pleased he was: "Joseph Wood Krutch must have left his chair unguarded by going and dying on us other natural historians or whatever."[34]* He let his true feelings shine when he told his family, as Luke recalled: "To be recognized by his peers would always mean more to him than critical acclaim or financial success, and the best had now anointed him as one of their own. He was proud, and I was happy for him."[35] Bill Styron was responsible for the nomination, or for seconding it, and Matthiessen was inducted alongside John Barth, James Wright, and Anaïs Nin.

The honor arrived at an interesting moment in his career. For the past nine years, ever since *At Play in the Fields of the Lord*, Matthiessen had published nothing but nonfiction. He made occasional mentions of his turtle novel in interviews ("a novel about a ship off the Nicaraguan coast"[36]), but a general reader could be forgiven for assuming he'd abandoned fiction in favor of sharks and shorebirds. Matthiessen, however, was just taking his time. The Grand Cayman project, which was based on material he'd held back from "To the Miskito Bank," his 1967 *New Yorker* article about Captain Cadie Ebanks and the *Lydia E. Wilson*, was a labor of love: "I had fun fooling with it, trying to make it work, trying to make the pieces resonate."[37] In March, after years of tinkering in tandem with journalistic projects, he had finally sold the promise of a manuscript to Random House. And when the news came through about the American Academy, in May, he was putting the finishing touches on a draft for Joe Fox. "I scarcely believe it," he added in his letter to Harrison. "It's a lot better than when you read it"—Harrison and Styron had been given sneak previews—"but I could put another year or two on it if I didn't sense I was hurting more than helping."[38]

The plot of *Far Tortuga* is relatively straightforward. In the spring of 1968, Raib Avers, a grizzled, gray-haired fifty-four-year-old sailing captain from Grand Cayman, finds that the industry which has defined his working life is now in a death spiral. Grand Cayman has been colonized by tourists, the wildlife is vanishing, and his ramshackle vessel, the *Lillias Eden*, is "de last of de old-time sailin fleet"[39]—the last of the top-sail schooners that once scoured the Caribbean for valuable green sea turtles, also increasingly rare. Raib is suspended between the old days and "de modern time," and the *Eden* reflects his discomfort. In a bid to fend off the inevitable, he has recently paid to have her converted with a diesel engine, but the job remains incomplete.

---

* Joseph Wood Krutch, the prolific drama critic, biographer, essayist, and nature writer of the Southwest, was elected to the American Academy of Arts and Letters in 1954. He died in 1970.

As one of the crew complains, "Since she got dose masts cut short, de *Eden* is ass over backward. All de riggin slack—you risk your neck just to climb up to de crosstrees."[40] Yet Raib is willing to risk his neck if it means sustaining himself in the face of so much socioeconomic and technological change. He is willing to risk the seven men (plus one stowaway) who submit to his command, too. They set out toward the Miskito Cays off the coast of Nicaragua. It is April, very late in the season to be hunting for green turtles, and the trade winds are unnervingly strong. "Dis is de worst April dat I remember!" Raib tells the men, giving voice to his gnawing desperation. "Take a fool to be a turtler!"[41]

"April Fool Day, mon."

"Dass exactly how I would express it—Fool Day! Every goddom day is Fool Day!"

Far Tortuga—the working title was "Fool Day"—follows the *Eden* as she sails between reefs and cays and outposts. The men work, then relieve one another from watch duties; unappetizing meals of rice and johnnycake are shared around the makeshift galley. Two catboats are launched, nets are thrown, a few stray turtles are hauled in to be stored upside-down on their shells. But much of the novel is concerned with what *doesn't* happen—the failures, disappointments, and foiled ambitions that drive the *Eden* further into the wilderness.

Matthiessen's main subject was not green turtles, or even an industry succumbing to globalization; it was the ways men contend with the ineffable power of an ocean on which they find themselves adrift. Raib (not so far from "Ahab") "confronts the empty sea."[42] His crew peer over coffee cups at "a great fire flow where the corona clings to the horizon."[43] They are often looking out across the stern, or down into the fathomless blue depths. But then a gale gathers force; the weather turns tempestuous. "The hull squeaks and bangs with strain. Where the ocean crashes on the reef, wind and waves are lost; there is no time, no space, but only the chaotic rush of the dark universe."[44] Then the men avert their eyes. They cower from their own smallness, "lie still in their berths." As the voyage progresses, they see omens everywhere—a shooting star, a wisp of cloud—and read them for meaning like tea leaves on a saucer. *Far Tortuga* is filled with the reassuring tales men conjure up to navigate the unknown when they're "way out on de edge . . . of de world."[45]

Raib is an experienced seafarer, but his voyage is doomed from the start. As Matthiessen once explained to a reader, "[Raib] will lose because he is a romantic who clings to the old ways . . . not only because the old ways seem to him more dignified and even honorable but also because he has great flaws of character, being proud, stubborn, and arrogant."[46] He pushes his increasingly uncooperative crew to search for Far Tortuga, an island at the aptly named Misteriosa Reefs. Far Tortuga appears on no nautical map, and while it is allegedly a turtle breeding ground kept secret by the old-time turtlers, it is also slightly unreal: a pastoral dream pulled briefly into existence by Raib's obsessive attempt to maintain control of his life, which is blowing away, as he laments to one of the men, on "Dis goddom wind."[47]

The climax is stunning: a moonless night, an invisible reef, a "shriek of twisting timbers,"[48] the *Eden* slipping beneath the waves with most souls still aboard. Yet what makes the novel so memorable is the *way* it is written:

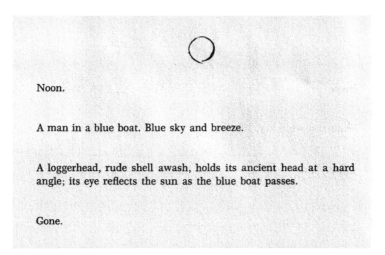

Noon.

A man in a blue boat. Blue sky and breeze.

A loggerhead, rude shell awash, holds its ancient head at a hard angle; its eye reflects the sun as the blue boat passes.

Gone.

All the furniture of the prose has been removed: transitions, connective tissue, conventional paragraphs. What remains is an assemblage of images, described with minimal embellishments and no sentimentality, like the flat, lean stage directions of a script. On other pages with dialogue, all of it written in various British West Indian and Honduran dialects, the speech is set off from third-person narration, without attribution: no "he said" or "she said," and no names, so it is not always clear who is even speaking. Words on a page can be physically scattered like fish, or arranged in the vague outline of a man, or inset to represent a seascape. Similarly, when characters speak in the wind, their voices shred into fragments: "By Jesus Christ it had blowed   not less den sixty-knot wind   blowed de hairs out of ye."[49] When characters whisper behind the captain's back, their voices are lower, literally smaller: "Raib treat dat poor woman so bad, she so scared of him, she don't know if she comin or goin. And dass de second wife, y'know—wore out de first one."[50] The text is punctuated by abstract drawings that resemble a setting sun, a bright star, swelling waves. And there is an enormous amount of negative space on each page; some feature only a few words ("first light"), or a single name with an ink splotch surrounded by white, to indicate a death. The cumulative effect is something like the poetry of Stéphane Mallarmé ("Un coup de dés jamais n'abolira le hasard"), or Ezra Pound, or modern concrete poetry—or something peculiarly Matthiessen; sui generis.

Far Tortuga was "the most exhilarating book I've ever written," Matthiessen said.[51] It was also the novel he discussed in the most detail, including in a dedicated *Paris Review* "Craft of Fiction" interview, conducted by George Plimpton as a favor to promote the novel's release. In every discussion over the years, Matthiessen's rationale for the unusual style remained consistent. What had struck him so keenly during his time aboard the *Lydia E. Wilson*, back in 1966, was "the stark quality of that voyage, everything worn bare by wind and sea—the reefs, the faded schooner, the turtle men themselves—everything so pared down and so simple."[52] It was not minimalism so much as the spareness that interested him: "A sense of the spareness and the fleeting quality of our existence."[53] When a thing was "pared down" to its elements, it seemed to reverberate with cosmic significance. "When you really pay attention to this moment," Matthiessen explained, "it just expands and expands and expands. And all the mystery is there. You suddenly see that mystery that's hiding behind everything."[54] As a writer, the possibility of capturing that spareness—and thus "mystery"—was why he felt compelled to translate the *Wilson* voyage from nonfiction into fiction: a straight report for *The New Yorker* would never allow him to evoke the "grit and feel of this present moment, moment after moment, opening out into the oceanic wonder of the sea and sky."[55] A magazine article could *tell* a reader, but how could it *show* spareness, make the reader feel it? As with *Under the Mountain Wall*, the impression he wanted to re-create demanded a more experimental approach.

The bones of Matthiessen's source material are still visible in *Far Tortuga*. Raib Avers and the ill-equipped *Lillias Eden* are clearly modeled on Cadie Ebanks and the *Lydia E. Wilson*; in an early draft it was "Raib Albury Ebanks." Other characters—Junior "Speedy" Bodden and Miguel "Brown" Moreno Smith—share the exact same nicknames, characteristics, and ambitions as real people Matthiessen encountered in Grand Cayman. Much of the novel's chronology corresponds to the weeks he spent sleeping on the *Wilson*'s deck; the turtle netting scenes are virtually identical to what he witnessed firsthand. The novel takes a hard turn into hallucinatory fiction, during the approach to Far Tortuga, right after Vemon is left on the dock at Bragman's Bluff, which is another name for Puerto Cabezas in Nicaragua—the place where Matthiessen himself disembarked the *Wilson*. Additionally, many of the stories the crew recount of shipwrecks and Obeah and ghostly black dogs were actual stories that he was told or overheard, which is why they sound so authentic.

Matthiessen had made audio recordings during his visits to Grand Cayman. He listened to these until he internalized the speech patterns of the seafarers. "I knew I couldn't write the book I wanted without hearing the language in my head night and day, for years," he said, although hearing it was not enough: "finally, you have to speak it, and writing *Far Tortuga* was like speaking it directly onto the page."[56] The sailors' dialect was almost "Chaucerian," and he noticed that each individual was "singing a song"—had tics and favored phrases that made their voice distinct. This determined the approach he used to craft dialogue for his characters, listed in a crew manifest near the start of the novel. A man like Speedy has a handful of refrains ("Modern time, mon"), which resurface so often that a reader, or so Matthiessen hoped, can identify who's speaking by words and cadence alone. "[The men] finally get fixed on one idea of what their life meant, or didn't mean, how it failed, or how it succeeded, and they don't much move off that spot. So what they're singing is a series of variations on the same theme throughout the book." Each voice is granted one or more solos, which fills in background and gives the character depth, but they're also part of the *Eden*'s chorus, harmonizing and clashing, "rising and falling . . . like waves." The dialogue, despite being frequently coarse, especially in the racism of Caymanians toward Jamaicans and "de domn Spoonish" Hondurans, used by them to establish and enforce social rank, has the deliberate quality of music.

When it came to the novel's form, Matthiessen was inspired by the concision of screenplays (and no doubt poetry, given his laments to Harrison). This made *Far Tortuga* a radical departure from *At Play in the Fields of the Lord*, a book as rhetorically lush as the Amazon jungle. To emphasize the spareness, Matthiessen eschewed metaphors and similes, which, he suggested, only insert a layer of abstraction between a reader and "the thing itself"[57] while also drawing attention to the presence of an author. He often thought about a cockroach's antennae, "these two extraordinary, delicate mechanisms," peeping out from the shadows of a ship's galley and catching the rays of the sun—"that light, and those things, to me is the echo of eons of evolution."[58] Who needed similes and metaphors when you already had something so evocative? Notably, one simile does exist in the published version of the novel, though: "A shadow in the eastern distance, under a sunken sky, like a memory in the ocean emptiness."[59] This sentence describes the first appearance of Far Tortuga, meaning the language becomes abstract, moving away from the thing itself, at the exact moment the *Eden* sails into what Matthiessen once described as "a mythical childhood place."[60]

As for the use of negative space on a page, he offered an elegant justification. "In Japanese *sumi* painting, in a drawing of a bamboo stalk, the brush moves upward, leaving a white space between strokes to suggest the nodes of the bamboo that separates sections of the stem; it's the emptiness that brings the rest to life. Similarly, the emptiness and silence represented by white spaces set up reverberations in what is written."[61] There is more than a little Zen in this explanation, but Zen was a strong influence on Matthiessen's process for *Far Tortuga*. Although he began writing before he even became involved with the Zen Studies Society, most of the work happened when he was fully committed to meditation practice. In fact, during zazen he sometimes found himself so distracted by "exciting insights" about structure that he asked Eido Roshi how to control his "creativity."[62] Eido Roshi advised him to embrace it, saying (as Matthiessen paraphrased in a letter): "Be entirely one with that activity, make it your *zazen* until rest period, when you can take notes and empty your mind of it for the next sitting period." This is how he managed to complete the manuscript while attending sesshins at Dai Bosatsu.

The earliest surviving fragment of "Fool Day," before it became *Far Tortuga*, is written in Matthiessen's LSD journal, and likely dates to sometime in early 1969. The fragment shows him playing with the arrangement of sounds ("bang") and dialogue ("What he doin?").[63] A full early draft, probably the same one mentioned to Jim Harrison in May 1974, gives a more detailed illustration of how he then refined the novel into its finished form. Most of the changes were cuts. There were originally dozens of similes and metaphors in the text. George Town looked from offshore "like a toy village." Brown was as still as "a giant growth on the blue oil drum."[64] These were removed, along with narration that commented on a character's feelings. Matthiessen preferred to show feeling through action: "Raib, half-smiling, is enjoying the discomfort of the crew" became, in the final version, "Raib, half-smiling, nods at Athens, who cannot meet his gaze; seeing the discomfort in the faces of his crew, he laughs aloud." Other details were excised to heighten ambiguity for the sake of mood. A white mass trailing the *Eden* was unquestionably a whale as first conceived; in the published book, it could well be a mirage. Several stories, like the sinking of the *Majestic*, were originally told by the crew in different, less thematically impactful places, and there were alternate endings that Matthiessen considered and discarded. In one, Raib abandons the *Eden* in a catboat to head for Far Tortuga; in another, the galley catches fire and the *Eden* burns.

But the most significant changes have to do with typographical layout. For example:

> White sails, white clouds, white morning sky.
>
> He's dead, Papa!

This, from an early draft, is fairly unremarkable. In Matthiessen's final version, however, a blazing sun looms over an immense white emptiness, silent until a small voice cries out in shock. The page contains very little, but that is exactly the point: Jim Avers is dwarfed on the surface of the ocean (in the bottom corner of the page), beneath the "white morning sky." Yawning space, combined with terse language and a simple pictogram, fosters an impression of loneliness, dread.

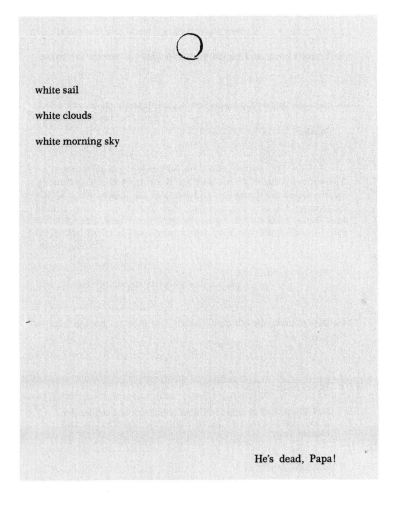

Far Tortuga is an unlikely accomplishment: the story of Caymanian turtle fishermen, written in dialect by an American WASP under the influence of Japanese Zen. It should not work, and yet it is humorous, elegiac, empathetic, and respectful, a testament to the research Matthiessen conducted and to the years he spent crafting his characters and their "songs." That its experimental, uncompromising nature can make it a challenging read probably goes without saying. As Jim Harrison once said, "It's never going to be an accessible book, any more than Melville's *Billy Budd* is."[65] When *Far Tortuga* was published in May 1975, the magazine editor Terry McDonell, a big fan of Matthiessen's work, rushed out to get a copy. "I could not wait, and I ran to my bookstore, and I bought *Far Tortuga*, and I took it home, and I opened it up, and I began to read, and I said, 'What the fuck?'"[66]

A NUMBER OF CRITICS had a similar first reaction. Thomas R. Edwards, writing in *The New York Review of Books*, sniffed at what looked suspiciously like "'poetic' self-consciousness," and wondered whether the novel was "some sort of Caribbean minstrel show."[67] But then he actually read the book and found it "enthralling." There were sentences that moved toward "the eloquence of Homeric or Old English epic," and dialogue that sounded "like the product of an acute ear and not of a superimposed literary sophistication." *Far Tortuga*, Edwards concluded, "is an adventure story of great purity and intensity, worth comparing to the best of Conrad or Stevenson."

After critics worked through the bewildering opening pages, the novel elicited remarkably extreme reactions. At one end of the spectrum, *Kirkus* called it "a sublime work of intense humanity."[68] Similar praise arrived in *The New Yorker*, *The New Republic*, *Texas Monthly*, *Newsweek*, *Time*, and *The Wall Street Journal*. In *The Atlantic Monthly*, Edward Weeks, the editor who had published Matthiessen's "Sadie" back in 1951, saw the book as a promise finally fulfilled: "Peter Matthiessen has lived with the potential that at some time he would write an exceptional novel. This is it. In its impressionistic form, with its humor, its melody, and its drama, *Far Tortuga* is a sea story the like of which I have not read since *Lord Jim*."[69] At the other end of the spectrum, the revulsion was equally extravagant. Anatole Broyard was withering in *The New York Times*. "Usually, an author who employs 'undeveloped' or 'primitive' people in fiction reaches for the humor or the 'poetry' in them, but I found very little of either," he wrote, declaring *Far Tortuga* "an unrelieved bore," especially compared to *At Play in the Fields of the Lord*, which Broyard had adored.[70] Going even further in *The Washington Post*, Larry McMurtry labeled the novel "drastically, indeed fatally flawed," and said it was filled with "a species of dialogue that is so bad that it completely destroys the book's credibility."[71]

Matthiessen bristled at "smart-ass critics."[72] And he found the *Washington Post* review unethical: McMurtry had a novel coming out (*Terms of Endearment*) that could theoretically compete with *Far Tortuga* for awards. But Matthiessen was reassured by the number of reviews that were, as he later recalled, "so excited and so good."[73] He liked to point out how many of the best came from other writers who, the implication went, actually knew what they were talking about: Edward Hoagland, Peter Benchley, and Robert Stone loved *Far Tortuga*. Arthur Miller sent a letter saying that the tragedy of Raib, the way he was broken by the world, reminded him positively of Ulysses.[74] "It is sonorous music you are making," Bill Styron said in his own note, "and I thought you brought it off beautifully. It's also quite unique, you know, a real original, and enormously haunting. I can still taste the sea and the wind."[75] Even Thomas Pynchon, whose *Gravity's Rainbow* had only recently been denied a Pulitzer Prize, emerged momentarily from wherever he was hiding to offer a rare endorsement: "I've enjoyed everything I've ever read by Matthiessen, and this novel is Matthiessen at his best—a masterfully spun yarn, a little otherworldly, a dreamlike momentum. . . . It's full of music and strong haunting visuals, and like everything of his, it's also a deep declaration of love for the planet."[76] In future years, Don DeLillo and Saul Bellow* would add their names to the list of admirers.

However, there was one reader who, much to Matthiessen's chagrin, felt far more ambivalent about the book: its editor at Random House. Almost all the editorial correspondence about *Far Tortuga* is now lost, but what little remains suggests that Matthiessen was not entirely joking when he described Joe Fox, in the book's acknowledgments, as an "adversary."

By the time Matthiessen sold *Far Tortuga* in March 1974, he had parted ways with Diarmuid Russell as his literary agent, largely because Russell had annoyed him with his "smug assumption that he is entitled to one tenth of my income simply because he leads a moral life out in the country."[77] Matthiessen was now represented by Candida Donadio, a chain-smoking, Brooklyn-born, Sicilian American with a tight bun and a penchant for colorful language. Donadio was renowned as a "grande dame sharky agent,"[78] but she was also motherly, adept at handling difficult male clients: Thomas Pynchon, John Cheever, Joseph Heller, Nelson Algren, Philip Roth. Mat-

---

* In January 1986, while Matthiessen was traveling in Zaire, Maria found herself seated next to Bellow at a New York dinner hosted by some friends. When Bellow figured out who Maria was, he turned to her and said of Peter Matthiessen: "Oh! I'm a great fan! I recently read *Far Tortuga*—terrific book." Maria dutifully reported this exchange in a letter dispatched to Africa, adding, "Naturally I beamed & blossomed in reflected glory." (Not only was she married to Peter by that point, but *Far Tortuga* was dedicated to her.)

thiessen trusted Donadio to get him a prime deal—he once watched her tell an attorney during negotiations, "We like you but we don't love you. You are not our brother!"[79]—yet *Far Tortuga* was beyond even her abilities. Joe Fox was not convinced the novel was commercially viable. Later, Matthiessen would claim that Fox "hated" the book, that he was "very offended by it,"[80] which was almost certainly an exaggeration; but the surviving contract suggests Fox did accept it only out of a sense of obligation to a valuable house author. The financial terms were not particularly favorable: an advance of $7,500, which was half what Matthiessen had received a decade earlier for *At Play*.[81] As a concession, Fox agreed to a royalty rate of 15 percent on hardcover sales—high, "but he thought we were only going to sell three hundred copies, so it wouldn't cost Random House anything," Matthiessen said. "He thought he'd pulled a fast one on me."[82]

The editing process was unpleasant. Fox petitioned Matthiessen to include name tags for the dialogue, but Matthiessen gruffly refused. Internally at Random House, Fox described Matthiessen's style as "obscure,"[83] and made biting reference to "typographical headaches"[84] for the book's designer, Kenneth Miyamoto. Matthiessen was perpetually dissatisfied with the layout, which messed up, as he put it, his "whole, exact choreography of space, language, time, and so forth."[85]

The book hit the *New York Times* Best Sellers list in June 1975. Random House was blindsided by the good reviews; there were not enough copies to satisfy demand. As Matthiessen recalled it—and this is perhaps unreliable—the second and third print runs were still too small, and Donadio had to pester the publisher to finally order a decent number. To make matters worse, Fox also came to Matthiessen and "tried to change the deal."[86] The advance had been insulting, Fox allegedly admitted ("we were unfair to you"), and Random House wanted to make things right. But they would need to take "a couple of points" back on the royalty percentage rate to do so. Matthiessen believed that Fox was getting heat from his bosses over the contract terms: "He'd blown it." This is impossible to corroborate, but whatever was said, Matthiessen and Donadio declined to renegotiate. When it came to *Far Tortuga*, Fox "was wrong. I felt he was wrong. And he was *very* wrong."

Few people could nurse a grudge like Peter Matthiessen. He never shook the suspicion that Random House had sunk his novel with its neglectful publication strategy. The book sold well but not exceptionally in the end, was nominated for no major awards, and soon slipped into an obscurity at odds with its achievement. (It would be adapted for screen by the writer-director Jonathan Demme but never produced because of the complexities of filming at sea.) A decade after publication, still brooding over the book, Matthiessen attended a dinner at Joe Fox's house. "There were eight of us," Fox once told the writer Michael Shnayerson—"he was at one end and I was at the other, and just as my wife was bringing the first course on, Peter said, 'Oh Jo Jo, did I tell you? Jason's just signed me up to do Men's Lives.'"[87] This celebratory announcement, like presenting a cake full of razor blades, was Matthiessen's way of telling Fox he was out as his editor, replaced by Fox's own boss, Jason Epstein. "It was so wildly inappropriate. I just gaped at him—I was stunned."

Another decade later, in 1995, Joe Fox attended a Thanksgiving dinner at the Matthiessens' house in Sagaponack. After the meal, Peter walked him out to the driveway to say goodbye. Twenty minutes later, Peter then returned inside to the table where Maria (long since married to him by this point) was sitting with their few remaining guests. He announced that he'd just had the "most awful row" about *Far Tortuga*.[88] Maria was aghast: "Peter, it's Thanksgiving!" She forced him to phone Fox, who lived just down the road, to offer an immediate apology. Matthiessen, whose apologies often included a reiteration of the perceived crime ("I am so sorry to have said those awful things, but . . .") went to the bedroom for another twenty minutes, and then returned to announce that he'd "made it worse."

Six days later, on November 29, 1995, at the age of sixty-nine, Joseph M. Fox died of a heart attack while resting on the couch in his office at Random House. Matthiessen was filled with remorse. Was he somehow responsible with his ridiculously long-running feud? Fox's children convinced him to set aside his reservations and speak at the memorial. In a prepared speech, Matthiessen quoted from the acknowledgments page in *Far Tortuga:* "we have been through hell together." He added, "I guess we were still in hell at the end, but he was [my] long-time friend of fifty years."[89]

18

Anthropology of the Unknown

> I felt that all my life, all my training and experience, had somehow been a preparation for the experience of Bigfoot, whose being seemed to draw into itself almost everything that intuitively I knew. And this was why Maria was a little worried: there was a discrepancy in my belief in the people I was working with and my belief in the something-unknown beyond; she felt that perhaps I wanted that too much, and was doomed to some profound disappointment in regard to life itself that I might not be able to cope with.
>
> —PM, Untitled bigfoot manuscript (c. late 1970s)[1]

HEMINGWAY MEETS the Dalai Lama," is how the filmmaker Susanna Styron liked to describe Peter Matthiessen—a perennial outsider "wrestling with the universe in some way."[2] But when the spirit possessed him, he could also be a generous uncle slipping money to a niece who had run off with her boyfriend to live in a van. He could be "Pete Pot," as his nephews nicknamed him for his penchant for smoking. He could be a surrogate father figure, stepping in to counsel Tom Styron when Bill proved incapable. He could be whimsical, dancing in front of Rue's friends to the Jackson 5's "Never Can Say Goodbye," an interpretive movement he called the "spidey." He could be so amusing at dinner, the observant raconteur, that he won the whole table over to his side. When he focused on somebody it was "like the sun comes out," said his friend Myrna Davis. "He could be very seductive, because he was so attractive *and* attracted."[3]

These were the kind of qualities that endeared him to Maria Koenig. Throughout the years she would make lists of other traits, too, as if to remind herself why she had chosen Peter over her husband.

In a poem: "There is a dryness, a dedication, / A purity, / An enviable discipline."[4]

On a scrap of paper: "Curious combination of manly achievement, responsibility, on-timeness. . . . [He] exercises—his body is beautiful, works ever so smoothly. I can never believe he aches, or groans, or hurts."[5]

During a speech she once gave, somewhat reluctantly, at the Sun Valley Writers' Conference: "He is delicious looking, has a sly, quick wit, and just when you are ready to throw in the towel because of his singular self-absorption, he is disarmingly self-deprecating. He also has good teeth and a lovely smile. All in all he is an interesting person to live with."[6]

MARIA VICTORIA ANTONIA KOENIG, née Eckhart, the woman who would live with Peter Matthiessen for the rest of his life, had a background very different to those of his first two wives. Both her parents were German, living in Heidelberg. But because her mother was also Jewish, they fled the Third Reich and moved to Tanganyika sometime around 1935, only to find that their relatives there—the ones who had invited them over in the first place—were Nazi sympathizers and anti-Semites. Gottlieb Eckhart, Maria's father, rode away on a horse to find somewhere more tolerant for his family to settle; this is how they ended up in Moshi, near Mount Kilimanjaro. Moshi may have been more accommodating to Jews, but as the world inched toward World War II, Germanness itself became a liability in Tanganyika, which had been ruled by the British since the end of the Great War. Maria's mother, Gertrude, refused to enter the British-run hospital to have the couple's fourth child for fear the staff would discriminate against her. Gottlieb, a doctor, delivered Maria himself on March 9, 1939. The first few years of Maria's life were spent in an internment camp, also British-run, set up for German settlers at a place called Oldeani. While living there, Gottlieb exposed a plot by the camp pharmacist to poison all the prisoners. Then he joined the British Army, having been deemed a "good German" by the camp administrators, and was dispatched to India. After the war ended, he returned to his family in Tanganyika to work in a different camp for Polish refugees, who had also fled from the Nazis in Europe. Maria had a Polish nanny, and she could soon speak German, Polish, English, and Swahili. Gottlieb was terrible with languages, so he would summon his daughter into his office to act as a translator for patients, who found themselves addressing a five-year-old girl.

At six, Maria was sent to boarding school in Arusha. It was an unusual childhood. One day an impala doe the girls had been nurturing for months was found "speared through its neck / in the changing cubicle / of the swimming pool," as Maria later recalled with a shudder in one of her poems.[7] A Maasai man brought her milk every day from her mother at the farm—ten miles each way on foot.

Maria's world, the settler community in Tanganyika, was almost exclusively white: all-white school, all-white club, "all-white everything."[8] The first time a Black African who was not one of the servants stepped foot in the family home was a momentous occasion. Gottlieb sat the children down and told them that a new doctor was coming for lunch, so they needed to behave. This landmark meal turned out to be uneventful—Dr. Kafamba was "perfectly delightful," although he refused, it later transpired, to allow Black patients into his own car. Gottlieb took them in his Land Rover instead.

When Maria was still a little girl, her parents divorced, and Gottlieb remarried. Gertrude, always prone to depression, committed suicide when Maria was thirteen—too young, she was told, to attend her mother's funeral. The loss was a defining trauma, and Maria reflected on it in a note written in 1976:

> She loved us as much as she could—she just couldn't stick around for the long haul. I remember well that feeling of wanting to please her too—to make her laugh, to light up her dark, sad eyes—and she gave back plenty—all she could, that was not embroiled in her insecurity, in her Jewishness—in being thrown out of her country for a freak of birth, in seeing her relatives killed, in living in a primitive country that didn't make sense to this woman who had had centuries of European culture—the rich, dark, antimacassared, stuffy, stultifying life of the rich, but stupid, bourgeoise.[9]

Being "abandoned" by her mother, Maria once told Peter, made her "an emotional refugee (and the circumstances of my life have made me even a physical one)."[10] Unlike Peter with his WASPy milieu, she had no fixed background to rebel against. "It is too dramatic, too scattered, too dark, too haphazard. I have to sit quiet in order not to unleash the whole mess."[11] Her way of coping was to steel herself, assuming a demeanor of unflappable stoicism. Privately, she also created "a metaphor for my past and future . . . An ideal or dream-self." She would measure her actual self against this dream-self and "wallow in the discrepancy."

At the time of Gertrude's death, Maria was boarding at the Kenya High School for Girls, in Nairobi, which local boys liked to refer to as the "heifer *boma*," or cow pen.[12] (Their school, the girls retorted, was the "cabbage patch" because of "smelly boys.") After graduating, she moved to England to attend the Oxford and County Secretarial College. But a job as somebody's assistant was not enough for her: "I wanted the big time."[13] By the age of nineteen, she was modeling in London, a profession she found degrading. Maria was astonishingly beautiful, with the bone structure of actress Merle Oberon, yet she had come to see her appearance as shameful, even slightly repellent. "Like all women who attract men easily, I always hoped that it was really because I was interesting or funny or both," she once told the poet William Merwin. "I always wished I had another way to be successful in the world. Certainly I used my looks to my advantage, and again, was always rather ashamed of it. In addition I was immensely self-critical about my looks. Not unusual in women."[14]

Success proved elusive as a model. To pay the rent, she went to a temp agency and looked through the Rolodex to find any job that was not secretarial. She ended up in television, selling time slots for advertisements; then she worked for a company *buying* time slots for advertisements—a promotion. Because so few women were doing this kind of "men's work," and because she was good at it, obsessively disciplined and organized, she was recruited by an upstart American ad agency, Papert, Koenig, Lois, which maintained an office in London. Instead of a model, Maria found her place as a media buyer at PKL responsible for millions of dollars, with two secretaries of her own.

Julian Koenig, the boss, was already a legend on Madison Avenue, having written the "Think Small" campaign for the Volkswagen Beetle in 1959. ("It takes a licking and keeps on ticking": also his, for Timex.) One day on a visit to the London office, he walked up to Maria's desk. "Will you marry me?" he asked.

"No," Maria said.

"Well, will you have lunch?"[15]

Then she married him. She was twenty-seven. He was forty-five.

Julian relocated Maria to New York, where they lived in the Plaza Hotel for three months until they found a satisfactory apartment; they were staying on the fifteenth floor during the Northeast blackout of 1965. It was an exciting start, and Maria expected the thrills to continue. She had given up her job to be with Julian: PKL didn't need more media buyers in America. "She thought she would be this New York hostess," said Antonia Koenig, their first daughter, born in 1966.[16] But Julian detested parties. He said he would rather die than see his clients outside the office. His primary interests were "smoking cigars, going to the racetrack, and worshipping Groucho Marx." The only people he wanted to see were the same friends he'd made as a boy on the Lower East Side, or at Camp Greylock (where he plausibly claimed to have invented thumb wrestling)[17] when he was fourteen years old—older Jewish men who now had grown children of their own. Maria found herself pushing a pram to the park and sitting there alone. "I became the sandbox nanny, while all the other mothers were chatting to one another," she recalled. "I would watch boys put sand in my sweet little daughter's mouth, and I couldn't stand it, really."[18] Making matters worse, Julian expected to be mothered as well. "I saw him as a father figure because he was eighteen years older. And then it turned out that *I* was in charge, and that disappointed me." Trying to make her happy, Julian bought a house in Bridgehampton so she could escape from a city she didn't like very much. Yet the underlying issue remained. "She had in mind a different kind of life," said Sarah Koenig, their second daughter, born in 1969. "I remember my dad saying something like, 'She wanted a salon'"—the kind frequented by literary figures and artists. "That was her ambition. She wanted to run a salon."[19]

Peter Matthiessen, just a mile down the road from Bridgehampton, held out the possibility of that different kind of life. He represented exotic travel, constant adventure, friends who were writers and film directors. More importantly, he seemed to offer a chance for Maria to shrink the discrepancy between her actual self and her idealized dream-self. She felt improved when he was paying attention to her. "You look at me and say / 'You are beautiful' / And I believe you for a minute," she told him in a poem.[20]

After Maria chose Peter over Julian at the start of 1974, she spent the next year in limbo, still living in Bridgehampton while she tried to convince her husband to file for divorce. Julian was devastated—her choice amplified neurotic insecurities he had about his own masculinity—and he held on to hope that she might change her mind. Antonia, now eight, sided "ferociously" with her father, which meant that she was "awful to Peter and Mom," as she recalled, "although they sort of deserved it. But Mom told me later that Peter admired me for it."[21]

As Maria wrangled with Julian, she was also negotiating with Peter about their future together. It soon became clear that it was going to be a more complicated arrangement than she'd anticipated. One day, they were cycling to the beach. "He said, 'Maria, you know, I've been married twice. And now it's the Seventies, and I don't want a conventional marriage, I want an open one.' I said, 'Well, what does that mean? You sleep with people and I sleep with people?' He said, 'Not *you!*' Like that. And I laughed so hard, I nearly fell off my bicycle."[22] Peter also laughed, and the conversation was dropped, but he was telling her something serious about his attitude toward monogamy.

In the spring of 1975, Maria accompanied him to Captiva, Florida, where his parents now owned a Spanish-style villa on a bayou near the Gulf after years of visiting the island for vacations. Maria observed him interacting with Matty, then took notes in a vacation journal: "The father is young-seeming, discreet, charming and skillful, and very amusing. He is complex and ambivalent about his son. P [is] a little stiff and ungiving—very polite. I assume they understand all those unspoken things about each other."[23] She kept notes on her own interactions with Peter, too, expressing how uncertain she was in her new role as his significant other: "Peter so happy and child-like. He gets up in the morning—very early, and creeps about and gazes out at the moon.... I am torn between leaving the man alone, or weakly wanting to be with him.... I am a little confused about how much attention or communication we can afford each other." Too much attention and he was liable to explode in an ornery outburst: "Peter and I quarrel, and I lie on the bathroom floor and wonder how I am going to get through the night. He says grimly, 'I won't stand for this for 30 years.'" Just as he could comfort her "whole being" with a touch of his hand, he could tear her to pieces with his tongue. "Words used as bludgeons," she wrote in another poem, before mimicking his voice:

> No hobbies, no interests, no contribution.
> What, in Buddha's name is your contribution?[24]

Maria was committed, but Peter made it difficult. He seemed uncertain, despite the ultimatums, about what he wanted from their relationship. One day in May, he phoned Bridgehampton and said he needed to talk. They arranged to meet on Rose Hill Road in Water Mill. Peter turned up wearing tennis whites. "He didn't like to waste time," Maria recalled. "He was going to play."[25] He said to her, "I can't do this. It's too much for me, the children and all of that." Maria was stunned. She fell silent. Then she went home to think. Soon afterward, a letter arrived from him that said something along the lines of, "You didn't fight very hard for me." He had underestimated how steely Maria could be in the face of adversity. "He must have known how I felt. I had already split my family in half." Yet because she didn't cry or plead at Water Mill for him to reconsider his decision, he was filled with self-doubt—actually, maybe he *did* need her.

Maria, Antonia, and Sarah moved into Sagaponack at the start of June 1975. Alex, having mostly lived alone with his father since Deborah's death, was beside himself with excitement. Rue, who spent most of her time at boarding school, had no idea what was happening. Antonia brooded unhappily. Sarah, too young to understand, asked Maria when they were going home to Bridgehampton.

The house was catastrophic: an overgrown garden, ugly rattan furniture, Indelible Ink staining all the sheets because Peter liked to write in bed. Maria set about fixing everything. Her strength of will was transformative. "When I take hold I make a very good show of it," she once reminded herself in a note. "People are impressed, or irritated, or overwhelmed by my toughness, my efficiency, my matter-of-factness, my outspokenness."[26] But these traits would help her endure the many challenges of living with Peter Matthiessen, who soon told Anna Puharich that he was now "domiciled with someone;

she has 2 lovely kids, and so there is a real household here again, and we are happy, well, and frantic, but it's great for my children, and me, too."[27]

JUST WEEKS BEFORE Maria and her daughters moved in, Matthiessen's work had begun to turn in a surprising new direction. Here is how he explained the shift in an untitled, unfinished manuscript of several hundred pages that nobody, not even Maria, knew he had written until after he died:

> In May of 1975, while working on an account of a foot journey I had taken with George Schaller across the Himalaya to the Tibetan Plateau, I received a letter from a stranger in California that read in part, "We have found Bigfoot. We have his location pin-pointed. . . . We can produce a skull." . . . As it happened—and this was the first of what was to become a long series of intriguing events—[Douglas] Blue's letter arrived as I was finishing my notes on evidence of the yeti in Nepal . . .[28]

Matthiessen was working on *The Snow Leopard*. More specifically, he was working on sections of the book where he digresses into speculation about the yeti. These sections would confuse (or amuse) skeptical future readers, but he included them because he believed the natural world was full of unfathomed mysteries. He had a longstanding interest in cryptozoology, the search for, and study of, unknown or extinct animals whose existence is disputed—a tiger in the Amazon; a heath hen in New England; an ancestor of the great white shark, swimming the seas as a living fossil—and the yeti was within the realm of scientific possibility.

Back in Kathmandu, Matthiessen had been fascinated by the plaster footprint Jeffrey McNeely made in the Arun Valley, not to mention McNeely's coauthored paper (with Edward Cronin Jr. and H. B. Emery), "The Yeti—not a Snowman," in the peer-reviewed journal of conservation science, *Oryx*.[29] While walking in Dolpo, he had then witnessed a "dark ~~animal~~ thing slip behind a boulder," as he wrote in his Himalayas journal; he had allowed himself to wonder if the "thing" was a yeti.[30] It helped that George Schaller was open to the possibility of an elusive relic ape hiding somewhere in the mountains. Matthiessen valued Schaller's opinion (best summed up as, "It's hard to prove something *doesn't* exist"),[31] and the hard-nosed field biologist, rather than snuffing out the spark of his friend's curiosity, helped fan it into a wildfire. Soon after Matthiessen departed Shey Gompa to head home to his children, Schaller had managed to gain entry into the locked monastery when someone turned up with a key. Inside, he discovered a painting on a large piece of old cloth: a hairy female hominid, bipedal, arms outstretched, surrounded by native animals like the wolf and blue sheep. Schaller had sketched the figure into his field journal, then copied his sketch into a letter to Matthiessen, where he labeled it "yeti."[32*]

Matthiessen was conducting a comprehensive literature review on the yeti, reading testimonials by explorers and primatologists, when the other letter arrived from a "stranger in California" about bigfoot. The timing was serendipitous, Matthiessen wrote in his manuscript: "It was hard not to take this as a sign that I should pay it some sort of attention."[33] If the yeti, sometimes derisively called the Abominable Snowman, was a Himalayan mystery, then bigfoot, also known to some as Sasquatch, was an equivalent mystery of the North American woods. The setting was different, but the essential details were the same.

The letter's author, Douglas Overton Blue, or Swami Atmatattwananda, was a Vedantist monk of the Ramakrishna Order who lived at a temple in Hollywood. He had decided to write after reading a profile of Peter Matthiessen in *Time* magazine; he recognized the name from his own time at Yale, and perhaps, Blue reasoned, the "naturalist-writer" might be a good ally. Like Blue himself, the letter was secretive bordering on paranoid, but it offered a few enticing crumbs. Blue mentioned potential "expeditions." He claimed his goal was to publicly reveal the existence of bigfoot, which he described as a kind of pre-Adamite man, while also safeguarding the creature from untrustworthy characters who might try to exploit it. "He was treating it like a military mission," recalled Hans Teensma, who was a twenty-four-year-old art student at California State University, Long Beach, when he met Doug Blue around the same time this letter was sent. Blue told Teensma what he told Matthiessen: "It's all about protecting the creature. You can't talk about it. You can't say where it is. We need hard evidence. We need to bring that evidence to the powers that be, to protect it."[34] Blue wrote and spoke with the charismatic conviction of a television evangelist.

Matthiessen read Blue's letter with a red pen in hand, underlining the reference to a bigfoot skull. Then he wrote back requesting more information. The floodgates opened. Between May and September, Blue sent at least

---

* In May 2022, I inspected the same cloth painting in a hidden room at Shey Gompa, where it has remained untouched for decades despite a devastating robbery at the monastery in 2015. A lama, Tenzin Choekyap, explained that the animals depicted on the cloth are "livestock of the deities." The hairy female hominid, which he called *medret*, has been sent by a deity to "monitor" the environment—to protect the mountain landscape as a guardian. Belief in the medret remains relatively widespread in Dolpo. Dorje Budha, a resident of Ringmo, told me he'd recently spotted one in the high alpine meadows. This medret, Budha claimed, was orangish-yellow, about four foot high, with elongated arms. He insisted it was *not* a bear, and other people in the camp at Phulbari, on the Ghyampokapawa Khola, supported him, attesting that they had also seen the medret. Budha had taken a photograph of the creature's footprints in mud using his smartphone, but the image to my eyes was inconclusive.

seventeen follow-up letters.³⁵ Matthiessen was invited to become a founding member of something called the "International Society for Research and Preservation of Bigfoot." A few letters discussed bigfoot's theoretical home range of Montana, Idaho, Washington, Oregon, California, British Columbia, and Alaska. Others considered evolutionary biology: was there a familial connection to *Homo sapiens*? Blue said yes. One letter even came with a sighting log kept by Blue's associate in the field, a man named Tom Willhoite. On July 25, 1974, for instance, a creature had allegedly knocked Willhoite down and backward some twenty feet.

Matthiessen, in his few written responses to Blue that survive, was comparatively restrained and cautious. The sightings log was "cryptic," he wrote noncommittally, though "I am fascinated, to say the least."³⁶ He ventured an opinion: "On the basis of my pseudo-scientific prudence and unscientific instinct I tend to agree . . . that the Himalayan forms [yeti] are probably not human; if Bigfoot is human, as you believe, then more than one species appears to be involved."³⁷ But what he wanted was the evidence: tape recordings, photographs, and a look at that skull, still exposed to the elements in Northern California.

For much of the summer, Matthiessen told nobody about his correspondence with Doug Blue. He monitored the fortunes of *Far Tortuga*, arguing with Joe Fox and complaining about Random House to Candida Donadio. He did a reading with Truman Capote to support the Marine Museum in Amagansett, sneaking out back to smoke a joint beforehand. He attended a Fourth of July celebration at George Plimpton's beach house, an event so enormous it featured in *The East Hampton Star*: "People streaming past lugging thermoses of martinis, hampers of pate and pastrami, coolers of daiquiris, Hammacher Schlemmer picnic tables. . . . Peter Matthiessen sails by and shouts that he's got another party first but he'll be back to help with the fireworks."³⁸

Before the end of summer, though, Matthiessen had signed a memorandum of understanding about who would receive credit—and payment—for the discovery of bigfoot if he published on the subject.* And then he'd scheduled an expedition to Northern California. This small gamble, through a "long series of intriguing events," would eventually lead to him writing *In*

---

* "I, Peter Matthiessen, in consideration of the best efforts of Tom Willhoite to provide me with the location of the creature known as Bigfoot, will try to take photographs, either motion picture or still or both, of said creature. All such photographs, both negatives and prints, will become the property of Tom Willhoite, to be released at his discretion only, at the time or times he designates; and we will split the (net) proceeds of such photographs in the following manner: 51% to me, Peter Matthiessen, and 49% to Tom Willhoite. In addition, the (net) proceeds of any first book I might write, with international rights including those on derivative material in other media, such as magazine articles, TV and motion pictures, will be similarly divided. . . . I also agree not to reveal the information given to me by Mr. Willhoite until it is officially released by him."

the Spirit of Crazy Horse, Indian Country, a trilogy of novels about the Florida Everglades, which he rewrote as the single-volume *Shadow Country*, and another novel, tentatively titled "Just at Dark," which he was tinkering with as late as 2010. In other words, the yeti and bigfoot were unlikely catalysts for the books that would define the rest of his career.

Before he left for California, Matthiessen went to see William Shawn at *The New Yorker* to ask for the magazine's financial support. As he wrote in his manuscript:

> From behind his huge desk in the corner of the building, with the flat bare city sunlight firing his ears, Mr. Shawn's round, kindly face gazed upon me with great sadness. Then he nodded in acquiescence, and he sighed. "If it was anybody but you, Mr. Matthiessen . . . I'd say No immediately. If there are three things I do not believe in, and have no patience with, they are U.F.O.s, the Loch Ness monster, and this 'Bigfoot.'" In his emphasis on this word, I detected a slight shudder of profound distaste. Nevertheless, Mr. Shawn underwrote this journey and another, and no doubt would have gone even further had I not ceased asking after that first year and found ways and means to pursue all my researches on my own.[39]

IN MID-SEPTEMBER 1975, Matthiessen flew west to San Francisco, and then north to Eureka, to meet up with Doug Blue's man in the field, who was working on a gold-dredging operation somewhere along the Klamath River. Sitting in the plane, Matthiessen looked down at "deep coastal fogs, the darkness of the raining mountains," and was "struck hard" by the "strange nature" of his quest.[40] He carried a new spiral notebook of 160 pages—the first of six he would fill over the following few years with thoughts and observations about bigfoot, and with searching questions to himself such as, "Where am I going?" and "Dread Bigfoot—why such a terrifying idea?"[41]

At a bend in the Klamath River near the town of Weitchpec, he met up with Tom Willhoite, who was accompanied by Hans Teensma, the art student Doug Blue had recruited to the cause. Matthiessen joined the two men in an inflatable Zodiac, and they motored upstream at sunset, then made their way by flashlight through dark trees to the gold-dredging camp.

Teensma had arrived several days earlier and been put to work on the rig. "I was in a wetsuit, hooked up to a hookah, in this raging river, drawing this giant suction hose, picking up rocks, and looking out for what they told me were dangerous sturgeons," he later recalled.[42] Matthiessen found the young man "exceptionally pleasant and polite, in the cool, ironic, tolerant style of Southern California."[43] For his part, Teensma was immediately drawn to Matthiessen as "a sane person, a person that I actually could talk to, because everybody else was a character out of a movie."[44] Tom Willhoite, for example, had spent time as a Green Beret, as a member of the United States Army Parachute Team, and as a clown in the Ringling Bros. Circus. Now thirty-eight, he had a black beard that was graying in patches, his hair was tied back with rawhide, and he wore a necklace of jade, shells, teeth, and bear claws given to him, he said, by a "spiritual leader" of the Karuk people.[45]

According to Matthiessen's notes, Willhoite claimed to have read none of the published literature about an undiscovered hominid in North America: "since he had personally observed these creatures, which the experts had not, he had no wish to clutter up his research data with their preconceptions."[46] Willhoite told Matthiessen that he had first seen the creature while prospecting for gold near Blue Lake, between the Eel and Russian Rivers in California. This was back in 1959—just one year after Gerald "Jerry" Crew, a worker for a local logging company, had famously found monstrous footprints near Bluff Creek and then posed with a plaster cast for *The Humboldt Times*. In the sixteen years since then, Willhoite said, he had spotted so many creatures while camping in the forested mountains, and at such close range, that he had twice been assaulted and opened fire "in panic and anger." As for the skull that Blue had mentioned in his original letter to Matthiessen (the carrot that lured the writer into correspondence), Willhoite said he had stumbled across it in a cave, where wildflowers were strewn about like at some kind of burial site. But now he'd forgotten the exact location. Maybe he could find it again with a little sniffing around Bee Mountain.

That first night, Willhoite let loose a "cascade" of stories by the campfire. "I must own," Matthiessen later wrote in the manuscript, which was based on his notebooks, "I found almost all of them enthralling; having come so far, I did not care as yet to ask the hard questions that were already occurring."[47] Wanting that evidence, however, he was anxious to begin investigating at the earliest opportunity. "Well, what are we going to do tomorrow? Where are we going to go?" Teensma heard him asking.[48] But Willhoite was committed to the dredging rig and refused to be rushed. To kill time, Matthiessen helped out a little, swam in the river, and snacked on wild grapes. "And then we realized things were a little crazy," Teensma recalled. "There were a lot of personality conflicts in the camp. I missed the shooting. What I heard is that somebody shot a toilet seat out of somebody's hand." Art Hammond, another rig operator, got into what Matthiessen would describe as "a foolish, dangerous, and very disagreeable confrontation" with Willhoite, who pulled out a .44 Magnum and fired at his colleague, though the gun jammed.[49] Teensma had already left to go back to school, and Hammond fled for his life.

The remainder of Matthiessen's notes about the short, chaotic expedition are both predictable and peculiar. Any intriguing detail that he pointed out to Willhoite—a foot-shaped depression in sand; a high-pitched squealing sound like a twelve-tire truck barreling around the curve of a mountain canyon—Willhoite automatically credited to bigfoot, while making comments like, "He looks kind of like the bark of them big trees, just standing there behind it, standing there watching you."[50] The man's willingness to ascribe *everything* to the creature made Matthiessen "uneasy," because it indicated a lack of critical judgment.

Eventually the gold-dredging operation was suspended, and Matthiessen accompanied Willhoite deeper into the forest. On the far side of Fish Lake, near Bee Mountain, they left the car to make camp by Serpentine Creek. Matthiessen's wariness only increased: "While chopping wood, [Willhoite] kept stopping to listen, and finally he said, 'Something is watching us; can you feel it?' I felt nothing at all, and said so."[51] This continued at another camp, then at a third, and the trip began to look like a waste of time. But Matthiessen wanted to believe he was on the right track. A rock thrown out of nowhere, a scent of ammonia on the air, prints that were "not so easy to dismiss"—perhaps they augured something significant just beyond the edge of his comprehension? One day he was possessed by an eerie feeling, "a great ringing . . . that made it impossible for either of us to eat our supper or even to sit still." This sense of "nameless apprehension" left him energized because it seemed to hint at a secret still waiting to be discovered here. Yet a feeling was not a sighting, not real evidence, and certainly not something he could offer up to *The New Yorker*.

A week later, back home in Sagaponack, Matthiessen wrote a muted assessment of the expedition in a letter to Doug Blue. "I suspect I am less suggestible and more critical of 'evidence' than most people that Tom takes into the woods, although we did find a half dozen or so weathered prints, in different locations, that Tom deemed 'highly probables'—and that impressed me very much, I must confess."[52] He cautioned Blue that his friends needed to be "impeccable in their methods," and more vigilant against "anything that might seem to be publicity seeking, sensationalism, or just plain campfire bullshit." Willhoite was far too credulous to convince the average person, let alone an expert like George Schaller. But maybe it didn't really matter how accurate Willhoite was being "moment to moment, in the linear Western sense," because there was still an "inner truth" to his stories about something inexplicable in the woods. Here Matthiessen was repeating, in a new context, his familiar argument about the ability of fiction to evoke an "intuitive absolute truth."

He explained his position to Doug Blue. And then wrote something that illustrates how completely Zen had infiltrated his thinking. Tom Willhoite "can't <u>show</u> me BF any more than a Zen roshi can <u>show</u> me satori; when I am ready, I shall see."

IN ONE SENSE, at least, Matthiessen did see bigfoot that fall and winter, and then repeatedly throughout the next year. The creature was a cultural fixation in 1975 and '76. It appeared in an advertising campaign for Canadian Club whisky, and in a double episode of *The Six Million Dollar Man*, looking, as Matthiessen quipped, "like God with His eyes rolled back, as if struck blind by human folly."[53] The "Sasquatch" earned its own page in the new *Washington Environmental Atlas*, a serious publication put out by the U.S. Army Corps of Engineers. In a sober, thoughtful article for *The New York Times*, Boyce Rensberger asked what everybody was wondering: "Is it Bigfoot, Or Can It Be Just a Hoax?"[54]

Before flying to California, Matthiessen had read "most of the serious material on BF," meaning books by the likes of John Napier, a British primatologist and paleoanthropologist who had set himself the unenviable task of disentangling "what is rational from what is irrational in current monster stories."[55] After the camping trip with Willhoite, Matthiessen now began to amass his own compendium of stories, many gathered through phone interviews that he documented in his notebook:

> Talk with Geraldine Watson, in Big Thicket [Texas]: around turn of century, her uncle Joe Simonbee, building r[ail].r[oad] thru Thicket, saw big brown hairy man who came each evening to firelight. This story confirmed many years later by another old timer who worked on r.r but did not know "uncle joe."[56]

At a literary conference in Salt Lake City, Matthiessen spoke with the young writer Howard Norman, who had recently earned a master's degree in folklore after spending years working with Arctic and Subarctic First Nations people in Canada. Matthiessen asked Norman, who would become a good friend in the years ahead, if the Witigo, or Windigo, a supernatural being that appears in the stories of multiple First Nations groups, might possibly be "a variation on 'Bigfoot.'" Norman thought not, but Matthiessen was intrigued by the idea that the creature he sought might have older names and identities in Indigenous knowledge. He struck Norman as "deeply curious and wonderfully obsessive" as he talked animatedly about "the sheer possibility of a primate other than human in North America."[57]

In early January, Matthiessen met up with George Schaller at the Bronx

Zoo, where they looked at the snow leopards together before going for lunch. ("Their luxuriant smoke-gray coats sprinkled with black rosettes convey an image of snowy wastes, and their pale, frosty eyes remind me of immense solitudes," Schaller later wrote of the enclosed animals.)[58] Matthiessen tentatively raised the subject of bigfoot, but he refrained from mentioning his recent foray in California. Schaller was already full of logical queries. Where was all the bigfoot scat, assuming the animal was primarily a vegetarian? "If there have been so many observations why isn't there more evidence?"[59] Matthiessen had asked himself the same thing; in his notebook, he described it as "the old question, and still a good one."

Later that same evening, he received two urgent phone calls from Doug Blue, who had just come across a disturbing news report. According to United Press International, a Manhattan lawyer named Michael Miller had purchased what he believed to be "a live 'Bigfoot.'"[60] Miller had reportedly paid $10,000, and he intended to have it evaluated by the Bronx Zoo and the Yerkes National Primate Research Center in Atlanta, Georgia. The UPI report was thin on specifics, but Blue was extremely alarmed by the talk of four-and-a-half-foot "Oliver," as somebody had christened the animal, which was said to resemble a cross between "a human and a chimpanzee."

Matthiessen made some general inquiries and notified Schaller, who was doubtful but intrigued. And then, at the end of January, Matthiessen was surprised to be contacted directly by Michael Miller; the appellate lawyer (of Landay and Miller) had been given his phone number by one of Blue's more dogged associates. Miller was familiar with Matthiessen's books, and he now explained that he had "never" thought Oliver was a bigfoot, as the media sensationally reported. Instead, he suspected Oliver was a missing link in human evolution—*Australopithecus*, perhaps—that had somehow fallen into the hands of a South African circus performer. Seeing this as a terrible waste, Miller had paid to rescue Oliver for *science*, he insisted. "I felt I was the fisherman who finds the coelacanth in his net, or the shepherd who discovers the Dead Sea scrolls," he later told the writer James Shreeve. "The earth has many secrets, and I was privileged to find a living one."[61] If Matthiessen promised, Miller continued, not to disclose Oliver's location or offer "any public opinion as to his true nature,"[62] he could come and take a look for himself. Agreeing to these terms, Matthiessen asked for permission to bring Schaller along to the clandestine meeting.

Less than a week later, Matthiessen and Schaller caught the Metroliner to Philadelphia together. Miller, appearing at the station with his girlfriend, had them sign confidentiality agreements. Then he drove them away, as Matthiessen wrote, "un-blindfolded into the bleak winter reaches of the New Jersey countryside."[63]

PM's trekking permit for Dolpo, Nepal, granting access in October and November 1973.

Alex and Deborah, not long before she died in January 1972.

Shey Gompa, the Crystal Monastery, on its snowy bluff—PM's destination in *The Snow Leopard* (1978). "[T]he emptiness and quiet are all one could wish for," he wrote.

PM crosses an icy torrent, perhaps the Suli Gad River in Dolpo, October 1973.

Transcribing notes from his pocket notebook to his journal while resting, boots off, in a mountain village.

The Ringmo porters, just before starting the steep ascent to the Kang La, 17,550 feet above sea level.

The kitchen hut at Shey Gompa: Gyaltsen, Jang-bu, George Schaller, and Phu-Tsering.

PM at Tsakang, in conversation with Karma Tupjuk (center), the incarnate Lama of Shey—with Jang-bu translating.

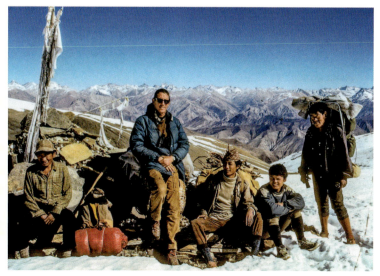

Homeward bound: Tukten, PM, Jang-bu, Gyaltsen, and Ang Dawa at the Saldang Pass, November 1973.

Eido Tai Shimano, also known as Tai-san, and (from 1972) Eido Roshi.

Soen Nakagawa, or Soen Roshi. "Swallow the stars," he commanded his students.

After a sesshin at Litchfield, Connecticut. PM is standing on the left in white robes. Roko Sherry Chayat—the future Shinge Roshi—is seated in the bottom row, third from right.

Maria Eckhart in her London days, early 1960s.

A new blended family in 1975: Maria, Antonia, Sarah on PM's shoulders, Alex, and Rue.

PM and Maria. "All in all he is an interesting person to live with," she wrote.

PM visits Alex, aged fifteen, at Rumsey Hall School in Connecticut, 1979.

Hans Teensma with Doug Blue, the "boyish, glad, enthusiastic man" who kindled PM's interest in bigfoot with a letter in 1975.

"Oliver" is exhibited by Frank Burger during a New York press conference in 1976.

Tom Willhoite searches for evidence of bigfoot in the Siskiyou Mountains, California, August 1976.

PM and Alan Gillespie inspect a tantalizing footprint near Deer Lick Lake, August 1976.

Frame 352 of the infamous Patterson-Gimlin bigfoot film, shot at Bluff Creek, California, in 1967. "[L]ike a primordial memory come to life," PM said of the film.

PM reenacts the film at Bluff Creek in 1976, playing bigfoot for Hans Teensma's camera.

Craig Carpenter, PM's "teacher and guide" through Indian country.

Leonard Peltier, the subject of *In the Spirit of Crazy Horse* (1983), is extradited from Canada to the United States in December 1976.

Peter Matthiessen, by Leonard Peltier, 1984.

PM joins a New York march demanding executive clemency for Peltier from President Clinton, December 10, 2000.

PM and Maria are married in a Zen ceremony on November 28, 1980.

PM prepares for Shukke Tokudo —"leaving home and entering the Way"—in October 1981, with Taizan Maezumi (center) and Bernie Tetsugen Glassman.

Shukke Tokudo.

PM and Glassman with a monk at Sōji-ji Temple in Yokohama, Japan, April 1982.

Converting an old stable on PM's Sagaponack property into a dedicated zendo.

The exterior door with its wooden han, worn from mallet strikes.

A walkway leads away from the zendo toward PM's karesansui—his Japanese rock garden.

The Ocean Zendo.

Edgar "Bloody" Watson, main subject of PM's Watson trilogy.

Watson's house at Chatham Bend in the Ten Thousand Islands, Florida, 1905.

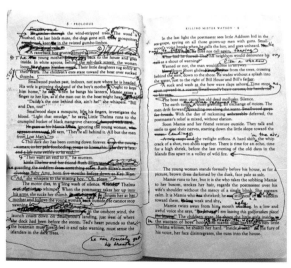

PM's handwritten edits to a published copy of *Killing Mister Watson* (1989). He substantially rewrote every page in the Watson trilogy of novels to produce the single-volume *Shadow Country* (2008), which won the National Book Award for Fiction and the William Dean Howells Medal.

Mamie and Ted Smallwood. Watson was executed by his neighbors next to their Chokoloskee store on October 24, 1910.

PM, Maria, and Tess the dog in Sagaponack, c. 1990s.

PM, notebook in pocket, holding a crane.

With a snow leopard cub.

With juvenile sandhill cranes. The glove puppet is used by biologists to train captive chicks how to behave without having them imprint on humans.

W. S. Merwin, Jim Harrison, and PM, friends and correspondents for decades.

PM with Kurt Vonnegut, Kris Kristofferson, and Norman Mailer.

Muryo Sensei weds Tom Styron and Phoebe Park in a Zen ceremony on May 21, 1994.

Birdwatching with Bill Styron in Gujarat, India, January 1993.

Victor Emanuel and PM visit the emperor penguins at Cape Washington, Antarctica, November 2001.

PM and Alex Matthiessen in Sagaponack, posing by a fin whale skull that was dragged by a tractor from Sagg Main Beach, 2009.

PM returns to Arctic Alaska for *The New York Review of Books*, reporting on Big Oil and "the dire threat of global warming," June 2006.

Bernie Glassman (center) leads the first Bearing Witness Retreat at Auschwitz-Birkenau, November 1996. PM is second from right.

Sitting between the train tracks in Birkenau, witness bearers chant Jewish names from the Sterbebücher—the Death Books compiled by the Gestapo.

Muryo Roshi and Joan Jiko Halifax, both Dharma successors of Bernie Glassman, c. 1999.

PM on March 5, 2014—exactly one month before he died—photographed by Damon Winter for *The New York Times Magazine*.

Oliver turned out to be residing in the town of Blackwood with his former owner, Frank Burger, who claimed, rather vaguely, to have acquired him via "agents" from an unspecified region near the Congo River in Africa. Miller was paying for Oliver's board with Burger until he figured out what to do next. Matthiessen and Schaller walked into the heated shed where Oliver was housed in a cage alongside several other animals. Burger led him out on a chain collar, held close, and sat him on a stool for inspection. As Matthiessen and Schaller looked at Oliver, he looked back at them: "he touched our faces and hair and clothing with his soft, gentle, ogre hands, and kissed and nuzzled us," Matthiessen wrote in his notebook.[64]

Schaller spent an hour conducting a physical exam. When he finished, he told Miller that what he had purchased was "a very interesting chimp." "Chimpanzees are very variable, and I see nothing that could not occur in any chimp excepting, of course, that habitual bipedal gait"—Oliver only stood and walked on two legs, never his knuckles.[65] Schaller would formalize this evaluation in a typed report that offered plausible explanations for Oliver's more atypical morphological features.[66] The sunken appearance of his face, for example, was due to a lack of teeth, which had all been deliberately extracted. Miller chose to ignore Schaller's deflating report; instead, he put "the ape-like creature" on display during a press conference at the Explorers Club in New York later that same month.[67]

On the return train from Philadelphia, Schaller reminded Matthiessen, perhaps as a consolation, that he was "very skeptical" by default. Matthiessen thought this was an appropriate stance for a biologist, and Schaller's physical exam had been unimpeachable. Still, he was more inclined toward ambivalence himself, more willing to leaven his commitment to science with faith or feeling, intuition, even imagination. "Like Michael Miller," he later wrote about the episode, "I had been strangely drawn to Oliver, and although I knew that George was right, I remained a little bothered."[68] That niggling sense that something was hidden, still unresolved, prevented him from declaring the case closed, just as he hesitated to dismiss Tom Willhoite's stories even as they failed to reflect empirical reality.

DOUGLAS BLUE LIKED to refer to Willhoite as a "pioneer" in the nascent area of bigfoot studies. He insisted that Willhoite's accounts were scrupulously accurate, *not* a matter of poetic license. But since Matthiessen had doubts, Blue was prepared to offer an alternative. He knew another pioneer by the name of Jean Fitzgerald, of Roseburg, Oregon, who was already something of a public figure, having featured in local newspapers making rather bold claims: "Mrs. Fitzgerald said that she first met the Sasquatch on Aug. 28th or

29th [of 1974] and since that time she has been feeding them Mound[s] bars and apples."[69] In one article disseminated nationally by UPI, she acknowledged rubbing out footprints to conceal the creatures from "Bigfoot hunters."[70] She also announced a plan to petition the government for protective legislation, seemingly on the assumption that bigfoot was an endangered species. In a photograph for the Salem *Capital Journal*, Fitzgerald, who was in her early to mid-forties, appeared with a large blond bouffant and neckerchief, smiling broadly as she held up a giant plaster foot for the camera.

Blue hinted that his new pioneer had access to color footage of bigfoot. This tantalizing prospect outweighed Matthiessen's misgivings, as he admitted in his manuscript: "I was hooked on the possibility of BF, no matter how remote; I was obsessed by it. I knew that I would have to check this lead, like it or not."[71] Blue provided a mailing address, and Matthiessen sent several of his nonfiction books along with a strategically obsequious letter. "I am sincerely concerned about the welfare and future of Bigfoot," he wrote. "I am equipped and ready to go into the wilderness. . . . I am willing to work under any restrictions or conditions. . . . I will even travel to and from your Bigfoot locations with a paper bag over my head."[72] Jean Fitzgerald responded enthusiastically in a letter of her own—the first of dozens.[73]

Matthiessen met with Fitzgerald on four separate occasions in Oregon over the course of a year. The first time, in December 1975, came on the tail end of a work trip to Los Angeles. He flew up to Medford and was greeted by Jean at the airport, along with her stiff, taciturn husband, Steve, and their two young children, Gloria and Danny. Despite having spoken to her on the phone, Matthiessen was surprised to find a woman with "a big face, big voice, and a big heart, set off by a hearty roadhouse style that included everything from wigs to winks."[74]

This initial visit was an introduction; he took notes while Fitzgerald told her story as though she was giving solemn testimony to a police detective. The saga, which would take many pages to recount in Matthiessen's manuscript, was centered on a small lake in Umpqua National Forest where the Fitzgeralds had camped every summer for the past thirteen years. Jean had first seen bigfoot near the lake in 1974; she had asked herself why "this man" was wearing "a dark suit and long sleeves in such hot weather." Over subsequent sightings, she had graduated from bafflement to dawning horror, to hysteria, to acceptance, to cautious curiosity, and finally to awe. Now fiercely committed to defending bigfoot from people like Grover Krantz, an anthropologist at Washington State University who was desperate to get his hands on a specimen, dead or alive, she was full of maternal desire to "make contact with the creatures so that she can take a young one and adopt it." This startling detail had also been reported by the *Capital Journal:* "Mrs. Fitzgerald says she intends to catch a Bigfoot for her very own."[75]

Matthiessen wrote down her story in meticulous detail. He found it, however, "very difficult to believe."[76] While Jean was "sincere," she also struck him as "immensely deluded." He was more impressed by the testimony of Steve Fitzgerald, in large part because it was given so reluctantly. Steve was visibly annoyed by his wife's claims, which had, he said, damaged their relationship and caused the children to be teased at school. And yet Steve, too, attested to having observed a creature in the Umpqua National Forest: "I've seen it, all right. I wish I hadn't."[77]

The second time Matthiessen saw Jean Fitzgerald, in January 1976, was even less promising than the first. (In the interim, he'd been forced to let her down gently after she confessed her love for him in letters: "you must be careful about making the wonderful new friendship that we have into something that it isn't. This is something we are all apt to do—I've done it myself—when there are problems with the person we live with, but in our case, it could lead to complications that might get in our way, and not only in our way but in the way of a project and a hope that is very big and important, perhaps the project of a lifetime.")[78] He met her in Portland, Oregon, without Steve or the children. They drove to Toledo, Washington, to interview Ray Wallace, a logger and building contractor who owned the color footage of bigfoot that Jean had sworn was authentic. In the car, she filled Matthiessen in on the full situation. "Mr. Wallace had a captive BF baby to go with two BF skulls and three skeletons. But he could show us neither bones nor Baby, since he was afraid of questions from the F.B.I."[79] These were some shocking claims, to say the least, and Matthiessen wondered if he was hallucinating—"what the hell am I doing?"[80] When they arrived in Toledo, Wallace's footage turned out to be risible: "hockey-glove type hand, too-small arm, fur cut off at wrist." Matthiessen was so appalled by the blatant hoodwinking that he drove to a café on the Cowlitz River and ordered a drink. As he tried to calm down, Fitzgerald tearfully defended herself by claiming she'd been duped.*

By May, Matthiessen had recovered from his "traumatic journey" to Toledo, and even "recouped" a little confidence in Jean. The third time they met, in June, was at the lakeside campsite in the mountains of Umpqua

---

* Ray Wallace was a notorious prankster whose hoaxes fooled many people over the decades. After he died in 2002, his children claimed their father had used a pair of wood-carved feet in the mud around a logging camp near Bluff Creek in 1958. This meant that Jerry Crew's infamous discovery of giant footprints—the discovery generally credited with triggering the modern craze for bigfoot—was likely Wallace's doing. "It's weird because it was just a joke, and then it took on such a life of its own that even now, we can't stop it," Michael Wallace told *The New York Times*.

National Forest. To be absolutely sure, he had decided to check her story "backwards and forwards" in the place where it supposedly began.[81] He invited Hans Teensma to accompany him for support, and they camped, along with Steve, Gloria, and Danny, for several days near the lake. (Jean reminded Teensma of Dolly Parton: "Boy, was that a surprise.")[82] But nothing happened with the Fitzgeralds, and Matthiessen wrote testily, "Jean has decided that the failure of BF to appear must be our fault."[83]

However, something *had* happened on his way to the national forest, during the drive north up the Redwood Highway, U.S. Route 199. Somewhere near the town of Gasquet, in California, he glimpsed a "fleeting silhouette" with a "<u>big</u> stride" run at full speed across the road and then vanish into trees:

> I assumed there must be some emergency—a child wandered into a farm pond, a house on fire—and I speeded up, then slowed to pull into his driveway. But there was no driveway, no sign of a road, not even a path, though I spent some time driving up and down the wall of forest. . . . The huge trees had been cut back from the shoulder of the road, and the roadside and ditches were a jumble of pits and stumps and gigantic twisted roots, that would have been difficult to clamber over, far less pass through at the dead run. . . . Suddenly out of breath, I pulled the truck onto the shoulder and turned the motor off; my skin was crawling. It just was not possible for a man to run as fast as that, not through that deadwood, straight into the forest! Where was he now? What had I seen, then[?][84]

This moment disturbed Matthiessen more than any other during all his bigfoot and yeti investigations. He would dwell on it for years, describing it to family and friends, to an archaeologist in British Columbia, and at dinner parties with "astonished" guests as Maria winced with embarrassment.[85] In an unfinished short story, "The Figure on the Road," Matthiessen would attempt to recapture the "primeval silence . . . an imminence of 'something there,' a presence inexplicable, uncanny."[86] Was this a genuine sighting on the outer reaches of the Pacific Northwest? Or had his mind played a sly trick, showing him something he desperately wanted to see?

FOR MUCH OF JULY, Peter vacationed with Maria in Tanzania. They left the children with her father and stepmother in Njombe, in the Southern Highlands, where Gottlieb Eckhart now ran a clinic, and set off with a few friends, including Maria's sister, in a Land Rover that had been previously damaged by a rhino. "The red roads under a blue sky evoke the Africa of childhood tales, the untouched colors of spontaneous life immediately lived"—Matthiessen's chronicle for *Audubon* about the trip, which covered some 1,600 miles through lesser-known parks and included a climb of Mount Kilimanjaro, made it sound spectacular.[87]

And yet the safari was, in Maria's words, punctuated by "immense pain and sadness."[88] After a year of living together, she and Peter were still getting used to each other's habits and moods. Peter thought Maria could be defensive, putting on a "front" to conceal her true feelings from him (which was true, as Maria admitted in some private notes: "my whole life goes on behind my eyes. . . . He knows nothing of it").[89] Maria, in turn, struggled to process Peter's biting criticism, and she had started keeping track of the negative attributes he ascribed to her during fights: "Paranoid . . . Childish . . . Repeating all these bad patterns over and over again, so that I am unable to 'grow.' NOT TO MENTION THE FACT THAT 'I HAVE LET MYSELF GO.' "[90] Maria also disliked how often Peter was absent from the family home, which was a complaint he was thoroughly acquainted with after years of hearing it from two former wives. "How have I got so attached and dependent in so little time—to a man who goes away all the time?" Maria had asked him in a letter. "I can't bear to look at your photograph anymore because a wave of sickness and sadness overwhelms me."[91] She pleaded with him to pay closer attention to Alex: "You must write more to him & ring. He misses you too—as do the girls."[92] On the Tanzanian safari, these simmering resentments now flared into confrontations, and threats were made. Then Peter left to answer the call of work, or perhaps to escape into his work; Maria lingered in Njombe with the children. He wrote her a conciliatory letter on the plane:

> As expected, am full of regret that we had no hugs this morning, and so little time to celebrate what we (really) knew all along, that we love each other deeply after all. (We must not get in this habit of threatening each other with willingness to abandon ship every time we reach a temporary sticking point.) And I realize how crazy I am to be so critical of (what seems to me) your "front" when the person behind is still attached to it by so many threads that cannot be torn all at once. I love you . . . and I am committed to you and maybe that scares me; maybe I've never been so committed before. And I think everything will work out, if we will let our defenses down, and work as the dear dear friends that we are. . . . A[lex] + A[ntonia] are both great children with temporary hang-ups—let's work with them together, all right? I do hope Alex will be a help (be open to his efforts, get angry but not cold + formal) (please) because you were already a great help to him, and he loves you almost as much as I do.[93]

This was reassuring, if not exactly an apology for his role in the conflict. Maria responded with mixed emotions: "Oh darling, I <u>do</u> love you. We have so many watersheds—but I feel clean and calm about us. I <u>miss</u> you and I am sad, but I am also at peace."[94]

By the middle of August, back in America, Matthiessen was on his way to the West Coast again. He stayed with the Fitzgeralds in Roseburg—a "pleasant evening," his fourth visit to see Jean—before driving two hundred miles south via Gasquet. At the approximate part of the Redwood Highway where he'd seen the eerie silhouette, he slowed down to take another look. But he found himself hopelessly disoriented: "The whole road looked changed."[95]

In Orleans, California, Matthiessen met up again with Tom Willhoite, having decided to give the gold prospector a final chance. Willhoite was accompanied this time by Rollin and Alan Gillespie. Rollin was a retired project engineer for NASA, where he'd been involved in devising a plan for manned interplanetary space travel. Alan, another of Doug Blue's recruits, was a twenty-eight-year-old geology student in the Jet Propulsion Laboratory at the California Institute of Technology, Pasadena. Both father and son were scientists, and both were interested in unexplained phenomena, though they held the bar for proof reassuringly high.

Willhoite and the Gillespies were already established at Louse Camp, twenty miles north of Orleans in the Siskiyou Mountains. Matthiessen joined them with his own tent, and Hans Teensma soon turned up from San Francisco, making five.

The collective focus of the trip was on finding footprints. The men scoured old logging roads for leads. "I found some prints in a jumble of burned snags and stumps and logs," Matthiessen wrote, "where I would have hidden had I been a big BF curious about what was going on down in Louse Camp, a few hundred yards below."[96]

One evening, he and Alan Gillespie hunkered down in the bushes near a spot where they'd found some promising tracks, hoping that whatever made them might pass back through again. They sat quietly for several hours, as Matthiessen wrote (and Alan Gillespie has substantially verified his account of the trip),[97] and then they noticed "flickering blue lights far up in the forest toward Blue Creek Mountain, and again a second time on or just above the logging road below us, no more than thirty yards away."* As if this wasn't baf-

---

* A month after the camping trip, Rollin Gillespie wrote a long, speculative letter to Matthiessen about the theory of electromagnetic vortices. He wondered if the Siskiyou Mountains were structured in a way that made them behave as a magnetic pole. Were the blue lights a product of collisions between ions and molecules in a charged atmosphere? Matthiessen underlined parts of the letter, but he found Rollin's explanation no more convincing than what Tom Willhoite had proposed: that the lights were "yewa demons," or "Yewaws," which his Native friends said could "envelop you, or lure you to your doom."

fling enough, another day, at Dry Lake near Burrill Peak while they investigated a forest clearing, a "silver object so studded with protuberances that we could not make out its shape" cruised across the sky. Rollin started yelling, and Alan ran through the clearing to get a better look. Everyone except Teensma, who was elsewhere at the time, was rattled by the spectacle. "I was sorry I had seen it," Matthiessen wrote, "and I tried to put it out of my mind as quickly as possible, before I lost the last vestiges of reasonableness in this account."[98] Other than these odd moments, however, which had nothing to do with bigfoot, the camping trip was fruitless. Willhoite had once again failed to deliver the goods. Sensing "a cynical, mutinous attitude about his leadership" in the other men, he turned petulant, insisted he was "not a liar," and drove back to Orleans to drink in a bar. "In some way Tom has lost his nerve," Matthiessen wrote; "Alan believes he is genuinely afraid of Bigfoot, and has chosen this bad camp site to lessen our chances of an encounter. Whatever the reasons, I feel sorry; I know I will not work with Tom again."[99]

On their last day in Louse Camp, Matthiessen and Teensma left the Gillespies and walked several miles up the north fork of Bluff Creek, taking pleasure in the "kingfishers and water ouzels and a red-tailed hawk that crossed the clear sky high over our heads,"[100] until they found a site that had become improbably famous, though few people knew the precise location. Eight years earlier, on October 20, 1967, Roger Patterson and Robert Gimlin, two rodeo riders who had decided to make a documentary about bigfoot, were heading upstream when they came upon a large fallen tree. As they guided their horses around the exposed roots, they spotted something staring directly at them. The horses panicked; Patterson tried to maintain control while pulling a film camera from a saddlebag. He then slid off his horse, which bolted, and ran toward a sandbar, where he fell to his knees and peered through the viewfinder. At least, that was the story the men later offered to explain some very shaky footage: a tall female figure covered in hair, glancing back as she strides purposefully away toward the trees. With her long swinging arms, this figure would become the most iconic image of bigfoot in history. Believers and skeptics have argued about her authenticity for decades, and even today, despite various claims of fraud, the Patterson-Gimlin film has never been definitively exposed as a hoax.[101]

Matthiessen was familiar with the footage, and he believed it was genuine: "the visible working of all the leg muscles seems impossible to fake, especially if seen through a fur suit," he once told Doug Blue in a letter.[102] In his manuscript, he confessed that whenever he watched the footage, "my temples tingle, the hair rises on my neck, because I know or think I know that I am seeing something absolutely astonishing, like a primordial memory come to life."[103]

Now, on the sandbar of Bluff Creek, he set out to conduct a curious exercise. Hoping to gauge how large the creature must have been, Matthiessen and Teensma set out to reenact the scene exactly so they would have a point of comparison. Teensma played the role of Roger Patterson, lying on the sandbar with his camera. And Matthiessen became the bigfoot. He peeled off his shirt, strode toward the trees, arms swinging in exaggerated arcs, and glanced backward to create an unforgettable image of obsession.

WHY DID MATTHIESSEN never publish anything about Doug Blue's pioneers? The obvious answer, of course, is because they never produced the creature. Matthiessen never found the conclusive proof that would shield him from a charge of gullibility.

But reading the original notebooks and the manuscript pages about his various travels in California and Oregon, one also gets the sense that Matthiessen withheld his material because he didn't fully understand it. What did bigfoot represent to him? Why was he so driven to establish its existence? While he floated various theories that would have answered these questions, he never fully settled on any one of them. Perhaps discovering bigfoot would force us to reimagine our relationship with the natural world. Perhaps bigfoot promised to renew our wonder at a moment when every part of the environment seemed to be in terminal decline because of humanity's selfish disregard. Perhaps bigfoot was a remnant of prelapsarian North America. "Daniel Boone once spoke of the wilderness as 'wild and horrid. . . . It is impossible to behold it without terror.' With BF in it, to replace the grizzlies, wolves, and savages now gone, the wilderness is 'terrible' again. Is that BF's attraction—the wilderness restored?"[104]

Or: "Need for innocence? A longing for a purer existence, something different from 'modern time'?"[105]

Matthiessen wondered. And yet, despite his demands for hard evidence from Tom Willhoite, Michael Miller, and Jean Fitzgerald, he was less interested in solving the mystery than he was in brushing up against mystery itself—what he called the "something-unknown beyond." Hans Teensma, discussing his friend's interest in bigfoot, once used the analogy of a Catholic confronted by a saint or angel: here was "a vision of the unknown, right in front of us, like a ghost."[106] To witness something so miraculous was to glimpse the true state of things beyond the limits of human comprehension. Perhaps it was not so different from an experience of satori, or kensho. And this, in fact, was what Matthiessen really hoped to find in the woods, as he admitted in the unpublished manuscript:

In the vastness of this forest, and especially when one is alone at dusk or daybreak, I feel as if I were invading the territory of *Homo nocturnus*, as Linnaeus called "the wild man," not his territory, exactly, but his realm in time, for there is something about him, some aspect of him, that lives between the dimensions known to *Homo sapiens* and formal science. And I perceive in him also something I knew earlier about the snow leopard, that to perceive him properly and fully was a kind of spiritual quest; that the preparation, the purification of the self, the training of mind and body, the trepidation, obstacles, the overcoming of fear was in some sense a true path to liberation.[107]

19

New Teachers

You refer to my "turning my back on (my) Buddhist gods." Not true. There are no Buddhist gods in the sense you mean (we are all Buddhas and/or Bodhisattvas), and even if there were, I can find no important conflict between Zen Buddhism and Indian teachings, and cannot imagine that any Zen master would object to what I am doing.

—PM to Craig Carpenter (April 1977)[1]

AROUND THE SAME TIME that Matthiessen began his investigations into the bigfoot phenomenon, a scandal erupted in the Zen Studies Society. Eido Shimano, a married man, was surreptitiously sleeping with a female student. One day this student decided to reveal the affair to another woman in the sangha. The second woman was stunned, not because of the impropriety but because she, too, had slept with Eido Roshi. Both women then made further inquiries, asking around, only to discover they were far from alone with their sexual relationships. "Many of us thought it was an experience that one of us may have had," recalled Shinge Roshi (Roko Sherry Chayat)—"and suddenly it was like, 'This is very widespread.' Soon it seemed as though there weren't too many of us who *hadn't* had that experience."[2]

Eido Roshi was seducing students in the dokusan room during one-on-one interviews. He was targeting women in sesshins, when they were at their most vulnerable. He was taking advantage of his position as roshi, the supreme spiritual authority, to lure whomever he desired and secure their complicit silence. When he lost interest, he was tossing them aside. Later, it would become clear that this was part of a longstanding pattern of predatorial behavior by Eido Shimano. Before migrating to New York, he had spent several years in Hawaii, at Robert Aitken's Koko An Zendo. His conduct during his time there had revolted Aitken Roshi, who believed the monk had indulged in a pathological exploitation that caused two women to be hospitalized with nervous breakdowns.[3]

Matthiessen learned about the scandal during a late-summer sesshin at Dai Bosatsu in 1975. Inside the new monastery, which still smelled of paint and freshly sanded wood, the atmosphere was "dark, distempered."[4] Word had spread quickly, and the students were unhappy. None of the allegations suggested Eido Roshi had done something criminal—the relationships were technically consensual, if dubious and manipulative—but he had violated trust, and, in the opinion of many, polluted the very idea of Zen. "[F]or idealistic American Zen students, seeking respite from our own disorderly lives, this practice had seemed a clear oasis where life could be kept pure, spare, and simple," Matthiessen wrote. "Now the image had been muddied, messy 'real life' had come flooding in, and we wrestled with 'oughts' and 'should' on our black cushions."[5] Eido Roshi's reaction to exposure only made his betrayal even more galling. He shouted, made vehement, implausible denials, and accused his accusers of conjuring oversexed fantasies. "He had no remorse," recalled Myoku Margot Wilkie in an interview with the writer David Chadwick. "He thought Americans were stupid and had no bones about saying it. We were crude and uncivilized. He thought nothing of women."[6]

Some students confronted him. A petition was circulated, and letters were sent to the Zen Studies Society Board of Directors demanding disciplinary action. But Eido Roshi had a small, powerful coterie of loyalists, and the board remained mute. In a despotic move, Eido Roshi then dissolved the sangha entirely: all members would need to apply to *him* for readmittance. Rather than submitting to his demand, more than sixty students chose to purge themselves instead—a choice, for many, that was utterly devastating. They had turned to the Zen Studies Society for guidance during a disillusioning decade; to now renounce it was like letting go of a life raft with no land in sight.

The scandal continued to unfold while Matthiessen traveled in California and Oregon. Then, at the start of July 1976, he drove to the Catskills for the grand opening of Dai Bosatsu Zendo Kongo-ji, which had been arranged to coincide with the bicentennial of American independence. At a preparatory sesshin before the ceremony, he met with Eido Roshi to talk things over. The man seemed "paranoid." His Dharma talks were "distracted, weak, and rambling."[7] Matthiessen was torn between anger and a sense of allegiance: "I cannot forget how strong he was at the time of Ho Ko's death, how much I owe him." And yet, Matthiessen was not convinced his teacher would ever concede fault; Eido Roshi insisted the real offense was student insubordination. Nor could Matthiessen move past the fact that a roshi had abused his position for sex, "preying"⁸ on the very same women who had looked after Deborah in her darkest hour, and then lying about it, as much to himself as to everybody else. Despondent, Matthiessen informed Eido Roshi that he was also withdrawing as a student once the grand opening was finished, joining the mass exodus. After the talk, he visited Deborah's grave and wondered what she would have thought about the sordid unravelling of her beloved sangha. (Had Eido ever made a move on Deborah? This question, too, must have crossed Matthiessen's mind.)

Having made a decisive break, why did he not then expose Eido Shimano in writing? Why did none of the disgruntled students, in fact, go to the media and prevent what became a decades-long pattern of abuse at the Zen Studies Society? Partly, there was a feeling of indebtedness to Eido Roshi, who was considered, despite his reprehensible conduct, a "purveyor of True Dharma"⁹ by many of the people who had followed him. "We felt," as Shinge Roshi put it, "a great gratitude to Eido Roshi, and great loyalty, even though we felt we had to leave."¹⁰ Partly the collective silence was due to a belief that the sangha was a family, with the scandal a "family thing,"¹¹ to be settled out of the public eye. Partly it was the era: men rarely got reprimanded for sexual misconduct. Matthiessen, for example, was not above wondering if the women owned "a larger share of the responsibility than they are accepting."¹² And partly there was a fear that disgracing Eido Roshi would fatally damage Zen in America, where its roots were still shallow enough to be ripped out. "You'd like to make it cut and dry. 'This guy's an asshole, get rid of him.' That would be lovely," said Adam Fisher, who chose to remain in the sangha. "But it wasn't that simple."¹³

Soen Nakagawa refused to attend the opening of Dai Bosatsu, a choice interpreted by many observers as a conspicuous rebuke of his disciple.¹⁴ But dozens of other guests ignored the rumors, prioritizing the future of Dai Bosatsu over the credible claims of the women who had helped build it from nothing. More than twenty roshis from Japan and America came—including Robert Aitken, who somehow managed to swallow his disgust—plus monks, Shinto priests, and dignitaries like the Tibetan Buddhist Chögyam Trungpa. In pouring rain, the crowd gathered on the monastery steps, and Matthiessen struck a huge iron *bonsho*, or temple bell, with a log wrapped in red, white, and blue.¹⁵

The opening ceremony on July 4, 1976, marked the end of Matthiessen's "early, infatuated days" with Zen.¹⁶ Having worked so hard to fund and construct the mountain retreat, he now abandoned it to others, and terminated his involvement with the Zen Studies Society back in New York. While he left the door open to a reconciliation—he was "(temporarily?) removed,"¹⁷ he told Jim Harrison in a letter—he would never again study under Eido

Roshi, who refused to reform even after further complaints were leveled against him in 1979, 1982, and 1995. Shimano would remain in his position as abbot until 2010, when yet more allegations of "clergy misconduct" and a damning article by the journalist Mark Oppenheimer in *The New York Times* finally led to his forced retirement.[18]

For the rest of the year, Matthiessen replaced the sesshins he would usually have attended with work on *The Snow Leopard*, a different kind of meditation practice. As he wrote, he also began to look around for a new teacher, other forms of spiritual guidance.

IN THE MID-1970S, Matthiessen spent far too much time ("I think of that energy wasted now with great regret")[19] as a screenwriter for Hollywood. Wanting to save some money to buy a few years for another novel, he collaborated with producers on a number of projects ("horrible ideas"), none of which ever made it to the silver screen: "Fair Angelica," about the Atlantic slave trade; "The Voyage of the Beagle," about Charles Darwin; "Leaping Whale Wind," about Hawaiian gods; and "The Disappearance," an ambitious double feature exploring what the world would be like if a) all the women suddenly vanished, and b) all the men did.

It was during a business trip to Los Angeles that Matthiessen finally saw Doug Blue in person, "a boyish, glad, enthusiastic man, somewhat removed from life."[20] They met at the intersection of Hollywood and Vine, then strolled up the hill to the Vedanta Society temple that Blue called home. After a long discussion about their mutual interest, Blue invited Matthiessen to a meeting at the nearby Immaculate Heart College, on North Western Avenue. This meeting was organized by a group called the Committee for Traditional Indian Land and Life, formed in 1967 to provide support for "Traditional Indians" against the scourge of American "progress." The scheduled speaker was a sixty-six-year-old Hopi man, Thomas Banyacya, an interpreter for the Hopi Traditionalists[*] who had attracted national attention for publicizing, in the wake of the Hiroshima and Nagasaki bombings,

---

[*] Self-described "Traditionals" who affiliated with groups like the Committee for Traditional Indian Land and Life, or the League of North American Indians, often defined themselves in opposition to what they called "progressives"—the Tribal Councils, for example, and Native people who had adopted Christianity. The truth, however, was not so tidy as "traditional" vs. "progressive," authentic vs. inauthentic. As the anthropologist Richard Clemmer has pointed out about the Hopi Traditionalists, "what the Hopi mean when they say *traditional* or *traditionalist* reflects a distinct political ideology that is not opposed to modernity but is part of it. . . . Hopi Traditionalism is an ideology that is constantly being constructed, created, recreated, and negotiated." Put another way, the "Traditionals" were not necessarily Native Americans living in pure continuity with the past. They were people engaged in a process of interpreting history and culture to assert a modern, reactionary identity. "Rather than resisting change," Brian Haley, another anthropologist, has written, "the Traditionalist movement was an agent of change."

grave prophecies concerning a "gourd of ashes" falling from the sky, to be followed by "Purification Day," when the world would be cleansed of pollution and evil.

The meeting began with a short film about strip-mining on Black Mesa in Arizona. Then Banyacya gave a passionate lecture, parts of which Matthiessen wrote down verbatim: "We are confused. We are searching, so that once again we may be one with the Great Spirit. When the sun comes up, traveling across the great sky, He will be crying, for we are dying away. No longer are we one with the birds and the grass, the wild creatures and the wind.... [T]he white man has built up this great pyramid of his progress and his needs, and now we are too high on the pyramid, and we had better come down off it slowly, or we are going to fall." Gesturing around the room, Banyacya added, "We don't need to have all this! Why aren't we sitting outside in the warm sunshine?"

Matthiessen thought Banyacya was an impressive orator: "his very stance suggests a weathered permanence: <u>we are here forever</u>." He was stirred by the speech, which echoed his own feelings about environmental ruin, the excesses of civilization, man's original unity with nature (a Zen teaching), and the need to return to simpler ways of living. During a break in the discussion, he spoke with Banyacya privately, along with several of Banyacya's associates. He had come to the meeting with Doug Blue, so the topic of conversation was unsurprising: he asked for their thoughts on bigfoot. Richard Kastl, an Osage man working with the Hopi Traditionalists, suggested there was a reference to "him" in the Hopi prophecies. Matthiessen pressed Banyacya for details, but the interpreter smiled, saying he should come to the Hopi Reservation in Arizona to question the elders instead. "They will talk to you about that. And we will show you Bigfoot." To conclude the meeting, Banyacya then led the crowd in a corn dance; Matthiessen held hands with a man named Felix Montoya. There was, he later wrote in his unpublished manuscript, "real power in the ceremony, accumulating as we danced, and the sense of an unspoken bond between this huge stern young Indian and myself."

The meeting at Immaculate Heart College would prove to be a turning point for Matthiessen in several key ways. When it came to the bigfoot investigations, his focus on empirical evidence would soon expand to encompass folklore, legends, and prophecies; science would make way for the consideration of religious beliefs.* In terms of his career, the "Land and Life"

---

* In his manuscript, Matthiessen wrote: "John Green [a Canadian journalist and prominent bigfoot researcher] once told me that he could not work with Indians because he could not trust what they told him, not because they were dishonest but because they drew no line between what white people thought of as 'reality' and another reality which whites thought of as 'supernatural.' But

meeting was a prologue to his affiliation with Native American people—an affiliation that would determine the next decade of his work. And more personally, the meeting hinted at, through Matthiessen's sympathetic attention to Banyacya's lecture, and through his earnest participation in the Hopi corn dance, his willingness to augment Zen practice with other forms of spiritual expression.

Less than six weeks later, returning to Los Angeles for more movie business, Matthiessen met up with Doug Blue again. This time they went to visit Felix Montoya (the "huge stern young Indian") and his wife, Stella, at their house near Glendale. "We do not call him 'creature' the way you do," Felix, who could be abrasive, told his guests during an uncomfortably tense dinner. "Bigfoot is our brother who can understand our tongues."[21] Though he had never seen one, he identified with bigfoot and suggested their fates were inseparable. "When Bigfoot goes, I go." Matthiessen, reflecting on these comments, came to suspect that Felix was "filling in the chinks of his shattered heritage" using the malleable symbol of bigfoot as a kind of caulking. What the Montoyas yearned to do, their vision of bigfoot still did: "He roams where he wishes on this continent, free of all laws or unnatural restraints, of highways, fences, property lines, and legal limits. He represents that part of the Indian—the spiritual part—which still roams free in the infinity and universality represented by great forests, mountains, sky."

In a letter to Felix and Stella, Matthiessen later described the idea that "this mysterious brother should become a symbol of a new and respectful treatment of our land (new to most white men, at least)" as both "exciting and moving."[22] Could bigfoot perhaps be used to encourage ecological consciousness, a new order of stewardship like the one he'd been agitating for since his work with Stewart Udall and Cesar Chavez? It sounded improbable, but he wanted to learn more.

A few days after the dinner, Felix called to offer a few words of caution. Matthiessen should proceed no further with his inquiries about the "Indian view" on bigfoot until he'd sought out the counsel of a man who lived on the Hoopa Valley Reservation, not far from Orleans in Northern California—a Mohawk turned Hopi messenger named Craig Carpenter.

AT THE END of August 1976, in a GMC truck fitted with a fiberglass camper, bought from a friend to ease his travels on the West Coast, Matthiessen drove onto the Hoopa Valley Reservation and asked around for directions to

---

for want of a better explanation, I had already begun to wonder if it wasn't just this concept of existence that might lead, if not to 'understanding,' at least to apprehension of this being."

Medicine Flat. After a few wrong turns, he pulled up near an old red cabin with papered-over windows, four guard dogs patrolling out front. Matthiessen settled down to wait. He did not feel like calling out, "although I had the feeling I was being watched."[23] A woman, Mary Hansen, appeared wearing a frayed bathrobe; she walked across the yard full of rusted-out cars, said nothing except, "Looking for Craig, huh?" and then returned to the cabin, where she lived with her children. Carpenter himself soon materialized out of the trees. He presented Matthiessen with fresh plums, "held ceremonially in both hands," and cut Matthiessen off when he tried to introduce himself: "We knew you would come today; she's been cleaning."

Craig Carpenter was lean, tall, and hawk-nosed, his profile reminding Matthiessen of the fifteenth-century Italian friar Girolamo Savonarola. He wore his dark hair tied back into a Diné chignon, turquoise earrings, and an unseasonable blue parka that was meant to hide the large sebaceous cyst growing on his right shoulder. Because news of Matthiessen's visit had preceded him, Carpenter was ready. Standing by the truck, he launched into a disquisition about the Hopi prophecies, and about the importance of contacting Indigenous people globally to share them. It was quite the introduction, as Matthiessen wrote in his manuscript:

> I had planned just to stop by and say hello, perhaps set up a longer meeting for a later date; it occurred to me now that I had taken him from his work, and apologized for the interruption. Craig Carpenter stopped talking long enough to look me over, indulgently but not without impatience. Nodding a little, holding my eye, he said in a very quiet voice, "Everything is right on schedule—you know that." Then he resumed what he had been saying, and this talk that had begun in the early morning went on unbroken after that until nearly midnight. I had meant to stay for fifteen minutes; instead I stayed there for three days.[24]

In *Indian Country* (1984), Matthiessen would credit Carpenter as his "teacher and guide on my first journeys into Indian Country, whose fierce encouragement of the last traditionals among his people is one good reason why they still exist."[25] Much of Matthiessen's initial contacts with Native Americans came via this man, making him a significant influence on the writer's early understanding of Native affairs and cultures. However, Craig Carpenter was not exactly who he presented himself to be.

By Carpenter's own account, he had been born in Temperance, Michigan, on April 28, 1927—just twenty-four days before Matthiessen—to parents who were so assimilated that they were no longer certain of their tribe and passed as members of the white middle class. With help from an aunt,

Carpenter had awoken to his Mohawk identity at the age of nineteen. In his twenties, he had then set off on a quest across the country, trying, in his words, "to find his way back to the real Indians."²⁶ He had ended up at the Hopi Reservation, and in 1955, after several futile attempts to gain an audience (being dismissed as "Chignon-White-Man"),²⁷ he had met David Monongye, the ascendent leader of the Hopi Traditionalists, and Thomas Banyacya, who decided to educate Carpenter about the prophecies and designate him a "messenger" entrusted with, as Matthiessen put it in *Indian Country*, "the correct presentation of the Hopi Message to other Indian nations and the outside world."²⁸ (In truth, Monongye and Banyacya, and thus Carpenter, only ever spoke for one faction of the Hopi Tribe.)

Carpenter had made a name for himself in Los Angeles, where he began printing newsletters and pamphlets to promote an Indian Rebirth Movement. During the 1960s, he had been a regular at countercultural concerts, pop festivals, rallies, and love-ins, where he often set up a tipi, like a Native information booth. His colorful appearance and "strong, messianic voice"²⁹ had attracted the attention of college students, hippies, writers, and artists, some of whom responded to his message by forming, among other organizations, the Committee for Traditional Indian Land and Life. By 1969, the year Carpenter moved to the Hoopa Valley Reservation, he had spent more than a decade disseminating the teachings of Hopi Traditionalists to Native and non-Native people alike. He was now tending his garden at Medicine Flat, quietly awaiting Purification Day, when "wrong-doers" would be annihilated and "the natural balance of the world" would be restored.³⁰

This was the personal history that Carpenter told Matthiessen—the personal history that, excepting a few shifting details and dates, Carpenter told everyone until the end of his life in 2006.³¹ But in 2018, Brian Haley, an anthropologist at the State University of New York at Oneonta, published an article telling a different story. According to Haley's extensive genealogical research, none of Carpenter's ancestors were "identifiable as American Indians or appear to have been affiliated with Indian communities."³² Haley labeled Carpenter a "neo-Indian," a man whose asserted Indigenous identity did not align with his actual ancestry, which can be traced back on both sides to early European settlers. Carpenter may not have known this himself: he did not seem to be "intentionally duplicitous" in claiming a Native background. When it came to his work as a Hopi messenger, however, Haley found that Carpenter had a habit of deliberately blending the Hopi Traditionalist teachings with Hawaiian-themed metaphysics (borrowed from David Kaonohiokala Bray) and from other "New Age precursors": "Rosicrucianism, Theosophy, and Faithism, a spiritual tradition begun by a New York dentist in the late nineteenth century." In other words, Carpenter's influential message of what it meant to be a "Traditional Indian" was something he crafted to suit his own interests.

Matthiessen, in both his published and unpublished writings about Craig Carpenter, gives no indication that he ever suspected his "teacher and guide" was anything other than a "half-baked detribalized"[33] member of the Kanien'kehá:ka, part of the Iroquois Confederacy of Nations. He sensed that Carpenter was touchy about identity: "Craig is impressive and sincere, but he is also judgmental, unforgiving, driven, and more self-conscious about his Indian-ness than these fullblood Indians."[34] Yet he accepted Carpenter at his word, perhaps because many Native people, from all around the country, took Carpenter as a Mohawk. And why would a non-Native outsider question their judgment?

For three days at Medicine Flat, Matthiessen helped irrigate crops and rake the ground clear for a planting of wheat. He was fascinated by his new acquaintance, who avoided paying taxes, refused to get a driver's license, declined to acknowledge U.S. citizenship, and rejected most modern technologies in favor of a spare existence that was similar to the one Matthiessen longed for:

> Except in bad weather, when he retreats into a battered trailer stuffed with books and pamphlets, Craig prefers to sleep outside; he has his bedroll on a raised platform under the great madrone tree on the east side of the yard. In the shade of this tree, in the afternoon, we prepare winter apples.... And sitting here in peace and silence in the golden colors and rich apple smells, amidst the soft voices of fruit bees and birds, I am overwhelmingly content, soft and easy with well-being, and filled with nostalgia for a bucolic life that I have never had.[35]

This kind of intoxicating "nostalgia" may have stifled any pangs of doubt he felt about Carpenter. That he had just abandoned the Zen Studies Society likely lowered his guard even further. Matthiessen was looking for a new direction; here was a man who seemed to offer privileged access to spiritual traditions and ways of thinking that had previously been off-limits.

Eventually, Carpenter opened up about bigfoot. A few years earlier, he said, he'd been given a plaster cast by a local Yurok leader named Calvin Rube—a duplicate of the cast made famous by Jerry Crew and *The Humboldt Times* in 1958. Carpenter had then made an additional forty copies in waterproof cement, and distributed them around the country through a network called the League of North American Indians. He had done this because bigfoot, he explained, was a messenger signifying that Purification Day was imminent. "[T]he increasing incidence of 'Bigfoot' [sightings] must be taken as a sign that people must return to the Creator's Life Plan," Matthiessen wrote in his notes.³⁶ In Carpenter's telling, bigfoot was a manifestation of "Bahana," or the "Lost White Brother," from the Hopi prophecies. Matthiessen would summarize this extraordinary claim in his introduction to *In the Spirit of Crazy Horse* (1983):

> My travels with Indians began some years ago with the discovery that most traditional communities in North America know of a messenger who appears in evil times as a warning from the Creator that man's disrespect for His sacred instructions has upset the harmony and balance of existence; some say that the messenger comes in sign of a great destroying fire that will purify the world of the disruption and pollution of earth, air, water, and all living things. He has strong spirit powers and sometimes takes the form of a huge hairy man; in recent years this primordial being has appeared near Indian communities from the northern Plains states to far northern Alberta and throughout the Pacific Northwest."³⁷*

Matthiessen knew how bizarre this all sounded, yet he found himself "relaxed and easy" at Medicine Flat, giving in to "calm acceptance of what is happening, or seems to be happening."³⁸ At one point Mary Hansen, a self-professed psychic, even schooled him about his "unseen helpers," four familiars who supposedly trailed behind him as ghosts: Lord Byron, Henry David Thoreau, Jean-Paul Marat, and Aesop.

Carpenter acknowledged the writer's seriousness by taking him to visit the Yurok leader Calvin Rube. No doubt Carpenter also, more quietly, recognized that Matthiessen might be useful, an effective promoter of the Indian Rebirth Movement were he to write something about it in one of his books. The men soon agreed to take a road trip together in the coming winter to Arizona, where they would consult with the elders on the Hopi Reservation.

In September, when Matthiessen got back to Sagaponack after a nephew's wedding in Seattle, he dashed off an excited letter to Doug Blue: "Am just home, and have had time to digest some of the experience of the past two

---

* Craig Carpenter is quoted telling the same story in Sandy Johnson and Dan Budnik's *Book of Elders* (1994): "Bigfoot is the super god of earth. There might be greater gods with more power, more intelligence, more compassion in outer space. But as far as we are aware, he is the most powerful deity on the surface of the earth. He is now coming down from the high mountains and appearing in broad daylight at the edges of villages. He is appearing to white people, and because they weren't observant enough to see him, he took the branch of a tree and waved it like a flag to get their attention. So he's really giving us every opportunity to bear witness to the fact that he's here, and from the Indian viewpoint it's the beginning of the fulfillment of his prophecies that he would come back to re-establish justice on this land."

weeks, which have been very rewarding despite my continuing state of virginity in regard to BF.... [S]uffice it to say that my understanding of the whole phenomenon is much deepened, to the point where I am getting glimmers of how shallow it has been up until now; and if the Indians permit it, I think I have found the path on which I wish to work."[39]

IN JANUARY OF the new year, 1977, Matthiessen left his family again to begin a semester-long engagement as a writing instructor at the University of California, Irvine. This was his first time running a seminar since he'd left Yale to join the CIA nearly three decades earlier, but he would quickly prove to be an excellent teacher. He was full of practical advice for students—no brand names in fiction if you want a story to survive the test of time—and he could be enormously encouraging when he saw raw talent. A young Cherokee student impressed him so much that he recommended his short stories to Candida Donadio for representation, to George Plimpton for *The Paris Review*, and to Daniel Halpern for Ecco Press.[40] This kind of generosity would characterize Matthiessen's future stints as a teacher, too. The novelist Amor Towles, who took a seminar with Matthiessen at Yale in 1986, recalled being pulled aside after class one day: "He said, basically, 'I don't know who you are. I don't know why you're here. I don't know what interests you, or what drives you. I don't know anything about you. But based on the work that you submitted, in my assessment, you're gifted, and so I would hope that you are taking this thing we're all doing here very seriously.' ... That would be right up there as probably one of the five most important moments of my life."[41]

Matthiessen found the city of Irvine "bare, grim, and inhospitable."[42] To avoid it as much as possible, he stayed with the poet Charles Wright and his wife, Holly, at their house in Laguna Beach, not far from the ocean. "We had a bedroom for him," recalled Wright, a colleague in the Department of English.[43] But Matthiessen was often absent as he pursued his own projects and extracurricular interests. (He would be away so often during the semester that Oakley Hall, another member of the faculty, assumed his Irvine seminar was a disaster until he read the "euphoric" student appraisals.)[44] "That was when he was on his way to get bigfoot," said Wright. "He was hoping to have some kind of entry into bigfoot. I don't know whether he believed in him or not."[45]

A week before classes were scheduled to begin, Matthiessen rented a car—his truck had broken down and was being repaired—and drove up to Manhattan Beach. Craig Carpenter was waiting for him at the home of screenwriter Silvia Richards (*Tomahawk*, 1951), a leading member of the Committee for

Traditional Indian Land and Life. The plan was to drive with Carpenter to the Hopi Reservation, meet the elders for a conversation, and then return to Irvine in time for the first writing seminar the following Tuesday.

The great California drought was finally breaking; torrential rain was turning to snow in the mountain passes between California and northern Arizona. At Avila Beach, they stopped to "purify" themselves with seawater, Carpenter thanking Massau'u, the Great Spirit, as Matthiessen observed. Then they headed inland to Coalinga, where Matthiessen exchanged the rental for his repaired truck, which (the mechanic told him) had been one screw away from losing its steering wheel. Before they could continue any further, a patrol officer informed them that the Tejon and Tehachapi passes were closed for at least the next day due to the heavy snowfall. This meant the path to Hopi was now blocked, and a visit to the elders would have to wait until another time. Carpenter decided it was fate—they were simply *not supposed to go there yet*—and Matthiessen agreed that the setbacks "seemed to be meaningful."[46]

With time to kill, they drove west to hike in Pinnacles National Park, and to visit Carpenter's ex-wife, Evelyn Winter, in nearby Greenfield. Along the way, Carpenter spontaneously shared a dream he'd had in which a street gang jeered at his spiritual beliefs before pushing him off a cliff to his death. Matthiessen listened thoughtfully, then suggested that the hostile cynics perhaps represented something he was familiar with himself: "the loud, brutal voice of our inner dread . . . [that is] awaiting the first faltering of faith in those on any spiritual quest." The same domineering voice of existential dread had threatened Matthiessen "more than once in the Himalaya, and not a few times since."[47]

Since they were being so candid with one another, he also shared a recent dream—one in which he'd appeared as "a hungry rat." Matthiessen wondered aloud if the dream meant he was "a greedy rat-like looter" of Carpenter's knowledge. Was he just another white man exploiting Native people for personal gain? Was he taking something that he had no right to even hear? To assuage his concern, Carpenter, at Evelyn Winter's house, gave him the gift of a tobacco kit and pipe. The next morning, they performed another purification ceremony together at dawn. "[T]his was the first time I had burned tobacco from my own medicine bundle, in a formal way," Matthiessen later wrote in his manuscript. "I wished for a simplification of my life, and a renewal, but mostly I listened to the world around. The sacred smoke that we cast to the four directions was the breath of life, and I was stirred as it disappeared into the sun that rose on the brown hills."[48]

ALONG WITH HIS tentative steps into something new with Carpenter, Matthiessen decided, in between his seminars at Irvine, that he needed to revivify his Zen practice, and that Los Angeles was the right place to do it. The previous summer at the grand opening of Dai Bosatsu, he had encountered a senior monk who went by the Dharma name of Tetsugen—"Iron Eye." Bernie Glassman was a thirty-seven-year-old Brooklyn-born Jewish sensei with a PhD in applied mathematics, and a former career as an aeronautical engineer at McDonnell Douglas, where he had helped develop plans for manned spaceflight expeditions to Mars. At Dai Bosatsu, Matthiessen had chatted with Glassman before the opening ceremony, confessing his intention to break with Eido Roshi. Glassman, offering sympathy, had encouraged him to visit his own teacher, Hakuyu Taizan Maezumi. "He wanted to continue his Zen training," Glassman later recalled of Matthiessen. "There wasn't much choice at that point. He would have probably preferred Soen Roshi, but Soen was in Japan."[49] Maezumi Roshi, the next best available option, was in Koreatown, Los Angeles.

Taizan Maezumi had been ordained as a monk at the age of eleven. In 1956, at twenty-five, he was sent to America because of his advanced language skills; he'd learned to speak English from the U.S. soldiers who had used his father's temple, in Otawara, to store antiaircraft missiles during the occupation of Japan.[50] Arriving in Los Angeles, Maezumi had first served as a priest at the Zenshuji Soto Mission. While he worked with the Japanese community, performing marriages and funerals, he had also continued his studies with Zen masters who had already made the leap from East to West, including Nyogen Senzaki, who eventually suggested to him that Zen might appeal to non-Japanese Americans beyond the walls of the Soto Mission. Inspired by the possibility, Maezumi had founded the Los Angeles Zendo in 1967, which was soon renamed the Zen Center of Los Angeles. Busshinji ("Buddha Essence Temple") was a converted clapboard house, with the zendo fashioned out of what was once the living and dining rooms, on a quiet stretch of South Normandie Avenue, in a neighborhood that was firmly immigrant and working-class.

The day Matthiessen pulled up in his truck, he would have seen a dedicated sangha house next door to Busshinji. Maezumi Roshi lived with his family in another house one street over, while Bernie Glassman lived with his wife, Helen, and their children at the end of the block. Each morning, Helen would walk up the avenue to a predawn liturgy at the zendo, and then walk home to send their kids to school. Other sangha members also lived on South Normandie, making up a tight community of dedicated students, or "weirdos," in Helen's affectionate phrase, who were "vaguely legitimized by this elegant Zen person whose father was the head of the Justice Department of Soto Zen Buddhism in Japan."[51] (Maezumi's father was Baian Hakujun Kuroda Roshi.) The remainder of the Los Angeles sangha, including many casual members, was comprised of perhaps a hundred people.

Matthiessen received a warm welcome from Maezumi Roshi, Glassman, and Dennis Genpo Merzel, another senior monk he'd briefly met at the Dai Bosatsu opening. He stayed for two days at the Zen Center, and then returned the following week for sesshin. This was Matthiessen's first training period in months, and he found it unexpectedly "disconcerting."[52] He was used to rigor and precision in Zen: barked orders, thwacks of the keisaku ("warning stick") across his shoulders, and a teacher who emphasized "one-pointedness—intense single-minded focus on the breath, on MU . . . with an eye to obliteration of the self in a sudden insight," meaning kensho.[53] These were the hallmarks of Rinzai Zen as taught by Eido Roshi, a practice that Matthiessen had come to rely upon like a penitent using a hair shirt. By contrast, Maezumi Roshi taught Soto Zen with only elements of Rinzai. (Unusually for a roshi, he had earned official recognition in both major schools, and in three distinct lineages.) Maezumi Roshi prescribed long periods of work practice—so long that Matthiessen worried they might sap too much energy from zazen. Maezumi also delivered "undramatic" lectures in a "murmur so soft that one could scarcely make out his words."[54] He referred to the keisaku as the *kyosaku* ("encouragement stick"), and rarely, if ever, shouted to exert his authority. He was not a "tough guy," said Glassman.[55] Under Maezumi's guidance, kensho, the flash of sudden insight, was less important than *shikantaza*, which means "just sitting." The practice Maezumi taught was a gentle "opening into" rather than a "seizing of." Since Matthiessen was used to the almost masochistic pursuit of mystical experience, this required a major adjustment in approach and expectations.

Matthiessen thought Maezumi Roshi was "handsome, and delicate too, without effeminacy, and he moved beautifully, leaving no trace, like a bird across the sky."[56] But one area where Maezumi could be "hard as nails,"[57] as another student put it, was in his traditional koan study, which he and Glassman oversaw according to the Harada–Yasutani system, a gauntlet of some five hundred stories, questions, or statements.[58] The dokusan room was an old upstairs bedroom. Students lined up outside to await the bell. When it rang, one would go in, bow deeply, and then pull up almost knee-to-knee with the teacher to present a koan answer. "That was probably the best laxative I ever had," recalled Charles Tenshin Fletcher, who was Maezumi's attendant for years. "He would keep you awake and aware. It was almost like being on the end of the sword, which he was turning."[59]

At the January sesshin, Maezumi tested Matthiessen's understanding of Zen using a famous koan by Hakuin Ekaku: "Two hands clap and there is a sound. What is the sound of one hand?" There are multiple "checkpoints" to this koan, variations of increasing difficulty and nuance. Matthiessen, snagging on the mental image of an actual hand, struggled to come up with an adequate response to the most basic checkpoint. Maezumi advised him not to be "imaginative," saying, "You are on the right track, but you must understand with your whole being."[60] The answer came in a fit of laughter as Matthiessen stood up to leave the room. What is the sound of one hand?

"Me, me, me! Peter, Peter, Peter! Tweet, tweet! Beep, beep!"[61]

This looks absurd on paper, but the point of a koan is not to elicit a rational answer. The intention is to make a student demonstrate "experiential insight, the noncerebral *knowing* that arises from the depths of profound samadhi."[62] A correct answer is a bodily response rather than an intellectual one; it should come like an arrow fired by an archer who gives, during the firing, no thought to their bow.

Whatever his feelings about the zazen at ZCLA, Matthiessen was exhilarated by the koan study. He would return in the fall to continue through the higher checkpoints with Maezumi Roshi and Bernie Glassman, keeping careful note of his accepted answers.

"Where did you hear [the hand], front or back?"[63]

Matthiessen turned in a circle.

"What did you intend to do after hearing it?"

He rubbed his stomach, saying, "Wonderful taste!" He intended to "swallow IT."

"The subtle sound of one hand?"

He exhaled lightly.

"What is the true state of one hand?"

He bowed.

"The source of one hand?"

"No source. No destination."

But Maezumi rejected this answer for being verbose. Matthiessen needed to find a more intuitive way to "express the inexpressible."

Later, when Matthiessen eventually passed the final checkpoint of this particular koan, Maezumi would throw him off-balance by immediately returning to an earlier one. "What is the true state of one hand?" he asked again. "In other words, what is the true state of your *self*?" This went straight to the heart of what Matthiessen was hoping to discover with Zen; it was, for him, the most difficult koan of them all. "That will be good for you to work on until we meet again," Maezumi advised.[64]

MATTHIESSEN'S SECOND ATTEMPT to visit the Hopi Reservation, in mid-March, at the end of the college semester, was derailed by a family crisis. He was scheduled to meet Carpenter after flying up the coast for a book reading, but he received a message at the Los Angeles airport from his film agent telling him to "call home at once."[65] Peter used a pay phone to reach Maria, who shared the shocking news: his mother had been in a car accident on Captiva Island. It was early afternoon when Peter hung up the phone, and the earliest flight to Florida did not leave until almost midnight. He booked a ticket, then went to the beach at Pacific Palisades to think. Mary Hansen, the psychic at Medicine Flat, had told him that "another obstacle" would prevent him from reaching the Hopi. Was this what she meant? Overcome at dusk by "a sudden sinking feeling," Peter drove to a friend's house in Bel Air to call Florida for an update. A housekeeper, answering, blurted out: "Your father just called from the hospital—your mother is dead."[66]

Betty Matthiessen had been driving alone on Captiva. On a blind curve, she slammed into a flatbed trailer that was coming from the other direction. Emergency services used hydraulic rescue tools—the Jaws of Life—to extricate her from the wreckage. A helicopter rushed her to an emergency room in Fort Myers, but she never regained consciousness.

Peter had tried repeatedly across the years to improve relations with his parents. After the early caustic novels, he had dedicated *Wildlife in America* to them "with love and many thanks," as though in apology. In 1975, he had taken what he called a "sentimental journey" with his aging father to South Carolina, where the Santee Gun Club, their old haunt, was being deeded to the Nature Conservancy. ("I just want to try to tell you once more just what this has meant to me," Matty wrote in a shy response to his son's article about the journey for *Audubon* magazine.)[67] Peter had also written an introduction to a short book about Bladensfield, the old Carey family seat in Richmond County, Virginia, as a tribute to Betty and her ancestry. These attempts at a rapprochement, however, had not really worked in any lasting way; there was always an unscalable wall of ice separating Peter from his parents. Perhaps the closest he'd ever come to reaching either of them on an emotional level had been during an uncharacteristically forthright conversation with his mother in the late 1960s. Peter had experienced a revelation during an LSD trip, and he wanted her to verify something. Was it true, as he suspected, that she'd loved him the least of her three children when they were young? Asked bluntly like this, without rancor, Betty had confessed that it *was* true: Peter had been a challenge ever since he was a baby biting her nipples while breastfeeding. This admission (Betty added, by way of consolation, that she'd always felt guilty about her favoritism) was distressing for him to hear—but a relief, too. The neglect was not just in his imagination. His neurosis had a source.

At their parents' house in Captiva, his sister was inconsolable. Mary had squabbled with Betty on the phone just a few hours before the accident. "Perhaps," Peter later wrote, "her grief was a little tainted with self-pity and drama, yet nonetheless it was genuine."[68] His brother, Carey, did not cry, and neither did he. In addition to his complicated feelings about Betty, Peter felt smothered by WASP decorum: "We could not express anything, we had no way of letting out that grief." His mother had already been cremated at a funeral home in Fort Myers; nobody saw the body except Matty. And her memorial service by the ocean—"the little Protestant Episcopalian funeral they rigged up down there," as Peter put it with unmistakable bitterness—showed "no sign of death, nothing but flowers and well-dressed, well-composed people who showed up for the occasion." There was no talk of what had happened, no mention of the Parkinson's disease or terrible depression that had plagued the last of Betty's seventy-three years, and that might have contributed to her death. No candid discussion disrupted the "lovely" atmosphere created by Matty. "No reality was permitted to enter."

Peter did what was expected of a dutiful son. Then he flew back to California to resume his plans with Craig Carpenter, brimming with "rage and pain, unfulfilled and incomplete."[69] In a letter to Maria, he wrote: "I miss my dear old Mum; I'd like to give her a hug goodbye, and a few tears. I am <u>wild</u> with restlessness over it."[70] But he would never get the maternal affection he wanted; the lack would remain for the rest of his own life. "More and more determined to understand ECM," he wrote in his notebook, giving the initials for Elizabeth Carey Matthiessen. "More and more sure that I must take my life in hand, live closer to silence."[71]

SEVEN DAYS AFTER his mother's death, Matthiessen drove east with Carpenter from Los Angeles to San Bernardino, then crossed the Cajon Pass and headed into the Mojave Desert. "[T]he road descended into a bare country of Joshua trees," he later wrote in his manuscript, "but near Barstow, the desert was carpeted with yellow flowers, and the winter chaparral was tossed by the wind."[72] In Nevada, they stopped in Overton to inspect Anasazi artifacts at the Lost City Museum, where Carpenter shared his firm belief "that traditional peoples once traveled far more widely than most white historians believe." Continuing on through cottonwoods, over rivers and hills, they entered Utah, the "brilliant towers" of Zion National Park looking to Matthiessen like the "city of God" the Mormons had once taken it to be. Heading south into Arizona, they crossed the ponderosa pineland of the

Kaibab Plateau, which he'd visited two decades earlier in search of white-tailed antelope squirrels for *Wildlife in America*. Past the Vermilion Cliffs, at a small trading post, Carpenter prevented Matthiessen from picking up a drunk Diné man who seemed at risk of exposure. ("He won't die; you don't know Indians. When he gets cold enough, he'll come to, and go on home.") They drove to Tuba City, and thus to the edge of the Hopi Reservation, where a sign warned them that alcohol and firearms were prohibited.

The Hopi Reservation covers more than 1.5 million acres of high, arid land in the northeast of Arizona. Most residents live in a dozen autonomous villages scattered around and on top of three imposing mesas. Matthiessen and Carpenter spent the night camped below Third Mesa, furthest to the west, under the village of Orayvi—possibly the oldest continuously occupied settlement in the United States, with structural woodwork dating back to 1150. But Carpenter was determined to follow what he termed the "proper traditional" process for entering Orayvi, and Hotevilla behind it. This meant starting at the villages on First Mesa in the east, "closest in all ways to the white world at Keams Canyon," another outpost. After that, Carpenter told Matthiessen, they could visit the villages on Second Mesa, where most of the leaders of the Coyote clan resided. Once they had been vetted and accepted by those leaders, only then could they ascend Third Mesa, where the "Hopi Way" was "maintained in its purest form." Carpenter intended to report back on his work as a messenger to elders of the Sun clan in Hotevilla. Matthiessen hoped to consult with leaders of the Coyote clan about bigfoot.*

The next few days were circuitous and frustrating. Polacca, a new government-funded settlement near First Mesa, struck Matthiessen as "nondescript, depressing, like any barren outskirts in America." Walpi, up on top of the mesa, was "probably the most picturesque of all the villages in Hopi," with sheer cliffs surrounding it and a magnificent view of the desert, although his eye drifted down to "the glint of tin and bright bad chemical colors that littered the rocks below"—trash. The village itself was mostly empty, and the few interactions with locals that Matthiessen and Carpenter did have were awkward. At Second Mesa, in Mishongnovi, they were invited inside the house of the village chief. But Guy Kolchaftewa was too deaf to

---

* In 1978, a narrative of this trip with Craig Carpenter was published by Matthiessen in *Rocky Mountain Magazine* under the title "Journey to Hopi: National Sacrifice Area." The fact-checked article was then reproduced as a chapter of *Indian Country* (1984). Both the article and chapter ("Mesas") were adapted from more than a hundred pages of the untitled manuscript—pages that include multiple references to bigfoot discussions at Hopi. Matthiessen deleted all of these references before publication. Readers of *Indian Country* might reasonably assume that he went to the Hopi Reservation in late March of 1977 specifically to report on strip-mining and corporate interests, and on the struggles of "Traditional" people versus the "progressives" involved with the Tribal Council. In truth, all of those issues were of secondary concern. Matthiessen kept his primary interest off the record.

answer their questions unaided, so he palmed them off to his nephew, Douglas Lomayaktewa, who "professed ignorance" of bigfoot. This, Carpenter explained, was just a test of sincerity: they would need to return several times in an elaborate, deferential performance that showed they were serious, "and not in a rude hurry like the white men." In between these visits, they camped below Second Mesa in the remains of a government school that had been torched by arsonists; Carpenter built a fire and baked buckwheat bread, and Matthiessen walked in the desert as drums beat provocatively in the distance—masked *kachina* dancers were trying to summon the rain. Beneath a juniper tree, he settled down to practice zazen.

On the day they went to Third Mesa, to Orayvi, they spent the morning and afternoon with a few of Carpenter's Traditionalist friends, who talked at length about their antipathy toward the modern world. After an early supper, Matthiessen then drove himself and Carpenter back to Second Mesa to attend a Coyote clan meeting in Shungopovi. Douglas Lomayaktewa was there, along with Chief Guy Kolchaftewa and several other men, all of them gathered around a large table in a tiny one-room house. Much of the meeting focused on perceived "excesses" and "abuses" of the Hopi Tribal Council. "They are the source of all the trouble here," one man insisted. Eventually, Matthiessen was invited to address the table with his questions. Relying on a translator named Will Mase to communicate with the older leaders, he explained, with a great show of respect, that he "wished to perceive Bigfoot as the Indians perceived him, since I believed that the concept of Bigfoot had been over-simplified and distorted by the white man." Now the fog of Lomayaktewa's "ignorance" suddenly lifted, according to Matthiessen's manuscript. "We know what you are talking about," Lomayaktewa admitted. As the other men nodded, Will Mase added that, while he thought Matthiessen was good and honest, they were "entering into religious matters that should only be discussed in our own societies." Nevertheless, the men appeared "very excited" about the subject; they were "eager to talk more," and Matthiessen was eager to listen.

Here, Carpenter interrupted with a booming voice: "If you're not supposed to speak about this, then don't do it." The meeting fell silent. Matthiessen was astonished. He was also, as he wrote in his notes, "very annoyed, for selfish reasons—hadn't we come all this distance to hear what these leaders had to say? And who was Craig to speak to them as if they were children—wasn't that the duty of Chief Guy or perhaps Will Mase?" He stared at Carpenter in disbelief. "Afterwards there was long talk, almost all of it by Craig; the subject of Bigfoot never came up again. I got the impression that Craig makes these people wary by talking too much and too fast about the Head-Chopper [Bahana] who will deal with the 'Wrongdoers' and how glad he is that the old government school where we are camped has been destroyed, and the too quick, too blunt criticism of Thomas Banyacya, who is, after all, the best known member of this Coyote Clan at Hopi." The meeting soon broke up. After so much anticipation, after three attempts to reach Hopi, Matthiessen was left to console himself with scraps: "At the very least, they had acknowledged Bigfoot's existence and his spiritual importance." He would get nothing more from the Coyote clan leaders.

Carpenter's erratic behavior (which reads like a power play: he cut the leaders off at the exact moment they threatened to take control of the narrative away from him) colored the rest of the visit to Hopi. He advised Matthiessen, without explanation, that the truck must not touch the branch tips of a peach tree. Finding some animal tracks in the desert, he insisted the prints were left specifically for the writer: "You are getting many signs. But you better be clean when the time comes. Mary [Hansen] says to tell you that she hopes your notes are legible, so all this work won't be wasted if you are wiped out." Wiped out? Carpenter was "only half-smiling" when he referenced Matthiessen's demise.

After a few more aimless days, they departed the reservation and made their way northeast to Cortez, Colorado. By the first of April, they were camping on a freezing alkali flat in Utah. Matthiessen's fingers were so numb that he had trouble lighting matches to burn the tobacco for a purification ceremony. Carpenter encouraged him to "summon" his unseen—those ghostly familiars Mary Hansen had told him about—"to bear witness to our journey to the Hopi leaders." Matthiessen now did so, yelling three times "with a startling force that seemed to come, not from me but rush <u>through</u> me." His notes contain no hint of skepticism or the suggestion this was a performance to humor his guide: Matthiessen was yelling for himself.

At Salt Lake City, he stopped at the airport to catch a flight home to New York. Carpenter, entrusted with the keys to the GMC truck, drove back to the Hoopa Valley Reservation in California, ferrying a small puppy they had rescued from a Hopi dump.

A FEW WEEKS LATER, Carpenter sent a rambling letter to Matthiessen that abruptly terminated their association. He had discovered a small bottle of "hard liquor" in the truck, he wrote. This was an unforgivable betrayal because it had put him at risk of arrest during the drive to California. More seriously, he also berated Matthiessen for abandoning his "Buddhist gods" in favor of "Redman gods," an act of apostasy, Carpenter insisted, that was both unwise and dangerous.[73]

Matthiessen was "very bothered" to receive such a testy letter, and he wrote one in return pointing out that the so-called liquor was a fruit preserve, not meant for drinking. As for the allegation that he was renouncing his "gods," he rejected the notion entirely: there was no Zen deity to abandon, and besides, he saw no irreconcilable conflict between Zen and Indian teachings. In fact, Matthiessen would later compile twelve pages of complementary beliefs under subheadings like "Religion as Everyday Life," "The Holy in Everything," and "Time as Space," juxtaposing quotes from roshis with those from various Native sources.[74] In *The Snow Leopard*, which he was just putting the finishing touches on, he would also digress about the "[i]nnumerable parallels"[75] between Eastern religions and Native American traditions, speculating that there might even be a shared prehistoric source, a single pool of lore (what Aldous Huxley called the "perennial philosophy") from which multiple streams had flowed during the centuries of human migration. The possibility of a "primordial intuition," expressed in similar ways by very different faiths on opposite sides of the world, was "a profound consolation" to Matthiessen—"perhaps the only one, to this haunted animal that wastes most of a long and ghostly life wandering the future and the past on its hind legs, looking for meanings, only to see in the eyes of others of its kind that it must die."[76]

He pleaded with Carpenter to reconsider his decision. "[I]t strikes me that we work together extremely well, and that the work we have in mind is exceptionally valuable, to others as well as to ourselves."[77] Carpenter muttered some more in a follow-up note, but then came around and allowed that their collaboration could continue *if* Matthiessen agreed to certain cleansing preparations. "I learn, I learn, slowly but surely," Matthiessen replied, desperate to repair the breach. "I shall <u>happily</u> observe a 3-day quarantine before and during any work we do together in the future on booze, dope, bad sex, shouting bad words, and blood (though I wish you would tell me <u>precisely</u> what the 'blood' restriction entails; I know that you are not quite sure what 'bad sex' is, and in the absence of a better interpretation, shall I take it to mean 'any sex that one feels guilty about'? I can't imagine what else 'bad sex' could be). Okay?"[78]

For the next few months, his attention was pulled elsewhere. In May, the novelist James Jones died from congestive heart failure; Matthiessen planned a memorial service with Irwin Shaw and hosted Jones's ashes in his upstairs zendo. He also buried his mother's ashes on Fishers Island, and, in the same week, marked his fiftieth birthday. "You are young, you are vibrant," Maria reassured him in a card. "Everyone loves you . . . but <u>no</u> one loves you more than I."[79] In July, he flew to Botswana for an ornithological safari with Victor Emanuel Nature Tours, an Austin-based company he would work with for decades as an occasional tour leader and host. He helped the guests spot birds—a Dickinson's kestrel, a painted-snipe—and found time to visit a camp of !Kung people in the Tsodilo Hills of the Kalahari Desert. (They were "serene in a way that we have lost.")[80] In August, he made his way to Tanzania, its borders with Kenya closed in an economic feud, and traveled to Ruaha National Park with Maria, her father and stepmother. "Dung smell, fresh heat, the brown glitter of the river," he wrote about the safari in *Audubon* magazine: "in a light wind I hear the fall of an acacia pod, bearing those seeds that will be devoured before a tree can grow."[81]

When he returned home to Sagaponack in the middle of September, he found another letter waiting for him from Craig Carpenter. This one gave a puzzling return address: "Somewhere in Paradise." The tone was manic. In a roundabout way, Carpenter explained that he was being forced to remove himself from civilization and retreat into the wilderness ("Paradise"), because he was now facing a criminal charge of kidnapping.

The story was very strange, even for Carpenter. At Medicine Flat, he had disagreed with Mary Hansen about the way she was raising her children. As Hansen soon told Matthiessen, Carpenter objected to her fourteen-year-old daughter "failing to behave as an Indian woman should," by dressing in midriff tops and tight "white man jeans."[82] Carpenter had reportedly grabbed the girl's hair and pulled her into the truck, and he'd convinced Hansen's twelve-year-old son to get in as well. Then Carpenter had driven away, Hansen said, but not before he threatened to kill her if she went to the police. Instead, she had gone to the reservation doctor to get something to calm her nerves; the doctor alerted the authorities. This had triggered a massive manhunt on Telescope Peak: twenty-five deputies, patrol vehicles, and a Coast Guard helicopter. An "Indian male" declared that he was going "to take [the children] to God," reported the *Eureka Times Standard*.[83] According to Hansen, this meant Carpenter had taken them to see "the Big Man"—Bahana, or bigfoot.[84] However, after just twenty-four hours in the woods, the children had reappeared at Medicine Flat, having been led back there by Carpenter, who immediately vanished. Matthiessen's truck was spotted by the helicopter on the top of Bald Mountain, poorly camouflaged with scrub. Carpenter was now a fugitive.

In his letter to Matthiessen, which was vague on all these details except the size and tenacity of the police pursuit, Carpenter found a silver lining. He was finally in "God's Country," he wrote, living off the land like a "real Indian."[85]

Matthiessen's response to the situation was swift and decisive. He phoned Mary Hansen and persuaded her to tell the police that she would *not* testify as a witness in any criminal proceedings against her friend and neighbor. Then he flew to California to retrieve his truck from the Eureka police pound. It was a "shambles," ransacked and hot-wired. "In this part of the world, one can't help but suspect that the vehicle was trashed because an Indian was thought to be the owner," he later wrote.[86] He had the truck repaired, then drove with Hans Teensma, who'd joined him in San Francisco for the ride, to speak to Hansen and her children at Medicine Flat, questioning them about the incident.

In October, Matthiessen tracked down Carpenter at his ex-wife Evelyn Winter's house in Greenfield. He now got the other side of the story—a side which corroborated Hansen's account, but which also involved "chipmunk messages," and a raven dropping salmon just as Carpenter was getting "zingy" from a lack of protein in the forest. "[Evelyn] kept glancing at me to see how I was taking all this," Matthiessen scrawled in his notebook.[87] He did not record how he was taking the evidence that Carpenter was unwell.

In *Indian Country*, there is only a passing mention of the kidnapping episode, though it would not be resolved for more than two years.* "Against their mother's will, [Carpenter] had taken two Indian children to a sacred mountain for religious purposes," Matthiessen writes, accurately enough; "when the children returned, the mother withdrew all charges and refused to sign any complaint"—also true, though he omits any reference to his own intercession with Hansen. But the next part is significant, because it suggests just how enamored he'd become with the idea of his "teacher and guide" as a man who has committed to a wild, unorthodox path in the pursuit of a more authentic life. Craig Carpenter made a mistake, Matthiessen implies, but his prosecution was never really about the kidnapping: "the authorities had no wish to forgive this seditious individual who grows most of his own food, owns almost nothing, and refuses to participate in 'the American Way of Life.'"[88]

---

* Carpenter was finally apprehended by police in Colusa, California, on September 10, 1979, on a seven-count warrant from Humboldt County for, among other charges, kidnapping, assault with a deadly weapon, and unlawful imprisonment. He sat in jail for three days, awaiting transportation, until the Humboldt County District Attorney's Office "caved," as Carpenter put it in a letter to Matthiessen, when the D.A. realized that Mary Hansen would never testify against him. Carpenter was set free—an appropriate conclusion to the whole episode, in his view, because the "whiteman court" had no jurisdiction over him anyway.

20

The Snow Leopard

> I remember saying to [George Schaller] early on, because I was just so stunned by what we were seeing and how everything was unfolding like a parable, I said, "If I can't get a good book out of this, I ought to be taken out and shot."
>
> —PM, in conversation with Michael Shapiro (2004)[1]

ELISABETH SIFTON, a brilliant thirty-seven-year-old senior editor at the Viking Press, was fed up with her job. She worked with some of the greatest writers in the world—Saul Bellow, for instance, who would sometimes pause their edit sessions to do "a five-minute yogic headstand against the bookcase"[2]—but the pay at Viking was lousy, and the boss, Tom Guinzburg, seemed "eccentric" to Sifton, running the business in a way that "wasn't really all that good."[3] (She would later revise her opinion after becoming a publisher herself and learning just how tough it could be.) Jason Epstein, over at Random House, got wind of her simmering dissatisfaction; he phoned and invited her out to lunch. As they ate, he suggested, in Sifton's memory, that she come and work at Random instead. There were follow-up meetings with him and Joe Fox, who also tried to win her over. They told her that Viking was in "the minor league," and that she could play in "the major league" if she was willing to defect. This was a tantalizing offer, but Sifton had a question: "What would you pay me?" Epstein replied, as she recalled, "You tell me you're going to come, and I'll tell you what I'm paying you." The first time he said this she shrugged it off, but she kept asking, and he kept saying it. Why wouldn't he tell her the salary? The offer started to taste a little sour. "He would never have said that to a man," Sifton thought.

She felt obliged to inform Guinzburg that she was considering leaving Viking for a competitor. He was sitting in his office when she confessed to the meetings. "Such a pity," he said. "I have this here"—he picked up a manuscript off his desk—"and I was going to give it to you to look after." Fresh from the mail room, it was titled *The Snow Leopard*.

Sifton was already an admirer of Peter Matthiessen. The year before, she had sent him advance proofs of *Humboldt's Gift*, fishing for a few lines of praise she might use in the marketing. She had also sent him a letter with a fawning postscript: "Tom is tiring of my continually popping into his office to tell him I've been reading P. Matthiessen and finding it marvelous. 'Don't you realize,' I said a while back, having just re-read Shore Birds, 'that he's the best writer of classic-romantic-modern prose in America?' Then I was back again to enthuse about Far T. 'Yes, yes,' said Tom, 'I think you should tell him!' So I take this post-scriptum opportunity to do so."[4]

Waving the new manuscript in her face, Guinzburg knew exactly what he was doing. Sifton planned to turn down Jason Epstein on principle, but when she told friends that she had decided to stay on at Viking, one of them said, "Boy, Tom Guinzburg really knows how to press your buttons."[5]

At that point, Matthiessen was still aligned with Random House as an author. But he was so irritated by the treatment *Far Tortuga* had received there that he'd concocted a plan to divide his output. All nonfiction would henceforth go to Guinzburg at Viking; fiction, whenever he got over *Far Tortuga* and wrote another novel, would remain at Random. This bifurcation was intended to mirror the two halves of his career: "nature writer/journalist" on the one hand, and "novelist" on the other. But the arrangement was nonsensical if one considered it too closely: Random House had already published *Blue Meridian*, and Dutton had published *The Tree Where Man Was Born*. The arrangement was really a "ruse,"[6] as Sifton once wrote in an internal memo, "invented" to get *The Snow Leopard* away from Joe Fox without causing the kind of wounded indignation that Matthiessen would later cause anyway.

Guinzburg handed Sifton the manuscript. She devoured it, growing increasingly excited by what she was reading. Then she went to lunch with "one of the most charismatic people I'd ever encountered."[7] Matthiessen wanted to know her opinion. Heart in her mouth, "trembling with fear," she told him "true things": that it was "perfectly wonderful," even magnificent. In her view, they could publish the book tomorrow with minimal changes. Matthiessen was stunned. "It won't do," he told her. "It's nowhere near ready for publication." What Sifton had read was only the rough draft.

After their meeting, Sifton sent him another flattering letter. "There's no reason I should be writing to you now, no operative reason: the decision as to how to proceed is yours, and Tom and you and Candida will keep each other posted as to all intents and particulars; but it seems discourteous not to pipe up and tell you how much I appreciated our lunch. The opulent pleasure of talking about your books spurred me on to the even more sensible activity of re-reading them, and that was terrific, though I nearly o.'d.'ed on the unrelieved excellence."⁸ She added, perceptively, "I liked to imagine that I saw the larger shape and pattern of which each volume was a component part." Compliments were always welcome, but Matthiessen was probably more impressed by her recognition of linkages and common themes between his fourteen books: a "larger shape and pattern" was something he'd started to notice himself. He also appreciated that Elisabeth Sifton was the daughter of the great theologian Reinhold Niebuhr—"the least of her many qualifications for this job," he told his friend William Merwin.⁹

After some fierce financial negotiations, Sifton won her prize. In February 1977, she typed up a memorandum of understanding so a rush contract could be produced for Candida Donadio's perusal. The advance was $80,000, to be paid in four installments by the end of the year. The royalty rate topped out at 17.5 percent—higher than even the controversial rate Matthiessen had secured at Random House for *Far Tortuga*. He was promised, too, the lion's share of paperback reprint earnings. There was one specific clause he requested for the contract, however, as a gesture of support for an old friend: Tom Guinzburg needed to be employed at The Viking Press. Facing cash-flow problems, the family-built company had been sold in 1975 to the British giant Penguin Books, which was owned by S. Pearson & Son. Should his childhood pal leave his role—or be pushed out—as president and CEO of Viking Penguin Inc. prior to *The Snow Leopard* being printed and bound, the author retained the right to take his book elsewhere.¹⁰

Before he mailed the manuscript to Guinzburg, Matthiessen had written more than a dozen potential titles on the cover of one of his Himalayan journals. "In the Secret of the Mountains." "A Walk into Autumn." "At Rest in the Present."¹¹ "Air Burial" might have worked, but the only one he ever seriously considered was "The Snow Leopard." Sifton thought it was perfect, and she protested when the book was described on the contract as "tentatively titled": "surely that glorious title is not tentative at all?"¹² Internally at Viking, there was concern that it was too opaque to be commercial. "There were a lot of discussions with, I think, not very top-drawer people in publicity and marketing who wanted there to be a nice explanatory subtitle," Sifton recalled.¹³ Her position was resolute. "No, and no, and no, because what are you going to say it's *about*?" It was about too many things to be distilled into a succinct, consumer-friendly phrase. And besides, she told her colleagues, "we're not going to need a subtitle." She was confident the book would become famous.

THE SNOW LEOPARD IS comprised of sixty-four dated journal entries, all first-person present tense. This creates an impression that one is reading what Matthiessen wrote each day in the Himalayas, a spontaneous, exquisitely observed account of his wildlife survey with George Schaller. In reality, *The Snow Leopard* is an artful construction, real life shaped into something almost mythic. Matthiessen's book reflects the vibrancy of his original notes: the wonder of a traveler seeing a sublime landscape for the first time; the enthusiasm of a man still relatively new to Zen, awed by the possibilities of his practice. Yet this wide-eyed freshness is supported, in the published book, by a degree of wisdom that he earned only in the years after the expedition. In effect, Matthiessen collapses his future (all that he will learn) and his past (all he has experienced) into the eternal present of a pilgrimage across the mountains of Dolpo, a place where, as he later said, "time dissolved, then space."[14] Despite the dated journal entries, the book is far from a simple foot march through chronological events. "Simultaneously, I am myself, the child I was, the old man I will be," he writes after noticing how his hands change texture in the high-altitude exposure.[15] A similar statement could be made about *The Snow Leopard*. It is a brilliant piece of nature writing: "a flock of vermilion minivets, blown through a wind-tossed tumult of bamboo."[16] It is also a carefully curated self-portrait of the author as he was, as he will be, as he really *is*, beyond the illusory veil of linear time.

Matthiessen was once asked during an interview for *The Missouri Review* to what extent *The Snow Leopard* was "a shaped creation." He answered, in part, that the guts of the book were already present in his field journals, but he "rewrote a lot": "I'm a terrific rewriter, I polish and polish and polish and polish."[17]

The rewriting began in the actual journals. Matthiessen had filled two notebooks in Nepal, scribbling on the right-hand pages while leaving the left almost entirely blank. For his first pass at a draft, he read back through these notebooks, marking several passages he'd written during the trek about his ultimate goals for the project: "Very important that for this book, details are chosen in such a way that effects transcend the mere parts, much as intuitive knowing transcends mere logic. . . . The NYorker chronicle can be quite straight, from these notes, but the book must be something else again: haiku, dreams, fragments, ritual."[18] As he read, he line-edited the entries, circled key phrases using colored pens (green for the richest material), crossed out hackneyed paragraphs, and inserted new sections using the blank left-hand pages. At the back of the two notebooks, and in a third used for drafting a prologue, he also compiled a reference index of what each page contained ("p. 180: disappointment at not being ready to 'let go'"), along with a list of the themes, concepts, and images he wanted to feature: Deborah Love "+death; ghats at Benares; light on snow peaks; ski trip." In this way, his original journals provided a blueprint for building *The Snow Leopard*.

At this point, Matthiessen made a series of strategic deletions. There are, in the original journals, multiple references to his adopted daughter, Rue, who, like Alex, had also lost her mother in 1972. Matthiessen chose to omit these references. He would include only a brief mention of Rue in the final book, preferring to focus his parental anxieties through the prism of his younger son. Years later, Rue would respond with remarkable equanimity to being written out of her own story. The lonely little boy yearning for his father is "archetypal," she said. "That's why he put it in there. It muddies the waters of the narrative to start gassing on about the daughter who is not biologically his. And then, he saw himself in his male children, too. He had more empathy, in an ordinary day-to-day way, for his male children than he did for his female children. We were in a different category in his mind."[19] Matthiessen also omitted the journal references to Maria Koenig, and skipped over entries that detailed his days with Jane Stanton in Italy. He once claimed that he "tried to be very honest" in *The Snow Leopard*, saying, "I put several episodes in there that, in a way, were embarrassing, because I'm a very private sort of person."[20] But there were limits to his candor. His long history of adultery vanished into the black hole of a single ambiguous phrase: he "behaved badly."[21]*

When it came to additions, Matthiessen relied on scholarly books by the British Tibetologist David Snellgrove, Anagarika Govinda, founder of the Arya Maitreya Mandala, and the American anthropologist Walter Evans-Wentz. He folded in new observations, as though they had occurred to him on the trek, about slash-and-burn agriculture and soil erosion, Tibetan Buddhism, the Bardo Thodol. Almost all the more substantial digressions spread throughout the manuscript were written after the expedition. A mild entry in the journals about pouring rain and Schaller's tetchy disposition was transformed, during the drafting process, into a wide-ranging meditation on the synchronicity of science and mysticism: "Today science is telling us what the Vedas have taught mankind for three thousand years, that we do not see the universe as it is."[22] Similarly, Matthiessen identified anchor points in his blueprint where he could tether discussions about Eastern teachings and Native American traditions, the psychological power of mountains, and, of course, the mysterious yeti, a subject heavily influenced by his bigfoot travels from 1975 onward. The single page for October 5 in the original notebooks contains little more of substance than "sphagnum + leeches."[23] In

---

* In a line cut from an early draft, Matthiessen acknowledged that he was "a faithless husband and poor friend to someone who deserved a great deal better." This was adapted from an original confession in his Himalayas journals: "D clung to . . . all she could find to excuse a faithless husband and poor friend. Once I told her that she was the best friend I had ever had—it's true—and that I was bitterly sorry she could not say the same."

The Snow Leopard, that same entry is the book's emotional core, a vulnerable confession of Matthiessen's "deep restlessness," and an outline of his lifelong search for a Way to apprehend the unity at the heart of the universe, and thus one's "true nature."[24]

Perhaps the most important additions, however, are Matthiessen's "moments of being," to borrow a phrase from Virginia Woolf. These are the moments when he seems to stop and marvel on the path through Dolpo, becoming acutely aware of himself in the world, attuned to the minutiae and meaning of some fleeting experience. The moments are largely inchoate in the journals. Polishing was also a process of creative excavation; Matthiessen dug past the surface of his field notes in pursuit of deeper truths below. For example: "There is a secret in these mountains, and it is right before me, I feel it," he wrote in his journal at Shey Gompa. "I ring, and the mountains ring—there is a ringing that we share, if I can tune it fine enough."[25] What secret? What was he really trying to say here? Later, on the left-hand page, he pushed himself to be clearer: "The 'secret' is: the mountains simply exist, as I do. The sun is round."

Then a blue pen edit: "without meaning, they are meaning."

And another attempt: "Secret of mtns is that they simply exist, as I do—they have no meaning, they are meaning."

And as the moment finally appears in *The Snow Leopard*:

> The secret of the mountains is that the mountains simply exist, as I do myself: the mountains exist simply, which I do not. The mountains have no "meaning," they *are* meaning; the mountains *are*. The sun is round. I ring with life, and the mountains ring, and when I can hear it, there is a ringing that we share.[26]

This lovely passage was the product of considerable effort over multiple drafts. But Matthiessen included another line, too, which suggests he was still a little unsatisfied with his final version: "I understand all this, not in my mind but in my heart, knowing how meaningless it is to try to capture what cannot be expressed, knowing that mere words will remain when I read it all again, another day." Futile or not, his attempts to "capture" the inexpressible using "mere words" are what animates *The Snow Leopard*; these brief moments, heightened but never overwrought, constitute some of the strangest, bravest, most radiant passages he would ever write.

Matthiessen worried about too much "Buddhist sentimentality" creeping into his prose. He was determined to avoid the woolly rhetoric of so many books about mysticism and mystical experience. "He kept talking about being precise," recalled Elisabeth Sifton. "There were lots of references to 'crystalline' versus 'muddy.'"²⁷

Sifton left comments on a manuscript draft, but she did not edit *The Snow Leopard* in a conventional sense. Instead, she traveled out from New York to Sagaponack and stayed for a few days with Peter and Maria. "You got up in the morning, you had a cup of coffee, and then you went to this cabin."²⁸ By 1977, Matthiessen had renovated the children's playhouse near the apple trees into his private writing studio, or "shed," as he called it. Sifton sat down beside him at the long L-shape desk, cluttered with sea rocks, coral, the vertebrae of an elephant. As she watched, he concentrated intently on his manuscript. "He would, as it were, review a page, and make changes, and say, 'This thing I find difficult about this is *blah blah blah*. What do you think?'" Then Sifton would offer her advice. Matthiessen would make some more changes—or not, depending on what he thought of her opinion. "And then we'd go on to the next page." While this was a curious arrangement, Sifton was used to being "the continuity girl,"²⁹ there to read a text closely and then offer support to the (invariably male) writer as requested. "I can remember at a cocktail party for Saul Bellow, Malamud said to me, 'Do you seriously edit Saul? I mean, do you *edit* him?' I said, 'No, I don't edit him! I just keep him company while he's going over his [pages].'"³⁰ So it was with Matthiessen in Sagaponack (and so it would be with Bruce Chatwin a few years later). The process took "quite a long time"—twenty-one hours in two days, according to an exhausted letter—and the atmosphere in the studio was intense. Matthiessen had written his journals in Dolpo as a Zen practice of close observation. He had produced the earliest draft as a replacement for sesshin. Now the editing, too, was a kind of zazen. "That's the way I felt," said Sifton.

To read *The Snow Leopard* is to read a record of all this meditation; thus, to some extent, the incantatory quality of Matthiessen's prose. It is worth noting that each of the book's four sections is prefaced by a title page featuring one or two Tibetan characters. Adding these characters together forms the six-syllable mantra of Avalokiteshvara: ཨོཾ (om) མ་ཎི (mani) པདྨེ (padme) ཧཱུྃ (hum). Turning the pages of the book is akin to turning a prayer wheel, ཨོཾ་མ་ཎི་པདྨེ་ཧཱུྃ—another form of meditation.

When the manuscript was in decent shape, Matthiessen, as he had with every project since *Wildlife in America*, forwarded copies to experts for comments and corrections: George Schaller for the science and general facts about the expedition; Bernie Glassman for the Zen; Robin Kornman, a student of Chögyam Trungpa, for "fine doctrinal points, transliteration of Sanskrit and Tibetan terms, and other matters on which no two scholars seem able to agree."³¹ Matthiessen sent a copy to Donald Hall, the first poetry editor of *The Paris Review*, for feedback on the language. Hall thought the book was "marvelous," and returned five pages of notes. "I strongly approve of the use of the present tense throughout," he wrote. "There is a sense of immediacy, of living in the present, which goes exactly <u>with</u> the current of Zen."³² Matthiessen may have felt trepidation as an "up-tight wasp" about baring his feelings for the world to see, but Hall told him to get over it. "No . . . there is <u>not</u> too much 'emotion' forced upon the text! Please don't be ashamed of your emotions! You are not just bleating or complaining. It is very beautiful, very strong, and totally appropriate. And it is artistically <u>fine</u>."

Hall did have a few small objections, though. There were a handful of clichés blemishing the pages. He was "skeptical" of the section about psychedelics as part of a "path," or "journey," or "way" to self-understanding: "I didn't take these drugs. So you can dismiss what I say." (Matthiessen mostly did on this subject.) Hall was also concerned about the presence—or absence, more accurately—of Deborah Love in the narrative. She was "absolutely central" to the book, he insisted. (As the poet and translator Christopher Merrill has pointed out, "If you add up the total number of pages about Deborah in *The Snow Leopard*, it's pretty much the same number of pages about the Virgin Mary in the New Testament, and yet she looms so large.")³³ However, in Matthiessen's early circulated draft, "D" all but disappeared toward the end of the manuscript. Hall argued that this was an unacceptable oversight. "I felt sad <u>for</u> her, that you were not thinking of her. And I felt a little annoyed with you," he wrote in another letter.³⁴ Hall's recommendation was an interesting one, because it speaks to how constructed *The Snow Leopard* was as an expedition journal: "I feel most strongly that you must remember her, must think about her again, within the last five pages of the book." Matthiessen seems to have taken Hall's advice seriously; he "remembered" his late wife more extensively on November 22, thirty-four pages from the end, offering closure for the reader with a brief scene of himself and Eido Roshi holding Deborah's hands and chanting the Four Vows as she died.

Matthiessen was not averse to massaging his material to make the book more thematically cohesive. Take, as another example, the eponymous snow leopard. The snow leopard in the original journals is elusive but real, *Panthera uncia*, the graceful great cat that Matthiessen and Schaller were hoping to glimpse as they conducted a scientific study of the blue sheep. The snow leopard of *The Snow Leopard* is something more literary: a malleable symbol of, among other things, the enlightenment Matthiessen seeks to attain before he realizes, in a flash, that aspiration is useless, and that he should open-heartedly accept whatever comes as "quite enough."

Have you seen the snow leopard?
No! Isn't that wonderful?[35]

This rhetorical question, Matthiessen muttering to himself, might be expressed in another way: "Have you found transcendence in the Himalayas, truly perceived reality? No! And I don't need to because this moment, right now, is already paradise."

Here is the shift in perspective that Matthiessen hinted at in *Far Tortuga* with Captain Raib, dreaming of building a shack on his Edenic island, and Speedy Bodden, rejecting dreams to find contentment with what he already has. ("I got fifty-five acres, mon, and cows. I go along every day, do what I got to do, and den I lays down to my rest.")[36] Here is the shift that Matthiessen tried to embrace when he left Eido Shimano, who emphasized the mystical experience of kensho, and turned to Taizan Maezumi, who advised "just sitting." Here is a shift that is not particularly discernible in the meandering entries of his unedited journals. Matthiessen's big revelation in *The Snow Leopard*, hard-won and even harder to hold on to, is one that was written with four years of clarifying hindsight.

"THE SNOW LEOPARD~I" appeared in *The New Yorker*, with some of the more mystical material edited out to fit the house style, on March 27, 1978. A second installment was published in the following issue, on April 3. Matthiessen was away in Africa at the time—a depressing journey with the primatologist Gilbert Boese, of Chicago's Brookfield Zoo, through Senegal, The Gambia, and the Ivory Coast, to survey what remained of West Africa's wildlife, and then a side trip to Zaire in search of the Congo peafowl*—so he missed the praise that immediately overwhelmed his mailbox. Edward Abbey sent a letter of congratulations. So did John Cheever (largely incoherent, possibly inebriated, about spiritual experience and the church bells of Ossining). Jim

---

* Both trips are recounted as two-thirds of the appropriately named *African Silences* (1991). Other than a single monkey, the survey with Gilbert Boese turned up no mammals outside a national park. Even mammals *within* the likes of Basse Casamance National Park, in Senegal, and Abuko Nature Reserve, in The Gambia, were few and far between. "I am encouraged by Senegambia conservation attitudes," Matthiessen wrote in a letter home to Maria, but evidence of poaching, livestock encroachment, and deliberate deforestation—fires glimpsed at night from a passing train—combined to form a bleak picture of ecological decline. The side trip to Zaire was only slightly more successful. Traveling with the British ornithologist Alec Forbes-Watson, and Sarah Plimpton, sister of George, Matthiessen failed to see the Congo peafowl, *Afropavo congensis*. He did see gorillas in the Kahuzi-Biega National Park, though, including an orphaned infant in the park office that requested to be held: "It was entirely relaxed, astonishingly so, a solid little coarsehaired thing of no more than twenty pounds that leaned its head quietly against my chest as it gazed about, eliciting an unfamiliar surge of maternal feeling."

Harrison, always reliable for a few words of heartening support, did not disappoint: "I think it is the best thing you ever wrote which is akin to saying the best thing anyone writes these days."[37]

Matthiessen worked on proofs of the book, making numerous changes until Sifton told him his tinkering needed to stop. "The job of an editor working with Mr. Matthiessen," she later said, "is partly one of making sure that physically the manuscript is legible so that the printer will be able to read it at the end of what is often a very lengthy process of revision."[38] He petitioned Viking's production department for a dust jacket without any blurbs or marketing copy, "which I think would fight the spirit of the book."[39] Unusually, and to his satisfaction, Viking acquiesced. When *The Snow Leopard* was published in August, its design was minimalist: nothing on the front or back cover except the title, the author's name, and a wrap-around photograph by George Schaller of snowy Shey Gompa, a few lamasery buildings barely discernible in a vast snowscape beneath a dome of blue sky.

More ecstatic letters arrived from Bill Styron ("plainly a masterpiece"),[40] William Merwin (trying to make it last, he said, like an ice cream cone in the old days when they'd only cost a nickel), Gardner Stout, Robert Aitken, Lewis Thomas, president of the Memorial Sloan-Kettering Institute where Deborah had died, and Francine du Plessix Gray, who actually swooned: "I went into a solitary room and shut out all light and lay flat on my back for a long while, eyes closed, partaking in some kind of sacramental substance issued forth by the book."[41]

There were a few tepid reactions, too, though these raised some legitimate points. One friend wrote a note wondering at Matthiessen's fixation on the "noble savage." Tukten, the Sherpa hired by Schaller in Kathmandu to support the expedition, is presented in *The Snow Leopard* as a mystical "teacher" for how he lives "in the moment," for his "freedom from attachments," and for the "simplicity of his everyday example."[42] Tukten's role was another literary device mostly manufactured during the writing process, and some of the passages about this "humble *tulku* of Kasapa"[43] with "guru's hands" and "yellow Mongol eyes"[44] are plainly orientalist, as are Matthiessen's more ill-tempered remarks about other porters and the Dolpo-pa, who are unfairly maligned in the book. *Orientalism*, by Edward Said, was also published in 1978, and *The Snow Leopard* does not escape Said's incisive critique of Westerners othering Eastern cultures and peoples.

Meanwhile, Matthiessen was challenged by two ex-lovers about his depiction of saintly "D" and his fraught relationship with her. Karen Yochim, the "Florida girl" he had hosted at Polgeto in 1969, was so sharp with her criticism during a phone call that he felt the need to defend himself in writing: "The book itself is pretty explicit about my very shaky marriage with D, talk of divorce, etc; that I also had a lot of respect and even love for her, despite all the incompatibility and fighting, is true, too, as you well knew."[45] Jane Stanton was even less impressed than Karen Yochim. She thought the book was, as she later recalled, an act of "wishful atonement."[46] Peter had been writing letters to her (and to Maria) in the Himalayas, yet a reader was supposed to believe he was consumed with grief for Deborah Love? "I think he felt that he should grieve. I think he felt that he wanted to grieve. And I think the artist in him knew that to have a great book, he would have to appear to grieve. But as I said to him, the more interesting book would have been if you had told the truth and said, 'Look, I'm having an affair, and I can't really grieve, and the two things are driving me crazy. And the snow leopard is me! I'm looking for me here, and I can't find me! Because I can't feel anything.'" Of course, Matthiessen did grieve for Deborah, including in Dolpo—his original journals are proof of that—but his ability to compartmentalize emotions is undeniable.

The Snow Leopard received more than eighty reviews across newspapers, magazines, and radio. Like those for *Far Tortuga*, they ran the gamut of critical assessment. Many reviews were rapturous: the book was "an exhilarating work of art";[47] "terrifyingly good";[48] "the genuine article in an era of ersatz wilderness travel books";[49] "as rarefied and sober as the remote northwest reaches of Nepal";[50] "fiercely felt and magnificently written, in which timelessness and 'modern time' are made to touch and join."[51] On the other side of opinion, the book was "didactic . . . predictable and finally impersonal";[52] "metaphysical self-indulgence";[53] bloated with "stiff pages of theology and history";[54] lacking "the lightness of touch that is absolutely necessary when jiggling the web of paradoxes nature has stretched across its secrets";[55] and maybe kind of pointless, according to Robert M. Adams in *The New York Review of Books*—did Matthiessen really need to "slog through the snows of Nepal" to figure himself out?[56] In Britain, where the book was published by Chatto & Windus, Colin Thubron declared it "a courageous, confessional, but high-flown pilgrimage, whose mystical perceptions evaporate under the discipline of words." He added, "It is sad that for its author the most important things are the least communicable; but a vividly individual journey none the less."[57]

Curiously, none of the reviews critiqued Matthiessen for abandoning his young son to go on an expedition in Nepal, the most common point of contention among future readers.

The Snow Leopard spent ten weeks on the *New York Times* Best Sellers list, peaking at number six. It might have stayed longer, or moved higher up the list, were it not for an unfortunate coincidence. In early August, Matthiessen received word that his book was the cover story of *The New York Times Book*

Review; an editor forwarded him a copy. Framing the review by Edward Hoagland was the illustration of a giant seated Buddha: two climbers ascended his right shoulder with rope, while a snow leopard perched regally on his head like a crown. It was an eye-catching drawing by Steven Guarnaccia, enchanting enough to counteract Hoagland's ambivalent verdict on a "radiant but rather fragile, flickering book."[58] Matthiessen was assured it was the sort of cover that got reproduced and put on display in bookstores—a guarantee of significant sales. He was "extremely gratified and excited."[59] However, the review was scheduled for August 13, 1978. On August 10, an industry-wide strike halted print production on the *Times*, the New York *Daily News*, and *The New York Post*. Some subscribers received early copies, but the Buddha never reached the newsstands. After the strike ended eighty-eight days later, the *Book Review* editors bumped Hoagland's piece to page four of a new issue, minus the illustration.

    In the four decades since then, *The Snow Leopard* has rightly attained the status of a modern classic. It has never sold as well as Robert Pirsig's *Zen and the Art of Motorcycle Maintenance*—"a hateful child-destroying egomaniac and an intelligent yet dull book," in Matthiessen's biting assessment[60]—to which it is sometimes compared, but *The Snow Leopard* is still frequently read and discussed. In 2021, Kathryn Schulz, in *The New Yorker*, suggested that it "looms over much of nature writing, enormous and immovable as Annapurna."[61] This is accurate, but it also looms over books about spiritual journeys, travel literature in general, and grief memoirs, too. Throughout the years it has inspired poetry, music, drama—David Chase cited it as an unlikely influence on the final season of *The Sopranos*[62]—and other literary treks to Dolpo: *Without Ever Reaching the Summit* by Paolo Cognetti. Pico Iyer was "so moved" by the book in his mid-twenties that he left his office at *Time* magazine, in Midtown Manhattan, "and went to live among the Zen monks of Kyoto."[63]

    For the rest of his life, Matthiessen would receive letters about *The Snow Leopard*, including heartfelt thanks from an English professor, undergoing chemotherapy for metastatic cancer, who found courage after reading the book to make peace with his impending death. And yet, while Matthiessen knew it was accomplished, it was nonfiction—artistically lesser, in his mind, than the novels he'd written. "I've come to a pretty pass where I kind of resent 'The Snow Leopard,'" he told the *San Francisco Chronicle* in 1997. "I don't disown the book, but I feel my fiction is the heart of my work."[64] He was still saying the same thing in 2014, in an interview recorded just weeks before he died. "I think it's a good book, but it really put me in a pigeonhole," he told Mark Adams. "It's been very hard to find a place for my fiction because I'm immediately thought of as the guy who wrote *The Snow*

Leopard."⁶⁵ Many writers would be thrilled to be associated with something so enduring, but Matthiessen saw it as bittersweet.

A FEW WEEKS BEFORE *The Snow Leopard* was published, Tom Guinzburg was fired from Viking Penguin. The publisher's parent company, S. Pearson & Son, was unimpressed with the annual earnings report, and unsympathetic when Guinzburg protested that a rough year in the book trade was often followed by a blockbuster one that balanced out the bottom line. Such thinking was old-school in publishing; a yearly profit was now nonnegotiable.

Matthiessen had that clause in his contract tying the *The Snow Leopard* to Guinzburg's employment status, but the book was too far along in the process to be derailed now. Still, his future with the imprint was suddenly uncertain. Irving Goodman, the replacement president, took him out to a "reassuring" lunch. Promises were made to reissue his backlist in uniform paperback Penguin editions, which was something he had already indicated he wanted. Elisabeth Sifton, too, stressed her "vigilance and support as an editor," soon to be editor-in-chief.⁶⁶ It was enough to keep Matthiessen on side—for now—although the ruthless treatment of his friend would not pass unacknowledged.

In the late afternoon of April 25, 1979, the National Book Awards were held at Carnegie Hall in New York. The favorite to win in the (now defunct) category of "Contemporary Thought" was Meyer Schapiro's *Modern Art: 19th and 20th Centuries*. The second favorite was *This House of Sky*, by Ivan Doig. In a surprising upset, the award went to *The Snow Leopard.** Matthiessen was not present for his moment of glory. Pointedly, he sent as his representative Tom Guinzburg rather than a current employee of Viking Penguin. Guinzburg walked onto the stage and read out a prepared statement on Matthiessen's behalf:

> Ladies and gentlemen of the committee: Thank you very much: I am honored indeed. It seems very ungracious, even ungrateful, not to be here in person to accept this award, presented by so distinguished a committee on behalf of so distinguished an organization. The only excuse I can offer for my disgraceful absence is the circumstance that I am away for a month on a research trip with traditional Indian people deep in the Nevada-Utah

---

* The category judges were Michael Arlen, Kenneth Clark, and Joyce Carol Oates. *The Snow Leopard* also won a second time, in 1980, in the category of "General Nonfiction (Paperback)," making it one of only three books that have won a National Book Award twice. The other two are John Clive's biography, *Thomas Babington Macaulay* (1973), and Lewis Thomas's *The Lives of a Cell* (1974).

desert, a hundred miles from an airport, from where, at this moment, on what I hope is a lovely Spring afternoon, I send warm desert greetings and sincere thanks.[67]

Matthiessen was near Tridell, Utah, with Craig Carpenter, who was still a fugitive because of the kidnapping. They were interviewing Carpenter's Ute contacts in the region about bigfoot, the Big Man, or "Zu-pitc'h," as an old chief called it as he leaned against a tractor—"kind of a hairy person."[68]

After the award ceremony, the New York literati toasted the winners at a cocktail reception in the Imperial Ballroom of the Sheraton. At the same time, Matthiessen and Carpenter were driving two hundred miles southeast from Tridell into Colorado. In the town of Montrose, Matthiessen proposed that they have their own celebration with dinner at a Chinese restaurant. Carpenter refused—he could not accept "expense money" food on a journey about "Indian Business," he said—so they marked the occasion, the biggest moment of Matthiessen's career thus far, with peanut butter sandwiches by the side of a road.

ON THE ACKNOWLEDGMENTS PAGE for *The Snow Leopard*, "Maria Eckhart" is thanked for her "sensible and constructive suggestions throughout the several drafts."[69] This is Matthiessen's earliest public recognition of a role—first reader—that Maria would occupy for decades, faithfully and tirelessly, on book after book for him. Maria read him better than almost anyone else, deftly identifying his tics and preoccupations. "I have been struck recently, in your writing, of how often you 'feel you have come home' or are 'homesick,'" she wrote about *The Snow Leopard* soon after its release. "In relation to the Bushmen, the Hadza, the Indians, at Crystal Mountain, and then perhaps with more childhood reasons, even Fishers Island. Your yearning is not appeased by here and now."[70]

"Sensible" and "constructive" were fitting adjectives for Maria Koenig. They describe how she approached almost everything in life, with good sense and practical attentiveness to what might be improved. In the few years since moving into Sagaponack with her two little girls, she had been sensible and constructive about the Matthiessen household. She had replaced the rattan furniture in the living room, making a cozy space beneath the wall-mounted spears from New Guinea. She had labeled Peter's drawers so he knew where his socks belonged, and got into the habit of tidying up in his wake—dropped clothes, cupboards left ajar, jars left open on the kitchen counter. She had made herself the point person for everything to do with the children, providing Alex with the support he so desperately needed. ("She was very loving and attentive," Alex recalled, though his friends quaked at her commands, this beautiful disciplinarian with a Sontag-like white stripe running through her dark hair.)[71]* Maria had already become known for literary dinners—attended by the likes of William Gaddis, Joseph Heller, Bruce Friedman, Kurt Vonnegut—and for instituting a German Christmas with real candles on a live tree, hand-painted name cards on the table. Friends found her dedication impressive, even intimidating. When Maria visited the Styrons with Peter, she reorganized their kitchen without saying a word, reminding Rose of her own "helter skelter" approach to domesticity.[72] "Maria raised homemaking to high art," said Myrna Davis. "Very few women could do it as well. I've spent my life feeling that I'm falling short."[73] Once, when Myrna sprained her ankle, Maria turned up unexpectedly on Thanksgiving morning to put her friend's turkey in the oven, then returned home to take care of her own.

Maria liked an ordered house. "It is the thing that makes me safe," she told Peter in a letter. "My home is my haven."[74] Yet the intensity of her effort was also due, by her own admission, to insecurities about their relationship: "I thought the more I did, the more he'd have to rely on me."[75] Patsy and Deborah chafed against Peter's expectations; Maria exceeded them to make herself indispensable. She prepared his lunch, which he returned from the writing studio each afternoon to eat, preferably in silence so he could remain in his head. She greeted his many guests and admirers, entertaining them until he was ready to be seen. (Not even Werner Herzog was permitted to disrupt the daily routine: Maria took him to wait at the beach.) She oversaw Peter's social calendar, balancing his contradictory desires to be reclusive and to go out drinking with friends. She also balanced his checkbook, paid all the bills, read through contracts, and answered phone calls as a first line of defense. After *The New York Times* revealed his involvement with the CIA in 1977, it was Maria who dealt with Richard Elman when the writer rang the house threatening further exposure in *Politicks* magazine. She wrote to Elman's editor condemning the "unprovoked hostility" of Elman's phone call, and requesting a forum for "Mr. Matthiessen" to respond to any allegations "if he wishes."[76] (He did not.)

Maria built a protective wall around Peter. With his every need taken care of, all he had to do was write. "She freed Peter," said her friend Ngaere Macray, "to live his life like Peter Pan—a Peter Pan who took on world

---

* Maria became so well known for her rules of etiquette, fiercely enforced, that her daughter Sarah Koenig eventually discussed them in a 2013 episode of *This American Life*, titled, in Maria's honor, "The Seven Things You're Not Supposed to Talk About." The "off-limit" topics of conversation included how you slept, your period, your health, your diet, your dreams, your finances, and "route talk"—how you traveled somewhere, the traffic, etc.

issues."[77] This came at a cost for the children, subordinated to his demands. When Antonia's cat started killing birds and leaving them at the door, Peter insisted they get rid of it. The cat vanished. "That sort of became the pattern of Mom sacrificing us to appease him," Antonia recalled.[78] But appeasing Peter came at a cost to Maria as well. Without intending to perform the role, she was transformed into "a handmaiden to the work."[79] Or, to use another of Maria's analogies, she provided "a sort of mothership, and mothers are resented one way or another." Peter rarely noticed the effort that went into making sure he never missed an appointment. He could be openly ungrateful. "When he complains about how he is surrounded by a million pin-prick irritations, I agree, sometimes with sympathy," Maria wrote in a diary—"but then I think about our days and realize a woman's day is like that <u>every</u> day, the world over. The fridge doesn't work, the plumber doesn't arrive, the dog shits on the carpet. . . . Every day, every day, the trick is how to deal with it. With indifference, with efficiency, with grimness—with whatever is at hand."[80] Sometimes, when Peter seemed especially oblivious to how the stars had been rearranged for his benefit, she wondered how she would deal with *him*. She felt "inadequate" to be his companion. Then she asked herself "who would do" as her replacement:

> In the back of my head I have a picture—nearly always the same picture—of a slim young girl with <u>long</u> dark hair—who would be free, free, to share his journeys. Quiet, subdued, smiling gently—deeply involved in studying—what? Botany, religion—Eastern of course—not too many friends—but knowing about Sixties music and drugs and baking bread and growing flowers. And never having any needs that would impinge on the work day—or on the closely hoarded emotions that cannot be dissipated or shared.

Maria was not that young girl—"I cannot be"—but she tried her best to be accommodating. She aimed to give Peter "enough freedom" so that he would "want to come back," she explained in a letter to him. "In principle, I hate those binding cords; in fact, it is hard to cut them free."[81]

Many of the letters Maria wrote to Peter in their first few years of cohabitation reflect this struggle between binding and letting go. She missed him terribly when he was away in Africa, or traveling out West with the bigfoot pioneers or Craig Carpenter. "It has been too long—our phone calls too hasty and dissatisfying," she wrote.[82] Yet she also tried to downplay her loneliness and anxiety. "I didn't get a letter from you & stupidly I went into a spin. Really we are too stupid," she sighed.[83] Or, in a Valentine message: "Bereft and restless—what is to become of us—so silly."[84] Peter grabbed his bag and headed out on another open-ended trip, and "my usual paranoia rushes to the fore and I assume I am abandoned, forgotten, disliked, unloved—have I forgotten something?"[85] Her words were dismissive, but the anguish behind them was real.

Peter's letters to Maria were filled with his own declarations of longing. "My head is all clogged, the air is heavy, my brain thick, and I am ingesting a jar of artichoke hearts at my desk by way of supper," he wrote from California during his semester at Irvine. "Maria, I love you, do you hear? I <u>need</u> you, I <u>want</u> you."[86] But his "<u>need</u>," often underlined like this, was just as often accompanied by reminders about the value of personal freedom. He needed Maria; he also needed his space away from Maria. They must learn to love "without killing each other's life with clinging," he advised.[87] While he professed a wish to be home more often (should they paint the house white, make it spare and airy?), his own struggle was between a desire to be settled and another "increasing" want: "to travel light, both spiritually + materially."[88] He knew this was selfish; his subconscious needled him about his impulse toward perpetual escape. In a journal he recorded a terrible nightmare: "idyllic life with Maria, kids . . . ruptured, obliterated by sudden explosion that rained 'rocks' on my home."[89] This was "depressing, just before a journey," but he left to go on the journey anyway.

For their third Christmas together, Maria asked for the modest gift of a poem that would articulate his feelings for her. She wrote these kinds of poems all the time; surely it was not too much to request one in return from a man who earned his living as a writer. Peter, however, found the assignment impossible:

> Why do you ask for proofs of love that are no proofs?—a Christmas poem, to order, indeed—one Christmas poem, coming up. I can't write that way, and I can't love you that way, either—the pressure dries me up. I have tried to write you your Christmas poem, several times now, and my mind goes into self-erase—maybe I will write you a birthday poem, an Easter poem, a poem of Spring, if you do not command it. Let me love you in my own way—you have all the proof of love you need, if only you could see it. You are my old lady, you are the woman of my life, you have only to come with me, you have only to let go. If you scan these sentences and stack them up, they will make a poem of return.[90]

NOT LONG AFTER *The Snow Leopard* won the National Book Award, an invitation arrived at the house for another expedition. The sponsor this time was Tom Arnold, a young British MP who had recently been appointed parliamentary private secretary to the secretary of state for Northern Ireland. Arnold wanted to take a team to the Selous, a game reserve in southern Tanzania that is four times larger than the Serengeti, encompassing three distinct ecological units and (at that point) some 750,000 large animals.[91] Its inaccessibility, tsetse flies, and relative lack of infrastructure meant the Selous was mostly undisturbed: Arnold framed his proposal as "the last safari into the last wilderness."[92] He would arrange everything for the expedition; Brian Nicholson, a former warden for the Selous, would lead the team; and all Matthiessen had to do was write a book that would be illustrated by the Dutch photographer Hugo van Lawick, Jane Goodall's ex-husband, to help recoup some of the considerable expense. Matthiessen had no real interest in writing yet another expedition record at the behest of a wealthy benefactor, but he longed to see the Selous. Both he and Baron van Lawick were willing "to sing for [their] supper."[93] It would, in effect, be a new installment of his long-running "Last Wilderness" chronicles. What made it unusual, however, was the generosity of Tom Arnold's invitation: Maria was included. Here was a trip that she and Peter could share.

In August 1979, Maria flew to Tanzania to visit her father and stepmother before the safari. Peter followed two weeks later via London, where he bought her butterscotch on Jermyn Street and wrote a note in anticipation, to be given to her when they convened in Dar es Salaam: "I think we are very lucky to have each other, and to have such good children, whom one day we may even deserve; and I am really looking forward to our safari together in the Selous, and discussing ideas for the book with you, and looking at birds with you, and being naughty in our tent to the accompaniment of tropical boubous."[94]

The month-long Selous expedition is recounted by Matthiessen in *Sand Rivers* (1981), which, much to his surprise—the book was a chore to draft—would go on to win a John Burroughs Medal for nature writing, and an African Wildlife Leadership Foundation Award. They assembled multiple camps in the roadless wilderness—near the Tundu Hills, in the Nahatu Valley, on the Luwegu River. The crew of seventeen people ate impala and drank red wine under the stars. It was slow and relaxing, full of "[q]uiet days watching the river, fishing and bathing, observing the local hippo herd, and walking out in the cooler hours to see what we might see."[95] Matthiessen kept detailed notes on wildlife—a pygmy mongoose, a civet cat, square-tailed nightjars—and went walking up hills to survey Miombo woodland from the high ridges. He joined van Lawick (whose pictures illustrate *Sand Rivers*) in a blue Land Rover, camouflaged with leaves to aid photography. Matthiessen also accompanied Brian Nicholson on a foot safari to an elliptical, unnamed mud pan in the middle of nowhere, a place of "resounding silence and expectancy, as if the creatures of the earth's first morning might come two by two between the trees at any moment."⁹⁶

Sand Rivers features extensive discussion about the epidemic of poaching that had already begun to devastate the Selous, with elephants slaughtered for ivory to fund the war in Uganda against Idi Amin.* The book shows, too, how Matthiessen's convictions about race had only hardened since *The Tree Where Man Was Born*. He was often at loggerheads with Nicholson, arguing against the ex-warden's "unpleasant" colonial mentality over a campfire: "Emboldened by drink, I concluded spiritedly that the white man judged Africans by the material standards of his own reckless civilization, by the 'progress' that was ruining the human habitat, and threatening the future of the earth."⁹⁷

Unsurprisingly, what *Sand Rivers* does not contain is any mention of Peter's affair, which he started with a young ecologist during the expedition, and which he continued afterward on a return stopover in London. Maria found out a few months later that their "safari together" was sullied while she was staying with him in a tent, interacting daily with the friendly young woman, unsuspecting all the while. At the start of December, she sat down to write Peter a melancholy letter. "I have taken this 'thing' very hard because I think we were both getting somewhere—flawed and stumbling as we are."⁹⁸ She would hate to lose him, she said—he knew her better than anybody ever had or ever would—but she needed to know where she stood once and for all. "Please be open and honest with me when you get back—it is of overwhelming importance to me—to us."

When he received this letter, Peter was in Florida conducting research with the Miccosukee Tribe of Indians, another bigfoot-related inquiry. He read through the letter several times. As well as being chastened, he thought it was a "fine" piece of writing. In response, he penned a long, abject apology that doubled as a confession of midlife crisis:

> I am not centered—have not been since I let my zazen slip, after eight intense years—and I feel sure these imbalances of feeling, of loss of oneness with my own aging, with a deep, quiet sadness about my children (and about myself vis-à-vis my children), with my increasing staleness as a writer (I hope it is just that I need a rest), with the no longer mistakable deterioration of my physical being—none of these are excuses . . . But

---

* The Selous Game Reserve was designated a UNESCO World Heritage Site in 1982, three years after "the last safari into the last wilderness." In recent years, however, that designation has been threatened by rampant industrial-scale poaching, which has caused wildlife to decline by almost 90 percent. Other concerns include newly built roads encroaching on the wilderness, loss of habitat via deforestation, and a massive hydropower dam project on the Rufiji River. Matthiessen describes most of these threats in *Sand Rivers*, making it one of his more prophetic books.

only to show you why I am perhaps a little more vulnerable these days to "romantic" twinges—the last little panic before stepping manfully forward to accept what I have made of my whole life, for the point of no return has surely come and gone, and now I must live with it, like it or not, and just be <u>damned grateful</u> I have a friend as true and dear and lovely as Maria Eckhart who loves me for worse as well as better.[99]

Why was he unable to "relinquish my (spurious) 'freedom' "? Why was he "so terrified," he asked himself, "of being 'pulled down' in my flight—flight from what?" These were hardly new questions; they had been dogging him for more than thirty years. Perhaps, Peter suggested, "it would be best if we were to marry."

Despite his words sounding like a lukewarm proposal, marriage had been Maria's idea first. She was thinking of security for herself and her daughters, of course, but she also wanted something else: proper recognition for her own hard work. While the *Snow Leopard* acknowledgment was appreciated, for several years now, in invitations sent to the house, and in fawning articles by journalists about the bestselling author Peter Matthiessen, she had been relegated to the uncertain status of his "friend." (In *The Washington Post*: "So the spookiness out here, which manifests itself most conspicuously as a kind of muscle-bound loneliness, doesn't bother him at all, he says a few minutes later, sitting down to a lunch of flat bread which he stuffs with avocado, cucumber and mushrooms fried in butter by his friend Maria Koenig. 'You're asking the wrong man about loneliness,' she says with rich exasperation.")[100] Given that she was the one who made the journalists lunch ("I would feed these bloody people"),[101] for all intents and purposes she was *already* Mrs. Matthiessen. She deserved to be formally identified as such if they were going to continue their relationship. When she put it like that, her own version of an ultimatum, Peter came around.

In the months after his "twinge" in the Selous, he went out of his way to demonstrate affection. He phoned Maria from South Dakota, where he'd gone for more "Indian business," and then, two hours later, wrote her a "custom-ordered" love letter reaffirming his belief that Maria was "the most wonderful girl in the world," and that he would be lucky indeed if she would "consent" to be his wife.[102] Maria did consent, choosing to put his affair behind them. For her part, she promised to try her best to leave him "loose and free—with a light heart."[103]

November 28, 1980, the day after Thanksgiving, was blustery on the East End of Long Island. Wind and rain grounded the Styrons, who had hired a plane to fly them down from Martha's Vineyard for the wedding. Maria assembled an altar in front of the fireplace in Sagaponack: an incense burner, a sprig of gorse, a Wedgwood vase. Chrysanthemums were arranged on the grand piano. A telephone rang incessantly. "It was like waiting for Godot, or like at an airport, unexplained delays," Gottlieb Eckhart wrote in a narrative account of the day; he had arrived from Tanzania to celebrate his daughter.[104] Maria wore a dusky pink Japanese kimono. Peter wore a black turtle-neck beneath a white linen shirt. Bernie Glassman conducted a Zen ceremony, with premarital meditation in the upstairs zendo. "When they came out Maria said it was wonderful, her beating heart was now quiet." The Heart Sutra was chanted, and vows were exchanged as the couple knelt before the altar. Afterward, the small family gathering joined a large group of friends at George and Freddy Plimpton's house. The guest list included Tom and Rusty Guinzburg, Joe Fox and Nora Ephron, Peter and Mary Stone, Dorothy and Roy Lichtenstein. Dinner was hosted by Piedy—Peter's old friend from his Junior Year in France days—and Sidney Lumet, the film director, her new husband. Peter had such a terrible hangover the following morning that he drove off with Maria to New York, en route to Venezuela, where they would honeymoon with the Styrons, without his rucksack or passport, "which had to be sent after them in some complicated way."

Marriage did bring Maria the recognition she deserved. But for every step Peter made toward commitment on the home front, there was an inevitable step away for himself. Within a year of the wedding, he had another major ceremony: a *Shukke Tokudo*, which means "leaving home and entering the Way." In Soto Zen, this is ordination as a priest, or monk—the terms "priest" and "monk" are somewhat fungible in American Zen—and it constitutes a sworn dedication not only to one's practice but to the sangha at large. Traditionally, Tokudo marks the beginning of a new monastic life of service.

Peter's Tokudo was attended by his eldest children, Luke and Sara Carey, some old associates from the Zen Studies Society, Maria, and a few bemused friends like Guinzburg, who thought the ceremony seemed to "go on all day."[105] In preparation, Peter had shaved his head to the scalp. He read out a statement before the sizable crowd: "Though my form is completely altered, I remain faithful to my purpose, parting with human attachment and thus renewing myself. Leaving home, I seek the Enlightened Way; I vow to free all creations."[106] There were other invocations and precepts, and then Peter, already wearing a white kimono, was dressed in a black *koromo*, or outer robe, and a *kesa*, a ceremonial shawl for Buddhist clergy. Taizan Maezumi, the presiding authority, gave him a new Dharma name: Muryo, which means "Boundless."*

---

* The name was taken from the third of the Four Great Bodhisattva Vows, HO MON MURYO SEI GAN GAKU—the same vow he'd been chanting in the hospital as Deborah Love drew her last breath.

Ishin Muryo Peter Matthiessen later wrote that he had "a crazy exhilaration, an airy feeling" about his "new blue head."[107] Maria was less enamored with the drastic haircut—was, in fact, "really pissed" about it, recalled Bernie Glassman.[108] But what bothered her more was something Maezumi Roshi told her that day. Tokudo, he said, was more important than a marriage. Peter's spiritual life, like his work, had always seemed to take priority over her and the children. Now, with much solemn bowing and the ring of a bell, the hierarchy was made official.

21

Indian Energy

> I believe in grit and passion. If you don't get mad and put feeling into things, those things are dead. Look, I care about saying I'm for the Native American people.
>
> —PM, in conversation with Nicholas Dawidoff (1990)[1]

For nearly three years, whenever he found a few days, a spare week, a slow month in the schedule, Matthiessen set off for some corner of North America to visit another tribal nation or Native community. "I was curious about researching the parallels between Indian spiritual attitudes and Buddhist attitudes,"[2] he later explained, though there was more to it than an exercise in comparative religion. "I actually was talking about the Big Man a lot," he confessed to his friend Howard Norman.[3] That-One-You-Are-Speaking-About; the monstrous Yeitso; the messenger Wa-ho-shi-hi—he would record many different names in his notebooks between 1978 and 1980. Matthiessen was "trying to grasp the essential nature of the seatko," he told Janet McCloud, a Tulalip activist in Yelm, Washington; "just how I will use this research, in what form, I'm not quite sure yet, but I have pledged to C[raig] and others—and yourself—that I will submit anything I do on the spiritual aspect for comment and correction before publication."[4]

Craig Carpenter, as Matthiessen freely acknowledged, was the catalyst for his travels in Indian country. In the spring of 1979, they drove across eight states together in search of bigfoot stories, "a long circular journey through the West,"[5] from the coast of California to the Uintah Mountains of northeastern Utah, down to the home of the Jicarilla Apache in New Mexico, then west once again to the Hopi Reservation. "As he has done with the greatest pains wherever we have gone," Matthiessen wrote in his unpublished manuscript, "Craig introduced me, describing my experiences in the Himalaya."[6] Carpenter led his diligent pupil to friends in the Pit River Tribe, where a man advised Matthiessen to keep searching for the elusive creature: "People have all got to where they don't believe anything; and that's where people have went wrong. When you can believe by faith, then you will see." At Fort McDermitt, on the Nevada-Oregon border, a Paiute man described the Ne-mud-zo-ho (as Matthiessen noted down the name): "He whistles at you at night, and if you go over there, he may crush you." A member of the Torres Martinez Desert Cahuilla Indians spoke of Na-kan-giansh Um-na-wett: "He came from the North about a hundred years ago or more, when the Indian was real close to God. Now he is separated from us. He does not come any more, only in dreams." Somebody at the Morongo Reservation in Banning, California, even suggested that what they called Taw-koosh should be protected as a "sacred being" under the new American Indian Religious Freedom Act.

"One group of people would send me to another," Matthiessen recalled. "It's very difficult for most white people to reach some of these [Native] people, so I felt I have to make the most of this opportunity."[7] Traveling without Carpenter in North Carolina, he took notes on Tsul 'Kalu, the Slant-Eyed Giant. He interviewed Tuscarora in New York, Miccosukee in Florida, a Cheyenne woman in Montana. "Cecile Horn, working in beaded moccasins . . . calls BF O-maki-tapé."[8] On the West Coast, he poked around Salish settlements on Vancouver Island, and examined wooden masks of Dzunuk'wa (the Wild Woman of the Woods) in the Royal British Columbia Museum. Returning to the Klamath Mountains, he encountered a Hupa man, Lee McCardie, who compared the creature to cold mountain water, an indelible part of the landscape. "He attaches a spiritual significance to Bigfoot," Matthiessen wrote of McCardie, "but his wife, who is a white woman, round and red-haired, outspoken and cheery, has her doubts. 'I accept some of this Indian stuff but not all of it. There's nothing "spiritual" about this thing, not smelling like that—like a sackful of dead cats left out in the sun for three weeks.' "[9]

Thomas Buckley, a young anthropologist who studied Yurok culture in Northern California, warned Matthiessen against overinterpreting the various stories he collected. It was possible, Buckley suggested, that some of Matthiessen's interviewees had contracted "bigfootmania" from the Anglo-American culture; it was possible his informants were retelling old tribal stories to conform with a popular legend, so that figures from disparate oral traditions seemed to merge into the single alluring specter of the Big Man. This idea bothered Matthiessen. "I was especially anxious," he wrote, "to talk to some elderly people who might have known of 'the big hairy man' before the white man made his late discovery [in 1958]."[10] But he refused to accept that the phenomenon might be nothing more than a mass delusion—or, even more troubling, that his contacts might simply be agreeing with his own suggestions. Forty people on Standing Rock testified "that they had seen Si-tanka, and it seemed most unlikely that all of them were drunks and liars."[11] There were too many coincidences, Matthiessen decided, as he compared the stories like a folklorist.

By 1980, he had started to conceptualize a nonfiction book, tentatively titled "Indian Energy." As he explained to a research assistant who spent hours searching library archives for material related to the Gwich'in, Tanaina, Mi'kmaq, and Chinook people, among other groups, he hoped to write something original about Native attitudes to land and life.[12] The call for a return to traditional ways, and these widespread stories of a spirit-being as harbinger of coming environmental catastrophe—it resonated with his own feelings about the need for a new American ethic, a shift in consciousness away from a destructive consumer culture and toward the ecological. The Big Man was, for Matthiessen, a productive symbol, and he was determined to use it in his work. He was unsure what "Indian Energy" should look like as a book, however, and he found himself, while he puzzled over the challenge, distracted by a related strain of social activism.

MORE THAN ONCE, after Matthiessen was finished asking his questions about spiritual beliefs and bigfoot, the Native person he was interviewing posed a question of their own. They had given him valuable information: what would he give them in return?

"What can you do for my people?"[13]

Matthiessen was aware that his inquiries could be construed as a kind of exploitation. Being a writer, he once said, meant feeling "like a terrible intruder because you're there to take something from the culture and sell it when you get home."[14] This arrangement was standard for journalists and social scientists, who swooped in to treat people as case histories, but it made him uncomfortable when the cultures in question had already been subjected to centuries of scrutiny and theft. Matthiessen was horrified by the poverty he witnessed on Indian reservations. He was appalled by accounts of disenfranchised communities pushed around by government and big business. With Cesar Chavez and the United Farm Workers, he had felt compelled to, in the words of Camus, "speak up, insofar as we can, for those who cannot do so." The situation for many Native groups was even more urgent; as a result, when somebody asked him for reciprocity—"Well, now we've told you our secrets, why don't you write about our problems?"[15]—Matthiessen was inclined to agree. Speaking up was an *obligation* for writers with significant national reach. "There are certain people," he once said, "who will read everything that Mailer and Styron and Vonnegut or Updike—writers of that type—write, no matter what. They've got a guaranteed audience. Let's talk about American Indians. It's high time."[16]

In the three years he spent roaming between reservations, Matthiessen produced nearly a dozen newspaper and magazine articles about the land and water disputes he would later term "the New Indian Wars."[17] These articles—his attempt to give something back—exposed large numbers of readers to ongoing battles that, because of disinterest, a lack of journalistic access, or structural racism, had received little attention in the mainstream press.

For *Audubon*, he wrote about the Siskiyou Mountains in California, and a proposed Gasquet–Orleans Road ("the GO Road") that would provide ruinous access for the Simpson Timber Company to cedar and Douglas firs that happened to stand in the sacred "High Country" of local tribes like the Yurok and Karuk.[18] For *Newsweek*, and then for *The New York Review of Books*, he wrote about the notorious Tellico Dam on the Little Tennessee River—"One of the oldest and most evil-smelling public works projects in the country"[19]—which had major ramifications not only for fauna (the snail darter) but for the Eastern Cherokee, who saw the soon-to-be-inundated valley as the source of their creation as a people. For *Geo*, Matthiessen turned his attention to Big Mountain, in Arizona, where Diné residents were being forcibly removed to make way for strip mines and power plants: "For Indians . . . mere 'access' to the mountain, as provided for in recent legislation, is of no use and not much interest to a people who conceive of themselves as not separable from this place."[20] Meanwhile, for *The Miami Herald*, Matthiessen focused on the Florida Everglades, forwarding a proposal that the Miccosukee be given free run of *Pa-hay-okee*, the "river of grass," as protective park wardens, before it was sucked dry by urban development.[21] Other long articles—some more than ten thousand words—also appeared in *Rocky Mountain*, *The Nation*, and *The New York Times Magazine*.

None of these pieces were particularly noteworthy in terms of style or form, and how much impact they had in the real world is debatable—nothing could have stopped the Tellico Dam gates from closing in November 1979. But this was environmental writing as polemic: cris de coeur meant to nudge a reader into the same moral outrage that Matthiessen felt. His efforts helped normalize what was then still a quietly radical notion, the idea that discussions about environmental conservation are incomplete unless they include the perspectives of Indigenous people.

The Native Americans that Matthiessen wrote about in his articles were mostly satisfied with how they were represented. Oren Lyons of the Onondaga and Seneca nations, part of the Iroquois Confederacy, which Matthiessen discussed in a detailed piece for *The Washington Post* about an armed standoff on the St. Regis Mohawk Reservation in New York, called him "a hero among my generation." In Lyons's view, when Matthiessen "saw injustice, serious injustice, he stood his ground."[22] Winona LaDuke, a member of the Mississippi Chippewa, who first met Matthiessen in South Dakota when she was a twenty-year-old environmental policy researcher, felt something similar. She understood what he was trying to do as a writer: "He was not a voyeur who came in. He was not an anthropologist. He didn't take something away and leave us with nothing. He is someone who was in an understanding with our community when he told those stories, and our people trusted him with those stories, and our people still respect and will always respect him for the way he told our stories."[23]

While Matthiessen never worried that he was wasting his time with ephemeral magazine pieces, he did lament how demanding they were to write. The "political work," he grumbled in a letter to Craig Carpenter, interfered with his research on the Big Man and his plans for "Indian Energy." Carpenter responded to the complaint with a reasonable suggestion. Rather than a distraction, he wrote, perhaps the political work *was* the "real work." Maybe this was what Matthiessen was meant to be doing with his skills in service to God, "the Real Coyote or Wolf"—defending Native Americans against the rapacious greed of his fellow white men.[24] Translated into Zen Buddhist terminology, what Carpenter suggested was that Matthiessen was engaged in Right Livelihood, compassionate work that also happens to be part of a spiritual discipline.

WHEN MATTHIESSEN FINALLY collected his advocacy journalism together in a book, *Indian Country*, he chose to frame the eleven chapters with an opening essay titled "Native Earth."[25] The essay is a kind of manifesto—and an abbreviated version, perhaps, of the argument he intended to make in "Indian Energy."

Published at a moment when America was gambling on neoliberal economics under the paternal hand of Ronald Reagan, it offered a full-throated endorsement of an alternate way of being in the world. Matthiessen made his case through the presentation of an unsubtle dichotomy. On the one hand is the white man, a tragic figure motivated by fear and guilt. The white man is still influenced by the frontier mentality (first articulated by Frederick Jackson Turner in 1893), still treating America as a "hideous and desolate wilderness" that needs to be domesticated. The white man is also the product of the scientific revolution, which makes him and his kind "observers, manipulators of the natural world, instead of unselfconscious participants." The white man is thus constitutionally alienated from nature, with a tendency to respond to his chronic solitude—the national sickness—with a "lunatic insistence on 'progress,' on 'growth.'"

In contrast, Matthiessen writes, there is the traditional man, "the Indian." This Indian does not see himself as divisible from nature; the concept of "wilderness" doesn't even exist for him. The Indian understands man as "an aspect of nature," and he considers no creature "superior to another." His is a "holistic vision" based on appreciation of the earth, a "respectful awareness" that results in "joyous humility, a *simplicity* that spares the Indian the great restlessness and loneliness that the alienated white men have brought down upon themselves"—upon *himself*, because of course Matthiessen was writing about his own alienation here.

In "Native Earth," he lays out a case he had been circling since *Wildlife in America*:

> Traditional people the world over have much to teach a spiritually crippled race which, as Lame Deer says, sees "only with one eye." This half-blindness has been the curse of Europeans as long as the Indians have known us, but we have not always been accursed; at one time, we, too, were at one with the *mysterium tremendum*. And we must feel awe again if we are to return to a harmonious existence with our own habitat, and survive; we must consider this life-essence that is all about us, manifesting in each moment—the music of the stars, the color of the wind, the dead stillness between tides at dead of night, the birds, trees, sea pearls and manure, the moment-by-moment miracle of our existence.

There are parts of this essay that are eminently sensible. The idea that man is a part of nature, rather than apart from it, recalls the biotic community of Aldo Leopold. The idea that wilderness does not exist except as a Western construct has been brilliantly explicated by William Cronin. And there is certainly something "lunatic" about an insistence on progress and unrestrained growth; the need for Western society to "return to a harmonious existence with our own habitat," partly by adjusting how we relate to the world around us, is undeniable in the age of man-made climate change. But "Native Earth" is less a rigorous argument than an airing out of Matthiessen's own desires. His white man is a stereotype. His Indian flattens more than five hundred Native tribes and nations into a Rousseauian abstract that ends up, ironically, representing nobody real. There is an unmistakable influence of Zen (that "moment-by-moment miracle"), and reference to the familiar "lost Paradise" as something that might be regained through a shift in consciousness. The white man has fallen, become dissociated, but if he can, like the traditional man, restore "his reverence for land and life," then "the Golden Age in the race memories of all people will come again, and all men will be '*in Dios*' [i.e., *Indios*, Indians], people of God." With its nod toward the idea of a perennial philosophy, this is, to put it mildly, an idealistic conclusion.

After Viking published *Indian Country* in 1984, the writer and anthropologist Peter Nabokov tore it to shreds in *The New York Review of Books*. (The review was so devastating that Nabokov, otherwise an admirer of Matthiessen's work, wrote a private letter trying to staunch the bleeding.) Taking issue with the author's "mystical romanticism," Nabokov wrote, "What is most interesting about Matthiessen's book is its unwitting perpetuation of the oldest images that whites have used to turn the Indians into symbols of their own deepest longings."[26] Nabokov questioned Matthiessen's "impassioned confusion," as he put it, about "America as Lost Paradise and the Indian as its Dispossessed Spirit." Indeed, Matthiessen's "purist sentimentality" had led him to embrace the mistaken assumption that Indian religious beliefs can be directly equated with "environmental ethics." This was a widespread canard, Nabokov continued, among "whites who are pious about ecology and would like to consider Indians as natural environmentalists."

By the mid-1980s, Matthiessen had established himself as an indefatigable champion of Native Americans. Many of the articles collected in *Indian Country* are well-intentioned attempts to expose genuine injustices—"to provide the voiceless with a voice, and sometimes to do no more than throw light into dark corners," as Barry Lopez recognized in a review for *Outside*.[27] At a time when few prominent journalists were conducting deep investigations into Native affairs (one notable exception being the fearless Kevin McKiernan, whose beat was Pine Ridge and the American Indian Movement for several years in the early 1970s, mostly for NPR), Matthiessen leveraged his influence and crossed barricades to report on the view from the inside.

However, the flaws in *Indian Country*, and "Native Earth" more specifically, are indicative of a paradox present in much of Matthiessen's writing about Indigenous people. He defended them. He frequently romanticized them, too. "Their values seem truer, their sensitivities better honed," he told a friend wistfully.[28] In an interview for the BBC, he once insisted that "a lot of what they can teach us is stuff we have forgotten, because of course our cultures were traditional too at a certain point, and we have lost—because we don't need them anymore—certain insights and spiritual values, and ideas of time and space."[29] The wise prelapsarian Indian of "Native Earth" makes cameos in a number of his fiction and nonfiction books, from *Race Rock* to *The Snow Leopard*. However, Matthiessen also frequently *denounced* romanticization. "Romanticizing is patronizing, and a form of racism," he said in another interview.³⁰ He made a similar point when speaking to Howard Norman: "We tend to get into a kind of sentimental thing about traditional people, especially American Indians. We say they're either drunken slobs, or they're environmental gurus who could save the world. . . . I think that they don't like being put in these romantic or sentimental categories, or these defamatory ones."³¹ Matthiessen would proclaim something like this, echoing Nabokov's argument, and then, in another book or article, espouse the same romantic primitivism that Nabokov condemned.

To extoll the wisdom of Indigenous perspectives without imbuing the people with mystical superiority—without making them into "environmental gurus," or paragons of longed-for "simplicity," or noble savages—was a needle Matthiessen attempted to thread for most of his career. Sometimes he recognized his own unsteady hand and subjected it to self-critique: "Like most people with more appreciation than understanding of the Indian vision, I clung to a romantic concept of 'traditional Indians,' aloof from activism and politics and somehow spiritually untouched by western progress."³² But sometimes he just slipped, his heartfelt admiration giving way to dreams and projections.

IN THE SPIRIT OF CRAZY HORSE, Matthiessen's monumental work of social justice advocacy, and the book that threatened to cost him everything—his reputation, his career, maybe his house—also began in an unlikely way, with inquiries about bigfoot. In November 1978, while visiting Santa Barbara for another teaching job at the University of California, he encountered a Lakota man of the Miniconjou band named Archie Fire Lame Deer, a self-styled shaman (and former Hollywood stuntman, rodeo rider, rattlesnake exterminator) who had cofounded the Santa Barbara Indian Center. Lame Deer told Matthiessen stories about *Waziya*; and in return Matthiessen, as they passed around a pipe in a sweat lodge assembled somewhere behind the town, promised to "find some way to help in the fight for Pt. Concepcion." Lame Deer was adviser to a band of Chumash, including his wife, who were protesting a liquefied natural gas terminal proposed for construction at Point Conception on California's Gaviota Coast. Humqaq, as this band preferred to call the landmark, was the "Western Gate," a portal through which souls were said to pass on their way to the land of the dead.³³

The following April, Matthiessen collected Lame Deer in Santa Barbara and drove up to Point Conception to take a closer look. They visited the remains of Shisholop, a Chumash encampment that had been disbanded by the energy companies two months earlier. They also climbed steep tracks into the flower-covered foothills for a broad view over the wild, windswept headland. Matthiessen would write about the fight for Point Conception in *The Nation* ("Tolakwe, Portal of Souls: Last Stand at the Western Gate"). But this visit was significant for another reason. While they walked, Lame Deer pointed out the Santa Ynez Mountains in the distance. On the far side, he said, was Lompoc Federal Correctional Institution, where he had recently established a sweat lodge for some Native prisoners. "Do you know about Leonard Peltier?" he asked.[34] Matthiessen said no, and Lame Deer told him that he should, because Peltier was "a true leader."

Leonard Peltier was a new inmate at Lompoc, having just been transferred there from Marion Penitentiary in Illinois. "I'm afraid they are trying to kill me," Peltier had apparently told Lame Deer during a sweat, and as Lame Deer now told Matthiessen, "they" being the federal authorities: "They are trying to set me up."[35] Peltier was a thirty-four-year-old Anishinaabe-Dakota man, born on a reservation in North Dakota and enrolled in the Turtle Mountain Band of Chippewa Indians. As a foot soldier in the American Indian Movement, he had been involved in several heated confrontations, including the 1970 takeover of Fort Lawton, outside Seattle, and the 1972 Trail of Broken Treaties caravan to Washington, D.C., which had led to the spontaneous occupation (and trashing) of the Bureau of Indian Affairs building. In 1975, after several more scrapes with the law, Peltier had participated in a shootout between members of AIM and the FBI near Oglala, on the Pine Ridge Reservation in South Dakota. Peltier was now serving consecutive life sentences for the murder of two FBI agents at Oglala. But this was a bogus conviction, Lame Deer told Matthiessen: Peltier was innocent. He had been railroaded into prison by corrupt government authorities who were intent on suppressing the bids of Native people for self-determination. "You ought to look into this," Lame Deer urged.

Matthiessen was unpersuaded by their conversation at Point Conception. "I didn't necessarily buy it," he later recalled. "Archie Fire Lame Deer is not an AIM person. He works with them a lot, but I just didn't know how much . . . was propaganda. It frankly wasn't very interesting to me at that time."[36] It wasn't interesting because the American Indian Movement was full, in his opinion, of "loud-mouth hipshooters." Founded in Minneapolis in 1968, AIM was a deliberately belligerent response to the bigotry, marginalization, and police brutality inflicted on Native people across the country. Matthiessen had "inherited"—his word—a hostile attitude toward AIM from Craig Carpenter, who dismissed urban militant groups as inauthentic. Matthiessen, clinging to his idealism, was interested in "Traditional Indians," in the so-called Old Ways, not in "young 'warriors' from the cities with their red wind bands, guns, and episodes of violence, who were sure to bring down further grief on a desperate people."[37]

At Point Conception, he wrote "Leonard Peltier/sweat" in his notebook, a reference to Lame Deer's lodge at Lompoc, and then pushed it out of his mind.[38]

That summer, Matthiessen drove through Manitoba and the Dakotas with Hans Teensma, his fellow bigfoot enthusiast, collecting more Native stories. In June, as a final stop in their travels, they visited Rapid City, just northwest of Pine Ridge in South Dakota, so they could inspect a new grassroots organization called the Black Hills Alliance. The BHA was a groundbreaking response to multinational mining companies, like the Union Carbide Corporation, who were planning to plunder the Black Hills for uranium, having already drilled thousands of exploratory bore holes. The Lakota people, who called the Black Hills Paha Sapa, "the heart of everything that is," vehemently objected to mines. So did environmentalists and a forward-thinking cattle rancher named Marvin Kammerer. The Lakota pointed out that they had never ceded Paha Sapa, which still belonged to them according to the Fort Laramie Treaty of 1868; the environmentalists spoke of inevitable water contamination and other kinds of pollution. The BHA united these very different groups in opposition to the energy companies. It was a "weird coalition,"[39] as one member called it, of white and Native people—something that was, until recently, unimaginable in the deeply racist atmosphere of South Dakota. Matthiessen thought it was marvelous. "I found the atmosphere at the BHA offices less zealous than exhilarating," he wrote. "I had not seen that interracial dedication, that *celebration* of hard work in a good cause, since working with Cesar Chavez in the late sixties."[40]

What made this visit significant, though, was the fact that many people in the BHA office were also involved with AIM. Madonna Gilbert, who showed Matthiessen around the "bare hectic offices" at 619 ½ Main Street, happened to be a cousin of the famous AIM leader Russell Means, as well as an active member herself. Meanwhile, one of the BHA cofounders, Bruce Ellison, had worked as a staff attorney for the Wounded Knee Legal Defense/Offense Committee, which was specifically created to defend AIM members from criminal prosecution after the Wounded Knee Occupation in 1973. A soft-spoken twenty-nine-year-old lawyer from Flushing, New York, who wore his hair in a braid as a sign of solidarity with his clients, Ellison had assisted on the defense team for Leonard Peltier following the shootout at Oglala. In fact, Ellison was one of Peltier's current attorneys. In July, Peltier would stage a desperate escape attempt from Lompoc in California—he had learned of a plot against his life, he later said, from another Native inmate—only to be recaptured after a dogged five-day manhunt. It was Bruce Ellison who would represent Peltier during the trial in November (where he would be sentenced to an additional seven years on top of his two life sentences).

Matthiessen may have come to learn about the Black Hills Alliance, but AIM and Peltier kept intruding into his field of view. He began to take what Lame Deer had said more seriously.

In April 1980, Matthiessen returned to Rapid City armed with a commission from *The New York Times Magazine*. His article, "High Noon in the Black Hills," would follow a Lakota man in the nearby town of Edgemont who had discovered that his family's house was built on radioactive tailings left over from an old mine—a cautionary horror story.[41] While reporting the piece, Matthiessen spent a great deal of time with the BHA, trying to get to the bottom of a century-old problem. "He started to get into the treaty, who really owned the Black Hills," recalled Mark Tilsen, another Alliance cofounder, "and that led to him trying to understand what had happened with AIM and Wounded Knee."[42]

One day Robert "Bob" Robideau appeared on the scene. Matthiessen would describe him vividly in *Crazy Horse:* "A taciturn, lanky, light-skinned man in his early thirties, Robideau was dressed in a red shirt, leather vest, jeans, boots, and a black cowboy hat with a buffalo-nickel hatband from which his long black hair fell straight down between his shoulder blades."[43] Like his cousin Leonard Peltier, Robideau had been charged with the murder of the two FBI agents at Oglala in 1975. Unlike Peltier, though, Robideau and a third man named Darrell "Dino" Butler had been acquitted by a jury. Robideau was newly released on parole from a sentence arising out of a different conviction, and he was back in Rapid City to see friends and revisit Pine Ridge for the first time since the infamous shootout. Matthiessen, now curious, decided to accompany him for a drive.

The Pine Ridge Indian Reservation sprawls across some 3,400 square miles, although this is just a fraction of the land promised in the Fort Laramie Treaty. (The Great Sioux Reservation once covered all of western South Dakota, plus parts of Nebraska, Wyoming, Montana, and North Dakota, before the government started taking big bites out of it for homesteaders and gold prospectors.) Matthiessen and Robideau drove onto Pine Ridge via Scenic, a blip of a town most notable for the unsavory Longhorn Saloon, with its sign announcing NO INDIANS ALLOWED. They passed through the Badlands Bombing Range, a parched landscape of eroded rock taken by the government, also without permission, from the Oglala Lakota during World War II for artillery training. In Porcupine, they stopped briefly so Robideau could visit the old AIM spokesman Ted Means, who declared that the "government has done one hell of a job in colonizing us."[44] Then they continued south past Wounded Knee, site of the seventy-one-day siege in 1973, and before that, in 1890, the massacre of more than 250 Lakota people by soldiers in the U.S. Army. They drove west, passing through the squat, unprosperous township of Pine Ridge, following Highway 18 as it snaked over sparsely wooded rangeland. Before reaching Oglala, another small community, they turned off the road onto a rude dirt track. At the end of the track were a few cabins and tar-paper shacks overlooking a pasture that sloped down toward cottonwoods by White Clay Creek—the Jumping Bull property.

It is impossible to say exactly what happened here on June 26, 1975.[45] The government has offered different versions during multiple court cases; Robideau and other participants have taken turns narrating their own versions for journalists and filmmakers, who have then written books and produced documentaries that forward competing interpretations.

By 1975, the Pine Ridge Reservation had descended into civil war. Richard "Dick" Wilson, the tribal chairman, dubiously elected, ruled it as his private fiefdom, inflicting a reign of terror through private militiamen who called themselves the "Guardians of the Oglala Nation"—the GOONs. Under Wilson's watch, Pine Ridge had the highest crime rate in the United States, with at least sixty-three homicides in the span of three years. People were shot, stabbed, raped, hanged, dismembered with axes, run over, and burned alive in their cars and houses. The FBI gave little indication of wanting to solve these horrific crimes—the FBI and the Bureau of Indian Affairs police seemed more interested in propping up Wilson—so some older locals, who considered themselves "traditionals," had taken things into their own hands by inviting AIM leaders to send in some people to form a kind of peacekeeping force that would protect them from the GOONs. This peacekeeping force had started out as a large and diverse crowd, as seen at the Wounded Knee occupation and siege. But by the middle of 1975, the force was reduced to a small group of well-armed AIM "warriors," who gathered in a log cabin on five acres of land belonging to Harry and Cecilia Jumping Bull. When the cabin became too crowded, the warriors erected what Leonard Peltier called "a spiritual camp, there to support Dennis [Banks, an AIM leader] and the Oglala people."[46] The camp was hidden in cottonwoods down by the creek.

Just before midday on June 26, two FBI agents, Jack R. Coler and Ronald A. Williams, drove their cars onto the Jumping Bull property and into the grassy meadow. The most widely accepted story is that they were chasing a van—or truck, or red Scout: one of the many unstable details—that they believed harbored James Theodore "Jimmy" Eagle, a young man wanted for the theft of some cowboy boots. The agents may also have been trying to get a look at the AIM encampment, which the FBI, as documents retrieved via the Freedom of Information Act would later show, was aware of and concerned about as a supposedly "secret AIM project," meaning, as the journalist Steve Hendricks once put it, "a popular revolt even bigger than Wounded Knee, or, failing that, scattered terrorist attacks."[47]

The cars stopped. Somebody took a shot, maybe in warning. Nothing is certain until Agent Williams radioed an urgent request for backup: "they are on a ridge above us and firing on us."[48] Williams and Coler exchanged more shots with the AIMers. Crouched behind his car with a .308 rifle he had managed to retrieve from the trunk, Coler was hit by a bullet that tore through the trunk lid and then much of his right arm, leaving it hanging by threads. He began to bleed out. Williams, after more frantic radio requests, seems to have taken off his shirt to make a tourniquet for his partner. Somebody—or somebodies—then approached the two cars. A first autopsy left open the possibility that both agents were killed in self-defense. A second autopsy, conducted by a more adept pathologist, found that Williams threw up his hand in a protective gesture, so the fatal bullet destroyed three of his fingers as it entered his forehead, and that Coler, who was either unconscious or already dead by that point, was shot in the back of the head where he lay in the grass.

In the chaotic retreat that followed, as FBI agents, BIA officers, and GOONs swarmed the property—a massive force soon joined by a SWAT team, U.S. marshals, state troopers, armored personnel carriers, helicopters, and spotter planes—a Native man, Joseph Killsright Stuntz, was killed by a sniper. Incredibly, the remaining AIM warriors managed to slip away along the creek, through a culvert and into the arid hills. The authorities set out to track them down, and in the meantime police fed a mostly cooperative media "clichés about ambushes and cold-blooded executions by bands of savage Indians," as the *Columbia Journalism Review* put it in an excoriating article.[49] (Later, the U.S. Commission on Civil Rights was similarly critical of the public messaging, as well as the "full-scale military-type invasion" by authorities who had seemed perfectly unbothered when it was just Indians being killed on Pine Ridge.)[50]

Who shot the FBI agents? This is where Matthiessen really began to pay attention. Although there were numerous individuals on the scene that day, in the months following the shootout, the Department of Justice narrowed its focus to four prime suspects: Bob Robideau, Dino Butler, Jimmy Eagle, and Leonard Peltier. Robideau and Butler were soon apprehended, and they were tried together in Cedar Rapids, Iowa. The prosecution mounted a shaky case using unreliable witnesses and circumstantial evidence; the agile defense team argued that the government, by infiltrating AIM with agents provocateurs and supporting Dick Wilson's brutal regime, had created a climate of such acute paranoia that the AIMers had merely acted in self-defense, regardless of who shot the agents. When it became clear that the jury agreed—Robideau and Butler were found "not guilty," a rare verdict against law enforcement—the federal government changed tactics. It dropped the case against Jimmy Eagle, which was essentially nonexistent (there was no evidence Eagle was even *present* at the shooting), and turned its full prosecutive attention toward Leonard Peltier.⁵¹

Using false affidavits as evidence, the U.S. extradited Peltier from Canada, where he had been picked up as a fugitive. He was put on trial in Fargo, North Dakota, before a far less sympathetic jury and an openly contemptuous judge, Paul Benson. Had Peltier stood trial with his friends, he would almost certainly have been acquitted alongside them. Instead, Judge Benson forbade Peltier's defense from pointing out FBI abuses: the fabricated affidavits, coerced testimony, and inconsistencies with ballistics data. The jury was shielded from a great deal of the material that had been used in the Cedar Rapids trial, but repeatedly exposed to gory photographs of the slain agents. On April 18, 1977, it found Peltier guilty on two counts of murder in the first degree. Before being sentenced, Peltier gave a furious speech in which he denounced Judge Benson as corrupt. "No, I'm not the guilty one here," he said. "I'm not the one who should be called a criminal—white racist America is the criminal for the destruction of our lands and my people."⁵²*

Now, three years later, Matthiessen and Robideau poked around the meadow where the agents had been killed. They worked through events step by step: the sequence of the shootout as Robideau presented it; the manhunts, extradition, and divergent trials. By the time Robideau had finished talking, Matthiessen was convinced there was no way the prosecution could have proved beyond a reasonable doubt that Leonard Peltier murdered Jack Coler and Ronald Williams. Did that mean Peltier was innocent, as Lame Deer claimed? "I wasn't so sure of that," Matthiessen later said. "But I was pretty sure he'd been framed."⁵³ The situation put him in mind of Nicola Sacco and Bartolomeo Vanzetti, the Italian anarchists executed for murder in 1927 after a compromised trial that reeked of anti-immigrant prejudice. Peltier's case had similar "historic reverberations"—an entire saga beyond Oglala came into focus through the story of this one man's extraordinary treatment.⁵⁴ "Somebody," Matthiessen thought, "has to write about this."⁵⁵

BUT NOT HIM. He had no intention of donating his time to Leonard Peltier. He was still leery of AIM, still resistant to "the Movement propaganda according to which 'AIM Warriors at Oglala were defending the Native People against Genocide,' as if the killings had somehow been sanctified by

---

* In September 1986, the U.S. Court of Appeals for the Eighth Circuit would conclude that the prosecution in Paul Benson's courtroom "withheld evidence from the defense favorable to Peltier," and that had this evidence been shown, there was "a possibility that the jury would have acquitted Leonard Peltier." Nevertheless, the appeals court declined to order a new trial.

the sacred pipe."[56] And he wanted to get away from advocacy journalism, which had started to consume his life, so he could return to writing fiction. It had been five long years since *Far Tortuga* was published by Random House, and he had been making notes for a promising new novel about the Florida Everglades.

He also felt this Oglala story was not his to tell; such a delicate subject should be handled by a Native writer. He queried Simon Ortiz, James Welch, and N. Scott Momaday, none of whom were prepared to drop everything and immediately act, which was what Matthiessen thought "this guy rotting away in prison"[57] really needed. Then he had a conversation with Russell Means on a flight from Rapid City to Denver. The AIM leader was renowned for aggressive bluntness, and he served it up straight. Coverage by an Indian writer would never get the same attention as something penned by the award-winning, and white, Peter Matthiessen. "Come on, you do it," Means reportedly told him with irritation.[58]

Matthiessen settled on another magazine article. He would give it a few months and move on. But impediments arose almost immediately. Editors at two "leading magazines in New York" told him that their readers didn't care about the plight of modern Indians: "They don't want to hear about them. They don't want to know about them."[59] One of these magazines was *The New Yorker*, which, despite being Matthiessen's primary outlet for decades, never published a word of his writing about Native Americans.[60] He had more luck at *The Atlantic Monthly*. However, it quickly became clear that the story was too complicated for a regular feature. Doing justice to the case required a book.

Hoping to share this unwanted burden, he invited Bruce Ellison, Peltier's attorney, to come onboard as cowriter. Ellison didn't feel up to the challenge ("I'm not capable"),[61] and he was already focused on a film project about his client with Lorenzo Semple Jr., screenwriter of conspiracy classics *The Parallax View* (1974) and *Three Days of the Condor* (1975). So Matthiessen was on his own. One day at a meeting with Ellison and Semple, he announced that if he was really going to write a book about AIM and the Oglala shootout, he wanted to share his earnings with the Leonard Peltier Defense Committee. This was another way of giving back: the offer was made "spontaneously and of my own accord,"[62] he later said, somewhat defensively, when questioned about the propriety of donating money or goods to his own subject—something he had previously done with Cesar Chavez. In October 1980, before he even had a publisher for the project, Matthiessen signed a contract with the Defense Committee that formalized a promise of more than 50 percent of any income from a book.[63] He retained complete control over the book's contents, however. While he "did not wish to profit from Peltier's desperate situation,"⁶⁴ he would write whatever he wanted, criticize AIM and Peltier as he saw fit, even if it damaged the cause. (This did not appease his critics, who would later seize on the contract as proof that he was hopelessly partisan.)

That same month, Matthiessen sent his first letter to U.S. Prisoner #89637-132, also known as Tate Wikikuwa, "Wind Chases the Sun":

> Dear Leonard,
> I'm the writer who will be doing the book that is being planned to accompany the movie, and just thought I'd introduce myself, and let you know that I'll do the best job I can. Meanwhile, I'm asking my publishers to send along copies of a couple of my earlier books so that you can get some sort of idea how my mind works, and also a couple of recent articles on transgression of Indian ground by big business and big government—the corporate state.⁶⁵

Peltier replied with an enthusiastic greeting. He had just received *The Snow Leopard*, he wrote, and other inmates were lining up to borrow it because of all the positive reviews. Peltier then offered three warnings that hinted at how difficult the road ahead would be for Matthiessen. Peltier's own family members had trouble securing visitation rights at the United States Penitentiary, Marion; a journalist should prepare for a mighty struggle. Peltier couldn't share any contacts in writing because all correspondence was screened; naming names in the past had led to his associates being "hassled" by authorities. And third, Matthiessen should take an escort to interviews he conducted for the book, "because of my people's reluctance to speak to strangers"—strangers, Peltier implied, had a habit of turning out to be snitches. Having imparted that advice, he signed off his letter with a distinctive flourish: "Take care, may the Great Spirit always protect you. In the Spirit of Crazy Horse, Leonard Peltier."⁶⁶

Crazy Horse, co-leading several thousand Lakota, Cheyenne, and Arapaho warriors, defeated Lieutenant Colonel George A. Custer and the 7th Cavalry at the Battle of the Little Bighorn in 1876. Although the Lakota Sioux war chief surrendered within a year of that battle, and although he was killed by a guard with a bayonet at Fort Robinson, Nebraska, he endured as a symbol of miraculous courage in the face of almost impossible odds. The "spirit of Crazy Horse" was Crazy Horse's ferocious defiance of an imperialist aggressor—his unwavering commitment to his people, the Lakota, regardless of the personal cost.

ONCE MATTHIESSEN DECIDED to take on the book, he mustered a staggering amount of energy for research. Another writer might have limited themselves to the Oglala shootout, plus a little of Peltier's biography. Matthiessen chose a more comprehensive approach. As he saw it, a limited purview was exactly why the Fargo trial had gone so poorly: Judge Benson disallowed any testimony that discussed the larger context of Pine Ridge, AIM, or subversive government tactics beyond the events of June 26. Matthiessen would investigate the wider context of the shootout—*all* the context, right back to the nineteenth century when white miners first invaded the Black Hills, "a sacred place at the center of the circle of the world."[67]

He spent much of the fall and winter immersed in reading everything from James Walker's *Lakota Belief and Ritual* (1980) to old issues of a Native newspaper called *Akwesasne Notes*. "Peter came to the story when the big parts were over, so he came to it with the eye of a historian," said Kevin McKiernan, who shared his audio recordings and photographs.[68] (McKiernan had been the only journalist to document the active crime scene at the Jumping Bull property.) Matthiessen also relied on Bill Hazlett, a veteran crime reporter at the *Los Angeles Times*, who had sniffed around the Peltier case and unearthed some "fishy" material. Then there were trial and hearing transcripts, and the voluminous papers from the Wounded Knee Legal Defense/Offense Committee; Matthiessen scoured all of it for pertinent material. Having filed requests under the Freedom of Information Act, Bruce Ellison began receiving a trove of twelve thousand pages from the FBI in late 1980, a selection of what the Bureau termed its "ResMurs" (Reservation Murders) investigation file; this "monument to bureaucratic zeal,"[69] as Matthiessen dubbed it, contained field notes, interviews, affidavits, teletypes, coroner and ballistics reports, letters, and government memos. Of the pages, maybe 5,500 were redacted beyond comprehensibility. Guided by Ellison and other attorneys, Matthiessen went through the rest. He concluded that the FOIA documents showed "how much effort was devoted to constructing a case in support of a preconceived idea of one man's guilt."[70]

Returning to Pine Ridge to survey the Jumping Bull property with Bob Robideau again, he used binoculars to test lines of sight, who would have seen what from where, and then inspected the culvert along the creek that had provided an escape route for the fleeing AIMers. He drove to the site near State Road 73 where Anna Mae Aquash, a Mi'kmaq woman who some AIM members suspected of being an informant—a rumor that may have been encouraged by the FBI to sow discord—had been found with a bullet wound at the base of her skull, in February 1976. "I mainly wanted a sense of the land," Matthiessen explained.[71]

His interviews were conducted in South Dakota, Minnesota, California, and British Columbia, where he tracked down Dino Butler serving time for other charges in Oakalla Prison. Matthiessen refrained from using a tape recorder after realizing people clenched up when he took it out of his bag. He adapted his methods to present himself as an ally. Peltier had a tic in his correspondence, writing "smile" in parentheses: (smile). Whether consciously or not, Matthiessen adopted the tic for his own letters to at least one of Peltier's associates, as one might use slang to win over a wary witness: "I've become very interested in your role, which I'd like to say I admire greatly; and perhaps a little media attention (smile) would not do you any harm just now either, in terms of easing any heat that might be on you."[72]

Peltier was not exaggerating when he warned that securing permission to see him in USP Marion might be difficult. Matthiessen was granted a single hour at the Illinois penitentiary in February 1981. His second visit, in June, would require a petition to Norman Carlson, director of the Federal Bureau of Prisons, and the persuasive intercession of Robert Redford, who was intrigued by Peltier's case and the possibility of a movie about it. (It appears prison authorities gave Redford preferential treatment.)* For the February visit, Matthiessen traveled to Marion with Bruce Ellison. "It was kind of a scary place," Ellison recalled.[73] Built to replace Alcatraz, the nation's highest-security prison was a different kind of island, all steel and concrete and insurmountable mounds of electrified barbed wire.† A water tower, Matthiessen observed, "loomed like a blue mushroom cloud on its long steel-blue stem, and guard towers like pylons jutted at random, dominating unseen yards full of captive men."[74] Somewhere out of sight, behind dozens of locked doors, a Control Unit threatened prisoners with behavioral modification programs—brainwashing, sensory deprivation, and Synanon attack therapy. Matthiessen and Ellison entered a spartan visitation room,

---

* Robert Redford also visited Leonard Peltier at USP Marion, and circled the film project involving Lorenzo Semple Jr. and Matthiessen's book. All the circling, however, eventually caused Matthiessen to lose his temper. He wrote Redford a brusque letter. "To be honest with you—and if I can't speak honestly, we're not going to be able to work together anyway, so here goes—I don't think these ongoing delays and postponements are fair to Leonard. Although I've repeatedly warned him—and others have, too—that you have many projects offered to you, that you need time before you can commit in a whole-hearted way, and that in the end you may decide not to involve yourself, a man in his desperate position can scarcely be blamed for wishful thinking. . . . I, for one, am tired of dancing around with all this indecision, and tired of watching that guy in prison talk himself into a precarious euphoria just when he needs to stay calm and cool, for his own safety." Redford was apparently unmoved by Matthiessen's boldness; he would continue to circle Peltier for another decade, until finally he executive-produced, and provided narration for, *Incident at Oglala*, Michael Apted's 1992 documentary about the shootout. Lorenzo Semple Jr.'s project was never realized.

† USP Marion was downgraded to a medium security prison in 2006—after twenty-three years of permanent lockdown, which was itself a response to the stabbing murder of two corrections officers in October 1983 by inmates aligned with the Aryan Brotherhood. Today, the country's highest security penitentiary is ADX Florence, a "supermax" prison in central Colorado comprised entirely of reinforced concrete single-occupancy cells.

then met Peltier inside a "small booth with glass windows, locked from outside and watched by a guard."[75] It was like being at the center of a set of menacing Matryoshka dolls.

There was little time for discussion, which was relegated to correspondence, but Matthiessen had come to Marion to form an impression of this shy, burly man with shaggy black hair and a "Zapata mustache."[76] Peltier recalled their brief introduction in 2000, for *The Independent*: "I was nervous as hell, afraid of saying something dumb that might hurt my case. . . . And also I knew Peter was trying to read me, read who I really was. At some point in the conversation, though, I happened to look into his eyes, and I thought, you can trust this man. Other Indian people, they notice it, too."[77]

Matthiessen's own account makes it clear why he liked Leonard Peltier. "What comes from him is a warm simplicity, a playful openness, a disarming lack of that arrogance and selfishness which many Indians still associate with the AIM leadership."[78] Here was the highest compliment one could hope to elicit from the writer: simplicity. On another visit, Peltier professed that he was just going to live "day by day," and Matthiessen, who had made similar promises to himself in recent years—who had written a whole book about aspiring to a state of contented immediacy—felt his temples "tingle with admiration" for "the courage and life-spirit of this man."[79]

Sympathy for Peltier was not something that Matthiessen ever tried to conceal. He openly declared his allegiance, just as he had with the United Farm Workers, wearing it like another armband. "I'm on the side of the Indians," he told Bill Hazlett in a letter.[80] Matthiessen would make this crystal clear in *Crazy Horse*; he would reiterate his position after the book's publication, too. He left absolutely no doubt he was partisan: "I felt the facts were so outrageous it was impossible to be unpartisan."[81] Writing from a particular corner, however, did not mean he felt free to manipulate facts. "I want this book to be as honest and accurate as possible," he reassured Hazlett. Matthiessen believed—although some powerful people would soon disagree with him—that you could take a side and still pursue objective truth.*

He mostly avoided interviews with the opposition. As far as he was concerned, the Department of Justice had already made its version of events widely known, a version that was, thanks to the media, the dominant narrative. Matthiessen saw his role as providing a counternarrative. He did make

---

* Barry Lopez believed something similar. After reading *In the Spirit of Crazy Horse*, which he considered "a work of intelligence, of courage, and of restraint," he sent a thoughtful note of support to Matthiessen. "In elucidating conditions of violent racism, abject poverty, disenfranchisement, and abuse of military or police authority, a journalist's special obligation is to provide a voice for those who have no voice. The other side already has a voice: it is insistent, loquacious, everywhere available, and represented by an abundance of material. The journalist's job on that side is to read and winnow."

two exceptions, though, when it came to the interviews. He wrote to Evan Hultman, special prosecutor in both the Cedar Rapids and Fargo trials, asking if Hultman would inspect his material for "accuracy," and perhaps "offer some general conclusions on the case."[82] Hultman rejected this request, perhaps because of Matthiessen's moralizing comments about his "duty as a leading citizen."

The other person Matthiessen approached was FBI Special Agent David Price, a controversial figure on Pine Ridge. Price had been involved in several incidents that would be minutely dissected in *Crazy Horse*, including the acquisition, from an impressionable woman named Myrtle Poor Bear (hospitalized eleven times in thirteen years), of the false affidavits that had facilitated Peltier's extradition from Canada; and in the perplexing saga and grim fate of Anna Mae Aquash. According to an outspoken lawyer who frequently worked with AIM, Price "must be the most evil living agent in an organization that trained thousands of agents in the practice of evil."[83] To hear many Native people speak of him, he personified "the most cynical abuses of the FBI's regressive attitudes toward Indians."[84] Was this reputation fairly earned? Matthiessen wanted to hear what the man had to say for himself. He phoned Price at his home in Rochester, Minnesota, and they spoke on the record for two hours and fifty-seven minutes. Their strange, looping conversation threw Matthiessen off-balance. He would write in his book that Price was "regarded wrongly as the villain of the tale."[85] He would also write this:

> I wondered how soon the Bureau would know about this phone call, how long before a new entry under my name would appear in those gigantic Bureau files. Because ever since the first few minutes of our conversation, I had been feeling paranoid myself. Why was Price telling me so often that I had to be careful, that I could expect harm from "them" if I told the truth? Was this his way of threatening me on the Bureau's behalf?[86]

Given how David Price reacted to the publication of *In the Spirit of Crazy Horse*, this paragraph is remarkably prescient. Price would offer his own disgruntled thoughts on the phone conversation in an affidavit filed with the U.S. District Court for the District of Minnesota in 1987. A copy of the affidavit, preserved in Matthiessen's archive, features the writer's annotations: "NOT SO," "disputed," and "?" scrawled angrily in the margins.[87]

BY MARCH 1981, Matthiessen was working "like the hammers of hell on the Book, and I think you'll like it,"[88] he wrote to Peltier, who responded with excitement: "After meeting you I'm convinced you will do more than your best on the book and can't wait to read the first draft."[89]

At some point that spring, Matthiessen went to see Elisabeth Sifton at Viking to make a verbal pitch. There was no written proposal, and she was given none of the manuscript to read as a sample. Sifton bought the project on trust: "It was virtually a foregone conclusion that we would want to publish a book by him."[90] In June, a contract between Peter Matthiessen and the Viking Press was drawn up for "THIEVES' ROAD," a working title, referencing the Bozeman Trail, that was soon superseded by *In the Spirit of Crazy Horse*. The advance was $250,000—three times more than *The Snow Leopard* had earned him, in recognition of his two National Book Awards. "Your price goes up after you have had a success like that," Sifton said. There were some notable stipulations in the contract, presumably at Matthiessen's request: a reaffirmation of his financial arrangement with the Leonard Peltier Defense Committee; a promise that all subsidiary payments would be disbursed much earlier than was usual for a new title, in time to meet, and help fund, Peltier's appeal; and a commitment by Viking to donate two hundred copies for distribution to "Indian friends."[91]

Matthiessen had the skeleton of a first draft by May, less than a year after beginning the project—an astonishing pace. Sifton got her first glance at pages in September. She visited Matthiessen in Sagaponack, where, once again, she sat beside him in the studio as they scrutinized paragraph after paragraph together. "We talked at length about the form the book would finally take," Sifton later recalled. "There was an enormous amount of material that was potentially includable. For a writer [with] his . . . highly developed sense of organization, of pace, of tone and color, how to use all of this material, whether he could use it at all, what would have to go, what would have to stay: all of these were issues of the greatest complexity and delicacy. I was frankly daunted by it, as I very frequently become daunted by Matthiessen's efforts, which strike me as amazingly big."[92]

By December, when Sifton returned to Sagaponack for another multiday conference in the studio, the book had grown to over a thousand manuscript pages. Sifton's "editorial anxiety" also ballooned. Matthiessen demanded "a general level of perfection" that would make even a slender pamphlet into an ultramarathon of labor, and this was nothing short of a tome.

Sifton carted the manuscript back to her office in New York. For the next three months, Matthiessen phoned her with fresh edits, sometimes daily, or dropped by in person to amend entire sections. "You have all of these revisions, all these little pieces of paper, cut and paste. This was not on a word processor. It was physically difficult to do," Sifton said. "I recollect that because there was still pending legal action involving some of the characters in the book, there were further legal developments anticipated or decisions to be handed down or papers to be obtained which might or might not encourage Matthiessen to alter what he had written."[93] It was the responsibility of Sifton and her assistant, Jennifer Snodgrass, to keep the master manuscript coherent, a stressful task given how much of it constantly shifted. Matthiessen needed "a lot of reassurance that . . . all of these moving parts would eventually be nailed down." As the months flew by and new material kept coming in, Sifton began to need some reassurance herself.

She implored him to make cuts. Did they really need three pages on X, four pages on Y? When Matthiessen resisted, she phoned Candida Donadio to discuss "Peter's psychological relationship to the Indians."[94] Sifton sensed that he was *unable* to make what seemed to her necessary edits. Donadio offered a theory. "She felt that in some respect they had spooked him," Sifton recalled. "And that he had given over some of his freedom as a writer to them, so that he felt obligated to do *this, this, this,* and *this* for them. She was aware of anxieties about positions he took in the book, or things that he said or wrote about the Indians, that she had never encountered before. Nor had I. I tended to take Candida seriously. She was a very, very wise woman."

Matthiessen's psychological relationship with the Indians was undoubtedly influenced by his soured relationship with Cesar Chavez. While he'd brought considerable attention to Chavez's union throughout the years, Matthiessen had continued to pursue his own projects at the same time; Chavez, succumbing to a monomania that caused him to institute purges in the union ranks, had gradually frozen him out as punishment. "I saw he didn't trust me," Matthiessen once recalled. "Why wasn't I there, if I cared so much about the cause, working for five dollars a week?"[95] Chavez's implicit accusation—Matthiessen had betrayed la causa by not giving his whole life to it—wounded the writer, who had given so much. Now, when it came to "the Indians," he made sure that nobody would ever be able to accuse him of abandoning Leonard Peltier. "I feel that it is a responsibility to maintain communication with Leonard and the Indian people," he affirmed during an interview in 1983. "You can't do a book like this, then walk away."[96] Like he had supposedly walked away from Chavez? "He didn't want to let him down," Maria said of her husband's feelings about Peltier. "Most writers like Mailer, or even Styron, they took up a cause and then . . . that was it. On to the next thing. Peter didn't do that. He kept in touch with Peltier until the day [Peter] died. And he *did* feel beholden. He felt that he had to do this, that America had done a dreadful thing."[97] He felt, in a sense, that he was atoning not only for his own privilege but for the entire culture, for all non–Native Americans.

Matthiessen declined to make Sifton's cuts because, as it had been with *Sal Si Puedes*, he did not consider *In the Spirit of Crazy Horse* to belong to him. He wanted it to be "an Indian book with Indian voices. . . . I didn't want my picture on the book, and if I had had my way, I would not have had my name on it."[98] Sifton, the editor-in-chief of a major publishing house that had just spent a quarter of a million dollars on this acquisition, would have blanched at the idea of effacing her author. What she wanted was a book that was short enough to be affordable for, and appealing to, a large number of potential customers.

Matthiessen had other ambitions, though he may not have shared them with the team at Viking. His post-publication comments about *Crazy Horse* make it sound almost willfully anti-reader. If *Sal Si Puedes* had been a book about hope, this was steeped in rage and bitterness, the loss of hope. He cut out "every bit of poetry."[99] He tried to write something "flat, hard-nosed, tough." He wanted "to hit people" with it. He aimed for "a brutalizing book because nothing else would make people wake up." The book was going to "make a lot of people upset," he told *The Philadelphia Inquirer*, sounding almost pleased.[100] At the same time, it was intended to serve as a "textbook for lawyers, or for anybody who wanted to bring in some sort of assistance for this man."[101] It was both a bludgeon and an exhaustive compendium for legal researchers—hardly an appealing prospect, either way, to a general audience.

In the Spirit of Crazy Horse is indeed formidable, a monument made up entirely of sharp edges. The first chapter surveys the big picture of indignities visited upon Native American people since the 1800s: treaties made and broken, "civilization" imposed using a "trusty mix of bibles and bullets,"[102] extermination of the bison, the Dawes Act, termination policy, the "weak and ambivalent"[103] Bureau of Indian Affairs. Then Matthiessen turns to AIM, a pride movement branded "extremist" by the FBI, which effectively declared a war of attrition on AIM's most prominent members after the Wounded Knee Occupation in 1973. Peltier may be the driving focus of *Crazy Horse*, but his story is just one among many—a shaggy collection of assaults, murders, cover-ups, and enforcement agency subterfuge. Matthiessen follows leads and falls down rabbit holes, then holes within holes, amassing piles of names and dates (some of them incorrect) that threaten to overwhelm all but the most diligent student. Some sections are virtuosic tours through conflicting accounts of the same event; other parts seem only tangentially relevant to Peltier, like footnotes accidentally left in the body of the text: a long analysis of a rape accusation, for instance, made in 1967 on the Rosebud Indian Reservation by Jancita Eagle Deer against a Legal Aid lawyer named Bill Janklow, a man who, eleven years later—three years after Eagle Deer was killed in an unsolved hit-and-run in southern Nebraska—happened to be elected the governor of South Dakota.

When *Crazy Horse* was published, a critic for *Vanity Fair* pointed out that the book seems "assembled rather than composed."[104] The authorial hand of Peter Matthiessen is unmistakable, though, in the splutters of indignant sarcasm ("The FBI agents, all suited up in war-games costumes");[105] in the repeated references to spirituality, the Great Spirit, an eagle that had supposedly guided the AIMers to safety at Oglala; and in the novelistic rendering of Coler's and Williams's hideous deaths: "The long black hair, the sweating forehead, the wild eye squinched by the rifle stock—*NO!*"[106] The book opens with an introduction less concerned with AIM and Peltier than it is with the Big Man, who then reappears, haunting the Jumping Bull property, the day before the shootout: "it was *plunk-plunk-plunk*, like that, big steady steps."[107] The book also ends with the Big Man: Sam Moves Camp describes his loud steps as "a sign, a warning."[108] *Crazy Horse* is framed by Matthiessen's obsession with bigfoot, a spectral figure thematically deployed as a symbol of impending doom.

Whether or not Peltier is also turned into a symbol, a romantic martyr, is something people began to argue about even before Matthiessen completed the manuscript. In 1981, after getting wind of the gestating project, Janet McCloud, the Tulalip activist, dashed off a letter challenging him for making Peltier out to be a "hero." Matthiessen rejected the charge. "This book does not attempt to 'heroize' Leonard, or prove his 'innocence'; I believe he was railroaded into jail and deserves a new trial, and I hope this book will help him get one."[109] Despite this objection, he certainly does paint a flattering portrait of Peltier in *Crazy Horse*, the hapless foot soldier forced by "ruthless persecution"[110] into the role of a leader—"everybody except possibly yourself thinks you come out as a great guy,"[111] he wrote Peltier directly—just as he brushes over some of the more violent conduct of the AIMers. While the book isn't propaganda, it is selective. For example, Joseph Killsright Stuntz, the only Native man killed at Oglala, was found wearing an FBI fatigue jacket taken from Agent Coler's car. Kevin McKiernan, the NPR journalist who had photographed Stuntz's body at the crime scene, offered two explanations for this detail when he spoke to Matthiessen: perhaps Stuntz had stolen the jacket as "war booty," or perhaps the jacket had been planted on Stuntz by government agents to further discredit AIM. Matthiessen quoted McKiernan proposing the second possibility (fingering the authorities) but, much to McKiernan's chagrin, chose to omit the first (fingering AIM).[112] At the same time, when the AIM leader Dennis Banks asked him to leave out other unflattering details about the Movement, Matthiessen demurred, saying he had to "draw the line a little."[113]

As for Peltier's innocence, Matthiessen eventually arrived at an "extreme"[114] position, as he once described it. "I'm not arguing," he told the writer Vine Deloria Jr., "that Leonard is 'innocent' of finishing off the two agents (though I think he is); I am arguing that he is innocent, for a whole century of reasons, whether he finished off those men or not."[115]

ONCE MATTHIESSEN HAD MOST of a polished draft, he circulated pieces of it to relevant parties for comments and suggestions. The response was mostly complimentary. "Everybody seems pretty excited," he informed Peltier.[116] Bruce Ellison thought the draft was a revelation. Ken Tilsen, formerly of the Wounded Knee Legal Defense/Offense Committee, called the chapters he read "unquestionably the best thing I have ever seen written in this area."[117] Peltier, however, was a little more circumspect after he finally inspected the manuscript. "I don't get the impression you like the book very much," Matthiessen wrote him in the summer of 1982, "but I feel confident you will by the time you see the printed version—at least I hope so, after all this goddamn work."[118] (In the decades after *Crazy Horse* was published, a few other Native people—children present at the Oglala shootout—would also respond to the book with ambivalence, or dissatisfaction, feeling that Matthiessen had spoken on their behalf without actually listening to them first.)

One letter of feedback would prove more consequential than the rest. Jim Leach was a young, meticulously thorough lawyer in Rapid City who had briefly worked for the Defense/Offense Committee, but he was not involved with Peltier's case and had enough critical distance to see the situation clearly. Recognizing that Leach was something of an impartial authority, Matthiessen invited him to review the manuscript in full. Leach agreed, and soon shared twenty-two pages of typed critiques. "In writing *In the Spirit of Crazy Horse*, Peter had many people trying to pull him in their direction. I thought of my role," Leach later recalled, "as pulling him back from some of the more unsupportable theories."[119]

Leach made a number of shrewd assessments. Matthiessen had argued that the real reason government agents had pursued AIM leaders so aggressively for years was because AIM stood between energy companies and Black Hills mineral deposits. Leach pointed out that there was, in fact, "no evidence whatsoever" to support this conspiratorial allegation.[120] And he raised an even bigger red flag over the multiple instances of potential defamation in the book. Leach wrote in his letter, one of several similar comments: "Saying

Janklow raped Jancita Eagle Deer is libel. Good luck trying to prove truth as a defense in a South Dakota court with a South Dakota jury. This one could easily be worth a few hundred thousand for Janklow." Matthiessen would be advised to avoid unproven claims about the touchy and litigious governor—claims which, in Leach's opinion, added little besides making the book even more lurid.

Matthiessen knew he was poking a bear when it came to "Wild Bill" Janklow. The baby-faced politician was known for abrasive theatricality. He attracted, and seemed to enjoy, rumors about his untamed behavior: that he had earned so many speeding tickets the police threatened to confiscate his license; that he'd slept with an M16 rifle by his pillow while he was South Dakota's attorney general. Supporters celebrated him as "one heck of a salesman." Opponents denounced him as a "two-bit demagogue." Janklow, who had once defended Native people in court, now spent a great deal of time trying to convict them. Indeed, he was said to refer to himself as an "Indian fighter."[121]

In a letter to Dennis Banks, Matthiessen wrote that he better go into hiding to avoid "legal suits from your pal Janklow."[122] This was meant as a joke; Banks, along with Russell Means, was Matthiessen's primary source of information about the accusations against Janklow, and Matthiessen himself felt relatively immune from the governor's wrath. Not only was he confident in the strength of his own reporting, but Viking had sent the manuscript to its counsel, Frankfurt, Garbus, Klein, & Selz, in New York, for a detailed legal read. Within days of receiving Leach's letter advising light-footedness around Janklow, Matthiessen also received a letter from Elisabeth Sifton that suggested Martin Garbus, the publisher's attorney, foresaw no "major problems" with the book—although there were a handful of "tricky points" that needed to be double-checked, including the rape allegations.[123] Matthiessen then sat down with Garbus's associate, Rick Kurnit, who had conducted the legal read and had extensive experience with libel law. "We would go back and forth," Kurnit said of the discussions conducted in his living room. "I remember when I would press Peter on some of the things, he made the strangest statement: 'Can't Viking verify this with a stringer out in South Dakota?' I had to resist his desire to have the publisher take care of the fact-checking"—a responsibility, then as now, of the author.[124]

To clear up the trickiest points about Janklow, Matthiessen obtained original court transcripts and documents from the Rosebud Indian Reservation; Kurnit then cross-checked the author's statements in *Crazy Horse* to ensure the accusations against Janklow were being reported accurately. As Martin Garbus later recalled, a decision was ultimately made that there were "sufficient facts . . . to allow Peter to say what he thought."[125] Perhaps this is why

Matthiessen was so bullish in his response to Leach's critiques: he figured he was legally in the clear. "This book," he wrote Leach in a note of appreciation, "is bound to be very controversial, even the Indians aren't going to like a lot of what it says, and as Bob R[obideau] says, 'There's no sense getting paranoid about what people <u>might</u> do.'"[126]

In the Spirit of Crazy Horse was printed by Viking at the start of 1983. Elisabeth Sifton was ecstatic to be finished after such an arduous production process. She invited Matthiessen to sign her personal copy; she had signed it herself "in blood and sweat," she said, adding, "I hope you are REALLY PLEASED with this book, cher maître."[127]

What happened next did so with dizzying speed, like the foundation of a building suddenly giving way. The book was released at the beginning of March. Many of the reviews were positive, if somewhat shellshocked by the magnitude of the subject matter. Carolyn See, in the *Los Angeles Times*, compared *Crazy Horse* "in intent if not in structure"[128] to *War and Peace*, while Page Stegner, writing in *The New York Review of Books*, called it "one of the most dramatic demonstrations of endemic American racism that has yet been written."[129] But other reviews were caustic—"damn near unreadable";[130] "an angry and naïve John Ford western reversed with mirrors"[131]—and two in particular struck Matthiessen as a "Saturday-Sunday-one-two-punch,"[132] both of them coming in the all-important *New York Times*.

On March 5, Christopher Lehmann-Haupt wrote a withering dismissal of the book. "So Indians on the Pine Ridge Reservation were attacked by members of the F.B.I., according to Mr. Matthiessen, and two agents were killed. So, he maintains, the F.B.I. fabricated evidence to discredit A.I.M. instead of going after the actual perpetrators.... So what else is new?" Lehmann-Haupt was "bored" by stories about the "alleged persecution of American Indians." He added, almost as an afterthought, "One does not like to be put in the position of yawning at murder, injustice, conspiracy and the railroading of innocent people."[133] Matthiessen was taken aback by these uncharitable comments; he thought Lehmann-Haupt was like "a white mouse" fleeing from reality.[134] Before he could get too indignant, though, the Harvard law professor Alan Dershowitz took another swing the following day, on March 6, in *The New York Times Book Review*. Matthiessen was a "good-hearted naïf," Dershowitz wrote. He was also "utterly unconvincing—indeed embarrassingly sophomoric—when he pleads the legal innocence of individual Indian criminals." AIM was a "militant fringe group," and the murdered FBI agents had only been doing their jobs. Indeed the "radicals of AIM," Dershowitz declared, in a line with the power of a nuclear bomb, had more in common with General Custer than they did with the "noble" and "selfless" Chief Crazy Horse.[135]

Now Matthiessen was stunned. He "lashed out bitterly" while speaking to journalists.[136] He fired off an incensed response to the *Times* accusing Dershowitz of "bias against the American Indian Movement," of "dutifully" swallowing the FBI's stories, and of writing the kind of adversarial hatchet job that might negatively impact Peltier's chance of appealing his conviction.[137] Letters of protest soon followed from other outraged readers. A rebuttal to Dershowitz's "insulting . . . slanderous . . . violent assault" appeared in *Wassaja*, a national newspaper of Indian America, co-signed by the likes of Russell Means, Oren Lyons, Madonna Thunder Hawk, and Ward Churchill.[138] Fifteen Native people also met—uninvited—with Dershowitz in his Harvard office to "voice their displeasure" with his presumptuous views. One of them reportedly informed Dershowitz that "violence was not the theoretical act of bashing in his face but rather his own 'rhetoric,' which would justify such actions."[139] Dershowitz stormed out of the room. "I remember," said Winona LaDuke, who helped organize the confrontation, "that he was probably a little shook up."[140] Matthiessen was pleased to hear that the professor had got what he deserved.

The same day, Martin Garbus was forced to write a carefully worded letter to Bill Janklow on behalf of Viking and its author. The South Dakota governor had, as Jim Leach predicted, not much enjoyed *In the Spirit of Crazy Horse* or his portrayal as (in Janklow's own words) "morally decadent, a drunkard," "a racist and a bigot,"[141] a gun-toting redneck running amok raping young women. Just because he was a public figure did not mean a writer had license to print "reckless" and "malicious" lies about him, Janklow said, hinting at possible legal action. Every new shipment of *Crazy Horse*, and every bit of advertising, would be considered a unique act of "malice," accumulating like a bill. He wanted the book withdrawn immediately to minimize "emotional harm."[142]

Over the next month, Garbus tried to negotiate with Janklow's office. Viking would be willing to amend the text if the governor supplied evidence that contradicted Matthiessen's reporting. But Janklow had already sued *Newsweek*, in February, for publishing the same rape allegations, and he seemed more intent on publicly raging than in privately resolving his grievances. (Matthiessen to Garbus: "If he truly wishes to spare his family further distress, as he states to the media at every opportunity, he is going about it in a very peculiar way.")[143] Viking's offers were mostly ignored; a phone call degenerated, on Janklow's side, into juvenile name-calling. Meanwhile, at a conference for South Dakota's Automobile Dealers Association, in front of two hundred people, the governor announced that he had been sorely tempted "to separate somebody's head from their shoulders."[144] Matthiessen assumed his head was the one in peril. "I've tried to do this in a very deliberate and responsible way," Janklow told *The Sioux City Journal*, at the end of April, about his campaign to phone every bookstore in his state to "persuade" them to stop selling *Crazy Horse*.[145] Sales only spiked as a result.[146] As the publicity manager for Viking pointed out in a statement, "There's nothing like someone telling you that you can't read something to make you want to go out and buy the book."[147]

In May, Janklow finally agreed to sit down with Viking's legal team to discuss the offending pages. Then he fell ominously silent; Garbus and Rick Kurnit sent letters and made phone calls trying to pin down a date, with no response. On May 19, instead of coming to the negotiating table in New York, Janklow went to South Dakota state court, in Pierre, and sued Peter Matthiessen, the Viking Press, and three bookstores that had "willfully refused"[148] to remove *Crazy Horse* from their shelves. He asked for $24 million in damages.[149] The bookstores in Sioux Falls, Hot Springs, and Rapid City reeled from this unprecedented bit of legal bullying—a "terrorist tactic," one journalism professor called it.[150] But Viking moved straight to the offensive. Six days later, on May 25, the publisher filed a countersuit charging that the governor was trying to interfere with their "constitutional right to publish and distribute" free speech.[151]

Where was Matthiessen during these extraordinary developments? The night the countersuit was filed, he was in Washington, in the Longworth House Office Building, at a book reception co-hosted by ten members of Congress.* Events had spun wildly out of control, but he tried to stay calm and on message. None of this was supposed to be about him. "I didn't want to do it," he told the assembled crowd. "I'm not a political writer. . . . I couldn't find anyone else to write it. . . . I think [Peltier] is not getting justice in the courts. . . . So that's why we're here—to get attention from Congress."[152]

WHILE JANKLOW'S LAWSUIT WAS not entirely a surprise, nobody anticipated the form a second one would take. In January 1984, Bruce Ellison was walking in downtown Rapid City when two federal agents appeared out of nowhere to shove a document into his hands. The summons named him as a codefendant: David Price was suing Peter Matthiessen and the Viking Press for defamation, and Ellison, too, for supposedly supplying the writer with the libelous material. Refusing to respond to what was obviously a provocation, Ellison thanked the men for personally delivering the news. They had

---

* All Democrats: Ron Dellums, Thomas Downey, Ed Markey, George Miller, Bruce Morrison, Robert Mrazek, John Seiberling, Fortney Stark, Chuck Schumer, and Pat Schroeder. The reception was additionally sponsored by Robert Blake, Jackson Browne, Max Gail, Jack Lemmon, Toby Moffett, Graham Nash, and Jon Voight.

big smiles on their faces. "I guess," Ellison then went and told *The Rapid City Journal*, "this lawsuit is the price one has to pay for exposing the truth about the FBI operations on the Pine Ridge Reservation."[153]

A few days earlier, Elisabeth Sifton had promised Matthiessen "that things are going to be better and different in 1984."[154] Once he got a summons of his own, Matthiessen scribbled his reply at the bottom of Sifton's letter, just below her signature: "Do you recall any <u>mention</u> of D. Price during libel check? I don't. (I can't believe this suit is Price's idea.)"[155] Back during his phone call with Price in Minnesota, he sensed that the agent was warning him like a dog starting to growl, but a libel suit had never crossed his mind as a possible reprisal. Unlike Janklow, who took issue with specific allegations in the book, David Price objected to *Crazy Horse* more generally. "The whole thing is rotten to me," he told the media.[156] His complaint cited thirty-four passages as examples of libel; some concerned his handling of witnesses, his relationship with members of AIM, but others didn't mention him directly at all. In a perplexed response to the court, Viking's lawyers pointed out that "the complaint quotes criticism of the FBI as defamation of Price."[157] Seemingly on behalf of all FBI agents, Price was challenging Matthiessen's version of history, a version that presented them as "corrupt and vicious" in their treatment of Native people on and beyond Pine Ridge.[158] Price sought $25 million in compensatory damages, and an unspecified amount in punitive damages. That meant Viking and Matthiessen, represented by Martin Garbus—a free speech absolutist who had once defended Lenny Bruce against an obscenity charge—were now facing down two major lawsuits adding up to more than $49 million.

By every measure, this was the worst possible scenario for *In the Spirit of Crazy Horse*. Matthiessen had written his book to draw attention to the plight of Leonard Peltier, yet the media was now more interested in the travails of its high-profile author than it was in Peltier's evidentiary hearing for a possible new trial, which Matthiessen attended in Bismarck, North Dakota, in October. He had intended to give a voice to the voiceless, yet the louder voices of Janklow and Price were dominating the conversation. Their lawsuits were attempts at intimidation, in Matthiessen's view: censorship by threat.[159]

And in this they were undeniably successful. Sometime in 1984, Viking preemptively withdrew the book from circulation and pulped all remaining inventory in the company's warehouse. Matthiessen was not consulted about this "panicky destruction," as he later grumbled to Sifton, "of 1700 copies of CRAZY HORSE that could just as well have been slipped out to the Indians."[160] Meanwhile, his UK publisher, Christopher MacLehose at Harvill, elected to hold off on a foreign edition despite considerable international interest in Peltier's case, which frustrated Matthiessen: "I shall play along with your mindless fear that these right-wing loonballs are poised to take their absurd case to England: all they really wish to do is squash smart-alecks here."[161] As Peltier wrote concerned letters from prison—he hoped Peter was holding up under the pressure—Matthiessen began to realize that he might not be able to help Leonard through a book, that all his hard work on *Crazy Horse* might have been for nothing.

A monograph could be written on the legal history of the twin lawsuits. Over the next few years they would bounce between different courts, from state to federal, South Dakota to Minnesota. One would be dismissed on the First Amendment doctrine of "neutral reportage," then appealed and reinstated.[162] A judge would recuse himself after discovering that some of his friends and former clients appeared in the book, along with himself, his wife's uncle, and the great-grandmother of his wife's nephew.[163] Settlement offers would be made, but to settle was to implicitly admit fault; Matthiessen and Viking would refuse. There would be days and days of depositions meant to wear the defendants down until they said something incriminating. Roger Magnuson, a fundamentalist minister and known defender of "right-wing causes,"[164] who was representing David Price, would grill Elisabeth Sifton about Matthiessen's use of LSD, and about his peculiar interest in cryptozoology:

> MR. MAGNUSON: I think I am entitled to ask her whether or not she at any time talked with Mr. Matthiessen about the credibility or believability of his descriptions of a big or big, hairy man as contained in the book. [To Sifton] Did you have such conversations with him?
> MR. GARBUS: Where in the book?
> MR. MAGNUSON: You know there is a story of the big hairy man in the book.[165]

"The whole thing was so corrupt," Sifton remembered. The aim of the depositions was to paint Matthiessen not only as a dodgy reporter but "very left, probably homosexual, probably a drunk ... a typical cliché of the FBI from the 1950s."[166]

As the process stretched on, Matthiessen became increasingly convinced of his early suspicion, shared by Ellison, that Price's lawsuit was covertly "sponsored" by the FBI in a bid to suppress *Crazy Horse*. How, Matthiessen wanted to know, could David Price with his modest agent's salary afford such expensive counsel?[167] Roger Magnuson was unlikely to have taken "a case of this magnitude on a contingency basis simply to embellish his reputation," Garbus said.[168] And then there was the matter of Price's first affidavit to the court, which seemed, in the reading of Viking's and Matthiessen's attorneys, to contain information unavailable to everyone *except* the FBI. Price claimed to be suing as a regular civilian, not as a special agent, yet his access to privileged materials suggested otherwise.[169] Garbus accused the Department of Justice of playing puppet-master behind the scenes. The DOJ, in a scoffing response sent straight to the judge, called Garbus a liar.[170]

For his part, Matthiessen couldn't help but recall something Craig Carpenter had told him before he even got involved with AIM: "those who stick with us too long or try to help us too much end up just as poverty-stricken and harassed as we have been, and ARE."[171] This was one prophecy that appeared to be coming true. "It's ugly," Matthiessen said, "when your own government is after you."[172]*

Over the years, he would find solace in the support of other writers, including Bill Styron, William Merwin, Gary Snyder, Susan Sontag (as president of PEN American Center), and Louise Erdrich, who had attended Peltier's murder trial in Fargo and found the verdict shameful. "My sense of sympathy with you over this awful nuisance in South Dakota is very strong," Barry Lopez wrote in another generous letter. "Although such a thought is at some level perfectly useless, you should know, and remind yourself, that your work, the record of your commitment, transcends all of this. The business of the courts and wounded egos takes place in the flattest dimension of history. Your worth is not contained there."[173]

While he mostly put on a brave face for the outside world, Matthiessen could not deny "a certain amount of depression" as a by-product of the lawsuits.[174] In fact, the emotional cost was significant. "I am determined to banish this depression and live out our lovely lives happily together," he vowed in a letter to Maria.[175] He made related confessions to friends over drinks or during late-night phone calls. "He began calling me up and asking if he should take antidepressants," recalled the writer Stuart Dybek, who sometimes spoke to Matthiessen at three or four in the morning.[176] (Insomnia was a lifelong struggle.) "Peter was a man of sensitivity," said Martin Garbus. "Plus, his credibility as a writer was at stake. His credibility and his accuracy

---

* After speaking to David Price on the phone, Matthiessen had wondered how long it would be before his name appeared "in those gigantic Bureau files." The question was still on his mind in 1987, when he clipped an article from *The New Yorker*—"Policing America's Writers," by Herbert Mitgang—about the FBI's habit of keeping tabs on literary folk it deemed subversive or troublesome. (This represented a somewhat ironic reversal, given Matthiessen himself had once kept tabs on literary folk in Paris for the CIA.) In 2018, for this biography, I submitted a Freedom of Information Act request for Matthiessen's file, which was declined by the FBI on the basis that "no main record files" could be located. However, the boilerplate letter came with multiple caveats that did not preclude the existence of classified records beyond the reach of my FOIA request. It seems highly improbable that not a single piece of paper exists on a man who wrote an enormous, widely discussed book defending AIM and Leonard Peltier—a book legally challenged by both a sitting governor and an active FBI agent.

were extraordinarily important to him, so he was very unhappy much of the time."[177] This unhappiness led to—or was perhaps exacerbated by, or both, in a feedback loop—the disintegration of his relationship with the Viking Press. In the wake of the Janklow suit, he felt "a bit estranged" from his publisher, he complained to Sifton.[178] With the Price lawsuit, he began to wonder if he was being fed to the wolves. Viking was not sufficiently supportive of his book; as Sifton noted in an internal memo, Matthiessen believed "Viking should do an ad for political reasons, as it were, to show that despite the slings and arrows of right-wing obscurantism, we thought him a hero and a star."[179] Sifton actually agreed with this—they *should* be propping up their embattled author, particularly when he was feeling so "dicey" about them— but her hands were tied at a moment when Viking Penguin was undergoing internal restructuring. And once they pulped *Crazy Horse*, perhaps nothing would have appeased him. *Indian Country* was published, in Matthiessen's opinion, with insufficient publicity, and at the end of 1984 he temporarily suspended plans to reissue his older books in uniform Penguin paperback editions. Sifton wrote in her memo, in January 1985:

> From his point of view, we are now a publishing house made up of people whom he has never met, who may for all he knows not want to meet him, and who view him as a nuisance because of the Crazy Horse litigation being such a pain in the ass. He asks me repeatedly whether this is the case.
>
> He says that he <u>knows</u> it was a nightmare, but that he also feels a subtle but large lack of moral support for him during the case. He was used, in the old days, as most authors are, to having his publisher and his publisher's attorney and his editor work with him in close collaboration on any problem or threat of a problem. He (rightly) imagined that in the new regime the legal matters were shunted off to the counsel's office, reported on to "management" . . . and then a decision made which the editors learned about ex post facto. I must say this is the way it felt to me, too.[180]

Sifton's ambivalence poured out in a long sigh: Matthiessen was "an immensely complicated, neurotic, charming, iron-willed, uncertain, demanding author," and his "quicksilver personality" left her "exhausted and rattled." He had just had a malignant melanoma removed from his left temple: "I have no doubt that the turbulent sense of mortality and urgency that such a development would induce has something to do with his recent difficult behavior."

Even after he healed from the operation, Matthiessen's behavior did not improve. In May, he sent a ferocious letter to Sifton that questioned her "over-work and perhaps unsuitability to simultaneous managerial and editorial roles and motherhood." He was "weary of all this talk," he said: "it's too much like a bad marriage, wouldn't you say?"[181] Sifton—in the midst of a nasty divorce—took a deep breath. She replied to the misogynistic tirade with a steely letter of her own that referenced their friendship in the past tense. Abashed, Matthiessen then apologized for his "out of order" motherhood insult: "Having seen you in action once, in Brooklyn Heights, I haven't the slightest doubt that you are a terrific mother, and I only meant—very sympathetically, au fond—that you had too much heat on you in recent years from too many directions."[182] He insisted, however, that his exasperation was justified. Communication had completely broken down with Viking, which, from his perspective, was a shadow of the publishing house once run by Tom Guinzburg. The old-school approach of boozy lunches and deals based on gut instinct had been replaced with the hierarchical coldness of a Wall Street bank crunching numbers. As Matthiessen complained to Christopher MacLehose:

> Elisabeth is somewhere beyond reach—my reach, anyway, and I am patronized by her ever-changing staff, which all but ignores my increasingly feeble and despairing voice. I am very fond of Elisabeth and respect her greatly as an editor, and I have made all the allowances I can muster for Viking's change of address, Viking's internecine tumult, Elisabeth's own domestic trauma, and my own famous paranoia, and still I conclude that, despite generally excellent reviews, INDIAN COUNTRY has been allowed to slip between the cracks and will do much more poorly than it need have done, had someone at Viking cared, or paid attention. "All authors say that, of course"—but in fact, I don't think I have said it before, and I shall make certain that I won't have to say it again.[183]

By 1985, it was clear to everyone involved that the lawsuits were not going to go away anytime soon. Matthiessen continued to do everything he could for Peltier, following his appeal process and appearing on the *Today* show to argue Peltier's case before the cameras. But he also made a major personal decision. He and Maria were shielded by Viking's insurance company, which was picking up the legal bills. While there was a ceiling to the coverage, they were not yet in danger of financial ruin. With this in mind, they came to an agreement. "We sat down together," Maria recalled, "and said, 'We've got to stop talking about it, and stop thinking about it, because otherwise it's going to ruin our life.'"[184] After so much anxious uncertainty, after being almost "papered to death," the lawsuit debacle was banished as a subject of discussion from the Matthiessen household.

The decision liberated Peter. He wrote to William Merwin as though he could hardly restrain himself from running out the door: "I worry about it no more, no more, having embarked at last, at last, on a new novel—wish me luck! I've been so taken up with 'Indian business' for the last 10 years that I've done no fiction at all. God, it feels good, too—I feel the juices seeping back into my batteries."[185]

In October, he signed a contract with Random House (another $250,000) for this untitled novel centered on the Florida Everglades. And then, having just received a Gold Medal for Distinction in Natural History Art, from the Academy of Natural Sciences in Philadelphia—an honor awarded to individuals whose work has contributed to "mankind's better understanding and appreciation of living things"—he took up nature writing again, too. In the final days of the year, he flew to Nairobi to meet David "Jonah" Western, a resource ecologist with the New York Zoological Society, for another eventful expedition (a forced bush landing in Zaire; an arrest by suspicious gendarmes; a sprained ankle, biting safari ants, Matthiessen "gasping in anger and shock")[186] in search of forest elephants in the remote tropical fastness of the Congo Basin.

22

Ten Thousand Islands

> Sometimes I rode all the way east to the Everglades, long silent days under the broad sky in the hard fierce light of Glades country, lost in the creak of my old worn-out saddle and my horse blowing and hot wind drying out the pines. For long years afterward I missed the stillness of the Big Cypress, the slow time of those horseback days, the hunting and fishing for the cow camp, the slow cooking fires, the simple sun-warmed tools of iron, wood, and leather, the resin scent of the pine ridges, the stomp of hooves and bawl of cattle, the glimpsed wild creatures, the echoing silence pierced far and near by the sharp cry of a woodpecker or the dry sizzle of a rattler, and always the soft blowing of my woods pony, a small short-bodied roan.
>
> —*Killing Mister Watson* (1990)[1]

O F ALL THE "LAST" wildernesses that Matthiessen wrote about during his life—remnants of a preindustrial world; regions not yet fully subdued and dominated by the hand of man—none haunted his imagination as deeply or persistently as the mosquito-infested backcountry of South Florida, "the last true wilderness in the nation,"[2] with its hardwood hammocks and roadless swamps, its river channels shifting through razor-edged sawgrass, like the Labyrinth of Greek mythology transposed to the American tropics and populated with panthers, alligators, parakeets.

As a boy, before the Everglades National Park was even established (in 1947), Peter accompanied his father on fishing trips down "jungly streams," past "green walls ornamented with white egrets and storks in the high trees."[3] One March when he was sixteen or seventeen, they motored northwest from the Florida Keys and Cape Sable, skirting the edge of the Ten Thousand Islands, a section of the coast that looks on maps as if someone has shattered it with a sledgehammer. Matty pointed out the islets and estuaries, then showed Peter a marine chart marked with evocative names like Rabbit Key and Lostmans River. A few miles up the Chatham River, Matty said, indicating another spot deep in the Islands, was a lonely house—two stories of Dade County pine, painted bone white, with hardwood floors and a formal dining room.[4] This incongruous construction in the middle of nowhere, long since abandoned, had once belonged to a man named Watson. As the boat continued toward Naples, Matty described Watson as "a famous killer" who was responsible for multiple murders before he was finally "shot to pieces" by a posse of his neighbors in 1910. Peter was gripped by the story of savage vigilante justice, of a solitary house built on an island made of clamshells collected by the old Calusa Indians. It stuck in his brain, he once recalled, "like a burr."[5]

A decade later, his mind was on Florida again as he started to craft some stories of his own. One of his earliest efforts, an unpolished piece titled "White,"* was written in Paris during his *Paris Review* days but set in the Ten Thousand Islands. The story follows a married couple from Massachusetts (Yankees on vacation) as they're forced to reckon with the moral outrage of racial authoritarianism in the South after the wife, without considering what might happen as a result, tells a bigoted sheriff their Black fishing guide has pilfered a pair of binoculars. Matthiessen heightened the Jim Crow atmosphere by rendering the landscape as suffocatingly hostile: "All around them, behind the night-time, lay the crawling white flats where even the fish were still and nothing was safe from the devilfish and barracuda but the huge white herons, waiting immobile in the two-foot water like one-legged ghosts."[6] The landscape is vigilant, swarming with predators; a ubiquitous wader bird becomes a symbol—a promise—of explosive violence.

In the 1960s and early '70s, Matthiessen's focus on Florida was mostly environmental. For Stewart Udall, he inspected the ecological consequences of the levees and canals built across the state, restricting the flow of freshwater down to the National Park. As a journalist for *Audubon*, he denounced a proposed Everglades Jetport, as well as the desecration of Kissimmee River, a meandering waterway straightened into a ditch "as rigid and ugly as a caved-in subway tunnel, and approximately as useful."[7]† He supported the National Audubon Society in its protective acquisition of land around the Corkscrew Swamp, penning passionate odes to a place whose majesty was not immediately apparent to most visitors. "[I]t is flat and swampy and inhospitable, and

---

* A version of this story appeared in *Esquire* in August 1985, substantially rewritten and retitled "On the River Styx," and then again in Matthiessen's short story collection of the same name in 1989.
† Since 1992, nearly half of the Kissimmee River has been restored to its original meandering state, which has rehydrated forty square miles of wetlands and led to a significant increase in biodiversity. Recognizing the remarkable transformation, Congress passed the Kissimmee River Wild and Scenic River Act in January 2023, which directed the secretary of the interior to complete a study of the river within three years for potential inclusion in the National Wild and Scenic Rivers System.

such big animals as it has left are rarely seen," Matthiessen conceded. But perhaps it was "the sense of something not quite known, of mystery withheld from the hard gaze of man," that attracted him back to Corkscrew again and again. "And then there are the birds."[8]

And then there was bigfoot, too. In 1975, almost from the start of his correspondence with Doug Blue in Los Angeles, Matthiessen had begun collecting material about Florida sightings of the creature. ("BF n. of St. Petersburg.... Description of shadow in rear window of car... as car slowed for crossing... then BF alongside, perhaps 30' away, the 'swinging' gait, but graceful.")[9] In 1977, he traveled to Florida to conduct interviews with eyewitnesses and to join a "Swamp Ape Expedition" run by Randy Wayne White, a young reporter with the *Fort Myers News-Press*. The expedition was a "farce" meant to titillate readers, in White's own account, but Matthiessen insisted on going anyway.[10] On their first day in the Everglades, White observed his new friend wading barefoot into a cypress swamp to catch a venomous cottonmouth: "He studied the snake closely, then let it swim free, grinning like a kid. In that instant the man who chose to spend much of his life in the world's backcountry seemed momentarily unveiled. It was neither the smile of a thrill-seeker nor that of some aloof visionary—it was the grin of a guy who was *enjoying* himself."[11]

So there were a number of threads about Florida in Matthiessen's life and work: frontier tales of a murderous desperado; racial attitudes entrenched since the days of slavery; a wilderness despoiled by the cult of progress; Native people pushed off ancestral lands; a strange shape stalking between the palmettos, between myth and reality. At the start of the 1980s, all these threads began to bunch together in a single project Matthiessen labeled "Florida (BF) Novel."[12] He wanted to "try something new," he told Howard Norman about his fiction. "I'd like to take a risk."[13] After writing novels set in South America and the Caribbean, he was contemplating something a little closer to home.

The surviving notes from this nascent project are fragmentary and elliptical. Most are dedicated to character sketches: poachers and Vietnam War veterans, shamans and con artists, a country singer ("cynically specializes in songs of parting"), and an anthropologist with the Bureau of Indian Affairs. A disgraced naturalist lives in a shack on a shell midden, the equivalent of a "Zen hermit." Meanwhile, the character Matthiessen most elaborately developed is a "halfbreed Seminole from Oklahoma," motivated to travel to the wilds of South Florida by an overwhelming "nostalgia for paradise." This man, named Blue and resembling Craig Carpenter, is committed (as Carpenter was) to an Indian Rebirth Movement, and he believes the Indians must "ally in common traditions" or risk cultural extinction. His idol is

Tecumseh, the Shawnee chief who once called for collective resistance to the European colonizers of Indigenous America.[14]

How these characters relate to each other is not entirely clear. The plot, only partially developed, seems to have revolved around efforts by the Army Corps of Engineers to construct a ruinous canal through Indian country, a repeat of the Kissimmee River catastrophe. Matthiessen had not figured out the exact details. "Developers + politics; drug smuggling?" he wrote to himself. "Novel takes place in 40s, before Park? In Sixties?" He considered including a sanctuary hidden at the heart of an inaccessible slough, a kind of waterlogged Brigadoon. He was determined to feature bigfoot, an "innocent, blind, random being, not primitive, but free as [an] atom." The entire story, in fact, hinged on unsettling encounters between characters and a "Lost Man" in the swamps, a creature "glimpsed, not conquered: still unknown," which Matthiessen likened in his notes to the white whale of *Moby-Dick*.

Matthiessen seems to have thrown everything he could think of into the pot of his Florida (BF) Novel. But the notes should be read less as a coherent plan than a miscellany of ideas to be kept or discarded as the project simmered in his mind. He typed adjectives, scenarios, quotes from Immanuel Kant onto little slips of hole-punched paper. He annotated his thoughts with a green pen, making emendations and additions. He filed the worthiest material into a ring binder. And then he stopped, his attention seized by Leonard Peltier and *In the Spirit of Crazy Horse*.

JUST AFTER *Crazy Horse* was published, Matthiessen announced that he was "sick of writing."[15] Fatigued by the demands of researching that enormous compendium and frustrated by its more severe critics, he told a group of students at Roger Williams College in Bristol, Rhode Island, that he'd said all he wanted to say as an author. Even before the $49 million in lawsuits, he was thinking of devoting himself full-time to environmental advocacy, and maybe his Zen practice. The "search" of writing, he said, "is less exciting as you go along." He was probably going to abandon his IBM for good—just as soon as he'd completed this one last novel. He declined to discuss the novel in any detail with the students, but conceded it would probably take him "years" to complete. By this he meant *several years*. He did not mean, could not imagine, what it would end up taking him, which was nearly three decades.

When Matthiessen returned to the Florida (BF) Novel sometime around the spring of 1984, he had amassed over seventy pages of notes. But something happened as he went back through them to gather up the threads. His father's old story about the outlaw Watson, living in a house on the Chatham River until he was executed by his neighbors, had been included as a minor episode, "a little vine in my environmental tableau."[16] The vine now revealed itself to be a stranger fig: "this thing began to grow and grow and grow."[17] As Matthiessen prepared a new set of notes to supersede the old ones, bigfoot dropped away, and so did all the original characters and the plot line involving the Army Corps of Engineers. The Watson vine flourished until it "circled and killed the other novel."

In interviews, Matthiessen professed bemusement about exactly why this happened. Who could explain the creative process? One reason, however, might be *Crazy Horse*. He had just finished a thorough investigation into a double homicide where the question of who pulled the trigger remained unresolved, and with many chapters of his book devoted to differing accounts of the circumstances leading up to the shootout. To now write about Watson was to do something strikingly similar. Watson's story also culminated in a shootout where guilt was difficult to assign, much of the contextual evidence coming from memories, hearsay, and compounding layers of gossip. Matthiessen had a habit of utilizing his fiction to reevaluate personal experiences: it is reasonable to wonder if a novel about Watson—a novel that would employ the conceit of a detective-like historian appraising testimonies in search of some fundamental truth—was perhaps a response to the ambiguities of his previous project.

Edgar Watson was an extraordinary figure, a folk legend like Jesse James or Butch Cassidy. During his lifetime he was nicknamed "Emperor" Watson, "Bloody" Watson, and, after a bullet from his gun grazed a man's mustache, "the Barber." His infamy was secured long before he died, in books such as S. W. Harman's *Hell on the Border* (1898), which Watson may well have read, smiling at the claim that he was killed during a prison escape. Because misinformation began to follow him early, almost everything concerning Watson must be qualified with "allegedly"—he *allegedly* grazed a man's mustache with a bullet from his gun. But a few basic details can be offered with confidence, including his birth on November 11, 1855, in Edgefield County, South Carolina. His father, Elijah, was an abusive drunk, so Edgar fled with his mother and sister to Columbia County in Florida, near Fort White. He found work on a plantation and started to put down roots; then he was accused of murder and fled west to Indian Territory, where he rented land from the "bandit queen" Maybelle Starr, in what is now Oklahoma.

When Belle Starr turned up dead, shot in the back in 1889, Watson was placed under citizen's arrest and put on trial across the border at Fort Smith, Arkansas. Because all the evidence was circumstantial, he got off—a questionable reprieve that only worsened an already poor reputation. Then, after maybe stealing some horses in Van Buren, he made his way back down to Florida, where he was implicated in yet another shooting in Arcadia. To keep ahead of the law, he continued south to the Everglades. In the 1890s, he acquired a claim in the Ten Thousand Islands, far from the surveilling gaze of sheriffs and marshals, built his white house on Chatham Bend near some poinsettia trees, and established a thirty-five-acre sugarcane plantation that produced a syrup he sold under the brand name Island Pride. The business turned out to be a tremendous success, but it was dogged by rumors that Watson was killing his Black field hands to avoid paying wages. It is true, at the very least, that several people died in suspicious circumstances on Chatham Bend, their corpses discovered in shallow graves or surfacing in the river currents. And there were documented instances of violence when Watson returned to Columbia County for a spell, and when he visited Key West in a schooner.

Finally, his neighbors at Chokoloskee, another shell midden sixteen miles to the north of Chatham River, grew tired of living in the shadow of Ed Watson and his menacing associate, a stranger named Leslie Cox. On October 24, 1910, Watson beached his boat on Chokoloskee by the Smallwood trading post, ostensibly to supply proof to the locals that he had killed Cox, the actual murderer, he claimed, of all those people at Chatham Bend. The most powerful hurricane in living memory had just devastated much of southwest Florida. A group of nearly two dozen men, strained and edgy, was waiting to confront him. Watson's answers were unsatisfactory: his body absorbed more than thirty-three of their bullets.

When it came to the sugarcane business, it occurred to Matthiessen that Watson had something in common with the titans of American industry: John Jacob Astor, John D. Rockefeller, Jay Gould. Those ruthless barons had all built their immense fortunes "on the blood of poor people, black people, Indian people,"[18] but they had done so at a remove, relying on overseers and lieutenants to do the dirty work for them. You could look at their piles of money and have no sense of how much human life was buried beneath. Watson, too, had abused his laborers to create a (comparatively tiny) fortune, but he had needed to do the dirty work himself. The violence perpetrated to further his ambitions was grimly conspicuous; the bodies were barely buried at all. This made him a vivid representative for the "entrepreneurial frontier spirit"[19] that steamrolled everything with a presumption of Manifest Destiny. To write about his deeds was to write about the cost and casualties, the full scope, of American capitalism—and thus, Matthiessen noted wryly, "our great American democracy."[20]

Even more intriguing, though, was the peculiar combination of characteristics attributed to Watson by various sources. He had three wives who adored him, along with a procession of willing lovers. He appears to have been an affectionate father to his numerous children, both legitimate and illegitimate. He maintained friendships with business and political leaders, including Napoleon Broward, the nineteenth governor of Florida. Watson's neighbors found him to be courtly, humorous, and a gifted storyteller. They also found him terrifying. He was something like Dracula—a malignant charmer. "My daughter-in-law," Matthiessen once said in an interview with *The Paris Review*, "who was raised in Brooklyn, told me that when she wouldn't go to bed, her mother would warn her, 'If you don't get in bed right now, Mister Watson will get you!'"[21] Matthiessen was drawn to the contradiction of a bogeyman that people seemed to have actually *liked*, right up until the moment they opened fire.

Ever since "Sadie" in 1950, Matthiessen had been writing characters who were perversely attractive. He had produced multiple portraits of the "specter escaped from the dark attic of the mind": Dewey Floyd, Cady Shipman, Raditzer, Lewis Moon. Watson, however, offered an opportunity to push much further than those earlier examples. How did a man like that think? What was the cadence of Watson's internal monologue? Here was a "challenge," as Matthiessen described it in some notes: "finding common ground with a sociopathic killer. Feeling my way deep into [the] interior of my mind in search for Watson's true nature and/or character, and through that discovery, confronting my self."[22] What exactly he would be confronting in himself is something he later hinted at in a Dharma talk: "Fully recognizing man's true nature, including its potential for great evil, is our only hope. Knowing the truth, knowing the nature of the real enemy within, we might take our first effective steps toward modifying our hidden, greedy, dark aggressive side."[23] Besides grist for a good novel, the "dark" charisma of Watson was a way for the author to reckon with those parts of himself that he instinctively shied away from.

Matthiessen began by compiling secondary sources, including Marjory Stoneman Douglas's *The Everglades: River of Grass* (1947), which contains a few error-filled pages on the enigmatic outlaw. But the crucial text was *The Story of the Chokoloskee Bay Country*, by the distinguished Florida historian Charlton W. Tebeau. Dedicated to "Chokoloskee Pioneers," Tebeau's monograph, published in 1955, featured the reminiscences of Charles Sherod "Ted" Smallwood, who had owned the trading post beside which Watson was executed. Smallwood had been friendly with Watson, and his recorded memories—"We heard guns going off and I heard Mrs. Watson say, 'My God, they have killed Mr. Watson,' and my wife started across the house to leave and I caught her and did not let her go"[24]—were a brilliant example of colloquial testimony. Smallwood's character came through the texture of his language and syntax. Matthiessen would use this uncorrected transcription of demotic speech as inspiration for the first section of his novel, which would also open with a prologue that was based, in part, on Smallwood's original words.

Matthiessen sat down with Ted Smallwood's daughter, Marguerite Williams, in the spring of 1985. (He also corresponded with Charlton Tebeau, who likely made the introduction.) Over the following few years he would visit Florida at least six times to conduct dozens of interviews; he eventually joked that he cornered everyone on the southwest coast over the age of ninety.[25] These old-timers offered insight into the way things used to be before urban development hemmed in the Glades, and they gave Matthiessen models of local dialect, which he carefully recorded in his notes: "Mr. Watson wasn't no maniac; I think he was a pretty good man. Wasn't no law here then; most of them people that he killed <u>needed</u> killin. . . . It's like he told my Grand-daddy House, 'I don't look for trouble; trouble comes to me.' He allus played honest with my dad, but there was just too many killed."[26]

Though more than seven decades had elapsed since Watson's death, the man remained a sensitive subject for some people. In the spring of 1986, Matthiessen was visiting Lake City, in Columbia County, to collect files from the courthouse; he was quoted by a local journalist offhandedly comparing Watson to Ted Bundy, who had just been given a date for execution. The comparison incensed Rosa C. Oliver, Watson's great-niece, and she sent a furious objection to Matthiessen. In response, he defended himself by blaming the journalist ("one is rarely quoted accurately in a newspaper interview"), but then added, in what sounds like back-pedaling: "if Edgar Watson was a Bundy-type killer—that is, a so-called 'serial killer,' seemingly functional in society but actually incapable of real relationships—I would not be interested in him."[27] Oliver cooled down and agreed to an interview. Other members of the Watson clan refused, however, or required a great deal more in the way of persuasion. To Ruby Palmer, Watson's daughter by his third wife, Edna Bethea, Matthiessen wrote:

> [Watson] was a very complex, able, and intelligent man, an excellent farmer, expert boatman, and generous neighbor, and his reputation to this very day among those who recall him, and their children, too, makes the way he died very mysterious, even if one can believe the usual accounts of how it happened. Needless to say, any light you could shed on your mother's decision never to speak of him (if that is true) would be extremely helpful in preparing a truthful and balanced account. I enclose a biographical summary, not to advertise myself, but to show you that I am not some fly-by-night reporter out for a scandalous story—quite the contrary.[28]

Ruby Palmer ignored this letter for months. Finally her grandson, Larry Owen—Watson's great-grandson—responded on her behalf, writing in a note that Ruby had decided to talk after all, but that she was "strongly opposed" to her name being used in any published book because none of her friends were aware of her father's "terrible alleged crimes."[29] (Years later, Owen would explain in another letter that his grandmother, despite fearing for her reputation, has been desperate to "find out who Edgar really was," to slice through the layers of myth so she could glimpse her own origins.)[30]

Besides Watson's relatives, Matthiessen ingratiated himself with as many of the old pioneer families as he could find. He spent countless hours scouring county libraries, census records, overgrown cemeteries. He camped at Chatham Bend—home to the worst mosquitoes he'd encountered "anywhere in the entire world"[31]—and explored the Ten Thousand Islands by boat. He was threatened by guard dogs, forced to shout questions through glass storm doors, and run off properties by people who suspected he was a federal drug agent.

He unearthed enough material on visits to Florida, South Carolina, Arkansas, and Oklahoma to fill boxes: affidavits, warrants, subpoenas, and a judge's orders regarding "Edgar A. Watson, a white man"; floor plans for Watson's house; meteorological records for Key West in 1910; vintage photographs labeled "the Old Watson Murder Farm"; and notes on how to hand-wash laundry using nothing but flour and starch. These were the hard facts of Watson's frontier existence. Matthiessen decided to treat them as a creative constraint. Nothing he wrote in his fiction, at least when it came to Watson and his contemporaries, would be "inconsistent" with "the very little that is actually on record."[32]

In an early draft of an author's note, he described his approach to the novel in terms that recall the work of a paleontologist. Research was a matter of excavating remains, then assembling the found bones into a plausible skeleton. Writing was gluing the bones together, intuitively filling in gaps, and then imagining an overlay of flesh, the way Edgar Watson might have looked and spoken, his behavior and motivations, his hopes and dreams.

MATTHIESSEN WAS LYING to the students at Roger Williams College, or lying to himself, when he suggested he was going to give up writing everything except this one last novel. In 1986, he paused the Watson research to publish two more books in support of causes close to his heart.

The first was *Men's Lives*, a mournful portrait and spirited defense of the Bonackers on the East End of Long Island, who were reeling from state legislation that effectively banned haul-seining for striped bass—the same centuries-old tradition Matthiessen had participated in during the mid-1950s. For decades, recreational sportsmen had been agitating for legal action under a dubious pretense of "conservation," and they had finally succeeded with the help of Governor Mario Cuomo.* *Men's Lives* paid tribute to yet another way of life seemingly doomed to fade away. "They're being forced out of their traditional livelihood," Matthiessen lamented.33 As a piece of advocacy journalism, the book was funded by the philanthropist and arts patron Adelaide de Menil, who owned a house in East Hampton with her husband, the anthropologist Edmund Carpenter. The project had been pitched to de Menil by Doug Kuntz, a photographer intimately acquainted with the Bonackers and their plight.34 Matthiessen was brought on to collaborate, and he requested a project fee equal to the minimum income a fisherman would earn over the same length of time it took him to write the book—$50,000 for approximately three years of seasonal labor.

His text, which included several chapters on his personal history with men like Captain Ted Lester, was paired with Kuntz's stormy, sea-drenched images of Bonackers (several of whom later committed suicide) at work on the beaches, or mending nets, or sawing ice in winter. The entire package was a work of "great beauty," as Joseph Heller wrote in a letter: "I can't remember when I've last been so engrossed in a book, unless it was The Snow Leopard."35 Reviews were effusive, and Matthiessen was "pleased," though he struggled to reconcile the critical acclaim with his own stern views on what constituted good writing. "Men's Lives, like the Indian books, etc., was written to achieve an end, and therefore comes from the wrong source," he told William Merwin. "I have little faith in its real merits from a literary or 'artistic' point of view . . . and I'm pretty sure that despite the double-barrelled raves in the NYT, Men's Lives is no better than the book that those smarties trashed."36

That "trashed" book, published just one month earlier, was *Nine-Headed Dragon River*. The motivation behind this one was Zen. At the end of 1979, Taizan Maezumi at the Zen Center of Los Angeles had assigned Bernie Glassman a formidable task: to establish a new group of students on the East Coast, expanding a Soto school they were calling the White Plum Asanga. Glassman had dutifully relocated his family to the Bronx, then begun building a local network with the assistance of Lex Hixon, a mysticism scholar

---

* The Australian art critic Robert Hughes, an East Hampton resident, deftly summed up the long-running conflict like this in *The New York Review of Books:* "A sport fisherman who has just spent several freezing hours up to his thighs in Montauk surf and sees, as he trudges empty-handed up the beach, a net full of flapping twenty-pound bass being winched ashore by a crew of taciturn Bonackers is not a happy man. He will seethe with jealousy and conclude that he caught nothing because the surf netters have caught everything. He will be apt to believe that the bass fishery is declining. And he will seek restrictive laws."

who hosted a weekly radio show on WBAI-FM. Glassman appeared as a guest on *In the Spirit*, reassuring listeners, when he was asked about it, that he was nothing like Jim Jones, and that his new Zen Community of New York was not another Jonestown.[37] The ZCNY had started life in a crumbling four-story building in Riverdale, slightly north of Manhattan. But Glassman soon discovered a nearby house for sale, fourteen thousand square feet, with twelve bedrooms and an industrial kitchen. "Greyston," an 1863 Gothic Revival mansion, was spectacular—and spectacularly expensive. Buying it for $600,000 was "a preposterous idea," recalled a member of the sangha.[38] Yet Glassman wanted a monastery to realize "the infinite possibilities of community practice," thus fulfilling Maezumi Roshi's mandate.[39] He had arranged to purchase Greyston despite the prohibitive cost, saddling the ZCNY with debt. *Nine-Headed Dragon River* was Matthiessen's attempt to raise some relief funds via royalties for "our beleaguered 'monastery' in Riverdale,"[40] which he had called home as Glassman's head monk for an intensive three-month training period in late 1982 ("one of the most moving experiences of my life").[41] Greyston, in the words of Helen Tworkov, another sangha member, "was a combination between a commune and *The Beverly Hillbillies*. We were just a bunch of rubes living in this mansion. One of the roles Peter played was that he legitimized the whole thing because he came from the same social class as our neighbors, who were sort of appalled by us."[42]

Unlike the beautifully sustained homage of *Men's Lives*, *Nine-Headed Dragon River* was an uneven book, meandering, esoteric, and occasionally mawkish as Matthiessen recounted episodes from his own Zen practice. After *Dragon River* was released, he admitted to being a little embarrassed himself about the contents. "One is always appalled by the idea of wearing your so-called spirituality on your sleeve," he told *Publishers Weekly*.[43] Even so, he was incensed when a reviewer in *The New York Times* dared to suggest that *Dragon River* was a weak effort compared to the rest of his oeuvre, filled, as the critic sneered, with "fools showing off."[44]

Matthiessen was also bothered by the lack of support *Dragon River* received from other Zen practitioners. Indeed, the only notable response of any kind was an eight-page diatribe from a reader in New York. This unnamed person, apparently a longtime fixture on the Zen scene, denounced Matthiessen's "great dishonesty"[45] (as Matthiessen characterized the complaint) when it came to abuses of power committed by authority figures such as Eido Shimano. *Dragon River* vaguely alludes to the sex scandal in 1975 that had triggered an exodus of students from the Zen Studies Society, but it flatly refuses to discuss Eido Roshi's "comportment," which is dismissed in a parenthetical aside as "not . . . the business of this book."[46] It avoids any mention whatsoever of a similar scandal from 1983, when news of Maezumi

Roshi's binge drinking and sexual relationships with female students had caused a rift in the sangha at the Zen Center of Los Angeles.*

Matthiessen tried to brush off the reader's discomforting criticism. *Dragon River* was hardly meant to be an exposé, he insisted in a letter to William Merwin. And Zen students needed to learn how to separate "the teacher from the teaching."[47] In truth, though, he was unwilling to accuse Zen leaders of sexual misconduct in print because it left him vulnerable to further charges of libel. "I couldn't do it," he protested to Merwin: "I'm still being sued for 49 million dollars!" Despite his agreement with Maria not to talk about the legal trouble, the threat still loomed over everything, impossible to forget.

IN THE WINTER, Matthiessen endured another deposition, this one at the offices of Dorsey & Whitney in New York. The line of questioning by David Price's lawyer was pugnacious and relentlessly recursive, covering the same material over and over. Matthiessen did his best to be as unhelpful as possible. Roger Magnuson complained that the writer was "quite cautious" with his answers, to which Matthiessen replied, icily: "You have taught me to be cautious in my answers. I read your brief from my last deposition."[48] The ordeal, which stretched over six days in December and January, was mind-numbing torture, and it left him depressed. He would later write that New York became intolerable around this time; perhaps through association, the city seemed to him "oppressive in its noise and filth."[49]

To escape "these pesky lawsuits,"[50] as he called them in a letter to Edward Hoagland, he scheduled further trips to Florida, escaping into cypress swamps and municipal archives. In March 1987, after yet another visit to the Lake City courthouse for records, he wrote to a woman who had proved to be a valuable source: "One gets so fascinated by research. I have to stop pretty soon and write the book!"[51] The research would continue on and off for years, but he seems to have started writing by May, the month he also turned sixty. Maria marked the occasion with an intimate party attended by close friends, including Joe and Anne Fox, and Robert and Victoria Hughes. "Never thought I'd reach 60 years," Peter told them in a bashful speech. "I mean, I don't know what there is to celebrate but I'm awfully glad to be

---

* Unlike Eido Shimano, Taizan Maezumi took steps to address his misconduct. He checked himself into an alcohol rehabilitation clinic. He apologized, repeatedly, for years, "to the point where you were sick of it," recalled Charles Tenshin Fletcher. "He tried, in a certain sense, to pay back for the suffering he'd caused in that period." His contrition perhaps explains why Matthiessen never formally broke with Maezumi, as he had with the defiant Eido Roshi seven years earlier. Matthiessen didn't expect an infallible teacher. He expected a teacher who could recognize his own shortcomings and turn them into teaching aids.

celebrating it with you."[52] Gesturing at George Plimpton and Sherry Lord, he added that everyone was probably sick of hearing how the three of them were in the second grade together, "and still haven't outgrown one another," but it never ceased to "astonish and delight" him. "Nobody else here has known me long enough to know how difficult I can be, although Maria may have had a glimpse or two."

That same month, in an interview for the American Audio Prose Library, he made another grand declaration about the future of his work. He was "so far behind in the fiction I want to do" that he was not going to produce "any nonfiction" until the novel was fully drafted.[53] He was determined to correct what he saw as an imbalance between the two halves of his career, and this time, at least, he mostly meant what he said. During the next two years, he traveled to Florida and Oklahoma for more novel research; he visited Germany to investigate his whaling ancestors on the island of Föhr; he taught a creative writing seminar at Yale; he ran a silent "Beginner's Mind" retreat at Greyston; he signed a letter of protest in *The New York Review of Books* against the government's treatment of Bernard "Buzz" Farbar, an editor imprisoned for smuggling hashish into the country from Lebanon; and he penned an introduction for the Penguin re-release of George Catlin's classic *North American Indians*. Compared to his usual schedule, though, this load was almost indolence. Matthiessen closed the door of his writing studio and focused intently on Edgar Watson.

While most of his writing from this period was left undated, a folder labeled "Earliest Draft" contains some hand-written pages that begin:

> Every family has a skeleton in the closet—you hear that a good deal in the Watson family. And our skeleton is really a skeleton now, there is no more meat on him at all.[54]

Nothing like this would appear in the final novel. For every published page about Watson, there are thousands more that Matthiessen discarded, aborted drafts which offer a glimpse of how the writing developed as he followed the currents of his imagination. He recycled many of the themes that had inspired the original Florida (BF) Novel: "the pollution of land and air and oceans, the obliteration of wilderness and the wild creatures, not to mention the more defenseless members of our own species."[55] He added others to the mix that were more transparently personal: fraught father-son relationships; anxiety about masculinity, about what it means to be a man; a bifurcated sense of self; and the longing for "paradise," simplicity, lost innocence, "home."

The Watson novel would undergo multiple structural transformations over the years. Matthiessen experimented with versions of the manuscript divided into two, five, eight, and ten distinct parts. In early 1989, when he rode a bicycle over to John Irving's Sagaponack house lugging a box that, as Irving recalled, "would have sufficed as the coffin for a Labrador retriever,"[56] he was planning on three. Matthiessen and the much younger Irving were friends, having met through Fox or Plimpton. There was a bit of mentorship involved ("He was very protective of me," Irving recalled),[57] but they also read each other's work in early draft—a screenplay for *The Cider House Rules*, for example—and offered constructive criticism. "We like to just stand and throw a ball at each other for an hour," Irving once told *The New York Times* about their casual arrangement. "It's a nice way to have a conversation."[58]

"He'll tell you the truth without being snotty," Matthiessen said.

The dog-sized box contained a manuscript of some 1,500 single-spaced pages. The first part was a chorus of voices—homesteaders, lawmen, a Civil War deserter—engaged in a process of communal mythmaking as they offered linked and sometimes speculative testimonies about Edgar "Bloody" Watson. The second part jumped decades ahead to follow Watson's descendants, damaged by his legacy and researching his life as a way of wringing meaning from their own. The third part was given over to Watson himself: a third-person account of his childhood in South Carolina, followed by an unreliable first-person memoir, offered from beyond the grave and covering everything up to the fatal moment on Chokoloskee.

Matthiessen had come to think of these three parts as "movements" in a symphony, "since the whole thing felt symphonic in its rhythms, rising and falling."[59] With this imperfect analogy in mind, he had written a prologue— Watson's execution on October 24, 1910—that was intended to function as a refrain for the full composition, arising repeatedly throughout: "the death of Mister Watson on that remote shore in the October dusk would remain the ending of all three of the so-called movements." He was more interested in the *feeling* of that ending than in the details of what exactly had happened to Watson: the plot, which he deliberately spoiled in the prologue. "I wanted to get that out of the way and penetrate the underlying mystery," he later said. "A powerful and respected man is shot to pieces by his neighbors: why? It is the *why* that matters." By approaching the "why" from different directions, the novel was meant to build for a reader emotionally, like music, so that the refrain was richer and more layered, more resonant, each time it struck up again.

John Irving looked at the tall stack of pages and expressed some skepticism. "I remember suggesting to Peter that I thought he'd written more than one novel."[60]

Matthiessen was not so sure. In an April 1989 letter to Kurt Vonnegut, he was still referring to a single "damnable dross-and-moss-filled, nonplussed, gross total-loss-of-a-boss novel."[61] By May, however, he had started to second-guess himself. "[It] may turn out to be two novels, or even three," he conceded to the writer Doug Peacock.[62]

Matthiessen knew Random House would flinch at the incredible length. His editor, having replaced Joe Fox in the role, was Jason Epstein, editorial director of Random since 1976. Epstein was another friend and East End neighbor—"I'd known him for years and years," Epstein recalled, "and we would talk all the time, so it was a natural situation"[63]—but Matthiessen decided to go easy on him, delivering just the first part of the novel as a work in progress.

Epstein loved the chorus of voices talking around the black hole of Edgar Watson, creating an unsteady outline of the man. Matthiessen, the editor thought, had discovered his muse: "Mr. Watson is LBJ and John Connally, Patrick Henry and Andy Jackson, someone who makes up his own rules as he goes along."[64] Epstein also thought this first part of the novel worked well enough to publish on its own. Matthiessen pointed out that he still needed to read the second and third parts, when Watson's ghostly outline would be filled in; Epstein said they could publish those as separate volumes.

A letter sent by Maria to Jim Harrison in October shows that Matthiessen was persuaded to view the trilogy idea as a net positive. "P in fine form as his mammoth book has turned into three! A writer's dream, so two more books in first draft"[65]—meaning two more sizable book advances. "I thought, I'm golden!" Matthiessen later remembered about the decision to break the manuscript up, a decision which would reverberate for years with unforeseen consequences.[66]

Jason Epstein was a canny conceptual editor: he could help with bigpicture problems a novelist might be facing. But he had little patience with, or interest in, line-editing prose. Because Matthiessen was obsessive about the quality of his sentences, he relied on Epstein's assistant, a young woman named Rebecca Saletan, who was happy to discuss every verb and comma. "One of the great things about Peter, from my standpoint, was that he had no sense of hierarchy," Saletan recalled. "He was really the first person in some ways to take me seriously, editorially speaking."[67] She would continue to work with him on the novel even after she was promoted away from Epstein to managing editor for Vintage Books.*

---

* Rebecca Saletan won Matthiessen's respect by solving structural problems that had been plaguing him in "Lumumba Lives," his short story about the CIA agent who returns from Africa to an old family estate in Westchester County. Saletan suggested, among other things, that "we shouldn't know so much about [Harkness] because he's a man who finds it impossible to let him-

The title, *Killing Mister Watson*, was borrowed from the testimony Ted Smallwood had given to Charlton Tebeau: "My God, they have killed Mr. Watson." It is typed on the cover page of the earliest surviving complete draft of part one, dated June 1989. What becomes immediately apparent, examining this draft, is how much Matthiessen revised the manuscript once the decision was made to publish it independent of the other two sections. "It was like palimpsests," Saletan said, "the amount of rewriting he would do."

Matthiessen rewrote the prologue numerous times, including the titular phrase, exclaimed by Edna Watson, which went through at least four variations.* He changed the tense of the prologue from present to past to present again, and heightened the tone of biblical apocalypse, the hurricane-ravaged landscape "broken, stunned, flattened to mud by the wild tread of God."[68] (One draft had the Everglades coast "sprawled in awful fever under a leaden sky, as if God had died"—a little *too* heightened.)[69] But perhaps the most transformative change had to do with the book's framing device. The published version of *Killing Mister Watson* consists of alternating testimonies from ten "pioneer Floridians." These testimonies are punctuated with brief italicized sections written by the historian who, in Matthiessen's fiction, had originally collected them; a historian modeled on Tebeau, who is supposedly sending all his research on Edgar Watson to an unnamed client in 1960. In manuscript drafts, this framing device is a meta mystery. "Would you be kind enough to clarify one question?" the historian asks his client. "Why are you curious about 'the man who killed Belle Starr'? Are you yourself a relative of Mr. Watson?"[70] As Matthiessen reworked the manuscript, he wisely trimmed this distracting puzzle, reducing the historian to an almost omniscient narrator who chimes in occasionally to point out facts and dates—

---

self be well known." Matthiessen took her advice, redrafted the story, and won second place in the O. Henry Prize, an honor that likely excited him only slightly less than the letter of praise he received from Don DeLillo about the story. "Lumumba Lives" appeared in *Wigwag* magazine in 1988. It was reprinted in Matthiessen's 1989 collection, *On the River Styx*, published by Random House. Saletan delivered the first copy of that book as Matthiessen was dining in New York with William Gaddis and Jim Harrison, their wives, and Maria. According to Matthiessen's memoir notes, Saletan strolled into the restaurant waving the book around: "Gaddis took it between thumb and forefinger, manifesting weary indifference if not open distaste, and was passing it to me across the table like a dead and smelly mouse held by the tail tip when Harrison lunged to intercept it, bawling, 'Here, let's see that!' Two very different men with enormous egos, both wonderful writers, exceptionally intelligent and stimulating, and I much enjoyed both, though I sometimes wondered why."

* " 'My God,' she repeated, quietly this time. 'They have killed Mr. Watson.' " (Earliest draft.)
" 'My God,' she says. 'They have killed Mr. Watson.' "
" 'My God,' she cries. 'They are killing Mister Watson!' "
" 'Oh Lord!' she cries. 'They are killing Mister Watson!' " (As it appears in *Killing Mister Watson*, 1990.)
" 'Oh Lord God,' she cries. 'They are killing Mister Watson!' " (As it appears in *Shadow Country*, 2008.)

landmarks, really, so a reader can navigate the testimonies, which are like the labyrinthine waterways of the Ten Thousand Islands, full of deceptive turns and dead ends.

These testimonies are frequently dazzling in *Killing Mister Watson*. Matthiessen had already proved himself an adept ventriloquist with *Far Tortuga*, but the dramatic monologues of his Floridians are a different order of achievement. The ten speakers range from Bill House, a gruff, penitent plume hunter—"Yessir, a lot of God's creation was left laying dead out there, it give me a very funny feeling even then"[71]—to thirteen-year-old Carrie Watson, whose diary reveals, through its tentative word choices ("Eddie and me—Eddie and I?"),[72] her aspirations to become a sophisticated woman. Sarah Hamilton entertains a liberalism heretical to many of her conservative neighbors. "This whole darn foolishness of blood will be the ruin of this country," she bravely declares.[73] Then there is Frank B. Tippins, the soft-spoken sheriff of Lee County, who may well have been a nature writer in another era given the way he lyrically evokes the Everglades. Tippins speaks with sympathy of the Seminole Indians, but with callous disregard of "nigras." He is simultaneously admirable and troubling—a convincing simulacrum of his historical counterpart.

Matthiessen knew he was taking a risk by presenting a tangled narrative through the *Rashomon*-style accounts of poor Florida whites and mixed-race outcasts living in a lonesome and inhospitable wilderness. He knew he was taking a risk with an enormously ambitious work about the American propensity to mythologize violence into a kind of secular religion. It is a difficult novel full of unpalatable truths. Yet as he later told Howard Norman, "I think serious writers stretch themselves, however subtly, and stretch their good readers, too—otherwise, why do it? . . . To keep that necessary edge, the writer must never feel quite comfortable, and never satisfied."[74] He was perennially *unsatisfied*; he made so many changes to the galleys for *Killing Mister Watson*, "tore [them] up so viciously,"[75] that Random House had to redo the typesetting. And even then, the version that was finally published in June 1990 and billed on the dust jacket as "Peter Matthiessen's masterpiece, the culmination of his writing life"—that version would not be the last one either.

" 'WATSON' IS GRAND," Jim Harrison wrote after getting his hands on a copy. "Euripides through Gogol, with Mr Faulkner leaning against a palm or hog pen with an actual smile. Totally engrossing. It is no wonder what we are now. This one really lifted the linoleum or carpet, also the floorboards, down to the cellar, and the cellar that is always beneath the cellar. Here are our bones so that we may understand them."[76]

Harrison's full-throated praise of *Killing Mister Watson* was soon echoed in letters from Don DeLillo, Thomas McGuane, Simon Ortiz, Rick Bass, Howard Norman, William Merwin, and Louise Erdrich. As for the critical reception, it was the warmest Matthiessen had ever received as a novelist. The book was "a marvel of invention,"[77] according to Ron Hansen in *The New York Times*. Other reviewers dubbed it "a tour de force,"[78] "somber, yet strangely exhilarating,"[79] and "stunning" as a political allegory, not to mention "first-rate" as a philosophical study of the "duality of human—and all—nature."[80] The prolific Joyce Carol Oates, in a review for *The Washington Post* that was syndicated widely, described it as "a nightmare of a novel, intricately structured, richly documented, utterly convincing."[81] *Killing Mister Watson*, Oates added, with considerable understatement, was obviously the product of a long-gestating obsession for its author. She also suggested that Matthiessen's "novel-prototype" was perhaps Faulkner's *Absalom, Absalom!*, about the damned plantation owner Thomas Sutpen: "like Sutpen, Watson is revealed solely by others' accounts—we are never brought into his consciousness, never allowed to know him intimately."*

For the few naysayers, this was the novel's main flaw: that we are not allowed to "know" Edgar Watson directly. Where was Watson's voice to counterbalance the gossip of his neighbors? Faulkner had let Addie Bundren speak as a literal corpse in *As I Lay Dying*, so why was Watson left silent, "a vacuum at the center of the book," as Patricia Storace put it in *The New York Review of Books*?[82] The irony of this was that Matthiessen had let Watson orate at length in part three of the novel—before it was broken into pieces. *Killing Mister Watson* felt incomplete to some readers because it *was* incomplete, although none of Random House's marketing explained there were two more books still on the way.

Matthiessen grumbled about the critics who labeled his novel "historical fiction," an accursed term denoting, in his mind, frivolous romances. And

---

* The comparison to *Absalom, Absalom!* is a good one. Both novels are about a redheaded, pale-eyed "demon," as Thomas Sutpen is described by Rosa Coldfield, and as Edgar Watson is presented by his awed neighbors. Both novels follow through testimonies, some second- or third-hand, the attempts of these Übermenschen to carve baronial splendor out of the American wilderness, to build ornate mansions and sprawling plantations using the bodies of Black people. To a considerable extent, both novels are also concerned with themes of race and racism. Matthiessen was "honored" to have his work compared to Faulkner's masterpiece, but he insisted the similarities were coincidental, "or at least subconscious"—he had not read *Absalom, Absalom!* since college. Perhaps, he suggested to one reader, "these wild figures (Thos. Sutpen and E. J. Watson) may be parallel incarnations of the many inspired ruthless entrepreneurs whose huge failings brought them to grief on our wilderness frontiers."

he hated the use of "docudrama," writing to Howard Norman: "isn't it clear that those interviews are made up?"[83] But the reviews that really got under his skin came from the people in Florida and South Carolina who had a vested interest in the Watson legend, descendants of the real-life figures he'd written about.

On the positive side were Edgar Watson's children. Ruby Palmer had died not long before the novel was published, but she was survived by a sister, Anna Metz Bonneman—aka Anna Metz Watson, born on Key West in May 1910. Unlike Ruby, Annie had refused to speak with Matthiessen during his research travels. She was a baby when Watson was shot, remembered little, and was so ashamed of the rumors about her father that she'd suppressed their connection. When her children asked for information, she told them her father had died because "his heart stopped"—not technically a lie (bullets tend to have that effect). Still, Annie bought and read *Killing Mister Watson* out of morbid curiosity. And she was so moved by the novel, so impressed by Matthiessen's care, that she then passed it on to her daughter, telling Barbara: "You want to know about your grandfather? Here's the book."[84] Barbara wrote a thank-you note to Matthiessen, marveling at her mother's change of heart; Annie suddenly felt "okay" about the family history. Barbara herself had wept while turning the final pages of the novel. Had Matthiessen not written it, she told him, she would probably never have learned anything more about her grandfather than his name.

The response from the Bonnemans (which thrilled Matthiessen: he visited them in Florida and kept in touch for decades) stood in stark contrast to another letter he received from a woman named Mary Hamilton Clark. As presented in the novel, the Hamilton clan is a group of humble fishermen living deep within the Ten Thousand Islands, not far from Watson at Chatham Bend. The (drawn from real life) family patriarch, Richard Hamilton, is a former buffalo soldier who has chosen to desert "white men and their ways" in favor of living like the "wild Mikasukis," self-sufficient in the backcountry.[85] Richard expresses spiritual views that are essentially Zen in substance, and the other Hamiltons are similarly open-minded. As a historical fact, Richard's racial makeup was somewhat ambiguous: he was part white, part Choctaw, and maybe part Black. This meant the Hamiltons, also as a historical fact, were subject to barrages of racist abuse whenever they emerged from their shacks in the Islands. At one point in the novel, Richard sardonically imitates his neighbors on Chokoloskee: "when it comes to white women, y'know, a nigger just can't help himself. Being an animal at heart, the poor devil just goes all to pieces."[86]

Matthiessen had based his characterizations on lengthy interviews with Mary Hamilton Clark, a living descendant of the clan. However, after she finally read the novel, she professed to be blindsided by the bigotry depicted in it with unflinching directness. *Killing Mister Watson* forces a reader to confront what the Hamiltons would have endured in all its brutality. Mary's letter claimed that, by exposing these old wounds, he had ruined her family's reputation and probably destroyed her life.

Matthiessen was "very sorry indeed" to hear this reaction, as he wrote in a typed reply:

> I believe I explained many times that I wanted to present a realistic picture of life in the Ten Thousand Islands around the turn of the century, including the ugly racism which ruled the South for a hundred years after the Civil War. In the Islands, as you yourself have told me, the main victims of that racism were the Richard Hamiltons.
>
> Based mostly on your information, I did my best to present the Hamiltons fairly and sympathetically as an outstanding and successful pioneer family in the Islands, the family that lasted in the Islands longer than any, and I gave them more space than anybody else. Richard, Leon, and Sarah Hamilton are all shown as exceptionally strong and appealing characters, with guts, wisdom, decency, and humor. If you can bring yourself to look at the book fairly, I believe you will acknowledge this. . . .
>
> So I don't think you are angry because I insulted your family. I didn't—quite the opposite. What upsets you is to see in print the references by Richard and others to the color prejudice against the Hamiltons that you yourself have told me about many, many times. And I warned you that I had to mention that prejudice in order to be able to attack it. . . . Would you really prefer that none of this prejudice be mentioned?[87]

In early drafts, he had called them the "Hardens." Ironically, it was Mary Hamilton Clark, insisting her family deserved recognition as pioneer Floridians, who had convinced him to abandon the pseudonym. Matthiessen had been so reluctant to do this that he'd asked her to sign a permission release form waiving any objection she might have to the novel, including claims of libel.[88] And now she was threatening to "get" him and his "garbage" book.

The issue was ultimately dropped; Mary Hamilton Clark would go no further than sending a few enraged letters. But her objection left Matthiessen flustered. He composed a "TO WHOM IT MAY CONCERN" disclaimer ("I made a mistake by not sticking to my original decision to change the names, and I sincerely apologize for any distress I may have caused"),[89] and he reverted to his original plan for the final two volumes of the Watson saga, the historical Hamiltons once again becoming the fictional Hardens.

A FEW WEEKS AFTER the publication of *Killing Mister Watson*, as the novel appeared on Best Sellers lists in the *New York Times*, *Washington Post*, and *San Francisco Chronicle*, Matthiessen hosted a party in Sagaponack for more than a hundred guests. John Irving, Kurt Vonnegut, and Edgar Doctorow stood in Maria's garden eating canapés prepared by members of the nearby Shinnecock Indian Nation. Loudspeakers blasted the AIM anthem, a rhythmic beat of drums and chanting. A television showed a looped thirteen-minute sizzle reel for *Warrior: The Life of Leonard Peltier*, a documentary being produced by the filmmaker Suzie Baer. "I'm not into benefits," Matthiessen told a lurking journalist. "It's not my style." But he'd made an exception to raise money for Baer's film, and he was in an unusually jubilant mood, having just been declared victor in the final lawsuit challenging *In the Spirit of Crazy Horse*. Indeed, the garden party doubled as an unofficial celebration after nearly seven years of litigation. Wearing jeans and a T-shirt, he offered some remarks to the crowd about Peltier. Then he asked a friend, playfully, if he had a future as a rabble-rouser. She replied, "You have a present and a past as a rabble-rouser."[90]

David Price's libel suit had been decided in January 1988. Diana Murphy, a federal district judge in Minnesota, ruled in favor of the defendants, Matthiessen, Viking, and Bruce Ellison, with an "elegant and eloquent"[91] (in Matthiessen's assessment) thirty-three-page discussion of an author's rights under the First Amendment. *Crazy Horse* deals with historical events, Judge Murphy wrote, but it does so "from a very pointed perspective," with "a mission of persuasion."[92] The book's "tone and style" make clear that it is substantially opinion about the government and its officers, not a straight recitation of facts. And it is precisely this form of speech, Murphy argued, that the framers of the Bill of Rights had sought to protect. "As criticism of government, the statements"—meaning the alleged libel Price had highlighted in *Crazy Horse*—"are entitled to the maximum protection of the First Amendment. They cannot provide the basis for a defamation action."

Price had disagreed, of course, and his attorneys had immediately turned to the United States Court of Appeals for the Eighth Circuit. In August 1989, a three-judge panel not only unanimously upheld Murphy's decision, it expanded her ruling with a generous read of *New York Times v. Sullivan*, the landmark case that put the onus on public officials to show defamation had been committed with "actual malice or reckless disregard for the truth." David Price insisted he was not a public figure; the appellate court determined that he was. "Sometimes it is difficult to write about controversial events without getting into some controversy along the way," Judge Gerald Heaney wrote. "In this setting, we have decided that the Constitution requires more speech rather than less."[93]

Disagreeing with this ruling, too, Price had then directed his attorneys to petition the U.S. Supreme Court. However, in January 1990, the court had declined to hear the case.

Meanwhile, Bill Janklow's suit had been decided in June 1989. In Sioux Falls, South Dakota, Gene Paul Kean—the same judge who had dismissed Janklow's complaint in 1984, only to have his decision overturned on appeal—also ruled in favor of the defendants, Matthiessen and Viking. In a familiar line of argument, Judge Kean wrote that Janklow had failed to show Matthiessen acted "with actual malice," and that while *Crazy Horse* might be biased toward the Indians, "First Amendment privileges of expression do not hinge on the basis of objectivity."[94] Janklow was outraged by Kean's audacity in ruling against him *twice*. He had appealed once again to the South Dakota Supreme Court. This time, though, the court proved far less sympathetic toward the now former governor, siding with Kean in a four-to-one[*] decision, passed down on July 18, 1990, two days before Matthiessen's garden party.

"I'm going to continue to use the judicial system as long as there's an avenue open to me," Janklow vowed to *The Sioux City Journal*. "It's not the money, and it isn't to clear my name. The important thing to me is that you don't have the right to do that to a human being. If Peter Matthiessen had taken a gun and shot at me and missed, he'd have gone to jail. But he can take his pen and point it at me, and hit me with it, and they say, 'Well, because the guy is a public figure it's OK.' "[95] This was all bluster by Janklow: the only avenue still open to him was the U.S. Supreme Court, but rather than petitioning it for a hearing, as Price had, he chose, in late October, to drop his case.[96]

The repeated rulings against Janklow and Price (eight in total since 1984) were significant votes in favor of greater press freedom in America. As Herbert Mitgang noted in *The New York Times* after Diana Murphy's decision, the verdict encouraged "less fear and suppression in publishing houses and broader availability of books on controversial subjects."[97] At least two of the rulings also affirmed, in what Martin Garbus described as "extraordinarily important"[98] precedents, that it was not libelous for authors to repeat unproven accusations about public figures as part of a historical survey. Several people had claimed Janklow was guilty of rape; Matthiessen, in reporting

---

[*] Judge Frank Henderson submitted a remarkable dissenting opinion that presented Janklow as a humble man embarked on an "odyssey in search of justice," a man simply asking for a jury trial: "Nothing more, nothing less." By contrast, the AIMers Matthiessen had defended in *Crazy Horse* were, in Judge Henderson's words, "convicted felons with long histories of crime and violence."

those claims in *Crazy Horse*, was providing the details of a complex situation, not claiming himself that Janklow assaulted Jancita Eagle Deer.

For Matthiessen on a more personal level, the rulings were a welcome vindication of his working methods. Still, he saw the result as "a Pyrrhic victory to put it very mildly."[99] Fighting the lawsuits had cost Viking's insurance company more than $2 million in legal fees; if the bill had crept above $3 million, he and Maria would have become directly liable. And what about the other costs? His book had been out of print for six years when it could have been helping Peltier as a "main organizing tool in his fight for justice."[100] During that time, Peltier had attracted the support of fifty members of Congress, as well as Jesse Jackson, Desmond Tutu, Willie Nelson, Joni Mitchell, Robin Williams, and Amnesty International. But he had also been denied a new trial in the federal district court and court of appeals; and, like the antagonistic David Price, he'd been refused a final hearing by the Supreme Court.

In the wake of the last Janklow decision, Viking Penguin committed to publishing an updated edition of *In the Spirit of Crazy Horse*, including a new epilogue that included a bombshell coda to the whole story of the Oglala shootout.

At the garden party in Sagaponack, Matthiessen told his guests that Peltier was innocent. "I had every reason to believe he was wrongly accused. Now I *know* he was wrongly accused."[101] As he paced across the lawn, he described an encounter he'd had a few months earlier with a Native man in disguise. "I spoke to him for five hours. This is the man who killed the agents. He has now come forward, and feels badly that Leonard has done fifteen years so far. However, he does not feel that he did anything wrong. He killed those men in self-defense."

In February 1990, Matthiessen had flown out West to see Bob Robideau, who'd shown him around the Jumping Bull property back in 1980. Somewhere in Oregon, probably Portland, Robideau introduced him to a "small, husky figure,"[102] faceless in black sunglasses and a blue woolen ski mask pulled all the way down to his collar. The man identified himself as "X," and he confessed to executing the two FBI agents at point-blank range. He was unwilling to go to prison, he said, but he wanted to stoke interest in Peltier's case by sharing his testimony. Matthiessen asked Robideau how he knew this man was telling the truth about his role in the shootings. Robideau replied, "I saw him do it."[103] Astounded by the revelation, Matthiessen then grilled the stranger for five hours. Their discussion was so thorough and specific that he emerged convinced he had just interviewed the true killer of Agents Coler and Williams.[104]

In August, en route to Siberia for a short expedition to Lake Baikal,* Matthiessen met with X again somewhere in Colorado, accompanied by a film crew and the director Oliver Stone, who was planning his own (never realized) movie about Leonard Peltier. Matthiessen and X, who kept a loaded AR-15 in the next room, spoke on camera for an additional eight hours, and this second conversation only strengthened Matthiessen's conviction that the masked figure was "persuasive and articulate, a man concerned for and committed to his people."[105]

In May 1991, Matthiessen wrote a cover story for *The Nation*, provocatively titled "Who Really Killed the F.B.I. Men." (The story was an abridged version of the new epilogue for *Crazy Horse*, which was republished in April.) Footage of the Colorado interview then aired on CBS's *60 Minutes* in September, lending Peltier invaluable publicity on the country's most prominent current affairs program, watched by an audience of some 26 million people.

However, a few years later, in yet another shocking twist, Dino Butler would expose X as a hoax. In a 1995 interview with *News from Indian Country*, Butler—who had been tried and cleared for his own involvement in the shootout—castigated Matthiessen for swallowing and then regurgitating a lie cooked up by Bob Robideau. After the interview was published, Matthiessen reportedly phoned Butler, "pissed-off" by his remarks. "Why did you say that? Don't you know that just attacks my credibility?" As Butler recalled their conversation:

> I said, "Peter, you put my life in jeopardy and you put the lives of my family in jeopardy by putting that bullshit out in your books. Why didn't you call me and ask me if that was true? Everything you said in that first book, you would call me; you would call Nilak [Butler]; you would call John [Trudell]; you would call all of us that were involved and ask us 'Is this true?' and we would tell you[,] but you didn't do this in the second edition. You went out and you put this Mr X in there when it was all lies." And he said, "Well, I didn't believe Bob would lie to me."[106]

In a misguided attempt to aid Peltier, Robideau had collaborated with a Choctaw man named David Hill—the man beneath the ski mask—to manu-

---

* Matthiessen traveled at the invitation of saxophonist Paul Winter. He described their journey in a long essay, "The Blue Pearl of Siberia," for *The New York Review of Books* (February 14, 1991). This essay was then published by Sierra Club Books as *Baikal: Sacred Sea of Siberia* (1992). "Baikal . . . has drawn me since the day, long years ago, that I first learned of a primordial lake of diamantine clarity that lay off to the north of the Gobi Desert," Matthiessen wrote. "Only recently has it been known how swiftly the lake's ancient ecology could unravel, and how close man has come to losing it forever."

facture an alternate story of what happened at Oglala on June 26, 1975. Matthiessen had suspended his critical judgment and blindly trusted his old contact. Worse, he had ignored the direct advice of AIM leader John Trudell, who had warned him to "stay away" from the "phony" confession.[107] Eager to believe in a deus ex machina that exonerated Peltier and perhaps validated his years of commitment, Matthiessen had dealt himself a humiliating blow, one that critics like Scott Anderson would point to ("the patent absurdity")[108] as proof of his myopia when it came to the American Indian Movement.

Matthiessen regretted his involvement in the hoax: he had been "set up" to "abet it," he wrote in some private notes.[109] He distanced himself from Robideau for more than a decade, and temporarily cooled his relationship with Bruce Ellison, Peltier's attorney, who had given him mixed signals about the legitimacy of the confession. "I should have expressed my doubts more forcefully to Peter," Ellison later reflected. "It's one of the greatest regrets of my life."[110]

Nevertheless, being played in an elaborate plot would have no lasting effect on Matthiessen's commitment to the cause. He had made a promise; he would continue to defend Leonard Peltier as though nothing had happened to shake his faith. Nor would the hoax alter his feelings about *Crazy Horse*, even with the largely discredited epilogue. At a Washington, D.C., rally held for Peltier in the summer of 1995, when the X fiasco was still fresh in his mind, and when a blistering attack by Scott Anderson had just been published in *Outside*, Matthiessen gave another rabble-rousing speech before a sizable crowd. "I stand by the integrity of *In the Spirit of Crazy Horse*, which is sort of like an old-fashioned hydrant in a rough neighborhood," he declared—"yes, scraped and battered from hard use, and stunk up by all these leg-lifters and ankle-biters, but still sturdy and still solid, still dependable, and still delivering the fresh water of the truth."[111]

PART IV

1991–2014

Five Cranes,
by Okuhara Seiko (1879).

23

Muryo Sensei

LAWRENCE SHAINBERG: What about doubt? Does any serious doubt about the practice come up anymore?
MATTHIESSEN: Practice? Or the teachings? I have no doubt about the practice. Doubts about myself as a teacher perhaps, about my ability to manifest the teaching.

—On Zen (1993)[1]

MOST MORNINGS IN SAGAPONACK in the early 1980s, before withdrawing to his writing studio for an uninterrupted day of work, Matthiessen stopped by the upstairs zendo to practice zazen. Sometimes he was alone, staring in silence at the wall, but often he was joined by a group of five or six other people who lived around the East End. These were not friends, exactly—outside the morning sessions "we really had very little contact with each other,"[2] recalled Dorothy Friedman, who had come to Zen via Vipassana meditation, and then met Matthiessen through another practitioner on Long Island—but they shared a commitment to the Dharma, and Matthiessen was happy to open his space to like-minded students for an hour or so before breakfast. Gradually, though, more people began to join, like the painter Connie Fox, and Rameshwar Das, who was closely affiliated with the yoga guru Ram Dass; the old tearoom proved too small to accommodate everyone. So Matthiessen moved the morning meditations out of the house, across the yard, into the ramshackle stable on the edge of his property. Now the students sat together in old horse stalls, "complete," he once said, "with manure smell and rats."[3]

One of the original students was a Swedish sculptor, woodworker, and furniture designer named Hans Hokanson, whose carved spirals and chiseled tree trunks are held in collections at the Smithsonian and the Metropolitan Museum of Art. When it became clear that the stable was a satisfactory alternative, Hokanson used a Japanese saw to fashion an altar and build raised wooden platforms for sitting. Matthiessen did the "crude work"[4] of tearing down the stalls and repurposing the wood for a new mid-wall, dividing the stable in two. One half was painted white, and tatami mats were taken from the upstairs zendo to furnish it. A wood-burning stove was installed for the colder months, when a crackle of fire was the only sound during zazen. Over time, other ornamentations were added to liven up the stable: a large bowl-shaped gong, which would reverberate "for almost as long as you can hold your breath," as a writer once noted;[5] floor vases filled with wildflowers; and a wooden *han*, rhythmically struck with a mallet at dawn and dusk. Outside the stable, a roadside Buddha, guardian of wayfarers, sat in a manicured clearing near a Japanese maple tree, all of it a short walk from the house porch where Matthiessen had placed the enormous crown of a fin whale skull, dragged by chain and tractor from the sand of Sagg Main Beach.

Now with a dedicated space, the morning group became more sociable; Dorothy Friedman arranged post-zazen discussions on topics such as "resistance, or jealousy, or ambition—something related to the precepts."[6] And more people continued to arrive, expanding the group further. Matthiessen would always welcome serious students of Zen, as well as anyone with a genuine curiosity about the practice, but he put his foot down when a photographer from *The East Hampton Star* was caught prowling around like a paparazzo. "For Zen training reasons I won't bore you with," he wrote to the newspaper's editor, Helen Rattray, in 1985, "I feel that our group is too fresh and unformed (this is also its strength) to be inviting attention to itself, especially in the feverish and faddish climate of the Hamptons, and perhaps we are not ready yet to handle in an harmonious way the attention and inquiry this sudden publicity is sure to bring."[7] Given his profile, of course, the attention was inevitable. On Mondays, Matthiessen convened a meditation group in the mid-afternoon, and one of the more seasoned students would eventually dub this "tourist day," because drop-ins came to gawk at "the famous writer" on his cushion.[8]

By 1989, ten to twelve students routinely showed up for daily 7 a.m. practice, with upward of thirty appearing on Monday afternoons. Matthiessen finished the second half of the stable, installing shoji screens and circular windows for natural light. Meanwhile, Hans Hokanson crafted new interior entry doors with redwood handles.

That year in October, as Matthiessen was revising the draft of *Killing Mister Watson*, he had a *Shiho* ceremony, receiving Dharma transmission from Bernie Glassman. After twenty years of study, Ishin Muryo Peter Matthiessen became Muryo Sensei, confirmed as a member of a Soto lineage—a spiritual bloodline—running backward through Glassman and Taizan Maezumi to countless predecessors in Japan and China, and all the way, theoretically, to the Buddha himself. Shiho was a way of rooting the lineage more firmly in

America, adding another homegrown authority to the ranks. It also empowered Matthiessen, as he irreverently put it, to "go nuts and teach any old thing any old way one wants."[9]

For his non-Zen friends, the most important change was that he was now permitted to conduct their marriages, christenings, and funerals. At one time or another, Muryo would officiate weddings for Doug Peacock, Terry McDonell, Jim Harrison's daughter, James Jones's daughter, and Bill and Rose Styron's son, Tom. For his sitting group in Sagaponack, though, the promotion meant something more: a formalization of their daily rituals and procedures. Before Shiho, Matthiessen was just another student, however renowned; after Shiho, he was the resident teacher, a symbolic embodiment of the Buddha sitting right alongside them in the stable. A journalist observed a practice in 1991:

> The gong strikes. Matthiessen-*sensei* kneels on the central cushion, the purple one, and begins offering incense. A woman chants a brief phrase in Japanese. Another woman across the way begins to drum on something that looks like a bone or a cracked melon. Suddenly the entire room is alive with resonant voices, chanting, "MAKA HANNYA [HARAMITA] SHIN GYO." Even in Japanese, Matthiessen's voice stands out: dark, full, patrician.[10]

In an "Introduction to Zen Practice" talk, Matthiessen would explain some of the ground rules for people visiting his zendo in Sagaponack:

> [W]e wear no loud clothes, perfume, jewelry, heavy make-up. Nothing to draw attention to ourselves. Nothing extra. This way, we forget our appearance, we forget our idea about ourselves. We forget the person. And very soon we forget the ego, and the self. We are just here! In our true nature. And in our true nature—which is our Buddha Nature—we are invisible, do you see? We have returned to the true ocean of being ... we have returned into Emptiness, the Void.[11]

Once he was sensei, responsible for nudging others toward the realization of their Buddha Nature, he turned the upstairs zendo into a dokusan room, a private chamber for interviews and koan study with his students. ("Be Lee," he would challenge Lee Carlson in one custom-made koan: express the original Lee uncorrupted by social pressures, financial woes, accumulated neuroses.)[12] During day-long retreats on one Saturday of each month, Matthiessen also began giving prepared addresses, a presentation of Zen insight called a teisho (*tei*, "to carry," *sho*, "to declare"), introduced with bells and chanting. His notes for some of these teishos, and for his more informal Dharma talks, survive in the archive, and they cover a wide variety of subjects. A few are concerned with specific koans, or with abstract concepts such as the Source, Oneness, the Absolute and Relative; others show him evoking Zen in discussions about troubling national events, like the Waco siege of 1993: "There were far better ways to take care of Waco. What got in the way? What blinded the perpetrators? Greed, anger, and folly."[13] After the terrorist attacks on September 11, 2001, he would even ask his students, "How are we to react as Buddhists?" In answer, he would cite the first precept as a "fundamental guide": abstain from killing, which meant, in this instance, abstain from acts of violent retribution in Afghanistan and Iraq. "[I]n the end, it would be seen as a great strength, even by the terrorist-sponsoring nations—[it would be] the greatest wisdom our country has shown since the Marshall Plan."[14]

These were unusually political topics for a Zen teacher. But Matthiessen was never entirely comfortable with being the authority figure. "I don't even think of myself as a teacher,"[15] he once admitted; ordination had simply been the logical next step in his practice after becoming a monk, and something Glassman encouraged him to do for the good of the Zen Community of New York. Matthiessen struggled to care about "all this priestly stuff." He didn't like the pomp of Dharma names, "which strike me as 'extra' in the context of American Zen."[16] He chafed against Soto hierarchy, the expectation that he would now conduct Jukai and appoint senior monks in Sagaponack. He was careless when it came to arranging his robes, occasionally becoming so tangled up in his koromo that he looked, in his own words, like "a sprung umbrella."[17] On one occasion, he surprised a visitor, while wearing full regalia, by expounding upon the defensive line of the New York Giants. "He was doing his best to be a formal Zen teacher, even though that was not his nature," recalled Dorothy Friedman.[18]

He could, like Taizan Maezumi, be formidable during dokusan when he rang his bell to curtly summon and dismiss. "You had butterflies in your stomach when you had to walk into that room," said Elizabeth Porebski, who, with her husband, Peter, traveled down from Toronto four or five times a year to visit the zendo.[19] But Matthiessen was admired precisely because he was less severe than some of his own teachers had been. "He was so personable and warm," said Megan Chaskey, another student alongside her husband, Scott. "There was none of the coldness of Zen you sometimes get in that lineage."[20] Matthiessen even welcomed their infant daughter, Rowenna, into the zendo during practice, nicknaming her "Buddha baby" and conducting a blessing ceremony. "Peter always carried kindness," remembered Linda Coleman, a former member of a Weather Underground–like revolutionary cell, who came to the group through the "totally Bodhisattva wacko poet" Allen Planz. Coleman saw symmetry between her student-teacher relationship with Matthiessen he encouraged her to write about her radical background—and the one she had with her father: "deep love, and a somewhat silent, wordless, kind of connection."[21]

For some students, like Mitchell Cantor, a monk in Sagaponack before he became a sensei himself down in Boca Raton, Matthiessen's very presence was a teaching: "There are people who just have a quiet elegance about them."[22] Saul Steinberg, the artist and frequent contributor to *The New Yorker*, turned up intermittently to practice, and he once started weeping as he listened to Matthiessen give a Dharma talk—"eyes wide as if liberated from those wintry glasses, he looked like an astonished child," Matthiessen later remembered of Steinberg's sudden kensho.[23] Afterward, during dokusan, Steinberg was still crying. "We rested in the other's eyes for a long while, unblinking, yet utterly natural, at ease. This silence, when trusted, is the most powerful form of interview. Finally, deeply moved, I murmured, 'I've never seen you before, Saul.' And knowing precisely what I meant, he nodded, wiped his tears, rose, bowed in the doorway, and went out. We never spoke of this event again."

Though he had reservations about his position, Matthiessen was devoted to what he affectionately dubbed his "slumgullion stew"[24] of spiritual seekers, this "sangha of scattered individuals and pesky loners."[25] And he cherished their converted stable as a refuge, which he officially named the Ocean Zendo. By the 1990s, it had become vital to his well-being, as he confessed one day during another Dharma talk:

> Every time I come home, I make a small pilgrimage of appreciation to two places: the Sagaponack zendo and the sea. Then I am home! Then I have come full circle, and everything is complete. There is always a great sense of wonder in the grandeur of the sea, which restores me endlessly—the Absolute?—but there is perhaps an even greater wonder in the common miracles of everyday life, even—or perhaps especially—in its humblest and most "ordinary" moments. When we pay attention to our life, appreciate our life, we feel that gratitude—it is inevitable!—because even the ordinary becomes extra-ordinary.[26]

MARIA MATTHIESSEN HAD less reverent feelings about the Ocean Zendo. The stable renovation was a lovely job, she conceded, but Peter's students could be a nuisance. "They sometimes frighten his third wife," a reporter observed, "as they peer into the windows or appear at the kitchen door."[27]

On *zazenkai* retreat days, when they came inside the house, they colonized the living room and formed a solemn line of seated figures below the staircase as they waited for Sensei's bell upstairs. Maria was forced to creep between their cushions to reach her bedroom, her office, and the kitchen, where she was prohibited from making any noise.

Maria hated the zazenkai days, which made her feel unwelcome in her own home. She hated when Peter assigned the students samu, work practice, around the garden she had labored so assiduously to cultivate over the years. He once decided to landscape a wild pond behind the house, ignoring Maria's pleas that he leave it alone because she already had more than enough to maintain. It was a "zendo project,"[28] he insisted—something the students would keep up. But none of his students knew how to garden ("hadn't a clue," said Maria), and the pond was soon overrun by phragmites, which suffocated everything. Maria was left to replant a muddy wallow. When Peter then decided to build a *karesansui*, a Japanese rock garden, bordered by a wooden walkway for kinhin meditation, she was understandably wary. A large hole ("a bloody mess") was excavated by the students, the first thing a visitor saw as they came in the driveway. It remained there for two years. The finished karesansui was undeniably stunning: pebble gravel in a tangle of beach rose and wild cherry, with a large glacial erratic and other "distinguished rocks"[29] lugged in from Connecticut and the Catskills. But Peter would then usher guests over to admire his handiwork, conspicuously ignoring the rest of the garden, Maria's labor of love, in what she recognized as an expression of his competitiveness.

Peter accused her of being a bad sport about the Ocean Zendo. "You're so ungenerous," he said in a recurring argument.

"I notice it's not at anybody else's house," Maria replied. "It's in *our* house, at *your* convenience."[30]

As a stubborn pragmatist, she had long been bemused by some of her husband's peculiar obsessions. His interest in bigfoot was disconcerting from the start—she "worried that he believed it"[31]—and the Florida Everglades struck her as "beastly."[32] Zen, however, was a particular point of disconnect between them, and it had been ever since his home-leaving ceremony in the wake of their wedding. In 1982, Peter had gone on a pilgrimage across Japan with Bernie Glassman, visiting sites associated with the thirteenth-century Soto master Dogen Zenji, while Maria had been left at home to hold the family together. He'd written her letters about his "spiritual and tantric life" in Kyoto, Nara, Tokyo, and Kamakura: "Up early every a.m. for morning service (and sometimes daisan w. Sensei), dead drunk every night."[33] She had written to him about her loneliness. "The house seems somehow meaningless and I wander around a bit. Don't exhaust yourself—although I know by this time you are absorbed and fascinated.... Sorry about this <u>exceptionally</u> dreary letter, but don't let it put you off writing to <u>me</u> & don't float off & leave your Mfupe"—a pet name—"(who loves you a <u>lot</u>, a <u>lot</u>) for a Zen dream."

That Peter might abandon her for a "Zen dream" had become a nagging worry once again during his three-month residence at Greyston as Glassman's head monk. He had written her letters portraying an idyllic existence in Riverdale ("the gray river, and the blue jays carrying silent autumn messages from tree to tree"),[34] and she was soon pleading with him for a "little note" to reassure her of his commitment to their life together. "I need something to hang on to ... I am a bit nervous of all of this—so that's why I'm writing—in case I <u>never</u> see you <u>again</u>."[35]

In 1986, when Peter published *Nine-Headed Dragon River*, Maria felt ambivalent enough about the subject matter to put off reading it for nearly six months. When she eventually did pick it up, the most she could muster was a bittersweet comment: "You have written a beautiful book, even though it is painful for me to read at times—and I hope, despite all the evidence within it, that you need me sometimes, as much as I need you."[36]

Peter often credited Zen with softening his temperament over the years. As a younger man, he had been consumed with anger at his parents and at the world. "He used to lash out at just about everything and everybody," his friend Sherry Lord recalled during an interview in 1990. "But Zen's given him much more balance."[37] The change was one his children could recognize. In conversation with the writer and filmmaker Jeff Sewald, Alex observed of his father "that Zen really did help him to become more compassionate, more understanding, more tolerant of people."[38] Zen "quieted a lot of demons," agreed Luke. "It certainly has generated a great deal of peace in him. It has, I think, helped him become far more accepting of himself, which is the main thing—that in the end it's okay to be simply who he is, rather than who he should be, or some ideal."[39] According to Rue, "the Zen saved him."[40]

And yet it did not save the people around him. Indeed, Luke later cited Zen as another example of his father's habitual leave-taking. "Zen practice, by definition, is very self-involved, a way of tuning everything else out.... To me, it was always a way of him escaping again."[41]

Maria, often alone in Sagaponack, devoted much of her energy to cultivating a three-acre sanctuary that blocked out the Hamptons crowd with tall privet hedges. Her extensive gardens attracted kestrels, cardinals, Canada geese, long-eared owls, and northern harriers. Peter enjoyed what she made for the family; he kept diligent lists of the many migrating birds. By adding the Ocean Zendo with its karesansui, however, he also carved out a corner of the property for himself, a spiritual island where he could float off and vanish into Emptiness, the Void.

IN MAY 1991, a few weeks before Peter's sixty-fourth birthday, Maria walked from the house to the Ocean Zendo to deliver some mail. Inside, forgotten in the corner, she found a woman's sweater. It could have belonged to anyone in the sangha; it was probably nothing significant. Still, a recent convergence of troubling signs—uncollected messages from a female caller on the answering machine; Peter's uncharacteristic decision to take a Tuesday afternoon off, despite being frantic about work—planted a seed of suspicion in her mind. Over the following few days, the seed was watered by an upsetting memory. Back during his three-month residency at Greyston, Peter had indulged in an affair with another student, a fling he apologized for when Maria, driving hours each weekend just to visit him in Riverdale, had finally found out about it.

Peter now flew to Jackson, Wyoming, to go fly-fishing with friends. When he was gone, Maria unlocked his office. She poked through the drawers of papers until she came across a file of correspondence from women she didn't know—women who seemed to know her husband very well. The shock was extreme. Reading all the correspondence "was so painful that I can't come up from under," she wrote Peter in a letter of her own. "I am in a deep depression, alternating with anger at you, but mainly at myself."[42] Maria continued:

> The most wounding letter was, I suppose, the latest letter from someone who signs herself [W].* You have been stringing this girl along for seven years? I have to reassemble my life backwards for that long? I noticed how careful you were not to have envelopes with postmarks, how carefully you blacked out the date, and yet you couldn't quite throw the letters away could you? If you had time enough, Peter, to read the whole romantic, moldy file you would see how very similar all these letters are. The same poems by Rilke, the same abject love, the same moment when you pull away and virtuously say you will stick with the wife of the moment. . . .
>
> You know what saddens me is that I was filled with a hope (just stupid complacency, I now realize) that we were trying to forge a long term relationship. . . . I had hoped that we would mature together in fits and starts and look back on a decent life. I hoped that the fact that I saw you <u>clearly</u>

---

* Name withheld for privacy.

would in the end be a comfort to you. I do, you know. I know every nook and cranny of you. The smallness, the meanness, the temper, the deep hole you carry in the center of your heart, the honour, the good, steady, talented, hard work, the willingness to take responsibility for your character defects. I know when you are scared by the future and I know your strength in unexpected and moving moments. I know your insatiable need for romance to make you feel better about yourself, and to fill that hole temporarily, even as you plan your escape. . . .

So, it has been sixteen years that I have lived with you, though I have known you for twenty three. It is a long time to love someone so passionately and singularly. I now regret not having an affair or two under my belt. But I felt deeply loyal to you, and in a way to your frailties. I knew how hurt you would be by the kind of betrayal you are so cavalier about imposing on me, and I couldn't do it. Perhaps that is putting too honourable a slant on it (I am trying to be scrupulously honest in this letter), and it was mere cowardice on my part. Perhaps I should be applauding your boldness. But in my heart I cannot. I never was willing to hurt you the way you are apparently willing to hurt me, and I hurt Julian. That wound will never heal. Hurting other people is so very damaging to oneself, something you seem unable to understand, although Zen must tell you that every single morning.

When Peter received this extraordinary letter in Wyoming, he was too stunned to compose a proper reply. Instead, he annotated Maria's sentences, underlining words and adding defensive comments in the margin. It was "not so" that he resented his long-suffering wife. It was "not so!" that he felt cavalier about betraying her. As for his frailties, he knew them all too well: "hence my profound doubt about being a Zen teacher."

Maria had ended her note with a Swahili rhyme ("instead of Rilke"), which she remembered hearing in Tanzania when she was a little girl. Beneath these melancholy lines, "Tuta kwenda safari . . . ," next to her glimmer-of-hope signature—"Love Maria"—Peter scrawled a final thought: "For all our quarreling—and now this—I have always loved you and admired you, and all the more so after this very painful and moving letter. You may find this too hard to believe (like the truth that I think you a fine writer)—all the same, it's true." The parenthetical compliment about her "fine" writing was a familiar one; he had offered the same consolation prize when apologizing for his affair in the Selous.

More than once over the years, Maria would contemplate divorce in response to his serial infidelity. But she loved him too much to just walk away; loved Alex too much to divide his loyalties; and felt, on a more practical level, that she had no way to earn an independent income, no viable career in the event of another separation. On this occasion, though, she would not easily recover from the magnitude of Peter's betrayal, particularly the revelation that he'd been using the fly-fishing trips with friends (Jim Harrison, Jack Zajac, Doug Peacock, David Karnos) as an opportunity to visit the same woman near Yellowstone National Park for *seven years*, a young wildlife activist who, in her own letters, also chided him for refusing to take responsibility for his choices.

Peter could mend almost any rift with his droll, self-effacing humor. "We made each other laugh, and that was one of the things that helped us along," recalled Maria.[43] However, something shifted after she found the file of correspondence hidden in his office. (He decried her snooping as a grave breach of trust. "Is it worse to read the letters or have the affairs?" she countered to him.)[44] The shift would manifest most clearly in the household finances. Though he was generous with charities, and sometimes made extravagant gestures, like buying a second house for Maria in Sag Harbor as retirement security, Peter had always been "frugal," as he put it, when it came to the little things; a carton of milk could scandalize him if he caught sight of the price. Maria had gone along with his penny-pinching ways since 1975. Now she found herself wondering why. *Why am I doing this?* Why was she depriving herself at home while he was out doing whatever he wanted? She decided to make an adjustment. His choices liberated her to spend money.

Maria also began to push back forcefully against Peter's more objectionable behavior, as she would a few years later when he accused her of burning cash "like a whore" after she booked an international flight, without consulting him first, to visit her aging father. Maria responded to the insult with a letter of tight-lipped defiance:

> I am perfectly aware that you "earn all the money" but as I have repeatedly told you, I also feel I earn the money, and hard though it is to convince you, I feel that I am a <u>full</u> partner in this relationship and I do not feel that I have to ask you or beg you to spend money that in fact I feel entitled to. . . . You must be aware that the work you do garners all the kudos and adulation of an admiring public (quite deservedly too and of which I am very proud), but you must also be aware that a great deal of the work that I do is sheer drudgery and gets no respect whatsoever, or even appreciation most of the time . . . and given these facts I may take a holiday whenever I want. I would be happy if it were with you more often, but it seems that this is not to be. You seem to get most of your enjoyment far from home, and this is a fact that I have had to accept.[45]

THE FREQUENT ARGUMENTS that flared between Peter and Maria often focused, in Sarah Koenig's recollection, on how excessive Peter thought their lives had become: "The household being too complicated, too much going on, too much purchasing, too much spending, too many parties, too many dinners, too many *things*."[46]

Peter claimed to want a simple life; it had been his constant refrain for half a century. He told Maria they should pack up and move to a shack in Montana. "He would terrify her," recalled their friend Steve Byers, "with the idea that she's going to have to go off and live in the goddamn woods."[47] Peter told a journalist, as he gestured around at the Sagaponack property, that "[s]ometimes, even though I love this place, in a way I wish I could burn it down and start from scratch."[48] It was an irony lost on nobody that a major source of the complications he wished to escape was the sensei himself. His un-Zen behavior "played havoc" with Maria's "always shaky" self-esteem.[49] She would not let him forget those "seven years."[50]

Peter sometimes drifted between the Ocean Zendo and the writing studio, his two islands, pausing briefly in between to observe his family from a distance. While he might smile and nod, taking pleasure in the domestic scene, it rarely occurred to him to sit down and join them as a participant. "He was so massively insecure," recalled Antonia, Maria's eldest daughter. "I think he thought we didn't want him there."[51] In Alex's view, his father was a man apart: "There was Maria, the girls, and me; and then there was Dad. He never quite fit in. He never felt at ease. He was a little bit like a stranger within the family. I think he always felt unloved, resented, judged, even in the household—and for good reason, because at least in the basic ways that a family operates and cooperates and spends time together, he didn't make the effort. We all kind of gave him a pass because he was the great artist who was out in the studio writing important books. But I think it did create some level of sadness for him, this feeling of being outside the family, a sense of loss, that the sacrifice for his work was human connection."[52]

If Peter did try to engage, every interaction, "no matter how small," said Sarah, involved some kind of internal struggle. "And it made him very complicated to communicate with, especially for his kids."[53] Her own strategy for dealing with Peter was to make him laugh ("he had a very juvenile sense of humor, very schoolboy"), and she could disarm him so thoroughly that he welcomed her into his writing studio, the inner sanctum, where he was "gracious and sweet." But then Sarah and Antonia—who had a tougher time during adolescence, her emotional outbursts at Maria triggering heated spars with Peter across the dinner table—were not really his children. Their father was Julian Koenig. To Sarah, Peter was just "an extra guy around," a guy whom she happened to like, especially when she was younger. "I became much more critical as I got older, because I started to understand things about his relationship with my mom."

When it came to Luke, Sara Carey, Rue, and Alex, communicating with Peter was a challenge with much higher stakes. He was their father, and they approached him as adults with varying degrees of longing and resentment.

For Sara Carey, the resentment was all-consuming by the 1990s. She had an unshakable belief that Peter had never atoned for abandoning her and Luke when he divorced her mother, Patsy Southgate. While her hurt was valid, it was exacerbated by mental illness, which she began to show symptoms of at an early age. Sara Carey could not come to Sagaponack without starting incendiary fights. She often canceled Christmas visits at the very last moment to inflict maximum inconvenience. She sought Peter's attention just to attack him, and to attack Maria (to hurt him). Peter was ill-equipped to respond to her provocations, which were not always rational. After Sara Carey confessed to manipulating him for money, he called her "Needy Daughter" in a wounded letter, while he was "Dumb Old Dad."[54] He then gave her more money—tens of thousands of dollars each year in financial support. He held on to the hope they might mend their relationship, but how to even begin? There was no solid ground on which to build a new foundation.

Luke, despite nursing similar feelings of abandonment, was more ambivalent about their father. When he was a teenager, Peter had spoken to him about his "vision" of a "grand threesome of Matthiessen writers": F. O. Matthiessen, Peter Matthiessen, and, the implication went, Lucas Conrad Matthiessen.[55] Luke had already spent his formative years believing himself inadequate in the eyes of his father, and this burdensome fantasy only made him feel worse. It "shaped a lot of my feelings and reactions to him for many years," Luke recalled. Over those years, Peter would suddenly appear in his son's life, attentive and concerned; then he would disappear again, becoming remote and inaccessible. In his twenties, Luke spiraled into alcohol abuse, and Peter swooped in to pay for therapy in New York, even accompanying Luke to a session to berate the therapist: "How can you accept your fee when Luke is doing so poorly? Haven't you been addressing his problems? Look at him. Hasn't it struck you that something is very wrong?"[56] After the appointment, as they rode downtown in a shared taxi, Peter warned "Lucassin" that he risked becoming an alcoholic. Luke was already downing a quart of vodka every day—was drunk, in fact, at that very moment—so the warning seemed "ironic and naïve, another indicator of how far apart we really were." Peter then flew to Japan for the Zen pilgrimage with Bernie Glassman. ("Like, that's what he does, you know?")[57] Within days, urinating blood, Luke was admitted to a hospital, where he was injected with a high dose of Valium and diagnosed with the early stages of cirrhosis. It was Maria who kept watch, writing updates to Peter in Japan: "I speak to Luke everyday. He is bored and a bit depressed but thinks that this was necessary."[58]

Another time, Peter, recognizing his son's advancing blindness due to the retinitis pigmentosa, took him on a trip to view nesting seabirds in the Midriff Islands off Baja California. Luke was moved by the gesture; he understood this was Peter's attempt to express his feelings through a medium (birdwatching) he felt comfortable with. The gulls and terns, brown and blue-footed boobies, were offered up as a gesture of love. "I watch Luke's face," Peter wrote in a magazine article about their voyage on a cabin cruiser named the *El Dorado*—"it is impressed, despite his indifference to birds, and I feel rather unreasonably happy."[59] It was a moment of genuine connection, perhaps, though Luke would continue to hold his father at arm's length for his own emotional safety.

Eight years later, in 1992, Luke's sight was almost fully gone when he picked up a copy of *Killing Mister Watson*. He had mostly avoided his father's books because reading them brought Peter "too close," and dredged up "a deep-seated suspicion that I had disappointed him."[60] However, he suspected he would never read another book—*any* book—with his eyes, so he swallowed his "disquiet," put the novel an inch from his face, and held it steady as he scanned each line. He soon concluded the novel was a masterpiece. "No longer just hearing about Peter Matthiessen's greatness, I had seen it for myself. To my mind he had achieved one of the highest goals imaginable, unattainable by all but the most gifted, and I was immensely proud of him."[61] Luke was sober by now, a therapist for other addicts, and he'd learned to stop measuring himself against his father, finding a healthy perspective. "Only later did it occur to me that charting an independent course had freed me from decades of defensive comparison." He would eventually write this in his own book, a candid memoir titled *First Light*.

As for Rue, she would also publish a memoir about, among other painful subjects, the mercurial interplay she had with her adoptive father: "It had been very difficult to get along with him after my mother had died. He did not respond well to need. In some ways we were always in opposition, though fond of each other at the same time, a strange and constant dichotomy."[62]

The twentieth anniversary of Deborah Love's death arrived on January 27, 1992. Rue happened to be visiting Sagaponack that day, and Peter suggested they go for a stroll. They ended up at Deborah's grave in the village cemetery. Rue was stunned; she had no idea Peter even thought about her mother anymore. Like the birdwatching with Luke, the walk together was his way of expressing something without using words, which seemed to fail him when it came to his family. You'd think Peter barely noticed you at all, Rue later marveled, "and then he'd turn around and say something, or *do* something that, for me at least, made it workable, and made me love him, and made me put up with the more difficult side."[63]

That left Alex—"Al," or "Bal Bal," as Peter sometimes called him. Of the four Matthiessen children, Alex had the most in common with his father: an uncanny physical resemblance, the same long face, high forehead, and curly hair; and mutual interests in politics, sports, travel, nature, and the outdoors. At the University of California, Santa Cruz, Alex majored in environmental studies and biology, "very much because of Dad."[64] He then found employment in wildlife conservation, before moving across to the Rainforest Action Network. He would later work for the deputy secretary of the U.S. Department of the Interior, and lead the Hudson Riverkeeper, an organization dedicated to defending the waterway from industrial polluters and protecting New York City's water supply.

Even-tempered and affable, Alex watched his older siblings scuffle fruitlessly with their father; he learned from them "what not to do." He understood that if wanted a good relationship, "a real relationship," he would have to let go of a great deal of his anger and resentment. If he could forgive Peter's flaws, Alex reasoned, he would get a father who was "more open, more willing to take chances, more intimate, more connected, because he wouldn't feel threatened by me, he wouldn't feel guilty in my presence,"[65] guilt being a common theme between Peter and each of his children. Alex just needed to find the right opportunity for an honest talk.

In the summer of 1993, at twenty-nine, Alex joined his father on an anthropological film expedition led by Peter Getzels and Harriet Gordon, two documentarians working for the BBC. The expedition had already visited the Faroe Islands and Iceland; Alex flew to Nuuk, the capital of Greenland, and then accompanied his father and the crew to a remote settlement called Qaanaaq, in the icy northwest of the country, where Inughuit people still used kayaks and handheld harpoons to harvest narwhal and beluga whales. Getzels and Gordon hoped to film the Inughuit going about their work; Peter Matthiessen was there to write a report for *The New Yorker*. To him, "the whale," like the black rhino, was "a metaphor for a paradise on earth already lost."[66] Nevertheless, his article would defend limited whaling by arguing it was a necessary practice if Inughuit culture "is to survive"—a controversial position that put him at odds with hardline conservation groups who wanted an end to whaling without exception. (Matthiessen thought "Green fundamentalism" was the wrong approach because it condescendingly overruled traditional peoples like the Inughuit.) To report the story, he and Alex joined one of the beluga hunts permitted by the International Whaling Commission, which made an exception from its member-state moratorium for "aboriginal subsistence whaling." Matthiessen would later describe the end of the hunt, after harpoons had been thrown, during a Dharma talk at the Ocean Zendo:

> At 4:30 in the morning, the sun is high and bright, and we watch the finish at a range so close that at one point the panicked cow, tended closely by her young one, swims just beneath our boat, her beautiful black-and-white marbled hide alight in the clear black water. Gideon dispatches her with a few rifle shots, much blood, and thrashing, then quickly harpoons and kills the young one. The hunters rig lines to the carcasses and tow them back in to the Narssaq beach.
>
> In old ceremony, the younger hunter cuts a slice of hide and blubber from the back of his whale's neck and each of us is presented with a piece of this whale skin delicacy known as mattak or "muktuk." It is rubbery and crunchy in the way of cartilage, and the taste is mild. . . . What kind of a Zen teacher is that, participating in killing, not only that but cow + calf, then eating meat raw[?] . . . The traditional hunter is far more aware of all life, being a part of it, and far more respectful and grateful to it—and therefore far more "Zen," in my opinion—than the angry, strident people who abuse him.[67]

One afternoon during the expedition, Alex hiked with his father above a picturesque fjord. When they rested at a spot overlooking the water, he decided the time had come to share his feelings. To stop Peter from getting immediately defensive, Alex told him, first of all, that he was here to offer forgiveness so they could move forward. "But for me to do that, I need to be honest with you about the ways in which you were a shitty father."[68] Peter started to protest, explaining himself—and then stopped, realizing what his son was trying to do. He sat down and listened as Alex calmly catalogued a lifetime of grievances. Peter had forgotten him in the aftermath of Deborah's death. Peter had never been seriously engaged in his life, either before or since then. Peter was not a mentor to his children; he never set aside his writing to offer paternal advice. To the contrary, he often needled Alex for not working as compulsively as he did, like a personification of the Protestant work ethic. ("Oh, a little more R&R, I see . . .") Above all, Peter had a habit of doling out emotional abuse within the family. This abuse, as Alex later recalled, was because Peter "couldn't get his own interior life straight," and it was easier to displace the frustration he felt about himself onto his wife and children.

528 · TRUE NATURE

Alex laid it all out for his father, who absorbed the blows with only minimal resistance. For both of them, this Greenland confrontation would be a turning point in their relationship, which dramatically improved from that point on. Alex was pleased at having achieved something that, in his view, none of his siblings had ever managed to do. "I became the one child who had formally forgiven him, and formally said, 'I'm not going to make this an issue anymore. We are now two adults and two equals. We are friends.'"

A FEW MONTHS BEFORE the whaling expedition, Matthiessen had sat down in the Sagaponack garden with the writer Lawrence Shainberg, who was interviewing him for *Tricycle*, a relatively new magazine, launched in 1991 by Helen Tworkov and Rick Fields, aimed at presenting the various schools and sects of Mahayana and Theravada Buddhism to an American audience.

Shainberg was interested in Matthiessen's personal history with Zen, and toward the end of the interview the questions turned to how Zen fit, or did not fit, with the different parts of his life. "How do writing and teaching conflict with each other?" Shainberg asked.[69]

"Time, in the main," Matthiessen replied as he nursed a cup of coffee.

When Shainberg urged him to elaborate—"Only in the concrete sense? What about the spiritual consequences of description, the separation of subject and object . . . ?"—Matthiessen offered a few stray thoughts about ego, the "trap of self," which can lead to "self-deception." But then he circled back to time, which was weighing on his mind. "I never have enough of it," he said. "One wants to help whenever one can, yet I find that it's very difficult to keep my own work going while trying to handle all these other matters and still be available to my students and my family. I travel a lot, and I'm constantly trying to catch up, all the while yearning for a simpler life."

"That's all through *Dragon River*, isn't it, your hunger for simplicity?"

"I dream of simplicity, but I'm as far from it as ever," Matthiessen said ruefully. "That is my practice, how to be in the world and remain simple. One day perhaps I'll accept the fact that I am never going to find the simple life. Maybe the first step toward simplicity will be to accept that my life will never be simple even if I go live in a cave and subsist on green nettles like Milarepa."

MATTHIESSEN MAY HAVE RECEIVED Dharma transmission from Bernie Glassman in 1989, but in Maezumi Roshi's lineage there was one final step beyond Shiho. Traditionally, the seal of *Inka* was bestowed on a disciple only when the teacher was satisfied on three counts: the maturity and integration of the disciple's character; the depth of their life experience, meaning their Zen experience; and their clarity—how clearly they actualize the teachings. A disciple chosen for Inka would ideally exceed their teacher in clarity of expression.

Matthiessen resisted Inka at first, believing himself too flawed to be ordained at the highest level of Soto. Yet Glassman would again insist otherwise, convincing him that it was also good for the Ocean Zendo and American Zen.

On July 6, 1996, during a ceremony conducted in Yonkers at a former Catholic convent being transformed, by Glassman, into a care center for people living with HIV/AIDS, Muryo Sensei would become Muryo Roshi. Almost immediately, Matthiessen confided to a niece that he did not "deserve" the title, and probably shouldn't have accepted it (though he was undoubtedly proud to have attained the rank of Zen master).[70] "You never feel like you're prepared, and anybody who says they are is an imposter," said Joan Jiko Halifax, who was ordained that same day as a priest, and who would go through Inka with Glassman a few years later, becoming a roshi herself. "Peter also had this sense of irony, a strange sense of humor, or sense of ambivalence, about everything in his life, whether it was Zen or his marriage or whatever. Everything was up for questioning, everything subject to doubt."[71]

The doubt would never go away, as he admitted during a Dharma talk in 2004: "Alas, the so-called 'roshi' who sits here before you, despite long years of practice, is still mired in the primordial mud from which the lotus of his true nature might or might not emerge, still deluded in his enlightenment. . . . After thirty-five years of practice, I remain to varying degrees greedy, angry, and foolish, and I break one or more of the precepts every day."[72]

In a letter to Craig Carpenter, his old teacher and guide, Matthiessen downplayed his progress in Zen entirely, offering his own version of a famous comment by Harry S. Truman. "I think you are too generous about my so-called spiritual attainment," he told Carpenter. "I'm more like that man whose tombstone in Pecos, Texas, reads, 'Here lies Bill Williams; he done his damndest.'"[73]

24

The Watson Years

> Slog it out across the desert of your own intuition.
>
> —PM, advice to a friend (1996)[1]

MATTHIESSEN SIGNED a contract for his Watson "continuation"—not a sequel, he was quick to point out—a few months after *Killing Mister Watson* was published in 1990. The advance for "WATSON II" was $375,000, and the deadline was February 1992: easy money and easily attainable, he figured, since there was already a full draft sitting on his desk. But after re-reading the pages he realized, in what must have been an alarming epiphany, that the decision to break up his Florida epic into three distinct parts had effectively crippled the middle one. As originally written, the part about Edgar Watson's heirs—how they were affected by his gruesome murder, and how history can transmute into a noxious myth—was "connecting tissue"; it lacked the "armature or bony skeleton"[2] required for a stand-alone novel, which, of course, it was never intended to be. In the summer of 1991, the journalist Michael Shnayerson, profiling Matthiessen for *Vanity Fair*, found the author in a pensive mood as he confronted the magnitude of his unexpected conundrum. "I've never tried anything as big as this trilogy," Matthiessen admitted. "I haven't gotten it under control, and really it's got me beat right now. I know the first book is strong, and I know the last book is strong. I was describing it to someone the other day, I was saying it's like throwing a stone, and this middle book, it doesn't have the support of the thrower or of the ground when it comes to rest. Those two structures are firm, but this is up in the air."[3]

As the deadline approached, he was "thrashing wildly" with his "monstrous" draft.[4] And for a moment, in January 1992, it seemed like he might have won the battle. All the "wonderful, funny, and colorful stuff" clicked together, and he glimpsed a viable whole with such excitement that he could barely contain himself, the next month, at a California Academy of Sciences talk in San Francisco. "I'm anxious to get back in and get to work on it," he told the audience.⁵ When he did return to his writing studio, though, the breakthrough turned out to be illusory. The manuscript remained a mess; the contract deadline came and went.

In May, Matthiessen started to contemplate a major overhaul of his book, "breaking it into short 'chapters' that would make a lot of the time jumps + flashbacks . . . a lot clearer."⁶ Still, what he desperately wanted before any more revisions was editorial guidance. As he told Maria in a letter: "Do please indicate to/reassure Jason that I consider him my editor, but that I also need some close structural advice—I've been too close to it for too long, can't see the forest for the trees—and would value a couple of responses . . . from people who did not read WATSON I."

He sent this letter from Nepal, where he had flown via France and Thailand. Matthiessen had a well-established habit, whenever something was not going well in his life, of filling the calendar with commitments that took him far away from home, and he would travel an extraordinary amount in the five difficult years it took him to finish "WATSON II," or "The Man Who Killed Belle Starr," which was eventually titled *Lost Man's River*.

THE NEPAL TRIP WAS the idea of Thomas Laird, a thirty-nine-year-old Kathmandu-based American correspondent and photographer. Matthiessen had never heard of him until Laird phoned up one day, on a "spirited impulse that recommended him right from the outset,"⁷ to make an attractive offer. The Government of Nepal had just granted the photographer a permit to visit Upper Mustang, or Lo, the "forbidden kingdom," bordered on three sides by Tibet, which had been closed for decades to outsiders due to the presence of Khampa guerrillas. An admirer of *The Snow Leopard*, Laird invited Matthiessen to join him on an expedition to Mustang with ten Sherpas and a government liaison officer. Matthiessen accepted the offer immediately "in the same out-of-the-blue spirit."

From Kathmandu, he flew to Pokhara, from where he had once set out on foot with George Schaller for the mountains of Dolpo. Much had changed here since 1973: a motor road now traced part of their original route, and airstrips connected remote villages to a rapidly urbanizing nation. Matthiessen and Laird caught a twin-engine Otter to the settlement of Jomsom. Then, over the next two weeks, they made their way on horseback north along the Kali Gandaki River to the royal capital of Lo Manthang, where they spoke with the king and observed the three-day Tiji Festival with its masked dancers. Along the way, Matthiessen meditated in a cave monastery, and Laird encouraged them to detour to a secluded valley, never visited by Westerners, where monk cells and a chapel were carved into cliffs. While they were there, a lama pointed out fresh footprints that had frightened the locals—*mehti*, the holy man claimed—and Matthiessen's obsession flared suddenly back to life. More than a dozen pages of his expedition account, *East of Lo Monthang*, would be dedicated to "the problematic creature derided in the West as the yeti, or Abominable Snowman."[8] (The footprints were later identified by George Schaller and another expert as likely left by a Tibetan brown bear, though Laird, like Matthiessen, found them "very seductive" as he photographed them: "For a moment you suspend knowing, and you open yourself up to the possibilities.")[9]

Matthiessen departed Nepal and headed home in early June. This was little more than a stopover, though, long enough to sort his mail and have his clothes laundered. He soon caught another series of flights west to Alaska, and then across the Bering Strait, "the rough gray shallow seas of the vanished land bridge between continents,"[10] to the Russian Far East. From the city of Khabarovsk, at the confluence of the Amur and Ussuri Rivers, he flew to a mining town near the Sikhote-Alin Biosphere Reserve, then hitched a ride 150 miles north to the fishing port of Terney, where he was met by the wildlife biologist Maurice Hornocker, a renowned authority on the world's big cats.

Affiliated with the University of Idaho, Hornocker was codirector of the Siberian Tiger Project, which had been running out of Terney for a little more than five months. Hornocker had invited Matthiessen to observe some early work in the field with the hope that he might write something about it, thus bringing the conservation project international attention. This was another offer Matthiessen gladly accepted, in part because he'd long wanted to see the wild province described by the Russian explorer Vladimir Arsenyev in *Dersu the Trapper* (1923), a province also closed to foreigners until very recently. Two days before Matthiessen arrived, Hornocker and his colleagues had tranquilized and radio-collared a mature female tiger; Matthiessen now accompanied the biologists as they tracked her movements through the taiga. Though they never glimpsed her directly, it was "exciting," he wrote Maria, "to be within 200 yards (on foot) of a grown tiger, in these beautiful woods of oak and birch, thrush song, and familiar flowers."[11] In an article for *The New Yorker*, he would later imagine the tiger "with her head raised and alert, her small, round white-spotted ears twitching in the greenish sunlight. In the fragmented sun shafts of the woodland, the head would be camouflaged by bold black calligraphic lines inscribed on frost-bright brows and beard and ruff, in a beautiful and terrifying mask of snow and fire."[12]

Matthiessen passed a few happy days hiking, camping, salmon fishing, and making reconnaissance scouts with Hornocker to monitor "Lena," as the biologists christened the tiger. They also attended an emergency conference about forest mismanagement in the "new Russia" (the Soviet Union having just collapsed), where timber leases were being handed out indiscriminately to multinational corporations, further threatening the already endangered *Panthera tigris altaica*. Then Matthiessen reluctantly returned to Khabarovsk—the visit was "unfortunately too brief," he grumbled[13]—with Hornocker promising to keep him updated on Lena and the Siberian Tiger Project.*

Rather than heading straight home, he joined an international crane conference that happened to be convening in Khabarovsk. For two weeks, dozens of delegates from China, Japan, South Korea, Russia, and the United States came together to discuss how the "best interests"[14] of migrating cranes might be reconciled with geopolitics and certain "national antagonisms."[15] Matthiessen was there because of his own curiosity, though he was eagerly welcomed by George Archibald, director of the International Crane Foundation and co-organizer of the conference. On a ship chartered by the ICF for a bargain rate thanks to Russia's shattered economy, Matthiessen accompanied the delegates seven hundred miles up the Amur River toward the floodplain breeding grounds of the rare red-crowned crane (*Grus japonesis*) and the white-naped crane (*Antigone vipio*). The conference was frequently heated, with much "Russo-Chinese skirmishing"[16] during daily discussion groups. But there were "some jolly vodka moments," too, as Peter wrote to Maria: "the other night, at midnight, I found myself on a horse, riding around in a swamp, alone, so drunk I could hardly recall how I had got there."[17]

After the voyage, he joined Jim Harris, deputy director of the ICF, on a side mission to Mongolia to verify reports of further breeding grounds for the white-naped crane. This "last leg of journey,"[18] as he promised his wife on a postcard, turned out to be unexpectedly stressful. A customs official at the border town of Kamen-Rybolov refused to honor his visa, which forced him to backtrack six hundred miles to Khabarovsk and bribe his way onto a plane. There were more dramas in China, and more bribery, though the stress and inconvenience turned out to be worth it. After transiting through Ulaanbaatar and then driving to eastern Mongolia along a rough dirt track— the national highway—he spent several exhilarating days with Jim Harris exploring the grassy reaches of the Daurian steppe. In a significant discovery

---

* Lena was killed just a few months later, her collar smashed and tossed aside by poachers. Project staff members managed to rescue four of her orphaned cubs; while two soon died of genetic abnormalities, two survived and were transferred to captive breeding programs in Omaha and Indianapolis zoos. The female cub, in Indianapolis, was also christened Lena, and later gave birth to cubs of her own.

for conservation science, they confirmed the reports of breeding territories for the white-naped crane in valleys east of the Hentei Mountains. They also chased juveniles in trucks and on horseback, to band them for research purposes; fled from a violent electrical storm; and visited nomadic herdsmen in white felt gers. These elegant tents struck Matthiessen as so "neat and spare, with nothing extra," that he indulged in an old daydream about living "permanently in such a dwelling, with no more possessions than such a space could comfortably contain."[19]

By early August, when he arrived home in Sagaponack, he had been traveling for the better part of three months. One evening at a dinner party, a guest challenged him about his extended absence. What the hell had he been doing all summer? He offered the "excuse," as he later termed it, of his fieldwork on endangered tigers and cranes, yet the guest was apparently unmoved. "'Cranes?!' she squawked. 'Who cares about cranes?'"[20]

Peter Matthiessen saw value in all animals, right down to the tsetse fly. But he cared about cranes in particular because they were often depicted in folklore as "semi-sacred messengers between heaven and earth,"[21] and in Chinese philosophy as "a manifestation of the yin-yang principle of bad and good, dark and light."[22] He cared because there was something spiritual about these graceful creatures; the bugle notes of their call could summon his attention "to our swift passage on this precious earth."[23] He cared because cranes were reminders of paradise lost, of the paradise *still* being lost. And he cared because the crane, like the tiger, was considered an umbrella species by conservationists: protecting the fifteen species of crane around the world would indirectly protect a wide range of flora and fauna that shared the same habitats.

Matthiessen cared so much that he now began to conceptualize a new book of environmental writing. "Tiger and Crane" would consider the mythic and spiritual dimensions of both animals, while simultaneously using them as focal points for a grounded discussion of global conservation challenges. Given that the decline in biodiversity only seemed to be accelerating as the millennium approached, he wanted to write something that might finally persuade "our consumer society to take responsibility for our fellow creatures while there is still time."[24] This was a lofty goal given the intransigence of human nature, but he saw it as his solemn responsibility to try.

THROUGHOUT ALL THIS, Edgar Watson waited in the writing studio. Just before leaving for Russia, Matthiessen had handed the latest draft of his novel to John Irving for another round of criticism. A six-page response arrived after he returned, and the verdict, from the very first sentence—

"I feel I've failed you as a reader"—only confirmed how much work he still had to do.[25]

Irving had received the novel in two boxes this time. He had made it halfway through the first box, interleaving his comments on green sheets of paper, before he became exasperated and abandoned that approach. "I found the new beginning very involving," he wrote in his letter; "if you read through my penciled comments on the green sheets, you'll see exactly when the manner of my responses changes from enthusiastic to peevish. Then I thought it best not to continue sounding peevish in the same way."

Irving's problem with *Lost Man's River* was a serious and intractable one. *Killing Mister Watson* had focused on a charming devil and his beguiled, resentful neighbors in the Ten Thousand Islands around the turn of the twentieth century. Yet Watson receded in the second installment, which, in the earliest drafts, was set in the 1980s and concerned with characters like Billy Watkins, Watson's great-grandson and a hotheaded Vietnam War veteran who had been involved in the My Lai massacre. *Killing Mister Watson* was structured as a collection of primary sources: the testimonies of people making history in the wild reaches of southwest Florida. The new volume shifted attention to descendants *discussing* that history: secondary commentary on an original text. Matthiessen's intention was to explore how Watson's legacy damaged his children, and his children's children, just as the country's violent, racist, and environmentally ruinous past continued to affect generations of Americans. Yet the time jump deprived the narrative of the vivid frontier setting and dramatis personae that had made the first novel so compelling. Instead of homesteaders and plume traders, there was a historian sleuthing across a blighted Florida of cane fields and condominiums ("a journey across tamed America")[26] to uncover a story the reader already knew, having previously read it in *Killing Mister Watson*. To compensate for this, Matthiessen had manufactured an extra layer of gothic family intrigue and machinations involving a sugar corporation. But Irving wasn't interested in digressions; he wanted to get back to Edgar Watson. In an astute diagnosis, Irving wrote: "When you inspire such interest in a character and his times, and such dread of the character, it's almost impossible to expect your poor reader to be interested in parallel but not equal information."[27]

How to *make* it equal for the reader? Matthiessen's challenge was to elevate the "parallel" material so *Lost Man's River* stood toe-to-toe with its predecessor. This was no easy task. His early draft had been rejected by Jason Epstein, who did not even finish reading it—"too many people" and "too much talking," the editor complained.[28] In December, Matthiessen wrote a note to Jim Harrison that was also an attempt to cheer himself up. "Am much enjoying my troublesome Watson 'continuation' . . . but all who have read it in MS early form have thrown up their hands, lunch, everything else. Actually, it's great. And as Wm [William] Kennedy said to me not long ago, 'Remember what the same people said about FAR TORTUGA? They hated that one, too!' (Easy for him to say, since he hasn't read it—but I was glad to be reminded, anyway.)"[29]

Matthiessen labored over the revisions for another few weeks in winter. Then he threw up his own hands, temporarily, and retrieved his passport again. With his old friend Victor Emanuel, whom Matthiessen called "Warbler"[*] (and "a sort of ornithological Zen master," because Emanuel liked to make pronouncements like, "Birds call us into the moment"),[30] he set off to track down the eight species of Asian cranes during a whirlwind three-week excursion. In January 1993, the two men were joined by thirteen other travelers through Victor Emanuel Nature Tours, including Bill and Rose Styron, George Plimpton, the photographer Inge Morath, and Maria. Their first stop was Gujarat, India, near the border with Pakistan, where the group spotted sarus and demoiselle cranes; their second stop was Keoladeo National Park in Rajasthan, where they found sarus, Eurasian, and Siberian cranes, like "wisps of desert cloud."[31] Matthiessen made a side trip to Ranthambore in search of tigers, but found none: a poaching ring had slaughtered roughly half the park's population over the previous three years. He then continued with the group to Bhutan—"In a world spinning out of ecological balance, this country is an oasis to environmentalists"[32]—crossing a high-altitude pass to reach black-necked cranes in the Phobjikha Valley. While the tour officially ended there, Emanuel and Matthiessen were not quite done. They continued on to Poyang Lake in China for Siberian, hooked, Eurasian, and white-naped cranes; and to Hokkaido in Japan for the red-crowned crane. "To observe it dancing in Hokkaido's snows," Matthiessen wrote, "is an ultimate pilgrimage for ornithologists."[33]

Returning to the trenches of his Watson draft in the spring of 1993, he decided to try something different. If the problem with the second novel was an absence of Edgar Watson, what if he combined the book with "WATSON III," which was mostly told from Watson's point of view? Matthiessen printed the second novel draft on white paper, the third on gray-blue paper, and devised a rough plan to intersperse them, producing a new contrapuntal whole that would move backwards and forwards through time. Then he sent the enormous pile to his agent with a letter announcing that "this is the book."[34] If Candida Donadio disagreed with his assessment, he requested a detailed explanation "telling me why." If she agreed that it was publishable,

---

[*] Matthiessen's own bird name, bestowed by Victor Emanuel, was "Curlew," because of his adoration for shorebirds.

she was instructed to send it all to Epstein, though Matthiessen was doubtful his editor would greet it with any real enthusiasm; they might, he acknowledged, need to take it to another editor at Random House, or perhaps even another publisher. "Because rightly or wrongly, I think it's potentially very strong, and I won't work with anybody who's just going through the motions just to hang on to PM as a writer or whatever." He would not be patronized under any circumstances. "Okay? It's a long book, you may not be through until late July, in which case you might want to consult with me before passing it along to Jason, as I'll be home on July 29. (Am off tomorrow.)"

Matthiessen was "off" for much of the remaining year, and for most of 1994, too. He was off to Greenland with Alex and the BBC filmmakers to visit the Inughuit whale hunters. He was off to New York for a retreat with Bernie Glassman, and to Los Angeles for a meeting of Taizan Maezumi's disciples. He was off "on a small winter speaking tour, financing my huge and baggy novel," as he informed the poet Gary Snyder.[35] He was off to a literature conference in Santa Monica; to give a craft lecture at the University of Virginia in Charlottesville. He was off to the International Crane Foundation headquarters in Baraboo, Wisconsin, where the director George Archibald took him to see the old writing shack of Aldo Leopold, and where Leopold's daughter, Nina, who lived nearby, told him it was the plight of sandhill cranes that had made her father into the passionate conservationist that Matthiessen had quoted so approvingly in *Wildlife in America*.

At home, Maria watched her husband's frantic activity with growing concern. He had always taken on more than an average person could handle, but she worried that he was overburdening himself with needless distractions. One morning before dawn, as he slept in the master bedroom, she sat down to write him a letter of gentle caution. "I think you are at a very important place in your life, and I can hear you say immediately, 'What <u>exactly</u> do you mean, explain it to me!' I can't really, it is just a thought that floats, but that I have a strong feeling about, so don't press me to death or it will wisp away."[36] Maria warned him not to lose sight of what was he was trying to achieve:

> You must not get splintered by diverse opportunities that will waft their siren song at you. Documentary deals, unless they <u>really</u> interest you, flattering offers of one sort or another because of your environmental, zen, literary gurism (is there such a word?) that will dilute your strength. You must beware of turning into an *eminence grise*, even though you are perfectly entitled to be one. You are far from ready for it, for your own mental health. There is untold coiled energy in you that must not be dissipated. That includes taking on more needy causes and eroding your time with small, helpful tasks, that in the end don't accomplish much. You have seri-

ous work to do, and in particular, the serious work you have done is of significant importance.

MATTHIESSEN ABANDONED HIS contrapuntal experiment, either of his own volition or at the urging of Candida Donadio, who found the whole thing overwhelming; he retreated to the plan of two separate volumes. By the start of 1995, he'd made major revisions to *Lost Man's River*, while maintaining his confidence that some "splendid winged thing may yet emerge from this crude nymph."[37] In January, he told Howard Norman that the manuscript was in good shape; Norman replied, "As Watson I strongly forecasted, this is a masterwork-in-progress, Peter, and I can't wait (but obviously must!) to read II."[38]

Norman was delighted when Matthiessen asked him to comment on the manuscript; he considered the honor "a once-in-a-lifetime gift of friendship."[39] He read the pages three times over the course of a month, writing in the margins and filling a notebook with questions. He then traveled to Sagaponack to spend two days discussing the novel (*not* a masterwork-in-progress) with Matthiessen, who turned out to be "irritable" at receiving any negative feedback. Norman was caught off-guard. Matthiessen snapped at him, "Maybe it was a bad idea to give this thing to you." Norman's comments were "less *seasoned* than those of others." This was an unprovoked insult—"Yeah, well, I had a great time reading the thing," Norman replied sarcastically—but it only got worse at dinner, where Matthiessen drank too much wine. At one point he turned to Maria and said, "Howard, here, fell quite short in his response to my book. But we're going to talk more about it tomorrow." Norman wrote Maria's biting defense down in his journal: "A month of reading, a notebook full of questions—that's what you consider 'falling short'?" Norman was offended by his host's patronizing hostility after he had put in so much effort, but it was a firsthand glimpse of how touchy Matthiessen had become about his troubled manuscript.

And not without reason. Over at Random House, a few of the senior editors were convinced that *Lost Man's River* was a disaster. Jason Epstein was no longer associated with the project. He "just lost interest"—that is how Matthiessen framed it, selectively, during a public talk at the Lannan Foundation: "He's been heard to say in literary circles in New York, 'Isn't Watson dead *yet*?' And I was amused, too, by that line from one's own editor."[40] When they agreed to part ways, or when Epstein announced that he was washing his hands of it all, Matthiessen told him that one of them was "very, very wrong"[41] about the quality of the pages, just as Joe Fox had once been very wrong about *Far Tortuga*. Then he turned for support to Bill Styron's longtime editor, Bob Loomis—who actually agreed with Epstein. Loomis thought Matthiessen was "kind of an amazing personality," but "difficult," too, and certainly wrong in his "overblown" regard for *Lost Man's River*.[42] In Loomis's reading, the manuscript was all but unpublishable. "It was just too extended, with too much about everything. The novel couldn't sustain itself." Nor could he see any way to fix it, and none of his colleagues were willing to try. "Nobody wanted to edit it."

Reluctantly, Loomis went to Sagaponack to share the bad news in person, which turned into yet another heated discussion that, in Loomis's memory, resulted in years of fraught silence between the two men. "I walked out of there absolutely devastated, and we didn't speak for a long time." (According to Maria, this was a big misunderstanding: "Bob thought Peter was very upset with him. Peter wasn't. He was sad that Bob didn't want to do the book, but he thought it was very gentlemanly of him to come to the house to say so.")[43] Whatever happened with Loomis, Matthiessen then appealed to Daniel Menaker, who had just joined Random after decades on *The New Yorker*'s fiction desk. Menaker also begged off *Lost Man's River*, sending a diplomatic letter that claimed the novel was so ambitious it simply exceeded his grasp as an editor.

That was in April 1995. With three strikes, Matthiessen was now ready to declare himself out of Random House. Harry Evans, the president and publisher (and husband to Tina Brown, Matthiessen's boss at *The New Yorker* these days), was not keen on canceling his contract, however, and asked him to hold on for a few months. In a written response to Menaker's polite evasion, Matthiessen explained that he "agreed—before making any drastic move away from Random—to go ahead with cutting and editing and clarification of the ms., after which, Harry says, he wants to read it, then 'assign it to the right person' in the house. (He might have meant you—watch out!)"[44] So there was still the sliver of a chance he might resolve things with Random, though Matthiessen was surely irked that his novel would need to be *assigned*, like a chore. To Jim Harrison, he wrote that he would "probably offer all 3 Watson books to another house" even after Evans's intervention, adding: "I have to conclude that writers and readers like my outlandish stuff a lot better than do editors and critics, which is as it should be, but their inability even to sense what I am after is still a pain in the ass after working on this thing for 17 years."[45]

In May, for a much needed break, he traveled to England to see the Eurasian crane in its breeding territory of East Anglia, joining a young ornithologist for a slow walk across dunes and meadows and marshland on the Norfolk coast.[46]

When he returned home again to continue work on the draft, he was guided by the judicious advice of Neil Olson. Candida Donadio was still officially Matthiessen's agent, but clients were handled communally at Donadio & Ashworth (in an unusual arrangement for a literary agency), and Olson, an ambitious thirty-year-old who was well on his way to becoming a name partner, had taken the lead on Matthiessen's dealings with Random House—"a slow-motion nightmare," as he would later describe it.[47] Olson and Donadio agreed that what *Lost Man's River* needed was some "serious, even brutal cutting."[48] And if none of the editors at Random House were willing to take on the task, Olson decided to do it himself. While Matthiessen was birdwatching in Europe, he went through the manuscript and typed up a long list of scenes that seemed extraneous, character inconsistencies, and anachronisms—references to big-screen TVs and serial killers, for instance—that existed because Matthiessen had recently shifted the time setting from the 1980s to the early 1960s.

"There is a whole world in this novel, rich in images and wonderful characters which inhabit the mind long after the reading is over," Olson wrote him on June 1. "And I'm pleased to see that beneath the layers of history and dialogue, there is a true trajectory, an arc of story that leads to a dramatic and satisfying climax, not an easy thing to achieve given all the elements you've put in play. Serious work remains, but 90% of it is cutting, from which a beautiful and compelling novel is sure to emerge."[49] This was exactly what Matthiessen wanted to hear: passion, hope, and a pathway forward. Olson earned his respect by taking the initiative; after Candida Donadio died from cancer in 2001, Olson would become his primary agent.

In later years, when Matthiessen spoke about the Watson trilogy, he often referenced an "Art of Fiction" interview Philip Roth had done with *The Paris Review* in 1984. Speaking with the biographer Hermione Lee, Roth mentioned that there was a "magnet" in each of his books, some theme or idea that drew him in, and around which everything in the narrative was then organized.[50] Matthiessen loved this analogy so much that he occasionally riffed on it: the magnet is "the navigational aide that keeps the writer on his course," he said, and losing it means "the book will wander, perhaps fatally."[51] That is what happened with *Lost Man's River*; somewhere in the process of expanding the middle part into a stand-alone novel, he had drifted away from his original intention. Ironically, and quite unintentionally, the final title—taken from the real Lostmans River in the Ten Thousand Islands—was more fitting than most readers would ever know.

Using the pages of advice from Neil Olson, Matthiessen sat down to find his way again. He edited through much of the summer, cutting or moving entire sections and characters. Olson had reminded him what the novel was supposed to be about: "Lucius Watson is near the end of a lifelong search to understand his father."[52] Matthiessen worked to prune away the details that had overgrown this central drama. By late August, he had trimmed the manuscript down to 1,089 pages. Olson pushed him to keep going: "I would ask you to consider how much info the reader can absorb at once, even when it's good."[53]

Matthiessen deleted more material in the fall. He reworked the opening so Lucius "sets off at once like a hunting dog following a scent."[54] By December, he had cut it down to 900 pages. This was still too long, but he declined to perform any more surgery until the editor question was resolved. "I believe that any editor who does not see the true nature of this book in its present form, or does not appreciate it, will not change his/her mind after a polish," he wrote to Olson and Donadio. In Matthiessen's opinion, the novel was just about "there." "I'm more excited about it than ever, for it seems to me a far more interesting book than KILLING MISTER WATSON, and [I] am convinced its readers will agree." They just needed to find someone who shared his vision enough to shepherd it through to publication.

"I DO HOPE you have a wonderful and productive journey, and I will keep the home fires burning, eagerly awaiting your return," Maria wrote on a postcard that showed an embroidered white crane from the Qing dynasty.[55]

Peter set off for another few months of restless travel. First he flew to Russia to revisit the Siberian Tiger Project. It was deep winter now, and "clapping your butt to an outhouse seat at -26 C is not everybody's idea of a grand time," he wrote home.[56] But the visit was a success, with days of tracking through the Sikhote-Alin Reserve and "two brief wonderful looks at a tiger in the snow."

He then flew to Seoul to meet up with George Archibald from the International Crane Foundation. Accompanied by a handful of scientists and birders, they drove to the edge of the Demilitarized Zone between South and North Korea, where red-crowned cranes and white-naped cranes had found an unlikely sanctuary. "To see such creatures in these sullen borderlands, skirting barbed-wire fences and embankments, highway construction and utility poles, in a ruptured landscape torn by loud and unnatural noises, is deeply saddening," Matthiessen later wrote of the experience. "One can only marvel at the endurance of wild animals and their strong instinct toward survival, which offer such hope as we have that these magnificent creations of our land and life can persist long enough for mankind to come to its senses and leave a place for them."[57]

With George Archibald, he continued to Australia, to an outback town 275 miles west of Cairns in northwest Queensland. At the Moor Moor Pastoral Company, a cattle station owned by Aboriginal Kurtijar people, brolgas (*Antigone rubicunda*) soared above a landscape of silent, sunburnt emptiness—precisely the antithesis of Korea.

In Bali, he was met by Alex, who also sent a dispatch home to Maria: "Dad + I having a grand ol' time . . . though in two days we've only left the hotel once! (It's very relaxing w/ pool, tennis court, and lots of croaking frogs)."[58] Saying goodbye to his son, Peter then continued to India on a last-minute detour to see Bengal tigers at Kahna National Park in Madhya Pradesh. For eight sublime days he observed horned gaurs, Indian leopards, the greater racket-tailed drongo—everything except a Bengal tiger, "the quintessential tiger of my imaginings,"[59] which remained frustratingly out of sight.

Finally, he headed to South Africa, driving northeast from Johannesburg to Dullstroom in Mpumalanga province. Not far from the small town, he observed two lovely blue cranes with a chick emerging from "golden grasses in the clear mountain light of the late austral summer,"[60] their long wingtip feathers trailing regally behind them. Of the world's fifteen crane species, *Grus paradisea* was the final one on Matthiessen's list: he had now, as of February 1996, seen them all in the wild. "I take a deep breath, content at last," he wrote of the achievement, "yet knowing already a vague regret that my search for the wild cranes of the world is at an end."

VERY EARLY ONE MORNING, Harry Evans phoned Neil Olson to announce that he'd found their solution to *Lost Man's River*. Deb Futter was a new executive editor at Random House, having just moved across from Doubleday with her assistant, Lee Boudreaux. Evans had asked Futter (or instructed her) to take on the novel as one of her first responsibilities, and Futter, partly out of a sense of obligation as a new employee with nothing else on her slate, had agreed to do so. While Matthiessen was looking for tigers in India, Neil Olson took Futter out to lunch to discuss the beleaguered project. "He liked her very much and thinks she is straight-forward and has clout," Maria reported afterward in a fax sent to Delhi. "Harry is very much in her corner. And she is quite unmoved by previous opinions of [the] book at Random House, and hinted that Jason's role there is somewhat reduced"—indeed, Epstein was no longer editorial director—"and she doesn't feel in the least intimidated by him. She is <u>very</u> enthusiastic about the book and is going to read it again before you get back to be really familiar with it."[61] This was cheering news for Matthiessen, who was excited to finally make some progress with a dedicated editor.

Within three weeks of getting home, however, he was stopped short by a terrible accident. On March 13, one of Luke's young sons was hit by a car near their house in Northport on Long Island. Peter was on his way to an author's appearance in Asheville, North Carolina, and Maria had to track him down (via "another girlfriend, the girl who ran that program for writers," as she later put it)[62] and tell him to turn around. Then she had to convince him to go and see Luke, because Peter was reluctant to confront the situation with his grandson. Christopher had died in the trauma unit at Stony Brook University Medical Center. "We are in shock here," he wrote to William Merwin—"8 yrs old, a dear gentle little boy."[63] At the funeral, Luke, who had heard the sickening collision while walking his guide dog, strained to see his son in the casket; he tucked some allowance money and a lucky blue marble into Christopher's pocket.[64] Peter was a pallbearer for the tiny coffin. It was "a sock in the heart," he told Jim Harrison, one of many friends who wrote or called with condolences . . . "and on we go, right?"[65] This comment in his letter to Harrison, followed by an abrupt turn to other subjects ("How is Key West? I saw the Siberian tiger") reveals the same unease around emotion that his own father once had, an awkward scramble for surer ground, because the alternative is to risk losing control. The following year, Peter would mark the anniversary of Christopher's death in another letter to Merwin: "we'll all be grateful when this date has passed."[66]

His first editorial meeting with Deb Futter came in June. Despite her enthusiastic comments to Olson, she had struggled with the unwieldy manuscript, in which every part seemed connected to so many others that any cut risked unraveling the entire tapestry. Yet she brought, as Matthiessen noticed, "a positive spirit and a lot of energy"[67] to the meeting, and she tried to reassure him with a few nice words about the novel, though these had the opposite effect to what she intended. Her comments were too vague to satisfy him: there was "not one mention of the smallest episode or scene or character or description that might have intrigued or interested or pleased [her]." He yearned for "specificity," he admitted in a frank follow-up note, and thus went into an "awful dip" after their conversation:

> Hearing only guarded abstractions, I am forced to wonder if you are simply turned off by or indifferent to the locale and subject matter, or the length, and might feel stuck with this project—with just another deluded writer who imagines he has written a (potentially) "great" book! I plead guilty to that, and cannot understand why editors are not excited about the potential of what I envision in this trilogy. I'm not complaining, mind, just fretting—I've been battling the tide for a long time, that's all.[68]

For the rest of the year, Futter worked to soothe his anxieties. She traveled out to Sagaponack and sat beside him in the studio, just as Elisabeth

Sifton once had. She offered structural and thematic edits, while Lee Boudreaux ("really the white knight in that whole mess," said Neil Olson)[69] spent countless hours line-editing pages of prose. Gradually, the manuscript shed some of its excessive bulk. Yet it was not enough for Matthiessen, who pushed Futter to do more, more. ("But I don't want to bully you.")[70] She did what she could, then handed a final edit back in January 1997. Matthiessen immediately "scrawled all over the damn thing on every page," he confided, somewhat spitefully, to Howard Norman. "Alas, she will have heart failure, but it's her own fault for giving it such a once-over-lightly and not being tough with it, as I requested."[71] He did the same thing with the galleys in May. He took umbrage, too, with her summary of the novel for the Random House marketing department, "which while effusive and no doubt effective went no deeper than the plot level." What of the grand themes he was tackling, "the old American knot of racism," the destruction of wilderness, the transformation of frontier entrepreneurship into the amoral capitalism of today? Futter was "taken aback" by his nitpicking. She patiently explained that a plot sketch was all the salespeople needed to do their jobs.

He recognized that he was being "exceedingly pompous"[72] with his ceaseless fretting and meddling. But Matthiessen couldn't help but lash out at what he saw, rather unfairly, as a lack of commitment. When his British publisher, Christopher MacLehose, made a lukewarm remark about the novel to Maria, Matthiessen accused him of jeopardizing their decades-long friendship. Then, acknowledging the overreaction, he apologized for his "black spirit and short temper."[73] A black spirit was something he had struggled with—and would continue to struggle with—for much of the Watson publication process: depressive episodes so acute that he'd already overcome an aversion to antidepressants, which he feared would blunt his creativity, and started taking Prozac. Maria noticed that Peter's depression was characterized by paranoia "about people not liking him, *me* not liking him."[74] He would bog down in a mire of sadness, anger, and pessimism, with everything interpreted through a glass darkly. This became especially pronounced around *Lost Man's River*, though the depression had been there since his boyhood days at Hotchkiss.

"This book has had such strange, dark karma that I wonder why I still believe it is the best thing I've done," Matthiessen wrote in another letter to Jim Harrison.[75] He finished his own edits, or had the proofs ripped away from him, during the summer months. And then miraculously it was complete. An excerpt from the novel appeared in *The Paris Review* Fall 1997 issue. Early reviews in *Kirkus*, *Booklist*, and *Publishers Weekly* were highly complimentary: "let that be a lesson to the likes of Jason Epstein," Matthiessen crowed.[76]

(Epstein sent a barbed congratulations saying he'd known there was a wonderful book waiting to be discovered in the manuscript "eventually.")[77]

The rest of the critics were considerably more mixed on *Lost Man's River*. When the novel was published in November, some notices were positive, several were negative, but the vast majority were ambivalent. The praise was often qualified by the same recurring adjectives: *complicated*, *demanding* on the reader. "Although incidental nuggets of information—how to make turpentine or how to gut an alligator—are riveting, the overall effect is of a writer who has lost his sense of selectivity," Michael Mewshaw wrote in *The Washington Post*.[78] A. O. Scott, in a thoughtful critique for *Newsday* that sums up the opinion of many reviewers at the time, deemed it a "large, flawed novel." While its "narrative incoherence" did not seem a fatal defect given the many rewards on offer, there was little suspense, Scott suggested, "in watching the unraveling of a mystery that has already been solved, in essence if not in detail."[79]

This was a fair assessment; *Lost Man's River* was far from the best thing Matthiessen had ever done. Years of rewrites had improved the novel but in no way fixed its underlying issues. Lucius Watson, twenty-one when his father was killed in 1910, now an old man, is an intriguing protagonist: a Hamlet-like figure "hobbled by introspection, guilt, and melancholy,"[80] who lives in self-imposed exile in a houseboat on Caxambas Creek. And the narrative setup is promising as well: Lucius receives an unexpected visit from a Miccosukee man carrying an urn full of ashes, which sets Lucius on a quest to gather facts and testimonies in order to write a whitewashing biography that will rehabilitate his father's name. Lucius is also searching for something "forever lost and far away—an innocence of 'home' that he himself had never known since leaving Chatham Bend decades before."[81] He is searching for a way back to the island, both literal and metaphorical, of untamed childhood.

And yet Lucius's road trip across Florida—a hunt that mirrors, at multiple points, Matthiessen's original research on Edgar Watson, with some of his own interviews and correspondence only thinly fictionalized in *Lost Man's River*—soon goes slack on the page. Reading about a spiritually broken man poking through cemeteries and courthouse records as he's egged on by a loud-mouthed drunkard (a long-lost brother in disguise) and dogged by a slimy Miami lawyer (a possible bastard half-brother), is like wading in circles through the Everglades. Stretches of the novel can feel interminable. Occasionally a patch of high ground appears in the narrative: an incendiary encounter between the brothers and a Black restaurant waiter ("Knock off this minstrel show, okay? Just carve that roast");[82] and a moving climax in which the Chatham house burns with one of them entombed inside. But much of the novel is a labyrinth of plot contrivances, meaningless names—one critic compared it to the book of Deuteronomy—and monologues that are far less convincing than any of those in *Killing Mister Watson*.

Even before the novel came out, Matthiessen groused (as he often did) about "urban Eastern reviewer critics" and their "snotty" opinions.[83] Over time, though, he would come to grudgingly concede the critics had a point about *Lost Man's River*. In 2008, after more than a decade of reflection, he was interviewed by Charles McGrath for *The New York Times*. The novel contained some of his best material, Matthiessen said, but it was also "weak": "It was too long in its time span, too long in every way."[84] For *Vanity Fair*, he had once compared it to a stone flying unsupported through the air, but the full Watson trilogy was really like a dachshund, Matthiessen had come to see. There was the head and the tail ends, both of which had "upright sturdy legs."[85] And then there was the middle section of this metaphorical wiener dog, an elongated belly sagging "woefully" in between.

COMPARED TO THE DRAMA that came before it, the edit of "WATSON III" was a reasonably short and tranquil affair. Most of the novel's elements were present in the early drafts, which were provisionally titled "Dead Reckoning," or "Homegoing," or simply "Hurt." Matthiessen started working on the rewrites as he finalized *Lost Man's River*—"WATSON III" was "already 'finished,'" he informed Deb Futter as early as May 1996, though his use of scare quotes around "finished" hinted at the tinkering still to come.[86] Neil Olson read the manuscript a few months later. "I feel [it] may be the strongest of the three works," he concluded brightly.[87] And Futter, too, found it wonderful when Matthiessen finally shared the pages in the spring of 1998. Her only significant concern was the novel's perspective. All of it was told from Edgar Watson's point of view *except* for the long first chapter, which used an omniscient narrator to document his traumatic upbringing in South Carolina. Futter thought this opening was dry and preachy, and she wished the whole novel was presented in Watson's voice. Neighbors had recounted his legend in *Killing Mister Watson*, and his sons had fought over the details in *Lost Man's River*; surely it was time to let the man tell his autobiography from the very beginning to the gruesome end? Matthiessen was "hellishly struggling"[88] with exhaustion by this point ("I've carried obsession to crazed lengths, I'm afraid—everyone's sick of it, most of all me," he confided to Harrison), but Futter was right about the voice. He reframed the opening of *Bone by Bone*, a final title for the novel borrowed from Emily Dickinson (poem 599; "There is a pain—so utter—").

The creative challenge Matthiessen had to overcome in this final volume—a challenge the previous two had only circled at a distance—was the black hole of Watson's character. How to convincingly evoke Edgar Watson's consciousness? And how to find a thread of humanity strong enough to make a reader stick by this man, even feel a "sneaking sympathy" for him, through terrible acts of violence? Matthiessen rejected the notion of a "natural-born killer." Nor was he interested in portraying what he called the "stunted criminal mentality." "My man was in fact very able and intelligent, by all accounts, which seems to eliminate the low i.q. road killer [theory]," he wrote to Tim Cahill, author of a book on John Wayne Gacy Jr. titled *Buried Dreams* (1986).[89] Instead, Matthiessen chose to dramatize an extreme version of an experience from his own life: a sensitive self becoming confused, estranged, and fractured at a formative moment of its development into an integrated whole. In *Bone by Bone*, to survive the unrelenting cruelty of his father, Edgar Watson imagines "a secret brother I called Jack, whom I confided in and raged and wept with through most of my childhood."[90] Trauma splits him in two—Watson presents "Jack" to the reader as an almost separate character—and much of the novel is preoccupied with the struggle between these competing aspects of his divided self. Jack is to Edgar as Mr. Hyde is to Dr. Jekyll. Whenever Watson does something ghastly, it is the spectral Jack, not Edgar—not "I"—who is saddled with the blame.

As the novel progresses, Edgar increasingly overlaps with Jack, the division between the two selves dissolving until even the narrator must admit that there is no real difference between them. At that point, Edgar Jack Watson comes up with a new justification for his escalating lawlessness. "On the Everglades frontier as the new century came in," he coldly explains, "rough methods were sometimes necessary in the name of progress. Any man standing in the way of progress in America was going to be knocked flat, and some were not so likely to get up."[91] History suggested it was permissible for the "great capitalists" like Jay Gould to expend a few lives in the name of profitable nation-building, so why not E. J. Watson, who is determined to transform the Florida wilderness into productive land? His schizophrenic character—scheming, racist, greedy, destructive, creative, brilliant—finally becomes a reflection of the national character, the American self.

Watson does horrendous things in *Bone by Bone*, but he never sheds his sensitivity. He sounds frightened when describing the murderous rage that sometimes overtakes him: a "taste of iron" seeps into his mouth, and he becomes like the coyote he once saw caught in an Arkansas tornado, "a pale dog spinning skyward, turning white against black clouds, then black against white, then lost into that apocalyptic funnel."[92] He tries to protect his family from the consequences of his mistakes, but when he fails to do so, he is remorseful about the "grievous sins" that have damned him, he knows, "beyond redemption."[93]

These embellishments by Matthiessen create a figure who is more sympathetic than he probably has any right to be, given the historical facts of the case. Yet it is the voice that makes him such engaging company for 410 pages. Matthiessen had invented many different voices before he wrote *Bone by Bone*; none, however, displayed the range of his Watson, who is both charming and dreadful, like Lucifer in *Paradise Lost*. The bravura performance is sustained right up until the moment Watson accepts his fate ("'Finish it,' I whispered, very tired now, and very calm"[94]) and is gunned down by the posse of his neighbors on hurricane-ravaged Chokoloskee. As his body is filled with lead, his speech breaks into sentence fragments on the page, scattered text that recalls the laconic poetry of *Far Tortuga*.

"I understand Watson (and myself) much better after all these years of frequenting his brain," Matthiessen once said in an interview—"and to some degree I find I can forgive him. He is a violent drunk and occasional killer, true, but he is also intelligent and persevering, with very sharp insights into human behavior, and he has dignity and courage, too, and can be very funny, at least by the lights of my own warped sense of humor. In the end, despite myself, I came to like him. But I think my task was to make the reader feel the humanity of a 'bad' man and even perhaps a twinge of regret at the waste of such ability when he is killed."[95]

BONE BY BONE WAS PUBLISHED in April 1999, just fifteen months after *Lost Man's River*, and the overall reception was far more positive. Not only were the critics kinder this time around, with only a few swipes about length and "artistic redundancy,"[96] but Matthiessen was also met with a flood of adulation from other writers. Howard Norman, John Irving, and Jim Harrison sent letters to Sagaponack, as did Joseph Heller, John Burnham Schwartz, and Annie Dillard, who declared the full Watson trilogy "a masterpiece of world literature."[97] Don DeLillo wrote the equivalent of a respectful nod between gentlemen, and Saul Bellow praised Matthiessen's use of language, his tactile descriptions of the pioneering life, by comparing him favorably to Robert Frost and Walt Whitman.[98]

Matthiessen replied to Bellow with giddy appreciation: "I don't have to tell you how much such support means from a reader whose own work one so much admires."[99] And yet, he was ultimately dissatisfied with the launch of *Bone by Bone*. Matthiessen felt Random House had committed insufficient resources to promoting his novel. "What more does Random need to have the courage of their own book and give it hell?" he wrote to Neil Olson. "It is not just any old offhand novel but a work twenty years in the making, a work that Random should be proud of."[100] A full-page advertisement had been run at considerable expense in the Sunday *New York Times*, but Matthiessen was sure the publicity team was holding out on him. "Forced," in his words, to become "a hateful old nag"[101] about the book, particularly because Deb Futter had suddenly returned to Doubleday just before publication ("she notified me, a bit too cutesomely, on the very day she cleaned out her office"), he waved the letters from DeLillo and Bellow at his publisher. To Matthiessen's astonishment, Random House paid for another ad in the *Times*—a "modest" one, he couldn't help but gripe to DeLillo.[102]

But perhaps the most important cause of his dissatisfaction was not Random House, or even the media's failure to fully recognize his efforts (*Newsweek*, *Harper's Magazine*, *The New York Review of Books*, and *The New Yorker* did not even run reviews); perhaps it was the work itself. The *works*, that is: the existence of three separate novels. Now the Watson trilogy was out in the world, Matthiessen began to speak more candidly about his compromised vision, the single novel that had been mutilated in a regrettable editorial misjudgment.

While out doing promotion duties for *Bone by Bone*, he floated the idea of restoring the trilogy to its original symphonic form. "I don't mind wasting the time," he told a reporter from *The Washington Post*. "I'd like it all of a piece."[103] In an interview for *The Boston Globe*, another journalist took this as a "dark joke," because it seemed preposterous to turn around and remake something that had just been completed. Still, Matthiessen kept talking: "It would be kind of a hobby, maybe leading to it being rediscovered 40 years later. Like 'Moby-Dick' was."[104]

His comments made the idea sound hypothetical. There was another interview, however, that also appeared that spring: "The Art of Fiction No. 157." For the first time since 1974, Matthiessen had sat down to reflect on his career and writing habits for *The Paris Review*. The actual interview was conducted over numerous sessions by his friend Howard Norman (who had recovered from their disagreement over *Lost Man's River*, and who now watched in horror as his painstakingly composited transcript was savagely mauled by the red pen of George Plimpton). At the very end of the published text in the *Review*, Matthiessen addressed the idea of "one work" about Edgar Watson:

> That's the way it was originally conceived and that will be its final form. As one novel, it will be considerably shorter and tighter, since much of the scaffolding required for setting up the three separate books will be dis-

mantled. Not that I can assume it will ever be published in its proper form. It's just that I need to reassemble it before putting it away, if only to know that it exists somewhere in its true nature.[105]

"Will be," and "I need"—there was nothing hypothetical here. He guessed it would take about a year to finish, eighteen months at most.

JUST AS MATTHIESSEN BEGAN to contemplate the gut renovation of his Watson trilogy, he received word from Teresa Heinz, widow of Senator John Heinz and chairwoman of the Heinz Family Foundation, that he was being awarded the Heinz Award in recognition of his literary achievements. This unexpected prize—"I am truly honored,"[106] he said in an acceptance speech on March 7, 2000—came with $250,000, which was enough to spare him "the necessity of so much travel, giving readings and talks all around the country, for that is the fate, and the real livelihood, of many writers such as myself whose acquaintance with the best-seller list is small and fleeting." At the ceremony in Washington, D.C., he told an audience how he would spend his unexpected bounty: some new clothes ("you're looking at my last remaining suit"), a new roof for the house (Maria's request), and the rest shared with his children, the Zen sangha, the Siberian Tiger Project, and the International Crane Foundation. "Perhaps most importantly in this election year, this award will help a twenty-year campaign to win justice for an imprisoned American Indian friend named Leonard Peltier," Matthiessen added. He invited everybody in the audience to inform themselves about "this painful case."

Leonard Peltier had been in prison for twenty-three years. Matthiessen had hoped that reissuing *In the Spirit of Crazy Horse* would help end his friend's incarceration, a hope that had been strengthened by the election of a Democrat as president shortly thereafter. In June 1993, the White House counsel Lloyd Cutler had "smuggled"[107] Matthiessen into the Oval Office, where the writer pressed a copy of his "flame-colored tome" into Bill Clinton's "big, white, friendly hands."[108] When nothing came of that encounter, he had then raised Peltier with Attorney General Janet Reno at a White House dinner in 1995. He had also appealed to her for a private meeting about the case in 1997. ("I hope you will take my word that this meeting, should you permit it, will be strictly off the record—I shall not tell anyone I am writing this letter.")[109] But the Clinton administration continued to shuffle its feet on Peltier's petition for executive clemency, and the delay had now, in 2000, reached a critical juncture. An election win by George W. Bush, "deep in debt to so many rich conservative Republicans,"[110] as Matthiessen put it, would be devastating for Peltier's chances at release: "Leonard Peltier may as well roll over on his cell cot and face the wall." Nor did Matthiessen have much faith that Al Gore would do the right thing if he won the race, lest it threaten his chances of reelection.

As the Bush and Gore campaigns hit the home stretch, Matthiessen became aware of an anti-Peltier propaganda campaign being quietly waged by the FBI at the Clinton administration. (Documents released through the Freedom of Information Act confirm that the FBI director and deputy director, Louis Freeh and Robert Bryant, were pressuring Reno to ignore Leonard Peltier.) Matthiessen responded to the revelation by throwing everything he could think of at the problem. As public rallies were held in New York and Washington in support of Peltier, he released a press statement declaring that "further persecution of this aging and ailing leader of his people can only demean our great nation."[111] In June, as members of Peltier's parole board prepared to convene, he sent a letter challenging their expectation that Peltier would express remorse for his supposed crime, which would be akin to an admission of guilt. The letter was co-signed by Bill and Rose Styron, Kurt Vonnegut, and E. L. Doctorow, all of whom then co-signed another letter for a July issue of *The New York Review of Books:* "to withhold parole because the prisoner won't admit to a crime that he denies committing is another unlawful violation of due process."[112]

After the election was over, and just days after the Supreme Court handed down its era-defining decision in *Bush v. Gore*, Matthiessen sent a final plea to Janet Reno. "[I]f you could spare me a few minutes," he wrote with desperation, "I would be happy to come to Washington and explain why I think this case is so important to our country and to the President's 'legacy'; as Judge [Gerald] Heaney said, it is time to begin the healing process between our federal government and the first Americans."[113]

Janet Reno could spare no minutes, although Matthiessen found himself in Washington anyway during Clinton's final week in office. In a lucky break, Peltier's attorney Bruce Ellison had a mutual friend with Bill and Hillary—a friend who happened to be interested in Peltier's case. An executive at DreamWorks Animation, this friend had previously helped Peltier get some medical attention in prison, and he now secured a last-minute meeting for his supporters at the White House. On January 8, 2001, as former FBI agents protested at the fence outside, Ellison, Matthiessen, and the film producer Jon Kilik met with White House counsel for several hours in the West Wing. The atmosphere was warm and receptive; Clinton's men seemed to be sympathetic to their arguments. "We had a wonderful meeting," Ellison later recalled.[114]

"We went out of there on a cloud," Matthiessen said.[115]

The next day, trying to seal the deal, he penned a follow-up note to President Clinton, who had not been present at the discussion:

> Mr. President, we understand and appreciate the very difficult political position in which you have been placed by the high emotions and outrage that inevitably surrounds the senseless destruction of human lives . . . but that tragedy cannot excuse an unethical prosecution and conviction and an endlessly vindictive attitude toward an unlucky scapegoat who has already served a quarter century of his life in federal prison. Under the circumstances, a thoughtful and principled grant of clemency seems to me the only just and honorable decision.[116]

On the morning of Inauguration Day, the White House released a long list of Clinton's final pardons and commutations. The list included Marc Rich, the fugitive financier indicted for federal tax evasion, whose wife had made sizable donations to Clinton's presidential library and to the Democratic National Committee campaign coffers. The list did not include Leonard Peltier. Matthiessen was appalled. Then he was furious. "Instead of all the hours and days and years, all the money spent, all the pro bono work from lawyers and artists and writers and movie people and everybody else, if we'd just stayed home and made our living and shipped in all our money [to the DNC], he'd have been out."[117]

Later that afternoon, the phone rang in Sagaponack. The call was coming from USP Leavenworth in Kansas. "They didn't give it to me," the prisoner mumbled in a dazed voice that Matthiessen barely recognized. It was, he later wrote, "the first time in twenty years of visits, letters, and telephone conversations that Leonard Peltier's strong spirit sounded broken."[118]*

MATTHIESSEN HAD BEEN working on "Tiger and Crane" since the early days of *Lost Man's River*. Several magazine pieces about his research travels had appeared in *Audubon*, *Harper's Magazine*, *Outside*, and *The New Yorker*, but no book appeared until early 2000, when North Point Press, an imprint

---

* On January 20, 2025, after nearly five decades in prison—after developing diabetes, and going partially blind, and suffering an aortic aneurysm and a stroke—Peltier was finally granted executive clemency by President Joe Biden. The extraordinary commutation of his life sentence was a response to appeals by tribal leaders, Democratic lawmakers, Nobel Peace laureates, human rights organizations, former law enforcement officials, and private citizens including Rose Styron and Alex Matthiessen, Peter's son. A White House statement noted that the commutation "will enable Mr. Peltier to spend his remaining days in home confinement but will not pardon him for his underlying crimes." "It's finally over," Peltier announced in his own statement—"I'm going home."

of Farrar, Straus & Giroux, published *Tigers in the Snow*. A separate volume, *The Birds of Heaven: Travels with Cranes*, appeared the following year; Matthiessen had divided his original idea into two complementary parts. In 2003, he would also publish another book of nonfiction, *End of the Earth*, which documented expeditions to Antarctica made as a field leader with his ornithologist friend Victor Emanuel and some of Emanuel's safari clients. The first of these voyages, from Ushuaia, Argentina, to South Georgia and then to islands down the northern arm of West Antarctica, had been a welcome break during the editing of *Bone by Bone*. The second voyage, coming at the end of 2001, offered an escape from Matthiessen's work on the trilogy overhaul, still barely begun at that point, as well as a respite from the strange new reality that had just been forged by the terrorist attacks in September of that year.*

This second voyage was on a leased polar icebreaker called the *Kapitan Khlebnikov*. The ship departed from Tasmania—not at all the "gloomy waste" he'd expected of "dark dripping trees from which most life has been extirpated, the traditional people included"[119]—and smashed its way south into the Ross Sea. The expedition's official goal was to observe a breeding colony of emperor penguins at Cape Washington, near the edge of the Ross Ice Shelf. But Matthiessen had a more personal motive, too. While it was difficult, he'd admit in *End of the Earth*, to explain precisely what his motive was, the polar explorer Apsley Cherry-Garrard had come close when he once wrote: "Why do men who have returned [from the Antarctic] always wish to go back to that hard and simple life? . . . I believe it to be this. . . . A man on such an expedition lives so close to nature, in whom he realizes a giant force which is visibly, before his eyes, carving out the world."[120] For Matthiessen, a voyage to reach emperor penguins in an inviolable wilderness of white and blue was yet another leg in his pilgrimage to "simplify my self,"[121] to "see and feel life clearly,"[122] and thus to glimpse something fundamental

---

* "I was flying over Pennsylvania when the attacks happened," Matthiessen recalled of September 11, 2001. "Traverse City was the nearest airport they could find with an open spot to land. The second building had just been hit when I landed in the airport. I remember people were yelling at the TVs—it was unreal. My God. So I was grounded there for six days. I mean, you couldn't get a horse out of town." When he did finally make it to Livingston, Montana, where he was expected to officiate at the marriage of Doug and Andrea Peacock, Matthiessen found himself having shell-shocked conversations with the other wedding guests, including Terry Tempest Williams. "My impulse is I want to take off my robes," he told her, meaning his Zen robes, "because I want to fight." But he knew that fighting was not the solution here. In some notes for a Dharma talk about the 9/11 attacks and the Bush administration's subsequent "war on terror," Matthiessen denounced the "old vicious cycle" of vengeful violence: "It appears to me that the richest and most powerful nation in history is the only one that can break that cycle; that it is morally and philosophically obliged to break that cycle, and that history will judge its leadership very harshly for yet another failure to do so."

about creation that can only be hinted at with the kind of language ("We had seen God in his splendour," said Ernest Shackleton) that "us poor moderns" instinctually shy away from.¹²³

Tigers, cranes, and a "longing for the Ice": these were the last nonfiction books Matthiessen would complete in his life. All three exhibit the qualities he had polished over decades as a writer preoccupied with the natural world: crystalline descriptions of animals and landscapes that combine hard facts with a light-footed lyricism; precise discussions of ecology and other sciences, segueing effortlessly into bold meditations on myth and belief; and serious attention paid to Native people and their wisdom.

At the same time, these final books are suffused with revulsion at "the American monoculture that spreads like a plastic sheet across the world, stifling the last indigenous whiffs and quirks and colors."¹²⁴ Matthiessen rails against overpopulation, biodiversity loss, poaching, the wildlife trade, industrial pollution, pesticides, deforestation, topsoil erosion, warfare, and the imprudent drainage of wetlands in countries rushing to imitate a Western conception of "progress." He is concerned about everything from power lines, which kill red-crowned cranes, to global climate change and the widespread refusal to confront its apocalyptic threat—a subject he also once discussed with Jim Harrison in a sarcastic letter:

> Never mind about that drought in Patagonia [Harrison's home in Arizona]. Don't mean a single thing, son. What's a few wildflowers? . . . Our state-of-the-art environmental authorities at Exxon have now advised us that global warming has never been proven mathematically, there is just no darn hard evidence for this so-called "global warming," which is some kind of a Jew-leftie plot back in the first place, right?¹²⁵

As long ago as *Wildlife in America*, Matthiessen had chafed against the label of "naturalist-writer." Four decades on, having observed so much senseless destruction and loss, he was now almost bitter in his skepticism of the genre. "It's too late for nature writing," he insisted. "You have to be an activist-ranter now, and a pain in the butt."¹²⁶

He was willing to be both in his books—and in the public lectures, too, that he was increasingly invited to give about his experiences. At a conference for the Orion Society, for example, he was preceded onstage by an executive from ARCO, the independent oil and mining company, who delivered a greenwashing address about how it was possible to drill diagonally to preserve wildlife habitat. Matthiessen listened politely, then stood up and altered his prepared remarks to dismiss the executive's words as specious bullshit. "There was this gasp," recalled Terry Tempest Williams, who was sitting in the audience and thrilled by his audacity. "Thank god someone told the truth."[127]

At another conference on sustainability at the Omega Institute in upstate New York, Matthiessen struck the artist Suzi Gablik as "a godly force of crabbiness."[128] He threw pages from his speech onto the floor, spouted denunciation after denunciation, and refused to stop speaking in time for lunch. "We have a great country and it pisses me off to see how we debase ourselves," he told the famished crowd. "It pisses me off to see how apathetic and spoiled we are."[129] What people needed—and he had been saying as much since his work with Stewart Udall and Cesar Chavez—was "spiritual rebirth." By this he did not mean a resurgence of organized religion so much as an ethical adjustment, a reorientation of consciousness toward what some traditional people called Land and Life. As Matthiessen argued in yet another forceful lecture, this one given at the Royal Albert Hall in London, "Our consumer culture, with its near-total loss of spiritual values, no longer takes responsibility for its activities, far less the wilderness, the air and oceans, or even the welfare of mankind."[130] This would need to change if humanity was to turn things around in time to avert climate catastrophe.

Such confrontational rhetoric could alienate some listeners, and Matthiessen's speeches had a tendency to become tirades. ("And now we want clones! Is that insane or what?")[131] But others found his words bracing, like buckets of ice water thrown from the podium to wake people up.

AT TWO DIFFERENT TALKS Matthiessen gave in 2001, in New York and Washington, D.C.—the latter a book launch for *Birds of Heaven* at the Smithsonian National Museum of Natural History—he was approached by a young Kolkata-born photographer named Subhankar Banerjee. Formerly a Boeing computer consultant, now a full-time conservationist, Banerjee was working on a project about the Arctic National Wildlife Refuge in Alaska, which was threatened by a new National Energy Policy that proposed opening 1.5 million acres to oil and gas exploration. Banerjee hoped Matthiessen might blurb a book of photographs he was assembling in defense of the Arctic Refuge, but Matthiessen had other ideas. He'd been interested in the area since he visited Alaska's North Slope for *Wildlife in America*, in 1957, three years before ANWR was even established by President Eisenhower. He had been following the drilling debate since the late 1980s, when he penned a foreword to *Tracking Arctic Oil: The Environmental Price of Drilling the Arctic National Wildlife Refuge*, a study published by the Natural Resources Defense Council. "The danger posed by destructive and inefficient drilling in the Arctic with irremediable loss to wilderness and wildlife is not an Alaska problem," Matthiessen had written. "It is a national problem, a world problem."[132] Now he told Banerjee that unfortunately he no longer did blurbs. Banerjee got the hint: "I said, 'Well, it sounds like you actually want to come to the Arctic.' And he said, 'If that's a possibility, I might consider it.'"[133]

On July 12, 2002, Peter flew to Fairbanks with his son Alex, and then northward to join a dozen other people on an expedition financed by Tom Campion, a self-made businessman and environmental activist from Everett, Washington. For ten days the group followed the Kongakut River on inflatable rafts, wading north from the Brooks Range toward the Arctic coast. Banerjee was traveling independently with a Gwich'in tracker, and he joined the camp for morning coffee before heading out to take photographs. The Matthiessens went birdwatching (sandhill cranes), fished for Arctic char, and admired grizzly bears in "one of the last pristine regions left on earth . . . indifferent to mankind, utterly silent."[134] After the river trip, they flew to the coastal village of Kaktovik, where Peter interviewed Iñupiat people about the impact of the oil industry. He saw some of the impact himself while looking out the Cessna window on a refueling flight to Prudhoe Bay: "Beyond the first wells, roads and land scars gouged by tracked vehicles begin accumulating; more drilling pads loom dimly through the fog, which mercifully shrouds the huge industrial site, one of the largest in the world."

Below the Brooks Range, the Matthiessens stopped in Arctic Village, a small Gwich'in settlement of spruce-log cabins. Peter was "[a]nxious to listen to the Indian point of view," to speak with elders of a village that had rejected the 1971 Alaska Native Claims Settlement Act because it would have required them to condone the construction of a pipeline. The people of Arctic Village, he later wrote admiringly, "held out for their original tribal land claim of 1.8 million acres, in the full knowledge that this brave commitment to the integrity of their ancestral lands and their traditional ways would condemn them to a life of bare subsistence." The elders, for their part, were just as anxious to speak with Peter Matthiessen. Arctic Village was home to Sarah James, a Neets'aii Gwich'in Athabascan activist who had just won the Goldman Environmental Prize for her advocacy in support of ANWR. James had a library in her tiny cabin, and one of the books was *In the Spirit of Crazy Horse*. Seemingly everyone in the village had borrowed it in preparation for the writer's visit. "It was a red-carpet treatment," recalled Banerjee. "I'd never seen anything like that. The respect that Peter had developed within the Indigenous communities was mind-blowing."[135]

After he returned home from Alaska, Matthiessen went on the offensive. He wrote a blistering article for *Outside* magazine. ("Can we really be so cowed by all the scare talk and false patriotism that we stand by watching our environment despoiled, our civil liberties eroded and our savings stolen, our children's future compromised by arrogant narrow men of totalitarian inclination and stunted vision?")[136] He hijacked his own acceptance speech for the Roger Tory Peterson Medal—"in recognition of his extraordinary contributions to naturalist literature, his unflagging commitment to environmental activism, and his advocacy on behalf of endangered wildlife and vanishing landscapes"[137]—to offer a lament about the Arctic Refuge. He lectured a journalist from the *Tampa Bay Times*, who was gamely trying to interview him, with "unexpected vehemence."[138] "It is a disgrace," he told her. "There are wonderful American Indian people up there and their culture will be wiped out. It's our last great wilderness, the last great stronghold for large Ice Age mammals . . . and these bastards want to trash it—for six months worth of oil at the most." The "bastards" included President George W. Bush, Vice President Dick Cheney, and virtually the entire Republican establishment.

Subhankar Banerjee published his book, *Arctic National Wildlife Refuge: Seasons of Land and Life*, in early 2003. Jimmy Carter wrote a foreword, and Matthiessen contributed a chapter focused on the Indigenous perspective. But then something remarkable happened. In March, during a Senate vote on drilling in the ANWR, California Democrat Barbara Boxer stood up and showed her colleagues one of Banerjee's photographs from the book—a polar bear stalking across sunlit ice—to prove the Arctic Refuge was not the "flat, white nothingness" oil and gas supporters liked to describe.[139] The stunt served its purpose: the Senate narrowly rejected the proposal to drill. Alaska Republican Ted Stevens was left fuming at Banerjee and what he later termed his "propaganda book."[140] Meanwhile, the Museum of Natural History, just down the National Mall, was preparing to open a temporary exhibition of Banerjee's images in its Beaux-Arts rotunda. In the aftermath of the Senate vote, museum staff suddenly relocated the exhibit into a basement gallery ("behind the cafeteria or the men's room or some place like that," Matthiessen noted wryly on *Charlie Rose*)[141] and censored many of the captions. A Smithsonian spokesman denied interference from Ted Stevens or the White House: "There was no pressure whatsoever."[142] Banerjee was skeptical. As a resident alien in a country that had recently adopted the Patriot Act, he was also "very scared."[143] His publisher, Helen Cherullo of Mountaineers Books, phoned Matthiessen for emergency advice. How could they protect Subhankar from further political retaliation? Matthiessen replied, according to Banerjee, "We have to make him famous overnight."

The writer made a few calls—"raised a fuss," as *The New York Times* soon put it in a news piece.[144] This prompted Senator Dick Durbin, Democrat of Illinois, to announce a plan to question Smithsonian management in a public hearing. "I want the world to see the caption of the little bird that the Smithsonian says is too controversial for the public," Durbin told the *Times*. "There was political pressure brought on this exhibition. And it's a sad day when the Smithsonian, the keeper of our national treasures, is so fearful."

Banerjee was amazed to find himself suddenly inundated with interview requests. "I was more famous than George W. Bush for a moment. There were like five pieces in *The Washington Post*, five pieces in the *Los Angeles Times*, editorials and op-eds in *The New York Times* . . . and the reason for that was Peter Matthiessen."[145] The exhibition was restaged, uncensored, by the California Academy of Sciences, which also sponsored a two-year national tour.

WHEN MATTHIESSEN FIRST began to talk about reassembling his Florida epic, just about everybody around him balked at the prospect. Neil Olson advised him to write something new; his "publisher," Matthiessen said, presumably referring to Harry Evans, went "white as this tablecloth" at the thought of going through it all over again.[146] So did Maria, who had already spent the better part of two decades living with Edgar Watson. Even Jim Harrison felt compelled to express reservations in a letter to his friend: "Why write the whole thing, then discard a goodly amount? . . . I am puzzled by your motive. . . . Aren't you immortal enough?"[147]

If Matthiessen had become immortal at all as a writer, it was, by his own estimation, for not quite the right reasons. His reputation rested mostly on his nonfiction books—*The Snow Leopard, The Tree Where Man Was Born, Wildlife in America, In the Spirit of Crazy Horse*. He resented this fact. "I feel, rightly or wrongly," he once said on a panel at the Key West Literary Seminar, "that my fiction will be seen eventually as my most significant work."[148]

The three Watson novels had been Matthiessen's big swing at literary greatness: a sprawling commentary on the nation's entrenched mythologies. "He recognized," said Amor Towles, who had read and offered feedback on the "problematic" *Lost Man's River* in early draft, "that if he was going to have a book on the fiction side that really held its place in the American canon, then it was probably going to be the Watson trilogy."[149] During the edit process for the second and third volumes, Matthiessen had spent hours talking with Deb Futter about how desperate he was to be taken seriously as a novelist. And when Random House had been slow to promote *Bone by Bone*, he had sent a handwringing note to Neil Olson: "I dearly hope it won't be allowed to just slip between the cracks, taking my hope of recognition as a fiction writer along with it."[150]

He decided to recombine the three novels—A New Rendering of the Watson Legend, as it would be officially described—to fulfill his original vision of a novel that drew together "in one work the themes that have absorbed me all my life,"[151] everything from the destruction of the wilderness and wildlife to the injustices inflicted on Native American people. But he also wanted another chance to make readers finally *see* Peter Matthiessen the way he'd come to see himself: as an artist who deserved to be named alongside the best of them. This was the motive that sustained him through year after year of fanatical labor on his magnum opus. "I will never let it go," he'd told Howard Norman for *The Paris Review*. "How could I?" The work was "a manifestation of my being."[152]

IT WAS SCOTT MOYERS, another senior editor at Random House, who first suggested the Modern Library as publisher for a consolidated Watson. Founded in 1917 to offer literary classics in attractive, inexpensive editions, the imprint was not exactly at the cutting edge of culture these days—not known for peddling the hottest new bestsellers—but it was respectable, a known repository for excellence overseen with care by the novelist David Ebershoff. After consulting with Moyers (who had stepped in to fill the editorial void left by Deb Futter, before moving on himself), Matthiessen became convinced it was an ideal home for his book. The Modern Library was willing to embark on a "suicidal quest" to publish his "forlorn project" in its final form, as he explained at a public talk in 2002; he was determined to seize the opportunity and "hasten forward" before anyone could get cold feet.[153]

Nevertheless, it was not until 2004 that he made any meaningful headway. Early that year, he wrote a seven-page master outline that listed characters to cut and repetitive material to cannibalize.[154] But almost immediately, he was faced with a familiar problem: *Lost Man's River*.

He sought some advice from his agent. How should he handle the weak link of his trilogy? Should he try to merge *Lost Man's River* and *Killing Mister Watson*, much as he had once attempted to combine the second and third volumes? The prospect was daunting, so Neil Olson volunteered to make the first attempt. Olson re-read the novels, spent weeks cutting them up and stitching them together, and then sent a letter with his verdict: "I do think this adds something fresh to the greater work and makes it a more cohesive whole, but I can't be certain that it's worth the great structural violence it will do."[155] Matthiessen was impressed by the prodigious effort of his agent. "He called me up in grand joy," Olson later recalled, "and said, 'This is extraordinary. I can't believe you did this. This is exactly what somebody needed to do. And now that you've done it, I see that it doesn't work.'"[156]

Matthiessen next turned to a young editor named Webster Younce, who proposed an even more radical reconfiguration of the books. What if they just deleted *Lost Man's River*? Younce suggested a Modern Library version of "Watson" that would consist of *Killing Mister Watson* and *Bone by Bone*—the sturdy head and tail sections without the sagging belly. This was a more severe cut than Matthiessen was willing to make, and he appears to have dismissed it out of hand.

In summer, he began working with Judy Sternlight at the Modern Library. While still relatively new as an editor—she had started at Random House in 2000 as a member of the sales department before becoming an editorial assistant and ascending the ladder—Sternlight quickly proved herself as a discerning reader, unintimidated by the magnitude of Matthiessen's ambition. She thought the trilogy was already a stunning accomplishment, so they had to be careful, she told him, not to inadvertently degrade it. She offered three theoretical approaches to *Lost Man's River*. Matthiessen could condense the middle book, streamlining an overcomplicated plot. He could rewrite the story from scratch, crafting an alternate narrative that focused on Edgar Watson rather than drifting away, as it currently did, into the tangential troubles of his heirs. Or he could transform *Lost Man's River* into a short bridge between the first and third books—keep a hundred pages, say, on the hit list Lucius Watson compiles of his father's killers, while jettisoning everything else. This third option was Sternlight's preference and recommendation; she encouraged Matthiessen to adopt it. He was happy to adopt *her* as his new editor—she was "exceptionally intelligent and insightful"[157]—yet he rarely took the easy path, and would instead pursue a hybrid of all three approaches: condensing, rewriting, bridging.

He passed the rest of 2004 deconstructing and rebuilding a version of what was now being called "Book II." Many of the most consequential changes were made at this point: the time frame was shifted (again) from the 1960s to the late 1920s; and whole stretches of Lucius Watson's road trip to North Florida were eliminated. The challenge, Matthiessen told a journalist in November, was to remove pieces that "unto themselves are lovely, but don't necessarily help tell us who E. J. Watson was."[158] In other words, the challenge was to kill his darlings. He kept at it through the new year, then submitted a revision to Sternlight in April 2005, after seven months of bloodletting in his studio. Sternlight rejected the draft. The trimming was welcome, she wrote in an apologetic response, but the story had spun even further out of focus. Neil Olson was horrified: "She went back to Peter and said, 'It's not good enough. It's not there yet.' I could have killed her."[159] But Matthiessen was energized by her response, which pushed him to do better. "Peter loved her for saying it because that's what he always felt about his work. Nothing was ever good enough."

By July, he had removed almost the entire second half of Book II, which, he belatedly acknowledged, "was perhaps self-indulgently too long."[160] He had also made substantial alterations to the first book, and more subtle tweaks throughout the third. "For reasons I won't bore you with," he wrote to Christine Jordis at Éditions Gallimard in Paris, trying to butter her up for a French translation, "the process of handling so much text, so many files, evolving across so many years—nearly thirty, in fact—and effectively rewriting it almost sentence by sentence out of obsession, has been so exhausting that I'm thinking of entitling it 'Killed By Mister Watson.' But miraculously I am still exhilarated and excited by the process, since the book is always deepening and because I believe the whole is so improved, with its thread of tragedy much stronger, more inevitable."

OF COURSE, there were other things he continued to do while "deepening" the manuscript: swimming, tennis, and bike rides to keep himself fit; zazen in the Ocean Zendo. He made several trips to Wyoming and Montana to go fishing with friends on rivers like the Bighorn. He traveled to the Cascade Range in Washington with Jeff Meldrum, a professor of anthropology at Idaho State University, and the ethnobotanist John Mionczynski, on yet another futile search for evidence of bigfoot. He also kept up his passionate defense of the Arctic National Wildlife Refuge. In June 2006, he accompanied Thomas Campion and Subhankar Banerjee to the National Petroleum Reserve, west of the refuge, to observe a migration of Western Arctic caribou; this trip provided material for a grave report in *The New York Review of Books* about what had become "the longest and most acrimonious environmental fight in American history."[161] Somehow, Matthiessen managed to maintain a pace so frenetic that the IRS finally audited him, suspicious that a man pushing eighty should claim such a high deduction for travel expenses on his Schedule C.

Every other moment was sacrificed on the altar of Watson. "This is my first letter in months," he wrote to a carefully anonymized lover ("dearest mistress") sometime in early 2007. "I am writing all day, often right through the evening, on this bloody machine until quite literally I can see no more through these blurred eyes. . . . I have no energy or imagination left."[162]

He had estimated it would take him twelve to eighteen months to "distill" the trilogy. In reality, it took nearly three years of work with Judy Sternlight—seven after the publication of *Bone by Bone*—before he reached a stage where he felt "confident" the draft might become something publishable.[163] Even then, he was getting a little ahead of himself. Further revisions consumed most of 2007. "I feel something—some plot element—has to go," he wrote after meeting with his editor in July, "but I seem to have lost my 'magnet' here."[164] This flailing admission came after the Modern Library had already produced a copyedited manuscript, which was supposed to be near the final text; Matthiessen defaced it with edits. He then assured Sternlight that his reputation for "brutalizing" galleys was "much exaggerated," only to cover every page of those with comments as well.[165] (The reputation was deserved.) He would rewrite the book's jacket copy supplied by the publisher—"It does seem a pity that no one in your office knew 'Watson' well enough . . . to take care of this properly"[166]—and critique the cover design down to the font size and title placement.

Sternlight handled his pedantic requests with unfailing grace, and he applauded her "honesty" and invaluable contributions. "At the same time," he added, somewhat undercutting the gratitude, "I sense that like all editors you are over-loaded with titles and probably over-worked and always rushed."[167] (Judy Sternlight declined to be interviewed for this biography. Collaborating with Matthiessen was "an intensely interesting and enlightening journey," she wrote in an email: "But somehow, as his editor, I prefer to keep my interactions with Peter private, even after his death.")[168]

By the time the Modern Library "Watson" was definitively finished, at the end of 2007, parts of it were almost unrecognizable. Gone were the historian's letters that had once provided a framing device in *Killing Mister Watson*. Gone was some 60 percent of *Lost Man's River*. Certain characters had been renamed, and their testimonies shuffled, blended, broken apart, and made strictly chronological. Major story beats had been rewritten in ways that dramatically altered their thematic impact. In *Killing Mister Watson*, to take one example, Edgar murders his ex-foreman when Wally Tucker makes a sudden lunge for his own gun in self-defense. Now it was Rob Watson, Edgar's eldest son, who shoots Tucker in an accident that psychologically scars the young man for life. In another example, Edgar guns down the psychotic Leslie Cox at the climax of *Bone by Bone*, before losing sight of his body in the strong current of Chatham River. Now Edgar wounds Cox, drags him onto the riverbank, and watches as Miccosukee Indians carry him off into the swamp to be executed. These changes were probably made to further humanize Watson; Matthiessen wanted to soften the monster into the kind of man who mourns his son's emotional damage even as he is the one responsible for inflicting it. ("I would have embraced Rob, squeezed his father's love into his bones and marrow, so fervently that never again would he doubt my feelings": all of this was new.)[169] In a similar fashion, Matthiessen's serious changes to the presentation of Henry Short—a mixed-race man who fires the first fatal shot at Watson on Chokoloskee in the prologue—were intended to spotlight Short as a moral center of the entire work, a pure soul in a society corrupted by racism.

There were many, many other changes; a full accounting would run as long as the novel itself (892 pages), because pretty much everything was at least tweaked. On the sentence level, Matthiessen's revisions could be a simple flip of "which" and "that," or they could be utterly transformative. Here is a passage about a hurricane from the original testimony of Sammie Hamilton in *Killing Mister Watson*:

> Seas come in off the horizon, crashing on the coast, couldn't hear one wave break no more, it was all thunder. And the rain slashing straight across in sheets, and that groaning wind twisting the trees when the gusts struck us. When the thatch tore off of our poor cabin, what few worldly goods we had was snatched away. By nightfall, we knew we was the last ones in the world, with the whole universe caving in on us poor lost souls.[170]

And here are the equivalent lines now spoken by Owen Harden, the same character renamed:

> At high tide, the seas washed over the shell ridge into the cabins. We floated the skiff right to the door and threw some stuff in. Something banged and something tore and the roof was gone and the storm exploded amongst the walls and the door frame was suddenly empty. Rain slashed straight across in sheets, whipping our faces. The sky caved in and the Gulf of Mexico crashed on our coast, so wild and heavy that the waves was lost, there was only roil and thunder.[171]

The writing was sparer and sharper by the time Matthiessen was done with it. The arc of Edgar J. Watson's life was clearer, too, with fewer digressions blurring the narrative. Whether all the changes added up to a superior novel is a matter of personal taste. The excess fat of the Random House trilogy was boiled away—"the books' rangy, Faulknerian essence is rendered more digestible,"[172] as Jonathan Miles put it in *Men's Journal*—but also boiled away was some of the world-building, black humor, and *strangeness* that had lent those earlier volumes their distinctive flavor.

With good reason, Matthiessen referred to the Modern Library version as a "NEW BOOK" in letters to Judy Sternlight.[173] What a new book needed was a new title, and he floated several in conversations with her and close friends. "A Dark Wild Metal." "In the Back Country." "Black Autumn."

"The Crocodile." Or did that latter choice sound too much like "another P.M. 'nature book'"?[174]

At a Thanksgiving dinner with extended family, he read through a list and solicited opinions from around the table. According to Luke Matthiessen, it was Mary Wheelwright, Peter's older sister, who offered another possibility. Peter would later deny it happened this way, but Luke was sitting next to his aunt when he heard her say, "Shadow Country."[175]

IN APRIL 2008, the same month *Shadow Country* was published by the Modern Library, Matthiessen was honored with the Hadada Award at *The Paris Review* Spring Revel, a lavish fundraiser held at Cipriani 42nd Street in New York. Established by George Plimpton, the Hadada is a lifetime achievement award given to a writer who has made a lasting contribution through his or her work. Awarding it to Matthiessen was like "saluting one of our founding fathers," said Philip Gourevitch, the *Paris Review*'s editor, adding: "Peter has led really one of the most accomplished and versatile and varied lives in American literature. He's really been a pioneer among American writers."[176]

Six months later, on October 15, Matthiessen was sitting in a board meeting for the magazine, in a conference room at the law firm of Debevoise & Plimpton, when he heard that *Shadow Country* had been shortlisted for the National Book Award. The critical reviews had been mostly superlative. Michael Dirda, writing in *The New York Review of Books*, had described it as "altogether gripping, shocking, and brilliantly told, not just a tour de force in its stylistic range, but a great American novel, as powerful a reading experience as nearly any in our literature."[177] Dirda compared the "magnificent, sad masterpiece" to Ralph Ellison's *Invisible Man*, Robert Penn Warren's *All the King's Men*, and mentioned Dostoevsky, Conrad, and "inevitably" Faulkner. Yet Matthiessen was shocked to receive an NBA nomination; he had accustomed himself to being overlooked when it came to the Watson books, and never imagined a recombined version might soar so high. Philip Gourevitch learned the news in a phone call and shared it with the board members, who broke into a round of cheers and applause.

In November, *The New York Times* published an article by Charles McGrath with a provocative headline: "Are 3 Novels, Revised as One, a New Book?"[178] There was a "small flare-up in the blogosphere," with some readers questioning whether *Shadow Country* was original enough to be named alongside *The Lazarus Project*, by Aleksandar Hemon; *Telex from Cuba*, by Rachel Kushner; *Home*, by Marilynne Robinson; and *The End*, by Salvatore Scibona. The executive director of the National Book Foundation, Harold Augenbraum, rolled his eyes at the minor controversy. "I can't give you a percentage of how much new writing there needs to be for a book to be eligible," he told the *Times*. "The issue is whether it's a different reading experience, and that's for the judges to decide."

Their decision was revealed on November 19, when the 59th Annual National Book Awards were held at Cipriani Wall Street, a Greek revival ballroom with seventy-foot ceilings and a Wedgwood dome that had once housed the New York Stock Exchange. Barack Obama had just been elected president (Matthiessen was "a great admirer"),[179] and the Dow Jones Industrial Average had just dropped below 8,000 points a few hours earlier. The mood was confused, and when the host, actor Eric Bogosian, cracked a joke about the ostentatious venue—"This was a bank once, and they built banks like this because banks never fail"—the audience of nearly seven hundred reacted with jittery laughter.[180]

Matthiessen was sitting at table fifteen with Maria, Neil Olson, Judy Sternlight, Bob Loomis, who had patched things up with the author, John Irving, who had followed the project from the start as an unwavering advocate, and several other people from Random House. Olson was sure the Fiction award would go to somebody else. And yet, when the writer Gail Godwin appeared on the stage, the name she read from a slip of paper was Peter Matthiessen for *Shadow Country*. "That was one of the best nights of my life, sitting there when his name was called out," Olson recalled. Peter's face was "pure joy."[181]

In a video recording of the victory, Matthiessen approaches the podium in an ill-fitting black suit, a pair of glasses hanging around his neck from a chain. He admits, a little sheepishly, that he has not prepared a speech for the occasion: he could not face the prospect of writing one and then finding it in his pocket after a loss. He rambles a few thanks to his friends and family and collaborators ("they very bravely saw me through this thing"), and gives some cursory backstory about the novel's difficult gestation. And then he gets to the heart of the matter, why this is such a "happy moment" for him. "I've had a hard time over the years persuading people that fiction was my natural thing, not nonfiction," he says. "So I've had this *neurotic* thing . . ." The audience begins to applaud again, and Matthiessen suddenly breaks off, hoisting the bronze sculpture above his head with wild eyes and a wild sound—*SOOO-aiiiiii*—that means: vindication![182]

MATTHIESSEN WAS NOW the only writer to have ever won the National Book Award for both Fiction and Nonfiction. It was a high summit in a mountain range of a career. It was not, however, the professional achievement that meant the most to him in his life. That would come eighteen months later, on May 19, 2010. The William Dean Howells Medal is bestowed once every five years by the American Academy of Arts and Letters to the "most distinguished" American novel published during that same period. *Shadow Country* was selected by a jury of Matthiessen's peers. A four-person committee—Charles Simic, Charles Wright, Richard Howard, Shirley Hazzard—had decided on a shortlist of three titles, and members of the Literature Department then cast their votes via postal ballots. The Howells Medal was exceptionally rare: only fifteen had been bestowed since 1925 (not counting the one declined by Thomas Pynchon for *Gravity's Rainbow*). In accepting the honor, Matthiessen joined an exalted list that included Willa Cather, William Faulkner, John Cheever, John Updike, and his friends Don DeLillo, E. L. Doctorow, and William Styron.

There was another improvised speech at an awards ceremony, but Matthiessen also prepared a written statement for the Academy, which ended like this:

> As somebody has famously said, "A work of art is never finished, it is simply abandoned." I agree. I spent thirty years [on] *Shadow Country* before I could let go, and even now I'd be content to polish it again. My instinct is that when the maker is truly satisfied that the damned thing is finished, it probably isn't really all that good.[183]

25

Homegoing

> This road with its shoulder of hard-pruned trees is the road he feels fated to travel to some final destination. *Heimgang*—the peculiar word hangs in his consciousness—is that a German word? These Germans have denied it, looking puzzled, yet in his poor brain it has an intimation that no other word seems to convey. Homegoing? The way home? It has fate in it, and that elusive homesickness.
>
> —*In Paradise* (2014)[1]

THERE IS A STRETCH of the Madison River, near the cowboy town of Ennis in southwest Montana, that is particularly wild and treacherous. The river flows north of the town, via myriad winding channels, into the shallow basin of Ennis Lake, which was first created by a timber-crib dam in 1906; then it crashes through a narrow eight-mile chute between rocky walls that tower up to two thousand feet overhead. Called Bear Trap Canyon, this stretch of river is infamous for rapids that reach Class IV—or even Class V after heavy rains—at a spot nicknamed the Kitchen Sink, where rafts tend to roll sideways or overturn in the sinister eddies, and where at least eight rafters have died in the past few decades.

Steve Byers suggested they portage around the canyon. As a close friend and longtime fishing pal, Byers regularly accompanied Matthiessen from the East Coast to Montana in search of trout. They would spend a day fly-fishing somewhere near Ennis, Matthiessen turning into a "blathering idiot"[2] whenever he finally caught something (usually to be thrown back), and then retire to the same Madison Valley motel, the same chairs out front, where they liked to sit and talk about Melville's *Billy Budd* as the sun went down. They had been making these fishing trips for years as a summer tradition. But now Matthiessen was eighty-two years old. Byers looked at the roiling chaos of Bear Trap Canyon, which he had twice failed to navigate on previous attempts. He warned his friend that, should something go wrong, "I'm not going to be able to save you."

Matthiessen was adamant about going through with it. Byers could take the portage path around the rapids with his wife, Heather, who was also present; but Matthiessen "wanted this adventure—*needed* it, in fact, before I shriveled like a grape on the autumn vine."[3] The afflictions of aging had started to plague him in recent years: a cataract in his left eye; a melanoma on his upper back; memory lapses; hearing loss; the distinct waning of endurance as he swam through the ocean surf at home. "I had to rise no less than 5 times last night, to monitor the subtle changes in the night ambience of the W.C.," he had complained in a letter to Jim Harrison.[4] To now shy away from Bear Trap was, in Matthiessen's mind, "to face the fact that a man I used to know was gone for good."[5]

Byers knew better than to argue, and Eric Shores, their fishing guide, reluctantly agreed to go down the river. Shores would do all the steering; Matthiessen's sole task was to sit in the back of the Zodiac and pass up a new oar ("pass it to me quick") if one of Shores's snapped in the unforgiving current.

The rapids themselves were over in a flash: "it was all rush and tumult and the thunder of white water, with hard loud *bangs* and jolts that came too close to catapulting the unbelted passenger right overboard." Yet for the few minutes they lasted, Matthiessen was ecstatic. It was like being back on the *Joseph T. Dickman* as waves slammed across the troopship bow; like being back in the Atlantic as Bonackers haul-seined for striped bass before dawn; like floating down the Pongo de Mainique as Agostino steered the flimsy balsawood raft. It was like being a young man again.

When the river was calm, he thanked Shores for the experience, and they paddled to shore to wait for Steve and Heather to catch up on foot. That evening, Matthiessen was still "on a high," he later wrote in an essay about his final feat of physical daring—"not only exhilarated but somehow *cleansed*, as if that passage had scoured off a rust of bad old stuff and perhaps the dust of oncoming decrepitude."

BEFORE HE CLIMBED into the Zodiac and headed for the Kitchen Sink, Matthiessen needled Byers about the impending loss to American literature for which Byers would inevitably be blamed. "Don't worry," he said. "My best work is behind me."[6]

There was truth in the joke: Matthiessen knew he was unlikely to produce another *Snow Leopard* or Watson trilogy. He thought that most writers, when they get older, "lose a certain elasticity and lyric energy and perhaps the ability to startle and astonish" with their writing; they reach a point beyond which there are only diminishing returns. It was a "conviction" of his ("based on the late work of almost all American novelists I truly admire") that one should get out while the words were still good. And yet he "obstinately failed" to accept this precept for himself. Who would Peter Matthiessen be if he gave up writing? The prospect of retirement filled him with dread. Writing was an "antidote," he once said, to the depression that could engulf his thinking like a poisonous gas; he was "dependent" on work to keep him clear and functional.[7] As he told the filmmaker Jeff Sewald in 2005, "Once you're really in that work, you are very different. Your mind's not wandering—at least, mine isn't. . . . [Writing] keeps me stable."[8] Even if his best work was behind him, he would keep writing to maintain a sense of equilibrium.

After he won the National Book Award for *Shadow Country*, Matthiessen initiated three new projects. These would occupy his final years, and he flitted between them depending on how he felt about his progress on each—or, as he explained in a letter to Jim Harrison, "I go back and forth according to which one I hate most."[9] One was the memoir he would never complete. Though suspicious of the genre—it was self-indulgent, unreliable, and worthless as serious literature, in his view—he had a huge number of personal anecdotes he wanted to preserve. As an indication of how dubious he was of memoir, his working title for the notes he began to keep was "Droppings," as in: "bird droppings, large and small."[10]

The second project concerned bigfoot, which Matthiessen had never been able to exorcise from his imagination. He pursued the creature yet again through a series of partial outlines labeled "SASQ-NOVEL" on his computer, in which he reexamined his bigfoot travels of the 1970s through the distorting lens of fiction. Douglas Blue, Tom Willhoite, Jean Fitzgerald, and Craig Carpenter were all depicted in the fragmentary drafts, as were many of Matthiessen's actual expeditions in California and Oregon, and his ambivalence about what had been some of the strangest events in his life:

> On way north through wilderness, X speculates again on human need to believe in mystery, ancient beings, or perhaps something on a grander time scale than the span of one human life. Attributes his own contradictory and erratic thoughts and actions to this need.[11]

Both "Droppings" and "SASQ-NOVEL" were less important, however, than the third project, which consumed the largest share of his attention. While this project was a surprising departure in many respects from anything he had yet written, it also turned out to be a poignant conclusion to familiar themes. The unlikely subject was the Nazi extermination camp of Auschwitz-Birkenau ("a poor idea, I'm told—I'm losing it, beyond a doubt").[12]

In 1996, Bernie Glassman had cofounded an organization called the Zen Peacemaker Order. Wanting to nudge American Zen in a bold new direction, Glassman took inspiration from the Vietnamese monk Thích Nhất Hạnh, who championed a practice of "engaged Buddhism" that united traditional Buddhist beliefs with social activism. Instead of hiding away in a silent zendo, Glassman had already sought, through the Zen Community of New York, to "harmonize meditation and livelihood and social action—to make them a model for living."[13] The Zen Peacemaker Order was meant to push this intention even further; it was a kind of think tank for techniques that could help, as Glassman put it, "all our brothers and sisters, from all cultures and traditions, experience the deep intimacy of no-separation, of the oneness that is our very own life."[14] Working alongside his second wife, Sandra Jishu Holmes (the other cofounder), Glassman devised three core tenets for the Peacemaker Order: *not-knowing*, which meant letting go of preconceived ideas and plunging into uncertainty; *bearing witness*, which entailed opening oneself up to the truth of a moment, however painful, "opening our hearts and letting it in,"[15] as Matthiessen put it; and *healing* as a result of this honest reckoning.

In 1994, Glassman had attended a large interfaith conference at Auschwitz-Birkenau in Poland. His experience at the death camp had been so profoundly shocking, a true plunge into an abyss of incomprehension, that he decided to make it a testing ground for the core tenets, and thus for the Zen Peacemaker Order more generally. He devised another conference: the Bearing Witness Retreat at Auschwitz-Birkenau. "I was determined," he later explained, "to bring people from different religions and nationalities to the very place where diversity had once been condemned to a terrible grave. There we would bear witness to our differences. Out of that, a healing would arise. How this would happen or what shape the healing would take, I had no idea."[16]

Matthiessen shared Glassman's enthusiasm for an American Zen that would confront social problems, rather than treat them, as Eido Shimano once had, as a needless distraction from the path to enlightenment. "Sometimes you just can't spend your life on a black cushion," Matthiessen said on *Fresh Air* in 1989. "There is great need or suffering outside your door, and you kind of have to deal with it. That's who you are in that moment. And that's an expression of yourself in the Zen way."[17] In the early 1990s, when Glassman had begun experimenting with "street retreats" alongside homeless New Yorkers—engaging them on their own terms to really *see* them and their plight—Matthiessen had joined him in the Bowery, jumping turnstiles, panhandling, and sleeping in cardboard boxes on Elizabeth Street.[18] He was a strong supporter of Glassman's unorthodox approach to spiritual practice. As another admirer of Thích Nhất Hạnh, he also believed "engaged Buddhism is the true nature of American Zen, so long as we approach it mindfully."[19]

In November 1996, Matthiessen had flown to Cracow, then caught a ride with two young Poles forty miles west to the town of Oświęcim, right up to the black gate with its infamous slogan, *Arbeit macht frei*. He was "astonished," he wrote in a journal, "that the camp is in the town, and must always have been at its edges—what can the townspeople have imagined? How can you build your new church beside it? Give a party? Raise your children?"[20]

Some 140 people convened for the Bearing Witness Retreat at Auschwitz-Birkenau, representing ten countries and four different faiths: Jewish, Christian, Muslim, and Buddhist. The retreat lasted six days, and Matthiessen stayed in a barracks that had once been occupied by the Schutzstaffel. ("There is bad power here. It is very hard to sleep.")[21] Each morning at dawn, a chime rang to summon the witness bearers to breakfast. Before gathering in the dining room, small groups met in the various cells for private discussion. As the photographer Peter Cunningham recalled, Matthiessen, to start the one he was responsible for leading, invited everyone to hold hands "silently in a circle until someone was moved to speak."[22] After a solemn meal, the participants would then trudge along a poplar-lined farm road to the neighboring camp of Birkenau. Much of each day was spent around the selection platforms in Birkenau, where SS doctors had sorted the prisoners imported in cattle cars on the train tracks: a few to the barracks to provide slave labor, and the rest to the "showers" to be immediately murdered. Forming an oval between the rails, the witness bearers set down their cushions to meditate in thirty-minute periods. Sometimes they took turns chanting Jewish names from the Sterbebücher—the Death Books of Auschwitz compiled by the Gestapo. (Matthiessen came across James Salter's family name of Horowitz: "I wondered if I should show him this list and decided against it.")[23] When they were not sitting or chanting, the participants lit candles and recited the Kaddish at the Death Wall, where thousands of prisoners had been lined up and shot. Or they offered Muslim prayers over the pits where countless others had been dumped out as ashes. Or they visited the crematoria—Matthiessen marveling at deer prints in the snow outside, life going on—and sang Christian hymns.

The Bearing Witness Retreat was almost too much of a plunge for some people. Stripping yourself bare and looking directly at the camp, without relief, was, in the words of Linda Coleman, like being "blown apart."[24] Some responded by weeping. Others were angry, ashamed, or "invaded by feelings of incomprehension, darkness, and cold," as one Swiss nun confessed in a diary she shared with Matthiessen.[25] According to his own notes and letters, he found it "<u>extraordinary</u>,"[26] though some of his emotion took the unexpected form of grief for his grandson Christopher, who had been killed by a car earlier that year: "The grief flows back into the grief of the world, and I can feel the seven-month burden of it lifting from my heart, as my head at last breaks the surface of the darkness."[27]

Each evening in the Auschwitz museum auditorium, people were encouraged to take the stage and share some thoughts about the retreat in an open forum. These discussions could be raw and confrontational, but on the first night a rabbi named Don Singer led the crowd in a soft rendition of "Oseh Shalom." Matthiessen watched as people began to join hands with the smiling rabbi—began to smile as well, self-consciously at first, and then, in an expanding circle of linked hands, including Matthiessen's, to dance, like a hora or like a childhood game of Ring Around the Rosie. A few people walked out in protest, seeing the dance as sacrilegious, but many others were transported by a surge of inexplicable joy as they moved clockwise up the aisle, across the stage, and down again, around and around before a statue depicting a camp inmate.

For Peter Cunningham, the dance was "an audacious act of laughing in the Nazis' faces, as if to say: you tried your best to wipe us off the face of the earth, but you failed miserably."[28] For Matthiessen, it was more metaphysical. Two months after the retreat, he spoke about the strange happening during a Dharma talk at the Ocean Zendo: "At first I thought this exhilaration derived from the energy and good will of so many good-hearted people. But this did not seem to account for it. . . . Now I think I am just beginning to understand that that exhilaration came from apprehension of a truth."[29] The precise nature of that "truth" was beyond easy articulation; it was like trying to describe kensho. Yet he believed he'd glimpsed something vital about human nature as he danced with the other witness bearers, and pondering what, exactly, became the central preoccupation of his final writing project. In early draft pages, Matthiessen asked himself: "Do we sense that, in a state of truth, we manifest the life essence? The One? Is this joy a kind of mystical experience . . . ?"[30]

By 2011, "Dancing at Auschwitz" had grown to more than forty thousand words. A nonfiction travelogue in a similar vein to *The Snow Leopard*, it combined Matthiessen's daily journal of bearing witness at the 1996 retreat, and at another he attended in November 2000, with philosophical reflections based on years of thought about the Nazi death camp:

In my opinion, we are very naive—and will remain ineffectual—so long as we think we can outgrow, far less "cure," the true nature of our species—its evolutionarily sensible propensity for violence and/or evil, for war and racism, through good works or traditional religion or even education (spiritual or otherwise). Politically, all we can do is institute wise international controls to save our species from itself—the U.N. Peace Force may be a crude start.... Perhaps insight into our own true nature is the other side of that strange "exhilaration": the liberation from false hope, from the delusion of human perfectibility on earth.[31]

But Matthiessen was not entirely comfortable with this kind of writing in the context of Auschwitz. Did he even have the *right* to address the subject? He was not the descendant of a prisoner or a concentration camp guard. He was not Jewish. He compared his work, unfavorably, to that of eyewitnesses like Primo Levi and Yehiel De-Nur. "How can you add anything when you weren't even there?"[32] His own experience at the camp seemed "insignificant," particularly when presented in the analytical language of a nonfiction chronicle.

In Poland he had met an artist, Marian Kołodziej, who'd somehow survived internment in Auschwitz-Birkenau as prisoner 432. After fifty years of silence, the painter had started working on a mural of his memories in the basement of a deconsecrated Franciscan chapel in neighboring Harmęże. Kołodziej told Matthiessen, in explanation of *The Labyrinth*, full of wide-eyed spectral figures, that "the only way to understand an evil is through art."[33] With this encounter in mind, Matthiessen took "Dancing at Auschwitz" and reimagined it as a novel. "I thought, with a novel, possibly, I could penetrate it, see something," he later explained.[34] He kept many details from the Bearing Witness Retreat, including the transcendental dance led by Rabbi Singer: "softly the silence implodes and awe arises, a sigh of bewilderment and gratitude, as with fulfilled lovers."[35] Yet he replaced himself in the narrative with David Clements Olinski, a Massachusetts-based professor of twentieth-century Slavic literature who discovers, not unlike the eponymous figure in W. G. Sebald's *Austerlitz*, that his Jewish mother was slaughtered by the Nazis—who has a direct, unambiguous connection to Auschwitz-Birkenau.

Matthiessen also decided, eventually, to replace the title. Taken out of context, "Dancing at Auschwitz" could seem disrespectful, like dancing on a grave, so he opted to use something a little more subtle. *In Paradise* was an original working name ("In Paradisum") for *At Play in the Fields of the Lord*, and another meaning of the phrase had been discussed in *The Snow Leopard*:

To the repentant thief upon the cross, the soft Jesus of the modern Bible holds out hope of Heaven: "Today thou art with me in Paradise." But in older translations, as Soen Roshi points out, there is no "today," no suggestion of the future. In the Russian translation, for example, the meaning is "right here now." Thus, Jesus declares, "You are in Paradise right now"—how much more vital! There is no hope anywhere but in this moment, in the karmic terms laid down by one's own life. This very day is an aspect of nirvana, which is not different from samsara but, rather, a subtle alchemy, the transformation of dark mud into the pure, white blossom of the lotus.[36]

Searching for paradise and learning to see it *right here now*: this was a recurrent theme in Peter Matthiessen's work. Perhaps it was the dominant theme of his life.

THE YEAR 2012, in which Matthiessen turned eighty-five, started out just as busy as the rest of them. He produced multiple drafts of *In Paradise*, while continuing to tinker with the other two projects on the side. He delivered the Iscol Distinguished Environmental Lecture at Cornell University, comparing climate change skeptics to "Holocaust deniers, people who fly in the face of incredible archives of fact."[37] He even appeared in a film by Terrence Malick about a screenwriter in spiritual crisis. Malick, a birder, was friends with Victor Emanuel—they both lived in Austin—and Matthiessen agreed, through Emanuel ("Terry had always wanted Peter in one of his movies"),[38] to do a day or two of filming for *Knight of Cups*. There was no script to speak of, but Malick cast Matthiessen as a Zen personage named Christopher whom the protagonist and his girlfriend, played by Christian Bale and Natalie Portman, visit in a Japanese garden. Making it up on the fly, "Christopher" instructed Portman how to kneel and how to bow. He regaled Bale with stories about his pilgrimage to Shey Gompa in 1973. "I remember when I came down out of the mountains with ambitions of being absolutely clear," he can be heard saying in the finished film. "Absolutely . . . if not enlightened, at least wiser than I had been . . ."

Matthiessen looks pale in *Knight of Cups*. His eyes are hooded, and his voice is a low, croaky rumble coming from deep within his chest. The filming was done in June 2012, which means he was already ill, though it would be several months before he understood why.

At home in Sagaponack, he had begun taking longer and longer afternoon naps. He had collapsed at a friend's house—"Peter's fainted,"[39] they announced on the phone to Maria—and collapsed at a party for the Ocean Zendo in front of some students. During a game of tennis with his son in

Sag Harbor, he wilted after just five or ten minutes of hitting a ball back and forth, then requested to sit down. The family doctor had already diagnosed anemia, and Peter was getting shots of vitamin B_{12}. He gave little thought to the treatment, but when Maria mentioned his "deficiency" to a friend who was also an orthopedic surgeon, the friend expressed doubt: nobody in well-fed America should be suffering from anemia. Something deeper might be wrong. He suggested they seek a second opinion.

Before Matthiessen got around to scheduling an appointment, he had another safari with Victor Emanuel in early October. Both of them had been invited by a Mongolian American entrepreneur, Jalsa Urubshurow, on an eleven-day tour through Mongolia. Alongside a dozen other guests, they would visit the westernmost province of Bayan-Ölgii for the famous Golden Eagle Festival, then Khustain Nuruu National Park, and finally Urubshurow's private ecolodge in the Gobi Desert. Matthiessen was feeling "strangely weak and out of breath,"[40] yet he insisted to friends that he *had* to go.[41]

The flights were an endurance test: New York to Toronto; Toronto to Beijing; Beijing to Ulaanbaatar. He arranged a layover to visit the Great Wall of China—until the authorities canceled his double-entry visa, perhaps because of criticisms he'd made of the country's environmental record in *Birds of Heaven*. He was forced to reroute through Seoul in South Korea instead.

Emanuel was waiting for him in the Blue Sky Hotel, the tallest building in Ulaanbaatar. Matthiessen shuffled into the glass lobby looking white as a ghost and shaky on his feet. "We thought, or hoped, he was recovering from a bad cold," Emanuel later recalled.[42] It took a day for Matthiessen to rally his strength. While the other travelers had a private audience with Hamba Lama, the highest Buddhist lama of Gandan Monastery, he excused himself to rest in his room, watching Barack Obama debate Mitt Romney at the University of Denver. "He was very upset," said Emanuel, who stayed behind to watch the first presidential debate with his old friend: "He felt Obama had done very poorly." The next morning, the group flew to Ulgii, and Matthiessen heroically pushed himself through the rest of the itinerary. A letter sent to a friend suggests he managed, despite some bad days, to even have a good time: "We went first to western Kazakh Mongolia to see these beautifully robed Kazakh horsemen compete with their trained golden eagles, stooping on wolf pelts dragged behind galloping horses: the horses are cow-pony size and the hunters are small men, too, and those huge eagles on their arms, riding in off the desert, look as big as they do. 61 hunters and 61 golden eagles!—about as many as I've seen altogether in the wild."[43]

And yet, by the time they reached the Gobi Desert, it was clear there was some undiagnosed problem beyond a bad cold. On October 14, Matthiessen returned to New York complaining of an exhaustion resembling jet lag that would not go away.

THE FAMILY DOCTOR, discovering an alarmingly low red blood cell count, sent him to the hospital for emergency tests. (Why not sooner? Why had the doctor let it get so dire? How, the Matthiessens would later ask, could he have misdiagnosed *anemia* in an eighty-five-year-old man?) Peter had blood transfusions, then a bone marrow biopsy, then signed himself out because he hated spending time in the hospital as an invalid.

On October 29, Hurricane Sandy ravaged the New York coast, bringing sustained winds that reached up to ninety-five miles per hour at Eatons Neck on Long Island. At least four people died in the historic storm, including one woman who washed ashore on Georgica Beach in East Hampton, more than sixteen miles from where she'd first slipped into the waves.[44] The ocean rose up and washed away most of the dunes along the East End. In the village of Sagaponack, the land between Peter's Pond Lane and Town Line Road was flattened, and houses bordering Sagaponack Pond were inundated with seawater.[45] Some two hundred homes were left for days without power—including the Matthiessens' place on Bridge Lane. Peter and Maria went to stay with Ngaere Macray and David Seeler, close friends who lived further inland and were thus spared from the blackout.

Alex Matthiessen dropped by Macray and Seeler's house to visit. When he arrived, Peter and Maria were at the hospital hearing the results of Peter's biopsy. "So I just hung out," Alex recalled. "Ngaere was preparing tea, everything was jolly; it wasn't like we were waiting for the results—or at least, we weren't concerned about them. I remember sitting there and the door opened. I think Maria walked in first, then Dad, and he had the most stricken expression. His face was almost paralyzed. And Maria looked worried. They came in and sat down and revealed pretty quickly that it was not good."[46] The biopsy had discovered acute myeloid leukemia, a cancer of the bone marrow where cells stop developing normally into the constituent parts of blood, remaining as immature white blood cells called myeloblasts that gradually crowd out any healthy cells. The prognosis, given Peter's age and the advanced state of his AML—stage four—was that it could be slowed but probably not stopped. He had maybe eighteen months left to live.

Peter was quiet after they shared the news. Alex was speechless. "It had just never occurred to me that my father was going to die from a disease. He seemed indomitable. He had never, other than a few melanomas, had health scares of any kind. He was always quite fit. He wasn't an exercise buff, but he walked and rode his bike to the beach every day, and swam, and went on expeditions. We had all thought that whatever the problem was, it would be a temporary nothing they would treat as an infection."

It took Alex a while to process the magnitude of what was coming. Peter had been "such a huge part of my life for so long. I always knew that, even when he was a shitty father, even when he was being neglectful or verbally abusive, underneath it all he cared. I always knew that Dad loved me. I never doubted that. That was something. That was comforting."

DEATH, IN PETER MATTHIESSEN'S WORK, IS sometimes associated with shorebirds. "To see a lone petrel arc across some desolate reach of ocean, as fleeting as the spray blown from wave crests," he writes in *End of the Earth*, "is to risk unnameable intuitions of mortal solitude and transience, one's own swift passage toward the void."[47] The whimbrel and curlew, he notes in *The Shorebirds of North America*, were once considered harbingers of death in English folklore: "Yet it is not the death sign that the curlews bring, but only the memory of life, of a high beauty passing swiftly, as the curlew passes, leaving us in solitude on an empty beach, with summer gone, and a wind blowing."[48]

To contemplate death was not, in his view, inherently morbid. "We can try to ignore death using repression or whatever means is at hand," he once said, "or we can confront it, try to penetrate it, try to be one with it, try to understand it for what it is, which is a part of our life."[49]

There was an exercise he liked to do with students in the Ocean Zendo. It was inspired by *chöd* practice in Tibetan Buddhism, where one attempts to rise above horror into a state of samadhi by confronting the horror directly—like Milarepa sitting with his mother's decomposed corpse for seven days and nights. ("Apparently it was a very illuminating experience.")[50] Matthiessen would direct his students to turn to the person sitting next to them. Take their face in your fingertips, he would say; look into their eyes. Now push the skin taut at their temples, and raise the person's upper lip, so their teeth are exposed. Feel and see the skull staring back at you, a symbol of death that is already with us at every moment of the day. "We can philosophize about death until we're blue in the face, we can say 'O Death, thou comest when I had thee least in mind,' but that's not nearly as powerful as *that*. That's the thing itself."[51]*

Matthiessen didn't need an exercise to remind himself of mortality: Death had been stalking his social circle since the early 1990s. The painter Sherry

---

* A very early version of this memento mori exercise appears in *Partisans* (1955): "'The teeth—' Marat said, 'notice the teeth, for they are the only part of the skeleton that shows, and should remind you of it. There is a skull behind those eyes, a death's head.'"

Lord, a friend since St. Bernard's, had succumbed to cancer in July 1994. ("With him will go a chunk of your understood and witnessed life, that no one else has knowledge of in the same way," Maria had written to Peter just days before.)[52] Taizan Maezumi had drowned in a bathtub, apparently drunk, in May 1995, his last Japanese Zen teacher. Hans Enku Hokanson—"Enku" was a Dharma name—his senior monk at the Ocean Zendo and cellmate at the Bearing Witness Retreat at Auschwitz-Birkenau, had died of a massive heart attack in August 1997. ("Enku! Speak! Where have you gone?" Matthiessen lamented at a zazenkai service.)[53] George Plimpton had died in September 2003—another unexpected heart attack—just two days after finishing the fiftieth-anniversary issue of *The Paris Review*. Matthiessen spoke at a memorial held by the American Academy of Arts and Letters, mourning his "friend of almost seventy years, and a very dear friend, too, for all our occasional petty strife over the Review."[54] Tom Guinzburg, another fixture since childhood and *Paris Review* cofounder, failed to survive complications of heart bypass surgery in September 2010. This was a particularly painful loss. "Skeptical sniff and twisty smile, hairy knuckles on big cupped hands, rolling shoulders," Matthiessen wrote in notes for another eulogy he had never dreamed of giving; "loyal, generous, smart, funny, lovely guy."[55] Most recently, the art critic Robert Hughes, a dependable fishing partner on the East End, had passed in August 2012 after spiraling into dementia—a "long illness," as *The New York Times* tactfully put it in Hughes's obituary.[56]

Matthiessen had outlived them all. And, perhaps most significantly, he had outlived Bill Styron. Over the decades, Styron had struggled with clinical depression; in 1984, he'd sent an anguished suicide note to Matthiessen: "I've gone through a rough time. I hope you'll remember me with love and tenderness. I wish I'd taken your way to peace and goodness. Please remember me with a little of that zen goodness, too. I've always loved you and Maria."[57] Styron had managed to survive that episode, but the depression had never fully abated, and his last few years were consumed by an unending battle he had no hope of winning. In October 2006, Matthiessen had traveled to Martha's Vineyard to see his friend for the last time. "My father was so afraid of death," recalled Susanna Styron.[58] "He was just terrified. And it was a self-fulfilling prophecy: fear of death contributed to his death. Peter witnessed that, and he told my father it was okay. My father actually asked him if it was okay to let go. Peter really helped him over that threshold. He died like three days later"—on November 1, 2006. In a tribute published in *The Paris Review*, Matthiessen described the death as "a true mercy."[59] "All the same," he added in a teisho for his Zen students, "it hurts."[60]

The day Styron died, Matthiessen invited James Salter around for a drink in his Sagaponack writing studio. He admitted that Bill was "the friend of his life." Salter hadn't known that, he later wrote: "I'd been with the two of them various times. They were easy with one another, easy enough to exchange insults. Styron was a southerner who didn't fish, hunt birds, or play tennis, and who lived in Connecticut, far away—but there had been some strong cord."[61]

Let go, Peter had told Bill on his deathbed. It was what he hoped to do when his own time came. "My ambition is to die the way ripe fruit lets go of a tree,"[62] he said; the way a mushroom disappears in a forest wind—*poof!*[63] The Buddha had taught that "all suffering comes from clinging,"[64] and it is the purpose of Zen to prize open the fingers of a desperately clutching hand, to help a person let go so they can end the suffering of all sentient beings.

At the end of 2012, Matthiessen wrote a letter to a friend about the grave situation he now found himself facing. "I'm just back from the hospital, in fact, after the first day of a five-day assault with chemo. I'm not complaining: I've had good health and a very adventurous life with all sorts of great people in it, you guys included, so I'm not going to cling to it past a certain point. I hope for the best but . . . anyway, wish me luck."[65]

NOT LONG AFTER he got his diagnosis of AML, Matthiessen asked Michel Dobbs for an unusual favor that recalled his comments to Craig Carpenter about the harmony, as he saw it, of Zen Buddhism and Native American spiritual teachings.

Michel Engu Dobbs was Matthiessen's Dharma heir. Dobbs had joined the Ocean Zendo in 1994, after moving with his family from Manhattan to the East End to manage a prominent bakery. A self-described "angry young man"[66] at the time, Dobbs had found calm in the city through Zen, and two different friends (Lawrence Shainberg and Allen Planz) had suggested Matthiessen could help deepen his practice in the Hamptons. Dobbs had been wary at first; the writer gave bizarre Dharma talks about whales and other seemingly irrelevant subjects. But after a few years of attending the Ocean Zendo, Dobbs had been persuaded to make a formal commitment by receiving the precepts. Then he had started koan study, a long process that brought him face-to-face with Muryo Roshi in meetings of "deep intimacy." At Matthiessen's encouragement, Dobbs had gone to a Bearing Witness Retreat at Auschwitz-Birkenau, which was "powerful" in ways that he hadn't anticipated. For a Tokudo ceremony in 2001, he had shaved his head and ascended to the rank of priest. Shiho, or Dharma transmission, had come about naturally in 2005, and it was now understood that Dobbs (who was temperamentally similar to his teacher: did Matthiessen see himself in this serious young man fighting to overcome greed, anger, and folly through Zen?) would shepherd the Ocean Zendo after Muryo Roshi was gone.

When Dobbs had first learned of the leukemia, he'd arranged a special service so the sangha could chant the Kannon Sutra thirty-three times. But now Matthiessen asked his Dharma successor to organize a different kind of ritual: a traditional Lakota healing ceremony called a *yuwipi*.

Dobbs, at a loss, phoned an acquaintance out West, who made some calls. And within surprisingly short order, a medicine man was on his way from Pine Ridge, South Dakota. Dobbs began receiving late-night phone calls from various rest stops across the country, all of them following a similar pattern: "We're in X. The car broke down. Can you send another $100 to the Western Union?"[67]

Matthiessen's nephew, Peter Matthiessen Wheelwright, was staying in Sagaponack on the night of the yuwipi. The Lakota healer and his entourage were very late, and everyone was waiting. "Maria was really fit to be tied," Wheelwright recalled. "She wanted Peter to go to bed—you could see how weak he was. But he didn't want to go. On the one hand, he felt Maria's pressure to kick everybody out of the house and just do it tomorrow, but it had to be done *that night* according to the ritual. So he insisted that he was going to wait until the Indians came."[68] When they finally arrived with Dobbs, who was hosting them in his basement, it was approaching midnight. The Lakota numbered four or five. They were casually dressed; one wore a Boston Red Sox baseball cap. Matthiessen introduced the medicine man to his nephew, and Wheelwright wished them well as he went to retire. "No," the healer said, stopping him: "We need as much of Peter in the room as we can get. We want you to come to the Zendo for the performance." Wheelwright was unenthusiastic ("You couldn't find a bigger apostate to go into Pete's zendo and sit cross-legged on the mats with all these believers"), but he agreed to do it for his uncle.

The sangha members, many of them purified after visiting a sweat lodge on the Three Mile Harbor Road, took their places along the walls. Peter was feeling weak, so he sat in a chair at the head of the zendo, and Maria sat slightly behind, monitoring him. "The Zendo gets darker, darker," Wheelwright recalled. "The Indians start arraying bones and hides and feathers, and there's smoke and flashing lights in the darkness, and there's chanting, and I'm sitting there in the dark suffocating on this incense." Two hours later, the lights slowly came back on. The medicine man chanted some more, and then Dobbs asked the Roshi how he felt. Matthiessen rose from his chair. As Wheelwright recalled, "He sort of threw his shoulders back and said—something like Peter would say—'*I'm feeling the spirit. I'm feeling fulfilled.*'"

Early the following morning, Wheelwright found his uncle sitting alone in the kitchen. He looked "150 percent better than he did the day before." They both laughed, Wheelwright because he was unexpectedly moved by the whole experience, and Peter because his atheist nephew had been forced to sit through an extraordinary fusion of Zen and Lakota belief. "It was all voodoo stuff to me," Wheelwright said, but it had clearly meant a great deal to Peter: "He was so *there*. He was so present with it."

THE DECITABINE, a chemotherapy drug, was administered intravenously during sessions over five consecutive days once a month at the Stony Brook Cancer Center. Maria drove Peter fifty miles each way from Sagaponack, a grueling commute down the Long Island Expressway that left her with so little time to cook or shop for him that family, friends, and members of the Ocean Zendo soon volunteered to take over the driving duties.

Peter read during his chemo appointments, which lasted for hours. He was "uncomplaining and gallant," said Maria; she was "stunned by his bravery."[69] He showed no fear even when the implantation of a chemo port in his chest caused unexpected complications. After each monthly cycle, he would be knocked flat for a day or two as the poison inhibited the production of more cancer cells; but then he would resume work on *In Paradise*. "He became singularly focused on the book," recalled Alex.[70] It kept his mind occupied, and Maria was grateful for the distraction.

How do you talk to somebody grappling with a terminal illness? Jim Harrison was uncertain, so he wrote Matthiessen about poetry and fish and yellow warblers, with only tentative references to the leukemia: "Hope you are feeling well. I'm a bit shy about asking."[71] For his own part, Matthiessen didn't avoid the subject of his condition, but nor did he make a fuss about it. The editor Terry McDonell, in a memoir, *The Accidental Life*, recalled sitting with Matthiessen in the Sagaponack garden after he had started treatment: "He was optimistic about the chemo, although it put him down for one week a month, and said he was looking forward to physical therapy. He was thinner but still looked strong. We talked about the touch football games with Jim Salter and other local writers played in the potato field behind the house, and how he used to sneak onto private golf courses for a quick round now and then and had been caught only once. And we talked too about Leonard Peltier, as we always did."[72] In phone calls with the writer Frederick Turner, Matthiessen would discuss his progress on *In Paradise*, and then passingly mention his red blood cell count. "That was volunteered and kind of matter-of-fact," Turner recalled, "as if every writer faces certain conditions when he or she is working on a book, and these were his."[73] The author and ecologist Carl Safina, who lived not far from the hospital in Stony Brook, was struck by Matthiessen's determination to go on as normal: "It was like a car that had blown two tires. You can't drive a car with two flat tires, but there's really nothing wrong with the car. That's the way his illness always seemed to me. Because what is a person as an individual? You are your mind, your memories, your relationships with other people. And in rare cases, you are also your body of work. None of that was affected by his illness as far as I could see."[74]

Matthiessen received blood transfusions, wrote out exercise routines, and intimated to at least one Zen student that he was on the upswing. Yet there were moments when his body belied his stubborn optimism—when he couldn't get up off the beach without assistance, or when he started to shuffle oddly in the kitchen, slur his words, and then fall unconscious just as a chair was pushed in to cushion his collapse. "I remember he was like, 'I could hear you guys . . . I knew I didn't need 9-1-1,' " recalled Sarah Koenig. "And I was like, 'You fucking did.' "[75]

In May, Peter celebrated his eighty-sixth birthday with a small family gathering. By now he had been on chemo for six months, and the drugs had aged him dramatically. Alex whispered to Luke, "He looks old, Luke, very old."[76] Due to his blindness, Luke hadn't been able to see his father for decades, and he struggled to imagine the man in his memory—six foot two, tan and fit, stalking an agitated rattlesnake in Baja California—as somebody physically smaller, "unable to walk more than a few hundred yards without tiring, and not at all without the cane Claire [de Brunner, Luke's wife] and I had given him."

Maria remained on standby to feed and clothe her husband, and to ensure he followed the doctor's guidelines. She could be fiercely protective on that point. When Peter lied to Steve Byers—yes, he was absolutely allowed to drink martinis—Maria was furious. "She blamed me for it," Byers said.[77] Maria had always run their affairs with no-nonsense rigor, and the rope was not about to slacken because of acute myeloid leukemia. To deal with the stress, she went for walks with her friend Ngaere Macray, who was struck by her "formidable courage and dignity."[78]

Yet there was another complication besides the cancer, and it was, for Maria, a much tougher trial to endure. Peter had a literary assistant, K*, a younger woman he'd met through the Ocean Zendo. By 2013, K had been his assistant for a decade, answering emails, coordinating with publishers, and typing up manuscripts. She had effectively become his first reader on *Shadow Country*, a usurpation that bothered Maria because that had always

---

* Name withheld and initial changed for privacy.

been *her* job, the one dependable access point she had to the fortress of Peter's working life. Over the years, his relationship with K had evolved into a mysterious kind of emotional dependency. Nobody was quite sure what to call it, though it didn't seem to be sexual. "He wasn't having an affair," Maria said, "but it was *something*."[79] It was enough to cause dissent in the Ocean Zendo: Dorothy Friedman, a member since the beginning, suddenly distanced herself from Muryo Roshi because "he did not walk his talk" as a moral guide for the sangha. "His behavior to Maria was just unbearable," Friedman said.[80] On the family front, Rue was appalled but not particularly surprised. "I think he was like a lot of these old lions in their later years. He felt the cold breath of mortality and wanted to have a young woman around. It's not like she was some femme fatale, but she was a writer to her core, and she loved his work, and loved *him*."[81]

Perhaps that was too much to resist for a man who was perennially insecure about his own status as a writer. "He just took whatever he wanted," Rue said. "He took that because he needed it. It was really shitty." Antonia Koenig was furious that, "even at the end, he couldn't give my mother the dignity of being a wife."[82] As Maria rushed around making him as comfortable as possible, Peter would be closing doors for intimate conversations he didn't want her to overhear. Maria went to the supermarket and returned to find K's car parked in the side driveway, as though the assistant had been waiting nearby until the coast was clear. "It was very hard," Maria said, "because Peter was dying, and I wanted to be closer to him and make the house calm. And instead it became this bad thing."[83]

The badness coalesced around *In Paradise*. After years of laboring over the manuscript, Matthiessen had finally shown it to Neil Olson. The novel was, Olson thought, not the best thing his client had ever written, but interesting, provocative, and more than publishable as Peter Matthiessen's final work. Olson arranged to sell it to Rebecca Saletan—who had worked on *Killing Mister Watson*, then edited the two books on cranes and tigers—at Riverhead Books, an imprint of Penguin, where she was now editorial director. Saletan soon realized that Matthiessen was still relentless when it came to his prose. ("I thought, Okay, this time he won't rewrite so much. I was wrong.")[84] She found herself in constant correspondence with K, who, like a project manager, kept track of the countless drafts flowing out of Sagaponack. In fact, K turned out to be a godsend to the team at Riverhead, yet her presence caused logistical awkwardness when Saletan and the publicity director wanted to see Matthiessen in person to discuss the novel's publication plan. "There was a very careful orchestration of when we came to the house," Saletan remembered. "We had to come on a Saturday, not a Sunday, because Maria wouldn't be there and [K] would be there, and we needed to deal with [K]."

To see the novel successfully through to bookshelves, the editor and publicist were forced to tiptoe around Maria, who had "basically washed her hands of it."

In October, Maria decided to wash her hands of everything. She had endured numerous affairs over the years. She had held the family together while Peter traveled the world unencumbered. She had given herself willingly, but now, in another frank letter, she announced that she was finally done:

> It is time to pass on the baton—truly.... You have been honest about telling me that you would resent me if you had to give [K] up. You have also made it plain that you need her and that you enjoy her company (I am sure beyond my own, and who could blame you?).... She could slot right into your life here and look after you well in all aspects of your current situation. You would feel so much freer.... I want you to be happy or happier in this time, and I had hoped it would be with me, but that, it is plain, cannot be. I am made too unhappy with this Shadow Person and it makes me cold and distant which in turn makes you unhappy.... The children would be fine too. They are all forgiving souls. And they are all sad that you are sick and would never abandon you. I don't feel I would be abandoning you really. I think I am leaving you in better hands, which is hard for me to admit, but I feel it to be true. I have always loved you very much, but I have not always liked you.... So let's talk about it as calmly as possible and see our way through this.[85]

Peter was "horrified" by this letter.[86] He did not want K to replace Maria; his devoted assistant performed a different role to that of wife. He did not want Maria to move into her property in Sag Harbor, which was the solution she proposed. He did not want to hear that she hadn't always liked him, a truth that surely touched some of the same nerves that had been raw since early childhood.

They both knew the coming Christmas was likely to be his last. Peter asked her to stay with him in Sagaponack. Recognizing how frail he'd become, Maria agreed to set aside her anger, resentment, and disappointment. Still, the letter made explicit the estrangement that had grown in their marriage, an emotional separation that would never be honestly addressed by Peter, who, even as he affirmed his love for Maria in a silly postcard ("You are at the pinnacle of my lifetime best-seller list and always have been"),[87] also guarded his connection with K, the Shadow Person.

ONE EVENING IN JANUARY 2014, after another appointment at the Stony Brook Cancer Center, Peter and Maria had dinner with Carl Safina. Following much good-natured prodding from both of them, Safina had finally married his longtime girlfriend, Patricia, and the dinner was a belated celebration. Meeting at Safina's house for an aperitif, Peter pinched his fingers together—"I can have a little"—and accepted a glass of wine. He ordered a second glass at the restaurant, then launched into a discussion about animal cognition and the wolves of Yellowstone. "If a wolf was here in the restaurant with us," Peter asked, "what would it be thinking?" As Safina attempted to answer as an ecologist, he noticed Patricia, out of the corner of his eye, engaged in a serious whisper with Maria. Later that night, Patricia revealed why Peter had been drinking despite the medical prohibition on alcohol: the chemo was no longer working. Maria said his treatments were being stopped.[88]

Decitabine was never going to cure the leukemia, but it gifted Matthiessen a relatively functional thirteen months in which to finish his novel. Now his oncologist, Michael Schuster, advised him to enjoy whatever little time he had left: "Anything you want."[89]

What Peter wanted was to keep working, though he'd been forced to abandon the writing studio due to creeping mold that threatened his compromised immune system. In an upstairs bedroom-turned-study, he tinkered with the memoir project. During February and March, he also consented to interviews with several journalists to promote the fast-tracked publication of *In Paradise*. These journalists made individual visits to Sagaponack, where they found, as Mark Adams put it in *Men's Journal*, "a wise owl dressed for comfort in a souvenir fleece from the 2006 U.S. Open."[90] Matthiessen was welcoming, even "rugged, vibrant, playful, encyclopedic, garrulous, rebellious,"[91] in the words of Alec Michod for the *Los Angeles Review of Books*. But he was clearly in decline, too. Jonathan Meiburg, writing for the *Believer*, needed to place his recorder close to Matthiessen just to pick up his "deep, conspiratorial rasp."[92] Ron Rosenbaum came for *Smithsonian*, and Jeff Himmelman visited for a profile in *The New York Times Magazine*, which also dispatched a photographer to document the adventures etched into Matthiessen's expressive face, now as craggy and worn as the Montauk cliffs.

The interviews surveyed nearly every aspect of his life, from childhood to psychedelics, Zen, the CIA, Africa, Auschwitz. But Matthiessen avoided talking about the decision he was making, right at that moment, that would determine the way his life would end.

Once the decitabine lost its efficacy, he had one final option available to him: a clinical trial. Sometime in winter or early spring, a friend of a friend who happened to be a renowned hematologist told the Matthiessens about an experimental immunotherapy that seemed to offer promising results for people with leukemia. When the Matthiessens mentioned the drug to Michael Schuster, he warned them that it had only ever been tested on younger patients, and Maria got the impression he was really saying, "Don't do it."[93] But Peter was intrigued. He asked Maria's opinion. Should he roll the dice? She declined to make a bet because, as she later recalled, "If I said no, it would be like I was trying to kill him. And I didn't want to say yes." At the same time, Linda Coleman from the Ocean Zendo, a registered nurse who read all the literature she could find about the trial, advised Peter that the risks involved for a man of his age and condition were extremely high. "This treatment is very likely going to kill you," she said.[94] Peter debated with himself and his family (and probably with K, whose influence remains unknown). "Initially he was leaning against it," recalled Luke.[95] By March, though, he had changed his mind and decided to go ahead with the treatment. To avoid the standard screening delay that would cost one or two of his precious remaining months, and that would likely disqualify him from participating anyway, he exploited "privilege" to sidestep the checkpoints: "the FDA helped to push it through," Maria said, so the "famous writer" could enroll in the clinical trial.[96]

Peter's decision surprised many of his closest friends. Taking an experimental drug seemed to contradict what he liked to preach about letting go gracefully. "Because Peter was a Zen priest, I thought—and maybe it was unrealistic—that he'd be philosophical about dying," said Myrna Davis. "But he wanted to fight."[97] Some saw his volte-face as evidence that he was more afraid than he let on. "Here's this guy who has dealt with death in every culture," said Antonia Koenig, "and then when it got down to it, he was so terrified of his own."[98] Or maybe it was less about fear than a belief he would ultimately prevail in his gamble on the drug trial. As Alex said, "I think he felt that if anybody could lick it, *he* could. He had a belief in his own physical health, because he had been a fairly prime specimen his whole life."[99] After all, his own father, Matty, had lived to the age of ninety-seven before prostate cancer finally killed him in 2000 ("in his own bed, without pain . . . and with all his marbles to the last," Peter wrote admiringly in a letter),[100] so surely he still had at least another decade of life ahead of him. The work, too, was undoubtedly a contributing factor. He was not quite finished as a writer. "There were still things he wanted to do," said Neil Olson.[101] There were still things he wanted to know about himself, suggested his nephew Jeff Wheelwright: "I can't die because I haven't figured out who I am!"[102]

But perhaps Peter's decision was not really that unexpected, even for a Zen master who rhapsodized about the evanescence of cherry blossoms. As his friend Frederick Turner artfully put it, "Every one of us has some kind of platonic ideal of how we're going to end up. And almost none of it ever happens the way we planned it." Peter's final choice to cling to life, to not die the way ripe fruit lets go of a tree, was "part of being a *Homo sapiens*."[103]

THE CLINICAL TRIAL STARTED in the last week of March. Within two days of his first treatment, blisters, like cold sores, appeared on his lips, and ulcers bloomed on the soft tissue of his mouth and throat. Speaking became difficult, and swallowing caused excruciating pain. It quickly became clear to Maria that this was more than she could handle by herself at home: "it was dreadful, dreadful, dreadful."[104] Once Peter was bedridden, Maria and Alex jointly made the decision to move him to Stony Brook until the doctors could stabilize his symptoms. Members of the Ocean Zendo, who had just started a sesshin on Shelter Island with the understanding that Muryo Roshi was doing okay, broke the retreat's silence to discuss the sudden crisis.

Maria phoned the other children and told them to come to the hospital immediately. Alex was joined by Luke, Rue, Sarah, and Antonia, who flew in from Seattle. For the first time since the initial leukemia diagnosis, Sara Carey was also told what was happening. Peter had intentionally withheld his condition from his eldest daughter. "We had wrestled over it together," recalled Alex. "He asked me what he should do. I think he was very torn, because on the one hand he didn't want to leave her out: she was one of his kids. But he was convinced she would abuse the privilege of knowing, and make it all about herself, and create a lot of drama and torture him."[105] Now Rue thought their sister *needed* to know, so they called and broke the depressing news. Sara Carey declined to visit the hospital, then changed her mind, then changed it again. According to Luke, instead of reconciling with him while there was still time, she sent her father "a vitriolic letter blaming him for ruining her life."[106] (After decades of struggling with mental illness, Sara Carey committed suicide in 2022.)

Peter was placed on morphine to mitigate the agony in his mouth and throat. Soon he was drifting in and out of delirium. He became incontinent, much to his horror. Rue watched as Alex and Maria tried to get answers from the doctors. The situation had deteriorated so rapidly that it was hard to understand what happened with the experimental drug. "I felt like they were trying to fix this," Rue said. "But it wasn't fixable. He was dying."[107] She held his hand and looked into his eyes, feeling very close to him. "He overflowed, with so much love coming out." Luke, too, took turns sitting by the bedside, though he was a little more reserved in his interactions. Back in Sagaponack before the hospital transfer, he'd asked Peter if he was afraid of dying. "I don't quite know what motived it. Maybe I was trying to invite him to be a little genuine or connect in some way." Peter had been enraged by the question: "It was as if I had insulted his masculinity."[108]

Peter would spend more than ten horrendously painful days at Stony Brook, but there were moments of grace amid the suffering. At one point a trio of musicians came through the ward taking requests for performances; Rue selected "Wichita Lineman" by Glen Campbell, and the Matthiessens sat around Peter as the band played. ("You run around your whole goddamn life," Rue said, "and then, at the end, what do you want to do more than anything? To listen to a song with your family.")[109] Another day, emerging from his morphine fog, Peter gestured at a nurse going about her duties, and whispered: "Look at this poor woman, how hard she's working."[110] Michel Dobbs visited on behalf of the Ocean Zendo, and he told Muryo Roshi that he was going to recite the Heart Sutra. As Dobbs ventured into the thicket of Japanese syllables—KAN JI ZAI BO SA GYO- JIN HAN- NYA HA RA MI TA JI—Muryo spontaneously joined him, chanting through to the end without missing a beat.[111]

"HOW CAN ONE DIE," Peter had once asked during a Dharma talk, "in a modern hospital with all that noise and all those tubes and people rushing back and forth? It's the greatest nightmare."[112]

Maria and Alex knew how he felt about hospitals. They knew he had talked about dying at home, watching birds in the garden. On April 4, they made another difficult decision to honor his wish and take him back to Sagaponack. Alex would later concede that it was probably the wrong decision, that if his father had been in his "right mind," perhaps he might have said: "It's not worth it. I'm here. I'm staying here."[113] Instead, Luke told him, "We're taking you home, Dad," and Peter mumbled, "Indeedy."[114] The ambulance ride took hours, and the bumpy road only magnified his pain and discomfort. Now his fear was undeniable: he no longer understood where he was or what was happening.

In Sagaponack, his king-sized bed, framed by bookshelves, had been removed to make way for the narrow hospital cot. The diminishment unsettled Alex, who associated the missing bed with happier times, all the football games he'd watched with his father on a bedroom television. Peter was unconscious when he was wheeled in and settled opposite the window. Still, a few people stopped in to say goodbye. Piedy Lumet, his old friend, thought he looked serene, "wrapped up in a way that was very becoming."[115] Jean Kennedy Smith came, Myrna and Paul Davis brought a pot of stew, and in a selfless gesture that shocked her daughters, Maria permitted K to enter the bedroom for a few minutes. As the young woman hovered near Peter's side, unable to speak freely while his children watched, Maria remained upstairs. "My mom was very graceful about it," Sarah recalled. "But I know it was heartbreaking for her."[116]

A hired nurse monitored him throughout the afternoon and evening. Around seven in the morning, she woke Maria, who had only gone to sleep at five, to announce that the end was imminent. The family gathered in the bedroom, but Peter's heart refused to stop beating. Alex quietly joked that he was waiting for "pub date on Tuesday"—*In Paradise* was about to come out. "That made us all laugh," recalled Maria. "You have to have some kind of humor otherwise you'll go mad."[117] At the same time, Peter had started making a humming sound that Linda Coleman, who relieved the nurse, described as a form of self-comfort. The "plaintive moan" reminded Luke of "the last note of the mourning dove's call."[118] Rue heard it as "surrender"— "here's this wave coming at me, and I have to dive into it"—as well as "an appeal for forgiveness."[119] Alex was disturbed by the noise; he broke down as his father gasped repeatedly. "It was," Alex said, "such an ignominious way for him to end, given who he was and how he saw himself and the kind of death he wanted to have."[120]

Peter survived through the morning and afternoon of Saturday, April 5. When his breathing slowed and the moaning finally ceased, Linda Coleman indicated that it really was time. Claire de Brunner, Luke's wife, put on a recording of Mozart's wind concertos. Michel Dobbs, who had spent the night holding a vigil in the house, lit some incense. Coleman encouraged everyone to speak soothing words, telling Peter—as he had once told Bill Styron—that he could let go, that he didn't need to hold on anymore. Unable to see, Luke concentrated on what he could hear of the scene, and the description in his memoir is stunningly vivid:

> Murmured prayers, the movement of my family closer to him, love and fatigue in their words, the room filling with audible anticipation. With a crescendo like that of approaching geese, the tree outside his window came alive with song, dozens of birds calling as if in a single voice, a cacophony I probably would have missed had I not been paying attention.[121]

Suddenly "the birds went away,"[122] and Peter Matthiessen died.

Led by Dobbs, the family would now chant the Kannon Sutra and wash the body in the Zen way, with each person applying themselves to a different limb or part of the torso. But in the immediate moments after Peter's final exhalation, everyone made space for Maria, who sat down next to her partner of more than forty years, and who said, in the ringing silence of an otherwise ordinary spring afternoon, "A mighty oak has fallen."[123]

Epilogue

News of Peter Matthiessen's death spread rapidly in the evening of April 5, 2014—a little *too* rapidly, in Luke's opinion. *The New York Times* posted an obituary online before he arrived home from Sagaponack: "we weren't to be allowed even a few hours of private mourning."[1]

The obituary, written by Christopher Lehmann-Haupt, described a "rugged, weather-beaten figure" who was "a man of many parts: littérateur, journalist, environmentalist, explorer, Zen Buddhist, professional fisherman and, in the early 1950s, undercover agent for the Central Intelligence Agency in Paris."[2] (But primarily a *novelist*, Matthiessen might have retorted.) The obit was quickly joined by a dozen other postscripts and lionizing tributes that attempted to make sense of an infinitely complicated icon. James Salter wrote perhaps the most clear-eyed reckoning for *The New Yorker:* "There were aspects of Peter that faced elsewhere—his spiritual life, his solitary travels, the intimate side of his past—and that you knew only by chance or from reading his books."[3]

Because *In Paradise* was published on April 9, just four days after Matthiessen died, the coverage for it took on an elegiac tone. Reviewers were respectful about the author, if somewhat more mixed about his novel, and the swirl of press attention helped propel it briefly to the Best Sellers list. *In Paradise* was a relatively minor achievement, but Matthiessen's literary reputation was already secured by *The Snow Leopard* and *Shadow Country*, not to mention *The Paris Review* (and *Far Tortuga*, perhaps, if it ever gets the reevaluation it deserves). Today, his legacy rests just as much on the writing as it does on his example, the precedents he set throughout an astonishing career. Here was a man who, coming at the forefront of the modern environmental movement, spent decades warning people about the accelerating loss of landscapes and wildlife to which he bore witness. Here was a man who insisted, vehemently, that Indigenous people be included, even prioritized, in discussion around conservation. Here was a man who answered Camus's challenge to speak up "for those who cannot do so" by normalizing the practice of advocacy journalism—who argued, in fact, that being an "activist-ranter" and "a pain in the butt" was a moral imperative given our alarming social and climatic circumstances. Here was a man who recognized early what more and more people are only now coming to understand: that we need a new way of thinking about the world around us, a new ethic based on justice, humility, dignity, and respect, if we are going to endure as a species. Matthiessen's trailblazing sensibility has already influenced a generation of writers and thinkers who followed in his footsteps, and his work, through the work he helped make possible, will continue to reverberate for years.

His memorial was held in Sagaponack on the brisk, cloudless morning of April 14. The Matthiessens walked together to the village cemetery, and Peter's ashes—Alex forgot the urn and had to run back for it—were interned next to Deborah Love, in a plot decorated with rocks and feathers and shells. Maria read out one of her poems, titled "4:40 AM":

> When I miss you it is the silent,
> remote, self-wrapped man.
> The one asleep on his stomach
> the one who holds me
> absently in his arms,
> who picks out an apple
> and walks bare footed
> across the luminous, wet grass.
> That is the person
> I try to delay
> when his thoughts are
> eons past me.
> He is the one
> I miss.[4]

Back at the house, a large group of friends and admirers had gathered on the patio. Many were residents of the East End, and a number were farmers and fishermen. Luke gave a speech, followed by Alex, Rue, and Sarah Koenig, and then friends including Carl Safina, Tom Styron, and Victor Emanuel spoke. Terry McDonell would later recall an older Russian man who lived nearby getting up to share a few words; the man announced that "he loved the dirt and just looking at the fields early in the morning, and that Peter had loved that too and in the same way."[5] His connection with the landscape and its creatures was what the locals seemed to appreciate most about their longtime neighbor.

Over the following few months, Maria packed up Peter's writing studio and office, a mammoth task of organizing files into archival boxes destined for the Harry Ransom Center in Austin, Texas. "She never laid flat on her face for a moment," said Ngaere Macray. "I think she must have paid a toll for it somewhere, but you never saw it."[6] The rest of the house, too, was packed up by Maria. Peter had left his children a sizable inheritance in the form of real estate, his $35,000 investment in 1960 now worth multiple millions. For financial reasons, and to generate the cash to pay the soon-to-be-due estate taxes, the family had to sell the developed half of the property. Maria moved her possessions to the Sag Harbor house. What she didn't take, and what the children didn't want, was offered to the public in a November estate sale managed by an outside agent. An enthusiastic announcement promised a "treasure trove of artifacts and mementos. Both indigenous and from the 4 corners of the Earth."[7]

On the day of the sale, a long line of fans, bargain hunters, collectors, and rubberneckers snaked along the driveway and down Bridge Lane. The scene, described by Sadie Stein for *The Paris Review*, was a spectacle. One man, offended by a woman who dared join her friend in the line ahead of him, exploded in a profanity-filled rant. When somebody chastised him for not behaving "in the spirit of Peter Matthiessen," the man screamed: *"Fuck Peter Matthiessen!"*

"There was a shocked gasp," Stein wrote.[8]

After the estate sale, with Maria now gone, the Sagaponack property fell quiet. Though it was almost immediately sold, the new owners removed a Japanese maple and left the rest to go fallow or fall into disrepair. The land was more a valuable investment than the ramshackle house, a converted garage dwarfed by the surrounding mansions in the state's most expensive zip code, 11962. A year passed. Then a second year. Then a third and a fourth year. The garden grew wild, brambles overtaking what had once been daffodils, columbines, hydrangeas, rhododendrons. Weeds invaded the rake-combed pebbles of Peter's karesansui, until it was all but invisible behind the abandoned zendo. A sea of grass swelled against the house, lapping at its shingles; vines curled around the front screen door as if to prize it open. Inside, mice and raccoons colonized rooms blanketed with mold, rooms smelling of earth and rot and stale air. Plaster flaked off the walls, dust collected in corners, and one of the upstairs bedrooms, perhaps after a heavy storm, opened to the elements when part of the ceiling caved in, leaving a fan dangling sideways over sodden carpet.

In August 2018, I visited the property with Alex Matthiessen and his young son, Theo—Peter's grandson—pushing past a wall of vegetation that hides the place from prying eyes. It was like getting a glimpse of the world without us: here is what would happen, in remarkably short order, if humanity suddenly vanished. I was reminded of *Lost Man's River* when a character returns to the old Watson house in the Ten Thousand Islands to find it "all gray and busted, jungled over."[9]

Alex guided me around his childhood home, pointing out the living room wall where Peter had once mounted the spears collected in Netherlands New Guinea, and the roof ledge outside the upstairs tearoom where he had once piled flat stones, like an elevated rock garden, to cheer up Deborah when she was sick. We inspected each room in the house, then made our way through an overgrown orchard to the small writing studio at the rear of the property, not far from the road that leads to Sagg Main Beach. The door was unlocked, and pushing it open, we were met with the putrid stench of animal scat, but I went in anyway. When my eyes adjusted to the gloom, I found two unmistakable traces of the writer who had once spent countless hours daydreaming in this former child's playhouse: a faded poster showing an artist's impression of bigfoot, or the Sasquatch; and a single issue of *The Paris Review*—No. 150, featuring Peter Matthiessen on the Art of Fiction.

Everything else had been reclaimed by nature.

"WE WONDER ALWAYS," Muryo Roshi once said during a Dharma talk in the Ocean Zendo, "what remains when we die? It would be comforting to know that something remains other than our jewelry, which our children are fighting over."[10]

He could never bring himself to believe in a heavenly afterlife. He was unconvinced by the Buddhist doctrine of reincarnation (though if he *was* reincarnated, he told Howard Norman during their final conversation, he hoped it would be as one of those rangers charged with protecting the last white rhinos on earth). But nor did he think dying just meant annihilation, the snuffing out of every aspect of "this aggregation known as PM."[11] Instead, he made another distinction between the relative and absolute. What disappears, in his view, is "the small relative mind"—thoughts and consciousness, along with all the empirical details that make up a person's lived experience, "these clothes, this place." All that stuff fades into darkness. What remains is something harder to pin down with language: Absolute Mind, Essential Mind, Buddha Mind. This is not, Muryo Roshi clarified for his students, the same thing as a *soul*, which is tethered to ego ("*my* soul"). Rather, it is the Emptiness at the heart of everything in the universe. "We are nothing but 'the behavior of water,' the manifestation of ether, no detail, no individual identity, not alienated from everything. All complete."

Acknowledgments

In early November 2017, I drove out to Sag Harbor to tell Maria Matthiessen, over cups of tea in her cozy kitchen, that I was thinking of writing a book about her late husband. Maria gave me her blessing that day—along with the warning that I was committing to something far larger than I realized, a vast labyrinth of a subject. She was right, and I thank her for remaining a dependable source of guidance and friendship during the nearly eight years the book took to write. This biography was not "authorized" by Maria, or by Peter Matthiessen's children—the final edit was mine alone—but I am grateful for the family's willing cooperation. Alex, Rue, and Luke (before he sadly died of cancer in 2022) fielded my nosy inquiries with extraordinary grace and openness, as did Maria's two daughters, Antonia and Sarah Koenig. I also want to thank Jeff Wheelwright for his sage advice over the years, and other members of the extended Matthiessen clan for talking to me at one time or another: Cis Matthiessen, Hope Matthiessen, Mary Wheelwright, Molly Wheelwright, Peter Matthiessen Wheelwright, and Claire de Brunner.

Although my name is the one on the cover, hundreds of people contributed to this book in different ways. It would be a far lesser work without Jeff Sewald, who shared the original transcripts of interviews he conducted for his 2009 documentary, *Peter Matthiessen: No Boundaries*. A quick glance at the endnotes reveals how valuable those interviews turned out to be. Thanks, Jeff. I also benefited from access to the private collections of Margaret Thomas Buchholz, George Schaller, Gay Talese, and Hans Teensma, among others. Wendy Morgan (née Burden), after showing me more than a hundred of her precious Matthiessen letters from the 1940s, agreed to donate them to the Harry Ransom Center—a gift that will benefit future researchers.

Speaking of the Ransom Center, it effectively became my office for almost a full year. I am grateful for the help I received there from Megan Barnard,

Michael Gilmore, Ancelyn Krivak, Kathryn Millan (who always brightened my day), Amy Wagner, and Rick Watson. I relied on numerous other librarians and archivists around the country, too, and they are all national treasures. To name just a few: Andrea Meyer and Mayra Scanlon at the East Hampton Library; Anders Winroth at the Elizabethan Club at Yale; Rosemary Davis at Hotchkiss; Sarah Pratt at the Howard Gotlieb Archival Research Center; Genie Henderson for some LTV recordings; Erin Schultz at the Minnesota Historical Society; Christine Nelson and María Isabel Molestina at the Morgan Library & Museum; Elise Fariello at the National Archives in Chicago; Thomas Lannon, Melanie Locay, Tal Nadan, Philip Sutton, and Carolyn Vega at the New York Public Library (more on that glorious institution in a moment); Mary Ann Quinn at the Rockefeller Archive Center; Juliette Monet at Sweet Briar College; and Michael Lotstein at the Yale University Archives.

I conducted hundreds of interviews for this book, some in person and many more via phone, email, CorrLinks, Zoom, or, in one case, Twitter DM. For sharing their thoughts and memories, my thanks go to Susan Abbot, Nelson W. Aldrich Jr., George Archibald, Subhankar Banerjee, Robert Bateman, Mary Morris Booth, Christopher Braider, Jackson Braider, Susan Braider, Barbara Brice, Jan Broekhuijse (with help from Gies Broekhuijse), Mark Bryant, Margaret Thomas Buchholz, Dan Budnick, Steve Byers, Mitchell Doshin Cantor, Lee Carlson, David Chadwick, Bill Chaliff, Megan Chaskey, Scott Chaskey, LeRoy Chatfield, Blair Childs, Lisa Choegyal, Jerry Cohen, Darrah Cole, Marshall Cole, Linda Coleman, Rachel Crespin, Peter Cunningham, Rameshwar Das, Myrna Davis, Paul Davis, Veronica Decanio, Michel Dobbs, Cile Downs, Louisa Drury, Nicholas Dujmovic, Stuart Dybek, Norma Edwards, Bruce Ellison, Victor Emanuel, Jason Epstein, James Fadiman, Polly Finn, Adam Fisher, Charles Tenshin Fletcher, Jill Fox, Dorothy Friedman, Deb Futter, Merete Galesi, Martin Garbus, Alan Gillespie, Bernie Glassman, Philip Gourevitch, Adam Green, Brian Haley, Joan Jiko Halifax, Helen Harkaspi, Karl Heider, Jane Stanton Hitchcock, Shirley Howard, John Irving, Pico Iyer, Marvin Kammerer, David Karnos, Doug Kuntz, Richard Kurnit, Winona LaDuke, Thomas Laird, Peter Lake, Jim Leach, Alvin Lederer, Marian Lindberg, Bob Loomis, Barry Lopez, Margaret Lord, Sid Lovett, Piedy Lumet, Ngaere Macray, Harry McCormick, Terry McDonell, Bill McKibben, Kevin McKiernan, Alexander McLanahan, Jeffrey McNeely, Jeffrey Meldrum, Christopher Merrill, David Michaelis, Payne Whitney Middleton, Wendy Morgan, Mira Nakashima, Jason Neimark, Howard Norman, Neil Olson, Doug Peacock, Leonard Peltier, Jesse Pollock, Elizabeth Porebski, Peter Porebski, Job Potter, Adele Pressman, Anton Prohaska, Betsy Gaines Quammen, Diana Rathbun, Serena

Rathbun, Robin Ridington, Carl Safina, Rebecca Saletan, George Schaller, Kay Schaller, Charles Schlesinger, Michael Schuster, Sheridan Segundo, Jeff Sewald, Lawrence Shainberg, Naomi Shihab Nye, Shinge Roshi (Roko Sherry Chayat), Elisabeth Sifton, Sarita Southgate, Gerry Spence, Renny Stackpole, Don Stap, Pat Stewart, Rose Styron, Susanna Styron, Tom Styron, Gay Talese, Nan Talese, Valerie Taylor, Hans Teensma, Mark Tilsen, Amor Towles, John Train, Frederick Turner, Helen Tworkov, Rusty Unger, Freck Vreeland, Christian White, Charles Wright, Karen Yochim, Jack Zajac, and a handful of people who asked to remain anonymous.

The unquestionable highlight of this entire project was my journey to the Crystal Monastery in May 2022, retracing much of the expedition Matthiessen describes in *The Snow Leopard*. This gigantic undertaking was made possible through the tireless effort (for *years*) of Gavin Anderson, whose trekking company, Nomadic Skies, should be a model for ethical tourism initiatives everywhere. Our walk together across the Himalayas was one of the greatest things I have ever done in my life, even with the unexpected illness. It was made special not only by Gavin, a true bodhisattva, as Matthiessen would say, but also by the fearless photographer James Appleton, by Nurbu Lama, and by our local team in Dolpo: Dawa Gyalpo Baiji, Ganesh, Keshar, Laxmi, and Dependra. I will never forget it.

Closer to home, Jim Leach arranged an illuminating visit to the Pine Ridge Indian Reservation in South Dakota. My thanks to Jim for his good company and legal knowledge, and to his lovely wife, Ann Trucano, for her warm hospitality. Pierce Rafferty showed me around the exclusive enclave of Fishers Island, where Hillary Schafer kindly granted me access to her property. Prudence Carabine shared the fascinating history of Springs and the East End Bonackers. Jeana Fucello, an avid birder, accompanied me to Aransas National Wildlife Refuge, in Texas, so I could figure out Matthiessen's obsession with cranes. To get acquainted with Zen, I spent time at Dai Bosatsu Zendo Kongo-ji in the Catskill Mountains; thanks to everyone at the Zen Studies Society for hosting me there, and to Kikko Maeyama, my fellow novice on the black cushion. Gassho.

An unfortunate fact of biography is that it is not only time-consuming but prohibitively expensive. I could not have finished this project without fellowships and grants. The first, in 2020, was the Hazel Rowley Literary Fellowship, a meaningful pledge of support from my country of origin. I am grateful for the faith of Della Rowley, Lynn Buchanan, John Murphy, Irene Tomaszewski, and the entire crew at Writers Victoria in Australia.

That same year, I was awarded another transformative fellowship through the Leon Levy Center for Biography. Kai Bird and Thad Ziolkowski have my gratitude for their long-distance encouragement during a global pandemic, as do my fellow Levy recipients: Nicholas Boggs, Miriam Horn, Susan Morrison, and Francesca Wade, all of whom have written excellent books.

For the Robert and Ina Caro Research/Travel Fellowship, I want to thank Deidre David, Marc Leepson, Steve Paul, and BIO International. For a month-long supported fellowship in late 2021, my thanks once again to the staff at the Harry Ransom Center. For a Public Scholar grant in 2021–22, I am grateful to the National Endowment for the Humanities.

During the 2023–24 academic year, I was the Janice B. and Milford D. Gerton/Arts and Letters Foundation Fellow at the Dorothy and Lewis B. Cullman Center for Scholars and Writers, at the New York Public Library. The Cullman Center is my own idea of paradise, an island of tranquility in the middle of Manhattan, and that is largely because of the people who run it. During my tenure that was Salvatore Scibona, Lauren Goldenberg, Paul Delaverdac, and Catherine Nichols. Thanks to Martha Hodes for making the initial offer (I nearly dropped the phone in shock), and to the rest of my beloved Cullman cohort: Seth Anziska, Jessica Bruder, Molly Crabapple, Caoilinn Hughes, Amitava Kumar, Catherine Lacey, Deborah Lutz, Stephanie McCurry, Sara McDougall, Suleiman Osman, Yasmine Seale, Nicole Sealey, Accra Shepp, and Brenda Wineapple.

For the gift of space and solitude when I needed it, my thanks to MacDowell, where I had the Eleanor Briggs Fellowship for five weeks; to Yaddo, where I passed half of a snowy December; and to the Key West Literary Seminar—to Arlo Haskell, Katie Leigh, and Katrin Schumann—for a delightful June stay filled with sunshine and bike rides. A substantial amount of the book was drafted in my hometown of Providence, Rhode Island, at a dedicated writer's space called LitArts RI, run by the powerhouse team of Susannah Morse, Jodie Vinson, and Jillian Winters. Providence is lucky to have them.

For some research assistance along the way, I want to celebrate the doggedness of Meghan Gunn and Ella Hester. In an act of astonishing generosity, David Smith wrote to *me* volunteering his services, for which I am very grateful. A number of other people read the manuscript either in whole or in part, and offered corrections that saved me from considerable embarrassment: Nicholas Boggs, Nicholas Dujmovic, Bruce Ellison, Alison Humes, Jim Leach, Neil Olson, Shinge Roshi (a kind and generous guide in Zen), Francesca Wade, and the Matthiessens. I am indebted to you all. My great friend Brooke Kroeger not only read chapters but taught me nearly everything I know about organizing an insane volume of research into something manageable. You are the best, Brooke. My special thanks also go to Howard Norman, who inspected the entire first draft, page by page, with diligent attention, and whose enthusiasm lifted me over some real low points.

For various favors and kindnesses, I want to acknowledge Mark Adams, Tim Cahill, Heather Clark, Benoit Denizet-Lewis, Matthew Evans, Liz Flock, Nona Footz, Todd Goddard, Anne-Marie Grant, Amanda Guinzburg, Brian Haley (again), Carl Hoffman, Ernst Karel, Daniela Kronemeyer, Veronika Kusumaryati, Claudia Lang, Ken Lopez, Megan Marshall, Rob Moor, Benjamin Moser, Tim Nye, Miriam Pawel, Amy Reading, Katie Roiphe, Kay Salter, Dennis Jerome Sears, Justin Spring, Daniel Stone, Bryant Urstadt, Randy Wayne White, and Robert Wolf of Tarter Krinsky & Drogin. It was Gemma Pitcher who lent me her paperback of *The Snow Leopard* all those years ago, so I suppose this is your fault, Gemma. (Thank you.) Sally Sparke inspired me to be a writer in the first place—the biggest favor of them all.

I was blessed to have Deborah Garrison as my editor on this project. Deb understood exactly what I was trying to do from the beginning, encouraged me the whole way, and approached my drafts, when she finally received them, with exquisite care of a brain surgeon. I never want to work with anyone else. Alongside Deb, Zuleima Ugalde made the publication process a pleasure, which is no mean feat. Everybody at Pantheon Books has my gratitude: Bill Thomas, Denise Oswald, Rose Cronin-Jackman, Juliane Pautrot, Stevie Pannenberg, Lisa D'Agostino, Felecia O'Connell, Fred Chase, Cassandra Pappas, and Amelia Zalcman. Thanks to Tyler Comrie for the perfect cover. I also want to single out Lisa Lucas, a brilliant, tireless advocate of books, for her support.

For shepherding the beautiful British edition of *True Nature* into print for Chatto & Windus, my thanks go to Molly Slight, Clara Farmer, Rose Tomaszewska, Asia Choudhry, Ellie Auton, Rhiannon Roy, Lucy Chaudhuri, Lucy Thorne, and Polly Dorner. Chatto published *The Snow Leopard* back in 1979, and I'm thrilled to add my book to the catalogue forty-six years later.

Of course, none of this would have happened without Sterling Lord Literistic: Jessica Friedman, Szilvia Molnar, and above all Flip Brophy, the best agent a writer could hope to have in his corner. Flip, I promise the next book will be shorter.

As for my family, a "thank you" feels insufficient, which is why I have dedicated this book to my wonderful parents, Murray and Donna Richardson, and to my partner, Theo Milonopoulos, who is probably very sick of hearing about Peter Matthiessen. I love you.

Notes

SOURCES

When I started work on this biography, the Peter Matthiessen Papers at the Harry Ransom Center in Austin, Texas, were spread across four discrete collections that had been acquired from the Matthiessen family in 1996, 2000, 2004, and 2014. The latter collection had not yet been processed by Ransom staff; I found it in the original cartons that had been delivered to the archive not long after Peter's death. In 2020, Ancelyn Krivak, an archivist, began the immense task of consolidating the four collections into one. She finished the project in 2022. This is excellent news for future researchers—the finding aid is a marvel—but I was too far along to update the new location of every scrap of paper across 227 manuscript boxes. References in this book to the Peter Matthiessen Papers therefore correspond to the older four-part arrangement.

ABBREVIATIONS

Names

- DL   Deborah Love
- ES   Elisabeth Sifton
- GP   George Plimpton
- GS   George Schaller
- HH   Harold "Doc" Humes
- HN   Howard Norman
- JF   Joe Fox
- JH   Jim Harrison
- KH   Karl Heider
- LR   Lance Richardson
- MK/MM   Maria Koenig / Maria Matthiessen (née Eckhart)
- PM   Peter Matthiessen
- PS   Patsy Southgate
- PWP   Payne Whitney Payson
- RG   Robert Gardner
- TG   Tom Guinzburg
- WB   Wendy Burden
- WS   William Styron
- WSM   William Stanley Merwin

Manuscript Collections and Archives

- AAB Anna Andreini-Brophy Papers, Walter P. Reuther Library, Wayne State University
- DHA Doc Humes Archive, Literary and Historical Manuscripts Department, The Morgan Library & Museum (MA 8492); purchased as the gift of The Buddy Taub Foundation, Dennis A. Roach and Jill Roach Directors, 2013
- ESP Elisabeth Sifton Papers, University Archives, Rare Books and Manuscript Library, Columbia University Libraries
- GPP George Plimpton Papers, Manuscripts and Archives Division, New York Public Library; Astor, Lenox, and Tilden Foundations
- GTC Gay Talese Private Collection
- HBR Harper & Brothers Records, Harry Ransom Center, The University of Texas at Austin
- HNC Howard Norman Collection, Howard Gotlieb Archival Research Center, Boston University Libraries
- JHP Jim Harrison Papers, Special Collections and University Archives, Grand Valley State University
- JSC Jeff Sewald Collection
- KWLS Key West Literary Seminar Audio Archives
- MMC Maria Matthiessen Collection
- NAC National Archives at Chicago
- NYR The New Yorker Records, Manuscripts and Archives Division, New York Public Library; Astor, Lenox, and Tilden Foundations
- PMP 1/2/3/4 Peter Matthiessen Papers, Harry Ransom Center, The University of Texas at Austin; 1 (1996 accession); 2 (2000); 3 (2004); 4 (2014)
- PRA The Paris Review Archives (1952–2003), Literary and Historical Manuscripts Department, The Morgan Library & Museum (MA 5040)
- PRH Penguin Random House internal records
- RGC Robert Gardner Collection, Harvard Film Archive, Harvard University
- RHR Random House Records, University Archives, Rare Books and Manuscript Library, Columbia University Libraries
- RV Russell and Volkening Records, Manuscripts and Archives Division, New York Public Library; Astor, Lenox, and Tilden Foundations
- UFW United Farm Workers Administration Department Files, Walter P. Reuther Library, Wayne State University
- WBC Wendy Burden Collection of Peter Matthiessen Letters, Harry Ransom Center, The University of Texas at Austin
- WSMP W. S. Merwin Papers, University of Illinois
- YAL Yale College Student Records (RU 587), Manuscripts and Archives, Yale University Library

Works by Matthiessen

- APFL *At Play in the Fields of the Lord* (1965)
- AS *African Silences* (1991)
- BAI *Baikal* (1992)
- BB *Bone by Bone* (1999)
- BM *Blue Meridian* (1971); page numbers refer to 1997 Penguin Books paperback
- BOH *Birds of Heaven* (2001)
- CF *The Cloud Forest* (1961)
- ELM *East of Lo Monthang* (1995)
- EOE *End of the Earth* (2003)
- FT *Far Tortuga* (1975)
- IC *Indian Country* (1984)
- IP *In Paradise* (2014)

ITSCH *In the Spirit of Crazy Horse* (1983); page numbers refer to the 1991 Penguin re-release edition
KMW *Killing Mister Watson* (1990)
LMR *Lost Man's River* (1997)
ML *Men's Lives* (1986); page numbers refer to the 1988 Vintage Books paperback
NHDR *Nine-Headed Dragon River* (1986)
OOM *Oomingmak* (1967)
OTRS *On the River Styx* (1989)
PAR *Partisans* (1955); page numbers refer to the 1987 Vintage Books paperback
RAD *Raditzer* (1961); page numbers refer to the 1987 Vintage Books paperback
RR *Race Rock* (1954); page numbers refer to the 1968 Avon paperback
SC *Shadow Country* (2008)
SL *The Snow Leopard* (1978)
SNA *The Shorebirds of North America* (1967)
SP *Seal Pool* (1972)
SR *Sand Rivers* (1981)
SSP *Sal Si Puedes* (1969)
TTS *Tigers in the Snow* (2000)
TWMB *The Tree Where Man Was Born* (1972)
UTMW *Under the Mountain Wall* (1962)
WIA *Wildlife in America* (1959); page numbers refer to the 1995 Penguin Books paperback

1. PM, "Foreword," in Anagarika Govinda, *The Way of White Clouds: A Buddhist Pilgrimage in Tibet* (Boston: Shambhala, 1988 [1966]), xiii.

INTRODUCTION

1. SL, 3.
2. Ibid., 58.
3. Ibid., 173–74.
4. Ibid., 244.
5. Ibid., 176.
6. PM, interviewed by Betsy Gaines Quammen for the Tributary Fund, 2010. See www.youtube.com/watch?v=xyrPhCim11A.
7. Helen Macdonald, *Vesper Flights* (New York: Grove Atlantic, 2020), 247–48.
8. Philip Hoare, *The Whale* (New York: Ecco, 2010), 198.
9. PM, "Poetry and Mysticism in Native American Teaching," Regents Lecture, UC Santa Barbara, November 15, 1978.
10. WS, "My Generation," *Esquire*, October 1968.
11. Bill McKibben, interviewed by LR, October 9, 2019.
12. Barry Lopez to PM, May 11, 1979. PMP 3, Box 24.
13. WS, "My Generation," *Esquire*, October 1968.
14. PM, quoted in "New Yorkers Aren't Interested in Stories About Swamp People," *The Observer*, May 10, 1998.
15. James Salter, introductory speech, February 10, 2000. PMP 3, Box 27.
16. Nicholas Dawidoff, "Earthbound in the Space Age," *Sports Illustrated*, December 1990.
17. Rosemary Goring, "Man with No Fame," *Scotland on Sunday*, May 3, 1998.
18. McKay Jenkins, "Introduction," in *The Peter Matthiessen Reader* (New York: Vintage, 2000), xiii.
19. Henry Allen, "Journeys into Meaning with Author Peter Matthiessen," *Washington Post*, December 13, 1978.
20. Terry McDonell, *The Accidental Life* (New York: Vintage, 2016), 31–32.
21. PM to JH, n.d. [April 1979]. JHP, Box 32.
22. PM, interviewed by Jeff Sewald, October 6, 2006. JSC.
23. Pico Iyer, "Laureate of the Wild," *Time*, November 1, 1993.

24. PM to JH, n.d. [April 1973]. JHP, Box 32.
25. *SL*, 118–19.
26. Ibid., 40.
27. Ibid., 171.

I · HOME WATERS

1. PM, Untitled teisho, September 26, 2000. MMC.
2. PM, interviewed by Mark Adams, February 14, 2014. Collection of Mark Adams.
3. *SL*, 37–38.
4. PM, Memoir notes. MMC. The final draft is dated March 15, 2014.
5. Matthiessen attributed the quote to "Anonymous" in his memoir notes, perhaps because he couldn't remember the source, which was a Paul Auster interview in *The Paris Review*, No. 167, Fall 1999.
6. "Fisher's [sic] Island Project," *New York Times*, May 21, 1925.
7. Permanent exhibition at the Henry L. Ferguson Museum, Fishers Island.
8. Quoted in Charles B. Ferguson and Pierce Rafferty, *The Fishers Island Club and Its Gold Links: The First Seventy-Five Years* (New York: Fishers Island Club, 1994), 13. Ferguson and Rafferty date the brochure to c. 1941.
9. See, for example: PM, "New York: Old Hometown," *Architectural Digest*, November 1989. Matthiessen originally claimed that Charles Lindbergh arrived in Paris the same day he was born, an error he corrected in his memoir notes. A more curious (and recurring) mistake was the hospital—he believed he was born at "the Le Roy Hospital, a small 'lying-in' establishment off Madison Avenue in the East Sixties." In fact, the LeRoy Sanitarium would not open on East 61st Street until 1928, and Matthiessen's own birth certificate states "Miss Lippincott's Sanitarium."
10. "May T. Lippincott, Sanitarium Head," *New York Times*, June 3, 1938.
11. "What Some People Are Doing in Society," *Chicago Inter Ocean*, July 6, 1913.
12. Erard Matthiessen joined the Fishers Island Club sometime between June 1926 and November 1927, when he first appears on the published "List of Members." Held by the Henry L. Ferguson Museum.
13. PM, Memoir notes. MMC.
14. Ibid.
15. Ibid. An abbreviated version of this anecdote appears in "Great River," Matthiessen's contribution to Joseph Barbato and Lisa Weinerman (eds.), *Heart of the Land: Essays on Last Great Places* (New York: Pantheon, 1994), 273–80.
16. *BM*, 11.
17. Matthiessen Family Record and Album, 2. PMP 4, Box 24.
18. Ibid.
19. PM, "The Captain's Trail," *Condé Nast Traveler*, January 1989.
20. Matthiessen Family Record and Album, 4. PMP 4, Box 24.
21. "The Long Journey: Zen and the Writing Life" (audio recording), San Francisco Zen Center, 1998.
22. Herman Melville, *Moby-Dick* (New York: Charles Scribner's Sons, 1902), 140.
23. "The Long Journey: Zen and the Writing Life" (audio recording), San Francisco Zen Center, 1998.
24. "F. O. Matthiessen Dies in His Paris Home," *New York Times*, March 10, 1901.
25. *Matthiessen & Hegeler Zinc Company: Our First Century of Service* (La Salle, IL: Matthiessen & Hegeler Zinc Company, 1958), 14. Matthiessen makes the observation about bullets in "New York: Old Hometown," *Architectural Digest*, November 1989.
26. This idea, which is not contradicted by anything in the family papers, was brought to my attention by Patrick Gilmartin in "The Remarkable Matthiessens," *The Roost*, Irvington Historical Society, Vol. 18, No. 1, Winter 2017.
27. "Yields Up His Salary," *Rich Hill Tribune*, August 24, 1905.
28. PM, "The Centerpiece," OTRS, 28.

29. *A History of the City of Chicago: Its Men and Institutions* (Chicago: The Inter Ocean, 1900), 467.
30. PM, "New York: Old Hometown," *Architectural Digest*, November 1989.
31. Ibid.
32. See "Trouble in the Big Corn Products Company," *Evening Star*, May 4, 1907; "Stockholder Liable in One State but Not in Another," *Arizona Republic*, February 27, 1912.
33. For Irvington-on-Hudson background, see Judith Doolin Spikes and Anne Marie Leone, *Irvington (Then and Now)* (Mount Pleasant, SC: Arcadia Publishing, 2009).
34. "F. O. Matthiessen Dies in His Paris Home," *New York Times*, March 10, 1901.
35. PM, "Lumumba Lives," *OTRS*, 172.
36. Ibid., 181.
37. Ibid., 177.
38. PM, Memoir notes. MMC.
39. PM, "The Captain's Trail," *Condé Nast Traveler*, January 1989.
40. Erard Matthiessen to Family, April 10, 1977. PMP 4, Box 36.
41. TG, interviewed by Jeff Sewald, November 29, 2006. JSC.
42. Piedy Lumet (née Bailey), interviewed by Jeff Sewald, December 5, 2006. JSC.
43. MM, interviewed by Jeff Sewald, n.d. [2006]. JSC.
44. Erard Matthiessen's transcript, January 2, 1942. YAL. For social activities, see the 1922 *Yale Banner*.
45. Mary Wheelwright, interviewed by LR, September 22, 2018.
46. PM, "Homegoing," in Evelyn D. Ward, *Children of Bladensfield* (New York: Viking, 1978), 116.
47. Evelyn D. Ward, *Children of Bladensfield*, 78.
48. Ibid., 112.
49. "A. O. H. Auxiliary Card Party Plans," *Perth Amboy Evening News*, October 22, 1923. "Miss Elizabeth Carey" is listed as an assistant to the organizers, and the "peanut jab" is singled out as an attraction. The game explanation comes from *Good Housekeeping*, January 1908.
50. Jeff Wheelwright, interviewed by LR, February 22, 2020.
51. "Miss Carey and E. A. Matthiessen Wed in Country," *New York Tribune*, October 12, 1924.
52. Elizabeth Matthiessen to Evelyn Ward, January 7, 1925. PMP 4, Box 40.
53. William A. Boring (director of the School of Architecture), quoted in "Architecture Has Record Enrolment," *Columbia Spectator*, November 9, 1927.
54. Erard Matthiessen to Family, April 10, 1977. PMP 4, Box 36.
55. Jill Lepore, *These Truths: A History of the United States* (New York: W. W. Norton, 2018), 440.
56. PM, "New York: Old Hometown," *Architectural Digest*, November 1989.
57. "44 Without Work Are Given Jobs Thru Relief Bureau," *Irvington Gazette*, December 11, 1931.
58. Editorial, *Irvington Gazette*, January 29, 1932.
59. "Irvington-on-Hudson," *New York Herald Tribune*, November 20, 1932.
60. "Woman 'Raffles' Steals $15,000 in Jewelry; Enters Irvington (N.Y.) Home, Posing as Guest," *New York Times*, October 27, 1930. See also "Woman Sought in $15,000 Gem Theft," *Irvington Gazette*, October 28, 1930.
61. "Police Prompt to Apprehend Woman Thief...," *Irvington Gazette*, October 31, 1930.
62. Ibid.
63. "Woman 'Raffles' Pleads," *New York Times*, October 31, 1930.
64. PM, Memoir notes. MMC.
65. Ibid.
66. St. Bernard's launch brochure, quoted in John S. Brodie et al., *Saint Bernard's School: The First Century, 1904–2004* (New York: St. Bernard's, 2004), 10.
67. PM, quoted in Nelson W. Aldrich Jr. (ed.), *George, Being George* (New York: Random House, 2008), 37.

68. PM to WB, February 10, 1946. WBC.
69. PM, Memoir notes. MMC.
70. PM, Tribute to GP at the American Academy, April 7, 2004. MMC.
71. *The Weekly Blues.* Matthiessen's copy has a note attached from GP, dated May 3, 1980: "This should take you back." PMP 4, Box 11.
72. PM, interviewed by Nelson W. Aldrich Jr., n.d. GPP, Box 240.
73. Ibid.
74. PM, "New York: Old Hometown," *Architectural Digest,* November 1989.
75. PM, "Foreword," *Saving Wildlife: A Century of Conservation* (New York: Harry N. Abrams, 1995), 24.
76. PM, Memoir notes. MMC.
77. "5,000 See Acrobat Injured at Circus," *New York Times,* April 13, 1935.
78. "Buys Stamford Estate," *New York Times,* March 20, 1937.
79. "E. R. [sic] Matthiessen Sells His Estate," *Irvington Gazette,* May 8, 1941.
80. Mary Wheelwright, interviewed by LR, September 22, 2018.
81. Elizabeth Matthiessen, quoted in the editorial, *Irvington Gazette,* March 3, 1933.
82. George H. W. Bush, quoted in Jon Meacham, *Destiny and Power: The American Odyssey of George Herbert Walker Bush* (New York: Random House, 2016), 44.
83. Cis Matthiessen, interviewed by LR, March 13, 2019.
84. "Foreword," *Saving Wildlife,* 24.
85. Shirley Howard, interviewed by LR, September 25, 2019.
86. TG, interviewed by Jeff Sewald, November 29, 2006. JSC.
87. PM, Acceptance speech for the Roger Tory Peterson Medal, April 12, 2003. MMC.
88. PM, Memoir notes. MMC.
89. Mary Wheelwright, interviewed by LR, September 22, 2018.
90. Erard Matthiessen to Family, April 10, 1977. PMP 4, Box 36.
91. Rue Matthiessen, interviewed by LR, September 25, 2018.
92. Peter Matthiessen Wheelwright, interviewed by LR, September 13, 2019.
93. PM, Memoir notes. MMC.
94. Ibid.
95. PM, interviewed by Mark Adams, February 14, 2014. Collection of Mark Adams.
96. PM, LSD Journal. PMP 4, Box 25. Matthiessen drew a direct line between this psychosomatic pang and the incident with the boat in his memoir notes.
97. PM, Memoir notes. MMC.

2 · THE CURLY GOD

1. *RR,* 54.
2. PM, Memoir notes. MMC.
3. Ibid.
4. Erard Matthiessen to PM, December 12, 1975. PMP 4, Box 36.
5. John Cole, *Away All Boats: A Personal Guide for the Small-Boat Owner* (New York: Henry Holt, 1994), 2–3.
6. Mary Wheelwright, interviewed by LR, September 22, 2018.
7. *RR,* 12.
8. Ibid., 123.
9. Ibid., 54.
10. PM, interviewed by Mark Adams, February 14, 2014. Collection of Mark Adams.
11. Mary Wheelwright, interviewed by LR, September 22, 2018.
12. "Class History," *Mischianza,* 1945, 74.
13. John A. Luke, quoted in Ernest Kolowrat, *Hotchkiss: A Chronicle of an American School* (New York: New Amsterdam Books, 1992), 262.
14. I am indebted to Ernest Kolowrat for his history of Hotchkiss, particularly its response to the Second World War. See *Hotchkiss,* pp. 262–64.
15. Blair Childs, interviewed by LR, February 5, 2019.
16. *Hotchkiss Annual* of 1893, quoted in Ernest Kolowrat, *Hotchkiss,* 78.

17. Walter Buell, quoted in Wendy Carlson, "Hotchkiss, The Place," *Hotchkiss Magazine*, Summer 2017. Also see a school booklet, Barbara M. Walker, "Hotchkiss, the Place: An Appreciation of the Hotchkiss School Campus," Spring 2011.
18. PM to WB, November 22, 1945. WBC.
19. PM to WB, September 18, 1944. WBC.
20. PM to WB, November 2, 1944. WBC.
21. PM to WB, May 2, 1945. WBC.
22. PM to WB, May 24, 1945. WBC.
23. Ernest Kolowrat, *Hotchkiss*, 26.
24. William M. Freeman, "George Van Santvoord Is Dead; Hotchkiss Principal 29 Years," *New York Times*, February 20, 1975.
25. Ernest Kolowrat, *Hotchkiss*, 201.
26. Zeph Stewart, quoted in Ernest Kolowrat, *Hotchkiss*, 277.
27. Blair Childs, interviewed by LR, February 5, 2019.
28. Ernest Kolowrat, *Hotchkiss*, 26.
29. George Van Santvoord, School Record (part of a Yale University application for Matthiessen), April 14, 1945. YAL.
30. "How the Class Voted," *Hotchkiss Record*, February 24, 1945.
31. PM to WB, February 19, 1945. WBC.
32. PM to WB, May 8, 1945. WBC.
33. PM to WB, April 25, 1945. WBC.
34. PM to WB, October 3, 1944. WBC.
35. PM to WB, October 9, 1944. WBC.
36. PM, interviewed by Scott Sherman, n.d. [c. 2007]. PMP 4, Box 11.
37. PM, "New York: Old Hometown," *Architectural Digest*, November 1989.
38. PM, interviewed by Jeff Sewald, December 2005. JSC.
39. PM, "New York: Old Hometown," *Architectural Digest*, November 1989.
40. PM to WB, May 20, 1946. WBC.
41. PM, "New York: Old Hometown," *Architectural Digest*, November 1989.
42. An archive of the *Social Register* can be found in the New York Public Library.
43. WS, quoted in Trip Gabriel, "The Nature of Peter Matthiessen," *New York Times Magazine*, June 10, 1990.
44. PM, interviewed by Jeff Sewald, December 2005. JSC. In addition to his memoir notes and the other sources listed here, Matthiessen tells this story in Hillel Italie, "The Absurdity of Life," Associated Press, November 14, 2004; "Writer's Symposium by the Sea," Point Loma Nazarene University, April 2005; and Michael Shapiro, *A Sense of Place: Great Writers Talk About Their Craft, Lives, and Inspiration* (San Francisco: Travelers' Tales, 2004), 332.
45. PM, quoted in "New Yorkers Aren't Interested in Stories About Swamp People," *The Observer*, May 10, 1998.
46. Mary Wheelwright, interviewed by LR, September 22, 2018.
47. PM, interviewed by Jeff Sewald, December 2005. JSC.
48. PM, interviewed for the National Writers Series, Traverse City, October 29, 2010.
49. PM, interviewed by Scott Sherman, n.d. [c. 2007]. PMP 4, Box 11.
50. PM, interviewed by Patty Satalia for "Conversations from Penn State," 2010.
51. PM, "'Jungle Book' Fever," *Salon.com*, March 1999.
52. Kenneth Grahame, *The Wind in the Willows* (Hertfordshire: Wordsworth Editions, 1998), 103.
53. PM, "'Jungle Book' Fever," *Salon.com*, March 1999.
54. PM, "Literature and Mysticism," Regents Lecture, UC Santa Barbara, November 9, 1978. See also PM, "How Does the Writer Catch Place?," 2002. KWLS.
55. PM, "'Jungle Book' Fever," *Salon.com*, March 1999.
56. *TTS*, 13.
57. PM to WB, April 18, 1945. WBC.
58. Ibid.
59. PM to WB, March 20, 1945. WBC.
60. PM to WB, February 15, 1945. WBC.

608 · Notes

61. PM, "The Spirit of Place," 2002. KWLS.
62. PM, interviewed by HN, December 15, 1997. 92Y/The Paris Review Interview Series.
63. John Hersey, quoted in Ernest Kolowrat, *Hotchkiss*, 174.
64. PM, "To the Beauty of Sun on Copper," *The Lit*, May 1945. Hotchkiss School Archives.
65. PM to WB, March 1, 1945. WBC.
66. PM to WB, February 19, 1945. WBC.
67. PM, "The Grave of Time," *The Lit*, May 1945. Hotchkiss School Archives.
68. See "Jersey Farmer Hires Five More Japanese," *New York Herald Tribune*, April 9, 1944; "Farm Revolt Against Japanese Threatens Violence in Jersey," *New York Herald Tribune*, April 14, 1944; and "Storm Subsides as 5 Japanese Quit N.J. Farm," *New York Herald Tribune*, April 14, 1944.
69. PM, "The Rousing of the Rabble," *The Lit*, May 1944. Hotchkiss School Archives.
70. "British Awards to Go to Four Connecticut Men," *Hartford Courant*, January 28, 1946. The honors were presented on February 18, 1946, at the Waldorf-Astoria in New York, by Sir Francis Evans, the British consul-general. A photocopy of the award (dated November 28, 1945) is in PMP 4, Box 33.
71. See *Office of Naval Operations: Arming of Merchant Ships and Naval Armed Guard Service* (United States Naval Administration in World War II, 1946), 94–95. Digitized at ibilio.org/hyperwar. The training device described was the Machine Gun Trainer Mark II, a modified version of the original Waller Trainer. "This was one of the finest training devices developed during the war," the history notes. "Four gunners could track and fire at planes as the four projectors threw a panoramic composite picture on the large spherical section of the screen." These details sync up with Matthiessen's vague descriptions of his father's work at the Gunnery School. Unfortunately, Erard Matthiessen's file at the National Military Personnel Records Center consists of nothing more than a notice of separation.
72. Ibid., 91.
73. PM, Memoir notes. MMC.
74. PM's "Application for Enrollment as a Temporary Member of the Coast Guard Reserve," signed June 3, 1944. The National Military Personnel Records Center.
75. See chapter six of Malcolm F. Willoughby, *The U.S. Coast Guard in World War II* (Annapolis, MD: United States Naval Institute, 1957), particularly pp. 75, 83–84.
76. PM to WB, July 28, 1944. WBC.
77. PM to WB, August 8, 1944. WBC.
78. PM to WB, April 16, 1946. WBC.
79. PM, "Great River," in Joseph Barbato and Lisa Weinerman (eds.), *Heart of the Land: Essays on Last Great Places* (New York: Pantheon, 1994), 274.
80. PM to WB, March 1, 1945. WBC.
81. PM to WB, July 28, 1944. WBC.
82. PM to WB, March 1, 1945. WBC.
83. PM, Memoir notes. MMC.
84. PM, quoted in Michael Shnayerson, "Higher Matthiessen," *Vanity Fair*, December 1991.
85. PM to WB, August 22, 1945. WBC.
86. PM to WB, April 11, 1946. WBC.
87. Ibid.

3 · AN OPENING

1. *RAD*, 69.
2. PM to WB, January 8, 1945. WBC.
3. PM to WB, February 5, 1945. WBC.
4. PM to WB, October 14, 1944. WBC.
5. PM to WB, January 8, 1945. WBC.
6. PM to WB, March 1, 1945. WBC.
7. PM to WB, January 8, 1945. WBC.

8. PM to WB, January 25, 1945. WBC.
9. W. Douglas Burden, *Dragon Lizards of Komodo: An Expedition to the Lost World of the Dutch East Indies* (New York: G. P. Putnam's Sons, 1927), 187.
10. Wendy Morgan (née Burden), email to LR, September 1, 2020.
11. PM to WB, February 15, 1945. WBC.
12. PM to WB, January 22, 1945. WBC.
13. PM to WB, January 25, 1945. WBC.
14. PM to WB, January 8, 1945. WBC.
15. PM to WB, January 25, 1945. WBC.
16. PM, "New York: Old Hometown," *Architectural Digest*, November 1989.
17. PM to WB, September 27, 1944. WBC.
18. PM to WB, May 8, 1945. WBC.
19. PM to WB, May 25, 1945. WBC.
20. Joseph Durso, "Joan Whitney Payson, 72, Met Owner, Dies," *New York Times*, October 5, 1975.
21. PM, Memoir notes. MMC.
22. PM to WB, August 2, 1945. WBC. Matthiessen's induction articles included a note that marked him out as "not qualified for subsequent enlistment in USN or USNR." See his service file (899–54–91) at the National Military Personnel Records Center.
23. Walt Gable, "Way Back When in Seneca County: A History of Sampson," *Finger Lakes Times*, November 13, 2016.
24. PM to PWP, August 6, 1945. PMP 4, Box 38.
25. PM to PWP, August 15, 1945. PMP 4, Box 38. The letter is postmarked for the 16th, but dated "Wednesday," which was the 15th.
26. PM to WB, August 15, 1945. WBC.
27. "Seabee History: Formation of the Seabees and World War II," Naval History and Heritage Command. See http://www.history.navy.mil/research/library/online-reading-room/title-list-alphabetically/s/seabee-history0/world-war-ii.html.
28. PM to WB, October 28, 1945. WBC.
29. PM to PWP, September 4, 1945. PMP 4, Box 38.
30. PM, Memoir notes. MMC. He called the graffiti "my high point in boot camp." The colorful detail also appears in *RAD*, 8.
31. PM to PWP, September 27, 1945. PMP 4, Box 38. Matthiessen's comments on Payson's response ("Ring-dang-doo of a lulapaloo") in a letter dated October 2.
32. PM to WB, January 1, 1946. WBC.
33. PM to WB, October 23, 1945. WBC.
34. PM to WB, n.d. [October 1945]. In 2018, when Wendy Morgan, née Burden, donated her Matthiessen letters to the Harry Ransom Center, she held several back for personal reasons, including this one.
35. PM to PWP, October 25, 1945. PMP 4, Box 38.
36. PM to WB, November 2, 1945. WBC. See also PM to PWP, November 2, 1945. PMP 4, Box 38.
37. PM to PWP, November 2, 1945. PMP 4, Box 38.
38. PM to PWP, November 8, 1945. PMP 4, Box 38. See also *Dictionary of American Naval Fighting Ships*, Naval History and Heritage Command (https://www.history.navy.mil/research/histories/ship-histories/danfs.html). In Matthiessen's memoir notes, he describes a "packed" troopship of "perhaps a thousand" men on a crossing that took "twenty slow days and nights"—all exaggerations or mistaken memories.
39. Ibid.
40. PM, Memoir notes. MMC.
41. PM to PWP, November 8, 1945. PMP 4, Box 38.
42. PM to WB, November 9, 1945. WBC.
43. Ralph Waldo Emerson, "Nature," *The Essential Writings of Ralph Waldo Emerson* (New York: Modern Library, 2000), 6.
44. Henry David Thoreau, *Walden and Civil Disobedience* (New York: Penguin Classics, 1983), 106.

45. Edward Abbey, *Desert Solitaire: A Season in the Wilderness* (New York: Touchstone, 1991), 6.
46. Ibid., 37.
47. Annie Dillard, *Pilgrim at Tinker Creek* (New York: Harper Perennial Modern Classics, 2013), 34.
48. Alan Watts, "This is It," *This Is It: And Other Essays on Zen and Spiritual Experience* (New York: Pantheon, 1960), 22.
49. Soen Nakagawa, in Kazuaki Tanahashi and Roko Sherry Chayat (trans.), *Endless Vow: The Zen Path of Soen Nakagawa* (Boston and London: Shambhala, 1996), 51.
50. See Lawrence Shainberg, "Emptying the Bell: An Interview with Peter Matthiessen," *Tricycle*, Fall 1993.
51. *SL*, 38.
52. *RAD*, 23.
53. PM, interviewed by Sedge Thomson, February 21, 1990, City Arts & Lectures.
54. PM quoted in Lawrence Shainberg, "Emptying the Bell: An Interview with Peter Matthiessen," *Tricycle*, Fall 1993. See also Jonathan Meiburg, "An Interview with Peter Matthiessen," *The Believer*, June 2014.
55. *RAD*, 24.
56. PM to PWP, November 15, 1945. PMP 4, Box 38.
57. See Gwenfread Allen, *Hawaii's War Years: 1941–1945* (Honolulu: University of Hawaii, 1950); and Joseph Feher, *Hawaii: A Pictorial History* (Honolulu: Bishop Museum Press, 1969).
58. Gavan Daws, *Shoal of Time: A History of the Hawaiian Islands* (New York: Macmillan, 1968), 353.
59. PM to WB, December 7, 1945. WBC.
60. Gwenfread Allen, *Hawaii's War Years*, 365.
61. Gwenfread Allen claims 500 sailors from the Honolulu Naval Air Station in *Hawaii's War Years*, p. 365. See also "1,000 Navy Men Riot in Honolulu," *New York Times*, November 14, 1945; and "1,500 Sailors Riot as False Rumor Pervades Honolulu," Associated Press, November 13, 1945.
62. PM to PWP, November 15, 1945. PMP 4, Box 38.
63. PM to WB, November 22, 1945. WBC.
64. PM to PWP, November 15, 1945. PMP 4, Box 38.
65. PM to WB, November 22, 1945. WBC.
66. PM to PWP, November 27, 1945. PMP 4, Box 38.
67. *RAD*, 33.
68. Ibid., 39.
69. Ibid., 68–69.
70. PM, Memoir notes. MMC.
71. PM to WB, January 5, 1946. WBC.
72. PM to WB, December 17, 1945. WBC.
73. PM to WB, January 11, 1946. WBC.
74. *RAD*, 70.
75. PM to PWP, January 13, 1946. PMP 4, Box 38.
76. See "Tsunami Historical Series: Aleutian Islands—1946," National Oceanic and Atmospheric Administration (sos.noaa.gov/datasets/tsunami-historical-series-aleutian-islands-1946); "1946 Aleutian Tsunami," USC Tsunami Research Group, archived on the Wayback Machine (web.archive.org/web/20160112224842/http://www.usc.edu/dept/tsunamis/alaska/1946/webpages); and L. A. Cotton, "The Pacific Ocean's Greatest Earthquake Wave," *Sydney Morning Herald*, April 5, 1946.
77. James Healy, quoted in "Alaskan Shoreline Installations 'Damaged,'" *Honolulu Advertiser*, April 1, 1946.
78. Richard MacMillan, "Noise 'Like Big Wind,'" *New York Times*, April 2, 1946.
79. Lorrin P. Thurston, "Tidal Wave Sidelights," *Honolulu Advertiser*, April 11, 1946.
80. "The Story of Hiromi Skeeter Tsutsumi," Pacific Tsunami Museum; see http://tsunami.org/survivor-narratives-1946-3.
81. PM to WB, April 1, 1946. WBC.

82. PM to WB, April 5, 1946. WBC.
83. "Army Barracks House 1800 Oahu Homeless," *Honolulu Advertiser*, April 2, 1946.
84. *RAD*, 103.
85. PM to PWP, May 6, 1946. PMP 4, Box 38.
86. PM to WB, March 18, 1946. WBC.
87. PM to WB, May 20, 1946. WBC.
88. PM to PWP, June 20, 1946. PMP 4, Box 38.
89. "Ike Patton, Stanford Navy's Two Big Guns," *Honolulu Advertiser*, June 21, 1946. The clipping can be found in PMP 1, Box 62.
90. PM to PWP, February 28, 1946. PMP 4, Box 38.
91. PM to WB, March 1, 1946. WBC.
92. PM to WB, June 5, 1946. WBC.
93. PM to PWP, June 20, 1946. PMP 4, Box 38.
94. PM to WB, June 5, 1946. WBC.
95. PM to WB, July 15, 1946. WBC.

4 · BIRD OF PASSAGE

1. PM, Paris notes, n.d. PMP 4, Box 11.
2. PM's "Application for Admission to the Freshman Class to enter in July 1945," February 12, 1945. YAL.
3. PM's "Memorandum of Personal Interview," September 28, 1946. YAL.
4. PM to WB, April 11, 1946. WBC.
5. PM, "New York: Old Hometown," *Architectural Digest*, November 1989.
6. Ibid.
7. PM, Memoir notes. MMC.
8. Ibid.
9. PM to WB, April 23, 1946. WBC.
10. "Dr. Florence Powdermaker, 71, Group Psychotherapist, Is Dead," *New York Times*, January 13, 1966.
11. PM, Memoir notes. MMC.
12. PM to WB, January 5, 1946. WBC.
13. PM to WB, February 10, 1946. WBC.
14. PM to WB, February 6, 1946. WBC.
15. Wendy Morgan (née Burden), interviewed by LR, November 29, 2018.
16. Jill Fox, interviewed by LR, August 28, 2020.
17. Wendy Morgan (née Burden), *A Long and Fortunate Life*. Self-published memoir.
18. PM to WB, May 6, 1947. WBC.
19. Red Smith, "Views of Sports," *Youngstown Vindicator*, December 23, 1951.
20. John Cole and PM, "Two in the Bush," *Yale Daily News*, December 4, 1947.
21. Payne Middleton (née Payson), interviewed by LR, December 18, 2018.
22. PM to PWP, April 16, 1947. PMP 4, Box 38.
23. TG, quoted in Michael Shnayerson, "Higher Matthiessen," *Vanity Fair*, December 1991.
24. Edward Boyes, quoted in Brooks Mather Kelley, *Yale: A History* (New Haven: Yale University Press, 1974), 403. The *Yale Daily News* was another invaluable source for understanding postwar changes at the college, as were interviews with alumni: Blair Childs, Sid Lovett, Alexander McLanahan, and Frederick Vreeland.
25. Brooks Mather Kelley, *Yale*, 403.
26. George Wilson Pierson, *A Yale Book of Numbers: Historical Statistics of the College and University, 1701–1976* (New Haven: Yale University Press, 1983), 10.
27. William F. Buckley Jr., *Miles Gone By: A Literary Autobiography* (Washington, DC: Regnery, 2005), 96.
28. TG, quoted in a "Class of '50" reunion brochure. PMP 4, Box 22.
29. TG, interviewed by Jeff Sewald, November 29, 2006. JSC.
30. Edward Boyes to PM, January 17, 1947. YAL.

31. PM to WB, n.d. [February 1947]. WBC.
32. PM to WB, n.d. [April 1947]. WBC.
33. John Cole, *Striper: A Story of Fish and Man* (Guilford, CT: Lyons Press, 1989), 11.
34. John Cole and PM, "Two in the Bush," *Yale Daily News*, October 9, 1947.
35. Frederick Vreeland, email to LR, February 28, 2019.
36. *SNA*, 22.
37. Peggy Lord, interviewed by LR, June 18, 2019.
38. Payne Middleton (née Payson), interviewed by LR, December 18, 2018.
39. PM, "Foreword," *Saving Wildlife: A Century of Conservation* (New York: Harry N. Abrams, 1995), 24. See also Dave Von Drehle, "Zen and the Art of Writing," *Miami Herald*, July 15, 1990; PM in conversation with Gary Snyder, February 23, 1994, City Arts & Lectures; and PM, "In Search of the World and Its Creatures," 2006. KWLS.
40. Wendy Morgan (née Burden), interviewed by LR, November 29, 2018.
41. PM to WB, July 29, 1947. WBC.
42. Wendy Morgan (née Burden), *A Long and Fortunate Life*.
43. Joseph A. Barry, "Americans in Paris," *New York Times*, August 15, 1948.
44. Gertrude Stein, *Paris France* (London: Peter Owen, 1971), 19.
45. Richard Wright, quoted in Joseph A. Barry, "Americans in Paris," *New York Times*, August 15, 1948.
46. Martha B. Lucas, Junior Year in France program booklet, 1948–49. JYF Collection at Sweet Briar College.
47. Information pack for 1948–49 program. JYF Collection at Sweet Briar College.
48. PM, Paris journal, 1948–1949. PMP 4, Box 25.
49. Janet Flanner, *Paris Journal, 1944–1955* (New York: Mariner, 1988), 92. See also "Avant La Grande Nuit de Paris," *Le Monde*, July 1, 1948; and "Paris Again the City of Light," *New York Times*, July 18, 1948.
50. Janet Flanner, *Paris Journal, 1944–1955*, 93.
51. Antony Beevor and Artemis Cooper, *Paris After the Liberation, 1944–1949* (New York: Penguin, 2004), 396, 402.
52. Janet Flanner, *Paris Journal, 1944–1955*, 83.
53. Arthur Miller, *Timebends: A Life* (New York: Grove Press, 2013), 157.
54. Art Buchwald, *I'll Always Have Paris: A Memoir* (New York: G. P. Putnam's Sons, 1996), 27.
55. PM to PWP, July 27, 1948. PMP 4, Box 38.
56. Ludwig Bemelmans, *My Life in Art* (New York: Harpers, 1958), 25–28.
57. Blair Fuller, "Where I Came to Live," *Zyzzyva*, Spring 2003.
58. PM, Paris journal, 1948–1949. PMP 4, Box 25.
59. Ibid.
60. PM, interviewed by Nelson W. Aldrich Jr., n.d. GPP, Box 240. A fictionalized version of this incident appears in *BB* (p. 18). Selden Tilghman shouts, "You are cowards! Betrayers of the South!" and repeatedly slams his fists down on the sharp points of a white picket fence until a man punches him in the jaw.
61. PM, Paris journal, 1948–1949. PMP 4, Box 25.
62. "Dr. Barker Reports on France, Junior Year Plan," October 27, 1948. JYF Collection at Sweet Briar College.
63. PM, Paris journal, 1948–1949. PMP 4, Box 25.
64. Mary Booth, interviewed by LR, April 24, 2019.
65. PM, Paris journal, 1948–1949. PMP 4, Box 25.
66. Jeanne de Salzmann, quoted in Margaret Croydon, "Getting in Touch with Gurdjieff," *New York Times*, July 29, 1979.
67. James Moore, *Gurdjieff: The Anatomy of Myth* (Boston: Element Books, 1999), 268.
68. Michel de Salzmann, quoted in Margaret Croydon, "Getting in Touch with Gurdjieff," *New York Times*, July 29, 1979. My summary of Gurdjieff's philosophy is based on Garrett Thomson, *On Gurdjieff* (Boston: Cengage, 2002); John Shirley, *Gurdjieff: An Introduction to His Life and Ideas* (New York: Jeremy P. Tarcher/Penguin, 2004); and Sophia Wellbeloved, *Gurdjieff: The Key Concepts* (London: Routledge, 2002).

69. PM, Paris journal, 1948–1949. PMP 4, Box 25.
70. *SL*, 39.
71. PM, Paris journal, 1948–1949. PMP 4, Box 25.
72. Ibid.
73. PM to WB, n.d. [September 1948]. WBC.
74. PM, Paris journal, 1948–1949. PMP 4, Box 25.
75. Blair Fuller, "Where I Came to Live," *Zyzzyva*, Spring 2003.
76. PM, Paris journal, 1948–1949. PMP 4, Box 25.
77. "Vienna Reds Hint Plot in Ross Death," *New York Times*, November 3, 1948.
78. PM, Notes on Jan Masaryk. MMC.
79. Ibid. The signed photograph survives in the Matthiessen family albums. MMC.
80. PM, Paris journal, 1948–1949. PMP 4, Box 25.
81. Ibid.
82. Payne Middleton (née Payson), interviewed by LR, December 18, 2018.
83. PM to PWP, September 29, 1948. PMP 4, Box 38.
84. PM, Paris journal, 1948–1949. PMP 4, Box 25.
85. Ibid.
86. Polly Kraft (née Winton), quoted in Michael Shnayerson, "Higher Matthiessen," *Vanity Fair*, December 1991.
87. Piedy Lumet (née Bailey), interviewed by LR, August 10, 2018.
88. Robert McGill Thomas Jr., "Patsy Southgate, Who Inspired 50's Literary Paris, Dies at 70," *New York Times*, July 26, 1998.
89. PM, Memoir notes. MMC.
90. PM, Paris journal, 1948–1949. PMP 4, Box 25.
91. Terry McDonell, *The Accidental Life: An Editor's Notes on Writing and Writers* (New York: Vintage, 2016), 199.
92. PM, Memoir notes. MMC.
93. PM to WB, n.d. [January 1949]. WBC.
94. PM, Paris journal, 1948–1949. PMP 4, Box 25. All quotes in this section come from this source unless otherwise noted.
95. *RR*, 11.
96. Ibid., 12.
97. Ibid., 28.
98. Ibid., 12.
99. PM to WB, n.d. [September 1948]. WBC.
100. PM, interviewed by Gay Talese, January 24, 1963. GTC.
101. PM to WB, n.d. [September 1948]. WBC.
102. PM, "Birds of Passage," April 12, 1949. PMP 4, Box 62.
103. PM to WB, n.d. [September 1948]. WBC.

5 · DAILY THEMES

1. "Peter Matthiessen: The Art of Fiction No. 157," *The Paris Review*, No. 150, Spring 1999.
2. PM, Yale notes. MMC.
3. Quoted in Calvin Trillin, "No Telling, No Summing Up," *The New Yorker*, June 11, 1966.
4. John Downey, "The Class I'll *Never* Forget," *Yale Alumni Magazine*, July/August 2012.
5. Frederick Vreeland, email to LR, February 28, 2019.
6. *SL*, 39.
7. PM, Memoir notes. MMC.
8. Ibid.
9. *Daily Themes: Nineteen Hundred and Forty-Nine*. YAL. The quotes are, respectively, from stories by F. Remington Ballou, Everett R. Castle Jr., and Scott Donaldson.
10. PM, *Daily Themes: Nineteen Hundred and Forty-Nine*. YAL.

11. Andrew Patten, quoted in Scott Donaldson, *Death of a Rebel: The Charlie Fenton Story* (Madison, NJ: Fairleigh Dickinson University Press, 2012), 7. Patten's article appeared in *Yale Daily News* on December 6, 1950.
12. Scott Donaldson, *Death of a Rebel*, 6.
13. TG, interviewed by Jeff Sewald, November 29, 2006. JSC.
14. PM, quoted in Scott Donaldson, *Death of a Rebel*, 51.
15. PM to Sandy McClatchy, n.d. MMC. In Donaldson's rendering of this episode in *Death of a Rebel*, the party entered the sewer with a flashlight, a candle, and a couple of cigarette lighters.
16. Wallace Stegner, quoted in "History of the Stanford Creative Writing Program." See https://creativewriting.stanford.edu/about/history-stanford-creative-writing-program.
17. Wallace Stegner, quoted in Scott Donaldson, *Death of a Rebel*, 43.
18. Matthew J. Bruccoli, "The Hemingway/Fenton Correspondence," in Matthew J. Bruccoli (ed.), *Dictionary of Literary Biography Yearbook* (Farmington Hills, MI: Gale, 2003), 282.
19. PM, "John Steinbeck, March 19, 2002." MMC.
20. PM to JH, April 1973. JHP, Box 32.
21. Matthiessen especially admired Faulkner's use of detail with his characters. "He would pick out one, or at most two, physical characteristics of somebody and then just repeat them over and over again, and the reader gradually builds up a whole character around that one physical detail because the detail is so well-chosen." See PM, *Fresh Air*, NPR, April 6, 1989. See also PM, "The Spirit of Place," 2002. KWLS.
22. PM, "The Long Journey: Zen and the Writing Life" (audio recording). San Francisco Zen Center, 1998.
23. PM, interviewed by HN, n.d. [multiple interviews, 1990s]. HNC, Box 2.
24. PM, "October in Valhalla" (typescript). PMP 4, Box 1.
25. PM, interviewed by HN, n.d. [multiple interviews, 1990s]. HNC, Box 2.
26. Shunryu Suzuki, *Zen Mind, Beginner's Mind* (Boulder, CO: Shambhala, 2011), 2.
27. PM, "Sadie," *Atlantic Monthly*, January 1951. All quotes are from this original version of the story.
28. Thomas R. Edwards, "Failed Journeys to the Wrong Place," *New York Times*, May 14, 1989.
29. Ibid.
30. John Farrar's letter to Edward Weeks is quoted in a short preamble to "Sadie," *Atlantic Monthly*, January 1951. Matthiessen neglected to thank Farrar for his help—a rudeness that Farrar held against him.
31. PM to WB, April 11, 1946. WBC.
32. PM to PWP, April 30, 1946. PMP 4, Box 38.
33. "Joan Mitchell," transcript Barney/Sandy interview, January 21, 2004. Barney Rosset Papers, Box 3, Columbia University Archives.
34. Beth Blaine, "By the Way—," *Evening Star*, May 2, 1939.
35. "Patsy Southgate" (obituary), *East Hampton Star*, July 1998.
36. Jane Freilicher, quoted in ibid.
37. PS, interviewed by Jeffrey Potter, May 14, 1980. Jeffrey Potter Oral History Collection, Pollock-Krasner House and Study Center.
38. Sarita Southgate, interviewed by LR, September 30, 2020.
39. Patti Smith, "Introduction," in Albertine Sarrazin, *Astragal* (New York: New Directions, 2013), x. Patsy Southgate translated *Astragal* into English in 1967.
40. Lucas Matthiessen, interviewed by LR, March 26, 2021.
41. PS, "My Night with Frank O'Hara," in Bill Berkson (ed.), *Homage to Frank O'Hara* (New York: Big Sky Books, 1988), 120.
42. Cis Matthiessen (née Ormsby), interviewed by LR, March 13, 2019.
43. PM, "The Making of an Adventurer," *Travel & Leisure*, April 1983.
44. PM, quoted in Jeff Himmelman, "Peter Matthiessen's Homegoing," *New York Times Magazine*, April 3, 2014.
45. PM, Memoir notes. MMC.
46. *WIA*, 26–27.

47. PM, Memoir notes. MMC.
48. PM, "The Making of an Adventurer," *Travel & Leisure*, April 1983.
49. Ibid. See also PM (with Milton Miller), interviewed by John Eilertsen, January 20, 1984. East Hampton Maritime Folklife Collection, East Hampton Library.
50. Edward Weeks to PM, October 31, 1950. PMP 1, Box 62.
51. PM, "The Long Journey: Zen and the Writing Life" (audio recording). San Francisco Zen Center, 1998.

6 · THE PARIS REVIEW

1. *PAR*, 6.
2. John M. Crewdson, "Worldwide Propaganda Network Built by the C.I.A.," *New York Times*, December 26, 1977. Regarding this article, Matthiessen wrote: "In December 1977, I acknowledged my past affiliation to reporter John Crewdson for his three-part report in the NY Times on CIA influence on artists and cultural organizations abroad. Because I was working at that time with Indian people, I requested Crewdson not to use my name. Without their trust, I explained, I would not be accepted, far less make friends: the few Indian friends I had confided in about that past CIA affiliation advised me strongly against mentioning it to others. Crewdson had honored the request for anonymity from a number of others but in my case he would not observe it, perhaps in the hope that dragging in The Paris Review and the name 'George Plimpton' (both well-known names by 1977) might pep up his long gray article." See PM, CIA notes. MMC.
3. David Michaelis, interviewed by LR, August 2, 2018. For further evidence of Matthiessen's combativeness around the topic, see his interactions with Immy Humes as recounted in Joel Whitney, *Finks: How the CIA Tricked the World's Best Writers* (New York: OR Books, 2016), 250–57.
4. The CIA denied my FOIA requests for information on PM in 2019 and 2021. The Agency also denied a FOIA request on *The Paris Review*, the Farfield Foundation, and Julius Fleischmann Jr., in 2020. Attempts to work directly with the CIA through its "entertainment liaison"—who consulted with Agency historians on my behalf—also led nowhere.
5. PM, CIA notes. MMC.
6. Ibid.
7. PM to Leonard Peltier, n.d. [c. June 2008]. MMC.
8. PM, quoted in Nelson Aldrich Jr. (ed.), *George, Being George* (New York: Random House, 2008), 86.
9. PM, quoted in Rachel Donadio, "The Paranoiac and The Paris Review," *New York Times*, February 17, 2008.
10. PM, CIA notes. MMC.
11. PM, quoted in Rachel Donadio, "The Paranoiac and The Paris Review," *New York Times*, February 17, 2008.
12. PM to Sandy McClatchy, n.d. MMC. See also PM, interviewed by Immy Humes, n.d. [2001]. Transcribed from unused footage for Immy Humes's *Doc* (2008). See tapes 085/086/087, DHA.
13. In his notes about Yale and the CIA, Matthiessen erroneously referred to the Elizabethan Club as the "Jacobean Club" (he was off by an era). His name can be found on the membership roll in Box 1 of the Elizabethan Club Records, YAL.
14. Michael Holzman, "The Ideological Origins of American Studies at Yale," *American Studies*, Vol. 40, No. 2, Summer 1999, 78.
15. Robin Winks, *Cloak and Gown: Scholars in the Secret War, 1939–1961* (New Haven: Yale University Press, 1996), 300.
16. Sid Lovett, interviewed by LR, February 4, 2019.
17. John B. Judis, *William F. Buckley, Jr.: Patron Saint of the Conservatives* (New York: Simon & Schuster, 2001), 79–80.
18. Frederick Vreeland, email to LR, February 28, 2019.

19. PM, interviewed by Patty Satalia for "Conversations from Penn State," 2010.
20. PM, CIA notes. MMC.
21. Ibid.
22. PM, interviewed by Gay Talese, January 24, 1963. GTC.
23. PM to Ben Bradlee, January 2, 1978. PMP 4, Box 11.
24. PM, CIA notes. MMC.
25. PM, quoted in Jeff Himmelman, "Peter Matthiessen's Homegoing," *New York Times Magazine*, April 3, 2014.
26. PM to WB, March 18, 1946. WBC.
27. PM, interviewed by Scott Sherman, n.d. [2007]. PMP 4, Box 11.
28. Ibid.
29. PM, CIA notes. MMC.
30. Ibid.
31. David Robarge, "Moles, Defectors, and Deceptions: James Angleton and CIA Counterintelligence," *The Journal of Intelligence History*, Vol. 3, Winter 2003.
32. Ed Welles, quoted in Evan Thomas, *The Very Best Men: The Daring Early Years of the CIA* (London: Simon & Schuster, 2007), 42. See also Scott Anderson, *The Quiet Americans: Four CIA Spies at the Dawn of the Cold War—A Tragedy in Three Acts* (New York: Doubleday, 2020), 251.
33. Peter Sichel, quoted in Evan Thomas, *The Very Best Men*, 42.
34. Joseph B. Smith, *Portrait of a Cold Warrior* (New York: G. P. Putnam's Sons, 1976), 66.
35. Scott Anderson, *The Quiet Americans*, 177. Matthiessen was "on the OPC payroll," Anderson writes, without providing any sources for this claim.
36. PM, Memoir notes. MMC.
37. PM, CIA notes. MMC.
38. Bernice Baumgarten to William Maxwell, August 15, 1951. NYR, Box 503; PM to "Jan," n.d. [February 1954]. HBR, Box MAT–MAY.
39. Cass Canfield to PM, January 3, 1951. HBR, Box MAT–MAY.
40. PM, "The Long Journey: Zen and the Writing Life" (audio recording), San Francisco Zen Center, 1998.
41. Charles Schlesinger, interviewed by LR, July 13, 2018.
42. Mary McCarthy, quoted in Matthew Bruccoli, *James Gould Cozzens: A Life Apart* (New York: Harcourt Brace Jovanovich, 1983), 290.
43. Bernice Baumgarten, quoted in Tom Hiney and Frank MacShane (eds.), *The Raymond Chandler Papers: Selected Letters and Nonfiction, 1909–1959* (New York: Grove Press, 2002), 182.
44. Shirley Jackson, quoted in Ruth Franklin, *Shirley Jackson: A Rather Haunted Life* (New York: Liveright, 2016), 315.
45. PM to Matthew Bruccoli, September 18, 1981. PMP 4, Box 39.
46. "Miss P. Southgate Married in Boston," *New York Times*, February 18, 1951. See also "Patricia Southgate to Be Feted," *New York Times*, January 12, 1951.
47. PM, CIA notes. MMC.
48. C. D. Edbrook, "Principles of Deep Cover," *Studies in Intelligence*, Vol. 5, Summer 1961.
49. Katharine White to Bernice Baumgarten, February 26, 1951. NYR, Box 503. White was talking about "Martin's Beach."
50. Bernice Baumgarten (quoting an editor) to PM, March 7, 1951. PMP 1, Box 62.
51. PM, "Wilderness" typescript, n.d. [1951]. PMP 4, Box 1.
52. PM told this anecdote numerous times in interviews about his career, always with the exact same wording. See, for example, PM to Matthew Bruccoli, September 18, 1981. PMP 1, Box 39; Kay Bonetti, "An Interview with Peter Matthiessen," *Missouri Review*, Vol. 12, No. 2, 1989; "No Boundaries" (audio recording), Gang of Seven, 1992; "The Long Journey: Zen and the Writing Life" (audio recording), San Francisco Zen Center, 1998; and "Peter Matthiessen: The Art of Fiction No. 157," *The Paris Review*, No. 150, Spring 1999.
53. PM, "No Boundaries" (audio recording), Gang of Seven, 1992.

54. 1951/06/16, "List of Outward-Bound Passengers" for the SS *Liberté*, tourist class, retrieved via Ancestry.com.
55. Janet Flanner, *Paris Journal, 1944–1955* (New York: Mariner, 1988), 118.
56. Ibid., 182.
57. Ibid., 183.
58. U.S. Department of State, *Intelligence Report No. 6140: The French Communist Party: Its 1952 Record and Prospects for 1953*, December 30, 1952.
59. See, for example, Janet Flanner, *Paris Journal*, 149; and Patricia Blake, "A Literary Letter from Paris," *New York Times*, October 19, 1952. There was even a sign on the stone wall surrounding Orly International Airport: "U.S. GO HOME BY AIR FRANCE."
60. Irwin M. Wall, *The United States and the Making of Postwar France, 1945–1954* (Cambridge: Cambridge University Press, 1991), 213. See also Susan M. Perlman, "Shock Therapy: The United States Anti-Communist Psychological Campaign in Fourth Republic France" (Thesis, Florida State University, 2006).
61. WS, "The *Paris Review*," *This Quiet Dust* (New York: Random House, 1982), 296. WS also discusses this in Paula Heredia (dir.), *The Paris Review . . . Early Chapters*, 2001.
62. PM, "William Styron," *The Paris Review*, No. 179, Winter 2006.
63. Gay Talese, "Looking for Hemingway," *Esquire*, July 1963.
64. PS, quoted in Michael Shnayerson, *Irwin Shaw: A Biography* (New York: G. P. Putnam's Sons, 1989), 205–6.
65. PM, CIA notes. MMC.
66. PM, quoted in Mark Adams, "The Many Lives of Peter Matthiessen," *Men's Journal*, May 2014.
67. Ron Rosenbaum, "Peter Matthiessen's Lifelong Quest for Peace," *Smithsonian*, May 2014.
68. GP, "Interview with George Plimpton," in Matthew J. Bruccoli (ed.), *Dictionary of Literary Biography Yearbook* (Detroit: Gale, 2000), 242.
69. PM, CIA notes. MMC.
70. PM, quoted in Jeff Himmelman, "Peter Matthiessen's Homegoing," *New York Times Magazine*, April 3, 2014.
71. PM and Charlie Rose, *Charlie Rose*, PBS, May 27, 2008. See https://charlierose.com/videos/15312.
72. PM, CIA notes. MMC.
73. Joel Whitney, *Finks*, 16–17.
74. Obtained by a FOIA request in August 2020. This specific document was declassified in response to a request from the FBI. The CIA declined to confirm or deny the existence of any further records on Wright's movements in Paris.
75. PS, quoted in Michael Shnayerson, *Irwin Shaw*, 215. James Salter witnessed a similar incident: "One night in St.-Jean-de-Luz, during an argument in a restaurant, [Marian] took off her wedding ring and threw it away in a fury. The next morning she went back to look but couldn't find it; as she left, miraculously she saw it in the street." See *Burning the Days* (New York: Vintage, 1997), 220.
76. PM, interviewed by Gay Talese, January 24, 1963. GTC. Talese describes Irwin Shaw as "a sort of pater familias" to the Tall Young Men in "Looking for Hemingway," *Esquire*, July 1963.
77. Irwin Shaw, quoted in GP, "The Paris Review Sketchbook," *The Paris Review*, No. 79, Spring 1981.
78. Irwin Shaw, "Playwright Says, 'Go East, Young Man,'" *New York Times*, November 2, 1947.
79. Michael Shnayerson, *Irwin Shaw*, 182.
80. PM, CIA notes. MMC.
81. Ibid.
82. *NHDR*, 26.
83. PM, Memoir notes. MMC.
84. Piedy Lumet (née Bailey), interviewed by LR, August 10, 2018.
85. *RR*, 5.

86. PM, CIA notes. MMC
87. TG to GP, February 14, 1955. PRA, Box 4.
88. Russ Hemenway, quoted in Nelson Aldrich Jr. (ed.), *George, Being George*, 87.
89. Immy Humes (dir.), *Doc*, 2008.
90. PM, quoted in GP, "The Paris Review Sketchbook," *The Paris Review*, No. 79, Spring 1981.
91. HH to Gay Talese, [1963]. GTC.
92. HH, quoted in "Patsy Southgate" (obituary), *East Hampton Star*, July 1998.
93. HH to PM, February 25, 1953. PMP 4, Box 39.
94. PM, CIA notes. MMC.
95. PM, interviewed by HN, n.d. [multiple interviews, 1990s]. HNC, Box 2. See also Nelson Aldrich Jr. (ed.), *George, Being George*, 92–93. PM mentions Baldwin's broken promise in PM to GP, n.d. [c. January 1954]. PRA, Box 6.
96. PM, "The Replacement," *Paris News Post*, Fall 1951. DHA, Box 2. A revised version of this story, renamed "A Replacement," also appeared in the first issue of *The Paris Review*, Spring 1953.
97. Katharine White to Bernice Baumgarten, September 7, 1951. NYR, Box 503.
98. Katharine White to Bernice Baumgarten, November 19, 1951. NYR, Box 503.
99. Katharine White to Bernice Baumgarten, November 27, 1951. NYR, Box 503.
100. PM to "Miche" [Michael Canfield], n.d. [1952]. PRA, Box 6. Of the story, GP once said, "It had a rattlesnake in it. But it wasn't very good." See David Remnick, "The Very Good Life of George Plimpton," *Washington Post*, November 4, 1984.
101. PM, quoted in "Postwar Paris: Chronicles of Literary Life," *The Paris Review*, No. 150, Spring 1999.
102. Ibid. See also GP, "The Paris Review Sketchbook," *The Paris Review*, No. 79, Spring 1981; and Nelson Aldrich Jr. (ed.), *George, Being George*, 94–95.
103. HH, interviewed by Gay Talese, January 12, 1963. GTC.
104. WS, "Peter Matthiessen," *This Quiet Dust*, 271.
105. WS, "The Paris Review," *Harper's Bazaar*, August 1953.
106. PM, quoted in Nelson Aldrich Jr. (ed.), *George, Being George*, 89.
107. PM, "William Styron," *The Paris Review*, No. 179, Winter 2006.
108. PM, eulogy for WS, n.d. [2006]. PMP 4, Box 40.
109. WS, interviewed by Gay Talese, January 25, 1963. GTC.
110. James L. W. West, *William Styron: A Life* (New York: Random House, 1998), 90.
111. WS, "Peter Matthiessen," *This Quiet Dust*, 272.
112. WS to Dorothy Parker, May 27, 1952, in Rose Styron and R. Blakeslee Gilpin (eds.), *Selected Letters of William Styron* (New York: Random House, 2012), 136.
113. WS to William Blackburn and Ashbel Brice, May 9, 1952, in ibid., 126.
114. WS to Dorothy Parker, May 27, 1952, in ibid., 136–37.
115. Nicolas Nabokov, quoted in Giles Scott-Smith, "The 'Masterpieces of the Twentieth Century' Festival and the Congress for Cultural Freedom: Origins and Consolidation 1947–1952," *Intelligence and National Security*, Vol. 15, No. 1, May 2000. See also Frances Stonor Saunders, *The Cultural Cold War: The CIA and the World of Arts and Letters* (New York: The New Press, 2001), 113–28; and Sarah Miller Harris, *The CIA and the Congress for Cultural Freedom in the Early Cold War* (London: Routledge, 2016), 98–110.
116. "Notes of Discord Mar Festival in Paris," *New York Times*, May 1, 1952.
117. Janet Flanner, "Letter from Paris," *The New Yorker*, February 9, 1952. For the CIA connection, see Frances Stonor Saunders, *The Cultural Cold War*, 126 (though Saunders confuses Fleischmann with his cousin, Raoul, who helped finance *The New Yorker*).
118. John Appleton to PM, May 14, 1952. HBR, Box MAT–MAY.
119. PM to John Appleton, May 23, 1952. HBR, Box MAT–MAY.
120. WS to William Styron Sr., May 1, 1952, in Styron and Gilpin (eds.), *Selected Letters of William Styron*, 122–23.
121. PM, quoted in Nelson Aldrich Jr. (ed.), *George, Being George*, 94.
122. HH, interviewed by Gay Talese, January 12, 1963. GTC.
123. Buzz Merritt, quoted in Nelson Aldrich Jr. (ed.), *George, Being George*, 51–52.

124. GP, "Interview with George Plimpton," in Matthew J. Bruccoli (ed.), *Dictionary of Literary Biography Yearbook*, 243.
125. GP, interviewed by Gay Talese, January 22–23, 1963. GTC.
126. PM to GP, n.d. [c. May 1952]. PRA, Box 6.
127. PM to GP, n.d. [c. May–June 1952]. PRA, Box 6.
128. Ibid.
129. TG, interviewed by Gay Talese, January 19, 1963. GTC.
130. Gay Talese, "Looking for Hemingway," *Esquire*, July 1963.
131. Ibid.
132. PM to GP, n.d. [c. July 1963]. PRA, Box 6.
133. Gay Talese to GP, September 8, 1963. PRA, Box 10.
134. PS, interviewed by Gay Talese, January 16, 1963. GTC.
135. Sarita Southgate, interviewed by LR, September 30, 2020.
136. Lucas Matthiessen, interviewed by LR, September 28, 2018.
137. PS, interviewed by Gay Talese, January 16, 1963. GTC.
138. Ibid.
139. Ibid.
140. PS, quoted in Gay Talese, "Looking for Hemingway," *Esquire*, July 1963.
141. Gay Talese to GP, July 19, 1963. PRA, Box 10.
142. Gay Talese to GP, September 8, 1963. PRA, Box 10.
143. GP to PM, March 11, 1981. GPP, Box 199.
144. WS, "The *Paris Review*," *This Quiet Dust*, 297–98.
145. HH, interviewed by Gay Talese, January 12, 1963. GTC. See HH to PM, February 25, 1953. PMP 4, Box 39. Evidence supporting Humes's claim, in the form of a dated receipt from the Parquet de Première Instance de la Seine, can be found in PRA, PR1 Box 12.
146. John Train, *The Paris Review: The Early Years* (Self-published, 2018). John Train, interviewed by LR, May 31, 2019.
147. PM, interviewed by Nelson W. Aldrich Jr., n.d. GPP, Box 240.
148. GP, quoted in "Postwar Paris: Chronicles of Literary Life," *The Paris Review*.
149. TG, interviewed by Gay Talese, January 19, 1963. GTC.
150. WS, "The *Paris Review*," *This Quiet Dust*, 296.
151. PM, interviewed by Gay Talese, January 24, 1963. GTC.
152. GP to Francis and Pauline Plimpton, n.d. [August 1952]. GPP, Box 177.
153. WS, "Letter to an Editor," *The Paris Review*, No. 1, Spring 1953. The letter was genuine: Styron was writing to the other editors after his initial preface was rejected for being overwritten. For the original, see PRA, Box 10.
154. "Foreign Origins: Expatriate Writers in Paris," *Times Literary Supplement*, May 27, 1955.
155. HH, interviewed by Gay Talese, January 13, 1963. GTC.
156. Art Buchwald, "Biarritz After Noon," *New York Herald Tribune*, August 30, 1952.
157. PM, Memoir notes. MMC.
158. PS, quoted in Michael Shnayerson, *Irwin Shaw*, 210.
159. PM to GP, n.d. [August 1952]. "Thanks for your racquet . . ." PRA, Box 6.
160. PM to GP, n.d. [August 1952]. "I have just sent you off another letter . . ." PRA, Box 6.
161. PM to Julius Fleischmann, n.d. [1952]. PRA, Box 6.
162. List of backers, n.d. [1953]. PRA, PR1 Box 12.
163. PM, CIA notes. MMC. See also Scott Sherman, "In His League," *The Nation*, January 15, 2009. In this article—an extended book review of the oral biography, *George, Being George*—Sherman publicly challenged Matthiessen's "silence and reticence" by posing a string of questions about his involvement with the CIA. In an annoyed response to the article, Matthiessen wrote that he had *already* gone over these "incriminating questions" with Sherman: "the answers . . . reside in his *Nation* files." (For an unfinished draft of the response, see PMP 4, Box 11.) On October 11, 2024, Sherman told me in an email that the material Matthiessen gave him was "evasive rubbish: junk."
164. Frances Stonor Saunders, *The Cultural Cold War*, 126.

165. PM, CIA notes. MMC.
166. Lillian von Nickern to GP, April 21, 1953. PRA, Box 10.
167. Frances Stonor Saunders, *The Cultural Cold War*, 177.
168. Office of Julius Fleischmann to GP, March 16, 1955. PRA, Box 3.
169. PM to GP, August 14, 1952. PRA, Box 6.
170. Ibid.
171. WS to PM, November 17, 1952. PMP 4, Box 40.
172. GP, "The Paris Review Sketchbook," *The Paris Review*, No. 79, Spring 1981.
173. Louisa Noble to *Esquire* Magazine, May 22, 1983. GPP, Box 200.
174. TG to PM, October 31, 1952. PRA, Box 4.
175. All quotes until the end of this section come from Matthiessen's CIA notes. MMC.
176. PM to GP, n.d. [c. May–June 1952]. PRA, Box 6.
177. My understanding of Tristan Tzara is based on Marius Hentea, *TaTa Dada: The Real Life and Celestial Adventures of Tristan Tzara* (Cambridge: MIT Press, 2014). Tzara would fall out of favor with the PCF in 1954 after speaking publicly about the revolutionary climate in Hungary and bemoaning "conformism and State dogmatism." See p. 279.
178. PM, CIA notes. MMC.
179. PM, "Lina," n.d. [1953: the title page features the rue de Chazelles address]. PMP 4, Box 1. A version of this story was published in *Cornhill*, Vol. 169, Fall 1956.
180. PM, interviewed by Nelson W. Aldrich Jr., n.d. GPP, Box 240.
181. HH to PM, February 25, 1953. PMP 4, Box 39.
182. PM, CIA notes. MMC.
183. Ibid.
184. Ibid.
185. Joseph B. Smith, *Portrait of a Cold Warrior*, 86. The CIA had a serious morale problem in 1953; Matthiessen was not alone in becoming disillusioned with the Agency's goals and methods. See Tim Weiner, *Legacy of Ashes: The History of the CIA* (New York: Anchor, 2008), 89.
186. PM, CIA notes. MMC.
187. John K. Hutchens, "On the Books," *New York Herald Tribune*, March 8, 1953.
188. WS, "The Paris Review," *Harper's Bazaar*, August 1953.
189. "Signs of Winter" publishing contract, April 3, 1953. Brandt & Brandt Contract Files, Princeton University Library, Box 11.
190. John Appleton to PM, March 27, 1953. HBR, Box MAT–MAY.
191. PM to John Appleton, n.d. [March 1953]. HBR, Box MAT–MAY.
192. Cynthia Cole, diary, April 5, 1953. Collection of Darrah Cole.

7 · PEOPLE FROM AWAY

1. PM, interviewed by HN, n.d. [multiple interviews, 1990s]. HNC, Box 2. See also *SL*, 261.
2. PM, interviewed by Nelson W. Aldrich Jr., n.d. GPP, Box 240.
3. PM, "William Styron," *The Paris Review*, No. 179, Winter 2006.
4. WS to PM, November 17, 1952. PMP 4, Box 40.
5. Rose Styron, interviewed by LR, November 27, 2018.
6. For the Styrons' wedding, see James L. W. West, *William Styron: A Life* (New York: Random House, 1998), 252–58; and Alexandra Styron, *Reading My Father: A Memoir* (New York: Scribner, 2012), 115–17.
7. WS to William Styron Sr., June 6, 1953, in Rose Styron and R. Blakeslee Gilpin (eds.), *Selected Letters of William Styron* (New York: Random House, 2012), 180–81.
8. WS to PM, November 17, 1952. PMP 4, Box 40.
9. WS to Mac Hyman, August 15, 1953, in Rose Styron and R. Blakeslee Gilpin (eds.), *Selected Letters of William Styron*, 185–87.
10. PM, quoted in James L. W. West, *William Styron*, 262.
11. PM, "William Styron," *The Paris Review*, No. 179, Winter 2006.
12. PM, address on WS for the Academy of Arts and Letters, April 4, 2007. MMC.

13. PM, CIA notes. MMC.
14. *PAR*, 163.
15. Ibid., 130.
16. Elizabeth Lawrence to PM, April 22, 1954. HBR, Box MAT–MAY
17. *PAR*, 84.
18. Ibid., 105.
19. Ibid., 182.
20. Ibid., 183.
21. PM to GP, n.d. [July 1953]. PRA, Box 6.
22. David Halberstam, *The Fifties* (New York: Villard, 1993), 195.
23. Ibid., 185.
24. PM to WB, April 11, 1946. WBC.
25. *ML*, 142.
26. PS, "The Eastern Long Island Painters," *The Paris Review*, No. 21, Spring/Summer 1959.
27. Ferris G. Talmage, *The Springs in the Old Days: An Eastern Long Island Town* (1970). This is a booklet published and sold by the East Hampton Historical Farm Museum. For my brief sketch of Springs, I relied on Talmage; on conversations with Prudence Carabine and Norma Edwards, both locals; and on The History Project, Inc., an extraordinary archive of hundreds of interviews documenting the history of the East End, held by the East Hampton Library.
28. See *ML*, 55–56.
29. Ibid., 51.
30. PS, interviewed by Jeffrey Potter, May 14, 1980. Jeffrey Potter Oral History Collection, Pollock-Krasner House and Study Center.
31. John Cole, *Away All Boats: A Personal Guide for the Small-Boat Owner* (New York: Henry Holt, 1994), 53.
32. Ibid., 89.
33. Ibid., 88.
34. Everett Rattray, "Long Island Books," *East Hampton Star*, November 23, 1978.
35. PM, quoted in Pico Iyer, "Laureate of the Wild," *Time*, November 11, 1993.
36. For Matthiessen's memories of the incident, see *ML*, 59–63. For Cole's, see *Away All Boats*, 106–14.
37. *ML*, 63.
38. GP to Irwin Shaw, n.d. [c. October 1953]. PRA, Box 8.
39. GP to PM, October 30, 1953. PRA, Box 8.
40. Ibid.
41. TG, quoted in Nelson Aldrich Jr. (ed.), *George, Being George* (New York: Random House, 2008), 143.
42. PM to GP, n.d. [c. September 1953]. PRA, Box 6.
43. GP to PM, October 30, 1953. PRA, Box 8.
44. TG to GP, December 9, 1953. PRA, Box 4.
45. GP to PM and TG, January 18, 1954. PRA, Box 8.
46. PM to GP, n.d. [c. January 1954]. "I think the Beckett is splendid . . ." PRA, Box 6.
47. PM to GP, n.d. [c. January 1954]. "Two pieces of bad news . . ." PRA, Box 6.
48. GP to PM and TG, February 1, 1954. PRA, Box 8.
49. PM to GP, n.d. [c. December 1953]. PRA, Box 6.
50. GP to WS, September 22, 1953. PRA, Box 8.
51. TG, interviewed by Jeff Sewald, November 29, 2006. JSC.
52. PM to GP, n.d. [c. December 1953]. PRA, Box 6.
53. Cynthia Cole, quoted in Steven Naifeh and Gregory White Smith, *Jackson Pollock: An American Saga* (New York: Harper Perennial, 1991), 734.
54. Cile Downs, interviewed by LR, June 21, 2019.
55. PS, quoted in Jeffrey Potter, *To a Violent Grave: An Oral Biography of Jackson Pollock* (New York: G. P. Putnam's Sons, 1985), 189.
56. Clement Greenberg, quoted in Mary Gabriel, *Ninth Street Women* (New York: Back Bay Books, 2018), 206.

57. Penny Potter, quoted in Jeffrey Potter, *To a Violent Grave*, 156.
58. PM, quoted in Gail Levin, *Lee Krasner: A Biography* (New York: HarperCollins, 2011), 294.
59. PS, interviewed by Jeffrey Potter, May 14, 1980. Jeffrey Potter Oral History Collection, Pollock-Krasner House and Study Center.
60. Ibid.
61. PS, quoted in Steven Naifeh and Gregory White Smith, *Jackson Pollock*, 549.
62. PS, quoted in Jeffrey Potter, *To a Violent Grave*, 198.
63. PS, interviewed by Jeffrey Potter, May 14, 1980. Jeffrey Potter Oral History Collection, Pollock-Krasner House and Study Center.
64. Ibid.
65. Cynthia Cole, quoted in Steven Naifeh and Gregory White Smith, *Jackson Pollock*, 735.
66. Elizabeth Lawrence to PM, August 25, 1953. HBR, Box MAT–MAY.
67. PM to GP, n.d. [March 1954]. PRA, Box 6.
68. PM to GP, n.d. [April 1954]. PRA, Box 6.
69. *RR*, 167.
70. Ibid., 16.
71. Ibid., 96.
72. Ibid., 76.
73. Ibid., 230.
74. Ibid., 238.
75. PM to Simon Bessie, n.d. [May 1953]. HBR, Box MAT–MAY.
76. PM to Elizabeth Lawrence, n.d. [October 1953]. HBR, Box MAT–MAY.
77. GP to Irwin Shaw, n.d. [c. October 1953]. PRA, Box 8. In this letter, Plimpton recounts a conversation he had with Matthiessen about *Race Rock*.
78. PM to Elizabeth Lawrence, n.d. [October 1953]. HBR, Box MAT–MAY.
79. *RR*, 9.
80. Ibid., 104.
81. Ibid., 222.
82. John K. Hutchens, "Book Review," *New York Herald Tribune*, March 31, 1984.
83. Joe Fox, "Signs of Winter" manuscript report, March 16, 1953. Alfred A. Knopf, Inc. Records, Harry Ransom Center, University of Texas at Austin, Container 1133.1.
84. "First Novelist on Right Track," *Boston Globe*, April 4, 1954.
85. Katherine Gauss Jackson, "Books in Brief," *Harper's Magazine*, April 1954.
86. Orville Prescott, "Book of The Times," *New York Times*, April 6, 1954.
87. PM to Norman Holmes Pearson, n.d. [1954]. Norman Holmes Pearson Papers, Yale Collection of American Literature, Beinecke Rare Book and Manuscript Library, Yale University, Box 77.
88. Randy Wayne White, "The Travels of Peter Matthiessen," *Outside*, April/May 1980.
89. *RR*, 25.
90. Ibid., 19.
91. Ibid., 53.
92. Ibid., 33.
93. *ML*, 69.
94. Ibid., 79. Lester's brothers also liked to say that he accepted foreigners because he could siphon off a larger share of the earnings for himself, though John Cole didn't believe it: "I never discovered any such imbalances." See *Away All Boats*, 90.
95. *ML*, 70.
96. For descriptions of haul-seining, see *ML*, 71–76; and John Cole, *Striper: A Story of Fish and Man* (Guilford, CT: Lyons Press, 1989), 69–85. PM also dramatizes the process (and an accident) in *RR*, 38–41.
97. *ML*, 124–25.
98. Ibid., 270–71.
99. Gay Talese to GP, September 8, 1963. PRA, Box 10.
100. Carol Southern, quoted in Steven Naifeh and Gregory White Smith, *Jackson Pollock*, 735.

101. PM, Memoir notes. MMC.
102. *ML*, 125.
103. See, for example, Michael Shnayerson, "Higher Matthiessen," *Vanity Fair*, December 1991; and "An Evening with Peter Matthiessen, February 12, 1992," City Arts & Lectures.
104. Margaret Lord, interviewed by LR, June 18, 2019.
105. Sarita Southgate, interviewed by LR, September 30, 2020.
106. Susan Braider, interviewed by LR, July 18, 2019.
107. *ML*, 100.
108. For PM's memories of chartering the *Merlin*, see *ML*, 100–14. For Cole's ("What a great way to make a living"), see *Away All Boats*, 121–31.
109. *ML*, 124.
110. PM, quoted in John Wakeman (ed.), *World Authors, 1950–1970* (New York: H. W. Wilson, 1975), 957.
111. PM to GP, n.d. [c. March 1954]. PRA, Box 6.
112. PM to GP, n.d. [c. April 1954]. PRA, Box 6.
113. PM to GP, August 9, 1954. PRA, Box 6.
114. PM to GP, n.d. [c. October 1954]. PRA, Box 6. Matthiessen quotes Plimpton in this letter.
115. Ibid.
116. GP interviewed by David Michaelis, quoted in Nelson Aldrich Jr. (ed.), *George, Being George*, 148.
117. PM to GP, n.d. PRA, Box 6.
118. Classifieds, September 8, 1955, *East Hampton Star*.
119. PM to Simon Michael Bessie, n.d. [March 1954]. HBR, Box MAT–MAY.
120. Elizabeth Lawrence to PM, April 22, 1954. HBR, Box MAT–MAY.
121. Elizabeth Lawrence to PM, May 20, 1954. HBR, Box MAT–MAY.
122. *Partisans* publishing contract, April 3, 1953. Brandt & Brandt Contract Files, Princeton University Library, Box 11.
123. PM, quoted in Rochelle Girson, "This Week's Personality," *Saturday Review*, October 1, 1955.
124. WS to PM, December 16, 1955, in Rose Styron and R. Blakeslee Gilpin (eds.), *Selected Letters of William Styron*, 215–17.
125. John Cole, *Away All Boats*, 145–46.
126. "Small Boy Killed on Way to School in Amagansett," *East Hampton Star*, June 2, 1955. Job Potter (Jeffrey's son), interviewed by LR, November 13, 2018.
127. Jeffrey Potter, interviewed by Tony Prohaska, May 16, 1998. The History Project, Inc., East Hampton Library.
128. Lucas Matthiessen, interviewed by LR, March 26, 2021.
129. PM, "Nightfall in Another Country." PMP 4, Box 1.
130. Anton Prohaska, *The White Fence: Icons and Legends in a Small Town* (Self-published, 2014).
131. PM, Memoir notes. MMC.
132. Lucas Matthiessen, interviewed by LR, September 28, 2018.
133. Joe LeSueur, *Digressions on Some Poems by Frank O'Hara: A Memoir* (New York: Farrar, Straus & Giroux, 2004), 177.
134. PS, "A Very Important Lady," *Evergreen Review*, Vol. 1, No. 3, 1957. In a remarkable coincidence, this issue features a cover photograph of Jackson Pollock by Hans Namuth, and PS's piece is preceded by poems by Frank O'Hara, with whom she would soon strike up the most important friendship of her life.
135. Lucas Matthiessen, interviewed by LR, March 26, 2021.
136. *ML*, 150.
137. PM, quoted in Michael Shnayerson, "Higher Matthiessen," *Vanity Fair*, December 1991. See also "An Evening with Peter Matthiessen, February 12, 1992, City Arts & Lectures.

8 · LOST AMERICANS

1. *WIA*, 232.
2. "Smog, Smaze, Smoze, Smag," *New York Times*, November 27, 1953.
3. Edith Evans Ashbury, "Smog Is Really Smaze; Rain May Rout It Tonight," *New York Times*, November 21, 1953.
4. Roy Popkin, "Two 'Killer Smogs' the Headlines Missed," *EPA Journal*, December 1986.
5. Quoted in Thomas Jundt, *Greening the Red, White, and Blue: The Bomb, Big Business, and Consumer Resistance in Postwar America* (Oxford: Oxford University Press, 2014), 67.
6. *WIA*, 21.
7. Dwight D. Eisenhower, quoted in Robert Gottlieb, *Forcing the Spring: The Transformation of the American Environmental Movement* (Washington, DC: Island Press, 1993), 39. Eisenhower's secretary of the interior, Douglas McKay, heartily agreed, and granted 274 lease grants on refuge land between August 1953 and December 1955, which "very nearly [equaled] the total number of leases in the previous history of the refuge system." See *WIA*, 227.
8. Stewart Udall, *1976: Agenda for Tomorrow* (New York: Harcourt, Brace & World, 1968), 17.
9. Thomas R. Dunlap, *Saving America's Wildlife* (Princeton: Princeton University Press, 1991), 102–3. See also PM's comments in *WIA*, 231–32.
10. Trailer available at www.youtube.com/watch?v=DwewijOin68.
11. Thomas R. Dunlap, *Saving America's Wildlife*, 100. A similar argument is made in Samuel P. Hays, "The Environmental Movement," *Journal of Forest History*, Vol. 25, No. 4, October 1981.
12. John Muir, *Nature Writings* (New York: Library of America, 1997), 755.
13. For an excellent breakdown of the Echo Park debate, see chapter twelve of Roderick Frazier Nash, *Wilderness and the American Mind* (New Haven: Yale University Press, 2014 [1967]). I also consulted Mark W. T. Harvey, *A Symbol of Wilderness: Echo Park and the American Conservation Movement* (Seattle: University of Washington Press, 2015).
14. Douglas McKay, quoted in *WIA*, 227.
15. Roderick Frazier Nash, *Wilderness and the American Mind*, 212.
16. Howard Zahniser, in Mark Harvey (ed.), *The Wilderness Writings of Howard Zahniser* (Seattle: University of Washington Press, 2014), 183.
17. "Naturalist-writer" is how PM styled it in the acknowledgments section of *WIA*.
18. PM, "Luis Buñuel and 'Travelin Man,'" *Zoetrope All-Story*, Vol. 9, No. 1, Spring 2005. It is likely that the island in "Travelin Man" was modeled on Murphy Island, part of the old Santee Gun Club, and that the main character was inspired by William Garrett, a Black guide at the club who took PM hunting for geese. In an interview in 2016, Garrett recalled PM's strict adherence to bag limits, and his habit of sketching while out in the field: "He used to draw pictures of stuff a lot. . . . After he'd come out to the island, he used to draw pictures. He don't hunt no quail, he don't hunt no deer, but he'd draw a picture, sit there." See William Garrett, interviewed by Bob Raynor, June 14, 2016, "Voices of the Santee Delta," Lowcountry Digital Library.
19. "Peter Matthiessen: The Art of Fiction No. 157," *The Paris Review*, No. 150, Spring 1999. See also Wendy Smith, "PW Interviews Peter Matthiessen," *Publishers Weekly*, May 9, 1986; PM, "The Long Journey: Zen and the Writing Life" (audio recording), San Francisco Zen Center, 1998; and Alec Michod, "Living on the Edge of Life: A Final Interview with Peter Matthiessen," *Los Angeles Review of Books*, April 6, 2014.
20. Ibid.
21. "Powerboat Cruising," *Holiday*, February 1957.
22. PM, "The Long Journey: Zen and the Writing Life" (audio recording). San Francisco Zen Center, 1998. See also "An Evening with Peter Matthiessen," February 12, 1992, City Arts & Lectures.
23. PM to William Shawn, April 28, 1956. NYR, Box 548.
24. Ben Bradlee, *A Good Life: Newspapering and Other Adventures* (New York: Simon & Schuster, 1995), 133–34.

25. PM to William Shawn, March 4, 1957. NYR, Box 548.
26. PM, "No Boundaries" (audio recording), Gang of Seven, 1992. PM claimed he sent the check back to Shawn, which may be an embellishment; there is nothing in the surviving letters to suggest he ever returned the money.
27. Ibid.
28. The original draft—which did indeed need a considerable amount of work—is in NYR, Box 1395.
29. PM, quoted in Rosemary Goring, "Man with No Fame," *Scotland on Sunday*, May 3, 1998.
30. PM, "Writer's Symposium by the Sea: Peter Matthiessen," April 2005. Recording held by Point Loma Nazarene University.
31. Rachel Carson (to Lois Crisler), quoted in *BOH*, xiv. Matthiessen referenced this letter several times over the years, but sometimes erroneously identified the recipient as Sally Carrighar. See "Writer's Symposium by the Sea: Peter Matthiessen," April 2005; and PM, interviewed by Jeff Sewald, March 2005. JSC. For more on Carson's correspondence with Crisler, the author of *Arctic Wild* (1958), see Linda Lear, *Rachel Carson: Witness for Nature* (New York: Henry Holt, 1997), 397.
32. Richard Johnston to PM, November 3, 1959. Johnston quotes the original commissioning letter from March 15, 1957. PMP 1, Box 58.
33. Contract for "Lost Americans," March 12, 1957. PRH, Box BX0902885, File 371866.
34. Alexander Wilson to William Bartram, August 4, 1809. *The Poems and Literary Prose of Alexander Wilson, the American Ornithologist* (Paisley, Scotland: Alex Gardner, 1876), 171.
35. PM came across Catlin's writings and paintings as part of his research for *WIA*. As he later wrote, "[Catlin's] one wish was faithfully to record American Indians before their 'native dignity and beauty and independence' were destroyed. This noble ambition, which seized George Catlin early in his career, has put us forever in his debt." See PM, "Introduction," in George Catlin, *North American Indians* (New York: Penguin Classics, 2004), viii.
36. Douglas Brinkley, *The Quiet World: Saving Alaska's Wildlife Kingdom, 1879–1960* (New York: Harper, 2011), 436.
37. PM, quoted in ibid.
38. *BOH*, 277.
39. *WIA*, 48–49.
40. Ibid., 265.
41. Ibid., 109.
42. PM, "Among the Griz," *Outside*, September 1990. See also *IC*, 171. Curiously, Matthiessen's notes about Yellowstone in *WIA* (p. 156) are focused on the black bears, which he calls "insolent and parasitic beggars."
43. PM, interviewed for the National Writers Series, Traverse City, MI, October 29, 2010.
44. PM, quoted in Rex Weyler, "Peter Matthiessen: The Search for Truth," *New Age*, August 1983. See also *IC*, 294–95.
45. *OOM*, 12.
46. PM, quoted in Douglas Brinkley, *The Quiet World*, 438.
47. *WIA*, 246.
48. PM, "Ovibos Moschatus," *The New Yorker*, February 5, 1966.
49. *WIA*, 247. See also PM, interviewed by Sedge Thomson, February 10, 1990, City Arts & Lectures.
50. PM, *Oomingmak* unused draft pages. PMP 1, Box 42.
51. Ibid.
52. *WIA*, 232.
53. PM, *Oomingmak* unused draft pages. PMP 1, Box 42.
54. *WIA*, 114.
55. Ibid., 178.
56. Richard Pough, "Introduction," *WIA* (1959 edition only), 13.
57. *WIA*, 64.

58. David S. Wilcove, *The Condor's Shadow: The Loss and Recovery of Wildlife in America* (New York: Anchor, 1999), 19.
59. *WIA*, 79.
60. Ibid., 25.
61. David S. Wilcove, *The Condor's Shadow*, 19–20.
62. *WIA*, 26.
63. Ibid., 64.
64. Ibid., 160.
65. William T. Hornaday, *Our Vanishing Wildlife: Its Extermination and Preservation* (New York: Charles Scriber's Sons, 1913), 8. To understand Hornaday, I also consulted Gregory J. Dehler, *The Most Defiant Devil: William Temple Hornaday & His Controversial Crusade to Save American Wildlife* (Charlottesville: University of Virginia Press, 2013).
66. *WIA*, 180.
67. Ibid., 70–71.
68. Ibid., 22. Matthiessen acquired his understanding of ecology during the research process for *WIA*.
69. Aldo Leopold, quoted in *WIA*, 22. The source is "Guacamaja," an essay in Leopold's *A Sand County Almanac* (New York: Oxford University Press, 1949), 137.
70. PM to Walter Isaacson, n.d. [1999]. MMC. For Matthiessen's thoughts on Carson, see PM, "Rachel Carson," *Time*, March 29, 1999; and "Introduction," in PM (ed.), *Courage for the Earth: Writers, Scientists, and Activists Celebrate the Life and Writing of Rachel Carson* (New York: Mariner, 2007). "Famed as a scientist whose timely book on chemical poisons had served as a warning to the world about the insatiable nature of corporate greed," Matthiessen wrote, "she was at the same time an important writer." At a City Arts & Lectures event in San Francisco, on May 3, 2009, he described her as "perhaps our foremost nature writer of all time."
71. Rachel Carson, quoted in Linda Lear, *Rachel Carson*, 221.
72. Rachel Carson, *The Sea Around Us* (New York: Oxford University Press, 2018 [1951]), 15.
73. *WIA*, 19–21.
74. PM, in conversation with Gary Snyder, February 25, 2002, City Arts & Lectures.
75. Ibid. On some undated notes for a lecture about his career, Matthiessen wrote: "W in A . . . 1959 . . . Even then, not a nature writer . . . environmental writer, already concerned with traditional people and social justice." PMP 4, Box 15.
76. Rae Eastman to PM, n.d. [1990]. PMP 4, Box 39.
77. Edward Weeks, *Atlantic Monthly*, March 1960.
78. Archie Carr, "The Need to Let Live," *New York Times*, November 22, 1959.
79. Alfred C. Ames, "An Impressive Memorial to Vanishing Wildlife," *Chicago Tribune*, October 18, 1959.
80. Rae Brooks, "Books in Brief," *Harper's Magazine*, November 1959.
81. Roger Tory Peterson, "Wildlife, Once Teeming, Still Under Big Threats," *Philadelphia Inquirer*, November 11, 1959.
82. Philip C. Freshwater, "Animals Waste Away as Americans Thrive," *Sacramento Bee*, December 2, 1959.
83. John H. Baker to PM, June 19, 1959. PMP 4, Box 39.
84. Richard Johnston to PM, November 3, 1959. PMP 1, Box 58. Johnston quotes PM referring to his drafts as "excellent material."
85. Ibid.
86. PM to Richard Johnston, November 7, 1959. PMP 1, Box 58.
87. PM, "Foreword," in Oren Lyons and John Mohawk (eds.), *Exiled in the Land of the Free: Democracy, Indian Nations and the U.S. Constitution* (Santa Fe, NM: Clear Light, 1992), xi.
88. *WIA*, 233.
89. Ibid., 230.
90. Ibid., 229.
91. For the original list, see "78 Species Listed Near Extinction," *New York Times*, March 12, 1967.

92. Terry Tempest Williams, interviewed by Jeff Sewald, August 31, 2006. JSC.
93. David S. Wilcove, *The Condor's Shadow*, xvii.
94. Kenneth V. Rosenberg et al., "Decline of the North American Avifauna," *Science*, Vol. 366, No. 6461, October 2019.
95. *WIA*, 22.

9 · UNSURVEYED AND UNFATHOMED

1. *APFL*, 2.
2. Decree of Divorce, August 5, 1958. District Court of Washoe County, Nevada.
3. Joe LeSueur, *Digressions on Some Poems by Frank O'Hara: A Memoir* (New York: Farrar, Straus & Giroux, 2004), 177.
4. Ibid., 178.
5. PS, quoted in Brad Gooch, *City Poet: The Life and Times of Frank O'Hara* (New York: Knopf, 2010), 307.
6. Lucas Matthiessen, interviewed by LR, August 30, 2019.
7. Rose Styron, interviewed by LR, November 27, 2018.
8. PM to Blair Fuller, n.d. [c. 2011]. MMC. See also Alexandra Styron, *Reading My Father: A Memoir* (New York: Scribner, 2012), 143.
9. PM, "No Boundaries" (audio recording), Gang of Seven, 1992.
10. For a sense of Diarmuid Russell, I relied on Michael Kreyling, *Author and Agent: Eudora Welty and Diarmuid Russell* (New York: Farrar, Straus & Giroux, 1992); and Harriet Wasserman, *Handsome Is: Adventures with Saul Bellow* (New York: Fromm International, 1997). Wasserman worked at Russell & Volkening.
11. Diarmuid Russell to PM, March 26, 1959. RV, Box 3.
12. PM to GP, n.d. [April 1960]. PRA, Box 6.
13. PM, "An Evening with Peter Matthiessen," February 12, 1992, City Arts & Lectures.
14. PM, in conversation with Gary Snyder, February 23, 1994, City Arts & Lectures.
15. PM repeats this claim in Kay Bonetti, "An Interview with Peter Matthiessen," *Missouri Review*, Vol. 12, No. 2, 1989; James Atlas, "To the Ends of the Earth," *Condé Nast Traveler*, October 1989; PM, "The Long Journey: Zen and the Writing Life" (audio recording), San Francisco Zen Center, 1998; Ben Naparstek, *In Conversation: Encounters with Great Writers* (Melbourne: Scribe Publications, 2009), 61; and Jonathan Meiburg, "An Interview with Peter Matthiessen," *The Believer*, June 2014.
16. PM, in conversation with Gary Snyder, February 23, 1994, City Arts & Lectures. See also Beth Baker, "When the World Was Wild," *AARP Bulletin*, February 1998.
17. PM, quoted in Nicholas Dawidoff, "Earthbound in the Space Age," *Sports Illustrated*, December 1990.
18. "Peter Matthiessen: Itinerary," n.d. [November 1959]. NYR, Box 564. "Approximate dates of arrival," Matthiessen noted: "freighter travel, etc. . . . is apt to be uncertain, and possibly I will arrive in Cairo as much as a month later than the proposed date below: the following dates will be amended by mail or cable as I go along."
19. PM, "Voyage of the Happy Days (Opening Section)." NYR, Box 1466.
20. WS, "Peter Matthiessen," *This Quiet Dust* (New York: Random House, 1982), 273.
21. John Wilcock, "Americans Abroad: Tourists Again Spend More Dollars Last Year than Ever Before," *New York Times*, June 21, 1959.
22. *CF*, 153–54.
23. PM, South America journal 1, November 1959–March 1960. PMP 4, Box 6.
24. PM, "Voyage of the Happy Days (Opening Section)." NYR, Box 1466.
25. Ibid. All quotes in this section come from Matthiessen's typed and lightly edited journal notes.
26. PM, "The Last Wilderness: Amazonas Journal," *The New Yorker*, July 8, 1961.
27. PM, South America journal 1, November 1959–March 1960. PMP 4, Box 6.
28. Ibid. Matthiessen also discusses Gauvin ("a young fellow") in an interview with Patty Satalia, "Conversations from Penn State," 2010. See www.youtube.com/watch?v=9cZFCdU6LWU&t=1535s. See also PM, interviewed by HN, n.d. [multiple

interviews, 1990s]. HNC, Box 2; "Peter Matthiessen: The Art of Fiction No. 157," *The Paris Review*, No. 150, Spring 1999; and PM, interviewed for the National Writers Series, Traverse City, MI, October 29, 2010.
29. PM, interviewed by HN, n.d. [multiple interviews, 1990s]. HNC, Box 2.
30. *CF*, 25.
31. Ibid., 26.
32. Ibid., 29.
33. Ibid.
34. Ibid., 27.
35. Ibid., 30.
36. Ibid., 38.
37. PM, South America journal 1, November 1959–March 1960. PMP 4, Box 6.
38. Ibid.
39. Ibid.
40. PM, "The Last Wilderness: Amazonas Journal," *The New Yorker*, July 8, 1961. In a line cut from the article, Matthiessen added: "Though I had travelled up the Amazon, this jungle had eluded me; I was a veteran only of its vapors, of that tropical *ennui* which makes the outside world and all its doings seem rather beside the point."
41. PM, South America journal 1, November 1959–March 1960. PMP 4, Box 6.
42. *CF*, 151.
43. Ibid., 24.
44. PM, South America journal 1, November 1959–March 1960. PMP 4, Box 6.
45. *CF*, 152.
46. PM, South America journal 1, November 1959–March 1960. PMP 4, Box 6.
47. *CF*, 152.
48. PM to William Shawn, February 14, 1960. NYR, Box 574.
49. *CF*, 117.
50. PM, South America journal 1, November 1959–March 1960. PMP 4, Box 6.
51. PM, "The Last Wilderness: Brazilian Chronicle," *The New Yorker*, August 12, 1961.
52. *CF*, 128.
53. Ibid., 127.
54. PM, South America journal 1, November 1959–March 1960. PMP 4, Box 6. In *CF* (p. 129), this passage is slightly expanded: "How serene these people are—as if religion were a state of shock, deep, peaceful shock, that good men like these are driven into by the spectacle of reality. Or is it that we, on the far side of the same abyss, do not wish to relinquish our tiny identities to a higher power? At least, I don't, and I'm just as aware as the next man that temporal ambitions are insane—not because we are immortal, though, but because we are so mortal, and because our ambitions will amount at best to a hill of beans."
55. *CF*, 140.
56. PM, South America journal 1, November 1959–March 1960. PMP 4, Box 6.
57. Ibid.
58. Ibid.
59. PM to GP, n.d. [April 1960]. PRA, Box 6.
60. Lisa Barclay Bigelow to PM, n.d. [April 1960]. PMP 4, Box 38.
61. PM to GP, n.d. [April 1960]. PRA, Box 6.
62. "The Cloud Forest," *Kirkus*, October 1, 1961.
63. Thomas Foster, "A South America Wilderness Journey," *New York Herald Tribune*, October 8, 1961.
64. Marston Bates, "Fortune Smiled on the Traveler in an Unmapped Part of the Earth," *New York Times*, October 15, 1961.
65. *CF*, 140.
66. Ibid., 122.
67. Ibid., 41.
68. Ibid., 75.
69. Ibid., 68.
70. Ibid., 152.

71. Ibid., 155.
72. Ibid., 167.
73. Ibid., 194.
74. Ibid., 199.
75. Ibid., 216.
76. PM, South America journal 2, April–May 1960. PMP 4, Box 6.
77. *CF*, 239–40.
78. Ibid.
79. PM, "Literature and Mysticism," Regents Lecture at UC Santa Barbara, November 9, 1978.
80. PM, Ayahuasca journal, May 1960. PMP 4, Box 7.
81. PM, "The Last Wilderness: Peruvian Journal," *The New Yorker*, September 9, 1961.
82. Don Stap to PM, September 20, 1987. PMP 4, Box 40. For a full account, see Don Stap, *A Parrot Without a Name: The Search for the Last Unknown Birds on Earth* (New York: Alfred A. Knopf, 1990), 19–25.
83. The "Matthiessen specimen of *Purussaurus*" was the subject of a panel at the seventy-fourth meeting of the Society of Vertebrate Paleontology, in Berlin, on November 7, 2014. See also Tito Aureliano et al., "Morphometry, Bite-Force, and Paleobiology of the Late Miocene Caiman *Purussaurus brasiliensis*," PLOS ONE, Vol. 10, No. 2, 2015.

10 · WAR GAMES

1. *UTMW*, 73.
2. RG to PM, July 5, 1960. RG, *Making Dead Birds: Chronicle of a Film* (Cambridge: Peabody Museum Press, 2007), 23.
3. Adele Pressman, interviewed by LR, March 31, 2020.
4. RG, *Making Dead Birds*, 5.
5. RG to Harold Coolidge, January 29, 1959. Ibid., 12.
6. RG, *Making Dead Birds*, 13.
7. RG and KH, *Gardens of War: Life and Death in the New Guinea Stone Age* (New York: Random House, 1969), xv.
8. PM and RG in conversation for the *New York Times*, 1996. See https://www.nytimes.com/video/obituaries/100000002999087/robert-gardner-and-peter-matthiessen.html.
9. RG, *Making Dead Birds*, 121.
10. Ibid., 15.
11. RG to Michael Rockefeller, April 20, 1960, in ibid., 19.
12. RG and KH, *Gardens of War*, xii.
13. Ibid., xiii.
14. Adele Pressman, interviewed by LR, March 31, 2020.
15. RG, *Making Dead Birds*, 22.
16. RG to PM, July 5, 1960, in ibid, 23.
17. A copy of the missionary eyewitness accounts that Matthiessen would have received from Gardner can be found in RGC, Box 2.
18. PM and RG in conversation for the *New York Times*, 1996.
19. *UTMW*, xiv.
20. KH, interviewed by LR, November 30, 2018.
21. RG, *Making Dead Birds*, 8–9.
22. Arthur Myers, "Versatile Author Matthiessen Stops Here Between South America and New Guinea," *Berkshire Eagle*, December 30, 1960.
23. *SNA*, 116.
24. PM, Ayahuasca journal, May 1960. PMP 4, Box 7.
25. *SL*, 39.
26. PM, interviewed by Immy Humes, n.d. [2001]. Transcribed from unused footage for Immy Humes's *Doc* (2008). See tapes 085/086/087, DHA.
27. The notecard can be found in PMP 4, Box 37.
28. Rose Styron, interviewed by LR, November 27, 2018.

29. PM, *The Snow Leopard* draft typescript. PMP 1, Box 48.
30. *SL*, 41.
31. Aldous Huxley, *The Doors of Perception* (New York: Harper Perennial, 2009 [1954]), 55.
32. *SL*, 203.
33. *RAD*, 43.
34. PM in Kay Bonetti, "An Interview with Peter Matthiessen," *Missouri Review*, Vol. 12, No. 2, 1989.
35. *RAD*, 64.
36. PM, "The Long Journey: Zen and the Writing Life" (audio recording), San Francisco Zen Center, 1998.
37. Gene Baro, "In the Society of Men at Sea a Romantic Comes to Self-Knowledge," *New York Herald Tribune*, January 29, 1961.
38. Charles Poore, "Book of the Times," *New York Times*, January 28, 1961.
39. Terry Southern, "Christ Seen Darkly," *The Nation*, February 25, 1961.
40. PM, "The Tree Where Man Was Born," *The Reporter*, June 1962.
41. *TWMB*, 22.
42. PM, interviewed by HN, n.d. [multiple interviews, 1990s]. HNC, Box 2.
43. DL to PM, February 13, 1961. PMP 4, Box 36.
44. *TWMB*, 32.
45. Ibid. See also PM, interviewed by Dean Nelson, "Writer's Symposium by the Sea."
46. PM, quoted in Joseph P. Kahn, "A Writer's Wide, Wide World," *Boston Globe*, June 1, 1999. See also Bruce Beans, "The Wilderness Within," *Philadelphia Magazine*, June 24, 1990.
47. *TWMB*, 8.
48. PM, interviewed by HN, n.d. [multiple interviews, 1990s]. HNC, Box 2.
49. *AS*, 74–75.
50. PM, interviewed by HN, n.d. [multiple interviews, 1990s]. HNC, Box 2.
51. Ruth Prawer Jhabvala to PM, March 31, 1961. PMP 4, Box 39.
52. *SL*, 40.
53. DL to PM, n.d. [February–March 1961]. PMP 4, Box 36.
54. PM, New Guinea journal, April–August 1961. PMP 1, Box 50.
55. Richard Archbold, "Unknown New Guinea," *National Geographic*, March 1941.
56. Extracts of Margaret Hastings's "Shangri-La Diary" are reproduced in Susan Meiselas, *Encounters with the Dani: Stories from the Baliem Valley* (New York: International Center of Photography, 2003), 17–21. I am indebted to Meiselas's book for a historical overview of early American and European contact with the Baliem Valley. I also referred to an unpublished essay by PM on Baliem history and anthropology: see PMP 1, Box 50. For further information about Hastings and the rescue, see Mitchell Zuckoff, *Lost in Shangri-La* (New York: Harper, 2011).
57. The pamphlet is reproduced in Susan Meiselas, *Encounters with the Dani*, 36–37.
58. Fritz Veldkamp, quoted in ibid., 45.
59. PM, New Guinea journal, April–August 1961. PMP 1, Box 50.
60. Ibid.
61. DL to PM, n.d. [April 1961]. PMP 4, Box 36.
62. *UTMW*, 17.
63. RG, New Guinea journal (typed), April–July 1961. RGC, Box 5.
64. PM, New Guinea journal, April–August 1961. PMP 1, Box 50.
65. Ibid.
66. RG, New Guinea journal (typed), April–July 1961. RGC, Box 5.
67. PM, New Guinea journal, April–August 1961. PMP 1, Box 50.
68. KH, New Guinea journal, April–August 1961. 2011. Dr. Karl G. Heider Papers, Peabody Museum of Archaeology and Ethnology, Harvard University.
69. Ibid.
70. RG, New Guinea journal (typed), April–July 1961. RGC, Box 5.
71. *UTMW*, 8.
72. RG, New Guinea journal (typed), April–July 1961. RGC, Box 5.
73. RG, *Dead Birds* (Contemporary Films and Mutual Distributors, 1963).

74. PM, New Guinea journal, April–August 1961. PMP 1, Box 50.
75. Ibid.
76. Ibid.
77. RG, *Making Dead Birds*, 58.
78. RG to J. O. Brew, April 21, 1961, in RG, *Making Dead Birds*, 62.
79. Quoted in RG, *Making Dead Birds*, 62.
80. Ibid., 121.
81. KH, interviewed by LR, November 30, 2018.
82. Jan Broekhuijse, *De Harvard-Peabody Expeditie: naar de Dani van de Baliem-vallei* (2019). Rough translations of passages from this memoir were provided by Broekhuijse's son, Gies, then edited for clarity.
83. KH, interviewed by LR, November 30, 2018.
84. Jan Broekhuijse, *De Harvard-Peabody Expeditie*.
85. *UTMW*, xiv.
86. RG, *The Impulse to Preserve: Reflections of a Filmmaker* (Cambridge: Peabody Museum Press, 2006), 65.
87. Jan Broekhuijse, *De Harvard-Peabody Expeditie*.
88. RG, Netherlands New Guinea journal (typed), April–July 1961. RGC, Box 5.
89. KH, *The Dugum Dani: A Papuan Culture in the Highlands of West New Guinea* (Chicago: Aldine Publishing Company, 1970), 14.
90. RG, "The More Things Change," *Transition*, No. 58, 1992.
91. RG, New Guinea journal (typed), April–July 1961. RGC, Box 5.
92. KH, *The Dugum Dani*, 14–15.
93. PM, interviewed by HN, n.d. [multiple interviews, 1990s]. HNC, Box 2.
94. Ibid.
95. RG, New Guinea journal (typed), April–July 1961. RGC, Box 5.
96. PM, interviewed by HN, n.d. [multiple interviews, 1990s]. HNC, Box 2.
97. RG, New Guinea journal (typed), April–July 1961. RGC, Box 5.
98. RG, *Making Dead Birds*, 76.
99. RG, New Guinea journal (typed), April–July 1961. RGC, Box 5.
100. For examples, see Homer Bigart, "Expedition Defended," *New York Times*, November 27, 1961; "Harvard Group Accused of Inciting Native War," *Los Angeles Times*, February 23, 1962. A collection of relevant clippings can be found in RGC.
101. Michael Rockefeller, quoted in RG, *Making Dead Birds*, 70.
102. Jan Broekhuijse, *De Harvard-Peabody Expeditie*.
103. PM and RG in conversation for the *New York Times*, 1996.
104. KH, interviewed by LR, November 30, 2018.
105. RG, *The Impulse to Preserve*, 56.
106. RG, New Guinea journal (typed), April–July 1961. RGC, Box 5.
107. This audio (and a transcript) was shared with me by Ernst Karel and Veronika Kusumaryati, who use it in their documentary about the Harvard-Peabody New Guinea Expedition of 1961, *Expedition Content* (2020). The original recording is in RGC.
108. PM, "Recognition," dated "June, 1961." PMP 4, Box 62.
109. DL to PM, May 19, 1961. PMP 4, Box 36.
110. PM to RG, summer 1963, in RG, *Making Dead Birds*, 124.
111. PM, quoted in Jonathan Meiburg, "An Interview with Peter Matthiessen," *The Believer*, June 2014.
112. DL to PM, May 30, 1961. PMP 4, Box 36. DL quotes Matthiessen in her letter.
113. PM, interviewed by HN, n.d. [multiple interviews, 1990s]. HNC, Box 2.
114. PM to James Jones, August 2, 1962. James Jones Papers, Harry Ransom Center, University of Texas at Austin, Box 68.
115. PM to William Shawn, July 11, 1961. NYR, Box 574.
116. KH to RG, October 4, 1961, in RG, *Making Dead Birds*, 105.
117. KH to RG, October 13, 1961, in ibid.
118. KH to RG, October 19, 1961, in ibid., 106.
119. KH to RG, November 2, 1961, in ibid.

120. KH to RG, November 15, 1961, in ibid.
121. *UTMW*, 10.
122. Ibid., 3.
123. Ibid., 13.
124. Ibid., 24.
125. Ibid., 51.
126. Ibid., 4.
127. Ibid., 183.
128. Ibid., 4.
129. RG, *The Impulse to Preserve*, 63.
130. Loren Eiseley, "Miniatures of Ourselves," *New York Times*, November 18, 1962.
131. Leopold Pospíšil, "Book Reviews," *American Anthropologist*, No. 66, 1964.
132. Paul Pickrel, "The New Books," *Harper's Magazine*, February 1963.
133. D. Carleton Gajdusek, "How 'Unspoiled' the Savage?," *Washington Post*, October 21, 1962.
134. PM to RG, November 7, 1962, in RG, *Making Dead Birds*, 121.
135. PM, interviewed by HN, n.d. [multiple interviews, 1990s]. HNC, Box 2. See also PM's interview on *Charlie Rose*, PBS, June 3, 1999 (https://charlierose.com/videos/9919); and Alec Michod, "Living on the Edge of Life: A Final Interview with Peter Matthiessen," *Los Angeles Review of Books*, April 6, 2014.
136. *UTMW*, vii.
137. Carl Hoffman, *Savage Harvest: A Tale of Cannibals, Colonialism, and Michael Rockefeller's Tragic Quest* (New York: William Morrow, 2014).
138. Adele Pressman, interviewed by LR, March 31, 2020.
139. PM, interviewed by HN, n.d. [multiple interviews, 1990s]. HNC, Box 2.
140. "An Evening with Peter Matthiessen," February 12, 1992, City Arts & Lectures.

11 · IN PARADISUM

1. PM, quoted in Jonathan White, *Talking on the Water: Conversations About Nature and Creativity* (San Francisco: Sierra Club Books, 1994), 241.
2. *SL*, 41–42.
3. DL, "LSD #2," n.d. PMP 4, Box 36.
4. *SL*, 42.
5. DL, quoted in Rue Matthiessen, "LSD and Zen," *Free State Review*, Issue 15, October 2022.
6. Ibid.
7. DL to PM, n.d. [January 1961]. "What a strange and good . . ." PMP 4, Box 36.
8. DL, *Annaghkeen* (New York: Random House, 1970), 107.
9. DL to PM, n.d. [February 1961]. "I'm thinking about the coldness . . ." PMP 4, Box 36.
10. Rue Matthiessen, interviewed by LR, March 25, 2021.
11. DL to PM, n.d. [January 1961]. "I see by your itinerary . . ." PMP 4, Box 36.
12. Rue Matthiessen, *Castles and Ruins: Unraveling Family Mysteries and Literary Legacy in the Irish Countryside* (Spokane, WA: Latah Books, 2024), 130.
13. "Pollock-Love Marriage Announced," *St. Louis Post-Dispatch*, November 22, 1957.
14. "The Victors," *Kirkus*, November 9, 1956.
15. Rue Matthiessen, interviewed by LR, September 25, 2018.
16. DL to PM, n.d. [February 1961]. "I'm thinking about the coldness . . ." PMP 4, Box 36.
17. DL to PM, n.d. [January 1961]. "Rue is taking a nap . . ." PMP 4, Box 36.
18. DL to PM, n.d. [February 1961]. "I'm thinking about the coldness . . ." PMP 4, Box 36.
19. DL, "One Winter" manuscript, n.d. RHR, Box 900. A version of this autobiographical story was published in *The Paris Review*, No. 50, Fall 1970.
20. DL to PM, n.d. [January 1961]. "What a strange and good . . ." PMP 4, Box 36.
21. DL to PM, n.d. [April 1961]. "I got a letter yesterday . . ." PMP 4, Box 36.

22. DL to PM, n.d. [March 1961]. "Please don't send me an avuncular kiss . . ." PMP 4, Box 36.
23. Ibid.
24. DL to PM, August 15, 1961. PMP 4, Box 36.
25. DL to PM, n.d., "Every time I wrote to you . . ." PMP 4, Box 36.
26. SL, 66.
27. DL to PM, April 9, 1961. PMP 4, Box 36.
28. SL, 40.
29. Ibid., 39.
30. Ibid., 40.
31. DL, *Annaghkeen*, 60.
32. SL, 40.
33. DL to PM, April 6, 1961. PMP 4, Box 36.
34. Alan Watts, *The Joyous Cosmology* (Novato, CA: New World Library, 2013 [1962]), 11.
35. DL to PM, April 9, 1961. PMP 4, Box 36.
36. SL, 41.
37. Alan Watts, *In My Own Way: An Autobiography* (Novato, CA: New World Library, 2007 [1972]), 323.
38. Ibid., 325.
39. DL to PM, April 9, 1961. PMP 4, Box 36.
40. Alan Watts, *The Joyous Cosmology*, 130.
41. PM, quoted in Nicholas Wrote, "Call of the Wild," *The Guardian*, August 16, 2002.
42. My overview of LSD history is based on Steven J. Novak, "LSD Before Leary: Sidney Cohen's Critique of 1950s Psychedelic Drug Research," *Isis*, Vol. 88, No. 1, March 1997; and Michael Pollan, *How to Change Your Mind* (New York: Penguin, 2018). I also interviewed James Fadiman about the International Foundation for Advanced Study on November 4, 2019.
43. See, for example, Douglas Brinkley, *The Quiet World: Saving Alaska's Wildlife Kingdom, 1879–1960* (New York: Harper, 2011), 440; PM, interviewed by Mark Adams, February 14, 2014. Collection of Mark Adams.
44. Timothy Leary, "Turning on the World," in Ann Charters (ed.), *The Portable Sixties Reader* (New York: Penguin, 2003), 331.
45. PM, interviewed by Mark Adams, February 14, 2014. Collection of Mark Adams.
46. PM, "Notes re hallucinogens > Zen practice," n.d. [1973]. PMP 4, Box 36.
47. SL, 42.
48. DL, "Even if It's Too Late," n.d. RHR, Box 900.
49. DL, "LSD #2," n.d. PMP 4, Box 36.
50. DL, "LSD #9," n.d. PMP 4, Box 36.
51. Ibid.
52. PM, quoted in Peter Damm, "Peter Matthiessen: Journeys of the Heart," *Berkeley Monthly*, July 27, 1978.
53. "Peter Matthiessen: The Art of Fiction No. 157," *The Paris Review*, No. 150, Spring 1999.
54. PM, quoted in "Sea Changes," *Time*, May 26, 1975.
55. APFL, 10.
56. Ibid., 154.
57. Ibid., 220.
58. Ibid., 16.
59. Ibid., 33.
60. Ibid., 129.
61. Ibid., 256.
62. PM, "Notes re hallucinogens > Zen practice," n.d. [1973]. PMP 4, Box 36.
63. APFL, 68–69.
64. Ibid., 232.
65. Ibid., 352.
66. Ibid., 79.

67. Ibid., 73.
68. Ibid., 100.
69. Ibid., 124.
70. Ibid., 186.
71. Ibid., 270.
72. Ibid., 372.
73. Ibid., 373.
74. PM to Diarmuid Russell, n.d. [May 1964]. RV, Box 18.
75. [No name; Scribner editor] to PM, May 18, 1964. RV, Box 18.
76. Paul Brooks to PM, June 2, 1964. RV, Box 18.
77. Robert Gutwillig to PM, May 22, 1964. RV, Box 18.
78. James Salter, *Burning the Days* (New York: Vintage, 1997), 361.
79. JF to PM, May 18, 1964. RHR, Box 1087.
80. JF to PM, May 19, 1964. RHR, Box 1087.
81. JF to PM, May 20, 1964. RHR, Box 1087.
82. JF to PM, May 22, 1964. RHR, Box 1087.
83. JF to PM, May 25, 1964. RHR, Box 1087.
84. JF to PM, May 27, 1964. RHR, Box 1087.
85. JF (quoting Irwin Shaw), quoted in Michael Shnayerson, *Irwin Shaw: A Biography* (New York: G. P. Putnam's Sons, 1989), 293.
86. JF to PM, June 17, 1964. RHR, Box 1087.
87. JF to Joseph Gies, August 17, 1965. RHR, Box 1087.
88. JF to PM, July 15, 1964. RHR, Box 1087.
89. PM to JF, July 27, 1964. RHR, Box 1087.
90. *APFL*, 3.
91. JF to PM, August 28, 1964. RHR, Box 1087.
92. JF, quoted in Michael Shnayerson, "Higher Matthiessen," *Vanity Fair*, December 1991.
93. "Peter Matthiessen: The Art of Fiction No. 157," *The Paris Review*, No. 150, Spring 1999.
94. PM, quoted in John Irving, "Fox Here . . . ," *The New Yorker*, December 25, 1995.
95. JF to PM, February 5, 1965. RHR, Box 1087.
96. Reader's Report for JF, May 14, 1965. RHR, Box 1087.
97. JF to Jim Silberman, June 1, 1965. RHR, Box 1087.
98. PM to JF, n.d. [June 1965]. RHR, Box 1087.
99. PM to Diarmuid Russell, July 13, 1964. RV, Box 18.
100. Lucas Matthiessen, interviewed by Jeff Sewald, n.d. [2006]. JSC.
101. Lucas Matthiessen, interviewed by LR, September 28, 2018.
102. PM to DL, March 17, 1964. Collection of Rue Matthiessen.
103. PM, interviewed by Patty Satalia for "Conversations from Penn State," 2010.
104. PM, quoted in Marty Berry, "Peter Matthiessen Looks to Nature for Inspiration," *Greenville News*, January 22, 1987.
105. Lucas Matthiessen, interviewed by LR, September 28, 2018.
106. DL to John Abbot, n.d. Collection of Rue Matthiessen.
107. Rue Matthiessen, interviewed by LR, September 25, 2018.
108. DL, *Annaghkeen*, 89. This book is a polished version of the journal she kept in Ireland during the summer of 1965.
109. Ibid., 4.
110. PM to JF, n.d. [July 1965]. RHR, Box 1087.
111. *SL*, 66.
112. DL, *Annaghkeen*, 203.
113. Ibid., 40.
114. Ibid., 140.
115. Ibid., 130.
116. Ibid., 203.
117. Ibid., 206.
118. Ibid., 215.

12 · A SIMPLE MAN

1. PM, "Simplicity" *teisho*, n.d. MMC.
2. Roderick Cook, "Books in Brief," *Harper's Magazine*, November 1965.
3. PM to John Fischer, October 28, 1965. RHR, Box 1087.
4. William Styron, "Reviewer Reviewed," *Harper's Magazine*, January 1966.
5. Pat Hanna, "Savages, Salvation and Cynics," *Rocky Mountain News*, October 31, 1965.
6. Victor Hass, "A Wide Range of Fiction," *Chicago Tribune*, December 26, 1965.
7. G. H. Pouder, "Unusual and Gripping," *Baltimore Sun*, November 7, 1965.
8. Peter S. Prescott, "Superior Novel of Man's Aspirations," *Chicago Daily News*, November 22, 1965.
9. PM, Washington notes, December 1965–February 1966. PMP 4, Box 10.
10. Ralph Metzner to PM, October 6, 1966. PMP 4, Box 40.
11. *ML*, 129.
12. DL to PM, n.d. [July 1961]. PMP 4, Box 36.
13. PM, "Even the Corps," *East Hampton Star*, February 24, 1966.
14. PM, Washington notes, December 1965–February 1966. PMP 4, Box 10. Unless otherwise noted, all quotes in this section come from these notes.
15. For an elegant overview of Stewart Udall's environmental legacy, see Michelle Nijhuis, *Beloved Beasts: Fighting for Life in an Age of Extinction* (New York: W. W. Norton, 2021).
16. PM, "The Last Great Strand," *Audubon*, March 1967.
17. PM to Stewart Udall, December 30, 1965. Stewart L. Udall Papers, University of Arizona, Box 55.
18. PM, "The Last Great Strand," *Audubon*, March 1967.
19. PM, in Immy Humes (dir.), *Doc*, 2008.
20. PM, quoted in Bryant Urstadt, "Paris, Paranoia, The CIA, Humes," *3 Quarks Daily*, December 29, 2008.
21. HH to GP, March 4, 1966. DHA, Box 10.
22. GP to HH, March 10, 1966. DHA, Box 10.
23. GP to HH, March 12, 1966. DHA, Box 10. This letter is also published in Joel Whitney, *Finks: How the CIA Tricked the World's Best Writers* (New York: OR Books, 2016), 223.
24. PM, Washington notes, December 1965–February 1966. PMP 4, Box 10.
25. PM, Memoir notes. MMC.
26. Matthiessen recalled this during his victory speech for the same award in 2008. See "At Play in a Book's Adulation," *East Hampton Star*, November 27, 2008.
27. PM, "To the Miskito Bank," *The New Yorker*, October 28, 1967.
28. Ibid.
29. PM to JF, n.d. [April 1965]. RHR, Box 1087.
30. PM, "To the Miskito Bank," *The New Yorker*, October 28, 1967.
31. Ibid.
32. Ibid.
33. Ibid.
34. Ibid.
35. PM, "History of Writing Development." PMP 4, Box 7.
36. PM described the conversation with his editor in a number of places. See, for example, Jonathan Meiburg, "An Interview with Peter Matthiessen," *The Believer*, June 2014; Michael Shapiro, *A Sense of Place: Great Writers Talk About Their Craft, Lives, and Inspiration* (San Francisco: Travelers' Tales, 2004), 337–38; and Ben Yagoda, *About Town: The New Yorker and the World It Made* (New York: Scribner, 2000), 332.
37. PM, quoted in GP, *Truman Capote* (New York: Nan A. Talese, 1997), 255.
38. Sherman L. Morrow, "The In Crowd and the Out Crowd," *New York Times*, July 18, 1965.
39. PM to JF, n.d. [July 1965]. RHR, Box 1087.
40. TG, interviewed by Jeff Sewald, November 29, 2006. JSC.
41. Recalled by PM in GP, *Truman Capote*, 255.
42. *SNA*, 21.
43. Alex Matthiessen, interviewed by LR, February 17, 2023.

44. Rue Matthiessen, interviewed by LR, March 25, 2021.
45. DL, "Even if It's Too Late," n.d. RHR, Box 900.
46. PM, LSD journal, 1968–1969. PMP 4, Box 25.
47. PM, Aves and Jamaica notes, May 1967. PMP 4, Box 19.
48. JF to Joseph Gies, August 17, 1965. RHR, Box 1087.
49. "For President and for Peace We Support Eugene McCarthy," *East Hampton Star*, March 28, 1968.
50. *SSP*, 29.
51. PM, "For McCarthy," *New York Review of Books*, July 11, 1968.
52. *SSP*, 30.
53. PM, "For McCarthy," *New York Review of Books*, July 11, 1968.
54. *SSP*, 30.
55. Ibid., 214.
56. Cesar Chavez, quoted in Miriam Pawel, *The Crusades of Cesar Chavez* (New York: Bloomsbury, 2014), 118. For my understanding of Chavez I am indebted to Pawel's excellent biography, and to Miriam herself for sharing her thoughts.
57. Ibid., 169.
58. *SSP*, 28.
59. Ibid., 42.
60. Ibid., 67.
61. Ibid., 83.
62. Ibid., 6.
63. Ibid., 109.
64. Ibid., 24.
65. Ibid., 27.
66. Ibid., 171.
67. Matthiessen was vocal about his "love" for Cesar Chavez. For interviews, see PM, interviewed by Sedge Thomson, February 10, 1990, City Arts & Lectures; PM, "No Boundaries" (audio recording), Gang of Seven, 1992; PM, in conversation with Gary Snyder, February 23, 1994, City Arts & Lectures; "An Evening with Peter Matthiessen," February 17, 1997, City Arts & Lectures; PM, interviewed by Samuel Taylor, May 3, 1999, City Arts & Lectures; and "Writers of the Land, with Peter Matthiessen," Wallace Stegner Center for Land, Resources and the Environment, February 5, 2001.
68. PM, interviewed by Jeff Sewald, May 2006. JSC.
69. *SSP*, 172.
70. PM, interviewed by Jeff Sewald, May 2006. JSC.
71. William Shawn to Bernice Baumgarten, December 7, 1956. NYR, Box 540.
72. William Shawn, quoted in Henry Finder (ed.), *The 60s: The Story of a Decade: The New Yorker* (New York: Random House, 2016), 265.
73. *SSP*, 318.
74. PM, "No Boundaries" (audio recording), Gang of Seven, 1992.
75. Ann Israel to PM, December 9, 1968. Anna Andreini-Brophy Papers, Wayne State University, Box 1.
76. PM to Dennis Banks, n.d. [1982]. PMP 4, Box 39.
77. Miriam Pawel, *The Crusades of Cesar Chavez*, 175. LeRoy Chatfield, email to LR, July 5, 2020.
78. *SSP*, 271.
79. PM to Cesar Chavez, n.d. UFW, Box 9. The attached article was Israel Shenker, "Man's Extinction Held Real Peril," *New York Times*, April 7, 1969. Matthiessen quotes from Richard Falk's speech more extensively in *SSP*, 357.
80. *SSP*, 30.

13 · LIONS AND SHARKS

1. *BM*, 117–18.
2. *NHDR*, 3.

3. Ibid., 4. In the first edition of the book, Matthiessen erroneously gave the date for this encounter as "an August day of 1969 . . . after a seven-month absence in Africa." The year was corrected to 1968 for subsequent editions, but the incorrect reference to Africa remained. In truth, he met the Zen masters five months before his Africa travels began. Matthiessen was generally reliable when it came to biographical details, but he was sometimes fuzzy with dates.
4. DL to Craig Burrell (Sandoz Pharmaceuticals), n.d. [April 1966]. Collection of Rue Matthiessen.
5. Mildred Johnstone, quoted in Patricia Peterson, "She Creates Her Own Style," *New York Times*, March 2, 1975.
6. Dorinne Kondo, "The Way of Tea: A Symbolic Analysis," *Man*, New Series, Vol. 20, No. 2, June 1985.
7. Mildred Johnstone to William Barbee, March 9, 1970. Collection of Margaret Thomas Buchholz.
8. Rick Fields, *How the Swans Came to the Lake: A Narrative History of Buddhism in America* (Boston: Shambhala, 1992 [1981]), 173.
9. See Eido Shimano, "The Way to Dai Bosatsu," in Louis Nordstrom (ed.), *Namu Dai Bosa: A Transmission of Zen Buddhism to America* (New York: Theatre Arts Books, 1976); and Rick Fields, *How the Swans Came to the Lake*, 238–39.
10. Shinge Roshi (Roko Sherry Chayat), quoted in "New York Zendo Shobo-Ji: The First 50 Years," Zen Studies Society, 2019.
11. Hakuun Yasutani, quoted in Philip Kapleau, *The Three Pillars of Zen* (New York: Anchor, 1980 [1965]), 31.
12. Merete Galesi, interviewed by LR, November 16, 2018.
13. *NHDR*, 4.
14. *SL*, 216.
15. PM, LSD journal, 1968–1969. PMP 4, Box 25.
16. DL to PM, n.d. [January 1970]. PMP 4, Box 36.
17. DL to PM, n.d. "Every time I wrote to you . . ." PMP 4, Box 36.
18. DL to PM, n.d. [February 1970]. PMP 4, Box 36.
19. DL to PM, n.d. [January 1970]. PMP 4, Box 36.
20. DL to PM, n.d. [January 1969]. PMP 4, Box 36.
21. DL, "The Sudden and Unexpected Flight of Love," January 1969. PMP 4, Box 36.
22. DL to PM, n.d. [January 1969]. PMP 4, Box 36.
23. DL to PM, January 17, 1969. PMP 4, Box 36.
24. DL to PM, February 4, 1969. Collection of Rue Matthiessen.
25. Merete Galesi, interviewed by LR, November 16, 2018.
26. Nancy Wilson Ross, quoted in DL, *Annaghkeen* (New York: Random House, 1970), jacket blurb.
27. *SL*, 66.
28. *TWMB*, 39.
29. GS, *Gold Shadows, Flying Hooves* (New York: Alfred A. Knopf, 1973), 4.
30. *TWMB*, 206.
31. PM, Memoir notes. MMC.
32. *TWMB*, 87.
33. Ibid., 7.
34. *SR*, 3.
35. *TWMB*, 128.
36. Ibid., 145.
37. GS, interviewed by Jeff Sewald, n.d. [2006]. JSC.
38. GS, *Gold Shadows, Flying Hooves*, 129.
39. GS, *A Naturalist and Other Beasts* (San Francisco: Sierra Club Books, 2007), 19–20.
40. GS, *Gold Shadows, Flying Hooves*, xvi. See also GS, *The Serengeti Lion: A Study of Predator-Prey Relations* (Chicago: University of Chicago Press, 1972).
41. GS, interviewed by Jeff Sewald, n.d. [2006]. JSC.
42. GS, *Stones of Silence: Journeys in the Himalaya* (New York: Viking, 1979), 208.
43. *TWMB*, 138.

44. GS, interviewed by LR, September 12, 2018.
45. *TWMB*, 138.
46. GS, *A Naturalist and Other Beasts*, 23.
47. *TWMB*, 138. GS gave a characteristically terse description of the incident in his own field journal: "I went out at noon and gave the lioness an overdose of drugs. She lay there twitching and licking her lips. Lamprey flew me and the lioness to Kirawira where Alan Young immediately started to autopsy her." GS, Serengeti journal, May 18, 1968–August 12, 1969. Yale Peabody Museum of Natural History.
48. Lucas Matthiessen, *First Light: A Journey Out of Darkness* (New York: Arcade Publishing, 2023), 219–20.
49. PM, "Desert Island" (unpublished), n.d. NYR, Box 1628. All quotes in this section come from the article draft.
50. PM to Susan and John Abbot, n.d. [c. 2010]. MMC.
51. Susan Abbot, interviewed by LR, October 26, 2018.
52. Karen Yochim to PM, October 29, 1966. PMP 4, Box 38.
53. Jeff Wheelwright, email to LR, July 9, 2019.
54. Karen Yochim, interviewed by LR, September 12, 2019.
55. PM, LSD journal, 1968–1969. PMP 4, Box 25.
56. PM to Susan and John Abbot, n.d. [c. 2010]. MMC.
57. PM, LSD journal, 1968–1969. PMP 4, Box 25.
58. Ibid.
59. Ibid.
60. Ibid.
61. Philip Kapleau, *The Three Pillars of Zen*, 69–70.
62. C. G. Jung, "The Development of Personality" (1934), in *The Collected Works*, trans. R. F. C. Hull, vol. 17, *The Development of Personality* (London: Routledge, 2014 [1954]).
63. PM, LSD journal, 1968–1969. PMP 4, Box 25.
64. C. G. Jung, "The Development of Personality," in R. F. C. Hull (trans.), *The Development of Personality: The Collected Works*, Volume 17.
65. *SL*, 41.
66. *BM*, 30–31.
67. Ibid., 161.
68. PM, quoted in Rosemary Goring, "Man with No Fame," *Scotland on Sunday*, May 3, 1998. Matthiessen said something similar to Terry Gross on *Fresh Air*, April 6, 1989: "I'm not in any way a Hemingway-esque person who loves adventure in that sense. I don't like being scared. . . . But sometimes you have to undergo certain risks to accomplish what you're after."
69. *BM*, 54.
70. Ibid., 115.
71. Ibid., 120.
72. Ibid., 114.
73. Ibid.
74. PM, "Kipahulu: From Cinders to the Sea," *Audubon*, May 1970.
75. *SSP*, 357.
76. LeRoy Chatfield, email to LR, July 5, 2020.
77. Miriam Pawel, *The Crusades of Cesar Chavez* (New York: Bloomsbury, 2014), 181.
78. PM to Ann Israel, n.d. [June 1969]. AAB, Box 1.
79. *SSP*, 31.
80. Ibid., 28.
81. Ibid., 250.
82. Ibid., 31.
83. Ibid., 173.
84. Ibid., 6.
85. Ibid., 248.
86. Ibid., 335.
87. PM, quoted in Jonathan White, *Talking on the Water: Conversations About Nature and Creativity* (San Francisco: Sierra Club Books, 1994), 233.

88. PM, quoted in Kay Bonetti, "An Interview with Peter Matthiessen," *Missouri Review*, Vol. 12, No. 2, 1989.
89. Cesar Chavez to Joanne Rosenshein (assistant to Joe Fox), January 9, 1970. UFW, Box 9.
90. *BM*, 181.
91. Valerie Taylor, interviewed by LR, October 18, 2018.
92. *BM*, 196.
93. PM to JH, February 8, 1970. JHP, Box 32.
94. *BM*, 203.
95. DL to PM, n.d. [January 1970]. PMP 4, Box 36.
96. DL to PM, n.d. [February 1970]. PMP 4, Box 36.
97. MM, interviewed by LR, November 16, 2018.
98. PM, "Peter's Matthiessen's Africa: Book Two: Tanzania," *Audubon*, May 1981.
99. MM, interviewed by LR, November 16, 2018.
100. Quotations come from a series of poems Maria Koenig wrote in August 1970. MMC.
101. MK to PM, n.d. [June 1970]. MMC.
102. Ibid.
103. DL to PM, June 16, 1970. PMP 4, Box 36.
104. *TWMB*, 163.
105. Ibid., 164.
106. MM, interviewed by LR, May 26, 2019.
107. Rue Matthiessen, interviewed by LR, March 25, 2021.
108. MK, "Our Final Farewell," August 6, 1970. MMC.
109. PM to Ann Israel, August 4, 1970. AAB, Box 1.
110. DL to PM, August 20, 1970. PMP 4, Box 36.

14 · HO KO

1. PM to DL, August 1971. PMP 4, Box 36.
2. Rue Matthiessen, *Castles and Ruins: Unraveling Family Mysteries and Literary Legacy in the Irish Countryside* (Spokane, WA: Latah Books, 2024), 139.
3. Rue Matthiessen, interviewed by LR, September 25, 2018.
4. Ibid.
5. Ibid.
6. Jackson Braider, "Peter Matthiessen—The Last Frontiersman," *The Arts Fuse*, April 19, 2014.
7. DL to Nan Talese, December 1, 1970. RHR, Box 900.
8. DL, "Even if It's Too Late," n.d. RHR, Box 900.
9. *NHDR*, 4. There is more of Matthiessen's fuzziness with dates around this significant event. In *NHDR*, he recalls accompanying Deborah to the New York Zendo in "December of 1970," just before he headed to Australia "in quest of the first film of the great white shark." But he actually went to Australia in January 1970, a full year earlier than he remembered, and more contemporaneous sources suggest he accompanied Deborah to the sesshin in January 1971.
10. *SL*, 79.
11. David Steindl-Rast, quoted in "New York Zendo Shobo-Ji: The First 50 Years," Zen Studies Society, 2018.
12. PM, "Deb Notes," seemingly written for *Nine-Headed Dragon River*, n.d. PMP 1, Box 56.
13. PM, quoted in Lawrence Shainberg, "Emptying the Bell," *Tricycle*, Fall 1993. See also PM, "No Boundaries" (audio recording), Gang of Seven, 1992.
14. PM, quoted in Lawrence Shainberg, "Emptying the Bell," *Tricycle*, Fall 1993.
15. *SL*, 67.
16. Ibid.
17. PM to DL, February 14, 1971. PMP 4, Box 36. Matthiessen enclosed a draft of the newspaper ad.

18. PM to JH, January 21, 1971. JHP, Box 32.
19. PM to Cesar Chavez, January 2, 1971. UFW, Box 9.
20. PM, "The Valley" (screenplay). PMP 4, Box 12.
21. PM to Cesar Chavez, February 26, 1971. UFW, Box 9.
22. Cesar Chavez to PM, March 12, 1971. UFW, Box 9.
23. PM, interviewed by Jeff Sewald, May 2006. JSC. See also Lawrence Shainberg, "Emptying the Bell," *Tricycle*, Fall 1993.
24. *SL*, 42.
25. PM to DL, February 14, 1971. PMP 4, Box 36. See Shunryu Suzuki, *Zen Mind, Beginner's Mind* (Boulder, CO: Shambhala, 2011), 112–13.
26. Ibid.
27. DL to PM, August 27, 1971. PMP 4, Box 36.
28. DL to Nan Talese, n.d. [March 1971]. RHR, Box 900.
29. DL to PM, August 27, 1971. PMP 4, Box 36.
30. Jane Stanton Hitchcock, interviewed by LR, May 30, 2019.
31. Jane Stanton Hitchcock, interviewed by LR, August 27, 2019.
32. PM to Joan Stanton, May 10, 1972. PMP 4, Box 38.
33. DL to PM, August 27, 1971. PMP 4, Box 36.
34. Eido Shimano, "The Way to Dai Bosatsu," in Louis Nordstrom (ed.), *Namu Dai Bosa: A Transmission of Zen Buddhism to America* (New York: Theatre Arts Books, 1976), 207.
35. Ibid., 208.
36. "A Preacher's Hermitage," *New York Times*, October 29, 1879.
37. Eido Shimano, "The Way to Dai Bosatsu," in Louis Nordstrom (ed.), *Namu Dai Bosa*, 212.
38. Gary Snyder, quoted in *NHDR*, 146.
39. Soen Nakagawa, in Kazuaki Tanahashi and Roko Sherry Chayat (trans.), *Endless Vow: The Zen Path of Soen Nakagawa* (Boston and London: Shambhala, 1996), 91.
40. PM, quoted in Lawrence Shainberg, "Emptying the Bell," *Tricycle*, Fall 1993.
41. *NHDR*, 48.
42. Ibid., 6.
43. Ibid., 5.
44. See Rick Fields, *How the Swans Came to the Lake: A Narrative History of Buddhism in America* (Boston: Shambhala, 1992 [1981]), 260–65. I also consulted a "Zen Mountain Center Report," San Francisco Zen Center, Fall 1967, which details the challenges facing the early residents.
45. DL to PM, August 27, 1971. PMP 4, Box 36.
46. PM, "Notes re hallucinogens > Zen practice," n.d. [1973]. PMP 4, Box 36.
47. *NHDR*, 214.
48. PM, Tassajara notes, n.d. [August 1971]. PMP 4, Box 37.
49. PM to DL, August 1971. PMP 4, Box 36.
50. DL to PM, August 27, 1971. PMP 4, Box 36.
51. *SL*, 67.
52. DL to Nan Talese, n.d. [March 1971]. RHR, Box 900.
53. Merete Galesi, interviewed by LR, November 16, 2018.
54. Rue Matthiessen, *Castles and Ruins*, 176.
55. PM, Aves and Jamaica notes, May 1967. PMP 4, Box 19. See also *SL*, 67: "For several years the certainty had deepened that my life was rushing toward a drastic change, and the strength of the premonition made me wonder if I was going to die."
56. Lucas Matthiessen, interviewed by LR, September 28, 2019.
57. Rue Matthiessen, interviewed by LR, September 25, 2018.
58. *NHDR*, 20. An almost identical telling appears in *SL*, 93.
59. Ibid., 21.
60. PM, "Death Practice" teisho, July 23, 2003. MMC.
61. *NHDR*, 21.
62. *SL*, 94.
63. Rue Matthiessen, *Castles and Ruins*, 177.
64. Shinge Roshi (Roko Sherry Chayat), interviewed by LR, April 1, 2019.

65. Mildred Johnstone to William Barbee, December 8, 1971. Collection of Margaret Thomas Buchholz.
66. PM, "Deb Notes," seemingly written for *Nine-Headed Dragon River*, n.d. PMP 1, Box 56.
67. Ibid.
68. PM to JH, n.d. [December 1971]. JHP, Box 32.
69. Jane Stanton Hitchcock, interviewed by LR, August 27, 2019.
70. Merete Galesi, interviewed by LR, November 16, 2018.
71. *NHDR*, 23.
72. Rue Matthiessen, *Castles and Ruins*, 180.
73. Nan Talese, interviewed by LR, July 25, 2018.
74. Piedy Lumet (née Bailey), interviewed by LR, August 10, 2018.
75. *SL*, 95.
76. Ibid., 68.
77. PM, *Nine-Headed Dragon River* early draft, January 1985. PMP 1, Box 40.
78. *NHDR*, 24.
79. Lucas Matthiessen, *First Light: A Journey Out of Darkness* (New York: Arcade Publishing, 2023), 63–64.
80. *NHDR*, 24.
81. Rue Matthiessen, *Castles and Ruins*, 178–79.
82. *NHDR*, 25.
83. PM, "Deb Notes," seemingly written for *Nine-Headed Dragon River*, n.d. PMP 1, Box 56.
84. *NHDR*, 25–26.
85. PM, "Third Vow" teisho, February 18, 1989. MMC.
86. PM, "Notes re hallucinogens > Zen practice," n.d. [1973]. PMP 4, Box 36.

15 · TWENTY MONTHS

1. *SL*, 114.
2. PM, Himalayas journal 1, September 11–November 10, 1973. PMP 1, Box 47.
3. Rose Styron, interviewed by Jeff Sewald, October 4, 2006. JSC.
4. Merete Galesi, interviewed by LR, November 16, 2018.
5. PM, "Deb Notes," seemingly written for *Nine-Headed Dragon River*, n.d. PMP 1, Box 56.
6. Rose Styron, interviewed by Jeff Sewald, October 4, 2006. JSC.
7. Shinge Roshi (Roko Sherry Chayat), interviewed by LR, April 1, 2019.
8. PM to Jane Stanton, May 10, 1972. PMP 4, Box 38. The letter was actually two letters: one addressed to Jane, and one addressed to Jane's meddling mother, Joan Stanton. Both letters were sent to (and really meant for) Jane: "perhaps you have the courage to give it to Joan yourself," Matthiessen wrote, not really expecting her to pass it along.
9. PM to JH, n.d. [May 1972]. JHP, Box 32.
10. PM to JH, n.d. [March 1972]. JHP, Box 32.
11. GS, *Stones of Silence: Journeys in the Himalaya* (New York: Viking, 1980), 4.
12. Ibid., 204.
13. *SL*, 3.
14. Ibid., 3–4.
15. GS to PM, August 6, 1972. PMP 1, Box 49.
16. PM, Himalayas journal 1, September 11–November 10, 1973. PMP 1, Box 47. See also *SL*, 110.
17. GS to PM, August 6, 1972. PMP 1, Box 49.
18. PM, *Charlie Rose*, PBS, December 9, 2003. See https://charlierose.com/videos/8293.
19. PM, "Citizens Versus Consumers" (unpublished), 1972. PMP 4, Box 11.
20. John Giumarra Jr., quoted in Miriam Pawel, *The Crusades of Cesar Chavez* (New York: Bloomsbury, 2014), 208.
21. PM to Cesar Chavez, July 6, 1970. UFW, Box 9.

22. PM, "Citizens Versus Consumers" (unpublished), 1972. PMP 4, Box 11. All remaining quotes in this section come from this source.
23. *SSP*, 357.
24. "Dharma Seasons," *The Zen Studies Society Quarterly*, Fall 1972.
25. *NHDR*, 31.
26. PM, "Deb Notes," seemingly written for *Nine-Headed Dragon River*, n.d. PMP 1, Box 56.
27. Roko Sherry Chayat, "Postscript: Where Is the Master?," in Kazuaki Tanahashi and Roko Sherry Chayat (trans.), *Endless Vow: The Zen Path of Soen Nakagawa* (Boston and London: Shambhala, 1996), 152.
28. *NHDR*, 34.
29. PM, "The Long Journey: Zen and the Writing Life" (audio recording), San Francisco Zen Center, 1998.
30. Ibid.
31. *NHDR*, 34.
32. PM to Anna Puharich, n.d. [September 1972]. AAB, Box 1.
33. Eido Shimano, *The Newsletter of the Zen Studies Society*, Spring 1996.
34. *NHDR*, 36.
35. PM, "In the Dragon Islands," *Audubon*, September 1973. Matthiessen also discusses this trip in his introduction to Tui De Roy Moore, *Galapagos: Islands Lost in Time* (New York: Viking, 1980).
36. PM to Eliot Porter, n.d. [December 1971]. PMP 1, Box 50.
37. Eliot Porter to PM, December 16, 1971. PMP 1, Box 50.
38. PM to JH, April 1973. JHP, Box 32.
39. *TWMB*, 22.
40. Ibid., 234.
41. Ibid., 108–9.
42. Ibid., 51.
43. Ibid., 215.
44. Ibid., 220.
45. Ibid., 143.
46. John Owen, quoted in PM to Jack Macrae, September 27, 1972. PMP 1, Box 50.
47. Elspeth Huxley to Jack Macrae, August 7, 1972. PMP 1, Box 50.
48. Nancy Hurxthal to PM, November 1972. PMP 1, Box 50.
49. Colin M. Turnbull to Jack Macrae, April 16, 1972. PMP 1, Box 50.
50. PM to Colin M. Turnbull, n.d. [April 1972]. PMP 1, Box 50.
51. Colin M. Turnbull to Jack Macrae, May 11, 1972. PMP 1, Box 50.
52. PM, interviewed by GP, October 30, 1996. GPP, Box 67.
53. PM to JH, n.d. [January 1970]. JHP, Box 32.
54. PM to JH, n.d. [September 1972]. JHP, Box 32.
55. PM to Jack Macrae, September 27, 1973. PMP 1, Box 50.
56. Peter Beard, unpublished review of *TWMB*, quoted in Graham Boynton, *Wild: The Life of Peter Beard* (New York: St. Martin's Press, 2022), 4.
57. PM to JH, April 1973. JHP, Box 32.
58. GS to Rajendra Rana, February 2, 1973. PMP 1, Box 49.
59. GS to PM, February 5, 1973. PMP 1, Box 49.
60. PM to GS, n d. [February 1973]. PMP 1, Box 49.
61. PM, "Deb Notes," seemingly written for *Nine-Headed Dragon River*, n.d. PMP 1, Box 56.
62. Chuck Thegze, "Putting a Passion for Nature into Words," *Los Angeles Times*, March 18, 1973.
63. PM, "Deb Notes," seemingly written for *Nine-Headed Dragon River*, n.d. PMP 1, Box 56. "These 'visitations,'" Matthiessen wrote, "if that is what they were, occurred in the first year to Alex, Eido-roshi, and several zendo friends, and all left a happy impression behind, as if Deborah's spirit was still in the state of beatitude of her last days."
64. PM, "Notes re hallucinogens > Zen practice," n.d. [1973]. PMP 4, Box 36.

65. *NHDR*, 41.
66. Ibid., 42.
67. Kathryn Schulz, "What Do We Hope to Find When We Look for a Snow Leopard?," *The New Yorker*, July 12 & 19, 2021.
68. These terms appear in a draft of Pico Iyer's 2008 introduction to *The Snow Leopard*, published by Penguin. After reading the draft, Matthiessen took umbrage in a letter to the editor in charge of the reissue: "I accept the rebuke for the original decision to leave my son behind—as [Pico Iyer] may recall, I was rebuking myself throughout the trip—and I do not ask or want that to be removed. However, in choosing such harsh terms, Pico may be forgetting that I left Alex in his own home in the loving care of his favorite friends . . . ," etc. (PMP 4, Box 62). The published version of Iyer's introduction, which Matthiessen otherwise found "exceptionally thoughtful, eloquent, and generous," was milder in its criticism.
69. PM, interviewed by Jeff Sewald, October 9, 2006. JSC.
70. PM to WB, October 10, 2008. MMC.
71. PM, interviewed by Jeff Sewald, October 9, 2006. JSC.
72. PM to GS, n.d. [February 1973]. PMP 1, Box 49.
73. *NHDR*, 26. Matthiessen found this line "very moving." So moving, in fact, that he borrowed it for a (never produced) screenplay. See "The Disappearance." PMP 4, Box 17.
74. Rue Matthiessen, *Castles and Ruins: Unraveling Family Mysteries and Literary Legacy in the Irish Countryside* (Spokane, WA: Latah Books, 2024), 182.
75. Diana Rathbun, interviewed by LR, May 14, 2020.
76. Alex Matthiessen, interviewed by LR, March 18, 2022.
77. PM, Himalayas journal 2, November 11–November 28, 1973. PMP 1, Box 47.
78. Rue Matthiessen, *Castles and Ruins*, 185–86.
79. PM, Himalayas journal 1, September 11–November 10, 1973. PMP 1, Box 47.
80. *SL*, 114.
81. PM to MK, December 21, 1972. MMC.
82. PM to MK, August 24, 1973. MMC.
83. MM, interviewed by LR, March 27, 2021.
84. PM to MK, September 18, 1973. MMC.
85. MM, interviewed by LR, March 27, 2021.
86. PM, Himalayas journal 1, September 11–November 10, 1973. PMP 1, Box 47.
87. PM to MK, September 25, 1973. MMC.
88. See J. A. McNeely, E. W. Cronin, and H. B. Emery, "The Yeti—Not a Snowman," *Oryx*, Vol. 12, Issue 1, May 1973; Edward W. Cronin Jr., "The Yeti," *Atlantic Monthly*, August 1975; and Edward W. Cronin Jr., *The Arun: A Natural History of the World's Deepest Valley* (Boston: Houghton Mifflin, 1979).
89. Jeffrey McNeely, email to LR, October 20, 2019.
90. PM, Himalayas journal 1, September 11–November 10, 1973. PMP 1, Box 47. Schaller mentions McNeely's plaster cast in his foreword to Jeff Meldrum, *Sasquatch: Legend Meets Science* (New York: Forge, 2006).
91. GS, Pakistan and Nepal journal, August 26–October 29, 1973. Yale Peabody Museum of Natural History.
92. PM to MK, September 25, 1973. MMC.
93. Alex Matthiessen to PM, n.d. [September 1973]. PMP 1, Box 49.
94. PM, Umbria fragment, possibly deleted pages from an early draft of *The Snow Leopard*. PMP 4, Box 63.

16 · AT CRYSTAL MOUNTAIN

1. PM, Himalayas journal 1, September 11–November 10, 1973. PMP 1, Box 47.
2. My descriptions of Dolpo are based on my own trek to Shey Gompa in May 2022. For background on Dolpo, I relied on Kenneth M. Bauer's excellent *High Frontiers: Dolpo and the Changing World of Himalayan Pastoralists* (New York: Columbia University Press, 2004). Given the age of the book, not all the information reflects the lived cir-

cumstances of the Dolpo-pa today, but it is a good place to start when read in conjunction with Kenneth M. Bauer, "High Frontiers: Dolpo Revisited," *The Tibet Journal*, Vol. 39, No. 1, Spring/Summer 2014. For another perspective on traveling in Dolpo—and for insight into some of the challenges faced by local people—see Rebecca Solnit, "Medical Mountaineers," *The New Yorker*, December 21 and 28, 2015. For wildlife, see Sonam Choekyi Lama (dir.), *The Snow Leopard Calling* (2021), a short film about snow leopard researcher Tshiring Lhamu Lama, who grew up in Dolpo. The beautiful artwork of Tenzin Norbu, a painter from Upper Dolpo, also gives evocative glimpses into traditional and contemporary life in the high valleys.
3. *SL*, 17.
4. GS, Pakistan and Nepal journal, August 26–October 29, 1973. Yale Peabody Museum.
5. PM, Himalayas journal 1, September 11–November 10, 1973. PMP 1, Box 47.
6. *SL*, 101.
7. Merete Galesi to PM, September 15, 1973. PMP 4, Box 38.
8. PM, Himalayas journal 1, September 11–November 10, 1973. PMP 1, Box 47.
9. *SL*, 98.
10. PM, Himalayas journal 1, September 11–November 10, 1973. PMP 1, Box 47.
11. "Peter Matthiessen: The Art of Fiction No. 157," *The Paris Review*, No. 150, Spring 1999.
12. PM, "Simplicity" teisho, n.d. MMC.
13. PM, Himalayas journal 1, September 11–November 10, 1973. PMP 1, Box 47.
14. PM to MK, n.d. [October 1973]. MMC.
15. PM to Alex and Rue Matthiessen, October 23, 1973. PMP 4, Box 30.
16. PM, Himalayas journal 1, September 11–November 10, 1973. PMP 1, Box 47.
17. Ibid.
18. GS, Pakistan and Nepal journal, October 30–December 31, 1973. Yale Peabody Museum.
19. PM, Himalayas journal 1, September 11–November 10, 1973. PMP 1, Box 47.
20. Ibid.
21. GS, Pakistan and Nepal journal, October 30–December 31, 1973. Yale Peabody Museum.
22. *SL*, 201.
23. PM, "Expedition Haiku," 1973. PMP 4, Box 62.
24. PM, Himalayas journal 1, September 11–November 10, 1973. PMP 1, Box 47.
25. Ibid.
26. PM, *The Snow Leopard* draft typescript. PMP 1, Box 48.
27. PM, Himalayas journal 2, November 11–November 28, 1973. PMP 1, Box 47.
28. PM, interviewed by HN, n.d. [multiple interviews, 1990s]. HNC, Box 2.
29. *SL*, 152.
30. PM, Himalayas journal 2, November 11–November 28, 1973. PMP 1, Box 47.
31. GS, Pakistan and Nepal journal, October 30–December 31, 1973. Yale Peabody Museum.
32. PM, Himalayas journal 2, November 11–November 28, 1973. PMP 1, Box 47.
33. GS, Pakistan and Nepal journal, October 30–December 31, 1973. Yale Peabody Museum.
34. PM, "Simplicity" teisho, n.d. MMC.
35. PM, Himalayas journal 2, November 11–November 28, 1973. PMP 1, Box 47.
36. Ibid.

17 · FOOL DAY

1. *FT*, 127.
2. JH to PM, n.d. [July 1974]. JHP, Box 32.
3. PM to JH, n.d. [January 1970]. JHP, Box 32.
4. JH to PM, January 29, 1970. JHP, Box 32.
5. PM to JH, February 8, 1970. JHP, Box 32.

6. JH to PM, n.d. [July 1974]. JHP, Box 32.
7. PM to JH, n.d. [April 1970]. JHP, Box 32. The profile was never published. A draft can be found in JHP, Box 4.
8. JH to PM, n.d. [July 1974]. JHP, Box 32.
9. Ibid.
10. PM, "Deb Notes," seemingly written for *Nine-Headed Dragon River*, n.d. PMP 1, Box 56.
11. *NHDR*, 47.
12. PM, "Deb Notes," seemingly written for *Nine-Headed Dragon River*, n.d. PMP 1, Box 56.
13. *NHDR*, 47.
14. PM to MK, n.d. [March 1974]. MMC.
15. PM to MK, September 25, 1973. MMC.
16. MK to PM, October 15, 1973. MMC.
17. PM, Himalayas journal 2, November 11–November 28, 1973. PMP 1, Box 47.
18. PM to MK, December 21, 1973. MMC.
19. MM, interviewed by LR, March 27, 2021.
20. MK to PM, November 15, 1973. MMC.
21. PM to MK, January 18, 1974. MMC.
22. Eido Shimano, quoted in Roko Sherry Chayat, "From Zen Community to Zen Monastery: The Transition Years," *The Newsletter of the Zen Studies Society*, Spring 1996.
23. See Luisa Kreisberg, "Buddhist Center Rises in the Catskills," *New York Times*, August 24, 1975. See also Eido Shimano, "The Way to Dai Bosatsu," in Louis Nordstrom (ed.), *Namu Dai Bosa: A Transmission of Zen Buddhism to America* (New York: Theatre Arts Books, 1976). For details of Dai Bosatsu, I also relied on notes taken during stays there in 2018 and 2023.
24. *NHDR*, 49.
25. Soen Nakagawa, in Kazuaki Tanahashi and Roko Sherry Chayat (trans.), *Endless Vow: The Zen Path of Soen Nakagawa* (Boston and London: Shambhala, 1996), 139.
26. *NHDR*, 53.
27. PM, "Deb Notes," seemingly written for *Nine-Headed Dragon River*, n.d. PMP 1, Box 56. For more about the "beaver episode," see *NHDR*, 53–54; and Pat van Boeckel (dir.), *Voorbij de tijd: een portret van schrijver Peter Matthiessen* (2015).
28. *NHDR*, 57.
29. PM, "Deb Notes," seemingly written for *Nine-Headed Dragon River*, n.d. PMP 1, Box 56.
30. Rockefeller Archive Center, Rockefeller Family General Files, RG 33, Box 155.
31. Shinge Roshi (Roko Sherry Chayat), interviewed by LR, April 1, 2019.
32. PM to Laurance Rockefeller, July 29, 1975. Rockefeller Archive Center, Rockefeller Family General Files, RG 33, Box 155.
33. Roko Sherry Chayat, Peter Matthiessen, and Myoku Margot Wilkie, "International Dai Bosatsu Zendo: A Mountain Retreat," 1975. Private Collection of the Zen Studies Society.
34. PM to JH, n.d. [May 1974]. JHP, Box 32.
35. Lucas Matthiessen, *First Light: A Journey Out of Darkness* (New York: Arcade Publishing, 2023), 16.
36. Chuck Thegze, "Putting a Passion for Nature into Words," *Los Angeles Times*, March 18, 1973.
37. PM, quoted in Wendy Smith, "PW Interviews Peter Matthiessen," *Publishers Weekly*, May 9, 1986.
38. PM to JH, n.d. [May 1974]. JHP, Box 32.
39. *FT*, 17.
40. Ibid., 304.
41. Ibid., 251.
42. Ibid., 98.
43. Ibid., 126.
44. Ibid., 223.

45. Ibid., 226.
46. PM to "Nicoletta," n.d. [c. 1998]. MMC.
47. *FT*, 202.
48. Ibid., 369.
49. Ibid., 200.
50. Ibid., 85.
51. "Peter Matthiessen: The Art of Fiction No. 157," *The Paris Review*, No. 150, Spring 1999.
52. "The Craft of Fiction in *Far Tortuga*," *The Paris Review*, No. 60, Winter 1974.
53. "Peter Matthiessen: The Art of Fiction No. 157," *The Paris Review*, No. 150, Spring 1999.
54. PM, "The Long Journey: Zen and the Writing Life" (audio recording), San Francisco Zen Center, 1998. See also PM, interviewed by Sedge Thomson, February 10, 1990, City Arts & Lectures; PM, "National Writers Series, City Opera House," October 29, 2010; PM, "The Spirit of Place: Wildlife and Land in Literature," 2002, KWLS; and Jonathan Meiburg, "An Interview with Peter Matthiessen," *The Believer*, June 2014.
55. "Peter Matthiessen: The Art of Fiction No. 157," *The Paris Review*, No. 150, Spring 1999.
56. PM, interviewed by HN, n.d. [multiple interviews, 1990s]. HNC, Box 2. See also Alec Michod, "Living on the Edge of Life: A Final Interview with Peter Matthiessen," *Los Angeles Review of Books*, April 6, 2014.
57. PM, "The Long Journey: Zen and the Writing Life" (audio recording), San Francisco Zen Center, 1998.
58. PM, quoted in Pico Iyer, "Laureate of the Wild," *Time*, January 11, 1993.
59. *FT*, 336.
60. "The Craft of Fiction in *Far Tortuga*," *The Paris Review*, No. 60, Winter 1974.
61. Ibid.
62. PM to John Daido Loori, n.d. [c. 2003]. MMC.
63. PM, LSD journal, 1968–1969. PMP 4, Box 25.
64. PM, "Fool Day" draft typescript. PMP 1, Box 7.
65. JH, interviewed by Jeff Sewald, n.d. [2006]. JSC.
66. Terry McDonell, interviewed by Jeff Sewald, n.d. [2006]. JSC.
67. Thomas R. Edwards, "Adventures of the Deep," *New York Review of Books*, August 7, 1975.
68. "Far Tortuga," *Kirkus*, March 1, 1975.
69. Edward Weeks, "The Peripatetic Reviewer," *Atlantic Monthly*, August 1975.
70. Anatole Broyard, "A Slow Boat to Symbolism," *New York Times*, May 6, 1975.
71. Larry McMurtry, "A Heavy Tale of Men and the Sea," *Washington Post*, June 2, 1975.
72. PM to Edward Hoagland, n.d. [1975]. Edward Hoagland Papers, Texas Tech University, Box 1.
73. PM, interviewed by Jeff Sewald, March 2005. JSC.
74. Arthur Miller to PM, July 5, 1975. PMP 1, Box 10.
75. WS to PM, January 24, 1975. PMP 1, Box 10.
76. Reproduced on the back cover of *FT*. See also www.pynchon.pomona.edu/uncollected/blurbs.html.
77. PM to JF, June 24, 1965. RHR, Box 1087. It is not clear when Matthiessen parted ways with Diarmuid Russell, but the correspondence dries up soon after *At Play in the Fields of the Lord*. Matthiessen may have spent a few years representing himself before signing with Candida Donadio.
78. Neil Olson, interviewed by LR, January 28, 2021.
79. PM, quoted in Daniel Simon, "Literature's Candida," *The Nation*, May 28, 2001.
80. PM, interviewed by Jeff Sewald, March 2005. JSC. Fox later claimed that Matthiessen had "proceeded to get himself worked up to truly believe I had hated *Far Tortuga*." See Michael Shnayerson, "Higher Matthiessen," *Vanity Fair*, December 1991.
81. "Fool Day"/*Far Tortuga* contract, March 14, 1974. PRH, Box 21026458, File 31024.
82. PM, interviewed by Jeff Sewald, March 2005. JSC.

83. JF to Selma Shapiro, April 1, 1975. RHR, Box 1212.
84. "Contract Proposal: Fool Day," March 1, 1974. RHR, Box 1212.
85. PM, interviewed by HN, n.d. [multiple interviews, 1990s]. HNC, Box 2.
86. PM, interviewed by Jeff Sewald, March 2005. JSC.
87. JF, quoted in Michael Shnayerson, "Higher Matthiessen," *Vanity Fair*, December 1991.
88. MM, interviewed by LR, November 16, 2018.
89. PM, Notes for Joe Fox's memorial, n.d. [1995]. PMP 4, Box 11.

18 · ANTHROPOLOGY OF THE UNKNOWN

1. PM, Untitled bigfoot manuscript, n.d. [c. late 1970s]. PMP 4, Box 29.
2. Susanna Styron, interviewed by LR, December 14, 2019.
3. Myrna Davis, interviewed by LR, March 28, 2021.
4. MK, "When I Was a Beginning Bird Person," February 1975. MMC.
5. MK, Notes on Captiva, April 10, 1976. MMC.
6. MM, Speech given at the Sun Valley Writers' Conference, 2000. PMP 4, Box 12.
7. Maria V. A. Eckhart, "The Buck," in *. . . until I write it* (Sagaponack: Sand Dune Press, 2009), 14.
8. MM, interviewed by LR, November 16, 2018.
9. MK, Notes on Fishers Island, October 1976. MMC.
10. MK to PM, "Meditations," n.d. MMC.
11. MK to PM, December 25, 1978. MMC.
12. *SR*, 7.
13. MM, interviewed by LR, November 16, 2018.
14. MM to WSM, December 18, 2001. WSMP, Sixth Accession, Correspondence, Box 1.
15. MM, interviewed by LR, November 16, 2018.
16. Antonia Koenig, interviewed by LR, October 2, 2020.
17. See Sarah Koenig, "Mad Man," *This American Life*, June 19, 2009.
18. MM, interviewed by LR, November 16, 2018.
19. Sarah Koenig, interviewed by LR, August 9, 2022.
20. MK, "When I Was a Beginning Bird Person," February 1975. MMC.
21. Antonia Koenig, interviewed by LR, October 2, 2020.
22. MM, interviewed by LR, May 26, 2019.
23. MK, Notes on Captiva, April 1975. MMC.
24. MK, "The Other Side of the Poetic Coin," February 1975. MMC.
25. MM, interviewed by LR, March 27, 2021.
26. MK, Notes on Fishers Island, October 1976. MMC.
27. PM to Anna Puharich, n.d. [1975]. AAB, Box 1.
28. PM, Untitled bigfoot manuscript, n.d. [c. late 1970s]. PMP 4, Box 29.
29. J. A. McNeely, E. W. Cronin, and H. B. Emery, "The Yeti—Not a Snowman," *Oryx*, Vol. 12, Issue 1, May 1973.
30. PM, Himalayas journal 1, September 11–November 10, 1973. PMP 1, Box 47. Matthiessen elaborated on the sighting in *The Snow Leopard:* "the deep forest across the torrent has been parted by avalanche, and on this brushy slope, a dark shape jumps behind a boulder. . . . It is much too big for a red panda, too covert for a musk deer, too dark for wolf or leopard, and much quicker than a bear. With binoculars, I stare for a long time at the mute boulder, feeling the presence of the unknown life behind it, but all is still, there is only the sun and morning mountainside, the pouring water." See *SL*, 121.
31. GS, interviewed by LR, September 12, 2018.
32. GS, Pakistan and Nepal journal, October 30–December 31, 1973. Yale Peabody Museum. See also GS to PM, n.d. [February 1974]. PMP 1, Box 49.
33. PM, Untitled bigfoot manuscript, n.d. [c. late 1970s]. PMP 4, Box 29.
34. Hans Teensma, interviewed by LR, March 21, 2019.
35. All of Douglas Blue's many letters are held in Matthiessen's archive. For the bulk of them, see PMP 4, Box 31. Doug Blue died on September 13, 2021, at the age of ninety-

one. I spoke to him briefly on the phone in 2019; he acknowledged his association with Peter Matthiessen but was reluctant to discuss bigfoot, which he believed still needed protection.
36. PM to Douglas Blue, n.d. [June 1975]. PMP 4, Box 31.
37. PM to Douglas Blue, July 2, 1975. PMP 4, Box 31.
38. Gaby Rodgers and Patsy Southgate, "The Biggest Bang in the Hamptons," *East Hampton Star*, July 17, 1975.
39. PM, Untitled bigfoot manuscript, n.d. [c. late 1970s]. PMP 4, Box 29.
40. Ibid.
41. PM, Bigfoot notebook 1, 1975–76. PMP 4, Box 12.
42. Hans Teensma, interviewed by LR, March 21, 2019.
43. PM, Untitled bigfoot manuscript, n.d. [c. late 1970s]. PMP 4, Box 29.
44. Hans Teensma, interviewed by LR, March 21, 2019.
45. PM, Untitled bigfoot manuscript, n.d. [c. late 1970s]. PMP 4, Box 29.
46. Ibid.
47. Ibid.
48. Hans Teensma, interviewed by LR, March 21, 2019.
49. PM, Untitled bigfoot manuscript, n.d. [c. late 1970s]. PMP 4, Box 29. Matthiessen's brief notes on the incident are corroborated by a letter from the man who was run out of camp: Art Hammond to PM, September 30, 1975. PMP 4, Box 27.
50. PM, Untitled bigfoot manuscript, n.d. [c. late 1970s]. PMP 4, Box 29.
51. Ibid.
52. PM to Douglas Blue, September 28, 1975. PMP 4, Box 31.
53. PM, Untitled bigfoot manuscript, n.d. [c. late 1970s]. PMP 4, Box 29.
54. Boyce Rensberger, "Is It Bigfoot, Or Can It Be Just a Hoax?," *The New York Times*, June 30, 1976.
55. John Napier, *Bigfoot: The Yeti and Sasquatch in Myth and Reality* (New York: E. P. Dutton, 1973), 14.
56. PM, Bigfoot notebook 1, 1975–76. PMP 4, Box 12.
57. HN, email to LR, August 13, 2022.
58. GS, *A Naturalist and Other Beasts* (San Francisco: Sierra Club Books, 2007), 209.
59. PM, Bigfoot notebook 1, 1975–76. PMP 4, Box 12.
60. "Oliver—Son of Bigfoot?," United Press International, January 2, 1976.
61. Michael Miller, quoted in James Shreeve, "Oliver's Travels," *The Atlantic*, October 2003.
62. PM, Untitled bigfoot manuscript, n.d. [c. late 1970s]. PMP 4, Box 29.
63. Ibid.
64. PM, Bigfoot notebook 1, 1975–76. PMP 4, Box 12.
65. PM, Untitled bigfoot manuscript, n.d. [c. late 1970s]. PMP 4, Box 29.
66. GS, "Evaluation of Oliver," February 8, 1976. PMP 4, Box 27.
67. A copy of Michael Miller's announcement letter—effectively a press release—is in PMP 4, Box 27.
68. PM, Untitled bigfoot manuscript, n.d. [c. late 1970s]. PMP 4, Box 29.
69. Phil Bishop, "Woman Encounters Family of Sasquatch," *Capital Journal*, November 14, 1974.
70. "Oregon Family Protecting 'Bigfoot' by Rubbing Out Monster's Footprints," United Press International, November 20, 1975.
71. PM, Untitled bigfoot manuscript, n.d. [c. late 1970s]. PMP 4, Box 29.
72. PM to Jean Fitzgerald, October 25, 1975. PMP 4, Box 31.
73. Most of these letters can be found in PMP 4, Box 31.
74. PM, Untitled bigfoot manuscript, n.d. [c. late 1970s]. PMP 4, Box 29.
75. Phil Bishop, "Woman Encounters Family of Sasquatch," *Capital Journal*, November 14, 1974.
76. PM, Untitled bigfoot manuscript, n.d. [c. late 1970s]. PMP 4, Box 29.
77. Hans Teensma was puzzled by Steve's attitude when he met the Fitzgeralds in June 1976: "One thing that Peter and I both couldn't explain is how mad [Jean's] husband was that bigfoot was around. He could easily dismiss it. Instead he showed fear or

annoyance, really, that this creature was around, really messing up their lives a lot. 'I wish it would go away!'" Hans Teensma, interviewed by LR, March 21, 2019.
78. PM to Jean Fitzgerald, n.d. [December 1975]. PMP 4, Box 31.
79. PM, Untitled bigfoot manuscript, n.d. [c. late 1970s]. PMP 4, Box 29.
80. PM, Bigfoot notebook 1, 1975–76. PMP 4, Box 12.
81. PM, Untitled bigfoot manuscript, n.d. [c. late 1970s]. PMP 4, Box 29.
82. Hans Teensma, interviewed by LR, March 21, 2019.
83. PM, Untitled bigfoot manuscript, n.d. [c. late 1970s]. PMP 4, Box 29.
84. Ibid.
85. Jeff Wheelwright, "The Wild Man Within: Peter Matthiessen's Bigfoot," *Yale Review*, July 2019. For the archaeologist in British Columbia, Grant Keddie, see an undated, untitled fragment by Matthiessen about their discussion in HNC, Box 30. Alan Gillespie, Hans Teensma, and Maria Matthiessen independently recalled him discussing the incident.
86. "The Figure on the Road" was seemingly drafted sometime in the 2000s. A copy is in PMP 4, Box 30.
87. PM, "Peter Matthiessen's Africa: Book Two: Tanzania," *Audubon*, May 1981.
88. MK to PM, September 13, 1976. MMC.
89. MK, Notes on Captiva, April 10, 1976. MMC.
90. MK, "LIST OF ASSETS ASCRIBED TO ME OVER THE LAST TWO OR THREE DAYS," December 16, 1975. MMC.
91. MK to PM, June 25, 1976. MMC.
92. MK to PM, June 7, 1976. MMC.
93. PM to MK, n.d. [August 1976]. MMC.
94. MK to PM, August 15, 1976. MMC.
95. PM, Untitled bigfoot manuscript, n.d. [c. late 1970s]. PMP 4, Box 29.
96. Ibid.
97. Alan Gillespie, email to author, February 19, 2020.
98. PM, Untitled bigfoot manuscript, n.d. [c. late 1970s]. PMP 4, Box 29. Alan Gillespie was so struck by the sighting that he would remember it for decades, and then describe it in a memorial for Tom Willhoite, who died on April 19, 2019.
99. Ibid.
100. Ibid.
101. For a comprehensive breakdown of Patterson and Gimlin's story—and for a good exploration of the scientific reactions to their footage—see Jeff Meldrum, *Sasquatch: Legend Meets Science* (New York: Forge, 2006), with a foreword by George Schaller.
102. PM to Douglas Blue, n.d. [May 1978]. PMP 4, Box 31.
103. At a conference on "humanoid monsters," "Anthropology of the Unknown: Sasquatch and Similar Phenomena," held at the University of British Columbia in 1978, Matthiessen would watch the footage again "slow and fast and [in] freeze-frame." He would also interview Robert Gimlin—"and I'll be damned if that man is a liar." For Matthiessen's extensive notes on the UBC conference and the Patterson-Gimlin film, see Bigfoot notebook 3, 1976–78, in PMP 4, Box 15. For his polished notes, see portions of the Untitled bigfoot manuscript [c. late 1970s], in PMP 4, Box 28.
104. PM, Untitled bigfoot manuscript, n.d. [c. late 1970s]. PMP 4, Box 29.
105. PM, Bigfoot notebook 1, 1975–76. PMP 4, Box 12.
106. Hans Teensma, interviewed by LR, March 21, 2019.
107. PM, Untitled bigfoot manuscript, n.d. [c. late 1970s]. PMP 4, Box 29.

19 · NEW TEACHERS

1. PM to Craig Carpenter, April 22, 1977. PMP 4, Box 27.
2. Shinge Roshi (Roko Sherry Chayat), interviewed by LR, April 1, 2019.
3. In addition to interviews with several people involved, my understanding of the Eido Shimano scandal is based on primary sources in the Shimano Archive (www.shimanoarchive.com), which contains, among other things, a large number of scanned and

authenticated documents from the Robert Aitken Archives at the University of Hawaii. The scandal was also the subject of a long exposé by Mark Oppenheimer: "The Zen Predator of the Upper East Side," *The Atlantic*, December 18, 2014.
4. NHDR, 61.
5. Ibid., 63–64.
6. Margot Wilkie, interviewed by David Chadwick, June 1999. See www.cuke.com/Cucumber%20Project/interviews/wilkie.html.
7. PM, "Deb Notes," seemingly written for *Nine-Headed Dragon River*, n.d. PMP 1, Box 56.
8. PM, interviewed by Mark Adams, February 14, 2014. Collection of Mark Adams.
9. Shinge Roshi (Roko Sherry Chayat), quoted in "New York Zendo Shobo-Ji: The First 50 Years," Zen Studies Society, 2018.
10. Shinge Roshi (Roko Sherry Chayat), interviewed by LR, April 1, 2019.
11. Ibid.
12. PM, "Deb Notes," seemingly written for *Nine-Headed Dragon River*, n.d. PMP 1, Box 56.
13. Adam Fisher, interviewed by LR, May 30, 2020.
14. Eido Shimano claimed disingenuously that he had no idea why Soen Roshi boycotted the opening of Dai Bosatsu: "I can only guess at his motivation for not coming. It could have been his illness, or his shyness about being the principal honored guest; it could have been to make a dramatic point through his absence. I was so eager to give Dai Bosatsu Zendo to him, but by not attending he gave it back to me." See Kazuaki Tanahashi and Roko Sherry Chayat (trans.), *Endless Vow: The Zen Path of Soen Nakagawa* (Boston and London: Shambhala, 1996), 45.
15. NHDR, 64–67. For details of the opening ceremony of Dai Bosatsu, see also Rick Fields, *How the Swans Came to the Lake: A Narrative History of Buddhism in America* (Boston: Shambhala, 1992 [1981]), 1–2.
16. Ibid., 64.
17. PM to JH, n.d. [November 1976]. JHP, Box 32.
18. Mark Oppenheimer, "Sex Scandal Has U.S. Buddhists Looking Within," *New York Times*, August 20, 2010.
19. PM, interviewed by HN, n.d. [multiple interviews, 1990s]. HNC, Box 2.
20. PM, Untitled bigfoot manuscript, n.d. [c. late 1970s]. PMP 4, Box 29. All remaining quotes in this section come from this manuscript.
21. Ibid. For Douglas Blue's six-page account of the dinner with Felix and Stella Montoya, see PMP 4, Box 15.
22. PM to Felix and Stella Montoya, n.d. PMP 4, Box 27.
23. PM, Untitled bigfoot manuscript, n.d. [c. late 1970s]. PMP 4, Box 29.
24. Ibid.
25. *IC*, i.
26. Craig Carpenter, quoted in ibid., 293.
27. *IC*, 81.
28. Ibid.
29. Ibid., 84. An audio recording of Craig Carpenter talking in his "messianic voice" about the Hopi prophecies and Purification Day can be found on Nat Freedland's *The Occult Explosion* (1973); see www.youtube.com/watch?v=BS3jQgyIDqA.
30. PM, Untitled bigfoot manuscript, n.d. [c. late 1970s]. PMP 4, Box 29.
31. See the long interview with Carpenter in Sandy Johnson (ed.), *The Book of Elders: The Life Stories of Great American Indians* (San Francisco: HarperCollins, 1994), 99–107.
32. Brian D. Haley, "Craig Carpenter and the Neo-Indians of LONAI," *The American Indian Quarterly*, Vol. 42, No. 2, Spring 2018. For more on Carpenter and the Hopi Traditionalists, see Brian D. Haley, *Hopi and the Counterculture* (Tucson: University of Arizona Press, 2024); and Brian D. Haley, "Ammon Hennacy and the Hopi Traditionalist Movement: Roots of the Counterculture's Favorite Indians," *Journal of the Southwest*, Vol. 58, No. 1, Spring 2016.
33. *IC*, 293.
34. PM, Untitled bigfoot manuscript, n.d. [c. late 1970s]. PMP 4, Box 29.

35. Ibid.
36. Ibid.
37. *ITSCH*, xxiii.
38. PM, Untitled bigfoot manuscript, n.d. [c. late 1970s]. PMP 4, Box 29.
39. PM to Douglas Blue, n.d. [September 1976]. PMP 4, Box 27.
40. PM to Daniel Halpern, n.d. [1977]. Ecco Press Records, Manuscripts and Archives Division, New York Public Library, Box 36.
41. Amor Towles, interviewed by LR, December 4, 2019. Matthiessen meant it when he advised Towles to take writing seriously. A few years later, he forwarded Towles's short fiction to *The Paris Review*, where it debuted in 1989. When Towles then found employment as an investment banker, Matthiessen made his disappointment known. Recalling his time teaching at Yale in 1950, he told Towles that everybody talented he'd taught who went off to Wall Street never came back: "That's it!" But Towles did come back, of course, finding enormous success as a novelist. Towles's classmate, Claire Messud, has also published a reflection of Matthiessen as a writing instructor: see John Irving and Claire Messud, "Our Hero: Peter Matthiessen," *Guardian*, April 11, 2014.
42. PM, Untitled bigfoot manuscript, n.d. [c. late 1970s]. PMP 4, Box 29.
43. Charles Wright, interviewed by LR, February 17, 2020.
44. Oakley Hall to PM, March 31, 1977. PMP 3, Box 24.
45. Charles Wright, interviewed by LR, February 17, 2020.
46. PM, Untitled bigfoot manuscript, n.d. [c. late 1970s]. PMP 4, Box 29.
47. Ibid.
48. Ibid.
49. Bernie Glassman, interviewed by LR, September 21, 2018.
50. Noa Jones, "White Plums and Lizard Tails: The Story of Maezumi Roshi and His American Lineage," *Lion's Roar*, March 1, 2004. See also Dale S. Wright, "Humanizing the Image of a Zen Master: Taizan Maezumi Roshi," in Steven Heine and Dale S. Wright (eds.), *Zen Masters* (New York: Oxford University Press, 2010); and Andrew Cooper, "The Good Fit," *Tricycle*, Winter 2015.
51. Helen Harkaspi, interviewed by LR, July 8, 2019.
52. *NHDR*, 119.
53. PM, "The Coming of Age of American Zen," keynote speech, the American Buddhist Conference, January 16, 1997. MMC.
54. *NHDR*, 119.
55. Bernie Glassman, interviewed by LR, September 21, 2018.
56. PM (as Muryo Sensei), "Remembering Maezumi Roshi," *Tricycle*, Fall 1995.
57. Charles Tenshin Fletcher, interviewed by LR, April 3, 2020.
58. *NHDR*, 242.
59. Charles Tenshin Fletcher, interviewed by LR, April 3, 2020.
60. PM, "Deb Notes," seemingly written for *Nine-Headed Dragon River*, n.d. PMP 1, Box 56.
61. PM, "Sound of One Hand" answers, 1977–1979. MMC.
62. *NHDR*, 57.
63. PM, "Sound of One Hand" answers, 1977–1979. MMC. Matthiessen's answers are not unusual; see Yoel Hoffman (trans.), *The Sound of the One Hand: 281 Zen Koans with Answers* (New York: Basic Books, 1975), 54–58.
64. *NHDR*, 132.
65. PM, Untitled bigfoot manuscript, n.d. [c. late 1970s]. PMP 4, Box 29.
66. Ibid. Peter Lake, the friend in Bel Air, recalled that Matthiessen was distraught. Peter Lake, interviewed by LR, March 28, 2024.
67. Erard Matthiessen to PM, December 8, 1975. PMP 4, Box 36. The article is "Happy Days," *Audubon*, November 1975.
68. PM, "Homegoing: Talks on Zen Buddhism, 1988–2003," unpublished manuscript. PMP 4, Box 25.
69. PM, Untitled bigfoot manuscript, n.d. [c. late 1970s]. PMP 4, Box 29.
70. PM to MK, March 25, 1977. MMC.
71. PM, Bigfoot Notebook 3, 1976–78. PMP 4, Box 12.

72. PM, Untitled bigfoot manuscript, n.d. [c. late 1970s]. PMP 4, Box 29. All quotes in this section come from the manuscript unless otherwise attributed. See also chapter three, "Mesas," of *IC*, 67–102.
73. Craig Carpenter to PM, April 6, 1977. PMP 4, Box 27. The bulk of Carpenter's correspondence is held in this box.
74. PM, "Zen and Indians," n.d. MMC. See also PM, "Poetry and Mysticism in Native American Teaching," Regents Lecture at UC Santa Barbara, November 15, 1978.
75. *SL*, 50.
76. Ibid., 51.
77. PM to Craig Carpenter, April 22, 1977. PMP 4, Box 27.
78. PM to Craig Carpenter, n.d. [April 1977]. PMP 4, Box 27.
79. MK to PM, May 22, 1977. MMC.
80. PM, "Peter Matthiessen's Africa: Book One: Botswana," *Audubon*, January 1981.
81. PM, "Peter Matthiessen's Africa: Book Two: Tanzania," *Audubon*, May 1981.
82. PM, Untitled bigfoot manuscript, n.d. [c. late 1970s]. PMP 4, Box 29.
83. "Kidnapped Children Found Safe," *Eureka Times Standard*, July 14, 1977. See also "Two Children Kidnaped [*sic*]," *Los Angeles Times*, July 15, 1977; and Associated Press, "Abducted Youngsters Safe," *Daily Oklahoman*, July 15, 1977.
84. PM, Untitled bigfoot manuscript, n.d. [c. late 1970s]. PMP 4, Box 29.
85. The original letter has not been preserved in Matthiessen's archive. However, he reproduces it in full in the bigfoot manuscript.
86. PM, Untitled bigfoot manuscript, n.d. [c. late 1970s]. PMP 4, Box 29.
87. PM, Bigfoot notebook 3, 1976–78. PMP 4, Box 12.
88. *IC*, 241.

20 · *THE SNOW LEOPARD*

1. PM, quoted in Michael Shapiro, *A Sense of Place: Great Writers Talk About Their Craft, Lives, and Inspiration* (San Francisco: Travelers' Tales, 2004), 339–40. Matthiessen often repeated this line when discussing *The Snow Leopard*. See also "Peter Matthiessen: The Art of Fiction No. 157," *The Paris Review*, No. 150, Spring 1999; PM's interview on *Charlie Rose*, PBS, December 9, 1999 (https://charlierose.com/videos/8293); PM, interviewed for the National Writers Series, Traverse City, October 29, 2010; and Jonathan Meiburg, "An Interview with Peter Matthiessen," *The Believer*, June 2014.
2. ES, "Editing Saul Bellow," *Slate*, April 8, 2005.
3. ES, interviewed by LR, July 24, 2018.
4. ES to PM, May 21, 1975. PMP 1, Box 10.
5. ES, interviewed by LR, July 24, 2018.
6. ES to Alan Kellock, January 4, 1985. ESP, Box 15.
7. ES, interviewed by LR, July 24, 2018.
8. ES to PM, November 17, 1976. PMP 3, Box 25.
9. PM to WSM, n.d. [March 1978]. WSMP, Sixth Accession, Correspondence, Box 14.
10. ES to "WWW," February 18, 1977. PRH, Box BX0902885, File 371868.
11. PM, Himalayas journal 3, n.d. PMP 1, Box 47.
12. ES to Candida Donadio, February 23, 1977. PRH, Box BX0902885, File 371868.
13. ES, interviewed by LR, July 24, 2018.
14. "Peter Matthiessen: The Art of Fiction No. 157," *The Paris Review*, No. 150, Spring 1999.
15. *SL*, 150.
16. Ibid., 33.
17. Kay Bonetti, "An Interview with Peter Matthiessen," *The Missouri Review*, Vol. 12, No. 2, 1989.
18. PM, Himalayas journal 1, September 11–November 10, 1973. PMP 1, Box 47.
19. Rue Matthiessen, interviewed by LR, September 25, 2018.
20. PM, interviewed by HN, n.d. [multiple interviews, 1990s]. HNC, Box 2.
21. *SL*, 66.

22. Ibid., 59.
23. PM, Himalayas journal 1, September 11–November 10, 1973. PMP 1, Box 47.
24. *SL*, 40.
25. PM, Himalayas journal 1, September 11–November 10, 1973. PMP 1, Box 47.
26. *SL*, 183–84.
27. ES, interviewed by LR, July 24, 2018.
28. Ibid.
29. ES, "Editing Saul Bellow," *Slate*, April 8, 2005.
30. ES, interviewed by LR, July 24, 2018.
31. *SL*, 282.
32. Donald Hall to PM, January 12, 1977. PMP 1, Box 62.
33. Christopher Merrill, interviewed by LR, September 14, 2019.
34. Donald Hall to PM, January 21, 1977. PMP 1, Box 62.
35. *SL*, 214.
36. *FT*, 331.
37. JH to PM, n.d. [May 1978]. PMP 4, Box 62.
38. ES, Deposition, *David Price v. Viking Press, Peter Matthiessen, and Bruce Ellison*, U.S. Dist. Ct., 4th Div. Minn., Civ. 4-85-819, October 8, 1986. NAC.
39. PM to MK, November 10, 1977. MMC.
40. WS to PM, December 24, 1978, in Rose Styron and R. Blakeslee Gilpin (eds.), *Selected Letters of William Styron* (New York: Random House, 2012), 529.
41. Francine du Plessix Gray published her own private letter to Matthiessen in *Commonweal*, December 8, 1978.
42. *SL*, 276.
43. Ibid., 233.
44. Ibid., 210.
45. PM to Karen Yochim, n.d. [c. 1978]. PMP 4, Box 38.
46. Jane Stanton Hitchcock, interviewed by LR, August 27, 2019.
47. James B. Steele, "Searching for More Than a Great White Cat," *Philadelphia Inquirer*, October 1, 1978.
48. John Walter, "A 'Terrifyingly Good Book' About Voyages," *Washington Star*, August 20, 1978.
49. Frank Graham Jr., "Wordviews," *Audubon*, August 1978.
50. "Expedition of the Spirit," *Horizon*, August 1978.
51. Terrence Des Pres, "Soul Searching in the Himalayas," *Washington Post*, August 20, 1978.
52. Paul Zweig, "Eastern Mountain Time," *SR*, August 1978.
53. Gerald Priestland, "Consciousness Raising—to 8,000 Feet," *Christian Science Monitor*, October 26, 1978.
54. Martin Levine, "In Search of Blue Sheep and of Tantric Wisdom," *Newsday*, August 20, 1978.
55. R. Z. Sheppard, "Zen and the Art of Watching," *Time*, August 7, 1978.
56. Robert M. Adams, "Blue Sheep Zen," *New York Review of Books*, September 28, 1978.
57. Colin Thubron, "High-Level Politics," *Sunday Telegraph*, April 8, 1979.
58. Edward Hoagland, "Walking the Himalayas," *New York Times*, November 11, 1978.
59. PM, interviewed by Jeff Sewald, March 2005. JSC.
60. PM to Donald Hall, n.d. [January 1977]. PMP 1, Box 62.
61. Kathryn Schulz, "What Do We Hope to Find When We Look for a Snow Leopard?," *The New Yorker*, July 12 & 19, 2021.
62. David Chase, quoted in Matt Zoller Seitz and Alan Sepinwall, *The Sopranos Sessions* (New York: Abrams, 2019), 383.
63. Pico Iyer, "Introduction: Ladders to the Roof," in PM, *The Snow Leopard* (New York: Penguin Classics, 2008), xix.
64. PM, quoted in Jerry Carroll, "Writer's Restless Mind Keeps Him Working," *San Francisco Chronicle*, November 22, 1997.
65. PM, interviewed by Mark Adams, February 14, 2014. Collection of Mark Adams.
66. ES to Alan Kellock, January 4, 1985. ESP, Box 15.

67. PM, "Acceptance Speech for the National Book Award," April 25, 1979. National Book Awards 30th Anniversary, Berg Collection, New York Public Library. An almost identical speech was read that same evening by Luke Matthiessen uptown at the Guggenheim, where his father was awarded the Brandeis University Creative Arts Award for *The Snow Leopard*. Luke added his own gloss to the speech: "I hope you will accept a surrogate, in the form of a son. I am proud to say that my father is, at this very moment, also being awarded the 1979 National Book Award in Contemporary Thought for THE SNOW LEOPARD. But he is not at that ceremony either. He is somewhere in the wilds of Utah or Nevada—we're not sure. The last time anyone heard from him was a call on Monday from a pay phone. He spoke to the housekeeper, the only person at his home in Sagaponack, who was to relay the message that he wouldn't be reachable for another three days, that he would call back then. He was calling to find out whether or not he had won the Award. As you can imagine, this took the form of a minor family tragedy—Dad unreachable in the desert while he was unknowingly receiving one of the most prestigious literary awards offered today. But that he is also receiving the Brandeis University Creative Arts Award on the same day is almost unbelievable. All of his family, his publishers and his friends are tremendously proud of him." See PMP 4, Box 51.
68. PM, Untitled bigfoot manuscript, n.d. [c. late 1970s]. PMP 1, Box 17.
69. *SL*, 281.
70. MK to PM, December 25, 1978. MMC.
71. Alex Matthiessen, interviewed by Jeff Sewald, n.d. [2006]. JSC.
72. Rose Styron, interviewed by Jeff Sewald, October 4, 2006. JSC.
73. Myrna Davis, interviewed by LR, March 28, 2021.
74. MK to PM, December 25, 1978. MMC.
75. MM, interviewed by LR, March 27, 2021.
76. MK to Thomas P. Morgan, April 3, 1978. PMP 4, Box 11.
77. Ngaere Macray, interviewed by LR, August 11, 2020.
78. Antonia Koenig, interviewed by LR, October 2, 2020.
79. MM, interviewed by Jeff Sewald, 2006. JSC.
80. MK, Notes on Fishers Island, October 1976. MMC.
81. MK to PM, December 25, 1978. MMC.
82. MK to PM, June 18, 1976. MMC.
83. MK to PM, August 15, 1976. MMC.
84. MK to PM, February 14, 1978. MMC.
85. MK to PM, March 18, 1978. MMC.
86. PM to MK, January 20, 1977. MMC.
87. PM to MK, n.d. [November 1978]. MMC.
88. PM to MK, November 10, 1977. MMC.
89. PM, Bigfoot notebook 1, 1975–76. PMP 4, Box 12.
90. PM to MK, December 1, 1977. MMC.
91. *SR*, 14.
92. Ibid., 4.
93. "Peter Matthiessen: The Art of Fiction No. 157," *The Paris Review*, No. 150, Spring 1999.
94. PM to MK, n.d. [August 1979]. MMC.
95. *SR*, 110–11.
96. Ibid., 178.
97. Ibid., 41.
98. MK to PM, December 2, 1979. MMC.
99. PM to MK, December 7, 1979. MMC.
100. Henry Allen, "Journeys into Meaning with Best-Selling Author Peter Matthiessen," *Washington Post*, December 13, 1978.
101. MM, interviewed by LR, March 27, 2021.
102. PM to MK, July 3, 1980. MMC.
103. MK to PM, May 22, 1980. MMC.
104. Gottlieb Eckhart, "Maria's Wedding to Peter Matthiessen," 1980. MMC.

105. TG, interviewed by Jeff Sewald, November 29, 2006. JSC.
106. PM to Mitchell Cantor, n.d. MMC.
107. *NHDR*, 246.
108. Bernie Glassman, interviewed by LR, September 21, 2018.

21 · INDIAN ENERGY

1. PM, quoted in Nicholas Dawidoff, "Earthbound in the Space Age," *Sports Illustrated*, December 1990.
2. PM, Deposition, *David Price v. Viking Press, Peter Matthiessen, and Bruce Ellison*, U.S. Dist. Ct., 4th Div. Minn., Civ. 4-85-819, October 9, 1986. NAC.
3. PM, interviewed by HN, n.d. [multiple interviews, 1990s]. HNC, Box 2.
4. PM to Janet McCloud, n.d. [July 1978]. PMP 4, Box 15.
5. *IC*, 241.
6. PM, Untitled bigfoot manuscript, n.d. [c. late 1970s]. PMP 1, Box 17.
7. PM, Deposition, *David Price v. Viking Press, Peter Matthiessen, and Bruce Ellison*, U.S. Dist. Ct., 4th Div. Minn., Civ. 4-85-819, October 9, 1986. NAC.
8. PM, Bigfoot notebook 6, c. 1979–80. PMP 4, Box 12.
9. PM, Untitled bigfoot manuscript, n.d. [c. late 1970s]. PMP 4, Box 29.
10. Ibid. Thomas Buckley's letter of warning, sent on May 25, 1978, is in PMP 4, Box 15. Matthiessen's response (June 10) is in the Thomas Buckley Papers, Humboldt State University Library, Box 3: "Probably you are right in yr interpretation of the BF phenomenon of recent times among the Klamath peoples, but I'm not positive about this yet; I'll let you know if I find out anything more. Don't leave out the possibility that BF 'Himself' has made a comeback, after being decimated by H. sapiens diseases in the 19th Century. Still, I'm glad you warn me."
11. PM, Untitled bigfoot manuscript, n.d. [c. late 1970s]. PMP 1, Box 15.
12. Most of the surviving correspondence with Matthiessen's bigfoot researcher, Janet Thiessen, can be found in PMP 4, Boxes 15 and 27.
13. This question was first posed by Felix Montoya in January 1976, but Matthiessen heard and recorded multiple variations of it over the following few years. "Wherever I went to talk to people, they had problems, and whenever I got through talking to people, they'd say, 'Hey, we need help here. How about publicizing the situation here on the rez, you know?' And I felt obligated to do that." PM, interviewed by HN, n.d. [multiple interviews, 1990s]. HNC, Box 2.
14. PM, quoted in Jonathan White, *Talking on the Water: Conversations About Nature and Creativity* (San Francisco: Sierra Club Books, 1994), 234.
15. PM, quoted in Jeff Sewald (dir.), *No Boundaries*, PBS, 2009.
16. PM, interviewed by HN, n.d. [multiple interviews, 1990s]. HNC, Box 2.
17. *IC*, xi.
18. PM, "Stop the GO Road," *Audubon*, January 1979.
19. PM, "How to Kill a Valley," *New York Review of Books*, February 7, 1980. See also PM, "The Price of Tellico," *Newsweek*, December 17, 1979.
20. PM, "A Land Sacred to Indians Is Despoiled by the White Man: Battle for Big Mountain," *Geo*, March 1980.
21. PM, "No Man's Land," *Miami Herald*, November 8, 1981.
22. Oren Lyons, interviewed by Jeff Sewald, October 24, 2006. JSC.
23. Winona LaDuke, interviewed by Jeff Sewald, November 16, 2006. JSC.
24. Craig Carpenter to PM, November 12, 1980. PMP 4, Box 27.
25. *IC*, 3–13. All quotes from "Native Earth" can be found in chapter one of *IC*. The essay was first published in the spring of 1981 in *Parabola*, a quarterly magazine about mythology and religious traditions.
26. Peter Nabokov, "Return to the Native," *New York Review of Books*, September 27, 1984.
27. Barry Lopez, "Books," *Outside*, June 1984.
28. PM, quoted in Randy Wayne White, "The Travels of Peter Matthiessen," *Outside*, April 1980.

29. PM, "The Wild World of Peter Matthiessen," *BBC World Service*, June 12, 2002. For similar comments by Matthiessen, see also Henry Allen, "Journeys into Meaning with Best-Selling Author Peter Matthiessen," *Washington Post*, December 13, 1978; Rex Weyler, "Peter Matthiessen: The Search for Truth," *New Age*, August 1983; Paul Rea, "Causes and Creativity: An Interview with Peter Matthiessen," *RE Arts & Letters: A Liberal Arts Forum*, Fall 1989; Trip Gabriel, "The Nature of Peter Matthiessen," *New York Times*, June 10, 1990; Eda Gordon, "Interview," *Crosswinds*, March 1991; and Patty Satalia, "Conversations from Penn State," 2010.
30. PM, quoted in Jonathan White, *Talking on the Water*, 241. Matthiessen also calls romanticization "revolting," and "kind of a reverse racism," in "No Boundaries" (audio recording), Gang of Seven, 1992.
31. PM, interviewed by HN, n.d. [multiple interviews, 1990s]. HNC, Box 2. In yet another interview, Matthiessen said: "I think we've had a very romantic idea about traditional people.... They're not wiser about traditional ways about the environment or anything like that." See PM in conversation with Gary Snyder, February 23, 1994, City Arts & Lectures.
32. *ITSCH*, xxiii.
33. Brian Haley, the anthropologist who wrote about Craig Carpenter as a "neo-Indian," has published a series of articles critiquing some of the assumptions in Matthiessen's article about Point Conception and the Chumash. Haley writes, for example, that the term "Western Gate" was only coined in 1978 "for its public relations value by the opposition organized against the construction of a liquefied natural gas receiving terminal at Coco Bay near Point Conception." See Brian D. Haley and Larry R. Wilcoxon, "Point Conception and the Chumash Land of the Dead: Revisions from Harrington's Notes," *Journal of California and Great Basin Anthropology*, Vol. 21, No. 2, July 1999. See also Brian D. Haley and Larry R. Wilcoxon, "Anthropology and the Making of Chumash Tradition," *Current Anthropology*, Vol. 38, No. 5, December 1997.
34. "How We Met: Peter Matthiessen and Leonard Peltier," *Independent*, November 5, 2000. Matthiessen also recounts his exchange with Lame Deer in *ITSCH*, xxv–xxvi; *IC*, 230–34; and Jonathan White, *Talking on the Water*, 231.
35. *ITSCH*, 381.
36. PM, Deposition, *David Price v. Viking Press, Peter Matthiessen, and Bruce Ellison*, U.S. Dist. Ct., 4th Div. Minn., Civ. 4-85-819, October 9, 1986. NAC.
37. *ITSCH*, xxiv.
38. PM, Bigfoot notebook 5, 1979. PMP 4, Box 12.
39. Mark Tilsen, interviewed by LR, April 24, 2020.
40. *IC*, 209.
41. PM, "High Noon in the Black Hills," *New York Times Magazine*, July 13, 1980.
42. Mark Tilsen, interviewed by LR, April 24, 2020.
43. *ITSCH*, 411.
44. Ibid., 423.
45. With so many conflicting accounts, only the barest details can be offered with any certainty. Besides *ITSCH*, my description of the 1975 shootout is based on Steve Hendricks, *The Unquiet Grave: The FBI and the Struggle for the Soul of Indian Country* (New York: Thunder Mouth Press, 2006); Michael Apted (dir.), *Incident at Oglala*, Miramax Films, 1992; and Kevin McKiernan (dir.), *From Wounded Knee to Standing Rock*, Access Productions, 2019.
46. Leonard Peltier, quoted in *ITSCH*, 148.
47. Steve Hendricks, *The Unquiet Grave*, 204.
48. Quoted in *ITSCH*, 174.
49. Joel Weisman, "About That 'Ambush' at Wounded Knee," *Columbia Journalism Review*, September 1, 1975.
50. The U.S. Commission on Civil Rights, quoted in Steve Hendricks, *The Unquiet Grave*, 211.
51. See *ITSCH*, 317.
52. Leonard Peltier, quoted in ibid., 363.
53. PM, "No Boundaries" (audio recording), Gang of Seven, 1992.

54. *ITSCH*, 469.
55. PM, interviewed by HN, n.d. [multiple interviews, 1990s]. HNC, Box 2.
56. *ITSCH*, 469.
57. PM, interviewed by Jeff Sewald, October 9, 2006. JSC.
58. PM, quoted in Jeff Sewald (dir.), *No Boundaries*, PBS, 2009.
59. PM, interviewed by HN, n.d. [multiple interviews, 1990s]. HNC, Box 2.
60. *The New Yorker* did buy Matthiessen's article on the Miccosukee of Florida, before it ran in *The Miami Herald;* see NYR, Box 1638. However, as Matthiessen recalled, the magazine killed it after copy-edits. "My young editor said, 'Nobody wants to read about Indians. Nobody cares about them. Nobody wants to read about them.'" See "A Side of Matthiessen," February 28, 1991. LTV Archives.
61. Bruce Ellison, interviewed by LR, November 1, 2022.
62. PM, "Mean Spirit," *Outside*, October 1995. Matthiessen was criticized for his profit-sharing arrangement by Scott Anderson in "The Martyrdom of Leonard Peltier," *Outside*, June 1995.
63. A copy of the contract between PM, the Leonard Peltier Defense Committee, and the Telos Film Corporation can be found in ESP, Box 15.
64. PM, "Mean Spirit," *Outside*, October 1995.
65. PM to Leonard Peltier, n.d. [October 1980]. PMP 4, Box 63.
66. Leonard Peltier to PM, October 23, 1980. PMP 4, Box 40.
67. *ITSCH*, 4.
68. Kevin McKiernan, interviewed by LR, March 28, 2020.
69. *ITSCH*, 469.
70. Ibid.
71. PM, Deposition, *David Price v. Viking Press, Peter Matthiessen, and Bruce Ellison*, U.S. Dist. Ct., 4th Div. Minn., Civ. 4–85–819, October 9, 1986. NAC.
72. PM to Richard Wilson, March 12, 1981. PMP 4, Box 9.
73. Bruce Ellison, interviewed by LR, November 1, 2022.
74. *ITSCH*, 502.
75. Ibid., 504.
76. Ibid.
77. "How We Met: Peter Matthiessen and Leonard Peltier," *The Independent*, November 5, 2000.
78. *ITSCH*, 507.
79. Ibid., 506.
80. PM to Bill Hazlett, n.d. [c. April 1982]. PMP 4, Box 63.
81. PM, interviewed by Jeff Sewald, October 9, 2006. JSC. PM made a similar statement in "The Long Journey: Zen and the Writing Life" (audio recording), San Francisco Zen Center, 1998: "I did become partisan. But I said so, at several places in the book."
82. *ITSCH*, 488. Hultman's reply is filed in PMP 4, Box 63.
83. Ken Tilsen, quoted in Steve Hendricks, *The Unquiet Grave*, 11. Tilsen told Matthiessen virtually the same thing: "In my opinion, David Price is one of the most corrupt and vicious agents in the FBI. I said this to two hundred agents in 1979, from the steps of the FBI Building in Washington, so you may as well quote me." *ITSCH*, 452–53.
84. *ITSCH*, 451.
85. Ibid., 464.
86. Ibid., 462.
87. Affidavit of David Price, March 30, 1987. PMP 4, Box 9.
88. PM to Leonard Peltier, n.d. [March 1981]. PMP 4, Box 63.
89. Leonard Peltier to PM, April 5, 1981. PMP 4, Box 40.
90. ES, Deposition, *David Price v. Viking Press, Peter Matthiessen, and Bruce Ellison*, U.S. Dist. Ct., 4th Div. Minn., Civ. 4–85–819, October 8, 1986. NAC.
91. Contract for "Thieves' Road," June 8, 1981. PRH, Box BX0902370, File 371864.
92. ES, Deposition, *David Price v. Viking Press, Peter Matthiessen, and Bruce Ellison*, U.S. Dist. Ct., 4th Div. Minn., Civ. 4–85–819, October 8, 1986. NAC.
93. Ibid.
94. ES, interviewed by LR, July 24, 2018.

95. PM, interviewed by Miriam Pawel, July 15, 2013. Collection of Miriam Pawel. Although Matthiessen's direct involvement with Chavez and the United Farm Workers ended sometime around 1975, he continued to admire Chavez for decades and wrote a tribute after his death. See PM, "Postscript: Cesar Chavez," *The New Yorker*, May 17, 1993: "Anger was part of Chavez, but so was a transparent love of humankind. The gentle mystic that his disciples wished to see inhabited the same small body as the relentless labor leader who concerned himself with the most minute operation of his union. Astonishingly—this seems to me his genius—the two Cesars were so complementary that without either, La Causa could not have survived."
96. PM, quoted in Rex Weyler, "Peter Matthiessen: The Search for Truth," *New Age*, August 1983.
97. MM, interviewed by LR, November 16, 2018.
98. PM, quoted in Sandra Cadwalader, "A Vision of Land and Life," *Indian Truth*, June 1983. See also Carla Hall, "A Spirit of Support for Indian Activists," *Washington Post*, May 26, 1983.
99. PM, quoted in Sandra Cadwalader, "A Vision of Land and Life," *Indian Truth*, June 1983.
100. PM, quoted in Stephan Salisbury, "Author Thinks FBI Framed an Activist Indian Leader," *Philadelphia Inquirer*, April 8, 1983.
101. PM, interviewed by Samuel Taylor, May 3, 1999, City Arts & Lectures.
102. *ITSCH*, 8.
103. Ibid., 26.
104. Kai Erikson, "New Indian Wars," *Vanity Fair*, March 1983.
105. *ITSCH*, 69.
106. Ibid., 546–47.
107. Ibid., 149.
108. Ibid., 554.
109. PM to Janet McCloud, n.d. [November 1981]. PMP 4, Box 39.
110. *ITSCH*, xx.
111. PM to Leonard Peltier, n.d. [July 1982]. PMP 4, Box 63.
112. Kevin McKiernan, interviewed by LR, March 28, 2020. For the offending passage, see *ITSCH*, 198.
113. PM to Dennis Banks, n.d. [1982]. PMP 4, Box 39.
114. "The Long Journey: Zen and the Writing Life" (audio recording), San Francisco Zen Center, 1998.
115. PM to Vine Deloria Jr., n.d. [May 1982]. PMP 4, Box 63. Matthiessen was not alone with this "extreme" opinion: see, for example, Ramsey Clark's preface to Leonard Peltier, *Prison Writings: My Life Is My Sun Dance* (New York: St. Martin's Griffin, 1999). Clark, a former U.S. attorney general, insisted Peltier was innocent, but said that even if Peltier did shoot the two FBI agents, "it would still have been in self-defense and in the defense not just of his people but of the right of all individuals and peoples to be free from domination and exploitation."
116. PM to Leonard Peltier, May 28, 1981. PMP 4, Box 63.
117. Ken Tilsen to PM, June 8, 1981. Wounded Knee Legal Defense/Offense Committee Records, Minnesota Historical Society, 147.K.19.8F.
118. PM to Leonard Peltier, n.d. [July 1982]. PMP 4, Box 63.
119. Jim Leach, email to LR, February 7, 2020.
120. Jim Leach to PM, April 20, 1982. PMP 4, Box 33. Matthiessen replied to Leach: "The circumstantial case there is so compelling that I guess I've taken the link for granted, like everyone else . . . but all along I've had an uneasy feeling of no-documentation, and yr letter forces me to deal with it. I do still find it hard to believe there is no connection. . . . Nevertheless, I think I should spike the gun by simply saying that there is no known documentation for the link, and invite the reader to account for the govt overkill in the area some other way." Even this would end up being too much conjecture for readers like Scott Anderson, who criticized Matthiessen's "über-conspiracy theory"—"that Peltier and AIM had to be destroyed in order to open up the uranium beds of western South Dakota for exploitation by energy industrialists"—in "The Mar-

tyrdom of Leonard Peltier," *Outside,* June 1995. Matthiessen felt compelled to respond to Anderson that same year, admitting he may have got a little carried away: "in hindsight, I would probably agree with lawyer Jim Leach, whose comments and criticisms I invited and Anderson exploited." See PM, "Mean Spirit," *Outside,* October 1995.
121. Bill Richards, "Prairie Promoter: Gov. Janklow Exhibits Strange Personal Style, but He Means Business," *Wall Street Journal,* March 29, 1984. See also Steve Hendricks, *The Unquiet Grave,* 143–57; and Martin Garbus, *Tough Talk: How I Fought for Writers, Comics, Bigots, and the American Way* (New York, Crown, 1998), 141–42.
122. PM to Dennis Banks, n.d. [1982]. PMP 4, Box 39.
123. ES to PM, April 28, 1982. PMP 4, Box 33.
124. Rick Kurnit, interviewed by LR, January 9, 2023.
125. Martin Garbus, interviewed by LR, May 15, 2020.
126. PM to Jim Leach, May 14, 1982. Collection of LR.
127. ES to PM, January 28, 1983. ESP, Box 15.
128. Carolyn See, "In the Spirit of Crazy Horse," *Los Angeles Times,* March 6, 1983.
129. Page Stegner, "Reds," *New York Review of Books,* April 14, 1983.
130. Peter S. Prescott, "Peltier's Last Stand," *Newsweek,* March 28, 1983.
131. J. D. Reed, "Black Hills," *Time,* March 28, 1983.
132. PM, interviewed by HN, n.d. [multiple interviews, 1990s]. HNC, Box 2.
133. Christopher Lehmann-Haupt, "The Troubled Indians," *New York Times,* March 5, 1983.
134. PM, quoted in Sandra Cadwalader, "A Vision of Land and Life," *Indian Truth,* June 1983.
135. Alan M. Dershowitz, "Agents and Indians," *New York Times,* March 6, 1983.
136. Sonya F. Gray, "A Cosmic Explorer Reports In," *Providence Journal-Bulletin,* March 20, 1983. Matthiessen was still talking about Dershowitz's review in April: "He doesn't deal fairly with my argument." See Stephan Salisbury, "Author Thinks FBI Framed an Activist Indian Leader," *Philadelphia Inquirer,* April 8, 1983.
137. PM, "American Indians," *New York Times,* March 20, 1983.
138. The rebuttal was reproduced in *Indian Truth,* June 1983.
139. Ric Kahn, "Dershowitz's Latest Stand," *Boston Magazine,* August 1983. A press release about the confrontation, and a letter sent to Dershowitz by the American Indian Law Students' Association on March 23, 1983, is in PMP 4, Box 25.
140. Winona LaDuke, interviewed by LR, July 10, 2020.
141. Quoted in Martin Garbus, "Afterword," *ITSCH,* 594.
142. See Bill Janklow to Martin Garbus, April 1, 1983. Wounded Knee Legal Defense/Offense Committee Records, Minnesota Historical Society, 147.K.19.8F.
143. PM to Martin Garbus, June 2, 1983. PMP 4, Box 9.
144. Bill Janklow, quoted in J. D. Ames, "Janklow Angered by Book," *Rapid City Journal,* May 14, 1983.
145. Bill Janklow, quoted in "Janklow Tries to Halt Sale of Book," *Sioux City Journal,* April 20, 1983.
146. "South Dakota librarians say they cannot keep copies on their shelves, and the Waldenbooks chain reported sales of the book jumped 50 percent across the nation in the week after stories about Janklow's attempts to stop several South Dakota bookstores from selling it." See Rogers Worthington, "Book and Rumors Dog Janklow; Is He the Indian's Friend or Foe?," *St. Paul Dispatch,* June 15, 1983.
147. Juliet Annan, quoted in David Egner, "Janklow's Attack on Book Boosts Sales," *Rapid City Journal,* June 2, 1983.
148. "S. Dak. Governor Sues Viking, Three Bookstores for Libel," *Publishers Weekly,* June 17, 1983.
149. A copy of Janklow's original complaint can be found in the Wounded Knee Legal Defense/Offense Committee Records, Minnesota Historical Society, 147.K.19.8F. Many of Janklow's and Garbus's early negotiation letters are also here. Garbus offers his take on the lawsuit in "Afterword," *ITSCH,* 594–96.
150. Donald Gillmore, quoted in Patrick Springer, "Janklow Suit Viewed as Legal Bullying Tactic," *Sioux Falls Argus Leader,* May 25, 1983.

151. Edwin McDowell, "Court Battle over Book: Viking and a Governor," *New York Times*, May 28, 1983.
152. PM, quoted in Carla Hall, "A Spirit of Support for Indian Activist," *Washington Post*, May 26, 1983. Matthiessen mentions the reception in *IC*, 199. See also Susan Kellam, "Book on Indians Touches Off Debate," *New York Times*, December 11, 1983. A copy of the reception invitation is in PMP 4, Box 63.
153. Bruce Ellison, quoted in Ken Baka, "Ellison Calls Libel Suit 'an FBI Lawsuit,'" *Rapid City Journal*, January 9, 1984.
154. ES to PM, January 4, 1984. ESP, Box 15.
155. Ibid. According to Rick Kurnit, during the legal read "there were definitely discussions with Peter about the accusations against the FBI." Despite PM retaining no memory of it, Kurnit is "pretty sure" there was also a discussion concerning Special Agent David Price: "I vaguely recall [Peter] saying something about Price having a trunk full of guns." Rick Kurnit, interviewed by LR, January 9, 2023.
156. David Price, quoted in Ken Baka, "FBI Agent Files $25 Million Suit," *Rapid City Journal*, January 7, 1984.
157. Memorandum of Law in Support of Defendants' Motion to Dismiss Complaint, March 8, 1984. Collection of LR.
158. A copy of Price's original complaint, filed in both state and federal court in South Dakota, can be found in PMP 4, Box 9. "Corrupt and vicious" came from a quote by Ken Tilsen in Matthiessen's book; see *ITSCH*, 452–53.
159. "[I]t was assumed that . . . both suits were intended mainly as chastisement and harassment as well as a means of keeping this book out of circulation," *ITSCH*, 561. See also PM, quoted in "In the Wake of 'Crazy Horse,'" *San Francisco Examiner*, March 15, 1987: "We think it's harassment . . . I have to be discredited and Viking Press has to be put out of business because we criticized the FBI."
160. PM to ES, May 21, 1985. PMP 4, Box 40. "I did not agree to the destruction of my books," Matthiessen told *The Nation*. "I didn't know about it. I felt they never should have withdrawn the book in the first place. It seemed to me overcautious. Martin Garbus, their lawyer, told me he didn't think Viking should have withdrawn the book until they had a judgement against them in court." See Jon Wiener, "Murdered Ink," *The Nation*, May 31, 1993. Garbus agreed with this during an interview with me (May 15, 2020). However, Elisabeth Sifton insisted it was not Viking's decision: "We hated that we couldn't continue to distribute it. We were thwarted. It's a very, very negative thing to have happen, to have an injunction against you for the distribution of a book until the legal issues are settled. . . . We were enjoined from further distribution." (Interviewed by LR, July 24, 2018). Despite Sifton's comments, there does not appear to have been a legal order forcing Viking to withdraw or halt publication of *In the Spirit of Crazy Horse*.
161. PM to Christopher MacLehose, August 8, 1984. PMP 4, Box 40.
162. The Second Judicial Circuit for South Dakota dismissed Janklow's lawsuit in June 1984. A copy of the order, issued by Judge Gene Paul Kean, is in PMP 1, Box 16. The State Supreme Court of South Dakota, rejecting the argument of "neutral reportage," reinstated the lawsuit in December 1985.
163. The judge was Roland E. Grosshans; he recused himself from presiding over David Price's lawsuit on March 13, 1984.
164. Martin Garbus, *Tough Talk*, 151.
165. ES, Deposition, *David Price v. Viking Press, Peter Matthiessen, and Bruce Ellison*, U.S. Dist. Ct., 4th Div. Minn., Civ. 4–85–819, October 8, 1986. NAC.
166. ES, interviewed by LR, July 24, 2018.
167. *ITSCH*, 561. At various times over the years, Matthiessen speculated that it was taxpayers who were funding the lawsuit without their knowledge. This eventually hardened into belief, presented as a proven fact at public talks: "And guess who was paying for those lawsuits? You guys. And me. This was all that tax money that was being marshaled against us." See PM, "The Long Journey: Zen and the Writing Life" (audio recording), San Francisco Zen Center, 1998; also PM, "National Writers Series, City Opera House," October 29, 2010.

168. Martin Garbus, *Tough Talk*, 150–51. "The FBI had as much a stake in the outcome as Price had," Garbus continued, "and it is not too far a stretch to think that the Bureau was ready to set up a fund to pay for the suit." Garbus made the same claims in "The FBI Men Who Cried Libel," *The Nation*, November 13, 1989, though he conceded that these were "rumors, never confirmed."
169. Viking's and Matthiessen's attorneys insisted that David Price's first affidavit included material that suggested Price had "surreptitiously reviewed FBI files that are not available to defendants." Price denied this. In a second affidavit, he insisted that "my practice in this litigation has been to obtain government files only through procedures that also were available to the author, such as FOIA requests and review of court transcripts and exhibits." Price also denied that he was being bankrolled by his employer: "Defendants have asserted repeatedly that it is the FBI that is behind this lawsuit. That is untrue. I am proceeding with this litigation to vindicate my personal reputation, and to seek damages from defendants for harm done to me personally. The federal government is not financially supporting me in this litigation." Second Affidavit of David Price, PMP 4, Box 9.
170. The correspondence between Martin Garbus, the Department of Justice lawyers, and Judge Diana Murphy is in the Wounded Knee Legal Defense/Offense Committee Records, Minnesota Historical Society, 147.K.19.8F. Perhaps it was paranoia, but Garbus and Matthiessen did have reasonable cause to distrust the Department of Justice. In a sworn affidavit, the DOJ had previously denied "the presence of any informer" planted with AIM—a lie, exposed when Douglas Durham admitted he was indeed a mole for the FBI. See *ITSCH*, 122.
171. Craig Carpenter to PM, November 12, 1980. PMP 4, Box 27. PM discussed this warning in an interview with HN, n.d. HNC, Box 2.
172. PM, interviewed by Jeff Sewald, October 9, 2006. JSC.
173. Barry Lopez to PM, May 10, 1984. PMP 4, Box 39.
174. PM, quoted in Bruce Beans, "The Wildness Within," *Philadelphia Magazine*, June 24, 1990.
175. PM to MM, January 23, 1984. MMC.
176. Stuart Dybek, interviewed by LR, August 28, 2021.
177. Martin Garbus, interviewed by LR, May 15, 2020.
178. PM to ES, June 20, 1983. ESP, Box 15.
179. ES to Alan Kellock, January 4, 1985. ESP, Box 15.
180. Ibid.
181. PM to ES, May 21, 1985. PMP 4, Box 40.
182. PM to ES, August 9, 1985. PMP 4, Box 40.
183. PM to Christopher MacLehose, August 8, 1984. PMP 4, Box 40.
184. MM, interviewed by LR, May 26, 2019.
185. PM to WSM, n.d. [1985]. WSMP, Sixth Accession, Correspondence, Box 14.
186. *AS*, 108. See also David Western, *In the Dust of Kilimanjaro* (Washington, DC: Island Press, 1997), 187–90, 199–201.

22 · TEN THOUSAND ISLANDS

1. *KMW*, 183.
2. *WIA*, 38.
3. PM to Priscilla Pizzolato, n.d. PMP 4, Box 14.
4. Matthiessen recalled this story about his father in numerous interviews. For example, *Charlie Rose*, PBS, November 26, 1997 (https://charlierose.com/videos/13799); *Charlie Rose*, PBS, June 3, 1999 (https://charlierose.com/videos/9919); "Peter Matthiessen: The Art of Fiction No. 157," *The Paris Review*, No. 150, Spring 1999; Jeff Sewald (dir.), *No Boundaries*, PBS, 2009; and PM, interviewed for the National Writers Series, Traverse City, MI, October 29, 2010.
5. PM, interviewed by HN, n.d. [multiple interviews, 1990s]. HNC, Box 2.
6. PM, "White," 1951. PMP 4, Box 1.

7. PM, "The River Eater," *Audubon*, March 1970.
8. PM, "The Last Great Strand," *Audubon*, March 1967. See also PM, "Lignumvitae," *Audubon*, January 1972.
9. PM, Bigfoot notebook 1, 1975–76. PMP 4, Box 12.
10. Randy Wayne White, "The Travels of Peter Matthiessen," *Outside*, April/May 1980.
11. Ibid. For a full breakdown of the Swamp Ape Expedition with Matthiessen, see Randy Wayne White, "The Swamp Ape," *Batfishing in the Rainforest* (New York: Lyons & Burford, 1991). PM's own notes on the expedition, titled "BF trips to Fla., Feb 17, 1977," are in PMP 4, Box 29.
12. PM, "Florida (BF) Novel," n.d. [c. 1980]. PMP 4, Box 10. Additional notes for the novel, which Matthiessen at some point labeled "NOTES FOR FLORIDA AMER-INDIAN NOVEL THAT EVENTUALLY EVOLVED INTO WATSON," can be found in PMP 4, Box 62. An elaborate chart breakdown for the unwritten novel is in PMP 4, Box 10.
13. PM, interviewed by HN, March 25, 1995. Private Collection of HN.
14. All quotes for this section come from the novel sources noted above.
15. PM, quoted in Sonya F. Gray, "A Cosmic Explorer Reports In," *Providence Journal-Bulletin*, March 20, 1983.
16. PM, interviewed by Jeff Sewald, May 2006. JSC.
17. PM, interviewed by HN, n.d. [multiple interviews, 1990s]. HNC, Box 2.
18. PM, quoted in Michael Sims, "A Series of Tiny Astonishments: An Interview with Peter Matthiessen," *BookPage*, 2000.
19. PM, quoted in Rosemary Goring, "Man with No Fame," *Scotland on Sunday*, May 3, 1998.
20. PM, quoted in Michael Sims, "A Series of Tiny Astonishments: An Interview with Peter Matthiessen," *BookPage*, 2000. See also PM, quoted in "New Yorkers Aren't Interested in Stories About Swamp People," *Observer*, May 10, 1998: "I saw this Watson as a metaphor for so much that's gone wrong. Racism, and entrepreneurialism and violence in our country."
21. "Peter Matthiessen: The Art of Fiction No. 157," *The Paris Review*, No. 150, Spring 1999.
22. PM, "FICTION v. NON-FICTION," n.d. MMC.
23. PM, Auschwitz teisho, n.d. MMC.
24. Charles Sherod Smallwood, quoted in Charlton W. Tebeau, *The Story of the Chokoloskee Bay Country* (Miami: University of Miami Press, 1955), 81.
25. See, for example, William K. Robertson, "Legend About Killing Had 'Stuck in My Brain,'" *Miami Herald*, June 24, 1990.
26. Robert Smallwood, quoted in Watson notes, from interviews in March 1984 and January 1985. PMP 1, Box 21.
27. PM to Rosa C. Oliver, n.d. [May 1986]. PMP 4, Box 5.
28. PM to Ruby Palmer, n.d. [1985]. PMP 4, Box 3.
29. Larry Owen to PM, February 11, 1986. PMP 4, Box 3.
30. Larry Owen to PM, April 17, 1991. PMP 4, Box 19.
31. PM, "The Spirit of Place," 2002. KWLS.
32. *KMW*, i.
33. PM, *Charlie Rose*, PBS, November 26, 1997. See https://charlierose.com/videos/13799.
34. For Doug Kuntz's memories of the project, see Jennifer Landes, "Photos from a Vanished World," *East Hampton Star*, February 29, 2024.
35. Joseph Heller to PM, July 15, 1986. PMP 3, Box 24.
36. PM to WSM, July 31, 1986. WSMP, Sixth Accession, Correspondence, Box 14.
37. Helen Harkaspi, interviewed by LR, July 8, 2019; Bernie Glassman, interviewed by LR, September 21, 2018.
38. Lawrence Shainberg, interviewed by LR, July 2, 2019.
39. Bernie Glassman, quoted in Lawrence Shainberg, *Ambivalent Zen* (New York: Pantheon, 1995), 264. Shainberg's book features a detailed narrative of the acquisition of Greyston: see pp. 257–65.
40. PM to WSM, n.d. [July 1986]. WSMP, Sixth Accession, Correspondence, Box 14.

41. PM, Ango talk, November 1982. PMP 2, Box 57.
42. Helen Tworkov, interviewed by LR, May 19, 2019.
43. PM, quoted in Wendy Smith, "PW Interviews: Peter Matthiessen," *Publishers Weekly*, May 9, 1986.
44. Janwillem van de Wetering, "In Short: Nonfiction," *New York Times*, April 6, 1986.
45. PM to WSM, July 31, 1986. WSMP, Sixth Accession, Correspondence, Box 14.
46. *NHDR*, 61.
47. PM to WSM, July 31, 1986. WSMP, Sixth Accession, Correspondence, Box 14.
48. PM, Deposition, *David Price v. Viking Press, Peter Matthiessen, and Bruce Ellison*, U.S. Dist. Ct., 4th Div. Minn., Civ. 4-85-819, December 17, 1986. NAC.
49. PM, "New York: Old Hometown," *Architectural Digest*, November 1989. Matthiessen claimed in this article to have spent a total of four days in New York in 1987.
50. PM to Edward Hoagland, March 2, 1987. Edward Hoagland Papers, Texas Tech University, Box 1.
51. PM to Winnie Collins, n.d. [March 1987]. PMP 4, Box 3.
52. PM, Sixtieth birthday speech, May 1987. PMP 3, Box 27.
53. PM, interviewed by Kay Bonetti, May 1987. American Audio Prose Library. An edited version of this conversation was published as "An Interview with Peter Matthiessen," *The Missouri Review*, Vol. 12, No. 2, 1989.
54. PM, Early Watson pages, n.d. PMP 1, Box 21.
55. "Peter Matthiessen: The Art of Fiction No. 157," *The Paris Review*, No. 150, Spring 1999.
56. John Irving (and Claire Messud), "Our Hero: Peter Matthiessen," *Guardian*, April 11, 2014.
57. John Irving, interviewed by LR, March 14, 2023.
58. John Irving, quoted in Trip Gabriel, "The Nature of Peter Matthiessen," *New York Times*, June 10, 1990.
59. "Peter Matthiessen: The Art of Fiction No. 157," *The Paris Review*, No. 150, Spring 1999. Matthiessen also refers to the "movements" during an appearance on *Charlie Rose*, PBS, November 26, 1997 (https://charlierose.com/videos/13799). In a letter to Neil Olson, sent in January 1996, he wrote: "In the author's very strong opinion, all three novels are in fact one large (dare I say 'symphonic'?) work. Such was the original concept, more than fifteen years ago, and I wrote all three in the first draft before going back to the second (and many more) drafts of BOOK I, then II, and now III." MMC.
60. John Irving (and Claire Messud), "Our Hero: Peter Matthiessen," *The Guardian*, April 11, 2014.
61. PM to Kurt Vonnegut, April 4, 1989. PMP 4, Box 40.
62. PM to Doug Peacock, May 7, 1989. PMP 4, Box 40.
63. Jason Epstein, interviewed by LR, November 16, 2018.
64. Jason Epstein, quoted in Bruce E. Beans, "The Wilderness Within," *Philadelphia Magazine*, June 24, 1990.
65. MM to JH, October 4, 1989. JHP, Box 32.
66. PM, interviewed by HN, November 21, 1996, for the Lannan Foundation.
67. Rebecca Saletan, interviewed by LR, September 3, 2020.
68. *KMW*, 3.
69. PM, *Killing Mister Watson* draft, n.d. PMP 1, Box 28.
70. PM, *Killing Mister Watson* draft, June 1989. PMP 1, Box 26.
71. *KMW*, 94.
72. Ibid., 67.
73. Ibid., 108.
74. "Peter Matthiessen: The Art of Fiction No. 157," *The Paris Review*, No. 150, Spring 1999.
75. PM to JH, n.d. [May 1990]. JHP, Box 32.
76. JH to PM, May 15, 1990. PMP 3, Box 25.
77. Ron Hansen, "Larger Than Life, Deader Than Dead," *New York Times*, June 24, 1990.
78. "Killing Mister Watson," *Kirkus*, April 15, 1990.
79. Wendy Smith, "A Powerful Novel from Matthiessen," *Chicago Sun-Times*, July 8, 1990.

80. Marianne Wiggins, "Killing Mister Watson," *Los Angeles Times*, August 5, 1990.
81. Joyce Carol Oates, "Was 1910 Fla. Slaying Murder, or Justice?," *Trenton Times*, October 14, 1990.
82. Patricia Storace, "Betrayals," *New York Review of Books*, January 31, 1991.
83. PM to HN, June 3, 1990. HNC, Box 13.
84. Barbara Brice, interviewed by LR, January 2, 2023.
85. *KMW*, 34.
86. Ibid., 36.
87. PM to Mary Hamilton Clark, July 26, 1990. PMP 4, Box 5.
88. A signed copy of the permission release form can be found in PMP 4, Box 5.
89. PM, "TO WHOM IT MAY CONCERN," August 15, 1990. PMP 4, Box 5.
90. David Streitfeld, "In the Spirit of Peter Matthiessen," *Chicago Tribune*, August 12, 1990. See also Steve Wick, "In the Spirit of Justice," *Newsday*, August 15, 1990.
91. PM, quoted in Linda Sherry, "Matthiessen Victor in Suit," *Washington Post*, January 1988.
92. Diana E. Murphy, Memorandum Opinion and Order, *David Price v. Viking Press, Peter Matthiessen, and Bruce Ellison*, U.S. Dist. Ct., 4th Div. Minn., Civ. 4–85–819, January 13, 1988.
93. Gerald Heaney, quoted in *ITSCH*, 599.
94. Gene Paul Kean, Memorandum Opinion and Order, *William Janklow v. Viking Press and Peter Matthiessen*, Circuit Ct., 2nd Circuit, Sioux Falls, Civ. 83–1385, June 2, 1989.
95. Bill Janklow, quoted in "Janklow Libel Suit Suffers Setback Before High Court," *Sioux City Journal*, July 20, 1990.
96. Elizabeth Mehren, "Suit Against 'Spirit of Crazy Horse' Ends," *Los Angeles Times*, November 16, 1990.
97. Herbert Mitgang, "'Crazy Horse' Author Is Upheld in Libel Case," *New York Times*, January 16, 1988.
98. Martin Garbus, interviewed by LR, May 15, 2020.
99. PM, quoted in Garry Abrams, "Last Shot in the Battle over 'Crazy Horse,'" *Los Angeles Times*, May 30, 1991.
100. *ITSCH*, 561.
101. PM, quoted in David Streitfeld, "In the Spirit of Peter Matthiessen," *Chicago Tribune*, August 12, 1990.
102. *ITSCH*, 576.
103. Bob Robideau, quoted in ibid.
104. A dot-matrix printout of Matthiessen's meeting with X, with pencil corrections, can be found in PMP 4, Box 8.
105. *ITSCH*, 584.
106. Darelle "Dino" Butler, "About Mr X . . . ," in Serle L. Chapman (ed.), *We, The People of Earth and Elders—Volume II* (Missoula, MT: Mountain Press Publishing, 2001), 248.
107. PM, Leonard Peltier parole hearing notes, July 2009. MMC.
108. Scott Anderson, "The Martyrdom of Leonard Peltier," *Outside*, June 1995.
109. PM, Leonard Peltier parole hearing notes, July 2009. MMC.
110. Bruce Ellison, interviewed by LR, November 1, 2022.
111. PM Statement for Peltier Weekend, July 1995. MMC. The rally statement was adapted from a draft of "Mean Spirit," *Outside*, October 1995, which was Matthiessen's angry response to Anderson's takedown of *Crazy Horse*, published in the same magazine four months earlier.

23 · MURYO SENSEI

1. See Lawrence Shainberg, "Emptying the Bell," *Tricycle*, September 1993.
2. Dorothy Friedman, interviewed by LR, May 26, 2019.
3. PM, "Dai-En" (Dorothy Friedman) Dharma talk, August 9, 1996. PMP 4, Box 14.
4. Ibid.

5. Charles McGrath, "Are 3 Novels, Revised as One, a New Book?," *New York Times*, November 11, 2008.
6. Dorothy Friedman, interviewed by LR, May 26, 2019.
7. PM to Helen Rattray, n.d. [August 1985]. PMP 4, Box 40.
8. Quoted in Trip Gabriel, "The Nature of Peter Matthiessen," *New York Times*, June 10, 1990.
9. PM, "Dai-En" (Dorothy Friedman) Dharma talk, August 9, 1996. PMP 4, Box 14.
10. Peter Becker, "Zen and the Art of Peter Matthiessen," *M inc.*, July 1991.
11. PM, "Introduction to Zen Practice, Ocean Zendo," n.d. MMC.
12. Lee Carlson, *Passage to Nirvana* (New York: Henry Chapin & Sons, 2010), 73.
13. PM, "Oklahoma City: Taking Care of Things," May 25, 1995. MMC.
14. PM, 9/11 Dharma talk, n.d. MMC.
15. PM, "Buddhism in America" keynote speech, January 1997. MMC.
16. *NHDR*, 148.
17. PM, "Gratitude" teisho, April 13, 1997. MMC.
18. Dorothy Friedman, interviewed by LR, May 26, 2019.
19. Elizabeth Porebski, interviewed by LR (with Peter Porebski), March 6, 2021.
20. Megan Chaskey, interviewed by LR (with Scott Chaskey), March 28, 2021.
21. Linda Coleman, interviewed by LR, May 27, 2019.
22. Mitchell Cantor, interviewed by LR, February 7, 2019.
23. PM, Memoir notes. MMC.
24. PM, Untitled Dharma talk, January 14, 1997. MMC.
25. PM, "Gratitude" teisho, April 13, 1997. MMC.
26. Ibid.
27. Margo Hammond, "An Examined Life Worth Sharing," *Tampa Bay Times*, October 29, 2002.
28. MM, interviewed by LR, May 26, 2019.
29. PM to Tom DeKay, n.d. MMC.
30. MM, interviewed by LR, May 26, 2019.
31. MM, interviewed by LR, November 16, 2018.
32. MM, "Introduction," speech given at the Sun Valley Writers' Conference, 2000. PMP 4, Box 12.
33. PM to MM, April 12, 1982. MMC.
34. PM to MM, November 1, 1982. MMC.
35. MM to PM, October 28, 1982. MMC.
36. MM to PM, n.d. [November 1986]. MMC.
37. Sherry Lord, quoted in Bruce Beans, "The Wildness Within," *Philadelphia Magazine*, June 24, 1990.
38. Alex Matthiessen, interviewed by Jeff Sewald, n.d. JSC.
39. Lucas Matthiessen, interviewed by Jeff Sewald, n.d. JSC.
40. Rue Matthiessen, interviewed by LR, September 25, 2018.
41. Lucas Matthiessen, interviewed by LR, September 28, 2018.
42. MM to PM, May 20, 1991. MMC.
43. MM, email to LR, September 25, 2023.
44. MM, interviewed by LR, March 27, 2021.
45. MM to PM, March 4, 1997. MMC.
46. Sarah Koenig, interviewed by LR, August 9, 2022.
47. Steve Byers, interviewed by LR, November 17, 2018.
48. PM, quoted in Bruce Beans, "The Wildness Within," *Philadelphia Magazine*, June 24, 1990.
49. MM to PM, July 21, 1994. MMC.
50. MM to PM, January 21, 1996. MMC.
51. Antonia Koenig, interviewed by LR, October 2, 2020.
52. Alex Matthiessen, interviewed by LR, February 17, 2023.
53. Sarah Koenig, interviewed by LR, August 9, 2022.
54. PM to Sara Carey Matthiessen, October 21, 1994. MMC.

55. Lucas Matthiessen, interviewed by LR, September 28, 2018.
56. Lucas Matthiessen, *First Light: A Journey Out of Darkness* (New York: Arcade Publishing, 2023), 107.
57. Lucas Matthiessen, interviewed by author, September 28, 2018.
58. MM to PM, April 11, 1982. MMC.
59. PM, "The Desert Sea," *Geo*, September 1984.
60. Lucas Matthiessen, *First Light*, 157.
61. Ibid., 158.
62. Rue Matthiessen, *Castles and Ruins: Unraveling Family Mysteries and Literary Legacy in the Irish Countryside* (Spokane, WA: Latah Books, 2024), 155.
63. Rue Matthiessen, interviewed by LR, September 25, 2018.
64. Alex Matthiessen, interviewed by LR, February 17, 2023.
65. Ibid.
66. PM, "Survivor of the Hunter," *The New Yorker*, April 24, 1995.
67. PM, "Zen and Whales" Dharma talk, n.d. MMC.
68. Alex Matthiessen, interviewed by LR, February 17, 2023.
69. Lawrence Shainberg, "Emptying the Bell," *Tricycle*, September 1993.
70. Molly Wheelwright, interviewed by LR, September 17, 2019.
71. Joan Jiko Halifax, interviewed by LR, January 21, 2020.
72. PM, "Zen and Iraq" Dharma talk, 2004. MMC.
73. PM to Craig Carpenter, n.d. MMC. Truman located the epitaph in Tombstone, Arizona, and credited it to "Jack Williams," who did his "damnedest."

24 · THE WATSON YEARS

1. PM to [Name withheld by request], December 9, 1996.
2. *SC*, iv.
3. PM, quoted in Michael Shnayerson, "Higher Matthiessen," *Vanity Fair*, December 1991.
4. PM to JH, December 12, 1991. JHP, Box 32.
5. "An Evening with Peter Matthiessen," February 12, 1992, City Arts & Lectures.
6. PM to MM, May 15, 1992. MMC.
7. *ELM*, 18.
8. Ibid., 62.
9. Thomas Laird, interviewed by LR, May 4, 2023.
10. *BOH*, 5.
11. PM to MM, June 30, 1992. MMC.
12. PM, "Tiger in the Snow," *The New Yorker*, January 6, 1997.
13. PM to MM, June 30, 1992. MMC.
14. *BOH*, 12.
15. Ibid., 20.
16. Ibid., 27.
17. PM to MM, July 11, 1992. MMC.
18. PM to MM, July 15, 1992. MMC.
19. *BOH*, 82.
20. Ibid., xiii.
21. PM, "Elephant Days" (unpublished manuscript), February 1996. MMC.
22. *BOH*, 184.
23. Ibid., 4.
24. Ibid., xiv.
25. John Irving to PM, August 16, 1992. PMP 4, Box 39.
26. PM, *Lost Man's River* draft, January 1, 1990. PMP 1, Box 28.
27. John Irving to PM, August 16, 1992. PMP 4, Box 39.
28. PM, "Watson: Critiques," n.d. MMC.
29. PM to JH, December 11, 1992. JHP, Box 32.

30. *EOE*, 9. See also Katy Vine, "The Birdman of Texas," *Texas Monthly*, May 2011. An amusing character sketch of Emanuel can be found in Lawrence Wright, *God Save Texas* (New York: Alfred A. Knopf, 2018), 238–41.
31. *BOH*, 126.
32. Ibid., 131.
33. Ibid., 164. Another perspective on the crane journeys can be found in Victor Emanuel, *One More Warbler* (Austin: University of Texas Press, 2017).
34. PM to Candida Donadio, June 29, 1993. Collection of LR.
35. PM to Gary Snyder, n.d. [November 1993]. Gary Snyder Papers, UC Davis, Box 2.
36. MM to PM, July 21, 1994. MMC.
37. PM to Bill Swainson, December 12, 1993. PMP 1, Box 6.
38. HN to PM, January 9, 1995. PMP 4, Box 40.
39. HN, email to LR, September 12, 2023.
40. PM, interviewed by HN, November 21, 1996, for the Lannan Foundation.
41. PM to JH, April 9, 1995. JHP, Box 32. Matthiessen recounts a conversation with Jason Epstein in this letter to Jim Harrison, and compares the situation to the prior one with Joe Fox and *Far Tortuga*.
42. Bob Loomis, interviewed by LR, May 19, 2019.
43. MM, interviewed by LR, August 10, 2018.
44. PM to Daniel Menaker, n.d. [April 1995]. MMC.
45. PM to JH, April 9, 1995. JHP, Box 32.
46. See *BOH*, 256–59.
47. Neil Olson, email to LR, May 16, 2023.
48. Neil Olson to PM, April 14, 1995. PMP 4, Box 3.
49. Neil Olson to PM, June 1, 1995. PMP 4, Box 3.
50. "Philip Roth: The Art of Fiction No. 84," *The Paris Review*, No. 93, Fall 1984.
51. "Peter Matthiessen: The Art of Fiction No. 157," *The Paris Review*, No. 150, Spring 1999. See also PM, "The Long Journey: Zen and the Writing Life" (audio recording), San Francisco Zen Center, 1998; PM, "The Problem of Reality," January 9, 1999. KWLS.
52. Neil Olson to PM, June 1, 1995. PMP 4, Box 3.
53. Neil Olson to PM, September 19, 1995. PMP 4, Box 3.
54. PM to Neil Olson and Candida Donadio, n.d. [December 1995]. MMC.
55. MM to PM, January 11, 1996. MMC.
56. PM to MM, January 25, 1996. MMC.
57. *BOH*, 209.
58. Alex Matthiessen to MM, February 11, 1996. MMC.
59. PM, "Elephant Days" (unpublished manuscript), February 1996. MMC. See also *TTS*.
60. *BOH*, 245.
61. MM to PM, February 12, 1996. MMC.
62. MM, interviewed by LR, March 27, 2021.
63. PM to WSM, March 26, 1996. WSMP, Sixth Accession, Correspondence, Box 14.
64. Lucas Matthiessen, *First Light: A Journey Out of Darkness* (New York: Arcade Publishing, 2023), 183.
65. PM to JH, n.d. [May 1996]. JHP, Box 32.
66. PM to WSM, March 13, 1997. WSMP, Sixth Accession, Correspondence, Box 14.
67. PM to Deborah Futter, June 26, 1996. MMC.
68. Ibid.
69. Neil Olson, email to LR, May 16, 2023.
70. PM to Deborah Futter, n.d. [August 1996]. MMC.
71. PM to HN, January 15, 1997. MMC.
72. Ibid.
73. PM to Christopher MacLehose, August 20, 1996. MMC.
74. MM, interviewed by Jeff Sewald, 2006. JSC.
75. PM to JH, n.d. [February 1997]. JHP, Box 32.
76. PM to JH, September 22, 1997. JHP, Box 32.

77. Jason Epstein to PM, November 4, 1997. PMP 4, Box 39.
78. Michael Mewshaw, "Mired in the Everglades," *Washington Post*, February 8, 1998.
79. A. O. Scott, "Sins of the Father," *Newsday*, December 21, 1997.
80. *LMR*, 28.
81. Ibid., 141.
82. Ibid., 233.
83. PM to JH, September 22, 1997. JHP, Box 32.
84. PM, quoted in Charles McGrath, "Are 3 Novels, Revised as One, a New Book?," *New York Times*, November 11, 2008.
85. *SC*, iv.
86. PM to Deborah Futter, May 24, 1996. MMC.
87. Neil Olson to PM, July 8, 1996. PMP 4, Box 3.
88. PM to JH, June 22, 1998. JHP, Box 32.
89. PM to Tim Cahill, n.d. [November 1986]. Collection of Tim Cahill.
90. *BB*, 29.
91. Ibid., 195.
92. Ibid., 190–91.
93. Ibid., 369.
94. Ibid., 409.
95. PM, interviewed by Bret Anthony Johnston, 2008, National Book Foundation.
96. Sven Birkerts, "Heart of the Swamp," *New York Times*, April 11, 1999.
97. Annie Dillard to PM, n.d. [c. August 1999]. PMP 4, Box 39.
98. Saul Bellow to PM, July 29, 1999. MMC.
99. PM to Saul Bellow, August 8, 1999. PMP 4, Box 39.
100. PM to Neil Olson, June 29, 1999. PMP 4, Box 12.
101. PM to John Burnham Schwartz, n.d. [July 1999]. MMC.
102. PM to Don DeLillo, June 16, 1999. Don DeLillo Papers, Harry Ransom Center, University of Texas at Austin, Container 100.8.
103. PM, quoted in David Streitfeld, "Book Report," *Washington Post*, May 9, 1999.
104. PM, quoted in Joseph P. Kahn, "A Writer's Wide, Wild World," *Boston Globe*, June 1, 1999.
105. "Peter Matthiessen: The Art of Fiction No. 157," *The Paris Review*, No. 150, Spring 1999.
106. PM, Heinz Award acceptance speech, March 7, 2000. PMP 3, Box 26.
107. PM to Bill Clinton, January 9, 2001. MMC.
108. PM, quoted in Jim Reilly, "Two Old Runners Bring Warnings About the Power of Money," Syracuse *Post-Standard*, April 20, 2001.
109. PM to Janet Reno, January 21, 1997. PMP 4, Box 25.
110. PM to "Mr. Lewis," n.d. [May 2000]. MMC.
111. PM, Press statement, May 17, 2000. MMC.
112. PM, Kurt Vonnegut Jr., William Styron, Rose Styron, E. L. Doctorow et al., "United States v. Leonard Peltier," *New York Review of Books*, July 20, 2000.
113. PM to Janet Reno, December 22, 2000. MMC.
114. Bruce Ellison, interviewed by LR, November 1, 2022.
115. PM, quoted in Jim Reilly, "Two Old Runners Bring Warnings About the Power of Money," Syracuse *Post-Standard*, April 20, 2001.
116. PM to Bill Clinton, January 9, 2001. MMC.
117. PM, quoted in Jim Reilly, "Two Old Runners Bring Warnings About the Power of Money," Syracuse *Post-Standard*, April 20, 2001.
118. PM, "The Tragedy of Leonard Peltier vs. the US," *New York Review of Books*, November 19, 2009.
119. PM to MM, n.d. [November 2001]. MMC.
120. Apsley Cherry-Garrard, quoted in *EOE*, 93.
121. *EOE*, 122.
122. Ibid., 179.
123. Ibid., 94.
124. *BOH*, 13.

125. PM to JH, March 28, 1999. JHP, Box 32.
126. PM, quoted in Suzi Gablik, "Morning Glory," *Resurgence*, No. 210, January/February 2002.
127. Terry Tempest Williams, interviewed by Jeff Sewald, August 31, 2006. JSC. A copy of Matthiessen's original speech, "Fire and Grit," given in June 1999, can be found in the Orion Society Papers, Texas Tech University, Box 4.
128. Suzi Gablik, "Morning Glory," *Resurgence*, No. 210, January/February 2002.
129. PM, Notes for Omega address, September 6, 2001. PMP 4, Box 11.
130. PM, "Human Nature Versus Nature," September 28, 1999. MMC. An extract of Matthiessen's lecture was published as "Get Down to Earth," *The Guardian*, October 30, 1999.
131. PM, quoted in Suzi Gablik, "Morning Glory," *Resurgence*, No. 210, January/February 2002.
132. PM, "Foreword," *Tracking Arctic Oil: The Environmental Price of Drilling the Arctic National Wildlife Refuge*, Natural Resources Defense Council, n.d.
133. Subhankar Banerjee, interviewed by LR, September 3, 2021.
134. PM, "In the Great Country," in Subhankar Banerjee, *Seasons of Life and Land* (Seattle: Braided River, 2003). All quotes about Matthiessen's July 2002 trip come from this essay.
135. Subhankar Banerjee, interviewed by LR, September 3, 2021.
136. PM, "Footprints in the Last Wild Place" draft, for *Outside*, 2003. See PMP 3, Box 22.
137. Roger Tory Peterson Medal citation, April 2003. PMP 3, Box 27.
138. Margo Hammond, "An Examined Life Worth Sharing," *Tampa Bay Times*, October 29, 2002.
139. The infamous words belonged to Interior Secretary Gale Norton. See "A Curious Commemoration," *Los Angeles Times*, March 17, 2003.
140. Ted Stevens, quoted in Joel Connelly, "In the Northwest: Arctic Photographer Gets a Cold Shoulder in D.C.," *Seattle Post-Intelligencer*, May 15, 2003. Subhankar Banerjee claims that Stevens called him a "liar" in the Senate.
141. PM, *Charlie Rose*, PBS, December 9, 2003. See https://charlierose.com/videos/8293.
142. Randall Kremer, quoted in Timothy Egan, "Smithsonian Is No Safe Haven for Exhibit on Arctic Wildlife Refuge," *New York Times*, May 2, 2003.
143. Subhankar Banerjee, interviewed by LR, September 3, 2021.
144. Timothy Egan, "Smithsonian Is No Safe Haven for Exhibit on Arctic Wildlife Refuge," *New York Times*, May 2, 2003.
145 Subhankar Banerjee, interviewed by LR, September 3, 2021. See, in addition to the articles referenced above, Patt Morrison, "Over at the Smithsonian, More Looting, of the Political Kind," *Los Angeles Times*, May 6, 2003; Elizabeth Olson, "Censorship and Politics? Views Differ over Exhibit," *New York Times*, May 21, 2003; Debbie S. Miller, "Bringing an Exhibit to Light," *SFGATE*, November 26, 2003; Robert Smith, "A Panorama of Alaska That Extends to the Senate," *New York Times*, October 13, 2004; and Regina Hackett, "Seattleite Subhankar Banerjee's Photos of Arctic 'Life and Land' Are Winning Hearts," *Seattle Post-Intelligencer*, June 24, 2005. A good retrospective overview of the full controversy, as well as its aftermath, is Finis Dunaway, "Did One Photograph Change the Fate of the Arctic Wildlife Refuge?," *Washington Post*, March 3, 2023.
146. PM, quoted in Joseph P. Kahn, "A Writer's Wide, Wild World," *Boston Globe*, June 1, 1999.
147. JH to PM, December 30, 2000. PMP 4, Box 39.
148. PM, "The Spirit of Place," 2002. KWLS.
149. Amor Towles, interviewed by LR, April 12, 2019.
150. PM to Neil Olson, June 2, 1999. PMP 4, Box 12.
151. SC, x.
152. "Peter Matthiessen: The Art of Fiction No. 157," *The Paris Review*, No. 150, Spring 1999.
153. PM, "The Spirit of Place," 2002. KWLS.
154. A copy of the master outline can be found in PMP 4, Box 3.

155. Neil Olson to PM, January 26, 2004. PMP 4, Box 3.
156. Neil Olson, interviewed by LR, January 28, 2021.
157. *SC*, iii.
158. PM, quoted in Hillel Italie, "The Absurdity of Life," Associated Press, November 14, 2004.
159. Neil Olson, interviewed by LR, January 28, 2021.
160. PM to Christine Jordis, July 7, 2005. MMC.
161. PM, "Inside the Endangered Arctic Refuge," *New York Review of Books*, October 19, 2006. See also PM, "Alaska: Big Oil and the Inupiat-Americans," *New York Review of Books*, November 22, 2007, based on yet another expedition with Subhankar Banerjee.
162. PM to "LL BB," n.d. [2007]. MMC.
163. PM to Judy Sternlight, n.d. [March 2007]. MMC.
164. PM, Notes on a July 12, 2007, meeting with Judy Sternlight. PMP 4, Box 3.
165. PM to Judy Sternlight, n.d. [June 2007]. MMC.
166. PM to Judy Sternlight, n.d. [August 2007]. MMC.
167. PM to Judy Sternlight, n.d. [June 2007]. MMC.
168. Judy Sternlight, email to LR, March 29, 2019.
169. *SC*, 694.
170. *KMW*, 284.
171. *SC*, 183.
172. Jonathan Miles, "Rebuilding a Classic, Bone by Bone," *Men's Journal*, March 2008.
173. PM to Judy Sternlight, n.d. [March 2007]. MMC.
174. PM to Judy Sternlight, n.d. [July 2007]. MMC.
175. Lucas Matthiessen, interviewed by LR, September 28, 2018.
176. Philip Gourevitch, quoted in Tom Clavin, "Paris Review Toasts Matthiessen at Revel," *East Hampton Press*, April 16, 2008.
177. Michael Dirda, "An Epic of the Everglades," *New York Review of Books*, May 15, 2008.
178. Charles McGrath, "Are 3 Novels, Revised as One, a New Book?," *New York Times*, November 11, 2008.
179. PM, *On Point with Tom Ashbrook*, WBUR, October 8, 2008.
180. Hillel Italie, "Matthiessen Wins Honor for Fiction," Associated Press, November 20, 2008. See also Motoko Rich, "Book Prizes Awarded with Nod to History," *New York Times*, November 20, 2008; Bob Thompson, "Hemings Saga Wins National Book Prize," *Washington Post*, November 20, 2008; and "At Play in a Book's Adulation," *East Hampton Star*, November 27, 2008.
181. Neil Olson, interviewed by LR, January 28, 2021.
182. PM, National Book Award speech, November 19, 2008. See https://vimeo.com/2423212.
183. PM, "Short Statement for AAAL Display," May 2010. PMP 4, Box 62.

25 · HOMEGOING

1. *IP*, 221. Matthiessen reflects on *Heimgang*, "the return to the lost paradise at the source of all man's yearnings," in *BOH*, 6. See also *SL*, 59, 201.
2. Steve Byers, interviewed by LR, November 17, 2018.
3. PM, "Bear Trap Canyon," in Don George (ed.), *Better Than Fiction: True Travel Tales from Great Fiction Writers* (London: Lonely Planet, 2012). The remaining quotes in this section come from this source. See also PM, interviewed by Patty Satalia for "Conversations from Penn State," 2010.
4. PM to JH, March 16, 2005. JHP, Box 32.
5. PM, "Bear Trap Canyon," in Don George (ed.), *Better Than Fiction*.
6. Ibid.
7. PM, interviewed by Jeff Sewald, May 2006. JSC.
8. PM, interviewed by Jeff Sewald, December 2005. JSC.
9. PM to JH, n.d. [2012]. JHP, Box 32.
10. PM, Memoir notes. MMC. The final draft dates to March 15, 2014.

11. PM, "SASQ-NOVEL," n.d. MMC.
12. PM to JH, n.d. [2001]. JHP, Box 32.
13. Bernie Glassman, quoted in Adam Gopnik, "Livelihood," *The New Yorker*, May 22, 1989.
14. Bernie Glassman, *Bearing Witness* (New York: Blue Rider Press, 1998), xiii–xiv.
15. PM, "Dancing at Auschwitz" draft, October 2010. MMC.
16. Bernie Glassman, *Bearing Witness*, 6.
17. PM, "Writer Peter Matthiessen 'On the River Styx,'" *Fresh Air*, April 6, 1989. See freshairarchive.org/segments/writer-peter-matthiessen-river-styx.
18. Matthiessen's notebook from a "street retreat" in April 1993 is held in PMP 4, Box 25. Matthiessen expanded these notes once he got back to his computer; a copy of those is in MMC.
19. PM, "The Coming of Age of American Zen," Keynote Speech at the Buddhism in America conference, January 1997. MMC.
20. PM, Auschwitz journal, November 1996. PMP 4, Box 23.
21. Ibid.
22. Peter Cunningham, "Bearing Witness: Notes from Auschwitz," *Tricycle*, Spring 1997.
23. PM, Auschwitz journal, November 1996. PMP 4, Box 23.
24. Linda Coleman, interviewed by LR, May 27, 2019.
25. PM, "Dancing at Auschwitz" draft, October 2010. MMC.
26. PM to JH, December 10, 1996. JHP, Box 32.
27. PM, Auschwitz journal, November 1996. PMP 4, Box 23.
28. Peter Cunningham, "Bearing Witness: Notes from Auschwitz," *Tricycle*, Spring 1997.
29. PM, Auschwitz Dharma talk, January 14, 1997. MMC.
30. PM, "Dancing at Auschwitz" draft, October 2010. MMC.
31. Ibid.
32. PM, quoted in Alec Michod, "Living on the Edge of Life: A Final Interview with Peter Matthiessen," *Los Angeles Review of Books*, April 6, 2014.
33. Ibid. A fictionalized account of his encounter with Marian Kołodziej ("Malan") can be found in *IP*, 188.
34. Ibid. See also Jonathan Meiburg, "An Interview with Peter Matthiessen," *The Believer*, June 1, 2014.
35. *IP*, 165.
36. *SL*, 261. The Bible reference is Luke 23:43.
37. PM, Iscol Distinguished Environmental Lecture, given April 23, 2012. MMC.
38. Victor Emanuel, interviewed by LR, September 11, 2023.
39. MM, interviewed by LR, March 27, 2021.
40. PM to Jinny Cardenas, n.d. [December 2012]. MMC.
41. James Salter, "Postscript: Peter Matthiessen (1927–2014)," *The New Yorker*, April 14, 2014. See also Terry McDonell, *The Accidental Life: An Editor's Notes on Writing and Writers* (New York: Vintage, 2016), 200–201.
42. Victor Emanuel, interviewed by LR, October 12, 2018.
43. PM to Jinny Cardenas, n.d. [December 2012]. MMC.
44. Russell Drumm, "Swept to Her Death by Sandy's Wrath," *East Hampton Star*, November 1, 2012.
45. Carrie Ann Salvi, "The Storm Damage Is Grim and Widespread," *East Hampton Star*, November 8, 2012.
46. Alex Matthiessen, interviewed by LR, February 17, 2023.
47. *EOE*, 109.
48. *SNA*, 129.
49. PM, "Homegoing: Talks on Zen Buddhism (1988–2003)," unpublished manuscript. PMP 4, Box 25.
50. Ibid. See also *SL*, 81.
51. Ibid. Matthiessen also discusses the exercise in "The Long Journey: Zen and the Writing Life" (audio recording), San Francisco Zen Center, 1998; and Jonathan White, *Talking on the Water* (San Francisco: Sierra Club Books, 1994), 244.
52. MM to PM, July 21, 1994. MMC.

53. PM, "Hans Hokusan Zazen-Kai Memorial," September 1997. MMC.
54. PM, George Plimpton memorial talk, 2003. MMC.
55. PM, Tom Guinzburg eulogy, 2010. MMC.
56. Randy Kennedy, "Robert Hughes, Art Critic Whose Writing Was Elegant and Contentious, Dies at 74," *New York Times*, August 6, 2012.
57. WS to PM, December 15, 1985, in Rose Styron and R. Blakeslee Gilpin (eds.), *Selected Letters of William Styron* (New York: Random House, 2012), 577.
58. Susanna Styron, interviewed by LR, December 14, 2019.
59. PM, "In Memory: William Styron," *Paris Review*, No. 179, Winter 2006.
60. PM, Rohatsu teisho, December 8, 2006. MMC.
61. James Salter, "Postscript: Peter Matthiessen (1927–2014)," *The New Yorker*, April 14, 2014.
62. PM, quoted in Jonathan White, *Talking on the Water*, 245.
63. Matthiessen made the comment about a forest mushroom in several conversations with various people, and in a letter to Jim Harrison: "I've lost too many precious friends in recent years, so I count on you to take care of yourself and hang in there. Also, to stifle any eulogies at my burial and let me 'blow away in the woods like an old mushroom' (the last ever-so-estimable wish of Nyogen Senzaki)." See PM to JH, September 22, 1997. JHP, Box 32.
64. PM, quoted in Jeff Himmelman, "Peter Matthiessen's Homegoing," *New York Times Magazine*, April 3, 2014. See also an interview he did with Howard Norman: "We can't hang on to the cherry blossoms. . . . The whole essence of Buddhist teaching is not to cling, not to hang on to things." HNC, Box 2.
65. PM to Jinny Cardenas, n.d. [December 2012]. MMC.
66. Michel Engu Dobbs, interviewed by LR, March 28, 2021.
67. Ibid.
68. Peter Matthiessen Wheelwright, interviewed by LR, September 13, 2019.
69. MM, interviewed by LR, March 27, 2021.
70. Alex Matthiessen, interviewed by LR, February 17, 2023.
71. JH to PM, October 17, 2013. PMP 4, Box 39. See also JH to PM, February 28, 2013, PMP 4, Box 39.
72. Terry McDonell, *The Accidental Life*, 201.
73. Frederick Turner, interviewed by LR, November 4, 2019.
74. Carl Safina, interviewed by LR, June 12, 2020.
75. Sarah Koenig, interviewed by LR, August 9, 2022.
76. Lucas Matthiessen, *First Light: A Journey Out of Darkness* (New York: Arcade Publishing, 2023), 209.
77. Steve Byers, interviewed by LR, November 17, 2018.
78. Ngaere Macray, interviewed by LR, August 11, 2020.
79. MM, interviewed by LR, March 27, 2021.
80. Dorothy Friedman, interviewed by LR, May 26, 2019.
81. Rue Matthiessen, interviewed by LR, March 25, 2021.
82. Antonia Koenig, interviewed by LR, October 2, 2020.
83. MM, interviewed by LR, March 27, 2021.
84. Rebecca Saletan, interviewed by LR, September 3, 2020.
85. MM to PM, October 28, 2013. MMC.
86. MM, interviewed by LR, March 27, 2021.
87. PM to MM, February 14, 2014. MMC. This note—possibly his last to anybody—was written on the back of a postcard showing Carel Fabritius's *The Goldfinch*. Donna Tartt's novel of the same name was at the top of the *New York Times* Best Sellers list at the time, thus the reference to his "lifetime best-seller list."
88. Carl Safina, interviewed by LR, June 12, 2020. See also Carl Safina, "Peter Matthiessen," *Audubon*, July/August 2014.
89. Quoted in PM, Notes on doctor's meeting, January 20, 2014. MMC.
90. Mark Adams, "Peter Matthiessen's Many Lives," *Men's Journal*, May 2014.
91. Alec Michod, "Living on the Edge of Life: A Final Interview with Peter Matthiessen," *Los Angeles Review of Books*, April 6, 2014.

92. Jonathan Meiburg, "An Interview with Peter Matthiessen," *The Believer*, June 1, 2014.
93. MM, interviewed by LR, November 17, 2018.
94. Linda Coleman, interviewed by LR, May 27, 2019.
95. Lucas Matthiessen, interviewed by LR, March 26, 2021.
96. MM, interviewed by LR, November 17, 2018.
97. Myrna Davis, interviewed by LR, March 28, 2021.
98. Antonia Koenig, interviewed by LR, October 2, 2020.
99. Alex Matthiessen, interviewed by LR, February 17, 2023.
100. PM to JH, April 15, 2000. JHP, Box 32.
101. Neil Olson, interviewed by LR, January 28, 2021.
102. Jeff Wheelwright, interviewed by LR, February 22, 2020.
103. Frederick Turner, interviewed by LR, November 4, 2019.
104. MM, interviewed by LR, May 26, 2019.
105. Alex Matthiessen, interviewed by LR, February 17, 2023.
106. Lucas Matthiessen, *First Light*, 211.
107. Rue Matthiessen, interviewed by LR, March 25, 2021.
108. Lucas Matthiessen, interviewed by LR, March 26, 2021.
109. Rue Matthiessen, interviewed by LR, March 25, 2021.
110. PM, quoted in Mark Adams, "Peter Matthiessen's Many Lives," *Men's Journal*, May 2014.
111. Michel Engu Dobbs, interviewed by LR, March 28, 2021.
112. PM, "Homegoing: Talks on Zen Buddhism (1988–2003)," unpublished manuscript. PMP 4, Box 25.
113. Alex Matthiessen, interviewed by LR, February 17, 2023.
114. Lucas Matthiessen, *First Light*, 212.
115. Piedy Lumet (née Bailey), interviewed by LR, August 10, 2018.
116. Sarah Koenig, interviewed by LR, August 9, 2022.
117. MM, interviewed by LR, November 17, 2018.
118. Lucas Matthiessen, *First Light*, 213.
119. Rue Matthiessen, interviewed by LR, March 25, 2021.
120. Alex Matthiessen, interviewed by LR, February 17, 2023.
121. Lucas Matthiessen, *First Light*, 215–16.
122. Lucas Matthiessen, interviewed by LR, March 26, 2021.
123. MM, email to LR, September 9, 2023. See also Lucas Matthiessen, *First Light*, 216.

EPILOGUE

1. Lucas Matthiessen, *First Light: A Journey Out of Darkness* (New York: Arcade Publishing, 2023), 219.
2. Christopher Lehmann-Haupt, "Peter Matthiessen, Lyrical Writer and Naturalist, Is Dead at 86," *New York Times*, April 5, 2014.
3. James Salter, "Postscript: Peter Matthiessen (1927–2014)," *The New Yorker*, April 14, 2014.
4. Maria V. A. Eckhart, "4:40 AM," in . . . *until I write it* (Sagaponack: Sand Dune Press, 2009), 83.
5. Terry McDonell, *The Accidental Life: An Editor's Notes on Writing and Writers* (New York: Vintage, 2016), 204.
6. Ngaere Macray, interviewed by LR, August 11, 2020.
7. Quoted in Sadie Stein, "Classified," *The Paris Review* (online), November 10, 2014.
8. Ibid.
9. *LMR*, 363.
10. PM, "Homegoing: Talks on Zen Buddhism (1988–2003)," unpublished manuscript. PMP 4, Box 25.
11. Ibid.

Index

Page numbers of illustrations appear in italics.

Key to abbreviations: DL = Deborah Love Matthiessen; MM = Maria Eckhart Koenig Matthiessen; PM = Peter Matthiessen; PS = Patricia Brigham "Patsy" Southgate

Note: Titles of Peter Matthiessen's books appear in italics followed by the publication date in parentheses. Titles of Peter Matthiessen's essays, articles, poems, and short stories appear in quotation marks followed by (PM).

Abbey, Edward, 53, 437
Abbot, John and Susan, 298, 299, 318
"Accident, The" (Southern), 131n
Accidental Life, The (McDonell), 581
Adams, Mark, 585
Adams, Robert M., 439
Africa
    Botswana ornithological safari (1977), 426–27
    Congo Basin expedition in search of forest elephants (1985–86), 485
    ecological destruction of, 437n, 447n
    Eritrea expedition (1969), 297–98
    PM in (1969, 1970), 291–98, 301–4, 311–12, 340
    PM surveying West African wildlife in The Gambia, Ivory Coast, and Senegal (1978), 437, 437n
    Selous expedition (1979), 445–47
    Sudan journey and standoff in Nimule (1961), 217–218.
    Zaire trip in search of Congo peafowl (1978), 437
    See also African Silences; Kenya; Tanzania; *Tree Where Man Was Born, The*
African Silences (1991), 294n, 437n
Aga Khan, Prince Sadruddin, 158
Aga Khan, Princess Andrée, 128
Agenda for Tomorrow (Udall), 272
Aitken, Robert, 408, 438

Alaska, 177–79
    Banerjee Arctic book and Smithsonian exhibit controversy, 557–58
    Iñupiat people, 39, 178, 556
    Kenai Peninsula, 177
    muskoxen, 177–78, 261
    Nunivak Island, 177–78, 261
    PM's alarm about oil exploration during visit (2002), 555–58, 561, 669n127
    PM's "Ovibos Moschatus" (later *Oomingmak*), 261, 261n
    PM's visit for *Wildlife in America* (1957), 177–79, 555
    village of Quinhagak, 178
    Yupik people, 177, 178
Allemand, Jeanne (Mme. Salzmann), 79, 89
Amazon/South America expedition (1959–60), 191–208
    as basis for *The Cloud Forest*, 202–8
    Belém, 195–96
    Brasília, 199
    deculturation of Indigenous people, 202, 202n
    drifter Gauvin, 195–96, 251, 627n28
    fellow traveler Templeton, 193–94, 196, 199–200
    funding for, 191
    inspiration for, 192
    journal, 192, 193, 628n54
    Karajá people, 200–201, 203
    Manaus, 196–97

676 · Index

Amazon/South America expedition (1959–60) *(continued)*
  New Yorker series "The Last Wilderness" and, 191–95, 197, 199, 202, 203, 628n40
  Orizona, Brazil, 193, 199–200
  At Play in the Fields of the Lord and, 251–52
  psychedelic ayahuasca, 206–7, 213–14
  in Pucallpa on the Ucayali River, 197–98, 206, 207
  "savage Canueiras," 201
  search for a prehistoric fossil jaw (*mandíbula*), 198, 203–8, 629n83
  search for self and, 200, 205
  travels in Tierra del Fuego, 199
  voyage on the freighter *Venimos*, 191–97, 627n18
American Anthropologist, review of *Under the Mountain Wall*, 239
American Audio Prose Library, 498
American Indian Movement (AIM), 102, 457, 459–61, 464–65, 469, 474–75, 510
American Museum of Natural History, 20, 344
  Archbold in New Guinea and, 220
  Burden's Komodo expedition, 45–46
  PM's Amazon expedition and, 207
  Stout as president, 277
American Ornithology (Wilson), 174
American Renaissance (F. O. Matthiessen), 103
Ames, Alfred, 184
Anderson, Gavin, xvi
Anderson, Scott, 510, 664n111
Andersson, Theodore, 73
Angleton, James, 106, 128
Annaghkeen (DL), 291, 319, 634n108
Antarctica expeditions (1999, 2001), 553–54
Appleton, James, xvi
Appleton, John, 120–21, 139–40
Aquash, Anna Mae, 467, 470
Archbold, Richard, 220, 227
Archibald, George, 533, 541
Arctic National Wildlife Refuge, 186, 555, 556, 561
Arctic National Wildlife Refuge: Seasons of Land and Life (Banerjee), 557
  PM's chapter in, 557
Arnold, Tom, 445–46
"artist-explorer," 174–75
Asian crane excursion (1993), 536
Assateague Island, Maryland, 261
Atlantic Monthly
  editor Edward Weeks at, 95, 100, 109, 184

  PM's "The Fifth Day" accepted, 109
  PM's "Sadie" and, 95, 100, 107, 184, 379
  PM's stories rejected, 109
  PM writing about Native Americans and, 465
  review of *Far Tortuga*, 379
  review of *Wildlife in America*, 184
At Play in the Fields of the Lord (1965), 195, 201, 251–61, 358
  book jacket and bio, 260
  concluding scene, 255–56
  as creative response to PM's travels in North and South America and New Guinea, 251
  critics and reviews, 265–66, 379
  dedication for, 261
  epigraph from Hesse, 254–55n
  film, 267, 267n
  financial success, 266–67
  Fox's editing, 258–60
  influence of *Ishi in Two Worlds*, 254–55n
  literary influences on, 256, 256n
  marketing of, 260
  National Book Awards and, 269, 272, 272n
  PM's spiritual evolution and, 345–46
  release date, 262
  response by publishing houses, 257
  sale to Random House, 257–58
  title of, 251
Auden, W. H., 65
Audubon, John James, 174, 179
  The Birds of America, 174
Audubon magazine
  PM pieces from "Tiger and Crane" research trips, 552
  PM's advocacy for Native Americans and, 454
  PM's article on Botswana ornithological safari, 427
  PM's article on the Nature Conservancy and Hawaii bird habitat, 304
  PM's article on Tanzania, 400–401
  PM's Galápagos Islands trip and, 339
Augenbraum, Harold, 564–65
Auschwitz-Birkenau, Poland
  Glassman and the Bearing Witness Retreat, 570, 573
  interfaith conference, 570
  PM at, 571–72
  Sterbebücher (the Death Books), 571
  See also In Paradise
Auster, Paul, 4, 604n5
Australia, xii, 639n9
  great white shark expedition (1970), 308–9
  PM in (1961), 236

PM's Queensland trip (1996), 541–42
Tasmania, 553

Badoud, Lucic "Youki," 112n
Baer, Suzie, 506
Baiji, Dawa Gyalpo, xvii
Baikal: Sacred Sea of Siberia (1992), 509n
Bailey, Mary "Piedy" (later Piedy Lumet), 84, 449, 588
Baker, John H., 184
Baldwin, James, 117
  "Everybody's Protest Novel," 116
Baldwin, Lois, 48
Banerjee, Subhankar, 555–56, 557, 561
  Arctic National Wildlife Refuge: Seasons of Land and Life, 557
  PM's advocacy and, 557–58
Banks, Dennis, 474–75, 476
Bannerman, Helen, 36
Banyacya, Thomas, 409–11, 413, 425
Barbados, 193, 194
Baro, Gene, 216
Barry, Ellen, 127
Barry, Joseph A., 72
Baruch, Bernard, 27
Bass, Rick, 503
Bates, Henry Walter, 192
  The Naturalist on the River Amazons, 165, 192, 196
Bates, Marston, 202
Baumgarten, Bernice, 107
  becomes PM's agent (1951), 107
  client list, 107
  Partisans and, 159
  PM and *The New Yorker*, 172–73
  PM's novel-in-progress rejected by, 109, 616n52
  PM's rejections from publishers, 109, 117
  retires, 190
  sells PM's first novel, *Race Rock*, 136–37
Beard, Peter, 343
Belém, Brazil, 193, 195–96, 267n
Bellow, Saul, 147, 380, 380n, 429, 435, 548
  Henderson the Rain King, 256n
Bemelmans, Ludwig, 75
Benchley, Peter, 380, 309n
Benedict, Ruth, 65, 211
  The Chrysanthemum and the Sword, 65
Bigelow, Lisa Barclay, 191, 201
bigfoot (Sasquatch), xiv, 383, 389–400, 402–5, 518, 561
  Carpenter and, 414–15, 415n, 423–24
  creature named "Oliver" and, 396–97
  Crew's plaster cast of a footprint, 393, 414
  as a cultural fixation, 395
  Everglades "Swamp Ape Expedition," 488
  Fitzgerald, Jean, and husband, 397–400, 399n, 402, 648–49n77
  Florida sightings, 488
  the Gillespies and, 402–3, 402n
  In the Spirit of Crazy Horse and, 474
  New Yorker funds PM's search, 392
  Patterson-Gimlin film, 403–4, 649n103
  PM and Douglas Blue, 389, 390–91, 394–95, 396, 402, 403, 415–16, 647–48n35
  PM focuses on bigfoot in Native American lore, 410, 411, 415, 423–25, 442, 447, 451–53, 460, 655n10
  PM's contract with Willhoite, 391, 391n
  PM's eight-state trip (1979), 451–53
  PM's "The Figure on the Road" (unfinished short story), 400, 649n85
  PM's literature survey for, 395
  PM's Northern California expedition (1975), 391–94, 648–49n77, 648n49
  PM's "SASQ-NOVEL," 569
  PM's second California trip (1976), 402–4
  PM's spiritual quest and, 404–5
  PM's strange sighting, 400, 402, 649n85
  PM's untitled, unfinished manuscript on bigfoot, 389, 404–5
  PM's Utah trip (1979), 442
  PM's visit to the Hopis (1977), 423–25
  Wallace hoax, 399, 399n
  Willhoite and, 391–95, 391n, 397, 402
"Bird of Passage" (PM), 87
Birds of America, The (Audubon), 174
Birds of Heaven, The: Travels with Cranes (2001), 553
  Amur River, Russia, voyage and search for cranes and (1993), 533
  Asian crane excursion in Far East and China and (1993), 536
  book launch (2001), 555
  concept for, 534
Black Hills Alliance (BHA), 460, 461
Blondin, Antoine, 136
Blower, John, 333
Blue, Douglas Overton, 389, 390, 394–95, 402, 403, 415–16, 647–48n35
  meets PM, 409, 410, 411
Blue Meridian (1971), 286, 304, 309n, 311
  Random House publishes, 308, 430
  whale hunt in, 309n
  on whale song, 7
"Blue Pearl of Siberia, The" (PM), 509n
Blue Water, White Death (film), 302, 308–9, 309n

678 · Index

Bly, Robert, 136
Bodmer, Karl, 175
Boese, Gilbert, 437, 437n
Bonaventure Island, Quebec, Canada, 98
  described in *Wildlife in America*, 98–99
  PM's birding expedition with Sherry Lord, 98–99
Bone by Bone (1999), 546–50, 553
  creative challenge of, 547–48
  critics and reviews, 548–49
  PM dissatisfaction with launch, 548–49, 558
  publication date, 548
  title of, 546
  as Watson "continuation" (Watson III), 546
Borges, Jorge Luis, 4
Botswana ornithological safari (1977), 426–27
Boudreaux, Lee, 542, 544
Bouvier, Lee, 41
Bowles, Paul: *The Sheltering Sky*, 256
Boyes, Edward, 69, 70
Bradlee, Ben, 105, 172, 173, 625n25
Braider, Donald and Carol, 157, 162
Brandt & Brandt literary agency, 107
Bray, David Kaonohiokala, 413
Brazilian Adventure (Fleming), 202
"Brazilian Chronicle" (PM), 199, 203
Brinkley, Douglas, 175
Broekhuijse, Jan, 211, 221–23, 225, 227, 231, 232, 234n
Bronx Zoo, 20, 22, 395–96
Brooks, Rae, 184
Brown, Tina, 539
Broyard, Anatole, 379
Buchwald, Art, 75, 126
Buckley, Thomas, 452, 655n10
Buckley, William F., Jr., 104
  God and Man at Yale, 69
Buell, Walter, 30
Buñuel, Luis, 170, 170–71n
Burden, Katherine "Babs," 45, 67
Burden, Wendy (later Wendy Morgan), 41, 44–47, 60, 66–67
  her mother suggests an affair with PM, 67
  marriage to Walter Sohier, 127–28
  PM–Payne Payson relationship and, 67, 72
  PM's letter of 1946, about search for self, 58
  PM's letters, 42–43, 48–51, 57, 61, 62, 66–67, 70, 85, 87, 105, 117, 609n31, 609n34
  relationship with PM ends, 71–72
  warnings about PM from his mother, 67

Burden, William Douglas, 45
  Komodo expedition, 45–46
Buried Dreams (Cahill), 546
Burroughs, William, 214n
Bush, George H. W. "Poppy," 21
Bush, George W., 550–51, 557
Butler, Darrell "Dino," 461, 463, 468, 509–10
Butz, Earl, 335
Byers, Steve, 523, 567–68, 582

Cahill, Tim: *Buried Dreams*, 546
Camp Endicott, Davisville, Rhode Island, 49–51
Campion, Tom, 556, 561
Camus, Albert, 307, 307n, 591
Canfield, Cass, 107
Cantor, Mitchell, 517
Capote, Truman, 119, 147, 240, 257, 276, 277, 292, 343, 391
Captiva Island, Florida, 22, 387, 421, 422
Carey, George (grandfather), 14, 23
Carey, Mary Seymour Jewett (grandmother), 14
Carlson, Dorris, 370
Carpenter, Craig, 406, 411–16, 451, 650n29
  bigfoot and, 414–15, 415n, 423–25, 451–52
  erratic behavior and break with PM, 425–26
  Haley's research on, 413–14
  Indian Rebirth Movement and, 413, 415, 488
  kidnapping episode, 427–28, 428n
  PM and eight-state trip, 451–52
  PM and Hopi Reservation trip, 422–25
  PM and Pinnacles National Park trip, 416–17
  PM and Utah trip, 442
  PM's *Indian Country* and, 412, 413
  PM's letter about Zen, 529
  warns of government retribution, 482, 482n
Carr, Archie, 184
Carson, Rachel, 174, 183, 185, 625n31, 626n70
  sea trilogy, 182
  Silent Spring, 169, 182, 186, 267, 307
Castaneda, Carlos, 345
  The Teaching of Don Juan, 345–46n
Catlin, George, 175, 183, 625n35
  North American Indians, 498, 625n35
Cayman Islands expeditions (1964, 1965, 1966), 273–76
  boat, *Lydia E. Wilson*, 273, 274–75
  Caymanian seafarers, 274–75

Ebanks, Cadie, 273, 274, 275, 276, 372
Far Tortuga and, 276, 372, 375–76
New Yorker funding, 273, 274, 276, 635n36
PM's interest in the green sea turtle, 272–76
"To the Miskito Bank" and, 276, 372
Chandler, Raymond, 107
Chapman & Son architects, 17, 22
Chaskey, Megan and Scott, 516
Chatfield, LeRoy, 305
Chavez, Cesar, xiv, 102, 280–85, 285n, 335–36, 411, 453
César E. Chávez National Monument, 337n
condolence call to PM, 334–35
PM's admiration for, 283, 636n67, 658n95
PM's *New Yorker* profile, 283–84, 305
PM's *Sal Si Puedes* and, 285, 285n, 305–8, 335
PM's screenplay for, 318
PM's soured relationship with, 472
PM's visits, 304, 335, 347
Chayat, Roko Sherry (Shinge Roshi), 332, 338, 371, 406
Cheever, John, 437
Cherullo, Helen, 557
Chicago Tribune, review of *Wildlife in America*, 184
Childs, Blair, 29, 31
Chrysanthemum and the Sword, The (Benedict), 65
CIA (Central Intelligence Agency)
Angleton and, 106, 128
Bay of Pigs and, 136
Congress for Cultural Freedom and, 120
coup d'état in Iran and, 136
cultural shift in, 136
Farfield Foundation and, 120, 128, 615n4
journal of, *Studies in Intelligence*, 108
magazines sponsored by, 128
monitoring Richard Wright, 113, 617n74
NYT exposes PM's role at, 101
Office of Policy Coordination (OPC) and Office of Special Operations (OSO), 106, 128, 129, 136
The Paris Review and, 120, 128–29, 131, 615n2, 615n4
PM as agent in Paris, 104–6, 108, 110, 112–16, 128–29, 131–36
PM exposed, 101, 270–72, 443, 615n2
PM quits, 135–36, 620n185
PM's involvement with, xiv, 101, 106–7, 615n4, 616n35
PM's political views and, 105
PM's recruitment, 102–5
PM's reticence about, 101–2, 112–13, 615n3
PM's training, 107, 108, 109–10
PM's unpublished notes, 102, 106, 131–32, 135
"Principles of Deep Cover," 108–9
Smith as director, 136
Wisner at, 106
Yale's Pearson and, 103–4
Cider House Rules, The (Irving), 499
Clark, Mary Hamilton, 504–5
Clark, Ramsey, 658n115
Clem, Robert Verity, 277
Clemmer, Richard, 409n
Clinton, Bill, 550–52
Cloud Forest, The: A Chronicle of the South American Wilderness (1961), 202–8, 235, 302
Amazon/South America expedition (1959–60) as basis for, 191–208
American Academy of Arts and Letters award, 250–51
critics and reviews, 202–3
foreign editions, 250
passage about the Quebrada Grasa, 205–6
publication date, 202
search for a *mandíbula*, 198, 203–8, 204n
Cohen, Herb, 217–218, 254
Cole, Cynthia Waterbury, 144, 148, 150, 161
Cole, John Nelson, 27, 70–71, 108, 144–45, 148, 161
PM's co-author, *Yale Daily News* column, 70–71
working for Ted Lester, 154–55, 622n94
Coleman, Linda, 516–17, 571, 586, 589
Coletti, Umberto, 108
Committee for Traditional Indian Land and Life, 409, 409n, 413, 416–17
Condor's Shadow, The (Wilcove), 186
Congo, Republic of the, 217–19
Connell, Evan S., 131
Conrad, Joseph, 58n, 256
Cooke, Joe, 62–63
Cornell Lab of Ornithology, 186
Cornell University
PM delivers Iscol Distinguished Environmental Lecture, 574
Cowley, Malcolm, 160
Cozzens, James Gould, 107
Crew, Gerald "Jerry," 393, 414
Crewdson, John M.: "Worldwide Propaganda Network Built by the C.I.A," 101, 615n2
Crisler, Lois, 174, 625n31

Cronin, Edward W., Jr., 351, 389
Cruz, César, 198, 203–7
Cultural Cold War, The (Saunders), 128
Cunningham, Peter, 571, 572
Cutler, Lloyd, 550
Czechoslovakia reporting trip (1948), 80–83
  PM's impressions in *Partisans*, 83, 141

Dabney, Bee, 131
Das, Rameshwar, 513
Davis, Myrna, 383, 443, 586, 588
Davis, Paul, 8, 588
Dawidoff, Nicholas, 451
Deacon, William T., III, 244
Dead Birds (film), 227–28, 239n
Dear Baby (Saroyan), 36–37
Death of a Rebel (Donaldson), 90–91, 614n15
de Bruijn, Jean Victor, 210
de Kooning, Willem, 263n
DeLamar, Alice Antoinette, 75
Delano (Dunne), 281
DeLillo, Don, 380, 503, 548
de Menil, Adelaide, 495
de Montherlant, Henry, 136
Dershowitz, Alan, 477–78, 659n136, 659n139
"Development of Personality, The" (Jung), 300–301
Didion, Joan, 306–7
Dillard, Annie, 53, 53n, 548
Dillion, Hope, 84
Dirda, Michael, 564
Ditman, Keith S., 248
Ditmars, Raymond Lee, 22
Dobbs, Michel Engu, 579–80, 588, 589
Doctorow, Edgar, 506, 551
Donadio, Candida, 472
  client list, 380–81
  death (2001), 540
  Far Tortuga and, 380–81, 391
  Lost Man's River and, 536–37, 538, 540
  PM signs with, 380, 646n77
Donaldson, Scott, 90, 91–92
  Death of a Rebel, 90–91, 614n15
Dostoyevsky, Fyodor, 56, 58n
Douglas, Marjory Stoneman: *The Everglades: River of Grass*, 492
Douglas-Hamilton, Iain, 293–94, 294n, 311–12
Downey, John, 88
Downs, Cile, 148
du Bois, William Pène, 122, 127, 136, 251n
Duhamel, Colette, 130
Dunne, John Gregory: *Delano*, 281
Dybek, Stuart, 482

Eagle, James Theodore "Jimmy," 462, 463, 464
Eagle Deer, Jancita, 473–74, 476, 508
East Hampton, Long Island, 142–43, 143n, 157
  Hurricane Sandy and, 576
  PM's environmental concerns, 267–68
  PM's *Men's Lives* and, 143, 143n
East of Lo Monthang (1995), 532
Ebanks, Cadie, 273, 274, 275, 276, 372
Eckhart, Gertrude, 384, 385
Eckhart, Gottlieb, 312, 384, 385, 400, 427, 446, 449
Eckhart, Meister, 300
Edwards, Thomas R., 379
Eiseley, Loren, 239
Eisenhower, Dwight D., 142, 168, 555, 624n7
1185 Park Avenue (Roiphe), 19n
Elisofon, Eliot, 212, 222, 224, 232–33, 241
Ellison, Bruce, 460–61, 465, 467, 468–69, 510
  Peltier clemency request and, 551
  Price defamation lawsuit and, 479–80
  In the Spirit of Crazy Horse and, 475
Elman, Richard, 443
Emanuel, Victor "Warbler," 536, 574, 591
  Golden Eagle Festival trip with PM, 575
  PM's Antarctica expeditions, 553
  PM's Asian crane excursion and, 536
  PM's bird name and, 536n
Emerson, Ralph Waldo, 52–53
Emery, H. B., 389
Enderlein, Peter, 340
End of the Earth (2003), 553, 577
environmental issues and PM's activism
  African wildlife and fate of elephants, 294n
  Africa's ecological decline, 437n, 447, 447n
  America in the 1950s, 167–68
  awakening of public awareness, 168–69
  bigfoot (Sasquatch) as a symbol and, 411
  Black Hills mining and, 460, 461, 467
  Chavez, United Farm Workers, and grape boycott, 280–85, 280n, 335
  Climate change (global warming), 554, 574
  Corkscrew Swamp Sanctuary acquisition, 270
  Disney nature documentaries and, 169, 169n
  Echo Park controversy, 169–70
  Eisenhower's policies and, 168, 169, 624n7
  Endangered Species Act of 1973, 186
  environmental movement begins, 169

Index · 681

Kissimmee River desecration, 487, 487n
Migratory Bird Treaty Act of 1918, 178
PM's Congo Basin expedition in search of forest elephants (1985), 485
PM's concerns about oil drilling and wildlife habitat, 554–58, 561, 669n127
PM's concerns about the future, 285, 636n79
PM's defense of the Arctic National Wildlife Refuge, 555–58, 561
PM's final nonfiction books and speeches, 554–58
PM's focus on ecological consequences of levees and canals in Florida, 487–88
PM's foreword to *Tracking Arctic Oil*, 555–56
PM's interest in cranes and *The Birds of Heaven*, 533, 534, 536, 539, 541–42, 552–53
PM's interest in tigers and *Tigers in the Snow*, 534, 541, 542, 552–53
PM's "orientation to doom," 314
PM's *Wildlife in America* and, 186
PM writing about insecticide abuse, 280
Reston, Virginia, and the Garden City movement, 269–70
Spectemur Agendo and, 280–81, 280n
Udall and, 186, 268–70
the whooping crane and, 169n, 175, 175n
Wilderness Act of 1964, 268
Zahniser's wilderness bill, 186
E. P. Dutton publishers
PM dissatisfied with royalties, 339
PM–Eliot Porter collaboration, 339
The Tree Where Man Was Born published by, 339, 430
Ephron, Nora, 449
Epstein, Jason, 429, 430, 500, 531
Killing Mister Watson and, 500, 667n41
Lost Man's River and, 537, 538, 544–45
as PM's editor, 500
Erdrich, Louise, 482, 503
Eritrea expedition (1969), 297–98
Espinouze, Henri, 112n
Esquire magazine
"Looking for Hemingway" (Talese), 122–23
"On the River Styx" (PM), 487n
Evans, Harry, 539, 542, 558
Everest, Mount, 351, 351n
Everglades, The: River of Grass (Douglas), 492
Everglades National Park, 486, 487
Evergreen Review, 162
"Everybody's Protest Novel" (Baldwin), 116

Falk, Richard Anderson, 285, 636n79
Farbar, Bernard "Buzz," 498
Farewell to Arms, A (Hemingway), 92
Farrar, John, 95, 614n30
Farrar, Straus and Company publishers, 95
Far Tortuga (1975), 276, 365, 372–82, 391, 590
  critics and reviews, 379–81
  dedication, 380n
  form and structure, 376
  influence of Zen, 377
  origins as "Fool Day," 377–78, 378
  plot, 372–74
  PM's anger at editor Fox, 381–82, 646n80
  PM's conversation with William Shawn and, 276, 635n36
  PM's dissatisfaction with Random House, 381, 430
  Random House contract, advance, and royalties, 380, 381, 431
  release date, 381
  sales, 381
  source material, 375–76
  style and voice of, 374–75
  use of negative space on a page, 377, 378
Faulkner, William, 92, 94, 103, 614n21
  Sanctuary, 92
Fawcett, Colonel Percy, 192
Fenton, Charles A., 90–92, 95
Fenton, Gwendolyn, 91
Ferguson, Alfred and Henry L., 5
"Fifth Day, The" (PM), 109
Fighting for Our Lives (film), 347n
"Figure on the Road, The" (PM, unfinished short story), 400, 649n85
Filler, John, 214
First Light (Lucas Matthiessen), 525
Fishers Island, New York, 4–5, 23, 41, 144
  Bernard Baruch and, 27
  dangerous reef of, 152
  defining event of PM's early life, 24–25, 606n96
  Hay Harbor Club, 6, 24
  influence of nature on PM, 6–7
  Matthiessen family and vacation home, 5, 6, 12, 24, 15, 604n12
  PM buries his mother's ashes on, 426
  PM saved from falling overboard, 6–7, 604n15
  PM's boat berthed on, 145
  PM's childhood rebellion and, 26
  PM's focus on birds, 71–72
Fitzgerald, F. Scott, 92
Fitzgerald, Jean, 397–400, 399n, 402, 404, 648–49n77

Five Cranes (Seiko), 511
Flanner, Janet, 74, 110, 617n59
Fleischmann, Julius, Jr., 120, 122, 127, 128, 129, 615n4
Fleming, Peter: *Brazilian Adventure*, 202
Fletcher, Charles Tenshin, 419
Florida Everglades, 270
  bigfoot sightings and "Swamp Ape Expedition," 488
  excerpt from *Killing Mister Watson*, 486
  as "the last true wilderness," 486
  National Audubon Society acquisition of land around the Corkscrew Swamp, 487–88
  PM's boyhood fishing trips, 486–87
  PM's contract for untitled novel centered in (1985), 485
  PM's research trips, 493–94, 497
  See also Bone by Bone; *Killing Mister Watson*; *Lost Man's River*; *Shadow Country*
Forbes-Watson, Alec, 437n
Forster, E. M., 122, 136
Foster, Thomas, 202
Foujita, Léonard Tsuguharu, 112, 112n
Fox, Anne, 497
Fox, Connie, 513
Fox, Jill Fuller, 67
Fox, Joe, 257–60, 273, 277, 309n, 449, 497
  At Play in the Fields of the Lord and, 257–60, 267n
  authors edited by, 257
  death of, PM's speech at his memorial, 382
  Far Tortuga and, 372, 381–82, 391, 538, 646n80, 667n41
  Naval service and PM, 257
  replaced by Epstein, 500
Freilicher, Jane, 96
Freshwater, Philip C., 184
Friedman, Dorothy, 513, 514
Fuller, Blair, 75–76, 81, 82, 107, 108, 117
Futter, Deb, 542, 543, 546, 549, 558

Gablik, Suzi, 555
Gaddis, Bill, 277n
Gaines Quammen, Betsy, xii
Gajdusek, Daniel Carleton, 240
Galápagos Islands, 339
Galbraith, John Kenneth, 142
Galesi, Merete, 288, 291, 324–25, 327, 328, 331–32, 348, 357
Garbo, Greta, 276
Garbus, Martin, 476–79, 481–83, 507, 660n160, 661n168, 661n170
Gardens of War (Heider), 239n
Gardner, Robert, 209–12, 240
  disappearance of Michael Rockefeller and, 241
  ethnographic cinema and, 209–10
  film, *Dead Birds*, 227–28, 239n
  Harvard-Peabody Expedition, 210–12, 221, 221n, 224, 225, 227, 230–32, 236
Gauvin, Jean Jacques, 195–96, 251, 252, 254, 627n28
Gellhorn, Martha, 292
Geo: PM's advocacy for Native Americans and, 454
Getzels, Peter, 526
Gide, André, 77
Gilbert, Madonna, 460
Gillespie, Rollin and Alan, 402–3, 402n, 649n98
Gimbel, Peter Robin, 301–4, 301n, 308–9
  Blue Water, White Death, 302
Gimlin, Robert, 403, 649n103
Ginsberg, Allen, 207, 214n
Glass, George, 200–201
Glassman, Helen, 418–19
Glassman, Bernie, 418, 419, 449, 514, 516, 528, 537
  Bearing Witness Retreat at Auschwitz-Birkenau, 570–72
  Greyston and, 495–96, 519, 662n39
  The Snow Leopard and, 435
  "street retreats," 570–71, 671n18
  Zen Peacemaker Order, 570
God and Man at Yale (Buckley), 69
God That Failed, The (Wright et al.), 105
Goldberg, Michael "Mike", 188–89, 213, 261, 263, 263n
Golden Eagle Festival trip (2012), 575–76
Goldman, Mab, 348, 367, 367n
Goodall, Jane, 446
Goodman, Irving, 441
Gordon, Harriet, 526
Gore, Al, 550–51
Gottlieb, Robert, 257–58
Gourevitch, Philip, 564
Govinda, Anagarika, 433
Grahame, Kenneth: *The Wind in the Willows*, 35–36, 52
Gray, Francine du Plessix, 438
"Great River" (PM), 604n15
great white shark expedition (1969, 1970), 298, 301–4, 308–9, 309n, 639n9
  Blue Water, White Death (film) and, 302, 308–9, 309n
  boat, *Terrier VIII*, 298, 303
  encounter with Veevers-Carter, 303
  Gimbel and, 301–4, 308
  PM on courage and risk, 302, 638n68
  PM rejoins in South Australia, 308–9

Index · 683

PM's *Blue Meridian* and, 303–4, 308
PM touches a great white, 308
 in the Seychelles, 303, 309n
Greenberg, Clement, 148
Greene, Graham, 131, 256
Greenland expedition (1993), 526–28, 537
 beluga hunt, 527
 PM reports for *The New Yorker* on whaling, 526–27
Griggs, Maitland, 27
Guinzburg, Tom, 22, 68–69, 88, 91, 108, 115, 122, 147, 160, 260n, 277, 449
 death of, 578
 The Paris Review and, 125, 130n, 131
 The Snow Leopard and, 430, 431
 The Snow Leopard and National Book Awards, 441–42
 Viking Press and, 429–30, 431, 441
Gurdjieff, G. I., 79, 80, 85, 89, 246

Haiti: PM in Port-au-Prince, 194
Halberstam, David, 142
Haley, Brian, 409n, 413, 656n33
Halifax, Joan Jiko, 528
Hall, Donald, 122, 136, 436
Hansen, Mary, 412, 415, 421, 425, 427–28, 428n
Hansen, Ron, 503
Harper & Brothers publishers, 107, 120, 150
 Race Rock, PM's first novel, published by, 136–37, 142
Harper's Bazaar: PM's "Travelin Man" published, 170
Harper's Magazine, 109
 PM's piece from "Tiger and Crane" research trips, 552
 review of *Race Rock*, 153
 review of *Under the Mountain Wall*, 240
 review of *Wildlife in America*, 184
Harrison, Jim, xv, 327, 333, 365, 372, 408, 500–501n, 522
 Bone by Bone and, 548
 Far Tortuga and, 377, 379
 Killing Mister Watson and, 500, 502–3, 667n41
 Legends of the Fall, xiv–xv
 opinion of PM's writing, 365
 PM on his final projects, 569
 PM on his own death, 672n63
 PM on problems with *Lost Man's River*, 535–36, 539, 544
 PM's cancer and final months, 581
 PM's concerns with global warming and, 554
 PM's grandson's death and, 543
 PM's Watson consolidation and, 558

 profile of PM for *Sports Illustrated*, 366
 The Snow Leopard and, 437
 Zen and PM and, 366
Hartmann, Ernst and Emma, 81
Harvard-Peabody Expedition to Netherlands New Guinea (1961), xiv, 209–41, 629n17, 630n56, 631n107
 Assuk-Palek raid, 234, 234n
 Broekhuijse's importance, 228
 camp at Homuak, 222, 224
 challenges/dangers, 223–26, 234
 conflict among members, 232–33
 Dugum Dani people, 221–22, 221n, 225, 230–31
 duration of, materials amassed, 232
 Dutch botanist Versteegh joins, 227
 end of the expedition, 236
 expedition interactions with Kurelu and Dugum Dani, 222–24, 223n, 228–30, 236
 fate of the Dugum Dani, 236–37
 funding for, 211
 Gardner as leader, 210–12, 221, 224, 225, 227, 228, 230–32, 236
 Gardner's film, *Dead Birds*, 227–28, 239n
 joint birthday of PM and Rockefeller, 233
 Life photographer Elisofon and, 212, 222, 224, 232–33
 missionaries' rumors and trouble with regional authorities, 231–32
 PM arrives in Wamena, 220, 221
 PM departs, 236
 PM joins the expedition, 212
 PM on medical assistance for the Dugum Dani, 229–30
 PM's accident, 234
 PM's account, approach to and style, 234–36
 PM's *At Play in the Fields of the Lord* and, 251–52, 255
 PM's circuitous route to New Guinea, 216–19
 PM's role/focus in the expedition, 212, 227
 PM's "startling" first impression of the Dugum Dani, 221
 PM's undercurrent of dread, 233–34
 PM's *Under the Mountain Wall* and, 237–41, 252
 translator Abututi, 222, 223, 228
 Wittaia as enemies of Dugum Dani, 223–26
Harvard University: Peabody Museum of Archaeology and Ethnology, Film Study Center, 209
Hastings, Margaret, 220, 630n56

Hazlett, Bill, 467, 469
Heart of the Land: Essays on Last Great Places (Barbato and Weinerman, eds.), 604n15
Hegeler, Edward C., 9, 9n
  Matthiessen & Hegeler Zinc Company, 9, 9n, 604n25
Heider, Karl, 212, 221n, 222, 224–227, 229, 236–37
  Gardens of War, 239n
Heller, Joseph, 495, 548
Hellman, Lillian, 209, 210
Hemingway, Ernest, 72, 76, 87, 91, 147
  A Farewell to Arms, 92
  PM on the style of, 92
Henderson the Rain King (Bellow), 256n
Hendricks, Steve, 462
Hersey, John, 37
Herzog, Werner, 204n, 276n, 443
Hesse, Hermann: *Steppenwolf*, 254–55n
"High Noon in the Black Hills" (PM), 461
Hill, David, 509
Hilo, Big Island, Hawaii, 59–60
Himalayas expedition (1973), xvi–xvii, 333–34, 344–52, 356–64
  account in *The Snow Leopard*, 334, 357, 429, 432–33, 647n30
  challenges/dangers, 357, 359
  in Duhnai, Rahagaon, and Ringmo, 358, 359
  guides, porters, and supplies, 344, 351–52, 359–60, 438
  as a pilgrimage, vii, xi, 334
  PM "abandons" his young son and, 346–47, 346n, 439, 642n68
  PM in Kathmandu, 350–52, 389
  PM leaves the expedition, 363–64
  PM purges himself of attachments, 357–58, 359, 362–63
  PM's concerns about, 344–45
  PM's emotional crash afterward, 366–67
  PM's encounter with the Lama of Shey, 362
  PM's hopes for revelation, 334, 359
  PM's journals, 349, 355, 361–62, 364, 432–34
  PM's letters, 358–59, 362–63
  PM's route to, stopovers in Italy and India, 350
  PM's search for spiritual insight, 334, 361–62, 366
  PM's Zen practice, 334, 338, 349, 358, 361, 362n
  Schaller and, 333–34, 344–52, 356–61, 363, 438
  Shey Gompa stay, 360–63
  snow leopard and, 333, 361
  sponsors for, 344
  yeti and, 351, 351n, 389, 647n30
Himmelman, Jeff, 585
Hines, Bob, 183
Hixon, Lex, 495
Hoagland, Edward, 380, 439–40
Hoare, Philip, xii
Hoffman, Carl, 240
Hokanson, Hans, 513–14, 578
Holiday magazine: "Powerboat Cruising" (PM), 171–72
Holmes, Sandra Jishu, 570
Hornaday, William Temple, 181, 183
  Our Vanishing Wildlife: Its Extermination and Preservation, 181–82
Horney, Karen: *Neurosis and Human Growth*, 299–300
Hornocker, Maurice, 532–33, 533n, 541
Hotchkiss School, 29–35, 39n
  Class of 1945 *Mischianza* (yearbook), 31–32
  headmaster's assessment of PM, 31
  The Lit literary journal, PM's pieces in, 38
  PM and nature at, 30
  PM begins writing, 37–39
  PM's classmates, 29, 62, 301
  PM's graduation and awards, 47
  PM's nicknames, 31–32
  PM's social conscience and, 33–35, 38–39
  St. Luke's Society, 34
  WWII and, 29
Howard, Shirley, 22
Hoyle, Rafael Larco, 203
Huerta, Dolores, 283
Hughes, Robert, 495n, 497, 578
Hughes, Victoria, 497
Hultman, Evan, 470
Humes, Harold Louis, Jr. "Doc," 115–16, 116n, 132, 134
  Doc documentary, 116n
  living in Greenwich Village, 213
  LSD and mental breakdown, 270–71
  The Paris Review and, 118, 118n, 121, 122, 125, 126, 130n, 619n145
  PM and mescaline and, 213–14
  PM's CIA involvement and, 270–72
  publisher of the *Paris News Post*, 116
  in Saint-Tropez, 126, 127
  The Underground City, 213
Humes, Immy, 116n
Hunters, The (Marshall), 210
Hurxthal, Lewis and Nancy, 312, 341
Huxley, Aldous, 215
  "perennial philosophy," 426
Huxley, Elspeth, 341

Idea of the Holy, The (Otto), 53n
India, 36, 384
  Asian crane expedition (1993), 536
  PM in (1973), 350
  PM's search for Bengal tigers (1996), 542
  Schaller's study of tigers in, 294, 333
Indian Country (1984), 392, 455–57, 656n31
  Carpenter and, 412, 413, 428
  chapter: "Journey to Hopi," 423n
  Nabokov's negative review, 457
  opening essay "Native Earth," 455–57
  Viking as publisher, 457
  Zen influence and, 456
In Paradise (2014), 567, 572–74, 581, 583, 585, 671n18
  critics and reviews, 590
  PM's cancer and fast-tracked publication, 585
  release date, 589, 590
  sales, 590
  title of, 573–74
  as a travelogue reimagined as a novel, 573
  working title "Dancing at Auschwitz," 572
International Crane Foundation, 533, 537, 541, 550
  Archibald as director, 533, 537, 541
  PM's Amur River and Mongolia trip (1992), 533–34
International Union for the Conservation of Nature, Red Data Book, 186
In the Spirit of Crazy Horse (1983), xiv, 14, 102, 391–92, 458–85, 506, 658–59n120
  bigfoot and, 415, 474
  book reception held for members of Congress, 479, 479n
  critics and reviews, 474, 477–78
  depiction of Peltier, 474
  emotional cost to PM, 482–83
  feedback on draft, 475–76
  Janklow and Eagle Deer section, 473–74, 476, 659n146
  lawsuits over, 476, 478–83, 506–8, 507n, 659n146, 660n155, 660n159, 660n167, 661n168, 661n169, 661n170
  PM's contract with the Leonard Peltier Defense Committee and, 465–66, 471
  PM's research for, 467–70
  PM's vision for, 473
  PM's voice in, 474
  republished and updated edition (1991), 508, 509, 550
  sales, 659n146
  Sifton as editor for, 471–73, 476, 480, 483–84, 660n160
  title of, 466
  Viking's attorneys and legal read of, 476–77, 660n155
  Viking's contract and advance, 471, 473
  Viking's release date, 477
  Viking withdraws the book, foreign edition halted, 480–81, 660n160
  "X" hoax confession by Robideau and Hill (1990), 508–10, 664n111
  See also Peltier, Leonard
Ireland
  Annaghkeen and DL's journals, 291, 634n108
  Mount Melleray Abbey, 264
  PM and family in (1965), 262–64
Irving, John, 499, 506, 548, 565
  The Cider House Rules, 499
  reading of *Lost Man's River*, 534–35
Irvington-on-Hudson, New York, 11, 12, 21
Ishi in Two Worlds (Kroeber), 254–55n
Israel, Ann (later Anna Puharich), 280, 281, 305, 310, 335, 336–37, 338, 388
Italy
  PM acquires a house near Polgeto, 318
  PM in Castello di Polgeto (1969, 1970), 298–300, 312–13, 318–19, 319n
  PM's LSD use and journal, 299, 300
  PM with lover Jane Stanton in (1973), 350
  PM with lover Karen Yochim in (1969), 298–99, 310n, 318
Iyer, Pico, xv, 440, 643n68

Jackson, Shirley, 107
Jallu, Marie-Claude, 76
James, Sarah, 556
James, William: *The Varieties of Religious Experience*, 52
Janklow, Bill, 473–74, 476, 478–79, 507–8, 507n, 659n146
Jarrell, Randall, 122
Jaws (Benchley novel and film), 309n
Jhabvala, Ruth Prawer, 219
Johnson, Lady Bird, 269
Johnson, Lyndon B., 272, 279
Johnston, Richard, 184–85
Johnstone, Mildred "Milly," 287, 287n, 310, 321–22, 328
Johnstone, William, 322
Jones, James, 235, 426
Jordis, Christine, 560
"Journey to Hopi: National Sacrifice Area" (PM), 423n
Joyous Cosmology, The (Watts), 247
Jung, Carl: "The Development of Personality," 300–301

Kakiay, Jusup, 222, 222n
Kammerer, Marvin, 460
Kapleau, Philip: *The Three Pillars of Zen*, 286, 300, 316
Karnos, David, 522
Kaufman, Sue: "Tea at Le Gord," 271
Kendall, Willmoore, 104
Kennedy, Jacqueline Bouvier, 41, 276, 343
Kennedy, Robert F., 269, 281, 282
Kenya, 292
  elephants of, 294n
  murder of Tom Mboya, 304, 304n
  PM expedition to Lake Rudolf, 340
  PM in Nairobi, 292, 301, 304, 310, 485
  PM researching *The Tree Where Man Was Born*, 311
  PM's safari with Lewis Hurxthal, 312
Kenyatta, Jomo, 304n
Kilik, Jon, 551
Killing Mister Watson (1990), 181n, 488–94, 497–506
  background on Edgar Watson, 490–92
  character of Smallwood, 492–93, 501
  critics and reviews, 503–4
  Edgar Watson as metaphor, 491, 662n20
  "Florida (BF) Novel" as precursor, 488–90, 498, 662n12
  folder: "Earliest Draft," 498
  Irving comments on original length, 499–500
  PM first hears about Edgar Watson, 486–87
  PM in Florida and interviews, 493–94, 497
  PM's approach to the novel, 494
  praise from other authors, 502–3
  Random House and editing, 500
  Rashomon-style accounts, 502
  research for, 492–94, 498
  response from PM's son Lucas, 525
  responses from Watson descendants and others interviewed, 504–5
  revisions and rewriting, 501–2, 501n
  sales, 506
  title of, 501
  vision for, three parts as movements, 499–500, 663n59
Kipling, Rudyard
  influence on PM, 36
  "Toomai of the Elephants," 36
Kirkus Reviews
  The Cloud Forest, 202
  Far Tortuga, 379
Kligman, Ruth, 162
Knight of Cups (film), 574
Koenig, Antonia, 386, 388, 523–24, 586, 587

Koenig, Julian, 310, 349–50, 367–69, 386–87, 521
Koenig, Maria Eckhart. *See* Matthiessen, Maria Eckhart Koenig
Koenig, Sarah, 387, 388, 523–24, 582
Koestler, Arthur, 105
Kolchaftewa, Guy, 423–24
Kołodziej, Marian, 573, 671n18
Kolowrat, Ernest, 37
Komodo, East Indies, 45–46
Kornman, Robin, 435–36
Krasner, Lee, 148, 149–50, 157, 162, 188–89
Kress, Margie, 323
Krishnamurti, 300
Kroeber, Theodora: *Ishi in Two Worlds*, 254–55n
Krutch, Joseph Wood, 372, 372n
Kruuk, Hans, 293
Kuntz, Doug, 495
Kurnit, Rick, 476–77, 479, 660n155

LaDuke, Winona, 455, 478
Laird, Thomas, 531–32
Lake, Peter, 309n
Lakota Belief and Ritual (Walker), 467
Lama, Nurbu, xvii
Lame Deer, Archie Fire, xii, 458–60, 464
Late George Apley, The (Marquand), 150
"Late in the Season" (PM), 146
Lawrence, Elizabeth, 150, 152, 159
Leach, Jim, 475–76, 477, 478, 658–59n120
Leary, Timothy, 248–49, 266, 270
Leatherbee, Frances Crane, 82
Lee, Hermione, 540
Legends of the Fall (Harrison), xiv–xv
Lehmann-Haupt, Christopher, 477, 590
Leonard, John, 343
Leopold, Aldo, 182, 183, 268, 537
  biotic community of, 456
Lester, Lewis, 163
Lester, Theodore Roosevelt "Ted," 154–55, 156, 157, 495, 622n94
LeSueur, Joe, 163, 189
Levy, Morton, 62
Lichtenstein, Dorothy and Ray, 449
Lie Down in Darkness (Styron), 119, 140, 150
Life magazine
  photographer Elisofon on the Harvard-Peabody Expedition, 212, 222, 224, 232–33, 241
  photographer Gimbel for the *Andrea Doria* wreck, 302
"Lina" (PM), 58n, 134
Lind, John "Jack," 304

"Literature and Mysticism" (PM, lecture), 206
Lomayaktewa, Douglas, 424
Long Island, New York, East End and town of Springs, 142–46, 245, 621n27
  artists Lee Krasner and Jackson Pollock on, 149–50, 149n
  Bonackers of, 143–44, 154, 155, 156, 163, 494–95
  Matthiessen family's Black housekeeper, 155–56
  Matthiessen family's move to Stony Hill Farm, Amagansett, 156–57, 161–62
  PM moves away from, 163
  PM's daughter Sara Carey born, 157
  PM's dog "Scoter," 146n
  PM's marriage to PS, 147–48, 156–57, 161–62
  PM's social circle, 157, 162
  PM's *Men's Lives* and, 494–95
  PM's satisfaction with the life, 157–58
  PM's seasonal jobs and writing, 144–46, 154–58
  PM's standing with the Bonackers, 155–56
  PM working for fisherman Ted Lester, 154–55, 156, 157–58, 622n96
  Pollock's fatal accident, 162
  PS's memories of, 144
  Yale roommate, John Cole and wife Cynthia on, 144–45, 148, 154–55
  See also East Hampton, Long Island; Sagaponack, Long Island
"Looking for Hemingway" (Talese), 122–23, 130n
Loomis, Bob, 539, 565
Lopez, Barry, xiii, 186, 457, 469n
Lord, Charlie "Ears," 32, 41, 48, 71, 108
Lord, Margaret Plunkett "Peggy," 71, 156
Lord, Sheridan "Sherry," 19, 41, 88, 108, 148, 277, 497
  death of, 577–78
  PM birding expedition with, 98–99
Los Angeles Times: *Crazy Horse* review, 477
Lost Man's River (1997), 190n, 530–31, 534–50, 558
  advance for "WATSON II" (1990), 530
  comments, reaction of Howard Norman, 538
  critics and reviews, 544–45, 546
  difficulties of length and cohesion, 530–31, 535–38, 543–44
  excerpt in *The Paris Review*, 544
  Irving's reading of and comments, 534–35
  Olson's work on, 540–41, 542, 544
  PM finding the "magnet," 540–41

PM's assessment of, 546
PM's depressive episodes and, 544
PM travels to escape dealing with, 531, 536, 537, 539, 541–42
publication date, 545
Random House editor Futter and, 542, 543
Random House's doubts about, 538–39
underlying issues with, 545–46
wife MM's concerns, 537–38
Love, John Allan, 243
Love, Kennett, 244
Love, Mary Chauncey Potter, 243
Lovett, Sid, 104
Lucas, Martha B., 73
Lumet, Sidney, 449
Lumumba, Patrice, 217, 219, 219n
"Lumumba Lives" (PM), 11–12, 500–501n
Lyons, Oren, 454–55
Lyttle, Thornton "Gus," 37

Macdonald, Helen, xii
Macedo, Victor, 205–7
MacLehose, Christopher, 484, 544
Macrae, Jack, 339, 342, 343
Macray, Ngaere, 443–44, 576
Madagascar, 301, 302–3
Maezumi, Hakuyu Taizan (Maezumi Roshi), 418, 419–20, 449, 495, 496–97, 497n, 514, 516, 537
  death of, 578
  Soto and Rinzai Zen and, 419
Magnuson, Roger, 481, 497
Mailer, Norman, 189–90, 306
Malick, Terrence, 574
Marquand, John, Jr., 131
Marquand, John P.: *The Late George Apley*, 150
Marshall, John: *The Hunters*, 210
Martha's Vineyard, 209, 210
Martin, Paul, 185
"Martin's Beach" (PM), 92, 92n, 145
Masaryk, Jan, 82
Mase, Will, 424
Matthiessen, Alexander Farrar Love (son), 261, 262, 310, 311, 312, 314
  Arctic Alaska trip with PM, 556
  cared for by Mab Goldman, 348, 367, 367n
  DL's death and, 327, 330, 332, 347–48, 643n73
  environmental studies and career, 526
  Greenland trip and confrontation with PM, 526–28, 537
  inheritance of, 592
  life with stepmother, MM, 388–89, 442–43, 521

Matthiessen, Alexander Farrar Love (son) *(continued)*
    PM and, in Bali, 542
    PM leaves to join the Himalayas expedition, 346–47, 346n, 352, 358–59
    PM's behavior at home and, 523
    PM's cancer and final months, 576–77, 581, 582, 587
    PM's death and, 588–89, 591
    relationship with PM, 401, 524, 526–28, 577
    response to PM's behavior, 348
    The Snow Leopard and, 433
    visit to Sagaponack home, in ruins, with Richardson, 592–93
    on Zen and PM, 519
Matthiessen, Carey (brother), 6, 15, 21, 24, 34, 41–42, 177
    death of his mother, 422
    marriage to Cis Ormsby, 21
    PM's "bad" influence on, 41–42
    PM's Himalayas expedition and, 352
Matthiessen, Cis Ormsby (sister-in-law), 21, 97–98
Matthiessen, Conrad Henry (grandfather), 9–11, 13
Matthiessen, Conrad Henry, Jr. (uncle), 10, 13, 15
Matthiessen, Constance Eda (aunt), 10–11, 12
Matthiessen, Deborah Love (wife), 23, 214–15, 242–50, 299, 309
    Annaghkeen (first book), 291, 319, 634n108
    antique Isfahan bowl and, 317–18, 320, 329
    background and family, 243–44
    birth of PM's son Alex, 261
    cancer (ovarian and then metastatic) and death, 315, 317, 320, 324–30, 642n63
    character and personality, other-worldliness, 243–44, 246, 263
    correspondence with PM, 218, 219, 222, 234, 245–46, 309, 311, 313, 314, 319, 319n, 323–24
    discussions of death and, 325
    European vacation, with PM, 317–18
    homelife with PM in Sagaponack, 277–78, 305, 319
    Ireland trip with PM, 262–64
    life of self-examination, 247–48, 278
    lover taken by, 320, 323
    marriages of, 244–45
    marries PM, 250
    meets PM in Sagaponack, 214–15, 244
    moves to Bridgehampton, 245
    parenting and self-centeredness, 262, 314–15
    picnic to dedicate her new tearoom, 310
    PM and, as "seekers," 215, 246, 262, 264, 291, 315
    PM introduced to Zen by, 315–17
    PM's infidelity and, 289–91, 298–99, 309–11, 312, 313, 318, 320, 327
    PM's search for "true nature" and, 246
    poetry of, 290
    psychedelics and, 215, 242, 243, 247, 248, 249–50, 278
    relationship with PM, 245–50, 263–65, 278, 289, 299, 309, 312–24, 324n, 328–29
    short story in *Paris Review*, 319
    Tanzania vacation with PM (1970), 312
    Zen and tea ceremony, 286–87, 287n, 310–13, 315–17, 319–24, 327–29, 346
    Zen class taught at New School, 319–20, 324, 328
Matthiessen, Eda Wilhelmina Sophie (grandmother), 9–13, 10n, 12–13, 604n26
Matthiessen, Ehrhard Adolph (great-grandfather), 8, 9
Matthiessen, Elizabeth "Betty" Bleecker Carey (mother), 12–16, 14n, 605n49
    character and personality, 14–15, 23–24, 25
    children of, 15
    death of, 421
    family's move to Stamford, 21, 23
    marriage of, 13, 15, 16, 21, 23
    parenting style, 15–16
    PM's birth, 5, 15, 604n9
    PM's conduct and, 28, 42–43
    PM's difficult relationship with, 421–22
    robbery of her jewels, 16–17
    values of, 33, 43
    warns Wendy Burden about PM's shortcomings, 67
Matthiessen, Erard Adolph "Matty" (father), 5, 6, 11–16, 604n12
    as an architect, 15, 17, 22–23
    birth, 11
    Captiva Island villa, 387, 421, 422
    character and personality, 13, 21, 23, 27–28
    childhood deaths of his siblings, 12
    childhood in Irvington-on-Hudson, 11, 12–13
    death of, 586
    death of his wife Betty and, 422
    defining event of PM's early life and, 24–25, 606n96
    family moved to Stamford, 20–21

home built in Irvington-on-Hudson, 12
leased apartments in New York City, 17, 19n
love of socializing, 16, 21, 23, 27
marriage to Betty Carey, 13–15, 21, 23
PM and, duck hunting, 170, 421
PM and, Florida fishing trips, 486–87
PM inducted into the Navy and, 48
PM's attempts to improve relations with, 421
PM's rebellion and misbehavior, 24–28
refusal to invest in *The Paris Review*, 147
relationship with his children, 15–16, 18, 23, 24–25, 26–27, 41, 42, 147, 387
values, 14, 27, 28, 33, 43
WWII and MBE award, 39–40, 41, 608n70, 608n71
Matthiessen, F. O. (second cousin), 103, 103n
American Renaissance, 103
Matthiessen, Franz Otto (great-great-uncle), 8, 9, 11
Matthiessen, Frederick Wilhelm (great-grandfather), 8–9, 9n
Matthiessen & Hegeler Zinc Company, 9, 9n, 604n25
Matthiessen, Johnson & Green architects, 23
Matthiessen, Lucas "Luke" Conrad (son), 58n, 134, 137, 139, 142, 147, 148, 161, 325, 347
in Africa with PM (1969), 296–97
alcoholism of, 524–25
death of son, Christopher, 542–43
degenerative eye disease, 367, 525, 543
Ireland trip with PM (1965), 263
life during the "Downtown" years, 189
memoir, *First Light*, 525
PM leaves his mother PS and, 162, 163
PM's cancer and final months, 582
PM's death and, 587–89
PM's habitual leave-taking, 519, 524–25
reads *Killing Mister Watson*, 525
relationship with PM, 189, 191, 261–62, 449, 524–25, 654n67
Seal Pool and, 251n
Shadow Country and, 564
stepfather, Mike Goldberg and, 261
wife, Claire de Brunner, 582, 589
Matthiessen, Maria Eckhart Koenig (wife), 3, 13, 347n
background and family, 384–86
beauty of, 385–86
character and personality, 388, 442–43
Crazy Horse lawsuits and, 484–85
daughters, 349, 386, 387, 388, 389, 442, 448

Far Tortuga and, 380n
final postcard from PM, 584, 672n87
given ultimatums by PM, 350, 368
gives PM an ultimatum for marriage, 448
homemaking as an art, 442–43
Killing Mister Watson and, 500
literary dinners given by, 443
marriage to Julian Koenig, 386–87
moves into PM's Sagaponack home, 388–89
PM and, before DL's death, 310–11, 312
PM's Asian crane excursion and (1993), 536
PM's cancer and final months, 576, 580–89
PM's correspondence, Himalayas expedition, 350, 352, 358
PM's death and, 589
PM's death: dealing with PM's files, papers, and property, 592
PM's interest in bigfoot and, 518
PM's letters from Russia (1992), 532, 533
PM's memorial service and her poem, 591
PM's needs versus her own, 443–45
PM's serial infidelity and, 350, 447–48, 520–23, 543, 582–85, 588–89
PM's Watson consolidation and, 558, 565
PM's Zen practice prioritized over their marriage, 450, 518–19
PM's Zen teaching and students as source of conflict, 518–19
qualities of PM and, 383–84
reactions to PM's relationship with "K," 582–85, 588–89
relationship and marriage to PM, 349–50, 367–69, 382–89, 400–402, 426, 442–45, 450, 498, 518–19, 522–23
role as reader for PM's writing, 442, 582–83
Sagaponack acreage and, 519–20
Sag Harbor house, 522, 584, 592
Selous, Tanzania, expedition (1979) and, 446
as stepmother to Alex, 388–89, 442–43, 521
wedding in Sagaponack (1980), 448–49
Matthiessen, Mary Seymour (sister). *See* Wheelwright, Mary Seymour Matthiessen
Matthiessen, Peter
alcohol and drinking, 42, 58, 84, 89, 91, 272, 276, 277, 518, 533
anger and temper, 250, 264, 278, 320, 519, 527, 544, 580
archives at the Harry Ransom Center, xvi, 592, 609n34

Matthiessen, Peter *(continued)*
  attractiveness to women, 68, 289, 314, 383
  birds, ornithology, and, 22, 22n, 23, 68, 70, 71, 81, 89, 98–99, 520, 525, 533, 534, 536, 536n, 541–42, 553 *(see also* Audubon magazine; *specific writings on)*
  birth, 5, 15, 604n9
  "black moods" and depression, paranoia, 61, 160, 367, 369, 482, 544, 569, 661n170
  characterizations of, xiv, 84, 116, 383, 555
  charisma of, 289, 430
  complexity and contradictions, xiv–xv, 333, 383–84, 483, 519, 522, 523–24
  death of, xvi, 589
  family, wealth, and patrician background, 7–15, 23, 33, 209, 277, 314, 604n26
  habitual leave-taking and desire to escape, 263, 278–79, 291, 299, 303–4, 309, 332, 361, 449–50, 519, 523, 524–25, 531, 536, 537, 539, 541–42
  infidelity, history of philandering, 289–91, 298–99, 301, 309–11, 310n, 313, 314, 318, 320, 324, 327, 332–33, 348, 349–50, 387, 433, 433n, 438–39, 447–48, 520–22, 543, 582–85
  insomnia of, 482
  legacy of, 590–91
  marijuana use and, 382, 391
  mystical experience and, 54, 54n, 326, 334, 346, 404–5
  name Conrad and, 58, 58n
  poor eyesight and glasses, 24, 34, 44–45
  rebelliousness of, 26–28, 32, 40, 49, 62, 91, 609n30, 614n15
  relationship with his children, 189, 191, 213–14, 261–62, 264, 296–97, 346–47, 352, 449, 523–28, 577
  search for "true nature," 25, 42–43, 58, 80, 87, 138, 200, 242, 246, 250, 286, 300–301, 325–26, 338
  self-centeredness, 262, 320, 326, 347, 519
  siblings, 6, 13, 15 *(see also* Matthiessen, Carey; Wheelwright, Mary Seymour Matthiessen)
  snakes as special interest, 21–22, 22n, 32, 488
  social activism and advocacy journalism, xiv, 35, 39, 135–36, 454–57, 461, 465, 494–95, 506, 508–10 *(see also* Chavez, Cesar; environmental issues and PM's activism; Peltier, Leonard; *specific works*)
  spirituality/spiritual evolution, xii, xiv, xvi, 9n, 30, 54n, 242, 334, 345, 345–46n, 410–11, 449–52 *(see also* Zen Buddhism: PM and)
  —*1927–1956*, 3–163
  appearance as a young man, 46, 64
  art collection, 112, 112n
  awakening of social conscience, 33–34, 38–39, 66
  birth of daughter Sara Carey, 157
  birth of son Lucas, 137
  boat, *Maudite (Vop-Vop)*, 99–100, 145, 157
  boat, *Merlin*, and charter business, 157, 158
  bogus novel created as CIA cover becomes *Partisans* (1955), 140–42, 145
  Captiva Island, Florida, family vacations, 22
  childhood in Irvington-on-Hudson, 12
  childhood in Stamford, 20–24
  CIA and, xiv, 101, 107–10, 112–14, 128–29, 131–36, 270–72, 615n2, 615n3, 615n4, 615n13, 616n35
  closest friends in early years, 108
  counselor, New Haven Boys Club, 34–35
  Czechoslovakia reporting trip (1948), 80–83
  death of his infant son, Thomas, 114
  defining traumatic event of his early life, 24–25, 606n96
  early experiences in nature, 6–7
  early political views, 105
  East End of Long Island with PS and days as a bayman, 142–63
  equestrian skills, 20
  first novel, *Race Rock* sold (1954), 136–37
  first published work, 107
  first writings of, 37–39
  Fishers Island and boyhood summers, 6, 12, 604n15
  friendship with Jackie and Lee Bouvier, 41
  girlfriends Payne Payson and Wendy Burden, 41–51, 57–58, 60–61, 67–68, 70–72, 83, 85
  at Greenwood Plantation (1947), 67–68
  involvement with Nathalie de Salzmann, 78–80, 84, 85–86
  lifelong friends from school, 19, 19n, 84, 118
  lifelong interest in nature and wild creatures begins, 20, 21–22
  mystical experience at sea, 52, 53n, 54–55, 54n, 152, 317
  New York City residence with PS, 108
  Oahu wartime experiences as basis for novel *Raditzer* (1961), 55, 57–60

in Paris, postwar (1948–49), 73–87
in Paris, with PS (1951–53), 110–37, 138
Paris News Post fiction editor, 116–18
The Paris Review and, xiv, *1*, 19, 118, 118n, 121–36, 146–47, 158–59, 270–72
post-Navy residence in New York, 65–66
PS marriage and break-up, 108, 161–63 (*see also* Southgate, Patricia Brigham "Patsy")
psychoanalysis and, 65–66
in Ravello, with the Styrons, 139–40
reading by, early years, 35–37
rebellion and misbehavior, 26–27, 28, 41–42, 163
rejection of convention, 142–43
rejection of *Social Register* status, 33–34
relationship with his parents, 24–28, 41, 42–43, 48, 64, 147
return from Europe (1953), 142
schools attended, 17–19, 21, 29–35
school years in the family's Upper East Side apartments, 17, 19–20, 19n
in Spain (1949), 87
stories published in *The New Yorker* as writing goal, 117
upbringing of, 15–20, 25, 27
U.S. Navy and, 48–52, 55–63, 609n22, 609n38
WWII and, 29, 34, 37, 40–41
Yale and, 47, 48, 64, 69–71, 88–96, 103, 615n13
—*1957–1973*, 165–352
advocacy journalism: *Sal Si Puedes* (1970) and Cesar Chavez, 102, 135, 280–85, 285n, 304–8, 318, 335–37, 337n, 347, 472, 473, 636n67, 636n79, 658n95
affair with Jane Stanton, 320, 324, 327, 332–33, 350, 368, 641n8
in Africa (1969, 1970) and nonfiction book *The Tree Where Man Was Born* (1973), 291–98, 301–4, 311–12, 340
in Alaska (1957), 177–79
Amazon/South America expedition (1959–60) and nonfiction book *The Cloud Forest* (1961), 191–208
anti–Vietnam War position, support for Eugene McCarthy, 279–80
in Asia, en route to New Guinea (1961), 219
Cayman Islands trip (1966) and the green sea turtle, 272–76 (*see also Far Tortuga*)
circle of friends, 277
commission for essays on shorebirds and *The Shorebirds of North America* (1968), 277
concerns about the future, 280, 285, 636n79
disappearance of Michael Rockefeller and, 241
discussions of death and morbidity of, 325, 640n55
DL relationship and marriage, 214–15, 218, 219, 222, 242–50, 263, 277–78, 289–91, 299, 305, 312–13, 317–20, 323–24, 324n, 327–29, 348–49
DL's cancer and death, PM's grief, and DL's visits as a "presence," xi, 325–35, 338, 345, 642n63
East End Long Island, property in Sagaponack (1960), 213, 250, 277, 305
in Egypt and Africa, en route to New Guinea (1961), 216–18
environmental concerns and Udall consultancy, 267–72, 284, 285, 636n79
Eritrea expedition (1969), 297–98
financial success and freedom as a writer, 266–67
"Florida girl," Karen Yochim, 290, 298–99, 310, 310n, 438–39
funds for alimony and child support, 171, 190
Galápagos Islands trip (1973), 339
great white shark expedition (1969, 1970) and nonfiction account, *Blue Meridian* (1970), 298, 301–4, 308–9, 309n
Hawaii trip (1969), 304
Himalayas expedition (1973), 333–34, 344–52, *353* (*see also Snow Leopard, The*)
Hurxthal safari in Kenya (1970), 312
Ireland trip (1965), 262–64
Italy, at the Castello di Polgeto (1969, 1970), 298–301, 310n, 312–13, 318–19
Netherlands New Guinea Expedition (April to August 1961) resulting in innovative nonfiction, *Under the Mountain Wall* (1962), xiv, 209–41
New York apartment, East 67th St., 325
New Yorker and William Shawn relationship begins with "Peut-être un Peu Excessif" (1957), 172–73
novel *At Play in The Fields of the Lord* written to process his travels (1965), 251–61
post-PS romances, 189–90, 190n, 191, 201
psychedelics and, 25, 206–7, 213–15, 214n, 216, 219, 219n, 242, 247–50, 278, 299, 318–19, 346, 421
reinvents himself as a nature writer, *Wildlife in America* (1957), 170–87
relationship with MM, 310–11, 312, 349–50, 352

—1957–1973 *(continued)*
  Reno divorce from PS (1958), 188–89, 191
  seeking a lost paradise, 246
  son Alexander born (1964), 261
  Tanzania trip with family (1970), 312
  travel/expeditions as escape from his marriage and family, 291
  writing projects (1962–64), 250–61
  writing projects (1969), 305
  Zen practice begins, 4, 286–91, 300, 315–17, 319–30, 337–39, 345–46, 349, 367, 639n9
—*1974–1990*, 353–510
  advocacy journalism: Peltier and *In the Spirit of Crazy Horse* (1983), 458–85, 506, 508, 509, 510, 658–59n120, 658n115, 664n111
  bigfoot and yeti obsession, 389–400, 402–5, 410, 414–16, 415n, 423–25, 442, 447, 460, 488, 647n30, 648n49
  birthday, fiftieth, 426
  birthday, sixtieth, 497–98
  Botswana ornithological safari (1977), 426–27
  Carpenter's kidnapping incident, 427–28, 428n, 442
  circle of friends, 449, 497
  Congo Basin expedition in search of forest elephants (1985–86), 485
  death of his mother, 421, 426
  death of James Jones and, 426
  declaration about the future of his work (1987), 498
  emotional crash following the Himalayas expedition, 366–67
  fame, recognition, and a modern classic published: *The Snow Leopard* (1978), 429–42, 654n67
  fatigue after *Crazy Horse*, 489
  Florida as literary focus: *Killing Mister Watson* (1985–90), 486–94, 497–505, 662n12, 662n20
  Germany trip in search of his ancestors on Föhr (1987), 498
  lawsuits and *Crazy Horse*, 479–85, 482n, 497, 506–8, 507n, 657n83, 660n155, 661n168, 661n169
  malignant melanoma (1983), 483
  Matthiessen family reunion, Yucatán, 367
  miscellaneous projects (1987–89), 498
  Native Americans and, 409–16, 410–11n, 421–26, 423n, 442, 451–85, 508, 655n13, 656n31
  nonfiction books following *Crazy Horse/Indian Country: Men's Lives* and *Nine-Headed Dragon River* (1986), 494–97

  Northern California expedition (1975), 391–94, 648–49n77, 648n49
  Random House contract for untitled novel on the Florida Everglades (1985), 485
  relationship with MM, 367–69, 382, 383–84, 387–89, 400–402, 426, 442–45, 449, 498
  return to fiction writing, *Far Tortuga* (1975), 372–82
  Selous, Tanzania, expedition (1979), 445–47
  Siberia expedition (1990) and nonfiction book *Baikal: Sacred Sea of Siberia* (1992), 509, 509n
  in Tanzania (1975, 1977), 400–402, 427
  thoughts of giving up writing (1984), 489, 494
  Utah trip (1979), 441–42, 654n67
  wedding to MM (1980), 448–49
  West African wildlife survey in The Gambia, Ivory Coast, and Senegal (1978), 437, 437n
  as writing instructor, UC Irvine, 416
  as writing instructor, Yale, 498
  Zaire trip in search of the Congo peafowl (1978), 437, 437n
  Zen commitment and the International Dai Bosatsu Zendo construction and fundraising, 369–71
  Zen disillusionment, 406–9
  Zen practice revival and ordination, 418–20, 449, 496, 498
—*1991–2014*, 511–89
  advocacy for Peltier clemency, 550–52, 552n
  Antarctica expeditions and nonfiction book *End of the Earth*, 553–54, 553n
  Arctic Alaska trip with Alex (2002), 556
  Asian crane excursion (1993), 536
  Auschwitz-Birkenau novel: *In Paradise*, 570–76, 581, 583, 589, 590, 671n18
  cancer and final months 2012–2014, 574–89
  circle of friends, 522, 567, 576, 581–82, 586–87, 588, 591
  continued interest in yeti and bigfoot, 532, 561, 569
  death, mushroom analogy and, 579, 672n63
  death of, media responses, 590
  death of Bill Styron, 578–79
  death of friends, 577–79
  death of grandson, Christopher, 542–43, 572

environmental activism and final nonfiction books, 554–58, 561, 574, 669n127
environmental book "Tiger and Crane" becomes *Tigers in the Snow* and *The Birds of Heaven* (2000, 2001), 534, 552–53
Eurasian crane excursion in East Anglia, England (1995), 539
Faroe Islands, Iceland, and Greenland anthropological film expedition (1993), 526–28, 537
fishing trip, Madison River rapids, Montana (2009), 567–68
Golden Eagle Festival trip (2012), 575–76
Heinz Award prize (2000) and use of the funds, 550
international crane conference and voyage on the Amur River, Russia (1992), 533
interviews during his final months, 585
Lakota healing ceremony (yuwipi), 580–81
magazine pieces on "Tiger and Crane," 552–53
in Malick film, *Knight of Cups*, 574
memorial service and reception, 591
MM reacts to his relationship with "K" and ensuing estrangement, 582–85, 588–89
Mongolia trip and white-naped crane (1992), 533–34
National Book Award for *Shadow Country* and vindication, 564–65
Nepal trip (1992) and expedition account, *East of La Monthang*, 531–32
projects of his final years, 569–76
Russian trips (1992, 1996), Hornocker's Siberian Tiger Project and, 532–33, 533n, 541
Shainberg interview (1993), 528
travels of 1996, Russia, Korea, Australia, Bali, India, and South Africa, 541–42
unfinished memoir (working title "Droppings"), 569, 585
Watson consolidation idea and *Shadow Country* (2008), 549–50, 558–65
Watson "continuation" (Watson II) *Lost Man's River* (1991–97), 530–31, 534–41, 542–46
Watson "continuation" (Watson III) *Bone by Bone* (1999), 546–50
Wyoming fly-fishing trip (1991) and MM discovers his serial infidelity 520–22
Zen and "engaged Buddhism," 570–71
Zen teaching and practice as Muryo Sensei/Muryo Roshi, 513–29, 577, 577n
—*literary career*
advocacy journalism and, 39, 454–57, 461, 465, 494–95, 506, 508–10, 554–58 (*see also* Chavez, Cesar; Peltier, Leonard; *specific works*)
African Wildlife Leadership Foundation Award, 446
on aging and writing, 568–69
American Academy of Arts and Letters awards, 250–51
American Academy of Arts and Letters induction, 371–72
approach to writing about animals and landscapes of East Africa, 296
beginning as a writer, 37–38
bifurcation of works between Viking and Random House, 430
book proposal that changed the direction of his life, 173–74
death associated with shorebirds in writing of, 577
desire for literary greatness and consolidation of Watson novels, 558–65
desire for peer recognition, 372
disinterest in realism, 151, 151n
dominant theme of life and works, 574
early rejections of his stories, 109, 616n52
earnings, 170–71n, 173, 216, 258, 261, 266–67, 381, 431, 471, 485, 495, 530
editor at Random House, Joe Fox, 257–60, 267n, 273, 277, 309n, 372, 381–82, 391, 438
editor at Viking, Elisabeth Sifton, 430–31, 434–35, 438, 471–73, 476, 480, 483–84
editors at Random House, Jason Epstein and Rebecca Saletan, 500, 531, 537
experimental approach and style of *Under the Mountain Wall*, 234–36, 239, 240
final nonfiction books and environmental activism, 554–58
first novel sold, published, 27, 136–37 (*see also Race Rock*)
first published work in *Atlantic Monthly*, 107
first writings of, 37–39
Florida in the life and work of, 487–505, 487n (*see also Bone by Bone*; *Killing Mister Watson*; *Lost Man's River*; *Shadow Country*)

—literary career (continued)
friendships with authors (*see* Harrison, Jim; Plimpton, George; Styron, William "Bill")
habit of forwarding edited books to experts for comments and corrections, 435–36
Hadada Award, 564
Howells Medal and statement on art, 566
ideas about the novel form, 215–16
impact of *In the Spirit of Crazy Horse*, 458
influence of Zen, 377
influences of other authors, 35–37, 58n, 256, 256n, 341, 614n21
influential reading, 299–300
innovations and themes in *At Play in the Fields of the Lord*, 256
"intuitive absolute truth" and, 276, 276n, 346n, 394
John Burroughs Medal, 446
legacy of, 590
life demands and conflict with his writing, 528
literary agents (*see* Baumgarten, Bernice; Donadio, Candida; Olson, Neil; Russell, Diarmuid)
literary ambitions as a young man, 46
"Literature and Mysticism" (lecture), 206
major works and literary reputation, 590
National Book Awards and nominations, xiv, 269, 272, 344, 441–42, 441n, 471, 564, 635n26, 654n67
National Geographic style of expedition writing, 235
as nature writer/"naturalist-writer," xiii–xiv, 170–87, 261, 485, 509n, 554, 626n75
as nature writer, awards, 485
nature writing, thoughts about, 183, 554
New Yorker as literary home, xiv, 107, 117, 172–73, 190–92, 194–95, 197, 199, 202, 203, 207, 212, 214n, 261, 273, 274, 276, 283, 292, 298, 305, 341, 372, 392, 394, 437, 446, 526–27, 532, 628n40, 635n36
O. Henry Prize, 170
"obscure longing" and, 206
paradox in his writing about Indigenous people, 457–58
reaction to criticism, xv, 538, 539, 544, 546
reading and criticism by and for John Irving, 499
reflection on his career and writing habits: interview for "The Art of Fiction No. 157," 88, 549–50
reputation resting on his nonfiction books, 372, 558
rising profile as a literary figure, media and, 277, 277n
Roger Tory Peterson Medal, 557
role of MM, 442, 443–44, 537
Roth's "magnet" in each book and, 540
Sal Si Puedes as a departure from previous books, 305–6
screenwriting, 335, 347n, 376, 409, 411
self-identifying as a fiction writer, xiv, 170, 183
singular power of perception, 340
style and experimentation of *Far Tortuga*, 374, 374–75, 376–77, 378
syncretic language of, xii
technical writing interspersed with poetry, *The Shorebirds of North America* (1968), 277
themes preferred, 215
value distinction between his fiction and nonfiction, 307, 440–41, 558, 565
value distinction within his nonfiction ("cause" books versus personal interest), 307–8
Viking Penguin estrangement, 483–84
Viking Press as his publisher, 55, 159–60, 174, 183, 202, 215, 237, 256
Watson "continuation" as career challenge, 530, 530–31, 534–50
wildlife as a metaphor, 37
work habits, 3, 513
on writers' need to "stretch themselves," 502
writing as an antidote, 569
Yale and Charles A. Fenton's class, 90–92
Yale's Daily Themes class and finding footing as a writer, 88–95
See also Paris Review, The; Random House; Viking Press; *specific works of fiction and nonfiction*
Matthiessen, Ralph Henry (uncle), 10, 12, 13
Matthiessen, Rue (adopted daughter), 23, 215, 244, 245, 261–62, 278, 288, 310, 311, 312
at British boarding school, 315, 317
determination to leave home, 314–15
DL's final illness and death, 326, 328–30, 332, 348
DL's morbidity, 325
impact of DL's death on brother, Alex, 347–48
Ireland trip with PM, 262–64
memoir of, 525
PM's death and, 587, 588, 589
PM's Himalayas expedition and, 358–59

Index · 695

psychotherapy and, 309
relationship with PM, 314–15, 329–30, 348–49, 524, 525–26
The Snow Leopard and, 433
on Zen and PM, 519
Matthiessen, Sara Carey (daughter), 157, 162, 191, 261, 263, 296–97, 449, 524
mental illness and suicide, 587
PM's death and, 587
Seal Pool and, 251n
Matthiessen, Thomas (son), 114
Maximilian of Wied-Neuwied, Prince, 174–75
Maxwell, William, 107
Mboya, Tom, 304, 304n
McCarthy, Eugene, 279–80, 280n
McCarthy, Mary, 107
McChesney, John "Mr. Mac," 37
McCloud, Janet, 451, 474
McDonell, Terry, xiv, 85, 379, 591
The Accidental Life, 581
McDougal, Charles, 351
McGrath, Charles, 546, 564
McGuane, Thomas, 503
McKibben, Bill, xiii
McKiernan, Kevin, 457, 467, 474
McMurtry, Larry, 379–80
McNeely, Jeffrey, 350–51, 389, 643n90
"The Yeti—not a Snowman," 389
Mead, Margaret, 211
Means, Russell, 460, 465, 476
Means, Ted, 461
Meiburg, Jonathan, 585
Meldrum, Jeff, 560
Menaker, Daniel, 539
Men's Lives (1986), 143, 143n, 155, 155n, 163, 494–95
as advocacy journalism, 495
critics and reviews, 495
funding for, 495
photography by Doug Kuntz, 495
plight of the Bonackers, 495, 495n
Merrill, Christopher, 436
Merwin, William, 386, 431, 438, 482, 484, 495, 497, 503, 543
Merzel, Dennis Genpo, 419
Messud, Claire, 651n41
Mewshaw, Michael, 545
Miami Herald: PM's advocacy for Native Americans and, 454
Michaelis, David, 101
Michaux, Henri, 214n
Michod, Alec, 585
"Midnight Turning Gray" (PM), 251
Midriff Islands, Mexico, 525
Millar, Stuart, 267, 267n
Miller, Arthur, 75, 380

Miller, Michael, 396–97, 404
Minot, Frank, 297
Mionczynski, John, 560
Mitgang, Herbert, 507
Modern Library, 559
editor Sternlight and, 560, 561–62, 563
PM's Watson consolidation *Shadow Country* and, 559, 560–63
Mongolia
Golden Eagle Festival trip (2012), 575–76
PM's trip to report on white-naped crane (1992), 533–34
Monongye, David, 413
Montoya, Felix and Stella, 411, 655n13
Mook, Charles, 207, 208
Morath, Inge, 536
Mountaineers Books, 557
Mountain Travel, Kathmandu, 344, 351
Moyers, Scott, 559
Muir, John, 169
Mumonkan (Wumen Huikai), 1, 300
Musée de la Reddition, Reims, France, 82

Nabokov, Nicolas, 120
Nabokov, Peter, 457
Nakagawa, Soen (Soen Roshi), 286, 288, 322, 337, 338, 369–70, 408, 650n14
Nangle, Benjamin, 88
Nation, The
PM and the CIA and, 128, 619n163
PM's advocacy for Native Americans and, 454
review of *Raditzer*, 216
"Who Really Killed the F.B.I. Men" (PM), 509
National Audubon Society, 184
PM and acquisition of land around the Corkscrew Swamp, Florida, 487–88
See also Audubon magazine
National Geographic Society, 344
Native Americans, 451–85
Chumash band, California, 458, 656n33
Cree nation, Manitoba, xv
Gwich'in and, 556
Hoopa Valley Reservation, California, 411, 413, 414, 425
Indian Country and, 455–57
Iñupiat people, 178, 556
Jicarilla Apache, 451
Lakota healing ceremony (yuwipi), 580–81
Lakota people, 460
Mississippi Chippewa, 455
Morongo Reservation, California, 452
Oglala Lakota, 461–62
Paiutes, 452

Native Americans (continued)
  Pit River Tribe, 451
  PM, Peltier, and *In the Spirit of Crazy Horse* and, 458–85, 506
  PM and Craig Carpenter, 411–17, 422–28, 451
  PM and Hopi Reservation, Arizona, 422–25, 423n, 451
  PM and parallels between Native American traditions and Zen, 426, 451
  PM at Medicine Flat, 414, 415
  PM begins affiliation with (1976), 409–16, 410–11n, 421
  PM concept for a book titled "Indian Energy," 453, 455
  PM eight-state trip (1979), 451–53
  PM focuses on bigfoot in Native American lore, 410, 411, 415, 423–25, 442, 447, 451–53, 460, 655n10
  PM's advocacy journalism and articles written, 453–57, 655n13 (*see also specific works*)
  PM's articles on "the New Indian Wars," 454–55
  PM's continuing relationship with, 472
  PM's Diné hitchhiker, 176–77, 195, 254
  PM's "Native Earth" and spirituality of, 456
  PM's psychological relationship to, 472
  PM's writing about the Miccosukee of Florida, 447, 452, 465, 657n60
  PM with Utes in Utah, 442
  Point Conception protests and "Western Gate," 458–59, 656n33
  poverty of, 453
  romanticizing of, 457–58, 655n13
  Salish settlements, 452
  Santa Barbara Indian Center, 458
  Shinnecock Indian Nation, 506
  St. Regis Mohawk Reservation, 455
  Tellico Dam and Eastern Cherokee, 454
  Torres Martinez Desert Cahuilla Indians, 452
  "Traditionals," 409, 409n, 412, 413, 424, 458, 459
  Tuscarora tribe, New York state, 452
  Wounded Knee Occupation, 460, 461
  Yupik people, 177, 178
  Yurok culture, 452
  See also Indian Country
"Native Earth" (PM), 456, 457, 656n31
Naturalist on the River Amazons, The (Bates), 165, 192, 196
Nature Conservancy, 179, 421
  Hawaii bird habitat and, 304
Naval Training Center, Sampson, New York, 48

Nepal
  Arun Valley, 351, 389
  Dolpo, ii, xi, 333, 334, 344, 351, 355, 389, 391n, 643–44n2
  Kathmandu, 350
  PM's 1992 trip and expedition account, *East of La Monthang*, 531–32
  Phoksundo Lake, xii, 356
  Pokhara, 352
  Richardson's expedition (2022), xii, xvi–xvii, 355–56, 643–44n2
  Shey Phoksundo National Park, 344, 344n
  Upper Mustang, or Lo, the "forbidden kingdom," 531
  yeti and, 389
  See also Himalayas expedition
Neruda, Pablo, 132
Netherlands New Guinea. *See* New Guinea
Neurosis and Human Growth (Horney), 299–300
"New Alchemy, The" (Watts), 248
New Guinea (Netherlands New Guinea), 210, 211
  Archbold Expedition, 220, 227
  Baliem Valley, 211–12, 220–21, 227, 237, 630n56
  Denison-Crockett Expedition (1937–38), 222, 222n
  Harvard-Peabody Expedition (1961), xiv, 209–41, 629n17, 630n56, 631n107
  Hollandia (now Jayapura), 216, 220, 223, 223n, 231
  Indonesian takeover, 237, 237n
  plane crash in "Shangri-La," 220, 630n56
New School for Social Research, New York, 65
  lectures by W. H. Auden and Ruth Benedict, 65
  PM's courses at, 65
  Zen class by DL, 319–20, 324, 328
Newsday review of *Lost Man's River*, 545
Newsweek, 478
  PM's advocacy for Native Americans and, 454
New Yorker magazine, 91, 184
  changes at (1960s), 283
  editor White's criticism of PM, 117
  Flanner on French anti-Americanism, 110, 617n59
  funding PM's Amazon and Africa trips, 191, 292
  funding PM's Grand Cayman trips, 273, 274, 276, 635n36
  funding PM's Northern California expedition to find bigfoot, 392, 394

Maxwell meets with PM, 107
"Peruvian Journal" (PM), 207, 214n
PM and Tina Brown at, 539
PM article about a Siberian tiger, 532
PM article about Eritrea expedition, 298
PM as "gentleman naturalist" for, 261
PM reports on whaling and the Inughuits of Greenland, 526–27
PM's Grand Cayman project and "To the Miskito Bank," 276, 372
PM's Harvard-Peabody Expedition and, 212
PM's literary ambitions and, 46
PM's pieces from "Tiger and Crane" research trips, 552
PM's profile of Cesar Chavez and, 283, 305
PM's series "The Last Wilderness," 190–92, 194–95, 197, 199, 202, 203, 446, 628n40
PM's *Snow Leopard* excerpts, 437
PM's stories rejected, 109, 117
PM's *The Tree Where Man Was Born* excerpts, 341
PM's writing about the Miccosukee of Florida rejected by, 465, 657n60
Salter on PM's death, 590
Schulz article on *The Snow Leopard*, 440
New York Herald Tribune
  review of *Raditzer*, 216
  review of *The Cloud Forest*, 202
"New York: Old Hometown" (PM), 604n25
New York Review of Books
  "The Blue Pearl of Siberia" (PM), 509n
  Peltier clemency petition and, 551
  PM's advocacy for Native Americans, 454
  PM's report on oil drilling in Alaska, 561
  protest against treatment of Farbar, 498
  review of *Crazy Horse*, 477
  review of *Far Tortuga*, 379
  review of *Indian Country*, 457
  review of *Killing Mister Watson*, 503
  review of *Shadow Country*, 564
  review of *The Snow Leopard*, 439
New York Times (*NYT*)
  article examining National Book Award nomination for *Shadow Country*, 564
  article on Falk's speech on man's risk of "irreversible catastrophe," 285, 636n79
  Barry on Americans and the dream of Paris, 72
  damning article on Eido Roshi, 409
  Dershowitz review of *Crazy Horse*, 477–78, 659n136, 659n139
  the "In Crowd" and PM, 276–77
  McGrath's interview with PM (2008), 546
  PM and CIA exposé, 101, 113, 443, 615n2
  PM obituary, 34, 590
  on Price lawsuit loss against Viking, 507
  PS obituary, 84
  Rensberger article on bigfoot, 395
  review of *The Cloud Forest*, 202
  review of *Crazy Horse*, 477
  review of *Far Tortuga*, 379
  review of *Killing Mister Watson*, 503
  review of *Men's Lives*, 495
  review of *Nine-Headed Dragon River*, 496
  review of *Race Rock*, 153
  review of *Raditzer*, 216
  review of *The Snow Leopard*, 439–40
  review of *The Tree Where Man Was Born*, 343–44
  review of *Under the Mountain Wall*, 239
  review of *Wildlife in America*, 184
  Wallace's bigfoot hoax article, 399n
New York Times Magazine
  "High Noon in the Black Hills" (PM), 461
  PM profile (2014), 585
  PM's advocacy for Native Americans and, 454
New York Zoological Society, 344, 371, 485
Nicholson, Brian, 446
"Nightfall in Another Country" (PM), 162
Nine-Headed Dragon River (1986), 495–97, 519, 528, 642n63
  death of PM's infant son and, 114
  PM encounters roshis and a monk in his Sagaponack driveway, 286, 637n3
  poor reception of, 496
  wife MM's response to, 519
Nixon, Richard, 335, 364
Noble, Louisa, 130–31n
Nonnie & Alex (film), 367n
Norman, Howard, 138, 169n, 229, 451, 458, 488, 502, 503, 504, 538, 544, 548, 672n64
  PM interview for "The Art of Fiction No. 157," 88, 549–50, 559
North American Indians (Catlin), 625n35
  PM introduction for re-release, 498
Northern California expedition (1975), 391–94
  New Yorker magazine funding, 392, 394
North Point Press
  The Birds of Heaven: Travels with Cranes (2001), 553
  Tigers in the Snow (2000), 553

Oahu, Hawaii, 55–63
  Aiea Barracks, 56, 61
  Japanese attack on Pearl Harbor and, 55

Oahu, Hawaii *(continued)*
  PM posted on, 55–63, 610n61
  PM's experiences as basis for novel *Raditzer* (1961), 55, 57–60
  PM's interaction with a fisherman, 59
  PM's mood swings and unhappiness, 60–61
  PM's reading during time on, 56
  PM writing for *The Honolulu Advertiser*, 61
  postwar discharge of troops from, 56
  transformation during WWII years, 55–56
  tsunami of 1946, 59–60
Oates, Joyce Carol, 503, 503n
O'Brien, Maisie (nanny), 20
"October in Valhalla" (PM), 92–93
O'Hara, Frank, 97, 189, 263n, 623n134
Olmsted, Frederick Law, Jr., 5
Olson, Neil, 549, 558, 586
  Lost Man's River and, 540–41, 542, 544
  PM's concerns about Random House, 558
  as PM's primary agent, 540
  PM's Watson consolidation and, 559–60, 565
  sale of *In Paradise*, 583
"One Winter" (DL), 319
"On the River Styx" (PM), 487n
On the River Styx (1989), 94n, 95, 500–501n
  "Horse Latitudes," 193n
  NYT's review, 95
Oppen, George, 4
Orientalism (Said), 438
Ortiz, Simon, 503
Otto, Rudolph: *The Idea of the Holy*, 53n
Our Vanishing Wildlife: Its Extermination and Preservation (Hornaday), 181–82, 183
Outside magazine
  Anderson attacks *In the Spirit of Crazy Horse*, 510, 657n62, 658n120, 664n111
  PM's piece on Alaska oil drilling, 556–57
  PM's pieces from "Tiger and Crane" research trips in, 552
  review of *Indian Country*, 457
"Ovibos Moschatus" (later *Oomingmak*) (PM), 261, 261n
Owen, James, 344
Owen, John, 291–92, 310, 341
  book proposal for PM and offer of quarters in the Serengeti, Tanzania, 292
  "Give a Lion a Home" campaign, 292, 310
  invites Schaller to study lions in the Serengeti, 294

Paget, Walter, 99
Paley, William, 276
Paris, France
  anti-Americanism in, 110, 111, 138, 617n59
  Barry on Americans and the dream of Paris, 72
  Buchwald's memories of postwar years, 75
  Grande Nuit de Paris, 74
  Hôtel Liberia, 119
  Humes and the *Paris News Post*, 115–16
  Jeu de Paume, 112
  Le Dôme, 115, 130n
  the Lost Generation in, 72
  magazines in postwar Paris, 116
  "Masterpieces of the Twentieth Century" festival, CIA and, 120
  PM and Gurdjieff's philosophy, 80, 85, 89
  PM and PS in (1951–53), 110–37, 138
  PM and women, 83–86
  PM residence, rue de Chazelles, 129
  PM residence, rue Perceval, 111–12, 118, 119, 120, 123–24, 127, 129
  PM's Atlantic crossing and arrival in, 74
  PM's CIA activity in, 112–14, 116, 120, 617n74
  PM's classes in, 78, 83
  PM's extracurricular activities, 83
  PM's friends: "Tall Young Men," 113
  PM's Junior Year in France, 1948–49, 73–87
  PM's side trips from his base in, 76, 87
  PM's son Lucas born, 137
  PM's writing inspired by, 87
  postwar Americans in, 72–73
  postwar arrival by Arthur Miller in, 75
  postwar rationing in, 73, 74–75
  Reid Hall as the center of student life, 77–78, 84, 119
  Styron comments on, 121
  Tristan Tzara in, 119–20, 120n
Paris News Post, 116–18, 116n
  PM as fiction editor, 116–18, 618n100
  as precursor to *The Paris Review*, 118, 118n
  sale of, 121
Paris Review, The, xiv
  Aga Khan as publisher, 158
  Aga Khan Prize for Fiction, 158
  "Art of Fiction" interview series, 125, 540
  "The Art of Fiction No. 157" (interview with PM), 88, 549–50, 559
  authors published by, 122, 126, 131, 131n, 136

chaotic workspace of, 130–31, 130–31n
concept of, 125–26, 619n153
contributions of PS ignored, 124
fiftieth-anniversary issue, 578
financial problems, 146–47
funding for, 127–29, 131
gérant (legal representative) for, 130
Hadada Award for PM and, 564
Humes and founding of, 118, 118n, 121, 125, 130n
inaugural issue, 136
managing editor Silvers, 158
"Miss Aptecker," 130, 130–31n
naming of, 124–25, 619n145
Paris headquarters for, 129–30
Plimpton and, 19, 121–23, 124, 126, 127, 130, 130n, 132, 146–47, 158
Plimpton interview with PM on *Far Tortuga*, 375
PM and, 121–36, 130n, 146–47, 158, 271, 271n
PM at rue Perceval and, 111–12
PM resigns, remains a board member, 158–59
PM's CIA involvement and, 101, 102, 120, 128–29, 131, 270–71, 615n2, 619n163
PM's move to Springs, Long Island, and, 146–47
PM's "self-portrait," *1*
seeds of planted at St. Bernard's, 19
staff for, 122, 125
Talese's "Looking for Hemingway" as a "painting" of the group, 122–23
wealthy backers for, 122, 126, 127
Partisan Review, 125
Partisans (1955), 101, 140–42, 145, 150, 153, 159–61, 251, 577n
CIA cover story and, 140
critics and reviews, 160
PM's Czechoslovakia trip and, 83, 141
published by Viking Press, 160
Styron's commentary on, 160–61
Patterson, Roger, 403, 649n103
Pawel, Miriam, 305
Payson, Charles Shipman, 68
Payson, Joan Whitney, 47, 67
Payson, Payne Whitney
breakup with PM, 83–84
PM's letters to, 49, 50–51, 57, 60, 61
PM vacations in Georgia with, 67–68
relationship with PM, 47–48, 68, 71
at Sarah Lawrence, 71
Peacock, Doug, 500, 522
Pearcy, Glen, 347n
Pearson, Norman Holmes, 103, 153
OSS and X-2, 103–4

Pelham-Clinton-Hope, Henry, 7
Peltier, Leonard, xiv, 102, 135, 658n115
AIM and, 459
attorneys for, 460–61, 465, 467, 468
background, 459
Baer documentary, 506
escape from Lompoc and capture, 460–61
executive clemency by Biden of, 552n
innocence of, 508–10, 658n115
in Lompoc Federal Correctional Institution, 459
Pine Ridge shootout and murder of two FBI agents, 459, 461, 462–64, 467, 474–75, 656n45
PM and, 459, 466, 475, 506, 508, 510
PM and *In the Spirit of Crazy Horse*, 458–85, 508, 658–59n120
PM and clemency bid from Clinton, 550–52
PM visiting in USP Marion, 468–69, 468n
political and international support for, 508
trial of, 464, 464n, 467
Penguin Books, 431
Pepper, George, 170, 170–71n
"Peruvian Journal" (PM), 207, 214n
Petersen, Matthias (ancestor), 7–8
Peterson, Roger Tory, 175, 184
review of *Wildlife in America*, 184
"Peut-être un Peu Excessif" (PM and Bradlee), 172–73, 190, 625n25
Pickrel, Paul, 240
Pine Ridge Indian Reservation, 461–62
PM and Robideau visit, 461, 464, 467, 508
shootout and murder of two FBI agents, 462–64, 474–75, 656n45
"X" hoax confession to executing the FBI agents, 508–10
Planz, Allen, 517
Plimpton, George Ames, 19, 19n, 85, 118, 449
career of, 121–22
complains about PM in Springs, 146
correspondence with PM, 150, 152, 201
death of, 578
Fourth of July celebration, 391
at Harvard and Cambridge, 121–22, 128
interviews PM on *Far Tortuga*, 375
Paris Review and, 19, 121–26, 130, 130n, 131n, 132, 146–47, 158–59
in Paris with PM, 122
PM's Asian crane excursion and (1993), 536

700 · Index

Plimpton, George Ames *(continued)*
   PM's lifelong friendship with, 190, 498
   at St. Bernard's School, 19
Plimpton, Sarah, 437n
Pough, Richard, 179
Points magazine, 116
Pollock, Clement W., Jr., 244–45, 314, 349
Pollock, Jackson, 148–50, 149n, 157, 623n134
   fatal auto accident and death of, 162
Poor Bear, Myrtle, 470
Poore, Charles, 216
Porebski, Elizabeth and Peter, 516
Porras Cáceres, Andrés, 203, 204
Porter, Eliot, 339, 343
Pospíšil, Leopold, 210, 239–40
Potter, Jeffrey, 156–57, 161–62
Potter, Penny, 157, 161
Powdermaker, Florence, 65–66
"Powerboat Cruising" (PM), 171–72
Price, David, 470, 482n, 657n83
   lawsuit against PM and Viking, 479–83, 497, 506–8, 657n83, 660n155, 661n168, 661n169
Prohaska, Anton, 162
psychedelics
   ayahuasca, 206–7, 213–14, 214n, 249
   Humes and mental breakdown, 270
   LSD history, 247–48, 286–87, 633n42
   manifestation of the *Mysterium tremendum*, 215
   mescaline and, 213–15, 216, 247, 249
   PM, DL, and, 215, 242, 243, 247, 249–50, 278
   PM and LSD, xiv, 25, 242, 247–50, 249n, 278, 299, 300, 421
   PM's interest in wanes, 318–19
   PM's LSD journal, 299, 377
   PM's spiritual evolution and, 346
   psilocybin "magic" mushrooms, 214
   psychotherapy and, 248–49
   Watts and, 247–48
Publishers Weekly: PM interview (1986), 496
Putnam, Samuel, 212, 224
Pynchon, Thomas, 380

Quammen, David, 186
Quiet Crisis, The (Udall), 268

Race Rock (1954), 26, 27–28, 28n, 142n, 145, 150–54, 151n
   critics and reviews, 153
   editor for, 150, 152
   Harper & Brothers buys, issues advance, 136–37
   idealization of the working class, 154
   nascent thoughts about the sublime, mortality, and transcendence, 152–53, 152n
   original title "Signs of Winter," 115, 137, 145, 152
   publication date, 150
   sales of, 153
   Salzmann's pregnancy and, 86–87
   title chosen, 152
Raditzer (1961), 44, 55, 190, 209, 215–16
   critics and reviews, 216
   PM's wartime experiences on Oahu and, 55, 57–58, 59, 60
   PM's mystical experience at sea, 54
   published by Viking Press, 55
   screen rights sold, 216
Random House
   advance for "WATSON II" (1990), 530
   Blue Meridian (1971), 308, 430
   Bone by Bone (1999), 545, 548–49, 558
   DL's *Annaghkeen* bought by Nan Talese, 291, 634n108
   Epstein and, 429, 430
   Far Tortuga (1974), 372, 381, 430, 538
   Futter leaves, 549, 559
   Killing Mister Watson (1990), 500, 500–501n, 502, 506
   Lost Man's River published (1997), 545
   Lost Man's River taken on by new executive editor, Deb Futter, 542, 543
   Lost Man's River thought unpublishable, 538–39
   Moyers suggests Modern Library for PM's Watson consolidation, 559
   At Play in the Fields of the Lord (1965), 257–58, 260, 266–67
   PM's fiction promised to, 430
   Sal Si Puedes (1970), 308
Ravello, Italy, 139–40
"Recognition" (PM), 234
Redford, Robert, 468, 468n
Reno, Janet, 550, 551
Rensberger, Boyce, 395
"Replacement, The" (PM), 117
Richards, Silvia, 416–17
Ripley, Sidney Dillon, 89, 222, 222n
Ritchey, Claire, 17
Robideau, Robert "Bob," 461, 463, 467, 477
   "X" hoax confession and, 508–10
Rockefeller, Laurence, 371
Rockefeller, Michael, xiv, 268, 371
   arrow wound of, 227, 231
   disappearance and fate of, 240–41
   Harvard-Peabody Expedition and, 212, 222, 226–27, 232–33, 236

nightmares and prescience of his death, 233
Rocky Mountain Magazine
  long PM environmental piece in, 454
Roger Williams College, Rhode Island, 489, 494
Roiphe, Anne
  1185 Park Avenue, 19n
Rolland, Romain, 52
Roosevelt, Franklin Delano (FDR), 31
  Infamy Speech, 29
Rosenbaum, Ron, 585
Roth, Philip: "Art of Fiction" interview in *Paris Review*, 540
Roueché, Berton, 149n
"Rousing of the Rabble, The" (PM), 38–39
Rube, Calvin, 414, 415
Russell, Diarmuid
  At Play in the Fields of the Lord and, 256–57, 258
  PM parts ways with, 380, 646n77
  PM signs with, 190
Russell & Volkening literary agency, 190
Russia
  Khabarovsk international crane conference and Amur River voyage (1992), 533
  PM's trips to Hornocker's Siberian Tiger Project (1992, 1996), 532–33, 541
  Siberia expedition to Lake Baikal (1990), 509n

Sacramento Bee review of *Wildlife in America*, 184
"Sadie" (PM), 68, 93–95, 94n, 107, 151, 492
  award for, 108
  character of Dewey Floyd and subsequent guises, 95
  effect on PM's career, 95
  published in *Atlantic Monthly*, 100
Safina, Carl, 582, 585, 591
Sagaponack, Long Island, 250
  Capote in, 240
  DL's grave in, 332, 338, 525–26, 591
  environmental concerns about, 267–68
  Harrison visits PM in, 366
  Hurricane Sandy and, 576
  Koenigs renting a summer house, 310
  PM garden party (1990), 506, 508
  PM in, after DL's death, 331–35
  PM in, after Harvard-Peabody Expedition, 250
  PM purchases property, 213
  PM's death in, 588–89
  PM's film rights money and home renovations, 277–78
  PM's home, 3, 4, 250, 277, 310, 514
  PM's home, MM and children move in, 388–89
  PM's home estate sale and fate of, 592–93
  PM's memorial service, internment, and reception, 591
  PM's "Ocean Zendo," 513–14, 517, 520, 523, 574
  PM's upstairs zendo, 366, 515
  PM's writing studio or "shed," 3–4, 435, 498, 513, 523, 585, 593
  PM's Zen students in, 515–18
Said, Edward: *Orientalism*, 438
Saletan, Rebecca, 500, 500–501n
  Killing Mister Watson editing and, 500–501
  In Paradise and, 583–84
Sal Si Puedes: Cesar Chavez and the New American Revolution (1970), 285, 285n, 305–8, 335, 473
  book jacket for, 308
  contrasted with Mailer and Didion, 306–7
  PM's editorial asides in, 306
  PM's "ethical imperative" and, 307–8
  techniques of New Journalism used in, 306
Salter, James, xiv, 257, 571, 578–79, 590
Salzmann, Alexandre de, 79
Salzmann, Michel de, 79
Salzmann, Nathalie de, 76, 78–79, 84, 86n
  Gurdjieffian philosophy and, 79, 86n, 89
  PM and, 78–80, 84, 85–86, 111
  pregnancy of, 85–86
Sanctuary (Faulkner), 92
"Sand and Wind and Waves" (PM), 261
Saroyan, William: *Dear Baby*, 36–37
Sand Rivers (PM), 294n, 446
  as account of the Selous expedition (1979), 446
  awards won, 446
  epidemic of poaching and, 447
  photos by van Lawick, 446
  PM's convictions about race and, 447
Saturday Review: PM interview (1955), 160
Saunders, Frances Stonor: *The Cultural Cold War*, 128
Schaller, George, xi, 294–96, 333
  discovery of a "yeti" painting, 353, 389–90, 391n
  friendship with PM, 363

Schaller, George *(continued)*
Himalayas expedition with PM (1973), xvii, 333–34, 350–52, 356–60, 363, 429, 531
PM and the dying lioness, 295–96, 638n47
PM's interest in bigfoot and yeti, 395–97, 532
PM's interest in Zen and, 334
The Serengeti Lion, 344
The Snow Leopard and, 363, 435
Schaller, Kay, 334
Schanker, Libby Holman, 370
Schultes, Richard Evan, 214n
Schulz, Kathryn, 440
Schuster, Michael, 586
Schwartz, John Burnham, 548
Scott, A. O., 545
Scott, Robert Falcon: *Terra Nova* Expedition to the South Pole, 263
Sea and the Jungle, The (Tomlinson), 192, 192n
Seal Pool (PM), 251, 251n
See, Carolyn, 477
Seeler, David, 576
Selous, Tanzania, expedition (1979), 445–47
as "the last safari into the last wilderness," 446
New Yorker "Last Wilderness" series and, 446
photographer for, 446
PM's infidelity and, 447–48
poaching epidemic in the reserve, 447, 447n
Sand Rivers based on, 446–47
size of the game reserve, 446
sponsor for, 445–46
team members, 446
Selver, Charlotte, 287
Semple, Lorenzo Jr., 465, 468n
Senzaki, Nyogen, 418
Serengeti Lion, The (Schaller), 344
Sewald, Jeff, xv, 147, 519, 569
Seymour, Horatio (ancestor), 14, 14n
Shadow Country (2008), 392, 558–65, 590
changes to original texts, 562–64
consolidation of Watson books, "one work" idea and, 549–50
critics and reviews, 564
editor Sternlight and, 560, 561–62, 563
Howells Medal, 566
National Book Award, 564–65
Olson's help with, 559–60
PM met with resistance to a Watson consolidation, 558
PM's motive for the consolidation, 558, 559

Younce's advice on, 560
See also Bone by Bone; *Killing Mister Watson*; *Lost Man's River*
Shainberg, Lawrence, 317, 513, 662n39
Shaku, Soyen, 9n
Shaw, Irwin, 113–14, 119, 126–27, 139, 146, 426
Shaw, Marian, 113, 119, 126, 139, 617n75
Shawn, William, 172, 173, 184
PM and Bradlee's "Peut-être un Peu Excessif" and, 172–73, 625n25
PM's account of the Dani and, 235–36
PM's South America expedition and, 190–91, 198, 199
PM's conversation about *Far Tortuga* and, 276, 635n36
PM's profile of Cesar Chavez and, 283
PM's search for bigfoot and, 392, 394
PM's *The Tree Where Man Was Born* and, 341
on PM's writing, 276n
Sheltering Sky, The (Bowles), 256
Shepard, Paul, 344
Sherman, Scott, 128, 619n163
Sherry, John and Dorothy, 245
Shey Gompa, the Crystal Monastery, xi, xvi–xvii, 333, 344
journey to reach, 355–60
PM at, 360–63
Schaller's discovery of a "yeti" painting, 391n
Shimano, Eido Tai (Eido Roshi), 286, 287–88, 289, 319, 321, 322, 327, 328, 330, 332, 337, 338, 339, 349, 369, 371, 377
"beaver episode" and PM, 370
Rinzai Zen and, 419
scandal and, 406–9, 418, 496, 497n, 650n14
Shipton, Eric, 351n
Shnayerson, Michael, 258, 382, 530
Shorebirds of North America, The (1967), 71, 277, 577
illustrations by Clem, 277
Shores, Eric, 568
Shreeve, James, 396
Siberian Tiger Project, 532–33, 533n, 541, 550
Sifton, Elisabeth, 429, 484
as admirer of PM, 430
as daughter of Reinhold Niebuhr, 431
lawsuit against PM and Viking and, 481
The Snow Leopard and, 429–31, 434–35, 438
In the Spirit of Crazy Horse and, 471–73, 476, 660n160

Viking and treatment of PM, 441,
    483–84
Silent Spring (Carson), 169, 186, 267, 307
Silvers, Robert B., 158
"Simplicity" teisho (PM), 265
Smith, Jean Kennedy, 588
Smith, Patti, 97
Smith, Walter Bedell, 136
Snellgrove, David, 433
Snow Leopard, The (1978), vii, xi–xiii, 366,
    409, 429–42, 590
  acknowledgment of "Maria Eckhart,"
    442, 448
  additions to his journal accounts, 433–34
  audiobook, xvii
  book jacket, 438
  book structure, 431–32, 435
  Brandeis University Creative Arts Award,
    654n67
  British edition, 439
  candor limited in, 433
  contract, advance, and royalties, 431
  contract clause about Guinzburg, 431,
    441
  on the cost of PM's choices, 347
  critics and reviews, 277n, 438–40
  date of publication, xii
  description of the Himalayas, 357
  DL and, 291, 318, 324, 436, 438–39
  elements borrowed from *Annaghkeen*,
    291
  endnotes on "intuitive absolute truth,"
    346n
  experts reviewing the manuscript,
    435–36
  Himalayas expedition (1973) and, 429,
    432
  influence of passage from *The Wind in the
    Willows*, 36
  influence on other authors, works, 440
  Iyer's 2008 introduction, 643n68
  "moments of being," 434
  National Book Award, 441–42, 441n,
    654n67
  Native American beliefs and, 426, 433
  as nature writing, 432
  newspaper strike and *NYT* review
    thwarted, 439–40
  New Yorker excerpts, 437
  PM's appraisal of, 440–41
  PM's Himalaya journals and, 432–34,
    433n, 647n30
  PM's mystical experience at sea, 54, 54n,
    152
  PM's rationale for his Himalayas
    expedition, 334
  PM's revelation in, 437
  praise and congratulatory letters, 437–38,
    440
  psychedelics and, 242, 248
  quotes from Jung in, 301
  Race Rock passage, 152
  readers' questions about PM's leaving his
    young grieving son, 346–47, 642n68
  Richardson and, xi, xvii
  sales, 439
  "secret of the mountains" passage, 434
  as "seeker," search for a Way, 215, 434
  "self-remembering" and, 80
  "the sickness of infinitude" and, 246
  Sifton as editor, 430–31, 434–35, 438
  the snow leopard and, 436–37
  status as modern classic, 440
  theme of self-understanding, xv–xvi
  as Thoreauvian, xii
  title of, 431
  Viking Press as publisher, 437–38
  yeti and, 389, 433, 647n30
  Zen and, 316, 331, 426, 432, 433,
    434–35, 436
Snyder, Gary, 183, 482, 537
Sohier, Walter Denegre, 83, 127
Solomos, George (aka Themistocles
    Hoetis), 116
Sontag, Susan, 482
South Africa
  great white shark expedition (1969), 298,
    301–4
  PM's sighting of *Grus paradisea* cranes
    (1996), 542
Southern, Carol, 156
Southern, Terry, 96, 118, 136, 156, 277
  "The Accident," 131n
  review of *Raditzer*, 216
  "The Sun and the Still-Born Stars," 118
Southgate, Lila, 96–97, 98, 114, 127, 142
Southgate, Patricia Brigham "Patsy" (wife),
    84–85, 86, 89, 104, 134
  affair with Jeffrey Potter, 161–62
  alcoholism of, 263, 263n
  artists Pollock, Krasner, and, 149–50,
    157, 162, 188
  aware of PM's CIA involvement, 109
  background and family, 96
  Black housekeeper for, 155–56
  character and personality, 96–97
  divorce from PM and unconventional
    marriage to Mike Goldberg, 188–89,
    213, 263, 263n
  engagement to PM and breakup, 98–100
  first pregnancy of, 110
  first short story published, 162–63,
    623n134
  lifelong resentment against PM, 163

Southgate, Patricia Brigham "Patsy" (wife) *(continued)*
  literary aspirations of, 123–24
  marriage to PM, dissatisfaction with, 156–57, 161–63
  marries PM, 108
  memories of PM and friends in Paris, 123–24
  O'Hara and, 189, 263n, 623n134
  Paris nightlife and social engagements with PM, 114
  The Paris Review and, 124
  PM and move to Paris (1951), 110
  PM and vacation in the South of France, 126–27
  PM as competitive with, 150
  with PM on Long Island's East End, loneliness and isolation, 142–46, 148–50, 157
  PM proposes, 96
  PM's Paris pals, his "boys club" and, 123–24
  pregnancy in Paris, birth of son Lucas, 129, 134, 137
  pregnancy on Long Island, birth of daughter Sara Carey, 156, 157
  premature labor and loss of child, 114, 123
  rebelliousness of, 97
  Rue Perceval apartment in Paris with PM, 112, 114
  travels with PM and the Styrons, 139–40
  U.S. return from Europe (1953), 142
Southgate, Richard, 96
Southgate, Sarita, 97, 114, 156
Spain, PM's travels in, 87
Sports Illustrated
  PM profile by Harrison, 366
  PM's American wildlife series and, 174, 184–85
Springs, Long Island. *See* Long Island, town of Springs and East End of
Spruce, Richard, 214n
SS *Andrea Doria*, 142, 167, 191, 302
Stamford, Connecticut
  Matthiessen family moves to, 20–21
  PM's childhood in, 21–24
  PM's communion with nature in, 21
Stanford Creative Writing Program, 91–92
Stanton, Jane, 320, 324, 327, 332–33, 350, 368, 641n8
Stap, Don, 207–8
St. Bernard's School, New York City
  curriculum and discipline at, 18
  PM attends, 17–19
  prominent classmates of PM, 18–19

Steele, Max, 131
Stegner, Page, 477
Stegner, Wallace, 91–92
Stein, Gertrude, 72
Stein, Sadie, 592
Steinbeck, John, 92
Steinberg, Saul, 517
Steppenwolf (Hesse), 254–55n
Sternlight, Judy, 560, 561–62, 563
Stevens, Ted, 557
Stevenson, James, 91
Stone, Oliver, 509
Stone, Peter and Mary, 449
Stone, Robert, 380
Storace, Patricia, 503
Story of Little Black Sambo, The (Bannerman), 36
Story of the Chokoloskee Bay Country, The (Tebeau), 492
Stout, Gardner, 277, 438
Stuntz, Joseph Killsright, 474
Styron, Rose Burgunder, 139, 189, 209, 214, 331, 332, 443, 448, 449
  Peltier clemency request and, 551
  PM's Asian crane excursion (1993), 536
Styron, Susanna, 383, 578
Styron, Tom, 591
Styron, William "Bill," xiii, 34, 132, 372
  commentary on *Partisans*, 160–61
  Crazy Horse lawsuits and, 482
  death of, 578–79
  Far Tortuga and, 380
  Lie Down in Darkness, 119, 140, 150
  marries Rose Burgunder in Rome, 139
  objects to mescaline use, 214
  The Paris Review and, 122, 124–26, 130, 136, 619n153
  Peltier pardon request and, 551
  PM in Paris and, 118–20, 121
  PM's Asian crane excursion (1993), 536
  PM's friendship and, 189, 191, 209, 277
  PM's wedding to MM and, 448, 449
  PM's writing and, 140
  Random House and PM's *At Play in the Fields of the Lord*, 258
  in Saint-Tropez, 126
  The Snow Leopard and, 438
  wins Prix de Rome, 119
Sulzberger, Arthur Ochs "Punch," 19
"Sun and the Still-Born Stars, The" (Southern), 118
Suzuki, Shunryu, 93, 319, 323
  Zen Mind, Beginner's Mind, 319, 334, 362n, 366
Sweet Briar College, 73, 83
  Junior Year in France (JYF), 73, 83
Symington, James W., 18, 19

Tai-san. *See* Shimano, Eido Tai
Talese, Gay, 112, 156, 291
   Humes and, 115–16
   "Looking for Hemingway," 122–23, 130n
   PM's response to, 123
Talese, Nan, 291, 315, 320, 328, 332
Tanzania
   Eckhart clinic in, 400
   Eckhart family in, 446
   elephants of, 293–94, 294n
   Hazda people, 340–41
   name of, 292
   Owen and wildlife protection, 291–92
   PM and George Schaller in (1969), 294–96
   PM and MM in (1975), 400–402
   PM and MM in (1977), 427
   PM and the dying lioness, 295–96, 638n47
   PM roaming the Serengeti (1969), 291–98
   PM's animal encounters (1970), 311–12
   PM's children Luke and Sara visit, 296
   PM's journey with Enderlein to the Yaeda Valley (1970), 340, 340n
   PM's safari to Ol Doinyo Lengai, 293
   PM's Selous expedition (1979), 445–47
   president, Julius Nyerere, 304, 304n
   Ruaha National Park, 427
   Serengeti Research Institute at Seronera, 291–92, 341
   as Tanganyika, 384
   See also Tree Where Man Was Born, The
Taylor, Ron and Valerie, 302, 303–4, 308
"Tea at Le Gord" (Kaufman), 271
Teaching of Don Juan, The (Castaneda), 345–46n
Teale, Edwin Way, 185
Tebeau, Charlton W., 493
   The Story of the Chokoloskee Bay Country, 492
Teensma, Hans, 390, 392–93, 400, 402, 403, 404, 428, 648–49n77
Tellico Dam, Tennessee, xv, 454
Templeton, Clayton, 193–94, 196, 199–200, 251
Ten Thousand Islands, Florida, 486–87
   Lostmans River, 540
   PM camping in, 494
   PM piece "White" (retitled "On the River Styx"), 487, 487n
   as setting for *Killing Mister Watson*, 494, 535
   story of Edgar Watson and, 487
Thacher, Peter, 75–76
Thích Nhất Hạnh, 570, 571

Thomas, Lewis, 438
Thoreau, Henry David, 53
   Walden, xii
Three Pillars of Zen, The (Kapleau), 286, 300, 316
Tigers in the Snow (2000), 552–53
   PM's concept for, 534
   Russian trip (1992), Hornocker's Siberian Tiger Project and, 533–34
Tilsen, Ken, 475, 657n83
Tilsen, Mark, 461, 475
Time magazine, 390
   At Play in the Fields of the Lord review, 266
   Far Tortuga review, 379
   Iyer leaves to live among Zen monks, 440
   "Laureate of the Wild" (Iyer), xv
Tomlinson, Henry Major, 202
   The Sea and the Jungle, 192, 192n
"Toomai of the Elephants" (Kipling), 36
"To the Beauty of Sun on Copper" (PM), 37
"To the Miskito Bank" (PM), 276, 372
"Tower of the Four Winds" (PM), 145–46
Towles, Amor, 416, 558, 651n41
Tracking Arctic Oil (Natural Resources Defense Council), PM's foreword, 555–56
Train, John P. C., 125, 130n
"Travelin Man" (PM), 170, 624n18
   film *The Young One* based on, 170, 170–71n
   O. Henry Prize, 170
Travers, Mary, 214
Tree Where Man Was Born, The (1973), 307, 311, 312, 315, 318, 326
   collaboration and photographs by Eliot Porter, 339
   critics and reviews, 341–43
   curious structure of, 340
   dedication, 339
   Dutton publishes, 339, 430
   excerpts printed in the *New Yorker*, 341
   National Book Award nomination, 344
   New York Times review and, 343–44
   PM and the dying lioness, 295–96, 638n47
   PM's evaluation of, 341
   PM's ideas about the autonomy of Native peoples, 340
   PM's vision for, 339
   title of, 339–40
   Turnbull–PM exchange over, 341–43
Tricycle magazine, 528
   Shainberg interview with PM (1993), 528
Trudell, John, 510
Truman, Harry, 111
Turnbull, Colin Macmillan, 341–42

Turner, Frederick, 581, 586–87
Tzara, Tristan, 119–20, 120n, 132, 620n177

Udall, Stewart, 168, 186, 268, 411
  Agenda for Tomorrow, 272
  PM and, 268–70, 271, 280, 284, 487
  The Quiet Crisis, 268
  Wilderness Act of 1964, 268
Underground City, The (Humes), 213
Under the Mountain Wall: A Chronicle of Two Seasons in the Stone Age (1962), 209, 237–41, 250, 252, 268
  American Academy of Arts and Letters award, 250–51
  based on the Harvard-Peabody Expedition, 250
  Capote on, 240
  critics and reviews, 239–40
  dedication of, 240
  note about Michael Rockefeller, 240
  PM's experimental approach and style, 234–36, 239, 240
  as a work of innovative nonfiction, 240
United Farm Workers of America, 102, 135, 280–85, 307, 308, 453, 469
  grape boycott and, 335
  PM as an advocate in search of a cause, 284
  PM's contributions to, 284
  PM's script for pro-union documentary, 347n
  staff for, 282
  See also Chavez, Cesar
University of California, Irvine, 416
  PM as writing instructor, 416, 651n41
University of California, Santa Barbara, Matthiessen lecture: "Literature and Mysticism," 54n
University of Texas at Austin, Harry Ransom Center: Peter Matthiessen Papers, xvi, 289, 592, 609n34
Urubshurow, Jalsa, 575
U.S. Fish and Wildlife Service, 177, 182
U.S. Navy
  Construction Battalions (Seabees, CBs), 49
  Naval Training Center, Sampson, New York, 48
  PM arrested by Shore Patrol, 62
  PM assigned to Recreation and Morale Activities, 61
  PM assigned to the Seebees, 49
  PM discharged (with docked pay), 62
  PM on Maui, 62–63
  PM on Oahu, 55–62, 610n61
  PM on the *Joseph T. Dickman*, 51–52, 55, 57, 152, 609n38
  PM reassigned to the regular Navy, 57
  PM's basic training, Camp Endicott, 49–51, 609n30
  PM's induction, 48, 609n22
  PM's novel *Raditzer* and, 190
Utah trip (1979), 441–42, 654n67

Vail, Sindbad, 116
Valdez, Luis, 347n
Vanderbilt, Sanderson, 173
Vanity Fair
  PM profile by Shnayerson, 530
  PM's assessment of *Lost Man's River*, 546
van Lawick, Hugo, 446
Van Santvoord, George, 29, 31, 32
Varieties of Religious Experience, The (James), 52
Veevers-Carter, Mark, 303
Venezuela
  Nathalie de Salzmann in, 86n, 111
  PM–MM honeymoon in, 449
Versteegh, Chris, 227
"Very Important Lady, A" (PS), 162–63, 623n134
Vesey-Fitzgerald, Desmond, 293
Vienna, Austria, 81
Vietnam War, 268, 272
  PM and Writers and Editors War Tax Protest, 279
Viking Press
  The Cloud Forest (1961), 202
  editor Sifton and PM, 429–30, 434–35, 438, 471–73, 480
  Guinzburg and, 13, 100, 429–30, 441
  Indian Country (1984), 457, 484
  lawsuits over *Crazy Horse*, 479–83, 497, 506–8, 507n, 660n155, 660n167, 661n168, 661n169
  Partisans (1955), 159–60
  PM at, 100
  PM parts ways with, 256
  PM's Harvard-Peabody Expedition and, 212
  PM's nonfiction promised to, 430
  PM's position as author at, 441, 471
  Raditzer (1961), 55, 215
  The Snow Leopard (1978), 430–31
  sold to Penguin Books, 431
  In the Spirit of Crazy Horse (1983), 471–80
  In the Spirit of Crazy Horse republished and updated edition (1991), 508, 509, 550
  In the Spirit of Crazy Horse withdrawn, 480–81, 660n160
  Under the Mountain Wall (1962), 237
  Wildlife in America (1959), 174, 183

Vonnegut, Kurt, 499–500, 506, 551
Vreeland, Frederick "Freck," 88, 104

Walden (Thoreau), xii
Walker, James: *Lakota Belief and Ritual*, 467
Wallace, Alfred Russel, 192
Wallace, Ray, 399, 399n
Walter, Eugene, 131
Ward, Michael, 351n
Warrior: The Life of Leonard Peltier (documentary), 506
Washington Post
  calls MM "friend" of PM, 448
  PM's advocacy for Native Americans and, 455
  review of *Far Tortuga*, 379–80
  review of *Killing Mister Watson*, 503, 503n
  review of *Lost Man's River*, 545
  review of *Under the Mountain Wall*, 240
Wassing, René, 240–41
Wasson, R. Gordon, 214n
Watt, James "Jim" Sutherland, 248–49, 249n
Watts, Alan, 54, 247–48, 278, 288
  influence on PM, 256
  The Joyous Cosmology, 247
  "The Marvelous Labyrinth" lecture, 247
  "The New Alchemy," 248
  The Wisdom of Insecurity, 300
Weeks, Edward, 95, 100, 109, 184, 379
Welty, Eudora, 190
Western, David "Jonah," 485
Wheelwright, Henry Jefferds, Jr. (brother-in-law), 61
Wheelwright, Jeff (nephew), 15, 586
Wheelwright, Mary Seymour Matthiessen (sister), 13, 15, 23, 24, 27, 45, 367, 564
  childhood in Stamford, Connecticut, 21, 22
  death of her mother, 422
  marriage of, 61
  WWII and, 34
Wheelwright, Peter Matthiessen (nephew), 580–81
"White" (PM), 487, 487n
White, Jonathan, 242
White, Katharine, 109, 117
White, Randy Wayne, 488
Whitney, Joel, 113, 122
Whitney, John "Jock" Hay, 23, 144
  Greenwood Plantation, 67–68
whooping crane (*Grus americana*), 169n, 175, 175n
"Who Really Killed the F.B.I. Men" (PM), 509
Wilcove, Davis S., 186
  The Condor's Shadow, 186

Wilderness Act of 1964, 186
Wildlife in America (1957), xiii, 167, 174–87, 180n, 423, 537, 554, 555
  catalogue of sins by colonizers, 180–81
  contemporary reading of, criticisms and kudos, 185–86
  contract with Viking, 174
  critics and reviews, 183–85
  debt to Rachel Carson, 182, 626n70
  dedication of, 421
  description of Bonaventure Island, 98–99
  elegies for extinct species, 181, 182–83
  endpapers, 183, 625n35
  as groundbreaking, 181–82
  illustrations for, 183
  insecticide abuse and, 280
  introduction by Richard Pough, 179
  lasting influence of, 186
  PM's somber introduction, 186–87
  PM's thoughts on nature, 178–79
  PM's travels for, 175–77
  PM's understanding of ecology and, 182, 626n68
  research and literature review for, 179
  as a story of paradise lost, 179–80
  style of writing, 182
  working title, 174
  Yellowstone National Park and, 176, 625n35
Wilkie, Myoku Margot, 371, 407
Willhoite, Tom, 391–95, 391n, 397, 402, 402n, 404, 649n98
William Dean Howells Medal, 566
  list of previous winners, 566
  PM's acceptance statement, 566
Williams, Terry Tempest, 186, 554–55, 669n127
Wilson, Alexander, 174, 179
  American Ornithology, 174
Wind in the Willows, The (Grahame), 35, 345
  "The Piper at the Gates of Dawn," 35–36, 52
Winks, Robin, 104
Winter, Evelyn, 417, 428
Winter, Paul, 509n
Winton, Polly, 84
Wisdom of Insecurity, The (Watts), 300
Wisner, Frank G., 106, 128
Woolf, Virginia, 434
World War II (WWII), 34
  atomic bombs and Japan's surrender, 48–49
  death of PM's friend, 37
  Hitler's suicide and V-E Day, 47
  Hotchkiss School students called to serve, 29

708 · Index

World War II (WWII) *(continued)*
  Japanese attack on Pearl Harbor, 29, 55
  OSS and X-2, 103–4
  PM inducted into the Navy, 48–51, 609n22
  PM in the Coast Guard Temporary Reserve, 40–41, 45
  PM's attempted enlistment, 44–45
  PM's father "Matty" Matthiessen in, 39–40, 41, 608n70, 608n71
Wright, Charles and Holly, 416
Wright, Richard, 36, 73, 105, 113, 617n74

Yale University
  Buckley at, 69
  Elizabethan Club, 103, 106, 615n13
  Guinzburg's memories of, 69–70
  Pearson at, 103
  PM accepted by, 47
  PM and Cole co-author *Yale Daily News* "Two in the Bush" column, 70–71
  PM and Daily Themes class, 88–95, 103
  PM attends, 69–71, 88–95
  PM defers enrollment, 48
  PM graduates, 95
  PM's CIA involvement and, 103–5, 615n13
  PM's engagement in sports at, 71
  PM's focus on birds and birdwatching, 71
  PM's "fondest memory of undergraduate life," 91, 614n15
  PM's interview for readmission (1946), 64
  PM's Junior Year in France (1948), 73–87
  PM's post-graduation position, 95–96, 100, 103
  PM's reading during time at, 92, 614n21
  PM's residence at, 70, 88–89
  PM's unusual program of study, 70
  PM's writing and Charles A. Fenton, 90–92, 95
  PM teaches creative writing (late 1980s), 498
  PM contributes specimens to the Yale Peabody Museum, 89
  postwar changes at, 69–70
  Ray Tompkins House, 69, 70
  students recruited into the CIA at, 104
  Tap Day, 91
Yamada, Hisashi, 310, 311
Yasutani, Hakuun (Yasutani Roshi), 286, 288
Yellowstone National Park, 176, 522, 585, 625n35
"Yeti, The—not a Snowman" (McNeely et al.), 389

yeti, xiv, 389
  Himalayas expedition (1973) and, 647n30
  McNeely's plaster cast of a footprint, 351, 643n90
  PM's investigation of, 389–90
  Schaller's discovery of a "yeti" painting at Shey Gompa, 353, 389–90, 391n
  Shipton and Ward photograph a footprint, 351n
Yochim, Karen "Florida girl," 290, 298–99, 310, 310n, 438–39
Younce, Webster, 560
Young One, The (film), 170, 170–71n

Zahniser, Howard, 169–170
Zaire
  PM expedition in search of forest elephants in the Congo Basin (1985–86), 485
  PM trip in search of the Congo peafowl (1978), 437, 437n
Zajac, Jack, 522
Zen Buddhism
  Dai Bosatsu Zendo Kongo-ji, 321–22, 323, 332, 418, 650n14
  Diamond Sutra, 371
  DL's ashes at Dai Bosatsu Zendo, 332, 369–70, 407
  DL's commitment to, 286–91, 311–13, 315–17, 319–21, 323–24, 327–28, 329–30
  DL's death and, 330, 337, 338, 449n
  DL's Dharma name and ordination, 328
  "Donors to the Dai Bosatsu Zendo," 370–71
  first roshi to travel and teach in America, 9n
  first U.S. Zen monastery, Tassajara, 322–23
  Heart Sutra, 288, 449, 588
  Indian Country and, 456
  Kannon Sutra, 331, 338
  kensho (mystical experience), 54, 54n, 326, 334, 346, 419
  koan study, Harada–Yasutani system, 419–20
  koan: what is the sound of one hand clapping, 419–20
  Mu koan, 300
  New York sangha, 288
  New York Zendo Shobo-ji, 316, 317, 321, 322, 326, 329, 332
  parallels with Indian spiritual attitudes, 426, 451
  shedding of ego and, xvi
  Shiho, 514–15
  shikantaza (just sitting), 419

shoshin (beginner's mind), 93
on suffering and clinging, 579, 672n64
teachers bringing Zen to the West, 288, 321, 418
zazen (sitting meditation), 288, 316–17
"true nature," xvi, 246, 338
See also Watts, Alan
Zen Buddhism: PM and, xiv, 54n
American Zen addressing social problems and, 570–71, 671n18
as another way to escape, 519, 524–25, 537
"beaver episode" at Dai Bosatsu, 370
"Beginner's Mind" retreat at Greyston, 498
death and Kannon Sutra, 589
Dharma heir Michel Engu Dobbs, 579–80
Dharma name "Ishin" (One Mind), 338
Dharma name "Muryo" (Boundless), 449
Dharma talk about Auschwitz-Birkenau experience, 572
Dharma talk about death, 325–26, 593
Dharma talk about doubt, 529
Dharma talk about Greenland beluga hunt, 527
disillusioned by Eido Shimano scandal and withdrawal from Zen Studies Society (1975), 406–9, 411, 414, 418–20, 650n14
embracing of (early 1970s), 4, 286, 319, 319n, 320–24, 330, 331–32, 338–39, 345
exercise with Ocean Zendo students on confronting death, 577
facing death and, 586–87, 588
haikus, 332, 337
Heart Sutra and, 588
help for his anger, inner conflict, 519
Himalayas expedition and, 338, 349, 358, 361, 362, 362n
influence on Jim Harrison, 366
Inka ceremony, PM becomes Muryo Roshi (1996), 528–29
International Dai Bosatsu Zendo project, 369–71, 407
"Introduction to Zen Practice" talk, 515
in Los Angeles, return to Zen and new teacher Maezumi, 418–20
meditation described in *The Snow Leopard*, 316

Nine-Headed Dragon River and, 495–97, 519, 528
officiating at marriages, christenings, and funerals, 515
reading and research on, 300
retreats and meetings (1994), 537
revival of practicing (1977), 418–20
Right Livelihood, 455
roshis and a monk in his Sagaponack driveway, 286, 637n3
Sagaponack sitting group and zendo in old stables, "Ocean Zendo," 513–14, 515
sesshin, Dai Bosatsu (1973), 345–46
sesshin, New York Zendo and introduction to Zen (1970), 315–17, 639n9
sesshin, Wisdom House, Litchfield, Connecticut (1972), 337–38
Shainberg interview (1993), 528
Shiho ceremony, PM becomes Muryo Sensei (1989), 514–15
The Snow Leopard and, 316, 432, 434–35
speech about his spiritual evolution (1973), 345–46, 345–46n
students of, 516–18
Tassajara Zen Mountain Center, visit to, 322
thinking infiltrated by, 395
three-month residency at Greyston, 519, 520
Tokudo, ordination as a priest (1981), 449–50, 449n
wedding to MM and, 449
work and teaching as Muryo Sensei, 515–29
writing and, 377
Zen Center of Los Angeles, 418, 495, 497
Zen Community of New York: "Greyston," 495–96, 498, 662n39
Zen Mind, Beginner's Mind (Suzuki), 319, 334, 362n, 366
Zen Peacemaker Order, 570
"engaged Buddhism" and, 570
three tenets of, 570
Zen Studies Society, 287, 377, 414
scandal and, 406–8, 418, 496
Zero magazine, 116
"Everybody's Protest Novel" (Baldwin), 116

ILLUSTRATION CREDITS

In-text Illustrations

p. ii: Photograph by George Schaller; courtesy of George Schaller

p. 1: Illustration by Peter Matthiessen; courtesy of the Estate of Peter Matthiessen

p. 165: Illustration by Josiah Wood Whymper; public domain

p. 353: Photograph by James Appleton; courtesy of James Appleton

p. 374: Detail from Matthiessen's *Far Tortuga* (1975); copyright © 1975 by Peter Matthiessen. Used by permission of Vintage Books, an imprint of the Knopf Doubleday Publishing Group, a division of Penguin Random House LLC. All rights reserved.

p. 378: Detail from Matthiessen's "Fool Day" manuscript; courtesy of the Estate of Peter Matthiessen, collection of the author

p. 378: Detail from Matthiessen's *Far Tortuga* (1975); copyright © 1975 by Peter Matthiessen. Used by permission of Vintage Books, an imprint of the Knopf Doubleday Publishing Group, a division of Penguin Random House LLC. All rights reserved.

p. 511: Illustration by Okuhara Seiko; public domain, sourced from Yale University Art Gallery

Insert Illustrations

All photographs are courtesy of the Estate of Peter Matthiessen with the exception of those indicated below.

ACME Newspictures, 1930: Photo by Acme Newspictures; courtesy of the Henry L. Ferguson Museum.

USS *Joseph T. Dickman:* Public domain; sourced from the United States Coast Guard Historian's Office

At the South Seas Club: Courtesy of the Harry Ransom Center

Wendy Burden: Courtesy of Wendy Morgan

On horseback at the Greenwood Plantation: Courtesy of Payne Middleton

Class of the Junior Year in France: Courtesy of Sweet Briar College

Patricia "Patsy" Southgate: Courtesy of Smith College Special Collections

Literary expats in Paris: Photo by Otto van Noppen

Harold Louis "Doc" Humes, Jr.: Courtesy of the Harold Louis Humes Estate

Plimpton, du Bois, and Connell: Photo by Otto van Noppen

The Paris Review, No. 1: Courtesy of *The Paris Review*

Patsy in Springs: Courtesy of Darrah Cole

Great Auk by Audubon: Public domain

The Harvard-Peabody New Guinea Expedition: Photograph by Eliot Elisofon, Gift of Jill and Elin Elisofon. © President and Fellows of Harvard College, Peabody Museum of Archaeology and Ethnology, 2006.37.1.57.5.

Elisofon takes a photo: Photograph by Karl G. Heider, Gift of Karl G. Heider. © President and Fellows of Harvard College, Peabody Museum of Archaeology and Ethnology, 2006.17.1.4.8.

The Dugum Dani: Photograph by Robert Gardner, Gift of Robert Gardner. © President and Fellows of Harvard College, Peabody Museum of Archaeology and Ethnology, 2006.16.1.1.9.

Cesar Chavez: Getty/Bettmann

Ann Israel and PM talk to Cesar Chavez: Courtesy of the Harry Ransom Center

PM suits up: Courtesy of Peter A. Lake

The *Blue Water* expedition: Getty/Michael Ochs Archives; reproduced with the permission of Peter A. Lake

PM's trekking permit: Courtesy of the Harry Ransom Center

Shey Gompa: Courtesy of George Schaller

PM crosses an icy torrent: Courtesy of George Schaller

Notes from notebook to journal: Courtesy of George Schaller

The Ringmo porters: Courtesy of George Schaller

The kitchen hut at Shey Gompa: Courtesy of George Schaller

PM at Tsakang: Courtesy of George Schaller

Homeward bound at the Saldang Pass: Courtesy of George Schaller

Eido Tai Shimano: Courtesy of the Zen Studies Society

Soen Nakagawa: Courtesy of the Zen Studies Society

After a sesshin at Litchfield, CT: Courtesy of the Zen Studies Society

Hans Teensma with Doug Blue: Courtesy of Hans Teensma

"Oliver": Getty/Bettmann

Tom Willhoite: Courtesy of Hans Teensma

PM and Alan Gillespie: Courtesy of Hans Teensma

Frame 352 of the Patterson-Gimlin film: Public domain

PM playing the role of bigfoot: Courtesy of Hans Teensma

Craig Carpenter: Courtesy of John Carpenter

Leonard Peltier extradited: Getty/Bettmann

Peter Matthiessen, by Leonard Peltier: Courtesy of the Harry Ransom Center and Leonard Peltier

PM prepares for Shukke Tokudo: Courtesy of Peter Cunningham

Shukke Tokudo: Courtesy of Peter Cunningham

PM and Glassman with a monk: Courtesy of Peter Cunningham

Interior conversion of the horse stable: Courtesy of Hans Teensma

Exterior door with its wooden han: Courtesy of Jaime Lopez

A walkway: Courtesy of Jaime Lopez

The Ocean Zendo: Courtesy of Jaime Lopez

Edgar "Bloody" Watson: Courtesy of the Harry Ransom Center

Watson's house at Chatham Bend: Courtesy of the American Museum of Natural History Library

Mamie and Ted Smallwood: Public domain; sourced from the State Library and Archive of Florida

PM's handwritten edits to a published *Killing Mister Watson:* Courtesy of the Harry Ransom Center

PM holding a crane: Courtesy of the Harry Ransom Center

With a snow leopard cub: Courtesy of Jesse Close

With juvenile cranes and puppet: Courtesy of the Harry Ransom Center

Muryo Sensei, Tom Styron, and Phoebe Park: Courtesy of the Estate of Peter Matthiessen and Tom Styron

Victor Emanuel and PM at Cape Washington: Courtesy of Birgit Freybe Bateman

PM and Alex Matthiessen: Courtesy of William Abranowicz/Art+Commerce

PM returns to Arctic Alaska: Courtesy of Subhankar Banerjee

Bernie Glassman leads the Bearing Witness Retreat: Courtesy of Peter Cunningham

Birkenau: Courtesy of Peter Cunningham

Muryo Roshi and Joan Jiko Halifax: Courtesy of Peter Cunningham

PM on March 5, 2014: Damon Winter/*The New York Times*/Redux

PERMISSIONS

All excerpts from the unpublished writings of Peter Matthiessen used by permission of the Estate of Peter Matthiessen.

Excerpts from "The Last Wilderness: Amazonas Journal," first published in *The New Yorker*, July 8, 1961; from "The Last Wilderness: Peruvian Journal," first published in *The New Yorker*, September 9, 1961; from "To the Miskito Bank," first published in *The New Yorker*, October 28, 1967; and from "New York: Old Hometown," first published in *Architectural Digest*, November 1989. All reprinted by permission of the Estate of Peter Matthiessen.

Excerpt(s) from *At Play in the Fields of the Lord* by Peter Matthiessen, copyright © 1966 by Peter Matthiessen. Used by permission of Random House, an imprint and division of Penguin Random House LLC. All rights reserved.

Excerpt(s) from *Far Tortuga: A Novel* by Peter Matthiessen, copyright © 1975 by Peter Matthiessen. Used by permission of Vintage Books, an imprint of the Knopf Doubleday Publishing Group, a division of Penguin Random House LLC. All rights reserved.

Excerpt(s) from *In the Spirit of Crazy Horse* by Peter Matthiessen, copyright © 1980, 1983, 1991 by Peter Matthiessen. Used by permission of Viking Books, an imprint of Penguin Publishing Group, a division of Penguin Random House LLC. All rights reserved.

Excerpt(s) from *Indian Country* by Peter Matthiessen, copyright © 1979, 1980, 1981, 1984 by Peter Matthiessen. Used by permission of Viking Books, an imprint of Penguin Publishing Group, a division of Penguin Random House LLC. All rights reserved.

Excerpt(s) from *The Cloud Forest: A Chronicle of the South American Wilderness* by Peter Matthiessen, copyright © 1961 by Peter Matthiessen. Used by permission of Viking Books, an imprint of Penguin Publishing Group, a division of Penguin Random House LLC. All rights reserved.

Excerpt(s) from *The Snow Leopard* by Peter Matthiessen, copyright © 1978 by Peter Matthiessen. Used by permission of Viking Books, an imprint of Penguin Publishing Group, a division of Penguin Random House LLC. All rights reserved.

Excerpt(s) from *The Tree Where Man Was Born* by Peter Matthiessen, copyright © 1972 by The New Yorker. Used by permission of Dutton, an imprint of Penguin Publishing Group, a division of Penguin Random House LLC. All rights reserved.

Excerpt(s) from *Wildlife in America* by Peter Matthiessen, copyright © 1959, revised and renewed © 1987 by Peter Matthiessen. Used by permission of Viking Books, an imprint of Penguin Publishing Group, a division of Penguin Random House LLC. All rights reserved.

Excerpts from *Nine-Headed Dragon River: Zen Journals 1969–1982* by Peter Matthiessen. Copyright © 1985 by the Zen Community of New York. Reprinted by arrangement with The Permissions Company, LLC, on behalf of Shambhala Publications Inc., Boulder, CO, shambhala.com.

Excerpts from *Sal Si Puedes* by Peter Matthiessen. Copyright © 1969 by Peter Matthiessen. Reprinted by permission of the University of California Press Books.

Excerpts from an unpublished letter by Lisa Barclay Bigelow. Used by permission of Lisa Edge.

Excerpts from an unpublished letter by Peter Benchley. Used by permission of Wendy Benchley on behalf of Benchley IP, LLC.

Excerpts from unpublished letters by Craig Carpenter. Used by permission of John Carpenter.

Excerpt from the unpublished journals of Cynthia Cole. Used by permission of Darrah Cole.

Selections from unpublished letters written by Annie Dillard in 1999 and 2006 reprinted with the permission of Russell & Volkening as agents for the author. Copyright © 1999 and © 2006 by Annie Dillard.

Excerpts from unpublished letters by Louisa Drury (née Noble). Used by permission of John and Kathryn Drury.

Excerpts from unpublished letters by Joe Fox. Used by permission of the Estate of Joe Fox.

Excerpt from an unpublished letter by Merete Galesi. Used by permission of Adriana Galesi.

Excerpts from an unpublished journal by Robert Gardner. Used by permission of the Estate of Robert Gardner.

Excerpts from unpublished letters by Tom Guinzburg. Used by permission of Amanda Guinzburg.

Excerpts from unpublished letters by Donald Hall. Used by arrangement with the Estate of Donald Hall, via Aevitas Creative Management.

Excerpts from unpublished letters by Jim Harrison. Used by permission of the James T. Harrison Trust.

Excerpt from an unpublished letter by Joseph Heller. Used by permission of the Estate of Joseph Heller.

Excerpts from unpublished letters by Harold Louis Humes Jr. Used by permission of the Estate of Harold Louis Humes Jr.

Excerpt from an unpublished letter by Nancy Hurxthal. Used by permission of Anwyn Hurxthal.

Excerpts from an unpublished letter by John Irving. Used by permission of John Irving.

Excerpts from unpublished letters by Mildred Johnstone. Used by permission of Margaret Buchholz.

Excerpts from an unpublished letter by Jim Leach. Used by permission of Jim Leach.

Excerpts from unpublished letters by Barry Lopez. Used by permission of the Estate of Barry Lopez.

Excerpts from the unpublished letters, journals, and poems of Deborah Love. Used by permission of Rue and Alex Matthiessen.

Excerpts from the unpublished letters, journals, and poems of Maria Matthiessen (formerly Koenig, née Eckhart). Used by permission of Maria Matthiessen.

Excerpts from an unpublished letter by Howard Norman, and selections from unpublished interviews conducted by Howard Norman with Peter Matthiessen. Used by permission of Howard Norman.

Excerpts from unpublished letters by Neil Olson. Used by permission of Neil Olson.

Excerpts from unpublished letters by George Plimpton. Used by permission of Sarah Dudley Plimpton.

Excerpt from an unpublished letter by Eliot Porter. © 1990 by the Amon Carter Museum of American Art. Used by permission of the Amon Carter Museum of American Art.

Excerpt from an unpublished letter by Diarmuid Russell. © 1959 by Russell & Volkening. Used by permission of Russell & Volkening.

Excerpt from an unpublished speech by James Salter. Used by permission of the Estate of James Salter.

Excerpts from unpublished letters and an unpublished journal by George Schaller. Used by permission of George Schaller.

Excerpts from unpublished interviews conducted by Jeff Sewald with various subjects for his documentary, *Peter Matthiessen: No Boundaries* (2009). Used by permission of Jeff Sewald. All rights reserved.

Excerpts from unpublished letters by Elisabeth Sifton. Used by permission of the Estate of Elisabeth Sifton.

Excerpt from an unpublished letter by Don Stap. Used by permission of Don Stap.

Excerpts from unpublished letters by William Styron. Used by permission of the Estate of William Styron.

Excerpts from unpublished letters by Gay Talese, and selections from unpublished interviews conducted by Gay Talese with various subjects. Used by permission of Gay Talese.

Excerpt from an unpublished letter by Ken Tilsen. Used by permission of the Estate of Kenneth Tilsen.

Excerpts from unpublished letters by Katharine White. Used by permission of White Literary LLC.

Excerpts from unpublished letters by Karen Yochim. Used by permission of Karen Yochim.

Other published sources

Excerpts from *Making Dead Birds: Chronicle of a Film* by Robert Gardner. © 2008 by Robert Gardner. Reprinted by permission of the Peabody Museum of Archaeology and Ethnology.

Excerpts from *Annaghkeen* by Deborah Love. © 1970 by Deborah Love. Reprinted by permission of Rue and Alex Matthiessen.

Excerpts from *First Light: A Journey Out of Darkness* by Lucas Matthiessen. © 2023 by Lucas Matthiessen. Reprinted by permission of Skyhorse Publishing.

Excerpts from "Peter Matthiessen, The Art of Fiction No. 157," first printed in *The Paris Review*, No. 150, Spring 1999. Reprinted by permission of *The Paris Review*.

Excerpts from "Emptying the Bell," an interview with Peter Matthiessen conducted by Lawrence Shainberg, first published in *Tricycle*, Fall 1993. Reprinted by permission of *Tricycle*.

Excerpts from "Higher Matthiessen," by Michael Shnayerson, first published in *Vanity Fair*, December 1991. Reprinted by permission of Michael Shnayerson.

Excerpts from "Looking for Hemingway," first published in *Esquire*, July 1963. Reprinted by permission of Gay Talese.

ABOUT THE AUTHOR

Lance Richardson's first book, *House of Nutter: The Rebel Tailor of Savile Row*, was a *New York Times* Editors' Choice and spotlighted on "The New Yorker Recommends." It was also named one of the notable books of 2018 by *The Sunday Times, The Mail on Sunday, Esquire*, and the American Library Association. He has been awarded the Hazel Rowley Literary Fellowship, a Leon Levy Center for Biography fellowship, and with residencies at MacDowell, Yaddo, the Harry Ransom Center, and the Key West Literary Seminar. In 2021, he was named a Public Scholar by the National Endowment for the Humanities. In 2023–24, he was the Janice B. and Milford D. Gerton/Arts and Letters Foundation Fellow at the Cullman Center for Scholars and Writers, New York Public Library. Richardson holds a master's degree in longform journalism from the Arthur L. Carter Journalism Institute, NYU. He teaches in the MFA in Writing program at Bennington College, Vermont, and lives in Providence, Rhode Island.

A NOTE ON THE TYPE

This book was set in Janson, a typeface long thought to have been made by the Dutchman Anton Janson, who was a practicing typefounder in Leipzig during the years 1668–1687. However, it has been conclusively demonstrated that these types are actually the work of Nicholas Kis (1650–1702), a Hungarian, who most probably learned his trade from the master Dutch typefounder Dirk Voskens. The type is an excellent example of the influential and sturdy Dutch types that prevailed in England up to the time William Caslon (1692–1766) developed his own incomparable designs from them.

Composed by North Market Street Graphics,
Lancaster, Pennsylvania

Designed by Cassandra J. Pappas